HANDBOOK ON THE HISTORY OF ECONOMIC ANALYSIS VOLUME III

Handbook on the History of Economic Analysis
Volume III

Developments in Major Fields of Economics

Edited by

Gilbert Faccarello

Professor of Economics, Panthéon-Assas University, Paris, France

Heinz D. Kurz

Emeritus Professor of Economics, University of Graz and Graz Schumpeter Centre, Austria

Cheltenham, UK • Northampton, MA, USA

Published by
Edward Elgar Publishing Limited
The Lypiatts
15 Lansdown Road
Cheltenham
Glos GL50 2JA
UK

Edward Elgar Publishing, Inc.
William Pratt House
9 Dewey Court
Northampton
Massachusetts 01060
USA

Paperback edition 2018

A catalogue record for this book
is available from the British Library

Library of Congress Control Number: 2015954313

This book is available electronically in the **Elgar**online
Economics subject collection
DOI 10.4337/9781785365065

ISBN 978 1 84980 112 6 (cased)
ISBN 978 1 78536 131 9 (cased 3-volume set)
ISBN 978 1 78536 506 5 (eBook)
ISBN 978 1 78897 239 0 (paperback)
ISBN 978 1 78897 240 6 (paperback 3-volume set)

Typeset by Servis Filmsetting Ltd, Stockport, Cheshire
Printed on FSC approved paper
Printed and bound in Great Britain by Marston Book Services Ltd, Oxfordshire

Contents

Figures and tables

Figures

Tables

Contributors

Michaël Assous, University of Paris I Panthéon-Sorbonne, France

Alberto Baccini, University of Siena, Italy

Antoinette Baujard, University of Saint-Étienne, France

Élodie Bertrand, National Centre for Scientific Research, France

Marcel Boumans, Utrecht University, The Netherlands

Jérôme de Boyer des Roches, University of Paris Dauphine, France

José Luís Cardoso, University of Lisbon, Portugal

Muriel Dal Pont Legrand, University of Nice Sophia Antipolis, France

Michel De Vroey, Université catholique de Louvain, Belgium

Sylvie Diatkine, Université Paris Est Créteil, France

Kurt Dopfer, University of Saint Gallen, Switzerland

Amitava Krishna Dutt, University of Notre Dame, USA and FLACSO, Ecuador

Ragip Ege, University of Strasbourg, France

Guido Erreygers, University of Antwerp, Belgium and University of Melbourne, Australia

Gilbert Faccarello, Panthéon-Assas University, Paris, France

Duncan Foley, New School for Social Research, USA

Rebeca Gómez Betancourt, University Lumière, Lyon, France

David Haas, University of Graz, Austria

Harald Hagemann, University of Hohenheim, Germany

Eiji Hosoda, Keio University, Tokyo, Japan

Herrade Igersheim, National Centre for Scientific Research, France

Alan Kirman, University of Aix-Marseille, France

Joern Kleinert, University of Graz, Austria

Hartmut Kliemt, Frankfurt School of Finance and Management, Germany

Heinz D. Kurz, University of Graz, Austria

Robert Leonard, University of Québec at Montreal, Canada

Pierre Malgrange, National Centre for Scientific Research, France

Andrea Maneschi, Vanderbilt University, USA

Perry Mehrling, Columbia University, USA

Simon Mohun, Queen Mary University of London, Great Britain

Manuela Mosca, University of Salento, Italy

Sergio Noto, University of Verona, Italy

Arrigo Opocher, University of Padova, Italy

Nicole Kathrin Palan, University of Graz, Austria

Fabio Petri, University of Siena, Italy

Andreas Rainer, University of Graz, Austria

Salvatore Rizzello, University of Piemonte Orientale, Italy

J. Barkley Rosser Jr, James Madison University, Harrisonburg, USA

Maurice Salles, University of Caen, France

Neri Salvadori, University of Pisa, Italy

Marlies Schütz, University of Graz, Austria

Rodolfo Signorino, University of Palermo, Italy

Anna Spada, University of Piemonte Orientale, Italy

Philippe Steiner, University of Paris-Sorbonne and Institut Universitaire de France, France

Antonella Stirati, Università di Roma Tre, Italy

Rita Strohmaier, University of Graz, Austria

Richard Sturn, University of Graz, Austria

Claudia Sunna, University of Salento, Italy

Jacques-François Thisse, CORE, Université catholique de Louvain, Belgium, Higher School of Economics at Saint Petersburg, Russia and CEPR

Paola Tubaro, CNRS, University of Paris-Saclay, France

Katsuyoshi Watarai, Waseda University, Tokyo, Japan

General introduction

The past is never dead. It's not even past. (William Faulkner)

The aim of this *Handbook on the History of Economic Analysis* is to provide a succinct overview of the development of economics since its systematic inception up until today. The *Handbook* has three volumes. Volume I deals with *Great Economists since Petty and Boisguilbert*. It provides short essays in biography of some of the most important economists in what is known as the "Western World". Volume II deals with *Schools of Thought in Economics*. A school is defined in terms of the analytical method(s) used, the approach chosen in tackling the problem(s) at hand, the results derived and the policy conclusions inferred. Volume III contains summary accounts of *Developments in Major Fields of Economics* reflecting the division of labour within the discipline.

There are different ways of approaching the history of economic thought. The focus of these volumes is on economic theories: their formation, including their philosophical and historical underpinnings, their conclusiveness and place within the field, and their possible use in formulating economic policies. We draw attention to those economists and their doctrines that we regard as especially significant. It hardly needs to be said that our choice unavoidably reflects a subjective element. We would have liked to include the portraits of several more important thinkers, but space constraints prevented us from doing so. The same applies *cum grano salis* to the schools of thought and developments in major fields covered.

Let us however acknowledge, at the outset, some of the important gaps in coverage. The focus is on European intellectual traditions and their continuation in the so-called Western World, but of course it is a fact that all advanced civilizations can point to notable achievements in the exploration of economic life – think of countries such as China or Japan, for example, or civilizations following philosophical or religious traditions such as Buddhism or Islam. In addition to geographic gaps, there are also some gaps in subjects covered, such as the omission of business administration and management theories.

Arthur Cecil Pigou once remarked that the history of economic thought is a history of the "wrong ideas of dead men". Certainly, it is partly also that, but not only, and moreover there is always much to learn from the alleged "errors". While there is progress in economics, there is also occasional regress. This should not come as a surprise: in a discipline dealing with as complex a subject matter as economics, it would be naive not to expect some intellectual "bubbles" that sooner or later burst, necessitating a fundamental re-orientation in the area of investigation under consideration. In the parlance of economists: the market for economic ideas is not a perfectly functioning selection mechanism that preserves all that is correct and valuable and discards whatever is wrong and useless.

This may also contribute to explaining the remarkable fact that certain ideas and concepts in economics, cherished at one time, get submerged and are forgotten afterwards, only to re-emerge in a new garb and liberated of their teething troubles at a later time. As Dennis Robertson once remarked with regard to the history of economics: "If you stand in the same place long enough, the hunted hare comes round again." Or, as Alfred Marshall put it: "We continually meet with old friends in new dresses." One of the most knowledgeable historians of economic thought ever, Joseph Alois Schumpeter, expressed the same view as follows: "Old friends come disguised to the party."

Modern economists frequently seem to believe that it not only suffices to know just the most recent economic doctrines and theories; they even seem to think, echoing Pigou's statement above, that it is detrimental to their intellectual development to expose themselves to the ideas and thoughts of earlier generations of economists. Since by assumption these must be partly or wholly wrong, or at least imperfect, it is not only a waste of time to study the "old masters", it may even be harmful to do so, because it may confuse readers and prompt them to deviate from the correct path to truth and wisdom. This position is a version of what the literary critic Norman Foerster called "provincialism of time", that is, "the measure of past literature by the ideas and moods of a narrow present". It is, among other things, based on the false presumption that it is the privilege of living economists to articulate only correct views.

Even a casual look at the history of economics, its various schools of thought and doctrines, shows that economics always lacked and still lacks a *unité de doctrine*, and that there is no reason to presume that this state of affairs will end any time soon. If economics were characterized by a relentless march towards ever-higher levels of knowledge and truthfulness, this fact would be difficult to explain.

There can be little doubt that the ideas of economists are important. John Maynard Keynes even insisted: "The ideas of economists and political philosophers, both when they are right and when they are wrong, are more powerful than is commonly understood. Indeed the world is ruled by little else." If this happens to be so, it is important to know the ideas of economists, especially when they are wrong. The history of economic analysis is not only a treasure trove of such ideas, it also informs about when and why certain ideas were challenged and some of them eventually rejected, at least in the form in which they were available at the time. Knowing the history of the discipline should help you to resist superstition, hysteria and exuberance in economic and social questions. And it should immunize you against falling victim to the ideas of some "defunct economist" (Keynes) all too easily.

The gestation period of the *Handbook on the History of Economic Analysis* was long – a great deal longer than originally planned. There are many factors that contribute to explaining the delays to the project. With some 140 authors, the probability was high that some of them could not deliver, for various respectable reasons, and had to be replaced. In some cases we had to act as writers of last resort. We also insisted that the three volumes should come out together, which necessitated the completion of them at roughly the same time. Bad health at different periods of time for each of the editors did not exactly help in propelling the project forward. Confronted with these and other difficulties, we are all the more pleased to be able to present the *Handbook on the History of Economic Analysis* to the scientific community. We take this opportunity to thank all of the contributors for their fine work. We are particularly grateful to those who delivered their entries in good time and for their patience thereafter. We also thank the referees we involved in assessing the different versions of the entries and for their useful comments, which helped to improve them.

May this *Handbook on the History of Economic Analysis* contribute to a better understanding of the path economics took over time up until today and substantiate William Faulkner's claim that "History is not was, it is".

GILBERT FACCARELLO AND HEINZ D. KURZ

A note on the cross-references sections: the volume in which the cross-references appear is listed as follows:

(I)   *Handbook on the History of Economic Analysis Volume I: Great Economists since Petty and Boisguilbert;*
(II)   *Handbook on the History of Economic Analysis Volume II: Schools of Thought in Economics;*
(III)   *Handbook on the History of Economic Analysis Volume III: Developments in Major Fields of Economics.*

Balance of payments and exchange rates

This entry briefly covers the analysis of the balance of payments and exchange rates from mercantilism to the 1980s' monetary approach to the balance of payments. The first section is devoted to the emergence in the eighteenth century of the concept of balance of trade equilibrium. The second section presents the distinction and connection between the balance of trade and the balance of payments developed and discussed in the first half of the nineteenth century. The third section studies the 1870–1930 period and the gold standard failure. The last section describes the open macroeconomic approach after the great depression.

Equilibrium versus Balance of Trade Surplus

Because they feared a currency shortage, mercantilists promoted policies – taxes, industrialization, creation of commercial companies, establishment of banks, colonization and wars – intended to achieve a balance of trade surplus. The entry of gold and silver coins was seen both as an accumulation of wealth and power and as the way to provide the economy with money to meet the needs of growing trade. The first break with this approach was made by John Locke, with *Some Considerations on the Consequences of the Lowering of Interest and the Raising of the Value of Money* (1691). In his view, because the levels of monetary prices in neighbouring countries are necessarily close to each other, the international stock of coined money will be distributed among countries in proportion to each country's level of internal trade. This leads to an equilibrium approach to the international distribution of gold and silver money, which assumes one property of the quantity theory of money previously expounded by Bernardo Davanzati in his *Lezione delle Monete*: "all these earthly things are, by the consent of nations, worth all the gold (and in this I include silver and copper) that is wrought" (1588: 32) and then by Geminiano Montanari in his *Della Moneta*: "all the commodities in commerce between men, taken together, are worth as much as the gold, silver, and copper, coined and in circulation" (1683 [1804]: 45). However, Locke did not address the problem of the stability of the equilibrium he defined, nor did he expound the quantity theory of money per se.

In the eighteenth century, the balance of trade surplus was understood as a stage in an equilibrium process. Any discrepancy in the proportions between quantities of money and commodities is removed: a relative redundancy (insufficiency) of money in a country results in an outflow (inflow) of money incurring a trade deficit (surplus). Trade deficit or surplus lasts until the equilibrium defined by Locke is reached; trade deficit and surplus correspond to temporary situations that only exist until equilibrium is attained. Isaac Gervaise deserves to be credited with having first described such a process in *The System or Theory of the Trade of the World* (1720). This was at the time of the Mississippi Bubble in France and the South Sea Bubble in England.

According to Gervaise, the proportion in a nation between the quantities of money – "the grand real measure or denominator of the real value of all things" (Gervaise [1720] 1954: 6) – on the one side, and the goods produced by labour on the other is at equilibrium when the expense of the rich is balanced by the labour of the poor. In this case, the nation has the appropriate "proportion of the grand denominator of the world" (ibid.: 7). If, however, the nation has "attracted a greater proportion [of the grand denominator] than its proper share, and the cause of that attraction ceases" (ibid.: 7) while production remains unchanged, then the increase of expense will result in a disequilibrium in the market for goods. Exports will decrease and imports increase in order to clear this market, thereby creating a balance of trade deficit. As payment of the balance reduces the quantity of money, it narrows the gap between consumption and production. Inasmuch as it restores the equilibrium, the outflow of money does not last long. If the nation has less than its just proportion of the grand denominator, the same mechanism will operate in the opposite direction. Then Gervaise explained that credit expansion has the same effect as the discovery of a "gold or silver mine" (ibid.: 9) in disturbing the equilibrium by increasing expense, thereby inducing an outflow of coins or bullion.

Gervaise's description of the stability of the balance of trade equilibrium did not involve either the quantity theory or any price process. By contrast, David Hume's theory did. In the 1752 edition of his *Moral, Political and Literary Essays*, Hume expounded the price specie flow mechanism (hereafter PSFM): any increase in the quantity of coined money in one country leads to an increase in the monetary prices of goods, which induces a decrease in exports and an increase in imports, that is, a balance of trade deficit. The payment of the balance consists in an outflow of specie, that is, a decrease in the quantity of money, which leads to a decrease in prices. This mechanism lasts until the initial equilibrium is restored. In a reciprocal way, if the quantity of goods increases in one country, the monetary prices of goods fall, inducing an increase in exports and a decrease in imports, that is, a balance of trade surplus. The inflow of money resulting from the payment of the trade balance leads to an increase in prices; again the process operates until the initial equilibrium is restored.

For example, consider France and England with respectively the franc FF and the sterling £ as monies of account. In France, 1 FF is the legal price of 0.290 grams of fine gold. In England, £1 is the legal price of 7.322 grams of fine gold. The ratio between the two legal prices of gold defines the par of exchange between the two monies of account:

$$\frac{7.32236 \text{ gr}/\pounds}{0.29032 \text{ gr}/FF} = 25.22 \text{ FF}/\pounds. \tag{1}$$

In France, the "20 francs or" coin, known as the "napoleon", containing 5.806 grams of fine gold, circulates with 20FF as legal tender. In England, the "guinea" coin, containing 7.688 grams of fine gold, circulates with £1.1s. as legal tender. The par of exchange between the two currencies is:

$$\frac{7.68848 \text{ gr/guinea}}{5.80645 \text{ gr/napoleon}} = 1.32413 \text{ napoleon/guinea} \tag{2}$$

Suppose that the gold price of the quantity Q of goods circulating is the same in both countries, 7688 grams. The prices of Q expressed in the monies of account and currencies are as in Table 1.

Now, consider the discovery of a gold mine which increases the quantity of gold circulating in England by 50 per cent, so that the gold price of Q becomes 11 532 grams in this country whereas it remains unchanged in France at 7688 grams. The prices are now as in Table 2.

Table 1   Money prices in France and England

Price of Q in	Money of account	Currency
France	26 482.55 FF	1324.13 napoleons
England	£1050	1000 guineas

Table 2   Money prices after the discovery of a new gold mine

Price of Q in	Money of account	Currency
France	26 482.55 FF	1324.13 napoleons
England	£1575	1500 guineas

Table 3   Situation after the adjustment

Price of Q in	Money of account	Currency
France	33 103.19 FF	1655.16 napoleons
England	£1312.5	1250 guineas

Considering the par of exchange between the guinea and the napoleon (that is, 1.32 napoleon/guinea), the purchasing power of 1500 guineas in France is equal to the purchasing power of 1986.19 napoleons, that is, 1.5 Q instead of Q in England. The guineas are melted, exported from England to France, coined in France, and then spent in the purchase of goods, which are imported into England. This gives rise to a decrease in the gold price of Q in England and an increase in France. The process stops when gold has the same purchasing power in the two countries, therefore when the following equilibrium is reached.

With the PSFM, Hume provides a description of the stability of the balance of trade equilibrium, which states the quantity theory as a central issue. The double and simultaneous price and quantity adjustment process shows as groundless the fear that a country's balance of trade deficit could last indefinitely and result in the outflow of all its precious metals. Equally, it refutes the idea that banks may be an unavoidable device to provide the country with money. First, thanks to the adjustment of prices, there cannot be a lack in the quantity of money: any quantity of money satisfies the needs of trade. Second, given the international price level, and thanks to the balance of trade adjustments, the quantity of money adjusts itself to enable the circulation of commodities at this price level. Hume's PSFM raises the fear that the development of banks will cause a pernicious substitution of paper money for coined money – that is, "banish the precious metals" (Hume 1752 [1972]: 72) – and ultimately provoke bankruptcies and public discredit. In his *Essai sur la nature du commerce en général* (written in 1728–30 and published posthumously in 1755; English translation 1959, *Essay on the Nature of Trade in General*), Richard Cantillon had already expounded a similar idea.

In *An Inquiry into the Nature and Causes of the Wealth of Nations* (Smith 1776), published 24 years after Hume's *Essays*, at a time when the Scottish banking experiment had showed its efficiency, Adam Smith did not share Hume's quantity theory and hostility to bank money. Furthermore, although Smith did not really focus on the balance of trade, he nevertheless developed an "anti-mercantilist" view on this matter, distinct from Hume's, which is worth noting. According to Smith, when banks issue their notes by discounting real bills rather than fictitious ones, they substitute these notes for gold and silver coins without either causing prices to rise or incurring a liquidity risk. Moreover, they allow to economize a costly means of circulation, that is, to save unproductive circulating capital and to increase investment in real capital. This occurs through the export of precious metals that is synonymous with an increase in the wealth of the nation.

Thus, these eighteenth-century authors converged in criticizing the mercantilist view of the balance of trade surplus; however, they conceived not one but two approaches to the balance of trade. Gervaise and Smith did not describe gold outflow with a price mechanism, whereas Cantillon and Hume did. Gervaise, Cantillon and Hume thought that the development of bank credit would result in bank illiquidity, whereas Smith rejected this view.

Balance of Trade or Balance of Payments?

In the context of the Napoleonic Wars, British classical economists developed two opposing views of the international flows of precious metals: the balance of payments approach, which takes into account transfers and capital flows, and the balance of trade approach, which does not.

Balance of payments approach, exchange rate and gold points
The balance of payments approach was introduced by Henry Thornton in *An Enquiry into the Nature and Effects of the Paper Credit of Great Britain* (1802) to explain the flows of precious metal (gold and silver) linked to financial transfers when bank notes are convertible into legal tender coins and the high price of bullion when the convertibility is suspended. To this end, Thornton developed the gold points mechanism (hereafter GPM), previously envisioned by James Steuart in his *An Inquiry into the Principles of Political Oeconomy* (1767). According to Thornton's GPM, gold and silver fulfil the function of international means of payment by seeking "like [other commodities] that country in which it is the dearest" (Thornton 1802 [1991]: 145). This function is achieved through an arbitrage performed by merchants between the legal price of precious metals in England, their legal price in foreign countries, the merchants' international trading costs and the market exchange rate of the pound sterling.

The legal prices of gold and silver define the par of exchange, while the supply and demand for pound sterling and foreign currencies determine the market exchange rates. When the exchange rates fall below (rise above) the par of exchange by an amount that exceeds the international trading costs of precious metals, "merchants . . . yield a profit" (ibid.: 145) by exporting (importing) gold and silver. The levels of exchange rates at which the gain of arbitrage between exchange rate and par of exchange equals its trading cost are called gold and silver export and import points. The gold export (import) point is the level of the exchange rate of the pound sterling, below (above) the par of exchange, at which it is profitable to buy (sell) British bank deposits by selling (buying) foreign bank deposits, then to buy gold – either specie or bullion – in London (in the foreign country) by selling the bank deposits – either at the bank at the legal price or in the market – then to export (import) gold to (from) the foreign country, incurring the trading cost, and to sell it by buying foreign (British) bank deposits (either at the bank at the legal price or in the market) in the foreign country (in London).

For example, consider the currency market between London and Paris, in which the par of exchange rate is 25.22 FF/£ and the gold transfer cost is 3.85 per cent. The gold import point in London (gold export point from Paris) is 26.19 FF/£, and the gold export point from London (gold import point in Paris) is 24.28 FF/£. Let us assume an equilibrium, then an export of £105 capital from England to France, with no other changes (in particular there is no change in the purchasing powers of the napoleon and the guinea). This export of capital provokes an excess supply of £105 and an excess demand for 2648.10 FF on the currency market, so that the exchange rate of sterling falls. When it reaches 24.28 FF/£, arbitrageurs supply 2549.40 FF and demand £105. Thereafter: (1) the £105 are exchanged in a London bank for 100 guineas; (2) the guineas are melted down, leave England, and are then coined in France for 132.4 napoleons whose value is 2648 FF, making a gain of 98.6 FF which covers the trading costs of the gold.

In the GPM, international flows of gold and silver are an effect of fluctuations in exchange rates, that is, the prices at which bank deposits are exchanged between countries. Within the levels of the gold and silver export and import points, there is no trading of precious metals, that is, no supply or demand in the currency market of sterling and foreign currencies to finance exports or imports of gold and silver. In this case, in the currency market, the supply and demand of bank deposits concern the trading of goods, except gold and silver, and financial flows. It is only when the forces of supply and demand in the currency market cause the exchange rate to reach the gold and silver import or export point that supply and demand are dominated by the arbitrage transactions, that is, the import and export of gold and silver.

Banking and interest rates

In Thornton's view, a full understanding of the export and import of precious metals, and of their effect on domestic gold and silver markets and bank liquidity, must take into account all the factors that intervene in the functioning of the law of supply and demand in the currency market beyond the GPM. On the one side, the trade balance varies with the money prices of goods and the exchange rate. On the other side, it also depends on events such as bad harvests or the suspension of trade routes as a consequence of wars. Above all, the exchange rate does not vary solely with the trade in goods but also with financial flows, such as the supply of sterling in the currency market from the British government in order to buy foreign currency and subsidize its allies in the war against France. Capital flows also arise from speculation on future exchange rates and from arbitrage between spot and anticipated exchange rates or between interest rates at home and abroad. All these factors operate simultaneously and the exchange rate may be within the gold import and export points, without any export or import of precious metals, although there may be a disequilibrium in the balance of trade. In this case, the balance of payments is said to be at equilibrium. On the other hand, if the exchange rate reaches a gold point (either import or export), whether there is a trade balance equilibrium or disequilibrium (either surplus or deficit), gold will move. In this case, the balance of payments is said to be in disequilibrium; the entry of gold means a surplus and the exit of gold means a deficit.

In the event of a deficit in the balance of payments, the gold reserve of the Bank of England diminishes and the exchange rate stabilizes at the gold export point. However, if the Bank of England is authorized not to pay its notes and/or deposits in gold at a fixed price, the exchange rate will fall below the export point and the excess demand for gold resulting from international arbitrage will drive up the market price of gold. Ricardo and his Currency School followers challenged Thornton's approach to the balance of payments and exchange rates. Instead Robert Malthus (1811) and subsequent leading authors of the Banking School – Thomas Tooke in his *History of Prices* (1838–56) and *Inquiry into the Currency Principle* (1844), and John Fullarton in *Regulation of Currencies* (1844) – adopted it.

One main feature of the balance of payments approach is that while the liquidity of the Bank of England is dependent on the balance of payments, this does not imply that the value of bank money is involved. This contradicts Hume's approach. In 1802, the debate was centred on the liquidity of the money market in the context of a deficit in the balance of payments. Thornton's balance of payments analysis complemented his theory of the Bank of England's function as lender of last resort. Furthermore, the balance of payments approach opens the door to a rejection of the quantity theory. Thornton did not reject it, but the Banking School did. In fact, the Banking School referred to both Smith and Thornton. It took from Thornton the currency and money markets analysis. It accepted Smith's real bills doctrine, his refusal of the quantity theory and his distinction between credit and money, that is, between "capital" and "currency". "Capital" refers to the transactions between traders, whereas "currency" refers to the transactions between traders and consumers, that is, the expense of money income. In the former, credit is used as means of circulation, while in the latter money is used. If a change in the quantity of money income can modify the price level (see the thirteenth proposition in Tooke 1844), a change in the amount of bank deposits and/or bank notes does not. The quantity of credit is determined by demand; it depends on the price level.

The Banking School made two contributions to the balance of payments approach. First, it extended the distinction between "capital" and "currency" to the analysis of the trade balance. Here, only "capital" is concerned, "currency" is not; in international trade, only credit is at work. Now, the flux and reflux of credit involved in financing exports and imports are not synchronized, so that the trade balance is often in disequilibrium, alternating periods of surplus and deficit. Tooke's diagnosis is that, when facing a balance of payments deficit, the Bank of England must accept the decrease in its gold reserve without changing its issuing policy, the aim of which is the liquidity of the London money market. The second contribution concerns interest rate policy. According to the Banking School, in the event of a lasting balance of payments disequilibrium, the solution consists in attracting or repelling foreign capital by changing the level of the Bank of England discount rate. To sum up, the rule for the Bank of England is to let the gold reserve fluctuate freely between a minimum and a maximum (£5 million and £15 million, according to Tooke), and to raise (lower) the discount rate when the reserve reaches the lower (upper) limit. The role of the Bank of England in regulating the international capital flows through its discount policy was re-stated by George Joachim Goschen in *The Theory of Foreign Exchanges* (1861) and Walter Bagehot in *Lombard Street* (1873).

Balance of trade approach and exchange rate

Ricardo (1810) criticized Thornton and rehabilitated the balance of trade approach. According to him, the flows of precious metals, and the high price of bullion in the context of inconvertibility, are not the effects of exchange rate fluctuations but the cause. He rejected the causality between gold flows and exchange rate specific to the GPM and improved the PSFM. Relying on the quantity theory, he explained that the value of gold fluctuates with its quantity and that gold is exported and imported according to this value. The discovery of a gold mine, like the establishment of a bank issuing notes convertible into gold, lowers the value of gold and silver, in the form of either coins or bullion, whereas they remain unchanged abroad, thus making them "articles of exportation" (Ricardo 1810 [1951–62]: 54). This export causes the balance of trade deficit, and the symmetrical balance of trade surplus in the foreign country: "In return for the gold exported, commodities would be imported" (ibid.: 54). According to Ricardo, only an excessive quantity of money can cause a deficit: "the temptation to export money in exchange for goods, or what is termed an unfavourable balance of trade, never arises but from a redundant currency" (ibid.: 59). By diminishing the quantity of money, the export of gold and silver remedies this cause, then gives rise to a balance of trade equilibrium. On the other hand, when the bank notes are inconvertible, or are convertible into degraded coins, the adjustment of the quantity of money is impeded. Without describing any market process, Ricardo concludes that, in this case, the temptation to export money results in the high price of bullion. Then this high price, through arbitrage, causes the exchange rate to fall: "the fall in the exchange, or the unfavourable balance of trade, is stated [according to Thornton] to be the *cause* of the excess of the market price above the mint price of gold, but to me it appears to be the *effect* of such excess" (Ricardo, ibid.: 64, n. 1, original emphases).

Therefore, when arguing in favour of the bullionist thesis, Ricardo did not simply take up Hume's PFSM. He stressed further that the export of gold defines a balance of trade deficit: "an exportation of bullion, in exchange for commodities . . . is called (I think very incorrectly) an unfavourable balance of trade" (Ricardo 1810 [1951–62]: 64). It is not the means to pay the deficit, it causes the deficit: "The exportation of the coin is caused by its cheapness, and is not the effect, but the cause of an unfavourable balance" (ibid.: 61). In fact, the export of gold does not occur through the need to pay a deficit, it results from the choice to export redundant currency: "We should not import more goods than we export, unless we had a redundancy of currency, which it therefore suits us to make a part of our export" (ibid.: 61). The idea that the balance of payments deficit results exclusively from a choice concerning money – that is, the choice to export money – would be dominant among the following classical and the first neoclassical economists in Europe until the First World War, and would be taken up and reshaped by the monetarists at the end of the twentieth century.

In the nineteenth century, Ricardo's approach reached its peak with the 1844 reform of the Bank of England. According to the Ricardian approach, in order to preserve the liquidity of the Bank, it was crucial to enable the corrective effect of gold exports that are caused by the excess of currency and which diminish the Bank's reserves. The Bank must stop issuing notes by granting credit at the moment when gold exporters demand the reimbursement of notes in gold. These new credits would maintain the excess of currency, causing the continuous export of gold. By prohibiting the Bank of England from issuing notes through credit, Parliament showed its adherence to the Ricardian quantity theory and balance of trade approach.

The Failure of the Gold Standard

Why and how to manage the gold standard?
From the 1870s and until the publication of Cassel's paper, "The present situation in the foreign exchanges" (1916), the efficiency of a gold standard system was questioned. The demonetization of silver in Germany (1871) and the United States (1873–79) brought about a crisis in bimetallism as an international monetary system. It gave rise to world deflation (1873–96) as well as frequent exchange crises in those countries that previously used the silver standard. Indeed, after demonetization, silver reserves were no longer useful to stabilize exchange rates.

The main neoclassical quantity theorists agreed that the shift from bimetallism to the gold standard caused a contraction of the monetary base, a phenomenon of relative scarcity of the currency and consequently deflation. In addition to Ricardo, these quantity theorists also referred to John Stuart Mill's *Principles of Political Economy* (1848) to explain that in a gold standard regime, even if the monetary unit is defined by a fixed quantity of gold, its value is variable; it is determined by the law of supply and demand. The demand for money depends on the quantity of goods to be traded, and the supply of money depends on its quantity, its velocity of circulation and credit. Moreover, they emphasized that the value of money is not linked to the price of gold but to the level of prices of all goods in the economy that gold allows to circulate. The variations in the value of the money may be measured by the fluctuation of a price index. Aiming to stabilize the level of prices, they developed theories of managed money like the coinage of silver token money (for example, the "billon d'argent régulateur" of Léon Walras 1884), the adoption of a joint silver and gold bullion standard (Alfred Marshall's symmetallism 1887), Aneurin Williams's (1892a, 1892b) and Irving Fisher's (1911, 1913) proposals for compensated sterling or dollar plans, and finally the gold exchange standard first conceived by Alexander Martin Lindsay in 1876.

The gold standard was no longer conceived of as an automatic system leading to monetary stability. It was rather seen as a system that has to be managed by cooperation between states. Thus, in *Interest and Prices* (1898 [1965]), Knut Wicksell suggested the implementation of international and symmetrical coordinated adjustments of bank rates by central banks; Irving Fisher (1911, 1913) called for an international implementation of compensated monies – dollar, sterling, franc, and so on – and Ralph Hawtrey explained in *Good and Bad Trade* (1913) that a metallic currency is not sufficient to remove the inherent instability of credit and that a discretionary management of paper money issued by the central bank is necessary.

Colonialism and the gold exchange standard
After certain leading countries adopted the gold standard, they were led to manage and organize a transition towards the gold standard of the countries under their influence, which were on a silver standard. For example, Great Britain for India, and the United States for the Philippines, sought a system that would allow to stabilize the exchange rate between the countries that were on the gold standard and those that were not. The

gold exchange standard (hereafter GES) was the solution. The idea was first introduced in 1876 by Lindsay in a letter to the *Calcutta Englishman* and developed thereafter in two pamphlets, *Ricardo's Exchange Remedy* (1892) and *How to Fix Sterling Exchange* (1898). England did not follow Lindsay's proposal but the United States did. Lindsay influenced the Conant–Jenks–Kemmerer mission (1903–04) to the Philippines, which resulted in the establishment of the first explicit GES in history. Kemmerer's articles (1904, 1905) set out its principle: it is a system in which, without itself buying and selling gold, and thus without holding gold, a country stands ready to buy and sell a foreign currency which is freely and fully convertible into gold. So the GES enables the international economy to economize on gold with respect to the gold specie standard; it is a mechanism for providing a country with the gold standard without a gold currency. In the case of the Philippines, the government controlled the minting of a token money (the silver peso, defined by a gold weight worth US 50 cents) which constituted the legal tender, and a fund was created to hold remunerated bank deposits in US dollars. This fund – the Gold Standard Fund – was financed by a loan in dollars granted by certain New York banks and guaranteed by the American Treasury. The Gold Standard Fund intervened on the exchange market as soon as the dollar exchange rates of the peso departed from the official rate of an amount equal to the costs of transfer of gold between Manila and New York. When the exchange rate of the silver peso fell to the gold export point, the fund bought pesos and sold dollars; conversely, it bought dollars and sold silver pesos when the exchange rate of the silver peso reached the gold import point, therefore stabilizing the dollar exchange rate of the peso between the gold import and export points. There was no need for the circulation of gold coins in the Philippines, thanks to the Gold Standard Fund and to the definition of the legal tender.

The gold exchange standard allowed a country to fix the value of its legal tender in terms of gold, even if there was no circulation of gold currency and even if the legal tender was not convertible into gold but into assets in dollars. The process of buying and selling Philippines pesos by the Gold Standard Fund was explained in accordance with Ricardian theory. Buying (selling) silver pesos by the fund results in a reduction (increase) in the quantity of money circulating inside the Philippines. On the other hand, this innovation in the management of the gold standard by American economists tells us that they had perfect mastery of the gold points mechanism.

Purchasing power parity

The young Keynes also participated in this debate on the exchange rate. In *Indian Currency and Finance* (1913), he brought to the light the fact that British management of the exchange rate of the Indian rupee was a kind of de facto GES, and argued for the creation of a central bank for India. In the *Tract on Monetary Reform* (1923), he introduced the principle known later as the theory of interest rate parity, which explains that there is a trend of adjustment in the spot exchange rate between two currencies according to the interest rates in each country and to the forward exchange rates. For example, noting R_{FF} and $R_£$, the respective interest rates in France and England, and e and e^f, the spot and forward exchange rates, one franc invested in France has the same return, $1\ FF.\ (1 + R_{FF})$, as one franc exchanged against $\frac{1\ FF}{e}$ sterling, then invested in England with a return of $\frac{1\ FF}{e}.\ (1 + R_£)$ sterling, then exchanged against $\frac{1\ FF}{e}.\ (1 + R_£).\ e^f$ francs. The equilibrium without arbitrage opportunity is:

$$(1 + R_{FF}) = \frac{1}{e} . (1 + R_{\pounds}). e^{f} \Leftrightarrow \frac{1 + R_{FF}}{1 + R_{\pounds}} = \frac{e^{f}}{e} \Leftrightarrow \frac{R_{FF} - R_{\pounds}}{1 + R_{\pounds}} = \frac{e^{f} - e}{e}$$

The gap between the French and the British interest rates is compensated by the gap between the forward and the spot exchange rates. For example, with $R_{FF} = 4\%$, $R_{\pounds} = 2.5\%$, $e = 25FF/\pounds$ and $e^{f} = 25.365FF/\pounds$:

$$\frac{R_{FF} - R_{\pounds}}{1 + R_{\pounds}} \equiv \frac{4\% - 2.5\%}{1 + 2.5\%} = \frac{1.5\%}{1 + 2.5\%} = 1.46\% \text{ and } \frac{e^{f} - e}{e} \equiv \frac{25.365 \text{ FF/}\pounds - 25 \text{ FF/}\pounds}{25 \text{ FF/}\pounds} = 1.46\%$$

(3)

Another improvement in the understanding of the gold standard emerged from Cassel's 1916 article and the subsequent discussion by Frank William Taussig (1917), Jacob H. Hollander (1918) and Wicksell (1918). It took place during the First World War, which had obliged most of the belligerents to suspend the convertibility of their money into gold. The issue was the determination of the new parities between currencies, therefore the legal prices of gold in francs, pounds, dollars, and so on after the war. Cassel's answer was that the new exchange rates must allow the parity of purchasing power of monies on goods in different countries, and thus the same purchasing power of gold in these countries. Cassel's purchasing power parity theory improved the balance of trade approach. By contrast, Taussig placed the emphasis on the impact of international capital flows between two countries, and the distinction between traded and non-traded goods. He explained that the adjustment process depends on whether countries are on the gold standard or not. He showed that an export of capital from one country that is on the gold standard to another where the gold standard is suspended modifies the exchange rate between the two countries, the gold premium in the second country and the relative prices of goods in both countries. This contradicts Cassel's purchasing power parity theory. Taussig used the gold point mechanism, being convinced that it was a well-known and accepted adjustment process in the case of two countries on the gold standard. Hollander and Wicksell criticized him for thinking that gold could exit a country without being in excess, and insisted that Ricardo would never have accepted this idea. As Jacob Viner showed in *Canada's Balance of International Indebtedness* (1924), Taussig was reviving Thornton's balance of payments approach. John H. Williams, another of Taussig's students, wrote his 1920 thesis on the effect of European private capital flows on the exchange rate regime, price of gold, quantity and purchasing power of money in Argentina between 1880 and 1900. This study strongly influenced the young Raúl Prebisch (1901–1986), the future first director (1950) of the Economic Commission for Latin America and theorist of the centre–periphery asymmetry.

After the First World War, when the return of European countries to the gold standard became the major question, the purchasing power parity theory was central. In European countries, there was a consensus that this theory allowed the determination of either the degree of deflation necessary to restore the pre-war gold parity, or the degree of devaluation necessary to avoid deflation. The controversies arose concerning the choice between deflation and devaluation, the short- and long-term effects of devaluation and the consequences of German transfers for the payment of war reparations.

More consensual was the acceptance of the conclusions of the Genoa Conference in 1922, the leading figure of which was Ralph Hawtrey. The conference proposed the return to an international gold standard system, with the leading European countries adopting a gold bullion standard and the other countries a gold exchange standard. The aim was not only to provide weak countries with a mechanism to manage their exchange rates without holding a gold reserve, but also to avoid an international scarcity of gold that could provoke international deflation. The United States, which did not join the League of Nations, implemented the gold exchange standard in several Latin American countries with Kemmerer's missions. Great Britain adopted a gold bullion standard in 1925 at pre-war parity, but abandoned it in 1931; France adopted a gold bullion standard in 1928 with an 80 per cent devaluation of the franc, but devalued again in 1936, with the other countries of the 1933 Gold Bloc (Belgium, Luxembourg, the Netherlands, Italy, Poland and Switzerland); the United States adopted a gold bullion standard with a 40 per cent devaluation of the dollar in 1933–34. The restoration of a gold standard in the interwar period failed. Nevertheless, Harry Dexter White, a third student of Taussig, became the senior American official at the 1944 Bretton Woods conference, which established the post-Second World War gold exchange standard.

The Open Macroeconomic Approach

Price level, exchange rate, income and interest rate
The effects of the flexibility of exchange rates, incomes and interest rates on the balance of payments and on exchange rates were introduced progressively, first by developing the partial equilibrium analysis of the balance of trade, and finally by exposing a general Keynesian equilibrium approach to the balance of payments.

The idea that a fall (increase) in the domestic price level, or in the exchange rate, improves (deteriorates) the balance of trade has been questioned since the period between the two World Wars. C.F. Bickerdike (1920), Alfred Marshall (1923), and Joan Robinson (1937) stressed that, in addition to its equilibrating effects on the volumes of exports and imports, exchange rate variation has an opposite effect in so far as it modifies the price of any volume of imports; a fall in the exchange rate increases the volume of exports and decreases the volume of imports, but increases the price of imports. Therefore, the global effect depends on the respective strengths of both price and volume effects. Abba P. Lerner (1944) showed that the price effect dominates the volume effect if the sum, in absolute terms, of the price elasticity of the quantity of imports and the price elasticity of the quantity of exports is greater than one. These critical conditions, called Marshall–Lerner conditions, gave rise to an "elasticity pessimism" and mistrust of a flexible exchange rate regime. This mistrust was reinforced at the end of the 1960s, when it was found that the price effect occurs before the volume effect, initially worsening the balance of trade and subsequently improving it, resembling a J curve drawn in a plane whose horizontal axis measures time and whose vertical axis measures the balance of trade.

In 1929, a controversy about German war reparations arose, opposing John Maynard Keynes on the one hand and Bertil Gotthard Ohlin and Jacques Rueff on the other. Keynes thought that Germany could not succeed in paying the reparations because the real transfer of goods – the German balance of trade surplus – following and clearing the monetary payment of war reparations, would necessitate an intolerable deflation in Germany. According to Keynes, any shift in the balance of trade requires a shift in the international terms of exchange. Ohlin and Rueff objected that, if financed by taxes in Germany, the payment would be a transfer in "buying power" from Germany to foreign countries. Therefore, the purchasing power becomes greater than income in foreign countries, and lower in Germany. Then, the domestic aggregate demand for goods increases in foreign countries, giving rise to a deficit in their balance of trade, and, symmetrically, the domestic demand for goods decreases in Germany, bringing about a balance of trade surplus. In this case, the real transfer occurs without involving a variation in price levels in either Germany or foreign countries. The adjustment process is similar to that described by Gervaise and relies on a spending effect.

The spending effect is also at work in Roy Harrod's analysis (1933) of the income multiplier effect of a variation in exports. An increase in exports gives rise to an increase in production, then in income, then in spending, and then in the demand for domestic-produced and imported goods. The demand for domestic goods induces new production, income and spending, whereas the demand for imported goods does not; imports, like saving and taxes, are a leakage in the multiplier process. The multiplier approach to the balance of trade enriches Keynesian macroeconomics: exports are included in the multiplicand; the propensity to import is included in the multiplier. The main result is that, given an initial equilibrium of the market for goods and the balance of trade, a shift in exports will induce shifts in both income and imports, which last until the market for goods is again at equilibrium. However, except for very special conditions, the balance of trade is either in deficit or in surplus. Therefore, in order to equilibrate the balance of payments and maintain the exchange rate, a shift of the interest rate, either up or down, has to occur. This shift may have an undesirable effect on investment and therefore on income. In his 1930 *Treatise on Money*, Keynes had already emphasized the conflict between the domestic and external objectives of economic policy.

The critical elasticities condition and multiplier analysis were synthesized in the absorption approach in the 1950s, mainly by Sidney Alexander (1952, 1959), in which absorption is the term used to designate domestic aggregate demand, that is, consumption and investment. Focusing on the equilibrium condition of the market for goods – income plus imports equals absorption plus exports – Alexander underlined that the gap between income and absorption equals the gap between exports and imports, that is, the balance of trade surplus or deficit. He concluded that the reduction of any balance of trade disequilibrium lies in the reduction of a disequilibrium between income and absorption. For example, a deficit, that is, income lower than absorption, would be removed by an increase in income, or a decrease in absorption, or an increase in income higher than the increase in absorption. A devaluation of the exchange rate would help to achieve this goal not only because it reduces the quantity of imports and increases the quantity of exports, but also because the increase in exports brings about an increase in production and then in income. Moreover, devaluation gives rise to an increase in the prices of imported goods, which causes a fall in the real balance and therefore in absorption. In addition, it gives rise to higher interest rates that will also lower the absorption. On the contrary, any increase in income increases absorption. Finally, several effects are at work and explain why the Marshall–Lerner conditions are satisfied or not. The introduction of the real balance effect and the interest rate underlined the need for a more general model. Robert Mundell (1960, 1961, 1962, 1963), a monetarist, and Marcus

Fleming (1962), a Keynesian, provided this by incorporating the exchange market into the IS–LM synthesis.

Keynesian and monetarist perspectives

The Mundell–Fleming model is Keynesian; that is, the labour market is not at equilibrium, the price level is given and nominal and real wage rates are determined by the level of income. It adds the exchange market to the IS–LM three-market model – goods, assets and money. The slope of the exchange market equilibrium curve is positive, meaning that a rise in the interest rate, which induces an entry of capital, is necessary to compensate the effect on the exchange market of a rise in the import of goods caused by a rise in income. The higher the mobility of international capital, the flatter the slope of this fourth curve. The four markets are interconnected by Walras's law and determine three variables: income, interest rate and either the exchange rate, if exchange rates are flexible, or the balance of payments, if exchange rates are fixed. According to the degree of international capital mobility and the exchange rate regime, fixed or flexible, the efficiency of monetary or budgetary policy is higher or lower.

Expansive monetary policy gives rise to an increase in imports and a decrease in the interest rate, both causing an excess supply of domestic currency on the exchange market. This causes a fall in the exchange rate if exchange rates are flexible, and a shrinkage of the money supply if they are fixed. In the first case, the exports are favoured, bringing about an increase of income, therefore strengthening the efficiency of monetary policy. In the second case, there will be a reduction in the quantity of money, which lasts until this quantity reaches its initial level, thus negating the efficiency of monetary policy.

The effects of expansive budgetary policy are more contrasted. On the one hand, this policy gives rise to an increase in imports, thereby increasing the supply of domestic currency on the exchange market. On the other hand, it brings about an increase in the interest rate, which favours entries of capital, thereby increasing the demand for domestic currency on the exchange market. The global effect on the exchange market depends of the degree of international capital mobility. If this mobility is high, there will be an excess demand for domestic currency. In this case, fixed exchange rates will cause an increase in the quantity of money, strengthening the efficiency of budgetary policy, whereas flexible exchange rates will cause an increase in the exchange rate, which deteriorates the balance of trade, weakening the budgetary policy. Symmetrically opposite results occur if international capital mobility is low. Thus, the choice of the exchange rate regime depends on various macroeconomic factors, including the respective efficiency of monetary and budgetary policies in closed economies.

Elsewhere, the sustainability of the Bretton Woods system, a gold–dollar exchange standard with pegged but adjustable exchange rates was questioned. In his 1953 article "The case for flexible exchange rates", Milton Friedman argued that this system encourages speculation as soon as an adjustment of the exchange rate is envisaged; a speculation that is risk-free. Speculators sell the domestic currency and buy dollars, then wait for devaluation. If it occurs, they make a profit, but they do not make a loss in the opposite case. Furthermore, Rueff (1961) brought to light a weakness of the gold exchange standard that he had already understood in 1931, along with Hawtrey in 1932, Kemmerer in 1944 and Robert Triffin in 1960. A country which is on the gold bullion standard is not limited in the accumulation of its bank debt, so that it takes a liquidity risk when countries on the gold exchange standard ask for the payment of their claims in gold. In this case, it would be obliged to suspend convertibility, bringing about a fall in its exchange rate. Therefore it appears that countries that are on the gold exchange standard face an exchange risk.

The monetary approach to the balance of payments, developed later by monetarist authors – Mundell (1968, 1971), Harry G. Johnson (1972), Jacob A. Frenkel and Johnson (1976) – uses a simplified version of the Mundell–Fleming model. It does not include the assets market and hypothesizes both full employment and that price levels are determined, according to purchasing power parity, by international price levels and the exchange rate. As a consequence, income and interest rates cease to be adjustment variables. As a consequence, only two markets are interconnected by Walras's law: the market for money and the exchange market. They determine one variable: either the exchange rate, if exchange rates are flexible, or the balance of payments surplus or deficit, if exchange rates are fixed.

In a fixed exchange rate regime, an increase in the demand for money gives rise to a decrease in the demand for goods, thereby inducing a decrease in imports and an increase in exports which clear the market for goods, finally resulting in a balance of payments surplus. Therefore, in order to clear the exchange market, the supply of money increases, also clearing the market for money. A symmetrically opposite result occurs in the case of a fall in the demand for money. Referring to Ricardo, the authors concluded that the choice concerning money causes the balance of payments surplus or deficit, that is, that the balance of payments is a monetary phenomenon. In the case of flexible exchange rates, an increase in the demand for money results in a rise in the exchange rate, which clears the exchange market and brings about a fall in price levels. Therefore, the real supply of money increases, clearing the market for money. A fall in the exchange rate and the real supply of money occurs when the demand for money decreases.

Even if, in itself, the monetary approach to the balance of payments does not imply a choice between fixed and exchange rate regimes, the authors adhered to Friedman's arguments and favoured a flexible exchange rate. However, Rüdiger Dornbusch (1976) called this conclusion into question by reintroducing the assets market and showing that the adjustment process in the exchange rate does not occur gradually. The level of the domestic interest rate is connected with the foreign rate according to the law of interest rate parity: a negative (positive) differential between domestic and foreign interest rates is hedged by an anticipated exchange rate appreciation (depreciation). Now, in the case of a domestic excess demand for money, the prices of goods decrease slowly, whereas the prices of assets decrease quickly. Then the interest rate rises, bringing about a rise in current and anticipated exchange rates. However, the positive differential between domestic and foreign interest rates must be compensated for by depreciation of the exchange rate. This means that the rise in the current exchange rate has to be higher than the rise in its anticipated equilibrium level. The exchange rate overshoots.

JÉRÔME DE BOYER DES ROCHES AND REBECA GÓMEZ BETANCOURT

See also:

Bullionist and anti-bullionist schools (II); Gustav Cassel (I); Milton Friedman (I); David Hume (I); International trade (III); Edwin Walter Kemmerer (I); John Maynard Keynes (I); Keynesianism (II); Macroeconomics (III);

Mercantilism and the science of trade (II); Monetarism (II); Money and banking (III); Robert Alexander Mundell (I); Open economy macroeconomics (III); David Ricardo (I); Henry Thornton (I); Thomas Tooke (I).

References and further reading

Alexander, S.S. (1952), 'Effects of a devaluation on a trade balance', *International Monetary Fund Staff Papers*, **2** (April), 263–78.

Alexander, S.S. (1959), 'Effects of a devaluation: a simplified synthesis of elasticities and absorption approaches', *American Economic Review*, **49** (1), 22–42.

Bagehot, W. (1873), *Lombard Street, a Description of the Money Market*, reprinted 1915, ed. H. Withers, London: John Murray.

Bickerdike, C.F. (1920), 'The instability of foreign exchange', *Economic Journal*, **30** (March), 118–22.

Boyer des Roches, J. de (2003), *La pensée monétaire, histoire et analyse*, Paris: Les Solos.

Cantillon, R. (1755), *Essai sur la nature du commerce en general*, English trans. H. Higgs (ed. and trans.) (1959), *Essay on the Nature of Trade in General*, London: Frank Cass.

Cassel, G. (1916), 'The present situation in the foreign exchanges', *Economic Journal*, **26** (101), 62–5.

Cesarano, F. (2007), *Monetary Theory and Bretton Woods: The Construction of an International Monetary Order*, New York: Cambridge University Press.

Davanzati, B. (1588), *Lezione delle Monete e Notizia de' Cambj*, ed. S. Ricossa, Turin: La Torre d'avorio. Fògola.

Dornbusch, R. (1976), 'Exchange rate expectations and monetary policy', *Journal of International Economics*, **6** (3), 231–44.

Dornbusch, R. (1980), *Open Economy Macroeconomics*, New York: Harper & Row.

Fetter, F.W. (1965), *Development of British Monetary Orthodoxy, 1797–1875*, Cambridge, MA: Harvard University Press.

Fisher, I., with H.G. Brown (1911), *The Purchasing Power of Money. Its Determination and Relation to Credit, Interest and Crises*, New York: Macmillan.

Fisher, I., with H.G. Brown (1913), *The Purchasing Power of Money. Its Determination and Relation to Credit, Interest and Crises*, 2nd edn, New York, Macmillan, reprinted in I. Fisher (1997), *The Works of Irving Fisher*, ed. W. Barber assisted by R. Dimand and K. Foster, consulting ed. J. Tobin, London: Pickering & Chatto, vol. 4.

Fisher, I. (1912), 'A more stable gold standard', *Economic Journal*, **22** (December), 570–76.

Fisher, I. (1997), *The Works of Irving Fisher*, 14 vols, ed. W. Barber assisted by R. Dimand and K. Foster, consulting ed. J. Tobin, London: Pickering & Chatto.

Fleming, M. (1962), 'Domestic financial policies under fixed and under floating exchange rates', *International Monetary Fund Staff Papers*, **9** (November), 369–79.

Frenkel, J.A. and H.G. Johnson (1976), *The Monetary Approach to the Balance of Payments*, London: George Allen & Unwin.

Friedman, M. (1953), 'The case for flexible exchange rates', in M. Friedman, *Essays in Positive Economics*, Chicago, IL: Chicago University Press, pp. 157–203.

Fullarton, J. (1844), *Regulation of Currencies of the Bank of England*, 2nd edn 1845, reprinted 1969, New York: Kelley.

Gandolfo, G. (1987), *International Economics*, Berlin: Springer-Verlag.

Gervaise, I. (1720), *The System or Theory of the Trade of the World, Treating of the different Kinds of Value, of the Ballances of Trade, of Exchange, of Manufactures, of Companies, and Shewing the Pernicious Consequences of Credit, and that it Destroys the Purpose of National Trade*, reprinted 1954, ed. J. Viner, Baltimore, MD: Johns Hopkins Press.

Goschen, J. (1861), *The Theory of Foreign Exchanges*, London: Effingham Wilson, Royal Exchange.

Harrod, R.F. (1933), *International Economics*, Cambridge: Cambridge University Press.

Hawtrey, R.G. (1913), *Good and Bad Trade, an Inquiry into the Causes of Trade Fluctuations*, London: Constable.

Hegeland, H. (1951), *The Quantity Theory of Money*, Gothenburg: Elanders Boktryckeri, reprinted 1969, New York: A.M. Kelley.

Hollander, J.H. (1918), 'International trade under depreciated paper: a criticism', *Quarterly Journal of Economics*, **32** (4), 674–90.

Hume, D. (1752), *Political Discourses*, Edinburgh: A. Kincaid and A. Donaldson, republished with intro. by E. Rotwein (ed.) (1955), *David Hume Writings on Economics*, Edinburgh: T. Nelson and Sons and the University of Wisconsin Press, reprinted 1972, New York: Books for Libraries Press.

Johnson, H.G. (1972), *Further Essays in Monetary Economics*, London: Allen & Unwin.

Kemmerer, E.W. (1904), 'A gold standard for the Straits Settlements', *Political Science Quarterly*, **19** (4), 636–49.

Kemmerer, E.W. (1905), 'The establishment of the gold exchange standard in the Philippines', *Quarterly Journal of Economics*, **19** (4), 663–98.

Kemmerer, E.W. (1944), *Gold and the Gold Standard – The Story of Gold Money, Past, Present and Future*, New York, McGraw-Hill Book Company.

Keynes, J.M (1913), *Indian Currency and Finance*, reprinted 1971 in *The Collected Writings of John Maynard Keynes*, vol. 1, London: Macmillan and Cambridge University Press.

Keynes, J.M. (1923), *A Tract on Monetary Reform*, reprinted 1971 in *The Collected Writings of John Maynard Keynes*, vol. 4, London: Macmillan and Cambridge University Press.

Keynes, J.M. (1930), *A Treatise on Money*, reprinted 1971 in *The Collected Writings of John Maynard Keynes*, vols 5 and 6, London: Macmillan and Cambridge University Press.

Laidler, D. (1991), *The Golden Age of the Quantity Theory, The Development of Neoclassical Monetary Economics 1870–1914*, New York: Philip Allan.

Laidler, D. (1999), *Foundations of Monetary Economics*, Cheltenham, UK and Northampton, MA, USA: Edward Elgar.

Lerner, A.P. (1944), *The Economics of Control*, New York: Macmillan.

Lindsay, A.M. (1876), 2 letters to the Editor of the *Calcutta Statesman*: Currency reform, 11 September 1876 and Currency reform, 23 October, 1876, reprinted as Appendix A and B in A.M. Lindsay (1879), *A Gold Standard without a Gold Coinage in England and India, a Step Towards an International Monetary System (Reprinted with Additions from the Calcutta Review of October 1878)*, Edinburgh: David Douglas, pp. 53–72.

Lindsay, A.M. (1877), Letter to the Editor of the *Calcutta Statesman*: A plan for maintaining the rupee currency at a fixed value relatively to sterling, 24th April, 1877, reprinted as Appendix C in A.M. Lindsay (1879), *A Gold Standard without a Gold Coinage in England and India, a Step Towards an International Monetary System (Reprinted with Additions from the Calcutta Review of October 1878)*, Edinburgh: David Douglas, pp. 53–72.

Lindsay, A.M. (1879), *A Gold Standard without a Gold Coinage in England and India, a Step Towards an International Monetary System (Reprinted with Additions from the Calcutta Review of October 1878)*, Edinburgh: David Douglas.

Lindsay, A.M. (1892), *Ricardo's Exchange Remedy*, London: Effingham Wilson.

Lindsay, A.M. (1898), *How to Fix Sterling Exchange*, Calcutta: Thacker, Spink & Co.

Locke, J. (1691), *Some Considerations on the Consequences of the Lowering of Interest and the Raising of the Value of Money*, reprinted 1824 in *The Works of John Locke in 9 Volumes*, vol. 4, London: C. and J. Revington.

Malthus, R. (1811), 'Publications on the depreciation of paper currency', *Edinburgh Review*, **17** (34), art. X.

Marcuzzo, M.C. and A. Rosselli (1986), *Ricardo and the Gold Standard, The Foundations of the International Monetary Order*, revd edn 1991, London: Macmillan.

Marshall, A. (1887), 'Remedies for fluctuations of general prices', *Contemporary Review*, March, reprinted in A. Marshall (1923), *Money, Credit and Commerce*, London: Macmillan, pp. 188–211.

Marshall, A. (1923), *Money, Credit and Commerce*, London: Macmillan.

Mill, J.S. (1848), *Principles of Political Economy*, London: Longmans, Green and Co.

Montanari, G. (1683), *Della moneta, trattato mercantile*, in P. Custodi (ed.) (1804), *Scrittori classici italiani di economia politica: parte antica*, Milan: Nella Stamperia e Fonderia di G.G. Destefanis a S. Zeno.

Mundell, R.A. (1960), 'The monetary dynamics of international adjustment under fixed and flexible exchange rates', *Quarterly Journal of Economics*, **74** (May), 227–57.

Mundell, R. (1961), 'A theory of optimum currency areas', *American Economic Review*, **51** (4), 657–65.

Mundell, R.A. (1962), 'The appropriate use of monetary and fiscal policy for internal and external stability', *IMF Staff Papers*, **9** (1), 70–79.

Mundell, R. (1963), 'Capital mobility and stabilization policy under fixed and flexible exchange rates', *Canadian Journal of Economics and Political Science*, **29** (4), 475–85.

Mundell, R. (1968), *International Economics*, New York: Macmillan.

Mundell, R.A. (1971), *Monetary Theory: Inflation, Interest and Growth in the World Economy*, Pacific Palisades, CA: Goodyear.

O'Brien, D.P. (1994), *Foundations of Monetary Economics*, London: Pickering & Chatto.

Pigou, A.C. (ed.) (1925), *Memorials of Alfred Marshall*, London: Macmillan.

Ricardo, D. (1810), *The High Price of Bullion, A Proof of the Depreciation of Bank Notes*, reprinted in D. Ricardo (1951–62), *The Works and Correspondence of David Ricardo*, ed. P. Sraffa with the collaboration of M.H. Dobb, Cambridge: Cambridge University Press, vol. III.

Ricardo, D. (1951–62), *The Works and Correspondence of David Ricardo*, ed. P. Sraffa with the collaboration of M.H. Dobb, Cambridge: Cambridge University Press.

Rist, Ch. (1938), *Histoire des doctrines relatives au crédit et à la monnaie depuis John Law jusqu'à nos jours*, Paris: Sirey.

Robinson, J. (1937), 'The foreign exchanges' in J. Robinson, *Essays in the Theory of Employment*, London: Macmillan.

Rueff, J. (1961), 'Un danger pour l'Occident: le Gold-Exchange Standard', *Le Monde*, June, 27–9.

Schumpeter, J. (1954), *History of Economic Analysis*, London: Allen & Unwin.

Smith, A. (1776), *An Inquiry into the Nature and Causes of the Wealth of Nations*, reprinted 1976, Oxford: Oxford University Press.

Steuart, J. (1767), *An Inquiry into the Principles of Political Oeconomy*, reprinted 1966, Edinburgh: Oliver & Boyd.

Taussig, F.W. (1917), 'International trade under depreciated paper: a contribution to theory', *Quarterly Journal of Economics*, **31** (3), 380–403.

Taussig, F.W. (1918), 'International freights and prices', *Quarterly Journal of Economics*, **32** (2), 404–14.

Thornton, H. (1802), *An Enquiry into the Nature and Effects of the Paper Credit of Great Britain*, reprinted 1839, F. Hayek (ed.), London: George Allen & Unwin, reprinted 1991 New York: Augustus M. Kelley.

Tooke, T. (1838–56), *A History of Prices and of the State of the Circulation from 1792 to 1856*, 5 vols, reprinted 1972, New York: Johnson Reprint Corp.

Tooke, T. (1844), *An Inquiry into the Currency Principle*, reprinted 1996, London: Routledge.

Triffin, R. (1960), *Gold and the Dollar Crisis: The Future of Convertibility*, New Haven, CT: Yale University Press.

Viner, J. (1924), *Canada's Balance of International Indebtedness*, Philadelphia, PA: Porcupine Press.

Viner, J. (1937), *Studies in the Theory of International Trade*, London: Allen & Unwin.

Walras, L. (1884), 'Monnaie d'or avec billion régulateur', *Revue de Droit International*, 1 December.

Wicksell, K. (1898), *Geldzins und Güterpreise*, English trans. R.F. Khan (1936), *Interest and Prices*, London: Macmillan, reprinted 1965, New York: Kelley.

Wicksell, K. (1918), 'International freights and prices', *Quarterly Journal of Economics*, **32** (2), 404–10.

Williams, A. (1892a), 'A fixed value of bullion standard. A proposal for preventing general fluctuations of trade', *Economic Journal*, **2** (6), 280–89.

Williams, A. (1892b), 'A fixed valued of bullion standard', *Economic Journal*, **2** (8), 747–9.

Williams, J.H. (1920), *Argentine International Trade under Inconvertible Paper Money. 1880–1900*, Cambridge, MA: Harvard University Press.

Behavioural and cognitive economics

Introduction

Behavioural economics and cognitive economics are two research programmes that emerged during the 1980s and 1990s, respectively. The adjective "behavioural" is introduced to stress the relevance recognized by behavioural economists to actual human behaviours, in contrast to traditional economics, criticized for employing unrealistic assumptions as a starting point for its models. As a consequence, behavioural economics attributes a large relevance to psychology. The adjective "cognitive" is introduced to stress a particular attention for the results of cognitive psychology and social cognition.

Both behavioural and cognitive economics have their roots in the 1950s. The main references are Herbert Simon, Maurice Allais, and George Katona. They innovatively contributed to the methodological perspective, with empirical and experimental works. Their work was also important for its theoretical perspective, with new conceptual tools; particularly, the ideas of bounded rationality (Simon 1947), the inconsistency of choices (Allais 1953), and the relevance of perception, expectations and motivations (Katona 1951). In the period until the end of the 1970s, these conceptual tools were developed, generating the ideas of procedural rationality and satisficing (Simon 1976), and many studies on the nature and kinds of psychological bias, and on perception and expectations (Kahneman and Tversky 1979). During the 1980s, several convergences allowed a systematization of these contributions, and behavioural economics emerged as a new research programme (Earl 1988; Gilad and Kaish 1986; Gilad et al. 1984). Successively, during the 1990s, some economists began to use the expression "cognitive economics" (Bourgine and Walliser 1992; McCain 1992; North 1996; Paquet 1998; Rizzello 1997; Viale 1997). The label "cognitive economics" is often used in the literature as a synonymous expression for behavioural economics. Although there are important differences between to the concepts, there are also a few common points: some shared references in the literature, and in particular to Simon's work; the importance given to psychology; the criticism of neoclassical economics; and the use of the experimental method.

Behavioural Economics

Some relevant changes in the concept of behavioural economics through time makes its definition difficult. Analysing and comparing the work of categorization proposed by Sent (2004) and Tomer (2007), a substantial difference between two periods in the history of behavioural economics development emerges. The first period is named by Sent (2004) "old" behavioural economics. The main references are the four schools that, according to Earl (1988), made the emerging of old behavioural economics possible, namely, the Carnegie School (with Simon), research teams from the University of Michigan (with Katona), the University of Oxford, and the University of Stirling. The second period is named "new" behavioural economics. The main references are to the work of C.F. Camerer, L.C. Babcock, C. Eckel, G. Loewenstein, and M. Rabin. D. Kahneman and A. Tversky are the primary referents of a transitional period, linking old and new behavioural economics. Old behavioural economics is characterized by a radical opposition to neoclassical economics; with this contrast diminished in new behavioural economics. The reasons why the definition of behavioural economics has drastically changed through time should not be a surprise, given the evolution that the concept has gone through from the old to the new period.

Simon, as an old behavioural economist, defines as a pleonasm the expression "behavioural economics" since, from his perspective, thinking of an economics that ignores effective behaviours is impossible (Simon 1987). He strongly criticizes the core of neoclassical economics and in particular concepts such as efficiency, maximization, and equilibrium (Simon 1989).

The core ideas of the old behavioural economics seem to be changed by the new behavioural economics. According to Camerer and Loewenstein behavioural economics "does not imply a wholesale rejection of the neoclassical approach to economics based on utility maximization, equilibrium and efficiency. The neoclassical approach is useful because it provides economists with a theoretical framework that can be applied to almost any form of economic (and even non economic) behaviour" (Camerer and Lowenstein 2004: 3).

The difference between old and new behavioural economics is thus mainly as regards a criticism of neoclassical economics. Some differences in the interpretation of Simon's concept of rationality made this change possible. Old behavioural economics considers bounded and procedural rationality as related concepts that radically modify economics. New behavioural economics maintains only bounded rationality, isolated from procedural rationality and satisficing (Augier 2003). Bounded rationality is compatible with maximization, and, in this way, it allows to preserve much of the neoclassical method. At the same time, bounded rationality is considered sufficient for behavioural economics.

Cognitive Economics

Cognitive economics is based on an interdisciplinary analysis of problem-solving, decision-making, and change processes. In explaining economic behaviours, and the nature and evolution of institutions and economic organizations, it acknowledges a great relevance to psychology, but also to all cognitive sciences (Rizzello 2004).

A detailed explanation of the notion of cognitive economics is provided by Walliser and Topol (2007). The term economics is related to the coordination of the exchanges among heterogeneous agents. It is called "cognitive" because the subjects are characterized by their capability to process information. The analysis of economic microfoundations is based on cognitive psychology, but also philosophy of mind and neurobiology. Cognitive economics refuses the conceptual instrument of *homo oeconomicus*, considered the principal source of the separation between theory and economic reality. The refutation is a consequence of the acknowledgement of the relevant differences between real man and economic man. Real man shows limitations, with respect to neoclassical assumptions, both in his rationality and in his capabilities of acquiring and using information. As regards the limits of rationality, Simon is the main reference. He introduced the concepts of bounded rationality, procedural rationality, and satisficing (Simon 1947). Each of these concepts is a critique and an alternative to the full rationality assumption of traditional economics. The analysis of the limits in information acquisition follows a different path, but it arrives at an analogous conclusion, equally connoted in a cognitive key. The main reference is to Friedrich August Hayek (Hayek 1937, 1945,

1952). Indeed, Hayek's contribution plays a central role in the rise of cognitive perspective. In particular, Hayek's work is based on the analysis of the similarities between the way the human mind works and the evolution of institutions (Rizzello 1997). However, while cognitive characterization of Simon's work has always been recognized, in the case of Hayek, the characterization as a cognitive key of its contribution emerged only later. His role in behavioural economics has been acknowledged later but not unanimously.

The cognitive dimension of the new analytical instruments introduced by Simon and Hayek are referable, directly or indirectly, to the concept of cognitive feedback, borrowed from cybernetics, and it represents the environmental answer to the cognitive behaviours of a subject. The relevance acknowledged to environment shows how cognitive economics includes some central ideas coming from social psychology and social cognition; an example of this is the idea of knowledge as a social result.

As a consequence, cognitive agents belong to a specific context and their behaviours can be understood only by taking this context into account. Choices and, more generally, economic behaviours depend on the characteristics of the individual, but also on the surrounding environment. At the same time, agents can shape and influence their environment. Preferences are not considered stable, invariant, and revealed in a univocal way through the choices, but neither are they accidental or only conditioned by psychological mechanisms (Walliser and Topol 2007). They are conditioned also by perceptive mechanisms, the social and institutional framework, and past direct or indirect experience. Therefore, although preferences are individual, patterns among subjects can be found. These regularities are emphasized by exchange, meant not just as economic exchange but in a wider sense.

A consequence of this approach is that an understanding of the economic phenomena requires an analysis of the context. The context is structured from the presence of institutions, necessary for the interaction. Institutions are characterized by a continuous evolution. Consequently, cognitive economics shows a strong relation with institutionalism and evolutionary economics.

The Ambiguities between Behavioural and Cognitive Economics

Old behavioural economics and cognitive economics

Cognitive economics shares a lot of literature with old behavioural economics. Both recognize a great relevance to the contribution of Simon. Katona also shows similar approaches for cognitive economics, for the importance recognized in psychology, but also in terms of the context in which subjects operate. In his words, a fruitful economic analysis "consist of the empirical investigations of the behaviour of businessmen and consumers in one country in one time. Generalization about economic behaviour emerges gradually by comparing behaviour observed under different circumstances" (Katona 1980: 3). The currents from the universities of Oxford and Stirling – whose contributions are considered fundamental to the birth of old behavioural economics – include topics that are central also in cognitive economics, such as uncertainty, knowledge, and interdisciplinarity. In particular, G.L.S. Shackle (Oxford) is also included in the tradition of cognitive economics (McCain 1992). B. Loasby (Stirling), another referent mentioned by Earl in the reconstruction of old behavioural economics, contributed in a meaningful way to the development of cognitive economics, in particular on knowledge, institutions, and evolution, often referring also to Hayek. Cognitive economics recognizes also some more ancient roots in A. Marshall, C. Menger, J.R. Commons, T. Veblen, F. Knight, R. Coase, J.M. Keynes, J.A. Schumpeter, W.B. Reddeway, K. Boulding, R.R. Nelson and S.G. Winter, and Shackle. An analogous history is recognized for old behavioural economics.

New behavioural economics and cognitive economics
The work of Simon is the common denominator of both new behavioural and cognitive economics, but whether his work is either a shared contact or a source of ambiguity between the two disciplines is uncertain. As seen above, Simon's analysis of rationality has been interpreted in different ways by new behavioural economics and by cognitive economics. An element that can be added is the effect of the work of Kahneman and Tversky (1979). With regard to their way of connecting psychology and economics, Sent underlines that according to Camerer (1999) "this sort of psychology provided a way to model bounded rationality which is more like standard economics than the more radical departure that Simon had in mind" (Camerer 1999, cited in Sent 2004: 743). Generalizing, he writes that "much of behavioural economics consists of trying to incorporate this kind of psychology into economics" (Camerer 1999, cited in Sent 2004: 743). This interpretation, shared by many new behavioural economists, confirms the aim to maintain a reference to Simon, but also to the neoclassical system (Augier 2003). Simon appreciates the work of Kahneman and Tversky. The appreciation could surely be motivated by the pluralism supported and demonstrated by Simon in various circumstances (Augier 2003). Probably, the same prospect theory assumes a different meaning if frame or prospect are intended just as some fixed, predictable and objective series of possible outcomes and probabilities, or if they are intended, like Simon, as a frame wide enough to include objectives, definition of the situations, resources of calculation and processes that generate the subjective representation of the decisional problem by an agent (Simon 1986).

Concluding Remarks

Behavioural and cognitive economics share various elements, the most important of which is the work of Simon. The evolution of behavioural economics can explain the ambiguities between (new) behavioural and cognitive economics. "Old" behavioural economics seems to be more similar to cognitive than to "new" behavioural economics. Consequently, the analogy between behavioural and cognitive economics is better referred to the old behavioural economics than the new.

SALVATORE RIZZELLO AND ANNA SPADA

See also:

Maurice Allais (I); Experimental economics (III); Game theory (III); Friedrich August von Hayek (I); Herbert Alexander Simon (I); Uncertainty and information (III).

References and further reading
Allais, M. (1953), 'Le comportment de l'homme rationnel devant le risque: critique des postulats et axiomes de l'école americaine', *Econometrica*, **21**, 503–46

Augier, M. (2003), 'The making of a behavioural economist: Herbert A. Simon and the early revolution of bounded rationality', in S. Rizzello (ed.), *Cognitive Developments in Economics*, London: Routledge, pp. 133–57.
Bourgine, P. and B. Walliser (eds) (1992), *Economics and Cognitive Science*, Oxford: Pergamon Press.
Camerer, C.F. (1999), 'Behavioral economics', *CSWEP Newsletter*, Winter, accessed 15 June 2012 at www.cswep.org/camerer.html.
Camerer, C.F. and G. Loewenstein (2004), 'Behavioral economics: past, present, future', in C.F. Camerer, G. Loewenstein and M. Rabin (eds), *Advances in Behavioral Economics*, Princeton, NJ: Princeton University Press, pp. 3–51.
Earl, P.E. (ed.) (1988), *Behavioural Economics*, Aldershot, UK and Brookfield, VT, USA: Edward Elgar.
Egidi, M. and S. Rizzello (eds) (2003), *Cognitive Economics*, vols 1 and 2, Cheltenham, UK and Northampton, MA, USA: Edward Elgar.
Gilad, B. and S. Kaish (eds) (1986), *Handbook of Behavioral Economics*, vols A and B, London: JAI Press.
Gilad, B., S. Kaish and P.D. Loeb (1984), 'From economic behavior to behavioral economics: the behavioral uprising in economics', *Journal of Behavioral Economics*, **13** (1), 1–22.
Hayek, F.A. (1937), 'Economics and knowledge', *Economica*, **4** (13), 96–105.
Hayek, F.A. (1945), 'The use of knowledge in society', *American Economic Review*, **35** (4), 519–30.
Hayek, F.A. (1952), *The Sensory Order. An Inquiry into the Foundations of Theoretical Psychology*, London, Routledge & Kegan Paul.
Heukelom, F. (2014), *Behavioral Economics: A History*, Cambridge: Cambridge University Press.
Kahneman, D. and A. Tversky (1979), 'Prospect theory: an analysis of decision under risk', *Econometrica*, **47** (2), 263–91.
Kao, Y.-F. and K.V. Velupillai (2015), 'Behavioural economics: classical and modern', *European Journal of the History of Economic Thought*, **22** (2), 236–71.
Katona, G. (1951), *Psychological Analysis of Economic Behavior*, New York: McGraw-Hill.
Katona, G. (1980), *Essays on Behavioral Economics*, Ann Arbor, MI: University of Michigan Institute for Social Research.
Loasby, B.J. (2004), 'Hayek theory of the mind', in R. Koppl (ed.), *Advances in Austrian Economics*, vol. 7, *Evolutionary Psychology and Economic Theory*, Amsterdam: JAI, pp. 101–34.
McCain, R. (1992), *A Framework for Cognitive Economics*, Westport, CT: Praeger.
North, D.C. (1996), 'Economics and cognitive science', accessed 13 September 2011 at http://econwpa.repec.org/eps/eh/papers/9612/9612002.pdf.
Paquet, G. (1998), 'Evolutionary cognitive economics', *Information Economics and Policy*, **10** (3), 343–53.
Rizzello, S. (1997), *L'economia della mente*, Rome and Bari: Laterza, English trans. 1999, *The Economics of the Mind*, Cheltenham, UK and Northampton, MA, USA: Edward Elgar.
Rizzello, S. (2004), 'Knowledge as path-dependence process', *Journal of Bioeconomics*, **6** (3), 255–74.
Sent, E.-M. (2004), 'Behavioral economics: how psychology made its (limited) way back into economics', *History of Political Economy*, **36** (4), 735–60.
Simon, H.A. (1947), *Administrative Behavior*, New York: Macmillan.
Simon, H.A. (1976), 'From substantive to procedural rationality', in S. Latsis (ed.), *Method and Appraisal in Economics*, Cambridge: Cambridge University Press, pp. 129–48.
Simon, H.A. (1986), 'Rationality in psychology and economics', *Journal of Business*, **59** (4), 209–24.
Simon, H.A. (1987), 'Behavioral economics', in J. Eatwell, M. Milgate and P. Newman (eds), *The New Palgrave: A Dictionary of Economics*, vol. 1, London: Macmillan, pp. 221–5.
Simon, H.A. (1989), 'The state of economic science', in W. Sichel (ed.), *The State of Economic Science: Views of Six Nobel Laureates*, Cambridge, MA: W.E. Upjohn Institute for Employment Research.
Tomer, J.F. (2007), 'What is behavioral economics?', *Journal of Socio-Economics*, **36** (3), 463–79.
Viale, R. (ed.) (1997), *Cognitive Economics*, Milan: La Rosa Editrice.
Walliser, B. (2008), *Cognitive Economics*, Berlin and Heidelberg: Springer-Verlag.
Walliser, B. and R. Topol (2007), 'Introduction', in R. Topol and B. Walliser, *Cognitive Economics: New Trends*, Amsterdam: Elsevier, pp. 1–12.

Business cycles and growth

For a long time business cycles and economic growth were considered to be strongly interconnected. During the interwar period, pioneering work in macroeconomics, by leading economists, offered deep theoretical reflections defining the fundamental purposes of the field, and elaborating different analytical frameworks and methodologies.

After the Second World War, when macroeconomics began increasingly to exploit mathematical tools, the analysis of growth cycles dynamics appeared a real and a mathematical challenge. The difficulty faced by economists in their various attempts to investigate the growth cycles interactions led to business cycles and growth theories being treated as independent research fields. On the one hand, business cycles theories tried to explain de-trended data movements; on the other hand, growth theory analysed the existence and uniqueness of a stable, long-run equilibrium. This dichotomy was strengthened by the then dominant monetary view, which insisted that monetary policy mattered only in the short run, and had no impact in the long run. However, it would be misleading to assume that all economists believed that business cycles and growth were independent phenomena.

As pointed out by Solow, this dichotomy is not founded on any serious theoretical argument but rather is the logical consequence of the discipline's shortcomings which should be challenged: "The problem of combining long-run and short-run macroeconomics has still not been solved" (Solow 1988: 310). The great majority of economists consider this (artificial) division not as a scientific choice but rather as a pedagogical dichotomy. While growth theory focuses on productivity-enhancing mechanisms and defines the "natural" path of aggregate activity, short-run analysis identifies the origins of output fluctuations around this path. Macroeconomists have always tried to straddle this artificial frontier and there is an extensive literature based on the numerous different attempts to bridge between those short-run and long-run dynamics.

Although this entry does not pretend to provide an exhaustive survey of the literature, it offers a comprehensive overview of the various approaches which were developed at different times, in order to provide a joint growth-cycles analysis. We identify the pioneering economists and summarize the more recent literature, focusing on those business cycles models that are based on the distinction between shocks and propagation. In what follows, we identify particular episodes in the development of macroeconomics when there was a convergence between analytical growth frameworks and business cycles analysis. These episodes are delimited mainly by Harrod's (1939) seminal essay on dynamics, Brock and Mirman's (1972) stochastic growth model, and the revival in the mid-1980s of growth theories, which opened new perspectives for growth-cycles analysis (see Stadler 1990).

The entry is organized as follows. First, we discuss theories, such as Schumpeter's theory of economic development in which cycle and trend are strongly intertwined. Next, we deal with the fundamental questions and methodological debates addressed by the pioneering authors in the field. We present Harrod's project and the reactions to his 1939 seminal paper, which strongly influenced the development of macroeconomics along two independent paths. The two types of instability in his model were at the origin of two types of research programmes: those involving economists who identified Harrod's "line of steady advance" as a growth path and saw its stabilization as a way to explain regular growth as it was observed after the Second World War, and those who saw the instability principle as an opportunity to develop a business cycles approach which contained instability within reasonable boundaries. The contributions of Kalecki, Kaldor and Goodwin and their contemporaries are discussed up to the emergence of post-Keynesian contributions.

In the second part of the entry, we analyse the theories that emerged from the modern growth theory starting with Brock and Mirman's (1972) seminal contribution. Their stochastic approach to growth combined with Lucas's (1972) counter-revolutionary approach to business cycles as equilibrium phenomena led to the emergence of real business cycles (RBC) models which eliminated the dichotomy between growth and cycles. We also discuss the potential of endogenous growth models to capture the impact of short-run fluctuations on (long-run) growth. The entry concludes with some comments on recent research agendas promoted by alternative approaches to the issue under consideration.

Growth and Cycles: From Schumpeter to Goodwin

Innovations as the impulse of growth and business cycles

> No problem in economics is more difficult than the one posed by the almost universal evidence that while capitalist economies grow, they do not expand steadily. . . .There is no obvious solution to this question, and I know of only one economist, Schumpeter, who has ever really constructed a unified theory of growth and cycle. (Goodwin 1953: 89)

From the start, Schumpeter emphasized the wave-like movement of capitalist development, and the important role of innovation (Hagemann 2003). Like Werner Sombart, he was strongly influenced by Karl Marx's analysis of the long-run development of capitalist economies and his emphasis on capital accumulation and technical progress. In Marx's view, crises and cycles were the very essence of the evolution of capitalist economies. For Schumpeter, studying business cycles "means neither more nor less than analyzing the economic process of the capitalist era" (Schumpeter 1939, vol. 1: v). Schumpeter considered capitalist development as a succession of prosperity and depression. Economic development in the sense of Schumpeter is endogenous and discontinuous, and it is the task of dynamic theory to explain the origin and effects of these processes which essentially are disturbances of the static equilibrium of the economy.

It is well known that innovations, pioneering entrepreneurs, and bank credit are the three main elements of Schumpeter's *Theory of Economic Development* in which, as Schumpeter (1911 [1934]: xiii) pointed out in his foreword to the fourth German edition, "any single page is dedicated to the problem of the business cycle". The pioneering entrepreneur is the agent of creative destruction in carrying out new combinations that include the five cases of introduction of new methods of production, new products, the opening of new markets, new sources of supply, and new forms of organization. The interaction between long-run growth and cyclical fluctuations, and particularly the role played by innovations, were the focus of Schumpeter's attention. However, in 1911 only the classical or Juglar cycle was known to him, the Kitchin, Kondratieff and Kuznets cycles not being discovered until the 1920s. This stimulated Schumpeter to elaborate his basic idea of the superposition of different waves. Thus, in *Business Cycles* he develops a three-cycle scheme in which Kondratieff long waves are combined with the classical Juglar and the shorter Kitchin cycles (see the famous diagram in Schumpeter 1939, vol. 1: 213). Schumpeter based his approach on a mono-causality argument in which both growth and business cycles result from innovation. Not only do innovations constitute the decisive impulse of cyclical fluctuations, the period of their implementation also determines the different lengths of the cycles. Thus, major innovations or fundamental technological breakthroughs cause Kondratieff long waves or growth cycles whereas medium and minor innovations lead respectively to Juglar and Kitchin cycles. According to Schumpeter (1939, vol. 1: 168), the Industrial Revolution "consisted of a cluster of cycles of various span that were superimposed on each other". Innovations tend not only to cluster but also lead frequently to a sequence of cycles which are not fully independent of each other. Railroadization, electrification, motorization (and we could add computerization) occur in steps and sequences. Thus for Schumpeter, business cycles and growth are inseparably linked. It can be excluded that Schumpeter would have become an adherent of the later neoclassical steady-state growth model in which the business-cycle problem was assumed away.

Harrod's project
Harrod's book *The Trade Cycle. An Essay* (1936) and his article "An essay on dynamic theory" (1939) set the agenda for research into formal business cycle and growth models in the 1950s. The point of departure was the possibility of reconciling the capacity and demand effects of investment. In a model with a fixed capital–output ratio C and a fixed saving–output ratio s, as long as a unit of capital producing $1/C$ unit of output (capacity effect of investment) generates s/C units of net savings (demand effect of investment), capital and output will grow at the same exponential rate s/C, which rate Harrod describes as the "warranted" rate of growth.

This raised two major issues. The first concerned the stability properties of that steady growth path, and the adjustment mechanism between the actual and warranted growth rates. Harrod's point was that forces will systematically drive the economy away from a steady growth path: any departure of the actual rate of growth from its warranted value will be self-aggravating rather than self-defeating so that cumulative growth at a constant warranted rate is unlikely. An illustration provided by Sen (1970) is of help here; it is a typically knife-edge interpretation which Harrod disliked (Harrod 1973). We treat the case of a saving rate of 20 per cent and a capital–output ratio of 2 so that the warranted growth rate is 10 per cent. Then let us suppose that current output is 90 so that a 10 per cent rate of growth will result in an output of 100, taking the growth rate as a proportion of the final output. How the actual rate behaves depends on the expectations that rule the investment behaviour. If entrepreneurs expect an output of 100 they will invest 20 units in the effort to create capacity for an additional 10 units of demand. This investment of 20 units will generate through the multiplier of 5 (implicit in a savings coefficient of 20 per cent) a demand level of 100, so that the expectation will be fulfilled. However, if they expect too much, say 101 units of demand, then investment will have 22 units to create capacity for 11 additional units to be produced, and through the multiplier the demand generated will be 110 so that investors will feel that they expected too little. The demand effect of investment will dominate the capacity effect. Similarly, if investors expect too little and anticipate 99 units of demand, investment will equal 18 units and actual demand will be 90 units, making the capacity effect stronger than the demand effect.

Harrod's view of the trade cycle was based on the argument that an actual movement away from the "warranted growth path" could be checked because the warranted rate would "chase" the actual rate upwards or downwards: "If the former eventually overtakes the latter a new equilibrium is achieved and if the former goes beyond the latter forces are generated setting up a reverse movement" (Harrod 2003: 1198–9). The way that expectations and income distribution were supposed to change during the adjustment process was essential to explaining the behaviour of the warranted rate of growth, and ultimately proposing a cycle theory endogenously generated along an endogenous trend (see Assous et al. 2014; Bruno and Dal Pont Legrand 2014). Tinbergen and Marschak were among the first to point out the difficulties inherent in modelling Harrod's theory of cyclical growth. In his review of *The Trade Cycle*, Tinbergen (1937) made it clear that Harrod's mathematical formulation only applied to exponential growth.

The second issue concerned the adjustment process between the warranted rate (assumed to remain equal to the actual growth rate) and the natural rate. Harrod assumed that the natural rate of growth is given by the maximum rate permitted by the rate of growth of the population, technology, and labour force participation. Thus, in a model with no technical progress and with a constant participation rate, the "natural" rate of growth is the maximum sustainable rate of growth in the long run measured as the rate of growth of the labour force. If the warranted rate of growth and the natural rate of growth are equal, the economy will exhibit steady growth at full employment. However, any change in the parameters which affect the equality among the warranted and natural rates results in a divergence in the capital and labour growth rates. For example, if the warranted rate exceeds the natural rate, redundant capital accumulates until the economy reaches equilibrium. On the other hand, if the warranted rate falls short of the natural rate, this will trigger a cumulative growth in the proportion of unemployment.

In focusing on the process of adjustment between the warranted (assumed to remain permanently equal to the actual growth rate) and the natural growth rates, neoclassical economists overlooked the issue of cyclical growth. This led to the out-of-equilibrium interpretation of observed growth being abandoned in favour of an equilibrium interpretation, and the widespread view that economic dynamics, rather than being essentially endogenously driven, was the response to continuous external forces. These developments led to the employment of two critical assumptions: (1) the development of growth models based on the assumptions of permanent full employment and equality of savings and investment with the result that the possibility of fluctuations vanished, and (2) the possibility of a steady and continuous increase in productivity.

Solow was aware that the neoclassical growth model had shunted aside all the rigidities and general (short-run) coordination problems likely to generate cyclical growth. In 1956, he expressed an interest in such questions, saying that "It is not my contention that these problems don't exist, nor that they are of no significance in the long run" (Solow 1956: 91; see also Hagemann 2009: 85). Later, he repeatedly tried to find a way to deal with Harrod's instability problem related to adjustment of the actual and warranted growth rates (Assous 2015). He concentrated mainly on finding a way to define a robust investment function capable of explaining the failed expectations of entrepreneurs who deviated from the equilibrium path. With no adequate fact-based treatment of representing expectations, and no solution to the sensitive problem of valuing durable capital in the context of an uncertain future, Solow doubted that a satisfactory solution was possible (Solow 2012). In his opinion, the dichotomy between cycles and growth analysis was no more than the unsatisfactory outcome of the difficulties faced by economists when dealing with growth and cycles simultaneously.

Kalecki and the problem of trend and cycle

Unlike Harrod, Kalecki did not believe that cycles arise along an endogenous trend. In order for growth to be self-perpetuating, investment, and therefore gross capital stock have to grow exponentially, at the same rate. This requires that via profits, gross investment must generate a larger gross investment in the next period. Kalecki's point was that this condition was unlikely to be met. First, a part of savings accrues outside enterprises, while firms are not in a position to indebt themselves sufficiently. Second, a capacity is created which depresses investment. Its strength will depend on the prevailing technique; a high capital coefficient providing relatively little capacity for a given investment, will favour the automatic increased growth, while a low capital-coefficient will have the reverse effect.

In addition, Kalecki's belief in the absence of an endogenous trend was connected to the issue of cycles. Frisch and Holme (1935) show that Kalecki's initial business cycle model could produce damped cycles but no trend or alternatively trend but no cycles. In discarding the trend solution, Kalecki could explain growth only as due to an exogenous stimulus which was able to propose an explanation for why cycles do not fade away. More generally, this approach was more relevant to an explanation of capitalist contradictions: "I believe that the antinomy of the capitalist system is in fact more far-reaching: the system cannot break the impasse of fluctuations around a static position unless economic growth is generated by the impact of semi-exogenous factors such as the effect of innovation upon investment" (Kalecki 1962: 134).

Kalecki considered that the main shocks were innovations. The effect of innovations on investment rests on the innovator's expectation of extraordinary profits, an expectation which is created not by the actual process of the cycle but is part of the circular system of demand and investment as extraneous factors which is based not on earnings experience but on the anticipation of something quite new. The trend-generating effect depends essentially on the assumption of a continuous stream of innovations: in other words, the stimulus has to be repeated again and again, so that the negative effect of creation of new capacity is compensated.

Kaldor's non-linear trade cycle theory

In 1940, Kaldor presented an ingenious graphical presentation of his business cycle theory based on Harrod's principle of instability. By means of S-shaped investment and saving functions, showing that if the investment curve intersects the saving curve three times, the stationary equilibrium might become unstable while, for a wide range of values of capital stock, the economy will stabilize to either a low or a high equilibrium. These considerations – under the assumption that the speed of quantity adjustment in the goods market is high, while real capital stock moves slowly – result in a self-sustained output and capital stock cycle model in which the economy moves from a stable, to an unstable, to a stable equilibrium. The model, though sufficient to obtain endogenous cycles around a static position does not address the issue of growth-cycle equilibrium values of income and capital. It produced local instability but only in a trendless economy. As Asada (2009) noted, in the 1950s Yasui and Morishima attempted to extend Kaldor's model through a mathematical formulation that would produce cyclical growth. However, in assuming that growth and cycles were linearly superimposed, their attempts were far from challenging Harrod's view that trend and cycle were indissolubly mixed.

In the 1950s, Goodwin engaged in efforts along similar lines to model Harrod's insights. With the help of his French Harvard colleague, Philippe Le Corbeiller, he attempted to determine how to exploit the Van der Pol–Raleigh limit-cycle theory of dynamics. In his 1951 pioneering contribution, he showed that this could be achieved within a non-linear formulation of the accelerator interacting with a stabilizing multiplier. However, like his Japanese contemporaries, Goodwin was unable to integrate both growth and cycles, assigning to trend only the role of a benchmark – a role that remained largely unexplained. It was not until the late 1960s that he succeeded in drafting a new approach.

Goodwin's growth cycle
Eschewing any reference to shocks as a way of modelling fluctuating growth, Goodwin carved out his own path towards an integration of Harrod and Marx's insights. In Goodwin's (1967) growth cycle, economic fluctuations in output, unemployment and wages are generated endogenously in a model that combines elements of Harrod's growth model and the Phillips curve. The key equations in the Goodwin model are the Lotka–Volterra equations for the rate of growth of the share of wages in output, and of capital. Goodwin adopts the Lotka–Volterra equations which are used in biology in order to model predator–prey interaction, to explain the dynamical contradictions of capitalism in a Marx–Kaleckian spirit. Due to innovations and productivity growth any upswing can carry the economy beyond the previous peak. Goodwin (1987) agrees with Schumpeter that economic growth is therefore likely to occur in waves. Goodwin's model has been discussed intensively and elaborated over the last decades (see, for example, Flaschel 2009: ch. 4). An important characteristic of the Goodwin model is that it can create economic fluctuations endogenously without relying on exogenous shocks – whether monetary or technological.

Modern post-Keynesian developments: growth, instability and cycles
A substantial literature emerged in the early 1980s on the interplay between economic growth and income distribution in economies in which failures of effective demand can have permanent effects on the utilization of productive resources. The model developed by Rowthorn (1981), Dutt (1984) and Taylor (1985) is characterized by the presence of an independent investment function. Assuming low sensitivity of accumulation to variations in utilization, with a given or changing mark-up, their models were able to address growth-cycles issues simultaneously. However, others – like Skott (2010) – argued that the integration of cycles and growth analyses was better explored by incorporating an Harrodian investment function likely to generate an unstable warranted growth path. An Harrodian investment function could be compatible with multiple steady growth solutions (some stable), allowing for new foundations for endogenous cycles along an increasing trend. For instance, Skott (2010) shows that destabilizing Harrodian effects

with stabilizing Marxian mechanisms can produce a combined understanding of growth and cycles.

New Classical Approach to Growth-Cycles Interaction(s)

Despite the contributions we just presented, up to the early 1970s, the great majority of economists had disregarded business cycles as a major issue (see Bronfenbrenner 1969).

Business cycles analysis resurfaced with the successive "oil shocks" and the inability of the then dominant approaches (namely, the Keynesian, Monetarist, and neoclassical synthesis views) to propose an efficient economic policy. The re-emergence was triggered by Lucas (1972), but the important point in our context is that this work was the starting point for a new macroeconomic approach which deeply affected the way economists analyse the interaction of business and growth cycles.

Introducing rational expectations in the sense of Muth (1961), Lucas developed an equilibrium business cycles theory in which the trend – defined as the optimum equilibrium position – is given, and where cycles – interpreted as temporary deviations from the trend – are always (non-optimal but) equilibrium positions. Although this model does not include any growth-cycles interactions, it was a first step in a new approach. In this model, business cycles disturbances are minimized and the necessity for stabilization policies is strongly questioned (see Dal Pont Legrand and Hagemann 2010). Indeed, stabilization policies are useless precisely because fluctuations are determined independently of the trend. Although Lucas's methodology came to dominate macroeconomics, his business cycles theory was heavily attacked for two main reasons. First, it was difficult to defend the idea that fluctuations could only be caused by (unexpected) monetary shocks, and second, the dynamics of his model could not mimic (or only on an ad hoc hypothesis) the persistence effect of shocks observed at that time.

Part of the solution to critiques addressed to Lucas's business cycles theory can be found in two papers by Lucas and Rapping (1969) and Brock and Mirman (1972). The former proposed an intertemporal substitution mechanism which acts as a propagation mechanism for shocks compatible with an equilibrium approach with the result that a single shock could initiate recurrent fluctuations, and those fluctuations would be the outcome of the optimal reactions of agents. Brock and Mirman (1972) introduced an intertemporal substitution mechanism but their contribution consisted mainly of providing the first optimal growth model for an economy with stochastic productivity shocks. They proposed a unified framework for growth and cycles (which we describe as shocks and propagation) dynamics, which was the first step towards their joint analysis.

Real business cycles: cycles interpreted as random walk
Real business cycles models are usually considered the second generation of models within the New Classical School founded by Lucas. These models were proposed to address some of the critiques of Lucas's model, and in a criticism of Lucas's business cycles theory made by Tobin (1980: 798), we can find an exact description of these future RBC models. Real business cycles models were presented as directly inspired by Frisch (1933) and Schumpeter – Frisch because RBC theory distinguishes between impulse and propagation mechanisms, and Schumpeter because it considers innovations (here

productivity shifts) as the main driving force of business cycles. However, for historians of economic thought, the links between these two literatures are rather tenuous.

Real business cycles models – the first of which was proposed by Kydland and Prescott (1982) – were an attempt to avoid the criticisms levelled at Lucas's model – mainly its inability to explain (and to reproduce) the persistence of shocks, and the exclusive reliance on the occurrence of regular monetary shocks (a somewhat doubtful hypothesis) in order to depict (recurrent) fluctuations. Real business cycles were built on optimal growth models in which fluctuations are driven by productivity shocks – either temporary or permanent– which have a direct impact on fully informed and rational agents' (optimal) decisions. Consequently, business cycles are expressed not only in equilibrium terms but are also the direct outcome of fully rational economic and perfectly informed agents. That is, they are also optimal positions. So the trend became both an equilibrium and optimal position, and cycles were interpreted as fluctuations of the trend. This can be considered as a sterilized version of business cycles, that is, a conception of cycles that is unrelated to the idea of disequilibrium or instability, in other words a totally new perspective on fluctuations.

Supported by Nelson and Plosser (1982), RBC models interpreted fluctuations of the level of productivity as a random walk (see Mata and Louçã 2009 for a history of "residual" interpretation). The main criticisms of these models were (1) the exclusive reliance of RBC models on technological shocks, a hypothesis which implied that recessions should be seen as periods of technological regress, which is a questionable interpretation, (2) their neglect of the role played by monetary and financial factors, and, more generally, that demand-side shocks could not, by definition, generate any consequences for long-run dynamics, and (3) their totally unrealistic reliance on the elasticity of substitution in order to generate fluctuations. These affected the credibility of their analysis of the persistence of fluctuations (for detailed critiques, see, for example, Summers 1986; Hoover 1988; Stadler 1994). The two generations of models (Lucas's and RBC) reveal a clear inclination among economists at that time to progressively exclude any sort of instability from the core of the model. Nevertheless, as in the interwar period, business cycles were analysed by a shock/propagation representation, and the notion of (endogenous) instability progressively disappeared to be substituted by a deeper analysis of shocks.

Thus, there is a sort of paradox in the RBC approach: while it relies exclusively on technological progress in order to generate fluctuations, it still considers it to be an exogenous factor. In addition, growth is also exogenous. The consequence of this is that despite growth and cycles being modelled jointly, this framework fails to explain business cycles and especially growth-cycles interactions. At best RBC models can only mimic observed fluctuations, a position for which RBC economists take credit but which remains controversial.

From business cycles to growth

In the mid-1980s new growth theory (NGT) emerged with Romer (1986) and Lucas (1988) as its main proponents. What is less well known is that this research contributed to the debate on business cycles and growth interactions, and, as a corollary, to arguments about the necessity (or not) of stabilization policy. The initial project of NGT was to endogenize technical progress and to take into account different elements (institutions, education, and innovation) that influence growth. This objective was supported by the existence of a substantial empirical and theoretical literature which documented the endogenous nature of technical progress. It should be noted that previous contributions had emphasized the importance of some of the mechanisms inherent in those models (for example, the well-known contributions by Arrow 1962 about learning by doing, and Eltis 1971 on the importance of research and development expenditures for economic growth), but the novelty certainly lay in the tractability of those models and in their capacity to be tested econometrically.

Because NGT models build on endogenous growth mechanisms, long-run trends are not predetermined, a characteristic which confers on them only a "relative stability" (Hénin 1994). More precisely, shocks affecting such a dynamics exhibit a – positive or negative – persistence. Indeed, Stadler (1990) proved that endogenous technical change acts as a strong propagation mechanism, whatever the nature (demand or supply) of the shocks: "real and monetary business cycles models with endogenous technology differ from the conventional models" (Stadler 1990: 764). Moreover, growth dynamics is characterized in these models by a kind of hysteresis phenomenon: an economy consecutively affected by two shocks, identical with the exception of the sign of their persistence, will not return to its initial rate of growth. With the inclusion of a learning by doing production function, the model exhibits a positive persistence of the shocks while models based on a learning or doing mechanism, claimed to be inspired by Schumpeter and dealing explicitly with the process of input reallocation between production and increased productivity (sort of research and development – R&D) sectors, exhibit a negative persistence of the shocks. The authors of the second category of models (Aghion and Saint Paul 1991, 1998; Saint Paul 1997) refer explicitly to Schumpeter's concept of the cleaning and restructuring effects both associated with periods of recession, in their emphasis (paraphrasing Schumpeter) that recessions are but temporary and that each occurrence represents the means to reconstruct the economic system according to a more efficient plan. Based on the "opportunity cost" approach, they consider that research and development activities that enhance productivity in the long run are nevertheless costly in the short run since they divert efforts (and the resources) from the productive sector. Thus, a recession can be seen as an opportunity to finance at low cost a productivity enhancing activity, and in this case, the persistence of the shock has a negative impact. Both endogenous mechanisms are interesting and contribute to our understanding of how growth may be affected by the nature of business cycles which means by their amplitude, frequency, and persistence. However, there is debate over the sign of persistence of shocks

Starting with the paper by Ramey and Ramey (1995), many contributions (see, for example, Barlevy 2004; Blackburn and Pelloni 2004, 2005) have tried – without success – to determine the sign of the relationship between growth and volatility; their conclusions are indeed oversensitive to the nature of the endogenous growth mechanism, and empirical investigations cannot tackle this issue. It is difficult then to draw sharp economic policy conclusions from these models, a weakness which certainly contributes to explaining the waning interest in these kinds of models. Along the same lines but within a different analytical framework is the paper by Stiglitz (1993) which proposes a complete growth-cycles model and analyses how recessions can negatively impact on growth if they lead to an interruption in the financing of research and development, a decision which has direct consequences on the (future) rate of growth.

Finally, Aghion and Howitt (1992, 1998, 2009) developed another generation of endogenous growth models, the so-called neo-Schumpeterian growth models. Aghion and Howitt started from a monopolistic market structure and introduced Schumpeterian features of innovation and growth; creative destruction, productive recessions (already discussed by Aghion and Saint Paul), cleaning effects, obsolescence of goods, and so on (see Aghion et al. 2013). While it was not their primary objective, Aghion and Howitt covered the different ways growth and cycles intertwine. Their starting point was the concept of general purpose technologies (GPTs), developed by Bresnahan and Trajtenberg (1995) and Helpman and Trajtenberg (1998). General purpose technologies are understood as raising productivity levels in the long run, and as being the cause of cyclical fluctuations due to their absorption into the economic system. Aghion and Howitt also examined how the nature of growth affects fluctuations. Focusing more specifically on firm dynamics, they emphasized that "misallocation of resources is a major source of productivity gap across countries" (Aghion et al. 2013: 36) and again tried to link cycles and growth dynamics.

Conclusions

Of course, there are other ways to organize this rather large literature including distinguishing between market clearing and non-market clearing approaches (as in Aghion and Saint Paul 1998).

We could have paid more attention to optimal growth models and their attempt to exhibit (endogenous) cyclical dynamics. However, we decided to focus in our assessment of the modern literature on the analysis of cycles based on impulse/propagation mechanisms. There are several fundamental contributions developed from that perspective: (1) Benhabib and Nishimura (1979, 1985) who show that multisectoral models can exhibit oscillating dynamics sometimes even with periodicity, and (2) Benhabib and Day (1982) and Grandmont (1985) who show in overlapping-generations models that under certain conditions optimal trajectories can be cyclical in nature.

Another interesting literature strand that we have not so far mentioned includes work that starts from the assumption of long-run growth as an exogenous trend and then examines how fluctuations could be generated endogenously (see Shleifer 1986) and those papers that try to endogenize both cycles and growth dynamics (see François and Lloyd-Ellis 2003).

Another (still) emerging field of research is founded on agent-based modelling (see Howitt and Gaffard 2007; Dosi et al. 2010). In this perspective, there is no doubt that the Schumpeterian idea that growth and cycles are indistinguishable dynamics, which so far has not been adequately modelled, is still of fundamental importance for modern research programs. What is less obvious is the extent to which those modern approaches can be interpreted as fully Schumpeterian contributions.

MICHAËL ASSOUS, MURIEL DAL PONT LEGRAND AND HARALD HAGEMANN

See also:

Growth (III); Roy Forbes Harrod (I); Clément Juglar (I); Michał Kalecki (I); Robert E. Lucas (I); Karl Heinrich Marx (I); New Classical Macroeconomics (II); Joseph Alois Schumpeter (I); Robert Merton Solow (I).

References and further reading

Aghion, P. and P. Howitt (1992), 'A model of growth through creative destruction', *Econometrica*, **60** (2), 323–51.

Aghion, P. and P. Howitt (1998), *Endogenous Growth Theory*, Cambridge, MA: MIT Press.

Aghion, P. and P. Howitt (2009), *The Economics of Growth*, Cambridge, MA: MIT Press.

Aghion, P. and G. Saint Paul (1991), 'On the virtues of bad times', Working Paper no. 578, CEPR, London.

Aghion, P. and G. Saint Paul (1998), 'Uncovering some causal relationships between productivity growth and the structure of economic fluctuations: a tentative survey', *Labour*, **12** (2), 279–303.

Aghion, P., U. Akcigit and P. Howitt (2013), 'What do we learn from Schumpeterian growth theory?', PIER working paper 13-026, Penn Institute for Economic Research, Department of Economics, University of Pennsylvania.

Arrow, K. (1962), 'The economic implications of learning by doing', *Review of Economic Studies*, **29** (3), 155–73.

Asada, T. (2009), *Japanese Contributions to Dynamic Economic Theories in the 1940s – the 1970s: A Historical Survey*, Tokyo: Chuo University.

Assous, M. (2015), 'Solow's struggle with medium-run macroeconomics: 1956–1995', *History of Political Economy*, **47** (3), 395–417.

Assous, M., O. Bruno and M. Dal Pont Legrand (2014), 'The "Law of Diminishing Elasticity of Demand" in Harrod's Trade Cycle (1936)', *Cahiers d'Economie politique/Papers in Political Economy*, **67** (2), 159–75.

Barlevy, G. (2004), 'The cost of business cycles under endogenous growth', *American Economic Review*, **94** (4), 964–90.

Benhabib, J. and R.H. Day (1982), 'A characterization of erratic dynamics in overlapping generations model', *Journal of Economic Dynamic and Control*, **4** (1), 37–55.

Benhabib, J. and K. Nishimura (1979), 'The Hopft bifurcation and the existence of stability closed orbits in multisector models of optimal economic growth', *Journal of Economic Theory*, **21** (3), 421–44.

Benhabib, J. and K. Nishimura (1985), 'Competitive equilibrium cycles', *Journal of Economic Theory*, **35** (3), 284–306.

Blackburn, K. and A. Pelloni (2004), 'On the relationship between growth and volatility', *Economics Letters*, **83** (1), 123–7.

Blackburn, K. and A. Pelloni (2005), 'Growth, cycles and stabilization policy', *Oxford Economic Papers*, **57** (2), 262–82.

Bresnahan, T.F. and M. Trajtenberg (1995), 'General purpose technologies: engines of growth?', *Journal of Econometrics*, **65** (2), 83–108.

Brock, W. and L. Mirman (1972), 'Optimal economic growth under uncertainty: the discounted case', *Journal of Economic Theory*, **4** (3), 479–513.

Bronfenbrenner, M. (1969), *Is the Business Cycle Obsolete?*, New York: Wiley.

Bruno, O. and M. Dal Pont Legrand (2014), 'The instability principle revisited: an essay in Harrodian dynamics', *European Journal for the History of Economic Thought*, **21** (3), 467–84.

Dal Pont Legrand, M. and H. Hagemann (2010), 'Théories réelles versus monétaires des cycles d'équilibre: une mise en perspective des travaux récents au regard des débats de l'entre-deux guerres?', *Revue Française d'Economie*, **24** (4), 189–229.

Dosi, G., G. Fagiolo and A. Roventini (2010), 'Schumpeter meeting Keynes: a policy-friendly model of endogenous growth and business cycles', *Journal of Economic Dynamics and Control*, **34** (9), 1748–67.

Dutt, A.K. (1984), 'Stagnation, income distribution and monopoly power', *Cambridge Journal of Economics*, **8** (1), 25–40.

Eltis, W.A. (1971), 'The determination of the rate of technical progress', *Economic Journal*, **81** (323), 502–24.

Flaschel, P. (2009), *The Macrodynamics of Capitalism. Elements for a Synthesis of Marx, Keynes and Schumpeter*, 2nd revised and enlarged edn, Berlin: Springer.

François, P. and H. Lloyd-Ellis (2003), 'Animal spirits through creative destruction', *American Economic Review*, **93** (3), 530–50.

Frisch, R. (1933), 'Propagation problems and impulse problems in dynamic economics', in K. Koch (ed.), *Economic Essays in Honour of Gustav Cassel*, London, Allen & Unwin, pp. 171–205.

Frisch, R. and H. Holme (1935), 'The characteristic solutions of a mixed difference and differential equation occurring in economic dynamics', *Econometrica*, **3** (2), 225–39.

Goodwin, R.M. (1951), 'The nonlinear accelerator and the persistence of business cycles', *Econometrica*, **19** (1), 1–17.

Goodwin, R.M. (1953), 'The problem of trend and cycle', *Bulletin of Economic Research*, **5** (2), 89–97.

Goodwin, R.M. (1967), 'A growth cycle', in C.H. Feinstein (ed.), *Socialism, Capitalism and Economic Growth, Cambridge*, Cambridge: Cambridge University Press, pp. 54–8, reprinted in R.M. Goodwin (1982), *Essays in Economic Dynamics*, Basingstoke: Macmillan, pp. 165–70.

Goodwin, R.M. (1987), 'Growth and cycles', in J. Eatwell, M. Milgate and P. Newman (eds), *The New Palgrave*, vol. 2, London: Palgrave Macmillan, pp. 574–6.

Grandmont, J.M. (1985), "On endogenous competitive business cycles", *Econometrica*, **53** (5), 995–1046.

Hagemann, H. (2003), 'Schumpeter's early contributions on crises theory and business-cycle theory', *History of Economic Ideas*, **11** (1), 47–67.

Hagemann, H. (2009), 'Solow's 1956 contribution in the context of the Harrod–Domar model', *History of Political Economy*, **41** (Supplement 1), 67–87.

Harrod, R.F. (1936), *The Trade Cycle. An Essay*, Oxford: Clarendon.

Harrod, R.F. (1939), 'An essay in dynamic theory', *Economic Journal*, **49** (193), 14–33.

Harrod, R.F. (1973), *Economic Dynamics*, London: Macmillan.

Harrod, R.F. (2003), 'An essay on dynamic theory [1938 draft]', in D. Besomi (ed.), *The Collected Interwar Papers and Correspondence of Roy Harrod*, vol. 3, Cheltenham, UK and Northampton.MA, USA: Edward Elgar, pp. 1188–212.

Helpman, E and M. Trajtenberg (1998), 'A time to sow and a time to reap: growth based on general purpose technologies', in E. Helpman (ed.), *General Purpose Technologies and Economic Growth*, Cambridge, MA: MIT Press, pp. 55–83.

Hénin, P.Y. (1994), 'L'impact à long terme des chocs de demande', *Revue Economique*, **45** (3), 883–96.

Hoover, K. (1988), *The New Classical Macroeconomics*, Aldershot, UK and Brookfield, VT, USA: Edward Elgar.

Howitt, P. and J.L. Gaffard (2007), 'Vers une macroéconomie fondée sur des agents autonomes et intelligents', *Revue de l'OFCE*, **2007/3**, 55–78.

Kaldor, N. (1940), 'A model of the trade cycle', *Economic Journal*, **50** (197), 78–92.

Kaldor, N. (1954), 'The relation of economic growth and cyclical fluctuations', *Economic Journal*, **64** (253), 53–71.

Kalecki, M. (1935), 'A macrodynamic theory of the business cycle', *Econometrica*, **3** (3), 327–44.

Kalecki, M. (1962), 'Observations on the theory of growth', *The Economic Journal*, **72** (285), 134–53.

Kydland, F.E. and E.C. Prescott (1982), 'Time to build and aggregate fluctuations', *Econometrica*, **50** (6), 1345–70.

Lucas, R. (1972), 'Expectations and the neutrality of money', *Journal of Economic Theory*, **4** (2), 103–24.

Lucas, R. (1988), 'On the mechanics of economic development', *Journal of Monetary Economics*, **22** (1), 3–42.

Lucas, R.E. and L. Rapping (1969), 'Real wages, employment, and inflation', *Journal of Political Economy*, **77** (5), 721–54.

Mata, T. and F. Louçã (2009), 'The Solow residual as a black box: attempt at integrating business cycle and growth theories', *History of Political Economy*, **41** (Supplement 1), 334–55.

Muth, J. (1961), 'Rational expectations and the theory of price movements', *Econometrica*, **29** (3), 315–55.

Nelson, C. and C. Plosser (1982), 'Trends and random walk in macroeconomic time series: some evidences and implications', *Journal of Monetary Economics*, **10** (2), 139–62.

Ramey, G. and V. Ramey (1995), 'Cross-country evidence on the link between volatility and growth', *American Economic Review*, **85** (5), 1138–51.

Romer, P. (1986), 'Increasing returns and long-run growth', *Journal of Political Economy*, **94** (5), 1002–37.

Rowthorn, B. (1981), 'Demand, real wages and economic growth', *Thames Papers in Political Economy*, Autumn, 1–39.

Saint Paul, G. (1997), 'Business cycles and long-run growth', *Oxford Review of Economic Policy*, **13** (3), 145–53.

Schumpeter, J.A. (1911), *Theorie der wirtschaftlichen Entwicklung*, Munich and Leipzig; Duncker & Humblot, 2nd edn 1926, English trans. 1934, *The Theory of Economic Development. An Inquiry into Profits, Capital, Credit, Interest, and the Business Cycle*, Cambridge, MA: Harvard University Press.

Schumpeter, J.A. (1939), *Business Cycles. A Theoretical, Historical and Statistical Analysis of the Capitalist Process*, 2 vols, New York: McGraw-Hill.

Sen, A.K. (ed.) (1970), *Growth Economics: Selected Readings*, Harmondsworth: Penguin Books.

Shleifer, A. (1986), 'Implementation cycles', *Journal of Political Economy*, **94** (6), 1163–90.

Skott, P. (2010), 'Growth, instability and cycles: Harrodian and Kaleckian models of accumulation and income distribution', in M. Setterfield (ed.), *Handbook of Alternative Theories of Economic Growth*, Cheltenham, UK and Northampton, MA, USA: Edward Elgar.

Solow, R.M. (1956), 'A contribution to the theory of economic growth', *Quarterly Journal of Economics*, **70** (1), 65–94.

Solow, R.M. (1988), 'Growth theory and after', *American Economic Review*, **78** (3), 307–17.

Solow, R.M. (2012), 'On Pasinetti and the unfinished Keynesian revolution', in R. Arena and P.L. Porta (eds), *Structural Dynamics and Economic Growth*, Cambridge: Cambridge University Press, pp. 267–75.

Stadler, G.W. (1990), 'Business cycle models with endogenous technology', *American Economic Review*, **80** (4), 763–78.

Stadler, G.W. (1994), 'Real business cycles', *Journal of Economic Literature*, **32** (4), 1750–83.

Stiglitz, J. (1993), 'Endogenous growth and cycles', NBER Working Paper No. 4286, National Bureau of Economic Research, Cambridge, MA.

Summers, L.H. (1986), 'Some sceptical observations on real business cycle theory', working paper, *Federal Reserve Bank of Minneapolis Quarterly Review*, Fall.

Taylor, L. (1985), 'A stagnationist model of economic growth', *Cambridge Journal of Economics*, **9** (4), 383–403.

Tinbergen, J. (1937), 'Review of Harrod, R.F., *The Trade Cycle*', *Weltwirtschaftliches Archiv*, **45** (3), 89–91.

Tobin, J. (1980), 'Are new classical models plausible enough to guide policy?', *Journal of Money, Credit and Banking*, **12** (4), 788–99.

Capital theory

Capital theory as intended in this entry is the study of the implications, for the functioning of market economies (centrally planned economies will not be discussed), of advances of produced means of production and/or of wages relative to the obtainment of a saleable output, advances on whose value a rate of return is obtained. The explanation of this rate (called rate of profits by the classical authors and later identified with the rate of interest by the marginalist authors) is the central problem of capital theory. There are deep differences between the capital theory of the two successive main approaches to value and distribution: the earlier Surplus approach called Classical by Karl Marx and undergoing nowadays a considerable revival, and the later marginalist or supply-and-demand approach (nowadays also called Neoclassical, or even Classical, a confusing terminology suggesting a continuity between the surplus and marginalist approach where in fact there is sharp opposition). In this survey of the historical development of capital theory in the two approaches, some reference to their overall structure will be indispensable to grasp the different difficulties encountered by them in the treatment of capital.

Capital Theory in the Surplus Approach

The classical or surplus approach starts with Petty, Cantillon and Quesnay, is dominant up to the 1830s, is resumed by Marx at a time when the main current of economic thought is already moving in a different direction, and is then nearly completely submerged by the marginalist approach and no longer well understood until the clarification of its structure by Sraffa (1951) and Garegnani (1960, 1987). It revolves around the notion of social surplus, that is, what is left of the yearly social product (that is, of the vector of all commodities produced during a year), after the replacement of the goods – inclusive of the subsistence of labourers – advanced and used up for production so as to permit the repetition of productive activity on an unchanged scale the subsequent year. Its origin lies in the perception of the labourers' subsistence as a production expense as necessary as fodder for horses, and nearly as fixed (although not only by physiological but also by social processes); this allows a determination of the excess over what is indispensable to the continuation of production as a residue. The size and the destination of the surplus determine the incomes of the social classes other than labourers, and the potential for economic growth as well as for state revenue (and hence for military and other state expenses).

The notion of surplus precedes the consideration of the advances as "capital" in the sense of a source of income; thus, strictly speaking, there is no capital theory in Quesnay's *Tableau*, where however important analytical distinctions are made between the components of advances, distinctions partly lost with Adam Smith but recuperated by Marx: (1) subsistence goods, (2) advances different from subsistence but also destined to disappear in a single yearly production cycle (for example, seed), and (3) advances destined to maintain durable tools, long-lived animals, structures. (A fourth type, once-and-for-all advances permanently modifying land, such as canals or dykes, is not part of the advances indispensable to reproduction and to be subtracted from the social product to obtain the surplus.) But in Quesnay the advances are not "capital" in the sense of a source of profits; there are no profits in the *Tableau*, the surplus (entirely agricultural) is absorbed by land rent, which induces the Physiocrats mistakenly to see the capacity to produce a surplus as pertaining to agricultural labour only.

Adam Smith

With Adam Smith the surplus includes manufactures too, and profit upon capital advances is recognized as a second source of appropriation of the surplus besides land rent, and as accruing tendentially at a uniform rate upon the value of capital, owing to competition. (Interest is viewed as a part of profit.) Capital theory is born: the advances are called "capital", and the magnitude of the rate of profits must be explained; its determination represents the main analytical problem of the surplus approach to value and distribution.

The determination of the surplus in classical authors rests on three groups of "intermediate" data (that is – see Garegnani 1987, 2007 – not exogenous to the overall theory, but treated as already determined when the purpose is the determination of incomes other than wages). The explanation of wages in terms of custom and of relative bargaining power of workers and "masters" (with a clear advantage, stressed by Smith, of the latter who can resist much longer in case of conflict) makes it legitimate, when one attempts to determine the rate of profits and its variations, to treat (1) the average real wage (and relative wages as well) as given or as an independently varying parameter.

The consideration of the social product as determined in its size and composition by the past accumulation of capital, by the dominant production methods that affect reproduction needs, and by the consumption habits of the social classes makes the same treatment possible for (2) the quantities produced, and for (3) the methods of production adopted, these latter viewed as depending on the "marginal" land and on the division of labour (in turn dependent on the extension of markets and on the stage of technical knowledge).

These three groups of data allow the determination of (4) the advanced capital physically specified, that is, the quantities of means of production and wage goods used up in order to produce the social product (these quantities are assumed adapted to the "effectual demands", according to the general classical method of concentrating on the "normal positions" toward which actual magnitudes tend to gravitate owing to competition); wages are included in the advances because of the importance of agriculture, where workers must be able to subsist for the year before the harvest. It is then possible to determine (5) the surplus as the difference between (2) and (4).

This simple analytical structure determines the physical surplus as well as physical capital advances and land use, but not yet the rates of the incomes other than wages: the rates of land rent, and the rate of profits. These rates, each one tendentially uniform owing to competition, enter normal prices (natural prices, in Smith's terminology: the centres of gravitation of market prices) in different proportions for different products, rendering relative exchange values dependent on these rates; this creates the main analytical problem of the approach: the rate of profits, being the ratio between exchange value of the surplus product net of land rents, and exchange value of the capital employed, requires for its determination the determination of the relative natural prices of commodities, which depend in turn on the rates of land rent and on the rate of profits. The question becomes whether data (1), (2) and (3) are sufficient to determine the value of capital and the rate of profits in spite of that reciprocal dependence or additional considerations are needed.

Let us see how the problem presents itself to Smith. The surplus approach makes it natural to attempt to determine the rate of profits through the "surplus equation":

$$r = \textit{value of surplus (net of rents) / value of capital advances (inclusive of wages)}$$

According to Marx's interpretation (followed also by Sraffa), Smith, although not endowed with the theory of differential rent which will allow Ricardo to "get rid of rent", nonetheless regards land rents as determinable independently of the rate of profits; but he still has the problem of determining the value of the surplus net of rents relative to the capital advances: these latter he essentially identifies with wage advances, because he replaces the value of the used-up non-wage capital goods in the natural price with the wages, profits and rents these goods have cost, but then forgets that these incomes were paid in previous periods, and views the value of the given social product as corresponding to current wages, profits and rents – which requires capital to consist of wage advances only. His conception of the natural price as resulting from the adding-up of wages, profits and rents at their natural rates makes him occasionally reason as if a rise in one of the three rates could be accommodated by a rise of the natural price without decrease of the other two rates. This slip may have been aided by his measurement of values in terms of labour commanded, which causes capital, but not the value of the social product nor therefore the surplus, to be known before the rate of profits: capital commands the amount of labour it employs, that is, is measured by the employment of productive labour; the excess of the social product net of rents over capital commands the more labour the greater the profits; it may then seem that there is a degree of freedom. Smith's solution is to admit an additional consideration in the explanation of the rate of profits: the competition of capitals. For individual commodities an increased supply decreases price and hence the rate of profits; Smith generalizes this to the whole economy:

> The diminution of the capital stock of the society . . . as it lowers the wages of labour, so it raises the profits of stock, and consequently the interest of money. By the wages of labour being lowered, the owners of what stock remains in the society can bring their goods at less expense to market than before, and less stock being employed in supplying the market than before, they can sell them dearer. Their goods cost them less, and they get more for them. Their profits, therefore, being augmented at both ends, can well afford a large interest. (Smith 1776 [1976], *Wealth of Nations*, I.ix.13)

Thus wage decreases tend to raise profits, but a given real wage does not suffice to determine the rate of profits, which also depends on the prices at which goods can be sold, that is, on aggregate supply relative to a purchasing power treated as independently determined.

According to a different recent interpretation which is gaining some following (O'Donnell 1990; Dome 1998), Smith does not lose sight of the constraint binding the rates of rent and the rate of profits, and determines rents residually; the key is how he envisages corn production, which he treats as utilizing the best ("improved") lands, and using essentially corn as advances (he treats the given real wage as if consisting of only corn, evidently taken, in the words of Petty, "to contain all necessaries for life, as in the Lord's Prayer we suppose the word Bread doth", Hull, 1899: 89); he views corn-producing land as yielding the highest rent rate (which determines the upper limit for other rates of rent too, by determining the maximum price of the products of other lands as the one that would permit replacing corn with them on corn land without lowering the rent rate); this rate is determined residually once the competition-of-capitals theory of profits allows taking the rate of profits as given in addition to the given wage; the independence of the rate of profits from the real wage is then not logically contradictory, a higher real wage without change of the rate of profits will imply a decrease of rent and a rise of the price (in terms of corn) of the goods in whose natural price rent does not enter.

Ricardo

Ricardo does not greatly progress relative to Smith on what capital is made of; very often he reasons as if capital advances consisted of wages only, and he inherits from Smith the mistake of conceiving the natural price as the sum of wages and profits (not rents, because the theory of differential rent allows him to exclude land rent from the natural price) forgetting about the value of the used-up non-wage capital: in the examples in which he discusses machines, these are produced by unassisted labour, are treated as if eternal (no depreciation), and use no non-wage circulating capital, so both their prices and the prices of their products still consist only of wages and profits. However, he progresses on the determination of the rate of profits. He realizes the mistake of Smith on the competition of capitals: it had escaped Smith that, since he assumed – like Ricardo – that all savings get invested, aggregate demand equals aggregate income and there is no reason why increased production should make it more difficult to sell at the old prices. Ricardo is then left with the sole influence of the wage on the rate of profits, and concludes that a given wage determines the rate of profits and the two are inversely related. At first, according to Sraffa (1951), Ricardo reaches this conclusion avoiding the need to determine relative prices, by noting that, in agriculture, capital advances and product are sufficiently homogeneous (corn produced by corn, like in Smith) as to render the rate of profits a material ratio, univocally determined once the real wage and the no-rent land are given; the rate of profits in other sectors will adapt. However, after Malthus's objection that wages include manufactures, Ricardo must face the problem of relative values; some examples in the *Principles* (Ricardo 1951–73, I: 50, 64–6) show that he continues to believe that the rate of profits can be seen as a material ratio (Kurz 2011); for the general case he determines it by adopting the labour theory of value as a sufficient approximation to actual exchange ratios. Ricardo knows that natural prices cannot be proportional to labours embodied (wages are advanced for different lengths of time in different productions), but he argues that the variations in relative prices caused by variations of the rate of profits are small, so one can neglect them. This neglect is further supported by a "compensation of deviations" argument implicit in Ricardo's considerations on an "invariable measure of value" (see Sraffa 1951: xliv–xlv). Exchanges in proportion to labour embodied render the ratio on the right-hand side of the "surplus equation" ascertainable before r. Ricardo concludes that the rate of profits depends on "the proportion of the annual labour of the country devoted to the support of the labourers" (1951–73, IV: 49), as if capital consisted only of wages and the rate of profits were determined by:

$$r = (N - V)/V = S/V \tag{1}$$

where total employment N is the labour embodied in the social product net of rent; V is the labour embodied in the capital advances, that is, in the wages (of productive labour); $S = N - V$ is surplus labour, that is, the labour embodied in profits; S/V, the ratio of surplus labour to "necessary" labour, is what Marx will later call rate of exploitation; and Ricardo's "proportion" is V/N which determines $S/V = (N/V) - 1$. A rise of real wages raises V/N and therefore reduces r. As to what keeps the "proportion" V/N less than 1 and therefore renders the rate of profits positive, Ricardo relies on the Malthusian population principle and appears less conscious than Smith of the importance of class coalitions and of the inferior bargaining power of workers vis-à-vis capitalists (he writes: "Like all other contracts, wages should be left to the fair and free competition of the market", 1951–73, I: 105); but no contribution of capitalists to production or to value is recognized. Thus it will be obvious to Bortkiewicz (1906–07) that Ricardo shares with Marx the view that profits have their origin in the "deduction" of part of the product of labour.

Equation (1) is a simplification of Ricardo's not fully consistent views. It treats all capital as wages advanced for one year, while Ricardo admits fixed capital; but he does not recognize the proportion of fixed to circulating capital as a further influence on the rate of profits besides the wage. Also, Ricardo correctly argues that only the production conditions of the "wage industries" (the ones that directly or indirectly produce the wage goods) influence the rate of profits; but then the "proportion" that determines r should not refer to the *whole* "annual labour".

Marx
The study of Quesnay's *Tableau* helps Marx to realize the presence, in the value not only of individual commodities but also of the social product, of a part corresponding to the value of the used-up non-wage capital goods, circulating and durable. On this basis he develops a disaggregation of capital into constant capital c (that is, non-wage capital goods) and variable capital v (wages) (I assume the reader is acquainted with Marx's $c + v + s$ formulas); his reproduction schemes in volume II of *Capital*, where different sectors produce constant capital, variable capital, and luxury goods, are at the origin of Leontief's input–output approach. This permits him a significant step forward relative to Ricardo: the recognition of the "organic composition of capital" c/v as a further determinant of the rate of profits besides the wage level. In Marx too the labour theory of value allows the determination of the aggregates of the "surplus equation" before the rate of profits. He reaches this conclusion before writing *Capital*, in the so-called *Grundrisse* (1858–59), on the basis of a "compensation-of-deviations" argument not unlike the one in Ricardo; this analytical motivation appears sufficient to explain his subsequent attachment to the idea that exchange value is created by labour, without need for the other motives often attributed him. Marx argues that the equalization of the rate of profits is brought about by an increase in price (relative to a starting point with prices proportional to labour-values) of the commodities produced with a higher-than-average organic composition of capital, and a decrease in price of the commodities with a lower-than-average organic composition of capital; these deviations, he concludes, will compensate one another and leave the aggregate value unchanged, if one chooses as

standard of value an "average commodity" produced with the average organic composition of capital – a property enjoyed, by definition, by the total social product which is then Marx's "average commodity" (this explains why Marx, *contra* Ricardo, considers the production conditions of *all* sectors to contribute to the determination of the rate of profits). But Marx does not realize that the same "average commodity" cannot leave the aggregate value of capital or of total profits unchanged because different aggregates have different average organic compositions, and concludes that the general uniform rate of profits is correctly determined by the "surplus equation" (assuming only circulating capital):

$$r = [(C + V + S) - (C + V)]/(C + V) = (N - V)/(C + V) = S/(C + V), \qquad (2)$$

where N is total employment (the labour embodied in the net product) and C, V, S are the labour embodied in, respectively, the constant capital, the variable capital, and the surplus of the entire economy. Marx also discusses durable capital and differences in rotation times, but is unable to go beyond the idea expressed by equation (2): the labour theory of value applied to the "surplus-equation" aggregates determines r correctly. Marx proceeds to argue that the r thus determined must be applied to the advanced capital of each industry to obtain the prices of production; he sees these prices as "transformed" labour values since they result from a redistribution of the given total surplus labour value. In volume III of *Capital* he has a numerical example of this determination of prices of production; he admits that the example needs correction because he has not "transformed" constant and variable capital from labour values to prices of production, but he argues that the question does not need further analysis because the compensation of deviations will operate for capital too, and does not attempt to implement the correction.

Dmitriev and Bortkiewicz

The moment scholars with greater mathematical competence than Marx, and accustomed by Walras to a complete disaggregation of production conditions and to simultaneous equations, are able to grasp the terms of the difficulty encountered by the surplus theorists in the determination of the rate of profits, a correct solution is quickly found.

The breakthrough is first performed in 1898, in Russian, in the form of a discussion of Ricardo. Dmitriev sees clearly the problem of apparent circularity that Ricardo confronted: "Thus, we are apparently trapped in a logical circle: profit must be known in order to determine value, but profit itself is dependent on value" (1974: 58). Dmitriev shows that one can surmount the problem through a "reduction" of the production cost of the given real wage basket to dated quantities of itself with the appropriate amount of profit on them (a "reduction" similar to the one to "dated quantities of labour" performed by Sraffa 1960: 35, except that Dmitriev takes the "reduction" to end in a finite number of steps), obtaining an equation where the sole unknown is r; the equation confirms Ricardo on the relevance of the "wage industries" only, and shows the irrelevance of labour values.

The importance of Dmitriev's contribution is realized by Bortkiewicz. In the first (1906–07) of two articles on Marx, he takes up Dmitriev's procedure as a way to surmount the erroneousness of Marx's equation (2), thus recognizing that Marx's problem is the same as Ricardo's. In the second much shorter article (1907) Bortkiewicz criticizes Marx's thesis of invariance of the aggregates in passing from labour values to prices of production; he uses a three-sector stationary economy whose sectors produce respectively the constant capital (assumed circulating), the variable capital, and the goods appropriated as profits; assuming that all goods produced in a sector have the same organic composition and can be treated as a single good, he applies the "transformation" as indicated by Marx but he also performs the correction indicated and not attempted by Marx, that is, he applies prices of production also to the constant and variable capital, obtaining the system:

$$(1 + \rho)(c_1 x + v_1 y) = (c_1 + c_2 + c_3)x$$

$$(1 + \rho)(c_2 x + v_2 y) = (v_1 + v_2 + v_3)y \tag{3}$$

$$(1 + \rho)(c_3 x + v_3 y) = (m_1 + m_2 + m_3)z$$

where c_i, v_i and m_i are the constant capital, variable capital and surplus value (in labour values) of sector i (all labour-value magnitudes are data); ρ is the rate of profits; x, y and z are the ratios of price to labour value, that is, the prices of production of the quantity of output of each sector that embodies one unit of labour. The equations determine rate of profits and relative prices simultaneously, and show the erroneousness of equation (2) (the first two equations suffice to determine r, independently therefore of the third sector; and the equality of labour value and price of production cannot be obtained simultaneously for more than one aggregate); but other implications are not made clear in the article (a fact that will negatively condition the debate on this article that starts 35 years later). In it Bortkiewicz does not stress that the stationariness assumption is superfluous, nor that – as is clear from the first article – labour values are not necessary for the determination of r, what is necessary is the complete disaggregation of production conditions. And it is only in the first article, not in the second, that Bortkiewicz insists that Marx's mistakes do not mean inconsistency of the idea, *common to Marx and to Ricardo*, and in fact clearer in Marx, of the rate of profits as resulting from the "deduction" of part of labour's product – "deduction" being the term Bortkiewicz prefers, but clearly expressing the same idea as Marx's "exploitation". But Bortkiewicz's first article remains unnoticed by Marxists even longer than the second one.

So by 1907 it has been proved twice (although the proof is essentially limited to circulating capital and no technical choice) that the classical analytical difficulty with determining the rate of profits is surmounted by a fully disaggregated description of capital, that is, of production conditions; so Jevons and Walras were mistaken when accusing Ricardo of trying to determine two variables – price and rate of profits – with one equation (the equation determining product price as equal to cost of production inclusive of the rate of profits). However, for many decades this achievement remains unrecognized, undiscussed by Marxists, and without any impact on the general development of economic theory.

In 1942 Bortkiewicz's second article is rediscovered by Sweezy, who presents equations (3) as confirmation that Marx was right: rate of profits and prices of production are determined, Sweezy argues, by labour values. A debate, slowed down by the limits of the article, takes many years to rediscover, with Seton (1957), that the full disaggregation needed in order correctly to determine prices of production and rate of profits shows that the only role of labour values is that of being one possible choice of units for the commodities (which refutes Sweezy). Because of lack of clarity on the structure of the classical approach, the importance of the demonstrated determinability of the rate of profits is not grasped; on the contrary, owing to the prevalent interpretation of the labour theory of value as essential to Marx's view of the origin of profits in the exploitation of labour, the erroneousness of Marx's equation (2) and superfluousness of labour values are perceived by many as undermining Marx.

Sraffa and von Neumann
The interpretation of the classics presented here first appears in Sraffa's 1951 introduction to Ricardo's *Principles* (1951–73: I); it subverts the Marshallian view of a continuity between Ricardo and marginalist theory, but its implications take time to be appreciated; important contributions to this effect are by Garegnani (1960, 1987, 2007). Garegnani's writings have the same aim as (and permit a better grasp of) Sraffa's analytically extremely rich but very concise (indeed, almost cryptic) 1960 *Production of Commodities*: namely, to prove, first, that the surplus approach is an approach *alternative* to the marginalist one, and *consistent* because its "main analytical problem", as we called it, is solvable; and second, that on the contrary the conception of capital as a single factor, indispensable to the marginalist approach, is untenable. Then it becomes important to check that a correct determination of the rate of profits is achievable within the surplus approach under sufficiently general hypotheses, one can then turn to this approach as an alternative to the defective marginalist one. A flood of contributions starts further to develop Sraffa's advances on technical choice, land rent, fixed capital, joint production.

To summarize an immense "Sraffian" formal literature up to the 1990s (among the many contributors one should mention at least Pasinetti, Garegnani, Schefold, Steedman, H.D. Kurz, Salvadori, Parrinello, Bidard), the consistency of the surplus approach's determination of r on the basis of data (1), (2) and (3) listed in the section on Adam Smith is fully confirmed for the cases of simple production, fixed capital (treated as a special case of joint production as suggested in the past by Torrens), and extensive differential land rent, without or with choice of techniques. Given the production methods among which firms can choose, the "effectual demands", the quantities and qualities of land, and either the real wage or the rate of profits, there is only one economically significant solution to the equations determining adopted methods, normal prices (prices of production), and the other distributive variables, such that no non-adopted method allows extraprofits; "truncation" of fixed capital (that is, when to discard durable capital goods) is also determined. There is a decreasing relationship between real wage and rate of profits. On general joint production and intensive differential rent, which in some cases can produce perplexing results (for example, technical choice need not lead to univocal results, and with some numéraires the real wage and the rate of profits need not be always inversely related), discussion continues, with some authors arguing that the treatment of the quantities produced as given should be reconsidered. On all these analytically complex issues we must refer to the excellent survey by Kurz and Salvadori (1995). In spite of the few perplexing special cases, it seems possible to conclude that the surplus approach can satisfactorily determine the composition of capital and the rate of profits for extremely general specifications of production methods. The road is thereby open to a full recuperation and development of the approach.

A result by Sraffa of particular interest to the historian of economic theory is that it is possible to determine the rate of profits as a material ratio, even when physical homogeneity between input and output is not obtained in any sector, by assuming a notional change of industry dimensions such that the economy produces a composite commodity with the composition required to render the rate of physical surplus (if wages are advanced and included in the production coefficients) or the rate of net product (if wages are paid in arrears) uniform for all basic commodities. When producing this Standard Commodity, product and capital are amounts of the same composite commodity, as in Ricardo's "corn model". The Standard Commodity, essential to Sraffa for several demonstrations because the Perron–Frobenius theorem was unknown to the mathematicians he consulted in Cambridge, renders explicit a mathematical property of the coefficients matrix, its dominant eigenvalue with the associated right and left eigenvectors, which determines the maximum rate of profits and of growth with the associated relative prices and relative industry proportions, as already noted in the past by long forgotten or misunderstood authors such as Charasoff, Remak or von Neumann (see Kurz and Salvadori 1995: ch. 13).

Of these the most important is von Neumann, who in a paper presented at a seminar at Princeton University in 1932 introduced inequalities and mathematical tools from game theory into a linear model of production and pricing (with given wages advanced and included in the technical coefficients), in order to admit joint production and choice among a number of linear alternative production methods. Von Neumann assumes the "rule of free goods" (price zero of commodities in excess supply, a possibility with joint production), determines the demand side by assuming that all profits are reinvested and that the growth rate is maximized, and proves that the rate of profits equals the growth rate. His paper, published in 1937 in German, was translated into English in 1945 with the greatly altered title "A model of general economic equilibrium" which helped its misinterpretation as a neoclassical general equilibrium model motivated by an interest in optimal growth; accordingly it gave rise to the studies culminating in "turnpike theorems". After the rediscovery, with Sraffa and Garegnani, of the structure of the classical approach, it became clear that von Neumann's paper was internal to the classical approach (as shown by the given wages included in the technical coefficients, by the absence of any substitution in consumer demand, and by the absence of any assumption of full labour employment), probably owing to an indirect influence of Bortkiewicz. The real purpose of the paper appears to have been to determine the rate of profits as a material ratio on the basis of a given real wage, while admitting technical choice and joint production: the very last sentence of the paper determines the rate of profits as equal to the previously determined maximum rate of growth; and, neglecting the commodities with zero price, the economy is producing a Standard Commodity.

Choice of techniques

Two results of the analysis of long-period technical choice deserve mention.

The enlargement of the analysis to consider the dependence of the long-period choice of production methods on income distribution modifies data (3) from given adopted

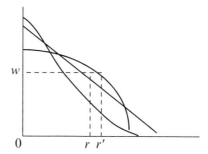

Figure 1 w(r) *curves of different techniques*

methods to (3′) given adoptable methods. Leaving aside some special cases of joint production, wage curves allow a graphical representation of how choice between alternative production methods operates (Figure 1). A wage curve, or $w(r)$ function, shows how the real wage depends on the rate of profits if the technique (that is, ensemble of methods of production, one for each industry) is given. Once a numeraire is chosen, a different $w(r)$ curve can be traced for each possible technique; they are all decreasing, and their North-East or "outer" envelope indicates the maximum real wage obtainable for each rate of profits (and vice versa). The main result is that the cost-minimizing choice of production methods will tend to reach this outer envelope.

This refutes Marx's claim of a secular tendency of the rate of profits to fall owing to the tendency of technical progress to replace labour with machines. Marx's idea was that the introduction of more mechanized methods of production that reduce average cost, while convenient at the old prices for the capitalist who first introduces these methods, ends up by lowering the average rate of profits when their adoption becomes generalized and raises the average organic composition of capital. However, the above result implies that new methods introduced because they are more convenient are associated with wage curves outside, at least locally, the old envelope (or leave it unchanged if not concerning a "wage industry"), so if the real wage stays constant the new uniform rate of profits cannot be lower, and will be higher, for example, from r to r' in the figure, if the change concerns a "wage industry". At least this, of Marx's reasons for pessimism on the future of capitalism, must be rejected. However, the result is a strengthening of the surplus approach, which is shown not to contradict the secular rise of real wages. A strengthening of the surplus approach, and therefore of Marx, is argued by Garegnani and others to be more generally entailed by the replacement of Marx's equation (2) with Sraffa's more correct equations that do not use labour values, because the role of the labour theory of value in Marx, as in Ricardo, was that of the imperfect tool – the only one available at the time – to determine the rate of profits surmounting the danger of circularity well grasped by Dmitriev; other aims traditionally attributed to the labour theory of value in Marx, such as proving exploitation or dispelling fetishism, are in fact achieved by the surplus approach's overall explanation of economic phenomena, and seem to depend, in Marx, on the labour theory of value only because of that theory's role in explaining the rate of profits. For example, on the fundamental issue of the origin of profits, the replacement of equation (2) with a more correct determination of r in no way questions Marx's explanation of why profits are positive, which is only another side of his classical approach to wages.

Sraffa proves another very important result, also shown in Figure 1: two wage curves can cross more than once, the "reswitching" phenomenon. The reason is that it is not true that if the rate of profits rises the relative normal price of two different commodities, or of the same commodity produced with two different methods, changes monotonically: it may at first rise, then decrease, and then rise again, owing to the complex influence of compound interest. (This had not been suspected even by Marx or Bortkiewicz.) This makes it impossible to see a commodity as produced by capital (conceived as a single factor) and labour combined in a proportion independent of income distribution, because if that were the case the change in the relative price of two commodities (or of the same commodity produced with two methods) would be monotonic, the commodity produced with the higher proportion of capital to labour always rising in relative price when the rate of profits rose. Sraffa notes: "The reversal in the direction of the movement of relative prices, in the face of unchanged methods of production, cannot be reconciled with *any* notion of capital as a measurable quantity independent of distribution and prices" (1960: 38). The implications for the marginalist approach are further discussed below in the section on the Cambridge controversy in capital theory.

It takes some years for attention to turn to the explanation of the "normal degree of utilization" of fixed capital implicitly assumed behind the technical coefficients that determine normal prices. Most fixed plants are not utilized 24 hours a day, seven days a week; since a faster consumption of durable capital reduces interest costs, the reason for not utilizing it maximally – apart from legal prohibitions – must be that some other cost, especially hourly wages, is higher for production outside normal hours. Marris (1964) is the first to raise this issue but not as part of the problem of determining prices of production; however, later it is seen (for example, Kurz 1990) that the issue can be studied as a problem of long-period choice of techniques, again dependent on income distribution (including now timetable wage differences).

Thereby it is made clearer that any tendency to identify normal and maximum utilization of capital is unwarranted. Maximum productive capacity is generally planned to be abundantly in excess of planned normal average production, not only because of higher wages for work in unusual hours but also because of regular periodic fluctuations in demand, of the desire to be ready to serve unexpected increases of demand without losing custom to competitors, and possibly of expectations of a trend of increase of demand that makes it convenient that new plants be bigger than necessary to satisfy initial demand. Therefore unexpected increases of demand will be generally easily met by increased utilization of existing plants. (The initial increase of production is made possible by the existence of inventories of intermediate goods, which are initially run down but are rapidly reconstituted by the increased production of the industries that produce them. The adaptability of production to decreases of demand of course poses no problem.) This, coupled with the general presence of overt and hidden unemployment and with the possibility of overtime, implies a considerable adaptability of production to demand not only for single industries, but also for the entire economy; this gives an essential role to aggregate demand in explaining aggregate output and growth of productive capacity, and denies that there is in general a trade-off between consumption and investment (Garegnani and Palumbo 1998).

The Marginalist Approach to Capital

Efforts to counter the view of the origin of profits emerging from the surplus approach are present already in Ricardo's time and increase afterwards. Around the middle of the nineteenth century, John Stuart Mill declares himself a Ricardian but accepts the combination of Senior's abstinence with a wage-fund approach to capital as a justification of profits. Abstinence determines savings, that is, the wage fund; the real wage results from the wage fund divided by labour employment, and if the real wage is fixed then labour employment results from the wage fund divided by the real wage, the first idea of an inverse relation between real wage and demand for labour. The weakness of the wage fund doctrine (which, as already argued by Ricardo, is unable to justify saving decisions preceding, and independent of, the level of real wages, see Stirati 1999) is admitted by J.S. Mill in 1869 after criticisms by Longe and Thornton (Stirati 1998), and the approach is abandoned. However, soon the claim that abstinence justifies profit finds a new analytical foundation in the marginalist approach.

The distinguishing element of the marginalist approach is the conception of production as the cooperation of "factors of production" substitutable one for the other through two mechanisms of substitution activated by changes in relative factor rentals: a direct or technological mechanism, based on the tendency of firms to change the proportion in which factors are combined in favour of the factor that becomes relatively cheaper; and an indirect mechanism, based on changes in relative industry dimensions due to the tendency of consumer demand (at least in the absence of "perverse" income effects) to shift in favour of the consumption goods that become relatively cheaper because their production employs in greater-than-average proportion the factor whose rental decreases. Owing to either mechanism the aggregate demand for each factor, assuming given employments of the other factors, is a decreasing function of its rental; this becomes the basis to argue that competition if allowed to work will push the rentals of all factors toward the levels ensuring equality, or equilibrium, between supply and demand simultaneously on all markets. The price of consumption goods measures their marginal utility, and the rental of a factor measures the indirect marginal contribution of the factor to utility.

Such an approach treats capital as another factor of production, whose reward, the rate of interest, is determined by the same substitution mechanisms that determine the reward of (each kind of) labour and land. However, capital is different in that it is physically heterogeneous and yet tending to a uniform rate of reward, so its insertion in the above theoretical structure is not easy; indeed it is done in a number of different ways that are distinguished below, all however having in common that capital is brought about and maintained by acts of saving, that is, of abstinence from immediate consumption; that more capital allows the same quantity of labour and land to produce more; that, because of this, abstinence has an indirect marginal utility which is what the rate of interest measures. This can be contrasted with the surplus approach, where the uniform rate of profits and prices of production have the sole function of allowing all units of capital equally to share in the total profits due to the capitalists' collective capacity to limit real wages – equally to share in the plunder, as a Marxist would put it.

The view of interest as the rental of a factor motivates its inclusion in the cost of production; "profit" is redefined to mean the excess of capital's net yield over the normal rate of interest, and therefore as tending to zero (apart from the reward for risk-taking) in the long period. We will maintain the classical meaning of "profit".

Comparison with the surplus approach

A comparison of what the marginalist approach takes as given to determine the rate of return on capital with what is taken as given for the same determination in the surplus approach is enlightening. In the marginalist approach the data are needed to determine the simultaneous equilibrium between supply and demand on all product and factor markets, that is (restricting analysis for simplicity to circulating capital):

1. preferences;
2. technical knowledge (the adoptable methods of production); and
3. endowments of factors of production and their allocation among consumers.

(Fixed capital would also require the specification of the age distribution of the several durable capital goods.) Comparison with data (1), (2), and (3) or (3') of the classical determination of the rate of profits reveals that the classical and the marginalist approach differ radically. The most glaring difference is that the surplus approach takes the real wage as already determined in another part of the overall analysis, while the marginalist approach determines it simultaneously with the rate of interest. (In what follows, land will be mostly assumed free, and neglected, because it is not in the treatment of land rents that the important differences between the two approaches reside.) The reason is the presence in the marginalist approach of the factor substitution mechanisms acting symmetrically on all factors, which imply a similar and simultaneous determination of all factor rentals. The idea of factor substitutability is on the contrary absent in the surplus theorists; this helps in understanding other differences too. In the absence of the premises for a decreasing demand curve for labour and hence for an adjustment toward equilibrium between supply and demand for labour, in the surplus authors a determination of the wage by political and social forces is indispensable to the explanation of wages, and therefore of profits. This is why classical theorists such as Adam Smith and Marx were also sociologists and political scientists, which is not generally the case with marginalist economists, owing to their view of the market as an essentially self-sufficient sphere that needs for its functioning little more than the respect of private property and contracts.

The political evaluation of capitalism is, of course, immensely influenced by the new approach: interest is now the reward for the sacrifice of abstinence, just as wages are the reward for the sacrifice of unpleasant labour; capital and labour cooperate rather than being in conflict (more capital raises the marginal productivity of labour and vice versa); both rates of reward reflect the marginal contribution to society of the "last unit" of sacrifice, for example, the wage equals what would be lost by society if an individual decided to supply one unit less of labour, so there is correspondence between individual contribution to social welfare and reward, which denies the exploitation of labour; a higher-than-equilibrium real wage damages society by reducing labour employment and thereby aggregate production.

Two problems with capital

The direct and the indirect substitution mechanisms are initially developed rather separately, and in the nineteenth century some authors appear conscious only or predominantly of the first one, others of the second one; but, with the singular exception (discussed later) of Walras and of his few followers (such as Pareto and Barone), capital is always conceived as a single factor "embodied" in the heterogeneous capital goods in proportion to their value. The reason is that the rate of interest is tendentially uniform on all capital, and therefore the logic of the theory obliges to see it as the rental of a single factor. One might think that each capital good could be seen as a separate factor, with its own contribution to production; but all founders of the marginalist approach as well as the second generation share with the earlier classical theorists the "method of normal positions", that is, the belief that it is fundamentally impossible (and also uninteresting) to explain the day-by-day market prices and quantities, influenced as they are by a multitude of accidental and transitory causes; what economic theory can and should try to explain is their averages and trends as determined by the gravitation toward persistent normal or long-period values. Then the treatment of each capital good as a different factor with its given endowment is made impossible by the rapid adaptability of the quantity in existence of each capital good to the demand for it, that deprives this quantity of the persistency required for its inclusion among the given factor endowments of an equilibrium determining normal prices. The quantities of the several capital goods must then be endogenously determined by the equilibrium, as the quantities associated with a uniform rate of interest on supply price. Therefore the only possibility is to view the several capital goods as "embodying" a single factor "capital" of endogenously determined "form", that is, composition. Now, the reward of capital, interest, is proportional to the value of capital, so if, like the rentals of other factors, it is to be proportional to the quantity of the factor "embodied" in the heterogeneous capital goods, this quantity must be proportional to the value of those capital goods; hence the value of capital measures the quantity of capital; nor is there any other physical way to specify this quantity: weight or volume of capital goods have no univocal connection with productivity or remuneration.

This poses two problems. A supply-side problem is how to specify the endowment of capital without logical circularity: the value of capital goods in terms of any numeraire depends on relative prices, but normal relative prices depend on the rate of interest, so a change in the rate of interest will change the normal value of the existing stock of capital goods even in the absence of any change in its physical composition, violating the need of the theory for data independent of what must be determined. A demand-side problem is that, even assuming the supply of capital to be somehow determinable without logical circularity, the theory needs to prove that the demand for capital is a decreasing function of the rate of interest, that is, that the two factor substitution mechanisms work for substitution between value capital and labour in the same way as for substitution between physically measurable factors; but this would require relative prices to be given, instead of being among the variables to be determined.

The direct factor substitution mechanism: from Thünen to Marshall

Awareness of these problems is initially nearly absent. First, this is shown for the economists who base their theory principally on the direct factor substitution mechanism. In such an approach, consideration of marginal utility is not indispensable; income distribution can be determined by marginal productivity even with a rigid composition of consumption demand and rigid factor supplies, and in fact the approach is born before the "marginal utility" revolution.

The starting point is the realization that, in the classical approach to intensive differential rent in the production of corn with corn, the role of land and the role of corn-capital (inclusive of advanced wages at a given wage rate and therefore also representing an input of labour) can be reversed because land rent, determined as a residue after the determination of profits as the "marginal product" of the last unit of corn-capital on a given quantity of homogeneous land, can also be seen as the "marginal product" of the last unit of land on the given quantity of corn-capital; both rent and profits can be seen as "marginal products" determined by a symmetrical mechanism; it is then concluded that the same intensive-differential-rent principle, which classical economists had used to determine only the division of the net product between land rent on one side and the *sum* of profits and wages on the other side, can be generalized to determine the division of this second part between wages and profits, a division that in the surplus approach was determined totally differently.

The first author to reach this conclusion is Heinrich von Thünen, whose influence upon Marshall, J.B. Clark, and indirectly upon the Austrian School through Roscher, is enormous. In *Die Isolierte Staat* (1850) von Thünen depicts an economy similar to Ricardo's corn sector in that rye is produced by rye (subsistence consists of rye); but land is assumed free, and Thünen uses intensive differential rent to determine the division of the product between interest and wages. The notion of marginal productivity is clearly formulated, and in some examples he also anticipates the idea of isoquants, as well as the idea that the optimal combination of capital and labour requires the equality between ratio of rentals and ratio of marginal products. In the same book he formulates detailed examples of a society where initially there is only production by unassisted labour, until someone by saving subsistence goods makes it possible to dedicate a year to produce tools first, which raise labour's subsequent productivity of consumption goods, so workers are ready to pay interest for the savings; when all workers producing consumption goods have been supplied with the most useful tools producible by one year of labour, further savings allow dedicating another year to the production of further and different tools, which add less to productivity since the most useful tools have been produced first, so the interest rate decreases and wages rise (see Leigh 1946, for a summary); thus Thünen also introduces the idea that savings allow a delay between application of labour and production of consumption goods that permits the productivity of labour to increase, the idea to be then found in Jevons and in the Austrian school. Heterogeneous capital is a value magnitude, equal to the wages paid to the labour that produces capital goods.

Clark studies Thünen, grasps the foundation of the new approach in a generalization of rent theory, and explicitly states that *all* incomes are determined by "a law of rent". But he does not notice the essential role of the physical homogeneity of corn-capital in permitting the symmetry between land and capital in classical intensive rent theory; he treats heterogeneous capital unproblematically as a quantity of value independent of income distribution, both in determining its total endowment, and in order to determine the factor proportions chosen by entrepreneurs. He does not realize that production functions or isoquants in which one factor is value capital can only be derived on the basis of given prices of the capital goods, and therefore cannot determine how optimal factor proportions change with changes in factor rentals, because the prices of capital goods will change, causing shifts of isoquants and of marginal product curves (as Wicksell 1934: 149 points out). The same mistake can be found in many other authors of the period.

Marshall, too, has read Thünen, but prefers a short-period approach where durable capital goods are given, and avoids an explicit reference to a value endowment of capital; but the value conception of capital as a factor of production emerges when he speaks of "free" or "floating" capital as what must be absorbed by new investments in a propor-tion to labour that depends negatively on the rate of interest. This "free" capital is the flow supply of savings, treated as measurable independently of income distribution, and entrepreneurs will demand it up to the point where the marginal value product of this investment becomes equal to the rate of interest. Thus although only at the margin of new investments, capital in Marshall is still the single factor produced by savings, an amount of value but analogous to physical factors in the marginalist factor substitution mechanisms. In determining the demand for the flow of savings, the dependence of prices on income distribution is neglected as much as in Clark. The short-period framework obscures but does not alter the basis of the theory, and the subsequent writings of his pupils Robertson or Pigou confirm this fact.

The Austrian approach: Böhm-Bawerk and Wicksell

The mistake of a measurement of capital as an amount of value in the specification of production methods is avoided in the "Austrian" approach of Böhm-Bawerk and Wicksell, a development of the analyses of Thünen and Jevons; but the total demand and supply of capital are still measured in value; and the negative interest elasticity of the demand for capital is obtained through the very restrictive assumptions justifying the average period of production.

Jevons supplies intuitions, more than a developed supply-and-demand theory, to sub-sequent authors. He argues that capital is a subsistence fund, an advancement of wages that permits a delay between work and enjoyment of the results, allowing for the produc-tion of useful capital goods first; the longer the average time for which the same total amount of labour is advanced, the greater the product (but less and less so), with the rate of interest reflecting the marginal increase. His conception of vertically integrated production processes as starting with unassisted labour will be called "Austrian" because it was adopted by Austrian authors, but in fact it is already in Smith. For the case of a given input of labour yielding some time later an output q of a consumption good that increases at a decreasing rate with the length of the intervening (or average) delay T, Jevons argues that the rate of interest must equal $q'(T)/q$. However, these intuitions are not developed into a complete theory; neither the supply side nor the demand side of the market that should determine the rate of interest are well specified.

Böhm-Bawerk (1891), like Jevons, assumes an "Austrian" structure of production, and adopts the conception of capital as a subsistence fund as well as the idea that labour productivity increases, but less and less, with a lengthening of the average delay between labour and final product, a lengthening that, for a given real wage and a given labour force, requires an increase of the subsistence fund. He introduces the period of produc-tion as a measure of how advanced wages are on average. Through numerical examples he shows that as the real wage rises, the optimal average period of production rises and the rate of interest decreases.

His verbal exposition is formalized by Wicksell (1893), who makes it clear that the average period of production allows the determination of the normal price of commodities and of a decreasing demand curve for capital if (1) capital goods are only circulating capital, (2) land is free (or always has exactly the same average period as labour), and (3) simple instead of compound interest is assumed (in Böhm-Bawerk this assumption is implicit in his numerical examples). A synthetic presentation of his model is in Garegnani (1990: 27). Wicksell shows that with simple interest at rate r the price (in terms of a representative basket of consumption goods) of a good produced by one unit of total direct and indirect labour advanced for an average period T is $w + rwT$, where w is the real wage, and the value of the capital employed in the vertically integrated sector producing that good as net product is wT. If r increases, the goods produced by processes with a greater T become relatively dearer; technical and consumer substitution then imply that as the rate of interest increases and the real wage decreases, the economy-wide weighted average of the T's of the several vertically integrated industries producing final goods, call it T^*, decreases, and thus one obtains an even greater decrease of wT^*. Letting A represent the total and fully employed labour supply, the value of the stationary net product if produced with the desired average periods is $wA + rwAT^*$, hence wAT^* is the demand for capital, a decreasing function of r, which if combined with a given supply of capital will allow a supply-and-demand determination of the rate of interest. Wicksell formalizes this last step by writing $\overline{K} = wAT^*$, where the value of capital $\overline{K}$ is a given number, with respect to which he writes that, in the process of achieving equilibrium, though "the forms of capital change, its total value remains unchanged, since, in place of the consumed capital goods, new ones of equivalent value enter successively" (1893: 103). This conception of the capital supply as a given amount of exchange value is taken from Böhm-Bawerk's conception of capital as a revolving subsistence fund, embodied in capital goods of value equal to the subsistence advanced to the labour that produced them (with simple interest, the value of a capital advance does not increase with the passage of time).

However, can one treat the subsistence fund as unchanged when income distribution changes? Following Garegnani (1960: 164–75), let us consider a stationary economy producing a single consumption good as net product, initially in equilibrium with full employment of labour and a value of capital equal to wAT^*. Now w increases to w', with – let us assume – no change in quantities produced nor production methods. The result is a revaluation of the capital goods in existence as prices adapt to the new normal prices; the value of capital rises to $w'AT^*$. There has been an increase of the subsistence fund owing only to the change in income distribution, without any net savings in any acceptable sense: the economy as a whole continues to consume as much as before. Every period the flow of wage advances has risen to $w'A$ but this does not require the community as a whole to have performed net savings; it is only another face of the income redistribution from interest to wages. Thus when income distribution is what must be determined, there is no right to treat the value of capital as given: any change in income distribution will alter it, showing that the value of capital reflects income distribution rather than being one of its determinants. This is a general conclusion, also valid with compound interest and with wages paid in arrears: the normal value of capital changes with changes in income distribution, even if physically nothing changes. To this basic problem can be added the short-period deviations of the values of existing capital goods from their normal values any time there is technical change or changes of demand.

Wicksell does not seem to be conscious of this problem in 1893, but he soon grows dissatisfied with the other limitations of the theory, and the attempt to surmount them makes him eventually realize the problem with the value endowment of capital too. In the *Lectures* (1934; first Swedish edition, 1900) he admits compound interest, drops the period of production, and adopts a representation of the production conditions of consumption goods via differentiable production functions with dated quantities of labour and of land as inputs, as if firms were vertically integrated (again Garegnani 1990: 29–31 offers a synthetic presentation of the model). Wicksell's preference for this representation (that requires "Austrian" production processes) derives from his continued belief that the key to the explanation of the rate of interest lies in the increase in production obtained by increasing the delay between use of "original" factors and final output; but now he admits problems. On the demand side, he notes that the rate of interest is generally not equal to the marginal product of capital, because of the revaluation of capital goods due to the change in income distribution associated with the employment of one more unit of capital; this revaluation, afterwards named "price Wicksell effect", makes him unsure whether a lower rate of interest will always cause a greater demand for value capital; at one point (Wicksell 1934: 183) he writes that the issue should be further studied (reverse capital deepening – see below – will show he was right to have doubts). For the same reason he admits problems on the supply side: after treating capital as a quantity of value in earlier chapters, when he must "close" the complete model of general equilibrium with the equality between supply and demand for capital, Wicksell cannot hide doubts on the legitimacy of taking the value of the capital endowment as given; he writes "it would clearly be meaningless – if not altogether inconceivable – to maintain that the amount of capital is already fixed before equilibrium between production and consumption has been achieved", because any change of relative prices during the tendency toward equilibrium would change the value of capital goods, with a consequent "indeterminateness" of the endowment of capital (1934: 202); still, although hesitatingly (he does not write down the equation), he finally takes the total value of capital as given (1934: 204). He has grown dissatisfied with a value endowment of capital but is unable to find an alternative.

The imputation approach: Menger, Wieser, Walras

Even less satisfactory is the treatment of capital by the authors who start from marginal utility and adopt an "imputation" approach in the sense that the market imputes to factor services the value of what they produce. The main authors are Menger, Wieser and Walras.

Carl Menger conceives production as a "downward" flow of services from inputs "of higher order", that is, employed earlier, toward goods of "lower order", and he insists that the value of the inputs derives from the value – the utility – of their final product; but hating mathematics and lacking the notion of marginal productivity he is unable to perform the derivation when there is more than one input; therefore his approach to income distribution remains disconcertingly vague. Understandably, he is also unable to reach a determination of the rate of interest: in 1888, at the end of a verbose and inconclusive article on what "capital" can mean, Menger states that a satisfactory theory of the yield of capital is still to come and expresses the hope that Böhm-Bawerk may soon redress the situation (so as better to counter the socialist propaganda, he explicitly writes).

Wieser eschews mathematics too, and proposes verbally an imputation method amounting to a system of equations, one for each consumption good, where technical coefficients are given, the values of consumption goods are given, the imputed rewards of factors are the unknowns to be determined, and for each consumption good the sum of the rewards imputed to its inputs equals its value. Besides problems of over- or under-determination of the system of equations, the method needs given values of the consumption goods so it remains incomplete. Furthermore capital, measured as an amount of value, is one of the factors in the imputation, and Wieser admits that this creates a problem, because the value of capital should derive from the imputation process, but if it is not known one does not know how much capital each process employs; the solution is clearly unsatisfactory: at each moment, Wieser argues, the value of capital can be taken as given (by previous calculations of economic agents).

When Wieser writes (his first contribution is in 1888), Walras has already (in the first edition of his *Eléments*, 1877, pt II) completed the "imputation" approach via a general equilibrium of production and exchange with fixed coefficients, with all factors physically specified and income distribution determined by the indirect factor substitution mechanism. In the Preface to the fourth edition, Walras summarizes: "the formula of the English school, in any case the school of Ricardo and Mill, must be reversed, for the prices of productive services are determined by the prices of their products and not the other way round". However, he too is unable to insert capital satisfactorily in the approach. Unique among the founders of the marginalist approach, Walras never glimpses the possibility of treating the several capital goods as "embodying" a single factor capital of variable "form"; he treats them as so many distinct factors, each one with its given endowment. Yet his conception of equilibrium fully belongs to the traditional method of normal positions. The equilibrium is described as: (1) a centre of gravitation to which the economy tends through slow adjustments (Walras 1954: 380); (2) persistent, allowing the treatment of equilibrium relative prices as if constant (for example, Walras determines the purchase price of land by dividing the land rental by the rate of interest, as if both variables could be assumed constant for ever); and (3) characterized by a uniform rate of return on the supply price of capital goods (URRSP), such as the classical natural prices or Wicksell's equilibrium prices. This clearly requires an endogenous determination of the composition of capital; but up to the third edition (1896) of his *Eléments* Walras appears not to be clear about the fact that his specification of the capital endowment prevents it. He argues that URRSP is reached by variations of the composition of investment because, if production of a new capital good rises owing to a higher-than-average rate of return on supply price, the increased production will significantly reduce its rental; but this can only be due to the increase of its endowment, which however Walras cannot admit because he treats the equilibrium's capital endowments as given. This contradictory view of URRSP as brought about by a process incompatible with the specification of the equilibrium's data reveals a confusion but it also reveals the origin of Walras's acceptance of URRSP in the traditional argument (explicitly accepted in one passage, 1954: 271) that URRSP is brought about by changes in the relative quantities in existence of the several capital goods. Walras seems confusedly to view the given endowments of capital goods as being adjusted by the process determining the quantities produced of new capital goods so as to yield URRSP.

With the fourth edition (1900), evidently having become clearer that he is taking the capital endowments' vector as arbitrarily given and not as adjusting, Walras introduces three changes whose importance is first stressed by Garegnani (1960). A first change (the only one Walras announces in the Preface) concerns the *tâtonnement*, which in the previous editions involved a repetition of actual productions and exchanges. Now Walras extends to the complete model the assumption he had until then restricted to pure exchange, that the adjustment toward equilibrium excludes actual disequilibrium productions and exchanges: it operates by means of provisional "bons" and production only starts when equilibrium is reached. Clearly, he has become conscious that he cannot allow disequilibrium productions to alter the endowments of capital goods. A second change reveals he has realized the mistake of his previous argument on what process achieves URRSP. Now the process relies only on the effect on the costs of production of new capital goods (the increase in the production of a capital good, Walras argues, raises the rentals of the factors more intensively utilized in that industry, so the cost of production rises relative to the rental – now assumed little affected – of that capital good). However, in a multiproduct economy changes in the quantity produced of a single product cannot greatly affect its cost of production; evidently having realized this fact, Walras introduces a third change: without modifying the equations, he inserts two new sentences (1954: 294, 308) where he states that URRSP is not always achievable and the capital goods unable to yield the same rate of return as the other ones will not be produced, which requires eliminating the equations imposing URRSP for these unproduced capital goods. This amounts to admitting a contradiction between the given vectorial capital endowment and the intent to determine a long-period equilibrium. As stressed by Garegnani, the implication is that, since the alternative conception of capital as a single value factor renders its endowment indeterminate as admitted by Wicksell, there is no way consistently to determine a long-period equilibrium.

Another little discussed aspect of Walras's approach to capital deserves mention. He distinguishes "capital proper", that is, durable capital goods, from raw materials, seed, and other circulating capital, and no endowments of the latter inputs appear among the data of equilibrium (1954: 238–41). He makes circulating capital disappear from the equations of equilibrium by replacing, in the equations determining the cost of production of goods, the cost of the raw materials and so on with the cost of the services of land, labour and "capital proper" that produced them. This is consistent only if production – imagining it to be in yearly cycles, with the equilibrium describing one cycle – is as follows: at the beginning of the year production starts with no circulating capital at all, only labour, land and durable capital goods; intermediate goods appear and are then totally used up during the productive process, so at the end of the year gross output consists only of consumption goods and new durable capital goods. The need for endowments of many circulating capital goods, for example, seeds, at the beginning of the year disappears from sight. Only with the fourth edition circulating capital is admitted, and only in a not very clear Part VI, but the picture of production of the earlier Parts influences later authors, contributing to a frequent erroneous identification of capital with only durable capital goods.

From the 1900s to the 1940s: disagreements and uncertainties
The period from 1900 to the 1940s witnesses the rise to practically complete dominance of the marginalist approach; but it also witnesses the paradox of economists who agree on interest as the reward, determined by a supply-and-demand equilibrium, of the factor "capital", but are unable to agree on how to make the idea rigorous; each different view is sharply criticized by others.

There is almost general agreement that the quantity of capital must be measured as a quantity of value; but the Clarkian conception of value capital as perfectly analogous to labour or land is criticized not only by Böhm-Bawerk (1907), who argues that it is indispensable to refer to the delay between inputs and output and to time preference to understand why advanced labour has a marginal product that pays not only its wages but also interest; it is also and more radically criticized by Veblen (1908: 160–67) who questions its value measurement noting that prices are not given. The given endowment of value capital is admitted to be problematical by Wicksell too, as we saw; a radical rejection comes from Irving Fisher who argues that the value of capital derives entirely from capitalization of its prospective returns, and that the rate of interest is determined, not by equality between supply and demand for capital, but by equality between supply and demand for savings, in turn determined by "impatience" and by the existence of "investment opportunities", which he treats as determinable independently of the rate of interest, as if there were just one aggregate commodity "income" that can be consumed or "transferred" across periods by being employed in investments that produce "income" in subsequent periods. In some passages Fisher admits the influence of the rate of interest on relative prices but (without proof) dismisses this effect as not affecting his conclusions. Fisher's approach is very unclear on the data it starts from, but it is rather similar to Marshall's (and is so judged by Keynes) in that the rate of interest is determined by the marginal rate of return (illegitimately assumed determinable independently of the rate of interest) over the investment absorbing the supply of savings.

Disagreements are strong also on the period of production, which is generally rejected (even, as we saw, by Wicksell) because of needing simple interest; but the idea that decreases of the rate of interest will induce the adoption of in some sense "longer" or "more roundabout" production processes is widely accepted: it is found, for example, in Fetter, Marshall, Hicks, and Kaldor. However, Knight criticizes this idea in a series of articles in the 1930s. He is answered by Hayek (1936) with an attack on all conceptions of capital as a single factor, a "fund", the Clarkian conception as well as the Böhm-Bawerkian one, all accused of needing the measurement in terms of value and therefore of suffering from logical circularity; capital, Hayek argues, can be described only through a complete enumeration of all physical capital goods. Knight (1936) replies that one does not need the "fund" capital to determine interest, which can be determined at the margin of new investment; but in so doing he follows Fisher in implicitly taking prices as given in determining the return to marginal investment; thus he too falls under the objection advanced, for example, by Lutz (1956 [1967]) that given prices imply a certain rate of interest, and therefore a determination of the rate of interest as the rate of return on marginal investment taking both present and future prices as given entails circularity. Actually Knight still believes in capital as the value factor, as shown, for example, by his 1946 entry "Capital and interest" in *Encyclopaedia Britannica*.

The uncertainties are confirmed by a tendency to limit the presentation of formalized general equilibrium theory to acapitalistic production. This is what Pareto does in the *Manuel* (1909) where he drops Walras's equations of "capitalization" he had initially accepted, without replacing them with anything else. Marshall too presents only (parts of) the acapitalistic general equilibrium model in the Mathematical Appendix of the *Principles*; Stackelberg, Zeuthen, and Wald, who in the 1930s try to give a more rigorous proof of existence of solutions to the general equilibrium equations, again limit themselves to the acapitalistic model. Apparently there is faith that the approach can be extended to include capital and interest, and therefore a limitation of the analysis to the acapitalistic model is not perceived as a decisive deficiency; but no one seems to know how rigorously to perform the extension.

Hayek, Lindahl, Hicks and neo-Walrasian equilibria

Hayek's attack reflects an important novelty, the birth of the belief that it is possible to maintain the supply-and-demand approach while abandoning the defective conception of capital as a single value factor, through a shift to a treatment of each capital good as a distinct factor with its given endowment. The different notion of equilibrium is sketched by Hayek in 1928 (see Gehrke 2003), but Lindahl (1929) is the first to develop it consciously as an alternative to value capital and long-period equilibria. Differently from Walras, both Lindahl and Hayek realize that the given vectorial endowment of capital goods implies that they are determining a very-short-period equilibrium, hence equilibrium prices may well be destined to change rapidly, and therefore agents must be admitted to take expected price changes into account in determining their equilibrium choices. This is done either by assuming a simultaneous determination of present and future equilibrium prices and quantities (a complete-futures-markets or perfect-foresight intertemporal equilibrium), or by introducing subjective and non-uniform expectations (temporary equilibrium). These notions of equilibrium are called Walrasian or neo-Walrasian, but they differ from Walras owing to their acknowledged very-short-period nature and admission of non-persistence of the relative prices that the equilibrium determines.

This new approach is made widely known by Hicks's *Value and Capital* (1939) where the temporary equilibrium method is advocated. Importantly, the justification Hicks provides for the shift misrepresents Marshall's static long-period equilibrium as a *secularly stationary* equilibrium (in the latter the rate of interest and the quantity of capital are endogenously determined so as to induce zero net savings and therefore no given quantity of capital appears among the data of equilibrium; in the former the quantity of capital is given and stationariness is assumed only for simplicity) and therefore too remote from actual economies; this allows Hicks to avoid a discussion of the true role and deficiencies of capital the value factor. The misrepresentation of the traditional notion of equilibrium as secularly stationary has dire consequences on the subsequent capacity of economists to understand previous economic theorists: the notion of normal position as distinct from steady growth is no longer understood, to this day many economists appear unable to grasp that the speed of variation of the composition of capital is sufficiently higher than the speed of the changes brought about by accumulation as to allow neglecting the latter changes in order to determine normal prices. Other aspects of the book are also perplexing. Hicks admits the need for instantaneous equilibration but is unclear on how to justify (after Keynes!) a very quick adaptation of aggregate demand to full-employment output; he avoids discussing the insufficient factor substitutability associated with a given "form" of capital, admitted by him in earlier writings, or the indeterminacy due to unknowable subjective expectations he had criticized in a 1936 review of Keynes's *General Theory*. (He will admit these weaknesses subsequently in what amounts to a full recantation of the temporary equilibrium method, see Petri 1991.)

The shift to neo-Walrasian equilibria is not intended to alter the marginalist view of how market economies work. In Hayek, Lindahl and Hicks one finds the same certainty as in Clark, Marshall or Wicksell that decreases of the rate of interest cause switches to production methods that require capital goods of greater value per unit of labour and therefore raise the flow demand for savings, ensuring stability of the savings-investment market; and that if real wages decrease, the demand for labour will rise, if not immediately for lack of substitutability, then through changes in the physical composition of capital over a succession of periods. The traditional marginalist factor substitution mechanisms are still believed to be operative although possibly over a sequence of temporary equilibria (or of periods of an intertemporal equilibrium): the traditional conception of capital is only apparently abandoned, it no longer appears in the specification of production methods nor of the economy's endowment of capital, but traditional capital-labour substitution is still present (although now without foundation since no solid argument makes up for the official rejection of value capital) in the assumed stability of the labour market and of the savings-investment market.

Lindahl, Hayek and Hicks open the way to an argument by Arrow and Debreu (1954) that capitalistic production can be dealt with by the acapitalistic model of general equilibrium without any need for formal modification, through a reinterpretation of goods as dated, of the model as describing an intertemporal equilibrium over a finite number of periods, of prices as discounted prices, and of some of the given factor endowments in the initial period as capital goods produced before the date when equilibrium is established. Koopmans (1957) notes the implausibility of complete futures markets, which imply the absurd assumption that future generations are present in the first period to communicate their desires, but without concluding that this notion of equilibrium must be discarded. Debreu's *Theory of Value* (1959) insists on the reinterpretability. No attention is paid to the fact that Maurice Allais had already developed the intertemporal-equilibrium model in the 1940s (with overlapping generations too in it) only to reject it as lacking sufficient persistency and incapable therefore of having the role of centre of gravitation of time-consuming disequilibrium adjustments.

The 1950s witness the coexistence of the acapitalistic general equilibrium model in textbooks, of the intertemporal model in specialist articles, and of the traditional treatment of capital as a single value factor in applications. The persuasion slowly takes hold that there is no incompatibility between the traditional and the neo-Walrasian treatments of capital. Solow is representative: in an answer to Joan Robinson's (1953–54) article that starts the Cambridge controversy in capital theory by asking in what units capital is measured, he admits problems with the notion of "quantity of capital" but argues that they can be surmounted through intertemporal equilibrium theory:

> [T]he real difficulty of the subject comes not from the physical diversity of capital goods. It comes from the intertwining of past, present and future, from the fact that while there is something foolish about a theory of capital built on the assumption of perfect foresight, we have no equally precise and definite assumption to take its place. (Solow 1955–56: 102)

In the same years he proposes his one-good growth model and even bases econometric estimates on it.

The Cambridge capital controversy

In 1960, Sraffa's *Production of Commodities* points out the possibility of reswitching of techniques, already hinted at by Joan Robinson in the mentioned 1953–54 article (on whose limits see Petri 2004: 227–33). This possibility, universally admitted after a 1966 Symposium in the *Quarterly Journal of Economics*, causes enormous surprise because it reveals that factor substitution need not work in the way until then unquestioned: a technique, abandoned in favour of others because the interest rate rises, may come back as being the most convenient as the rate of interest rises further; which means that if one switch of technique is in a direction supportive of marginalist theses, the other switch contradicts them. Thus, whatever way one measures the capital–labour proportion of different techniques, a rise of the interest rate need not cause a switch to a less capital-intensive technique. The impossibility of deciding unambiguously which techniques are more capital-intensive puts a final nail in the coffin of the idea that the observed methods of production entail the presence in the economy of a "quantity of capital" independent of distribution. Furthermore, a decrease of real wages may cause a switch to methods of production that decrease the amount of labour employed per unit of net product, and it may raise the normal relative price of the goods using more labour per unit of (value) capital: both the direct and the indirect factor substitution mechanisms are questioned. In value terms, a decrease of the rate of interest can cause the switch to a technique with a lower value of capital per unit of labour; this reverse capital deepening undermines the traditionally assumed negative interest elasticity of the demand for capital, and hence of investment too. Garegnani, in an influential article on Keynes (1964–65), argues that this possibility undermines faith in the rate of interest as capable of bringing investment into equality with savings; as a consequence one must reject Keynes's investment function and the "neoclassical synthesis". This, he concludes, strengthens Keynes's principle of effective demand and the thesis that wage flexibility does not guarantee the tendency to full employment, and that growth depends on the evolution of the autonomous components of aggregate demand.

One line of defence against the "Sraffian" criticisms is the argument that the likelihood of reswitching and of reverse capital deepening is low so their possibility can be neglected, as for Giffen goods. However, this attempted rehabilitation of traditional capital–labour substitution, besides being based on underestimation of the "likelihood" of reswitching (Petri 2011a), relies on a mistaken analogy: different from income effects, reswitching does not indicate a reason for multiple solutions in an otherwise consistent system of equations; it destroys the logical consistency of the conception of capital as a single factor and thus it destroys all legitimacy of determining equilibria based on capital treated as a single factor. The problem is not the likelihood of multiple or unstable such equilibria but the impossibility of determining them.

For this reason, the treatment of capital as a single value factor, still widely accepted in the early 1960s, undergoes a loss of theoretical legitimacy, and the main reaction to reswitching quickly becomes the claim that the "rigorous" versions of marginalist theory (by now more often called neoclassical theory) are the neo-Walrasian general equilibrium models that do not need capital the single factor; the one-good models (the sole versions by now that treat capital as a single factor, hiding its conception as a value factor under the thin disguise of the physical homogeneity obtained with the one-good assumption) are argued to be only simplifications, shortcuts to results that the "rigorous" theory would confirm, such as factor rentals inversely related to factor abundance, or supply-side-determined growth. This line of defence abounds with misunderstandings. Bliss (1975) and Hahn (1982) take it for granted that neo-Walrasian intertemporal equilibria are the only conceivable disaggregated theory of value and distribution. The notion of long-period disaggregated equilibrium such as Wicksell's is totally forgotten; the problems with "capital aggregation" are misunderstood as identical with those posed by aggregation (in production functions) of heterogeneous labour or land, without perceiving the fundamental difference consisting of the insufficient persistency of the endowments of the several capital goods that makes it nonsensical to take them as given, a problem not arising for different qualities of land or of specialized labour, whose quantities are persistent and accordingly can be treated as different factors. The possibility of a theory of income distribution not based on factor supply-and-demand equilibration is not considered at all. This makes Hahn present Sraffa's prices as a very special case of intertemporal general equilibrium prices (the case when initial endowments cause equilibrium relative prices not to change from one period to the next), to be contrasted with the capacity of general equilibrium theory to deal with any given initial endowments: absent is any recognition that Sraffa is not assuming full employment, or that his prices are the same normal prices that not only Ricardo but also Wicksell tried to determine, necessarily associated with an endogenous determination of the composition of capital.

This helps to explain why the undermining of the notion of capital the single factor does not bring about an abandonment of the entire supply-and-demand approach. Hicks's misrepresentation of long-period equilibria as secularly stationary equilibria has favoured an inability to understand the long-period method; the new generations of economists, acquainted only with neo-Walrasian equilibria, have grown accustomed to the auctioneer, are unaware that, for example, in Wicksell complete disaggregation has gone together with the treatment of capital as a single value factor of variable "form", and do not understand the reasons for such a treatment of capital; the impossibility to treat capital as a single factor is viewed as questioning only the use of aggregate production functions. Garegnani's 1960 book, that discusses Wicksell at length, concluding that the impossibility of determining the capital endowment of long-period equilibria undermines the entire marginalist approach, is not very widely read (it is not translated into English), but above all it is not found decisive because neo-Walrasian equilibria do not require – it is argued – capital the single factor.

Garegnani (1976, and then in greater detail in 1990) tries to re-establish an understanding of the evolution of neoclassical capital theory, remembering the method of normal positions, and the marginalist need for a given endowment of capital the single value factor of variable "form" in spite of complete disaggregation if the aim is to determine a normal-position (that is, a long-period) equilibrium, because the several endowments of capital goods must then be variables. He argues that the shift to the neo-Walrasian treatment of the capital endowment was due to the indefensibility of the value–capital factor, with an example from Hicks. He proceeds to stress three new problems of neo-Walrasian equilibria owing to the vectorial specification of the capital endowment:

1. *Impermanence problem.* Some of the data determining the equilibrium (endowments of the several capital goods and also, in temporary equilibria, expectation functions) lack persistence, being changed by disequilibrium decisions; the auctioneer is only a fairy tale; therefore before the repetition of transactions may correct or compensate the deviations from equilibrium, the equilibrium's data may have changed considerably; then, since the theory is silent on what happens in disequilibrium and therefore offers no reason to exclude a cumulation of deviations of the actual path from the path traced by the sequence of equilibria (even assuming this sequence does not itself suffer from indeterminacy), the actual path remains undetermined.
2. *Substitutability problem.* There is almost no substitutability among factors, because different production methods generally require different capital goods, not the same goods in different proportions; thus the demand for labour will be extremely inelastic and the equilibrium real wage may easily be totally implausible.
3. *Price-change problem.* Since equilibrium relative prices cannot be assumed persistent, consideration of price changes must be allowed but only two equally indefensible roads are available: intertemporal equilibria require the absurdity of complete futures markets or perfect foresight, which means that, clearly, real economies will behave differently; temporary equilibria suffer from an indefiniteness problem because the single equilibrium as well as the path followed by a sequence of temporary equilibria come to depend upon arbitrary assumptions on unknowable initial expectations and on how these evolve over time.

However, Garegnani (1990) continues, these new problems, that drastically undermine the capacity of these equilibria to indicate the behaviour of actual economies, are incurred to no avail, because the need for the traditional conception of substitutability between labour and capital the value factor has not been removed. A persistent change in the rate of interest necessarily causes a tendency of prices over time toward the corresponding long-period relative prices, and hence it causes changes in technical choices and in consumer choices tending to those studied by long-period analysis. The full employment assumed by neo-Walrasian equilibria requires that these changes be such as to ensure that, if the value of decisions to save were to exceed that of decisions to invest, a reduction of the rate of interest would induce firms to absorb the excess savings by coupling the existing labour supply with capital goods of greater value. This is what the validity of the conception of capital as an amount of value and yet behaving like a technical factor would ensure, but reverse capital deepening refutes it. So the shift to the neo-Walrasian versions represents a cosmetic change only; the old conception of capital is still implicitly and illegitimately assumed to be valid if it is claimed that neo-Walrasian equilibria mimic tendencies of actual economies.

Recent trends: a paradox
Only brief hints can be given on trends after 1990. Garegnani's criticisms (1), (2) and (3), then taken up by numerous other economists (for example, Petri 2004), have remained unanswered so far by neoclassical economists, a continuation of the attitude started by Hahn (1982), who had taken no notice of Garegnani (1976). Neoclassical capital theory continues to be based on intertemporal equilibria (temporary equilibria without perfect foresight have been abandoned owing to grave difficulties with

formalization and existence), extended now to cover the infinite future, with display of impressive mathematics but little discussion of the legitimacy of such a step. A debate on whether reswitching and reverse capital deepening cause problems of instability and multiplicity of intertemporal equilibria has been started by Garegnani (2000), but with unclear results for the moment (Petri 2011b). Complaints about the lack of realism of intertemporal equilibria are frequent; furthermore the Sonnenschein–Mantel–Debreu results, and problems of equilibrium indeterminacy with overlapping generations, have greatly increased discomfort among general equilibrium specialists, with instances (for example, Alan Kirman) of outspoken rejection of general equilibrium theory as a positive theory. However, paradoxically neoclassical macroeconomic theory has become dominated by continuous-full-employment equilibrium models (real business cycle models and dynamic stochastic general equilibrium models), often one-good models, that are justified as simplified intertemporal general equilibrium models. Among neo-classical macroeconomists there seems to be little doubt about the legitimacy of assuming continuous equilibrium, with perfect foresight (or "rational expectations") in place of the obvious absence of complete futures markets. The so-called "Hahn problem" (Hahn 1987), that points out that, with heterogeneous capital, correct myopic foresight leaves room for a continuum of alternative equilibrium paths, is set aside through an assumption of coincidence of equilibrium path and optimal path, obtained by assuming an infinitely lived representative consumer with perfect foresight over the infinite future, an incredible assumption (for example, how can one foresee technical progress?).

The key to explaining this paradox would appear to lie in recognizing that the same a priori certainties pointed out apropos Lindahl, Hayek and Hicks still rule among neoclassical macroeconomists. Evidently, a faith remains strong in the existence of the tendencies traditionally postulated by the marginalist approach: since in real economies there is no auctioneer and no perfect foresight, the implicit view of these theorists must be that time-consuming disequilibria do not cause the actual path of the economy to differ drastically from the one traced by intertemporal equilibria, because there are adjustment mechanisms that bring the economy back toward a full-employment equilibrium path when it strays away from it. What seems to be missing is consciousness of the fact that neo-Walrasian general equilibrium theory, owing to its inability to indicate actual paths, offers no support to such views. Rather, one must believe in the time-consuming adjustments, involving actual disequilibrium productions and exchanges, originally postulated by the marginalist approach and crucially relying (also in their reformulation by the "neoclassical synthesis" after Keynes) on a decreasing demand curve for labour and on an interest-elastic investment function, notions developed on the basis of the conception of capital as a single value factor, and lacking foundation outside that admittedly indefensible conception.

In conclusion, in the light of the historical evolution of the marginalist/neoclassical approach to capital, its problems appear insurmountable: the conception of capital as a single factor is unacceptable; the treatment of each capital good as a distinct factor brings sterile notions of equilibrium, silent on the behaviour of actual economies. As these are the two possible treatments of capital in the approach, what seems to emerge is the impossibility of the marginalist approach to distribution satisfactorily to insert produced means of production in its analytical structure. The surplus approach to capital, with its different, socio-political determination of income distribution, appears to encounter no comparable difficulty.

FABIO PETRI

See also:

Ladislaus von Bortkiewicz (I); British classical political economy (II); British marginalism (II); General equilibrium theory (III); German and Austrian schools (II); John Richard Hicks (I); Marxism(s) (II); Neo-Ricardian economics (II); François Quesnay and Physiocracy (I); Piero Sraffa (I); Value and price (III); Marie-Esprit-Léon Walras (I); Knut Wicksell (I).

References and further reading

Arrow, K.J. and G. Debreu (1954), 'Existence of an equilibrium for a competitive economy', *Econometrica*, **22** (3), 265–90.

Bliss, C.J. (1975), *Capital Theory and the Distribution of Income*, Amsterdam: North-Holland.

Böhm-Bawerk, E. von (1891), *The Positive Theory of Capital*, London: Macmillan.

Böhm-Bawerk, E. von (1907), 'Capital and interest once more: II. A relapse to the productivity theory', *Quarterly Journal of Economics*, (February), 247–82.

Bortkiewicz, L. von (1906–07), 'Wertrechnung und Preisrechnung im Marxschen System', *Archiv für Sozialwissenschaft und Sozialpolitik*, **23** (1906), 1–50, **25** (1907), 10–51, 445–88.

Bortkiewicz, L. von (1907), 'Zur Berichtigung der grundlegenden theoretischen Konstruktion von Marx im 3. Band des "Kapital"', *Jahrbücher für Nationalökonomie und Statistik*, **34**, 319–35.

Debreu, G. (1959), *Theory of Value*, New York: John Wiley & Sons.

Dmitriev, V.K. (1974), 'The theory of value of D. Ricardo, an attempt at a rigorous analysis', in V.K. Dmitriev, *Economic Essays on Value, Competition and Utility* (transl. of 1904 book in Russian), Cambridge: Cambridge University Press, pp. 37–95; first published 1898 in *Ekonomicheskie Ocherki*.

Dome, T. (1998), 'Adam Smith's theory of tax incidence: an interpretation of his natural-price system', *Cambridge Journal of Economics*, **22** (1), 79–89.

Eatwell, J.L. and M. Milgate (eds) (1983), *Keynes's Economics and the Theory of Value and Distribution*, London and New York: Duckworth and Oxford University Press.

Eatwell, J.L., M. Milgate and P. Newman (eds) (1987), *The New Palgrave Dictionary of Economics*, London: Macmillan.

Garegnani, P. (1960), *Il capitale nelle teorie della distribuzione*, Milan: Giuffrè.

Garegnani, P. (1964–65), 'Note su consumi, investimenti e domanda effettiva. Parte I, Parte II', *Economia Internazionale*, reprinted in P. Garegnani (1979), *Valore e domanda effettiva*, Turin: Einaudi, English trans. (with modifications), *Cambridge Journal of Economics*, Part I in **2** (4), 335–53, Part II in **3** (1), 63–82, both parts reprinted in J.L. Eatwell and M. Milgate (eds) (1983), *Keynes's Economics and the Theory of Value and Distribution*, London and New York: Duckworth and Oxford University Press, pp. 21–69.

Garegnani, P. (1976), 'On a change in the notion of equilibrium in recent work on value and distribution', in M. Brown, K. Sato and P. Zarembka (eds), *Essays in Modern Capital Theory*, Amsterdam: North-Holland, pp. 25–45; reprinted in J.L. Eatwell and M. Milgate (eds) (1983), *Keynes's Economics and the Theory of Value and Distribution*, London and New York: Duckworth and Oxford University Press, pp. 129–45.

Garegnani, P. (1987), 'Surplus approach', in J.L. Eatwell, M. Milgate and P. Newman (eds), *The New Palgrave Dictionary of Economics*, London: Macmillan.

Garegnani, P. (1990), 'Quantity of capital', in J.L. Eatwell, M. Milgate and P. Newman (eds), *The New Palgrave: Capital Theory*, London: Macmillan, pp. 1–78.

Garegnani, P. (2000), 'Savings, investment and capital in a system of general intertemporal equilibrium', in H.D. Kurz (ed.), *Critical Essays on Sraffa's Legacy in Economics*, Cambridge: Cambridge University Press, pp. 392–445.

Garegnani, P. (2007), 'Professor Samuelson on Sraffa and the classical economists', *European Journal of the History of Economic Thought*, **14** (2), 181–242.

Garegnani, P. and A. Palumbo (1998), 'Accumulation of capital', in H.D. Kurz and N. Salvadori (eds), *The Elgar Companion to Classical Economics*, Cheltenham, UK and Northampton, MA, USA: Edward Elgar.

Gehrke, C. (2003), 'On the transition from long-period to short-period equilibria', *Review of Political Economy*, **15** (1), 85–106.

Hahn, F.H. (1982), 'The neo-Ricardians', *Cambridge Journal of Economics*, **6** (4), 353–74.

Hahn, F.H. (1987), 'Hahn problem', in J.L. Eatwell, M. Milgate and P. Newman (eds), *The New Palgrave Dictionary of Economics*, London: Macmillan.

Hayek, F.A. (1936), 'The mythology of capital', *Quarterly Journal of Economics*, **1** (February), 199–228.

Hicks, J.R. (1939), *Value and Capital*, Oxford: Clarendon Press.

Hull, C.H. (ed.) (1899), *The Economic Writings of Sir William Petty*, vol. 1, Cambridge: Cambridge University Press.

Knight, F.H. (1936), 'The quantity of capital and the rate of interest: I', *Journal of Political Economy*, **44** (4), 433–63.

Knight, F.H. (1946), 'Capital and interest', *Encyclopaedia Britannica*, vol. 4, Chicago and London: Encyclopaedia Britannica Inc., pp. 779–801, reprinted in American Economic Association (1946), *Readings in the Theory of Income Distribution*, Toronto: American Economic Association.

Koopmans, T. (1957), *Three Essays on the State of Economic Science*, New York: McGraw-Hill.

Kurz, H.D. (1990), 'Effective demand, employment and capital utilisation in the short run', *Cambridge Journal of Economics*, 14, 205–17.

Kurz, H.D. (2011), 'On David Ricardo's theory of profits: the laws of distribution are "not essentially connected with the doctrine of value"', *History of Economic Thought*, **53** (1), 1–20.

Kurz, H.D. and N. Salvadori (1995), *Theory of Production*, Cambridge: Cambridge University Press.

Leigh, A.H. (1946), 'Von Thünen's theory of distribution and the advent of marginal analysis', *Journal of Political Economy*, **54** (6), 481–502.

Lindahl, E. (1929), 'The place of capital in the theory of price', originally published in Swedish, English trans. in E. Lindahl (1939), *Studies in the Theory of Money and Capital*, London: George Allen & Unwin, reprinted 1970 by Augustus Kelley, New York, pp. 271–350.

Lutz, F.A. (1956), *Zinstheorie*, Tubingen: Mohr, English trans. 1967, *The Theory of Interest*, Dordrecht: Reidel.

Marris, R. (1964), *The Economics of Capital Utilisation*, Cambridge: Cambridge University Press.

Menger, C. (1888), 'Zur Theorie des Kapitals', *Jahrbücher für Nationalökonomie und Statistik*, pp. 1–49.

Neumann, J. von (1937), 'Über ein ökonomisches Gleichungssystem und eine Verallgemeinerung des Brouwerischen Fixpunktsatzes', *Ergebnisse eines mathematischen Kolloquiums*, **8**, pp. 73–83, English trans. 1945, 'A model of general economic equilibrium', *Review of Economic Studies*, **13**, 1–9.

O'Donnell, R. (1990), *Adam Smith's Theory of Value and Distribution: A Reappraisal*, New York: St Martin Press.

Pareto, V. (1909), *Manuel d'Economie Politique*, 2nd edn, reprinted 1963, Paris: R. Picon and R. Durand Auzias.

Petri, F. (1991), 'Hicks's recantation of the temporary equilibrium method', *Review of Political Economy*, **3** (3), 268–88.

Petri, F. (2004), *General Equilibrium, Capital and Macroeconomics*, Cheltenham, UK and Northampton, MA, USA: Edward Elgar.

Petri, F. (2011a), 'On the likelihood and relevance of reswitching and reverse capital deepening', in N. Salvadori and C. Gehrke (eds), *Keynes, Sraffa and the Criticism of Neoclassical Theory. Essays in Honour of Heinz D. Kurz*, London: Routledge, pp. 380–418.

Petri, F. (2011b), 'On the recent debate on capital theory and general equilibrium', in V. Caspari (ed.), *The Evolution of Economic Theory. Essays in Honour of Bertram Schefold*, London: Routledge, pp. 55–99.

Ricardo, D. (1951–73), *The Works and Correspondence of David Ricardo*, ed. P. Sraffa, 11 vols, Cambridge, Cambridge University Press, vol. 1: *On the Principles of Political Economy and Taxation* (1823, first edn 1817) with an introduction by P. Sraffa, and vol. 4: *Pamphlets and Papers, 1815–1823*.

Robinson, J.V. (1953–54), 'The production function and the theory of capital', *Review of Economic Studies*, **21** (1), 81–106.

Seton, F. (1957), 'The "transformation problem"', *Review of Economic Studies*, **24** (June), 149–60.

Smith, A. (1776), *An Inquiry into the Nature and Causes of the Wealth of Nations*, 2 vols, London: Strahan and Cadell, reprinted in R.H. Campbell, A.S. Skinner and W.B. Todd (eds) (1976), *Adam Smith. An Inquiry into the Nature and Causes of the Wealth of Nations* (Glasgow Edition of the Works and Correspondence of Adam Smith, vol. 2), 2 vols, Oxford: Clarendon.

Solow, R.M. (1955–56), 'The production function and the theory of capital', *Review of Economic Studies*, **23** (61), 101–8.

Sraffa, P. (1951), 'Introduction', in D. Ricardo (1951–73), *The Works and Correspondence of David Ricardo*, ed. P. Sraffa, vol. 1, Cambridge, Cambridge University Press, pp. 13–62.

Sraffa, P. (1960), *Production of Commodities by Means of Commodities*, Cambridge: Cambridge University Press.

Stirati, A. (1998), 'Wage fund doctrine', in H.D. Kurz and N. Salvadori (eds), *The Elgar Companion to Classical Economics, L–Z*, Cheltenham, UK and Lyme, NH, USA: Edward Elgar, pp. 522–8.

Stirati, A. (1999), 'Ricardo and the wages fund', in G. Mongiovi and F. Petri (eds), *Value, Distribution and Capital. Essays in Honour of Pierangelo Garegnani*, London: Routledge, pp. 204–29.

Sweezy, P. (1942), *The Theory of Capitalist Development*, New York: Monthly Review Press.

Veblen, T. (1908), 'Professor Clark's economics', *Quarterly Journal of Economics*, **22** (2), 147–95.
Walras, L. (1954), *Elements of Political Economy*, Homewood, IL.: Richard D. Irwin.
Wicksell, K. (1893), *Über Wert, Kapital und Rente*, Jena: G. Fischer, English trans. 1954, *Value, Capital and Rent*, London: Allen & Unwin.
Wicksell, K. (1934), *Lectures on Political Economy*, vol. 1, London: Allen & Unwin, 1st Swedish edn 1900, trans. from the posthumous 3rd edn 1928.

Competition

> Only through the principle of competition has political economy any pretension to the charac-
> ter of a science. So far as rents, profits, wages, and prices are determined by competition, laws
> may be assigned for them. Assume competition to be their exclusive regulator, and principles
> of broad generality and precision may be laid down, according to which they will be regulated.
> (Mill 1848 [1973], vol. II: 242)

This oft-quoted passage by John Stuart Mill highlights the fact that, ever since economics acquired the status of an autonomous scientific discipline, competition has
been one of its basic concepts. This is particularly true as regards the theory of value:
the analysis of competition carried out by a few late seventeenth–mid-eighteenth
century authors, such as William Petty, Pierre Le Pesant de Boisguilbert, François
Quesnay, Richard Cantillon, Anne-Robert-Jacques Turgot and David Hume, provided the crucial breakthrough in order to free the theory of price determination
from previous scholastic and Middle Ages influences. These authors established the
view that competition imposes a discipline on the ebb and flow of market outcomes:
the workings of competition enforces the gravitation of market prices towards
some definite theoretical magnitudes, subsequently christened as natural prices, prices
of production or long-run normal prices. As stressed by McNulty (1967), Adam
Smith's

> contribution with respect to the concept of competition was the systematization of earlier
> thinking on the subject and, more importantly, the elevation of competition to the level of
> a general organizing principle of economic society ... After Smith's great achievement, the
> concept of competition became quite literally the *sine qua non* of economic reasoning. (McNulty
> 1967: 396–7)

It is not an overstatement to claim that the historical evolution of the concept of competition largely overlaps with that of economic theory itself. This may help explain the
reason why, in the course of time, the same word "competition" "has taken on a number
of interpretations and meanings, many of them vague" (Vickers 1995: 3). Such a situation is not uncommon in the history of economics: other basic economic notions such as
value, equilibrium, income distribution and so on have undergone substantive shifts of
meaning. Yet, what is peculiar of "competition" is that "the new meaning of competition
precludes the old; that the perfect competition of modern analysis is incompatible with
the competitive behaviour of the classical and early neoclassical periods" (High 2001:
xiv). It is certainly paradoxical that:

> the single activity which best characterized the meaning of competition in classical economics
> – price cutting by an individual firm in order to get rid of excess supplies – becomes the one
> activity impossible under perfect competition. And what for the classical economists was the
> single analytical function of the competitive process – the determination of market price –
> becomes, with perfect competition, the one thing unexplained and unaccounted for. (McNulty
> 1968: 649)

By drastically simplifying, the following is a tentative and by no means exhaustive
taxonomy of the different notions of competition.

Competition as Rivalry in a Race

Historically, the first notion of competition developed in modern economic literature is that of free competition or competition without restraint. Competition is viewed as a kind of rivalry in a race. What is at stake here is to get limited supplies or to get rid of excess supplies: competitors consciously underbid or overbid each other, that is, make deliberate use of prices as their main competitive weapon. The "rivalry in a race" notion of competition is endorsed by almost all the classical and early neo-classical authors, most notably Marshall whose "treatment of competition was much closer to Adam Smith's than to that of his contemporaries" (Stigler 1957: 9). As noted by Richardson (1975), in Adam Smith (but the same holds true for Karl Marx) competition plays a significant role in two very different contexts, which may be termed static and dynamic. The static context is devoted to the determination of market prices, given technology and the vector of effectual demands. The dynamic context is devoted to the explanation of structural change and technological development driven by the process of division and specialization of labour and its relation to the extent of the market.

Classical economists generally base their analysis of competition on Book I, chapter vii of *The Wealth of Nations* (Smith 1776 [1976], hereafter *WN*). The data from which the Smithian argument starts are the natural rates of wages, profits and rents which, sectoral specificities apart, basically depend on the conditions of prosperity of the economic system under scrutiny, its "advancing, stationary, or declining condition" (*WN* I.vii.1). The natural price of (re)production of the various commodities springs from the summation of these three elements. Accordingly, the natural price is a magnitude whose genesis lies outside the market, but that, given some well-specified conditions, may come true in the market. Natural prices provide scholars with a clue to the explanation of the dynamic path followed by market prices:

> The natural price, therefore, is, as it were, the central price to which the prices of all commodities are continually gravitating. Different accidents may sometimes keep them suspended a good deal above it, and sometimes force them down even somewhat below it. But whatever may be the obstacles which hinder them from settling in this center of repose and continuance, they are constantly tending towards it. (*WN* I.vii.15)

In particular, natural prices play the role of market price floors in the sense that market prices cannot remain for long below their natural level without seriously jeopardizing commodity reproduction:

> The competition of the different dealers obliges them all to accept of [the natural price]; but does not oblige them to accept of less. . . . The natural price, or the price of free competition . . . is the lowest which can be taken, not upon every occasion, indeed, but for any considerable time together . . . is the lowest which the sellers can commonly afford to take, and at the same time continue their business. (*WN* I.vii.11 and 27)

To study the genesis of market price and its relationship with natural price in a given market Smith introduces the concept of effectual demand, that is, "the demand of those who are willing to pay the natural price of the commodity". It is to be stressed, first, that the match between the quantity brought to the market and the effectual demand determines only the market price of a commodity and not its natural price and, second, that "demand" and "supply" are treated by Smith as given quantities and not as functional relationships between price and quantity characterized by well-defined formal properties (Garegnani 1983).

Given the unplanned nature of market economies, classical analysis requires the specification of an adjustment mechanism powerful enough to bring about an effective convergence to a situation in which the produced quantity coincides with the effectual demand: in the absence of such a mechanism, natural prices would hardly constitute a reliable guide to explain market prices dynamics. Following the lead of Smith's famous example of a public mourning which raises the market price of black cloth while sinks the market price of coloured silks and cloth (*WN* I.vii.19), the adjustment mechanism envisaged by classical authors may be reconstructed as follows. At the end of a productive cycle, entrepreneurs bring to the market a given quantity of the produced commodity resulting from the production decisions taken at the beginning of the cycle which has just concluded. This quantity cannot be modified to adjust to the effectual demand. Thus, the adjustment variable is constituted by the selling price of the commodity. Smith assumes that, in the presence of a gap between actual production and effectual demand, a sort of auction starts among the agents that happen to be on (what we today would call) the long side of the market: such agents are prepared to offer higher and higher prices (in case of excess demand) or lower and lower prices (in case of excess supply). Once the market price of any commodity happens to be different from its natural price, this causes an imbalance in the distributive sphere in the sense that the earnings of those people that have contributed to the production of the commodity prove different from their respective natural values. In the absence of entry/exit barriers, the difference between the market price and the natural price brings about (1) an intersectoral reallocation of economic resources in search of the highest market remuneration and (2) a variation in the produced quantity of the commodity in the following periods. This process comes to a halt only when the produced and demanded quantity balance in correspondence of the natural price and the market values of wages, profits and rents equal their respective natural values. Therefore, the imbalance in the sphere of circulation (discrepancy between the natural and market price of a commodity) spills over to the sphere of distribution (discrepancy between the natural and market values of wages, profits and rents) and, finally, to the sphere of production (intersectoral reallocation of productive resources and variation in the quantities produced in the following periods).

The assumed tendency of market values towards their respective natural values is based on two broad assumptions: (1) economic agents choose where to allocate their economic resources taking into account, *inter alia*, their opportunity costs and (2) there are but negligible barriers to the intersectoral mobility of economic resources:

> When the price of any commodity is neither more nor less than what is sufficient to pay the rent of the land, the wages of the labour, and the profits of the stock employed in raising, preparing, and bringing it to market, according to their natural rates, the commodity is then sold for what may be called its natural price. The commodity is then sold precisely for what it is worth, or for what it really costs the person who brings it to market; for *though in common language what is called the prime costs of any commodity does not comprehend the profit of the person who is to sell it again, yet if he sells it at a price which does not allow him the ordinary rate of profit in his neighbourhood, he is evidently a loser by the trade; since by employing his stock in some other way he might have made that profit. . . .* Though the price, therefore, which leaves him this profit is

not always the lowest at which the dealer may sometimes sell his goods, it is the lowest at which he is likely to sell them for any considerable time; at least where *there is perfect liberty, or where he may change his trade as often as he pleases.* (*WN* I.vii.4–6, emphasis added)

The above quotation shows that Smith devotes much care to the determination of natural values and to the explanation of the gravitation process of market magnitudes towards their natural counterparts. The same cannot be maintained as concerns the question of market price determination, particularly in the presence of market imbalances. Taking stock of Smith's sparse hints on this subject it is possible to point out what follows. Where competition is free and industrial secrets absent, price-undercutting starts as soon as at least two competitors are present in the market. This process is amplified by increasing the number of competitors since effective collusion among competitors becomes more and more unlikely:

The quantity of grocery goods, for example, which can be sold in a particular town is limited by the demand of that town and its neighbourhood. The capital, therefore, which can be employed in the grocery trade cannot exceed what is sufficient to purchase that quantity. If this capital is divided between two different grocers, their competition will tend to make both of them sell cheaper than if it were in the hands of one only; and if it were divided among twenty, their competition would be just so much the greater, and the chance of their combining together, in order to raise the price, just so much the less. (*WN* II.v.5)

By contrast, in those markets in which competition is not free (for example, because of a legal monopoly and/or the presence of a guild, a collusive agreement, a rule that somehow reduces economic agents' freedom as to the intersectoral allocation of their resources) or where there are industrial secrets, entrepreneurs voluntarily curb the produced quantity so that the market is left understocked and the market price may stay artificially high even "for ages":

A monopoly granted either to an individual or to a trading company has the same effect as a secret in trade or manufactures. The monopolists, by keeping the market constantly understocked, by never fully supplying the effectual demand, sell their commodities much above the natural price, and raise their emoluments, whether they consist in wages or profit, greatly above their natural rate. . . . The exclusive privileges of corporations, statutes of apprenticeship, and all those laws which restrain, in particular employments, the competition to smaller number than might otherwise go into them, have the same tendency, though in a less degree. They are a sort of enlarged monopolies, and may frequently, for ages together, and in whole classes of employments, keep up the market price of particular commodities above the natural price, and maintain both the wages of the labour and the profits of the stock employed about them somewhat above their natural rate. (*WN* I.vii.26 and 28)

Whenever the agents on one side of the market are few (for example, thanks to an entry barrier artificially created by the law) and able to communicate (for example, because they operate in the same place such as a town) while the agents on the other side of the market are many and unable to communicate (for example, because they are scattered in the countryside) the bargaining from which the market price springs will obviously be more favourable to the former. Thus, the relative number of the sellers in relation to the buyers, their relative ability to make a binding agreement and the presence and significance of entry barriers may be crucial elements determining a market price permanently above its natural level. The classical notion of competition is percolated into modern literature with the label of "Bertrand competition" (Salvadori and Signorino 2013).

Competition as a Specific Market Structure

Smith considered free competition as a synonym of the "obvious and simple system of natural liberty" (*WN* IV.ix.51), an ideal benchmark against which various socio-political arrangements may be compared and assessed (Aspromourgos 2009: ch. 5). Therefore, his notion of competition is far removed from the contemporary notion of competition as a specific market structure, alongside pure monopoly, monopolistic competition, duopoly *à la* Cournot, *à la* Bertrand, *à la* Stackelberg, and so on. In this latter context, the various market structures are defined in terms of well-defined assumptions concerning the characteristics of the goods produced, the technology of production, the elasticity of demand, the number and size of existing firms, the nature and significance of entry/exit barriers, the type of firms' conjectures on rivals' reactions etc. In particular, a perfectly competitive market is characterized by the assumption that each competitor faces a perfectly horizontal demand curve, that is, she takes market price as a parametric datum when she chooses the profit-maximizing quantity to produce. (As noted by Arrow 1959 and now acknowledged by some contemporary advanced textbooks, the price-taking assumption drastically reduces the theoretical domain of the perfect competition model just to Walrasian equilibrium states. In fact, consumers and producers have no incentive to quote a price different from the ruling market price if and only if the ruling market price is the Walrasian market-clearing price: see Mas-Colell et al. 1995: 314, fn. 1, and 315.) The price-taking behaviour by each competitor is usually justified by the further assumptions that (1) competitors are so many as to make a collusive agreement unfeasible and (2) each competitor is "small" in relation to the extent of the market. (Formally, the market is inhabited by a continuum of traders: see Aumann 1964.) As is well-known, the "negligibility" assumption was first introduced into the economic literature by Antoine-Augustin Cournot in chapter 8, "Of unlimited competition", of his *Recherches sur les Principes Mathématiques de la Théorie des Richesses*:

> The effects of competition have reached their limit, when each of the partial productions D_k is *inappreciable*, not only with reference to the total production $D = F(p)$, but also with reference to the derivative $F'(p)$, so that the partial production D_k could be subtracted from D without any appreciable variation resulting in the price of the commodity. (Cournot 1838 [1897]: 90, original emphasis)

Cournot justifies his "negligibility" assumption on the basis of two different arguments, one empirical and one formal: he claims that the assumption holds true for "a multitude of products, and, among them, for the most important products" and "[i]t introduces a great simplification into the calculations" (ibid.). Cournot does not further elaborate the empirical argument; while he investigates at length the formal argument. In fact, Cournot writes down the profit-maximizing equation for the *k-th* firm as:

$$D_k + [p - \phi_k'(D_k)]dD/dp = 0 \qquad (1)$$

where D_k is the quantity produced by the *k-th* firm, p the market price (goods are homogeneous to the effect that there is just one market price), $D = D_1 + \ldots + D_n = F(p)$ the market demand function and $\phi'_k(D_k)$ the marginal cost function of the *k-th* firm, respectively. The above equation, with some manipulation, turns out to be the now familiar marginal revenue-marginal cost equality. (As noted by Magnan de Bornier (1992), with the single notable exception of section 43 where the famous duopoly model is introduced, Cournot consciously uses p and not D as the independent variable in the maximization problem.) Thanks to the negligibility assumption the above equation boils down to:

$$p - \phi'_k(D_k) = 0 \qquad (2)$$

which is the price-marginal cost equality of any textbook model of perfect competition.

It may be worth stressing that Léon Walras too endorses an empirical argument similar to Cournot's but he defends it at length. Walras is ready to admit that markets best organized from the point of view of competition are auction markets, where there are "stockbrokers, commercial brokers or criers acting as agents who centralize transactions in such a way that the terms of every exchange are openly announced and an opportunity is given to sellers to lower their prices and to buyers to raise their bids" (Walras, 1874 [2003]: 84); but he insists that his view of competition is not in the least confined to auction markets and he goes on enumerating a series of real world markets where competition works quite adequately, notwithstanding the absence of centralized transactions. And he concludes by saying that: "the whole world may be looked upon as a vast general market made up of diverse special markets where social wealth is bought and sold" (ibid.).

Some decades after Cournot's path-breaking but long-neglected contribution, the notion of competition as a specific market structure has been refined and enriched by the analyses of the Law of Indifference (Jevons 1871), the recontracting (Edgeworth 1881) and *tâtonnement* (Walras 1874) processes, the role of returns to scale and the optimal dimension of competitive firms (Wicksell 1901–06 [1934]), the stationary state (J.B. Clark 1902) and the relationship between (extra)profits and uncertainty (Knight 1921). Finally, the market structure notion of competition has been codified in the course of the imperfect/monopolistic competition revolution of the early 1930s launched by Joan Robinson (1933) and Edward Chamberlin (1933). (Stigler 1957, Backhouse 1990 and High 2001 provide excellent historical reconstructions of the notion of perfect competition, while Tsoulfidis 2009 explores the issue of monopolistic competition as a failed revolution in the field of value theory. For a stimulating reformulation of the perfect competition model without the price-taking assumption see Makowski and Ostroy 2001.)

Competition as a Discovery Procedure

Cournot's complaint that economists before him "have not in the least improved on popular notions [on the effects of competition leaving such notions] as ill-defined and ill-applied in their works, as in popular language" (Cournot 1838 [1897]: 79) may be taken to mark the distance between the classical and the contemporary notion of competition. Yet, as some commentators have recognized, Cournot's complaint is not groundless: the rivalry-in-a-race notion of competition is very akin to the layman notion of competition

(Kirzner 1973: ch. 3). Should we conclude that the transition from the ancient to the modern notion of competition is but a telling example of progress in economics? The answer to such a question is controversial (as is controversial the very notion of progress in economics: see Boehm et al. 2002). The price-taking notion of competition and the cognate analysis of different market structures are considered by some economists as a remarkable example of theoretical progress. Yet, a few others have questioned that these theoretical developments imply empirical progress too. For example, Demsetz (1982) claims that the perfect competition model is a valuable tool to understand the workings of the price system in a fully decentralized economy; but it is highly unsuited to understand any form of competitive activity. Within the perfect competition model, in fact:

> firms and households increasingly represented mere calculating machines whose inner workings were of little interest. Markets became empirically empty conceptualizations of the forums in which exchange costlessly took place. The legal system and the government were relegated to the distant background by the simple device of stating, without clarification, that resources were "privately owned". . . . [The perfect competition model] also encouraged the neglect of those islands of authority, firms and households, which, by exercising limited authority in a sea of prices, could translate [their] special knowledge into goods and services. (Demsetz 1982: 6–7, 8)

Accordingly, Demsetz proposes to rechristen the perfect competition model as the "perfect decentralization model" since it "adds much to our understanding of coordination through price, nothing to our understanding of coordination through authority, and only little to our understanding of competitive actions" (Demsetz 1982: 6).

The idea that an understanding of the actual workings of competition requires the abandonment of the perfect competition model has been forcefully advocated by neo-Austrian and evolutionary economists (see McNulty 2008 and Witt 2008, respectively). Neo-Austrian economists have generally looked at the price-taking notion of competition with a critical eye since the latter depicts "a state in which all essential conditions are assumed to be known – a state that theory curiously designates as perfect competition, even though the opportunity for the activity we call competition no longer exists. Indeed, it is assumed that such activity has already performed its function" (Hayek 1968 [2002]: 13). Accordingly, for the neo-Austrians, competition is basically "a procedure for discovering facts which, if the procedure did not exist, would remain unknown or at least would not be used" (ibid.: 9). In the evolutionary scenario, economies seldom or never are in a situation of Walrasian equilibrium. Accordingly, analytical attention is devoted to non-equilibrium processes engendered by the interaction of intrinsically heterogeneous agents, endowed with idiosyncratic information and bounded rationality. Neo-Austrian and evolutionary economists put great emphasis on the active role of entrepreneurs who strive to get both static and dynamic profit differentials. The former arise from the discovery of arbitrage opportunities (Kirzner 1997), the latter from the process of creative destruction depicted in chapter 7 of Joseph Alois Schumpeter's *Capitalism, Socialism and Democracy* (1942), namely, the discovery of new consumers' goods, new methods of production or transportation, new markets, and new forms of industrial organization created by capitalist enterprises. From this point of view, the analysis of competition is intimately tied with that of economic development: the two "are isomorphic by virtues of being examples of the phenomenon of economic evolution" (Metcalfe et al. 2004: 59).

Competition as Class Struggle

While neo-Walrasian general equilibrium theory endorses a notion of competition as an (intertemporal) equilibrium end-state where any potential for Pareto-improving real-location is fully exhausted, classical, neo-Austrian and evolutionary economics describe competition as an intrinsically dynamic process of technological innovation and struc-tural change (Blaug 2003; Machovec 1995). Yet, notwithstanding their different notions of competition, classical, neo-classical, neo-Austrian and evolutionary economists basi-cally agree on the view that a competitive market economy is an economic system which promotes long-run growth and provides ample scope to the benign action of Adam Smith's invisible hand. By contrast, Karl Marx and Marxian economists consider capi-talism and free markets as economic systems in which the process of capital accumula-tion goes hand in hand with the proletarianization of the masses, on the one side, and the concentration of social wealth into the hands of an elite controlling big corporations, on the other:

> The battle of competition is fought by cheapening of commodities. The cheapness of commodi-ties depends, *cæteris paribus*, on the productiveness of labour, and this again on the scale of production. Therefore, the larger capitals beat the smaller. It will further be remembered that, with the development of the capitalist mode of production, there is an increase in the minimum amount of individual capital necessary to carry on a business under its normal conditions. The smaller capitals, therefore, crowd into spheres of production which modern industry has only sporadically or incompletely got hold of. Here competition rages in direct proportion to the number, and in inverse proportion to the magnitudes, of the antagonistic capitals. It always ends in the ruin of many small capitalists, whose capitals partly pass into the hand of their conquerors, partly vanish. Apart from this, with capitalist production an altogether new force comes into play – the credit system. In its beginnings, the credit system sneaks in as a modest helper of accumulation and draws by invisible threads the money resources scattered all over the surface of society into the hands of individual or associated capitalists. But soon it becomes a new and formidable weapon in the competitive struggle, and finally it transforms itself into an immense social mechanism for the centralisation of capitals. (Marx 1906 VII.XXV.18–19)

Moreover, Marx emphasized that competition determines a falling rate of profits (Marx 1909 III.III). As a consequence, capitalist economies are plagued by recursive crises of realization. This aspect of Marxian contribution has been developed by Baran and Sweezy (1966). The two authors explore the way competition works in monopoly capitalism and argue that the law of the falling rate of profits does not apply to modern capitalism. In particular, they emphasize the role of stagnation, which is only inter-rupted by violent crises. Since Marx and Marxian authors generally view capitalism as an economic system characterized by deep-routed and violent contradictions, the literature on "Marx and Marxists on crisis" is huge. Sweezy (1946) keeps its status as a classic, while a recent assessment is provided by Clarke (1994). John E. Roemer (1982) provides a modern presentation of how society is partitioned into different classes by competition.

From Competition Theory to Competition Policy: Pugnacity or Complacency?

The fact that different schools of thought attach different meanings to the same word, "competition", has obvious consequences at the policy level. As just a trivial but telling example, consider the case of a firm earning persistent and substantial extra-profits (that is, profits above its opportunity costs). In the competition-as-market-structure scenario, such a situation is explained in an outright way by claiming that the firm under scrutiny is endowed with persistent and substantial market power. Such an explanation obviously entails a prima facie case for an aggressive antitrust action (even a divestiture) in order to restore the minimal conditions for perfect competition to obtain. On the contrary, in the neo-Austrian or evolutionary scenario, the above situation may be explained by claiming that the firm under scrutiny is a successful innovator with imitators constantly lagging behind. The latter explanation entails that an aggressive antitrust action is definitely unwarranted. In short, the origin of the liveliest debates as concerns competition policy may be traced back to the different notions of competition assumed by the participants in the debate.

By drastically simplifying, it may be claimed that, at the normative level, an illuminating distinction is that introduced by Blaug between competition as an end state and competition as a process (Blaug 1997). Economists adopting the notion of competition as a process are usually very prudent before condemning as anti-competitive many of the current business practices:

> When competition is analytically considered as a process, pure integration, mergers and acquisitions, cooperation and alliances may become integral parts of the normal functioning of competitive markets. These inter-firm relations which are perceived as collusion within the traditional vision of competition can be legitimated for some periods and for specific purposes. (Krafft 2000: 1–2)

As a consequence, these economists generally are distrustful towards active antitrust policies. Commenting on the puzzle noted by Stigler (1982), namely, the US economists' lack of enthusiasm towards the Sherman Act, DiLorenzo and High claim:

> There is no doubt that economists at the turn of the century looked upon competition as a process of enterprise and rivalry, and that they disapproved of antitrust law. These two views were not merely coincidental. Although viewing competition as rivalry does not necessitate opposition to antitrust law, it surely encourages such opposition. (DiLorenzo and High 1988: 432)

By contrast, economists adopting the end-state notion of competition and the related Pareto-optimality theorems are likely led to focus on the number and size of competitors in a given market as the two crucial variables which (together with entry barriers) determine the distance between the actual workings of the market under scrutiny and the ideal of perfect competition. As a consequence, these economists are generally much less reluctant to endorse active antitrust policies.

Provided that workable competition is assumed as the antitrust benchmark instead of perfect competition (Van den Bergh and Camesasca 2001: ch. 1.4), the structure–conduct–performance approach to industrial organization theory, developed in the course of Mason's seminar at Harvard, may be singled out as an obvious candidate for aggressive antitrust. At the opposite end of the spectrum stands the Chicago School of antitrust economics. As noted by Reder (1982), Chicago economists usually assume that "one may treat observed prices and quantities as good approximations to their long-run competitive equilibrium values" (1982: 12) and that "most of what appears to be monopoly is ephemeral, being eliminated by free entry" (ibid.: 15). Thus, within Chicago style of economics, standard (neoclassic) price theory happily coexists with a bold distrust towards active government intervention in market outcomes: only explicit price fixing and mergers to monopoly are worthy of serious antitrust concern (Posner 1979: 933). In the extreme version of the Chicago school theory of markets, the theory of contestable markets (Baumol et al. 1982), even a single seller-market may be considered as competitive, provided that it is subject to the "hit and run" competition of external firms.

An interesting though not yet fully acknowledged third way between Harvard pugnacity and Chicago complacency is represented by the German ordoliberalism, the so-called Freiburg school of Walter Eucken, Franz Böhm, Hans Grossmann-Doerth and Wilhelm Röpke, to mention just a few. Freiburg scholars thought that both laissez-faire and direct government intervention into market outcomes were wrong answers to the problem of creating and maintaining a competitive economy. Rather, they opted for a policy aimed at improving the existing economic order in an indirect way, through a deliberate reformulation of the rules of the game. Therefore, they approached antitrust issues as a problem of constitutional choice. The constitutional dimension of the Freiburg school represents an original and brilliant solution to the classical liberal dilemma of calling for government action to prevent the abuse of private market power while, at one and the same time, acknowledging that government action itself may heavily interfere with and overturn market processes (Giocoli 2009). (Gerber 1998, chapters 7 and 8 provide a full-scope analysis of the role played by German Ordoliberalism and social market economy into shaping European competition law and practice.)

NERI SALVADORI AND RODOLFO SIGNORINO

See also:

British classical political economy (II); British marginalism (II); Edward Hastings Chamberlin (I); Antoine-Augustin Cournot (I); Francis Ysidro Edgeworth (I); Formalization and mathematical modelling (III); General equilibrium theory (III); Friedrich August von Hayek (I); Industrial organization (III); Lausanne School (II); Alfred Marshall (I); Karl Heinrich Marx (I); Marxism(s) (II); Joan Violet Robinson (I); Adam Smith (I); Theory of the firm (III); Marie-Esprit-Léon Walras (I).

References and further reading

Arrow, K.J. (1959), 'Toward a theory of price adjustment', in M. Abramovitz (ed.), *The Allocation of Economic Resources*, Stanford, CA: Stanford University Press, pp. 41–51.
Aspromourgos, T. (2009), *The Science of Wealth. Adam Smith and the framing of political economy*, London and New York: Routledge.
Aumann, R. J. (1964), 'Markets with a continuum of traders', *Econometrica*, **32** (1/2), 39–50.
Backhouse, R.E. (1990), 'Competition', in J. Creedy (ed), *Foundations of Economic Thought*, Oxford: Basil Blackwell, pp. 58–86.
Baran, P.A. and P.M. Sweezy (1966), *Monopoly Capital. An Essay on the American Economic and Social Order*, London and New York: Monthly Review Press.
Baumol, W.J., J.C. Panzar and R.D. Willig (1982), *Contestable Markets and the Theory of Industry Structure*, New York: Harcourt Brace Jovanovich.
Blaug, M. (1997), 'Competition as an end-state and competition as a process', in M. Blaug, *Not Only an Economist. Recent Essays by Mark Blaug*, Cheltenham, UK and Lyme, NH, USA: Edward Elgar, pp. 66–86.
Blaug, M. (2003), 'The formalist revolution of the 1950s', *Journal of the History of Economic Thought*, **25** (2), 145–56.
Boehm, S., C. Gehrke, H.D. Kurz and R. Sturn (2002), *Is there Progress in Economics? Knowledge, Truth and the History of Economic Thought*, Cheltenham, UK and Northampton, MA, USA: Edward Elgar.
Chamberlin, E.H. (1933), *The Theory of Monopolistic Competition: A Re-orientation of the Theory of Value*, Cambridge, MA: Harvard University Press.

Clark, J.B. (1902), *The Distribution of Wealth: A Theory of Wages, Interest and Profits*, New York: Augustus M. Kelley.

Clarke, S. (1994), *Marx's Theory of Crisis*, London: Macmillan.

Cournot, A.A. (1838), *Recherches sur les Principes Mathématiques de la Théorie des Richesses*, English trans. N. Bacon (1897), *Researches into the Mathematical Principles of the Theory of Wealth*, London: Macmillan.

Demsetz, H. (1982), *Economic, Legal, and Political Dimensions of Competition, the De Vries Lectures in Economic Theory*, Amsterdam: North Holland.

DiLorenzo, T.J. and J.C. High (1988), 'Antitrust and competition, historically considered', *Economic Inquiry*, **37** (3), 423–35.

Edgeworth, F.Y. (1881), *Mathematical Psychics: An Essay on the Application of Mathematics to the Moral Sciences*, London: Kegan.

Garegnani, P. (1983), 'The classical theory of wages and the role of demand schedules in the determination of relative prices', *American Economic Review*, **73** (2), 309–13.

Gerber, D.J. (1998), *Law and Competition in Twentieth Century Europe. Protecting Prometheus*, Oxford: Oxford University Press.

Giocoli, N. (2009), 'Competition vs. property rights: American antitrust law, the Freiburg School and the early years of European competition policy', *Journal of Competition Law and Economics*, **5** (4), 747–86.

Hayek, F.A. (1968), 'Der Wettbewerb als Entdeckungsverfahren', lecture sponsored by the Institut für Weltwirtschaft, University of Kiel, published as no. 56 in the Kieler Vorträge series, English trans. 2002 'Competition as a discovery procedure', *Quarterly Journal of Austrian Economics*, **5** (3), 9–23.

High, J. (2001), 'Introduction. split personality: a brief history of competition in economic theory', in J. High (ed), *Competition*, Cheltenham, UK and Northampton, MA, USA: Edward Elgar, pp. xiii–xlv.

Jevons, W.S. (1871), *The Theory of Political Economy*, London: Macmillan.

Kirzner, I.M. (1973), *Competition and Entrepreneurship*, Chicago, IL, and London: University of Chicago Press.

Kirzner, I.M. (1997), 'Entrepreneurial discovery and the competitive market process: an Austrian approach', *Journal of Economic Literature*, **35** (1), 60–85.

Knight, F.H. (1921), *Risk, Uncertainty and Profit*, New York: Houghton Mifflin.

Krafft, J. (2000), 'Introduction', in J. Krafft (ed.), *The Process of Competition*, Cheltenham, UK and Northampton, MA, USA: Edward Elgar, pp. 1–9.

Machovec, F.M. (1995), *Perfect Competition and the Transformation of Economics*. London and New York: Routledge.

Magnan de Bornier, J. (1992), 'The "Cournot–Bertrand Debate": a historical perspective', *History of Political Economy*, **24** (3), 623–56.

Makowski, L. and J.M. Ostroy (2001), 'Perfect competition and the creativity of the market', *Journal of Economic Literature*, **39** (2), 479–535.

Marx, K. (1906), *Capital*, vol. I, Chicago, IL: Charles H. Kerr & Co., English trans. by S. Moore and E. Aveling of F. Engels (ed.) (1890), *Das Kapital*, vol. 4th edn, Hamburg: Meissner. In the text quoted as part number, chapter number, and paragraph number.

Marx, K. (1909), *Capital*, vol. III, Chicago, IL: Charles H. Kerr & Co. English trans. by E. Untermann (1894), *Das Kapital*, Hamburg: Meissner.

Mas-Colell, A., M.D. Whinston and J. Green (1995), *Microeconomic Theory*, New York: Oxford University Press.

McNulty, P. (1967), 'A note on the history of perfect competition', *Journal of Political Economy*, **75** (4), 395–9.

McNulty, P. (1968), 'Economic theory and the meaning of competition', *Quarterly Journal of Economics*, **82** (4), 639–56.

McNulty, P. (2008), 'Competition, Austrian', in S.N. Durlauf and L.E. Blume (eds), *The New Palgrave Dictionary of Economics*, 2nd edn, vol. 2, London: Macmillan, pp. 61–3.

Metcalfe, J.S., R. Ramlogan and E. Uyarra (2004), 'Competition, innovation and economic development: the instituted connection', in P. Cook, C. Kirkpatrick, M. Mingue and D. Parker (eds), *Leading Issues in Competition, Regulation and Development*, Cheltenham, UK and Northampton, MA, USA: Edward Elgar, pp. 58–91.

Mill, J.S. (1848), *Principles of Political Economy: With Some of Their Applications to Social Philosophy*, London: John W. Parker, reprinted 1973, New York: Augustus M. Kelley.

Posner, R.A. (1979), 'The Chicago School of Antitrust Analysis', *University of Pennsylvania Law Review*, **127** (4), 925–48.

Reder, Melvin W. (1982), 'Chicago economics: permanence and change', *Journal of Economic Literature*, **20** (1), 1–38.

Richardson, G.B. (1975), 'Adam Smith on competition and increasing returns', in A.S. Skinner and T. Wilson (eds), *Essays on Adam Smith*, Oxford: Oxford University Press, pp. 350–60.

Robinson, J. (1933), *The Economics of Imperfect Competition*, London: Macmillan.

Roemer, J.E. (1982), *A General Theory of Exploitation and Class*, Cambridge, MA: Harvard University Press.

Salvadori, N. and R. Signorino (2013), 'The classical notion of competition revisited', *History of Political Economy*, **44** (1), 149–75.

Schumpeter, J.A. (1942), *Capitalism, Socialism and Democracy*. London: George Allen & Unwin.

Smith, A. (1776), *An Inquiry into the Nature and Causes of the Wealth of Nations*, vol. II of The Glasgow Edition of the Works and Correspondence of Adam Smith, ed. by R.H. Campbell and A.S. Skinner. Oxford: Oxford University Press. (In the text quoted as *WN*, book number, chapter number, paragraph number.)

Stigler, G.J. (1957), 'Perfect competition, historically contemplated', *Journal of Political Economy*, **65** (1), 1–17.

Stigler, G.J. (1982), 'The economists and the problem of monopoly', *American Economic Review*, **72** (2), 1–11.

Sweezy, P. (1946), *The Theory of Capitalist Development*, London: Dobson.

Tsoulfidis, L. (2009), 'The rise and fall of monopolistic competition revolution', *International Review of Economics*, **56** (1), 29–45.

Van den Bergh, R.J. and P.D. Camesasca (2001), *European Competition Law and Economics: A Comparative Perspective*, Antwerp: Intersentia.

Vickers, J. (1995), 'Concepts of competition', *Oxford Economic Papers*, **47** (1), 1–23.

Walras, L. (1874), *Éléments d'économie politique pure, ou Théorie de la richesse sociale*, Lausanne: L. Corbaz and Paris: Guillaumin et Cie. English trans. 2003, *Elements of Pure Economics or The Theory of Social Wealth*, London: Routledge.

Wicksell, K. (1901–06), *Forelasningar I Nationalekonomi*, 2 vols, Lund: C.W. Gleerups Vorlag, English trans. 1934, *Lectures on Political Economy*, 2 vols, London: Routledge.

Witt, U. (2008), 'Evolutionary economics', in S.N. Durlauf and L.E. Blume (eds), *The New Palgrave Dictionary of Economics*, 2nd edn, vol. 3, London: Macmillan, pp. 67–73.

Corporatism

Corporatism is probably the most common system of economic organisation in both the Eastern and Western worlds. As in the case of, for example, mercantilism, we should not look for the foundations of corporatism in the writings of eminent thinkers. There are certainly some remarkable theories that offer a theoretical basis, but in reality corporatism is indubitably based for the most part on historical facts. It has a history of more than 2000 years and this thus prevents us from defining it simply as being somewhere in between capitalism and socialism or as the economic doctrine of some authoritarian regimes.

Definition

If we consider how corporatism has taken shape over the years, historical experience is more relevant than any theoretical foundations. During the course of its history, scholars of economics have spoken of several instances of corporatism, largely different and often labelled with different names. Nevertheless, these come from the same origin and must all be considered as true corporatism. Just as we accept that there are several varieties of capitalism, we must also acknowledge that corporatism is a multi-faceted phenomenon comprising many features. Also we must realise that it is necessary to connect all the different aspects and characteristics that have shaped the historical process behind corporatism in order to understand its theoretical structure.

The Latin word *corpora* refers to groups that are legally recognised, but it can also be interpreted more broadly. For instance, the term also encompasses the "vital" nature of these groups and hints at their "biological" structure, which is made up of various articulated functions and parts that are inextricably connected. We can thus define corporatism as a series of actions related to an economic policy which is not necessarily supported by an articulated theory. By means of the establishment of economic institutions, these actions aim to direct economic factors according to precise objectives that have been acknowledged by groups of varying sizes.

The word "corporatism", however, is frequently used in different ways. For instance, an act that pursues limited interests connected to a single group is invariably considered to be corporatist. The lexical origin of the word seems to indicate that any act follows the general interest of a number of groups, but we argue that there is no contradiction between these two apparently contrasting uses. Corporatism is indeed an attempt to pursue general aims by means of supporting some more limited interests and is not simply a fight between public versus private interest. It is quite often a struggle to correct market and driving economic factors on the basis of private goals which are presented as being of general interest.

The essence of corporatism may be found in the method used (that is, an alteration of the natural dynamics of economic processes) and not the purpose, which can change according to the situation. Corporatism may support and "drive" ethical rather than economic, political or social values, but in any case it will be identified as such by the means employed to achieve the aim. Furthermore, it should be noted that corporatism is neither merely a set of pure options nor just a type of behaviour associated with the ruling classes (collectively or otherwise). Corporatism requires institutions and laws to be defined as such. Many aspects of corporatism are listed by Siaroff (1999: 177–9) in order to rate the current level of corporatism. These structures are largely adopted as a temporary solution to an economic crisis, but severely limit economic freedom and market dynamics (Hayek 2004).

There are three different versions of corporatism, two traditional and one which is perhaps less well known but equally significant. (1) Ethical corporatism – the purpose of this is to pursue ethical objectives (for example, religious goals). To some extent any corporatism is grounded on an ethical basis, but in some cases ethical purposes are clearly predominant. Medieval corporatism and the Christian social doctrine are the forerunners of this kind of corporatism. (2) Political corporatism – this was popular in Italy, France and Germany in the 1930s, and there are more recent examples in Scandinavia and the United Kingdom after the Second World War (Siaroff 1999: 184–5, tables 2 and 3). Its objective is political and the aim is to achieve greater control over political processes and consensus. (3) Economic corporatism – here the aim is to achieve certain economic goals (public/private wealth, production, prices, salary). Known as neo-corporatism, it is often the primary objective of a country. It is the most frequent and recent type of corporatism and is mainly the result of the introduction of laws or measures (for example, privatisation), which have been presented as being of general interest. In effect it refers to certain influencing groups pursuing their own interests.

These three versions of corporatism are invariably intertwined since it is not always easy to identify the prevailing goals of corporatist economic choices. We may also argue that corporatism (as it aims to pursue collective interests through limited groups) is in itself contradictory and may often be the source of additional problems. This is the case for some countries, for example, which, with the purpose of achieving certain economic goals, potentially supported the interests of some influencing groups without these being explicitly endorsed by the population.

Historical Notes

As far as we know, corporatism originated during the Roman period, at least as regards the Western world. The Roman economy, like most other ancient civilisations, was based on compulsory work and on a particular concept of society. Using Weberian concepts, it was actually closer to the concept of *Gemeinschaft* (as compared to *Gesellschaft*) and was quite separate from the idea of the market being the ideal allocator (Holton and Turner 1989: 111–13). According to Max Weber, *Gemeinschaft* relates to an organisation that is based on subjective, traditional feelings; *Gesellschaft* is based on a rational agreement by mutual consent (Temin 2004). In a similar way, corporative structures were established in Rome during the Republican era and subsequently in the Imperial era. The *Lex Iulia de Collegiis* is officially considered to constitute the foundation of Western corporatism. The exact date of this legal act is uncertain but presumably it was issued between 49 BC and 44 BC (De Robertis 1973: 204). It is a fact that Roman corporatism was born during the Republican era as a result of the already existing practice of association and it was only subsequently coded so that it became part of the prolific Roman judicial system. The most important characteristic of ancient corporatism is that it was established as a form of voluntary organisation, and it was not until much later that it became obligatory. This was because the principal objective of Roman law was to safeguard public interest. According to the original regulations, every association had to draw up a statute and appoint those in charge. It had to possess its own assets and administer the law according to the regulations established. Fulfilling the expected legal prescriptions would lead to full recognition on the part of the State and to the acquisition of some advantages available only to practices, which were regulated by economic activities. Between the fourth and fifth centuries AD, corporatism declined and the rules and constraints on which it was based became less binding. The Justinian code that followed conceded even more individual freedom to developing businesses. Hence, the decline of the Roman corporatist structure (Waltzing 1895, vol. II: 320) was not the result of it becoming too rigid. On the contrary, it became too lax in a period of serious economic decline (De Robertis 1973, vol. 2: 231–2).

The real triumph of corporatism occurred in medieval times, so much so that the economic recovery that took place in the twelfth and thirteenth centuries coincides with the first examples of Medieval and Christian corporatism. The combination of some elements (among which, the predominantly religious view of the world), the lack of power in the government and the relatively low rate of economic exchanges all benefited the development of an economic corporatist practice. This was subsequently described by a number of writers: from Thomas Aquinas to Antonio Pierozzi, from Uguccione da Pisa to Francesco Zabarella, from Pietro Lombardo to Gaetano (Tommaso da Vio) in addition to various theologians and doctors of Canon law. Finally, a group of merchants all concurred to make up an imposing doctrinal corpus, which subsequently became the social Christian doctrine. This, to all effects, was corporatism (Nuccio 1987).

Medieval Christian corporatism is a form of organisation the main objectives of which were religious. It encompassed practical-institutional aspects and had a very solid theoretical framework based on an organic vision of society and on the theory of *bonum commune*. It was also based on just prices as well as on the principle of the transience of possessions. For at least three centuries, these features contributed towards economic development and to the creation of important centres of wealth such as Venice, Florence, Bruges and Lyon. Decline followed or, rather, a change in economic conditions meant that the corporatist system gradually became inadequate in terms of solving new problems related to labour, production and the accumulation of capital. However, its influence remained at least until the eighteenth century and the Napoleonic reforms, above all in the city centres. Note that voluntarism, one of the distinct features pertaining to both mercantilistic and physiocratic theories, also had much in common with the basic corporatist concept of economic life.

The main concept persisted even during the Industrial Revolution and while in the nineteenth century numerous forms of associationism and corporatism (without religious objectives) drew unconditionally from medieval corporatism, the Catholic Church introduced the encyclical *Rerum Novarum* in 1891 deliberately harking back to the main themes of the medieval doctrines. The rebirth of Catholic corporatism at the end of the nineteenth century involved all Catholic countries and influenced other Christian religions until it became an international phenomenon. Among many other writers, it is worth remembering that Karl von Vogelsang (1818–1890) in Austria, René de la Tour du Pin (1834–1924) in France, Giuseppe Toniolo (1845–1918) in Italy, and Charles Périn (1815–1905) in the Catholic University of Louvain renewed the scholastic thought on associationism and are considered prominent predecessors of social catholicism

(Misner 1991: 446–50). Probably the most remarkable contribution to the modern reassessment of medieval Catholic principles was offered by the German Jesuit Heinrich Pesch (1854–1926). His work was also translated into English and is rightly considered a comprehensive treatise on Catholic corporatism and the foundation of all the other encyclical documents.

Corporatism in the 1930s and 1940s

The idea of corporatism was radically conditioned by the fact that during the 1930s and 1940s, corporatist economic policies were widely adopted by authoritarian regimes. Corporatist economic organisations were claimed to be limited to specific experiences such as these and were identified exclusively with an authoritarian use of power. There is no doubt that Italian fascism, some aspects of National Socialism in Germany, in addition to the fascism of Franco in Spain and the Zaibatsu in Japan all represented a significant range of corporatist theories. It might be that these countries had a weaker tradition of market-oriented theories and had not long been established as democratic institutions. However, the practice of corporatism during the Great Depression was not limited to only a few nations.

Between 1930 and 1945, while in certain areas the corporatist doctrine became the official economic policy of illiberal regimes, many fundamental corporatist principles were also applied on a large scale to the economic programmes of nearly every country in the Western world. Severe criticism of the market system was widespread in mainstream economics (Åkerman 1936: 99–101). The economic concept of corporatism reached wide consensus among intellectuals and was even well received in those countries not politically in favour of it. There is proof of this in the acclaimed book, eloquently entitled *Le Siècle du corporatisme*, written by the governor of the National Bank of Romania, Mihail Manoïlesco and published in France in 1938. In Montreal on 19 November 1945, Joseph Schumpeter presented an address during which he openly declared that corporatism was the economic theory of the future (translated from the French and published in Prime and Henderson 1975; also Cramer and Leathers 1981; Solterer 2005). In the meantime, in France and England, and even in the United States (see the group of Jesuits who were followers of Father Dempsey at St Louis University), ideas on corporatism were well received and this gave rise to many publications (Noto 2008).

From an analytical point of view, it was probably a group of Italian economists in the 1930s, who achieved the most significant results in the development of the theoretical corporatist system. One in particular was Luigi Amoroso (1886–1965) who was a mathematician and a follower of Pantaleoni and Pareto. He was an economist of international stature, and together with Schumpeter and Spiethoff, many issues concerning international economics in the 1930s were discussed. He aimed to prove that corporatism could potentially represent a challenge to economics and be accepted by the community of economists as a legitimate contribution to macroeconomics. Amoroso moved on from the notion of stable Paretian distributions and suggested that there are two different levels: an analytical level where economic processes are dynamic, and an economic policy level according to which the economy is totally subservient to political objectives. From an analytical point of view, the most original aspects of his theory are concerned with methodology, the business cycle and the dynamics of money.

We take a quick look at some of the issues discussed by Amoroso, since he was probably the person who made the most significant effort in terms of grounding corporatism on analytical economics, namely, on a "corporatist" business cycle theory. Methodologically, Amoroso is worth noting for his attempt to include non-economic factors in his analyses, for example, psychological, political and social factors. He thus enriched (but also complicated) the hypothesis relating to stable distributions. However, he was not confident that economic analyses alone could produce scientifically valid results and so he used mathematics as a more suitable means to express economic phenomena in exact terms. Consider also that Amoroso used the descriptive (not deductive) function of mathematics, following a long-standing Italian tradition that had started with Angelo Messedaglia and continued up to Corrado Gini (Pomini and Tusset 2009).

Amoroso divides the economic system into three sectors: industrial, commercial and banking, their respective aims being production, exchange and currency (Amoroso and De' Stefani 1933). The business cycle is the result of two basic parts, cyclic and evolutionary. Their interaction determines the structural characteristic of economics, conceived as a dynamic, not static, system. The time frame in which the cycle manifests itself gives rise to simultaneous actions, albeit distributed in successive moments (leads and lags). Amoroso's cycle theory does not envisage a clear separation between the various phases, nor does it envisage separation between different monetary, productive or commercial factors. Consequently, money cannot be separated from production; money is not neutral except when there are some particularly unstable conditions. Price fluctuations are determined both by monetary actions and by productive actions and exchange, which affect relative prices. Inflation is determined by the expansion of monetary circulation, while deflation is not due to monetary causes and does cause monetary effects because it is determined by excessive capital assets. Therefore, it is up to politics to conciliate the needs deriving from contrasting interests. Inflation benefits the producers, whereas deflation tends to safeguard private savings. Corporatism, with its focus on balancing contrasting interests, appears to be a necessary solution to internal economic problems.

Fascist corporatism was analysed by Amoroso in his scientific work but there have also been many other scholars working on various different, alternative trends. It is well worth remembering Ugo Spirito's work on corporatism, which was both philosophically and epistemologically oriented. He claimed that there was a correspondence between the state's general interest and the individual's interest. He eventually came to several conclusions that many economists found interesting, particularly regarding the limitations he introduced to the law of individual material property rights. These rights were only to be considered legitimate where they were included in a legal and economic corporatist system. Also worth noting was a more radical branch of Italian corporatism, which suggested a social and economic revolution and was promoted by Luigi Razza, among others. Edmondo Rossoni's (1884–1965) corporatism, on the other hand, had no strong theoretical basis, but it is a remarkable variety of fascist corporatism that went against the mainstream in its effort to bring the unions to the foreground in the corporatist process. Finally, we should also remember Gino Arias, the main representative of a political trend promoting a predominantly juridical type of corporatism, which, through an articulated system of laws, aimed to regulate the market and production (Rasi 2009: 26–9).

Political corporatism

The development of studies on economic corporatism and the achievement of greater awareness of the implications of this in the field of economics were made possible thanks to studies carried out in the political field, particularly that done by Andrew Shonfield and Philippe Schmitter in the 1970s. Despite the fact that politics and economics are interwoven and often overlap, it should be noted that a deep conceptual awareness of the meaning of corporatism arose as a result of research carried out within the sphere of political science. It was Philippe Schmitter who revealed the inconsistency of interpretations that confined corporatism to certain authoritarian regimes in the 1930s, and who disclosed the deep bonds and similarities between certain characters such as J.-C.L. Simonde de Sismondi, Pierre-Joseph Proudhon, Wilhelm Emmanuel Von Ketteler, Albert de Mun, Francesco Vito, Émile Durkheim, Charles Maurras, A. de Oliveira Salazar, Walter Rathenau, Georges Sorel, Pierre Mendes-France and John Maynard Keynes. He also emphasised the fact that corporatism affected many different countries (Schmitter 1974: 87–8, 99).

Shonfield was the first to state that post-war corporatism came in two main different forms: (1) an intellectual, technocratic approach towards economic problems, paving the way to planned interventions, and (2) a new form of public ownership of the means of production which was fully controlled and widespread. As first proposed by Manoïlesco and subsequently developed by Schmitter, we can see that there is a clear distinction between two main types of corporatism: (1) pure corporatism – in which the legitimacy and the functioning of a state mainly depend on the activities of a single, non-competitive and hierarchically ordered "corporation"; and (2) subordinate corporatism – in which structures resembling "corporations" are created and maintained as auxiliary bodies within a state which owes its legitimacy to other bodies and functions. The former may be identified as state corporatism (as in Spain, Brazil, Chile, Peru, Mexico and Greece, as well as in Italy during the fascist period, in France at the time of Petain and in Austria at the time of Dollfuss). The latter can be seen as social corporatism with well-known examples in Holland, Sweden, Denmark, Switzerland, Norway, Germany, Great Britain, Canada and the USA (Manoïlesco 1938; Shonfield 1965; Schmitter 1974).

Manoïlesco was an engineer and professor of political economy, as well as a banker and a minister, who devised a modern, lay theory of corporatism based on an analysis of the needs of populations. His theory went beyond the idea of corporatism as a pure intra-class system. He pictured corporatism as a system of peace and harmony, promoting a supranational European institution, which aimed to overcome national egoism and economic individualism.

In the context of political corporatism, some of John Maynard Keynes's ideas should also be taken into account among the formulations of social corporatism described earlier. In particular, there are certain extracts in *The End of Laissez-Faire* (1926) which provide evidence of a widespread need for correctives in order to give a social objective to capitalism. Furthermore, he admitted that there were things that had to be done or not done in economic policy. Finally, there are some explicitly corporatist statements, for example, "I propose a return, it may be said, towards medieval conceptions of separate autonomies" (Keynes 1926 [1972]: 289). All this attests that Keynes was not explicitly anti-corporatist, as had already been acknowledged by two of his contemporaries, Joseph Schumpeter and Friedrich von Hayek.

Contemporary Corporatism

Starting from the 1950s, what, historically speaking, had been defined as pure corporatism was completely dismissed after the fall of the political regimes that had endorsed it. However, this was precisely the moment that social corporatism became extremely widespread and there is evidence of this in many seminal contributions (for example, Schmitter 1974; Alesina and Perotti 1997; Siaroff 1999; Hicks and Lane 2003). This renewed interest in corporatism – at least in its "social" version – proves that corporatism itself cannot be limited to a certain period or to the ideology of certain authoritarian nations. Moreover, there has been a conceptual development, which, according to its keenest representatives, goes so far as to identify corporatism with capitalism itself in its most recent forms (Siaroff 1999: 183–7). Therefore, we consider the term "neo-corporatism" to be inadequate and incomplete for the many corporatist structures that emerged in a number of countries in the post war period. This would mean disregarding the historical continuity and adaptability of corporatism, that is, its most significant characteristic.

Let us briefly examine the case of one country in particular. Germany (that is, initially West Germany and then the whole of Germany after 1989) deserves attention not only for its high degree of corporatism but also for its extraordinary economic performance. Wolfgang Streeck (1983) emphasised the significance of the relationship between the government and certain important German associations such as the Deutscher Industrie- und Handelskammertag (DIHT), the Bundesverband der Deutschen Industrie (BDI) and the Zentralverband des Deutschen Handwerks (ZDH). These associations safeguarded their members' interests and thus played an important role in terms of defining economic policies and obtaining juridical, self-regulating acknowledgement from the state. The structure of the German economy probably went well beyond the balanced dynamics of the Soziale Marktwirtschaft and demonstrated a propensity for corporatism. Likewise, there are a number of other very similar empirical studies related to many economically developed countries.

In a broader perspective, note that economic growth in the 1970s and the beginning of the 1980s was supported in many developed countries by corporatist policies of a social democratic kind (Hicks 1988). This was so much so that some studies (for example, Alesina and Perotti 1997) demonstrated that welfare policies had significantly distorted competitiveness, particularly as far as taxes for redistribution and the role of trade unions were concerned.

Remarkable results derive from an empirical analysis of the rate of corporatism. A study carried out on 24 industrialised countries (Siaroff 1999) identified 22 factors, which affect the level of corporatisation in a country's economy. These factors can be divided into four main groups relating to: (1) structure; (2) roles performed; (3) behavioural structures and (4) environment/conditions. As far as structures are concerned, examples of corporatism can be found in a high level of union participation, a relatively small number of unions, an entrepreneurial community dominated by large companies specialised in exports and highly centralised wage bargaining. We might also consider: the crucial role of both entrepreneurs and workers cooperating in programmes regarding education, training and social commitment; consensus reached between unions and companies; a low rate of strikes; voluntary or consenting policies regarding wage restraints;

low military expenditure; an effort to achieve consensus by means of pacts rather than a majority vote and, finally, a high level of social expenditure along with successful economic performance. In more general terms, it is quite possible to assess the degree of corporatism in each individual country, measuring it in terms of the degree of deviation from the pure dynamics of a free market. Surprisingly, in this way, it becomes clear that nearly all developed countries have implemented varying degrees of corporatist policies. Corporatism was and still is vital. Since the beginning of the twenty-first century it seems to have paradoxically become not so much a third option, but rather to represent the most developed and adopted form of Western capitalism (Hicks and Kenworthy 2003; Streeck 2010).

SERGIO NOTO

See also:

Business cycles and growth (III); Historical economics (II); Friedrich List (I); Mercantilism and the science of trade (II); Political philosophy and economics: freedom and labour (III); Pierre-Joseph Proudhon (I); Joseph Alois Schumpeter (I); Arthur Spiethoff (I).

References and further reading

Åkerman, J. (1936), 'Annual survey of economic theory: the setting of the central problem', *Econometrica*, **4** (2), 97–122.
Alesina, R. and R. Perotti (1997), 'The welfare state and competitiveness', *American Economic Review*, **87** (5), 921–39.
Amoroso, L. (1999), *Ciclo, Circolazione, Politica Monetaria, a cura di L. Venturi, introduzione di S. Vinci*, Rome: UTET-Bancaria Editrice.
Amoroso, L. and A. De Stefani (1933), 'La logica del sistema corporativo', *Rivista internazionale di scienze sociali*, Serie III, **4** (fasc. 4), 393–411.
Cramer, D.L. and C.G. Leathers (1981), 'Schumpeter's corporatist views: links among his social theory, *Quadragesimo Anno*, and moral reforms', *History of Political Economy*, **13** (4), 745–71.
De Robertis, F.M. (1973), *Storia delle Corporazioni e del regime associativo nel mondo romano*, Bari: Adriatica.
Halevi, J. (1987), 'Corporatism', in J. Eatwell, M. Milgate and P. Newman (eds), *The New Palgrave Dictionary of Economics*, vol. 1, London: Macmillan, pp. 677–8.
Hayek, F. (2004), *The Road to Serfdom: Text and Documents: The Definitive Edition (The Collected Works of F.A. Hayek)*, ed. B. Caldwell, London: Routledge.
Hicks, A. (1988), 'London: democratic corporatism and economic growth', *Journal of Politics*, **50** (3), 677–704.
Hicks, A. and L. Kenworthy (2003), 'Varieties of welfare capitalism', *Socio-Economic Review*, **1** (1), 27–61.
Holton, R.J. and B.S. Turner (1989), *Max Weber on Economy and Society*, London: Routledge.
Keynes, J.M. (1926), *The End of Laissez-Faire*, London: Hogarth Press, reprinted in J.M. Keynes (1972), *The Collected Writings of J.M.K.*, vol. IX: *Essays in Persuasion*, ed. D. Moggridge, London and Basingstoke: Macmillan and Cambridge University Press, pp. 272–94.
Manoïlesco, M. (1938), *Le siècle du corporatisme. Doctrine du corporatisme intégral et pur*, new edn, Paris: Félix Alcan.
Misner, P. (1991), 'The predecessors of Rerum Novarum within Catholicism', *Review of Social Economy*, **49** (4), 444–64.
Noto, S. (2008), 'Beyond the business cycle and socialism: the late Schumpeter's corporatist view', accessed 11 January 2016 at SSRN http://ssrn.com/abstract=1261910 or http://dx.doi.org/10.2139/ssrn.1261910.
Nuccio, O. (1987), *Il Pensiero Economico Italiano*, Sassari: Gallizzi.
Padovano, F. (2003), 'Corporatism', in J. Mokyr (ed.), *The Oxford Encyclopedia of Economic History*, vol. 2, New York: Oxford University Press, pp. 8–11.
Pesch, H. (2002), *Lehrbuch der Nationalökonomie/Teaching Guide to Economics*, trans. R.J. Ederer, Lewiston, Queenston and Lampeter: Edwin Mellen Press.
Pomini, M. and G. Tusset (2009), 'Habits and expectations: dynamic general equilibrium in the Italian Paretian School', *History of Political Economy*, **41** (2), 311–42.
Prime, M.G. and D.R. Henderson (1975), 'Schumpeter on preserving private enterprise', *History of Political Economy*, **7** (3), 293–8.

Rasi, G. (2009), 'Introduzione', in U. Spirito, *Il Corporativismo. Edizione Nazionale delle Opere di Ugo Spirito*, Soveria Mannelli, Italy: Rubbettino, pp. 13–32.

Schmitter, P.C. (1974), 'Still the century of corporatism?', *Review of Politics*, **36** (1), 85–131.

Shonfield, A. (1965), *Modern Capitalism. The Changing Balance of Public and Private Powers*, London: Oxford University Press.

Siaroff, A. (1999), 'Corporatism in 24 industrial democracies: meaning and measurement', *European Journal of Political Research*, **36** (2), 175–205.

Solterer, J. (2005), 'Quadragesimo Anno: Schumpeter's alternative to the omnipotent state', *Review of Social Economy*, **63** (3), 357–68.

Streeck, W. (1983), 'Between pluralism and corporatism: German business associations and the state', *Journal of Public Policy*, **3** (3), 265–83.

Streeck, W. (2010), 'Taking capitalism seriously: towards an institutionalist approach to contemporary political economy', *Socio-Economic Review*, **9** (1), 137–67.

Temin, P. (2004), 'The labor market of the Early Roman Empire', *Journal of Interdisciplinary History*, **34** (4), 513–38.

Toniolo, G. (1947–53), *Opera Omnia*, Vatican City: Comitato Opera Omnia di G. Toniolo.

Waltzing, J.-P. (1895), *Étude historique sur les corporations professionnelles chez les Romains depuis les origines jusqu'à la chute de l'Empire d'Occident*, 4 vols, Leuven: Charles Peeters.

Development economics

The history of development economics is as old as that of economics itself, with contributions ranging back to the mercantilists, the Physiocrats and the classical economists. However, the systematic and specialized study of the entire range of problems of less-developed countries (LDCs) did not begin until just after World War II. The purpose of this chapter is to provide a brief overview of the evolution of the field of development economics by viewing this history in terms of four slightly overlapping phases and by drawing some general conclusions. However, given the early roots of the field, it will also provide a brief discussion of some relevant aspects of the contributions of earlier economists. The next section discusses the ideas of the precursors of development economics. The following sections discuss the four phases in the history of development economics. The final section concludes.

Precursors of Development Economics

As noted above, the study of economic development has a very long history, with economists analysing the development process and problems of countries which are now economically developed and occasionally writing about countries which are still economically underdeveloped. We may provide a sampling of these past contributions by examining three themes in the history of economic thought which are of particular relevance to modern development economics (see also Vaggi 2008 for further discussion and references).

The first concerns the general issues of growth, stagnation and income distribution. Pre-classical French economists, such as the Physiocrats and Turgot, examined issues such as agrarian structure and the relationship between agriculture and industry. Around the middle of the eighteenth century Quesnay, for instance, examined the interaction between the industrial and agricultural sectors in his analysis of how the two sectors created markets for each other's products, emphasizing the productive role of the agricultural sector. This focus on growth in the pre-classical economists was taken further by the classical economists. There were some common features to their approach. Smith, Ricardo and Marx focused on the importance of saving and capital accumulation in the growth process and took the view that labour supply was not a constraint on economic growth; since they assumed that saving arose mainly out of profits, they emphasized the positive relation between the inequality of income distribution (as measured by the profit share) and accumulation. However, individual classical economists emphasized some specific ideas and differences from the general approach. Smith emphasized productivity growth owing to the increasing division of labour. Smith, and more explicitly McCulloch, examined the role education played in increasing the skills and productivity of workers thereby contributing to economic growth. Ricardo examined the interaction between agricultural and industrial sectors, and analysed the tendency of diminishing returns in agriculture to squeeze industrial profits and bring about the stationary state. While Ricardo believed that this state was in the distant future and could be pushed by technological changes, he thought its effects were pernicious; John Stuart Mill, however, was more favourably disposed towards it, in part because of the environmental damage done by endless economic growth. In explaining the absence of labour supply constraints on growth, the earlier classical writers invoked the Malthusian endogeneity of population, according to which, when capital accumulation and employment growth makes the wage rise above the subsistence level (usually broadly defined), population and labour supply expand and drive the wage back towards subsistence. Marx argued against this Malthusian approach, and instead viewed the wage as being kept down by the existence of the reserved army of the unemployed, which was replenished by those who lost their jobs in the pre-capitalist sectors owing to competition from the growing capitalist sector and by labour-saving technological change in the capitalist sector. Although the classical writers generally emphasized the role of saving in the process of capital accumulation, some of them recognized the possibility of aggregate demand problems which reduce investment incentives. Thus, Malthus discussed the problem of a general glut due to excessive saving, and Marx analysed the possibility of a realization crisis which could reduce production and growth because producers could not find markets for all their products. From the last quarter of the nineteenth century, the marginalist economists, such as Walras, Jevons and Menger, turned their attention to the problems of resource allocation and the full employment of resources, including labour, and away from the dynamics of growth and distribution. However, an interest in the questions of growth, stagnation and development continued in the writings of Schumpeter, the followers of Marx, and Keynes and his followers, who stressed the role of aggregate demand.

A second theme concerns international issues. The mercantilist writers who flourished during the period from the sixteenth century to the late eighteenth century emphasized the importance of having foreign trade surpluses to make precious metals flow into their country, to attain the twin related goals of power (by increasing the availability of precious metals to finance the military) and plenty (by increasing the demand for their products and hence production and employment). The classical economists, however, departed from this position by emphasizing the benefits of trade owing to specialization and increasing both exports and imports according to absolute and comparative advantage, rather than by increasing the trade surplus. Ricardo's theory of comparative advantage showed – using the England and Portugal example with clothing and wine – how both countries gained from trade. His dynamic theory of trade and growth also showed how imports of food prevented the price of wage goods from rising due to capital accumulation, and, by counteracting the tendency of the rate of profit to fall because of this, postponed the stationary state for food-importing countries such as England. However, it is interesting to note that if the country in question exports, rather than imports, food, the tendency of the price of food to increase and the profit rate to fall is exacerbated, bringing closer the onset of the stationary state. Marx took a more ambiguous view of international economic relations. On the one hand, the spread of capitalism around the globe in search of higher profits played a positive role not only for rich countries by obtaining cheaper inputs and higher profits abroad, but also for poor countries by fostering capitalist development. On the other hand, the incorporation of backward countries into the world economy also had a destructive effect by exposing their industries to foreign competition and by siphoning off their economic surplus, themes which were stressed by later Marx-inspired scholars of imperialism and dependency. Nationalist writers in colonies and elsewhere stressed the problems of surplus transfers from colonies and other backward countries to rich countries – for instance, the "drain theory" of

Indian nationalist writers such as Dadabhai Naoroji (1901) – and the dangers of foreign competition for their nascent industries.

A third theme concerns the role of the state in economic development. Since, as noted above, the mercantilist writers were concerned with increasing employment and foreign trade surpluses with a view to increasing the economic and political power of nations, they were in favour of trade policies which promoted exports and provided protection against imports. They therefore wrote extensively about themes which are relevant for the LDCs of today, including foreign exchange constraints, state intervention and planning and protection. The classical writers such as Smith and Ricardo, who favoured free trade, were generally in favour of laissez-faire policies and argued against state involvement in the economy because of the monopolies it created and the impediments it imposed on the free exchange of goods. Malthus even argued against efforts to help the poor because such measures simply increased population growth and failed to help the lot of the poor. However, they were not entirely against government intervention either. Smith, for instance, was concerned about the deleterious effects of the division of labour on the conditions of workers, and supported government provision of primary education. Economists concerned with the development problems of relatively backward countries envisioned a much more active role for the state. When writers of colonial theory and policy studied the economic problems of their colonies and discussed the problems resulting from cultural attitudes and climate, some with concern for the well-being of the subjected people, they recommended government action to address these problems. Alexander Hamilton in the United States and, following his lead, Friedrich List in Germany argued for active government support, including protection for domestic industry to allow them to withstand foreign competition from producers in more technologically advanced countries. List was in favour of national systems which, with the help of government intervention and protectionism, would improve technology especially in the manufacturing industry, and allow countries with nascent industrial sectors to develop and compete in world markets. List was critical of the attitude of advanced countries which had used such interventionist policies for their own development and then tried to "kick away the ladder", promoting free trade and laissez-faire, forcing such policies on relatively backward countries when they were able to do so, for instance, through colonization (Chang 2002).

Despite such early beginnings, however, this early history can be called a prehistory because the systematic and specialized study of the entire range of problems of LDCs did not begin until after World War II. The rise of the study of economic development as a separate field of enquiry around this time was caused by the conjunction of several powerful influences (see Hirschman 1981). At one level the rise of Keynesianism paved the way for state intervention, for the development of analytical concepts such as unemployment, for the focus on macroeconomic aggregates, and generally for departures from neoclassical orthodoxy; the consequent development of growth theory by Keynesians and neoclassicals, input–output analysis, and optimal programming also helped the growth of the subject. At other levels, the wartime experiences with active state intervention and planning, the experience of planning in the Soviet Union, the political independence of several LDCs and the consequent desire of – and pressures on – new nationalist governments to prove their capabilities, the advent of international agencies fostering development, and the spectre of communism all strengthened the need for development with active state intervention (see also Meier 1984). The combination of these factors helped to create a tremendous enthusiasm for, and interest in, the development of LDCs. The subsequent history of development economics will now be considered by examining four phases.

Low Level Equilibria, Dualism and Sectoral Interaction

The first phase, from 1945 to the mid-1950s, emphasized a number of major (and more or less related) themes. First, underdevelopment was characterized as a low-level equilibrium caused by factors such as low savings, high rates of population growth, and low investment incentives due to market failures arising from indivisibilities in investment and externalities, ideas that were explored in classic early works by Rosenstein-Rodan (1943) and Nurkse (1953), among others. Rosenstein-Rodan (1943) argued that a big push, through the simultaneous establishment of a number of industrial enterprises which would generate income flows and provide consumer demand to the products of these different enterprises, could overcome the problem of investment incentives. Nurkse (1953) discussed the problems both of low income and low savings, and low income and low levels of demand, which created vicious cycles from the sides of both saving supply and investment incentives. Early development economists also examined how the effects of increases in income and living standards would be reversed by reductions in mortality rates and consequent population along Malthusian lines, and argued for at least a critical minimum level of expansion of saving and growth in order to produce a demographic transition, due to declines in fertility rates brought about by social changes (such as the desire for economic improvement and upward social mobility).

Second, the economy was characterized as a dual economy with a backward sector, predominantly agricultural, and a modern industrial sector. The classic formulation was that of Lewis (1954), who analysed how the backward sector, characterized by surplus labour which was disguisedly employed in family farms and enterprises, provided labour to the modern capitalist sector at a fixed real wage and allowed the expansion of the latter through the investment of saving from the profits made in it. The product wage in this modern sector was held down both by the existence of surplus labour in the backward sector, and by the absence of an upward pressure in the price of agricultural goods, which could squeeze modern sector profits by requiring higher industrial wages, because the existence of disguised unemployment implied that the withdrawal of labour from agriculture did not reduce agricultural output. Lewis's writings resulted in a bias towards seeing the industrial sector as the engine of growth and the agricultural sector as a source of surplus labour, although Lewis himself recognized the importance of the balanced expansion of both sectors.

Third, intersectoral interactions and changes in sectoral composition, related to this agriculture–industry distinction, and to the distinction between consumption and capital goods sectors were emphasized. For instance, the need for increasing the share of total investment allocated to the capital goods sector to make saving and investment physically possible (with limited access to imported capital goods, given foreign exchange constraints) was stressed; see Mahalanobis (1953). Arguments were made in favour of balanced growth to prevent the growth process faltering due to the stagnation of some sectors, and to increase the demand for other sectors, as noted by Rosenstein-Rodan. However, given the shortage of resources, some authors also made the case for unbalanced growth – concentrating energies on some key sectors to stimulate other sectors through backward linkages, by creating a demand for inputs for them, and forward linkages, by supplying inputs to them (see Hirschman 1958).

Structuralism, Import Substitution and State-Led Development

A second phase extended from the early 1950s to the late 1960s. The major contributions – from structuralists in the South, such as the group of economists working at the United Nations (UN) Economic Commission for Latin America with Raul Prebisch – and in the North, such as Chenery, maintained the earlier themes but moved further away from neoclassical economics (and from its generally optimistic and problem-solving mind-set) in at least two different ways.

First, there was a general recognition that many kinds of structural rigidities existed in LDCs which made these countries very different from what were then perceived as relatively smoothly functioning advanced economies. For instance, supply rigidities in particular sectors, such as the agricultural sector owing to conditions of land tenure and the balance of payments due to a rigid import–gross domestic product (GDP) ratio – an idea formalized in the two-gap model (Chenery and Strout 1966) incorporating both saving and foreign exchange problems – were emphasized, and inflation was seen to be the result of supply rigidities and distributional conflicts in the economy (Noyola 1956; Sunkel 1960).

Second, there was a general belief that trade could not be relied on as an engine of growth, and that attempts to increase exports were likely to be met with inelastic world demand and hence worsening terms of trade (see Singer 1950; Prebisch 1959). The interaction between rich and poor countries through trade and factor movements, in particular, was argued to give rise to uneven international development. Myrdal (1957), who discussed both spread (which made rich country growth pull up poor countries) and backwash (which created divergence) effects, argued that, without deliberate redistributive mechanisms (in the absence of a world government), the latter would dominate.

The recognition of market failures, as in the first phase, together with that of rigidities and "export pessimism" led to the view that development and growth could not be left to the market. Major reliance was therefore placed on state-led development planning and, in particular, there was general support for protectionist import-substituting trade policies to promote industrialization and to overcome balance of payment problems, echoing the views of the mercantilists and nationalist writers of earlier times.

This is not to say that there was unanimity on these views. An important dissenting voice was that of Bauer (see Bauer and Yamey 1957), who emphasized the corrupting influence of the politicization of economic life as a result of state intervention. Moreover, Marxist writers such as Baran (1952) took a broader view of development by emphasizing political and social factors which, among other problems, led to the transfer of the economic surplus from LDCs to developed countries, rather than narrowly focusing on economic factors related to capital accumulation and industrialization, and also drew attention to the inefficiency of, and corruption in, the capitalist state.

Challenges to "Old" Development Economics

The third phase, starting around the mid-1960s, resulted from different reactions to views rife during the first and second phases.

The major challenge came from the resurgence of neoclassical economics, which criticized a number of pet themes of development economics of the earlier phases, including surplus labour, export pessimism, the focus on capital accumulation, and the benefits of state-led planned industrialization (see Lal 1985). This resulted partly from changes in intellectual currents in economics as a whole, reflected in the ascendancy of different forms of monetarism over Keynesianism. It was also due to the actual experiences of LDCs: the blame for development failures in many LDCs was laid at the door of development economics for its focus on dirigiste and autarkic industrialization policies, and the emergence and rapid growth of the East Asian economies was perceived by neoclassical economists as resulting from export-oriented and free-market policies (see Little et al. 1970). The policy of import-substituting industrialization, in particular, was singled out for criticism, for promoting inefficient capital-intensive industries and diverting resources away from labour-intensive sectors in which LDCs had a comparative advantage, and for promoting rent-seeking and other kinds of directly unproductive activities rather than productive and innovative activity. The successful developers of East Asia were seen as promoting exports and removing the import-protecting distortionary biases and following market-friendly policies which exposed their economies to foreign competition. Although, as we shall see later, this interpretation of the reasons for the success of these economies is flawed, it had an effect on the nature of development economics.

A second challenge came from those who argued that the focus of development economics on growth and capital accumulation resulted in the neglect of the human dimension of development and of income distribution and poverty (see Little 1982: ch. 11). This view was bolstered not only by cases of rapid growth and increasing inequality in some LDCs, but also because, in the wake of growth failures, it was believed that the urgent priority should be the satisfaction of the basic needs of the poor. To some extent this was a reorientation of the objectives of development – although it can be argued that the early proponents of growth viewed growth as a means to human development and poverty removal – but it also reflected a change in the strategy of development, from a focus on saving, investment and industrialization, to an emphasis on employment creation and direct methods of poverty alleviation. The basic needs approach pioneered by Paul Streeten (1982) and others was developed, focusing on the consumption of basic goods such as food, clothing, shelter and health care, and it led to a focus on poverty, inequality and human development.

A third challenge came from radical quarters, especially with the rise of the dependency school (see Palma 2008). This school, although echoing many of the concerns addressed in early development economics, saw the root cause of underdevelopment not in the problems of capital accumulation and internal rigidities and market failures, but in the relations of LDCs to rich countries. Some argued that underdevelopment was not the absence of development but, rather, a process just like development; in other words, underdevelopment developed. Moreover, development and underdevelopment were seen as two sides of the same coin, part of an overall common process of global uneven development according to which the very process which led to development in some parts of the world led to the underdevelopment of other parts. Marxist and other radical writers focused on the problems created by trade and aid dependence and, most importantly, by the activities of transnational corporations. International trade locked in countries into their traditional roles – the rich as producers of advanced industrial goods and the poor as producers of primary products and simple consumer goods – and allowed technological development in rich countries and caused stagnation in poor countries. The activities of transnational corporations, by adversely affecting domestic entrepreneurship in LDCs and by causing the transfer for large monopoly profits to rich countries – often facilitated by transfer pricing between branches to hide actual profit transfers – also impoverished poor countries as a whole while supporting local elites and widening income distribution, and politically subjugated poor country governments. Foreign aid also created dependence and reduced domestic saving while supporting repressive regimes.

New Directions in Development Economics

These challenges were interpreted by some as reflecting a decline in the discipline of development economics (Hirschman 1981). However, from the middle and late 1980s there has occurred a revival of interest in development economics, which may be interpreted as ushering in a fourth phase in the history of the discipline.

This phase continues to be dominated by the neoclassical approach which emphasizes the policies of liberalization, privatization and globalization – the so-called Washington Consensus view – and locates the problems of development in the allegedly misguided policies of interventionist and protectionist governments (see Meier 2005). According to this approach, the solution lies in rolling back the state by reducing government regulation of the economy and privatizing state-owned enterprises, reducing restrictions on trade, reducing financial regulation and reducing restrictions on international capital movements. These policies coupled with those which impose austerity measures involving fiscal and monetary contraction continue to be enthusiastically and vigorously supported by the International Monetary Fund when it provides external financing to countries with payments problems, and by the World Bank, as part of its structural adjustment programs when it provides development assistance to LDCs. The World Trade Organization has also promoted free trade, in addition to reducing regulations that LDCs can impose on the activities of transnational corporations and imposing intellectual property rights protections internationally. Even when policies of this type have had disastrous consequences, the policy of getting the prices right through such measures has not lost favour. Rather, the sequencing of reforms, the incompleteness of reforms (for instance, not liberalizing labour markets), and not having proper institutions in place have taken the blame. Some shifts in emphasis – such as increasing attention to poverty alleviation, governance and democracy – have occurred, arguably without changing the basic approach. Despite the dominance of this approach in policy circles, development economics during this most recent phase actually reflects a rich variety of approaches of which six strands may be usefully distinguished.

The first strand refers to new neoclassical approaches that examine issues such as agrarian relations, income distribution, the causes of poverty, and general institutional issues. While applications of neoclassical microeconomic theory to development economics – with its ubiquitous optimization agent – have a long history, the recent flowering in this literature applying the tools of industrial organization, game theory and information economics – reviewed, among others, by Ray (1998) – is unprecedented in volume and scope. A flavour of the analysis can be gleaned from the following examples. First, if an economy with imperfect competition in goods markets has different production technologies available to it, it can be caught in a low-level equilibrium trap using constant returns to scale technology rather than using the increasing returns technology which requires a higher level of production. This analysis uses neoclassical methodology to formalize Rosenstein-Rodan's argument for a big push. Second, in the presence of asymmetric information in which lenders possess incomplete information about the actions of borrowers, it is argued that credit is rationed to poor borrowers with smaller endowments of wealth and collateral, resulting in an inefficient allocation of resources and the perpetuation of inequality. A similar logic explains why capital, rather than flowing from rich to poor countries with an allegedly higher marginal productivity of capital and profitability, can flow the other way, implying growth divergence. Third, in agricultural sectors with sharecropping tenure systems, land reforms granting tenants greater security of tenure and regulating the tenant share can strengthen the bargaining position of tenants, increase their share of output, increase their incentives and effort and thereby improve efficiency. Fourth, if there are search costs in labour markets which prevent workers and firms from finding suitable matches after they are separated due to exogenous shocks, and firms can choose to incur the cost of adopting new technology and workers can choose to acquire training to productively use new technology, the economy can be trapped at an equilibrium without training and innovation, despite the existence of an equilibrium in which all firms innovate and all workers train; with imperfect competition in the labour market the worker's return to training is lower, which further reduces incentives for training. Fifth, if information problems in choosing technologies and network externalities are present, the benefits to economic agents of choosing a technology depend positively on the number who have already adopted that technology, and multiple equilibria are possible, some in which the economy is locked into choosing inefficient technologies. Finally, in the presence of increasing returns to scale and learning by doing, new neoclassical models of international trade theory imply that import protection which expands scale and results in greater efficiency can subsequently expand exports.

Two, in the macroeconomic sphere, an empirical and theoretical literature on long-term growth has expanded rapidly, triggered in the late 1980s by the revival of neoclassical growth economics in the form of new growth theories. Cross-country and panel growth regressions have examined factors explaining variations in growth rates across countries (Temple 1999). The role of numerous variables, including the rates of investment and saving, the level of human capital formation, research and development expenditures, political stability, financial variables, inequality, the extent of openness to international trade, and foreign direct capital inflows, have been explored. The robustness of these results, however, has been called into question, with only a few variables – such as investment rates – being found to have a positive and significant effect. Questions have also been raised about the way in which different independent variables (such as economic openness) have been measured, and about whether cross-country methods, which assume that countries have a basically similar structure (apart from those which are captured using country dummies in panel equations), are useful for understanding growth dynamics over time. There has also been an attempt to distinguish between what have been referred to as proximate and fundamental (or ultimate) determinants of growth, with geography and institutions, being singled out as fundamental determinants, with a consensus forming around the notion that institutions – understood to include not only legal frameworks and organizations but also social norms – are the key (Rodrik 2007). Aside from the fact that it is not clear why institutions, which have been found to depend endogenously on other supposedly proximate factors (like saving and investment rates) which affect growth, are considered to be fundamental determinants, the literature is not very persuasive about what institutions work best, the excessive and simplistic focus on private property rights and market freedoms appearing to be unwarranted. Although cultural norms and political organizations as stressed, they are not as resilient in the face of economic and policy changes as sometimes believed (Chang 2008). Despite the problems with the empirical literature, it does suggest that long-run growth seems to depend on economic and other determinants, rather than on exogenous factors as implied by the old neoclassical models such as Solow's (1956) with diminishing returns to capital. The so-called "new" neoclassical growth models, which typically assume away diminishing returns to capital by introducing learning by doing, profit-seeking research and development expenditures and education, are better placed to examine the role of endogenous economic and policy-related determinants of long-run economic growth (see Romer 1988). While these models raise important issues related to externalities, scale economies, the division of labour, and imperfect information, and imply a role for government policies for economic growth and development, their ability to explain actual development successes and make specific policy recommendations can be questioned (Pack 1994). Moreover, while this literature runs parallel to – rather than being closely integrated with – development economics, it has recently emphasized some classic themes in development theory such as the role of income inequality, natural resources and increasing returns in the process of economic growth (for a review and evaluation of this literature, see Ros 2000).

Three, also in the macroeconomic sphere, there has developed what can be called the neo-structuralist approach, which blends macroeconomic approaches drawn from the classical economists, Marx, Keynes and Kalecki, with early structuralist contributions from the second phase described above, to analyse the determinants of growth and income distribution (see, especially, Taylor 1983). This approach uses mathematical methods involving accounting identities and behavioural and equilibrium equations, and uses dynamic equations to examine the time path of the economy. Several features of this approach can be noted. First, aggregate demand determines capacity utilization and the rate of growth with the price level determined by a fixed money wage and a given mark-up set by firms. While early development economists argued that LDCs were mainly constrained by saving, foreign exchange and other supply-side bottlenecks, this approach places aggregate demand issues at centre stage, given the many sources of uncertainty present in the economy (see Dutt 1996). Second, the approach examines how the distribution of income between wages and profits affects capacity utilization and growth. Growth can be wage-led – because a redistribution of income towards wage earners from profit recipients who save a higher fraction of their income increases consumption demand, capacity utilization, and investment, which depends positively on capacity utilization – thereby formalizing a long tradition which argues that inequality causes economic stagnation. However, this is not a necessary outcome, if the economy is close to full capacity, in which case increases in growth require higher savings through income distributional shifts towards profits, or if investment depends positively on the profit share; in these cases growth is profit-led as in classical growth theory. Third, the approach has been extended to introduce asset market complications and interest rates, and inflation owing to conflicting claims. An important implication is that monetary contraction, which raises the interest rate, can reduce investment demand by increasing the cost of borrowing, and increase the mark-up of firms which try to pass on higher interest costs to higher prices, which shifts income distribution away from wages and increases inflation; thus macroeconomic austerity as recommended by the IMF can be stagflationary as well as inequalizing. The approach is also able to integrate the analysis of what is generally considered short-run economic phenomena, such as financial crises, with long-run analysis of growth and distribution. Fourth, since LDCs usually have large agricultural sectors, the approach has been extended to have two sectors, an industrial fixprice sector and an agricultural sector with a flexible market-clearing price; it has been used to show how the economy experiences balanced growth in the long run with different assumptions about agricultural growth such as, for instance, growth depending on the terms of trade or growth being determined by exogenous institutional factors. The models show how the agricultural sector can provide a market for industrial goods, and how agricultural stagnation, by turning the terms of trade against industry, can reduce industrial growth. Fifth, although aggregate demand plays a major role, the models introduce other constraints on growth, including foreign exchange constraints and fiscal constraints. Finally, the approach has been used to develop models of the global economy to analyse the interaction between the North and the South, at times taking into account structural differences between the two economies. These models examine conditions under which uneven development and North–South terms of trade changes occur, confirming – though not in all cases – the informal analyses of earlier structuralist and dependency writers.

Four, less formal literatures have re-examined the actual experience of developing economies, especially the successful East Asian newly industrialized countries (NICs) and, more recently, China, and drawn broad general conclusions from this analysis. Going beyond the boundaries of economics narrowly defined to incorporate and develop ideas from sociology, political science, and other disciplines, this study of the NICs experiences has shown that the success of these countries cannot be interpreted as an accomplishment of free market economics, and that the state played an active role in the development process (see Wade 1990; Amsden 1991; Stiglitz 2002; Chang 2008). The experience of these countries seems to be no different from those of late development in backward countries of the past, as argued in the early historical analysis of Gerschenkron (1962). In countries such as Korea and Taiwan, the state intervened in the economy, established state-owned enterprises, provided import protection, and allocated credit to particular sectors and firms. However, when it provided protection and credit it demanded that the recipients meet performance criteria in terms of eventual export success, without which the help they received was withdrawn. The recent interdisciplinary work suggests that markets and states can play a synergistic role in the development process, and that the nature of markets and of the state are more important than whether the state or the market is allowed a greater role. Markets push producers to become more competitive, but only after they have overcome initial handicaps against more technologically advanced foreign producers, as stressed earlier by List. The state can guide the market to get the best out of firms, playing a strategic role. Successful developmental states which have promoted economic development have been relatively autonomous from civil society and not become captive to powerful groups who act in their narrow self-interest, but have also been embedded within society – through Weberian bureaucracies and political parties – to obtain appropriate information and develop trust with private partners (see Evans 1995).

Five, also using an empirical approach, several mainstream economists are looking carefully at institutions and behaviours, and designing policies, that affect development and poverty (see, for instance, Banerjee and Duflo 2011). This approach examines historical evidence, econometric studies often using survey data, and randomized experiments to study how people actually behave, how norms and other institutions affect their behaviour and how their behaviour reacts to policy interventions. Although this approach generally takes a microeconomic perspective, it draws on the ideas of behavioural economics rather than using the neoclassical optimizing agent.

Six, following the early focus on growth in per capita income and the criticisms which gave rise to the interest in poverty and basic needs, a strand in development economics focuses on the meaning and measurement of economic development. Sen (1999) distinguishes between opulence (or income and production), utility and functionings and capabilities. While opulence – for countries as a whole or for individuals, for instance, in the measurement of poverty – refers to the means of development, it cannot be considered an end. Utility – which is now measured in happiness studies by surveys of subjective well-being – can be considered an end, but is subjective because it depends on individual feelings, and may reflect the fact that people adapt to changes in their circumstance; thus, for instance, the poor may get used to their impoverished conditions and not feel too unhappy. Thus, Sen prefers to emphasize functionings – the extent to which people are obtaining and achieving goods that they justifiably value, such as nutrition, healthy lives, education and dignity – and even more, capabilities, that is, whether people have the ability to achieve these valued goods (without necessarily achieving them). Despite the difficulties in compiling lists of such goods and of measuring and aggregating over them, there have been attempts to construct such measures of development, including the Human Development Index which takes into account achievements in education and health in addition to income. While many of these concepts examine how individuals are doing, others may refer to overall societies, for instance, regarding environmental issues, which have received increasing attention not just because of what it does for growth and health, but also as an end. Aside from the fact that this strand clarifies the meaning of development, it also leads to an examination of how different people in an economy are doing relative to each other – for instance, people of different genders and ethnic groups – and how the different elements of development affect each other – for instance, how growth and poverty, and the environment and poverty, interact. On the last issue, although it is possible to have growth without improvements in distribution and average levels of functionings, the experience of LDCs analysed in the previous strand, suggests that sustained growth seems to be required for such improvements.

Conclusion

Rather than summarizing our summary of a large literature, we conclude with three comments.

First, the field of development economics seems to be alive and well. Hirschman's (1981) obituary, written at the end of the third phase, seems to have vastly exaggerated the rumours of its demise, as is suggested by the outpouring of research in the different strands of the most recent phase. Some observers seem to disagree. Krugman (1995 7), for instance, has written more recently that "Once upon a time there was a field called development economics ... That field no longer exists". However, Hirschman and Krugman's judgements are based on what the former referred to as the rejection of monoeconomics claim – that there is one economics which applies everywhere – in the early days of the field in order to stress the differences between economically advanced countries and LDCs, each with their own distinctive structures. Scholars working on LDC now use methods and approaches very similar to those employed in analysing economically advanced countries. This is true for orthodox approaches, where many methods and insights of standard neoclassical economic theory – including game theory, growth theory, econometrics and information economics – have been applied to LDCs, as discussed under the first and second strands of the final phase. In fact, Krugman (1995) finds in some of these formal contributions the resurrection of earlier development economics insights. It is also true for heterodox approaches, where case study methods, broad political economy approaches and heterodox mathematical theories – as discussed in the third and fourth strands of the final phase – have been applied to LDCs as well as to general economic analysis. It should be noted, however, that this does not imply that there is only one kind of economics – to be applied everywhere, since it is not obvious that economics is a monolithic subject, an issue to which we will return in our next comment. It is also worth pointing out that even if there has been a convergence in the methods and analyses of the economics of rich and poor countries, this is not due to one-way traffic from the analysis of rich countries to that of poor countries. Many neoclassical ideas that were developed in the analysis of LDCs (see Bardhan 1993) – such as efficiency wages and increasing returns – have entered general economic analysis, and the same has been true for heterodox neo-structuralist macroeconomic models.

Second, there exists a fair amount of pluralism within development economics, arguably more so than is in existence in other fields of economics. Chenery (1975), for instance, distinguished between neoclassical, Marxist and structuralist approaches, where the first two attempt to adapt systems of thought initially applied to developed economies to less developed economies, and the last "attempts to identify specific rigidities, lags and other characteristics of the structure of developing economies" (ibid.: 310) which are generally ignored in the neoclassical approach. Bardhan (1988) partitions the subject in a similar manner, distinguishing between neoclassical, Marxist and structuralist-institutionalist approaches, recognizing that each is a portmanteau category. In Bardhan's view, the neoclassical approach analyses economic behaviour in terms of maximizing individuals, the Marxist emphasizes structural constraints and the importance of class, and the structuralist approach stresses the structures of particular economies (for instance, the importance of oligopoly and sectoral divisions) and structural differences between economies. There are, in fact, many ways in which one can divide the sub-discipline, according, for instance, to differences in: method (for instance, using mathematical models using the optimizing agent, or broad political economy analysis emphasizing the role of class differences); views of the economy (for instance, whether the markets work efficiently or the economy is rife with structural rigidities); strategies (for instance, whether free market or government intervention is the best approach) and meanings of development, as discussed in the sixth strand of the most recent phase (see Dutt 1992). Differences in these different dimensions also exist in economics more generally – although alternatives are not as widely represented as in development economics.

Third, despite this greater pluralism, there are some convergent tendencies, in at least three senses. One, in policy discussions, there is the overwhelming dominance of the neoclassical free market view, although with some recognition of government intervention to reduce poverty and provide infrastructure. Two, in terms of methods, there seems to be the dominance of the neoclassical optimization and formal econometric approaches. Despite this dominance, there are also vibrant heterodox literatures which have adopted broader political economy analysis and neo-structuralist modelling methods. Three, in both orthodox and heterodox literatures, there seems to be convergence in the sense of movement away from extreme views in debates concerning state intervention versus free market policies (with growing recognition of the synergistic role of markets and the state), and concerning growth versus distribution, poverty and human development, and on the need for incorporating broader institutional and political economy issues beyond narrowly economic ones. It is to be hoped that the convergence towards neoclassical methodology and policy will give way to convergence of the third kind rather than to the sharp pendulum swings of the past in terms of views of the economy, strategies and goals of development. That, and greater methodological pluralism, are arguably the best means of ensuring that development economics continues to flourish and focus on the vitally important task of facilitating development in poor countries and improving the lot of the poor.

AMITAVA KRISHNA DUTT

See also:

Balance of payments and exchange rates (III); British classical political economy (II); Economic geography (III); Economic sociology (III); Growth (III); Income distribution (III); Institutional economics (III); International trade (III); Michał Kalecki (I); John Maynard Keynes (I); Paul Robin Krugman (I); Friedrich List (I); Thomas Robert Malthus (I); Karl Heinrich Marx (I); Marxism(s) (II); Mercantilism and the science of trade (II); Gunnar Myrdal (I); Population (III); Post-Keynesianism (II); Poverty (III); François Quesnay and Physiocracy (I); Resource and environmental economics (III); David Ricardo (I); Amartya Kumar Sen (I); Adam Smith (I); Robert Merton Solow (I); Joseph Eugene Stiglitz (I); Technical change and innovation (III).

References and further reading

Amsden, A. (1991), *Asia's Next Giant: South Korea and Late Industrialization*, New York: Oxford University Press.
Banerjee, A.V. and E. Duflo (2011), *Poor Economics*, New York: Public Affairs.
Baran, P. (1952), 'On the political economy of backwardness', *Manchester School*, **20** (January), 66–84.
Bardhan, P. (1988), 'Alternative approaches to development economics', in H.B. Chenery and T.N. Srinivasan (eds), *Handbook of Development Economics*, vol. 1, Amsterdam: North Holland, pp. 39–71.
Bardhan, P. (1993), 'Economics of development and the development of economics', *Journal of Economic Perspectives*, **7** (2), 129–42.
Bauer, P.T. and B.S. Yamey (1957), *The Economics of Under-Developed Countries*, Chicago, IL: University of Chicago Press.

Chang, H.-J. (2002), *Kicking Away the Ladder: Development Strategy in Historical Perspective*, London: Anthem Press.

Chang, H.-J. (2008), *The Bad Samaritans*, New York: Bloomsbury Press.

Chenery, H.B. (1975), 'The structuralist approach to development policy', *American Economic Review*, **65** (2), 310–16.

Chenery, H.B. and A.M. Strout (1966), 'Foreign assistance and economic development', *American Economic Review*, **56** (4), 679–733.

Dutt, A.K. (1992), 'Two issues in the state of development economics', in A.K. Dutt and K. Jameson (eds), *New Directions in Development Economics*, Aldershot, UK and Brookfield, VT, USA: Edward Elgar, pp. 1–34.

Dutt, A.K. (1996), 'The role of Keynesian policies in semi-industrialized economies: theory and evidence from India', *International Review of Applied Economics*, **10** (1), 127–40.

Dutt, A.K. and J. Ros (eds) (2008), *International Handbook of Development Economics*, 2 vols, Cheltenham, UK and Northampton, MA, USA: Edward Elgar.

Evans, P. (1995), *Embedded Autonomy*, Princeton, NJ: Princeton University Press.

Gerschenkron, A. (1962), *Economic Backwardness in Historical Perspective*, Cambridge, MA: Harvard University Press.

Hirschman, A.O. (1958), *The Strategy of Economic Development*, New York: Norton.

Hirschman, A.O. (1981), 'The rise and decline of development economics', in A.O Hirschman, *Essays in Trespassing: Economics to Politics and Beyond*, Cambridge: Cambridge University Press, pp. 1–24.

Krugman, P. (1995), *Development, Geography and Economic Theory*, Cambridge, MA: MIT Press.

Lal, D. (1985), *The Poverty of 'Development Economics'*, Cambridge, MA: Harvard University Press.

Lewis, W.A. (1954), 'Economic development with unlimited supplies of labour', *Manchester School*, **22** (2), 131–91.

Little, I.M.D. (1982), *Economic Development*, New York: Basic Books.

Little, I.M.D., T. Scitovsky and M. Scott (1970), *Industry and Trade in Some Developing Countries*, Oxford: Oxford University Press.

Mahalanobis, P.C. (1953), 'Some observations on the process of growth of national income', *Sankhya*, **12** (4), 307–12.

Meier, G.M. (1984), 'The formative period', in G.M. Meier and D. Seers (eds), *Pioneers in Development*, New York: Oxford University Press, pp. 3–22.

Meier, G.M. (2005), *Biography of a Subject. An Evolution of Development Economics*, Oxford and New York: Oxford University Press.

Myrdal, G. (1957), *Rich Lands and Poor Lands*, New York: Harper Brothers.

Naoroji, D. (1901), *Poverty and Un-British Rule in India*, London: Swan Sonnenschein.

Noyola, J.F. (1956), 'El desarrollo económico y la inflación en México y otros países latinoamericanos', *Investigación Económica*, **16** (4), 603–48.

Nurkse, R. (1953), *Problems of Capital Formation in Underdeveloped Countries*, Oxford: Oxford University Press.

Pack, H. (1994), 'Endogenous growth theory: intellectual appeal and empirical shortcomings', *Journal of Economic Perspectives*, **8** (1), 55–72.

Palma, J.G. (2008), 'Theories of dependency', in A.K Dutt and J. Ros (eds), *International Handbook of Development Economics*, vol. 1, Cheltenham, UK and Northampton, MA, USA: Edward Elgar, pp. 125–35.

Prebisch, R. (1959), 'Commercial policy in underdeveloped countries', *American Economic Review*, **49** (2), 251–73.

Ray, D. (1998), *Development Economics*, Princeton, NJ: Princeton University Press.

Rodrik, D. (2007), *One Economics Many Recipes*, Princeton, NJ: Princeton University Press.

Romer, P.M. (1986), 'Increasing returns and long-run growth', *Journal of Political Economy*, **94** (5), 1002–37.

Ros, J. (2000), *Development Theory and the Economics of Growth*, Ann Arbor, MI: University of Michigan Press.

Rosenstein-Rodan, P.N. (1943), 'Problems of industrialisation of eastern and south-eastern Europe', *Economic Journal*, **53** (210/211), 202–11.

Sen, A.K. (1999), *Development as Freedom*, New York: Anchor Books.

Singer, H. (1950), 'The distribution of gains between borrowing and investing countries', *American Economic Review*, **40** (2), 473–85.

Solow, R.M. (1956), 'A contribution to the theory of economic growth', *Quarterly Journal of Economics*, **70** (1), 65–94.

Stiglitz, J.E. (2002), *Globalization and Its Discontents*, New York: W.W. Norton.

Streeten, P. (1982), *First Things First: Meeting Basic Human Needs in the Developing Countries*, Oxford: Oxford University Press.

Sunkel, O. (1960), 'Inflation in Chile: an unorthodox perspective', *International Economic Papers*, **10**, 107–31.

Taylor, L. (1983), *Structuralist Macroeconomics. Applicable Models for the Third World*, New York: Basic Books.

Temple, J.R.W. (1999), 'The new growth evidence', *Journal of Economic Literature*, **37** (1), 112–56.

Vaggi, G. (2008), 'Historical antecedents of development economics', in A.K Dutt and J. Ros (eds), *International Handbook of Development Economics*, vol. 1, Cheltenham, UK and Northampton, MA, USA: Edward Elgar, pp. 97–110.

Wade, R. (1990), *Governing the Market. Economic Theory and the Role of the Government in East Asian Industrialization*, Princeton, NJ: Princeton University Press.

Econometrics

Notwithstanding a few more general perspectives on the history of econometrics (Darnell 1984; Morgan 1990; Qin 1993; Hendry and Morgan 1995; Morgan and Qin 2001; Gilbert and Qin 2006; Louçã 2007), writing the history of an entire discipline is complicated because a scientific discipline consists of several interacting layers, such as a layer of tools and techniques, one of models and theories, one of methodologies, and so on. Moreover, econometrics has not emerged historically as a unified field. Any attempt to write the history of econometrics is bound to fail. An entry on econometrics will have to consist of several histories or perspectives.

The overarching framework, therefore, that will be used for providing these histories is Thomas Kuhn's (1970) "disciplinary matrix". This notion reflects nicely the multi-layered character of a discipline. According to Kuhn a discipline consists of four elements: symbolic generalizations, metaphysical parts, values and paradigms.

Symbolic generalizations are expressions, deployed without question or dissent by group members, which can readily be represented in logical or mathematical form. They are the formal or the readily formalizable elements of the disciplinary matrix. An example of such symbolic generalization in econometrics is the commonly used Durbin–Watson statistic:

$$d = \frac{\sum_{t=2}^{T}(\hat{e}_t - \hat{e}_{t-1})^2}{\sum_{t=1}^{T}\hat{e}_t^2}, \tag{1}$$

where $\hat{e}_t$ is the tth ordinary least squares residual from the general model $Y = X\beta + \varepsilon$ based on T observations. This perspective will not be given here. It implies a history of econometric tools and techniques, which cannot be but a very detailed account, too large for a *Handbook* entry.

The metaphysical parts are the shared commitments to beliefs in particular models, including their heuristic value. These models help to determine what will be accepted as an explanation and as a puzzle-solution; conversely, they assist in the determination of the roster of unsolved puzzles and in the evaluation of the importance of each. An example of this metaphysical part in econometrics is the vector autoregression (VAR) approach. In this approach each time series variable is explained by a linear function of its own lagged (past) values and the lagged values of all other variables in the system.

Values are shared more widely among different communities than either symbolic generalizations or models. Though they are present in the background at all times, their particular importance emerges when the members of a particular community must identify a crisis, or, later, choose between incompatible ways of practicing their disciplines. One of these values is the role of economic theory in econometrics. However, what econometrics is all about is also one of these shared values.

The fourth and final sort of element in the disciplinary matrix are the paradigms, used here in its original sense of exemplars, that is, the concrete solutions to problems that students encounter from the beginning of their scientific education, whether in laboratories, in examinations, or in their textbooks. These shared exemplars can be supplemented by some of the technical problem-solutions found in the periodical literature that scientists encounter during their post-education careers. These include classic publications, like Trygve Haavelmo's (1944) "The probability approach in econometrics".

It appeared that the disciplinary elements of metaphysics and paradigms are so entangled in econometrics that their histories cannot be given separately. Therefore, the two perspectives for setting out the history of econometrics will be a history of econometric values and a history of metaphysics and their paradigms.

A History of Econometric Values

Ragnar Frisch (1895–1973) (Bjerkholt 1995) coined the term (in French) econometrics in his very first paper in economics, "Sur un problème d'économique pure" (1926); the term signified the unification of economic theory, statistics, and mathematics (Bjerkholt and Dupont 2010):

> Intermediate between mathematics, statistics, and economics, we find a new discipline which, for the lack of a better name, may be called econometrics. Econometrics has as its aim to subject abstract laws of theoretical political or "pure" economics to experimental and numerical verification, and thus to turn pure economics, as far as possible, into a science in the strict sense of the word. (Frisch 1971: 386)

Frisch was also the initiator of the foundation of the Econometric Society on 29 December 1930. The 16 founding members were: Frisch, Charles F. Roos, Joseph A. Schumpeter, Harold Hotelling, Henry Schultz, Karl Menger, Edwin B. Wilson, Frederick C. Mills, William F. Ogburn, J. Harvey Rogers, Malcolm C. Rorty, Carl Snyder, Walter A. Shewhart, Øystein Ore, Ingvar Wedervang and Norbert Wiener. The first president was Irving Fisher (Divisia 1953; Christ 1983; Bjerkholt and Qin 2011). The Econometric Society sponsors the academic journal *Econometrica*, the first issue of which was published in 1933. Frisch was its first editor, from 1933 to 1954.

In his first "Editorial" of *Econometrica*, Frisch gave an explanation of the term econometrics:

> Its definition is implied in the statement of the scope of the Econometric Society, in Section I of the Constitution, which reads: "The Econometric Society is an international society for the advancement of economic theory in its relation to statistics and mathematics. The Society shall operate as a completely disinterested, scientific organization without political, social, financial, or nationalistic bias. Its main object shall be to promote studies that aim at a unification of the theoretical-quantitative and the empirical-quantitative approach to economic problems and that are penetrated by constructive and rigorous thinking similar to what has come to dominate in the natural sciences". (Frisch 1933: 1)

While today, econometrics is often seen as something which "began as an offshoot of the classical discipline of Mathematical Statistics" (Granger 2006: xi), it is of interest to see that Frisch's original idea was the unification of statistics, economic theory and mathematics:

> Experience has shown that each of these three view-points, that of statistics, economic theory, and mathematics, is a necessary, but not by itself a sufficient, condition for a real understanding of the quantitative relations in modern economic life. It is the *unification* of all three that is powerful. And it is this unification that constitutes econometrics. (Frisch 1933: 2, original emphasis)

It is apparent that the underlying motivation for this "new discipline," from its beginning, was to turn economics "into a science," that is, to penetrate economics by the "constructive and rigorous thinking" dominant in the natural sciences.

It appeared that the term itself – though having a different meaning – was used previously in relation to accounting. In *Grundriss einer Oekonometrie und die auf der Nationaloekonomie aufgebaute natürliche Theorie der Buchhaltung* by Pawel Ciompa (1910), "oekonometrie" was described as a geometrical representation of the values, a natural theory of bookkeeping based on macroeconomics (Mattessich 2003). According to Frisch (1936), Ciompa emphasized too much the descriptive side of what Frisch himself meant by econometrics (see also Tintner 1953).

Subsequent debates shaped the ideas of what econometrics entails, or is supposed to entail. It should be noted that these debates also reflected the then contemporary notions of what it meant for econometrics to be a science.

The Keynes–Tinbergen debate
The first two macro-econometric models were constructed by Jan Tinbergen (1903–1994) (Jolink 2003; see Morgan 1990 for a discussion of both models). Tinbergen's first model was of the Dutch economy, published in 1936 (Tinbergen 1959). In the same year Tinbergen was commissioned by the League of Nations to perform statistical tests on business-cycle theories. The results of this later study were published in a two-volume work, *Statistical Testing of Business-Cycle Theories* (1939). The first contained an explanation of this new method of econometric testing as well as a demonstration of what could be achieved, based on three case studies. The second volume developed a model of the United States, the second macro-econometric model in the history of econometrics.

Tinbergen's first League of Nations study provoked a great deal of controversy. It was circulated in 1938 prior to its publication, and generated lively discussions about the role that econometrics could play in the testing of economic theory. It was John Maynard Keynes's (1939) critique of Tinbergen's first volume that sparked off the debate about the role of econometrics and what it might be able to achieve.

According to Keynes, the technique of multiple correlation analysis which had been adopted by Tinbergen was solely a method for measurement. It contributed nothing in terms of either discovery or criticism. The implication was that if the economic theorist does not provide the modeller with a complete set of causal factors, then the measurement of the other causal factors will be biased. Moreover, Keynes argued that some significant factors in any economy are not capable of measurement, or may be interdependent.

Another of Keynes's concerns was the assumed linearity of the relations between these factors. He also noted that the determination of time-lags and trends was too often based on trial and error, and too little informed by theory. Finally, there was the problem of invariance: would the relations found also hold for the future?

Tinbergen's response (1940) was technical, rather than methodological. He gave a very detailed description of how he had solved each problem by explaining the techniques he had employed. He assumed that through the adoption of these techniques he had overcome any of the methodological problem listed by Keynes.

Tinbergen's reply was largely dismissed by Keynes. Taking into account all these concerns, Keynes came to the conclusion that econometrics was not yet a scientific approach:

> No one could be more frank, more painstaking, more free from subjective bias or *parti pris* than Professor Tinbergen. There is no one, therefore, so far as human qualities go, whom it would be safer to trust with black magic. That there is anyone I would trust with it at the present stage or that this brand of statistical alchemy is ripe to become a branch of science, I am not yet persuaded. But Newton, Boyle and Locke all played with Alchemy. So let him continue. (Keynes 1940: 156)

The measurement-without-theory debate

Another of the early econometric debates started with a lengthy book review written in 1947 for *The Review of Economic Statistics* by Tjalling C. Koopmans (1910–1985). In 1949, under the general heading "Methodological issues in quantitative economics", a number of publications advancing the debate appeared in the journal: a response from Rutledge Vining (1949a) was followed by a "Reply" from Koopmans (1949), and finally a "Rejoinder" from Vining (1949b).

The subject of Koopmans's review was *Measuring Business Cycles*, by Arthur F. Burns and Wesley C. Mitchell (1946), and published by the National Bureau of Economic Research (NBER), of which Mitchell was the director between 1920 and 1945. At this time Koopmans was a senior research figure, and midway through the debate (1948) he became director of the Cowles Commission. So, his original article was more than a book review. Koopmans was mounting a full critique of the NBER empirical approach while simultaneously defending the Cowles Commission's econometric approach.

Koopmans's critique was based on Haavelmo's "Probability approach" (1944). He accused Burns and Mitchell of trying to measure economic cycles in the absence of any economic theory about the workings of such cycles: "The toolkit of the theoretical economist is deliberately spurned" (Koopmans 1947: 163).

Koopmans put forward three arguments to explain the implications and limitations of the NBER's "empiricist position". His first argument is that for the purposes of systematic and large-scale observation of a many sided phenomenon such as the business cycle, "theoretical preconceptions about its nature cannot be dispensed with, and the authors do so only to the detriment of the analysis" (Koopmans 1947: 163). He compared this empiricist position with Kepler's discovery of the more superficial empirical regularities of planetary motion, which fell short of the deeper "fundamental laws" later discovered by Newton. Newton's achievement was based not only on the regularities observed by Kepler, but also on experiments conducted by Galileo.

However, Koopmans believed that economists are unable to perform experiments on an economic system as a whole, and that it is therefore impossible for many economic problems to separate causes and effects by varying causes one by one, and studying the separate effects of each cause. According to Koopmans, instead of experiments, economists possess "more elaborate and better established theories of economic behavior than the theories of motion of material bodies known to Kepler" (1947: 166), because the evidence for these theories is based on introspection, on interviews, and on inferences from the observed behaviour of individuals.

In general, economic variables are determined by the simultaneous validity of a large number of structural equations describing behaviour and technology. Any observed empirical regularity between a number of variables may be the result of the working of several simultaneous structural relations. Because so many empirical relations are valid simultaneously, it may be difficult – or even impossible – to uncover the more fundamental structural relationships. In the absence of experimentation, the identification of these structural relations is possible only if the set of variables involved in each equation, and perhaps also the manner in which they are combined, is specified by economic theory.

Koopmans's second argument against the NBER's empiricist position was that it offered no evidence for the assumption that the empirical relations found would be invariant across time. As long as the dynamics of economic variables are not based on structural relations of behaviour and technology, it was difficult to know how reliable they would be for the purposes of prediction or as a guide for economic policy.

Koopmans's third argument against a purely empiricist approach is that statistical analysis of the data requires additional assumptions about their probabilistic characteristics that cannot be subject to statistical testing from the same data. These assumptions need to be provided by economic theory and should be tested independently.

In a defence of "empiricism as a fundamental part of scientific procedure", Vining replied by offering three points that challenged Koopmans's arguments. His first point is that he doubted whether "the method of Koopmans's group" would lead to the uncovering of the fundamental invariant relationships:

> Is it not something of a mighty jump to imply that the postulated preference function of an individual is in some sense analogous to the general laws of thermodynamics, the dynamics of friction, etc., etc.? Is the Walrasian conception not in fact a pretty skinny fellow of untested capacity upon which to load the burden of a general theory accounting for the events in space and time which take place within the spatial boundary of an economic system? (Vining 1949a: 82)

He asserted that the theory about the behaviour of economic agents had not been given in sufficient detail. Vining stated that the Cowles model was therefore a "pretty skinny fellow" upon which to base so much high-powered statistical estimation.

He questioned the position that empirical research should be evaluated from the point of view of social usefulness. However, Vining did not offer any further discussion of this point.

The third point was that Cowles' version of statistical economics, if it includes only the estimation of postulated relations, had little or no role to play in the discovery of economic hypotheses. According to Vining, statistical theory should play a similar role in economic research to that played by microscopy in biology.

The science or alchemy debate
After 1950 econometrics became a mature field and the Cowles Commission (henceforth, CC) approach was the dominant practice. But after two decades, 1950s and 1960s, of high expectations of econometrics as producer of reliable predictions and policy advice, in the 1970s these expectations were increasingly doubted. David F. Hendry especially, in his London School of Economics (LSE) inaugural lecture "Econometrics – alchemy or science?" (1980), used the opportunity to revisit the Keynes–Tinbergen debate as a backdrop to reiterate the scientific possibilities of econometrics.

Hendry labelled Keynes's list of concerns as "problems of the linear regression model", which, according to him, consisted of using an incomplete set of determining factors (omitted variables bias); building models with unobservable variables (such as expectations), estimated from badly measured data based on index numbers; obtaining spurious correlations from the use of proxy variables and simultaneity, being unable to separate the distinct effects of multicollinear variables; assuming linear functional forms not knowing the appropriate dimensions of the regressors; misspecifying the dynamic reactions and lag lengths; incorrectly pre-filtering the data; invalidly inferring causes from correlations; predicting inaccurately (non-constant parameters); confusing statistical with economic significance of results; and failing to relate economic theory to econometrics. To Keynes's list of problems, he added stochastic misspecification, incorrect exogeneity assumptions, inadequate sample size, aggregation, lack of structural identification, and an inability to refer back uniquely from observed empirical results to any given initial theory.

Hendry admitted that "it is difficult to provide a convincing case for the defence against Keynes's accusation almost 40 years ago that econometrics is *statistical alchemy* since many of his criticisms remain apposite" (1980: 402, original emphasis). The ease with which a mechanical application of the econometric method produced spurious correlations suggests alchemy, but, according to Hendry, the scientific status of econometrics can be regained by showing that such deceptions are testable. He, therefore, comes up with the following simple methodology: "The three golden rules of econometrics are test, test and test" (ibid.: 403). In his view, rigorously tested models, which offer adequate descriptions of the available data, take into account previous findings, and are derived from well-based theories justify the claim that they are scientific.

Hendry referred to Keynes's use of the term alchemy to discuss the scientific nature of econometrics. Another way to denote this discussion is to see how much econometrics differs from "economic tricks" (or "econo-mystics" or "icon-ometrics"; see Hendry 1980: 388). This was the kind of denotation Edward Leamer (1983) used to contribute to the debate about the scientific character of econometrics under the title "Let's take the con out of econometrics".

Leamer's paper is very much about the "myth" of science that empirical research is (randomized controlled) experimentation and scientific inference is objective and free of personal prejudice. The problem of nonexperimental settings (usually the case in economics) compared with experimental settings ("routinely done" in science) is that "the misspecification uncertainty in many experimental settings may be so small that it is well approximated by zero. This can very rarely be said in nonexperimental settings" (Leamer 1983: 33). Protecting the image that econometrics is like agricultural experimentation (randomized controlled experimentation) is "grossly misleading" (ibid.: 31).

In addition, "the false idol of objectivity has done great damage to economic science" (Leamer 1983: 36). If we want to make progress, according to Leamer, "the first step we must take is to discard the counterproductive goal of objective inference" (ibid.: 37). Inference is a logical conclusion based on facts, but because "the sampling distribution and the prior distribution are actually *opinions* and not *facts*, a statistical inference is and must forever remain an *opinion*" (ibid., original emphasis). Moreover, Leamer considers a fact as "merely an opinion held by all, or at least held by a set of people you regard to be a close approximation to all" (ibid.).

The problem with using opinion, however, is its "whimsical nature". An inference is not "believable" if it is fragile, if it can be reversed by a minor change in assumptions. It is thus the task of the econometrician to withhold belief until an inference is shown "to be adequately insensitive to the choice of assumptions" (Leamer 1983: 43).

A History of Econometric Metaphysics and their Paradigms

In the 1950s and 1960s, the dominant approach in econometrics was the CC approach (Hildreth 1986; Epstein 1987; Christ 1952, 1994). The Cowles Commission for Research in Economics (CC) was set up in 1932, being funded by Alfred Cowles (1891–1984) specifically to undertake econometric research. In 1939, it moved to the University of Chicago, and in 1955 it moved to Yale University where it was renamed as the Cowles Foundation for Economic Research. The Econometric Society's journal, *Econometrica*, was published by the Commission. The CC's econometric approach, developed in the 1940s and 1950s, became the standard approach found in most econometric textbooks; this approach is also known as the simultaneous equation modelling (SEM) approach.

One of the most popular of these textbooks, Jack Johnston's *Econometric Methods*, identifies the basic task of econometrics as being "to put *empirical* flesh and blood on theoretical structures" (Johnston 1984: 5, original emphasis). For Johnston, this involves three distinct steps:

1. The model must be specified in explicit functional – often linear – form.
2. Decide on the appropriate data definitions, and assemble the relevant data series for those variables included in the model.
3. Form a bridge between theory and data through the use of statistical methods. The bridge consists of various sets of statistics, which help to determine the validity of the theoretical model.

The most important set of statistics consists of numerical estimates of the model's parameters. Further statistics enable an assessment to be made of the reliability or precision with which these parameters have been estimated. Further statistics and diagnostic tests will help to assess the performance of the model.

Trygve Haavelmo's 1944 paper, "The probability approach in econometrics", laid the groundwork upon which the CC developed a more advanced methodology for macroeconometric modelling than Tinbergen's (1936, 1939). Haavelmo (1911–1999) had been a student of Frisch and later his research assistant. The Haavelmo paper moved the emphasis of econometrics from the measurement of parameters (for example, demand elasticities) and the problem of the quality of statistical data, to the testing of theories. It introduced the probabilistic approach into econometrics by showing how to use the Neyman and Pearson statistical theory of hypothesis testing. It became the "blueprint" of an approach which is now identified with the CC approach, and which emerged via two monographs (Koopmans 1950; Hood and Koopmans 1953) published by the Commission.

From the mid-1970s onwards, there was a growing scepticism towards the value of the more theoretical CC approach for applied econometric research. There was a gap between what theoretical econometricians were developing and what applied econometricians actually needed. These discussions lead to Hendry's (1980) "Alchemy or science?" paper and Leamer's (1983) "Let's take the con out of econometrics" paper, but also to Christopher Sims's (1980) "Macroeconomics and reality".

A result of these publications, for the first time, a special invited symposium on econometric methodology was held in 1985 at the Fifth World Congress of the Econometric Society. The invited speakers were Hendry, Leamer and Sims. Adrian R. Pagan (1987) was invited as discussant and published an "appraisal" of this debate (see also Hendry et al. 1990). To prevent econometrics from becoming statistical alchemy, Hendry, Leamer and Sims developed their own methodologies: the general-to-specific approach (Hendry and Richard 1982), the Bayesian approach (Leamer 1978), and the vector autoregression (VAR) approach (Sims 1980), respectively.

The VAR approach arose as an answer to the growing criticism of the CC structural approach with its assumptions of zero restrictions to achieve identification of a model and the division of the variables into endogenous and exogenous ones. The questioning of the role of zero restrictions had already started in the 1960s, due to the work of Ta-Chung Liu (1914–1975) (Chao and Huang 2011). Liu (1960) had noticed that the number of restrictions needed to identify large-scale macro-econometric models far exceeded the number that economic theory could be confidently relied upon to provide. The danger is that models may be formulated and estimated with some variables added to equations without much economic justification and other variables deleted (that is, zero restrictions imposed), in order to achieve identification. The a priori restrictions imposed on structural simultaneous equation models were viewed by Sims as "incredible".

Sims's proposal was to remove the pretence of applying theoretical structure to the data and, instead, to use unrestricted systems of reduced form equations or vector autoregressions to model the responses of variables to shocks. This does not mean however that the VAR approach should be considered as "atheoretical macroeconometrics". Stimulated by the rational expectations movement in macroeconomics, the VAR approach offers a systematic procedure to tackle the issue of model choice. It shifted the focus from measurement of given theories to identification of data-coherent theories (Qin 2011).

The model of James E.H. Davidson, Hendry, Frank Srba and Stephen Yeo (1978) of UK aggregate consumption expenditure, published in 1978 was a major influence on the way econometricians now use time series data to model economic relationships. One of its main methodological innovations was the general-to-specific approach to deal with time series data. General-to-specific modelling is the formulation of a fairly unrestricted dynamic model which is subsequently tested, transformed and reduced in size by performing a number of tests for restrictions (Hendry 1995). This approach also came to be known as the LSE approach and is in the spirit of the Box–Jenkins approach.

The approach proposed by Box and Jenkins (1970) introduced a number of concepts that were either missing or neglected in the CC approach: the principle of parsimony in model formation, diagnostic checks on model adequacy, and a data-led identification procedure.

Leamer observed a wide gap between the formal textbook approach and its practised variant, which Leamer called "cookbook econometrics" (Leamer 1978):

As it happens, the econometric modeling was done in the basement of the building and the econometric theory courses were taught on the top floor (the third). I was perplexed by the fact that the same language was used in both places. Even more amazing was the transmogrification of particular individuals who wantonly sinned in the basement and metamorphosed into the highest of high priests as they ascended to the third floor. (Leamer 1978: vi)

He therefore suggested the making of more "honest" modellers out of cookbook econometricians by formalizing their ad hoc procedures using informal Bayesian procedures such as extreme bounds analysis. This should expose the possible fragility of estimated relationships by testing their robustness to changes in prior information (Leamer and Leonard 1983).

Further Reading

A survey of the literature on the history of econometrics showed that interest in the history of econometrics has arisen primarily from within econometrics itself and that its histories have been written mainly by econometricians (Boumans and Dupont-Kieffer 2011). This tradition started with the very first issue of *Econometrica*. From 1933 until the 1960s, *Econometrica* regularly published articles on denominated forerunners: Emile Borel, Augustin Cournot, Francis Ysidro Edgeworth, Francesco Fuoco, William Stanley Jevons, Hans von Mangoldt, Johann Heinrich Von Thünen, Vilfredo Pareto, Léon Walras, and Knut Wicksell. Also, from 1939 onwards, articles on "founding fathers" were published whenever the occasion arose (anniversary or death): Oskar Anderson, Bernard Chait, Clément Colson, Georges Darmois, François Divisia, Luigi Einaudi, Irving Fisher, Eraldo Fossati, Ragnar Frisch, Yehuda Grunfeld, Leif Johansen, John Maynard Keynes, Oskar Ryszard Lange, Ta-Chung Liu, Henri L. Moore, Hans Peter, Charles Frederick Roos, Henry Schultz, Joseph A. Schumpeter, Eugen Slutsky, Abraham Wald, and Frederik Zeuthen.

This tradition of bringing the history of econometrics to the econometrician's attention and awareness almost died out in the 1960s. It was *Econometric Theory*, established in 1985, that continued this tradition.

The first issue of *Econometric Theory* contains an explanation of the objectives of the journal's editorial policy. Besides the obvious objectives, the editor Peter C.B. Phillips added two historical aims: "to publish historical studies on the evolution of econometric thought and on the subject's early scholars" (Phillips 1985: 4) and "to publish high-level interviews with leading econometricians" (ibid.). As a result of this latter objective, interviews with the following econometricians have been published: Takeshi Amemiya, Theodore W. Anderson, Albert Rex Bergstrom, Gregory C. Chow, Manfred Deistler, Phoebus J. Dhrymes, James Durbin, Robert F. Engle, Arthur S. Goldberger, Clive Granger, Edward James Hannan, Michio Hatanaka, David F. Hendry, Alan T. James, Joseph B. Kadane, Lawrence R. Klein, Jan Kmenta, G.S. Maddala, Edmond Malinvaud, Marc Nerlove, C.R. Rao, Olav Reiersøl, John Denis Sargan, Richard Stone, George C. Tiao, Jan Tinbergen, James Tobin, H.O.A. Wold, and Arnold Zellner.

Beside the more general histories mentioned in the first paragraph of this section, the following publications should be mentioned as they provide collections of more specific histories of econometrics: De Marchi and Gilbert (1989) and Boumans et al. (2011).

MARCEL BOUMANS

See also:

Irving Fisher (I); Ragnar Anton Kittil Frisch (I); John Maynard Keynes (I); Jacob Marschak (I); Wesley Clair Mitchell (I); Joseph Alois Schumpeter (I); Jan Tinbergen (I); James Tobin (I).

References and further reading

Bjerkholt, O. (1995), 'Ragnar Frisch, the originator of econometrics', in O. Bjerkholt (ed.), *Foundations of Modern Econometrics. The Selected Essays of Ragnar Frisch*, Aldershot, UK and Brookfield, VT, USA: Edward Elgar, pp. xiii–lii.

Bjerkholt, O. and A. Dupont (2010), 'Ragnar Frisch's conception of econometrics', *History of Political Economy*, **42** (1), 21–73.

Bjerkholt, O. and D. Qin (2011), 'Teaching economics as a science: the Yale lectures of Ragnar Frisch', in O. Bjerkholt and D. Qin (eds), *A Dynamic Approach to Economic Theory*, London: Routledge, pp. 1–28.

Boumans, M. and A. Dupont-Kieffer (2011), 'A history of the histories of econometrics', *History of Political Economy*, **43** (supplement), 5–31.

Boumans, M., A. Dupont-Kieffer and D. Qin (eds) (2011), *Histories on Econometrics*, Durham, NC: Duke University Press.

Box, G.E.P. and G.M. Jenkins (1970), *Time Series Analysis: Forecasting and Control*, San Francisco, CA: Holden-Day.

Burns, A.F. and W.C. Mitchell. (1946), *Measuring Business Cycles*, New York: National Bureau of Economic Research.

Chao, H.-K. and C.-H. Huang (2011), 'Ta-Chung Liu's exploratory econometrics', in M. Boumans, A. Dupont-Kieffer and D. Qin (eds), *Histories on Econometrics*, Durham, NC: Duke University Press, pp. 140–65.

Christ, C.F. (1952), 'A history of the Cowles Commission, 1932–1952', in *Economic Theory and Measurement*, Chicago, IL: Cowles Commission for Research in Economics.

Christ, C.F. (1983), 'The founding of the Econometric Society and Econometrica', *Econometrica*, **51** (1), 3–6.

Christ, C.F. (1994), 'The Cowles Commission's contributions to econometrics at Chicago, 1939–1955', *Journal of Economic Literature*, **32** (1), 30–59.

Ciompa, P. (1910), *Grundriss einer Oekonometrie und die auf der Nationaloekonomie aufgebaute natürliche Theorie der Buchhaltung*, Lviv: Poeschel Verlag.

Darnell, A.C. (1984), 'Economic statistics and econometrics', in J. Creedy and D.P. O'Brien (eds), *Economic Analysis in Historical Perspective*, London: Butterworths, pp. 152–85.

Davidson, J.H., D.H. Hendry, F. Srba and S. Yeo (1978), 'Econometric modeling of the aggregate time-series relationship between consumers' expenditure and income in the United Kingdom', *The Economic Journal*, **88** (352), 661–92.

De Marchi, N. and C. Gilbert (eds) (1989), 'History and methodology of econometrics', *Oxford Economic Papers*, **41** (1), special issue.

Divisia, F. (1953), 'La société d'économétrie a attient sa majorité', *Econometrica*, **21** (1), 1–30.

Epstein, R.J. (1987), *A History of Econometrics*, Amsterdam: North-Holland.

Frisch, R. (1926), 'Sur un problème d'économique pure', *Norsk Matematisk Forenings Skrifter*, **1** (16), 1–40, English trans. 'On a problem in pure economics', in J.S. Chipman, L. Hurwicz, M.K. Richter, and H.F. Sonnenschein (eds) (1971), *Preferences, Utility, and Demand: A Minnesota Symposium*, New York: Harcourt Brace Jovanovich, pp. 386–423.

Frisch, R. (1933), 'Editorial', *Econometrica*, **1** (1), 1–4.

Frisch, R. (1936), 'Note on the term "Econometrics"', *Econometrica*, **4** (1), 95.

Frisch, R. (1971), 'On a problem in pure economics', in J.S. Chipman, L. Hurwicz, M.K. Richter, and H.F. Sonnenschein (eds), *Preferences, Utility, and Demand: A Minnesota Symposium*, New York: Harcourt Brace Jovanovich, pp. 386–423.

Gilbert, C.L. and D. Qin. (2006), 'The first fifty years of modern econometrics', in T.C. Mills and K. Patterson (eds), *Palgrave Handbook of Econometrics. Volume 1 Econometric Theory*, Basingstoke: Palgrave, pp. 117–55.

Granger, C.W.J. (2006), 'Foreword', in T.C. Mills and K. Patterson (eds), *Palgrave Handbook of Econometrics. Volume 1 Econometric Theory*, Basingstoke: Palgrave, pp. xi–xii.

Haavelmo, T. (1944), 'The probability approach in econometrics', *Econometrica*, **12** (supplement), i–viii, 1–118.

Hendry, D.F. (1980), 'Econometrics – alchemy or science?', *Economica*, **47** (188), 387–406.

Hendry, D.F. (1995), *Dynamic Econometrics*, Oxford: Oxford University Press.

Hendry, D.F. and M.S. Morgan (1995), 'Introduction', in D.F. Hendry and M.S. Morgan (eds), *The Foundations of Econometric Analysis*, Cambridge: Cambridge University Press, pp. 1–82.

Hendry, D.F. and J.-F. Richard (1982), 'On the formulation of empirical models in dynamic econometrics', *Journal of Econometrics*, **20** (1), 3–33.
Hendry, D.F., E.E. Leamer and D.J. Poirier (1990), 'The ET dialogue: a conversation on econometric methodology', *Econometric Theory*, **6** (2), 171–261.
Hildreth, C. (1986), *The Cowles Commission in Chicago, 1939–1955*, Berlin: Springer-Verlag.
Hood, W.C. and T.C. Koopmans (eds) (1953), *Studies in Econometric Method*, New York: Wiley.
Johnston, J. (1984), *Econometric Methods*, Singapore: McGraw-Hill.
Jolink, A. (2003), *Jan Tinbergen. The Statistical Turn in Economics: 1903–1955*, Rotterdam: Chimes.
Keynes, J.M. (1939), 'Professor Tinbergen's method', *The Economic Journal*, **49** (195), 558–68.
Keynes, J.M. (1940), 'Comment', *The Economic Journal*, **50** (197), 154–6.
Koopmans, T.C. (1947), 'Measurement without theory', *Review of Economic Statistics*, **29** (3), 161–72.
Koopmans, T.C. (1949), 'A reply', *Review of Economics and Statistics*, **31** (2), 86–91.
Koopmans, T.C. (ed.) (1950), *Statistical Inference in Dynamic Economic Models*, New York: Wiley.
Kuhn, T.S. (1970), *The Structure of Scientific Revolutions*, 2nd enlarged edn, *International Encyclopedia of Unified Science*, vol. 2, no. 2, Chicago, IL and London: University of Chicago Press.
Leamer, E.E. (1978), *Specification Searches: Ad Hoc Inferences with Nonexperimental Data*, New York: Wiley.
Leamer, E.E. (1983), 'Let's take the con out of econometrics', *American Economic Review*, **73** (1), 31–43.
Leamer, E.E. and H.B. Leonard (1983), 'Reporting the fragility of regression estimates', *Review of Economics and Statistics*, **65** (2), 306–17.
Liu, T.C. (1960), 'Underidentification, structural estimation, and forecasting', *Econometrica*, **28** (4), 855–65.
Louçã, F. (2007), *The Years of High Econometrics: A Short History of the Generation that Reinvented Economics*, London and New York: Routledge.
Mattessich, R. (2003), 'Accounting research and researchers of the nineteenth century and the beginning of the twentieth century: an international survey of authors, ideas and publications', *Accounting, Business & Financial History*, **13** (2), 125–70.
Morgan, M.S. (1990), *The History of Econometric Ideas*, Cambridge: Cambridge University Press.
Morgan, M.S. and D. Qin (2001), 'Econometrics, history of', in N.J. Smelser and P.B. Baltes (eds), *International Encyclopedia of the Social & Behavioral Sciences*, Amsterdam: Elsevier, pp. 4065–9.
Pagan, A. (1987), 'Three econometric methodologies: a critical appraisal', *Journal of Economic Surveys*, **1** (1), 3–24.
Phillips, P.C.B. (1985), 'Editorial', *Econometric Theory*, **1** (1), 1–5.
Qin, D. (1993), *The Formation of Econometrics: A Historical Perspective*, Oxford: Clarendon Press.
Qin, D. (2011), 'Rise of VAR modelling approach', *Journal of Economic Surveys*, **25** (1), 156–74.
Sims, C.A. (1980), 'Macroeconomics and reality', *Econometrica*, **48** (1), 1–48.
Tinbergen, J. (1936), 'Kan hier te lande, al dan niet na overheidsingrijpen, een verbetering van de binnenlandse conjunctuur intreden, ook zonder verbetering van onze exportpositie?', *Prae-adviezen voor de Vereeniging voor de Staathuishoudkunde en de Statistiek*, The Hague: Nijhoff, pp. 62–108, English trans. in J. Tinbergen (1959), 'An economic policy for 1936', in L.H. Klaassen, L.M. Koyck and H.J. Witteveen (eds), *Jan Tinbergen – Selected Papers*, Amsterdam: North-Holland, pp. 37–84.
Tinbergen, J. (1939), *Statistical Testing of Business-Cycle Theories*. Volume I: *A Method and its Application to Investment Activity*; Volume II *Business Cycles in the United States of America*. Geneva: League of Nations.
Tinbergen, J. (1940), 'On a method of statistical business-cycle research: a reply', *The Economic Journal*, **50** (197), 141–54.
Tinbergen, J. (1959), 'An economic policy for 1936', in L.H. Klaassen, L.M. Koyck and H.J. Witteveen (eds), *Jan Tinbergen – Selected Papers*, Amsterdam: North-Holland, pp. 37–84.
Tintner, G. (1953), 'The definition of econometrics', *Econometrica*, **21** (1), 31–40.
Vining, R. (1949a), 'Koopmans on the choice of variables to be studied and the methods of measurement', *Review of Economics and Statistics*, **31** (2), 77–86.
Vining, R. (1949b), 'A rejoinder', *Review of Economics and Statistics*, **31** (2), 91–4.

Economic dynamics

"Economic dynamics" is a large topic. In the space allotted here it is impossible to fully cover it. So, I shall begin by clarifying what will not be covered in this entry. While the focus will be more on macroeconomic than microeconomic dynamics, long-run growth will not be a main topic, although it will enter in as it is connected to economic fluctuations.

Also, there will be less focus on models of dynamics that rely mainly upon exogenous shocks as their main driver, sometimes argued to represent classical approaches. It must be recognized that much of current modelling in macroeconomics follows such an approach, with Frisch's (1933) "rocking horse model" the archetype for much of what followed in this vein (Lucas and Sargent 1981; Kydland and Prescott 1982; Long and Plosser 1983). Business cycles arise from shocks to productivity or to the desire to work on the part of labour. Little effort is made to model these shocks, and the result is that such models have performed poorly in explaining such events as the crisis of 2008 and the events following it. However, it must be recognized that the wisecrack of William "Buz" Brock that the only truly exogenous force in the economy is the sun (personal communication 1985) contains considerable truth.

All this means that we shall mostly be concerned with fluctuations that arise endogenously from an economy, or with models that exhibit such endogenously driven fluctuations, even as there may be stochastic noise ultimately driving the system. Though we shall not be focusing on growth per se, we shall consider fluctuations that may occur over longer periods of time than short-period business cycles, which may indeed involve supply-side processes and effects.

Another issue that will not be focused on is that of microfoundations of macroeconomics. This is not an unimportant issue, but models that arise from microfoundations or directly from the macro level will not be distinguished. Probably most macro fluctuations either resemble or arise from micro phenomena, with such examples as lags in production leading to cobweb dynamics or speculative bubbles that usually initially appear in particular markets but can spread to affect an entire economy. However, there are sources of macro fluctuations that arise largely directly at the macro level, particularly related to monetary and financial markets as well as fiscal policies, even though this entry will not focus on policy issues either. This entry draws heavily on several other works, especially Haberler (1963), Freeman (1996), Rosser (1999, 2000, 2004), Gandolfo (2009), and Venkatachalam and Velupillai (2012).

The Early History of Macroeconomic Fluctuation Models

The history of debates about the sources of macroeconomic fluctuations began with the first appearance of actual fluctuations within the newly industrializing economies after the Napoleonic Wars. There had always been economic fluctuations, but before the Industrial Revolution they were driven by agricultural production fluctuations that were in turn clearly driven by exogenous forces, particularly those related to climate – although these were sometimes seen as having elements of periodicity, such as the Jevons (1878) sunspot theory or the much earlier Joseph story, from Genesis in the Bible, about the seven fat years followed by the seven lean years. What was missing in these earlier

117

phenomena was any sort of endogeneity of the cycles that might be there or not. The idea that such might be the case arose with the fluctuations of the industrializing economies where capital investment would play the leading role.

There had been commercial crises prior to the post-Napoleonic wars recession, but they had not led to major disruptions of employment, nor did they lead any economists to discuss where they came from, although the discussion of speculative bubbles in particular had gotten the attention of such figures as Cantillon (1755) and Adam Smith (1776: 703–4) owing to the large-scale and dramatic nature of the linked Mississippi and South Sea bubbles of 1719–20. However, these discussions focused more on the stupidity of those participating in such events than on any underlying processes or broader economic repercussions, although Cantillon (1755: ch. 10) particularly emphasized the need for bullionism in order to avoid speculation. As it was, the post-Napoleonic Wars years after 1815 saw considerable disruptions and the appearance of unemployment in several core nations involved, particularly Britain and France. These events triggered a debate between Malthus and Ricardo over its causes that also involved such figures as Sismondi and Say on the sidelines.

Ricardo (1817: 265) argued that the disruptions were temporary adjustments arising from exogenous shocks, in particular, the beginning or ending of major wars that engender a microeconomic intersectoral misallocation. Given the time needed to make adjustments, this can lead to a "distress in trade", with this later being understood to possibly involve chaotic dynamics (Bhaduri and Harris 1987).

> It changes in a great degree the nature of employment to which the respective capitals of countries were before devoted; and during the interval while they are settling in the situations which new incentives have made most beneficial, much fixed capital unemployed, perhaps wholly lost, and labourers are without full employment. (Ricardo 1817: 165)

While this is the foundation for modern classical views, it is also perhaps more in the spirit of the Austrian School, which argues that fluctuations in interest rates lead to intersectoral misallocations. In any case, the disruption is temporary, and the system should adjust on its own in some reasonable time without any tendency to a longer-term general glut due to demand being insufficient to supply. On this latter point, the "law of markets" identified with J.B. Say (1803) would be invoked throughout the nineteenth century, even if the discussion by Keynes (1936) of "Say's Law" and its role can be argued to be misguided, and Say himself did not see his law as universally holding and supported public works spending during the post-Napoleonic war recession.

On the other hand, Malthus argued for the possibility of general gluts owing to an insufficient aggregate demand, ultimately pointing to income inequality as a source of the underconsumption. "Commodities would be everywhere cheap. Capital would be seeking employment, but would not easily find it; and the profits of stock would be low. There would be no pressing and immediate demand for commodities" (Malthus 1836: 415). Ricardo and Malthus would go back and forth on this in their correspondence, but other elements came into the discussion.

In particular Sismondi (1819) became the first to hint at the possibility of endogenous cycles, or to be more precise, periodic crises that were linked, with one laying the groundwork for the next. His argument had many similarities to that of Malthus, particularly emphasizing the role of income inequality more than Malthus, even coining the term "class struggle" in this emphasis, but he made more of an effort to build a broader model with these general gluts chronically appearing without the need for some exogenous shock such as the beginning or end of a war.

Probably the most thorough codifier of the Ricardian defence against this Malthus–Sismondi critique was John Stuart Mill (1871). More than Ricardo he invoked Say, but he also allowed for temporary disruptions that could lead to temporary unemployment and output decline. He brought in other factors that could serve as sources of exogenous shocks besides war, such as bad crops or obstructions to imports. The major element he added to Ricardo was to emphasize the role of the financial sector and to see speculative bubbles as bringing about the disruption of the financial sector when they crash, thus leading to a fall in real investment that reduces output and employment temporarily. Many would say that speculative bubbles contain a strongly endogenous component, and once started a particular speculative bubble will clearly feed upon itself. However, Mill retained his classical perspective by emphasizing that the speculative bubble would be triggered by some initial shock to supply that would push up prices, this then triggering the bubble dynamic (Mill 1871: 526). After the crisis and crash, it would be simply a matter of time for the financial sector to reorganize and revive for things to return to normal. There would be no need for a "diminution of supply" but rather for "the restoration of confidence" (Mill 1871: 561). Each such event stands on its own with no cyclical aspect linking it to others.

Curiously, while Malthus did not pose a cyclical model in his response to the events after the Napoleonic wars, he had earlier posed the possibility of longer-run fluctuations tied to relations between population growth and the broader economy, although with these fluctuations possibly being erratic and combining both exogenous and endogenous elements, with Day (1983) and Day and Walter (1989) showing how a model based on this might produce longer run chaotic dynamics. Thus, from the first edition of his *Essay on the Principle of Population* (Malthus 1798: 33–4) we get:

> Such a history would tend greatly to elucidate the manner in which the constant check upon population acts; and would probably prove the existence of the retrograde and progressive movements that have been mentioned; though the times of their vibration must necessarily be rendered irregular, from the operation of many interrupting causes; such as, the introduction or failure of certain manufactures; a greater or less prevalent spirit of agricultural enterprise; years of plenty, or years of scarcity; wars and pestilence; poor laws; the invention of process for shortening labour without the proportional extension of the market for the commodity; and particularly the difference between the nominal and the real price of labour; a circumstance, which has perhaps more than any other, contributed to conceal this oscillation from common view.

Marx drew on elements from both Mill and Malthus, although by way of Sismondi for the latter given his intense dislike of Malthus, particularly in volume III of *Das Kapital* (Marx 1894) and in part II of his *Theories of Surplus Value* (Marx 1969). While in volume I Marx laid out a vision of collapse of capitalism as a whole leading to revolution and socialism, volume II concentrated more on equilibrium models of steady state or expanded reproduction in which the consumption and capital goods sectors remain in balance. It was in volume III where Marx concerned himself more with the matter of the periodic outbreak of crises and the resulting pattern of repeated fluctuations. He expressed doubt that one ever sees equilibrium in micro markets except accidentally for a second as a market moves from excess demand to excess supply and back again. Malthus was muddled in his formulation of the general glut, nevertheless, the problem of "surplus realization" periodically arose, and he dismissed Mill's dismissal of the possibility of general gluts. Like Mill, he was aware of the problem of speculative bubbles appearing in capitalist financial markets and how they could lead to "regular and periodic" crises (Marx 1969: 500). Ultimately the problem would be that "the demand for the general commodity, money, exchange-value, is greater than the demand for all particular commodities" (Marx 1969: 505). A particular idea that he first developed which has reappeared since in many models of macro fluctuations, even in modern real business cycle models, is that of the echo boom, wherein a wave of investment at one time leads to the wearing out of that capital stock at the same time which then engenders another wave of replacement investment (Kydland and Prescott 1982).

Haberler's Taxonomy of Business Cycle Models in the Early Twentieth Century

The appearance of depressions in the 1870s and 1890s (with some arguing for the entire period to have been a depression), along with more crises in the early twentieth century and finally the Great Depression, led to many further developments in the theory of how macroeconomic fluctuations could occur. One year after Keynes (1936) published his most important work attempting to explain the Great Depression as arising from failures of aggregate demand, Gottfried Haberler (1937) published the first edition of his *Prosperity and Depression*. Whereas Keynes sought to lay out a specific theory that incorporated a number of ideas that had been developed earlier by others, such as the multiplier effect (Johansen 1903; Kahn 1931), Haberler reviewed broad schools and views that had been developing since the end of the nineteenth century, some of them also adopted by Keynes, but some of them disagreeing with him to various degrees.

The theories reviewed by Haberler are the purely monetary theory, the over-investment theories (three of them), changes in cost or horizontal maladjustments or over-indebtedness, underconsumption, psychological theories, and harvest theories (which largely amounts to a discussion of the already mentioned sunspot theory of Jevons in 1878). Of these he spends the most time on the three over-investment theories. It must be noted also that not all of these theories are mutually exclusive and that in any particular fluctuation the effects described by more than one of them may be simultaneously at work.

For Haberler, the leading exponent of the purely monetary theory was R.G. Hawtrey (1913, 1932) who relies upon the quantity equation of exchange of Irving Fisher (1911) that Humphrey (1984) documents was developed by others earlier (Lubbok 1840), but who more strongly emphasizes the role of credit and interest rates and their impact on merchants. He believed that there was instability in the credit system that led to cumulative movements away from equilibrium in either direction, accompanied by either deflation or inflation. Indeed, in his earliest writing he recognized the possibility of a complete freezing of credit in a sufficiently deflationary situation, in which monetary policy will be ineffective to stimulate the economy, rather resembling the liquidity trap of Keynes. Later the greatest champion of Hawtrey's approach would be Milton Friedman

(1956; Friedman and Schwartz 1963). While Friedman agreed with Hawtrey about shorter-term impacts of money on the economy, he also strongly emphasized the longer-run neutrality of money associated with the monetarist approach.

The leaders of the monetary theory of over-investment tended to be of the Austrian School, notably von Mises (1934) and Hayek (1933), although they drew on the work of the Swedish economist Wicksell (1898), who also inspired the alternative to Keynes, the Swedish sequence analysis school (Lundberg 1937). While there is overlap with the monetarist theory, there is even greater emphasis on interest rates and their control by central banks. So, Wicksell posed the idea of the natural rate of interest. If interest rates were held below this rate, then there would be over-investment, particularly of longer time horizon projects, with this being followed by interest rates above the natural rate, which would lead to a crisis and decline of output while there was a shutting down of many now unprofitable projects.

The non-monetary over-investment theory's leading advocate was Spiethoff (1902), who saw investment in fixed capital respond to a rise in demand for final goods, but that the boom that develops runs into an outright shortage of capital goods as that sector hits capacity limits. There is something of a production lag element to this such as one finds in the cobweb theorem dynamics of microeconomics (Cheysson 1887; Ezekiel 1938) with the crucial lag being in capital investment in the capital goods sector. However, this theory has roots in some of Marx's arguments, and one of his followers, Tugan-Baranovsky (1901), argued for a periodicity and regularity to such a cycle, likening it to a steam engine.

The third over-investment theory depends on the acceleration principle that has investment responding to changes in consumer final goods demands, but overshooting the increase in capacity. Among those developing and applying this would be Carver (1903), Aftalion (1913), Clark (1917) and Harrod (1936). The related multiplier concept due to Johansen (1903 (under the pseudonym, "J.J.O. Lahn")) and Kahn (1931) would be combined in the form of multiplier-accelerator models to show mathematically complete models of periodic and endogenous macroeconomic fluctuations (Samuelson 1939a, 1939b), with nonlinearity in the consumption function in the latter version making it susceptible to endogenously erratic fluctuations.

The horizontal maladjustment theory, or "error theory," much resembles the explanation by Ricardo of what happened after the Napoleonic Wars. As argued by Mitchell (1924), this involved over-investment in particular sectors, and did not necessarily lead to general decline, although it could.

Irving Fisher (1933) developed the debt-deflation theory, which has influenced Minsky (1986) and Bernanke et al. (1996) since. Fisher did not support any ideas of periodicity of cycles, but saw each as an individual event. A deflation could expand the real value of debt, which in turn could drive down output as firms fail due to their rising real indebtedness. For later writers this would become the "financial accelerator".

We have already encountered the under-consumption theory earlier from the work of Malthus and Sismondi. A later more detailed presentation was due to Hobson (1909), who placed special emphasis on the role of income inequality leading to the poor being unable to buy consumer goods. Haberler notes that at least conceptually this theory is similar to the over-investment theory, although the emphasis in the latter tends to be on the behaviour of the capitalists making overly large investments, whereas the under-consumption view focuses on the would-be consumers who do not buy enough to justify the investments that have taken place.

Finally, we have the psychological theory. Many observers mention psychological factors, including Spiethoff and Mitchell. But the main developers of this theory were Pigou (1927) and Keynes (1936). This theory more directly confronts the issue of expectations formation, with waves of mania and depression driving investment up and down, Keynes adopting the term "animal spirits" for these oscillations of mood. This theory also plays an enormous role in the work of Minsky (1986), who sees the swelling of optimism in an initially favourable equilibrium situation to destabilize it as a bubble develops leading to a crash. Kindleberger (1978) and Shiller (2015) have been followers of this approach, which easily fits in with some of the other theories, particularly the over-investment theories. An unresolved issue with this approach is the degree to which the psychological factors are exogenous or endogenous, with them conceivably exhibiting both characteristics. The modern theory of psychological variations being driven by arbitrary exogenous effects that themselves do not directly affect production are the sunspot theories of dynamic fluctuations (Azariadis 1981; Cass and Shell 1983), which contrast to the Jevons theory of direct influence on agricultural production from sunspot cycles.

The Question of Periodicity

While many models of fluctuation patterns suggest possible mechanisms for endogenously driven repetition, if only through "echo effect" bunching of investments in similarly depreciating capital stocks, probably a majority of economists are sceptical regarding regular periodicities occurring with respect to most macroeconomic fluctuations. The general problem is that even when such endogenous cycling happens, it is often argued that there are sufficient variations from recession to recession of the mechanisms involved that strictly regular periodicities are unlikely or are likely to break down or change over time if there is a tendency for them to exist. Thus, it may be that previously observable inventory cycles, usually viewed as the shortest of periodic cycles, may have largely disappeared from more advanced economies in recent decades due to improved, "just-in-time," inventory management systems tied to computerization and improved information transmission. However, there has long been a fascination with the possibility of periodic cycles, with different periodicities being proposed and studied.

Although he would be followed soon by Jevons (1878) with his exogenously driven but regular sunspot cycles working through agriculture, the first to identify a possible regular periodic macroeconomic cycle was Juglar (1862). He argued that these were driven by cycles of fixed capital investment along echo boom lines, replacement waves of investment coinciding with a periodicity of about 7–11 years, depending on time period and place. Kitchin (1923) would label this the "major cycle" and posited a shorter 40-month cycle that he called the "minor cycle". He found this looking at commodity prices, interest rates, and bank clearings, and explained it as due to mass psychology, and argued that the major cycle was simply an aggregation of two or three minor cycles. Later observers would argue that inventory fluctuations due to cobweb-like lags were more likely to be responsible (Metzler 1941), with these being examples of the acceleration principle at work.

Cobweb models themselves (Ezekiel 1938) usually focused on agricultural cycles such as 5–6 year corn-hog cycles and 14–17 year cattle cycles, with Rosen et al. (1994) finding the cattle cycle to hold empirically for 1875–1990 in the US. Ezekiel also recognized the possibility that such cycles might be erratic, and Artstein (1983) showed they could be chaotic. Hommes (1991) has studied chaotic dynamics in macroeconomic cobweb models based on the Hicks (1950) nonlinear-accelerator model that assumes floors and ceilings for investment.

Next up in periodicity is the "long swing", first argued for by Simon Kuznets (1930), with a period of 15–17 years, possibly twice the length of a Juglar major cycle. Kuznets focused on demographics and residential construction as the main sources of this hypothetical cycle, although infrastructure investments have been suggested as well.

Probably the most controversial of hypothesized cycles is the "long wave", usually associated with Nikolai D. Kondratieff (1926), although he was preceded by van Gelderen (1913), with others making vague arguments along such lines even earlier (van Duijn 1983). Kondratieff would be executed by the Soviet government, at least partly for his work on this idea. The cycle was argued to be about 50 years in length, and Kondratieff focused on prices and interest rates like some others in looking for cycles, with these variables more observable than gross domestic product (GDP), which was not being estimated officially prior to the early twentieth century. From the beginning there was debate about what might be a driving mechanism, with many arguing that even if it was there in the data it was an artefact with no clear basis for a consistent regularity (Kuznets 1940). Some argued that it was a monetary phenomenon, with the major discoveries of gold in California and Alaska a half-century apart responsible for it, or even a sort of long period accelerator tied to investment waves in the capital goods sector responding slowly to those in the consumer goods sector (Forrester 1977). However, the major argument put forward by Kondratieff and strongly supported by Schumpeter (1939) and most later discussants of the cycle (Freeman 1996) has been technological change, particularly the idea that major innovations bunch together during major downturns. Schumpeter (1939) went further and argued that the Kondratieff was constructed out of the two lower cycles, the Kitchin and the Juglar (ignoring the Kuznets long swing), although few have supported this view even among those who argue for the reality of the Kondratieff. Many have spent much effort identifying particular innovations associated with particular Kondratieffs, such as cotton textiles and steam power during a 1787–1800 boom, followed by a railroadization boom in 1843–1857, and an electricity and automobile boom in 1898–1911 (Kuznets 1940: 261).

Unsurprisingly, the empirical debate on this has been lengthy itself without a clear conclusion. Typical is the exchange between Solomou (1986) and Bieshaar and Kleinknecht (1986) with many issues involved in this. One of the most recent efforts to consider these matters has been by Korotayev and Tsirel (2010) who test for all four of the hypothetical cycles mentioned above at the level of global GDP. They claim to find both the Juglar and the Kondratieff, but neither the Kitchin nor the Kuznets.

While they emphasize elements that go beyond economics, and economists have largely ignored their work, others have posited even longer cyclical patterns. Modelski (1987) sees economic developments tied to larger political ones, particular the rise and fall of hegemonic powers at the global level, with the economies of the hegemons rising and falling along with their power. He argues that such a cycle may be around 120 years.

Even longer is the "longue durée" or "geographical cycle" of Fernand Braudel (1949). Associated with the Annales school of history, he sees deep cycles driven by demographic forces in relation to the geographical environment that work themselves out on a scale of 300–400 years, with collapses in Europe in the sixth, the tenth, the fourteenth, and the seventeenth centuries. Note that the dynamics described by Braudel are somewhat similar to those modelled by Day and Walter (1989). Note also that if one wishes to be pessimistic about future economic growth in the coming decade or so, some have argued that we could be experiencing a simultaneous downturn of the fifth Kondratieff wave since the Industrial Revolution (Korotayev and Tsirel 2010) with a downturn of a Braudel *longue durée* that began its early upturn in the late seventeenth century, with the pessimists pointing to a possibly substantial slowdown of serious new innovations as the key to this secular stagnation (Cowen 2011).

Endogenous Irregular Fluctuations

We have already noted that probably the vast majority of economists do not accept that macroeconomic fluctuations exhibit definite periodicities of any length, including many of those who accept that such fluctuations are substantially endogenous in character, with only a few of those stressing exogenous sources seeing any possibility of this, notably Jevons (1878) who saw sunspots as the periodic exogenous driver. However, gradually many came to realize that if crucial relationships, particularly those involving capital investment, are nonlinear, then endogenous fluctuations can arise that may be not only periodically regular, but aperiodically erratic in a variety of ways. Venkatachalam and Velupillai (2012) argue that the first to realize this possibility was Hamburger (1930), who was inspired by the physics models of relaxation oscillations of van der Pol (1926), drawing on the earlier work of Poincaré (1908).

Hamburger was followed by Le Corbeiller (1933), who in turn personally influenced the crucial work of Goodwin (1951) whose nonlinear accelerator model was shown by Strotz et al. (1953) to be capable of generating endogenous erratic fluctuations that could possibly be chaotic. However, probably the first to develop a model capable of generating chaotic dynamics was Palander (1935) whose regional dynamics model exhibited three-period cycles, shown by Sharkovsky (1964) and Li and Yorke (1975) to be sufficient in one-dimensional models to produce chaotic dynamics. While none of these realized at the time what they had shown, Goodwin (1990) would later become a committed student of endogenous chaotic dynamics in nonlinear economic models. Chaotic dynamics exhibit sensitive dependence on initial conditions, known popularly as the "butterfly effect", in which small changes in a control parameter or a starting point can lead to large changes in the dynamic pattern (Rosser 2000: ch. 2).

Independently, various economists associated with Keynesian economics developed models with nonlinearities that they realized could endogenously generate periodic cycles (Kalecki 1935; Kaldor 1940; Metzler 1941; Hicks 1950), with later economists understanding that these models could generate various forms of complex aperiodic dynamics. Variations on the Kaldor model, particularly by Chang and Smyth (1971) have been shown to exhibit a wide variety of complex dynamics, including catastrophic discontinuities (Varian 1979; Rosser 2007). Zeeman (1974) applied this to stock market crashes (drawing on Thom 1972), chaotic dynamics (Dana and Malgrange 1984), and

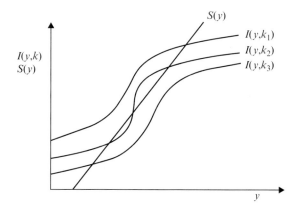

Figure 2   Shifting Kaldorian nonlinear investment functions

transient chaos as well as fractal basin boundaries with multiple attractors (Lorenz 1992). Key to the Kaldor model dynamics is a nonlinear sigmoid function relating output with investment, with this investment function shifting over the course of a business cycle as the capital stock varies. As the investment function shifts, discontinuous changes in investment happen. This is depicted in Figure 2.

Full recognition of how wide the conditions are under which deterministic chaotic dynamics can happen only came about in the 1980s (Rosser 2000). Among the first to be explicitly studied in this way were overlapping generations models (OLG) that followed the formulation of Gale (1973). Benhabib and Day (1980) showed that a sufficient degree of substitutability in the intergenerational offer curves can lead to endogenous chaotic dynamics, although presumably these would be fluctuations more along Kuznetsian long-swing time periods rather than shorter-term fluctuations. Grandmont (1985) extended this, bringing in risk aversion and interest rates (and thus implicitly potentially monetary policy) to show that chaotic dynamics can arise if older agents have a sufficiently higher marginal propensity to consume leisure than younger agents. Keeping in mind that in one-dimensional systems a three-period cycle is a sufficient condition for the existence of chaotic dynamics, Figure 3 depicts such a cycle where μ represents real balances today and $x(\mu)$ real balances tomorrow.

Chaotic dynamics have been shown to be possible in neoclassical models of agents with multiple sectors and infinitely lived agents, hence not just OLG models where things can happen (such as rational speculative bubbles) that do not in representative agent models. Day (1982) provides one such example that involves an upper limit on the capital–labour ratio, suggested by him to be due to a pollution limit. This leads to a standard Solow growth model turning into one with a logistic function determining the dynamics of the sort shown to exhibit chaotic dynamics by Robert May (1976). This model by Day can serve as a driver for a model of much greater financial volatility through the mechanism of "flare attractors" (Rosser et al. 2003) as first posed by Rössler and Harmann (1995).

Another take on this without any "ad hoc" variation from the neoclassical approach is to find that with a sufficiently high discount rate, "every possible" sort of behaviour can happen in a conventional growth model (Boldrin and Montrucchio 1986; Mitra 1996;

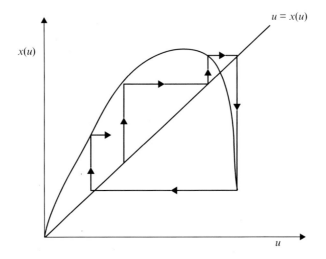

Figure 3   Chaotic Grandmont monetary dynamics

Nishimura and Yano 1996). We note that these models all assume full optimization as well as perfect knowledge by an infinitely lived agent. However, generally the discount rates at which chaos appear are very high, although lower as the number of factors of production increases.

Returning to the world of more post-Keynesian models without representative infinitely lived fully informed and rational agents, more complex dynamics have been observed in other variations of models. Goodwin (1967) proposed a model of endogenous regular business cycles driven by class struggle dynamics using Lotka–Volterra predator–prey equations, with the workers ironically performing the role of the "predators" in the model as their wages fluctuate over the course of the cycle. Pohjola (1981) showed that a discrete version of this model could produce chaotic dynamics and Soliman (1996) shows that it can also lead to fractal basin boundaries between multiple basins of attraction.

Goodwin's (1951) version of the nonlinear accelerator has also been shown capable of being modified to produce dynamics that exhibit both catastrophic discontinuities along with chaotic dynamics in a phenomenon dubbed "chaotic hysteresis" initially by Abraham and Shaw (1987). More particularly Puu (1997: ch. 8) posits that the investment function be non-monotonic rather than merely nonlinear. An example of chaotic hysteretic dynamics can be seen in Figure 4 that holds for certain parameter values of the Puu model, with the horizontal axis being output and the vertical one being the change of output.

Another route by which complex endogenous dynamics can arise in economic models is through the self-organized criticality phenomenon (Bak 1996). Bak et al. (1993) present such a model, which depends on a lattice structure of multiple pathways and stages of production in a sandpile model. This can allow a Gaussian distribution of exogenous shocks (sand dropping on the sandpile) to generate non-Gaussian distributions of final outcomes.

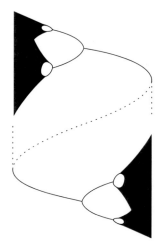

Figure 4   Chaotic hysteresis in a Puu nonlinear accelerator model

Unsurprisingly adding a financial sector to many of these models simply increases the likelihood that one can observe some form of complex dynamics. Among those finding chaotic dynamics include Foley (1987), Woodford (1989), and Delli Gatti et al. (1993). A variation on these models involves the role of speculative bubbles in the financial sector, which harks back to our earlier discussions of the role that such can play in macro-economic dynamics going back to Mill and even to the origins of economic dynamics discussions with Cantillon. This links to more modern post-Keynesian concerns such as those involving financial fragility following the work of Minsky (1986). That bubbles might be chaotic was first shown by Day and Huang (1990), and Keen (1995) has shown this in the context of a model more directly based on Minsky.

Where Do We Stand Now?

The financial market crash of 2008 and the subsequent Great Recession have substantially altered the discussion of economic dynamics. The long Great Moderation beginning in the mid-1980s (at least for a set of the higher income market capitalist economies) had underpinned the rise to dominance of the use of dynamic stochastic general equilibrium (DSGE) models based on rational expectations and real business cycle approaches emphasizing stochastic exogenous shocks (Woodford 2003). These models would be modified by the introduction of various frictions such as sticky prices to lead to New Keynesian variants that came to be widely used (Smet and Wouters 2002). However, the complete failure of these models to either model or to forecast showed up their severe limitations. While there is no clear successor (and sufficiently modified versions of these may well yet continue to dominate policy discussions), several alternatives drawing on some of the traditions discussed above have emerged as possible contenders for replacements. We note three of these to conclude this entry. All of these clearly involve great emphasis on the financial sector.

One of these involves drawing together elements from the models of Marx, Keynes,

Metzler, Goodwin, and occasionally even Schumpeter. This has been done principally by economists either based at or visiting Bielefeld University over the past couple of decades, with a series of articles and substantial books, a group that can arguably be called the "Bielefeld School". It is not simple to label these models, but their elements do include emphasis on financial sector dynamics in connection with the real economy, lags and inventory dynamics, nonlinear accelerators affecting investment decisions, along with concerns about distributional effects, with their models able to show the full array of complex dynamics discussed above. An incomplete list of works includes Asada et al. (2003), Chiarella et al. (2005), Flaschel (2009), and Semmler and Bernard (2012).

While they have not been worked out much formally, some argue for a revival of the Austrian School approach, arguing that the role of the overvaluation of housing in the crash initiating the Great Recession may be explained by focusing on Austrian misallocation across sectors, with low interest rates playing the role of putting too much financing and investment in the long time horizon residential real estate sector. Garrison (2001) provides a discussion of Austrian approaches to modelling macrodynamics.

The other approach more specifically tries to model heterogeneous agents from the ground up and their interactions. One branch of this has followed on a more explicitly econophysics approach focusing on statistical mechanical stochastic processes in the presence of nonlinearities (Aoki 1996). The other has moved to more explicitly model individual parts of the economy in an effort to build up a microfoundation to obtain macroeconomic results, although without tying that microfoundation to a rational or optimizing model of agents in the DSGE tradition (Delli Gatti et al. 2008). While there have been efforts to introduce heterogeneity into DSGE models (Krusell and Smith 1998), these have usually taken the form of assuming a distribution of characteristics over an interval, with the interval then in effect behaving as a homogeneous agent. The agent-based approach attempts to more specifically model the interactions of the agents directly to find how extreme outcomes can endogenously arise from within an economy, with Gallegati et al. (2011) showing how such models can lead to more specifically Minskyan financial dynamics.

J. Barkley Rosser Jr

See also:

Albert Aftalion (I); British classical political economy (II); Business cycles and growth (III); Evolutionary economics (III); Financial economics (III); Formalization and mathematical modelling (III); Growth (III); William Stanley Jevons (I); Clément Juglar (I); Michał Kalecki (I); Robert E. Lucas (I); Macroeconomics (III); Alfred Marshall (I); Karl Heinrich Marx (I); John von Neumann (I); Frank Plumpton Ramsey (I); Paul Anthony Samuelson (I); Joseph Alois Schumpeter (I); Joseph Eugene Stiglitz (I); Technical change and innovation (III).

References and further reading

Abraham, R. and C.D. Shaw (1987), 'Dynamics: a visual introduction', in E.F. Yates (ed.), *Self-Organizing Systems: The Emergence of Order*, New York: Plenum Press, pp. 543–97.
Aftalion, A. (1913), *Les Crises Périodiques de Surproduction*, Paris: Rivière.
Aoki, M. (1996), *New Approaches to Macroeconomic Modeling: Evolutionary Stochastic Economics, Multiple Equilibria, and Externalities as Field Effects*, Cambridge: Cambridge University Press.
Artstein, Z. (1983), 'Irregular cobweb dynamics', *Economics Letters*, **11** (1–2), 15–17.
Asada, T., C. Chiarella, P. Flaschel and R. Franke (2003), *Open Economy Macrodynamics: An Integrated Disequilibrium Approach*, Heidelberg: Springer.
Azariadis, C. (1981), 'Self-fulfilling prophecies', *Journal of Economic Theory*, **25** (3), 380–96.

Bak, P. (1996), *How Nature Works: The Science of Self-Organized Criticality*, New York: Copernicus Press for Springer-Verlag.

Bak, P., K. Chen, J. Scheinkman and M. Woodford (1993), 'Aggregate fluctuations from independent sectoral shocks: self-organized criticality in a model of production and inventory dynamics', *Ricerche Economiche*, **47** (1), 3–30.

Benhabib, J. and R.H. Day (1980), 'Erratic accumulation', *Economics Letters*, **6** (2), 113–17.

Bernanke, B., M. Gertler and S. Gilchrist (1996), 'The financial accelerator and the flight to quality', *Review of Economics and Statistics*, **78** (1), 1–15.

Bhaduri, A. and D.J. Harris (1987), 'The complex dynamics of the simple Ricardian model', *Quarterly Journal of Economics*, **102** (4), 893–901.

Bieshaar, H. and A. Kleinknecht (1986), 'Kondratieff long waves? Reply to Solomou', *Konjunkturpolitik*, **32** (3), 185–93.

Boldrin, M. and L. Montrucchio (1986), 'On the indeterminacy of capital accumulation paths', *Journal of Economic Theory*, **40** (1), 26–39.

Braudel, F. (1949), *La Méditerranée et le Monde Méditerranéan à l'Époque de Philip II, Tome I, La Part d Milieu*, Paris: Armand Colin.

Cantillon, R. (1755), *Essai sur la Nature du Commerce en Général*, London: Fletcher Gyles.

Carver, T.N. (1903), 'A suggestion for a theory of industrial depression', *Quarterly Journal of Economics*, **17**, 457–500.

Cass, D. and K. Shell (1983), 'Do sunspots matter?', *Journal of Political Economy*, **91**, 193–227.

Chang, W.W. and D.J. Smyth (1971), 'The existence and persistence of cycles in a nonlinear model: Kaldor's 1940 model re-examined', *Review of Economic Studies*, **38** (1), 37–44.

Cheysson, É. (1887), *La Statistique Géometrique Méthode pour la Solution des Problèmes Commerciaux et Industrièles*, Paris: Legenie Civil.

Chiarella, C., P. Flaschel and R. Franke (2005), *Qualitative Analysis and Quantitative Assessment*, Cambridge: Cambridge University Press.

Clark, J.M. (1917), 'Business acceleration and the law of demand: a technical factor in business cycles', *Journal of Political Economy*, **25** (3), 217–35.

Cowen, T. (2011), *The Great Stagnation*, New York: Penguin.

Dana, R.-A. and P. Malgrange (1984), 'The dynamics of a discrete version of a growth model', in J.P. Ancot (ed.), *Analysing the Structure of Econometric Models*, Boston, MA: Martinus Nijhoff, pp. 115–42.

Day, R.H. (1982), 'Irregular growth cycles', *American Economic Review*, **72** (3), 406–14.

Day, R.H. (1983), 'The emergence of chaos from classical economic growth', *Quarterly Journal of Economics*, **98** (2), 201–13.

Day, R.H. and J.-L. Walter (1989), 'Economic growth in the very long run: on the multiple interaction of population, technology, and social infrastructure', in W.A. Barnett, J. Geweke and K. Shell (eds), *Economic Complexity: Chaos, Sunspots, Bubbles, and Nonlinearity*, Cambridge: Cambridge University Press, pp. 253–89.

Day, R.H. and W. Huang (1990), 'Bulls, bears, and market sheep', *Journal of Economic Behavior and Organization*, **14** (3), 299–329.

Delli Gatti, D., E. Gaffeo, M. Gallegati, G. Giulioni, and A. Palestrina (2008), *Emergent Macroeconomics: An Agent-Based Approach to Business Fluctuations*, Milan: Springer.

Delli Gatti, D., M. Gallegati and L. Gardini (1993), 'Investment confidence, corporate debt and income fluctuations', *Journal of Economic Behavior and Organization*, **22** (2), 161–88.

Ezekiel, M. (1938), 'The cobweb theorem', *Quarterly Journal of Economics*, **52** (2), 255–80.

Fisher, I. (1911), *The Purchasing Power of Money, its Determination and Relation to Credit, Interest and Prices*, New York: Macmillan.

Fisher, I. (1933), 'The debt-deflation theory of great depressions', *Econometrica*, **1** (4), 337–57.

Flaschel, P. (2009), *The Macrodynamics of Capitalism: Elements for a Synthesis of Marx, Keynes, and Schumpeter*, 2nd edn, Heidelberg: Springer.

Foley, D.K. (1987), 'Liquidity-profit cycles in a capitalist economy', *Journal of Economic Behavior and Organization*, **8** (3), 363–77.

Forrester, J.W. (1977), 'Growth cycles', *De Economist*, **125** (4), 525–43.

Freeman, C. (ed.) (1996), *Long Wave Theory*, Cheltenham, UK and Brookfield, VT, USA: Edward Elgar.

Friedman, M. (1956), *Studies in the Quantity Theory of Money*, Chicago, IL: University of Chicago Press.

Friedman, M. and A. Schwartz (1963), *A Monetary History of the United States 1867–1960*, Princeton, NJ: Princeton University Press.

Frisch, R. (1933), 'Propagation problems and impulse problems in dynamic economics', in G. Cassel (ed.), *Economic Essays in Honour of Gustav Cassel*, London: George Unwin & Allen, pp. 171–206.

Gale, D. (1973), 'Pure exchange equilibrium of dynamic economic models', *Journal of Economic Theory*, **6** (1), 12–36.

Gallegati, M., A. Palestrina and J.B. Rosser Jr (2011), 'The period of financial distress in speculative markets: interacting heterogeneous agents and financial constraints', *Macroeconomic Dynamics*, **62** (1), 96–121.

Gandolfo, G. (2009), *Economic Dynamics*, 4th edn, Heidelberg: Springer.

Garrison, R. (2001), *Time and Money: The Macroeconomics of Capital Structure*, London: Taylor & Francis.

Goodwin, R.M. (1951), 'The nonlinear accelerator and the persistence of business cycles', *Econometrica*, **19** (1), 1–17.

Goodwin, R.M. (1967), 'A growth cycle', in C.H. Feinstein (ed.), *Socialism, Capitalism and Economic Growth: Essays Presented to Maurice Dobb*, Cambridge: Cambridge University Press, pp. 54–8.

Goodwin, R.M. (1990), *Chaotic Economic Dynamics*, Oxford: Oxford University Press.

Grandmont, J.-M. (1985), 'On endogenous competitive business cycles', *Econometrica*, **53** (4), 995–1045.

Haberler, G. (1937), *Prosperity and Depression: A Theoretical Analysis of Cyclical Movements*, Cambridge, MA: Harvard University Press.

Haberler, G. (1963), *Prosperity and Depression: A Theoretical Analysis of Cyclical Movements*, 4th edn, New York: Atheneum.

Hamburger, L. (1930), 'Een nieuwe weg voor conjunctuur-onderzoek, een nieuwe richtlijn voor conjunctuur-politik', *De Economist*, **79** (1), 1–38.

Harrod, R.F. (1936), *The Trade Cycle*, Oxford: Oxford University Press.

Hawtrey, R.G. (1913), *Good and Bad Trade*, London: Constable.

Hawtrey, R.G. (1932), *The Art of Central Banking*, London: Longmans.

Hayek, F.A. (1933), *Monetary Theory and the Trade Cycle*, trans. from German, London: Jonathan Cape.

Hicks, J.R. (1950), *A Contribution to the Theory of the Trade Cycle*, Oxford: Oxford University Press.

Hobson, J.A. (1909), *The Industrial System: An Enquiry into Income Earned and Unearned*, London: Longmans Green.

Hommes, C.H. (1991), *Chaotic Dynamics in Economic Models: Some Simple Case-Studies*, Groningen: Wolters-Noordhoff.

Humphrey, T.M. (1984), 'Algebraic quantity equations before Fisher and Pigou', *Federal Reserve Bank of Richmond Economic Review*, **70** (5), 3–12.

Jevons, W.S. (1878), 'Commercial crises and sun-spots', *Nature*, **19** (November), 33–7.

Johansen, N.A.J.L. (aka J.J.O. Lahn) (1903), *Der Kreiselauf des Geldes und des Mechanismus des Soziallleben*, Berlin: Putkammer und Mülbrecht.

Juglar, C. (1862), *Des Crises Commerciaux et leur Retour Périodique en France, Angeterre et aux États-Unis*, Paris: Guillaumin.

Kahn, R.F. (1931), 'The relation of home investment to unemployment', *Economic Journal*, **41** (162), 173–98.

Kaldor, N. (1940), 'A model of the trade cycle', *Economic Journal*, **50** (197), 78–92.

Kalecki, M. (1935), 'A macrodynamic theory of business cycles', *Econometrica*, **3** (3), 327–44.

Keen, S. (1995), 'Finance and economic breakdown: modeling Minsky's "financial instability hypothesis"', *Journal of Post Keynesian Economics*, **17** (4), 607–35.

Keynes, J.M. (1936), *The General Theory of Employment, Interest and Money*, London: Macmillan.

Kindleberger, C.P. (1978), *Manias, Panics, and Crashes: A History of Financial Crises*, New York: Basic Books.

Kitchin, J. (1923), 'Cycles and trends in economic factors', *Review of Economics and Statistics*, **5** (1), 10–16.

Kondratieff, N.D. (1926), 'Die Langen Wellen der Konjunktur', *Archiv für Sozialwissenschaft und Sozialpolitik*, **56** (3), 573–609, abbreviated English trans. 1935, 'The long waves in economic life', *Review of Economics and Statistics*, **17** (6), 105–15.

Korotayev, A.V. and S.V. Tsirel (2010), 'A spectral analysis of world GDP dynamics: Kondratieff waves, Kuznets swings, Juglar and Kitchin cycles in global economic development and the 2008–2009 economic crisis', *Structure and Dynamics*, **4** (1), 3–57.

Krusell, P. and A.A. Smith Jr (1998), 'Income and wealth heterogeneity in the macroeconomy', *Journal of Political Economy*, **106** (5), 867–96.

Kuznets, S. (1930), *Secular Movements in Production and Prices*, New York: Houghton Mifflin.

Kuznets, S. (1940), 'Schumpeter's business cycles', *American Economic Review*, **30** (2), 257–71.

Kydland, F.E. and E.C. Prescott (1982), 'Time to build and aggregate fluctuations', *Econometrica*, **50** (6), 1345–69.

Le Corbeiller, P. (1933), 'Les Systèmes autoentretenus et les oscillations de relaxation', *Econometrica*, **1** (3), 328–32.

Li, T.-Y. and J.A. Yorke (1975), 'Period three implies chaos', *American Mathematical Monthly*, **82** (10), 985–92.

Long, J.R. and C.I. Plosser (1983), 'Real business cycles', *Journal of Political Economy*, **91** (1), 39–69.

Lorenz, H.-W. (1992), 'Multiple attractors, complex basin boundaries, and transient motion in deterministic economic systems', in G. Feichtinger (ed.), *Dynamic Economic Models and Optimal Control*, Amsterdam: North-Holland, pp. 411–30.

Lubbock, J.W. (1840), *On Currency*, London: J.C. Knight.

Lucas, R.E. Jr and T.J. Sargent (ed.) (1981), *Rational Expectations and Econometric Practice, Volume I.* Minneapolis, MN: University of Minnesota Press.

Lundberg, E. (1937), *Studies in the Theory of Economic Expansion*, London: P.S. King & Son.

Malthus, T.R. (1798), *An Essay on the Principle of Population*, London: J. Johnson.

Malthus, T.R. (1836), *Principles of Political Economy*, 2nd edn, London: W. Pickering.

Marx, K. (1894), *Das Kapital, Kritik der Politischen Öpkonomie, Buch III: Der Gesamtprozess der Kapitalischen Produktion*, Hamburg: Verlag von Otto Meissner.

Marx, K. (1969), *Theories of Surplus Value, Part II*, English trans. by R. Simpson, London: Lawrence & Wishart.

May, R.M. (1976), 'Simple mathematical models with very complicated dynamics', *Nature*, **261** (5560), 459–67.

Metzler, L.A. (1941), 'The nature and stability of inventory cycles', *Review of Economics and Statistics*, **23** (3), 113–20.

Mill, J.S. (1871), *Principles of Political Economy*, 7th edn, London: Longmans Green.

Minsky, H.P. (1986), *Can 'It' Happen Again: Essays on Instability and Finance*, Armonk, NY: M.E. Sharpe.

Mises, L. von (1934), *The Theory of Money and Credit*, trans. from German, London: Jonathan Cape.

Mitchell, W.C. (1924), 'Competitive illusion as a cause of business cycles', *Quarterly Journal of Economics*, **38** (4), 631–57.

Mitra, T. (1996), 'An exact discount factor restriction for period three cycles in dynamic optimization models', *Journal of Economic Theory*, **69** (2), 281–305.

Modelski, G. (1987), 'The study of long cycles', in G. Modelski (ed.), *Exploring Long Cycles*, London: Frances Pinter, pp. 1–16.

Nishimural, K. and M. Yano (1996), 'On the least upper bound of discount factors that are compatible with optimal period-three cycles', *Journal of Economic Theory*, **69** (2), 306–33.

Palander, T.F. (1935), *Beitrage zur Standortstheorie*, Uppsala: Almqvist & Wiksell.

Pigou, A.C. (1927), *Industrial Fluctuations*, London: Macmillan.

Pohjola, M.T. (1981), 'Stable, cyclic, and chaotic growth: the dynamics of a discrete time version of Goodwin's model', *Zeitschrift für Nationalökonomie*, **41** (1–2), 27–38.

Poincaré, H. (1908), *Science et Méthode*, Paris: Ernest Flammarion, English trans. 1956, *Science and Method*, New York: Dover.

Puu, T. (1997), *Nonlinear Economic Dynamics*, 4th edn, Heidelberg: Springer-Verlag.

Ricardo, D. (1817), *On the Principles of Political Economy and Taxation*, London: John Murray.

Rosen, S., K.M. Murphy and J. Scheinkman (1994), 'Cattle cycles', *Journal of Political Economy*, **102** (3), 468–92.

Rosser, J.B. Jr (1999), 'The prehistory of chaotic economic dynamics', in M.R. Sertel (ed.), *Contemporary Economic Issues: Proceedings of the Eleventh World Congress of the International Economic Association, Tunis*. New York: St Martin's Press, pp. 207–24.

Rosser, J.B. Jr (2000), *From Catastrophe to Chaos: A General Theory of Economic Discontinuities: Mathematics, Microeconomics, Macroeconomics, and Finance, Volume I*, 2nd edn, Boston, MA: Kluwer.

Rosser, J.B. Jr (ed.) (2004), *Complexity in Economics, Vols I–III: The International Library of Critical Writings in Economics 174*, Cheltenham, UK and Northampton, MA, USA: Edward Elgar.

Rosser, J.B. Jr (2007), 'The rise and fall of catastrophe theory applications in economics: was the baby thrown out with the bathwater?', *Journal of Economic Dynamics and Control*, **31** (10), 3255–80.

Rosser, J.B. Jr, E. Ahmed and G.C. Hartmann (2003), 'Volatility via social flaring', *Journal of Economic Behavior and Organization*, **50** (1), 77–87.

Rössler, O. and G.C. Hartmann (1995), 'Attractors with flares', *Fractals*, **3** (2), 285–96.

Samuelson, P.A. (1939a), 'Interactions between the multiplier analysis and the principle of acceleration', *Review of Economics and Statistics*, **21** (2), 75–8.

Samuelson, P.A. (1939b), 'A synthesis of the principle of acceleration and the multiplier', *Journal of Political Economy*, **47** (6), 786–97.

Say, J.-B. (1803), *Traité d'Économie Politique*, Paris: Deterville.

Schumpeter, J.A. (1939), *Business Cycles: A Theoretical, Historical, and Statistical Analysis of the Capitalist Process*, New York: McGraw-Hill.

Semmler, W. and L. Bernard (2012), 'Boom-bust cycles: leveraging complex securities, and asset prices', *Journal of Economic Behavior and Organization*, **81** (3), 442–65.

Sharkovsky, A.N. (1964), 'Coexistence of cycles of a continuous map of a line into itself', *Ukrainskii Matemacheskii Zhurnal*, **16** (1), 61–71, originally in Russian.

Shiller, R.J. (2015), *Irrational Exuberance*, 3rd edn, Princeton, NJ: Princeton University Press.

Sismondi, J.-C.L. Simonde de (1819), *Nouveaux Principes d'Économie Politique*, Paris: Delaunay.

Smet, F. and R. Wouters (2002), 'An estimated stochastic general equilibrium model of the euro area', European Central Bank Working Paper No. 171, ECB, Frankfurt am Main.

Smith, A. (1776), *The Wealth of Nations*, London: Strahan & Cadell.

Soliman, A.S. (1996), 'Transitions from stable equilibrium points to periodic cycles to chaos in a Phillips curve system', *Journal of Macroeconomics*, **18** (1), 139–53.

Solomou, S. (1986), 'Kondratieff long waves in aggregate output', *Konjunkturpolitik*, **32** (3), 179–84.

Spiethoff, A. (1902), 'Vorbemerkungen zu einer Theorie der Überproduktion', *Jahrbüch für Gesetzgebung, Verwaltung und Volkswirtschaft im Deutschen Reich*, **26**, 721–59.

Strotz, R.H., J.C. McAnulty and J.B. Naines Jr (1953), 'Goodwin's nonlinear theory of the business cycle: an electro-analog solution', *Econometrica*, **21** (3), 390–411.

Thom, R. (1972), *Stabilité Structurelle et Morphogenèse: Essai d'une Théorie Générale des Modèles*, New York: Benjamin, English trans. 1975, *Structural Stability and Morphogenesis: An Outline of a Theory of Models*, New York: Benjamin.

Tugan-Baranovsky, M. (1901), *Studien für Geschichte der Handelskrisen im England*, Jena: Verlag von Gustav Fischer.

Van der Pol, B. (1926), 'On relaxation oscillations', *The London, Edinburgh and Dublin Philosophical Magazine*, Series 7, **2** (11), 978–92.

Van Duijn, J.J. (1983), 'The discovery of the long wave', in J.J. van Duijn, *The Long Run of Economic Life*. London: George Allen & Unwin, pp. 59–72.

Van Gelderen, J. (aka 'J. Fedder') (1913), 'Springvloed: Beschouwingen over Industrieële Ontwikkeling en Prijsveweging', *Die Nieuwe Tijd*, **18**, 369–84, 445–64, English trans. 'Springtide: reflections on industrial development and price movements', in C. Freeman (ed.) (1996), *Long Wave Theory*, Cheltenham, UK and Brookfield, VT, USA: Edward Elgar, pp. 1–56.

Varian, H.R. (1979), 'Catastrophe theory and the business cycle', *Economic Inquiry*, **17** (1), 14–28.

Venkatachalam, R. and K.V. Velupillai (2012), 'Origins and early development of the nonlinear endogenous mathematical theory of the business cycle', *Economia Politica*, **24** (1), 45–80.

Wicksell, K. (1898), *Geldzins und Güterpreise*, Jena: Verlag von Gustav Fischer, English trans. 1936, *Interest and Prices*, London: Macmillan.

Woodford, M. (1989), 'Imperfect financial intermediation and complex dynamics', in W.A. Barnett, J. Geweke and K. Shell (eds), *Economic Complexity: Chaos, Sunspots, Bubbles, and Nonlinearity*, Cambridge: Cambridge University Press, pp. 309–34.

Woodford, M. (2003), *Interest and Prices: Foundations of a Monetary Policy*, Princeton, NJ: Princeton University Press.

Zeeman, E.C. (1974), 'On the unstable behavior of the stock exchanges', *Journal of Mathematical Economics*, **1** (1), 39–44.

Economic geography

Ever since the emergence of civilization, human activities and standards of living have been unevenly distributed among both the continents and their territories. Economic life is concentrated in a fairly limited number of human settlements (cities and clusters), which are gathered under the heading of "economic agglomerations". Furthermore, there are large and small agglomerations with very different combinations of firms and households. Economic geography – or geographical economics – aims to explain why economic activities choose to establish themselves in some particular places, with the result that some places fare better than others.

The purpose of this chapter is to provide a bird's-eye overview of the main contributions made by economists and regional scientists in understanding how the space-economy is organized. There is a wide agreement that the space-economy may be viewed as the outcome of a trade-off between different types of scale economies in production and the mobility costs of goods, people and information. Although it has been rediscovered many times (including in recent periods), this trade-off is at the heart of economic geography ever since the work of Lösch (1940). It implies that the location of economic activities is the result of a complicated balance of forces that push and pull consumers and firms in opposing directions.

I want to stress from the outset the influence of three major scientists who epitomize the main questions raised in economic geography: Johann Heinrich von Thünen (1783–1850), Harold Hotelling (1885–1973) and Paul Krugman (1953–). Their contributions have paved the way to large flows of high-quality research. Thünen (1826) is the founding father of land use theory and his work has served as the corner-stone for the development of modern urban economics. Hotelling (1929) deals with a very different but equally fundamental issue, namely the nature of competition across space and the way firms choose their location in a strategic environment. Last, Krugman (1991) has highlighted the microeconomic underpinnings of both spatial economic agglomerations and regional imbalances at national and international levels. He has achieved that by building a full-fledged general equilibrium model, which is able to explain why the economic activity is agglomerated in a few places.

Ironically enough, none of those three authors is a "spatial economist" per se. They turned their attention to spatial issues for reasons that are not directly related to the location of economic activities. Thünen was interested in the allocation of resources and the determination of prices. He emphasized space because land was an essential production factor in the main sector of his time. Hotelling aimed to build a theory of product selection by oligopolistic firms. To achieve his goal, he used space as a metaphor. As for Krugman, he was mainly interested in the interplay between increasing returns and imperfect competition in globalizing markets, commodity trade and production factor mobility being the two fundamental ingredients.

A last warning is in order. Even though Krugman gave new life to the field of economic geography, many ideas and concepts have been around for a long time. However, they were fairly disparate and in search of a synthesis ranging from the small to the large, which Fujita and Thisse (2013) have endeavored to develop. To a large extent, the history of economic geography may be viewed as a process that has gradually unified various bodies of knowledge, as shown by the different names given to the field (regional and urban economics, location theory, and spatial economics), within a theoretical framework in which the focus has shifted from perfect competition to imperfect competition and various types of market failures. In what follows, I will only discuss the fundamental contributions made in economic geography through the lenses of modern economic theory. This choice will lead me to put aside a wide range of contributions that have not passed the test of time.

Thünen and Land Use Theory

The location of agricultural activities

Thünen (1826) sought to explain the pattern of agricultural activities surrounding cities in pre-industrial Germany. Each location in space is characterized by various factors such as soil conditions, relief, geographical position, and the like. Both land rent and land use vary across locations depending on these characteristics. Among them, the most important for location theorists is the transport-cost differential over space. Whereas Ricardo concentrated on fertility differences in his explanation of the land rent, Thünen constructed a theory focusing on the transport-cost differentials across locations. To this end, he used a very simple and elegant setting in which space is represented by a plain on which land is homogeneous in all respects except for a market town in which all transactions regarding agricultural goods must occur. The location of the market town is supposed to be given and the reasons for its existence are left outside of the analysis. By allocating an acre of land near the town to some crop, the costs of delivering all other crops are indirectly affected as they are forced to be grown farther away. Hence, determining which crops to grow where is not an easy task. Though simple, this setting is rich enough to show how a competitive land market can structure the use of land across space by perfectly divisible activities.

The principles underlying his model are so general that Thünen can be considered the founder of marginalism (Samuelson, 1983). In addition, the importance of Thünen's analysis for the development of location theory is twofold in that space is considered as both an economic good and as the substratum for economic activities. In his framework, the allocation of land to the different economic activities is shown to emerge as the equilibrium outcome of a perfectly competitive land market. The assumption of a competitive land market can be justified on the ground that land in a small neighborhood of any location belonging to a continuous space is highly substitutable, thus making the competitive process for land very fierce. Very ingeniously, Thünen imagined a process in which each farmer makes an offer based on the surplus he can generate by using one unit of land available at any particular location. This has led him and his successors to develop the concept of bid rent function, which describes the maximum price an agent is willing to pay to occupy each location.

This approach is probably what makes Thünen's analysis of land use so original. In a sense, it rests on the idea that land at a particular location corresponds to a single commodity whose price cannot be obtained by the textbook interplay between a large number of sellers and buyers. Specifically, land at any point is allocated to an activity according to a bidding process in which the producer offering the highest bid secures the corresponding lot. A farmer's bid depends on the transportability of his output and the amount of land needed to produce one unit of the good. Land being allocated to the highest bidder, economic activities are distributed according to the famous pattern of concentric rings, each of them being specialized in one crop. The land rent decreases with distance from the market town at a rate which is constant in each ring and decreasing from one ring to the next.

The model can be closed by assuming that all agricultural activities use land and labor while a manufactured good is produced in town by using labor alone, typically under the form of craftsmanship. Such a specialization of tasks reflects the traditional division of labor between cities and the countryside. Workers are perfectly mobile and land-lords reside in town; they all have identical preferences. The solution to such a general spatial equilibrium model, in which the real wage common to all workers as well as the prices of agricultural and manufactured goods are endogenous, has been obtained by Samuelson (1983).

Yet, despite his monumental contribution to economic thought, Thünen's ideas languished for several decades. Blaug (1985: ch. 14) attributes the subject's neglect to Thünen's cumbersome style. Indeed, one had to wait for Launhardt (1885 [1993]: ch. 30) to have a formal treatment of his ideas in the special case of two crops. The first model with *n* crops is due to Dunn (1954), while Schweizer and Varaiya (1976) have provided the complete solution to the general model with a Leontief technology in which goods may be used both in the final and intermediate sectors. Whatever their use, goods are either shipped toward the marketplace or used locally. It was not until Beckmann (1972a) that the Thünen model was extended to cope with a neoclassical production function.

It took even more time to explain how and when a market town, which imports agricultural goods from and exports manufactured goods to its rural hinterland, may emerge as an equilibrium outcome. More precisely, the key question that has been at the heart of economic geography for decades may be stated as follows: what binds together manufacturing firms and workers within the city? Using the new economic geography framework discussed below, Fujita and Krugman (1995) have identified sufficient conditions for a monocentric economy to emerge as an equilibrium outcome. Specifically, when (1) the transport cost of the agricultural good is low relative to that of the manufactured good and (2) when the total population is small enough, all manufacturing firms, which operate under increasing returns, agglomerate within a single district together with their workers, while farmers are dispersed across the agricultural hinterland. When one of these two conditions does not hold, shipping goods from and to a single market town is so costly that several cities emerge and generate an urban system.

Urban economics
In his doctoral dissertation, Alonso (1964) succeeded in extending Thünen's concept of bid rent curves to an urban context in which a marketplace is replaced by an employment center (the central business district – CBD). In this context, the only spatial characteristic of a location is its distance from the city center, while the land available for raising crops is now used for housing and transportation infrastructure. The main objective of urban economics is to explain the internal structure of cities, that is, how land is distributed among various activities and why cities have one or several employment centers. The basic concept of urban economics is the land market, which serves to allocate both economic agents and activities across space. Alonso (1964) and Mills (1967) may be considered as the founders of this field. Treading in these authors' footsteps, several economists

and regional scientists have developed the model of the monocentric city. The main focus is on the households' trade-off between the desire to consume more space and to make shorter trips to the CBD. Ever since the 1970s, urban economics has advanced rapidly. The reason for this success is probably that the model of the monocentric city can take leverage on the competitive paradigm of economic theory.

In equilibrium, identical consumers establish themselves within the city so as to equalize utility across space. In such a state, no one has an incentive to change location, the land rent at a particular location being equal to the largest bid at that location. Building on this idea, urban economists have endeavored to explain the internal structure of cities, that is, how land is distributed across activities and economic agents around the CBD. Though very simple, the monocentric city model has produced a set of results consistent with the prominent features of cities. In particular, it explains the decrease in the urban land rent with distance away from the city center as well as the fall in the population density as one move away from the center. The model also explains how the development of modern transportation means (cars and mass transportation) has generated both suburbanization and a flattening of urban population densities, an evolution known as urban sprawl. The best synthesis today of the results derived within the monocentric framework remains the landmark book of Fujita (1989).

Very much as in the Thünen model which does not say why transactions take place in a given market town, the monocentric city model is silent on the reasons that would explain the existence of a district where jobs are available. So, we are left with the following question: why do city centers exist? Or, more generally, why do cities exist? This question has haunted economic geography for decades.

Beckmann (1976) views personal relations as the essence of societies, even though the consequences of relations are often double edged. The propensity to interact with others has a gravitational nature in that its intensity increases with the number of people living in each location and decreases with the distance between two locations. Beckmann then focused on the trade-off between the desire of an individual to interact with others and her need to consume a large plot of land. Under such preferences, the spatial equilibrium exhibits a bell-shaped population density supported by a similarly shaped land rent curve, and thus face-to-face contact supports urbanization. This provides an illuminating explanation for the existence of cities, which combines the natural gregariousness of human beings together with their desire to consume more space.

Although very suggestive, this approach does not explain the existence of an employment center because firms are left aside. Thus, beyond the standard market transactions in which firms are involved, one may wonder what the interactions that would foster their concentration are. The reason here is very different from what Beckmann assumed in that it refers to the role of information as a basic input in firms' activities, a kind of information difficult to codify because it is tacit and which can be collected through face-to-face communications only. The exchange of information between firms generates externality-like benefits for each of them. Provided that firms own different pieces of information, the benefits of communication generally increase as the number of firms rises. The quality of the information is also better when firms are gathered in that the number of intermediates is smaller. Because communications typically involve distance-decay effects, the benefits are greater if firms locate within the same district.

The seminal contribution in this respect is due to Ogawa and Fujita (1980) who explored the implications of spillovers, the intensity of which is affected negatively by a distance-decay effect. Specifically, the agglomeration force finds its origin in the existence of the exchange of information which allows companies to learn from each other how to do things better. The transmission of tacit knowledge and information often requires face-to-face communication between agents, which typically involves distance-sensitive costs. Hence the benefits of information are larger when firms locate closer to each other. On the other hand, the clustering of many firms into a single area increases the average commuting distance for their workers which, in turn, leads to higher wages and land rent in the area surrounding the cluster. Such high wages and land rents tend to discourage the agglomeration of firms and acts as a dispersion force. Consequently, the equilibrium distributions of firms and households/workers are determined as the balance between these two opposite forces.

Ogawa and Fujita showed that high commuting costs lead to a completely mixed configuration, that is, a pattern with no land specialization and no commuting. As commuting costs fall while the intensity of communication between firms rises (two fairly general trends observed since the development of the Industrial Revolution), one moves from backyard capitalism to a monocentric city with complete specialization of land. In other words, low commuting costs and/or strong spatial externalities foster the emergence of a monocentric city in which firms gather to form a central business district.

Despite many progresses in urban economics, the most enduring problem, that is, the existence of an urban hierarchy involving large and medium-sized cities as well as towns and villages, remains unsolved. Although Christaller (1933) has forcefully argued that the number of goods supplied in a city rises with its size, with the manufactured goods supplied in a low-rank city being also supplied in cities of higher rank, there is still no comprehensive microeconomic model explaining the urban hierarchy. So far, the most elegant proposal to describe how cities having different sizes emerge has been provided by Henderson (1974, 1988). In each city, there is again a tension between two forces. On the one hand, there are external economies associated with the agglomeration of firms at the city center. On the other hand, there are diseconomies generated by the need to commute to the city center. Hence, in equilibrium, each city has a well-defined size that depends on the type of firms it accommodates. As cities vary in their industrial mix, they have different sizes because industries differ in the external economies they are able to create. The setting remains incomplete, however. Cities are like floating islands because nothing is said about their relative locations. Furthermore, the model is silent on why and how cities get specialized in particular activities, whereas a few real-world cities are diversified.

The Nature of Competition in Space

The debate about whether the general competitive equilibrium model is comprehensive enough to fully reflect the working of the spatial economy has a long history. Arrow and Debreu have made an interesting attempt to integrate space within general competitive analysis. Specifically, they assume that a commodity is defined not only by its physical characteristics but also by the place where it is made available. This implies that the same good traded at different places is treated as different economic commodities. In addition, the above approach integrates spatial interdependence across markets into general equilibrium in the same way as other forms of interdependence: location choices are contained in the specification of the production or consumption plans selected by firms and households. Hence, the Arrow–Debreu model seems to obviate the need for a space-specific theory of prices and markets. Indeed, standard general equilibrium theory has proven to be very useful for the study of commodity flows across space provided that both firms and households have exogenously given locations. However, things become more problematic once agents are free to choose their locations.

The spatial impossibility theorem
I begin the discussion by considering the assignment problems introduced by Koopmans and Beckmann (1957). Assume that n firms are to be assigned to n locations. Each firm is indivisible, and the amount of land available at each location is such that a single firm can be set up there. Hence, every firm must be assigned to a single location, and every location can accommodate only one firm. Each firm produces a fixed amount of goods and uses one unit of land. Suppose further that the technology used by each firm is not affected by the chosen location. Koopmans and Beckmann first considered the linear assignment problem in which firms receive revenues from the rest of the world, which are location specific. They showed that this problem can be expressed as a linear program, the solution of which is given by integer numbers. Since the shadow prices generated by the dual of this program are location specific, these prices have the nature of land rents. Thus, a competitive equilibrium exists since the optimal solution may be decentralized through a competitive land market, very much as in Thünen.

Koopmans and Beckmann then turned to the quadratic assignment problem in which each firm uses the goods produced by the others and bears the corresponding transportation costs. Because of the exchange of goods, this problem cannot be expressed as a linear program anymore. When locations generate similar revenues, Koopmans and Beckmann showed that no feasible location pattern of firms can be sustained as a competitive equilibrium, thus implying that there exists no competitive equilibrium. Revisiting the quadratic assignment problem, Heffley (1972) showed that decentralization is possible when sites have very different comparative advantages. Hence, as Hamilton (1980: 38) put it: "Stability is lent to the system by having plants differ from one another in their preferences for the sites *qua* sites, and instability arises from a large volume of trade among plants."

In the long debate concerning the comprehensiveness of general equilibrium theory for the spatial economy, Starrett (1978) has made the fundamental contribution. The question is whether the competitive price mechanism is able to explain the endogenous formation of economic agglomerations and the existence of large trade flows. Because they are not perfectly divisible, agents are not ubiquitous and, therefore, must choose an "address". Space is then said to be homogeneous if (1) the utility function of each household is identical no matter what its location and (2) the production function of each firm is independent of its location. In other words, the location choice made by a consumer or a producer does not affect her preferences or the technologies that are available. The spatial impossibility theorem may then be stated as follows:

Theorem 1   Consider an economy with a finite number of locations. If space is homogeneous, transport is costly, and preferences are locally non-satiated, then there exists no competitive equilibrium involving the transport of goods between locations.

Consequently, the perfectly competitive price mechanism alone is unable to deal simultaneously with cities and trade. This has a fundamental implication for economic geography: if the purpose is to build a theory explaining the formation of economic agglomerations, then such a theory must depart from general competitive analysis. What is the meaning of this result? Whenever economic activities are perfectly divisible, the spatial impossibility theorem implies that the mobility of production factors is a perfect substitute for trade. Such a result is hardly surprising because every activity can be carried out on an arbitrarily small scale in every possible place, without any loss of efficiency. Firms and households are then induced to suppress all distance-related costs by producing exactly what they need where they are. In contrast, as pointed out by Starrett (1978: 27), "so long as there are some indivisibilities in the system (so that individual operations must take up space) then a sufficiently complicated set of interrelated activities will generate transport costs". In this case, the spatial impossibility theorem tells us something really new and important: whenever agents have to choose an address, there is no competitive equilibrium (hence the term "impossibility" in the name of the theorem) such that places trade goods. In other words, factor mobility and interregional trade are incompatible in the standard neoclassical world. This result is especially meaningful in so far as it is internal to the theory itself.

Intuitively, the reason for this is that the only location factor that matters to an agent is its position with respect to the others. In this case, the price system must play two different roles: (1) it must allow trade between locations while guaranteeing that all local markets clear and (2) it must give firms and households the incentives not to change location. Once the economy is competitive and space homogeneous, the spatial impossibility theorem tells us that it is impossible to kill two birds with one stone: prices that sustain commodity flows between places send incorrect signals from the point of view of the stability of locations, and vice versa. The fundamental reason for the spatial impossibility theorem is the non-convexity of the set of feasible allocations caused by positive transport costs and the fact that agents have an address in space, even though the individual land consumption is endogenous. Hence, in the absence of external factors that drive firms' and households' locations, such as the existence of a market town or of spatial externalities, a sound spatial economic theory cannot be built within the competitive general equilibrium framework by differentiating goods through their locations and adding land as a new commodity.

Spatial competition theory

Because consumers are dispersed across space, they differ in their access to the same firm. In such a context, firms anticipate accurately that each consumer will buy from the firm posting the lower full price, namely, the price at the firm's gate, called mill price, augmented by the travel costs that consumers must bear to go to the firm they patronize. As a consequence, firms have some monopoly power over the consumers located in their vicinity, which enables them to choose their price. Of course, this choice is restricted by the possibility that consumers may decide to supply themselves from competing firms. This process of competition among spatially dispersed firms has been described by Launhardt (1885 [1993]) who proposed a model of price formation, in which he anticipated the concept of Nash equilibrium. In particular, he was the first to show what came to be known as the principle of differentiation in industrial organization: "the improvement of means of transport is dangerous for costly goods: these lose the most effective protection of all tariff protections, namely that provided by bad roads" (p.150 of the English translation). In other words, firms want to be separated to relax price competition.

Launhardt's contribution remained ignored outside the German-speaking scientific community until recently. Hotelling (1929), more than 40 years later, has had more impact although the path-breaking nature of his paper was more fully recognized when economists became aware of the power of non-cooperative game theory. The value and importance of Hotelling's contribution was brought to light in the 1980s by showing that its use exceeds the original geographical interpretation to accommodate various dimensions that differentiates firms and consumers. To be precise, the spatial framework may serve as a powerful metaphor for dealing with issues involving heterogeneity and diversity across agents in a host of economic, political and social domains. In addition, Hotelling's paper may be viewed as one of the prototypes of the modern economic literature: it is self-contained and focuses on a specific problem, which is studied by means of a simple and elegant model.

Because any single consumer is negligible to firms, Hotelling assumed that consumers are continuously distributed along a linear and bounded segment – think of Main Street. Two stores, aiming to maximize their respective profits, seek a location along the same segment. Each firm being aware that its price choice affects the consumer segment supplied by its rival, spatial competition is, therefore, inherently strategic. This is one of the main innovations introduced by Hotelling who uses a two-stage game to model the process of spatial competition: in the first stage, stores choose their location non-cooperatively; in the second, these locations being publicly observed, firms select their selling price. The use of a sequential procedure means that firms anticipate the consequences of their location choices on their subsequent choices of prices, thus conferring to the model an implicit dynamic structure. The game is solved by backward induction. For an arbitrary pair of locations, Hotelling starts by solving the price sub-game corresponding to the second stage. The resulting equilibrium prices are introduced into the profit functions, which then depend only upon the locations chosen by the firms. These functions stand for the payoffs that firms will maximize during the first stage of the game. Such an approach anticipates by several decades the concept of sub-game perfect Nash equilibrium introduced by Selten in the 1960s.

Hotelling's conclusion was that the process of spatial competition leads firms to agglomerate at the market center. If true, this provides us with a rationale for the observed spatial concentration of firms selling similar goods (for example, restaurants, movie theaters, and fashion cloth shops). Unfortunately, Hotelling's analysis was plagued by a mistake that invalidates his main conclusion: when firms are sufficiently close, the corresponding sub-game does not have a Nash equilibrium in pure strategies, so that the payoffs used by Hotelling in the first stage are wrong (d'Aspremont et al., 1979).

This negative conclusion has led d'Aspremont et al. (1979) to modify the Hotelling setting by assuming that the travel costs borne by consumers are quadratic in the distance covered, instead of being linear as in Hotelling. This new assumption captures the idea that the marginal cost of time increases with the length of the trip to the store. In this modified version, d'Aspremont et al. show that any price sub-game has one and only one Nash equilibrium in pure strategies. Plugging these prices into the profit functions, they show that firms choose to set up at the two extremities of the linear segment. Firms do so because this allows them to relax price competition and to restore their profit margins. Therefore, the slight change made by d'Aspremont et al. leads to conclusions that completely differ from those obtained by Hotelling.

In his review of Chamberlin's book, *The Theory of Monopolistic Competition*, Kaldor (1935) forcefully argued that, once it is recognized that firms operate in space, each one competes directly with only a few neighboring firms regardless of the total number of firms in the industry. The very nature of competition in space is, therefore, oligopolistic, thus casting serious doubt on the relevance of monopolistic competition as a market structure. Beckmann (1972b) has developed a full analytical treatment of spatial competition in a well-crafted paper that went unnoticed, probably because it was published in a journal having a low visibility in the economics profession. In addition, Beckmann's main results were rediscovered by Salop (1979) in a paper that became famous in industrial organization. These two authors show how free entry may determine the equilibrium number of firms operating under increasing returns and competing oligopolistically with adjacent firms. Among other things, their analysis shows in a very precise way how the market solves the trade-off between increasing returns (internal to firms) and transport costs.

Building respectively on Kaldor and Hotelling, Eaton and Lipsey (1977) and Gabszewicz and Thisse (1986) have provided syntheses that help to clarify what spatial competition theory is about and what it can accomplish. This work was timely. Indeed, Salop was not aware of the contributions made by his four predecessors (Launhardt, Hotelling, Kaldor, and Beckmann), who all had a clear understanding of the nature of competition in space. This list of unrelated contributions, which cover almost one century, provides evidence of the very dispersed and fragmented nature of research in spatial economics until the emergence of new economic geography, which has served as a catalyst.

Increasing returns and strategic competition are, therefore, the basic ingredients of a relevant theory of spatial equilibrium. The difficulty of the task has put off more than one scholar. Exaggerating a little, we may say that the inability of the competitive model to tackle various issues as well as the absence of alternative models have generated a lock-in effect that economists had a lot of trouble escaping. It is, therefore, not totally surprising that the surge of new economic geography took place a few years after the revival of monopolistic competition.

As seen above, when firms sell a homogeneous good, they want to avoid spatial clustering because price competition has devastating effects upon them. It should be kept in mind, however, that this result is based on an extreme price sensitivity of consumers: if two firms are located side by side with identical prices, a small price reduction of one firm will attract all the customers. Such an extreme behavior seems unwarranted. When the product is differentiated and when consumers like product variety, the aggregate response to a price cut will not be so abrupt because the quality of product match matters to consumers. By turning the picture around, this observation suggests that firms selling differentiated goods may want to gather at some central market location, because price competition is now weakened (de Palma et al., 1985).

When transport costs are low, the benefits of geographical separation are reduced and prices are lower. Firms then choose to reconstruct their profit margins by differentiating their products along some non-geographical characteristics that are tangible or intangible. Stated differently, product differentiation is substituted for geographical dispersion. In this case, firms no longer fear the effects of price competition and strive to be as close as possible to the consumers with whom the fit is the best. Because these consumers are spread all over the market space, firms set up at the market center and, therefore, minimize their geographical differentiation.

New Economic Geography

The existence of interregional inequalities has long attracted the attention of economists, especially in the area known as "regional economics". For a long time, however, regional concepts, models and techniques were a mere extension of those used at the national level, with an additional index identifying the different regions – think of interregional input–output matrices. Despite valuable earlier contributions, no one before Krugman (1991) had been able to show how regional imbalances could arise within the realm of economic theory.

In the 1950s, several development theorists put forward a principle that allowed them to uncover the underpinnings of unequal development – a principle that has been ignored, however, for several decades – that of circular or cumulative causation. Myrdal (1957: 13) sums up these ideas in the following paragraph:

> The idea I want to expound in this book is that . . . there is no such tendency towards automatic self-stabilization in the social system. The system is by itself not moving towards any sort of balance between forces, but is constantly on the move away from such a situation. In the normal case a change does not call forth countervailing changes but, instead, supporting changes, which move the system in the same direction as the first change but much further. Because of such circular causation a social process tends to become cumulative and often to gather speed at an accelerating rate.

Applied to economic geography, this principle says that regional disparities are driven by a "snowball" effect, which results in its continuous reinforcement once it is set in motion. Krugman (1991: 486) states the same idea when he writes: "manufactures production will tend to concentrate where there is a large market, but the market will be large where manufactures production is concentrated".

The core–periphery structure
It is by marrying the Dixit and Stiglitz (1977) model of monopolistic competition with the iceberg transport technology that Krugman (1991) may find out when and why Myrdal's prediction materializes. The Dixit–Stiglitz model of monopolistic competition relies on product differentiation and increasing returns at the firm's level, as in spatial competition. Unlike spatial competition, however, monopolistic competition involves weak interactions among firms, which respond to aggregate market statistics only. The iceberg cost means that only a fraction of good shipped between two places reaches the destination, the missing share having "melted" on the way. This ingenious modeling trick allows one to integrate positive shipping costs without having to deal explicitly with a transport sector.

As for the other ingredients of his model, Krugman considers a standard setting that involves two regions, two sectors, and two types of labor. The former sector produces a homogeneous good under constant returns and perfect competition, using one type of labor which is spatially immobile. The latter sector supplies a horizontally differentiated good under monopolistic competition and increasing returns, using the other type of labor which is mobile across space. Shipping the homogeneous good is costless. This assumption, which guarantees the equalization of earnings across regions, is made for the immobile workers to have the same demand for the differentiated good. In contrast, shipping the differentiated good requires scarce resources, and thus the demand for this good varies with the location choices made by those workers.

When workers move to a new region, they bring with them both their production and consumption capabilities. As a result, their movements affect the size of labor and product markets in both the origin and destination regions. These effects have the nature of pecuniary externalities because migrating workers do not take them into account in their decisions. Moreover, such externalities are of particular importance in imperfectly competitive markets, where prices fail to reflect the true social value of individual decisions. Hence, the effects of migration are best studied within a general equilibrium framework, where one can capture not only the interactions between spatially separated (product and labor) markets, but also the dual role of individual-as-worker and individual-as-consumer. The great accomplishment of Krugman (1991) was to integrate all these effects within a single framework and to determine precisely the conditions under which the cumulative process predicted by Myrdal occurs or not. Turning next to the specific conditions for agglomeration, Krugman has shown that the value of transport costs is the key determining factor.

If transport costs are sufficiently low, then all footloose firms will concentrate in a single core region, whereas the peripheral region supplies only the standardized good. In this way, firms are able to exploit increasing returns by selling more goods in the larger market without losing much business in the smaller market. It is worth stressing here that the core–periphery structure is the involuntary consequence of decisions made by a large number of economic agents pursuing their own interests. By contrast, if transport costs are sufficiently high, then interregional shipments of goods are discouraged. Hence the economy displays a symmetric regional pattern of production that focuses on local markets. The core–periphery model thus allows for the possibility of convergence or divergence between regions, whereas the neo-classical model, based on constant returns and perfect competition in the two sectors, would predict convergence only. Consequently, it is fair to say that Krugman has presented a synthesis of the polarization and standard neo-classical theories.

The bell-shaped curve and regional growth
The core–periphery model has triggered a huge flow of extensions, which have contributed to make new economic geography one of the most lively research topics of the 1990s. Fujita et al. (1999) is the first place to go, whereas Neary (2001) remains the best critical review of the canonical model. One of the main criticisms is that the model ignores the congestion costs generated by the gathering of people and firms within the same territory. In particular, armchair evidence shows that a human settlement of a sizable scale almost inevitably takes on the form of a city. As a consequence, a growing concentration of people intensifies competition for land and, therefore, leads to higher housing costs and longer commuting. In other words, even when nominal wages increase

with employment density, housing and commuting costs, as well as pollution and crimes, make such large agglomerations less attractive.

As transport costs steadily decrease, the spatial economy now moves through three phases instead of two: dispersion, agglomeration, and re-dispersion of the mobile sector (Helpman 1998). Agglomeration arises in the second phase for the reasons highlighted in the core–periphery model. The dispersion in the first and third phases emerges for very different reasons. In the first phase, firms are dispersed because shipping their output is expensive whereas, in the third phase, dispersion occurs because housing and commuting costs are too high for the agglomeration to be sustainable. Put differently, beyond some threshold congestion prompts firms and workers to re-disperse in order to alleviate the corresponding costs. At the limit, high commuting costs are sufficient to prevent the formation of a large city and guarantee the continuation of industrial activities within several small cities, a situation fairly characteristic of pre-industrial economies.

Another major shortcoming of the core–periphery model is that it overlooks the importance of intermediate goods. Yet, the demand for consumer goods does not account for a very large fraction of firms' sales, often being overshadowed by the demand for intermediate goods. Therefore, in making their location choices, it makes sense for intermediate-goods producers to care about the places where final goods are produced; similarly, final-goods producers are likely to pay close attention to where intermediate-goods suppliers are located. Giving intermediate goods a prominent role is a clear departure from the core–periphery model, which allows one to focus on other forces that are at work in modern economies. To this end, note that, once workers are immobile, a higher concentration of firms within a region translates to an increase in wages for this region. This gives rise to two opposite forces. On the one hand, final demand in the core region increases because consumers enjoy higher incomes. As in Krugman, final demand is an agglomeration force; however, it is no longer sparked by an increase in population size, but by an increase in income. On the other hand, an increase in the wage level generates a new dispersion force, which lies at the heart of many debates regarding the deindustrialization of developed countries, that is, their high labor costs. In such a context, firms are induced to relocate their activities to the periphery when lower wages more than offset lower demand (Krugman and Venables, 1995).

Finally, the vast majority of economic geography models rely on a fairly naive assumption regarding migration behavior: individuals care only for real wages. Leaving aside migratory movements triggered by wars, people are heterogeneous in their perception of the non-economic attributes of the different regions, and this heterogeneity affects the nature and intensity of migration flows, very much as it shapes consumers' shopping behavior. Because labor mobility is also driven by non-economic variables, workers do not react to economic inequalities in the same way. In such a context, the bell-shaped curve emerges again: workers move to the core when spatial inequalities are large but stay put when they are small (Tabuchi and Thisse 2002). This is because workers bestow increasing relative weight on non-economic factors affecting the quality of their life once they have achieved a sufficiently high material welfare. If this premise is correct, both economic growth and the development of the welfare state combine to slow down individuals' mobility by allowing them to satisfy their needs for socializing and/or their attachment to a certain environment.

The benefits of using the Dixit–Stiglitz model of monopolistic competition are reaped when we turn to regional growth because new economic geography and endogenous growth theories have been built on the same setting, thus making it easier to combine these two bodies of research within a unified framework. The contributions reviewed by Baldwin and Martin (2004) emphasize the possible geographical concentration of the innovation sector. Innovation being one of the main sources of the long-term growth of the economy, this innovation-driven concentration supplements the core–periphery effect to generate long-run patterns characterized by persistent and sizable income differences. That is, the predominant centers would retain the high value-added activities, whereas the routine activities would be relocated into the periphery. This challenges the unfolding of the bell-shaped curve and keeps open the debate on the spatial diffusion of economic development. However, thanks to new economic geography, we understand much better the various forces at work.

Concluding Remarks

The (relative) absence of space in economic theory lies in the attempt made by economists to develop a rigorous theory of markets and prices. This attempt has led them, through a series of simplifications and shortcuts taken long ago, to zero in on the combination of "constant returns and perfect competition" with consequences for economic geography that are comparable to those for growth theory. While the lack of interest manifested by many economists about spatial issues is regrettable, the opposite attitude (disinterest in economic theory as a whole on the grounds that it is a-spatial) is untenable. This attitude long characterized traditional regional economists, and it largely explains the stagnation of this field.

The present state of the art in economic geography is the outcome of a two-sided process. The first side involves regional scientists who felt the need to root their field in economic theory. For a long time, because the emphasis was on city and regional planning, regional science focused more on optimization techniques than on equilibrium analyses. Despite some mutual ignorance between economists and regional scientists, most of the main contributions in regional science have been incorporated into the realm of economic theory, often after some delay. Among the community of regional scientists, one scholar stands out, namely, Masahisa Fujita whose contributions have been acclaimed by the economics profession. The second side involves the few economists who faced the challenges posed by the introduction of space in economic theory, such as Martin Beckmann and Edwin Mills. Their task was not an easy one since space is plagued with all the difficulties that one may encounter in standard economic theory: non-convexities, externalities and imperfect competition.

For a long time, the contributions to economic geography made by economists have been confined to a small circle of isolated specialists. The situation has vastly changed. Whereas most old contributions to economic geography were often poorly related to mainstream economic theory, Krugman's work has drawn space from the periphery to the center stage of economic theory, making new and already existing ideas more amenable to both theoretical and empirical scrutiny. While new economic geography is closely related to trade theory, it is also very much connected to industrial organization. It is, therefore, not totally surprising that the surge of new economic geography took place a few years after the revival of monopolistic competition and industrial organization, from which it borrows many ideas and concepts. There are also strong links to new growth theories, where many scholars see cities as the engine of growth. Thus, it is fair to say that new economic geography has contributed to the development of a new and large flow of high-quality research and to the gradual emergence of a unified field. All of this highlights the integrative power of modern economic theory.

JACQUES-FRANÇOIS THISSE

See also:

General equilibrium theory (III); International trade (III); Paul Robin Krugman (I); Johann Heinrich von Thünen (I).

References and further reading

Alonso, W. (1964), *Location and Land Use*, Cambridge, MA: Harvard University Press.
Arrow, K. and G. Debreu (1954), 'Existence of an equilibrium for a competitive economy', Econometrica, **22** (3), 265–90.
Baldwin, R.E. and P. Martin (2004), 'Agglomeration and regional growth', in J.V. Henderson and J.-F. Thisse (eds), *Handbook of Regional and Urban Economics*, vol. 4, Amsterdam: North Holland, pp. 2671–711.
Beckmann, M.J. (1972a), 'Von Thünen revisited: a neoclassical land use model', *Swedish Journal of Economics*, **74** (1), 1–7.
Beckmann, M.J. (1972b), 'Spatial Cournot oligopoly', *Papers and Proceedings of the Regional Science Association*, **28**, 37–47.
Beckmann, M.J. (1976), 'Spatial equilibrium in the dispersed city', in Y.Y. Papageorgiou (ed.), *Mathematical Land Use Theory*, Lexington, MA: Lexington Books, pp. 117–25.
Blaug, M. (1985), *Economic Theory in Retrospect*, Cambridge: Cambridge University Press.
Christaller, W. (1933), *Die zentralen Orte in Süddeutschland*, Jena: Gustav Fischer Verlag.
D'Aspremont, C., J.J. Gabszewicz and J.-F. Thisse (1979), 'On Hotelling's "Stability in Competition"', *Econometrica*, **47** (5), 1045–50.
De Palma, A., V. Ginsburgh, Y.Y. Papageorgiou and J.-F. Thisse (1985), 'The principle of minimum differentiation holds under sufficient heterogeneity', *Econometrica*, **53** (4), 767–81.
Dixit, A.K. and J.E. Stiglitz (1977), 'Monopolistic competition and optimum product diversity', *American Economic Review*, **67** (3), 297–308.
Dunn, E.S. (1954), 'The equilibrium of land-use pattern in agriculture', *Southern Economic Journal*, **21** (1), 173–87.
Eaton, B.C. and R.G. Lipsey (1977), 'The introduction of space into the neoclassical model of value theory', in M. Artis and A. Nobay (eds), *Studies in Modern Economics*, Oxford: Basil Blackwell, pp. 59–96.
Fujita, M. (1989), *Urban Economic Theory. Land Use and City Size*, Cambridge: Cambridge University Press.
Fujita, M. and P. Krugman (1995), 'When is the economy monocentric? Von Thünen and Chamberlin unified', *Regional Science and Urban Economics*, **25** (4), 505–28.
Fujita, M. and J.-F. Thisse (2013), *Economics of Agglomeration. Cities, Industrial Location and Globalization*, 2nd edn, Cambridge: Cambridge University Press,
Fujita, M., P. Krugman and A.J. Venables (1999), *The Spatial Economy. Cities, Regions and International Trade*, Cambridge, MA: MIT Press.
Gabszewicz, J.J. and J.-F. Thisse (1986), 'Spatial competition and the location of firms', in J.J. Gabszewicz, J.-F. Thisse, M. Fujita and U. Schweizer, *Location Theory*, Chur: Harwood Academic, pp. 1–71.
Hamilton, B.W. (1980), 'Indivisibilities and interplant transportation cost: do they cause market breakdown?', *Journal of Urban Economics*, **7**, 31–41.
Heffley, D.R. (1972), 'The quadratic assignment problem: a note', *Econometrica*, **40** (6), 1155–63.
Helpman, E. (1998), 'The size of regions', in D. Pines, E. Sadka and I. Zilcha (eds), *Topics in Public Economics. Theoretical and Applied Analysis*, Cambridge: Cambridge University Press, pp. 33–54.
Henderson, J.V. (1974), 'The sizes and types of cities', *American Economic Review*, **64** (4), 640–56.
Henderson, J.V. (1988), *Urban Development. Theory, Fact and Illusion*, Oxford: Oxford University Press.
Hotelling, H. (1929), 'Stability in competition', *Economic Journal*, **39** (March), 41–57.
Kaldor, N. (1935), 'Market imperfection and excess capacity', *Economica*, **2** (5), 35–50.
Koopmans, T.C., and M.J. Beckmann (1957), 'Assignment problems and the location of economic activities', *Econometrica*, **25** (1), 1401–14.
Krugman, P. (1991), 'Increasing returns and economic geography', *Journal of Political Economy*, **99** (3), 483–99.

Krugman, P.R. and A.J. Venables (1995), 'Globalization and the inequality of nations', *Quarterly Journal of Economics*, **110** (4), 857–80.

Launhardt, W. (1885), *Mathematische Begründung der Volkswirtschaftslehre*, Leipzig: B.G. Teubner, English trans. B.G. Teubner (1993), *Mathematical Principles of Economics*, Aldershot, UK and Brookfield, VT, USA: Edward Elgar.

Lösch, A. (1940), *Die räumliche Ordnung der Wirtschaft*, Jena: Gustav Fischer.

Mills, E.S. (1967), 'An aggregative model of resource allocation in a metropolitan area', *American Economic Review*, **57** (2), 197–210.

Myrdal, G. (1957), *Economic Theory and Underdeveloped Regions*, London: Duckworth.

Neary, J.P. (2001), 'Of hype and hyperbolas: introducing the new economic geography', *Journal of Economic Literature*, **39** (2), 536–61.

Ogawa, H. and M. Fujita (1980), 'Equilibrium land use patterns in a non-monocentric city', *Journal of Regional Science*, **20** (4), 455–75.

Salop, S.C. (1979), 'Monopolistic competition with an outside good', *Bell Journal of Economics*, **10** (1), 141–56.

Samuelson, P.A. (1983), 'Thünen at two hundred', *Journal of Economic Literature*, **21** (4), 1468–88.

Schweizer, U. and P.V. Varaiya (1976), 'The spatial structure of production with a Leontief technology', *Regional Science and Urban Economics*, **6** (3), 231–51.

Starrett, D. (1978), 'Market allocations of location choice in a model with free mobility', *Journal of Economic Theory*, **17** (1), 21–37.

Tabuchi, T. and J.-F. Thisse (2002), 'Taste heterogeneity, labor mobility and economic geography', *Journal of Development Economics*, **69** (1), 155–77.

Thünen, J.H. von (1826), *Der isolierte Staat in Beziehung auf Landwirtschaft und Nationalökonomie*, Hamburg: Perthes.

Economic sociology

Economic sociology is the study of economic activity considered as a set of social events related to other dimensions of social life, such as family, gender, morals, law, and politics. The history of economic sociology is deeply intertwined with the history of political economy, as a scientific endeavour and as an academic discipline.

When the social sciences were not divided into separate provinces and disciplines were not institutionalized, there was no reason for an "economic sociology" to exist. Accordingly, one finds a mix of economic and sociological approaches – as we now understand these domains – within the work of major economists of the nineteenth century. Nevertheless, the ongoing process of specialization within the social sciences changed the situation toward the end of the nineteenth century and then economic sociology began to appear explicitly, either as a sub-discipline of political economy or as a challenge to economics. This tension remains after more than a century of difficult and sometimes fruitful relations between economists and sociologists.

Before 1870

Adams Smith's work is of relevance to the broad view of the subject when both *The Theory of Moral Sentiments* and *The Wealth of Nations* are taken into account. The Smithian approach to wealth and social behaviour demonstrates that he did not consider economic activity without inquiring into many other dimensions of the social fabric. His famous analysis of the political, social and economic development of Europe in book III of the *Wealth of Nations* is a case in point. A few decades later, Jean-Charles Léonard Simonde de Sismondi followed the same path when he added to his works on political economy a collection of studies of the social sciences (*Études sur les sciences sociales*, 1836), two volumes being specially devoted to political economy (published as *Études sur l'économie politique*, 1837–38), because he was dissatisfied with the "scholasticism" of political economists who persisted in treating wealth at a very high level of abstraction. This is still true of Karl Marx's *Capital*, in which capital is not simply a set of material goods and services necessary for the production of commodities but also a social relation thanks to which the accumulation of wealth is made possible and profitable to capitalists. Furthermore, Marx's study of the development of the capitalist order, from manufacturing to major industrial enterprises, can still be considered a major achievement in which social issues (political struggles between landlords and capitalists, enactment of legal regulations, changes to the production process and the like) are connected to the economic development in England.

However, none of these major political economists claimed to be economic sociologists. The reason is plain: in order to create such a label, sociology had first to come to existence, and this did not happen before Auguste Comte's lectures on positive philosophy at the end of the 1830s (Comte 1830–42 [1975]). Sociology, or the study of complex social facts was the final layer in his classification of the sciences. According to Comte's views on the progress of scientific knowledge, sociology could not appear before existing domains of knowledge (mathematics, astronomy, physics, chemistry and biology) had reached the status of positive sciences. Consequently Comte dismissed eighteenth-century political economy purely as a premature endeavour to create a social science capable of dealing with the issues raised by an industrial society emerging from the political, scientific and cultural changes brought by the American and the French revolutions. While Comte was himself a competent mathematician, he thought, contrary to Condorcet's essay in social mathematics, that mathematics would be of no use to the social sciences. He believed mathematical thinking to be at the root of the abstract reasoning of political economists, conceiving men as rational calculating machines – what would soon be known as *homo œconomicus.*

Given Comte's views on the role of the government and his strong argument that egoism had to be contained by altruism, which was the principal challenge that industrial society confronted (Comte 1851–53 [1895], II: ch. 2), he initially placed sociology in opposition to political economy as a more comprehensive and balanced view of the functioning of societies, permitting adequate moral ideas (altruism) to be fostered. This had immediate consequences: Marx, Pierre-Joseph Proudhon and French liberal economists all agreed on rejecting Comte's philosophy of sciences and sociology.

English thinkers were more receptive to Comte's views. The first to play a positive role was John Stuart Mill, who was greatly impressed by Comte's broad views on sciences and societies, even if his defence of an abstract science of wealth based on the behaviour of a *homo œconomicus* set a limit to his enthusiasm. Nevertheless, Mill's *Principles of Political Economy* (1848) opened the road to a form of cooperation between the sociological approach and political economy, even if sociology is never mentioned within that book. First, in the first pages of book II (Distribution) Mill explained that "the distribution of wealth is a matter of institutions solely" (1848 [1900], I: 197) and thus gave a leading role to "the opinions and feelings of mankind . . . consequences of the fundamental laws of human nature, combined with the existing state of knowledge and experience, and the existing condition of social institution and intellectual and moral culture" (1848 [1900], II: 210). Secondly, he endorsed the Comtean distinction between the static and the dynamic in book IV (The influence of the progress of society on production and distribution), pointing out the role of collective action as the major source of progress.

Finally, Herbert Spencer was instrumental in legitimizing the sociological approach in nineteenth-century social science. He explicitly admitted his debt to Comte in the very essay in which he explained his disagreement with several general principles related to the classification of the sciences. Among the points of agreement that he considered as "sundry minor views" were the distinction between statics and dynamics, the concept of social consensus (that is, interdependency between the various parts of the society), and the necessity of a class of scientists devoted to synthesizing the local achievements of the specialists. Finally, he adopted the word sociology, and wrote a series of volumes (*Descriptive Sociology*, 1873; the multivolume *Principles of Sociology* that appeared from 1876 to 1896) that were widely read among the educated classes by the end of the nineteenth century. Among his differences with Comte, Spencer firmly rejected the idea that the government may have a larger and positive role in the future, and he claimed that in the future a minimal state would afford the largest freedom to citizens contracting with each other. This view of sociology made it much more palatable to economists.

Finally, sociology was made a part of political economy by William Stanley Jevons. In 1876, celebrating the publication of Smith's landmark book, he proposed dividing the domain of political economy into several branches so that economists could specialize and keep in touch with developments in that part of the science with which they were concerned. One aspect of this was directly connected to Spencer's views on sociology, understood as a dynamic approach to societies, political economy being found wanting in this domain: "We must take into account the long past out of which we are constantly emerging. Whether we call it sociology or not, we must have some scientific treatment of the principles of evolution as manifested in every branch of social existence" (Jevons 1876: 195). This was more than lip service paid to the crisis in the political economy of his time. Three years later, in the preface to the second edition of his *Theory of Political Economy*, he proposed a division of political economy into five branches: commercial statistics, the mathematical theory of economics, systematic and descriptive economics, economic sociology and fiscal science (Jevons 1879 [1965]: xvii). He was therefore the first political economist to suggest that economic sociology should play a part in the development of economics. The lesson was not lost with the tragic death of Jevons: given the continuing intellectual crisis within political economy, three great social scientists of the next period pushed the idea further.

The 'Great Decades': 1890–1940

By the end of the nineteenth century, political economy was in a critical situation. First, a debate on method was started by the German Historical School, whose centre was in Germany but which, since German universities attracted many scholars from Europe and the United States, had international influence. Furthermore, a historical orientation was then common among economists – Alfred Marshall's work is a good illustration of this influence (Marshall 1890). Second, the development of an economics based upon more abstract reasoning and mathematical methods was at this time in its early stages. Some leading scholars, such as Vilfredo Pareto, relentlessly repeated that pure political economy had a very limited power of explanation and should be complemented by other approaches. Finally, the period was marked by a series of attempts to institutionalize political economy within universities and to create specialized journals in which economists could publish the result of their research.

It is in this context that economic sociology appeared to be a possible solution. Three different strategies were then proposed: Emile Durkheim (1858–1917), a French philosopher by training and sociologist, suggested a strategy in which political economy would be superseded by economic sociology. Pareto (1848–1923), trained as an engineer, became the successor of Léon Walras in Lausanne. He proposed a strategy of progressive complexification, going from pure political economy to applied political economy and then to economic sociology. Finally, Max Weber (1864–1921), an economist from Schmoller's *Verein* who became a sociologist in the very last part of his life, suggested a strategy which would connect abstract theory to the empirical data given by history. Each strategy was grounded on a complex set of methodological and theoretical statements on the one hand, and empirical research on the other.

Durkheim had initially oriented his research on issues related to economic life. His dissertation was on the division of labour (*On the Division of Social Labour*, Durkheim 1893). He then devoted his attention to corporations and their regulatory functions in order to find a solution to what he saw as the unsatisfactory situation of industrial society, which was riven by periodic crises. He also lectured on socialism, a topic of great interest to economists of the time, and on the role of government in industrial society. At the end of the nineteenth century he turned from economic issues to the sociology of religion, pointing out that economic events should also be connected to their religious underpinnings – but he did not himself explore this hypothesis (Steiner 2011: chs 2 and 5). As a philosopher he was well versed in the methodological problems that plagued political economy at the end of the nineteenth century, as illustrated by the German debate on method. Concepts and abstraction are necessary tools in social sciences, explained Durkheim, and sociology should develop its own abstract conceptualization and follow specific rules on method (definition, classification, comparison of series of facts in order to reach an explanation of social facts according to the sequence set up in his *Rules of Sociological Method*, 1895). Nevertheless, Durkheim was not satisfied with the concepts used by economists: these concepts were not inductively grounded, and therefore they were nothing but normative statements. They expressed what a rational actor should do in order to be rational, not what these actors actually do in their economic life. A second fundamental critique appeared in one core chapter of his dissertation, where Durkheim criticized Spencer's view of industrial society, in which social intercourse would be primarily founded upon free contractual relationships. This was impossible, argued Durkheim, since the increasing number of contractual relations would exceed the capacity of individuals to bargain and monitor contracts; instead, individuals had to rely upon ready-made contracts in which duty would, to a great extent, impinge upon contractual freedom. This means that there are non-contractual elements in a contract, and these elements do not come from nowhere: they are social facts or institutions that impose themselves on individuals. The institutional embeddedness of economic exchanges became a key point for understanding economic activity.

Durkheim did not develop these methodological critiques; instead the task was taken up by two of his disciples, François Simiand (1873–1935) and, to a lesser extent, by Maurice Halbwachs (1877–1945), who were at the head of the "Economic Sociology" section of the Durkheimian journal, *L'Année sociologique* (1897–1913). Simiand had a polemical turn of mind that led him to criticize both the German Historical School for its lack of clear theoretical underpinnings, and also the neo-classical school, mathematical economics included, which was found wanting in its approach to empirical data (Simiand 1912). Rejecting "theories without facts and facts without theories", he tried to fill the gap with a theory of economic action (effort versus routine and increase of profit versus status quo) which he put at the basis of his work on business cycles (Simiand 1932). He became a leading French economist of the so-called *économie positive* school, arguing for a political economy founded upon statistics and history on the one hand, and sociological theory on the other.

Pareto is mainly known for his outstanding achievements in the domain of pure political economy. However, throughout his academic life he warned his colleagues of the epistemological pitfalls that he thought plagued political economy considered as a separate science. This twofold dimension of Pareto's thinking was clearly present in the introduction to his *Manuale di economia politica* (1906, translated into French in 1909 with a substantial appendix on mathematical economics) where he explained that pure political economy was a powerful but limited tool of enquiry, in the sense that its subject matter was strictly limited to the behaviour of rational actors considering nothing but the economic aspect of the social world. In Pareto's own words, these actions are "logical" in the sense that they meet three criteria: (1) there is a subjective goal for the actor; (2) there is an objective one for a scientifically qualified observer and (3) that these two goals coincide. Beyond logical action, there is a large set of non-logical actions that do not fit into any of the three criteria. Pareto maintained the idea of an applied political economy based upon a broader view of an economic man who, while considering only the economic side of the social world, was subject to passion – something Pareto had witnessed with Italian monetary and banking policy at the end of the nineteenth century. To this, Pareto added a sociology which had to deal with a large number of non-logical actions. Pareto's emphasis on the circulation of various elites (governing and non-governing elites) lent a major role to political sociology. Nevertheless, the economic dimension of this sociology is very important, as one can see in the two last chapters of Pareto's *Trattato di sociologia generale* (1916, French translation 1917). One example will make clear the significance of economic sociology for Pareto. Throughout his life Pareto fought against protectionism (Steiner 1995). His position was clearly founded upon pure political economy – not to mention Pareto's adhesion to the liberal credo of the time – since he used a general equilibrium approach to international trade in demonstrating that any form of protection would prevent societies from achieving the best allocation of productive resources, and thus the largest output possible. Subsequently, Pareto explained the existence of protectionism and the "demand for protectionism" in terms of the economic passions of both entrepreneurs and politicians. This was conceptualized in terms of what is now called "the free rider" mechanism: to fight against protectionism could be more costly than passive acceptance of this form of spoliation, unless all the citizens paid the cost of a campaign against industrial protection. The other solution is to be found in the moral or political commitment of citizens willing to act against protection, even if such struggle is not economically rational. In the final part of his work Pareto added a final component to his analysis of protectionism. Confronted with the rise of protectionist policies in Europe, Pareto explained that protectionism could provide a larger output than free trade. Does it mean that pure political economy is wrong? No, answered Pareto. This means that protectionism has both direct and indirect economic consequences: the former are those negative consequences demonstrated by political economy; the latter are the possible positive economic consequences of the social changes following the implementation of protectionism. Such policy changes the relative positions of members of the governing elites, so that more innovative and economically effective elites would gain power; in the long run, this political change offered more possibilities to entrepreneurs and, ultimately, greater economic output. Economic sociology is therefore the most complicated part of the Paretian view of social sciences, since it involves economic and social interdependencies in providing a better explanation of economic events.

Weber was trained as an economist and a jurist, and was not formally appointed as a sociologist before 1919, when he accepted a chair in Munich, one year before his death. Schumpeter's view was that Weber made no contribution to economic theory, but had important methodological views on the work that economists did, as can be seen in his comments on the debate over "value freedom" in political economy. Nonetheless, his contribution to economic sociology was of very first order in designing a strategy combining economic history and economic theory. Weber always considered that economic theory, at least the Austrian version of neo-classical economics with which he was familiar, was crucial to the understanding of empirical data – those who were not happy with it, he wrote, have to provide a better theory – and to causal imputation. Nevertheless, connecting theory and historical events is not an easy task, and Weber suggested that economic sociology could provide an intermediary conceptualization to make such a connection possible. For example, Weber accepted Eugen von Böhm-Bawerk's views on the existence of a positive interest rate between present and future goods, based upon the rationale of a preference for the present. Nevertheless, he wrote, the sociologist would like to know when and how such rational behaviour can really be implemented. Weber was very familiar with financial markets from his study of stock and commodity exchanges (Weber 1894), the institutions in which merchants, capitalists, and financiers gather and give reality to this rational economic behaviour. Accordingly, part I of *Economy and Society* (Weber 1922) offers the most comprehensive conceptual framework in the domain of economic sociology.

Weber did not only provide this conceptual apparatus. His famous essay on *The Protestant Ethic and the Spirit of Capitalism* is a case in point: he explained the birth of the rational economic ethos (that is, economic behaviour based upon deeply internalized values) through a careful analysis of the religious reformation of the seventeenth century, before Puritanism came "to its dissolution into pure utilitarianism" (Weber 1920 [2002]: 122). In this essay, Weber explained how religious change in the sixteenth century (primitive Puritanism) created an economic ethos fitted to the development of modern capitalism. The religious dimension of this explanation came from the idea that many Protestant sects considered that Christians must continuously look for confirmation of their religious status in the daily business of their life. Accordingly, owing to their value-rational behaviour, the Protestant ethos legitimized behaviour that fostered the accumulation of wealth and, finally, the instrumental rationalization of the entire life of believers to the point where Weber considered that "[. . .] the Quaker is a kind of 'walking law of marginal utility'" (Weber 1920 [2002]: 116). This essay is thus a remarkable demonstration of the interconnection between the various spheres of social life and of the role of (religious) institutions in the development of crucial elements of economic activity and theory, namely utility maximizing behaviour.

These three scholars died in the early years of the twentieth century. Who was to continue the work that they had begun as founders of modern sociology, and also of economic sociology?

In the case of Durkheim, the heirs came from the group of scholars created around his journal *L'Année sociologique*. Simiand, Halbwachs, and Marcel Mauss (1872–1950) devoted a large part of their scientific work to economic sociology in the interwar period. Simiand was very active in the domain of the economic theory of wages and business cycles, whereas Halbwachs focused on consumption and demography (Halbwachs 1912). Mauss should also be acknowledged here for his pathbreaking contribution on the gift (Mauss 1925).

In the case of Pareto and Weber, the situation was quite different, since they did not create a "school" in the way that Durkheim had done. Pareto was certainly the less fortunate and had no direct followers. His approach may be pragmatically considered to be a dead end, even if Talcott Parsons (1934, 1935) made him one of the four pillars of his general theory of action (Weber, Durkheim and Alfred Marshall being his three other references), aiming at a general approach to economy and society. Weber fared much better; he became the reference-point par excellence for the sociological domain, and a large part of the research conducted in contemporary "new economic sociology" is influenced by Weber's method and approach. Joseph Schumpeter's own approach to economic sociology complements that of Weber, as his definition of the subject in his famous *History of Economic Analysis* (Schumpeter 1954) makes clear. After distinguishing economic history, statistics and theory as techniques of political economy, he added a fourth element:

> It is easy to see that when we introduce the institution of private property or of free contracting or else a greater or a smaller amount of government regulation, we are introducing social facts that are not simply economic history but are a sort of generalized or typified or stylized economic history . . . Borrowing from the German practice, we shall find it useful, therefore, to introduce a fourth fundamental field to complement the three others, although positive work in this field also leads us beyond mere economic analysis: the field that we shall call Economic Sociology (*Wirtschaftssoziologie*). (Schumpeter 1954: 20–11)

Furthermore, Schumpeter himself devoted a large part of his work to studying connections between economic and social events, whether in the domain of monetary theory, fiscal policy or of the entrepreneur. This last concept deserves a specific comment, for while it is crucial, economists have had difficulty using the idea. The entrepreneur is central to the evolution of a market economy, but his behaviour does not enter easily into the economic man's rigid form of rationality. Schumpeter thought that the entrepreneur was led by a "super rationality" and the desire to create an economic empire; Pareto for his part had suggested that the entrepreneur acted in a non-logical way, since his action, guided by the desire to make a profit, brings the economy to an equilibrium in which profits are nil; Marshall (1907) emphasized the "chivalric" dimension of the entrepreneur, and suggested that they should be honoured with rewards for their contribution to the progress of societies. In brief, the entrepreneur is a central character of economic theory, and also a central one for economic sociologists when they claim that non-economic motives and ultimate values must be taken into account for explaining the behaviour of key economic actors.

The emphasis put on institutions by Durkheim and the Durkheimians, on the one hand, and by Schumpeter, on the other, makes it necessary to introduce an important development of American political economy at this point. The old institutionalist school, elaborated first by Thorstein Veblen, then by John Commons and Wesley Mitchell, has striking similarities to economic sociology (Gislain and Steiner 1995). Mitchell translated and summarized various passages from Simiand's book on the critique of the method of "orthodox" political economy, and pointed out many similarities between the Durkheimian approach and Veblen's views. Later, Commons toyed with the idea of labelling his main book "Economic Sociology" instead of *Institutional Economics* (Commons 1934 [1959]: introduction).

However, as the "years of high theory" spread over political economy in the 1930s, economic sociology lost its grip on the profession. The disciplinarization of the social sciences compounded this situation and for some decades created a major divide between economists and sociologists. This was acknowledged in the opening pages of Talcott Parsons and Neil Smelser's essay:

> The work of Marshall and Weber, considered together, constituted a level of rapprochement between economics and sociology which has not been matched since. From a somewhat different point of view, Pareto also made a notable attempt at synthesis which has greatly influenced our thinking . . . But the initiative of these men failed to gain momentum. Indeed, we feel that there has been, if anything, a retrogression rather than an advance in the intervening half century. (Parsons and Smelser 1956: xvii)

Lost Decades

The so-called Americanization of economics in the European countries and a focus on the technical potentialities of "high theory", on the one hand, and the pressing problems related to the reconstruction of Europe and then the process of decolonization, on the other, channelled intellectual efforts in directions other than economic sociology. While economists had claimed that the future of political economy lay in its connection with other social sciences, they failed to realize this; as exemplified in the case of France by the group of economists who created a new journal – the *Revue économique* – in order to strengthen the sociological dimension of political economy. By the end of the 1960s their project had clearly been unsuccessful, with young generations of French economists orienting themselves either towards neo-classical economics with its growing emphasis upon formalization, or towards Marxism.

The Keynesian revolution appeared as a further blow to economic sociology, since macroeconomic approaches were not easily assimilated with economic sociology. In his reviews of the *General Theory* Halbwachs was unable to understand the potentialities of the Keynesian approach, with its emphasis on the economic behaviour of specific social and economic classes. When shortly after the Second World War Georges Lutfalla went in that direction in *L'Année sociologique*, he seemed to make no impact at all, which could be explained by the fact that at that time Keynesianism was not well received in France. In the famous comparison between the functioning of the financial market and the beauty contest in chapter 12 of Keynes's *General Theory*, he compared a financial market with a beauty contest, where a competitor should choose not what that competitor thinks to be the prettiest faces, but "those faces which he thinks likeliest to catch the fancy of other competitors, all of whom are looking at the problem from the same point of view" (Keynes 1936 [1973]: 156). This point was not grasped by Halbwachs, despite the way that it suggests a connection between the functioning of the financial market and the Durkheimian approach to social economic representations.

Keynesianism was taken up by Takata's (1956) "sociological economics", focusing on the issue of money wage stickiness. The main thrust of his approach was to give power its full dimension within political economy, reassessing Friedrich von Wieser's approach to social economy in which asymmetries of power, states and the constraints of the world economy were taken into account (Wieser 1914). The same impetus was also at the root of the work of François Perroux in the same period as Takata, with a series of studies – *Économie et société: contrainte, échange, don*, 1960, *Pouvoir et économie*, 1973 and *Unités actives et mathématiques nouvelles*, 1975 – on power within the economy and within economics (see Perroux 1994). Later, this issue was central to James Coleman's endeavour to provide a general theory of social behaviour grounded on utility maximization and control over the relevant resources (Coleman 1990).

However, two important works appeared in that period. *Economy and Society* was written as a result of the encounter between Parsons, then a major sociologist in Harvard, and Smelser, a young scholar at the London School of Economics (LSE), who tried to connect Parsons's sociology to recent development in economic theory, and Keynesianism in particular. Their approach was based upon Parsons's general theory of the social system, with his famous distinction of four functional imperatives – the so-called AGIL (adaptation, goal gratification, integration, and latent-pattern maintenance) variables – and a new hypothesis according to which economics is the theory of processes occurring within a specific sub-system – the economy – differentiated from the other sub-systems but in which, contrary to Pareto's views, the same basic variables (AGIL) are as relevant for the economy as they are for the social system in general. As a result, they focused on the interchanges between the economy and other sub-systems. Beyond these general statements, they insisted on the social dimension of many economic data: for example "propensities" are not natural phenomena but resulted from values internalized by individuals during the process of socialization. These values thus underpin the Keynesian labour market in which workers refuse to accept a lower money wage; accordingly, "many empirical areas such as market imperfections can be attained only by supplementing economic theory with other elements of the general theory of social systems" (Parson and Smelser 1956: 84). Social behaviour being driven by values and economic behaviour by utility, the task of economic sociology was to link together these dimensions of action in order to provide a better understanding of the functioning of social life.

Karl Polanyi is the second key author in this period. His landmark study published towards the end of World War II – *The Great Transformation* – is now acknowledged as a major achievement in the domain of economic sociology, introducing the concept of embeddedness (Polanyi 1944). Polanyi stressed that the general rule until the nineteenth century was to regulate markets by norms coming from other social spheres (political, religious and moral). The introduction of the New Poor Law of 1834 marked the abrogation of workers' protection dating back to the Elizabethan period; Polanyi considered this to be the landmark decision that opened the door to a fully self-regulated market system. He added that the spread of the classical political economy of Ricardo and Malthus had been instrumental in that political decision. As a consequence, labour (human beings), land (nature) and money (politics) were treated as commodities – or pseudo-commodities in Polanyi's parlance –no longer regulated by any social norms, but instead by supply and demand and the price mechanism: a situation of dissembeddedness, or the domination of society by the market system. In later work (Polanyi and Arensberg 1957), he omitted this binary distinction (embedded/disembedded economies) suggesting a more flexible approach, according to which several economic integrating principles are simultaneously at work within any given society: household (or self-sufficiency), reciprocity (social exchanges between equals), redistribution (wealth being centralized and then redistributed) and the market. A balance between these four forms of economic organization was the basis for political freedom.

The Parsonsian approach petered out and was never in a position to gain momentum among sociologists and economists; the Polanyian approach went its way but mainly among economic anthropologists, notably through the long debate opposing the substantive and the formalist view of the economy in pre-modern societies. The change came from a new generation of sociologists and economists in the 1970s.

The Rise of "New Economic Sociology"

In the United States, Parsons's approach to sociology was challenged by a group of young sociologists, notably those who studied network analysis under the supervision of Harrison White (then in Columbia), a major contributor to the development of that new form of mathematical sociology. There was a second reason for this renewal of economic sociology, with sociologists reacting to the so-called "economic imperialism" threat. The "invasion" of their domain came from Gary Becker's work, notably his claim that economic theory could provide relevant explanation for any rational action, be it labelled "economic", "social" or "political". It came as well from the favourable sociological reception for Oliver Williamson's (1981) transaction cost economics, with his powerful distinction between organization (power relations) and the market (contractual arrangements).

In this situation, Parsons's emphasis upon the internalization of values during the socialization process was considered to be an over-socialized view of the economic agent which was as irrelevant as the under-socialized view held by economists. Instead, Mark Granovetter used network analysis to explain how flows of information could be channelled to some agents and not others, studying empirically the structure of an agent's contact network, and how these flows could explain the fact that some people find a job without looking for it (Granovetter 1974). Then, he further elaborated his approach and suggested that the network could be treated as an empirical measure of the social embeddedness of economic action (Granovetter 1985), turning to the Polanyian concept, but giving a theoretical new departure to this approach. Network analysis was then implemented in a large number of areas, such as financial markets (Baker 1975), producer's markets (White 2002), credit markets (Uzzi and Lancaster 2004), and is now a very active field of research at the crossroads of economics and sociology (Rauch and Casella 2001). It also has close relations with some heterodox school in contemporary economics, such as the "economy of convention" school in France (Eymard-Duvernay et al. 2002). Coming from the field of cultural sociology, Viviana Zelizer offered a different approach, arguing that the distinction between society and the economy was of little use and, instead of the domination of market over social life, stressing the capacity of social actors to give meaning to market activity, as was the case with the growth of the life insurance market (Zelizer 1979) and the use of money (Zelizer 1994). In Europe, Pierre Bourdieu developed a theory of the market for symbolic goods – that is, goods that have a strong cultural component, such as fashion clothes, art, and literature (Bourdieu 1971). According to Bourdieu, these goods are exchanged for the sake of their symbolic dimension and not according to their utility/price ratio. Bourdieu studied the production of such symbolic goods; more recently, Lucien Karpik (2010) has considered the consumption side, explaining how these markets worked, despite customers facing a high degree of uncertainty.

In any case, sociologists were actively providing a sociological approach to the functioning of the market, able to counter the so-called "economic imperialism" developed by economists trying to give an economic explanation of the social fact, as claimed by Gary Becker (1976; Becker and Murphy 2000); whereas others were pushing in that direction, but with a more subtle and respectful approach to social sciences (Akerlof 1984).

Conclusion

Although it has had a tortuous history, the idea that economic events are social events is taking its place within the academic world. This does not prevent contemporary economic sociologists from referring to different currents of thought, and thus offering a variety of research programmes provided by recent handbooks (Smelser and Swedberg 2005, Beckert and Zafirowski 2006, Steiner and Vatin 2009).

One final point should be stressed, of particular interest to historians of economic thought. From the outset, and exemplified by Durkheim and Weber, economic sociologists have had a particular interest in the sociology of economic knowledge; this holds true for contemporary research on economists as professionals in various countries and the evolution of their connections to the market and policy (Fourcade 2008), the different forms of rationalization of their science (Steiner 1998) or the political consequences of the symbolic dimension of their "science", even when their prognosis went plainly wrong, as was the case with the subprime financial crisis in 2008–09. This is still true with the development of a pragmatic approach to economics, according to which economists do not describe economic activity, but perform it (Callon 1998); creating the devices and arrangements thanks to which actors in the markets implement what economic theory considers to be rational economic behaviour (Muniesa et al. 2007). This approach is gaining momentum, since it has provided fruitful explanations in the case of the creation of derivatives markets (McKenzie and Milo 2003), the carbon market or some matching markets as developed by Alvin Roth, a laureate of the Sveriges Riksbank Prize in Economic Sciences in Memory of Alfred Nobel. More generally, the sociology of economics acknowledges the changes brought about by the development of the engineering approach to economics, and the turn to what is known as "market design".

PHILIPPE STEINER

See also:

Historical economics (II); Institutional economics (III); Institutionalism (II); Alfred Marshall (I); Vilfredo Pareto (I); Karl Polanyi (I); Georg Simmel (I); Thorstein Bunde Veblen (I); Max Weber (I).

References and further reading

Akerlof, G. (1984), *An Economic Theorist's Book of Tales*, Cambridge: Cambridge University Press.
Baker, W. (1975), 'The social structure of a national securities market', *American Journal of Sociology*, **89** (4), 775–811.
Becker, G. (1976), *The Economic Approach to Human Behavior*, Chicago, IL: University of Chicago Press.
Becker, G. and K. Murphy (2000), *Social Economics: Market Behavior in a Social Environment*, Cambridge, MA: Harvard University Press.
Beckert, J. and M. Zafirowsky (eds) (2006), *International Encyclopædia of Economic Sociology*, London: Routledge.
Bourdieu, P. (1971), 'Le marché des biens symboliques', *L'année sociologique*, **22** (1), 49–126.
Bourdieu, P. (2000), *Les structures sociales de l'économie*, Paris: Le Seuil.
Callon, M. (1998), 'Introduction: the embeddedness of economic markets in economics', in M. Callon (ed.), *The Laws of the Market*, Oxford: Blackwell, pp. 1–47.

Clark, J.M. (1936), *Preface to Social Economics. Essays on Economic Theory and Social Problems*, reprinted 1967, New York: Kelley.

Coleman, J.S. (1990), *Foundations of Social Theory*, Cambridge, MA: Harvard University Press.

Commons, J.R. (1934), *Institutional Economics. Its Place in Political Economy*, reprinted 1959, Madison, WI: University of Wisconsin Press.

Comte, A. (1830–42), *Cours de philosophie positive*, reprinted 1975, Paris, Hermann.

Comte, A. (1851–53), *Système de politique positive*, reprinted 1895, Paris: Larousse.

Durkheim, E. (1893), *De la division du travail social*, Paris: Alcan.

Eymard-Duvernay, F., O. Biencourt and O. Favereau (2002), 'Were do markets come from? From (quality) conventions!', in O. Favereau and E. Lazega (eds), *Convention and Structure in Economic Organizations. Markets, Networks and Hierarchies*, Cheltenham, UK and Northampton, MA, USA: Edward Elgar, pp. 253–81.

Fourcade, M. (2008), *Economists and Societies. Discipline and Profession in the United States, Britain and France 1890s to 1990s*, Princeton, NJ: Princeton University Press.

Gislain, J.-J. and P. Steiner (1995), *La sociologie économique (1890–1920). Durkheim, Pareto, Schumpeter, Simiand, Veblen et Weber*, Paris: Presses Universitaires de France.

Granovetter, M. (1974), *Getting a Job. A Study of Contact and Careers*, Chicago, IL: Chicago University Press.

Granovetter, M. (1985), 'Economic action and the problem of embeddedness', *American Journal of Sociology*, **91** (3), 481–510.

Halbwachs, M. (1912), *La classe ouvrière et les niveaux de vie. Recherches sur la hiérarchie des besoins dans la société industrielle*, reprinted 1970, Paris and New York: Gordon and Breach.

Jevons, W.S. (1876), 'The future of political economy', in H. Higgs (ed.), *The Principles of Economics: A Fragment of a Treatise on the Industrial Mechanism of Society*, New York: Kelley.

Jevons, W.S. (1879), *The Theory of Political Economy*, 2nd edn, reprinted 1965, New York: Kelley.

Karpik, L. (2010), *Valuing the Unique. The Economy of Singularities*, Princeton, NJ: Princeton University Press.

Keynes, J.M. (1936), *The General Theory of Employment, Interest and Money*, in D. Moggridge (ed.) (1973), *The Collected Writings of John Maynard Keynes*, vol. 7, London, Macmillan and Cambridge, University Press.

Mackenzie, D. and Y. Milo (2003), 'Constructing a market, performing theory. the historical sociology of a financial derivatives market', *American Journal of Sociology*, **109** (1), 107–45.

Marshall, A. (1890), *Principles of Economics*, variorum edn, reprinted 1961, London: Macmillan.

Marshall, A. (1907), 'The social possibilities of economic chivalry', in A.C. Pigou (ed.), *Memorials of Alfred Marshall*, reprinted 1925, London: Macmillan, pp. 323–46.

Mauss, M. (1925), *The Gift: Forms and Functions of Exchanges in Archaic Societies*, reprinted 1954, New York: Free Press.

Mill, J.S. (1848), *Principles of Political Economy, with Some of its Application to Social Philosophy*, reprinted 1900, New York: Colonial Press.

Muniesa, F., D. McKenzie and L. Siu (eds) (2007), *Do Economists Make Markets?*, Princeton, NJ: Princeton University Press.

Pareto, V. (1909), *Manuel d'économie politique*, in G. Busino (ed.), *Œuvres complètes de Pareto*, vol. 7, reprinted 1981, Geneva: Droz, first published 1906.

Pareto, V. (1917), *Traité de sociologie générale*, in G. Busino (ed.), *Œuvres complètes de Pareto*, vol. 12, reprinted 1968, Geneva: Droz, first published 1916.

Parsons, T. (1934), 'Sociological elements in economic thought, I', *Quarterly Journal of Economics*, **49** (3), 414–53.

Parsons, T. (1934), 'Sociological elements in economic thought, II', *Quarterly Journal of Economics*, **49** (3), 645–67.

Parsons, T. and N.J. Smelser (1956), *Economy and Society. A Study in the Integration of Economic and Social Theory*, London: Routledge and Kegan.

Perroux, F. (1994), *Pouvoir et économie généralisée*, in R. Di Ruzza and P. Berthaud (eds), *Œuvres complètes*, vol. 5, Grenoble: Presses Universitaires de Grenoble.

Polanyi, K. (1944), *The Great Transformation. The Political and Economical Origins of Our Time*, reprinted 2001, Boston, MA: Beacon Press.

Polanyi, K. and C. Arensberg (1957), *Trade and Markets in the Early Empires. Economies in History and Theories*, New York: Free Press.

Rauch, J. and A. Casella (eds) (2001), *Network and Market*, New York: Russell Sage Foundations.

Schumpeter, J. (1954), *History of Economic Analysis*, London: George Allen and Unwin.

Shionoya, Y. (1995), *Joseph Schumpeter and the Idea of Social Science. A Metatheoretical Study*, Cambridge: Cambridge University Press.

Simiand, F. (1912), *La méthode positive en sciences économiques*, in F. Simiand (2006), *Critique de l'économie politique*, Paris: Presses Universitaires de France, pp. 31–144.

Simiand, F. (1932), *Le salaire, l'évolution sociale et la monnaie*, Paris: Alcan.

Smelser, N.J. and R. Swedberg (eds) (2005), *Handbook of Economic Sociology*, 2nd edn, Princeton, NJ: Princeton University Press.

Steiner, P. (1995), 'Pareto et le protectionnisme: l'économie pure, l'économie appliquée, et quelques paradoxes', *Revue économique*, **46** (5), 1241–63.

Steiner, P. (1998), *Sociologie de la connaissance économique. Essai sur les rationalisations de la connaissance économique (1750–1850)*, Paris: Presses Universitaires de France.

Steiner, P. (2011), *Durkheim and the Birth of Economic Sociology*, Princeton, NJ: Princeton University Press.

Steiner, P. and F. Vatin (eds) (2009), *Traité de sociologie économique*, Paris: Presses Universitaires de France.

Swedberg, R. (1990), *Economics and Sociology. Redefining their Boundaries: Conversations with Economists and Sociologists*, Princeton, NJ: Princeton University Press.

Swedberg, R. (1998), *Max Weber and the Idea of Economic Sociology*, Princeton, NJ: Princeton University Press.

Takata, Y. (1956), *An Introduction to Sociological Economics*, Economic Series, no. 13, Tokyo: The Science Council of Japan.

Uzzi, B. and R. Lancaster (2004), 'Embeddedness and price formation in the corporate law market', *American Sociological Review*, **69** (June), 319–44.

Weber, M. (1894), 'Stock and commodity exchange', trans. S. Lestition (2000), *Theory and Society*, **29** (3), 305–38.

Weber, M. (1920), *The Protestant Ethic and the "Spirit" of Capitalism*, reprinted 2002, London: Penguin Books.

Weber, M. (1922), *Economy and Society. An Outline of Interpretative Sociology*, reprinted 1980, Berkeley, CA: University of California Press.

White, H. (2002), *Markets from Network. Socioeconomic Models of Production*, Princeton, NJ: Princeton University Press.

Wieser, F. von (1914), *Social Economics*, reprinted 1967, New York: Kelley.

Williamson, O. (1981), 'The economics of organization: the transaction cost approach', *American Journal of Sociology*, **87** (3), 548–77.

Zelizer, V. (1979), *Markets and Morals. The Development of Life Insurance in the United States*, New York: Columbia University Press.

Zelizer, V. (1994), *The Social Meaning of Money*, New York: Basic Books.

Economics and philosophy

The man of system . . . is apt to be very wise in his own conceit; and is often so enamoured with the supposed beauty of his own ideal plan of government, that he cannot suffer the smallest deviation from any part of it. He goes on to establish it completely and in all its parts, without any regard either to the great interests, or to the strong prejudices which may oppose it. He seems to imagine that he can arrange the different members of a great society with as much ease as the hand arranges the different pieces upon a chess-board. He does not consider that the pieces upon the chess-board have no other principle of motion besides that which the hand impresses upon them; but that, in the great chess-board of human society, every single piece has a principle of motion of its own, altogether different from that which the legislature might chuse to impress upon it. If those two principles coincide and act in the same direction, the game of human society will go on easily and harmoniously, and is very likely to be happy and successful. If they are opposite or different, the game will go on miserably, and the society must be at all times in the highest degree of disorder. (Smith 1759 [1982]: 233–4)

Philosophers and economists alike tend to think of Adam Smith as the founding father of economics and of his *Wealth of Nations* as its founding document. Yet Adam Smith was a prescient critic of assuming rational *homo œconomicus* behaviour across the board, not a supporter of this explanatory strategy. The economic philosophy underlying neo-classical economics and the so-called economic imperialism that arose from it is Hobbesian rather than Smithian. It rests on and still expresses Thomas Hobbes's vision of a universal social theory that should, first, be unfolded by spelling out the implications of the *homo œconomicus* model "more geometrico" and, secondly, restrict normative argument and practical advice to pointing out means to the ("given") ends of its addressees.

The subsequent discussion of "economics and philosophy" starts by addressing the Hobbesian model of *homo œconomicus*. Rejecting the claim that empirically relevant insights can be derived "more geometrico" from "*homo œconomicus*" in an a priori way, it emphasizes that an evidence-based empirical account of human (inter-)action must be based on nomological knowledge of law-like regularities. The discussion will turn then to "economics as a discipline" and some surprisingly "Kantian" ideas of interpersonal respect that many economists seem to endorse. It will be argued that normative economics, nevertheless, has to restrict itself to the study of "technological relationships" (in the sense of Hans Albert 1985) based on nomological economic knowledge. Economic advice has to restrict itself to pointing out means to potential ends (Robbins 1935).

Neoclassical as Hobbesian Economics

Since the 1940s economics has been increasingly dominated by purely analytical concerns of a mathematical nature and a behavioural model akin to "*homo œconomicus*". At the same time it insisted on being an empirical science. Without being aware of it, neo-classical economics went back to the ideas of its true founding father, Thomas Hobbes.

The *homo œconomicus* in Hobbes

Interpreting the theory of Thomas Hobbes – in particular the core passages sections 10–13 of *Leviathan* (1651 [1968]) – as an extended effort to provide explanations for all social behaviour in terms of the *homo œconomicus* model is not an anachronistic ("hindsight-biased") projection of modern rational choice thinking. As the following citation shows, Spinoza's seventeenth-century "rational choice" interpretation of Hobbesian "economic philosophy" is strikingly modern:

> Now it is a universal law of human nature that no one ever neglects anything which he judges to be good, except with the hope of gaining a greater good, or from the fear of a greater evil; nor does anyone endure an evil except for the sake of avoiding a greater evil, or gaining a greater good. That is, everyone will, of two goods, choose that which he thinks the greatest; and of two evils, that which he thinks the least. I say advisedly that which he thinks the greatest or the least, for it does not necessarily follow that he judges right. This law is so deeply implanted in the human mind that it ought to be counted among the eternal truths and axioms.
>
> As a necessary consequence of the principle just enunciated, no one can honestly forego the right which he has over all things, and in general no one will abide by his promises, unless under the fear of a greater evil, or the hope of a greater good . . . Hence though men make promises with all the appearances of good faith, and agree that they will keep to their engagement, no one can absolutely rely on another man's promise unless there is something behind it. Everyone has by nature a right to act deceitfully, and to break his compacts, unless he be restrained by the hope of some greater good, or the fear of some greater evil. (Spinoza 1670 [1951]: 203–4)

As Spinoza clearly indicates, according to the Hobbesian model, actors will comply with (legal) norms if and only if the expected negative sanctions are even more costly than the expected "profitability" of violating the norm in the case at hand. That is, "people would act *economically*; when an opportunity of an advantage was presented to them they would take it" (Hicks 1979: 43, original emphasis). This conception of case-by-case opportunity taking behaviour has far reaching consequences. It gives rise to the so-called (Parsons 1968) "Hobbesian order problem" of explaining the existence and the workings of social/legal institutions solely in terms of opportunity taking individual behaviour. Economists believe that *homines œconomici* could create social order while other social theorists deny this.

According to the economic model a norm as such has never weight in the opportunity-seeking calculus of the individual. The "norm" is "announcing" future causal consequences of behaviour as triggered by it as a response. To the extent that the announcement is credible, it enters the expected value calculation of the individual when considering an action. Yet, beyond shaping the perception of likely ("predicted") future consequences, the information contained in a norm is irrelevant for the rational actor. As clearly stated already by Spinoza, the rational actor chooses exclusively in view of the expected causal negative or positive external consequences of each act taken separately. Neither falling under a rule nor the evaluative intention behind the rule matter when deciding on an act.

Fully rational actors are not intrinsically motivated by rules. Norms operate only as external and not as internal constraints on maximizing behaviour of rational Hobbesian (wo)men.

Rationality of strategists

The anti-speculative climate of the interwar period of the last century was quite hospitable to the Hobbesian focus on expected (observable) consequences of action. Within the broadly behaviourist framework of the time it appeared as a great achievement that economists could show that, independently of any intention to maximize, individual behaviour can be described "as if" maximizing a utility function. Provided that certain consistency and continuity axioms are fulfilled, an increasing function (monotone on the underlying implied ordering of the set on which it is defined) will summarily describe the choice-making of an actor who is rational in the sense of the axioms. In short, on sets of potential choices the function represents a rational individual's choice-behaviour. From any feasible set the individual will choose an alternative to which maximal utility is assigned. However, this choice takes place without the utility value of the function being among the reasons for making it.

Although the preceding characterization of "representative utility" is a banality, it is still frequently mixed up with (classical) "motivating utility". To prevent confusion, the absolutely central concept of modern representative utility deserves to be spelled out somewhat more formally: If for two choices, A, B, the (order representing) utility function u(.) assigns values such that the relation $u(A) < u(B)$ applies then this indicates that, whenever both A, B are present in a set of behavioural alternatives, A is not chosen from that set. The behaviour B is not shown because $u(B)$ is greater than $u(A)$. It is just the other way around. The expression $u(B) > u(A)$ is simply shorthand to inform about "predicted" choice behaviour. Yet it does not provide a reason or an explanation for that behaviour in terms of motives. In particular, modern utility u is not a measure of, say, pleasure or satisfaction. Maximization of u can be diagnosed from an external point of view but there is no motive, selfish or other, concerning "u" involved. Overt choice behaviour is only "as if" maximizing u but not brought about by an intention to maximize.

The representation of choice behaviour by a (representative) utility function was extended to choices among lotteries and many powerful representation theorems for risky choices could be proven (see, for example, von Neumann and Morgenstern 1944; Savage 1954). Expected value formation – that is, "linear" probability weighting – on the basis of utilities representing risk attitudes is viable without distorting the representation of choices among lotteries. Risk is included from the beginning by using a basic reference lottery ticket (BRLT), (see Raiffa 1968, on such BRLT) instead of the measuring rod of (risk-free) money to assign order-representing numbers.

Owing to the representation theorems the formal apparatus of expected value formation and "maximization under constraints" remains intact under the re-interpretation of the concept of "utility". The maximization under constraints approach of economists is not anymore restricted to those aspects of behaviour that are brought about by selfish pecuniary motives under the assumption of risk-neutrality. Provided that they fulfil certain consistency and continuity axioms, arbitrary motives and attitudes to risk can be represented such that behaviour can be described as if maximizing an expected value function "linear in probability". However, for valid explanations of real choice-making "as if" is not good enough. For empirical explanations some kind of causal rather than logical "if-then" is required.

If nomological regularities of motivational processes are used to explain choice-making, reliance on psychology seems unavoidable. Yet neo-classical economists try to avoid this by almost all means. Most of them resent any move away from *homo oeconomicus* or "rational expecting maximizing man" (see Meckling 1976) towards truly empirical science. This move is indeed subversive for their desire to derive insights "more geometrico" according to a "logic" – rather than a "psychology" – of action. Economists take to either "eductive" (mindful) or to "evolutionary" (mindless) game theoretically inspired a priori models (see, in particular, Binmore 1987, 1988).

Table 4   Battle of the sexes

She He	Boxing	Cinema
Boxing	(2, 1)	(0, 0)
Cinema	(0, 0)	(1, 2)

Mindful strategists

As one of the founding fathers of modern game theory, Oskar Morgenstern was interested in how theories about the world can conceivably influence the world. If, for instance, an economist predicts that the business cycle will turn towards growth, this may support that it will become true. More theoretically speaking, self-supporting theories can become commonly known without undermining their own "predictions". They are "absorbable" (see Morgenstern and Schwödiauer 1976; Dacey 1976; Morgenstern 1972).

Absorbability of a theory is a surprisingly strong requirement. To see why, imagine the most simple case of the classical "2 × 2" battle of the sexes (Table 4).

For instance, a "theory" of rational play that recommends that players should be heading for the option that may lead to the best possible result for them is not absorbable. According to such a theory's advice "He" should go to watch boxing and "She" should watch the film, but if the theory advice becomes known, both have good reason to deviate from it. That is, it cannot become commonly known that the "theory" implying the advice of "going for the best" is guiding actors without providing actors with reasons to deviate from the theory's guidance.

Although von Neumann and Morgenstern did not explicitly use the concept of a Cournot–Nash equilibrium, its central role was implied by their "reasoning about knowledge" approach to interactive-decision making (see Buchanan et al. 2001; Fagin et al. 1995; and for a comparison with homoeostatic classical conceptions of equilibrium, Walsh and Gram 1980). Their view had the advantage of giving a clear reason why "equilibria" are important: A theory recommending some sort of play as rational must pick equilibria if the type of rationality embodied in the theory is to become common knowledge and operative among the actors whose behaviour is captured and guided by the theory (see for this in a bounded rationality context, Güth and Kliemt 2004).

To the extent that the theory is meant to be presenting the "decision logic" rather than the "decision psychology" of choice, absorbability is the central coherence criterion. A Cournot–Nash equilibrium is present only if the interaction "generates messages which do not cause agents to change the theories which they hold or the policies which they pursue" (Hahn 1973: 59) However, this is not sufficient for deriving clear action guiding advice from the theory. In the standard fully symmetric 2 × 2 battle of the sexes game of Table 4, alternative theories, each suggesting a different equilibrium, could conceivably be absorbable.

For instance, a theory that would recommend the strategy combination leading to the result that the female player prefers most could as a matter of fact become common knowledge and could be observed by minimally rational individuals in view of their own payoffs. Yet, in this case, a theory is singled out by some contingent historical circumstance. It applies only to 2×2 games in which female players are present. It would not be universally applicable – not even to all 2×2 interactions. It cannot be commonly known rationality or decision logic per se that favour one theory of rational play over the other. An empirical fact is decisive where reason alone is insufficient.

As the preceding simple example already shows, there is no way to resolve strategic uncertainty in terms of rationality and reasoning alone. Common knowledge of rationality cannot serve as a sufficient "correlating signal" (see Aumann 1987). Some extra-rational clue – rendering one of the possible theories "focal" – is needed to coordinate successfully on a single equilibrium (see Sugden 1991, for this critique of Harsanyi and Selten 1988)).

To put it slightly differently, those who intend to engage the challenge of construct-ing theories only under the constraints of consistency and absorbability will not be able to solve the equilibrium selection problem "more geometrico". Even what is rational is in some sense contingent and dependent on something in the real world that cannot be inferred by reason alone but requires knowledge of facts that typically emerge in a "path dependent", contingent way from human practices. If mindful strategists cannot be guided by their reason alone, would a theory about mindless strategists (see Gul and Pesendorfer 2008) do any better?

Mindless strategists

In Hobbes's *Leviathan* the competition of individuals who can choose on the basis of a model of the situation and in view of the expected causal consequences of each act taken separately takes place under a scarcity constraint. Hobbesian "power" or "present means, to obtain some future apparent good" (Hobbes 1651 [1968]: first sentence of s. 10) under such a constraint is relative. It matters to have relatively more of it than com-petitors. Under certain conditions, only strategists who behave as if they were pursuing optimal plans will survive.

> The assumption that conduct is prompt and rational is in all cases a fiction. But it proves sufficiently near to reality, if things have time to hammer logic into men. Where this has hap-pened, and within the limits it has happened, one may rest content with this fiction and build theories upon it . . . and we can depend upon it that the peasant sells his calf just as cunningly and egoistically as the stock exchange member his portfolio of shares. But this holds good only where precedents without number have formed conduct through decades and, in fundamentals, through hundreds and thousands of years, and have eliminated unadapted behavior. Outside of these limits our fiction loses its closeness to reality. (Schumpeter 1959: 80)

Armen Alchian (1950), in an argument concerning firms competing on "open markets", argued in the same vein. Only "well-adapted" firms would survive in a (suitably speci-fied) competitive process. Their behaviour would look like that of a "corporate" *homo oeconomicus* since, firstly, better than choosing optimally is impossible, secondly, the factual evolutionary process will, under certain conditions, weed out less than optimal behaviour and therefore, thirdly, whenever the conditions are met, selection will generate the behaviour that would have been generated by a fully rational corporate *homo oeco-nomicus* (see in detail Gintis 2000).

Arguments like those of Schumpeter and Alchian raise, however, a foundational problem stated with exemplary clarity by Robert Aumann:

> When there is a formal relationship between two interpretations, like the rationalistic conscious maximization and evolutionary interpretations of Nash equilibrium, then one can say, "Oh, this is an accident, these things really have nothing to do with each other." Or, one can look for a deeper meaning. In my view, it's a mistake to write off the relationship as an accident. (Aumann, 1998: 192)

Philosophically we should indeed seek for the deeper meaning envisioned by Aumann. This is a central philosophical question concerning the "make up" of the (economic) world. Yet, even if we could find such a deeper philosophical meaning it would not reinstate the *homo oeconomicus* model in its explanatory role. For, even then it would not be the model of *homo œconomicus* that explains phenomena. Quite on the contrary, the fact that behaviour is "as if maximizing" is explained on some ultimate level. We encounter an explanandum (something to be explained) rather than being provided with an explanans (something that explains).

Towards Behavioural Economics

Although the (cognitive) psychologist Daniel Kahneman was awarded the Sveriges Riksbank Prize in Economic Sciences in Memory of Alfred Nobel, this does not mean that modern economics has turned into a special branch of cognitive psychology. Economists still insist on starting with representations of overt choice behaviour (or preferences) rather than concepts that explain what brought these choices (or preferences) about. Although economics would gain in empirical content and validity by re-introducing the mind as an "order-imposing organ", a move towards cognitive psychology is not the path neo-classical economics has taken. Neo-classical economists love the peace of doing a priori behavioural geometry in their armchair better than the trench war of gathering empirical evidence.

Economics as "logic" of rational behaviour
The Cowles Commission series of books that defined the paradigm of modern neo-classical economics unwillingly paved the way for upholding the claim to analytical truth and empirical validity at the same time. Despite the fact that many of the Cowles Commission series of texts were written in the Bourbaki style of mathematical formalism, the books were understood to be claiming to present self-evident truths about the real world. To name just two prominent examples, the papers in *Activity Analysis of Production and Allocation* edited by Tjalling C. Koopmans (1951) or Gérard Debreu's (1959) *Theory of Value* were interpreted by neo-classical economists as theories about the world, that is, they were not treated as examples of mathematical formalism but, in the spirit of classical Euclidean geometry, as expressing undeniable truths about the real world.

In this regard, modern economists repeated the philosophical blunder of Hobbes and philosophical rationalists who also believed that they could make empirical claims for theories developed "more geometrico". Only an empirical turn of economics away from a rationalist Hobbesian "logic" ("*Entscheidungslogik*") to an empiricist social psychology of decision-making in interactive situations ("*Marktsoziologie*") can heal this deficiency (see Albert 1967 [1998]).

Nomological hypotheses about real economic behaviour can, of course, be represented by systems of axioms that can then be studied analytically with logical and mathematical methods. However, the truth of such theories that make a nomological claim is tested (a posteriori) through their implications rather than justifying the implications by the (a priori) truth of the axioms.

As far as this is concerned the practice of neo-classical economic theory is still much closer to the older Hobbesian/Euclidean tradition of reasoning more geometrico than to modern empirical science. That the misconceived ideals of behavioural geometry linger on to the present day is mostly due to the fact that economics is still conceived as dealing with a normative conception of "rational" behaviour rather than with empirical behaviour per se.

Economics as psychology of rational behaviour

Whatever is used as a criterion to classify behaviour as "rational", it must be distinguished between (1) substantive rationality of (the results of) choice making as observed from an outside observer's ("external") point of view; and (2) procedural rationality from the ("internal") point of view of the choice-making entity.

1. The first point of view broadly corresponds to that of a behaviourist psychologist who observes how rats in a maze respond to various stimuli. Along these lines, economists have studied adaptive behaviour of animals in broadly speaking micro-economic settings (see Kagel 1995). In such studies, the utility functions can, under certain minimum conditions of consistency, represent the choices that individuals are assumed to make from choice sets. Actors – rats, men, corporate actors and so on – frequently behave as if maximizing.

    For the reasons indicated above, it is a mistake to drop the "as if" condition and to transfer the external description to motives in the internal mental model of the actor without a nomological theory justifying this move. Motives can be ascribed on the basis of overt behaviour only as theoretical terms of some underlying empirical theory of cognitive processes. The theory must link behaviour and motives by nomological hypotheses. The form of the utility function representing observed behaviour must be explained by the theory as well. Unless such a theory is presented the common practice of economists to put all sorts of concerns into the utility functions – "to make them more realistic" – remains "ad hoc". Without systematically testing theories justifying such inclusions it is but another variant of "revelations" that are supported merely by plausibility. A possible remedy emerges if we leave the "mindless economy" and go from substantive to procedural accounts of rational choice making.

2. In the second, procedural, sense (minimally) rational actors choose on the basis of some mental model of the action situation. In forming such a model, rational actors will try to distinguish between what is and what is not subject to the causal influence they can exert through choices they make (see Kliemt 2009). Against the background of the distinction between what is and what is not subject to the causal influence of the acting entity, there are two ways to come to terms with stronger rationality requirements.

    (a) Choice makers can rank states of the world along several value dimensions (according to desires and so on). Taken separately, these dimensions rank the states of the world to be influenced by choices. If this kind of evaluation allows for aggregation (corresponding to the formation of a decathlon table on the basis of its ten performance measures), an overall function comprising all dimensions of value may possibly be formed (see MacKay 1980). Then the choice maker might be seen as a person who seeks to make choices that will maximize the value of that aggregate function intentionally (see Broome 1991). This will come very close to the classical utilitarian model that assumed that humans would not merely behave as if maximizing a function but would indeed be guided by the intention to act such as to maximally fulfil their desires and some value criterion like, say, "aggregate happiness".

(b)   One might want to avoid the assumption that there is a maximand guiding intentional action. Individuals who do not intend to maximize nevertheless evaluate the expected consequences of possible choices and have certain aspirations that they want to fulfil (see Simon 1957). They intentionally satisfy aspirations rather than intentionally maximizing value. A theory of boundedly rational economic behaviour that does away with the necessity to describe behaviour as if maximizing could conceivably emerge from this move.

To explicate what the attribute "rational" – as an evaluative term – in the context of the two competing forms of procedural rationality – "2(a)" intentional maximization and "2(b)" intentional satisficing – means, it will be unavoidable to evaluate the results of the procedures. This evaluation will in the end have to have some relationship to the substantive success of those who act according to the evaluated processes or procedures. As in the Alchian argument cited above, the bottom line will provide an ultimate evaluation in terms of success and survival of the proximate causes of action.

More concretely, if actors guided by, say, a decision support procedure conforming with alternative "2(a)" would "on average" be substantively better off compared with actors who decide according to some decision support procedure corresponding to "2(b)", then this would count as an argument in favour of procedure "2(a)". However, even though this comes rather close to providing a tentative answer to Aumann's question it does not explicate rationality fully in substantive terms. Substantive criteria on the ultimate level do not translate into substantive criteria on the proximate level of behaviour. On the contrary, behavioural procedures that are proximately neither maximizing nor satisficing may ultimately be the most successful and in that sense substantively rational.

The Disciplines of Economics

Hume described the aim of his path-breaking *A Treatise of Human Nature* as "being an attempt to introduce the experimental method of reasoning into moral subjects" (see Hume 1739 [1978] subtitle). As used by Hume the term "experimental" should not be interpreted in the sense of controlled experiments but more broadly in the sense of "experiental" or "experience based".

Economics is a "moral science" to the extent that it is experiental. However, what kind of experience matters and how this experience itself is constituted is open.

Economics as "moral science"

In the introduction of his *Treatise on Human Nature* (1739 [1978]: xv f.) Hume states:

> 'Tis evident, that all the sciences have a relation, greater or less, to human nature; and that however wide any of them may seem to run from it, they still return back by one passage or another. . . .
>
> Here then is the only expedient, from which we can hope for success in our philosophical researches, to leave the tedious lingering method, which we have hitherto followed, and instead of taking now and then a castle or village on the frontier, to march up directly to the capital or center of these sciences, to human nature itself; which being once masters of, we may every where else hope for an easy victory. From this station we may extend our conquests over all those sciences, which more intimately concern human life, and may afterwards proceed at leisure to discover more fully those, which are the objects of pure curiosity. There is no question of importance, whose decision is not compriz'd in the science of man; and there is none, which can be decided with any certainty, before we become acquainted with that science. In pretending, therefore, to explain the principles of human nature, we in effect propose a compleat system of the sciences, built on a foundation almost entirely new, and the only one upon which they can stand with any security.

This passage exhibits certain similarities with Kant's Copernican turn towards the knowing subject. However, the "moral science" Hume envisions is devoid of Kant's claims to a priori knowledge. Its epistemology is broadly speaking a sub-discipline of the psychology of knowledge. Likewise Hume translates the "logic of inter-active choice making" into a specific type of social-institutional psychology. Yet, much of what economists actually do is a far cry of the fact finding and hypothesis-testing mission of empirical science. Practical concerns of making the world a better place seem to play a much greater role in economics than in natural sciences. Beyond experiments (field and laboratory), econometric studies (including their focus on identifying causal factors), the new economic history and so on, economics addresses basic normative concerns as in welfare economics.

Economics as political theory

For instance, the modern welfare economic focus on Pareto improvements does not make sense within a Hobbesian means to ends framework. Hobbesians who seek means to pursue their own ends have good reason to impose their own values on others if they can. If they can get their way only if others are interested in it as well, they have a good reason to bring together a sufficiently powerful winning coalition. Yet they cannot have other rational reasons than prudential ones to restrain themselves from searching for Pareto improvements. Only if all individuals can, as a matter of fact, block change will Hobbesian/Robbinsian normative economists have a reason to suggest that they behave as if Kantian.

Kantian political economy

The welfare economic focus on Pareto improvements indicates that economists hesitate to endorse the Hobbesian ruthlessness of a true *homo oeconomicus* who is treating the whole environment including other human persons as means to ends. A deep philosophical concern with human autonomy and norms of interpersonal respect seems built into economics as a practical discipline. For instance, in his 1956 United Nations Educational, Scientific, and Cultural Organization (UNESCO) report on the state of economic science in America, Rutledge Vining stated:

To require of each individual that he takes no action which impairs the freedom of any other individual is to accept the moral principle that no individual should treat another simply as means to an end. Each individual chooses the rules and principles for the guidance of his conduct, but he does so under the general principle that no rule of action will be adopted which could not be universally adopted by all individuals. In deciding whether an action is compatible with the assumption of freedom for all, he will apply a test to the rule which would call for this action under the contemplated conditions, asking, not how the rule will work from the point of view of his own personal interests, but how the rule will work if all individuals adopted it as a principle of action. (Vining 1956: 19)

The norms of Kantian interpersonal respect expressed in this citation are incompatible with the "Hobbesianism" of neo-classical economics. While Lionel Robbins's *Essay on the Nature and Significance of Economic Science* (1935) seems to suggest that the Hobbesian view on the limits of rational normative argument is endorsed by modern economics, Vining's statement seems to indicate just the opposite.

Of course, you could dismiss the preceding quote and the views expressed in it as the personal opinion of Vining. Yet this would be a mistake. Owing to, rather than despite, their own scepticism concerning the epistemic status of value judgements (that is, their status as knowledge claims beyond means to given ends arguments), economists have always been and still are psychologically inclined to respect plural values (if for the wrong reasons of the impossibility of making inter-personal comparisons) and to regard this kind of interpersonal respect as constitutive for their discipline.

Most economists understand that the substantial respect-norm expressed by Vining is not a logical conclusion of value scepticism. After all, if all inter-subjectively accessible value judgements are hypothetical imperatives concerning prudent choices of means to given ends, showing Kantian respect is justified for the addressee of the justification only if this furthers aims, ends or values he or she as a matter of fact endorses (if you intend to achieve x you should do y since we know that – empirically speaking – y will enhance the probability of x). Using somebody as a means to one's own ends will be commendable if this, as a matter of fact, is the course of action most suitable to reaching the ends of the actor.

Vice versa, economists who reflect on the matter also understand that the claim to objective knowledge of value judgements does not "logically" entail the desire to impose what is held to be "objectively" right on others. For, on the one hand, claims to knowledge of values will be as prone to error as claims to knowledge of facts – which suggests allowing for competing views in search of truth, and, on the other hand, even a "value sceptical" economist can understand that a Kantian can believe to know that tolerance is morally right. Indeed, the norm to respect other individuals as ends in themselves is regarded by Kantians as part and parcel of the objective a priori normative knowledge supported by the categorical imperative.

In short, neither tolerance nor intolerance have any "logical" relation to knowledge claims concerning value judgements. Yet, if norms of interpersonal respect cannot be justified without going beyond the officially accepted limits to legitimate normative economic argument as formulated in their canonical form by Robbins, this leaves the focus on Pareto dangling in the air. This lack of a "logical foundation" does, of course, not rule out psychological relations between meta-ethical or meta-normative and substantive normative claims.

Within the meta-ethical position that is regarded as constitutive for economics, at least since Robbins's (1935) essay on "the nature and significance of economic science", it is not the task of the economist to tell people what they should desire. An advice-giving economist has to respect whatever his or her advisees desire. He or she can rationally tell advisees how, but not that, they should reach certain aims, ends or values.

Economics as study of catallaxy

It seems that some economists believe that rational individuals must conceive of themselves as living in a world of "Crusoes" who all pursue what they desire "against" other "Crusoes" rather than as part of a community of individuals. Then, according to the Hobbesian hypothetical "means to given ends" imperatives, rational individuals should treat other individuals always as means and not as "purposes in themselves". However, it should be noted well that this imperative of prudent behaviour is based on an empirical thesis about which ways of world making as a matter of fact prevail among humans. As a matter of fact human actors need not conceive of their interaction with other human actors as a so-called game against nature. The presence of human minds who are aware of the presence of other human minds may be "a game changer" (see more extensively Kliemt 2009).

Perhaps, humans naturally perceive themselves as not involved in a game against other "parts of nature" but rather as "members of a community of rational beings" who look at the world primarily in terms of mutual rather than of their unilateral advantage.

> Man might be defined, "An animal that makes *Exchanges*": no other, even of those animals which in other points make the nearest approach to rationality, having, to all appearance, the least notion of bartering, or in any way exchanging one thing for another. . . . For, the *things* themselves of which the science treats, are immediately removed from its province, if we remove the possibility, or the intention, of making them the subjects of exchange; and this, though they may conduce, in the highest degree, to happiness, which is the ultimate object for the sake of which wealth is sought. A man, for instance, in a desert island, like Alex. Selkirke, or the personage his adventures are supposed to have suggested, Robinson Crusoe, is in a situation of which Political-Economy takes no cognizance; though he might figuratively be called rich, if abundantly provided with food, raiment, and various comforts; and though he might have many commodities at hand, which would *become* exchangeable, and would constitute him, strictly speaking, rich, as soon as fresh settlers should arrive. (Whately 1831: 7–10, original emphases)

The Sveriges Riksbank Prize in Memory of Alfred Nobel laureate, James M. Buchanan (like Rutledge Vining, student of Frank Knight) has been, arguably, the most prominent modern economist endorsing the norm that economists should restrict their policy advice to what furthers mutual advantage (as opposed to getting their way). In his essay on "what economists should do", Buchanan (acknowledging Whately) says:

> Crusoe's problem is, as I have said, essentially a computational one, and all that he needs to do to solve it is to program the built-in computer that he has in his mind. The uniquely symbiotic aspects of behavior, of human choice, arise only when Friday steps on the island, and Crusoe is forced into *association* with another human being. The fact of association requires that a wholly different, . . . behavior take place, that of "exchange", "trade", or "agreement". Crusoe may, of course, fail to recognize this new fact. He may treat Friday simply as a means to his own ends, as a part of "nature", so to speak. (Buchanan 1985: 35, original emphasis)

Crusoe, after the arrival of Friday, should and as a rule will perceive of interaction with another human being in terms other than those he would apply to the interaction with a distant relation in the animal kingdom like a chimpanzee. Crusoe would adopt what the philosopher Frederick Strawson (see Strawson 1962) called a participant's point of view to the interaction with Friday. He would therefore naturally be inclined to perceive the interaction in an other-respecting way (see MacKabe et al. 2001 for experimental evidence on the empirical presence of the participant's point of view in the human psyche).

The nature and significance as an advice-giving, as a prudentially prescribing rather than merely describing, discipline are deeply influenced by non-Hobbesian background intuitions concerning a community of rational beings. That economists such as, in particular, Buchanan think that economists should regard such a framing of interaction as constitutive for their discipline may on the whole be a good thing. Yet it must be clearly admitted that the restriction of (constitutional political economy) policy advice by universalistic – contractarian – principles of mutual respect, mutual agreement and mutual advantage is based on a value judgement itself (see on mutualism as an ethical principle, Hazlitt 1964).

To promote some conception of general rather than particular interests is in itself expressive of an ethical rather than an epistemic ideal. As long as it is clearly understood that the underlying value judgement does not influence what is regarded as a fact but only fixes which kind of questions are asked in a regular fact-finding mission, it is as innocuous a value judgement as can be found in any discipline. It determines which kinds of social technologies – namely, those involving mutual advantage – are explored. It is not by chance that Buchanan was also a driving force of the non-normative public choice movement that tried to understand the actual workings of politics in the Hobbesian/Robbinsian tradition. It should, however, also be acknowledged that Buchanan himself rather unashamedly and rightly saw himself as being a contractarian ally of John Rawls.

Conclusion

There seems a much stronger philosophical streak in economics than in many other fields of social theory. This may in part be due to the fact that economics is still in the process of preparing fields of inquiry to treatment by specialized disciplines (see on this, Schlick 1986). This philosophical process within economics may lead to yet unforeseeable results. However, it seems clear that empirical psychology and experimental science – including experimental economics in particular – are incompatible with a priori conceptions of how rational individual behaviour must be modelled and understood. Yet it seems almost inconceivable that the neo-classical insistence on "explaining" human behaviour in terms of ("as if") maximizing some objective function under constraints will survive. Even though it is nowadays still a prevalent selection criterion of leading economic journals that papers submitted to them do endorse this aspect of the Hobbesian rational choice framework, it is empirically bordering on the absurd.

The foundational controversy concerning the maximization framework needs no further comment here since what may be called the "experiential turn" of modern economics will take care of it anyway. This turn is exactly what David Hume would have required had he ever been specifically asked about economics as a specialized domain of enquiry.

Economists who accept basic insights of empiricist philosophy of science should at least most of their time go on with empirical work relying on "everything from experiments to econometrics". At the same time economists should also be aware that the practice of economics as a discipline contains many aspects that are, properly speaking, economic and moral philosophy rather than empirical fact finding.

The writings that come out of the, strictly speaking, non-science activities of economists are legitimate as long as they do not blur the distinction between what has and what has not the backing of empirical or analytical scientific argument. To accomplish this, economists should be much clearer about what they are doing. They should indicate when they are acting as philosophers, when as analytical scientists, when as empiricists. They also might want to stop spreading confusion about the status of basic concepts like that of a utility function, maximization and Pareto efficiency. This being said, for the philosophical enterprise of exploring the limits and powers of means to given ends rationality, economic and in particular game and decision-theoretic insights remain invaluable. In this regard economists have been the leading practical philosophers ever since economics split off from philosophy in the nineteenth century.

HARTMUT KLIEMT

See also:

James M. Buchanan (I); Game theory (III); Political philosophy and economics: freedom and labour (III); Public choice (II); Scottish Enlightenment (II); Social choice (III).

References and further reading

Albert, H. (1967), *Marktsoziologie und Entscheidungslogik. Zur Kritik der reinen Ökonomik*, reprinted 1998, Tübingen: Mohr.
Albert, H. (1985), *Treatise on Critical Reason*, Princeton, NJ: Princeton University Press.
Alchian, A.A. (1950), 'Uncertainty, evolution, and economic theory', *Journal of Political Economy*, **58**, 211–21.
Aumann, R.J. (1987), 'Correlated equilibrium as an expression of Bayesian rationality'. *Econometrica*, **55** (1), 1–18.
Aumann, R. (1998), 'On the state of the art in game theory: interviewer Eric van Damme', *Games and Economic Behavior*, **24**, 181–210.
Binmore, K. (1987), 'Modeling rational players: part I', *Economics and Philosophy*, **3** (2), 179–214.
Binmore, K. (1988), 'Modeling rational players: part II', *Economics and Philosophy*, **4** (1), 9–55.
Broome, J. (1991), *Weighing Goods. Equality, Uncertainty and Time*, Oxford: Basil Blackwell.
Buchanan, J.M. (1985), *What Should Economists Do?*, Indianapolis, IN: Liberty Fund.
Buchanan, J.M., W. Güth, H. Kliemt, G. Schwödiauer and R. Selten (2001), *John von Neumanns und Oskar Morgensterns "Theory of Games and Economic Behavior"*, Düsseldorf: Verlag die Wirtschaft.
Dacey, R. (1976), 'Theory absorption and the testability of economic theory', *Zeitschrift für Nationalökonomie*, **36** (3–4), 247–67.
Debreu, G. (1959), *The Theory of Value: An Axiomatic Analysis Of Economic Equilibrium*, Cowles Commission Monograph 17, New Haven, CT.
Fagin, R., J.Y. Halpern, Y. Moses and M.Y. Vardi (1995), *Reasoning About Knowledge*, Cambridge, MA and London: MIT Press.
Gintis, H. (2000), *Game Theory Evolving*, Princeton, NJ: Princeton University Press.
Güth, W. and H. Kliemt (2004), 'Bounded rationality and theory absorption', *Homo Oeconomicus*, **21** (3–4), 521–40.
Gul, F. and W. Pesendorfer (2008), 'The case for mindless economics', in A. Caplin and A. Schotter (eds), *The Foundations of Positive and Normative Economics: A Handbook*, Oxford; New York: Oxford University Press, pp. 3–43.
Hahn, F. (1973), *On the Notion of Equilibrium in Economics*, Cambridge: Cambridge University Press.
Harsanyi, J.C. and R.A. Selten (1988), *General Theory of Equilibrium Selection in Games*, Cambridge, MA: MIT Press.
Hazlitt, H. (1964), *The Foundations of Morality*, Princeton, NJ: University Press of America.

Hicks, J. (1979), *Causality in Economics*, Oxford: Blackwell.
Hobbes, T. (1651), *Leviathan*, reprinted 1968, Harmondsworth: Penguin.
Hume, D. (1739), *A Treatise of Human Nature*, reprinted 1978, Oxford: Clarendon.
Kagel, J.H. (1995), *Economic Choice Theory: An Experimental Analysis of Animal Behavior*, Cambridge: Cambridge University Press.
Kliemt, H. (2009), *Philosophy and Economics I*, Munich: Oldenbourg.
Koopmans, T.C. (1951), *Activity Analysis of Production and Allocation*, Cowles Commission Monograph 13, New Haven, CT.
MacKay, A.F. (1980), *Arrow's Theorem. The Paradox of Social Choice. A Case Study in the Philosophy of Economics*, New Haven, CT.
McCabe, K., D. Houser, L. Ryan, V. Smith and T. Trouard (2001), 'A functional imaging study of cooperation in two-person reciprocal exchange', *Proceedings of the National Academy of Sciences*, **98** (20), 11832–5, doi:10.1073/pnas.211415698.
Meckling, W. (1976), 'Values and the choice of the model of the individual in the social sciences', *Schweizerische Zeitschrift für Volkswirtschaft und Statistik*, **112** (4), 545–65.
Morgenstern, O. (1972), 'Descriptive, predictive and normative theory', *Kyklos*, **25**, 699–714.
Morgenstern, O. and G. Schwödiauer (1976), 'Competition and collusion in bilateral markets', *Zeitschrift für Nationalökonomie*, **36** (3–4), 217–45.
Neumann, J. von and O. Morgenstern (1944), *Theory of Games and Economic Behavior*, Princeton, NJ: Princeton University Press.
Parsons, T. (1968), 'Utilitarianism: sociological thought', in D. Sils and R.K. Merton (eds), *International Encyclopedia of Social Sciences*, New York and London.
Raiffa, H. (1968), *Decision Analysis*, Boston, MA: Addison-Wesley.
Robbins, L. (1935), *An Essay on the Nature and Significance of Economic Science*, London: Macmillan.
Savage, L. (1954), *The Foundations of Statistics*, New York: Dover.
Schlick, M. (1986), *Die Probleme der Philosophie in ihrem Zusammenhang*, Frankfurt: Suhrkamp Verlag.
Schumpeter, J.A. (1959), *The Theory of Economic Development*, Cambridge, MA: Harvard University Press.
Simon, H.A. (1957), *Models of Man*, New York: John Wiley and Sons.
Smith, A. (1759), *The Theory of Moral Sentiments*, in D.D. Raphael and A.L. Macfie (eds), *The Glasgow Edition of the Works and Correspondence of Adam Smith*, reprinted 1982, Indianapolis, IN: Liberty Classics.
Smith, A. (1776), *An Inquiry into the Nature and Causes of the Wealth of Nations*, vol. 1, Indianapolis, IN: Liberty Press.
Spinoza, B. de (1670), *A Theologico-Political Treatise. A Political Treatise*, reprinted 1951, New York: Dover.
Strawson, P.F. (1962), 'Freedom and resentment', *Proceedings of the British Academy*, **48**, 187–211.
Sugden, R. (1991), 'Rational choice: a survey of contributions from economics and philosophy', *The Economic Journal*, **101** (7), 751–85.
Vining, R. (1956), *Economics in the United States of America. A Review and Interpretation of Research*, Paris: UNESCO.
Walsh, V. and H. Gram (1980), *Classical and Neoclassical Theories of General Equilibrium*, Oxford: Oxford University Press.
Whately, R. (1832), *Introductory Lectures on Political Economy*, delivered in Easter Term, 2nd and enlarged edn, London: B. Fellowes.

Evolutionary economics

The last three decades have seen an upsurge in the number of publications addressing themes that have come to be grouped under the heading of "evolutionary economics", paralleled by the foundation of new journals and new scientific societies devoted to the subject matter. It was a great moment for the science of economics, and for evolutionary economics in particular, when *An Evolutionary Theory of Economic Change* was published, in 1982, by Richard R. Nelson and Sidney G. Winter – a work that served as an icebreaker and, arguably, gave the early stages their critical momentum.

In a recent bibliometric account comprising the abstracts of articles published in all economic journals over the past half-century, Sandra Silva and Aurora Teixeira have been documenting the impressive magnitudes and structural dynamic of this trend – a trend that has accelerated tremendously in the last two decades, considering that 90 per cent of this body of research is recorded as having been published since 1990 (Silva and Teixeira 2009).

The aim of this entry is to present evolutionary economics as a particular school of thought. To this end, it is necessary to keep the analysis general enough to highlight the major differences from other schools of thought, but it is also necessary to frame the general exposition in such a way that it allows the main lines of current research to be accommodated systematically. Inevitably, the choice of general exposition can be expected to differ substantially from author to author, and as a consequence any choice of research fields and works is bound to be subjective.

The best approach in these circumstances is to follow the Popperian postulate of falsification and to make the premises upon which the choice of exposition and of research fields is based as explicit as possible. Specifically, this entry proposes that (evolutionary) economics should be conceived of as rule-based economics.

Turning to the particular sources used, the discussion of ontological foundations draws on Dopfer (2005), as does that about rule taxonomy and the architecture of micro–meso–macro, which also draws on Dopfer and Potts (2008) and Dopfer et al. (2004). All scientific thinking and advance rests on the shoulders of giants, as Newton has remarked famously, which in the present case suggests referring to – as major pioneers of an evolutionary approach to economics – Thorstein B. Veblen, Joseph A. Schumpeter, Alfred Marshall, and Friedrich August von Hayek.

Realism of Perception

It was Veblen (1898) who introduced the term "evolutionary economics" into the discipline, and he did so in recognition of the fundamental fact that the nature of the modern economy may be captured most adequately by referring to its dynamics (1909: 621): "To the modern scientist the phenomena of growth and change are the most obtrusive and most consequential facts observable in economic life. For an understanding of modern economic life the technological advance of the past two centuries – e.g., the growth of the industrial arts – is of the first importance." Turning to "neoclassical" economics, as he called it, Veblen continues: "but marginal utility theory does not bear on this matter, nor does this matter bear on marginal utility theory" (ibid.).

Although Joseph Schumpeter's theoretical work differed from Veblen's in fundamental ways, the two pioneers of the evolutionary school found themselves in entire agreement when it came to the recognition that continual change is the hallmark of modern capitalism. As Schumpeter (1942 [1976]: 82) puts it, "Capitalism . . . is by nature a form or method of economic change and not only never is but never can be stationary".

The engine of the system of "restless capitalism" (to use Stanley Metcalfe's felicitous phrase) is the energetic-dynamic entrepreneur, who carries out new combinations in every province of the economy. Schumpeter designates the entrepreneur as the dynamic alter ego of Vilfredo Pareto's static *Homo oeconomicus*. He portrays the particular functions of this agent in his *Theory of Economic Development* (Schumpeter 1912 [1934]), and describes their withering away in the managerial large-scale enterprise of late capitalism in his *Capitalism, Socialism and Democracy* (1942). The institutional conditions of the engine of change of modern capitalism have seen a number of metamorphoses, but at no time in its historical course has its engine come to a halt.

There is a distinct difference between the kind of dynamics at work in a traditional system and that in a modern one. Change may well occur in the former on account of altered external factors and data, but this does not represent the evolutionary change that is characteristic of modern capitalism; see Schumpeter (1942 [1976]: 82–3).

Schumpeter did not consider extant neoclassical theory to be deficient in its treatment of static (non-changing) aspects – in fact, he went so far as to praise Léon Walras's static equilibrium theory as the magna carta of the discipline – but, rather, that it lacked a dynamic element (Schumpeter 1908: 182–3).

Schumpeter was well aware that a theoretical programme dealing with dynamic issues would encounter major conceptual and methodological challenges, for which statics could not provide any answers (1908: 183): "Statics and Dynamics are completely different fields; they concern not only different problems but also different methods and different materials".

Alfred Marshall, another heroic member of the "hall of fame" of the evolutionary school, shared Veblen's and Schumpeter's fundamental perceptions about modern capitalism. He too acknowledged the fact that change – continuous, novelty-driven, qualitative and structural change – was the distinctive feature of the modern regime. Arguably, however, he was more reluctant than Schumpeter to make compromises when it came to method and formalisation and, in general, to the use of technique. Schumpeter (1997: 93, 101) emphasises Marshall's pioneering contribution to the understanding of the dynamic nature of modern capitalism:

> Marshall was one of the first economists to realize that economics is an evolutionary science. . ., in particular that the human nature he professed to deal with is malleable and changing, a function of changing environments. . . . His thought ran in terms of evolutionary change – in terms of organic, irreversible process.

Marshall emphasises repeatedly in his works the endogenous dynamics of modern capitalism. Like Schumpeter, he considered change not simply as an alteration of quantitative data or of external influences but, rather, as a history-dependent process of "organic growth" (Marshall, 1898: 42–3).

To Marshall, the nature of this process was very similar to the ideal found in modern evolutionary biology, eschewing that of classical mechanics – a position well epitomised in the familiar passage in the foreword to the eighth edition of his *Principles* (1920

[1972]: xii): "The Mecca of the economist lies in economic biology rather than in economic dynamics". However, Marshall saw formidable hurdles in the way of actually undertaking the journey to Mecca:

> But biological conceptions are more complex than those of mechanics . . . This fact, combined with the predominant attention paid in the present volume to the normal conditions of life in the modern age, has suggested the notion that its central idea is "statical", rather than "dynamical". But in fact it is concerned throughout with the forces that cause movement: and its key-note is that of dynamics, rather than statics. (Ibid.)

The work of Marshall – more than that of any other pioneer of the evolutionary approach – demonstrates the conflicting priorities between realism and method. Schumpeter's (1997) appraisal of Marshall's work is itself a portrayal of this difficult journey, which alternates between statics, in honouring the demands of method, and dynamics, in satisfying those of realism given the ever-changing nature of the system.

This difficult course, alternating between the conflicting demands of method and of realism, has characterised much of the history of theory formulation in evolutionary economics right from its very inception.

Finally, there is Friedrich Hayek's contribution as the fourth pillar of the exegetically construed edifice of evolutionary economics. He saw the essence of the modern market economy in the distinctive complexity and accelerated evolution of knowledge. For him, the European Enlightenment of the seventeenth and eighteenth centuries had not only changed the meaning and the significance of human knowledge for society at large, it had also altered radically the conditions in which the economy in particular operated. Hayek rejected a deterministic notion of societal or economic development and instead held the view of a future-open development, informed by the vision of what Adam Smith has called "the Great Society" and Karl Popper "the Open Society" (Hayek 1973: 2). All the theoretical concepts that Hayek went on to develop in great detail may be traced back to his realisation of the significance of knowledge. Synchronically, market order shows up as a problem of coordinating divided knowledge; diachronically, economic evolution originates with a process of growth and of complexification of knowledge.

Hayek's emphasis on the role of knowledge in the process of coordination brought him, inevitably and naturally, into opposition to the mainstream doctrine, which largely neglects knowledge (Hayek 1945: 532):

> Clearly there is here a problem of the division of knowledge, which is quite analogous to, and at least as important as, the problem of the division of labour. But, while the latter has been one of the main subjects of investigation ever since the beginning of our science, the former has been as completely neglected, although it seems to me to be the really central problem of economics as a social science.

The knowledge problem is "central", embracing not only the particular provinces of price theory but also, more generally, the way in which the different commodities are obtained and used (ibid.: 532).

There is, therefore, a "narrow" aspect to knowledge, referring to current prices or price expectations, and a "wider" aspect, referring to knowledge about the generation and use of the knowledge upon which price formation is based. Generally, there is knowledge that pertains to the knowhow required to perform economic operations, on the one hand, and factual knowledge that relates to an understanding of the circumstances of the environment in which operations are performed, on the other. The former may be called generic knowledge and the latter operant knowledge – a distinction that is at the core of the theoretical exposition to be introduced subsequently.

The evolution of the knowledge that governs economic operations and outcomes works out in a process in which, first, "knowledge bits" originate in a group and, subsequently, those variants that have a selective advantage are retained. The evolutionary course of knowledge follows the logic of a Darwinian trajectory – specified in biology by the phases of mutation, selection and retention (Hayek 1973). Hayek joins in the chorus with Veblen, Marshall and other proponents of an evolutionary approach in advocating biology rather than mechanics as the economist's Mecca.

In Hayek's theoretical efforts to specify the notion of knowledge, the concept of rule plays a pivotal role. At the micro level, the term shows up as "rules of conduct"; at the macro level, it appears as social rules coordinating individual activities under the premise of man-made or spontaneous organisation. The conceptual term "rule" may carry either a positive or a normative meaning. In a positive mould, a rule is a "knowledge bit", providing individuals with the potential to carry out operations; here, "rules . . . follow from their desires and their insights into relations of cause and effect" (Hayek 1973: 45). In turn, "[f]or the resulting order to be beneficial, people must also observe some conventional rules"; here, rules "are normative and tell them what they ought to or ought not to do" (ibid.).

Although rules may come in different guises, they share a common syllogistic structure. Whether individual, social, positive or normative, they are all anchored in an "if–then" logic. Given its general format, the rule concept may serve as key device for constructing the overall theoretical framework of evolutionary economics. On top of this, the concept is instrumental as a bridging concept, connecting the domain of theorising with that of modelling and computational analysis, in which the concept of the "rule" is widely used.

The early pioneers of evolutionary economics perceived the economy as a highly dynamic system. This fundamental perception of reality informed their theorising and their methods substantively. The neoclassical economists after them had a different perception, and their ways of theorising and their methods differ accordingly.

Evolutionary ontology
Addressing economic change theoretically requires, first, identification of the fundamental premises on which the theoretical statements are to be based. A mechanistic world view can provide us with a set of premises that would allow a theory of rest and equilibrium to be constructed, but not one that would explain endogenously continuous change. Ever since the early days, evolutionary economics has been confronting the problem of proper ontological foundations to provide guidance for the construction of a theory explaining the phenomenon of change.

Looking for new foundations, biology was seen to be of primary interest. Recently, philosophers of biology have proposed that Charles Darwin's explanatory principles attain universal significance, suggesting that they may be of scientific interest not only for biologists but for students of other disciplines as well. This persuasive idea has found advocates among economists, who have been proposing that "universal Darwinism" may inform theory construction in economics in a fundamental way (Hodgson and Knudsen 2010).

At a more general level, philosophers and biologists have considered continuity of change (not one of rest) to be of ontological significance. After he had inspected geological and paleontological evidence, Gottfried Leibniz proposed a "principle of continuity"; Darwinians such as Thomas Huxley defended their "continuity theory" against creationists; and Charles Peirce made the "principle of continuity" a centrepiece of his process philosophy. More recently, Witt (2003) has proposed to premise economic theorising on a continuity thesis, which views evolution as a natural history of increasingly more complex behaviours and production regimes (Witt, 2003). In line with this proposition, a naturalist approach to economics has been advocated.

The two strands of discussion have provided valuable insights into various theoretical topics (Darwinian principles explaining the dynamic of institutions, the continuity thesis shedding light on cross-level dependence and transition analysis), but it is fair to say that these endeavours have not yet provided a systematic exposition of what may represent the ontological foundations for a theory that deals with change in an economic system.

Exploring the field of ontology further, we arrive at a rich legacy handed down from philosophers of science such as Alfred Whitehead, Charles Peirce and Henri Bergson. Drawing on findings from disciplines such as physics, biology and the social sciences, they have advanced important ontological statements that, together, may be considered to represent an evolutionary ontology.

The task to be faced in this analysis is not a detailed exegesis of these works but, rather, the extracting from them what may represent the essentials of an evolutionary ontology. Three ontological propositions are submitted. Being ontological, the propositions represent generalisations about reality, and therefore they are subject to falsification. The propositions also represent the premises for the lower, theoretical, level, however, and at this level they are no longer questioned. They are taken to be "worth" (Greek *axio*) not to be questioned. In the process of theorising, the ontological propositions thus attain the status of axioms. Challenging the axioms means challenging the validity of the evolutionary ontology proposed.

In a nutshell, the three axioms are as follows:

Axiom 1 All existences are physical actualisations of information in time and space. There is bimodality, meaning that their complete representation requires an acknowledgement of both physical (matter and energy) and non-physical (information) categories of existence.

Axiom 2 Existences have a propensity to associate; given (thermodynamic) conditions, they emerge into structure.

Axiom 3 Structures unfold as processes. There are repeatable and non-repeatable processes. In a regime of repeatable processes, structural characteristics or functional attributes are retained; in one of non-repeatable processes, they change (evolvability).

Analytical Ontology: New Concepts of Representation

Although adequate ontology is an elementary requirement for theorising, scientific progress also depends crucially on the improvement of formal-analytical weaponry, such as mathematical representation or modelling techniques. Schumpeter and Marshall both deplored the lack of adequate techniques for representing economic dynamics, but things have changed since the 1980s.

Advances in computing power have opened up entirely new possibilities for dealing with masses of data and information, and the computational sciences have provided an arsenal of new methods for analysing or modelling the complex phenomenon of economic change. The radical novelty of these developments lies not in the improvement of the received tools such as calculus, topology or descriptive statistics (which are all suitable for the purposes of an analysis cast in a mechanistic mould) but, rather, in furnishing entirely new analytical tools and modelling techniques meeting the requirements of an evolutionary ontology.

The radical turn in analytical representation is well demonstrated by the fact that, in the computational sciences, this development is considered as being ontological, and in fact the term computational ontology is widely used nowadays. Various ontological issues have been surfacing in many of the works on analytical representation inspired by the digital age: e-science tools, computational automation and cyber-infrastructures (Kishore et al. 2004). Given the significance that ontology attains in this domain, we may assemble studies addressing computational and other kinds of analytical representation under the umbrella of analytical ontology.

Theoretical developments concurring with advances in analytical ontology abound. Multi-agent models have become standard for numerous special theoretical models (Grebel and Pyka 2006). An array of network models connects with multi-agent and related models highlighting the connective complexity (Potts 2000). Models featuring multidimensional fitness landscapes allow for the dynamic of differential adaptation and selection; path dependence and lock-in models posited in network structures have been designed to highlight the interconnectivities of non-ergodic paths (David 2005; Arthur 2013).

Models applying the (physics) synergy master equation have been introduced to give analytical precision to Veblen's venerable proposition that there is circular causality between individual and social behaviour (Weidlich 2000). Models featuring kernel density distribution methods have shed new light on the structure of income distribution, given dynamic knowledge differentials (Cantner et al., 2001).

Complexity economics has re-emerged from the 1950s as a general branch featuring new forms of analytical exposition, new tools and new modelling techniques (Arthur et al. 1997; Colander et al. 2010; Foster and Metcalfe 2012). Many of the analytical approaches have been producing offspring in the form of more special models, referring to particular theoretical problems (Kwasnicka and Kwasnicki 2006; Safarzyńska and van den Bergh 2010).

The theoretical concept of rule has been specified analytically as requiring a deductive format. For any rule R_j it holds that, "if condition C_j obtains, then operations Op_j" occur/are possible. While syllogism also applies to "laws" (as nomological rules), a rule in, for example, a classifier system has generic characteristics expounding variety, plasticity and evolvability. A special category inspired by biology deals with rules as genetic algorithms, adaptive genetic algorithms or hybrid genetic algorithms, paralleled by its sister branch of genetic programming.

Taking an overview, the contours of a unified programme may be seen to emerge in which analytical and semantic ontology combine – epitomised in the view of evolution as a form of computation (Beinhocker 2011).

Rule Taxonomy

The main branches of modern biology, such as genetics and epigenetics, investigate the nature of biological rules. Many of the recent scientific advances in biology have occurred in these branches. In economics, however, unlike biology, there does not yet exist any corresponding general research area to deal with economic rules.

However, the concept of the rule has at least been applied in various specialised areas in economics, for example, in the guise of social, technical, behavioural and cognitive rules. The aim is to combine them into a unified rule taxonomy.

The broad distinction between biological and cultural rules is critical for drawing the boundaries of the discipline. Economics belongs to the cultural level of the evolved hierarchy of natural history. Its subject matter is neither the analysis of the structure and evolution of biological rules nor the more narrowly conceived analysis of the coevolution of biological and cultural rules.

The rules of the cultural level – cultural rules – may be used for both economic and non-economic operations. Differentiation on the basis of the kind of operation sets economics apart from other social sciences. Thus we arrive at the definition: economics is the study of cultural rules for economic operations. Economic operations include production, transaction and consumption.

Biological rules describe the innate capacity of *Homo sapiens* (HS) to make and to use rules. Our focus being on rules for economic operations, we are interested specifically in *Homo sapiens oeconomicus* (HSO).

The neoclassical *Homo oeconomicus* is a particular "species" of HS equipped with a single invariant rule: the maximisation of expected utility under constraints. This HS rule is taken to represent a universal "law" (not subject to further scrutiny), and the subject matter of neoclassical analysis is economic operations obeying to this law. In contrast, evolutionary economics highlights HSO: explaining economic operations on the basis of a scientific understanding of the structure and evolution of cultural rules.

Analytically, we have two levels of investigation:

1. Generic level: rules for economic operations.
2. Operant level: economic operations based on these rules.

To summarise, neoclassical economics occupies the operant story in this analytical edifice, evolutionary economics the generic one, putting in centre stage investigations into the rule knowledge that enables economic operations.

Homo sapiens oeconomicus generates cultural artefacts. Economics deals with cultural artefacts under the special premise of scarcity. Looking for the constituent characteristics of the two prime categories – HSO and economic artefacts – there should be little in the way of objection if we associate the former with the concept of subject and the latter with that of object. Introducing the general concept of the carrier, we get HSO as the carrier of subject rules and economic artefacts as the carriers of object rules.

Table 5   Rule taxonomy

Generic rules			
Subject rules		Object rules	
Cognitive rules	Behavioural rules	Social rules	Technical rules
e.g. mental models and schema	e.g. behavioural heuristics	e.g. organisation of a firm, rules of a market	e.g. technologies

The validity of economic theory depends crucially on the giving of proper emphasis to "subjective" (subject-related) and "objective" (object-related) factors. Evolutionary economics eschews monist interpretations and views change in/of the economy generally as a process of coevolution between subject rules and object rules. A good example of a monist position that relates to "subjectivism" is radical Austrian economics, and one that relates to "objectivism" is radical Marxian economics.

The usefulness of rule taxonomy depends largely on its ability to delineate a scope wide enough to embrace all the relevant rule categories and pinpoint them in a way that they may be used as building blocks for theorising. To this end, subject rules may be subdivided into cognitive/mental rules and behavioural rules, on the one side, and object rules may be differentiated into social rules (for organising subjects) and technical rules (for organising physical artefacts), on the other side (see Table 5). Evolutionary (or generic, rule-based) economics is, then, the study of the structure and evolution of the economy in terms of these rules.

The four rule categories correspond to major research areas and are represented by large bodies of publications. Although this is, in general, a sign of scientific progress, the further task is to investigate the specific aspects that are relevant for explaining the structure and evolution of the economy. This immediately brings back into focus the economic agent as a rule maker and rule user. At the level of micro-foundations, the evolutionary programme calls essentially for a reconstruction of the economic agent as HSO (Davis 2010; Gerschlager 2012).

The generic programme of cognitive and behavioural economics deals specifically with aspects of rule processes. Topics covered by the two broad agendas include the creation of novel rules, selective adoption, generic learning, the adaptive accommodation of novel rules in the extant knowledge base and retaining them in a meta-stable process for recurrent operations (Witt 2003; Dosi et al. 2005; Hodgson 2006; Herrmann-Pillath 2012).

The nature of object rules may be highlighted by making reference to four rule categories: rules expressing product characteristics; industry or manufacturing rules; Nelson–Winter (N–W) organisational routines; and Ostrom social rules. While these rules may relate to quite different kinds of operations, as object rules they all share the feature of being rules for organising entities of the external world.

Traditionally, a product (commodity, good) is defined as a "quantil", following Jevon's phrasing (number of units times price). There are no rules that would "inform" the product of its qualitative characteristics. In the 1970s Kelvin Lancaster initiated a discussion by proposing to augment the neoclassical utility function with factorials of product attributes. This was a major step forward, and a generic approach has now been employed in evolutionary economics by defining Lancaster's characteristics as rules that expound plasticity and evolvability (Saviotti and Metcalfe 1984; Saviotti and Pyka 2004;).

At a global scale, a taxonomy of object rules has been developed for manufacturing systems and industrial sectors. Traditionally, classifications such as the Standard Industrial Classification (SIC) have followed the template of Carolus Linnaeus, who assumed morphological characteristics to be immutable and who posited them in a grand classificatory schema on the basis of their similarity. This kind of taxonomy may prove helpful for making statements about structure.

The rules of biology and of economics are in a continual state of flux, however, which calls for a taxonomy that accounts for this fact. Based on Darwinism, cladistics and similar taxonomies have been devised to reckon with the phenomenon of change. They integrate aspects of the genealogy of rules with morphological attributes reconciling the demands of structure and of change when charting empirical data. Cladistic taxonomy has inspired novel taxonomies in evolutionary economics, as in the form of cladograms for manufacturing systems or phylogenetic trees for industrial sectors (McCarthy et al. 2000; Andersen, 2003;), or particular aspects of evolutionary taxonomy such as classifying technology policy (Cantner and Pyka, 2001).

Up until this point, the focus has been on object rules for organising physical entities. In contradistinction, Nelson–Winter routines and Ostrom social rules are for organising agents – subjects, not physical entities. N–W organisational routines are especially interesting from a conceptual point of view, since they combine the concept of rule with that of actualisation (axiom 1).

Generally, a routine is a rule that has passed through a process of routinisation. An N–W routine is a rule that has attained the specific informational content of a social organisational rule. Other rules, not related to the process of organising, may also be the subject of routinisation.

The process of routinisation is part of an overall process of rule actualisation. The entire process of rule actualisation involves the generation, adoption and retention of a rule. These may be conceived of as constituting three distinct phases of a micro-trajectory of rule actualisation:

Phase 1 – generation of novel rule.
Phase 2 – adoption of rule by carrier.
Phase 3 – retention of rule for recurrent operations.

The routinisation process relates to the second and third phases of the trajectory. Routinisation presupposes a rule.

Routinisation – being a mental process – takes place at the locus of an individual. Veblen has called this process habituation and its outcome habit (Hodgson 2006; Brette and Mehier 2008). Individual routines and habits may therefore be taken to be identical. An individual Nelson–Winter routine is an organisational habit of an individual agent as a member of an organisation, such as the firm.

The Nelson–Winter concept of routine has led to various discussions, which have furnished valuable building blocks for reconstructing the evolutionary micro-foundations of economics, and in turn they have stimulated discussions in the management sciences (Becker 2008; Lazaric and Oltra 2012).

The work of Elinor Ostrom and her collaborators represents a milestone in the construction of a taxonomy of social rules (Ostrom 2005, Ostrom and Basurto 2011). On the basis of dozens of empirical studies and having inspected about 100 empirically recorded social rules, she has devised a "universal" rule taxonomy. This general result is particularly interesting, as Ostrom links it up with major theoretical approaches, thereby demonstrating its great usefulness for theory making. She connects the rule categories of choice rules, pay-off rules or scope rules with game theory and those of positional rules, entry rules or boundary rules with the organisation theory featured in the concept of Nelson–Winter routines.

System Science and Evolutionary Science

The subject matter of evolutionary economics is the economy as an evolving system. The central scientific focus of this approach lies in investigating the theoretical nature of the system and that of evolutionary dynamics. From the perspective of extant science programmes, economics may thus be seen as being built on two pillars. These are (1) system science and (2) evolutionary science.

Early pioneers of modern evolutionary economics, such as Nicholas Georgescu-Roegen (1972) and Kenneth Boulding (1980), featured expressly an evolutionary system approach. There are surprisingly few references to these pioneers in evolutionary economics today, which may reflect the fact that the systemic aspect of evolutionary analysis has been generally neglected in the community.

The archetypical domain to start with is a network, defined as an ensemble of many elements and their connections. A network is said to constitute a system (to have systemic properties) if all or some of the elements have functional or similar systemic attributes connecting into a whole. The distribution of the systemic elements represents a structure brought about by a process of coordination. A system is said to change when one or several of the component parts of the structure change and, as a consequence, the structure of their connections changes.

The theoretical key problem lies in furnishing an analytical unit that in one breath explains both: the theoretical features of structure and of its evolution as a process of continual change. The core of the theoretical explanation of the evolution of an economic system resides thus in a unit composed of a structure component and of a process component. Neoclassical economics conspicuously lacks both (structure and process), and as a consequence, its theoretical programme fails to provide any cues for an endogenous explanation of an evolving – continuously restructuring – economy.

The analytical concept dealing with structure – the structure component – is well exemplified in Adam Smith's famous case of the division of labour in pin manufacturing. The whole process of producing a pin is divided into structure components stated in terms of special (and possibly specialised) production steps of the total production sequence. This example is important as it highlights the power of "downward" scale economies, but it is not the only kind of structure component characteristic of a product and its production. For instance, for a car to qualify as such it is necessary for it to be composed of various component parts independent of whether or not their production involves Smithian division of labour or scale economies. The constituent criterion in this case is *e contrario* the "upward" complementarity of the component parts. The relative importance of this kind of division of labour will increase as the number of new consumer products increases or as factorial inputs (as structured wholes) are substituted increasingly by new ones (as in the digital economy, Beinhocker 2006). Brief as this account may be, it leads to the identification of the two essential building blocks of a general theory of division of labour: there are derived, *ex-post* downward (Smith type) and original, *ex-ante* upward (non-Smith type) kinds of complementarity defining the nucleus of a general theory of the division of labour.

How does change occur in the economy? Enquiring into this issue, it is helpful to return to evolutionary ontology, which proposes that information changes continuously. This has led to a bimodal representation of existences distinguishing between semantic information or the content of a rule and its physical actualisation in historical time and space (axiom 1). Structure and change (rest representing temporary non-change) are defined with respect to these two existential categories.

At the level of semantic information, we have rules as component parts of a rule structure. The subject of analysis at this level is the nature of the complementarities, which calls for the methods of mereology and hermeneutics. Both are analytical branches that are entirely absent in the neoclassical canon and hardly touched upon in evolutionary economics. Information or semantic content being invisible, we may conceive of the rule level as the "deep" level of the economic system.

In turn, rule actualisation occurs as a process in time and space. Being physical instantiations, rule actualisations are observable. They may be interpreted as representing a "surface" level of the economic system.

The ontological posture backing up the theoretic terms – structure (axiom 2) and process (axiom 3) – has far-reaching consequences for the nature of economic methodology. In its very core, there is a deep level of structure that relies essentially on qualitative analysis and a surface level of process that is amenable to observation and quantification. Combining the two into a single set of analytic or theoretic statements makes for the art of an evolutionary economic methodology.

Activities at the operant level – the level at which rules are assumed to be given – are also observable; as a result, dealing with particular topics in economic analysis may suggest a need to distinguish between the generic and the operant surface level. In what follows only the former are dealt with.

Evolutionary (generic) change occurs as change in the rules at both the deep and the surface levels. While this exposition excludes some interpretations, it still leaves much room for competing propositions as to how change occurs, or what its causes and systemic consequences are. In Smith's model, change occurs in the course of an increase of production steps and specialisation in a particular kind of product. The crucial point with this interpretation of change is that the novelty-generating engine comes to a halt once the optimal regime of decomposition has been reached and the benefits from economies of scale have become exhausted. Smith's model is reminiscent of that of Jean-Baptiste Lamarck. Lamarck proposed that organisms adapt to their environment and that the characteristics acquired by an organism during its lifetime can be inherited by future generations. Once the organism is perfectly adapted to its environment, evolution comes to a halt (ignoring Lamarck's spontaneous procreation of novel variants).

Darwin, by contrast, proposed that change comes about in the process of sexual reproduction, suggesting a continuity of change, which therefore did not require Lamarckian "learning" (though Darwin did appreciate Lamarck's views). Various mechanisms, such as recombination, mutation and others, incessantly generate novel generic variants (today we talk of genes or genomes). The various organisms produce offspring, leading to a variety of organisms in a population. Learning from Thomas Malthus that resources are scarce, Darwin conjectured that only those organisms would survive – and retain temporarily their heritable information – that could cope with environmental constraints through adaptation. He argued that nature "selects" much more powerfully than humans do when practising artificial selection, and thus he used for the proposed mechanism the metaphor "natural selection".

The micro-trajectory introduced earlier is reminiscent of Darwin's trajectory, with the crucial difference that a Darwinian trajectory features in the second (selection) phase and the third (retention) phase the concept of population. For economic illustration, the mentioned N–W routines are now not adopted by a single carrier (micro) but rather by a population of them (meso). Darwin's notion of population represents thus an entirely new concept. There was, of course, the concept of species defined by a genus and a population, as with the taxon in Linnaeus's taxonomy, but in that concept the genus was assumed to be pre-given and fixed. In Darwin's model, a population is assumed to come into existence only if new information is generated. Linnaeus's taxa of species featured "typological thinking", Darwin's "population thinking" (Metcalfe 2001).

From the viewpoint of the present analysis, it is essential to acknowledge not only that a population is an ensemble of many members but also that it represents a process of rule actualisation along a population trajectory of origination, selection and retention. Summarily,

Phase 1 – generation of novel rule.
Phase 2 – adoption of rule by population of carriers in selective environment.
Phase 3 – retention of rule by population of carriers for recurrent operations.

Theoretical Architecture: Micro–Meso–Macro

How shall we posit the analytical unit of a population in an architecture that, traditionally, is composed of micro and macro? The unit is difficult to associate with either micro (organism; agents), or with macro (nature; economy); it clearly assumes, as indicated above, an intermediate position. In acknowledgement of this, the term meso (as a neologism) is being proposed. We get thus a new theoretical architecture which comprises the levels of Micro–Meso–Macro.

The concept of rule structure exemplified by Smith's division of labour lacks a Darwinian type of self-generating (meso) trajectory that would drive endogenously a continuous evolutionary dynamic. Smith's model is proto-evolutionary; to allow for a theoretical statement about the evolution of economic structure, we require Darwin.

The question is whether or in what way a Darwinian approach may help us in the task of connecting the process units into a structure in order to explain the evolution of the economy as a change in its structure. We have defined structure by its complementarities, such as heterogeneous agents performing complementary production tasks. The structure of knowledge and labour in an economy is generally based on complementarities.

It is quite clear that, in nature, nothing like a Smithian kind of division of labour exists. In nature there are, of course, hunter–prey relationships, co-variation among species and interdependences between them in the use of resources and so on, but there is no structure in a sense of complementary tasks or functional assignments aimed at common ends. Not only have we never seen a dog exchanging bones with another but also has there been no empirical indication that dogs would cooperate on the basis of assigned tasks for a common result. The evidence becomes much more robust as we extend the observation to the whole of nature, considering cooperation among various species, say dogs, cats and chimpanzees. While Smith cannot explain process, Darwin cannot explain structure. The most challenging task for evolutionary economics lies in integrating Smith and Darwin.

Analytically, we have a structure component (Smith) and a process component (Darwin). The structure component is a single rule (or rule composite) that relates to other rules as part of a structure. The process component is a trajectory that tells the "life story" of that rule as a process of physical actualisation in an agent population. Both combined represent the basic analytical unit: the meso unit.

To ease the procedure of falsification with respect to this proposition, let the conclusion be stated explicitly: without meso neither structure nor process can be explained endogenously. Neoclassical economics is a most conspicuous case in point expounding the ineptitude to cope endogenously with structure and evolutionary change.

Evolutionary Microeconomics

Conventionally, microeconomics is the study of the decisions made by individual agents or agencies in the market. In it, producers and consumers exchange a certain quantity of a product at a price. When referring to a single market, the study is usually called partial equilibrium analysis. Further, demand and supply functions may in their entirety be represented as a system of simultaneous equations. The study of the totality of all markets is usually called general equilibrium analysis. In this case, we have a model that contains all producers, all consumers, all products, all quantities supplied, all quantities demanded and all exchange prices. We are dealing with the total produce in an economy stated in terms of many individually allocated resources. Having included everything that constitutes a market economy, one might expect that this ought to make for macroeconomics, but still it is called microeconomics.

The obvious misnomer can be explained only by considering its intellectual history. John Maynard Keynes suggested not looking at the relative allocation but, instead, at the aggregates of all production and of all consumption, and relating these to other aggregates such as investment, employment and money volume. The decision making of individual agents now does not refer to the relative choice in a commodity space but, rather, involves choices (translated into propensities) referring to the variables of the macro model. This alternative position led to the divide into micro and macro after World War II.

The "new macroeconomics" argues that better results may be obtained on the basis of microeconomics, for instance, by considering the individuals' relative choice between more employment or more leisure – suggesting that properly understood macro-economics can be interpreted as "applied" microeconomics. What remains as a distin-guishing criterion for macroeconomics today is the money side, namely the variables of money volume, price level, circulation velocity and related variables. The entire real side of the economy is left to the received canon of microeconomics, leaving in limbo the important questions of its endogenous structure and its endogenous change. Post-Keynesian economics has identified major weak spots in the treatment of the money side, but it is not unfair to say that it has largely failed to furnish a theoretical exposition that would allow us to deal with structure and change.

Evolutionary economics aims to construct "micro-foundations" that will enable us to explain endogenously structure and change in the economy (Blind and Pyka 2014). The term "microeconomics" will be adopted from the received canon for ease of com-munication in the following. Also the proposition of bimodality in the interpretation of microeconomics is retained. We have thus a rule (or rule composite), on the one side, and its carrier and a population of carriers that have adopted this rule, on the other side.

This stance may be identified as typically Marshallian. Marshall saw the single market or industry as a single unit comprising several integrated markets of a kind, as the major building block for constructing the macro of the economy. His building block was designed as a component part of the economy's structure and as a process unit for explaining how it changed over time and, concomitantly, the structure it was part of. In the dichotomy between Keynesianism and neoclassicism, this central aspect of Marshall's work got lost entirely.

This aspect has previously been captured with the notion of meso, distinguishing it from micro, as the single agent or socially organised micro-entity such as the firm, and macro, as the domain of the whole economy. The term microeconomics is redefined in this way, allowing us to address structure and change – in both the agent and the population. Evolutionary microeconomics is composed of a micro-unit (agent, firm or household) posited in a meso context (population, industry or institution; as structure/process component).

Drawing on the concepts of rule trajectory and rule taxonomy, as introduced earlier, an exposition of the theoretical building block that captures the features of a single market can be attempted. At its simplest, we have supply and demand for a product in a market. The magnitudes of these depend on the demand and supply behaviour of the agents. In a neoclassical model both demand and supply behaviour depends on a single, uniform and invariant decision rule, the familiar maximisation of expected utility (with preferences, and so on, given). In a generic model, all operant behaviour is rule-based; specifically, demand behaviour depends on demand rules, and supply behaviour depends on supply rules. Rules evolve along a meso trajectory; they originate (phase 1), are selectively adopted (phase 2) and retained as institutions, facilitating the efficient performance of recurrent operations (phase 3). Market change represents a process of co-evolution between supply rules and demand rules; a market institution (phase 3) is a meta-stable co-evolutionary process composed of these rules.

The market is the locus where demand and supply meet – as rules and operations – but the way this happens depends on the distinct organisational rules of the market. Until the breakdown of the centrally planned Soviet system prevailing in eastern European coun-tries, the question of market organisation was part of the broader issue of centralisation versus decentralisation for all economic activities. Today the issue is more narrowly construed, with the focus on rules for organising capitalist markets. The design pertains to the various kinds of organisation of markets (market rules) given a market economy, not to the design of the market economy itself (system rules). Following the former line of inquiry, various types of market design or market rules have been discussed (Mirowski 2007; Roth 2007; Storbacka and Nenonen 2011).

The object of exchange is a product. It may be a money (finance) product or a real sector product. Demand and supply in real product markets relate, contrary to money markets, to producers and to consumers (of real products). Therefore, supply and demand operations depend on producer rules and consumer rules. The real product itself is not homogeneous, like money or corn as standard, but it does have particular characteristics. To allow for the heterogeneity of products, it is necessary to specify them in terms of product rules.

The example par excellence for producer rules is Nelson–Winter organisational routines, but they run through the whole gamut of rules assembled in the rule taxonomy. Consumer rules relate to new ways of consuming, to learning to consume and to retaining them as habits and institutions for recurrent consumptive operations (Bianchi 1998; Witt 2001; Potts et al. 2008; Nelson and Consoli 2010; Lazaric and Oltra 2012).

At a price, where the quantity supplied equals that of demand, the market is cleared. The operations governing supply and demand depend on producer and consumer rules, however, and reallocation at the operant level can in an evolutionary model take place only within a domain determined by the matching of producer rules and consumer rules. Thus, for market clearing, besides the equilibrium condition at the operant level we have the condition of rule correspondence at the generic level. The domain of the rule correspondence is not defined by Jevon's "quantil" (number of units times price) of the product exchanged but, instead, by particular rule-defined product characteristics. It is not the operant but, rather, the locus of generic intersection – the rule-matching domain – that determines the exchange value and quantity of a product at the "deep" level.

The duality (producer versus consumer) of the generic characteristics of a product has been discussed in terms of technical rules (producer) and service rules (consumer) as a condition for establishing the afore-mentioned rule correspondence (Saviotti and Metcalfe 1984; Saviotti and Pyka 2004; Windrum et al. 2009).

An exposition of a generic market model in which producer (firm) rules and consumer (household) rules are in a state of rule correspondence, thus yielding the product rule, is provided in Table 6.

The dynamics of markets is the process of coevolution of the rules defined by the taxa stated.

Table 6   Firm and household rules map into product rule

Carriers	Producers (Firms)		Product		Consumers (Households)
Rules by carrier	**Producer rules** (Firm rules)	→	**Product rule**	←	**Consumer rules** (Household rules)
Rule types	*Nelson–Winter*		*Metcalfe–Saviotti–Pyka*		*Nelson–Consoli–Witt*

Evolutionary Macroeconomics

Students of evolutionary economics have traditionally dealt with microeconomic issues, and it is only recently that macroeconomic issues have received particular attention. The general aim of the models is to integrate evolutionary behavioural assumptions with approaches that emphasise structural economic dynamics.

In some models, the theoretical arguments have been developed along a Marshall–Kaldor–Fabricant–Pasinetti lineage or related ones, highlighting the evolutionary relationships between production, productivity and consumption structures (Metcalfe et al. 2006). In another strand, Lotka–Volterra, selection, percolation and related models have been utilised to explain the evolutionary nature of economic growth (Silverberg and Verspagen 2005). Along Keynesian lines, attempts have been made to substantiate the Keynesian money and real aggregates by integrating the novelty-driven dynamic, with its effect on changing income distribution and structures, into output, investment, consumption and employment aggregates (Verspagen 2002; Dosi et al. 2008).

The basic aim of evolutionary economic policy may be described with reference to the works on the concept of the "national system". Traditionally, the economy has been a domain defined by microeconomics and macroeconomics, with a linkage to governmental policy informed by these. In contrast, evolutionary economic policy views the national system of the economy in its distinct evolutionary characteristics, and designs economic policies in consideration of these. Appreciating the national system as a complex evolving system, various suggestions have been put forward with a view to reconfiguring economic policy along evolutionary lines, such as highlighting the national economy (or analogous politico-economic unit) as a "national system of innovation", a "national knowledge system", a "national R&D (research and development) system" or a "national learning system" (Freeman, 2002; Nelson, 1993; Lundvall, 1992).

Outlook

The modern economy has been called – with much justification – a knowledge economy. This may be misleading, however, as knowledge is required in a traditional economy as well to perform operations for solving the scarcity problem. What the statement means is that, at the present and in the future, it may not be possible to acquire an adequate understanding of economic phenomena without due recognition of the significance of knowledge – beyond prices and quantities.

Central to our analysis has been the recognition that knowledge enables economic operations. Simple as it is, this tenet allows an important distinction to be drawn between two major levels of economic enquiry. One is the level of knowledge for economic operations, the other that of operations under the assumption of given knowledge. Evolutionary economics deals with the former, neoclassical mainstream economics with the latter.

Analysing the structure and change of economic knowledge calls for the adoption of an evolutionary ontology; in turn, theoretical enquiry into the phenomena of the operant level may be conducted validly on the basis of mechanistic ontology (constant knowledge may attain the status of immutable "law"). Evolutionary economics considers the problem of economic knowledge to be centre stage, and it aims to reconstruct economic theory on the basis of – semantic and analytical – evolutionary ontology.

By addressing the knowledge level, evolutionary economics opens up the problem space required to identify and – possibly – contribute to solving the most pressing problems of a modern economy. In its grand theoretical design, it is heading towards an integration of Smith (structure) and Darwin (process).

KURT DOPFER

See also:

Behavioural and cognitive economics (III); Competition (III); Development economics (III); Economic dynamics (III); Experimental economics (III); German and Austrian schools (II); Friedrich August von Hayek (I); Institutionalism (II); Alfred Marshall (I); Joseph Alois Schumpeter (I); Adam Smith (I); Thorstein Bunde Veblen (I).

References and further reading

Andersen, E.S. (2003), 'The evolving tree of industrial life: an approach to the transformation of European industry', paper presented at the second 'Economic transformation of Europe' workshop, Turin, 1 February.

Arthur, B.W. (2013), 'Complexity economics: a different framework for economic thought', Institute for New Economic Thinking (INET) Research Notes 33, New York.

Arthur, B.W., S.N. Durlauf and D.A. Lane (eds) (1997), *The Economy as an Evolving Complex System II*, Reading, MA: Addison-Wesley.

Becker, M. (2008), *Handbook of Organizational Routines*, Cheltenham, UK and Northampton, MA, USA: Edward Elgar.

Beinhocker, E.D. (2006), *The Origin of Wealth. Evolution, Complexity, and Radical Remaking of Economics*, Cambridge, MA: Harvard Business Review Press.

Beinhocker, E.D. (2011), 'Evolution as computation: integrating self-organization with generalized Darwinism', *Journal of Institutional Economics*, **7** (3), 393–423.

Bianchi, M. (ed.) (1998), *The Active Consumer: Novelty and Surprise in Consumer Choice*, London: Routledge.

Blind, G.D. and A. Pyka (2014), 'The rule approach in evolutionary economics: a methodological template for empirical research', *Journal of Evolutionary Economics*, **25** (2), 1085–105, doi 10.1007/s00191-014-0382-4.

Boulding, K. (1980), *Ecodynamics: A New Theory of Societal Evolution*, Thousand Oaks, CA: Sage.

Brette, O. and C. Mehier (2008), 'Building on the "micro–meso–macro" evolutionary framework: the stakes for the analysis of clusters of innovation', in W. Elsner and H. Hanappi (eds), *Varieties of Capitalism and New Institutional Deals: Regulation, Welfare and the New Economy*, Cheltenham, UK and Northampton, MA, USA: Edward Elgar, pp. 227–49.

Cantner, U. and Pyka, A. (2001), 'Classifying technology policy from an evolutionary perspective', *Research Policy*, **30** (5), 759–75.

Cantner, U., B. Ebersberger, H. Hanusch, J.J. Krüger and A. Pyka (2001), 'Empirically based simulation: the case of twin peaks in national income', *Journal of Artificial Societies and Social Simulation*, **4** (3), http://jasss.soc.surrey.ac.uk/4/3/9.html.

Colander, D., R.P.F. Holt and J.B. Rosser (2010), 'The complexity era in economics', Working Paper no. 1001, Middlebury College, Middlebury, VT.

David, P.A. (2005), 'Path dependence in economic processes: implications for policy analysis in dynamical systems contexts', in K. Dopfer (ed.), *The Evolutionary Foundations of Economics*, Cambridge: Cambridge University Press, pp. 151–94.

Davis, J.B. (2010), 'Neuroeconomics: constructing identity', *Journal of Economic Behavior and Organization*, **76** (3), 574–83.

Dopfer, K. (ed.) (2005), *The Evolutionary Foundations of Economics*, Cambridge: Cambridge University Press.

Dopfer, K. and J. Potts (2008), *The General Theory of Economic Evolution*, London: Routledge.

Dopfer, K., J. Foster and J. Potts (2004), 'Micro–meso–macro', *Journal of Evolutionary Economics*, **14** (2), 263–79.

Dosi, G., G. Fagiolo and A. Roventini 2008), 'Schumpeter meeting Keynes: a policy-friendly model of endogenous growth and business cycles', Working Papers 50/2008, University of Verona, Department of Economics.

Dosi, G., L. Marengo and G. Fagiolo (2005), 'Learning in evolutionary environments', in K. Dopfer (ed.), *The Evolutionary Foundations of Economics*, Cambridge: Cambridge University Press, pp. 255–338.

Foster, J. and J.S. Metcalfe (2012), 'Economic emergence: an evolutionary economic perspective', *Journal of Economic Behavior and Organisation*, **82** (2), 420–32.

Freeman, C. (2002), 'Continental, national and sub-national systems of innovation', *Research Policy*, **31** (2), 191–211.

Georgescu-Roegen, N. (1972), *The Entropy Law and the Economic Process*, Cambridge, MA: Harvard University Press.

Gerschlager, C. (2012), 'Agents of change', *Journal of Evolutionary Economics*, **22** (3), 413–41.

Grebel, T. and A. Pyka, (2006), 'Agent-based modelling: a methodology for the analysis of qualitative development processes', in F.C. Billari, T. Fent, A. Prskawetz and J. Scheffran (eds), *Agent-Based Computational Modelling: Applications in Demography, Social, Economic and Environmental Sciences*, Heidelberg: Physica, pp. 17–36.

Hayek, F.A. (1945), 'The use of knowledge in society', *American Economic Review*, **35** (4), 519–30.

Hayek, F.A. (1973), *Law, Legislation and Liberty*, vol. 1, *Rules and Order*, Chicago, IL: University of Chicago Press.

Herrmann-Pillath, C. (2012), 'Institutions, distributed cognition and agency: rule-following as performative action', *Journal of Economic Methodology*, **19** (1), 21–42.

Hodgson, G.M. (2006), 'What are institutions?', *Journal of Economic Issues*, **40** (1), 1–25.

Hodgson, G.M. and T. Knudsen (2010), *Darwin's Conjecture: The Search for General Principles of Social and Economic Evolution*, Chicago, IL: University of Chicago Press.

Kishore, R., R. Sharman and R. Ramesh (2004), 'Computational ontologies and information systems: I. foundations', *Communications of the Association for Information Systems*, **14**, 158–83.

Kwasnicka, H. and W. Kwasnicki (2006), 'Evolutionary modeling and industrial structure emergence', in J.-P. Rennard (ed.), *Handbook of Research on Nature Inspired Computing for Economy and Management*, vol. 1. Hershey, PA: IGI Global, pp. 281–300.

Lazaric, N. and V. Oltra (2012), 'Sustainable consumption in an evolutionary framework: how to foster behavioral change', in B. Laperche, N. Levratto and D. Uzunidis (eds), *Crisis, Innovation and Sustainable Development: The Ecological Opportunity*, Cheltenham, UK and Northampton, MA, USA: Edward Elgar, pp. 67–95.

Lundvall, B.-Å. (1992), *National Systems of Innovation: Toward a Theory of Innovation and Interactive Learning*, New York: Pinter.

Marshall, A. (1898), 'Distribution and exchange', *The Economic Journal*, **8** (29), 37–59.

Marshall, A. (1920), *Principles of Economics*, vol. 1, 8th edn, reprinted 1972, London: Macmillan.

McCarthy, I.P., K. Ridgway, M. Leseure and N. Fieller (2000), 'Organisational diversity, evolution and cladistic classifications', *Omega – International Journal of Management Science*, **28** (1), 77–95.

Metcalfe, J.S. (2001), 'Evolutionary approaches to population thinking and the problem of growth and development', in K. Dopfer (ed.), *Evolutionary Economics: Program and Scope*, Dordrecht: Kluwer Academic, pp. 141–64.

Metcalfe, J.S., J. Foster and R. Ramlogan (2006), 'Adaptive economic growth', *Cambridge Journal of Economics*, **30** (1), 7–32.

Mirowski, P. (2007), 'Markets come to bits: evolution, computation and markomata in economic science', *Journal of Economic Behavior and Organization*, **63** (2), 209–42.

Nelson, R.R. (1993), *National Systems of Innovation: A Comparative Analysis*, Cambridge, MA: Harvard University Press.

Nelson, R.R. and D. Consoli (2010), 'An evolutionary theory of household consumption behavior', *Journal of Evolutionary Economics*, **20** (5), 665–87.

Nelson, R.R. and S.G. Winter (1982), *An Evolutionary Theory of Economic Change*, Cambridge, MA: Harvard University Press.

Ostrom, E. (2005), *Understanding Institutional Diversity*, Princeton, NJ: Princeton University Press.

Ostrom, E. and Basurto, X. (2011), 'Crafting analytical tools to study institutional change', *Journal of Institutional Economics*, **7** (3), 317–43.

Potts, J. (2000), *The New Evolutionary Microeconomics: Choice, Complexity and Adaptive Behaviour*, Cheltenham, UK and Northampton, MA, USA: Edward Elgar.

Potts, J., J. Hartley, J. Banks, J. Burgess, R. Cobcroft, S. Cunningham and L. Montgomery (2008), 'Consumer co-creation and situated creativity', *Industry and Innovation*, **15** (5), 459–74.

Roth, A.E. (2007), 'The art of designing markets', *Harvard Business Review*, October, Reprint R0710G.

Safarzyńska, K. and J.C.J.M. van den Bergh (2010), 'Evolutionary modelling in economics: a survey of methods and building blocks', *Journal of Evolutionary Economics*, **20** (3), 329–73.

Saviotti, P.P. and J.S. Metcalfe (1984), 'A theoretical approach to the construction of technological output indicators', *Research Policy*, **13** (3), 141–51.

Saviotti, P.P. and A. Pyka (2004), 'Economic development, variety and employment', *Revue économique*, **55** (6), 1023–49.

Schumpeter, J.A. (1908), *Wesen und Hauptinhalt der theoretischen Nationalökonomie*, Leipzig: Duncker & Humblot.

Schumpeter, J.A. (1912), *The Theory of Economic Development: An Inquiry into Profits, Capital, Credit, Interest and the Business Cycle*, trans. R. Opie (1934), Cambridge, MA: Harvard University Press.

Schumpeter, J.A. (1942), *Capitalism, Socialism and Democracy*, 5th edn 1976, New York: Harper & Brothers.

Schumpeter, J.A. (1997), 'Alfred Marshall's principles: a semi-centennial appraisal' in *Ten Great Economists: From Marx to Keynes*, reissued with new introduction by M. Perlman, London: Routledge.

Silva, S.T. and A.A.C. Teixeira (2009), 'On the divergence of evolutionary research paths in the past 50 years: a comprehensive bibliometric account', *Journal of Evolutionary Economics*, **19** (5), 605–42.

Silverberg, G. and B. Verspagen (2005), 'Evolutionary theorizing on economic growth', in K. Dopfer (ed.), *The Evolutionary Foundations of Economics*, Cambridge: Cambridge University Press, pp. 506–39.

Storbacka, K. and S. Nenonen (2011), 'Scripting markets: from value propositions to market propositions', *Industrial Marketing Management*, **40** (2), 255–66.

Veblen, T.B. (1898), 'Why is economics not an evolutionary science', *Quarterly Journal of Economics*, **12**, 373–97.

Veblen, T.B. (1909), 'The limitations of marginal utility', *Journal of Political Economy*, **17** (9), 620–36.

Verspagen, B. (2002), 'Evolutionary macroeconomics: a synthesis between neo-Schumpeterian and neo-Keynesian lines of thought', *Electronic Journal of Evolutionary Modelling and Economic Dynamics*, accessed at www.e-jemed.org/1007/index.php.

Weidlich, W. (2000), *Sociodynamics: A Systematic Approach to Mathematical Modelling in the Social Sciences*, Amsterdam: Harwood Academic.

Windrum, P., C. Diaz and D. Filiou (2009), 'Exploring the relationship between technical and service characteristics', *Journal of Evolutionary Economics*, **19** (4), 567–88.

Witt, U. (2001), 'Learning to consume: a theory of wants and the growth of demand', *Journal of Evolutionary Economics*, **11** (1), 23–36.

Witt, U. (2003), *The Evolving Economy: Essays on the Evolutionary Approach to Economics*, Cheltenham, UK and Northampton, MA, USA: Edward Elgar.

Experimental economics

Introduction

Experimental economics is based on applying laboratory methods to economics. Experimental economists consider the experimental method applicable to the economy and innovative because it allows a level of realism that has been impossible for economic analysis. Experimental economics is not only a methodological change, as it also challenges some assumptions commonly accepted by traditional economic theory, in particular, the concepts of full rationality and perfect information. As a result, since the 1950s experimental economics plays a relevant role in the debate on the nature and validity of these assumptions.

Experimental economics started to be developed in the late 1940s and early 1950s (Davis and Holt 1993), and it grew in the subsequent decades and in particular in the 1960s (Roth 1995), up to the 1980s, when economic experiments were very popular. Von Neumann and Morgenstern's work (1944) is considered the milestone for the emergence of experimental economics: their expected utility and game theory required a formalization of assumptions and implications of rational choice and so made possible their experimental verification. Although the role of von Neumann and Morgenstern's work has been important for experimentation on decisions (both individual and strategic), it has had less of an impact on market experiments. Two different contributions are often cited as precursors of experimentation in economics: Thurstone (1931) for experiments on choices and Chamberlin (1948) for experiments on markets.

An economic experiment requires the involvement of real people who are asked to take choices in a controlled environment. Just as with experiments in natural sciences, it is possible for the economist to isolate one (or more) variable(s) and to check its (or their) impact on the choices taken by the subjects and replicate his or her experiments. During an economic experiment, a series of rules, called the experimental protocol, must be followed to ensure the validity of data.

The experimental method has been applied in particular to individual and strategic decisions and to market theory. Currently, the work of Daniel Kahneman and Amos Tversky is considered the landmark for conducting experiments on decisions, whereas the experiments on markets have as major landmark the work of Vernon Smith. The Sveriges Riksbank Prize in Economic Sciences in Memory of Alfred Nobel awarded in 2002 to Kahneman and Smith (Tversky died in 1996) is cited by many economists as a pivotal moment for the acknowledgement of the experimental method in economics.

Together with its spread, there has also been a diversification in the ways of conceiving and applying the experimental method. Some economists are, however, still not convinced about this method; their main criticisms focus on the difficulty of reproducing the complexities of the real world in a laboratory.

What is an Economic Experiment?

An experiment in economics is based on the possibility to reproduce one part of a real economic behaviour in a laboratory. In this way, the experimenter can control and replicate the observed behaviour in order to identify the role played by one or more definite elements, named variables. So, an economic experiment is similar to a scientific experiment.

Carrying out an experiment requires subjects and tools; for the experiment to be effective, a protocol of rules needs to be strictly followed. In economics, the experimental subjects are the economic behaviours. As a result, usually the experimental subjects are real people. So, economic experiments can be viewed as a "synthetic" economic reality. Tools can be divided into material tools and conceptual tools. Material tools include a laboratory (physical location), a group of subjects, and a set of techniques (mainly computer based, sometimes on paper, rarely oral). Conceptual tools can vary according to the kind of experiment, but a common denominator is the possibility of "comparison" whereby the importance of a particular variable is studied by comparing behaviours with and without the studied variable. So, an economic experiment requires different subjects experiencing different situations, which are called treatments. It may happen that two (or more) treatments are experienced by two (or more) groups (between-subjects procedure); or it may happen that two (or more) treatments are experienced by a single group (within-subjects procedure). In any case, only one of the treatments includes the variable under examination, so that the environment is isolated and controlled).

Moreover, an economic experiment requires strict consistency with precise procedures, named protocols. In particular, instructions, incentives and fairness towards experimental subjects are considered compulsory. Instructions must be clear and complete. Incentives should be monetary and well balanced to the required efforts. This is considered to be important to ensure an adequate motivation in experimental subjects; the practice of paying participants emerged as early as the 1950s and, according to Roth (1995), it can be read as the answer to Wallis and Friedman's (1942) criticisms. According to these criticisms, the hypothetical nature of experimental choices made experimental results weak. Recently, the idea emerged that if it is true that the reliability of experimental data requires a good motivation, at the same time, it is also true that a good motivation does not necessarily require monetary incentives.

The diffusion of economic experiments has also brought some criticisms about the relationship between experiments and reality (Sugden 2005). It is a problematic relationship in both directions: when one tries to reproduce reality in the laboratory and when one tries to apply the laboratory results to reality. The central issue of this relationship is the basic difference between the simplicity of experimental situations and the complexity of the correspondent reality.

Three Objectives and Three Strands in Experimental Economics

Aims and objectives
Economic experiments have the general aim of transforming the economy using realistic science and it is underpinned by three main objectives: testing existing economic theories; identifying useful elements (and in particular some constants that characterize human behaviours in order to develop new theories); applying the experimental results to the real world through a dialogue with policymakers – or, in the words of Roth (1995: 22), "whispering in the ears of princes" – with the aim to help people to improve their performance of choice (Davis and Holt 1993; Roth 1995).

The role of experiments in testing theories is described below. The main result of the second aim – the identification of regularities – finds its widest and most complete formulation in the identification and classification of some biases characterizing experimental men respect to economic man. Finally, the application of experimental results to reality is the basis of market design, which simulates market strategies and policies to predict their effects on economic behaviours (Roth 2002).

Strands
These aims are pursued by applying the experimental method to three specific areas (strands) of economic theory: individual decisions, strategic decisions and markets (Davis and Holt 1993; Roth 1995). Each objective can be achieved in one specific area, or strand; although, when experimental economics was developed, in every strand researchers focused on testing theories and only successively the other two objectives became important.

Experiments on individual decisions aim to analyse, in a laboratory, individual decision-making processes. In economics, the starting point is the theory of rational choice: individuals make choices following criteria of perfect rationality with the goal to maximize utility (or profits). In 1944, von Neumann and Morgenstern's expected utility theory provided rational choice with a more specific and formalized configuration. With respect to individual decision-making, experimental economics first highlighted the lack of realism in expected utility theory, showing that subjects are characterized by bounded rationality and, as a consequence, that their choices are not necessarily maximizing choice: key contributions are Allais's paradox and prospect theory. Following these core contributions, a large literature has shown some bias (from traditional economic assumptions) that characterize human behaviour: they occur with regularity and therefore, according to experimental economics, can be used to build a model of economic behaviours standardized but closer to reality.

Experiments on strategic decisions aim to analyse those decision-making processes where the results of a choice taken by each subject also depend on the choices made by the others (therefore called strategic). The starting point is game theory, introduced in economics by von Neumann and Morgenstern (1944). In particular, a dominant strategy, defined as the best choice that an individual can take regardless of the choice taken by the others, is the equivalent in strategic decision-making of what maximization is in individual decision-making. A key contribution is, in particular, the "prisoner's dilemma". It shows that, following expected utility theory and dominant strategies, the subject reaches a suboptimal equilibrium, named a Nash equilibrium, and not a Paretian equilibrium. The prisoner's dilemma is central for experimental economics because when it is submitted to experimental individuals they tend to carry out behaviours characterized by a level of social cooperation with greater respect to the assumptions of rational choice. Similar results stem from the ultimatum game. It is a game that analyses strategic choices in which subjects do not choose simultaneously but in different and immediately subsequent moments.

The third strand of experimental economics is the experiments on markets. The typified experiment is the "double auction" one (Smith 1962, 1964), which reproduces in a laboratory a market situation where experimental subjects are divided into buyers and sellers, both provided with incomplete information. The experimental results are that the quantity of goods exchanged and the price of exchange approximate those predicted by the theory of Walrasian equilibrium.

Concluding Remarks

Experimental economics raised the issue of the relationship between models and reality. The review of leading experimental economists reveals many steps forward. With this in mind, it is useful to return to the difference between experiments on decisions, which deny the traditional theory, and experiments on markets, which instead confirm it. Combining these findings, experimental economics shows that real man is different from economic man. Experimental man is closer to real man than to economic man and he can perform efficient exchanges on markets without requiring the acceptance of the unrealistic assumptions of full rationality and perfect information.

SALVATORE RIZZELLO AND ANNA SPADA

See also:

Maurice Allais (I); Game theory (III); Herbert Alexander Simon (I); Uncertainty and information (III).

References and further reading

Binmore, K. (1999), 'Why experiment in economics?', *The Economic Journal*, **109** (453), F16–F24.
Chamberlin, E.H. (1948), 'An experimental imperfect market', *Journal of Political Economy*, **56** (2), 95–108.
Davis, D.D. and C.A. Holt (1993), *Experimental Economics*, Princeton, NJ: Princeton University Press.
Roth, A.E. (1995), 'Introduction to experimental economics', in A.E. Roth and J.H. Kagel (eds), *The Handbook of Experimental Economics*, Princeton, NJ: Princeton University Press, pp. 3–109.
Roth, A.E. (2002), 'The economist as engineer: game theory, experimentation, and computation as tools for design economics', *Econometrica*, **70** (4), 1341–78.
Smith, V.L. (1962), 'An experimental study of competitive market behavior', *Journal of Political Economy*, **70** (2), 111–37.
Smith, V.L. (1964), 'Effect of marketing organization on competitive equilibrium', *Quarterly Journal of Economics*, **78** (2), 181–201.
Sugden, R. (2005), 'Experiment, theory, word: a symposium on the role of experiments in economics', *Journal of Economic Methodology*, **12** (2), 177–84.
Thurstone, L.L. (1931), 'The indifference function', *Journal of Social Psychology*, **2** (2), 139–67.
Von Neumann, J. and O. Morgerstern (1944), *Theory of Games and Economic Behavior*, Princeton, NJ: Princeton University Press.
Wallis, W.A. and M. Friedman (1942), 'The empirical derivation of indifference functions', in O. Lange, F. McIntyre and T.O. Yntema (eds), *Studies in Mathematical Economics and Econometrics in Memory of Henry Schultz*, Chicago, IL: University of Chicago Press, pp. 175–89.

Financial economics

Financial economics is both an ancient subject, with origins in business practice, and one of the newest, with origins in applied mathematics. From the former perspective, it seems closest to accounting, and to money and banking, both of which arise from the attempt by practitioners to codify their own experience (Poitras 2000; Goetzmann and Rouwenhorst 2005). From the latter perspective, it seems closest to forms of engineering, where tools of dynamic programming and modern probability theory, for example, are deployed to solve practical problems facing businesses and consumers (Cont 2010).

In both of these guises, financial economics has always maintained an uneasy relationship with economics proper, for which the implied audience is typically some state actor with instrumental goals of its own. Until very recently, public finance and monetary economics were considered finance enough for economics, these subjects being attempts to provide the conceptual framework needed to guide government policy, fiscal and monetary policy respectively. (See, for example, Musgrave 1959 and Gurley and Shaw 1960.) Corporate finance and investment management were left to the schools of business, and it was therefore in those schools of business that modern finance first grew up. The initial impetus for that growth came from developments in business practice, specifically the revival of private capital markets in the decades after World War II. This revival happened first in the United States, which helps to explain why the field of modern finance was initially largely an American invention.

The Capital Asset Pricing Model

On the supply of funds side, burgeoning pools of private investment capital inside pension funds and insurance companies cried out for scientific management, and portfolio theory developed to meet that demand. By treating the returns on individual securities as random variables, Markowitz (1952) was able to provide a framework for thinking about efficient portfolio diversification, and for actually calculating the portfolio weights that would achieve minimum risk for any given expected return target. (See also Roy 1952, writing outside the US.)

On the demand for funds side, increased scarcity of investment funds inside corporations forced new attention to focus on capital allocation decisions, as well as on decisions about external funding in capital markets; corporate finance theory developed to guide these decisions. By abstracting from taxation and bankruptcy, Modigliani and Miller (1958) were able to provide a framework for thinking systematically about the problem of the appropriate capital structure of a firm, a framework that clarified not only the choice between debt and equity finance, but also the choice between internal and external funding.

These two different material origins of modern finance help to explain the different versions of the capital asset pricing model (CAPM) that emerged at more or less the same time, as well as the mutual incomprehension with which they initially received one another. Bill Sharpe's (1964) CAPM built on the portfolio theory pioneered by Harry Markowitz, as did the CAPM of Jan Mossin (1966). By contrast, the CAPMs of Jack Treynor (1962) and John Lintner (1965) both built on the corporate finance theory pioneered by Franco Modigliani and Merton Miller. The eventual 1990 Nobel prize (the

Sveriges Riksbank Prize in Economic Sciences in Memory of Alfred Nobel) that recognized these achievements was shared by Markowitz, Sharpe and Miller, thus recognizing both versions, and hence both origins.

Nevertheless, for teaching purposes, the canonical CAPM became that of Sharpe, which made its way into textbooks as the following formula:

$$ER_i = R_f + \beta_i(ER_m - R_f). \tag{1}$$

This says that the expected return on asset i is equal to the risk-free rate of interest R_f plus the amount of risk in the asset β_i times the price of risk. According to CAPM, portfolio diversification implies that risk is properly measured by the covariance of an asset with the diversified market portfolio (not by the asset's own variance), and that the price of risk is the excess expected return on that diversified market portfolio, $(ER_m - R_f)$.

The two origins shared the CAPM Nobel prize, but that prize did not come for 25 years, a delay that in retrospect can be understood as reflecting the time it took for the new finance to be recognized as a contribution to economics proper. To most economists, CAPM just did not seem that important; it was about private finance not public finance, and also about finance not money. At the beginning, the new finance entered economics only to the extent that it seemed to bear on the traditional fiscal and monetary policy concerns of economics.

Thus, Sharpe was not initially seen as the main road leading from Markowitz; first there was Tobin (1969) whose contributions to portfolio theory fed directly into the economists' project of building large-scale econometric models of the economy, the better to calibrate fiscal and monetary policy interventions. Similarly, Lintner and Treynor were not the main road leading from Modigliani and Miller; first there was Ando and Modigliani (1969) whose "Econometric analysis of stabilization policies" actually implemented the necessary parameterization. Thus Tobin and Modigliani got their Nobel prizes first, in 1981 and 1985, respectively. Initially, the work of Tobin and Modigliani was considered finance enough for economics.

Finance and General Equilibrium

To understand better the resistance of economics to modern finance, it is necessary to appreciate the role played by general equilibrium theory in orienting economists' sense of their intellectual project in the years after World War II, and to appreciate the place of finance in that theory.

Famously, the canonical Arrow–Debreu model (Arrow and Debreu 1954) extended general equilibrium from one period to many, and from the case of certainty to the case of risk, by imagining markets in state-contingent commodities, each with its own price. In the real world, of course, such markets are noticeably absent, except in a very few cases of generic raw commodity inputs such as wheat, cotton, and oil. However, crucially, Arrow (1953) also showed how financial instruments that promise state-contingent payoffs (so-called Arrow–Debreu securities) could substitute for those missing commodity markets, and how the price of those financial instruments could substitute for state-contingent commodity prices. In effect, he argued that a world of complete financial markets would be equivalent to the idealized Arrow–Debreu world of complete state-contingent commodity markets, and either world would provide the institutional basis for full general economic equilibrium.

In this way of thinking, the role for policy intervention, both fiscal and monetary, arises from institutional imperfections of one kind or another that prevent the economy from achieving full general economic equilibrium. If the institutions were perfect, the economy would already be at that equilibrium, and there would be no need for policy intervention. However, the institutions are not perfect, so policy intervention is needed to push the economy closer to the ideal. Finance enters the picture because proper calibration of policy intervention requires an understanding of how any particular intervention is transmitted through financial markets into the broader economy. Public finance and monetary economics were finance enough for economics, but as real-world financial markets developed, public finance and monetary economics had to adapt to those developments by bringing in relevant bits of modern financial theory. That is what Tobin and Modigliani, among others, thought they were doing.

For both men, the key link between the ideal world of Arrow–Debreu and the large-scale econometric modelling project they were conducting was the theory of "monetary Walrasianism". Also, the key figure who set the agenda for monetary Walrasianism was Jacob Marschak, initially in his pre-war "Money and the theory of assets" (1938). The story of intellectual transmission from these origins has only recently begun to surface, but a central chapter clearly involves Marschak's role, during 1943–48, as Research Director of the Cowles Commission. (See Mehrling 2010; also Hagemann 2006; Cherrier 2010.)

Crucially, it was Marschak, before anyone else, who took the pre-World War II work of Irving Fisher as his starting point, especially Fisher's 1930 *The Theory of Interest as Determined by Impatience to Spend Income and Opportunity to Invest It*. Subsequently, post-war macroeconomics became a project of bringing the sensibility of Irving Fisher to bear on post-war problems, using updated analytical tools that had been developed in the meanwhile, many of them under the pressure of war. James Tobin, himself Research Director of the reconfigured Cowles Foundation from 1955 to 1961 and 1964 to 1965, can be viewed as the standard bearer of this neo-Fisherian American-style Keynesianism (Tobin 1985; Dimand 1997).

Marschak–Tobin was the first road leading from Irving Fisher, but CAPM and modern finance was the next, and this second road led in a much more radical direction. The Marschak–Tobin monetary Walrasian project was about providing a scientific basis for government policy intervention to steer the economy closer to the full general equilibrium ideal. By contrast, the finance project was about changing financial institutions themselves to eliminate the imperfections and frictions that were the putative source of policy leverage. The goal was nothing less than to make the world ever more like the complete-markets ideal, and so also presumably ever less in need of expert policy guidance. If finance were to be successful, economics would become irrelevant.

This second road leading from Irving Fisher to modern finance is clearest in the life and work of Fischer Black, who from the first interpreted CAPM as the broader macroeconomic construct that arises when we retrace the steps of Irving Fisher but with risk, time, and equilibrium built in from the beginning. (See Mehrling 2005: 93–8.) Black's particular view has not (so far) prevailed, but the larger transformative finance project that he anticipated certainly has. In my view, future historians will see developments after about 1970 in these more fundamental terms as a struggle between old economics versus new finance, and the contemporary quarrelling between Keynesianism and monetarism within economics will come to seem much less important. To the generation of Tobin and Modigliani, and also Milton Friedman, "financial economics" meant applications of economics to financial topics. To the generation of today, it means applications of modern finance to economic topics.

Efficient Markets

Historically, the origin of the audacious finance project can be traced to the much more modest idea that stock market prices follow a random walk. Initially little more than an empirical characterization of the data, the "random walk theory" developed into a powerfully evocative theoretical construct called the efficient markets hypothesis (Fama 1965, 1970, 1991), and then even further into a theory of the economy as a whole. Arrow's general equilibrium framework had envisioned the economy fundamentally as a system of real commodity exchange, with financial markets serving as a kind of subordinate mechanism to facilitate that exchange. By contrast, modern finance came to see the economy fundamentally as a system of asset pricing, with commodity exchange conceived as a kind of special case. As one measure of the intellectual distance travelled since Arrow (1953), consider the changing fortunes of the lowly option. The apparently esoteric state-contingent security of Arrow and Debreu is today seen as the fundamental building block of all of finance, and the problem of option pricing as the key to understanding asset pricing more generally.

The efficient markets hypothesis originated as an attempt to explain a startling empirical fact. If you draw a chart showing how the price of a stock (or stock index) has moved over some period of time, it will typically bear a striking resemblance to similar charts showing the movement of variables that we know to be random, such as coin flips. If you keep track of a series of coin flips, counting heads as $+1$ and tails as -1, the cumulative sum will go up and down in a way that is hard to distinguish from the movement of a stock price. Harry Roberts (1959), a statistician at the Graduate School of Business at the University of Chicago, convinced himself of this "random walk theory" by showing charts of stock prices and cumulative coin flips to stock market analysts, who could not tell the difference. In succeeding years Roberts' students, most notably Eugene Fama, applying more sophisticated statistical techniques to the data, came to more sophisticated versions of more or less the same conclusion.

This new statistical way of thinking about the data focused attention on two questions: the independence of successive price changes over time, and the shape of the probability distribution of price changes at a point in time. For most economists, the independence question seemed the more important of the two, since statistical independence would imply zero expected speculative profit, which economists recognized as a characterization of equilibrium in competitive markets. Thus the random walk theory, initially only a statistical characterization of the data, came to be endowed with economic content, got renamed as the efficient markets hypothesis (EMH), and then adopted as the centrepiece of a distinctive Chicago-style approach to finance (Fama and Miller 1972).

The random walk formulation of EMH was soon shown to be not entirely correct (Samuelson 1965, Mandelbrot 1966); the correct statistical consequence of assuming zero expected speculative profit was a "martingale" not a random walk. What is important is not that successive increments are statistically independent, but only that current price is the conditional expectation of future price. As Samuelson stated it (under the simplifying assumption of a zero discount rate):

$$P_t = E(P_{t+1}|P_t).$$ (2)

Notwithstanding this correction – and notwithstanding also the branding effort of Cootner's *Random Character of Stock Prices* (1964) which sought to establish a distinguished ancestry for this approach in the person of Louis Bachelier (1900; Davis and Etheridge 2006) – the EMH became the brand of Chicago rather than of the Massachusetts Institute of Technology (MIT), if only because Chicago wanted the brand while MIT did not. At MIT, efficiency was merely an idealization, unlikely to hold reliably in the real world, hence not an attractive null hypothesis and certainly not a useful maintained hypothesis (Mandelbrot 1971). Chicago went the other way.

This intellectual split, right at the origin of the modern field, would have continuing reverberations throughout the subsequent decades, as fledgling finance grew to be an enormous field in its own right. One immediate consequence showed itself in dispute over the proper interpretation of statistical tests of asset pricing theories such as CAPM. Such tests were always joint tests of both the theory and the efficient markets hypothesis, so negative results could be met either by rejecting CAPM or by rejecting efficiency (Roll 1977). Chicago reliably chose the former, while MIT reliably chose the latter (Shiller 2000).

From this point of view, the importance of the Samuelson–Mandelbrot results was not so much to correct a technicality in the mathematical formulation of EMH, but rather to endow the formulation with a deep economic interpretation, namely, no arbitrage. Once no arbitrage was placed at the centre of finance, the new field could grow essentially unhindered by any further intellectual inheritance from economics, no utility curves or production functions, no supply and demand. So it did, for more than a decade.

No Arbitrage

The reason that finance could make progress from such minimal economic foundations is that for finance the empirical relevance of no arbitrage is high, for two simple reasons: there are many actors (speculators) actively searching for arbitrage opportunities, and it is relatively costless for them to exploit any opportunities they find. It follows that, for finance, the principle of no arbitrage is not merely a convenient assumption that makes it possible to derive clean theoretical results, but even more an idealization of observable empirical reality, and a characterization of the deep and simple structure underlying multifarious surface phenomena.

Crucially, it is the principle of no arbitrage that lies behind the fundamental theorem of asset pricing which asserts the existence of a positive linear pricing rule (Ross 1976b, 1978). The most important practical implication of this theorem is that assets that are not yet traded can be priced simply by reference to the price of assets that are already traded, and without the need to invoke any particular theory of asset pricing. This feature opened the possibility of creating new assets, such as options but also other financial derivatives, that would in practical terms "complete" markets, and so help move the economy closer to the ideal characterized by Arrow (1953). This possibility subsequently served as the legitimation for the entire field of financial engineering (Ross 1976a). However, the first use of the principle of no arbitrage, and to this day its most resoundingly successful use, was to solve the previously intractable problem of pricing options. The story of how that happened is instructive.

A call option, the right to purchase a given security at a given exercise price on or before a given maturity date, is clearly a risky security, and so in principle should be amenable to pricing by means of the CAPM. Such was the idea of Fischer Black when he first started to work on the problem, having been initially introduced to CAPM through the work of his colleague Jack Treynor. What made the problem hard was that the amount of risk in the option changed over time, and in a non-linear way, as the price of the underlying referenced security changed. Nevertheless, by characterizing these price dynamics, Black was able to obtain a differential equation and then, working with Myron Scholes, solve it for the famous formula:

$$W(x, t) = xN(d_1) - ce^{-r(t^* - t)}N(d_2) \qquad (3)$$

where x is the stock price, $N(d)$ the cumulative normal density function that describes the distribution of the stock price, c the exercise price, r the rate of interest, t^* the expiration date, and d_1 and d_2 are functions of these data and the variance of the stock return (Black and Scholes 1973).

Black and Scholes came to the correct formula using CAPM, but in the end it turned out that the formula did not depend on CAPM at all, or indeed on any other theory of asset pricing either. Robert Merton (1973) came to the same formula in a different way, by thinking about the option as a portfolio of stock and riskless debt, with portfolio proportions that changed over time as the price of the stock changed. (That proportion is called the hedge ratio; it is a number indicating how many shares of the referenced security should be held to hedge the risk in the option.) Assuming continuous and costless trading, the portfolio could exactly replicate the payoff from the option. Since we know the price of the replicating portfolio, it follows that we also know the price of the option. One problem with Merton's formulation was the crucial but implausible assumption of continuous and costless trading; in practice exact replication was simply impossible. To the rescue came the principle of no arbitrage, since it allows us to price the option even if replication is not possible in practice.

The solution of the option pricing problem was just the beginning. An entire field of financial engineering was the result. Notwithstanding Merton (1990), instead of calling that field "continuous time finance" and so conceptualizing it as a field of applied mathematics, as an economist I would rather emphasize the principle of no arbitrage as the essential foundation for the field, and the source of its continuing link to economics. Crucially, it was the principle of no arbitrage that made it possible for developments in finance to re-enter economics in the 1980s, through the unlikely mechanism of the martingale equivalence theorem (Harrison and Kreps 1979). The story of how that happened is also instructive.

In Samuelson's original work on the connection between no arbitrage and the martingale property, he assumed an exogenously fixed discount rate, and limited his attention to asset prices. As a consequence, it was not at all clear how general his result was, since in a more general economic model the discount rate should be endogenous and should fluctuate with the economy as a whole. That means, as LeRoy (1973) and Lucas (1978) pointed out, that there is no reason to suppose that the martingale property will necessarily be a general feature of efficient asset market prices; in other words, Samuelson's results were a special case. From this point of view, Harrison and Kreps (1979) was crucial, rehabilitating the foundational place of the martingale property, by shifting attention to risk-neutral pricing under a martingale equivalent probability measure. In doing so, they also made it possible to treat no arbitrage and the martingale property as foundational for economics, as well as finance.

Finance and General Equilibrium, Redux

Therefore, we can understand the work of Cox et al. (1981, 1985a, 1985b) as an attempt to connect the insights of no arbitrage back to economic "fundamentals".

> In work on contingent claims analysis, such as option pricing, it is common, and to a first approximation reasonable, to insist only on a partial equilibrium between the prices of the primary and derivative assets. For something as fundamental as the rate of interest, however, a general equilibrium model is to be preferred. (Cox et al. 1981: 773)

To do this, the authors built on Ross's own arbitrage pricing theory (Ross 1976b) to produce a general equilibrium model driven by a k-dimensional vector of state variables. In the end they were forced to specialize the model considerably in order to achieve definite results for the dynamics of interest rates and the term structure, and as a consequence economics did not pick it up.

A more successful attempt to do essentially the same thing was the real business cycle literature which started from the other end, with its foundations in economics, and then imported no arbitrage under the disarming name of rational expectations. The connection to finance was made through the Euler equation of consumption that lies at the heart of both modern finance and modern macroeconomics. Economists like to write the equation like this:

$$U'(C_{it}) = E_t[\delta U'(C_{it+1})R_{jt+1}]. \tag{4}$$

In this equation C_{it} is the consumption of consumer i at time t, U is a function that translates consumption into utility terms, δ is the subjective discount rate, and R_{jt+1} is the gross return on asset j in the period between t and $t+1$.

For finance, this equation is about how asset prices depend on time and risk preference, the equation is called the "consumption CAPM", and the asset in question is typically equity or long term bonds (Breeden 1979). But the same equation can be used to talk about the intertemporal fluctuation of income, and as such is at the core of both real business cycle theory (Kydland and Prescott 1982) and its new Keynesian variants (Woodford 2003) that see the economy through the lens of the so-called dynamic stochastic general equilibrium (DSGE) model. In this application, the asset is typically capital, or a rate of interest.

The link to finance, and the foundational role of no arbitrage and the martingale, comes clear when we write the Euler equation instead as:

$$1 = E_t[M_{it+1}R_{jt+1}] \tag{5}$$

where M is a stochastic discount factor treated as a free variable that must fit the cross section pattern of asset returns R. (Note how the characteristic utility foundations of economics disappear in this finance formulation.) Under the martingale equivalent measure, this equation can equivalently be written as:

$$1 = E^M_t[R_{t+1}] \text{ or } P_t = E^M_t[P_{t+1}], \tag{6}$$

the latter formulation being exactly analogous to Samuelson (1965).

Thus it is that modern finance, having grown up outside of economics and independent from almost all of the intellectual inheritance of the field, re-entered economics and in doing so quite completely transformed it. The monetary Walrasianism of Tobin and Modigliani survives in elementary textbooks, and in policy discussion circles, but hardly a trace can be found in the advanced academic literature. Originally conceived as an account of how government can make use of imperfections in markets as leverage for moving the economy closer to the complete markets ideal, monetary Walrasianism has in the past 40 years had its institutional and intellectual foundations cut out from under it by a combination of financial innovation and deregulation, both domestically and internationally. The audacious finance project has come to pass; is economics irrelevant?

The Future of Finance

The consequence of financial innovation and de-regulation has quite clearly not been the achievement of the full general equilibrium ideal posited in Arrow (1953). Indeed, the global financial crisis of 2007–09 has brought with it widespread questioning of both the DSGE model (in economics) and the EMH (in finance). Arrow himself was prescient about the limitations of both, insisting repeatedly in print that the problems of risk and time are not really addressed within the intertemporal general equilibrium model (Arrow 1978: 159; see also Arrow 1981). Indeed, as Frank Hahn, among others, has repeatedly emphasized, the model has no place in it for money (Hahn 1965).

That is the fundamental reason that academic economics and finance had so little to say when the crisis struck. The crisis was essentially about money and liquidity, matters from which both economics and finance had resolutely abstracted (Mehrling 2011). Before the crisis, most people thought that efficient markets would be liquid markets, because there would always be a buyer willing to step forward when price fell even a little bit below fundamental value. "Not so", is the verdict of history, and "Why not so?" is the question now confronting the field of financial economics.

This reading of history suggests that the road forward, both for finance and for economics, and hence a fortiori for financial economics, will involve a shift of focus to matters of money and liquidity. The crisis has made clear that the modern real world is in important ways not like the ideal world posited long ago by intertemporal general equilibrium theory. As a consequence, public finance and monetary economics that are orientated around that ideal world are simply not finance enough for modern economics. During the crisis, states were called upon to act and they did so, but without much help from economics. Public entities, just as much as private entities, confronted the problem of managing their affairs in the face of the "dark forces of time and ignorance". As in the past, we can expect the future fertility of financial economics to arise from attempts to respond to practical problems, both public and private, in the real world.

PERRY MEHRLING

See also:

Kenneth Joseph Arrow (I); Louis Bachelier (I); Business cycles and growth (III); Gérard Debreu (I); Irving Fisher (I); General equilibrium theory (III); Robert E. Lucas (I); Macroeconomics (III); Jacob Marschak (I); Richard Abel Musgrave (I); New Classical Macroeconomics (II); Paul Anthony Samuelson (I); James Tobin (I); Value and price (III).

References and further reading

Ando, A. and F. Modigliani (1969), 'Econometric analysis of stabilization policies', *American Economic Review*, **59** (2), 296–314.

Arrow, K.J. (1953), 'Le role des valeurs boursieres pour la repartition la meilleure des risques', in *Econometrie*, Colloques Internationaux du Centre National de la Recherche Scientifique, vol. 11, Paris: CNRS, pp. 41–7.

Arrow, K.J. (1978), 'The future and the present in economic life', *Economic Inquiry*, **16** (2), 157–69.

Arrow, K.J. (1981), 'Futures markets: some theoretical perspectives', *Journal of Futures Markets*, **1** (2), 107–15.

Arrow, K.J. and G. Debreu (1954), 'Existence of an equilibrium for a competitive economy', *Econometrica*, **22** (3), 265–90.

Bachelier, L. (1900), *Théorie de la speculation*, reprinted in M. Davis and E. Etheridge (2006), *Louis Bachelier's Theory of Speculation*, Princeton, NJ: Princeton University Press, pp. 15–79.

Black, F. and M. Scholes (1973), 'The pricing of options and corporate liabilities', *Journal of Political Economy*, **81** (May–June), 637–54.

Breeden, D.T. (1979), 'An intertemporal asset pricing model with stochastic consumption and investment opportunities', *Journal of Financial Economics*, **7** (3), 265–96.

Cherrier, B. (2010), 'Rationalizing human organization in an uncertain world: Jacob Marschak', *History of Political Economy*, **42** (3), 443–67.

Cont, R. (ed.) (2010), *Encyclopedia of Quantitative Finance*, Chichester: John Wiley & Sons.

Cootner, P.H. (ed.) (1964), *The Random Character of Stock Prices*, Cambridge, MA: MIT Press.

Cox, J.C., J.E. Ingersoll Jr and S.A. Ross (1981), 'A re-examination of traditional hypotheses about the term structure of interest rates', *Journal of Finance*, **36** (4), 769–99.

Cox, J.C., J.E. Ingersoll Jr and S.A. Ross (1985a), 'An intertemporal general equilibrium model of asset prices', *Econometrica*, **53** (2), 363–84.

Cox, J.C., J.E. Ingersoll Jr and S.A. Ross (1985b), 'A theory of the term structure of interest rates', *Econometrica*, **53** (2), 385–407.

Davis, M. and A. Etheridge (2006), *Louis Bachelier's Theory of Speculation*, Princeton, NJ: Princeton University Press.

Dimand, R.W. (1997), 'Irving Fisher and modern macroeconomics', *American Economic Review, Papers and Proceedings*, **87** (2), 442–44.

Fama, E. (1965), 'The behavior of stock-market prices', *Journal of Business*, **38** (1), 34–105.

Fama, E. (1970), 'Efficient capital markets: a review of theory and empirical work', *Journal of Finance*, **25** (2), 383–417.

Fama, E. (1991), 'Efficient capital markets: II', *Journal of Finance*, **46** (5), 1575–617.

Fama, E. and M. Miller (1972), *The Theory of Finance*, Hinsdale, IL: Dryden Press.

Fisher, I. (1930), *The Theory of Interest as Determined by Impatience to Spend Income and Opportunity to Invest It*, New York: Macmillan.

Goetzmann, W.N. and K. Geert Rouwenhorst (2005), *The Origins of Value; the Financial Innovations that Created Modern Capital Markets*, New York: Oxford University Press.

Gurley, J.G. and E.S. Shaw (1960), *Money in a Theory of Finance*, Washington, DC: Brookings Institution.

Hagemann, H. (2006), 'Marschak, Jacob (1898–1977)', in R.B. Emmett (ed.), *The Biographical Dictionary of American Economists*, vol. 2: J–Z, New York: Thoemes, pp. 596–603.

Hahn, F.H. (1965), 'On some problems of proving the existence of an equilibrium in a monetary economy', in F.H. Hahn and F.P.R. Brechling (eds), *Theory of Interest Rates*, Houndmills: Macmillan, pp. 126–35.

Harrison, J.M. and D.M. Kreps (1979), 'Martingales and arbitrage in multiperiod securities markets', *Journal of Economic Theory*, **20** (3), 381–408.

Kydland, F.E. and E.C. Prescott (1982), 'Time to build and aggregate fluctuations', *Econometrica*, **50** (6), 1345–70.

LeRoy, S.F. (1973), 'Risk aversion and the martingale property of stock returns', *International Economic Review*, **14** (2), 436–46.

Lintner, J. (1965), 'The valuation of risk assets and the selection of risky investments in stock portfolios and capital budgets', *Review of Economics and Statistics*, **47** (1), 13–37.

Lucas, R.E. Jr (1978), 'Asset prices in an exchange economy', *Econometrica*, **46** (6), 1429–45.

Mandelbrot, B.B. (1966), 'Forecasts of future prices, unbiased markets, and "martingale" models', *Journal of Business*, **39** (1), 242–55.

Mandelbrot, B.B. (1971), 'When can price be arbitraged efficiently? A limit to the validity of the random walk and martingale model', *Review of Economics and Statistics*, **53** (3), 225–36.

Markowitz, H. (1952), 'Portfolio selection', *Journal of Finance*, **7** (1), 77–91.

Marschak, J. (1938), 'Money and the theory of assets.' *Econometrica*, **6** (4), 311–25.

Mehrling, P. (2005), *Fischer Black and the Revolutionary Idea of Modern Finance*, New York: John Wiley & Sons.

Mehrling, P. (2010), 'A tale of two cities', *History of Political Economy*, **42** (2), 201–19.

Mehrling, P. (2011), *The New Lombard Street; How the Fed became the Dealer of Last Resort*, Princeton, NJ: Princeton University Press.

Merton, R.C. (1973), 'Theory of rational option pricing', *Bell Journal of Economics and Management Science*, **4** (Spring), 141–83.

Merton, R.C. (1990), *Continuous Time Finance*, revised 1992, Cambridge, MA: Basil Blackwell.

Modigliani, F. and M.H. Miller (1958), 'The cost of capital, corporation finance, and the theory of investment', *American Economic Review*, **48** (3), 261–97.

Mossin, J. (1966), 'Equilibrium in a capital asset market', *Econometrica*, **34** (4), 768–83.

Musgrave, R. (1959), *The Theory of Public Finance: A Study in Public Economy*, New York: McGraw-Hill.

Poitras, G. (2000), *The Early History of Financial Economics*, Cheltenham, UK and Northampton, MA, USA: Edward Elgar.

Roberts, H.V. (1959), 'Stock market "patterns" and financial analysis: methodological suggestions', *Journal of Finance*, **14** (1), 1–10.

Roll, R. (1977), 'A critique of the asset pricing theory's tests', *Journal of Financial Economics*, **4** (2), 129–76.

Ross, S.A. (1976a), 'Options and efficiency', *Quarterly Journal of Economics*, **90** (1), 75–89.

Ross, S.A. (1976b), 'The arbitrage theory of capital asset pricing', *Journal of Economic Theory*, **13** (3), 341–60.

Ross, S.A. (1978), 'A simple approach to the valuation of risky streams', *Journal of Business*, **51** (3), 453–75.

Roy, A.D. (1952), 'Safety first and the holding of assets', *Econometrica*, **20** (3), 431–49.

Samuelson, P.A. (1965), 'Proof that properly anticipated prices fluctuate randomly', *Industrial Management Review*, **6** (2), 41–9.

Sharpe, W. (1964), 'Capital asset prices: a theory of market equilibrium under conditions of risk', *Journal of Finance*, **19** (3), 425–42.

Shiller, R. (2000), *Irrational Exuberance*, Princeton, NJ: Princeton University Press.

Tobin, J. (1969), 'A general equilibrium approach to monetary theory', *Journal of Money, Credit, and Banking*, **1** (1), 15–29.

Tobin, J. (1985), 'Neoclassical theory in America: J.B. Clark and Fisher', *American Economics Review*, **75** (6), 28–38.

Treynor, J.L. (1962), 'Toward a theory of market value of risky assets', in R.A. Korajczyk (ed.) (1999), *Asset Pricing and Portfolio Performance*, London: Risk Books, pp. 15–22.

Woodford, M. (2003), *Interest and Prices: Foundations of a Theory of Monetary Policy*, Princeton, NJ: Princeton University Press.

Formalization and mathematical modelling

Claims that economics is close in spirit and principle to mathematics have been reiterated many times; a well-known one is William S. Jevons's "*our science must be mathematical, simply because it deals with quantities*" (1871 [1888]: 1.5, original emphasis). The use of mathematics is now widely recognized as an essential ingredient of both research and teaching in economics, and attempts to build mathematical accounts of economic phenomena are as old as the discipline itself (Theocharis 1961 [1983]).

The history of mathematical modelling in economics has not been a linear one. The profession privileged the verbal form for long, and even when the formal approach gradually gained ground, it often had to defend itself against hefty criticisms. Today's widespread consensus around formalization does not prevent doubts from occasionally resurfacing.

Formalization and mathematical modelling in economics need to be distinguished from quantification, or the systematic effort to measure reality for purposes of administrative intervention, for instance, by counting the population in a census or by devising accounting rules to estimate national income. Quantification dates back to the very origins of government and received substantial impulse in the seventeenth century, with the seminal contributions of William Petty and Charles Davenant; it remains a necessary support of economic policy today. More deeply intertwined with the development of economic thought, formalization is an approach to theory-building which, starting from the definition of theoretical constructs and of linkages between them, allows deriving logical conclusions from given premises. It does not even require its objects to be measurable or quantifiable, in so far as they can be expressed as variables or functions of variables, and they can be compared (larger/smaller, more/less, positive/negative, and so on). Advocating this approach, Jevons wrote that "The data are almost wholly deficient for the complete solution of any one problem", yet "we have mathematical theory without the data requisite for precise calculation" (Jevons 1871 [1888]: 1.9).

Because formalization purports to develop hypotheses and explanatory arguments independently of, or prior to, confrontation with empirical data, it is not to be confused with a third and more recent use of mathematics, namely, empirical validation and verification, testing (formal) theory against (quantitative) data according to some version of the scientific method. It is with the rise of econometrics (see this entry) in the twentieth century that the latter approach has blossomed.

The history of formalization is a succession of trials and errors, of failures and successes, and of difficulties that needed to be surmounted for mathematical models to provide relevant economic insight. At the beginning, only loose analogies were established between mathematical symbols or diagrams and economic concepts, so that the former could at most vaguely illustrate or summarize the latter, but could not guide reasoning. It took a long time to understand how symbols and formulas could be made to embody economic content in such a way that any conclusion reached mathematically – for example, by solving a system of equations – allows substantive economic interpretation.

The history of formalization is also a history of inter-disciplinary exchange and influence: far from being a set of ready-made tools for the economist to apply, mathematics is an independent discipline with its own constructs and modes of reasoning, whose use may contribute to forging economic ideas. It matters which mathematics is used: for example, do the assumptions of continuity and derivability required for calculus excessively constrain the choice of appropriate forms for the production and/or utility function? Is the assumption of linearity a reasonable approximation, or a deceptive misrepresentation of a more complex reality? Notice, also, that the choice of a particular branch of mathematics at a given point in time also depends on the state of mathematics at that time, so that its implications for economic theory may change with the further progress of mathematics (see also Weintraub 2002). For example, the continuity assumption was introduced in economics to authorize the use of calculus, before the discovery that it is a necessary but not a sufficient condition for derivability; it remained widespread afterwards, supporting use of other mathematical techniques. Another example is the notion of limit, which was formed after the first applications of calculus to economics and required reinterpretation of existing results.

A related issue is the relationship between economics and physics, the first example of a successful mathematical science. To name just two, Jevons himself and another founding father of mathematical economics, Léon Walras, made systematic use of mechanical analogies in justifying their theories and methodological choices. Even leaving aside the empirical dimension to focus on formalization alone, the questions arise of how physics may have influenced economics through mathematics and of the extent to which economics can meaningfully imitate physics in its choice of mathematical methods and procedures. Economists' use of calculus is a case in point, as this area of mathematics was originally developed in close relation with Newtonian mechanics.

The next sections outline the history of formalization and mathematical modelling in economics, in two phases (up to 1925 and since 1925); a third part on recent developments has been added to this basic scheme. There is insufficient room here to cover all aspects of the intellectual reflection in mathematical economics over such a long time span. For this reason, the presentation is limited to a sketch of what each period contributed to the formal study of two foundational issues that, more than others, have lent themselves to mathematical treatment – namely, the theories of individual economic behaviour and of the market mechanism as a coordinating device.

Mathematical Economics up to 1925

The use of formalisms was infrequent in the early stages of the discipline, but some attempts at framing economic concepts and theories in mathematical terms appeared from the beginning. Initially rudimentary, they steadily gained in sophistication, explanatory power, and creative potential. Despite their limited diffusion, these undertakings contributed to shaping some of the essential principles of economics and influenced its development, both substantively and methodologically. What follows is an overview of the main phases of development of mathematical economics at this stage, with its first steps in the eighteenth century, its improvements in the early nineteenth century, the subsequent blooming of marginalism, and the first formal models of the market mechanism.

The eighteenth century: a marriage not consumated
The making of economics in the eighteenth century was accompanied by enthusiasm for mathematics and some attempts at formalization. Most of the latter seem naive today;

they mainly used elementary arithmetic and few went as far as to apply some algebra. In Italy, for example, (see Bianchini 1982), Cesare Beccaria (1764 [1804]) used algebra to determine customs duties based on a fine analysis of the choice of a merchant and the opportunity to smuggle goods. Pietro Verri (1771 [1772]) and others proposed a price determination formula in which they summarized demand and supply by taking the ratio of the number of buyers to the number of sellers. The formula, which had a certain echo at the time, admittedly conveys some appropriate intuitions, in particular that prices tend to rise with an increase in demand, and to diminish with an increase in supply, and that relative to a monopoly a higher number of sellers signal a more competitive market and therefore lower prices. However, it is a coarse form that includes unjustified auxiliary assumptions (why a ratio?) and fails to distinguish the questions of how to calculate the price level with given supply and demand, and how to assess its variations in case of changes in supply or demand.

Other contributions made more advanced use of mathematics. In 1772, Paolo Frisi endeavoured to complete Verri's price formula with an optimization calculation, using differentials and even – barely ten years after their introduction into mathematics – Lagrange multipliers. In France, Achilles-Nicolas Isnard (1781 [2009]) represented the economy as a system of simultaneous equations which, despite some rough simplifications that ensured tractability, prefigures later efforts to account for interdependencies across markets (Van den Berg 2006). Charles-François Bicquilley's 1804 attempt to formulate a wide-ranging mathematical theory of the economy that could cover a range of aspects – from market price determination to insurance – is unique for its extensive use of probability theory (Crépel 1998). There are even outliers, most prominently Daniel Bernoulli who, as early as 1738, relied on the theory of functions to anticipate what would be later known as expected utility theory and provided a first version of the decreasing marginal utility principle.

The success of all these attempts was, however, limited. One reason is that many of them dealt with circumscribed questions, without developing a comprehensive approach to individual behaviour or market coordination. For all its originality, Bernoulli's formalization simply related utility to monetary income, where the latter is first allocated to buy the most necessary things, then the less and less necessary, until the superfluous ones; that is, wealth can satisfy a series of hierarchically ordered needs, an idea that others had already expressed at the time (though only verbally). It does not prove decreasing marginal utility for one good only and does not open the way to a general theory of utility; therefore, it cannot constitute the basis of a theory of demand, let alone of market price formation.

Another reason is the imperfect correspondence between economic principles and mathematical symbols or equations. Italian writers' ratio of the number of buyers to sellers is a clear example of how mathematics had an evocative, illustrative function but did not serve as a guide for building compelling arguments. Even Frisi's differential calculus, in the absence of a theory of economic behaviour backing his calculations, turned out to provide little, if any, economic insight (Tubaro 2002).

Reactions to these attempts were varied, but rarely enthusiastic. Vehement attacks were directed against Frisi's mathematics, and Verri dropped the mathematical notes from subsequent editions of his book. Bicquilley and Isnard were less overtly criticized but fell rapidly into oblivion; and Bernoulli's formalization found an echo among mathematicians but, until more than a century later, contributed very little to economists' debates on utility.

The early nineteenth century: building economics through geometry and calculus
In the nineteenth century the old-style, approximate use of mathematics as an illustration gradually lost ground: a notorious example is Nicolas-François Canard, who won an Institut de France contest in 1801 and enjoyed celebrity for some time, but subsequently attracted torrents of criticisms. A new generation of mathematical economists were distancing themselves from their predecessors to develop a new, more sophisticated approach.

Initiated by the work of David Ricardo and the so-called English "classical" school, a large part of the reflection of this time emphasized the differential impact of conditions of production on individuals according to their position as workers, capitalists, or landowners. Though most contributions were verbal, some ventured into tackling income distribution and the possible tension between wages and profits with the help of mathematics. In England, the so-called "Whewell group" – see, for example, Whewell (1829–50 [1871]), and Henderson (1996) – of mathematical economists used algebra to represent, cultivate and develop Ricardo's theory. One of them, John E. Tozer, proposed in 1838 a model of the social effects of substitution of capital for labour through the introduction of machinery, which Ricardo had judged "often very injurious to the interests of the class of labourers" (Ricardo 1817–21 [1951]: 388). While apparently critical of Ricardo, Tozer's equations in fact refine his views by bringing to light the specific conditions under which labourers' loss occurs (Tubaro 2008).

While these authors primarily used algebra the use of calculus also progressed significantly. A Prussian landlord, Johann H. von Thünen (1850 [1960]), concocted the concept of marginal productivity and the idea that, at an optimum, the marginal productivity of a factor must equal its remuneration. Not only did he use differential calculus to prove his result, but he derived the very economic notion of marginal productivity from the mathematical concept of partial differential (Tubaro 2006). Mathematics, then, played an essential creative role as it contributed to shaping a fundamental economic construct. Unfortunately, this intellectual achievement was obfuscated by Thünen's cumbersome notation, together with much-ridiculed enthusiasm for his own results (he claimed to have found the formula for the "natural wage" and had it engraved on his tombstone).

The early nineteenth century also saw efforts to move forwards in the understanding of utility. Reflection on this topic had already appeared, with the idea that the problem of political economy and the ultimate purpose of all productive activities, is to satisfy human wants at best. However, it seemed difficult to integrate utility into economic analysis, not least because at first glance it appears as a subjective, qualitative notion devoid of any objective, let alone quantifiable, attribute. Mathematics offered a solution: another German writer, Hermann H. Gossen (1854 [1983]), was the first to apply the idea that, even without actual measurements, formalization can support theory-building at a more abstract level, "to develop the possibilities that may occur in enjoyment and place them in mutual relation" (Gossen 1854 [1983]: 10). He used the mathematical notion of a function to reinterpret utility not as an absolute but as a relative magnitude, varying from one individual to another and for each individual, depending on the available quantity of a good. Gossen considered individual goods and the feelings of satisfaction they yield to the individual, thereby liberating himself from the older postulate of a universal, hierarchical ordering of needs defined with respect to monetary wealth. He also provided graphical methods to determine a maximum of utility, which he interpreted in a purely normative sense – what people ought to strive for in order to live a satisfactory life – without suggesting that they actually maximize. Gossen's contribution remained unknown and was only rediscovered towards the end of the century, but in the meantime others independently proposed similar solutions.

Economists' understanding of the market also made significant progress in this time period. The older, rudimentary formula of price determination, expressed simply as the ratio of demand to supply, was gradually replaced by the idea that demand and supply can be conceptualized as two different schedules and that what matters is their point of intersection, where they are equal. Price-quantity diagrams in which demand decreases and supply increases with price appeared from the 1830s onwards, in particular with Augustin Cournot (1838 [1960]) and Karl H. Rau (1841 [1997]). Verri's version of the eighteenth-century demand/supply formula, based on the number of buyers and sellers, also intuitively conveyed the idea that in monopoly situations prices are higher and quantities are lower than in cases in which several sellers compete. It was Cournot (1838 [1960]) who first gave an analytical account of this idea, while also pioneering the use of mathematics (including algebra, calculus and diagrams) to guide reasoning. He illustrated how the sole seller of a good controls the entire market and extracts a monopoly rent; with two or more sellers, decisions are interdependent and the market is in equilibrium when each firm's output maximizes its profit given the output of others; as the number of sellers rises, the weight of each diminishes until no one exerts any influence on prices, and the quantity produced is such that its market price equals (what would be later called) its marginal cost.

Overall, these attempts had limited resonance, and the use of mathematics remained confined to a small minority. Even Cournot, who was otherwise a well-known scientist, did not enjoy any success and reverted to verbal form in later economics writings (1863). Also, when his 1838 book is later rediscovered and eventually gains the recognition it deserves, it is often believed to be an isolated accomplishment. The other early mathematical economists remain little known today. Especially the German contribution is insufficiently appreciated, partly shadowed by the Historical School which, in the second half of the nineteenth century, loudly dismissed all efforts to identify universal regularities in the name of empirical and inductive reasoning. Nevertheless, a growing literature on the topic may lead to a more balanced appreciation in future (see, for example, Theocharis 1961 [1983], 1993; Baumol and Goldfeld 1968; Mirowski 1989; Ingrao and Israel 1990; Darnell 1991; Baloglou 1995).

Marginal variations, limits, and the continuum

The second half of the nineteenth century saw growing interest for utility interpreted as in Gossen: a relative notion, depending on the available quantity of a good. Emphasis was on the distinction between the total amount of utility and "marginal" utility, namely, the change in the level of utility that results from a given increase in the quantity of the good. With this solution, utility became tractable and gained right of citizenship into economic theory.

The importance of thinking in terms of marginal variations rather than total magnitudes proved so useful to account for utility and demand that it was subsequently extended to supply. Notions of marginal productivity and marginal cost had already been sketched, notably by Cournot and Thünen, but were rediscovered independently, refined and generalized in the 1890s by, among others, John B. Clark, Philip H. Wicksteed, and Knut Wicksell. Originally grounded in distinct traditions of thought, models of consumer demand based on utility and models of producer supply based on productivity/cost began to be seen as two symmetric poles, sharing a similar formal structure. On the whole, marginal reasoning seemed so important that the economic thought of this time is often referred to as "marginalism".

At the beginning, many adopted a discrete framework of analysis and focused on small but finite changes in quantities and the resulting changes in levels of utility or profit. Use of differential calculus initially built directly on this view, taking into account progressively smaller units until they could be said to be "infinitesimally small" – an ambiguous notion that dated back to the Leibnizian origins of differential calculus. A sounder approach saw the light in mathematics towards the mid-nineteenth century, when the notion of limit was forged and calculus was entirely rebuilt on this basis. Economic thought was affected by these results in that emphasis gradually shifted towards the assumption of continuity (also based on the notion of limit) with a continuous representation of the objective function. Eventually, insistence on the effects of marginal increments was replaced by a more straightforward determination of the optimum as the point where the partial derivative is zero.

Though obviously inconsistent with the physical properties of many real-world goods, the continuum appeared as a reasonable approximation of situations in which there is a finite but very large number of elements. The main reason to adopt this approximation was to allow for use of calculus, more powerful and elegant than the finite methods available at the time. Notice, also, that the difference between continuity and differentiability was unknown in mathematics until the late nineteenth century, and the two were taken as equivalent.

Understanding markets: diagrams or equations?
Towards the end of the nineteenth century, different approaches to the study of supply and demand came into sight, relying more heavily upon mathematics than before. Of the many contributions of this period, only the approaches of Alfred Marshall (1890) and Walras (1874 [1988]) are sketched here as they are illustrative of methodological and substantive issues of great import for formalization. Marshall took up the supply-and-demand diagrams of Cournot and other predecessors to develop a "partial equilibrium" approach, focusing on a single market. Partial equilibrium admits a simple solution where supply equals demand, but is only an approximation, based on the restrictive assumption that changes in the price of a good have repercussions on the quantity of that good only. In contrast, Walras emphasized interdependencies among markets and developed a notion of "general equilibrium" corresponding to equality between supply and demand on each market. A related, though distinct, question is whether and how actual trade practices will drive prices and quantities towards equilibrium; again, Marshall and Walras provided different answers. In Walras's "tâtonnement" process, transactions take place simultaneously, at equilibrium, so that the same prices apply to all traders. Instead, Marshall had in mind bilateral transactions that occur sequentially, in disequilibrium, at prices that may differ from a pair of traders to the other.

Neither Marshall nor Walras identified the most appropriate combination of theoretical constructs and mathematical techniques. Marshall's supply and demand geometry was a static tool that could not account for a dynamics of sequential transactions, and failed to convey the richness and depth of his thought. Its inconsistencies opened the way to criticism, most prominently with a famous attack by Piero Sraffa (1925). Walras, in turn, was unable to answer the question of whether his system admits a solution that is meaningful both mathematically and economically, that is, an equilibrium in which demand equals supply for scarce goods (that is, with positive prices) and demand does not exceed supply for free goods (that is, with a price of zero). Because his proofs were merely based on counting equations and unknowns, they could not rule out negative equilibrium prices or quantities; therefore, the very notion of equilibrium of a system of interrelated competitive markets remained vacuous.

The classical tradition
The tradition of using algebra to develop the classical theory of Ricardo (and, after him, Karl Marx) was revived towards the end of the century, most prominently with the contributions of Vladimir K. Dmitriev (1974, first published 1898) and Ladislaus von Bortkiewicz (1906–07 [1952]). Using systems of equations, Dmitriev defended Ricardo against Walras's accusation of circular reasoning by demonstrating that the current conditions of production are sufficient to determine prices and the rate of profit in a logically consistent way – without any need for a "historical regress" to determine the quantities of labour embodied in the capital goods used in production, as was believed to be necessary. Dmitriev also made precise Ricardo's intuition of a negative relationship between the rate of profit and the real wage rate at given conditions of production. Bortkiewicz built on, and extended, Dmitriev's framework of analysis to solve the Marxian problem of the transformation of values into prices of production.

By disambiguating and making more explicit the pillars of the classical theory of prices and distribution, these first contributions laid the foundations for richer developments in the twentieth century, from Wassily Leontief's input–output framework for applied analysis (Leontief 1966), to the more theoretical contributions of Sraffa (1960), John von Neumann whose well-known growth model (1945) shares a classical filiation (Kurz and Salvadori 1993, 2000), and the recently re-discovered Maurice Potron (Bidard et al. 2009). The interested reader is invited to consult relevant entries of this volume for more information.

Some concluding remarks on pre-1925 mathematical economics are in order. In spite of remaining weaknesses, the economic thought of this time placed greater emphasis on mathematics than before, and showed mounting enthusiasm about its use; indications of this tendency are the re-naming of the discipline, from the older "political economy" to "economics", rhyming with "mathematics" and primarily due to the initiative of Marshall; and the first bibliographies of mathematical economics, established by Jevons (1879 [1888]) and Irving Fisher (1892).

A possible explanation of the increased penetration of mathematics into economics may be found in Philip Mirowski's controversial claim that the economists of this time period deliberately tried to imitate physics (1989). It is certainly true that some marginalist writers explicitly mentioned physics as a source of inspiration; yet some of these mentions are misleading and fail to convey the real originality of the economic thought of these authors (see, for example, Donzelli 1997). Others refrained from using mechanical analogies and Marshall, in particular, privileged biological metaphors. Notice that at the time, mathematical methods – even those ultimately based on physics too, specifically those of Newton – were often taught and researched independently of any physical application (see Weintraub 2002: ch. 1).

It must also be mentioned that many economists of this time still privileged the verbal form, some overtly criticizing the use of mathematics (the most prominent example being the German Historical School), and even the most motivated mathematical economists were cautious, preferring to communicate in literary form wherever possible. Towards the end of his life, Marshall himself recommended prudence:

> (1) Use mathematics as a shorthand language, rather than as an engine of inquiry. (2) Keep to them till you have done. (3) Translate into English. (4) Then illustrate by examples that are important in real life. (5) Burn the mathematics. (6) If you can't succeed in (4), burn (3). (Marshall 1925 [1966]: 427)

Mathematical Economics since 1925

The twentieth century, chiefly after World War II, can be said to be the golden age of mathematical economics. Formalization allowed systematizing different concepts and ideas in a consistent, unified body of knowledge. Mathematics became a central part of economists' training and shared knowledge, for the first time dominant over the traditional literary form. What follows is an account of the main areas of development at this stage, including optimization models of individual behaviour, general equilibrium theory, game theory, and first attempts to develop formal, but non-mathematical models of the market.

Optimization and its discontents

Already outlined towards the end of the nineteenth century, the constrained maximization model was refined and extended to the study of both consumers and firms, with, respectively, utility and profit as objective functions. Its enhancement opened the way to a conception of economics based on two pillars: optimizing behaviour of agents, interpreted as individual rationality, and equilibrium of markets, interpreted as consistency of individual choices. Paul Samuelson (1947) gave a major boost to these developments by rewriting many problems of economics as optimization problems, with extensive use of mathematics. The discipline gained unity and coherence as apparently diverse subjects appeared to share the same underlying structure and to allow use of the same mathematical techniques.

Maximization did not remain confined to the normative character that it had with Gossen, and over time came to be seen as an interpretation of actual behaviours too. The revealed preference approach developed by Samuelson (1938) and others aimed precisely to reformulate the model in a way that allowed checking it against empirical data; among others, Hal Varian (1982) performed tests using US consumption data.

The optimization model has not been beyond dispute, though: at least since the 1950s, Herbert Simon and others contended that actual decision makers lack the cognitive capacities to solve maximization problems and, rather, content themselves with "satisficing" behaviour, choosing options that are acceptable though not optimal. Along these lines, they developed a "bounded rationality" approach as an alternative to the seemingly strong requirements of the individual maximization model. Yet it was difficult to identify universal principles enabling economists to devise general models of non-maximizing behaviour, so that bounded rationality hypotheses maintained an ad hoc character, in that they represented specific types of behaviours but were hardly robust to changes, however small, in their characterization. Partly for this reason, the optimization model retained its prominence until very recently.

Away from calculus? The rise and fall of general equilibrium theory

Regarding market models, it was Walras's general equilibrium approach that experienced the most extraordinary developments during this time period. After being taken up by members of the so-called Vienna Colloquium in the 1930s, it blossomed in the US after World War II, and enjoyed particular support from the Cowles Commission in the 1940s and 1950s. Its successes were largely due to the introduction into economics of topology, convex set theory and fixed-point theorems, with an entirely new way of thinking about mathematics that was based on axiomatization and originated in Bourbakist France (Weintraub 2002). A feeling of dissatisfaction with calculus was increasingly widespread, while, according to Nobel prize winner Gérard Debreu, reformulation of the theory in set-theoretical terms "forced a reexamination of several of the primitive concepts of the theory of general economic equilibrium. This was of great value" (1984: 269). From their Vienna experience, Oskar Morgenstern and John von Neumann also brought a view that the discipline needed "mathematical methods which diverge considerably from the techniques applied by older or by contemporary mathematical economists" (Morgenstern and von Neumann 1944: 1). Interestingly, they put the blame on the traditional linkages of calculus with physics: "the emphasis on mathematical methods seems to be shifted more towards combinatorics and set theory – and away from the algorithm of differential equations which dominate mathematical physics" (Morgenstern and von Neumann 1944: 45). Similarly, Debreu absorbed from Bourbakism the view that axiomatic mathematical structures must be seen as fully separated from any physical model, almost taking on a life of their own (Weintraub 2002).

The new mathematics allowed for a sophisticated refinement of Walras's approach, which goes beyond the simple count of the number of equations and number of unknowns, and may be named the Arrow–Debreu–McKenzie model after its main contributors. One of its major achievements in the 1950s was a formal proof of existence of equilibrium, establishing that Walras's notion of a set of prices that clear all markets is consistent. It showed that the system of simultaneous equations representing equality between supply and demand in all markets has a solution, with non-negative prices and quantities (Arrow and Debreu 1954; Debreu 1959; McKenzie 1959). Another success was the mathematical proof of the so-called two theorems of welfare economics. The first theorem states that a general equilibrium corresponds to a socially optimal allocation of resources, and the second states that, under some conditions, any socially optimal allocation of resources can be sustainable by a general equilibrium. These results amounted to rigorously establishing the desirable properties of the free market mechanism that earlier economists had put forward only intuitively. In sum, the new approach completely transformed general equilibrium theory, allowing to make it "rigorous, to generalize it, to simplify it, and to extend it in new directions" (Debreu 1984: 267).

The new mathematics did not completely discard old-style tools, though. On the one hand, the assumption of continuity had always been preserved, only derivability being eliminated. A well-known criticism of this property is that it is just as unrealistic, approximate, and unable to tackle the question of indivisibilities, as in traditional models. Besides, continuous but not derivable functions are rare and ad hoc constructs, so that excluding them hardly leads to any gain in generality. On the other hand, and more importantly, Debreu himself felt the need to reintroduce differential calculus to rule out the possibility of a continuum of equilibria, which would have rendered the existence result void. In the 1970s, differentiable functions provided the "suitable conditions" (Debreu 1984: 271) to prove that the set of economies with a continuum of equilibriums is negligible. Samuelson summarized well the failure of the project to completely replace the mathematical apparatus of economics: "I must agree that the Age of Debreu sees new and fruitful tools being used by mathematical economists . . . However, I do not honestly perceive any basic newness in the so-called non-physics mathematics . . . We benefit from the Debreu–von Neumann novelties and still operate in Isaac Newton's style" (Samuelson 1989: 112).

Still, the mix of set theory and calculus seemed to have the potential to provide the whole of economics with strong mathematical foundations. Problems started with attempts at proving two other properties of equilibrium, namely, stability and uniqueness. The former is meant to ensure that after an exogenous shock, the market mechanism can generate endogenous forces that bring it back to equilibrium; and uniqueness is needed to know where an adjustment process will drive the system after a shock. Yet proofs of stability and uniqueness under "tâtonnement", relying on systems of differential equations, could not be obtained under general conditions and required additional, excessively restrictive assumptions (Sonnenschein 1972; Mantel 1974; Debreu 1974).

Despite this ultimate failure, the project to rebuild economic theory on mathematical bases (admittedly, with varied methods and approaches) continued to be pursued for a long time, and the decline of general equilibrium theory as a major research programme only started in the 1990s after a few decisive attacks (Kirman 1989; Ingrao and Israel 1990). Still, general equilibrium theory long remained an important part of economists' education (Mas-Colell et al. 1995) and the purely verbal style without any formalism, used by many of the forefathers of the discipline until the mid-twentieth century, has now virtually disappeared.

Game theory: from the "invisible hand" to the "prisoner's dilemma"
Another reason why the hegemony of general equilibrium theory and its underlying mathematical form has been largely reduced is a shift in emphasis towards new and different questions, requiring different methods. The idea that individuals make decisions in reaction to exogenous variables has progressively given way to a more active view of decisions as strategic reactions to other agents' own actions. In parallel, fascination for the idea that the market mechanism reconciles *ex post* the autonomous decisions of a myriad of individuals, has been replaced by a "prisoner's dilemma" viewpoint, placing emphasis on inconsistencies between individual strategies and socially optimal outcomes, which can be recognized and anticipated *ex ante*. Game theory has proven to be the appropriate technique to explore the structure of strategic interactions and the effects of individual decisions on one another. Initiated in the 1940s with, among

others, the above-mentioned seminal contribution of Morgenstern and von Neumann (1944), game theory experienced a rapid development and an extraordinary expansion of its application to economics in the 1980s and 1990s. By the end of the twentieth century, it had become the essential mathematical structure and support of all economic analysis, from the theory of individual behaviour to the study of markets and policies.

Partial equilibrium and the advent of non-mathematical quantitative methods
Marshall's partial equilibrium approach remained in the shadow for long after Sraffa's 1925 critique, but did not entirely disappear. The static supply-and-demand diagram was used in some applied studies, while the dynamic conception of sequential transactions between pairs of buyers and sellers, underdeveloped in Marshall's own time, was refined with the help of novel, non-mathematical techniques. It underpinned the pioneering laboratory experiments on markets that were implemented by Edward Chamberlin (1948) and Vernon L. Smith (1962). Although experimental research remained a tiny niche within economics for a long time, it kept alive the Marshallian approach in its dynamic connotation. Today, partial equilibrium experimental markets are still of great interest and the properties of the exchange dynamics that they generate are often referred to in the literature as "Marshallian dynamics" (Friedman and Rust 1993).

Interestingly, the first experimental markets inspired by Marshall's dynamic orientation were being devised at the same time in which set-theoretical mathematical techniques were being implemented to model Walrasian systems. These tools were rudimentary at the beginning (Chamberlin simply relied on his students and a blackboard to perform his market experiment), but they became more powerful over time with the increased availability of software for computer-based experiments and the possibility to perform parallel experiments with human and artificial (simulated) agents (Gode and Sunder 1993). They correspond to a view of economics that gives less weight to the logical rigour of formalization than to the theory's fit with empirical data, assessed with objective, well-defined and replicable measures. While Walras's approach and its mathematical bases experience a slow but neat decline, experimental and computational approaches are on the rise, transforming the discipline.

Formalization is Dead – Long Live Formalization!

Since the time of Chamberlin and Vernon Smith, use of experiments and other non-mathematical techniques to test theories against data has blossomed. In part, this change has been triggered by advancements in statistics, increases in computing power, and availability of higher-quality data; in part, it is also explained by growing dissatisfaction with the mathematics that had imposed itself as primary mode of economic investigation with Samuelson and Debreu. At the end of the 1990s, even the media echoed a widespread feeling that economics was devolving into a technical discipline for mathematical *virtuosi*, incomprehensible to the public and unable to answer the crucial questions facing contemporary societies (Cassidy 1996). Thus in recent years, growing emphasis has been placed on the need for procedures allowing validation of theories against data, rather than (or in addition to) abstract, deductive mathematics. Econometrics, experiments, randomized trials, computer simulation and even brain scans have progressively gained ground; empirical research has earned a central place in the discipline, and today's economists often pride themselves on their superior capacity to extract information from data. New (though still uncommon) interactions with physics have taken place, most notably in the field of complexity studies and with the help of computer simulation rather than formal theorems. Although a detailed account of these developments would be beyond the scope of this entry, it is worth mentioning their repercussions on the issues that are of import here.

Substantively, the new tendency changes the interpretation of many inherited theoretical constructs. For example, behavioural economics challenges the individual optimization model as a description of reality, but preserves it as a normative benchmark: policies, then, have to induce real-world individuals to make choices that are as close as possible to the optimum (Thaler and Sunstein 2009). In a sense, the new approach reverts to the original, primarily normative interpretation of optimization put forward by Gossen.

Methodologically, critics may contend that today's non-mathematical methods include some elements of induction, thereby lowering the standards of rigour that the deductive mathematics of Samuelson and Debreu had spread. Yet some of the main attainments of formalization have been preserved in that the new methods are all directly or indirectly based on some form of mathematical or game-theoretic reasoning, and the pursuit of rigour continues, affecting all phases of scientific reasoning from the initial formulation of hypotheses to their final empirical test. To some extent, the new approaches synthesize aspects of both quantification and formalization.

As a matter of fact, today's methods are as sophisticated and demanding as mathematics in terms of the technical and methodological skills needed to apply them. This is a reason that partly explains their rising status, but also raises concerns that they might turn once again into forms of virtuosity unrelated to the discipline's capacity to work on relevant social issues – somehow renewing with older worries about formalization becoming an end in itself.

While further developments are likely to occur in the near future, the three-century long history of formalization will continue to make its presence felt. It has contributed to shaping economics and its debates in the past, raising methodological and substantive issues that recurrently reappear even under changed historical and intellectual circumstances. It has left its indelible mark on the discipline, and all evidence indicates that its influence is here to stay.

PAOLA TUBARO

See also:

Daniel Bernoulli (I); Marie-Jean-Antoine-Nicolas Caritat de Condorcet (I); Econometrics (III); Experimental economics (III); Game theory (III); General equilibrium theory (III); Russian School of Mathematical Economics (II).

References and further reading

Arrow, K. and G. Debreu (1954), 'Existence of an equilibrium for a competitive economy', *Econometrica*, **22** (3), 265–90.
Baloglou, C.P. (1995), *Die Vertreter der mathematischen Nationalökonomie in Deutschland zwischen 1838 und 1871*, Marburg: Metropolis.

Baumol, W.J. and S.M. Goldfeld (1968), *Precursors in Mathematical Economics: An Anthology*, 6 vols, London: LSE Press.

Beccaria, C. (1764), 'Tentativo analitico sui contrabbandi', *Il Caffè*, reprinted in P. Custodi (1804), *Scrittori classici italiani di economia politica*, vol. 12, Milan: Stamperia G.G. Destefanis, pp. 235–41.

Bernoulli, D. (1738), 'Specimen theoriae novae de mensurea sortis', *Commentarii Academiae Scientiarum Imperialis Petroplitanae*, **5**: 175–92, English trans. in L. Sommer (1954), 'Exposition of a new theory on the measurement of risk', *Econometrica*, **22** (1), 23–36.

Bianchini, M. (1982), *Alle origini della scienza economica*, Parma: Studium Parmense, French trans. 2002, *Bonheur public et méthode géométrique: enquête sur les économistes italiens (1711–1803)*, Paris: INED.

Bicquilley, C.F. (1804), *Théorie élémentaire du commerce*, reprinted 1995, P. Crépel (ed.), Lyon: Aléas éditeur.

Bidard, C., G. Erreygers and W. Parys (2009), 'Our daily bread: Maurice Potron, from Catholicism to mathematical economics', *European Journal of the History of Economic Thought*, **16** (1), 123–54.

Bortkiewicz, L. von (1906–07), 'Wertrechnung und Preisrechnung im Marxschen System', English trans. 1952, 'Value and price in the Marxian system', *International Economic Papers*, **2**, 5–60.

Cassidy, J. (1996), 'The decline of economics', *The New Yorker*, 2 December, p. 50.

Chamberlin, E.H. (1948), 'An experimental imperfect market', *Journal of Political Economy*, **56** (2), 95–108.

Cournot, A.A. (1838), *Researches into the Mathematical Principles of the Theory of Wealth*, trans. N.T. Bacon (1897), reprinted 1960, New York: A.M. Kelley.

Cournot, A.A. (1863), *Principes de la théorie des richesses*, Paris: Hachette.

Crépel, P. (1998), 'Mathematical economics and probability theory: Charles-François Bicquilley's daring contribution', in G. Faccarello (ed.), *Studies in the History of French Political Economy, From Bodin to Walras*, London: Routledge, pp. 78–119.

Darnell, A.C. (ed.), (1991), *Early Mathematical Economics: Journal Articles and Pamphlets from 1800 to 1900*, 6 vols, London: Pickering and Chatto.

Debreu, G. (1959), *Theory of Value. An Axiomatic Analysis of Economic Equilibrium*, New Haven and London: Yale University Press.

Debreu, G. (1974), 'Excess demand functions', *Journal of Mathematical Economics*, **1** (1), 15–24.

Debreu, G. (1984), 'Economic theory in the mathematical mode', *American Economic Review*, **74** (3), 267–78.

Dmitriev, V.K. (1974), *Economic Essays on Value, Competition and Utility*, D.M. Nuti (ed.), Cambridge: Cambridge University Press.

Donzelli, F. (1997), 'Pareto's mechanical dream', *History of Economic Ideas*, **5** (3), 127–78.

Fisher, I. (1892), 'Bibliography of mathematico-economic writings', in I. Fisher (1925), *Mathematical Investigations in the Theory of Value and Prices*, New Haven, CT: Yale University Press, app. IV, pp. 120–24.

Friedman, D. and J. Rust (eds), *The Double Auction Market: Institutions, Theories, and Evidence*, Reading, MA: Addison-Wesley.

Gode, D.K. and S. Sunder (1993), 'Allocative efficiency of markets with zero-intelligence traders: market as a partial substitute for individual rationality', *Journal of Political Economy*, **101** (1), 119–37.

Gossen, H.H. (1854), *The Laws of Human Relations and the Rules of Human Action Derived Therefrom*, trans. R.C. Blitz (1983), Cambridge, MA and London: MIT Press.

Henderson, J.P. (1996), *Early Mathematical Economics. William Whewell and the British Case*, Boston, MA: Rowman & Littlefield.

Ingrao, B. and G. Israel (1990), *The Invisible Hand. Economic Equilibrium in the History of Science*, Cambridge, MA: MIT Press.

Isnard, A.-N. (1781), *Traité des richesses*, reprinted 2009, Whitefish, MT: Kessinger.

Jevons, W.S. (1871), *The Theory of Political Economy*, 3rd edn 1888, London: Macmillan.

Jevons, W.S. (1879), *The Theory of Political Economy*, 2nd edn, 3rd edn 1888, London: Macmillan.

Kirman, A.P. (1989), 'The intrinsic limits of modern economic theory: the emperor has no clothes', *The Economic Journal*, **99** (395), 126–39.

Kurz, H.D. and N. Salvadori (1993), 'Von Neumann's growth model and the "classical" tradition'. *European Journal of the History of Economic Thought*, **1** (1), 129–60.

Kurz, H.D. and N. Salvadori (2000), 'Classical roots of input–output analysis: a short account of its long prehistory', *Economic Systems Research*, **12** (2), 153–79.

Leontief, W. (1966), *Input–Output Economics*, New York: Oxford University Press.

Mantel, R. (1974), 'On the characterization of aggregate excess demand', *Journal of Economic Theory*, **7** (3), 348–53.

Marshall, A. (1890), *Principles of Economics*, London: Macmillan.

Marshall, A. (1925), *Memorials*, A.C. Pigou (ed.), reprinted 1966, New York: A.M. Kelley.

Mas-Colell, A., M. Whinston and J. Green (1995), *Microeconomic Theory*, Oxford: Oxford University Press.

McKenzie, L. (1959), 'On the existence of general equilibrium for a competitive economy', *Econometrica*, **27** (1), 54–71.

Mirowski, P. (1989), *More Heat than Light. Economics as Social Physics: Physics as Nature's Economics*, Cambridge: Cambridge University Press.

Morgenstern, O. and J. von Neumann (1944), *Theory of Games and Economic Behavior*, Princeton, NJ: Princeton University Press.

Neumann, J. von (1945), 'A model of general economic equilibrium', *Review of Economic Studies*, **13** (1), 1–9.

Rau, K.H. (1841), *Grundsätze der Volkswirthschaftslehre*, 4th edn, reprinted 1997, Hildesheim, Zurich and New York: Olms-Weidmann, first published 1826.

Ricardo, D. (1817–21), 'On the principles of political economy and taxation', reprinted in P. Sraffa (ed.) (1951), *The Works and Correspondence of David Ricardo*, vol. 1, Cambridge: Cambridge University Press.

Samuelson, P. (1938), 'A note on the pure theory of consumer's behavior', *Economica*, **5**, 61–71.

Samuelson, P.A. (1947), *Foundations of Economic Analysis*, Cambridge, MA: Harvard University Press.

Samuelson, P.A. (1989), 'A revisionist's view', in M. Dore, S. Chakravarty and R. Goodwin (eds), *John Von Neumann and Modern Economics*, Oxford: Clarendon Press, pp. 100–122.

Smith, V.L. (1962), 'An experimental study of competitive market behavior', *Journal of Political Economy*, **70** (2), 111–37.

Sonnenschein, H. (1972), 'Market excess demand functions', *Econometrica*, **40** (3), 549–63.

Sraffa, P. (1925), 'Sulle relazioni fra costo e quantità prodotta', *Annali di economia*, **2** (1), 277–328.

Sraffa, P. (1960), *Production of Commodities by Means of Commodities*, Cambridge: Cambridge University Press.

Thaler, R.H. and C.R. Sunstein (2009), *Nudge: Improving Decisions About Health, Wealth, and Happiness*, Harmondsworth: Penguin.

Theocaris, R.D. (1961), *Early Developments in Mathematical Economics*, 2nd edn 1983, London: St Martin's Press.

Theocharis, R.D. (1993), *The Development of Mathematical Economics: The Years of Transition, from Cournot to Jevons*, London: Macmillan.

Thünen, J.H. von (1850), *The Frontier Wage: the Economic Organization of Free Agents*, vol. 2, trans. B.W. Dempsey (1960), Chicago, IL: Loyola University Press.

Tubaro, P. (2002), 'A case study in early mathematical economics: Pietro Verri and Paolo Frisi, 1772', *Journal of the History of Economic Thought*, **24** (2), 195–214.

Tubaro, P. (2006), 'Mathématiques et économie dans la détermination du "salaire naturel" de J.H. von Thünen', *Cahiers d'économie politique*, **50** (1), 59–85.

Tubaro, P. (2008), 'Producer choice and technical unemployment: John E. Tozer's mathematical model (1838)'. *European Journal of the History of Economic Thought*, **15** (3), 433–54.

Van den Berg, R. (2006), *At the Origins of Mathematical Economics. The Economics of A.N. Isnard (1748–1803)*, London and New York: Routledge.

Varian, H.R. (1982), 'The nonparametric approach to demand analysis', *Econometrica*, **50** (4), 945–72.

Verri, P. (1771), *Meditazioni sulla economia politica*, 6th edn 1772, Livorno:Nella Stamperia dell'Enciclopedia.

Walras, L. (1874), *Eléments d'économie politique pure*, reprinted in L. Walras (1988), *Œuvres économiques complètes*, vol. 8, Paris: Economica.

Weintraub, E.R. (2002), *How Economics Became a Mathematical Science*, Durham, NC: Duke University Press.

Whewell, W. (1831–50), *Mathematical Exposition of Some Doctrines of Political Economy*, reprinted 1871, New York: Augustus M. Kelley.

Game theory

In August 1941, at Princeton University, while working on the introductory chapter of what was to become the *Theory of Games and Economic Behavior* (von Neumann and Morgenstern 1944 [1947]), Oskar Morgenstern confided to his diary: "Johnny called me; he likes my manuscript . . . I am very happy about this. After all, it wasn't easy for me to simplify his mathematical theory, and to represent it correctly. He is working continuously without a break; it is nearly eerie" (Morgenstern Papers, Diary, 7 August 1941, translation by author). Like other entries in his journal at the time, Morgenstern's reflection revealed the awe inspired in him by von Neumann and the gulf that lay between the two men. The first was a Viennese economist of critical, philosophical inclination, with little or no mathematical training, while the second was a Hungarian mathematician of first rank, contemptuous of philosophy, and boundlessly confident in the application of mathematics across the scientific domain. Yet, their differences notwithstanding, the two émigrés at Princeton managed to forge a productive intellectual partnership, writing – in the middle of World War II, no less – a 500-page book on mathematical social science that would prove influential in various fields, and secure their joint renown.

Beneath those arid chapters of combinatorial mathematics lies a rich scientific, social and personal history, embracing developments as diverse as the rise to cultural prominence of chess at the turn of the century; the politics of anti-Semitism in Central Europe; debates between the Formalists and Intuitionists on the foundations of mathematics; disputes over the relationship between politics and social science; and arguments over the relevance of mathematics to the pursuit of economic understanding. These developments formed the background against which von Neumann and Morgenstern were led to write their big book. In what follows, we present the history of the *Theory of Games*, and a brief synopsis of the book and its impact. (For a fuller account, the reader is referred to Leonard 2010, and, for related treatments, Mirowski 2002 and Giocoli 2003.)

From "Struggle" to "Balance": Von Neumann's Minimax Theorem of 1928

Born to a wealthy banking family of assimilated Hungarian Jews, John von Neumann (1903–1957) was a privately tutored mathematical prodigy. It is not insignificant for the present subject that, during his formative years, he was witness to not only the upheaval of the Great War but also, in Hungary, the 1919 Communist revolution of Béla Kun and its subsequent brutal suppression. He watched too the growth of anti-Semitism, which would increasingly restrict the opportunities available to even well-integrated Jews such as himself. In the mid-1920s, he completed degrees in mathematics and chemical engineering at Budapest and Zurich, during which time he wrote several papers in the areas of axiomatic set theory and the consistency of mathematics, and in 1926 he became postdoctoral fellow at the University of Göttingen. Then a world centre in mathematics, Göttingen provided a vibrant intellectual setting, where he was able to work close to its leader David Hilbert and other mathematical luminaries such as Richard Courant and Hermann Weyl. During this period, he continued working on set theory and foundations and, in particular, the mathematical theory of quantum mechanics (see von Neumann 1932). While these works reveal features that would ultimately characterize von Neumann's approach to economics, in particular the emphasis on axiomatic description, in the short-term it was not social science that drew his attention. His minor interest at Göttingen was, rather, the analysis of parlour games, activities then very much part of the culture.

The background to von Neumann's first paper on games was twofold. First, there was the great prominence of chess in cultural life at the time, with the game capturing the imagination not only of the general public but also of writers, psychologists and mathematicians. (For psychological perspectives on chess during the period, see Binet 1894, and Djakow et al. 1927; or Nabokov's chess novel *The Defense* 1930 [1964]). At the centre of the chess world stood mathematician Emanuel Lasker, who not only wrote about chess tactics, but also speculated on the possibility of a more general science of strategy and conflict. Secondly, quite unconnected to chess, and located in the French rather than German mathematical community, there was in the 1920s a series of papers on the theory of games by eminent French mathematician Emile Borel. Let us consider first Lasker and then Borel.

With a 1902 doctorate in mathematics from Erlangen, and counting Hilbert and Max Noether among his mentors, Emanuel Lasker came from the same world of German mathematics into which von Neumann would later make his entry. As a student, turning to chess in order to pay his bills, Lasker took the world championship from Wilhelm Steinitz in 1897, and gradually attained mythical status by going on to hold the title for the next 24 years. Denied an academic post in mathematics, the rabbi's son wrote prolifically, providing counsel on chess strategy and also speculating about a possible science of "struggle", applicable to the many realms in which strategic interaction was important. Most significant here was his 1907 pamphlet, *Kampf*, which presented an embryonic, discursive "game theory", with discussion of "strategy", the "economy principle" (achieving strategic effect with minimum effort), and "equilibrium and dominance". Lasker felt that chess, although a complex game, with many moves available at any given moment, could, by virtue of the limited number of relevant moves, be inevitably made subject to scientific analysis. Similarly, he speculated that the struggles evident in economic and social life could also eventually be analysed scientifically, in terms of strategy and equilibrium, and he even emphasized the importance of focusing on expected payoffs, in order to allow for the riskiness of outcomes associated with different strategies.

Of the same generation as Lasker, and also a student of Hilbert, Ernest Zermelo was one of the first mathematicians to consider chess as a mathematical object. His 1913 paper, "Über eine Anwendung der Mengenlehre auf die Theorie des Schachspiels" ("On the application of set theory to the theory of the game of chess"), presented to the International Congress of Mathematicians at Cambridge, asked whether it was possible to characterize an arbitrary position in a game in mathematical terms, that is, what does it mean to be in a winning position, and is it possible to determine the number of moves necessary in order to secure victory? Zermelo supplied purely technical answers to these questions, in terms of the necessity and sufficiency of the emptiness and non-emptiness of certain strategic sets, and his paper gave rise to further discussions after World War I, involving Hungarian mathematicians Dénes König and László Kalmár. Each of them produced a paper offering a refinement of Zermelo's, and they cited discussions with their contemporary, von Neumann (see König 1927; Kalmár 1928–29).

As for Emile Borel, the relevant papers were inspired, not by chess, but by his experience as a player of card games. Indeed, Borel followed Poincaré in the view that chess, being confined to a chessboard that was 8×8, was never generalizable to $n \times n$, and therefore was not a truly mathematical object. In a series of mathematical notes written throughout the 1920s, Borel presented in precise form the notion of strategy and the principle of random play (that is, the deliberate use of a mixed strategy), and investigated the range of two-person, zero-sum games in which the latter could be employed profitably (see Borel 1921, 1924, 1927). Having shown that an equilibrium was possible for games of three, five and seven strategies, he wondered if this would always be the case for increasingly "large" games. Not unlike Lasker, Borel also later speculated about the existence of a science of strategy, applicable to war, and economic and financial speculation (see Borel et al. 1938).

Presented at Göttingen in December 1926 and published two years later, von Neumann's "Zur Theorie der Gesellschaftsspiele" ("On the Theory of Games of Strategy") provides an answer to Borel's question in the form of a theorem. Given the subsequent history, the paper may be retrospectively viewed as the beginning of the "science" of strategy sought speculatively by the Frenchman and Lasker. Citing chess, baccarat, roulette and poker as examples, von Neumann considers the generic two-person, zero-sum game, which he defines by the strategies available to both players and their associated payoffs, and gives a tortuously difficult proof of the existence of a minimax equilibrium: a preferred way to play, possibly requiring the use of mixed strategies, that allows each player to minimize the amount ceded to the other. Such a game, says von Neumann, in the language of Lasker, is "well-balanced", and it "makes no difference which of the two players is the better psychologist, the game is so insensitive that the result is always the same" (Von Neumann, 1928b: 23). (Further on, he promises to publish numerical examples of such two-person games as baccarat and a simplified poker, the "agreement of the results [of which] with the well-known rules of thumb of the games (for example, proof of the necessity to 'bluff' in poker) may be regarded as an empirical corroboration of the results of our theory", ibid.: 42).

Closing the paper with preliminary suggestions about how to extend the analysis to games of three players, he notes that the possibility of coalition-formation marks the reappearance in the game of something quite foreign to the two-person one, namely "struggle" – again, in the language of Lasker. He concludes with the suggestion that a similar approach could be taken with games of four and, ultimately, any number of players, the result of which would be a "satisfactory general theory" of all such games.

In May 1928, presumably when he became aware of Borel's papers on the subject, von Neumann sent him a note, indicating that he had been independently working on the problem of existence of an equilibrium, and announcing the proof (see von Neumann 1928a). This Borel presented later to the Académie des Sciences. In university courses given in 1936–37, and published in 1938, Borel commented on von Neumann's theorem, insisting that it was unlikely to prove at all useful to the actual playing of games of strategy, where the presence of innovation and cycles in ways of playing made the practical application of mathematical calculation very difficult: "Perhaps [these remarks] will make clear . . . to those who would wish to turn games into an occupation how futile is the search for a perfect formula which is forever likely to elude us" (Borel et al. 1938: 117).

After his 1928 paper, however, von Neumann went no further with the theory of games, essentially putting it aside for a decade. In 1930, he took a half-time appointment at Princeton's Department of Mathematics, at the initiative of topologist Oswald Veblen, and, for two years, alternated between Berlin and Princeton, sharing the latter position with mathematical physicist and fellow Hungarian, Eugene Wigner. Gauging that his opportunities in Europe were limited, he then moved permanently to the US, becoming, along with Albert Einstein, one of the first members of the newly founded Institute for Advanced Study, which although located at Princeton was independent of the university. It was here that he would eventually be led back to game theory, when stimulated by both political developments and his eventual encounter with Oskar Morgenstern.

Economics and Mathematics in Interwar Vienna

The Viennese with an active interest in economics can be grouped into three partially overlapping communities. First and foremost were "the economists", who gravitated variously around the Vienna Economics Association and the seminars of Ludwig von Mises and Hans Mayer, and who included, among others, Friedrich Hayek, Fritz Machlup, Gottfried Haberler, Paul Rosenstein-Rodan and Alexander Gerschenkron. Second was that small group of mathematicians, including Abraham Wald and Franz Alt, who developed an interest in economic theory in the early 1930s, and met at the mathematical colloquium organized by Karl Menger, son of the founder of the Austrian School of Economics. Third were the philosophically inclined members of the Vienna circle, surrounding Moritz Schlick, and including Hans Hahn, Philip Frank and Otto Neurath, with the latter being the one most actively involved in economic debates.

Although he was an occasional observer at the Menger Colloquium and had some familiarity with the Schlick Kreis, Oskar Morgenstern (1906–1976) was, above all, part of the first group. After his 1928 Habilitation at the University of Vienna, he in time succeeded Hayek as director of the Rockefeller-financed Institut für Konjunkturforschung (Business Cycle Institute), and remained an influential figure in the city until his departure from Austria in late 1937. It is worth mentioning that while von Neumann would visit Vienna during the 1930s when sailing back to Hungary for the summer, and knew the work in mathematical economics of Menger and Abraham Wald, there is no evidence that he had any significant relationship with the economics community of which Morgenstern was part.

At the outset, Morgenstern was, in many respects, an economist in the "Austrian" mould, and his early work reflected the critical stance of his Viennese mentors, especially Ludwig von Mises and Hans Mayer. The former was sceptical of the contribution of mathematics to economic analysis, believing that theoretical insights were always achieved through reasoned reflection, without recourse to formalism. To present a theory in mathematical terms, said Mises, was, at best, a kind of decorative embellishment; at worst, a mechanical presentation of a distinctly non-mechanical field (see von Mises 1960). Because of his belief that economic truths were discoverable a priori, Mises also placed limited value on empirical work, and he was particularly critical of quantitative attempts to predict the economic future. So great was the flux of valuations and information in the economic sphere, he claimed, that it rendered impossible any attempt at numerical prediction. Although less guided by a faith in economic liberalism than Mises, and although somewhat forgotten today, Hans Mayer too provided an important critique of the mathematical economics of equilibrium, again with a typically "Austrian" emphasis on time and flux (see Mayer 1932). Thus he insisted that the effect of assuming stable utility functions was to rule out essential characteristics of real economic life, namely, the complete satisfaction and disappearance of certain wants and the emergence of new ones. This critical refrain of Mises and Mayer is echoed in Morgenstern's Habilitation thesis of 1928, which concerned the impossibility of prediction of economic events, and in his philosophical papers of the 1930s on time, knowledge, beliefs and expectations (see Morgenstern 1934b, 1935).

At the same time, over the course of the 1930s, Morgenstern began to distinguish himself from his Austrian economist peers in two regards; first, in the interest he showed in mathematics and mathematicians; secondly, in the emphasis he placed upon cleansing economic "science" of all political or normative influence. In this, he was very much influenced by his contact with the above mentioned Karl Menger, and it was largely under the latter's influence that he was steered away from his Viennese economist mentors and ultimately became someone open to collaboration with von Neumann.

The citizens of "Red Vienna" were exposed to a great deal of social and political upheaval. In 1927, the city became the theatre of political violence between the Austrian Right and the Socialists in charge of the city. In 1934, there was essentially civil war, when the conservative Chancellor Dollfuss, with the encouragement of Mussolini, resorted to artillery barrage to crush the municipal regime. It was in this difficult setting that Menger retreated from his normal mathematical work and wrote his 1934 book, *Moral, Wille und Weltgestaltung. Grundlegung zur Logik der Sitten* (*Morality, Decision and Social Organization. Towards a Logic of Ethics*): an exploratory mathematical analysis of the social compatibility of individuals, based on their stance with regard to various norms.

Morgenstern, for his part, was particularly concerned with what was assumed about the knowledge and predictive capacities of the agent in neoclassical economics. Here, he was also motivated by his reading on paradox and antimony in the work of Bertrand Russell and other logicians. Thus, for example, the assumption in general equilibrium theory that the agent had "perfect foresight" could, if interpreted literally, lead to paradoxical situations in which such agents could all outguess each other, thereby destroying any possibility for equilibrium. Morgenstern was thus particularly interested in Menger's embryonic analysis, in so far as it seemed to begin, at least, to address the question of knowledge specification and interaction between economic agents.

Another effect of Menger on Morgenstern was the general stimulus he provided by emphasizing the need for theoretical rigour. Following his experience in the debates on the foundations of mathematics, and particularly his negative experience in Amsterdam with Intuitionist mathematician, L.E.J. Brouwer, Menger became allergically sensitive to any intrusion into the scientific domain of the "normative", that is, expressions of political or personal preference. In time, he developed the same critical attitude towards von Mises, whom he regarded as not fully capable of separating his politics from his economic theory. He already thought the same of Otto Neurath, to the political left. At Menger's side, Morgenstern learned to share this attitude so that, by the mid-1930s, for both of them, the use of mathematics had become a way to ensure logical argument, and to prevent the smuggling into economics of political biases. In short, it provided a method of "purification" (see Morgenstern 1934a). Thanks to his alliance with Menger, Morgenstern soon learned to see Mises, and, in time, Hayek as propagandists, rather than true economic "scientists". This meeting of minds reflected itself too in their institutional relationship, with Menger's students Wald and Alt providing mathematics tutorials to Morgenstern at his institute, in return for much needed financial support.

The political upheaval of the decade reached its zenith in 1938, when Hitler annexed the country, thereby ensuring the demise of one of interwar Europe's most intellectually and culturally active centres. Many, including Menger, had already left, and Morgenstern found himself ousted from his institute. Leaving Austria, he took a position at the Department of Economics at Princeton, where he soon got to know many of the European émigrés, at both the university and the Institute for Advanced Study.

Von Neumann and the Struggles of the 1930s

The political tumult after 1933 was as important for von Neumann as it was for the Viennese. Indeed, the evidence suggests that it was his observation of the social upheaval and shifting political alliances of the period that brought him back to game theory, after a 10-year hiatus.

In Germany, in April 1933, the Restoration of Civil Service Act marked the beginning of the "purification" of the universities, and the end of the academic world von Neumann had known. From then on, his correspondence shows him to have been greatly preoccupied with events, worried about the European political "balance", and soon predicting a catastrophic conflict. In early 1935, in response to Nazi mathematician Ludwig Bieberbach's campaign for a properly German, non-Jewish mathematics, von Neumann cut the ropes further with that country, resigning in protest from the German Deutsche Mathematiker Vereinigung. He was never to set foot in Germany again.

As of late 1937, when his wife left him, and he found himself going through a divorce and remarriage in Hungary, he spent increasing amounts of time back in his own country. One effect of this was to bring him in direct contact with Hungarian politics, and with its contamination of national life. May 1938 saw the passage of Hungary's infamous "Balance Law", which sought to reduce to 20 per cent the proportion of Jews in the professions and in financial, commercial and industrial enterprises of 10 employees or more. Von Neumann was struck forcefully by the emergence of the radical Right, and the turning of Hungarians against the Jews – the "internal Nazification" of the country, as he called it. By late 1938, he and his fiancée, Klara Dán, were preparing to get out of the country and beginning to think of persuading their families to do the same. The following year, Hungary was preparing further anti-Semitic legislation, and von Neumann's letters continued to dwell on questions of rationality, politics and social equilibrium. By late 1939, both families had left Hungary for the US, but the trauma continued with the suicide of von Neumann's father-in-law, Charles Dán, near Princeton close to Christmas of that year. So difficult was this period for von Neumann that, in 1938 and 1939, his scientific output essentially collapsed.

It was in early 1940 that von Neumann got to know Morgenstern, and they began what would eventually become a sustained discussion on economics, knowledge and games. In mid-May 1940, amid continued correspondence with Hungarian friends, von Neumann and his wife sought respite by driving across to the University of Washington, where he was to deliver a series of lectures on games. While these appear to have been mainly on chess and his 1928 paper, the sojourn was clearly pivotal for, immediately upon returning to Princeton that August, he threw himself into the development of a new theory of coalition-formation and stability. Discussing everything with Morgenstern, he produced "Theory of Games I (General Foundations)" (Morgenstern Papers, File: John von Neumann, 1940–1948). A key feature of the solution concept developed therein, the stable set, is the role played by arbitrary forms of discrimination, between players – or between social groups, with each acting as one player – with such discrimination having no justification other than its being accepted for reasons of history or tradition. To a Hungarian Jew, observing European political unrest, the social motif of arbitrary, historically contingent discrimination was an essential one.

By mid-1941, on the foot of continued discussions, and the study of von Neumann's early draft, Morgenstern could report that he and "Johnny" had started working on a treatise together. Energized by this, and particularly by von Neumann's scathing criticism of mathematical economics, Morgenstern wrote a corrosive review of Hicks's 1939 *Value and Capital*, and produced a draft paper titled "Quantitative implications of maxims of behavior" (see Morgenstern 1941a, 1941b). The latter was a qualitative attempt to develop ideas on interdependent decision among economic agents, drawing on both Menger (1934) and these new discussions with von Neumann. In the meantime, the latter ploughed ahead with the work on games, producing "Theory of Games II" in January 1941, which, among other things, extended the theory to cover non-zero-sum games. By December 1942, their book was well under way – tentatively titled *Theory of Games, and its Applications to Economics & Sociology* – and the manuscript finally went to Princeton University Press in April of the following year, its entire technical apparatus being the work of von Neumann, and the introduction and general orientation that of Morgenstern.

It is important to note that while they were writing the book, von Neumann's attention to the project on games was already facing great competition from other uses of his time. He had by then become a very active, indeed peripatetic, mathematical adviser to various military organizations, on matters that included the use of game theory in certain conflict situations. In early 1943, he departed to England for a long stint as advisor to the Navy. By 1945, he was playing a central role at Los Alamos, in the development of the atomic bomb.

A New Mathematics of Society

Morgenstern's introductory chapter of *Theory of Games and Economic Behavior* (von Neumann and Morgenstern 1944 [1947]), as the book was finally titled, is the volume's most accessible and most widely read part. It is at once a defence of the use of mathematics in social science and a critique of the current state of mathematical economics. Von Neumann's influence, and almost religious faith in the supremacy of mathematical formalism, is clear throughout. There is nothing intrinsically different about social science, they say, that renders it inimical to mathematical treatment. Natural phenomena, whether they concern human behaviour or not, are potential repositories of mathematics, the richness of which is likely to be correlated with the empirical prominence of the field. Social and economic activity is of such great worldly importance that it is likely to require a new mathematics all of its own.

The most prominent extant treatment of the field, general equilibrium theory, is, in the authors' opinion, merely the imitative grafting of physical science methods onto social science. The importation of rational mechanics brings with it assumptions about the underlying continuity of change, whereas the social domain likely requires attention to discretely separate structures and discontinuities, and thus recourse to mathematics of a different kind. General equilibrium theory has also failed to account for the properly interactive nature of social behaviour, particularly that which is manifest in situations involving "small" numbers of agents, be they involved in the exchange of goods or in the distribution of gains through the formation of social and political groups. Throughout the book, von Neumann's preference for "modern", discrete mathematics (that is, set theory and combinatorics) over the "outdated" differential and integral calculus, is evident. Several pages are devoted to defending the use of cardinal, or numerical, utilities, with the axiomatic proof of the existence of a cardinal utility function being included in an appendix to the second edition, published in 1947.

Chapter 2 of *Theory of Games and Economic Behavior* (von Neumann and Morgenstern 1944 [1947]) lays out the mathematical structure of a game, introducing the concepts of sets and partitions and describing the game axiomatically in these terms. The whole is presented as a piece of modern mathematics, in the spirit of Hilbert: although the axioms are stimulated by the common sense features of games, the latter are soon allowed to recede into the background and the theory pursued in a spirit of relative abstraction. While the mathematics is being followed through, the empirical is held at arm's length and everyday terms are introduced in inverted commas. Hence, "class", "discrimination", "exploitation" and so on. Only during periodic returns to the heuristics is the vocabulary of the everyday re-invoked, and the "common sense" meaning of the results discussed. The minimax theorem is proved in the next chapter, using, not von Neumann's earlier proof, but a modification of the elementary 1938 proof by Borel's student Jean Ville, based on the theory of convex sets. From here on, chapter upon chapter, von Neumann systematically goes through the zero-sum game for three, four and more players, exploring the combinatorial possibilities for coalition-formation and compensations (side payments). Each game is described in terms of its characteristic function, which shows the maximal payoff available to each possible coalition of the game, assuming that the coalition plays minimax against its complement and that utility is transferable between players. In chapter 9, von Neumann introduces the concept of strategic equivalence to show how the move from the zero-sum restriction to a constant sum retains the basic features of the game, thus allowing it to be solved by the same means. In the eleventh chapter, von Neumann drops the zero (or constant-) sum restriction, moving to the "general game".

As already mentioned, the central theoretical contribution of the *Theory of Games* is the stable set, von Neumann's solution to coalitional games. It is a "complicated combinatorial catalogue", indicating the minimum each participant can get if he behaves rationally. He may, of course, get more if the others behave "irrationally", that is, make mistakes. Were the solution to consist of a single imputation – a unique vector of the amounts to be received by each player – then the "structure of the society under consideration would be extremely simple: there would exist an absolute state of equilibrium in which the quantitative share of every participant would be precisely determined" (von Neumann and Morgenstern 1944 [1947]: 34). However, such a unique solution does not generally exist – a given society can be organized in various ways – so the notion needs to be broadened. The solution is thus a set of possible imputations.

Any particular alliance describes only one particular consideration which enters the minds of the participants when they plan their behaviour. Even if a particular alliance is ultimately formed, the division of the proceeds between the allies will be decisively influenced by the other alliances which each one might alternatively have entered . . . It is, indeed, this whole which is the really significant entity, more so than its constituent imputations. Even if one of these is actually applied, i.e., if one particular alliance is actually formed, the others are present in a "virtual" existence: Although they have not materialized, they have contributed essentially to shaping and determining the actual reality. (Ibid.: 36)

In an *n*-person game, therefore:

[a] solution should be a system of imputations possessing in its entirety some kind of balance and stability the nature of which we shall try to determine. We emphasize that this stability – whatever it may turn out to be – will be a property of the system as a whole and not of the single imputations of which it is composed. (Ibid.)

This stability is based on the notion of "dominance". One imputation, x, is said to dominate another, y, "when there exists a group of participants each one of which prefers his individual situation in x to that in y, and who are convinced that they are able, as a group – i.e. as an alliance – to enforce their preferences" (von Neumann and Morgenstern 1944 [1947]: 38). Since the demurring coalition may be different in each case, the dominance relation is not a transitive ordering. Von Neumann defines the solution to an *n*-person game as a set of imputations, S, with the following characteristics: (1) no imputation y contained in S is dominated by an imputation x contained in S; (2) every y not contained in S, is dominated by some x contained in S.

A solution is thus a set of possible imputations, stable in so far as none of its member imputations dominates each other and every non-member imputation outside the set is dominated by at least one member. Not only is a solution comprised of possibly many imputations, linked by these stability criteria: a given game may have many solutions. To take a simple example, consider the fixed-sum game in which a "pie" of value 1 has to be divided among three people. It has the following four solutions:

1. $(1/2, 1/2, 0)$ $(1/2, 0, 1/2)$ $(0, 1/2, 1/2)$
2. (x_1, x_2, c) where $0 \leq c \leq 1/2$ and $x_1 + x_2 + c = 1$
3. (c, x_2, x_3) where $0 \leq c \leq 1/2$ and $x_2 + x_3 + c = 1$
4. (x_1, c, x_3) where $0 \leq c \leq 1/2$ and $x_1 + x_3 + c = 1$

Here, not only are there multiple solutions, but three of them actually admit an infinite number of possible imputations. Note also that the observation of a given imputation, such as $(1/2, 1/2, 0)$, says nothing about which solution obtains, as that imputation could occur in any of the four solutions possible.

The question of which solution will obtain in a given situation, the authors say, can be broached only by considering "standards of behaviour", the various rules, customs or institutions governing social organization at the time. These are extra-game considerations, not contained in the information provided by the characteristic function. To understand the analogy, von Neumann and Morgenstern advise the reader to "temporarily forget the analogy with games and think entirely in terms of social organization" (von Neumann and Morgenstern 1944 [1947]: 41, n. 1):

Let the physical basis of a social economy be given, – or to take a broader view of the matter, of a society. According to all tradition and experience human beings have a characteristic way of adjusting themselves to such a background. This consists of not setting up one rigid system of apportionment, i.e. of imputation, but rather a variety of alternatives, which will probably express some general principles but nevertheless differ among themselves in many particular respects. This system of imputations describes the "established order of society" or "accepted standard of behaviour". (Ibid.: 41)

Thus, in the above game, in solution 2, player 3 is held to an amount, c, that may be as small as zero, or as high as 1/2. The actual value of c would reflect the social norms governing that player's social standing. Depending on tradition, the marginal member might be completely exploited or might not. As von Neumann and Morgenstern write: "A theory which is consistent at this point cannot fail to give a precise account of the entire interplay of economic interest, influence and power" (ibid.: 43).

When one considers the social and political backdrop against which von Neumann developed this theory, the *Theory of Games*, with its emphasis on stability and its pervasive reference to norms, discrimination and power, appears as an attempt not simply to replace general equilibrium theory, but to achieve a mathematical description of social organization, much more broadly defined. And, after the publication of the book, von Neumann continued to speak of game theory in these terms. In 1953, when Harold Kuhn wrote to him, asking what he thought of the experimental games then being conducted at the RAND Corporation, von Neumann replied:

I think that nothing smaller than a complete social system will give a reasonable "empirical" picture [of the stable set solution]. Here, over reasonably long periods of time, one can meaningfully assert that the "system" has not changed, while the positions of various participants within it may have changed many times. This would seem to me to be the analogue of a single solution and an "exploration" of the imputations that belong to it. After relatively long times, there occur discontinuous changes, "revolutions" which produce a different "system". (Von Neumann to Harold Kuhn, 14 April 1953, Von Neumann Papers, Library of Congress, Washington, DC, Container 24, File: Kuhn, H.W.)

In 1955, at a Princeton conference on game theory, when the young John Nash objected to the great multiplicity of solutions to cooperative games, von Neumann replied that "this result was not surprising in view of the correspondingly enormous variety of observed stable social structures; many differing conventions can endure, existing today for no better reason than that they were here yesterday" (in Wolfe 1955: 25).

Reception and Impact of the Book

Notwithstanding the ambitious quest for a new social mathematics embodied by the book, the concrete influence of the *Theory of Games* was initially felt, not in social theory, but in the domain of military strategy. During the early 1940s, when the book was being written, through von Neumann's influence at the Princeton branch of the Statistical Research Group and at the Boston-based Anti-submarine Warfare Operations Research Group, game theory became an element in mathematical models of military engagements, such as submarine-search and bombing strategy. For example, a submarine navigating a channel is pursued by an overhead spotter-plane, the former trying to minimize the probability of contact, while the latter strives to maximize it. Such models involved the application of a very small part of the mathematics – usually centred on the minimax theorem – to specific, confined problems. Concerned with facilitating interventions in the world, game theory *qua* operations research was far-removed from the broad abstract representation of the social order that von Neumann had sought in the *Theory of Games*. Nonetheless, it was the perceived success of operations research during World War II that provided the impetus for the Army Air Corps' creation of the RAND Corporation in the late 1940s, where models of this kind continued to be developed and game theory was given strong institutional support. While there is little evidence that these game-theoretic models were of anything other than very limited influence in quantitatively shaping particular strategic decisions, it is incontestable that the language, terminology and "thought framework" of game theory became important to the strategic mind-set that dominated the Cold War, helping shape such books as Herman Kahn's (1962) *Thinking about the Unthinkable* and Thomas Schelling's (1960) *The Strategy of Conflict*.

The *Theory of Games* also set new standards for mathematical rigour in the field of economic theory. For example, before leaving France to move to the US, mathematical economist, Gérard Debreu, read the book in Salzburg, Austria, at a summer school run by Harvard University. Though Debreu would never work on game theory, the book shaped his thinking. His pathbreaking *Theory of Value* (1959), an axiomatic treatment of Walrasian general equilibrium theory, refers to the outstanding influence of von Neumann and Morgenstern (1944 [1947]: x) "which freed mathematical economics from its traditions of differential calculus and compromises with logic". Debreu's Hilbertian stance, too, on the relationship between the mathematics of general equilibrium and the empirical economic substrate went even further than that of von Neumann on games: "the theory, in the strict sense, is logically entirely disconnected from its interpretations" (Debreu 1959: x). This austerity shaped the views of an entire generation of economists from the 1950s till the 1980s, during which general equilibrium theory represented the pinnacle of intellectual achievement in the discipline. The irony, of course, is that it was precisely their dissatisfaction with Walrasian general equilibrium theory that provoked von Neumann and Morgenstern in the first place.

It was in the post-war military-academic milieu that a new generation of game theorists came of age. Whether at Princeton or the RAND Corporation, or alternating between the two, young mathematicians such as Harold Kuhn, Lloyd Shapley and John Nash developed new lines of analysis. Shapley, a towering influence in the game theory community from the 1950s onwards, produced, among other things, the Shapley Value, which described the solution to a coalitional game in terms of the amount brought by each player to an average, randomly formed coalition. For his PhD thesis, Nash sought to provide for n-person games a solution that was as restricted as von Neumann's minimax for the two-person game. Introducing the conceptual division of games into co-operative, in which coalitions are permitted, and non-cooperative, in which players act in isolation, he proved the existence for the latter, under specific conditions, of what he called an "equilibrium point", later known as the Nash Equilibrium (see Nash 1950a, 1950b; 1951; Leonard 1994). That von Neumann found this non-cooperative approach to be rather trivial is understandable in the light of his own aims for the theory. Subsequent work on non-cooperative game theory by Harsanyi, Selten, Aumann, Kreps and others has contributed to the transformation of the microeconomic canon and shaped modelling in industrial organization, international trade and a range of areas. The field of behavioural economics, which has recently enjoyed great expansion, owes its existence in part to the appearance of game theory. Although von Neumann replied sceptically to Kuhn concerning the ability of laboratory experimentation to shed light on the stable set, game theory did provide a structured basis for empirically testing the theory of individual decision, via its utility axioms, and various solution concepts, both cooperative and non-cooperative. This experimentation, too, began at the RAND Corporation (see Kalisch et al. 1954). Under the influence of John Maynard Smith, the theory of games has had a significant impact on the field of evolutionary biology (see Maynard Smith 1988).

In short, although it quickly attained the status of a classic, which is to say that it was cited by many but read by few, the *Theory of Games and Economic Behavior* set in motion developments that deeply affected the economics discipline. From the recasting of the economic agent as a strategic player to the reshaping of entire fields of economic analysis; from the introduction of axiomatics into general equilibrium and social welfare theory to the rise of experimental economics, the direct and indirect influence of von Neumann and Morgenstern's wartime book has been profound and long lasting.

ROBERT LEONARD

See also:

Behavioural and cognitive economics (III); Experimental economics (III); General equilibrium theory (III); German and Austrian schools (II); Friedrich August von Hayek (I); Ludwig Heinrich von Mises (I); John Forbes Nash Jr (I); John von Neumann (I); Non-Marxist socialist ideas in Germany and Austria (II).

References and further reading

Binet, A. (1894), *Psychologie des grands calculateurs et des joueurs d'échecs*, republished in 1981 with an introduction by F. Le Lionnais, Paris and Geneva: Slatkin.
Borel, E. (1921), 'La théorie du jeu et les équations intégrales à noyau symétrique', *Comptes Rendus, Académie des Sciences*, **173** (25), 1304–8, trans. in M. Fréchet (1953), 'Emile Borel, initiator of the theory of psychological games and its application', *Econometrica*, **21** (January), 95–127.
Borel, E. (1924), 'Sur les jeux où l'hasard se combine avec l'habilité des joueurs', *Comptes Rendus, Académie des Sciences*, **178**, 24–5.
Borel, E. (1927), 'Sur le système de formes linéaires à déterminant symétrique gauche et la théorie générale du jeu', *Comptes Rendus de l'Académie des Sciences*, **184.2** (10 January), pp. 52–4, trans. L.J. Savage, 'On systems of linear forms of skew symmetric determinants and the general theory of play', *Econometrica*, **21** (January), pp. 116–17.
Borel, E. and J. Ville (1938), *Traité du Calcul des Probabilités et de ses Applications*, vol. 4, fasc. 2, Applications aux Jeux de Hasard, Paris: Gauthier-Villars.
Debreu, G. (1954), *Theory of Value: an Axiomatic Analysis of Economic Equilibrium*, a Cowles Foundation Monograph, New Haven, CT and London: Yale University Press.
Djakow, I.N., N.W. Petrowski and P.A. Rudik (1927), *Psychologie des Schachspiels*, Berlin and Leipzig: Walter de Gruyter & Co.
Giocoli, N. (2003), *Modeling Rational Agents: From Interwar Economics to Early Modern Game Theory*, Cheltenham, UK and Northampton, MA, USA: Edward Elgar.
Kahn, H. (1962), *Thinking about the Unthinkable*, New York: Avon.
Kalisch, G., J.W. Milnor, J. Nash and E.D. Nering (1954), 'Some experimental n-person games', in R.M. Thrall, C.H. Coombs and R.L. Davis (eds), *Decision Processes*, New York: Wiley, pp. 301–27, originally RAND report, RAND RM-948, 25 August.
Kalmár, L. (1928–29), 'Zur Theorie der abstrakten Spiele' ('On the theory of abstract games'), *Acta Litterarum ac Scientiarum, Regiae Universitatis Hungaricae Francisco-Josephinae*, s. Scientiarum Mathematicarum, Szeged, **4**, 65–85.

Kirzner, I. (ed.) (1994), *Classics in Austrian Economics: A Sampling in the History of a Tradition*, London: W. Pickering.

König, D. (1927), 'Über eine Schlussweise aus dem Endlichen ins Unendliche' ('On a method of conclusion from the finite to the infinite'), *Acta Litterarum ac Scientiarum, Regiae Universitatis Hungaricae Francisco-Josephinae*, s. Scientiarum Mathematicarum, Szeged, **3**, 121–30.

Lasker, E. (1907), *Kampf*, New York: Lasker's Publishing Co.; reprinted 2001 with foreword by Lothar Schmidt, Potsdam: Verlag für Berlin-Brandenburg.

Leonard, R. (1994), 'Reading Cournot, reading Nash: the creation and stabilization of the Nash equilibrium', *Economic Journal*, **104** (May), 492–511.

Leonard, R. (1995), 'From parlor games to social science: von Neumann, Morgenstern, and the creation of game theory, 1928–1944', *Journal of Economic Literature*, **33** (June), 730–61.

Leonard, R. (1998), 'Ethics and the excluded middle: Karl Menger and social science in interwar Vienna', *Isis*, **89** (1), 1–26.

Leonard, R. (2010), *Von Neumann, Morgenstern and the Creation of Game Theory: From Chess to Social Science, 1900–1960*, New York and Cambridge: Cambridge University Press.

Mayer, H. (1932), 'Der Erkenntniswert der funktionellen Preistheorien', in H. Mayer (ed.), *Die Wirtschaftstheorie der Gegenwart*, vol. 2, Vienna, pp. 14 239b, English trans. and reprint 1994, 'The cognitive value of functional theories of price, critical and positive investigations concerning the price problem', in I. Kirzner (ed.), *Classics in Austrian Economics: A Sampling in the History of a Tradition*, London: W. Pickering, pp. 55–168.

Maynard Smith, J. (1988), *Games, Sex and Evolution*, New York and Toronto: Harvester-Wheatsheaf.

Menger, K. (1934), *Moral, Wille und Weltgestaltung. Grundlegung zur Logik der Sitten*. Vienna: Julius Springer, English trans. 1974, *Morality, Decision and Social Organization. Towards a Logic of Ethics*, Dordrecht: Reidel.

Mirowski, P. (2002), *Machine Dreams: Economics Becomes a Cyborg Science*, New York and Cambridge: Cambridge University Press.

Mises, L. von (1960), *Epistemological Problems of Economics*, Princeton, NJ: van Nostrand, first published 1933.

Morgenstern, O., Diary, Oskar Morgenstern Papers, Special Collections Library, Duke University, Durham, NC.

Morgenstern, O. (1934a), *Die Grenzen der Wirtschaftspolitik*, Vienna: Julius Springer, English trans. V. Smith and revised (1937), *The Limits of Economics*, London: Hodge, pp. v, 151.

Morgenstern, O. (1934b), 'Das Zeitmoment in der Wertlehre', *Zeitschrift für Nationalökonomie*, **5** (4), 433–58, English trans. 'The time moment in economic theory', in A. Schotter (ed.) (1976), *Selected Economic Writings of Oskar Morgenstern*, New York: New York University Press, pp. 151–67.

Morgenstern, O. (1935), 'Vollkommene Voraussicht und wirtschaftliches Gleichgewicht', *Zeitschrift für Nationalökonomie*, **6** (3), 337–57, English trans. F. Knight, mimeo, University of Chicago, IL, reprinted in A. Schotter (ed.) (1976), *Selected Economic Writings of Oskar Morgenstern*, New York: New York University Press, pp. 169–83.

Morgenstern, O. (1941a), 'Professor Hicks on value and capital', *Journal of Political Economy*, **49** (3), 361–93.

Morgenstern, O. (1941b), 'Quantitative implications of maxims of behavior', unpublished manuscript, Princeton University, Princeton, NJ.

Nabokov, V. (1930), *Zaschchita Luzhina*, Berlin: Slovo, English trans. 1964, *The Defense*, New York: G.P. Putnam's and Sons.

Nash, J. (1950a), 'Equilibrium points in n-person games', *Proceedings of the National Academy of Science*, **36** (1), 48–9.

Nash, J. (1950b), 'Non-cooperative games', PhD dissertation, Princeton University, Princeton, NJ.

Nash, J. (1951), 'Non-cooperative games', *Annals of Mathematics*, **54** (2), pp. 286–95.

Neumann, J. von (1928a), 'Calcul des Probabilités – Sur la Théorie des Jeux' presented by E. Borel, *Comptes Rendus Hebdomadaires des Séances de l'Académie des Sciences*, **186** (25), 1689–91.

Neumann, J. von (1928b), 'Zur Theorie der Gesellschaftsspiele', *Mathematische Annalen*, **100**, 295–320, English trans. S. Bargmann (1959), 'On the theory of games of strategy', in A.W. Tucker and R.D. Luce (eds), *Contributions to the Theory of Games*, vol. 4, Princeton, NJ: University Press, pp. 13–42.

Neumann, J. von (1932), *Mathematische Grundlagen der Quantenmechanik*, Berlin: J. Springer, English trans. R. Beyer (1955), *Mathematical Foundations of Quantum Mechanics*, Princeton, NJ: Princeton University Press.

Neumann, J. von and O. Morgenstern (1944), *Theory of Games and Economic Behavior*, reprinted 1947, Princeton, NJ: Princeton University Press.

Schelling, T. (1960), *The Strategy of Conflict*, Cambridge, MA: Harvard University Press.

Schotter, A. (ed.) (1976), *Selected Economic Writings of Oskar Morgenstern*, New York: New York University Press.

Schwalbe, U. and P. Walker (2001), 'Zermelo and the early history of game theory', *Games and Economic Behavior*, **34** (1), 123–37.

Wolfe, P. (ed.) (1955), 'Report of an informal conference on recent developments in the theory of games', mimeo, Logistics Research Project, Department of Mathematics, Princeton University, Princeton, NJ.

Zermelo, E. (1913), 'Über eine Anwendung der Mengenlehre auf die Theorie des Schachspiels', *Proceedings of the 5th International Congress of Mathematicians, 22–28 August 1912, Cambridge*, vol. 2, Cambridge: Cambridge University Press, pp. 501–4, English trans. U. Schwalbe and P. Walker (2001), 'On an application of set theory to the theory of the game of chess', U. Schwalbe and P. Walker (2001), 'Zermelo and the early history of game theory', *Games and Economic Behavior*, **34** (1), 133–6.

General equilibrium theory

When, in some discipline, we arrive at a fully fledged, internally consistent model, we have a tendency to assume that such a model was the inevitable consequence of progress in that discipline. Einstein, quoted by Hahn (1974: 23), observed that:

> Creating a new theory is not like destroying an old barn and erecting a skyscraper in its place. It is rather like climbing a mountain, gaining new and wider views, discovering new connections between our starting point and its rich environment. But the point from which we started still exists and can be seen, although it appears smaller and forms a tiny part of our broad view gained by the mastery of the obstacles on our way up.

This suggests that there was only one mountain to climb and that each hard-won vertical metre gave us a better and fuller understanding of the world. Yet general equilibrium theory and its evolution illustrates perfectly the difficulties with this view. What do we mean now by general equilibrium theory? A concise definition might be the study of those states of an economy where "rational" optimizing, and isolated individuals and firms make choices subject to constraints, where the constraints are determined by the prices of goods and factors, where these prices are known to all agents, and where no agent has an incentive to change his choice. Furthermore, the states are described as "equilibria" if the quantities of goods demanded are equal to the quantities of goods or resources produced or naturally available. The questions that then arise are: do such states exist and what are their properties? How many are there? Will the economy reach them?

The usual observation in economics textbooks is that this formulation originated with Léon Walras and that Vilfredo Pareto and his successors, culminating with the contribution of Kenneth Arrow and Gérard Debreu, honed this vision to perfection until they produced the beautiful and complete mathematical formulation that we know today. What ought to be mentioned briefly at the beginning of this entry is that the modern notion of equilibrium evolved with Walras from a complicated and intertwined intellectual inheritance. Furthermore, it is far from clear that the route followed by his successors was the obvious one, nor that the result fully reflects the more complex, and perhaps less well-defined, ideas that Walras, his predecessors and contemporaries developed. The evolution of the theory since Walras will be traced and some of the problems that have been encountered on the way indicated.

Economic Equilibrium: The Pre-Walrasian Background

A recurrent theme in economics was, well before Walras and already developed by Adam Smith (1776), the notion that somehow out of the disparate activities of many relatively disconnected individuals a great deal of coordination emerges. This is the idea behind the often quoted and frequently misinterpreted phrase of Smith in which he refers to the "invisible hand". There are a number of aspects of this vision that are worth examining. The usual idea, attributed to Smith, is that the result of the unconscious coordination of individuals leads to some sort of social optimum. Even a casual reading of Smith reveals that this is not what he had in mind but once again this is a projection of ideas developed subsequent to Walras. Nevertheless there was clearly present in Smith's work the idea that an economy self-organizes into states, which have, possibly positive, attributes. However, the underlying argument in Smith was that capital would flow from activities with low rates of profit to those yielding higher rates and that this would finally result in a uniform rate of profit (that is, zero extra profit) situation, which could now, with hindsight, be thought of as some sort of long-period position or equilibrium. David Ricardo developed the analysis and also included demographic changes and emphasized the importance of land but also envisaged a point of gravitation (see Kurz and Salvadori 1995: ch. 1).

If one accepts the idea that the simple process of interpersonal trading would lead to a situation in which there was no more extra profit to be made from trade and that this could be considered as an equilibrium, then this had much earlier origins as Arrow observed:

> The idea that traders will respond to profit opportunities by increasing their activities and, by doing so, tend to wipe them out must have been recognized whenever there was trade. A 12th century rabbinical commentary argues that if someone charges "too high a price", others will offer the good at a lower price and thereby bring it down. (Arrow 2007: 1)

This idea was developed by Antoine-Augustin Cournot (1838), who defined markets as being places, not necessarily geographically defined, where all units of the same good are sold at the same price. How this would happen was not specified but the argument that the gains from trade would be arbitraged away had a direct influence on Walras who was familiar with, and influenced by, Cournot's work. Thus Cournot had this early sort of equilibrium notion in mind.

Yet the problem that Walras addressed, and which has come to be called the general equilibrium problem, was not whether economies would settle to some sort of general state from which individuals would not want to deviate, but whether in an economy with many goods it was possible that all these markets would clear simultaneously. He also posed the important but different question: would there be some natural tendency for this to happen? The first and less ambitious question can be phrased as: could one find prices for each of the goods even when the demand and supply for each good depends on the prices of the other goods, such that there would be no excess demand or supply for any good? That is, if you could write down the aggregate demand and supply for the goods as a function of the prices of all goods could you solve this system for an equilibrium?

In this respect there is, it has been suggested, some evidence that Walras was influenced by Achilles-Nicolas Isnard (1781), a French engineer and economist who defined an equilibrium notion and was considered to be a follower (whereas, he was more of a critic) of Quesnay. Isnard has been credited by Ingrao and Israel (1990) with seeing economic equilibrium as a solution of a system of equations and claiming that a solution could be found if the number of equations were equal to the number of unknowns. The same claim was made by Jaffé (1969: 25), who went as far as to say, "Walras worked out the mathematical framework of his general equilibrium theory with Isnard's *Traité des Richesses* at his elbow". (See also Screpanti and Zamagni 1993.) What is suggested by Jaffé is that the essential framework for Walras's work was already laid out by Isnard, and that what was lacking was the derivation of demand from the maximization of utility and it was this that Walras added to move the theory forward. Indeed, it has also been suggested that Isnard, as an engineer, was not particularly interested by what motivated individuals to make their choices and that Walras's contribution was a natural way to fill the gap. All of this is an *ex post* construction. As Misaki (2009) points out, there is little concrete evidence that Walras actually studied Isnard's work in detail, contrary to Jaffé's assertion, and furthermore, as van den Berg (2007) indicates, Isnard developed, at some length, arguments as to the psychological factors influencing people's choices. As van den Berg (2007: 94) says,

> Isnard developed sophisticated views about human decision-making processes. While he claimed that producers and consumers make decisions on the basis of personal interests, he qualified these as being supported by unreflective, impulsive, or habitual action and concluded that only conduct motivated by an "interested" choice that is "fortified by virtuous habits" leads to socially desirable outcomes. This concern with the motivations of humans engaged in social transactions stands in strong contrast with modern economic equilibrium theory.

The point here is a simple one, in order to trace a direct progressive path in the development of theory we tend to ignore the other possible routes that could have been taken. If Walras had been more interested in the alternative ways of formulating motivations, for example, by taking various psychological considerations into account, his theory might have evolved quite differently.

However, there are good reasons as to why he took the path he did. Walras had three projects, which he referred to as pure economics, applied economics and social economics. The only one of these that was pursued fully was the first. While, as he himself insisted, no theory has any value if not consistent with empirical evidence, his pure economics and those who followed in that tradition reflect little concern for the inductive approach.

Walras himself was persuaded by the idea that, even though we are dealing with internal feelings and sentiments when talking about what satisfies people, once we establish what these preferences are we can have full recourse to the weapons of the natural sciences. Indeed, in a letter to Hermann Laurent he said:

> All these results are marvels of the simple application of the language of mathematics to the quantitative notion of need or utility. Refine this application as much as you will but you can be sure that the economic laws that result from it are just as rational, just as precise and just as incontrovertible as were the laws of astronomy at the end of the 17th century. (Letter no. 1454 to Hermann Laurent, in Jaffé 1965)

In this connection, Mirowski (1989) has developed a complete account of the dependence of Walras on the physics of the time. It is not surprising therefore that he insisted on developing what he came to call *l'économie mathématique* at the expense of a more general framework. Indeed, Walras continually manifested the desire to be appreciated and approved of by mathematicians. Yet, Walras was far from convincing the mathematicians on many points. For example, late in his life Walras, unjustifiably claimed the unqualified support of Henri Poincaré and wrote, "in 1906 I was in contact with certain eminent French mathematicians who had seen at first glance that my mathematical economics was well founded and who made a declaration to this effect at the St. Louis Exhibition" (Walras letter 1642 to Charles Gide, in Jaffé 1965) – this, as Jaffé remarks, despite the explicit denial by Henri Poincaré that he had mentioned mathematical economics in the address to which Walras referred (Poincaré letter no. 1639, in Jaffé 1965).

Thus there were many forces at play in the evolution of Walras's work, and although he claimed that the only economists to whom he owed anything were Cournot and his father, Auguste Walras, this is far from being the whole story. He chose the route that he did in part because of his natural inclination to develop what he thought of as an economic science and his fascination with the mathematical approach, but also because of the heritage of ideas of his many intellectual predecessors, such as Quesnay, Isnard, Descartes and J.S. Mill, to name but a few. The extent of their influence is open to discussion but its existence can hardly be denied.

Walrasian General Equilibrium

The basic problem that Walras wished to analyse was that of finding prices and the corresponding inputs and outputs of firms and allocations to consumers in a many goods economy such that all markets clear, that is that excess demand for every good is zero. It was the passage from a single good to many goods that was the challenge. Before accepting any definition of equilibrium, one has to specify what motivates the choices made by the individuals in the economy or market. In other words, in the Walrasian context we have to specify the demands and supplies of all the agents in the economy. For firms the idea adopted by Walras in line with earlier writers is simply that they wish to increase the profitability of their activity and the same idea was often attributed to traders. However, the objectives of consumers are less clear and this was the subject of vigorous debate. Walras had in mind that consumption bundles yielded utility, a cardinal or measurable concept for which he was criticized by Poincaré (1901) and Laurent (1900), and that individuals maximized their utility subject to their budget constraints. (Incidentally, both Laurent and Poincaré disagreed with the idea that satisfaction or utility could be measurable. Walras cites Laurent as having said in his address to the Institut des Actuaires français in 1900, "How can one accept the notion that satisfaction can be measured? No mathematician could agree to this." However, in his 1901 letter Poincaré tried to soften what Walras regarded as being unjustifiably harsh criticism but still balked at the idea of utility as a measurable entity.) The latter was defined by the prices which individuals took as given. The informal justification for another assumption, that of price taking behaviour, as the number of individuals became large, had already been given by Cournot (1838) whose influence Walras acknowledged. (In fact within the Walrasian framework we had to wait until the 1960s when Aumann 1964 provided a rigorous argument for price taking behaviour by introducing a continuum of individually insignificant agents.) Having specified the choices made by individuals at any prices, the equilibrium was then simply defined as the vector of prices for the l goods in the economy for which the excess demand for all goods was 0. Since the level of prices is indeterminate in the Walrasian system we can fix one price so that it is the numeraire. Thus, we only need $(l-1)$ prices. However, if $l-1$ markets clear, at equilibrium so must the remaining market. Thus we have a set of equations with the same number of equations as unknowns and this Walras claimed was enough to show that there was a solution. It was not (see below).

However, before proceeding, what has just been described is part of the Walrasian legacy but does not correspond to what Walras really did. It would be convenient to assume that Walras adopted Cournot's ideas and used them to justify price-taking behaviour. If so, then the question is where do the prices come from? The way to answer this has been to suggest that there is an auctioneer who cries out the prices and this figure is regularly referred to as the "Walrasian auctioneer". However, if there is one thing that we owe to Donald Walker (1996), it is to insist on the fact that Walras never, in fact, saw the market or economy as one in which there was free competition, in the sense that all the participants were price takers. He argues, and even his opponents agree, that the agents in Walras's models could not have been viewed as "price takers" since nothing was specified about whom they were supposed to be taking prices from. Rather, he argues, Walras had in mind a notion of free or perfect competition as corresponding to a situation in which large numbers of individuals interact with each other freely but they are not passive price takers since they themselves quote the prices at which they are prepared to buy or sell. Walras also saw pure or perfect competition as an ideal rather than a reality. Walker quotes Walras, in a letter to Ladislaus von Bortkiewitz, as saying: "Free competition is the principle mode of exchange in the real economy, practiced on all markets with more or less precision and therefore with less or more efficiency" (Walras to von Bortkiewicz, 1891, letter 999, in Jaffé 1965).

Hence Walras believed in the idea that individuals quoted prices and exchanged goods with each other and that this would drive prices to some sort of equilibrium. There is a major problem with this in that we have to know, or rather the agents in the economy have to know, when to stop. This requires a great deal of information and Alfred Marshall (1920) argued that this was implausible for the minor players in the economy.

De Vroey (2003) has put forward an alternative argument to explain the emergence of the Walrasian auctioneer as a standard idea in economic theory. He suggests that the only way of completing the Walrasian story convincingly is to introduce an auctioneer. Thus he claims that the auctioneer is a logical necessity rather than an assumption made directly by Walras. As he says, "the auctioneer hypothesis is part and parcel of Walrasian theory. Without it, the latter would lack any scenario about the institutional dimension of its price formation mechanism" (De Vroey 2003: 469).

Two Visions of Equilibrium

The preceding discussion reveals a fundamental problem with general equilibrium theory. Are we talking about a state in which all agents' choices are consistent or are we talking about the resting point of a dynamic system, which adjusts towards such a state?

Walras discussed both, and, in the end, seemed to settle for the mathematically more tractable, and less complex, vision which is the first. The second brings up the problem of stability which turned out much later to be the *bête noire* of the theory. If we adopt the first approach then all that needs to be shown is that there are such states. There could, indeed, be many of them and we do not have to be concerned with the process by which they are achieved. This view has led to what Backhaus and Maks (2006) suggest is the caricature of what they describe as "the common university trained scholar's" under-standing of the Walrasian model, which is, "Walras developed the general economic equilibrium model, but did not care about uniqueness and stability of an equilibrium. It is a model with exchange and production only and it assumes an auctioneer who announces price vectors to establish the equilibrium" (Backhaus and Maks 2006: 1).

Walras had an ambiguous view, although this has been the subject of vigorous debate (see, for example, Walker 1996, 1999; De Vroey 1999). On the one hand he pursued his "scientific" view, which consisted in showing that a solution to the system of excess demand functions existed. In this, he advanced the explanation that it was sufficient to count the number of equations and unknowns and that, since in his model the two were equal, the problem was solved. In fact it was Abraham Wald (1936) much later who showed that equilibrium did exist and for this it was necessary to use a fixed point theorem which was not proved till after Walras's death. (The first fixed point theorem was proved by Brouwer 1912 and there were later generalizations by, for example, Kakutani 1941 which have been widely used in economics.) The alternative view, that of a system which would converge to an equilibrium state, invokes the problem of stability (see below).

However, before embarking on this subject, a number of remarks are in order. The idea that the essential problem was that of showing that equilibrium exists was far from being universally accepted, and yet what is often regarded as the apogee of General Equilibrium theory, the results of Arrow and Debreu (1954), do no more than this.

Furthermore, the vision of economic equilibrium as the solution of a set of simultaneous equations was criticized by a number of leading economic theorists and this is well illustrated by the observation of John Hicks (1939: 60) who remarked, disparagingly,

> To some people (including no doubt Walras himself) the system of simultaneous equations determining a whole price-system seems to have vast significance. They derive intense satisfaction from the contemplation of such a system of subtly interrelated prices; and the further the analysis can be carried (in fact it can be carried a good way) . . . the better they are pleased, and the profounder the insight into the working of a competitive economic system they feel they get.

Nevertheless, the idea of finding a solution to a set of equations, which was, in large part, solved by Wald (1936), was in the spirit of the Bourbaki tradition and it is not surprising that it should have been Debreu who pushed Walrasian theory in this direction. He was following on from Maurice Allais, his mentor, who was clearly oriented in the direction of mathematical purity rather than realism. Allais said, "The fundamental Anglo-Saxon quality is satisfaction with the accumulation of facts. The need for clarity, for logical coherence and for synthesis is, for an Anglo-Saxon, only a minor need, if it is a need at all. For a Latin, and particularly a Frenchman, it is exactly the opposite" (Allais 1952: 58). However, in thinking in this way Allais was encouraging the distancing of economics from reality. Indeed this was exactly in the Bourbaki tradition for as Bourbaki (1949: 2) said:

> Why do applications [of mathematics] ever succeed? Why is a certain amount of logical reasoning occasionally helpful in practical life? Why have some of the most intricate theories in mathematics become an indispensable tool to the modern physicist, to the engineer, and to the manufacturer of atom-bombs? Fortunately for us, the mathematician does not feel called upon to answer such questions.

Although to many economists this was not the appropriate route to follow, it is worth observing that considerable progress was made along the way in weakening the assumptions on individual characteristics necessary to achieve this result. Pareto (1906) showed that only an ordinal representation of preferences was necessary. A result of Shapley and

Folkman could be used to show that the highly contestable assumption of the convexity of preferences was not necessary, if one was satisfied with a close approximation of the true equilibrium. (The lemma is stated and the original proof given in Starr 1969.) Incomplete preferences and other relaxations of the traditional axioms of rationality are discussed in Chipman et al. (1971).

A second and very important result of this line of thought was the demonstration by Vilfredo Pareto (1906), Walras's successor at the University of Lausanne, that a competitive equilibrium is what is now referred to as a Pareto optimal state. This should be regarded essentially as an efficiency criterion. In such a state no individual can be made better off without making another worse off. This has widely, and often erroneously, been used to justify the market mechanism as a solution to society's economic allocation problems. However, even before Pareto showed that a competitive equilibrium was efficient, in this sense Walras himself was at lengths to point out that there were no distributional considerations involved in defining such an equilibrium. Thus, ideas of equity and fairness nowhere figure in the standard general equilibrium framework. (This does not mean that such considerations cannot be included in the model as shown by Kolm 1968, Feldman and Kirman 1973 and Foley 1967. However, this literature is usually considered as an intriguing but unimportant side road.) Nevertheless, the importance attached to this result, which has come to be called the First Fundamental Theorem of Welfare Economics, can be measured by the disproportionate emphasis that has been given to the mathematical appendix to Pareto's work (see Kirman 1998, 2013).

However, the very foundations of the analysis that led to this result are dependent on the notion of rational, optimizing agents, and Pareto in his later sociological work expressed a great deal of skepticism about this. He even went as far as to suggest that people spend a little part of their time taking non-rational decisions and the rest of their time rationalizing them!

Equilibrium and the Adjustment to It

In the end we have arrived at a situation where we can show the existence of an equilibrium under certain, rather strong, restrictions on the characteristics of individuals, and that equilibrium satisfies a minimal efficiency criterion.

But what about the other concept of equilibrium, that of the resting point of a process of adjustment from an out of equilibrium position? If we consider what Arrow (2007) has to say about this, even though his name is inextricably linked with the proof of the existence of such a state, then it is clear that he, like Walras, has kept in mind a process, which would bring the economy to an equilibrium. It is worth observing that Debreu never ventured into the field of stability analysis, with the exception of his contribution to the literature (Debreu 1974), showing that, in the Arrow–Debreu model, stability could not be guaranteed, whereas Arrow wrote a number of papers on the subject. Despite the attention Walras paid to the equilibrium as a solution of a set of equations, he never completely abandoned his idea of the economy as self-organizing into such a state. For example, he observed, when describing the evolution of an economy, that it is "like a lake stirred by the wind, in which the water continually seeks its equilibrium without ever achieving it" (Walras 1877: 310). Or as Arrow himself said recently:

The very concept of equilibrium, economic or otherwise, presupposes a dynamic system which determines change as a function of state variables. An equilibrium is a vector of state variables for which no change occurs. In economics, this is interpreted as a set of quantities and prices for which there is no incentive on anyone's part to change. The dynamics runs in terms of profit opportunities or incentives to outbid others for scarce commodities or for market opportunities. (Arrow 2007: 1)

Again, Walras when he developed his market models (see Walker 1996) was explicitly concerned with the stability of an adjustment mechanism. Walras himself tried two approaches to this problem. In one he explained that the price of one good could be adjusted until the equilibrium, for the market for that good, was reached while holding the prices of the other goods constant. Then one would fix that price and move on to the next good adjusting the price of that good, and repeat the process. Walras seems to suggest that this would automatically converge to an equilibrium situation. Yet, any student of first-year economics can point out the flaw in this argument. If the cross-effects on the excess demand for other goods are sufficiently strongly affected by the adjustment mechanism, then the process may lead to prices exploding or cycling indefinitely, for example. This anticipates one of the standard conditions for the stability of equilibrium, which is that called the "dominant diagonal" condition. This says, in brief, that if the own effect of a change in the price of a commodity outweighs the sum of all the cross effects of that change on other markets then equilibrium will be stable. (This is a little bit of a finesse since the dominant diagonal condition was used in connection with the "tâtonnement process" (see next paragraph).

The alternative approach suggested by Walras was the so-called "tâtonnement" process. Here prices adjust whenever markets are not in equilibrium and they do so in proportion to the level of excess demands for the commodities. However, in doing this, we encounter a problem with the adjustment approach. If the process of adjustment to equilibrium is a process which happens in the real economy, it must take time, in particular when the production of goods is involved. Alternatively, you could think of the process as a virtual one which happens instantaneously and does not take any time at all. This could be thought of as akin to certain arguments in physics where one thinks of something moving slowly along a surface but adjusting instantaneously back to the surface whenever it leaves it. This is discussed by Donzelli (2009: 15) who says:

> Among the epistemological inconsistencies, the most evident is revealed by the dualistic character of the Walrasian theoretical system: in fact, in the versions of this system developed in the second (and third) edition of the *Eléments*, one can find, side by side, two alternative interpretations of the *tâtonnement*, the virtual and the effective; these two kinds of processes evolve in two distinct time sets, the "logical" and the "real", lead to alternative notions of equilibrium, the "instantaneous" and the "stationary", and finally pertain to different models, the pure-exchange model, on the one hand, and the models with production, on the other.

As Donzelli rightly points out, it is production which makes the Walrasian concept of adjustment in real time implausible. The conflict over the interpretation of the Walrasian price adjustment process is apparent in the acrimonious debate that Walras had with Edgeworth, often through von Bortkiewicz as intermediary (see Walker's 1996 very complete discussion of the debate between Edgeworth and Walras). The latter asserted in a review of Walras's *Eléments* that Edgeworth was convinced that Walras had described a system which was not functional and that what Walras was describing was a virtual adjustment, and in his review he came down on Edgeworth's side when he said:

> Well, the way to solve the equilibrium equations analysed by M. Walras is absolutely consistent with the idea that Jevons had about the nature of these equations. As to the exchange problem, M. Walras thinks about this in a purely static way, in the sense that the quantities of goods available are fixed, preferences are unchanging and he simply solves the equations by increasing and decreasing prices. (Bortkiewicz 1890: 86)

Edgeworth was evidently convinced that the process described by Walras was virtual since there was none of the "higgling" that he described in his recontracting process. Furthermore, the quantities to be traded and the preferences were not modified while the process was taking place. This makes little sense when physical production is analysed. However, it is also true that in *Mathematical Psychics* (Edgeworth 1881) the nature and timing of the bargaining process are not discussed in detail. Indeed Edgeworth himself admitted as much 10 years later in his reply to von Bortkiewicz, at least as far as the "time" factor is concerned (Jaffé 1965). However, Edgeworth came to be convinced that the stability problem did not have a general solution and that, at best, a solution could be found for particular institutional arrangements. He discussed various forms of auctions, for example. Walras, still persuaded that he was working towards some sort of general science, reacted angrily, for Edgeworth, he felt, was convinced that,

> I am engaged in absolutely useless exercises in my efforts to demonstrate that the operations of the raising and lowering of prices, of the increases and decreases of the quantities of products produced, etc. on the markets are nothing other than the solution by tâtonnement of the equations of exchange, of production and of capital formation. (Letter no. 927 to von Bortkiewicz, in Jaffé 1965)

His conviction that his view was a general one made him object particularly strongly to the idea that adjustment processes could only be applicable in specific institutions. He seemed to assimilate the notion of "free competition" to the tâtonnement process and once again he complained to von Bortkiewicz:

> I take the almost universal regime of free competition in regard to exchange, that which was described by John Stuart Mill, and which consists in raising the price in the case of the quantity demanded exceeding the quantity supplied and lowering it in the case of the quantity supplied exceeding the quantity demanded, and I demonstrate that the process leads to equilibrium by establishing the equality of the quantities supplied and demanded. Whereupon there is thrown at my head the market for English public debt, the system of English auctions, the system of Dutch auctions etc., etc. (Letter no. 999 to von Bortkiewicz, in Jaffé 1965)

Of course, unfortunately Walras had done nothing of the sort. Indeed, much later it became clear that what he tried to do was not possible. There is a long history of what might be called "centralized" adjustment processes in which all individuals take prices as given and somehow these prices are adjusted as a function of aggregate excess demand for various goods (see, for example, Arrow and Hurwicz 1958; Arrow et al. 1959).

It is this that led De Vroey, as mentioned earlier, to assert that the only idea that was compatible with this sort of mechanism was to have some sort of auctioneer. Here, an important gulf between what was needed to ensure some sort of stability and what were typically made as assumptions on the individual participants in the economy becomes clear. The conditions that guarantee stability, at least of the tâtonnement process, are conditions on the aggregate excess demand of the economy. For example, a condition that guarantees both stability and uniqueness of equilibrium is that all goods be "gross substitutes", if the price of one good increases the demand for none of the other goods decreases. This is of course not a reasonable empirical condition, everyone can immediately think of goods which are complementary, cars and tyres, for example. Worse, this is a condition on aggregate excess demand while theoretical macroeconomists continued, and continue, to insist that one should limit oneself to assumptions on the rationality of individuals. However, the basic problem is that the structure that we impose on individual firm and consumers' choices does not carry over to the aggregate.

To take a simple example, Samuelson (1938) introduced the notion of "revealed preference", that is, rather than make rather abstract assumptions about the underlying preferences of consumers one could impose a simple axiom of consistency on their choices. This, it was thought, would rid us of the unverifiable structure that had been imposed by Walras and Pareto and would mean that we could verify empirically the consistency of individual choices. The simplest expression of the axiom is what is called the weak axiom of revealed preference. It simply says that if an individual chooses alternative x when he could have chosen y he will never choose y when x is available. Unhappily it was easily shown that the aggregate choices of two individuals, each of whom satisfy this assumption, do not necessarily do so. This was particularly unfortunate since Uzawa (1960) showed that satisfying the axiom of revealed preference was equivalent, for an individual, to satisfying all of the restrictive and artificial assumptions that mathematical economists had imposed on individuals. (To be precise it should be observed that what is needed is the strong axiom of revealed preference which assumes that there is no cycle of preferred bundles of goods.) There was clearly a problem with the passage from individual behaviour to aggregate behaviour.

The fruitless search for showing that reasonable conditions on individual preferences for consumers or for technologies for firms that would guarantee stability of some plausible price adjustment process was brought to a halt by the results of Sonnenschein (1972), Mantel (1974) and Debreu (1974) himself. (For simplicity, the reference will be to the SMD results from here on.)

What did they show? This needs a little background. It was well established long before these results that aggregate excess demand, that is, aggregate demand minus aggregate supply which we can denote by $Z(p)$, satisfies four conditions:

1. $Z(p)$ is a continuous function of the prices of the l goods in the economy.
2. $Z(p)$ satisfies Walras' Law that is $p \cdot Z(p) = 0$, that is, the value of what is sold at any prices must be equal to the value of what is bought.
3. $Z(p)$ is homogeneous of degree 0. Changing the price level, that is, multiplying all prices by a constant does not change excess demand.
4. If the price of any good goes to zero, average aggregate demand $\|Z(p)\|$ becomes infinite.

Each of these conditions is easily derived from the standard assumptions on individuals. In particular, the first reflects the condition that individuals have continuous preferences, they do not suddenly switch their preferences when faced with small changes in the choices with which they are faced. The second comes from the fact that individuals are assumed to satisfy their budget constraints. The third reflects the fact that only relative prices matter for individual choices. The last, for which Walras was mildly criticized by Poincaré, comes from the assumption that individuals always prefer more of any good, as Poincaré (1901) said, they are assumed to be "infinitely greedy".

Now, there was a latent idea that the conditions for uniqueness and stability of equilibrium were somehow related. This was, no doubt, due to the fact that the known sufficient conditions on aggregate excess demand for uniqueness also implied stability. However Scarf (1960) gave an example of an economy with a unique but unstable equilibrium. Furthermore, it was not difficult to construct examples of economies with multiple equilibria. Therefore, the hope was to use the standard assumptions and to show that they ruled this sort of phenomenon out.

What the SMD results showed was that the only conditions imposed on aggregate excess demand by the standard assumptions on individuals were the four mentioned above. Since we can find economies satisfying these conditions which have multiple and/or unstable equilibria there was no hope of guaranteeing uniqueness or stability. This meant that simply constructing models on the basis of assumptions on individual rationality does not lead to any empirically meaningful restrictions on aggregate behaviour. Indeed many distinguished economists have claimed that uniqueness and stability are minimal requirements for a satisfactory model of an economy. For example, Schumpeter (1939) argued that a satisfactory model must, of necessity, generate a unique equilibrium to be considered as scientific:

> The first and foremost task of economic analysis is to explore the properties of that system . . . What we want to learn before anything else is whether or not the relations known to subsist between the elements of the system are, together with the data, sufficient to determine these elements, prices and quantities, uniquely. For our system is logically self contained only if this is the case: we can be sure that we understand the nature of economic phenomena only if it is possible to deduce prices and quantities from the data by means of those relations and to prove that no other set of prices and physical quantities is compatible with both the data and the relations. The proof that this is so is the magna charta of economic theory as an autonomous science, assuring that its subject matter is a cosmos and not a chaos. (Schumpeter 1939: 41)

Even if we can handle the problem of multiple equilibria, and this poses serious problems for those who are interested in analysing the comparative statics of their model, the stability problem seems much more important. For as Morishima (1984: 68–9) remarked:

> If economists successfully devise a correct general equilibrium model, even if it can be proved to possess an equilibrium solution, should it lack the institutional backing to realise an equilibrium solution, then the equilibrium solution will amount to no more than a utopian state of affairs which bear no relation whatsoever to the real economy.

The SMD results put an end to any hope of showing that there is a mechanism which would provide such an institutional backing, at least if one insists on building a general equilibrium model based solely on assumptions about individuals. Hahn (2002) pointed out that, worse, these results that undermined Walrasian general equilibrium theory came from within the group of distinguished theorists who had so successfully promoted the formalization of the theory and who were responsible for perfecting it. Perhaps strangest of all, the SMD results did not arise from a discussion as to whether an economy would converge from an out-of-equilibrium position to such a state. As Hahn observed: "The enterprise was doomed not to be capable of reaching general conclusions in the Walrasian setting. A theorem not directly related to or connected with dynamics did the damage" (Hahn 2002: 24).

Information

Despite these difficulties the Walrasian model, perfected by Arrow and Debreu, remains "the benchmark model" of modern economics. However, it is not obvious where precisely the difficulty revealed by the SMD results comes from. One way to see this is to consider the role of information. It should, by now, be clear that, in the general equilibrium model, prices have a very particular informational role. In the perfectly competitive world it is the price system that coordinates the activity of all the agents. As we have seen and contrary to statements often made, the only information that an individual requires is the current vector of prices of all commodities (goods or services). He or she knows his or her own endowments and has preferences (in the case of the consumer) or technological possibilities (in the case of the producer). Each individual acting independently makes his or her own choices within the constraints determined by current prices and an equilibrium is a situation in which these choices are compatible (aggregate supply is equal to aggregate demand). Such an equilibrium exists under the standard assumptions on the characteristics of the economic agents.

Given this, it is worth noting an important result due to Jordan (1982), which is the key to understanding the problem posed by the SMD results. What Jordan shows is that if you are interested in designing a mechanism to achieve an efficient allocation of resources in an economy, then the competitive mechanism uses less information than any other mechanism. What is more, there is no other mechanism that uses so little information.

To explain this result, which it is worth dwelling upon, consider the following very simple case: a simple barter economy in which there are n individuals each owning a bundle of l goods. We wish to design a mechanism to allocate these goods efficiently, that is, which achieves a Pareto optimum and which, at equilibrium, uses as little information as possible. A mechanism is understood as associating with each economy a set of messages, these messages induce actions by the agents in the economy which lead to an efficient outcome. How would the competitive mechanism fit into this scheme?

With each economy the messages that will be required are the vector of prices and the vector of trades each agent wishes to make. For each economy then we need a vector of $l - 1$ prices (the last one can be dropped since we can normalize prices) and for each of the n individuals a vector of "excess demands" or "net trades". Since each individual satisfies Walras's law (what he or she purchases must have the same value as what he or she sells) we only need to know $l - 1$ of these quantities. Furthermore, since we are considering an equilibrium the aggregate excess demand or net trade must be zero for each commodity, therefore we can drop one of the individuals. Thus we have $1 \cdot (l - 1) + (n - 1) \cdot (l - 1)$ "pieces of information", that is, the messages we use must contain $n(l - 1)$

pieces of information or, put more technically, "the dimension of the message space" of this mechanism is $n(l-1)$.

The remarkable fact is that any other mechanism satisfying certain minimal requirements can only achieve an efficient outcome by using more information than this. In other words, the use of a price mechanism limits dramatically the amount of information required to achieve a desirable result.

All of this seems very positive and the idea that the Walrasian equilibrium is informationally efficient is very appealing. However, the very same analysis shows why the SMD results are so destructive. Suppose that we come back to the idea of adjusting from an out-of-equilibrium position to an equilibrium. That is, suppose we take the stability issue seriously and, instead of just trying to solve a system of simultaneous equations, we wish to study how equilibrium is achieved. Even if we accept that all the individuals in the economy observe the same prices for all goods, we have to be able to specify the mechanism that adjusts prices towards equilibrium values.

The first suggestion to solve this problem was that the price adjustment process, which we have typically considered, was inadequate and by modifying it we might be able to get out of the dilemma posed by the SMD results. Yet, what became immediately clear after the innovative work of Smale (1976) was that stability could only be achieved at the price of an enormous increase in the amount of information.

Smale's global Newton method is an extension of the standard tâtonnement process for finding the equilibria of an aggregate excess demand function. However, unfortunately it uses a great deal of information. Without entering into technical details, let me just mention that what is needed is a knowledge of all the partial derivatives of the aggregate excess demand function and this greatly increases the size of the messages necessary to make the mechanism function. Worse, despite this increase in the information required, although the process leads to equilibria from a large set of starting prices, it still does not guarantee convergence from any arbitrary starting point. An additional problem is with the economic content of the process. While the original tâtonnement process has a very natural interpretation, despite valiant efforts by some economists, this is not the case for the Newton method. Furthermore, all the alternative adjustment processes in order to solve the stability problem that have been constructed to date have no natural economic interpretation. The informational problem posed by the Newton problem turns out to be unavoidable, for what Saari and Simon (1978) showed was that any process that would always take the economy from any starting prices to an equilibrium would use an infinite amount of information. Thus, while at equilibrium the competitive process is extremely informationally parsimonious, as soon as we consider the Walrasian idea of an economy moving from an out-of-equilibrium position to an equilibrium, the amount of information necessarily explodes. This shows where one of the fundamental problems exposed by SMD comes from.

Three Ways Out

Given this situation, three ways out have been proposed. First, there was the feeling that perhaps the basic problem lay with the adjustment process itself. Despite the Saari and Simon result, various ingenious attempts have been made to construct globally and universally stable price adjustment processes. Although, some of these attempts, Kamiya

(1990), Flaschel (1991) and Herings (1997), seem, in a certain sense, to have been successful, if one looks closely at these results there is always some feature which is open to objection. There is, in general, no natural economic interpretation and, furthermore, in one case the adjustment process depends on the particular parameters of the economy in question. It seems implausible to assume that when something changes in the economy the way in which prices adjust when out of equilibrium should also change.

A second route was to argue that there was no particular reason to suppose that when out of equilibrium, in a market, all the individuals should be faced with the same prices. This is what Rothschild's (1973) seminal contribution on searching for lower prices in markets considered. Were we to make the assumption, implicit in Arrow–Debreu, that the price for any good, in particular labour, is the same across the whole economy, the whole literature on search for lower prices (see, for example, Mortensen 1986; Diamond 1987; Pissarides 1990) would lose any significance. In that literature there is a distribution of prices for the same good or of wages, and individuals match with others in their search for the best opportunity. Indeed, pursuing this line of thought and looking at the evolution of the price distribution, rather than have some sort of centralized price adjustment mechanism, you could just think of individuals bargaining and that the prices at which the goods were exchanged would vary between individuals. There would, it was argued, be some sort of force which would drive the economy to an equilibrium where prices for the same good were equalized and, furthermore, any excess demand for any particular good would be arbitraged away. This is what lay behind Edgeworth's (1925) "higgling" and Hayek's (1945) informal suggestions as to how individuals might react to some change in the economic situation and how prices would be modified accordingly. This is what the latter had in mind when criticizing Walras's idea of central price adjustment and the idea that there is some central figure that will adjust prices if the economy is out of equilibrium. As Hayek (1945: 519, original emphasis) said:

> This, however, is emphatically *not* the economic problem which society faces. And the economic calculus which we have developed to solve this logical problem, though an important step toward the solution of the economic problem of society, does not yet provide an answer to it. The reason for this is that the "data" from which the economic calculus starts are never for the whole society "given" to a single mind which could work out the implications and can never be so given.

Hayek's famous informal example of a change in the use of tin and resultant price changes was in the spirit of the idea of different agents trading initially at different prices, launched by Edgeworth. This led to a number of efforts culminating in Frank Fisher's (1989) heroic attempt to build a general model. Yet, as Fisher (2011) himself observes in a recent survey, a favourable answer to the question of stability is still "by no means assured".

The last route is that which has been widely followed in macroeconomics and consists in assuming directly from the outset that the average behaviour of individuals satisfies the same conditions of consistency, or rationality, that we impose on individuals. It is of little value here to pass in review, yet again, the difficulties with this assumption (see Kirman 1992). Let it just be said that there is widespread dissatisfaction with models based on the representative agent, and that proposals to introduce heterogeneity and individual interaction which undermine traditional macroeconomic analysis have come from many quarters, (see, for example, Trichet 2010; Turner 2010).

Conclusion

It would hardly be appropriate to end a discussion of general equilibrium theory without assessing its status today and its future. Many still believe that the Walrasian model is still the basic foundation on which we should build our economic theory. They argue that by introducing imperfections or frictions we can recover the Keynesian or other features which are absent from the basic model. They argue against trying to develop alternative models with a non-degenerate distribution of characteristics and where agents acting on simple rules generate the sort of aggregate phenomena that we observe. This, they claim, leads us into the "wilderness of bounded rationality". Thus studying agent-based models such as those proposed by Stiglitz and Gallegati (2011) or Colander et al. (2008) is condemned as being "ad hoc" and "non scientific", that is, as John Moore once remarked, we should stick as closely to Walras as we can. Yet when you look more closely at the favourite macroeconomic model of our day, the "dynamic stochastic general equilibrium" model, it typically makes many "ad hoc" assumptions on the technologies of firms or the utility functions of individuals. These are deemed acceptable mainly because we are familiar with them. The assumption of homogeneous production functions or concave utility functions are not based on meticulous observation of individuals and firms, but on the introspection of economic theorists. What we have done, in trying to stay on the path that Walras set us on, is to succumb to the temptation that Solow (2006: 234) has convincingly described, when he said: "Maybe there is in human nature a deep-seated perverse pleasure in adopting and defending a wholly counterintuitive doctrine that leaves the uninitiated peasant wondering what planet he or she is on".

On the one hand, the assumptions made have become more and more restrictive and the models more mathematically sophisticated. On the other, the modifications made to be able to calibrate the models with some success lead us very far from the scientific foundations claimed for the models. For example, building a general equilibrium model and then including a large number of individuals who each period simply spend all that they have and never save or borrow seems totally artificial and not in the spirit of the overall theory that Walras and his successors wished to develop. If we adhere to the basic tenet of the general equilibrium model that macro or aggregate behaviour must be derived from underlying rational microfoundations, then we have to explain how the characteristics of the aggregate are determined by those of the individuals. It is here that the general equilibrium model has let us down, because, as the SMD results showed, we can say very little about aggregate behaviour in that model. Holding rigidly to the very specific axioms underlying the model of the "rational" individual and ignoring the problems of aggregation and interaction has led us into a cul-de-sac.

However, if we are prepared to move forward and to argue that there is more interaction between individuals than that foreseen in the general equilibrium approach, then we have to take account of the interaction between the individuals and how this is organized. Looking at the economy as a complex interactive system (see Kirman 2010) opens new horizons but deviates in an essential way from the path that those, who claim to have inherited the general equilibrium tradition, have followed.

In my view, we came to the end of the Walrasian general equilibrium road in the 1970s and since then have persisted with that structure more out of a desire to protect our human capital than out of a genuine desire to use the model to give a satisfactory explanation of the economic phenomena that we actually observe. More importantly, to adequately explain the movements of economic variables we need to envisage a non-equilibrium process and its evolution. Those who think of themselves as the rightful successors to Walras seem to have strayed far from the sort of model he had in mind and might rightly be thought of as heretics who have left the pure Walrasian church. The structure that they have constructed in a desire to remain relevant lacks the beauty and generality of the Walras–Arrow–Debreu model. Those who think that economic theory must be built on new foundations have not, as yet, constructed an edifice as impressive or beautiful as that which Hildenbrand (1983, 29) described as the "cathedral" of general equilibrium theory of which Walras was the architect and Debreu the master builder. However, that monument is now, at best, filled with admiring tourists and very few true believers.

ALAN KIRMAN

See also:

Kenneth Joseph Arrow (I); Competition (III); Antoine-Augustin Cournot (I); Gérard Debreu (I); Francis Ysidro Edgeworth (I); Evolutionary economics (III); Formalization and mathematical modelling (III); Game theory (III); David Hume (I); Lausanne School (II); John Forbes Nash Jr (I); Vilfredo Pareto (I); Paul Anthony Samuelson (I); Scottish Enlightenment (II); Adam Smith (I); Value and price (III); Marie-Esprit-Léon Walras (I).

References and further reading

Allais, M. (1952), *Traité d'économie pure*, Paris: Imprimerie Nationale.
Arrow, K. (2007), 'Getting to economic equilibrium: a problem and its history', in D. Xiaotie and F.C. Graham (eds), *Internet and Network Economics*, Berlin and Heidelberg: Springer Verlag, pp. 1–2.
Arrow, K. and G. Debreu (1954), 'Existence of an equilibrium for a competitive economy', *Econometrica*, **22** (3), 265–90.
Arrow, K. and L. Hurwicz (1958), 'On the stability of competitive equilibrium I', *Econometrica*, **26** (4), 522–52.
Arrow, K., H.D. Block and L. Hurwicz (1959), 'On the stability of competitive equilibrium II', *Econometrica*, **27** (January), 82–109.
Aumann, R (1964), 'Markets with a continuum of traders', *Econometrica*, **32** (1–2), 39–50.
Backhaus, J. and H. Maks (eds) (2006), *From Walras to Pareto, European Heritage in Economics and the Social Sciences*, vol. 4, Berlin, New York and Vienna: Springer Verlag.
Billette de Villemeur, E. (1999), 'Aggregation of demand and distribution of characteristics: a difficulty in modelling behavioural heterogeneity', THEMA Working Papers 99-38, THEMA, Université de Cergy-Pontoise.
Bortkiewicz, L. von (1890), 'Compte rendu des *Éléments d'économie politique pure*', *Revue d'économie politique*, **4** (1), 80–86.
Bourbaki, N. (1949), 'The foundations of mathematics for the working mathematician', *Journal of Symbolic Logic*, **14** (1), 1–8.
Brouwer, L.E.J. (1912), 'Uber Abbildungen von Mannigfaltigkeiten', *Mathematische Annalen*, **71**, 97–115.
Chipman, J.S., L. Hurwicz, M.K. Richter and H.F. Sonnenschein (eds) (1971), *Preferences, Utility and Demand*, New York: Harcourt Brace, Jovanovich.
Colander, D., P. Howitt, A. Kirman, A. Leijonhufvud and P. Mehrling (2008), 'Beyond DSGE models: toward an empirically based macroeconomics', *American Economic Review*, **98** (2), 236–40.
Cournot, A (1838), *Recherches sur les principes de la théorie des richesses*, Paris: Librairie Hachette, English trans. N.T. Bacon (1897), *Researches into the Mathematical Principles of the Theory of Wealth*, New York: Macmillan.
Debreu, G. (1959), *Theory of Value: An Axiomatic Analysis of Economic Equilibrium*, New York: Wiley.
Debreu, G (1974), 'Excess demand functions', *Journal of Mathematical Economics*, **1** (1), 15–21.
De Vroey, M. (1999), 'Transforming Walras into a Marshallian economist: a critical review of Donald Walker's *Walras's Market Models*', *Journal of the History of Economic Thought*, **21** (4), 413–35.

De Vroey, M. (2003), 'Perfect information à la Walras versus perfect information à la Marshall', *Journal of Economic Methodology*, **10** (4), 465–92.

Diamond, P. (1987), 'Consumer differences and prices in a search model', *Quarterly Journal of Economics*, **102** (2), 429–36.

Diamond, P. (1989), 'Search theory', in J. Eatwell, M. Milgate and P. Newman (eds), *The New Palgrave: A Dictionary of Economics*, Macmillan, London, pp. 273–9.

Dillmann, R. and H. Frambach (2006), 'Economic equilibria an the balancing act between total and partial analysis', in J. Backhaus and H. Maks (eds), *From Walras to Pareto, European Heritage in Economics and the Social Sciences*, vol. 4, Berlin, New York and Vienna: Springer Verlag, pp. 103–16.

Donzelli, F. (2009), 'Walras v. Edgeworth on equilibrium and disequilibrium', Working Paper no. 2009-47, Università degli Studi di Milano.

Edgeworth, F.Y. (1881), *Mathematical Psychics: An Essay on the Application of Mathematics to the Moral Sciences*, London: C. Kegan Paul and Company.

Edgeworth, F.Y. (1925), 'Higgling', in H. Higgs (ed.), *Palgrave's Dictionary of Political Economy*, London: Macmillan.

Feldman, A. and A. Kirman (1973), 'Fairness and envy', *American Economic Review*, **64** (6), 995–1005.

Fisher, F.M. (1989), *Disequilibrium Foundations of Equilibrium Economics*, Cambridge: Cambridge University Press.

Fisher, F. (2011), 'The stability of general equilibrium – what do we know and why is it important?', in P. Bridel (ed.), *General Equilibrium Analysis: A Century after Walras*, London and New York: Routledge, pp. 34–45.

Flaschel, P. (1991), 'Stability – independent of economic structure?', *Structural Change and Economic Dynamics*, **2** (1), 9–35.

Foley, D.K. (1967), 'Resource allocation and the public sector', *Yale Economics Essays*, **7** (1), 45–98.

Hahn, F. (1974), *On the Notion of Equilibrium in Economics: An Inaugural Lecture*, Cambridge: Cambridge University Press.

Hahn, F. (2002), 'On the possibility of economic dynamics', in. H. Hommes, R. Ramer and C.A. Withagen (eds), *Equilibrium, Markets, and Dynamics: Essays in Honour of Claus Weddepohl*, Berlin: Springer-Verlag.

Hayek, F.A. (1945), 'The use of knowledge in society', *American Economic Review*, **35** (4), 519–30.

Herings, J.-J. (1997), 'A globally and universally stable price adjustment process', *Journal of Mathematical Economics*, **27** (2), 163–93.

Hicks, J. (1939), *Value and Capital*, Oxford, Oxford University Press.

Hildenbrand, W. (1983), 'Introduction', to G. Debreu, *Mathematical Economics: Twenty Papers of Gerard Debreu*, Cambridge: Cambridge University Press, pp. 1–29.

Hildenbrand, W. (1994), *Market Demand: Theory and Empirical Evidence*, Princeton, NJ: Princeton University Press.

Ingrao, B. and G. Israel (1990), *The Invisible Hand*, Cambridge, MA: MIT Press.

Isnard, A.-N. (1781), *Traité des Richesses*, published anonymously by the author in London and distributed by Grasset et cie, Lausanne.

Jaffé, W. (ed.) (1965), *Correspondence of Leon Walras and Related Papers*, 3 vols, Amsterdam: North Holland.

Jaffé, W. (1969), 'A.N. Isnard, progenitor of the Walrasian general equilibrium model', *History of Political Economy*, **1** (1), 19–43.

Jordan, J.S. (1982), 'The competitive allocation process is informationally efficient uniquely', *Journal of Economic Theory*, **28** (1), 1–18.

Kakutani, S. (1941), 'A generalization of Brouwer's fixed point theorem', *Duke Mathematical Journal*, **8** (3), 457–9.

Kamiya, K. (1990), 'A globally stable price adjustment process', *Econometrica*, **58** (6), 1481–5.

Kirman, A. (1992), 'What or whom does the representative individual represent?', *Journal of Economic Perspectives*, **6** (2), 117–36.

Kirman, A. (1998), 'Vilfredo Pareto', in F. Meacci (ed.), *Italian Economists of the 20th Century*, Cheltenham, UK and Lyme, NH, USA: Edward Elgar.

Kirman, A. (2010), *Complex Economics: Individual and Collective Analysis, the Graz Schumpeter Lectures*, Abingdon: Routledge.

Kirman, A. (2013), *Il padre dell'economia scientifica? Indagine su Vilfredo Pareto*, Rome: Luiss University Press.

Kolm, S.-C. (1968), 'The optimal production of social justice', in J. Margolis and H. Guitton (eds), *Public Economics*, London: Macmillan, pp. 145–200.

Kurz, H. and N. Salvadori (1995), *Theory of Production*, Cambridge: Cambridge University Press.

Laurent, H. (1900), 'Lettre 1452 à Walras', in W. Jaffé (ed.) (1965), *Correspondence of Leon Walras and Related Papers*, 3 vols, Amsterdam: North Holland.

Mantel, R. (1974), 'On the characterization of aggregate excess demand', *Journal of Economic Theory*, **7** (3), 348–53.

Marshall, A. (1920), *Principles of Economics*, London: Macmillan.
Mirowski, P. (1989), *More Heat than Light: Economics as Social Physics, Physics as Nature's Economics*, Cambridge: Cambridge University Press.
Misaki, K. (2009), 'Walras and Isnard: continuity and discontinuity in the history of economic thought', *Cahiers du Centre d'études interdisciplinaires Walras Pareto*, December.
Morishima, M. (1984), 'The good and bad uses of mathematics', in P. Wiles and G. Routh (eds), *Economics in Disarray*, Oxford: Basil Blackwell, pp. 51–73.
Mortensen, D.T. (1986), 'Job search and labor market analysis', in O. Ashenfelter and R. Layard (eds), *Handbook in Labor Economics*, Amsterdam: North Holland, pp. 849–919.
Pareto, V. (1906), *Manuale di economia politica con una introduzione alla scienza sociale*, Milan: Società editrice libraria, nuova edizione critica 2006, A. Montesano, A. Zanni and L. Bruni (eds), Milan: Università Bocconi Editore.
Pareto, V. (1916), *Trattato di sociologia generale*, 2 vols, Florence: Barbera, 2nd edn, 3 vols, Florence, 1923, English trans. A. Bongiorno and A. Livingston (1935), *The Mind and Society*, 4 vols, London: Cape.
Pissarides, C.A. (1990), *Equilibrium Unemployment Theory*, Oxford: Basil Blackwell.
Poincaré, H. (1901), Letter to L. Walras, 30 September, in Collection de la Bibliotheque Universitaire et Cantonale de Lausanne.
Rothschild, M. (1973), 'Models of market organisation with imperfect information: a survey', *Journal of Political Economy*, **81** (6), 1283–301.
Saari, D. and C.P. Simon (1978), 'Effective price mechanisms', *Econometrica*, **46** (5), 1097–125.
Samuelson, P.A. (1938), 'A note on the pure theory of consumer's behaviour', *Economica*, **5** (17), 61–71.
Scarf, H. (1960), 'Some examples of global instability of the economic equilibrium', *International Economic Review*, **1** (3), 157–72.
Schumpeter, J.A. (1939), *Business Cycles. A Theoretical, Historical and Statistical Analysis of the Capitalist Process*, New York, Toronto and London: McGraw-Hill.
Schumpeter, J.A. (1954), *History of Economic Analysis*, New York: Oxford University Press.
Screpanti, E. and S. Zamagni (1993), *An Outline of the History of Economic Thought*, Oxford: Oxford University Press.
Smale, S. (1976), 'Exchange processes with price adjustment', *Journal of Mathematical Economics*, **3** (3), 211–26.
Smith, A. (1776), *An Inquiry into the Nature and Causes of the Wealth of Nations*, London: W. Strahan and T. Cadell.
Solow, R.M. (2006), 'Reflections on the survey', in D. Colander (ed.), *The Making of an Economist Redux*, Princeton, NJ: Princeton University Press, ch. 12.
Sonnenschein, H. (1972), 'Market excess demand functions', *Econometrica*, **40** (3), 549–63.
Starr, R. (1969), 'Quasi-equilibria in markets with non-convex preferences', *Econometrica*, **17** (1), 25–38.
Stiglitz, J.E. and M. Gallegati (2011), 'Heterogeneous interacting agent models for understanding monetary economies', *Eastern Economic Journal*, **37**, 6–12, doi:10.1057/eej.2010.33.
Stoker, T.M. (1993), 'Empirical approaches to the problem of aggregation over individuals', *Journal of Economic Literature*, **31** (December), 1827–74.
Trichet, J.-C. (2010), 'Reflections on the nature of monetary policy non-standard measures and finance theory', speech by President of the ECB, opening address at the ECB Central Banking Conference, Frankfurt, 18 November.
Turner, A. (2010), 'The crisis, conventional economic wisdom and public policy', *Industrial and Corporate Change*, **19** (5), 1317–29.
Uzawa, H. (1960), 'Preference and rational choice in the theory of consumption', in K.J. Arrox, S. Karlin and P. Suppes (eds), *Mathematical Models in the Social Sciences, 1959: Proceedings of the First Stanford Symposium*, Stanford Mathematical Studies in the Social Sciences 4, Stanford, CA: Stanford University Press, pp. 129–49.
Van den Berg, R. (2007), 'Economic equilibrium in the French Enlightenment: the case of A.N. Isnard', in V. Mosini (ed.), *Equilibrium in Economics: Scope and Limits*, Abingdon: Routledge.
Wald, A. (1936), 'Uber einige Gleichungssysteme der mathematischen Okonomie', *Zeitschrift fur Nationalokonomie*, **7** (December), 637–70.
Walker, D. (2006), *Walrasian Economics*, Cambridge: Cambridge University Press.
Walker, D.A. (1996), *Walras's Market Models*, Cambridge: Cambridge University Press.
Walker, D.A. (1999), 'Some comments on Léon Walras's health and productivity', *Journal of the History of Economic Thought*, **21**, 437–48.
Walras, L. (1877), *Elements d'economie politique pure ou Theorie de la Richesse Sociale*, Lausanne: L. Corbaz.

Growth

Ever since the inception of systematic economic analysis at the time of the classical economists from William Petty to David Ricardo the problem of economic growth – its sources, forms and effects – has been high on the agenda of economists. In the real world the problem and the fact of economic growth are, of course, of much longer standing. Even in the more or less stationary economies of antiquity the possibility, if not the fact, of economic expansion lingers at the back of certain considerations. Brick plates from Mesopotamia provide information about social productivity by means of a simple input–output calculation in terms of barley. The main question concerned the surplus product of barley that the ancient society was able to generate, that is, the excess of total output in a year with a normal harvest over the amount of input of barley as seed or as means of subsistence of labourers plus any other inputs needed in the society measured in terms of barley. From the surplus rate, that is, the ratio of surplus product to necessary input, it is obviously only a small step intellectually, but a huge step historically, to the concept of the rate of growth.

Adam Smith on Growth

Adam Smith viewed the growth process as strictly endogenous (see also Lowe 1954 [1987]: 108; Eltis 1984: 69; Rostow 1990: 34), placing special emphasis on the impact of capital accumulation on labour productivity. He began his inquiry into the *Wealth of Nations* (Smith 1776 [1976], hereafter *WN*) by stating that income per capita "must in every nation be regulated by two different circumstances; first, by the skill, dexterity, and judgment with which its labour is generally applied; and, secondly, by the proportion between the number of those who are employed in useful labour, and that of those who are not so employed" (*WN*, I.3). According to Smith there is no upper limit to labour productivity. This is why Smith maintained that an investigation of the growth of income per capita is first and foremost an inquiry into "The causes of this improvement, in the productive powers of labour, and the order, according to which its produce is naturally distributed among the different ranks and conditions of men in the society" (*WN* I.5).

Smith's attention focused accordingly on the factors determining the growth of labour productivity, that is, the factors affecting "the state of the skill, dexterity, and judgment with which labour is applied in any nation" (*WN* I.6). At this point the accumulation of capital enters into the picture because of Smith's conviction that the key to the growth of labour productivity is the division of labour which in turn depends on the extent of the market and thus upon capital accumulation. "The greatest improvement in the productive powers of labour", we are told, "seem to have been the effects of the division of labour" (*WN* I.i.1), both within given firms and industries and, even more significantly, between them. In the first three chapters of book I of *The Wealth of Nations* Smith established the idea that there are increasing returns, which are largely external to firms, that is, broadly compatible with the classical hypothesis of a uniform rate of profits. (Here we set aside the reasons put forward by Smith and Ricardo, why profit rates may permanently differ between sectors; see therefore Kurz and Salvadori 1995: ch. 11). In the first chapter he made clear how powerful a device the division of labour is in increasing labour productivity, and analysed in some detail its major features: (1) the improvement of the dexterity of workers; (2) the saving of time which is otherwise lost in passing from one sort of work to another; and, most importantly, (3) the invention of specific machinery (cf. *WN* I.i.6–8). In the second chapter he argued that there is a certain propensity in human nature "to truck, barter and exchange one thing for another", which appears to be rooted in "the faculties of reason and speech", that gives occasion to the division of labour (*WN* I.ii.1–2). In the third chapter the argument is completed by stressing that the division of labour is limited by the extent of the market (cf. *WN* I.iii.1): a larger market generates a larger division of labour among people and, therefore, among firms, and a larger division of labour generates a larger productivity of labour in all firms.

Despite the presence of increasing returns, Smith retained the concept of a general rate of profits. His argument appears to be implicitly based on the hypothesis that each single firm operates at constant returns, while total production is subject to increasing returns. Even though some examples provided by Smith relate more to the division of labour within firms than to the division of labour among firms, Smith appears to be correct in sustaining that some of the activities which were originally a part of the division of labour within the firm may eventually become a different "trade" or "business", so that the division of labour within the firm is but a step towards the division of labour among firms. In the example of pin making at the beginning of chapter i, Smith pointed out that "in the way in which this business is now carried on, not only the whole work is a peculiar trade, but it is divided into a number of branches, of which the greater part are likewise peculiar trades" (*WN* I.i.3).

Smith's analysis foreshadows the concepts of induced and embodied technical progress, learning by doing, and learning by using. The invention of new machines and the improvement of known ones is said to be originally due to the workers in the production process and "those who had occasion to use the machines" (*WN* I.i.9). At a more advanced stage of society making machines "became the business of a peculiar trade", engaging "philosophers or men of speculation, whose trade it is, not to do any thing, but to observe every thing; and who, upon that account, are often capable of combining together the powers of the most distant and dissimilar objects". Research and development of new industrial designs becomes "the principal or sole trade and occupation of a particular class of citizens" (ibid.). New technical knowledge is systematically created and economically used, with the sciences becoming more and more involved in that process. More than two centuries before the invention of the term "knowledge society" Smith insists that "the quantity of science" available to a society decides its members' productivity and wealth (*WN* I.i.9). The accumulation of capital propels this process forward, opens up new markets and enlarges existing ones, increases effectual demand and is thus the main force behind economic and social development (*WN* V.i.e.26).

Did Smith expect the endogenous growth factors to lose momentum as capital accumulates? He considered three potential limits to growth: an insufficient supply of workers, the scantiness of nature, and an erosion of the motives of accumulation. Smith saw that the scarcity and potential degradation of renewable and the depletion of exhaustible resources may constrain human productive activity and the growth of the economy (*WN* I.xi.i.3; see also I.xi.d). However, at the time when he wrote, the limits to growth deriving from nature were apparently still considered far away.

Smith also saw no danger that the process of accumulation might come to an end because of an insufficient supply of labour and any diminishing returns to capital.

He rather advocated a view, which was to become prominent among the classical economists: the supply of labour is generated within the socio-economic system, that is, endogenously. He drew an analogy between the multiplication of animals and that of the inferior ranks of people (cf. *WN* I.viii.39–40). Smith envisaged the growth of the labour force as endogenous, the determinant being the rate of capital accumulation. Real wages are higher, the more rapidly capital accumulates. As to the impact of high and rising real wages on the rate of profits, it appears that we cannot say anything definite, given Smith's opinion that "the same cause . . . which raises the wages of labour, the increase of stock, tends to increase its productive powers, and to make a smaller quantity of labour produce a greater quantity of work" (*WN* I.viii.57).

Adam Smith explained economic growth thoroughly as an endogenous phenomenon. The growth rate depends on the decisions and actions of agents, especially their saving and investment behaviour, and the creativity and innovativeness they come up with in given social and historical conditions and institutional settings. Special emphasis is placed on the endogenous creation of new knowledge that can be used economically. New technical knowledge is treated as a good, which is or in the long run tends to become a public good. There are no clear and obvious limits to growth. The additional work force needed in the process of accumulation is generated in that process itself: labour power is a commodity the quantity of which is regulated by the effectual demand for it. Diminishing returns due to scarce natural resources are set aside or seen to be of little significance vis-à-vis increases in productivity due to the division of labour.

While Smith saw "improvements" to take place in all major sectors of the economy – agriculture, manufacturing, commerce and trade (see *WN* I.x.b.43) – he was convinced that manufacturing was most susceptible to an ever deeper division of labour and thus a rapid growth of labour productivity. Alas, he vastly underrated the importance of the manufacturing sector as an engine of growth by assuming that it produces only amenities and luxuries. The idea that necessities, raw materials, tools and machines are produced by means of necessities, raw materials, tools and machines is not yet to be found in Smith. Mentally he was still rooted in the age of corn and had only glimpsed the dawn of the upcoming age of coal and iron. Others coming after him had seen more of the new age triggered by the Industrial Revolution and began to understand better the crucial role of machinery and industry. These included authors such as David Ricardo, Charles Babbage and Karl Marx.

David Ricardo on Diminishing Returns

Ricardo in much of his reasoning set aside what may be called statically and dynamically increasing returns. The beneficial effects of capital accumulation on productivity mediated through the extension of the division of labour, which assumed centre stage in Smith's analysis, play hardly any role in Ricardo's. In modern parlance, the problems of externalities are given only sparse attention. This does not mean that Ricardo was of the opinion that they are of negligible importance, certainly not. Recall that Ricardo explicitly subscribed to much of Smith's analysis and set himself the moderate task of correcting views of the Scotsman he deemed wrong. These concerned especially Smith's view of the long-term trend of profitability as capital accumulates and the role of scarce natural resources in it. Ricardo was keen to show that, given the real wage rate, the rate of profits cannot fall as a consequence of the "competition of capitals", as Smith had argued, but only because of diminishing returns due the scarcity of land(s). Much of Ricardo's argument therefore was developed in terms of the explicit and often implicit assumption that the set of (constant returns to scale) methods of production from which cost-minimizing producers can choose is given and constant. In such a framework the question then is how scarce natural resources affect profitability as capital accumulates. The resulting vision is reflected in what Ricardo called the "natural course" of things.

As capital accumulates and population grows, and assuming the real wage rate of workers given and constant, the rate of profits is bound to fall; due to extensive and intensive diminishing returns on land, "with every increased portion of capital employed on it, there will be a decreased rate of production" (Ricardo 1817 [1951], hereafter *Works*, I: 98). Since profits are a residual income, based on the surplus product left after the used up means of production and the wage goods in the support of workers have been deducted from the social product (net of rents), the "decreased rate of production" involves a decrease in profitability. On the assumption that there are only negligible savings out of wages and rents, a falling rate of profits involves a falling rate of capital accumulation. Hence, Ricardo's "natural course" of things will necessarily end up in a stationary state.

This path must not be identified, however, with the actual path the economy takes because technical progress, which is set aside in the argument under consideration, will repeatedly offset the impact of the "niggardliness of nature" on the rate of profits (see Ricardo *Works* I: 120). Ricardo is frequently presented as a technological pessimist, who believed in the overwhelming importance of diminishing returns in agriculture in combination with the Malthusian law of population and who saw the stationary state around the corner; see, for example, Blaug (2009) and Solow (2010). This interpretation does not do justice to him. As early as in the *Essay on Profits* of 1815 he expressed the view that there are no signs pointing in the direction of a falling rate of profits in the foreseeable future: "we are yet at a great distance from the end of our resources, and . . . we may contemplate an increase of prosperity and wealth, far exceeding that of any country which has preceded us" (see Ricardo *Works* IV: 34). This view is confirmed in a letter to Hutches Trower of 5 February 1816, in which he concluded from the fall in grain prices since 1812 that "we are happily yet in the progressive state, and may look forward with confidence to a long course of prosperity" (Ricardo *Works* VII: 17).

So let us see more clearly the way in which Ricardo approached the difficult problem of capital accumulation and growth. The assumptions of a given real wage rate and the absence of technical progress represent a first logical step in an approach to the problem of capital accumulation and income distribution, which proceeds in terms of distinct analytical stages (see Garegnani 1990). The attention focuses first on abstract and general principles, which are then gradually attuned to the concrete case or specific historical circumstances under consideration. Economic theory is combined with historical analysis. Here we focus only on the first stage and set aside its historical part. The reader will therefore not be misled thinking that in our view classical political economy is co-extensive with or can be reduced to this first stage. It reaches far beyond it.

Like Smith, Ricardo thought that savings and investment, that is, accumulation, would largely come from profits, whereas wages and rents played a negligible role. Hence, as regards the dynamism of the economy attention should focus on profitability.

Assuming that the marginal propensity to accumulate out of profits, s, is given and constant, a "classical" accumulation function can be formulated:

$$g = \begin{cases} s(r - r_{min}) & \text{if } r \geq r_{min} \\ 0 & \text{if } r \leq r_{min} \end{cases}$$

where $r_{min} \geq 0$ is the minimum level of profitability which, if reached, will arrest accumulation (see *Works* I: 120).

Ricardo saw the rate of accumulation as endogenous. The demand for labour is seen to depend on the pace at which capital accumulates. As regards the long-term supply of labour Ricardo in some of his analysis adopted some form of the "Malthusian law of population". However since, contrary to Malthus, Ricardo was no technological pessimist, he did not share the latter's pessimism as regards the development of real wages. Real wages, he insisted, may rise, that is, the "market price of labour" may rise above the "natural" wage rate. This is the case in a situation in which capital accumulates rapidly, leading to an excess demand for labour. As Ricardo put it, "notwithstanding the tendency of wages to conform to their natural rate, their market rate may, in an improving society, for an indefinite period, be constantly above it" (*Works* I: 94–5). If such a constellation prevails for some time a ratchet effect may make itself felt: it is possible, Ricardo observed, that "custom renders absolute necessaries" what in the past had been comforts or luxuries. Hence, the natural wage is driven upward by persistently high levels of the actual wage rate. Accordingly, the concept of "natural wage" in Ricardo is a flexible one and must not be mistaken for a physiological minimum of subsistence.

Assuming for simplicity a given and constant real wage rate, Ricardo's view of the long-run relationship between profitability and accumulation and thus growth (in the absence of technical progress) can be illustrated in terms of Figure 5, which is a diagram used by Kaldor (1955–56). The curve *CEGH* is the marginal productivity of labour-cum-capital; it is decreasing since land is scarce: when labour-cum-capital increases, either less fertile qualities of land must be cultivated or the same qualities of land must be cultivated with processes which require less land per unit of product, but are more costly in terms

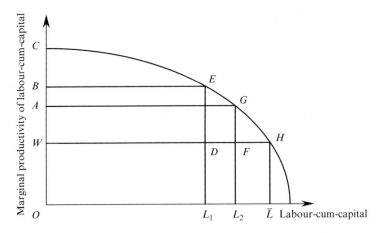

Figure 5   Land as an indispensable resource

of labour-cum-capital. Let the real wage rate equal OW. Then, if the amount of labour-cum-capital applied is L_1, the area $OCEL_1$ gives the product, $OWDL_1$ gives total capital employed, and BCE total rent. Profit is determined as a residual and corresponds to the rectangular $WBED$. As a consequence, the rate of profits can be determined as the ratio of the areas of two rectangles which have the same basis and, therefore, it equals the ratio WB/OW. Let us now consider the case in which the amount of labour-cum-capital is larger, that is, L_2. Then $OCGL_2$ gives the product, $OWFL_2$ the capital, ACG the rent, and $WAGF$ profits. The rate of profits has fallen to WA/OW. Obviously, if a positive profit rate implies a positive growth rate (that is, $r_{min} = 0$), the economy will expand until labour-cum-capital has reached the level $\bar{L}$. At that point the profit rate is equal to zero and so is the growth rate. The system has arrived at a stationary state. Growth has come to an end because profitability has.

For both Smith and Ricardo the required size of the work force is essentially generated by the accumulation process itself. That is, labour power is treated as a kind of producible commodity. It differs from other commodities in that it is not produced in a capitalistic way in a special industry on a par with other industries, but is the result of the interplay between the generative behaviour of people and socioeconomic conditions. In the most simple and abstract conceptualization possible, labour power is seen to be in elastic supply at a given and constant real wage basket. Increasing the number of baskets available in the support of workers involves a proportional increase of the work force. In this view, the rate of growth of labour supply adjusts to any given rate of growth of labour demand without necessitating a variation in the real wage rate. In a more sophisticated conceptualization, higher rates of growth of labour supply presuppose higher levels of the real wage rate. However, the basic logic remains the same: in normal conditions the pace at which capital accumulates regulates the pace at which labour, a non-accumulable factor of production, grows. (For a more detailed presentation, see Kurz and Salvadori 2006.)

Thus labour cannot put a limit to growth because it is generated within the growth process. The only limit to growth can come from other non-accumulable factors of production. That is, there is only endogenous growth in Ricardo. This growth is bound to lose momentum as the system hits its natural barriers, especially as soon as extensive and intensive diminishing returns make themselves felt and are not counteracted by a sufficient technical progress.

Ricardo contemplated the implications for income distribution and the rate of expansion of the economic system in the hypothetical case in which land of the best quality is available in abundance. In one place he wrote:

> Profits do not necessarily fall with the increase of the quantity of capital because the demand for capital is infinite and is governed by the same law as population itself. They are both checked by the rise in the price of food, and the consequent increase in the price of labour. If there were no such rise, what could prevent population and capital from increasing without limit? (Ricardo *Works* VI: 301)

If land of the best quality was available in abundance it would be a free good and no rent would be paid for its use. In this case the curve of the graph showing the marginal productivity of labour-cum-capital would be a horizontal line and the rate of profits would be constant whatever the amount of labour-cum-capital employed. As a consequence, other things equal, the growth rate would also be constant: the system could grow for ever at a rate that equals the given rate of profits times the propensity to accumulate. There are other possible interpretations of a horizontal marginal productivity of labour-cum-capital: either workers consume only non-agricultural commodities, which are produced without using land either directly or indirectly (D'Alessandro and Salvadori 2008) or the economy is small and open and the economy is so large that any increase in the pace of the accumulation process is obtained through an increase in the production of the industrial commodities (Salvadori and Signorino 2015).

To conclude, two observations are apposite. First, vis-à-vis a widespread misconception it deserves to be emphasized once again that Ricardo was no technological pessimist. In the above we cited some passages from his work in support of this. Here is another. In his entry on the "Funding system" for volume IV of the *Supplements to the Encyclopædia Britannica*, published in September 1820, he stressed that "the richest country in Europe is yet far distant from that degree of improvement", that is, the stationary state, and that "it is difficult to say where the limit is at which you would cease to accumulate wealth and to derive profit from its employment" (Ricardo *Works* IV: 179). Secondly, in the new chapter 21 "On machinery" added to the third edition of the *Principles* (1823) Ricardo responded to the movement of the Luddites and a pamphlet by John Barton, in which the introduction of machinery was taken to be responsible for unemployment and workers' distress. Ricardo admitted that a particular form of improved machinery, the one that decreases the gross produce, is harmful to workers and that there is no presumption of an automatic compensation of the displacement of workers. Ricardo's chapter inspired Marx to his concept of an "industrial reserve army of the unemployed" and is the starting point of an extended debate on "technological unemployment". The chapter contains also a clear statement of the fact that the use of machinery is not limited to the production of luxury goods, as in Smith, but plays an increasingly important role also in the production of "necessaries" and of machinery itself. Interestingly, Ricardo even contemplated the extreme case of a fully automated production and pointed out: "If machinery could do all the work that labour now does, there would be no demand for labour. Nobody would be entitled to consume any thing who was not a capitalist, and who could not buy or hire a machine" (Ricardo *Works* VIII: 399–400).

Linear Classical Models of Production

Central elements of classical analysis are the concept of production as a circular flow and the related concept of surplus product left after the wage goods and what is necessary for the replacement of the used-up means of production have been deducted from the annual output. This surplus can be consumed or accumulated. With constant returns to scale and setting aside the problem of scarce natural resources, the notion of an economy expanding at a constant rate of growth was close at hand. In this section we shall mention some contributions to what may be called linear growth theory with a classical flavour.

Robert Torrens in his *Essay on the External Corn Trade* (1815) clarified that the concept of surplus provides the key to an explanation of the rate of profits. Growth in the model by Torrens is both linear and endogenous; the rate of growth depends on the general rate of profits and the propensity to accumulate. The same can be said of Marx's theory of expanded reproduction in chapter 21 of volume II of *Capital* (Marx 1885 [1956]). In it Marx studied the conditions under which the system is capable of reproducing itself on an upward spiralling level: the economy expands at an endogenously determined rate of growth. This rate depends on the proportion of the surplus value ploughed back into the productive system to increase the scale of operation. Marx stressed that the accumulation of capital is "an element *immanent* in the capitalist process of production" (ibid.: 497, emphasis added). For, "the aim and compelling motive of capitalist production" is "the snatching of surplus-value and its capitalisation, i.e., accumulation" (ibid.: 507). In Marx's analysis, this theory is only a first logical step toward a proper theory of accumulation. Here we cannot deal with the latter and Marx's "law" of a falling tendency of the rate of profits in volume III of *Capital*. There Marx argues that a tendency of the real wage rate toward a socially and historically defined subsistence level is not due to a population mechanism, but due to the presence of an "industrial reserve army of the unemployed", which is continually filled and re-filled by labour saving technical progress. This form of technical progress Marx takes to involve an increase in the "organic composition of capital", that is, the ratio of "dead labour" incorporated in the capital goods employed, or "constant capital" C, and of "living labour" L hired by capitalists with the "variable capital" V. The inverse of the organic composition for the economy as a whole is seen to be equal to the maximum rate of profits, which obtains in the case in which wages (variable capital) vanish. The form of technical progress, which according to Marx dominates capitalism, thus translates into a falling maximum rate of profits.

The Russian mathematician Georg von Charasoff elaborated on Marx's analysis and was possibly the first to provide a clear statement of the fundamental duality relationship between the system of prices and the rate of profits on the one hand, and the system of quantities and the rate of growth on the other (see Charasoff 1910). He developed his main argument within the framework of an interdependent model of (single) production exhibiting all the properties of the later input–output model, and which is fully specified in terms of use values (rather than labour values as in the case of Marx) and labour needed per unit of output (see Kurz and Salvadori 1995: ch. 13).

John von Neumann (1945) in a paper first published in German in 1937 and then translated into English in 1945 elaborated the by far most sophisticated linear model of endogenous growth. In it von Neumann assumed that there are n goods produced by m constant returns-to-scale production processes. There is a problem of the choice of technique, which consists of establishing which processes will actually be used and which not, being "unprofitable". Von Neumann (1937 [1945]: 1–2) took the real wage rate, consisting of the "necessities of life", to be given and paid at the beginning of the uniform period of production, that is, he considered wages as a part of the capital advanced and thus as a part of the physical real costs of production. In addition, he assumed "that all income in excess of necessities of life will be reinvested". In von Neumann's model the rate of growth is determined endogenously. He set aside the problem of scarcity of all non-accumulable factors of production: while all primary factors other than labour (that is, all natural resources) were taken to be available at whichever amount was needed at zero price, labour was assumed to be available at the required amount at a given real wage rate.

Models of Exogenous Growth

The marginalist or "neoclassical" school of economic thought seeks to explain income distribution in a symmetrical way via the relative scarcities of the factors of production, labour, "capital", and land. Interestingly, the idea of exogenous growth which classical theory did not entertain is the starting point of important early works in the marginalist tradition.

The idea of an economic system growing exclusively because some exogenous factors make it grow has variously been put forward in the history of economic thought as a standard of comparison. For example, in chapter 5 of book V of his *Principles*, first published in 1890, Alfred Marshall (1890 [1977]: 305) introduced the "famous fiction of the 'Stationary state' . . . to contrast the results which would be found there with those in the modern world". By relaxing one after another of the rigid assumptions defining the stationary state, Marshall sought to get gradually closer to the "actual conditions of life". The first relaxation concerned the premise of a constant (working) population:

> The Stationary state has just been taken to be one in which population is stationary. But nearly all its distinctive features may be exhibited in a place where population and wealth are both growing, provided they are growing at about the same rate, and there is no scarcity of land: and provided also the methods of production and the conditions of trade change but little; and above all, where the character of man himself is a constant quantity. For in such a state by far the most important conditions of production and consumption, of exchange and distribution will remain of the same quality, and in the same general relations to one another, though they are all increasing in volume. (Marshall (1890 [1977]: 306)

The resulting economic system grows at a constant rate which equals the exogenous rate of growth of population. Income distribution and relative prices are the same as in the stationary economy. In modern parlance: the system expands along a steady-state growth path.

We encounter essentially the same idea in Gustav Cassel's (1918 [1932]) *Theory of Social Economy*. The model of exogenous growth delineated by Cassel can be considered the proximate starting point of the development of neoclassical growth theory. In chapter 4 of book I of the treatise, Cassel presented two models, one of a stationary economy, the other of an economy growing along a steady-state path.

In his first model Cassel assumed that there are z (primary) factors of production. The quantities of these resources and thus the amounts of services provided by them are taken to be in given supply. General equilibrium is characterized by the equality of supply and demand for each factor service and for each good produced and the equality of the price of a good and its cost of production. The resulting sets of equations constitute what is known as the "Walras–Cassel model" (Dorfman et al. 1958: 346). It satisfies the then going criterion of completeness: there are as many equations as there are unknowns to be ascertained.

Cassel (1932: 152–3) then turned to the model of a uniformly progressing economy. Although described only verbally, he introduced the model in the following way:

> We must now take into consideration the society which is progressing at a uniform rate. In it, the quantities of the factors of production which are available in each period . . . are subject to

a uniform increase. We shall represent by [g] the fixed rate of this increase, and of the uniform progress of the society generally.

In Cassel's view this generalization to the case of an economy growing at an exogenously given and constant rate does not cause substantial problems. The previously developed set of equations can easily be adapted appropriately, "so that the whole pricing problem is solved". Cassel thus arrived at basically the same result as Marshall.

The neoclassical growth models of the 1950s and early 1960s differ from the growth version of the Walras–Cassel model in the first five of the following six important respects:

1. They are macro-models with a single produced good only which could be used both as a consumption good and as a capital good.
2. The number of primary factors of production is reduced to one, homogeneous labour (as in Solow 1956, 1970; Swan 1956), or two, homogeneous labour and homogeneous land (as in Swan 1956; Meade 1961).
3. The all-purpose good is produced by means of labour, capital, that is, the good itself, and possibly land.
4. There is a choice of technique, where technical alternatives are given by a macro-economic production function, which is homogenous of degree one with positive and decreasing marginal productivities with respect to each factor of production.
5. Savings are proportional to net income, that is, a "Keynesian" saving function is assumed.
6. Say's law holds, that is planned savings are taken to be equal to planned investment at all times. There is no separate investment function.

Focusing attention on the models with a single primary factor (labour), in steady-state equilibrium:

$$sf(k) = gk,$$

where s is the (marginal and average) propensity to save, $f(k)$ is the per unit of labour or per capita production function, k is the capital–labour ratio (where labour is measured in terms of efficiency units), and g is the steady-state growth rate of capital (and labour, and income, and so on). In steady-state equilibrium output expands exactly as the exogenous factors make it grow. Note that assuming $s > 0$ presupposes that the exogenous factors are growing at some positive rate. In these models the steady-state rate of growth is exogenous. Outside steady-state equilibrium the rate of growth can be shown to depend also on the behavioural parameter of the system, that is, the propensity to save (and invest), but that parameter plays no role in determining the long-term rate of growth.

While these models are aptly described as models of exogenous growth, they can also be described as models of endogenous profitability. Since in the one-good framework adopted by the authors under consideration the rate of profits r equals the marginal productivity of capital,

$$r = f'(k),$$

the two equations are able to determine a relationship between the rate of profits and the steady-state rate of growth.

Keynes and Keynesians

It is remarkable that whereas growth was at the centre of the concerns of the classical political economists, and then of Karl Marx, it moved to the periphery in the aftermath of the so-called "marginal revolution". Léon Walras (1874 [1954]) still tackled the problem in terms of his theory of "capitalization", that is, of credit and capital accumulation (see Morishima 1977 and Knut Wicksell 1893 [1954]) in terms of his theory of capital formation. Thereafter it moved largely to the background of economic theory. The field was revitalized when attempts were made to extend Keynes's 1936 short-run analysis to the long run by taking into account not only the income effect of investment in terms of the multiplier, but also the capacity effect of investment. Evsey Domar (1946) showed that productive capacity and effective demand grow in step with one another, if and only if investment grows at a rate that is equal to the ratio of society's propensity to save, s, and the capital-to-output ratio (which is taken to be constant), v, that is: $g = s/v$. Roy F. Harrod (1939, 1948) sought to carry Keynes's principle of effective demand over to the long run by studying the interplay of a proportional savings function and an investment function relying on the "acceleration principle", which takes investment to react on changes in effective demand in the past and thus on changes in the degree of utilization of capital equipment. Within such a framework Harrod was able to show that the accumulation path is unstable: deviations of the actual growth rate of investment from the "warranted rate" (which is essentially the one Domar had shown to guarantee the continuous full utilization of productive capacity) leads either into a boom or a recession. This has become known as Harrod's "knife-edge problem" in the literature. The instability results because if the actual rate of growth of investment exceeds (falls short of) the warranted rate, the income effect of investment exceeds (falls short of) the capacity effect, which is reflected in a growing (falling) rate of capital utilization. This can in turn be expected to lead to an acceleration (deceleration) of investment growth, which increases the upwards (downwards) deviation of the actual from the warranted rate and exacerbates the disequilibrium: the economy is bound to run into a boom (a depression), because market signals are read by single firms which leads to a collective behaviour that destabilizes the economy. Harrod saw the "instability principle" as an integral part of a theory of the business cycle, which had to explain, first and foremost, if and why there are upper and lower turning points giving rise to cyclical behaviour of output and employment.

The papers by Solow (1956) and Swan (1956) mentioned in the previous section sought to answer not only Harrod's (short-run) knife-edge problem, but also to do away with the possibility Harrod had contemplated of economic growth in the presence of cyclically fluctuating, but persistent unemployment. This was effectuated in terms of (1) the introduction of ample possibilities of substitution among factors of production etched in a macroeconomic production function and (2) the invocation of Say's law by abandoning an independent investment function and assuming that each and every act of saving will always and instantaneously lead to an act of investment of the same magnitude. By this token both kinds of problems Harrod had analysed were made to disappear and the attention could focus on full employment–full capacity growth. Solow justified this approach in terms of the assumption that Keynesian stabilization policy would accomplish the job, in case the market economy would not. It deserves to be stressed that while Solow was perfectly aware that his model reflected an idealized world in which the problem of effective demand was deliberately shunted aside, many of his followers tended to mistake the model for a description of the real world.

However, there was not only a neoclassical response to the challenges Keynes and then Harrod had put to the profession. Another response came from Nicholas Kaldor (1955–56) and Joan Robinson (1956), who worked in the Keynesian tradition. Kaldor's contribution became known as the Neo-Keynesian model of growth and distribution.

Kaldor distinguished between wage-earners and profit-earners, noticing that the propensity to save of the first group can be assumed to be smaller than that of the second group simply as a consequence of the fact that the bulk of profits accrues in the form of company profits and a high proportion of these profits are retained by firms in order to finance investment (see Kaldor 1955–56: 95 fn.). In a later contribution Kaldor (1966: 310–11) confirmed his intention to model the role of a large share of undistributed profits to favour self-finance. Kaldor assumed the following saving function:

$$S = s_\omega W + s_\pi P,$$

where S is total savings of a given economy, and W and P are total wages and total profits. Since, in equilibrium, planned saving equals planned investment and since wages plus profits equal the national income, we have:

$$I = (s_\pi - s_\omega)P + s_\omega Y,$$

where I is net investment and Y is net national income. Finally, because of "the 'Keynesian' hypothesis that investment, or rather, the ratio of investment to output, can be treated as an independent variable" (Kaldor 1955–56: 95),

$$\frac{P}{Y} = \frac{1}{s_\pi - s_\omega}\frac{I}{Y} - \frac{s_\omega}{s_\pi - s_\omega} \tag{1}$$

The rate of profits, r, is then obtained by multiplying equation (1) by the output–capital ratio, Y/K, which Kaldor (1955–56) assumed to be constant with respect to changes in distribution:

$$r = \frac{P}{K} = \frac{1}{s_\pi - s_\omega}\frac{I}{K} - \frac{s_\omega}{s_\pi - s_\omega}\frac{Y}{K}, \tag{2}$$

where I/K is the rate of capital accumulation. Since he considered a fairly constant capital-to-output ratio, K/Y, as a "stylized fact" of economic history, the rate of growth of output equals the rate of capital accumulation.

In contradistinction to Kaldor, Luigi L. Pasinetti (1962) dealt with *classes* (capitalists and workers) rather than with income groups, suggesting the use of the following

saving functions which assume that the propensity to save out of the profits earned by
the capitalist class differs from the propensity to save out of the profits earned by the
working class:

$$S_w = s_w(W + P_w),$$

$$S_c = s_c P_c$$

Further, Pasinetti explicitly introduced the dynamic equilibrium conditions, according
to which capitalists' and workers' capitals, like all variables changing through time,
must, in the steady state, grow at the same rate as the economy as a whole. In addition,
he pointed out that, since those who save out of wages must receive a part of the profit
as interest for what they lend to capitalists, to determine the rate of profits it is necessary to specify the relationship between the money rate of interest and the rate of profits
in steady growth. He maintained that "in a long-run equilibrium model, the obvious
hypothesis to make is that of a rate of interest equal to the rate of profit" (Pasinetti
1962: 271–2). Then workers' and capitalists' capitals grow at the same rate *g*. That is, the
following constraints hold:

$$s_w(W + P_w) = gK_w \tag{3}$$

$$s_c P_c = gK_c, \tag{4}$$

where K_w is workers' capital loaned to capitalists, and K_c is capitalists' own capital
$(K_w + K_c = K)$.

If it is assumed that interest and profit rate coincide, then $P_c = rK_c$ and $P_w = rK_w$. If,
moreover, $K_c > 0$, then the rate of profits is immediately obtained from equation (4):

$$r = \frac{g}{s_c} \tag{5}$$

This is the "Pasinetti theorem", which gave rise to a huge debate on the limits of Pasinetti's
result and involved, among others, Franco Modigliani and Paul A. Samuelson. For a
detailed account, see Kurz and Salvadori (2010). For a more complete discussion of
Keynesian contributions to the study of economic growth, see Commendatore et al.
(2003) and Setterfield (2010).

Endogenous Growth Theory

The debate in the 1960s and 1970s between neoclassical and Keynesian economists and
the criticism of the neoclassical concept of capital as a quantity that could be ascertained independently of, and prior to, the determination of relative prices and the rate
of profits (see in particular Kurz and Salvadori 1995: ch. 14) sent growth economics into
a slumber. It was only in the second half of the 1980s that it was awakened again. The
proponents of the revival of growth economics dubbed their theories "new" or "endogenous", henceforth NGTs, drawing attention to the fact that long-run growth was not

taken to be given from the outside, as in Solow, but was explained from within the economic system, that is, endogenously.

One of the key properties of the NGTs is intensive growth, that is, an increase in income per capita, another is the elimination or at least the limitation of any tendency of the returns to capital and the rate of profits to diminish. The first generation of models of NGT defined the confines within which subsequent contributions to NGT were carried out. The attention focuses on the mechanism that prevents the returns to capital from falling (below a certain level). For a more detailed treatment of these models, see Acemoglu (2009), Aghion and Howitt (1998), Barro and Sala-i-Martin (2003), Jones (1998) and Kurz and Salvadori (1998, 1999).

The first class of NGTs (in terms of simplicity, not in chronological terms) set aside all non-accumulable factors of production, such as labour and land, and assumed that all inputs in production are themselves producible and accumulable, that is, "capital" of some kind. The simplest version of this class is the so-called "AK model", which assumes that there is a linear relationship between total output, Y, and a single factor capital, K, both consisting of the *same* commodity:

$$Y = AK, \tag{6}$$

where $1/A$ is the amount of that commodity required to produce one unit of itself. K is said to be able to comprise both physical and human capital and it is assumed that the two can be aggregated without further ado. The rate of return on capital r is given by:

$$r + \delta = \frac{Y}{K} = A,$$

where δ is the exogenously given rate of depreciation. There is a large variety of models of this type in the literature. In the two-sector version in Rebelo (1991) it is assumed that the capital good sector produces the capital good by means of itself and nothing else. It is also assumed that there is only one method of production to produce the capital good. Therefore, the rate of profits is determined by technology alone. Then the saving-investment mechanism jointly with the assumption of a uniform rate of growth, that is, a steady-state equilibrium, determines a relationship between the growth rate, g, and the rate of profits, r. Rebelo (1991: 504, 506) obtains either:

$$g = \frac{A - \delta - \rho}{\sigma} = \frac{r - \rho}{\sigma} \tag{7}$$

or

$$g = (A - \delta)s = sr \tag{8}$$

Equation (7) is obtained when savings are determined on the assumption that there is an immortal representative agent maximizing the following intertemporal utility function:

$$U = \int_0^\infty e^{-\rho t} \frac{c(t)^{1-\sigma} - 1}{\sigma} \, dt,$$

subject to constraint (6), where ρ is the discount rate, or rate of time preference, and $1/\sigma$ is the elasticity of substitution between present and future consumption ($1 \neq \sigma > 0$), and where $Y = c(t) + \dot{K}$. (A dot above a variable refers to the differentiation of the variable with respect to time – in the present case to dK/dt.) Equation (8) is obtained when the average propensity to save s is given. Hence, in this model the rate of profits is determined by technology alone and the saving-investment mechanism determines the growth rate.

King and Rebelo (1990) essentially followed the same avenue. Instead of one kind of "capital" they assumed that there are two kinds, real capital and human capital, both of which are accumulable. There are two lines of production, one for the social product and the real capital, which consist of quantities of the same commodity, and one for human capital. The production functions relating to the two kinds of capital are assumed to be homogeneous of degree one and strictly concave. As in Rebelo's model the rate of profits is uniquely determined by the technology (and the maximization of profits which, because of the non-substitution theorem, implies that only one technique can be used in the long run); the growth rate of the system is then endogenously determined by the saving-investment equation. The larger is the propensity to accumulate human and physical capital, the larger is the growth rate.

The second class of models preserve the dualism of accumulable and non-accumulable factors but restrict the impact of an accumulation of the former on their returns by a modification of the macroeconomic production function. Jones and Manuelli (1990), for example, allow for both labour and capital and even assume a convex technology, as the Solow model does. However, a convex technology requires only that the marginal product of capital is a decreasing function of its stock, not that it vanishes as the amount of capital per worker tends towards infinity. Jones and Manuelli assume that:

$$h(k) \geq bk, \quad \text{each } k \geq 0,$$

where $h(k)$ is the per capita production function and b is a positive constant. The special case contemplated by them is:

$$h(k) = f(k) + bk,$$

where $f(k)$ is the conventional per capita production function. As capital accumulates and the capital–labour ratio rises, the marginal product of capital will fall, approaching asymptotically b, its lower boundary. With a given propensity to save, s, and assuming that capital never wears out, the steady-state growth rate g is endogenously determined: $g = sb$. Assuming, on the contrary, intertemporal utility maximization, the rate of growth is positive provided the technical parameter b is larger than the rate of time preference ρ. In the case in which it is larger, the steady-state rate of growth is given by equation (7) with $r = b$.

Finally, there is a large class of models contemplating various factors counteracting any diminishing tendency of returns to capital. Here we shall be concerned only with the following two sub-classes: human capital formation and knowledge accumulation. In both kinds of models positive external effects play an important part; they offset any fall in the marginal product of capital.

Models of the first sub-class attempt to formalize the role of human capital formation in the process of growth. Elaborating on some ideas of Uzawa (1965), Lucas (1988) assumed that agents have a choice between two ways of spending their (non-leisure) time: to contribute to current production or to accumulate human capital. With the accumulation of human capital there is said to be associated an externality: the more human capital society as a whole has accumulated, the more productive each single member will be. This is reflected in the following macroeconomic production function:

$$Y = AK^{\beta}(uhN)^{1-\beta}h^{*\gamma}, \tag{9}$$

where the labour input consists of the number of workers, N, times the fraction of time spent working, u, times h which gives the labour input in efficiency units. Finally, there is the term h^*. This is designed to represent the externality. The single agent takes h^* as a parameter in his or her optimizing by choice of c and u. However, for society as a whole the accumulation of human capital increases output both directly and indirectly, that is, through the externality represented by $h^{*\gamma}$, where $\gamma > 0$.

Lucas's conceptualization of the process by means of which human capital is built up is the following:

$$\dot{h} = \upsilon h(1 - u), \tag{10}$$

where υ is a positive constant. (Note that equation (10) can be interpreted as a "production function" of human capital.)

Interestingly, it can be shown that if the above mentioned externality is not present, that is, if γ in equation (9) equals zero, and therefore returns to scale are constant and, as a consequence, the non-substitution theorem holds, endogenous growth in Lucas's model is obtained in essentially the same way as in the models of Rebelo (1991) and King and Rebelo (1990): the rate of profits is determined by technology and profit maximization alone; and for the predetermined level of the rate of profits the saving-investment mechanism determines the rate of growth. Yet, as Lucas himself pointed out, the endogenous growth is positive independently of the fact that there is the above mentioned externality, that is, independently of the fact that γ is positive. Therefore, while complicating the picture increasing returns do not add substantially to it: growth is endogenous even if returns to scale are constant. If returns to scale are not constant then the non-substitution theorem does not apply, implying that neither the competitive technique nor the associated rate of profits are determined by technical alternatives and profit maximization alone. Nevertheless, these two factors still determine, in steady states, a relationship between the rate of profits and the rate of growth. This relationship together with the relationship between the same rates obtained from the saving-investment mechanism determines both variables.

Models of the second sub-class attempt to portray technological change as generated endogenously. The proximate starting point of this kind of model was Arrow's (1962) paper on "learning by doing". Romer (1986) focuses on the role of a single state variable called "knowledge" or "information" and assumes that the information contained in inventions and discoveries has the property of being available to anybody to make use of it at the same time. In other words, information is considered essentially a non-rival good. Yet, it need not be totally non-excludable, that is, it can be monopolized at least for some time. It is around the two different aspects of publicness – non-rivalry and non-excludability – that the argument revolves. Discoveries are made in research and development departments of firms. This requires that resources be withheld from producing current output. The basic idea of Romer's (1986: 1015) model is "that there is a trade-off between consumption today and knowledge that can be used to produce more consumption tomorrow". He formalizes this idea in terms of a "research technology" that produces "knowledge" from foregone consumption. Knowledge is assumed to be cardinally measurable and not to depreciate: it is like perennial capital.

Romer stipulates a research technology that is concave and homogeneous of degree one:

$$\dot{k}_i = G(I_i, k_i),$$ (11)

where I_i is an amount of foregone consumption in research by firm i and k_i is the firm's current stock of knowledge. (Note that the foregone consumption good is a capital good utilized in the production of "knowledge".) The production function of the consumption good relative to firm i is:

$$Y_i = F(k_i, K, \mathbf{x}_i),$$ (12)

where K is the accumulated stock of knowledge in the economy as a whole and $\mathbf{x}_i$ are all inputs different from knowledge. The function is taken to be homogeneous of degree one in k_i and $\mathbf{x}_i$ and homogeneous of a degree greater than one in k_i and K. Romer (1986: 1019) assumes that "factors other than knowledge are in fixed supply". This implies that "knowledge" is the only capital good utilized in the production of the consumption good. Spillovers from private research and development activities increase the public stock of knowledge K.

Assuming, contrary to Romer, that the above production function (12) is homogeneous of degree one in k_i and K involves a constant marginal product of capital, the diminishing returns to k_i are exactly offset by the external improvements in technology associated with capital accumulation. In this case it can be shown that, similar to the models of NGT previously dealt with, the rate of profits is determined by technology and profit maximization alone, provided, as is assumed by Romer, that the ratio K/k_i equals the (given) number of firms. The saving-investment relation then determines endogenously the growth rate. Once again endogenous growth does not depend on an assumption about increasing returns with regard to accumulable factors. Growth would be no more endogenous if increasing returns were to be assumed (but the analysis would be a good deal more complicated).

Since the publication of the papers mentioned, a huge literature has built up in which the several aspects dealt with have been studied more thoroughly and new aspects have been brought into the picture. Here we can draw attention only to some of the contributions to this literature; for a more comprehensive treatment see the summary accounts referred to in the above. Romer (1990) tried to enrich the model by introducing a "product-diversity" specification of physical capital: in a research sector "new designs" for intermediate products are being invented, which are then used in another sector by monopolistic firms to produce these intermediate products. The sector producing the final product then employs the latter and is taken to be the more productive the greater is the product diversity of its capital inputs. Aghion and Howitt (1992) and Grossman and Helpman (1991) incorporate imperfect markets and research and development (R&D) in the growth model in seeking to formalize what Joseph A. Schumpeter called "creative destruction". Martin L. Weitzman (1998) followed a different route by taking his inspiration from agricultural research stations, in which new "hybrid ideas" are generated by cross-breeding known ideas. Oded Galor (2005) put forward a "unified growth theory" designed to boldly interpret the entire history of mankind in terms of NGT. David de la Croix (2013) explored the role of fertility and education in generating growth. The economic historian Joel Mokyr (1990) used arguments forged in the recent growth literature to reconsider economic history and especially the origins and consequences of the Industrial Revolution for the growth performance of industrializing countries.

The interesting thing to note by way of conclusion is that, the NGTs' occasionally great complexity notwithstanding, in the steady state they all replicate in one form or another a characteristic feature of the AK model: its linearity. As Romer (1990: S84) put it: "Linearity in [the number of intermediate products] is what makes unbounded growth possible, and, in this sense, unbounded growth is more like an assumption than a result of the model." And Weitzman (1998: 345) concludes that in his model "everything comes full circle to steady-state growth rates being linearly proportional to aggregate savings", just as in the models of Harrod and Domar and, we may add, in the AK model.

HEINZ D. KURZ AND NERI SALVADORI

See also:

British classical political economy (II); Business and growth cycles (III); Capital theory (III); Development economics (III); Economic dynamics (III); Roy Forbes Harrod (I); John Richard Hicks (I); Income distribution (III); Nicholas Kaldor (I); Michał Kalecki (I); John Maynard Keynes (I); Robert E. Lucas (I); Macroeconomics (III); Karl Heinrich Marx (I); James Edward Meade (I); John von Neumann (I); New Keynesianism (II); Post-Keynesianism (II); David Ricardo (I); Adam Smith (I); Robert Merton Solow (I).

References and further reading

Acemoglu, D. (2009), *Introduction to Modern Economic Growth*, Princeton, NJ: Princeton University Press.
Aghion, P. and P. Howitt (1992), 'A model of growth through creative destruction', *Econometrica*, **60** (2), 323–51.
Aghion, P. and P. Howitt (1998), *Endogenous Growth Theory*, Boston, MA: MIT Press.
Arrow, K.J. (1962), 'The economic implications of learning by doing', *Review of Economic Studies*, **29** (3), 155–73.
Barro, R. and X. Sala-i-Martin (2003), *Economic Growth*, 2nd edn, Boston, MA: MIT Press.
Blaug, M. (2009), 'The trade-off between rigor and relevance: Sraffian economics as a case in point', *History of Political Economy*, **41** (2), 219–47.
Cassel, G. (1918), *Theoretische Sozialökonomie*, Leipzig: Deichert, English trans. 1932, *The Theory of Social Economy*, New York: Harcourt Brace.
Charasoff, G. (1910), *Das System des Marxismus: Darstellung und Kritik*, Berlin: H. Bondy.
Commendatore, P., S. D'Acunto, C. Panico and A. Pinto (2003), 'Keynesian theories of growth', in N. Salvadori (ed.), *The Theory of Economic Growth: A 'Classical' Perspective*, Cheltenham, UK and Northampton, MA, USA: Edward Elgar, pp. 103–38.
D'Alessandro, S. and N. Salvadori (2008), 'Pasinetti versus Rebelo: two different models or just one?', *Journal of Economic Behavior & Organization*, **65** (3–4), 547–54.

De la Croix, D. (2013), *Fertility, Education, Growth, and Sustainability*, Cambridge: Cambridge University Press.

Domar, E. (1946), 'Capital expansion, rate of growth and employment', *Econometrica*, **14** (2), 137–47.

Dorfman, R., P.A. Samuelson and R. Solow (1958), *Linear Programming and Economic Analysis*, New York, Toronto and London: McGraw-Hill.

Eltis, W. (1984), *The Classical Theory of Economic Growth*, London: Macmillan.

Galor, O. (2005), 'From stagnation to growth: unified growth theory', in P. Aghion and S. Durlauf (eds), *Handbook of Economic Growth*, Amsterdam: Elsevier, pp. 171–293.

Garegnani, P. (1990), 'Quantity of capital', in J. Eatwell, M. Milgate and P. Newman (eds), *The New Palgrave. Capital Theory*, London: Macmillan, pp. 1–78.

Grossman, G.M. and E. Helpman (1991), 'Quality ladders in the theory of growth', *Review of Economic Studies*, **58** (1), 43–61.

Harrod, R.F. (1939), 'An essay in dynamic theory', *Economic Journal*, **49** (March), 14–33.

Harrod, R.F. (1948), *Towards a Dynamic Theory*, London: Macmillan.

Jones, J.E. (1998), *Economic Growth*, 2nd edn 2002, New York: W.W. Norton.

Jones, L.E. and R. Manuelli (1990), 'A convex model of equilibrium growth: theory and policy implications', *Journal of Political Economy*, **98** (5), 1008–38.

Kaldor, N. (1955–56), 'Alternative theories of distribution', *Review of Economic Studies*, **23** (2), 83–100.

Kaldor, N. (1966), 'Marginal productivity and the macro-economic theories of distribution', *Review of Economic Studies*, **33** (4), 309–19.

King, R.G. and S. Rebelo (1990), 'Public policy and economic growth: developing neoclassical implications', *Journal of Political Economy*, **98** (5), 126–50.

Kurz, H.D. (2010), 'Technical progress, capital accumulation and income distribution in classical economics: Adam Smith, David Ricardo and Karl Marx', *European Journal of the History of Economic Thought*, **17** (5), 1183–222.

Kurz, H.D. and N. Salvadori (1995), *Theory of Production. A Long-Period Analysis*, Cambridge: Cambridge University Press.

Kurz, H.D. and N. Salvadori (1998), '"Endogenous" growth models and the "classical" tradition', in H.D. Kurz and N. Salvadori, *Understanding 'Classical' Economics*, London: Routledge, pp. 66–89.

Kurz, H.D. and N. Salvadori (1999), 'Theories of "endogeneous" growth in historical perspective', in M.R. Sertel (ed.), *Contemporary Economic Issues. Proceedings of the Eleventh World Congress of the International Economic Association, Tunis. Volume 4 Economic Behaviour and Design*, London: Macmillan, and New York: St. Martin's Press, pp. 225–61.

Kurz, H.D. and N. Salvadori (2006), 'Endogenous growth in a stylised "classical" model', in G. Stathakis and G. Vaggi (eds), *Economic Development and Social Change*, London: Routledge, pp. 106–24.

Kurz, H.D. and N. Salvadori (2010), 'The post-Keynesian theories of growth and distribution: a survey', in M. Setterfield (ed.), *Handbook of Alternative Theories of Economic Growth*, Cheltenham, UK and Northampton, MA, USA: Edward Elgar, pp. 95–107.

Lowe, A. (1954), 'The classical theory of economic growth', *Social Research*, **21** (July), 127–58, reprinted in A. Lowe (ed.) (1987), *Essays in Political Economics: Public Control in a Democratic Society*, Brighton, UK: Wheatsheaf Books.

Lucas, R.E. (1988), 'On the mechanics of economic development', *Journal of Monetary Economics*, **22** (1), 3–42.

Marshall, A. (1890), *Principles of Economics*, 8th edn 1920, reprint and reset 1977, London: Macmillan.

Marx, K. (1885), *Das Kapital*, vol. II, ed. F. Engels, Hamburg: Meissner, English trans. I. Lasker (1956), *Capital*, vol. II, Moscow: Progress.

Meade, J.E. (1961), *A Neoclassical Theory of Economic Growth*, London: Allen and Unwin.

Mokyr, J. (1990), *The Lever of Riches: Technological Creativity and Economic Progress*, Oxford: Oxford University Press.

Morishima, M. (1977), *Walras' Economics. A Pure Theory of Capital and Money*, Cambridge: Cambridge University Press.

Neumann, J. von (1937), 'Über ein ökonomisches Gleichungssystem und eine Verallgemeinerung des Brouwerschen Fixpunktsatzes', *Ergebnisse eines mathematischen Kolloquiums*, **8**, 73–83, English trans. 1945, 'A model of general economic equilibrium', *Review of Economic Studies*, **13** (1), 1–9.

Pasinetti, L.L. (1962), 'Rate of profit and income distribution in relation to the rate of economic growth', *Review of Economic Studies*, **29** (4), 103–20.

Rebelo, S. (1991), 'Long run policy analysis and long run growth', *Journal of Political Economy*, **99** (3), 500–521.

Ricardo, D. (1817), *On the Principles of Political Economy and Taxation*, 3rd edn 1821, in P. Sraffa (ed.) with the collaboration of M.H. Dobb (1951), *The Works and Correspondence of David Ricardo*, vol. I, Cambridge: Cambridge University Press.

Robinson, J. (1956), *The Accumulation of Capital*, London: Macmillan.
Romer, P.M. (1986), 'Increasing returns and long-run growth', *Journal of Political Economy*, **94** (5), 1002–37.
Romer, P.M. (1990), 'Endogenous technological change', *Journal of Political Economy*, **98** (5), S71–102.
Rostow, W.W. (1990), *Theorists of Economic Growth from David Hume to the Present*, Oxford: Oxford University Press.
Salvadori, N. and R. Signorino (2015), 'From stationary state to endogenous growth: international trade in a mathematical formulation of the Ricardian system', *Cambridge Journal of Economics*, online, 1 April, doi:10.1093/cje/bev018.
Setterfield, M. (ed.) (2010), *Handbook of Alternative Theories of Economic Growth*, Cheltenham, UK and Northampton, MA, USA: Edward Elgar, pp.95–107.
Smith, A. (1776), *An Inquiry into the Nature and Causes of the Wealth of Nations*, London: Methuen, reprinted in 1976 in *The Glasgow Edition of the Works and Correspondence of Adam Smith*, 2 vols, Oxford: Oxford University Press.
Solow, R.M. (1956), 'A contribution to the theory of economic growth', *Quarterly Journal of Economics*, **70** (1), 65–94.
Solow, R.M. (1970), *Growth Theory. An Exposition*, London: Oxford University Press.
Solow. R.M. (2010), 'Stories about economics and technology', *European Journal of the History of Economic Thought*, **17** (5), 1113–26.
Swan, T.W. (1956), 'Economic growth and capital accumulation', *Economic Record*, **32** (2), 334–61.
Torrens, R. (1815), *An Essay on the External Corn Trade*, London: Hatchard.
Uzawa, H. (1965), 'Optimum technical change in an aggregate model of economic growth', *International Economic Review*, **6** (1), 18–31.
Walras, L. (1874), *Eléments d'économie politique pure*, Lausanne: Corbaz, English trans. W. Jaffé (1954), *Elements of Pure Economics*, London: Allen and Unwin.
Weitzman, M.L. (1998), 'Recombinant growth', *Quarterly Journal of Economics*, **113** (2), 331–60.
Wicksell, K. (1893), *Über Wert, Kapital und Rente*, Jena: Gustav Fischer, English trans. 1954, *Value, Capital and Rent*, London: Allen and Unwin.

Income distribution

The distribution of output among the members of society is one of the oldest and most important topics of economics. The technical use of the term "distribution" dates back to the Physiocrats and appears in the very title of Anne-Robert-Jacques Turgot's *Réflexions* (1766). The first book of the *Wealth of Nations* (Smith 1776 [1976], hereafter *WN*) concerns "the Order, according to which [the] Produce is naturally distributed among the different Ranks of the People" (*WN*, see title of book I); David Ricardo regarded this distribution as "the principal problem in Political Economy" (Ricardo 1951–73, hereafter *Works*, I: 5). Even though distribution has not always been on top of the agenda of economic theory, the measure and explanation of the shares of profits and wages, their international differences and their evolution through time are still a lively object of investigation, both by academics and by international organizations (a recent survey is in Atkinson 2009). Likewise, household inequality and wage differentials are widely investigated in current literature (for example, Atkinson 2007; Checchi and García-Peñalosa 2008). The distribution among different kinds of labour, capital owners and rent seekers, on one side, and the distribution among individuals (households), on the other, are usually referred to as "functional" and "personal" distribution, respectively.

In a long span of time, quite naturally, a series of different (and sometimes contrasting) approaches have evolved. It is hardly possible to fit them along a line of cumulative scientific progress and, at any rate, this is not the aim of the present brief historical account. If there is a clear element that embraces such an evolution, it is variety.

A broad distinction must be made from the outset between analyses of the general problem of income distribution, which are deeply integrated into an overall theory of production and prices, and analyses which are designed to clarify specific aspects. The early theories of rent were perhaps of the second kind, like certainly most of the contemporary studies: the Lorenz curve, the 80/20 Pareto distribution, wage differentials, the return to human capital, intergenerational distribution, the role of imperfect information or trade unions in wage setting, and so on are all topics which need a specialized analysis. An excellent survey of the main current fields of research can be found in Atkinson and Bourguignon, who admit – and complain – that "no unified theory of income distribution actually exists" (Atkinson and Bourguignon 2000: 5).

We concentrate, therefore, on the theories of the first kind. They are themselves characterized by a good deal of variety. The distribution of output according to Adam Smith, Thomas Robert Malthus, David Ricardo or Karl Marx followed principles which are completely different from those of William Stanley Jevons, Philip Henry Wicksteed or Knut Wicksell. Interest theory in Carl Menger or Eugen von Böhm-Bawerk has few points of contact with that of John von Neumann or with the post-Keynesian theory of Nicholas Kaldor, Joan V. Robinson and Luigi L. Pasinetti. The distribution theory based on the works of Piero Sraffa is normally considered a radical alternative to that embedded in supply and demand theories. Yet, at the cost of sacrificing historical detail, we shall present a description of these theories which reduces contrast to a minimum, with the aim of underlying both their most fundamental differences and what is still alive and agreeable in all of them.

The Distribution among Social Classes: The Classical Economists

The unprecedented growth of output and productivity which characterized the aftermath of the first Industrial Revolution posed a new challenge to human civilization: not only could improvements and successful business yield great fortunes for investors; by their extension and persistence, they also offered the opportunity of decent standards of comfortable living for the great bulk of the population. Enlightenment philosophers such as Nicolas de Condorcet and William Godwin diffused optimistic views, and passed on to economists the difficult task of proving or disproving their own claims. The theories of distribution of Smith, Malthus, Ricardo and John Stuart Mill (just to mention the leading authors of the classical period) were precisely aimed at assessing the extent to which the social and economic mechanisms at work in the new age allowed for a permanent improvement in the living condition of the working classes. Does economic progress increase the "natural" wages as estimated in food and necessaries? Is this increase permanent? Is indefinite economic progress possible? The answers provided by Smith, Malthus and Ricardo were in the main similar despite some differences in theoretical details. They shared the conclusion that, in the economic conditions of their age, the real wages normally rose in phases of economic progress, but returned to about previous levels as soon as growth slowed down. It is true that Smith and Ricardo stressed the fact that the "natural" wage was not absolutely fixed but varied through time and materially differed in different countries according to habits and customs (for example, *Works* I: 96–7); nonetheless the historically determined minimum had in their understanding a fatal power of attraction. In the end, no significant rise in wages was expected. Enlightenment enthusiasms were therefore much softened by the "dismal science".

The relation of economic activity (particularly in agriculture) to population growth was their central argument. According to Smith:

> the demand for men, like that for any other commodity, necessarily regulates the production of men; quickens it when it goes on too slowly, and stops it when it advances too fast. It is this demand which regulates and determines the state of propagation in all the different countries of the world. (*WN* I, viii: 40)

The "demand for men", in turn, increased with the scale of economic activity and the "production of men" increased with real wages. As a consequence, the real wages tended to be higher than mere subsistence in periods of sustained economic growth, but they were bound to be kept down to a minimum in a stationary state. Hence Smith concluded that "it is not the actual greatness of national wealth, but its continual increase, which occasions a rise in the wages of labour"; (*WN* I, viii: 22).

The analysis of the actual proportion between the provision of food and population growth has been greatly extended in Malthus's theory of population. He argued in favour of a natural tendency of population growth, if unchecked, to grow far faster than the provision of food (see Malthus 1826 [1986]: 7–13): in the absence of moral, preventive checks, there was no hope that the condition of the working classes could be permanently improved, even in the presence of some economic growth and productivity increase. The tortoise would never catch the hare unless the latter could be set to sleep. Of course, Malthus did not overlook the benefits of technological improvements in agriculture.

Nor did he neglect those for the workers of an individual country arising from the importation of food and emigration. Yet, in his view, the effects of such changes – remarkable as they were in given contingencies – were temporary. The only possibility of a permanent improvement was a widespread adoption of a preventive check based on moral qualities, which unfortunately were not yet in sight during his lifetime, but he thought they could be slowly cultivated.

By contrast, J.S. Mill, who lived two generations after Smith and witnessed a material change in the social climate around the mid-nineteenth century, foresaw the possibility that the working classes may take a full and lasting advantage from the increase in productivity. The diffusion of the Malthusian moral restraint through the skilled artisans first and then to factory workers was the essential condition for this to happen (Mill 1871 [1965] bk IV: ch. VII; see Schwartz 1972; Opocher 2010).

Obviously, the theory of wages was not complete until it was integrated with a theory of rents and profits. Only then there emerged a proper theory of distribution. A series of pamphlets in 1815 by Sir Edward West, Malthus and Ricardo were precisely aimed at explaining the formation of rents and profits, assuming wages as broadly given at subsistence levels. It is a matter of debate whether Ricardo has been the first to develop such a theory, but certainly he is commonly credited with priority (cf. Sraffa 1951: 4–7). His typical mode of reasoning was to isolate single aspects of the question, and then integrate them into a realistic overall picture. In particular, he first isolated the peculiar effects of economic growth on income distribution; then he focused on the countervailing effects of technological improvements and the removal of trade restrictions; finally, he could isolate the specific effect of increasing or diminishing real wages on the rate of profits. Ricardo's 1815 *Essay on Profits* (*Works* IV) contains the main ingredients of the theory of distribution that he later developed in his *Principles* (*Works* I). He considered an agricultural activity (corn production) in which wages, profits and rents were all measured in terms of the output itself. The main argument, consisting of the explanation of extensive rent, assumes that there are qualities of land of different fertilities. Let an acre of land (of any quality) be cultivated by a team of a workers, each paid in advance a corn-wage equal to w. Let there be s different qualities of land; the output of an acre of quality i is q_i. Needless to say, there can be many acres of the same quality. Different lands can be ordered in such a way that $q_i > q_j$ if $i < j$. The rent on each acre of quality i, r_i, is simply the *difference* between that land's output and the output of the cultivated land of the worst quality, j, with $j \leq s$. Hence:

$$r_i = q_i - q_j, \, i \leq j \tag{1}$$

Since $r_j = 0$, the whole product of the cultivated lands of the least good quality is distributed to wages and profits. Denoting by π the profit per acre of such a land, we have $q_j = \pi + wa$. Moreover, if wages are the only form of capital, and i is the profit *rate*, we have $\pi = i(wa)$. Now competition forces i and w to be uniform on all lands (as well as in the other sectors of the economy). It follows that the rate of profits and the wage rate in the economy as a whole must satisfy the following equation:

$$q_j = (1 + i)wa \tag{2}$$

Equations (1) and (2) determine the rent and profit rates, assuming the margin of cultivation and the wage rate as given. It should be stressed that, since *wa* is the amount of corn anticipated to the workers employed in an acre of land, then the rate of profits corresponds to the rate of surplus on the least fertile quality of land among all lands cultivated.

A series of important results follow at once: (1) an economic expansion, represented here by an increase of index *j*, per se increases each rent rate and total rents, while the profit rate falls, assuming the wage rate is constant; (2) at a given total output, significant technological improvements in agriculture reduce the index *j*, thereby diminishing rents and increasing the profit rate, at constant wages; (3) a similar effect follows from the removal of restrictions on the importation of corn, which reduces the domestic output of corn; (4) at a given total output and technical and trade conditions, an increase in wages is always at the expense of profits, and not of rents.

If this "corn model" is referred to, as in Ricardo, an economic system in which there are other sectors, we must say very clearly how a "corn" measure of capital (and notably wages) is to be interpreted. For if all capital literally consists of corn, the above model of income distribution is self-contained and determines the rents and the rate of profits without involving commodity prices. However, if there are components of capital other than corn (for example, when the significant wage basket contains a variety of commodities), then a theory of relative prices is necessarily involved. If labour receives a constant basket of commodities, including manufactured goods, the extension of cultivation to less fertile lands must reduce the corn-value of wages, because the relative price of corn has increased; the same is true of the manufactured components of capital (such as fixed capital). It follows that a change in relative prices naturally modifies the surplus of corn, to be divided between profits and rents. Ricardo correctly argued that his qualitative results hold even in the presence of non-corn components of capital, provided that the change in relative prices is governed by labour inputs per unit of output. It was all a matter of measure and not of principle: the higher the share of the non-corn component, the lower the fall in the rate of profits associated with economic growth (see *Works* IV: 16–17, fn; for a general interpretation of the corn model, see the debate between Hollander 1973 and Eatwell 1975).

In the second edition of the *Principles* Ricardo was clear that prices are not exactly proportional to labour inputs per unit of output: much depends on the composition of capital, which generally differs across sectors. He saw that there was an intimate relation between prices and distribution, which was highly complex, and that it was beyond his capability of providing a theoretically satisfactory discussion of it. He believed that the main qualitative conclusions remained true as sound approximations, but did not prove them on logical grounds. Nor did his immediate followers substantially improve on the state in which the question was left by him.

Marx, in particular, claimed that hidden in the labour theory of value was the proof that profits were based on the exploitation of labour: he argued that they consisted in a positive difference ("surplus value") between the quantity of labour hired by employers and the quantity of labour embodied in the goods received by workers as wages (and forming the bulk of circulating capital). He took pains to prove that this concept of profits could be retained even when relative prices differed from relative labour values and that the general rate of profits, which was given by the ratio between aggregate surplus value and total capital, tended to decrease, owing to the increase of "constant capital" (means of production) relative to "variable capital" (wages). His theory of distribution, however, important as it is on historical and philosophical grounds, did not add substantially to the Ricardian idea that, in real terms, profits and rents originate in the commodity surplus generated in the economic system and in the inability of workers to appropriate it (for an assessment of Marx's theory of value and distribution, see Steedman 1977).

Some proper mathematical developments of the "surplus" theory of interest were discussed later, in the early twentieth century, especially in German-speaking countries. Meanwhile the "marginal revolution" set the Ricardian themes aside, in favour of a different approach.

The Distribution among Factors of Production: The Marginalist Approach

Ricardo emphasized the extension of cultivation to new lands more than the intensive cultivation of a given land, even though his theory contemplated both cases (*Works* IV: 14). By contrast, the complete recasting of the theory of distribution, which characterized the "marginal revolution" (started in the 1870s) distinctly focused on a variable intensity of cultivation of a given land and this ultimately led to an altogether different distribution theory.

A formal statement of marginal conditions in wage setting is due to Jevons (1871 [1970]: 194), while the basic principle can be traced back to Johann Heinrich von Thünen. An early neat and rigorous account of distribution along marginal lines is in Wicksteed (1894 [1992]); Wicksell's *Lectures* (1901 [1934]) are generally recognized to be the best synthesis of the formal arguments put forward by Léon Walras, Menger, Böhm-Bawerk, Wicksteed and by his own original work (Wicksell 1893 [1954]) (see Stigler 1941: ch. 10).

The first logical step was a rethinking of rents in terms of differential calculus. Let there be only two factors of production, labour and land (in private ownership and entirely cultivated). The landlord acts as entrepreneur and hires labour. He pays labour in kind when output becomes available; the limit of increasing returns to labour "has long been passed" (Wicksell 1901 [1934]: 110) and diminishing returns (to labour) prevail. In such circumstances:

> to the landowner, it can evidently never be economically advantageous to pay an additional labourer *more* in wages than the additional product obtained from employing him. But [by competition] none of the labourers previously engaged can claim higher wages than the last one engaged. . . . On the other hand, if there is perfect competition between employers, wages cannot sink materially *below* [that amount]. (Wicksell 1901 [1934]: 111–12; emphasis in the original)

> If the number of labourers is a, then the gross product . . . may be represented algebraically as a function $f(a)$ of the number a. The wages of the last labourer, as of every other labourer, is then represented approximately by the differential coefficient $f'(a)$. (Wicksell 1901 [1934]: 116)

The rent and wage rate (in kind) are, therefore, respectively:

$$R = f(a) - af'(a) \qquad (3)$$

$$w = f'(a) \tag{4}$$

In equation (3), rent is a residual. It can be easily seen that it rises as employment rises, so long as $f''(a) < 0$. Wicksell carefully stressed that this conforms with the Ricardian theory of (intensive) rent (Wicksell 1901 [1934]: 116; see also the models of Pasinetti 1960, and Samuelson 1978). An even closer similarity with the Ricardian theory of intensive rent is when "a" is an index of capital-plus-labour, as in the case of Wicksteed (1894 [1992]: 66).

The equations above were only a first step, however. A "residual theory of rent" was not a theory at all, according to our authors. Rather, it was "simply a statement that when all other factors of production have been payed off, the "surplus" or residuum can be claimed by the land-owner" (Wicksteed (1894 [1992]: 66). For, by the same token, one can formulate a "residual theory of wages", as Wicksteed (1889: 312) himself did a few years earlier; a masterly illustration of this symmetry is in Wicksell (1901 [1934]: 124–5).

Further steps were to be made in order to explain all remunerations by the same principle. There should not be separate "laws" of rent, wages and profits, but a single law for all of them. The main problem with which Wicksteed dealt was precisely whether a single principle existed, such that the sum of the remunerations "cover the product and be covered by it" (cf. Steedman 1992: 13–14) without any surplus or deficit. Aiming at this, the new theory completely abandoned the classical "surplus approach".

The keystone was the assumption of constant returns to scale, and the consequent properties of homogeneous functions of the first degree. It is notorious that Wicksteed dedicated many pages to a cumbersome proof of Euler's theorem, which he appeared not to know. Yet, as noted by Flux (1894: 311), "Euler's equation gives at once the result". If **a** is the (column) n-vector of input use, including land, and **w** is the (row) n-vector of the input rentals, including land rent, in terms of the output, and $f(\mathbf{a})$ is the production function homogeneous of degree one, we have:

$$w_i = \frac{\partial f}{\partial a_i}, \; i = 1, 2, \cdots, n \tag{5}$$

$$f(\mathbf{a}) = \mathbf{wa} \tag{6}$$

There was no need to express any reward as a residuum, because the residuum was identically equal to the factor's partial derivative multiplied by the amount of that factor used.

Wicksell acutely observed that this important property was satisfied not only when "large-scale and small-scale operations are equally productive" (Wicksell 1901 [1934]: 126), but also "at the point of transition from "increasing" to "diminishing returns" (relatively to the scale of production)" (ibid.: 129). He also argued that "the firm must always, economically speaking, gravitate" (ibid.) towards this point, which he called "full equilibrium".

A specific merit of Wicksteed must also be mentioned: he insisted on the fact that the new theory was inconsistent with an aggregate view of labour, capital and land. In fact, marginal productivity is a technological phenomenon, which concerns physically specified inputs:

we must regard every kind and quality of labour that can be distinguished from other kinds and qualities as separate factors; and in the same way every kind of land will be taken as a separate factor. Still more important is it to insist that instead of speaking of so many £ worth of capital we shall speak of so many ploughs, so many tons of manure, and so many horses, or foot-pounds of "power". (Wicksteed 1894 [1992]: 83–4)

The focus of distribution theory shifted, therefore, from big social classes to the owners of technically specified inputs and new basis for the analysis of wages and wage differentials was provided. This appeared to be more adequate than the classical theories not only on logical grounds but also in consideration of the fact that the Malthusian pressure on wages gradually relaxed, and productivity increase proved to be the main permanent source of the increase in real wages and in leisure time, which characterized the second half of the nineteenth century. This link was reinforced by a reverse causation, from wages to productivity. Wicksell, perhaps inspired by Alfred Marshall, noted that "the mental and physical health and strength of the worker, and consequently the efficiency of labour, are largely dependent on the wages received and, within certain limits, rise and fall with the wage" (Wicksell 1901 [1934]: 104; see also Marshall 1920 bk VI: ch. XIII).

Equations (5) and (6), however, still do not provide a complete theory of income distribution. First, they formulate conditions that input rentals must satisfy (under differentiability assumptions), but do not determine them. At most, they offer a theory of input demand. Second, given their disaggregate nature, they do not involve explicit conditions for the rate of profits or interest.

As to the next steps, there are important differences between Wicksteed and the authors of general equilibrium orientation, like Wicksell. While the former basically remained within the boundaries of a partial equilibrium theory of the price-taking enterprise (see Steedman 1992: 35), Wicksell went somewhat further.

He assumed, as a first approximation, a fixed supply of the factors of production. By market clearing, he could say that wages, for instance, were determined by "the marginal productivity of labour *as it is when all labourers are employed*" (Wicksell 1901 [1934]: 121, emphasis added). If we ignore for a moment the presence of capital (as he did in a first step), Wicksell's argument clearly anticipated the logical structure of the Heckscher–Ohlin–Samuelson theory of trade for the small open economy: with two industries facing internationally given prices and characterized by smooth, constant-returns production functions and two primary factors in fixed supply and fully employed; factor prices are known to be uniquely determined. In this setting one can study the same problems which attracted the interest of the classical economists, such as the effect of increasing population or of technological progress on wages and rents.

In a second step, Wicksell removed the assumption of constant commodity prices, which in a closed economy are related to output levels, and presented a sketch of a general equilibrium model with given factor supplies, which he claimed was "completely determinate" (Wicksell 1901 [1934]: 205).

His argument, however, is far less conclusive and satisfactory than the analysis based on given prices. This is partially due to the fact that, even in the simple case with two primary inputs, many other elements should be taken into account, such as the "distribution [of factors] among individuals, and personal preferences in consumption" (Wicksell 1901 [1934]: 201) – and this notoriously reduces the ability of the theory to provide definite conclusions. But the argument was also obscured by the fact that Wicksell's equations allowed for capital and interest, which introduced further complex and controversial aspects.

Wicksell carefully noted that the "analogy between interest, on the one hand, and wages and rent, on the other, is incomplete" (Wicksell 1901 [1934]: 148) and that the principle of marginal productivity cannot be immediately applied to capital: "whereas labour and land are measured each in terms of its own *technical* units . . . capital, on the other hand . . . is reckoned, in common parlance, as a sum of *exchange value*", which "disturbs the correspondence which would otherwise exist between all the factors of production"(ibid.: 149; emphases in the original). Given the "varied and changing forms which productive capital assumes in reality" (ibid.: 144), the principle of marginal productivity should be applied to each item individually, but in so doing one can only obtain marginal conditions for the individual rentals, and not for the rate of interest. On the other hand, the conception of capital stock given in terms of a "sum of exchange value" was, according to Wicksell, a "theoretical anomaly" (ibid.: 149), which could not provide a theory of interest, because commodity prices depend themselves on the rate of interest. Moreover, he thought that interest had an "enigmatic nature": the presence of capital increased productivity, but it was far from clear on what grounds the owners of capital goods can claim a share of the increased output: capital goods can be reproduced at will and no threat of withdrawal can support such a claim (cf. ibid.: 146). The theory of income distribution was at a very critical point: the new principles excluded a surplus theory of interest, yet they did not provide, in the same form as applied to wages and rents, a new explanation.

Marginal Productivity and Interest

The Austrian attempt developed by Wicksell consisted in tracing back the different capital goods to a common origin. For this purpose, he elaborated on the time dimension of capital, as theorized by Böhm-Bawerk (whom he praised for his magnificent overall picture, which, alas, lacked analytical precision):

> All capital goods, however different they may appear, can always be ultimately resolved into labour and land; and the only thing which distinguishes these quantities of labour and land from those which we have previously considered is that they belong to *earlier years*, whilst we have previously been concerned only with current labour and land directly employed in the production of consumption-goods. (Wicksell 1901 [1934]: 149–50, emphasis in the original)

Capital consists therefore in saved-up labour and land and one need only consider dated quantities of these factors, whose marginal productivities can conceptually be defined in the ordinary way. Wicksell, like Menger and Böhm-Bawerk, assumed a finite number of "layers" of saved-up resources (which excludes mutual input–output relations). Let (l_j, t_j) $(j = 0, 1, \cdots, n)$ denote the amounts of labour and land used j periods before the consumer good stage; (l_0, t_0) denotes therefore the direct use of labour and land in this final stage. In a certain vertically integrated firm, the current output of a consumption good is $f(l_0, t_0, l_1, t_1, \cdots, l_n, t_n)$, where f is a production function characterized by constant returns to scale. As before, let i denote the rate of profits (uniform across stages), that Wicksell and the Austrians called "interest". The rental on saved-up labour of j periods before, equal to $\partial f/\partial l_j$, must satisfy:

$$\frac{\partial f}{\partial l_j} = (1 + i)^j w, j = 0, 1, \cdots, n$$

It follows at once that:

$$(1 + i) = \frac{\partial f / \partial l_j}{\partial f / \partial l_{j-1}} \tag{7}$$

Similar relations hold for land. This ratio is supposed to be greater than one and to be uniform across firms and industries. We have here the basis for a theory of factor demand, including the demand for (heterogeneous) capital.

In order to determine the rate of interest, a solution proposed by Wicksell as a first approximation was to assume, by analogy with the case without capital, a given supply of saved-up labour and land in the various periods. It must be remarked, however, that this naturally refers to the short period rather than to the long, and in this case it is not clear why the rate of interest should be uniform. The analogy, therefore, is not complete. Wicksell oscillated between this "solution" and a conception of capital as an aggregate, whose precise composition was determined as a long-run phenomenon (see Kurz 2000). Yet by so doing it is clear that the "theoretical anomaly" comes back again.

Wicksell recognized that the marginal productivity of a given capital endowment is not a well-defined concept, but unfortunately his ingenious idea of reducing capital to "dated" primary inputs was of no use for a long-period distribution theory. Nor did the following literature provide better solutions: there simply is no microeconomic foundation for a scalar measure of heterogeneous capital, independent of income distribution, except for very special cases. The real situation of an economic system which can combine qualitatively different produced means of production with each other and with primary inputs is not equivalent to an imaginary situation in which a single capital good is combined with primary inputs. The lack of generality of Paul Samuelson's "surrogate production function" is expressive of this dead end (see Samuelson 1962; Garegnani 1970).

Back to a Surplus Theory of Interest

The conception of economic activity as a circular flow and the "surplus approach" to interest surfaced again at the turn of the nineteenth century, especially in German-speaking countries, partly in opposition to marginal productivity theories. A leading figure was Friedrich von Wieser, Böhm-Bawerk's colleague and brother in law. He adopted a view of production as a circular flow right from his *Ursprung* of 1884, maintaining that unidirectional production is characteristic of primitive societies, whereas circular production pertains to developed societies (Wieser 1884: 50; see Kurz and Sturn 1999: 83). In his more mature work (Wieser 1889), he built on the observation that there is simultaneously a certain consumption of means of production, and a certain production of them, with a positive surplus. In value terms (irrespective of the price theory adopted) "the subtrahend is somewhat less than the minuend, and the required residue of interest must be the result" (Wieser 1889: 142; see Opocher 2005). More generally, he was convinced that the "imputation" of output to each factor should be ascertained not using marginal variations, but under the assumption of undisturbed, actual input use (see Rothschild 1973) and that such an imputation is the solution of a system of equations. Vladimir Karpovich Dmitriev (1904 [1974]) and Ladislaus von Bortkiewicz (1906–07 [1952]) also tried to explain interest on the basis of a given system of production, even though they started from unidirectional processes of finite length, like the leading Austrians (see Kurz and Gehrke 2006: 115–16, n. 22): implicit in a system of production there was a rate of interest, which can be calculated on the basis of a mathematical description of all the economic processes in use.

The main formal contribution, however, is that of von Neumann. He presented a theory of interest in an economy in which "goods are produced . . . in the first place from each other" (Neumann 1937 [1945–46]: 1) in conditions of constant returns to scale; differently from Dmitriev and Bortkiewicz, and, like Wieser, he considered reciprocal input–output relations. He introduced technological alternatives in each sector and universal joint production (which includes fixed capital as a special case), in the sense of a finite number of potential processes. Accordingly, the determination of the rate of interest and of relative prices is placed in the framework of a wider problem of the choice of technique and optimization in which also the rate of economic expansion and the activity levels are determined. This has been an important development, since Wieser had been criticized for his failure to explain how input choices come about (see Wicksell 1893 [1954]: 24–5). His model follows a general equilibrium logic, but marginal productivities, preferences, and factor supplies have no role in it. Assuming m processes and n goods, let $\mathbf{A}$ be the $n \times m$ matrix of input coefficients when processes are run at unit level; likewise, let $\mathbf{B}$ be the $n \times m$ matrix of output coefficients. The net profit from each process, evaluated at price vector $\mathbf{p}$, is $[\mathbf{pB} - (1 + i)\mathbf{pA}]$. The total balance of each commodity, calculated at activity levels $\mathbf{x}$, is $[\mathbf{Bx} - (1 + g)\mathbf{Ax}]$, where $(1 + g)$ is the growth factor. It is assumed that no process can make positive net or extra profits and that no commodity can be produced short of its use; that a process, which makes losses, is not activated and that a good produced in excess has a zero price. Hence, denoting by $\mathbf{e}^j$ the jth unit vector, we have:

$$\mathbf{pB} \le (1 + i)\mathbf{pA} \text{ and } \mathbf{Bx} \ge (1 + g)\mathbf{Ax}$$

$$x^j = 0 \text{ if } \mathbf{pBe}^j < (1 + i)\mathbf{pAe}^j, \mathbf{p} \ge \mathbf{0}$$

$$p^j = 0 \text{ if } (\mathbf{e}^j)^T\mathbf{Bx} > (1 + g)(\mathbf{e}^j)^T\mathbf{Ax}, \mathbf{x} \ge \mathbf{0}$$

Equilibrium is determined as a pair of vectors $(\mathbf{p}, \mathbf{x})$ and of scalars (i, g) satisfying the above inequalities: it is shown that, on the assumptions employed by von Neumann, the solution is a saddle point where $g = i$.

A similar logic, it must be briefly said, can also be applied to the determination of the rewards of primary factors available in fixed supply, as in Knight (1925), Samuelson (1958), Uzawa (1958) and Dorfman et al. (1958). Wieser, again, is credited with having had an inspiring role in it. Activity levels and factor prices are determined by a system of inequalities in which the value of production (at any given vector of commodity prices) is maximum and the cost of employing the available factors is minimum. A fact that has attracted the interest of some authors is that in this model one can define a "purely physical quasi-social marginal productivity" (Samuelson 1958: 315) of each factor (by marginally changing its supply) and that in equilibrium this equals the real reward of this factor (Knight's theorem).

About ten years before von Neumann, Piero Sraffa explored the idea that socio-technical conditions alone may suffice to determine simultaneously the rate of profits (interest) and relative prices as solutions of a system of equations. This has been part of an ambitious project of rethinking the old problems of value and distribution paving the ground for new analytical solutions, which will be completed in Sraffa (1960). What are now known as Sraffa's "second equations" (see Kurz and Gehrke 2006 for details) were drafted in 1928 (the 1927 "first equations" referring to the limiting case of production without a surplus). Sraffa assumed, like von Neumann after him, that the production of each commodity required the consumption of several commodities, either as means of subsistence of workers or as means of production, and that there was an overall surplus of some (or all) commodities and a deficit of none. For each commodity, the value of the output should be equal to the value of all the commodities consumed plus a profit (interest) component, at a uniform rate. Denoting now by $\mathbf{A}$ the square matrix of all material inputs per unit of output (as calculated at specific output levels), including workers' sustenance, we have:

$$\mathbf{p} = (1 + i)\mathbf{p}\mathbf{A} \text{ or } \mathbf{p}\left[\mathbf{A} - \frac{1}{(1 + i)}\mathbf{I}\right] = \mathbf{0} \tag{8}$$

All depends on the properties of matrix $\mathbf{A}$: the equilibrium vector of commodity prices is an eigenvector of $\mathbf{A}$, while the profit (interest) factor $(1 + i)$ is the reciprocal of the dominant eigenvalue. By the Perron–Frobenius theorems of linear algebra, there is a unique largest eigenvalue, associated with an eigenvector with positive elements, which is unique up to a scalar factor. A solution therefore exists if the dominant eigenvalue is lower than one. (The Perron–Frobenius theorems are central for Sraffa's theory of distribution just as Euler's theorem was central for Wicksteed's theory and it is curious to note that none of them appeared to know the relevant mathematical theorem, but both were able to "see" the necessity for them and had been assisted for a proof by a mathematician, Frank P. Ramsey and John Bridge, respectively.)

As in the case of von Neumann's model, labour and wages do not appear explicitly: they are "mixed together" by the assumption that a unit of labour receives the anticipation, not of a wage of a certain value, but of an "inventory" of commodities. It follows that an increase, say, in the amounts forming this inventory or an increase in the amount of labour per unit of output in all sectors are indistinguishable: both determine an increase in the consumption of commodities per unit of output and a fall in the rate of profits (interest). This is quite consistent with the main conclusions that Ricardo reached in his "corn model".

The Post-Keynesian Theory of Growth and Distribution

We must now give a succinct account of another approach stemming from the London–Cambridge milieu and elaborated by Nicholas Kaldor and Joan Robinson in the 1950s. They applied the Keynesian apparatus of thought to the problem of distribution on the basis of a breakdown of aggregate real income (aggregate output) into wages and profits and the assumption that the propensity to save from profits was higher than the propensity to save from wages. In a simple limiting case, let there be no saving from wages, and let the propensity to save from profits be s_p. Denoting by Y the real income (the aggregate output), by W and P, respectively, the total amounts of wages and profits and by I the investment (in terms of the output) the equality between savings and investment implies:

$$\frac{P}{Y} = \frac{1}{s_p} \frac{I}{Y}$$

Assuming the capital/output ratio, K/Y as constant, defining $i = (P/K)$ as the rate of profits and $g = (I/K)$ as the rate of growth, we have:

$$i = \frac{g}{s_p}$$

This is known as the "Cambridge equation". It should be stressed that the saving–investment equality is *not* regulated here by price adjustments in competitive markets; rather, it is regulated by output formation and its distribution between profits and wages.

This basic model admits a number of variants. Kaldor's original version (Kaldor 1955–56) includes a positive propensity to save from wages. In Pasinetti's version (Pasinetti 1962) the propensities to save were referred not to wages and profits but to workers and capitalists (whether or not workers had any share in profits); also, Pasinetti took g to represent an exogenous rate of population growth, under full employment: in this understanding, the Cambridge equation has a normative nature.

The "Real Wages–Rate of Interest Frontier"

Let us return to the "surplus" theories of interest. Further developments are required to introduce labour as an explicit input, and to express the wage rate in value (whatever the chosen numeraire), rather than as a vector of physical commodities. This Sraffa did in his "third equations" (see Kurz and Gehrke 2006: 106–7). There are at least two good reasons to do so. The first is that there is no strict "recipe" for the sustenance of workers and their families; the second and more important reason is that the secular tendency for real wages has been to increase, and not to remain constant, and any conception of a radial, say, expansion of a given inventory of goods would violate the principle that the composition of consumption changes along with real income (Engel's law). Sraffa's "third equations" formalized an inverse relationship between the real wage and the rate of profits (interest) along Ricardian lines. A more complete analysis required further steps, including the introduction of a variety of methods of production amongst which the firms in the various industries can choose. This aspect, which of course was present in Ricardo, established also a link with the marginal theory of capital and interest. For Sraffa's mathematical model (Sraffa 1960) has been the basis both of a revival of the Ricardian approach and of a critique of the marginalist theory of capital and interest.

The original model assumed a finite number of potential processes in each industry, as in von Neumann's model and in activity analysis. Also, successive developments normally kept this assumption (two classical reference books are Pasinetti 1977 and

Kurz and Salvadori 1995). Nonetheless, for a neat comparison with the marginalist approaches, it is convenient here to assume a continuum of technical alternatives, as in Salvadori and Steedman (1985). This is not to downplay the non-differentiability case, but just to make some other and less obvious differences more transparent.

Let us describe the individual firm in terms of a twice differentiable unit cost function, so that the "marginal conditions" are automatically satisfied for each individual input in each firm.

Assuming identical firms in each industry, the unit cost function in industry j is $c^j((1 + i)\mathbf{p}, w)$, homogeneous of degree one. By Shephard's Lemma we have:

$$c^j_{(1+i)\mathbf{p}} = \mathbf{a}^j((1 + i)\mathbf{p}, w),$$

$$c^j_w = l^j((1 + i)\mathbf{p}, w) \tag{9}$$

where $(\mathbf{a}^j, l^j)$ are, respectively, the cost minimising use of produced inputs and of labour per unit of output in industry j. The partial derivatives $\partial a^{tj}/\partial((1 + i)p^t)$ $(t = 1, 2, \cdots, n)$ and $\partial l^j/\partial w$ are no doubt (semi-)negative, since the cost function Hessian is negative semidefinite. This is the logical ground for downward sloping marginalist input demand curves. However, when (9) is satisfied, extra profit must be zero, implying also:

$$1 = \frac{1}{p^j}(1 + i)\mathbf{p}\mathbf{a}^j + \frac{1}{p^j}wl^j \tag{10}$$

Equations (9) and (10) are the dual representation of the Wicksteed–Wicksell marginal productivity conditions corresponding to the individual firm, in a specific point of long-period equilibrium.

Now considering the comparative statics of such an equilibrium, we see at once that it is impossible to change just one price in (9) without violating (10): at least two prices must change and we can draw no conclusion on the input use–input price relation from the mere sign of the curly derivatives of marginalist partial equilibrium analysis (cf. Opocher and Steedman 2015: ch. 1.4).

The fact that some inputs are produced introduces further complications, because vector $\mathbf{p}$ in (10) cannot be simply "given", unless we consider an "isolated" industry which imports its material inputs at given terms of trade. Equation (10) must hold for all industries. Therefore:

$$\mathbf{p} = (1 + i)\mathbf{p}\mathbf{A} + w\mathbf{I} \tag{11}$$

Since only relative prices matter in any genuine microeconomic argument, let us express all prices in terms of a real composite numeraire, $\mathbf{s}$, so that:

$$\mathbf{p}\mathbf{s} = 1 \tag{12}$$

Equations (9), (11) and (12) define the "real wage–rate of interest frontier". It should be stressed that in our formulation $(\mathbf{A}, \mathbf{I})$ are continuous functions of relative prices. Within the limits of the microeconomic assumptions made, no long-period theory of income distribution can violate it. Of course, it only determines a trade-off between the real wage and the rate of interest and not a pair of specific equilibrium values. Yet it is very useful in itself. First it permits a coherent theoretical analysis of the relation between input use and input prices both in each individual industry and in the economy as a whole. For let us consider a point on the frontier, however determined. How does a small increase, say, in the rate of interest affect input use per unit of output in each industry? The wage certainly falls both in numéraire and relative to each produced-input rental $(1 + i)p_t$ $(t = 1, 2, \cdots, n)$; but the latter may either increase or fall relative to each other. It follows that, even under differentiability assumptions, the industry-level use of an individual commodity per unit of output in (9) need not be inversely related to the rate of interest. Nor need its total value be inversely related, unless relative commodity prices in (11) are "frozen". In the long period, to which distribution theories typically refer, we are left with no microeconomic foundation for a "demand for capital", inversely related to the rate of interest. Things are different as far as labour use per unit of output is concerned: under differentiability assumptions, and if all pairs of inputs are Hicksian substitutes (that is, all the off-diagonal terms of the cost function Hessian are positive), then the industry-level input use per unit of output is in fact inversely related to the wage. It should be remarked, however, that the symmetry among inputs which characterized the upsurge of the marginal productivity theory of distribution is here broken without remedy. Moreover, it has been shown that, without the differentiability assumption, also this regularity would disappear (for a full-length discussion, the reader is referred to Opocher and Steedman 2015: chs 4, 5).

The Sraffian critique of the marginalist theory of distribution supports the view that, in a long-period perspective, the rate of profits (interest) and the real wage are hardly determined by a general principle of "factor demand and supply": primary and produced inputs behave in different ways and they obey no general "law of demand" either at the firm/industry level or at the aggregate level. Rather, the theory of distribution should be "open ended" and admit some degrees of freedom.

The real wage(s)–rate of interest frontier has been used also in applications: a change in technology, in international prices and taxation can be analysed on the basis of proper modifications of equations (9) to (12) (see, for example, Steedman 1983; Mainwaring 1974; Metcalfe and Steedman 1971, respectively; see also Opocher and Steedman 2015: chs 7, 8). A positive (negative) shock ultimately increases (reduces) the maximum real wages and rate of interest that can be paid and determines a complex and often counter-intuitive effect on relative prices. Also, it determines a redistribution of income. If we consider, then, the change in an individual real earning rate, it would be useful to distinguish between two components: one due to the income enhancing (reducing) effect of the shock, the other due to a redistribution effect. Using the frontier, we may conceptually distinguish between them: the first can be measured by a shift of the whole frontier, the other by a movement on it (see Opocher and Steedman 2015: ch. 8.1).

The Theories of Distribution and the Empirics of Inequality

Current empirical studies show an overwhelming evidence of an increasing inequality since the late 1970s in many advanced economies and notably in Anglo-Saxon countries: the labour share decreased and at the same time both wage dispersion and household inequality increased (for example, Checchi and García-Peñalosa, 2008: 604). Confronted with this evidence, the reader may wonder what the explanatory power of the main theories of distribution that we have reviewed is.

The recent, highly successful book by Thomas Piketty (2014), while referring to no mathematical (or econometric) model nor to any formalized theory of distribution, can be instructive in this respect. A big issue on which he insists is the excess of the "rate of return to capital" over the output growth rate for long periods of time, which is an automatic driver of an ever increasing capital share and an ever decreasing labour share (ibid.: 232–3). Even though this evidence is broadly consistent with the "Cambridge equation" referred to above, more should be said on the reasons why profits have been so high relative to growth and average wages could obtain such small advantages from technological progress. Another important issue concerns the modes of the increasing earnings inequality, which displayed in past decades a fanning out of the upper tail of the distribution and a relative fall at the middle (ibid.: 304–10; also Atkinson 2007; Autor et al. 2006). A marginal productivity theory of labour demand cannot explain these wage developments: a more nuanced view should include some other elements.

It is hardly possible, we suggest, to explain the main stylized facts of income distribution without integrating economic arguments with arguments relating to other spheres of social life. The distribution of wealth and power among individuals and social groups, the advantages and disadvantages that they can get from specific technological developments, the institutions that regulate labour and capital markets, and so on, cannot be without effect on income distribution and its changes through time. In this respect, the open-ended analyses of income distribution have some advantages over the self-contained theories.

ARRIGO OPOCHER

See also:

Eugen von Böhm-Bawerk (I); British classical political economy (II); British marginalism (II); Capital theory (III); William Stanley Jevons (I); Neo-Ricardian economics (II); John von Neumann (I); Post-Keynesianism (II); Population (III); David Ricardo (I); Piero Sraffa (I); Value and price (III); Knut Wicksell (I); Philip Henry Wicksteed (I); Friedrich von Wieser (I).

References and further reading

Atkinson, A.B. (2007), 'The distribution of earnings in OECD countries', *International Labour Review*, **146** (1–2), 41–60.
Atkinson, A.B. (2009), 'Factor shares: the principal problem of political economy?', *Oxford Review of Economic Policy*, **25** (1), 3–16.
Atkinson, A.B. and F. Bourguignon (2000), 'Income distribution and economics', in A.B. Atkinson and F. Bourguignon (eds), *Handbook of Income Distribution*, Amsterdam: Elsevier, pp. 1–58.
Autor, D.H., L.F. Katz and M.S. Kearney (2006), 'The polarization of the US labor market', *American Economic Review*, **96** (2), 189–94.
Bortkiewicz, L. von (1906–07), 'Wertrechnung und Preisrechnung im Marxschen System', *Archiv für Sozialwissenschaft und Sozialpolitik*, **3**, English trans. 1952, 'Value and price in the Marxian system', *International Economic Papers*, **2**, 5–60.
Checchi, D. and C. García-Peñalosa (2008), 'Labour market institutions and income inequality', *Economic Policy*, **23** (56), 601–49.
Dmitriev, V.K. (1904), *Ekonomicheski ocherki*, Moscow, English trans. by D. Fry, *Economic Essays on Value, Competition, and Utility*, edited with an introduction by D.M. Nuti, Cambridge: Cambridge University Press, 1974.

Dorfman, R., P.A. Samuelson and R.M. Solow (1958), *Linear Programming and Economic Analysis*, New York: McGraw-Hill.

Eatwell, J. (1975), 'The interpretation of Ricardo's essay on profits', *Economica*, **42** (166), 182–7.

Flux, A.W. (1894), 'Review of: Essay on the co-ordination of the laws of distribution, by P.H. Wicksteed', *The Economic Journal*, **4** (14), 305–13.

Garegnani, P. (1970), 'Heterogeneous capital, the production function and the theory of distribution', *Review of Economic Studies*, **37** (3), 407–36.

Hollander, S. (1973), 'Ricardo's analysis of the profit rate, 1813–15', *Economica*, **40** (159), 260–82.

Jevons, W.S. (1871), *The Theory of Political Economy*, reprinted 1970, ed. and introduction by R.D. Collison Black, Harmondsworth: Penguin Books.

Kaldor, N. (1955–56), 'Theories of distribution', *Review of Economic Studies*, **23** (2), 83–100.

Knight, F.H. (1925), 'A note on Professor Clark's illustration of marginal productivity', *Journal of Political Economy*, **33**, 550–53.

Kurz, H. (2000), 'Wicksell and the problem of the "missing" equation', *History of Political Economy*, **32** (4), 765–88.

Kurz, H. and C. Gehrke (2006), 'Sraffa on von Bortkiewicz: reconstructing the classical theory of value and distribution', *History of Political Economy*, **38** (1), 91–149.

Kurz, H. and N. Salvadori (1995), *Theory of Production. A Long-Period Analysis*, Cambridge: Cambridge University Press.

Kurz, H.D. and R. Sturn (1999), 'Wiesers "Ursprung" und die Entwicklung der Microökonomik', in *Vademecum zu einem Klassiker der österreichen Schule*, Dusseldorf: Verlag Wirtschaft und Finanzen.

Mainwaring, L. (1974), 'A neo-Ricardian analysis of international trade', *Kyklos*, **27** (3), 537–53.

Malthus, T.R. (1826 [1986]), *An Essay on the Principle of Population*, in E.A. Wringley and and D. Souden (eds), *The Works of Thomas Robert Malthus*, vol. 2, London: Pickering.

Marshall, A. (1920), *Principles of Economics*, 8th edn, London: Macmillan.

Meek, R.L. (ed.) (1973), *Turgot on Progress, Sociology and Economics*, Cambridge: Cambridge University Press.

Metcalfe, J.S. and I. Steedman (1971), 'Some effects of taxation in a linear model of production', *The Manchester School*, **39** (3), 171–85.

Mill, J.S. (1871 [1965]), *Principles of Political Economy*, in J.M. Robson (ed.), *Collected Works of John Stuart Mill*, Toronto: University of Toronto Press.

Neumann, J. von (1937 [1945–46]), 'A model of general economic equilibrium', *Review of Economic Studies*, **13** (1), 1–9.

Opocher, A. (2005), 'Formalizing Wieser's theory of distribution: consistent imputation in alternative theoretical perspectives', *Metroeconomica*, **56** (2), 200–220.

Opocher, A. (2010), 'The future of the working classes: a comparison between J.S. Mill and A. Marshall', *European Journal of the History of Economic Thought*, **17** (2), 229–53.

Opocher, A. and I. Steedman (2015), *Full Industry Equilibrium. A Theory of the Industrial Long Run*, Cambridge: Cambridge University Press.

Pasinetti, L.L. (1960), 'A mathematical formulation of the Ricardian system', *Review of Economic Studies*, **27** (2), 78–98.

Pasinetti, L.L. (1962), 'Rate of profit and income distribution in relation to the rate of economic growth', *Review of Economic Studies*, **29** (4), 267–79.

Pasinetti, L.L. (1977), *Lectures on the Theory of Production*, London: Macmillan.

Piketty, T. (2014), *Capital in the Twenty-First Century*, Cambridge, MA: The Belknap Press of Harvard University Press.

Ricardo, D. (1951–73), *The Works and Correspondence of David Ricardo*, 11 vols, ed. P. Sraffa with the collaboration of M. Dobb, Cambridge: Cambridge University Press. In the text referred to as *Works*, volume number and page number.

Rothschild, K.W. (1973), 'Distributive aspects of the Austrian theory', in J.R. Hicks and W. Weber (eds), *Carl Menger and the Austrian School of Economics*, Oxford: Clarendon Press, pp. 207–25.

Salvadori, N. and I. Steedman (1985), 'Cost functions and produced means of production: duality and capital theory', *Contributions to Political Economy*, **4** (1), 79–90.

Samuelson, P.A. (1958), 'Frank Knight's theorem in linear programming', *Zeitschrift für Nationalökonomie*, **18** (3), 310–17.

Samuelson, P.A. (1962), 'Parable and realism in capital theory: the surrogate production function', *Review of Economic Studies*, **29** (3), 193–206.

Samuelson, P.A. (1978), 'The canonical classical model of political economy', *Journal of Economic Literature*, **16** (4), 1415–34.

Schwartz, P. (1972), *The New Political Economy of J.S. Mill*, London: Weidenfeld and Nicolson.

Smith, A. (1776 [1976]), *An Inquiry into the Nature and Causes of the Wealth of Nations*, in R.H. Campbell,

A.S. Skinner and W.B. Todd (eds), *The Glasgow Edition of the Works and Correspondence of Adam Smith*, vol. II, Oxford: Clarendon. In the text referred to as *WN*, book number, chapter number, (section number), paragraph number.

Sraffa, P. (1951), 'Note on "Essay on Profits"', in D. Ricardo (1951–73), *The Works and Correspondence of David Ricardo*, vol. IV, Cambridge: Cambridge University Press, pp. 3–8.

Sraffa, P. (1960), *Production of Commodities by Means of Commodities. Prelude to a Critique of Economic Theory*, Cambridge: Cambridge University Press.

Steedman, I. (1977), *Marx after Sraffa*, London: NLB.

Steedman, I. (1983), 'On the measurement and aggregation of productivity increase', *Metroeconomica*, **35** (3), 223–33.

Steedman, I. (1992), 'Introduction', in P.H. Wicksteed, *The Coordination of the Laws of Distribution*, Aldershot, UK and Brookfield, VT, USA: Edward Elgar.

Stigler, J. (1941), *Production and Distribution Theories. The Formative Period*, New York: Macmillan.

Turgot, A.-R.-J. (1766), *Réflexions sur la formation et la distribution des richesses*, in R.L. Meek (ed.) (1973), *Turgot on Progress, Sociology and Economics*, Cambridge: Cambridge University Press.

Uzawa, H. (1958), 'A note on the Menger–Wieser theory of imputation', *Zeitschrift für Nationalökonomie*, **18** (3), pp. 318–34.

Wicksell, K. (1893), *Über Wert, Kapital und Rente*, Jena: G. Fischer, English trans. S.H. Frowein (1954), *Value, Capital and Rent*, London: Allen and Unwin.

Wicksell, K. (1901), *Lectures on Political Economy*, English trans. E. Classen (1934), ed. and intro. by L. Robbins, London: Routledge.

Wicksteed, P.H. (1889), 'On certain passages of Jevons's "Theory of political economy"', *Quarterly Journal of Economics*, **3** (3), 293–314.

Wicksteed, P.H. (1894), *The Coordination of the Laws of Distribution*, revised edn 1992 with intro. by I. Steedman, Aldershot, UK and Brookfield, VT, USA: Edward Elgar.

Wieser, F. von (1884), *Über den Ursprung und die Hauptgesetze des wirtschaftlichen Wertes*, Vienna: Hölder.

Wieser, F. von (1889), *Der natürliche Wert*, English trans. 1893, *Natural Value*, London: Macmillan.

Industrial organization

> Are you seriously proposing that we abandon the concept of perfect competition, the theory of general equilibrium and the New Welfare Economics associated with perfectly competitive general equilibrium? Yes, that is precisely what I am proposing . . . But what are we then left with? We are left with the content of every chapter in every textbook on imperfect or monopolistic competition, on oligopoly, duopoly and monopoly, in short, on Industrial Organization as a sub-discipline in economics. (Blaug 1997: 79–80)

As one can see from Mark Blaug's quotation, industrial organization (IO) deals with imperfectly competitive markets. The discipline was founded in the 1930s, but before reconstructing its history it is useful to identify in detail its content, its tools, and its aims in the tables of contents of the three volumes of the *Handbook of Industrial Organization* (Schmalensee and Willig 1989; Armstrong and Porter 2007). They are:

> Technological determinants of firm and industry structure – The theory of the firm – Transaction cost economics – Vertical integration – Non-cooperative game theory for IO – Theories of oligopoly behavior – Cartels, collusion, and horizontal merger – Mobility barriers and the value of incumbency – Predation, monopolization, and antitrust – Price discrimination – Vertical contractual relations – Product differentiation – Imperfect information in the product market – The timing of innovation – The theory and the facts of how markets clear – Inter-industry studies of structure and performance – Empirical studies of industries with market power – Empirical studies of innovation and market structure – Applications of experimental methods – Industrial organization and international trade – International differences in industrial organization – Economic perspectives on the politics of regulation – Optimal policies for natural monopolies – Design of regulatory mechanisms and institutions – The effects of economic regulation – The economics of health, safety and environmental regulation – The theory of regulation – Advertising – Empirical models of entry and market structure – Applied dynamic analysis in IO – Coordination and lock-in: competition with switching costs and network effects – Auctions – Foreclosure – Price discrimination and competition – Market structure – Antitrust policy toward horizontal mergers.

This list gives the topics of today's IO. This entry, as some other histories of the discipline (De Jong and Shepherd 2007; Bianchi 2013), will go no further than the early 1980s, so only some of these topics will be dealt with. However, other issues that today no longer belong to this field will be included. Specifically, apart from the occasional reference to later developments, all the subjects examined here are dealt with prior to the revolution in the discipline due to the introduction of game theory in the 1980s. To start with, a review of the economists' ideas before the foundation of IO in the 1930s will help to find its historical roots.

Pre-History (before 1890)

The first considerations on some of the topics just listed were already present in the Scholastics or especially in Richard Cantillon. We start with the classical economists here, but before examining their ideas it must be recalled that the present notion of perfect competition was fully defined only in the 1930s (Machovec 1995): before that, competition was treated as an activity, and competing meant undertaking strategies to obtain monopoly power, that is, the power to set prices so as to make positive extra profits. As we shall see, this conception of competition largely corresponds to the content of today's IO.

Classical political economy

In the classical economists' works there are many descriptions of the ways firms compete, of the obstacles they encounter in competing, and of the sources of their monopoly power (Backhouse 1990). A brief review of the classical ideas on these topics starts in 1776 with Adam Smith, who regarded competition as a race among rivals. He showed that if the number of entrepreneurs is small this facilitates coalitions, and highlighted their propensity to contrive to raise prices; he also suggested that secrets and collusion could be used to compete and to obtain market power. In particular, he saw imperfect factor mobility and inelastic input supply as sources of monopoly power that cannot be removed (Salvadori and Signorino 2013). In 1803 Jean-Baptiste Say brought the primacy of the entrepreneur's role both as a risk taker and as a manager into focus. In 1815 Thomas Robert Malthus introduced the expression "natural monopoly", applied to cases where natural inputs are in limited supply, while Samuel Bailey (in 1825) defined "monopolies" as the markets with restricted entry and one or more competing sellers; he also identified the markets in which the incumbents have a cost advantage over the new entrants, and highlighted the role of potential competition. In 1836 Nassau W. Senior saw the introduction of innovations as a way of competing, and considered the unavailability of information on profits as a source of market power. Although the literature insistently recalls that in classical thinking the restraints on competition not created by the government had importance only in the short run, John Stuart Mill believed that certain obstacles would last longer: in 1848 he identified situations of natural monopoly in the modern meaning, agreed with Smith that the small number facilitates collusion, and described many restraints on competition in practice, the best known of which are customs. However, he was confident that a certain amount of competition would take place even among a few producers, and saw innovation as due to the entrepreneur's effort to survive. In 1867 Karl Marx foresaw that in capitalism competition would lead to an increasing concentration and centralization of capital, forming large firms with growing monopoly power, while John Elliot Cairnes (in 1874) was interested specifically in cases of "non-competing groups", that is, producer groups within which there could be competition, but between which competition was impossible.

To sum up, classical economists had singled out a series of strategies for competing, as well as some obstacles to the competitive process. As they believed in the ability of markets in conditions of free competition to self-regulate, they usually considered the monopoly power resulting from firm's strategies as threatened by competition, both actual and potential. Competition was considered a very widespread phenomenon, as long as the market was free from legal restraints. This conception is further confirmed by the fact that in their writings comparatively little room is devoted to the specific subject of monopoly as such.

Pre-marginalism

In the writings of the so-called pre-marginalists the foundations are laid for competition considered as the specific market structure in which prices rapidly converge towards production costs. They determined the equilibrium prices and quantities in monopoly and duopoly markets. Before looking at the thought of Antoine-Augustin Cournot, who can be credited with most of the formal basis of the discipline, the pioneering contribution to urban economics made in 1826 by Johann Heinrich von Thünen should be mentioned, although today spatial economics no longer belongs to IO, but to economic geography. In 1838 Cournot started his analysis with the monopolist profit-maximization problem, then elaborated a duopoly model in which firms compete in quantity. Adding more firms to his model, he showed that "unlimited" competition (*concurrence indéfinie*) is reached if the number of firms becomes infinite. He also stated that, if the marginal cost function is decreasing, a monopoly will occur. The pre-marginalist era was dominated by engineer-economists (Ekelund and Hébert 1999): in 1839 Charles Ellet developed a duopoly model with price conjectures; in 1844 Jules Dupuit calculated the deadweight loss due to monopoly pricing, initiated the theory of price discrimination, indicated a number of deterrents to entry in the transport sector, and identified the transport network as a natural monopoly (Mosca 1998); in 1850 Dionysius Lardner represented the model of monopoly profit maximization in a diagram. The lawyer Edwin Chadwick must also be mentioned here for proposing and supporting (in 1859) the principle of "competition for the field" (competitive bedding) in those cases where competition within the market was considered impossible.

The Historical School
The second half of the nineteenth century was a kind of crossroads for a variety of methodological positions. One controversy took place between classical thought and the German historical school, which applied the historical method to economic research. Its members denied the universality of economic laws, rejected any theoretical approach to knowledge, and supported empirical analysis. At the level of economic policy they advocated an active role for the government. This doctrine became the dominant economic paradigm in many European countries before the spread of marginalism. In those years many American economists studied in European universities and became historicists, deeply influencing the birth of the American Institutionalist School. As will be seen below, some historicists, such as John Bates Clark and Richard T. Ely, played a role in the foundation of IO (Hovenkamp 1991). For a long time classical and pre-marginalist theories coexisted with historical studies based on historical and empirical analysis.

Marginalism
In the 1870s and 1880s the controversy between the classical and the historical school also had to face the challenge of the marginalist paradigm that was slowly gaining ground (Steedman 1995). As for its contribution to the field of IO, it has to be remembered that in 1871 William Stanley Jevons defined a perfect market as a market in which there is perfect knowledge, "perfectly free" competition (in the meaning of free entry), and no conspiracies by sellers. In contrast, in the same year Carl Menger, the founder of the Austrian school, regarded monopoly as one of the expressions of the competitive process, just like the classical thinkers. One significant aspect of this period concerns the history of the analytical tools used by economists: von Thünen, Cournot, Ellet, Dupuit and Lardner had used mathematics, leaving an inheritance of methods, tools and results to those who came after them; therefore some of the theoretical developments in IO came about through the logical necessity imposed by the formal tools they employed. This is

the case of Francis Y. Edgeworth, who in 1881, following up on Cournot, set out the first duopoly model of price competition with product homogeneity. Edgeworth was also the first to list certain conditions needed in order to compete, namely, free communication, divisibility of goods, and a large number of sellers. Joseph L.F. Bertrand is also linked to Cournot: he is credited with the formulation in 1883 of the price undercutting mechanism as an alternative to quantity competition. Actually, Bertrand wrongly attributed to Cournot a confusion between quantity and price competition; but in fact the paternity of the formal treatment of price competition is to be attributed to Wilhelm Launhardt in 1885, whose duopoly model with horizontal differentiation produces a price equilibrium which encompasses the so-called Bertrand paradox (Lambertini and Mosca 2015). In 1889 Rudolf Auspitz and Richard Lieben, who also built on the mathematical work of the previous generation, incorporated monopoly into a general equilibrium framework (Niehans 1990). To sum up, in this decade the idea of different market structures made headway, without however crowding out the classical idea of competition as a dynamic process.

Proto-History (from 1890 to 1930)

From the point of view of the history of IO, 1890 was a very important year both in Europe and in the US. In Europe it was the year when Alfred Marshall's *Principles of Economics* was published, giving rise to neoclassical economics; in the US it was the year of the introduction of the Sherman Act, the first antitrust law. From 1890 to 1930 the focus on issues that today belong to IO increased for two different kinds of reason. The first concerns the economic situation: new phenomena like trusts, cartels, mergers, the vertical integration of firms, public utilities, and the railways, raised new problems. Compared with the world of the classical economist, the provisional character of the obstacles to competition no longer seemed to apply; in certain cases entering a market turned out to be very difficult even in the absence of legal barriers; market power, whether generated by strategies or obstacles, proved to be long lasting. Faced with these new phenomena, economists tried to understand why in certain markets there were few firms, if they should be worried about their size, whether this was on the contrary an advantage, or whether one could count on their reciprocal rivalry. The second kind of reason is linked to method: in the light of the emerging neoclassical notion of perfect competition, all strategic behaviours of firms were interpreted as a sign of monopoly, and no longer as an expression of competitive behaviour; as such, once again, though for other reasons, it caused concern.

Marshall

In 1890 Alfred Marshall, like the classical economists, was still confident that the race of competition could take place, on condition there was a sufficient degree of knowledge and no agreements among firms. However, his biological analogy of the firm, that is, the metaphor of the young trees of the forest struggling with their older rivals, was unsuitable for dealing with the phenomenon of the big industrial concentrations. In fact, in later editions of his *Principles* he was less optimistic about competition: for instance, he recognized the effect of economies of scale on the size of big business units, and described some firms' strategies to drive competitors out of the market. Most of the topics that belong to today's IO, such as vertical and horizontal integration, innovation, the behaviour of oligopolistic firms and regulation, can be found in his 1919 *Industry and Trade* (Phillips and Stevenson 1974). It should also be remembered that it was from Marshall that we got the concept itself of industry, which is the basis of the discipline; as a matter of fact, without the Marshallian conception of industry "the field of Industrial Organization is a wilderness" (Mason 1957, 5). Marshall is important in this context not only directly, but also indirectly because he inspired some criticisms from Piero Sraffa, which opened the way to the theory of imperfect competition. Marshall's importance can also be seen from the fact that we talk about a Marshallian approach to IO, as juxtaposed to the American line. It includes the concept of industrial districts, which brings sociological and cultural aspects to bear on economic theory (Becattini 1990), while a different approach to clusters is today part of economic geography. In Europe the field of IO even had a different name, which was inspired by Marshall, namely, industrial economics.

Scale, scope and network economies

In the same year of Marshall's *Principles*, the Italian public economist Antonio De Viti de Marco, in dealing with the telephone industry, recognized for the first time in the literature the network effects: he wrote that utility increases with the number of subscribers with whom consumers can communicate; he also saw this phenomenon as a source of monopoly power. In 1896–97 Vilfredo Pareto defined competition as the situation in which firms are price-takers, and monopoly as the situation in which firms are price-setters. He also analysed the spontaneous formation of industrial combinations, and was convinced that without the support of government (which he decidedly opposed) they could not last. In 1896 Arthur T. Hadley, in the US, dealt with the effects of the time needed to enter a market, developed the theory of "ruinous competition" for firms with high fixed costs, and described the process by which price competition between two firms in a natural monopoly leads to the survival of a single firm. In 1899 J.B. Clark added two more conditions to those suggested by Edgeworth, in the direction of defining perfect competition: the instantaneous mobility of resources and the identification of competition with a stationary equilibrium. He was a specialist on trusts, which he analysed with the historical as well as the marginalist method. At first he very much believed in the effectiveness of the threat of entry by new firms, and on this basis he criticized antitrust laws; but later he recognized the dangerous role of firms' strategies designed to eliminate potential competition and called for more government control.

Strategies and market structures

In the 1910s further competition strategies were discussed, and the features typifying different market structures were identified with growing precision. In 1900 Ely grasped the monopolistic nature of trademarks, stated that substitute goods reduce market power and that economies of scale are a deterrent to entry. He dealt with natural monopoly and consolidated the use of this expression in its modern meaning. His studies in Germany influenced his favourable view of an active economic role of the government. In the same year William M. Collier understood the strategic role of excess capacity, while in 1901 Knut Wicksell advanced a great deal further along the path towards defining perfect competition; he also provided an example of imperfect competition due to large overhead costs, joint supply, and location. In 1903 Maffeo Pantaleoni put forward an articulate analysis of horizontal as well as vertical integration, and regarded the latter with approval; he was against antitrust laws, considering them an unfair persecution of firms. In 1909 Pantaleoni also analysed in depth the effect of overhead costs on the size of firms. The American economist Henry Ludwell Moore, in 1906, in the first article explicitly devoted to the issue of competition, provided a new list of necessary prerequisites for defining a perfectly competitive market. As for the identification of market structures, a crucial role was played in 1908 by Enrico Barone: he gave the analytical definition of the minimum efficient scale and the optimal number of firms. He was also the first to work out a rigorous description of the characteristics of costs and demand that give rise to a situation of natural monopoly (Mosca 2008). The drawing of the first diagram with U-shaped cost curves was owed in 1911–13 to Edgeworth, and he showed for the first time in the literature how, in the case of natural monopoly, the demand function intersects the average cost curve in its downward sloping portion. In 1912 Irving Fisher discussed the idea of a separate market for each seller, while in the same year Arthur Cecil Pigou introduced the idea of "monopolistic" competition as opposed to "simple" competition. Henry Carter Adams, after having (in 1887) analysed the effects on market structure of different returns to scale, in 1918 stated that firm size is the cause of monopoly power. He was in favour of state intervention, the role of which he defined in detail. While market structures were being identified with growing precision, competition continued to be treated mostly in behavioural terms, as had been the case since the beginning of economic thought.

The emergence of the concept of perfect competition

Finally, the credit of making the first effort to set down a set of conditions for perfect competition goes to Frank Knight (in 1921), and it should also be noted that he himself did not believe in it. He prepared the way for the definition of perfect competition, as well as for the reaction in the 1930s against the theory of perfectly competitive markets. In 1923 John Maurice Clark emphasized that the presence of scale economies due to overhead costs would weaken potential competition and criticized the "ruinous competition" theory. He was so strongly in favour of a considerable state intervention that in 1912, in the revised edition of his father's book, now co-authored by both of them, the previous criticisms of antitrust action disappeared. As already mentioned, in 1926 Sraffa criticized Marshall, showing the incompatibility of scale economies with perfect competition, and suggested abandoning the hypothesis of perfectly competitive markets: in the 1930s his criticism opened the way to Joan Robinson's (1933) imperfect competition revolution. Just before this revolution, the history of the attempts to determine equilibrium prices and quantities in imperfectly competitive markets went on with Harald Hotelling (in 1929), who built a model of spatially differentiated duopoly. To sum up, before 1930 the economists' treatment of hybrid situations between monopoly and perfect competition was much broader than that of the two extreme cases, one of which (perfect competition) had not yet been put forward.

Policy implications

As for the policy implications of the theories just surveyed, the economists' reactions to the antitrust laws have already been mentioned. When the Sherman Act was passed in 1890, with the intention of defending small businesses from the price policies of the trusts that had formed in the previous 20 years, there was a critical reaction from the economists (DiLorenzo and High 1988). Many of them welcomed large-size firms for their efficiency gains; as already seen, they very much believed in the effectiveness of the threat of entry by new firms. However, in the following decades the economists acknowledged that exclusionary practices played a dangerous role; this mitigated their faith in potential competition, and led them to call for greater government intervention in controlling firms' strategies against potential competition, and in regulating public utilities and transportation.

In summary, although the real history of the discipline had not yet officially begun, we find here a great number of issues that today are part of the realm of IO. They were intensely debated in Europe as well as in the US. As the notion of perfect competition was worked out, the boundary of IO was defined, and the classical idea of competition was shifted into this "new" discipline.

The Official Birth of IO (from 1930 to 1950)

The history of IO officially began in the 1930s. There are three places that can be considered the most significant birthplaces of the discipline: one was Cambridge (UK) with J. Robinson (in 1933), and the other two were in the US, at Harvard with Edward H. Chamberlin (in 1933) and Edward S. Mason (in 1939), and at Chicago with Henry C. Simons (in 1934).

The revolution of imperfect competition

In the UK, Joan Robinson's theory of non-perfect competition arose from the criticism that Sraffa had made of Marshall's theory in 1926. She developed her new theory assuming that every firm faces a downward sloping demand curve owing to the monopoly power given by product differentiation. At Harvard in the same period, independently of Joan Robinson, Chamberlin came up with a similar theory, the theory of monopolistic competition, based on totally different roots, namely the literature on railroad economics. Joan Robinson and Chamberlin's recognition of the importance of product differentiation marked the shift of their theory away from a concept of perfect competition that they themselves had worked out. According to this concept, which was far more restricted than Knight's, perfect competition was the market structure in which a seller faces a perfectly elastic (horizontal) demand curve. This was how the boundary between perfect and imperfect competition was established, giving rise to a new discipline dealing with the latter. However, as seen above, essentially the notion of imperfect competition has always existed, although mainly informally, right from the beginning of economic thought.

The structure–conduct–performance approach

Still at Harvard, in the 1930s and 1940s, Mason adopted an approach based on case studies. From this applied approach there emerged an analytical framework known as Structure–Conduct–Performance (S–C–P) which dominated IO studies until the early 1970s. This paradigm explained the working of imperfectly competitive markets by means of the hypothesis that industry structure (concentration) affects the firm's conduct (pricing behaviour), which in turn influences the industry performance (profits).

To verify the hypothesis of a causal relation between market structure and performance, Mason and his group of scholars classified many industries into different market structures. Thanks also to the concept of "workable competition" expressed by J.M. Clark in 1940 as a useful operational instrument for the measurement of the strength of real competition, the S–C–P paradigm led to a great many cross-industry studies. On grounds of economic policy, this approach, with its emphasis on market structures, provided a persuasive theoretical justification for antitrust interventions designed to reduce firms' market shares. In these years alone, many antitrust actions based on this approach were undertaken with the aim of enforcing de-concentration policies (Kovacic and Shapiro 2000).

Chicago

Besides Cambridge (UK) and Harvard, the third birthplace of IO was Chicago: in the 1930s and 1940s its main exponents were Simons, Knight, and Jacob Viner. Relative to their time, they were laissez-faire oriented economists, in the sense of being opposed to collectivism and government planning. They considered competition desirable for reasons political and social, not just economic. However, these scholars advocated a positive role for the government, although strictly confined to the preservation of competition conditions in the markets. So at this time it was not just Harvard, but also Chicago that advocated an active antitrust role.

Other approaches

Apart from these approaches, there were some other interesting developments. One was the attempt in 1940 to work out a general equilibrium theory under monopolistic competition by Robert Triffin. Unlike Mason, he worked on the more theoretical aspects of Chamberlin's revolution (Corley 1990), but his generalization of the Walrasian theory was considered too abstract to deal with the problems of IO, which revolved around the Marshallian category of industry. Owing to its great abstraction, it is still the general equilibrium theorists who work on this line of research today, rather than industrial economists. A second development taking place outside the structuralist and the Chicago approaches was Joseph Alois Schumpeter's dynamic theory of competition, in which competition comes about through the introduction of innovations. The 1942 version of this theory states that the main sources of innovation are large-size firms, because it is their monopolistic position which favours innovations. The theory of dynamic competition lets us envisage a role for the antitrust policy that is very different from what was current at that time: to enhance economic welfare, in fact, the monopolistic power of large-scale enterprises should have been regarded favourably. The last development, to mention it briefly, is the innovative theory of the nature of the firm by Ronald H. Coase (in 1937), a British economist who in the 1960s was to become a leading exponent of the Chicago school.

Harvard versus Chicago (from 1950 to 1970)

In the 1950s and 1960s the scene was dominated by the Harvard approach: consequently government interventions intensified, taking the forms of nationalization, regulation and antitrust action. In the meantime, the Chicago position became more radical, giving rise to a clash between the two schools of thought. These two decades also saw important developments in the theory of oligopoly.

The dominance of the S–C–P approach

Joe Bain was one of those scholars who, in the 1930s at Harvard, had belonged to Mason's group (Grether 1970). Thanks to Bain, the S–C–P approach became the dominant paradigm in IO. In Bain's studies the incumbents' above-normal profits do not induce potential competitors to enter a market because of the presence of barriers to entry: in his statistical results entry barriers were positively correlated with high profits. As shown in the previous sections, the concept of barriers to entry was not a novelty for the discipline, but Bain is usually considered its originator (Mosca 2009). In 1956, he identified three sources of entry barriers, that is, scale economies, absolute-cost advantages, and product differentiation, the latter being the most significant. If monopolistic power depends on market structure, and if the market is concentrated due to entry barriers, then competition policies are needed. The impact on antitrust policy of Bain's structuralist theory of markets was pervasive: these two decades are often called the golden era for antitrust de-concentration policies.

The new Chicago School

In the same period, in Chicago a new free-market oriented school was strongly opposing the Harvard structuralist view. The exponents of the new Chicago School, like Milton Friedman and George J. Stigler, by comparison to the previous generation, had radicalized their emphasis on the desirability of competition, and attacked the S–C–P paradigm advocates on several points. They suggested a different interpretation of the data, claiming that the link between concentration and profitability put forward by the S–C–P paradigm had to be interpreted differently: for them firms were large and profitable because they were more efficient; the new Chicago scholars interpreted the high profit rates in industries supplied by a small number of firms as an effect of efficiency, and not of monopoly power. The direction of the causal mechanism from market structure to performance attributed to the S–C–P paradigm was reversed: it is the performance of firms which affects their behaviour and modifies market structure, not vice-versa. For them entry conditions are endogenous, and change according to a firm's behaviour, so market structure spontaneously adjusts to its most efficient configuration. The S–C–P approach was also criticized by advocates of the new Chicago School for another reason: not only did they claim that the Harvard interpretation of the data was wrong, but also that the empirical method in itself needed to be replaced by a rigorous theoretical approach. The approach they adopted was the neoclassical theory of perfect competition, and they accordingly treated most of the real markets as if they were at their perfectly competitive equilibrium values – the so-called "good approximation assumption". A very important bone of contention between the two schools was antitrust policy, as on this ground the new Chicago School deeply diverged not only from Harvard position, but even from the positive role for the government advocated by Simons and the first Chicago School. On the basis of their trust in the efficiency of the markets, the new Chicago scholars attacked all kind of de-concentration policies previously adopted, and starting from the 1970s their influence on antitrust decisions was increasingly strong (Martin 2007).

Oligopoly theories

After Chamberlin's 1929 model of "mutual dependence recognized", after Heinrich von Stackelberg's 1934 duopoly model, after Paul M. Sweezy's 1939 "kinked-demand curve" theory, and after the influential book *Competition Among the Few* (1949) by William Fellner, a ground-breaking approach to oligopoly theory emerged between 1956 and 1958 from Bain, Paolo Sylos-Labini, and Franco Modigliani. Sylos-Labini had denounced the lack of a rigorous theory of oligopoly; he claimed that the monopolistic nature of giant firms had always been regarded as a problem by the economists of the past, but that the imperfect competition revolution had shifted the focus towards the market power of very small firms, distracting theoretical research from the question of monopoly power in concentrated industries. With its "limit pricing" model, the new approach assumed that a monopolist, or a number of oligopolists, can set a price sufficiently low to deter the entry of new firms. Here not only actual, but also potential competition affects a firm's conduct, which in turn determines market structure. In this model we find a formalization of the old idea that the threat by potential competitors disciplines the incumbent's behaviour.

Another important contribution to the theory of oligopoly came from Stigler (in 1964), the most influential economist of the new Chicago school, who attributed a crucial role to information in oligopolistic markets: he emphasized that when information about firms' behaviour is lacking, collusion cannot be effective, because it is difficult to detect "secret price-cutting". Stigler's article greatly contributed to the change in the antitrust attitude, especially in the merger area. Before Stigler, in 1950 Tibor Scitovsky had already stressed the importance of asymmetric information as a source of market power; but it was after Stigler that information started to play a pivotal role, which is still central today in the new IO.

The 1950s and 1960s were also very important for the development of game theory, a branch of mathematics used to model strategic behaviour. Its earliest applications to economics were made in the 1940s by John von Neumann and Oskar Morgenstern, and then by John Nash in 1950 who introduced his famous notion of equilibrium, but as we shall see, it was only after its extensions and refinements by Reinhard Selten (in 1965) and John C. Harsanyi (in 1967–68) that John F. Nash's concept of equilibrium was definitely adopted by industrial economists (Giocoli 2009).

The New IO Theory (from 1970)

As seen above, in the previous two decades there were many different theories of oligopoly. However, a unified approach was about to be adopted, thanks to the extraordinary spread of game theory, eventually employed by economists to model the strategic interdependence characterizing oligopolistic markets.

Game theory applied to economics became the standard tool of IO only in the late 1970s. Various reasons have been given as to why it took this branch of mathematics over 30 years to become the general analytical framework for dealing with the strategic interaction of firms (Giocoli 2009; Lambertini 2011: ch. 1). Whatever the real cause of this delay, the new method adopted after the game theory revolution made a decisive contribution to re-establishing the theoretical foundations of the discipline. It made it possible to move on from both the S–C–P paradigm and the Chicago school theories through the use of models of strategic interaction in which firms' behaviour is explained as the outcome of their rational choices. Here it is firms' conduct that has the pivotal role: it affects both performances and market structures. Focusing on the strategic contexts in which the potential entrants and the incumbents operate, its main concern is with endogenous, not exogenous barriers to entry. Thanks to game theory, imperfect competitive markets can finally be investigated with the use of a unified formal method.

The success of game theory has also led to a change on the policy side. In the 1970s and 1980s antitrust policy was dominated by the laissez-faire orientation of the new Chicago school. As we have seen, its advocates claimed that concentration is dictated by efficiency rather than by market power. Therefore, many practices were considered to be pro-competitive, and government intervention unnecessary. At the end of the 1970s this free-market orientation was also strengthened by the contestable market theory (elaborated by William Baumol, John C. Panzar and Robert D. Willig in 1982), whose fundamental idea was that the threat of new entry compels firms to behave according to the principles of the perfect competitive model. Hence, its policy implication was that monopoly power has no damaging effects in contestable markets, and there is no need for government intervention. Consequently, a wave of deregulation started in the 1980s, in airlines and in the telecommunication industry.

However, during the same decade, the game theory approach to IO showed that monopoly power might persist under free entry "if sunk costs are important, if consumers have switching costs, if there are network externalities, and if a monopolist can engage in anti-competitive practices" (Motta 2004: 71). This perspective, also called the post-Chicago approach, confirmed many structuralist prescriptions, re-stating that high profit rates in concentrated industries may be a sign of monopoly power, not only of efficiency (Grillo 2006).

Conclusion

In 1954, many years before game theory was adopted by industrial economists, Schumpeter had defined as "the principle of excluded strategy" the assumption of price-taking behaviour which had been adopted at one point in the history of economic thought to characterize competition. This implies that for him the previous concept of competition included strategy. This is what we intended to show here: the idea of competition as strategic behaviour used by IO is among the oldest notions in the history of economic thought, and game theory has supplied some tools to deal formally with an idea that has always existed.

MANUELA MOSCA

See also:

Enrico Barone (I); British classical political economy (II); British marginalism (II); Cambridge School of Economics (II); Edward Hastings Chamberlin (I); Chicago School (II); John Bates Clark (I); Competition (III); Antoine-Augustin Cournot (I); Economic geography (III); Francis Ysidro Edgeworth (I); Game Theory (III); Historical economics (II); Institutionalism (II); Frank Knight (I); Alfred Marshall (I); John Stuart Mill (I); John Forbes Nash Jr (I); John von Neumann (I); Joan Violet Robinson (I); Adam Smith (I); Piero Sraffa (I); Heinrich von Stackelberg (I); Theory of the firm (III).

References and further reading

Adams, H.C. (1887), *Relation of the State to Industrial Action*, reprinted in J. Dorfman (ed.) (1969), *Two Essays by Henry Carter Adams*, New York: A.M. Kelley.

Adams, H.C. (1918), *Description of Industry*, New York: Holt.

Armstrong, M. and R. Porter (2007), *Handbook of Industrial Organization*, 3 vols, Amsterdam: North-Holland, III.

Auspitz, R. and R. Lieben (1889), *Untersuchungen über die Theorie des Preises*, Leipzig: Verlag von Duncker & Humblot.

Backhouse, R.E. (1990), 'Competition', in J. Creedy (ed.), *Foundations of Economic Thought*, Oxford, Blackwell, pp. 58–86.

Bailey, S. (1825), *A Critical Dissertation on the Nature, Measures and Causes of Value*, reprinted 1931, London: London School of Economics.

Bain, J.S. (1956), *Barriers to New Competition*, Cambridge, MA: Harvard University Press.

Barone, E. (1908), *Principi di economia politic*, reprinted 1936 in *Le opere economiche*, vol. 2, Bologna: Zanichelli.

Baumol, W., J.C. Panzar and R.D. Willig (1982), *Contestable Markets and the Theory of Industry Structure*, New York: Harcourt Brace Jovanovich.

Becattini, G. (1990), 'The Marshallian industrial district as a socio-economic concept', in F. Pyke, G. Becattini and W. Sengenberger (eds), *Industrial Districts and Inter-form Cooperation in Italy*, Geneva: IILS, pp. 37–51.

Bertrand, J.L.F. (1883), 'Théorie des Richesses: revue de Théories mathématiques de la richesse sociale par Léon Walras et Recherches sur les principes de la théorie des richesses par Augustin Cournot', *Journal des Savants*, **68**, 499–508.

Bianchi, P. (2013), 'Bain and the origins of industrial economics', *European Review of Industrial Economics and Policy*, **7**, accessed 18 January 2016 at http://revel.unice.fr/eriep/index.html?id=3608.

Blaug, M. (1997), 'Competition as an end-state and competition as a process', in M. Blaug, *Not Only an Economist*, Cheltenham, UK and Brookfield, VT, USA: Edward, Elgar, pp. 66–86.

Cairnes, J.E. (1874), *Some Leading Principles of Political Economy*, London: Macmillan.

Cantillon, R. (1755), *Essai Sur la Nature du Commerce en Général*, English trans. H. Higgs (2001), *Essay on the Nature of Commerce in General*, New Brunswick, NJ: Transaction.

Chadwick, E. (1859), 'Results of different principles of legislation and administration in Europe; of competition for the field, as compared with competition within the field, of service', *Journal of the Statistical Society of London*, **22** (3), 381–420.

Chamberlin, E.H. (1929), 'Duopoly: value where sellers are few', *Quarterly Journal of Economics*, **44** (November), 63–100.

Chamberlin, E.H. (1933), *The Theory of Monopolistic Competition*, Cambridge, MA: Harvard University Press.

Clark, J.B. (1899), *The Distribution of Wealth: A Theory of Wages, Interest and Profits*, reprinted 1908, New York: Macmillan.

Clark, J.B. and J.M. Clark (1912), *The Control of Trusts*, New York: Macmillan.

Clark, J.M. (1923), *Studies in the Economics of Overhead Costs*, Chicago: University of Chicago Press.

Clark, J.M. (1940), 'Towards a concept of workable competition', *American Economic Review*, **30** (2), 241–56.

Coase, R.H. (1937), 'The nature of the firm', *Economica*, **4** (16), 386–405.

Collier, W.M. (1900), *The Trusts: What Can We Do with Them – What Can They Do for Us?*, New York: The Baker and Taylor Company.

Corley, T.A.B. (1990), 'Emergence of the theory of industrial organization, 1890–1990', *Business and Economic History*, **19**, 83–92.

Cournot, A.A. (1838), *Recherches sur les principes mathématiques de la théorie des richesses*, Paris, English trans. N.T. Bacon (1897), *Researches into the Mathematical Principles of the Theory of Wealth*, New York: Macmillan.

De Jong, H.W. and W.G. Shepherd (2007), *Pioneers of Industrial Organization*, Cheltenham UK and Northampton, MA, USA: Edward Elgar.

De Viti de Marco, A. (1890), 'L'industria del telefoni e l'esercizio di Stato', *Giornale degli Economisti*, September, 279–306. English trans. 'The telephone industry and state exercise of Said', in M. Baldassarri and P. Ciocca (eds) (2001), *Roots of the Italian School of Economics and Finance: From Ferrara (1857) to Einaudi (1944)*, vol. 3, New York: Palgrave, pp. 505–29.

DiLorenzo, T.J. and J.C. High (1988), 'Antitrust and competition historically considered', *Economic Inquiry*, **26**, (July), 423–35.

Dupuit, J. (1844), 'De la mesure de l'utilité des travaux publics', *Annales des Ponts et Chaussées*, s. II, 2nd semester, 332–75, English trans. R.H. Barback (1952), 'On the measurement of the utility of public works', in *International Economic Papers*, no. 2, London: Macmillan.

Edgeworth, F.Y. (1881), *Mathematical Psychic*, London: Kegan Paul.

Edgeworth, F.Y. (1911–13), 'Contribution to the theory of railway rates', *The Economic Journal*, **21** (83), 346–70, **21** (84), 551–71, **22** (86), 198–218, **23** (90), 206–26.

Ekelund, R.B. and R.F. Hébert (1999), *Secret Origins of Modern Microeconomics*, Chicago, IL and London: The University of Chicago Press.

Ellet, C. (1839), *An Essay on the Laws of the Trade in Reference to the Works of Internal Improvement in the United States*, Richmond, VA: P.D. Bernard, reprinted 1966, New York: A.M. Kelley.

Ely, R.T. (1900), *Monopolies and Trusts*, New York: Macmillan.

Fellner, W. (1949), *Competition among the Few*, New York: Knopf.

Fisher, I. (1912), *Elementary Principles of Economics*, New York: Macmillan.

Giocoli, N. (2009), 'Three alternative (?) stories on the late 20th-century rise of game theory', *Studi e Note di Economia*, **14** (2), 187–210.

Grether, E.T. (1970), 'Industrial organization: past history and future problems', *The American Economic Review*, **60** (2), 83–9.

Grillo, M. (2006), 'The theory and practice of antitrust: a perspective in the history of economic ideas', *Storia del Pensiero Economico*, **3** (2), 33–63.

Hadley, A.T. (1896), *Economics: An Account of the Relations between Private Property and Public Welfare*, New York: G.P. Putnam's Sons.

Harsanyi, J.C. (1967–68), 'Games with incomplete information played by "Bayesian"' Players, *Management Science*, **8**, 159–82, 320–34, 486–502.

Hotelling, H. (1929), 'Stability in competition', *Economic Journal*, **39** (153), 41–57.

Hovenkamp, H. (1991), *Enterprise and Americal Law 1836–1937*, Cambridge, MA: London: Harvard University Press.

Jevons, W.S. (1871), *Theory of Political Economy*, London: Macmillan.

Knight, F.H. (1921), *Risk, Uncertainty and Profit*, Boston, MA and New York: Houghton Mifflin.

Kovacic, W.E. and C. Shapiro (2000), 'Antitrust policy: a century of economic and legal thinking', *The Journal of Economic Perspective*, **14** (1), 43–60.

Lambertini, L. (2011), *Game Theory in the Social Sciences. A Reader-Friendly Guide*, London: Routledge.

Lambertini, L. and M. Mosca (2015), 'The Bertrand paradox, the useless auctioneer and the Launhardt model', *Australian Economic Papers*, **53** (3–4), 170–83.

Lardner, D. (1850), *Railway Economy*, New York: Harper & Brothers, reprinted 1968, New York: A.M. Kelley.

Launhardt, W. (1885), *Mathematische Begrundung der Volkswirtschaftslehre*, English trans. J. Creedy (ed.), (1992), *Mathematical Principles of Economics*, Aldershot, UK and Brookfield, VT, USA: Edward Elgar.

Machovec, F.M. (1995), *Perfect Competition and the Transformation of Economics*, London and New York: Routledge.

Malthus, T.R. (1815), *An Inquiry into the Nature and Progress of Rent, and the Principles by Which It Is Regulated*, reprinted 1969, New York: Greenwood Press.

Marshall, A. (1890), *Principles of Economics*, London: Macmillan.

Marshall, A. (1919), *Industry and Trade*, London: Macmillan.

Martin, S. (2007), 'Remembrance of things past: antitrust, ideology, and the development of industrial economics', in V. Ghosal and J. Stennek (eds), *The Political Economy of Antitrust*, Amsterdam: Elsevier, pp. 25–57.

Marx, K. (1867), *Capital; a Critique of Political Economy*, vol. 1, *The Process of Capitalist Production*, reprinted 2008, Chicago, IL: C.H. Kerr & Co.

Mason, E.S. (1939), 'Price and production policies of large-scale enterprise', *American Economic Review*, **29** (1), 61–74.

Mason, E.S. (1957), *Economic Concentration and the Monopoly Problem*, Cambridge, MA: Harvard University Press.

Menger, C. (1871), *Grundsätze der Volkswirthschaftslehre*, Vienna: Braumüller. English trans. *Principles of Economics*, New York: New York University.

Mill, J.S. (1848), *The Principles of Political Economy: With Some of their Applications to Social Philosophy*, reprinted 1849, London: John W. Parker.

Modigliani, F. (1958), 'New developments on the oligopoly front', *Journal of Political Economy*, **66**, 215–32.

Moore, H.L. (1906), 'Paradoxes of competition', *Quarterly Journal of Economics*, **20** (2), 211–30.

Mosca, M. (1998), 'Jules Dupuit, the French 'Ingénieurs-Économistes' and the Société d'Économie Politique', in G. Faccarello (ed.), *Studies in the History of French Political Economy: From Bodin to Walras*, London: Routledge, pp. 254–83.

Mosca, M. (2008), 'On the origins of the concept of natural monopoly', in *The European Journal of the History of Economic Thought*, **15** (2), 317–53.

Mosca, M. (2009), 'The sources of monopoly power before Bain (1956)', Department of Economics, Working paper Paper no.112/46, University of Salento.

Motta, M. (2004), *Competition Policy. Theory and Practice*, Cambridge: Cambridge University Press.
Nash, J.F. (1950), 'The bargaining problem', *Econometrica*, **18** (2), 155–62.
Neumann, J. von and O. Morgenstern (1944), *Theory of Games and Economic Behavior*, Princeton, NJ: Princeton University Press.
Niehans, J. (1990), *A History of Economic Theory*, Baltimore, MD and London: The Johns Hopkins University Press.
Pantaleoni, M. (1903), 'Alcune osservazioni sui sindacati e sulle leghe', *Giornale degli Economisti*, March, 236–65; April, 346–78; December, 560–81. English trans. 'Some observations on syndicates and associations', in M. Baldassarri and P. Ciocca (eds) (2001), *Roots of the Italian School of Economics and Finance: From Ferrara (1857) to Einaudi (1944)*, vol. 1, New York: Palgrave, pp. 131–214.
Pantaleoni, M. (1909), 'Di alcuni fenomeni di dinamica economica', *Giornale degli Economisti*, September, 211–54. English trans. 'Some phenomena of economic dynamics', *International Economic Papers*, no. 5. London: Macmillan, pp. 26–57.
Pareto, V. (1896–97), *Cours d'Économie politique*, Lausanne: F. Rouge.
Phillips, A. and R.E. Stevenson, (1974), 'The historical development of industrial organization', *History of Political Economy*, **6** (3), 324–42.
Pigou, A.C. (1912), *Wealth and Welfare*, London: Macmillan.
Robinson, J. (1933), *The Economics of Imperfect Competition*, 2nd edn 1969, London: Macmillan.
Salvadori, N. and R. Signorino (2013), 'The classical notion of competition revisited', *History of Political Economy*, **45** (1), 149–75.
Say, J.B. (1803), *Traité d'économie politique, ou, Simple exposition de la manière dont se forment, se distribuent et se consomment les richesses*, Paris: De Chapelet, English trans. C.R. Princeps (1821), *A Treatise on Political Economy*, Boston, MA: Wells and Lilly.
Schmalensee, R. and R. Willig (eds) (1989), *Handbook of Industrial Organization*, vols 1 and 2, Amsterdam: North-Holland.
Schumpeter, J.A. (1942), *Capitalism, Socialism and Democracy*, New York: Harper and Brothers.
Schumpeter, J.A. (1954), *History of Economic Analysis*, reprinted 1986, London: Allen & Unwin.
Scitovsky, T. (1950), 'Ignorance as a source of oligopoly power', *American Economic Review*, **40** (2), 48–53.
Selten, R. (1965), 'Spieltheoretische Behandlung eines Oligopolmodells mit Nachfragetragheit', *Zeitschrift für die gesammte Staatswissenschaft*, **121** (2), 301–24, (4) 667–89.
Senior, N.W. (1836), *An Outline of the Science of Political Economy*, London: W. Clowes and Sons.
Simons, H.C. (1934), *A Positive Program for Laissez Faire*, Chicago, IL: University of Chicago Press.
Smith, A. (1776), *An Inquiry into the Nature and Causes of the Wealth of Nations*, London: W. Strahan and T. Cadell.
Sraffa, P. (1926), 'The laws of returns under competitive conditions', *Economic Journal*, **36** (144), 535–50.
Stackelberg, H. von (1934), *Marktform und Gleichgewicht*, Vienna: Julius Springer.
Steedman, I. (ed.) (1995), *Socialism and Marginalism in Economics 1870–1930*, London and New York: Routledge.
Stigler, G.J. (1964), 'A theory of oligopoly', *Journal of Political Economy*, **72** (1), 44–61.
Sweezy, P.M. (1939), 'Demand under conditions of oligopoly', *Journal of Political Economy*, **47** (4), 568–73.
Sylos Labini, P. (1957), *Oligopolio e Progresso Tecnico*, Milan: Giuffrè. English trans. E. Henderson (1962), *Oligopoly and Technical Progress*, Cambridge, MA: Harvard University Press.
Thünen, J.H. von (1826), *Der isolierte Staat in Beziehung auf Landwirtschaft und Nationalökonomie*, Hamburg: Perthes.
Triffin, R. (1940), *Monopolistic Competition and General Equilibrium Theory*, Cambridge, MA: Harvard University Press.
Wicksell, K. (1901), *Forelasningar I Nationalekonomi*, Lund: C.W. Gleerups Vorlag, English trans. E. Classen (1934), *Lectures on Political Economy*, reprinted 1938, London: Routledge.

Input–output analysis

Input–output analysis is a technique developed for the study of interdependencies between sectors or industries of an economy. It is based on a system of linear equations which describe the existing relations between the inputs (or means of production) and outputs (or products) of all sectors of an economy. The framework has proved very successful in applied economic research. Nowadays, input–output economics covers a very broad area of research. Good overviews of the literature can be found in the collection of articles edited by Kurz et al. (1998), in Miller and Blair's (2009) textbook, and in Ten Raa (2005). The International Input–Output Association (IIOA), founded in 1988, is the main network of economists working in the field (www.iioa.org). It publishes the journal *Economic Systems Research*.

The Origins of Input–Output Analysis

It is customary to trace the origins of input–output analysis to the work of Nobel laureate Wassily Leontief (1905–1999). Leontief wrote a PhD dissertation at the University of Berlin under the supervision of Ladislaus von Bortkiewicz (1868–1931). In 1928 he published part of his work (in German) as an article with the title "The economy as a circular process". After moving to Harvard University he further elaborated his model, and started to collect the data for the first input–output table of the United States economy. This led to the 1936 article "Quantitative input–output relations in the economic system of the United States" and then to his 1941 book *The Structure of American Economy, 1919–1939. An Empirical Application of Equilibrium Analysis*.

Leontief himself referred to the Physiocrats and their *Tableau Œconomique* as his main source of inspiration. The genealogy of input–output analysis is actually quite long and diverse. Kurz and Salvadori (2010) and Kurz (2011) focused on the roots of input–output analysis in the classical political economy tradition. They pointed out that the notions of production as a circular process and of interdependency between sectors were already present in the work of William Petty (1623–1687) and of Richard Cantillon (1697–1734). In the hands of François Quesnay (1694–1774), the leader of the Physiocratic movement, these notions got shaped into the *Tableau Œconomique*, a stylized representation of the economy of a country. The model involves two sectors of production: a productive sector, agriculture, and a sterile sector, industry, which need one another to be able to keep production going. The net product generated by agriculture ends up in the pockets of the class of property owners. In equilibrium, the system is able to reproduce itself year after year. Related constructions can be found in the writings of Achilles-Nicolas Isnard (1748–1803) and of Robert Torrens (1780–1864). It was, however, Karl Marx (1818–1883) who seems to have benefited most from the Physiocratic ideas. His numerous and elaborate schemes of reproduction were obviously inspired by the *Tableau Œconomique*. Marx used these schemes also to shed light on the transformation of labour values into prices of production. Around the turn of the century, the labour value theory came under the scrutiny of Vladimir Dmitriev (1868–1913) and Ladislaus von Bortkiewicz (1868–1931), with the latter focusing on the transformation problem. Georg von Charasoff (1877–1931), a mathematician born in Georgia, also developed a highly original input–output model inspired by Marx's schemes of reproduction.

Since Leontief wrote his PhD dissertation under the supervision of von Bortkiewicz, it is tempting to conclude that input–output analysis can be seen as the culmination of an evolutionary line linking Quesnay via Marx and von Bortkiewicz to Leontief. This view has been challenged by William Baumol (2000), who argued that Leontief's work constitutes a revolutionary departure from earlier approaches. Moreover, Leontief himself suggested that his work was related to "the neo-classical theory of general equilibrium" (Leontief 1966: 134), where he obviously had economists such as Léon Walras (1834–1910) and Gustav Cassel (1866–1945) in mind.

Prior to or roughly at the same time as Leontief, several authors formulated models which were in many respects similar to Leontief's input–output models. The most important of these are Maurice Potron (1872–1942), Robert Remak (1888–1942), John von Neumann (1903–1957) and Piero Sraffa (1898–1983). As early as 1911, the French Jesuit engineer and mathematician Potron independently developed a complete input–output model in order to find out whether prices and quantities exist which satisfy four basic principles of a just social order. He was the first to apply the Perron–Frobenius results on non-negative matrices in an economic setting (Bidard and Erreygers 2010). The German mathematician Remak, who wrote his dissertation under the supervision of Frobenius, published an input–output-based analysis of what he called "superposed" prices in 1929. In 1937 the Hungarian mathematician von Neumann used a fixed-point theorem to show the existence of an equilibrium in a linear economic model. Also, in 1960 the Italian economist Sraffa published his book *Production of Commodities by Means of Commodities*, which proved to be very influential in the capital controversy debates of the 1960s. It must be noted, however, that Sraffa had started working on his model in the 1920s. (A thorough comparison of the approaches of Leontief and Sraffa has been made by Kurz and Salvadori (2006). This was published in a special issue of *Economic Systems Research* "The history of input–output analysis, Leontief's path and alternative tracks", edited by Bjerkholt and Kurz (2006), which one should consult for a more detailed exploration of the roots of input–output analysis.)

The Closed and Open Leontief Models

The standard input–output analysis is based upon a number of simplifying assumptions with regard to the productive structure of an economy. It is assumed that the economy can be divided into n sectors of production, each of which is uniquely associated to a specific product (for example, the steel producing sector). In addition, all production processes are characterized by constant returns to scale, and all production functions are of the fixed proportions type. This means that it is possible to describe the relations between the sectors of production by means of a square matrix of technical coefficients, habitually designated by A. The j-th column of A ($j = 1$, $2, \ldots, n$) describes the amounts of goods $1, 2, \ldots, n$ required as inputs to produce one unit of good j as output.

In the so-called closed Leontief model the inputs are defined in such a way that they include the consumption of goods by those who have contributed to production. This implies that there is no net output: on the level of the economy as a whole, the inputs are exactly equal to the outputs. In mathematical terms, this can be expressed as:

$$\mathbf{A}x = x \tag{1}$$

where x represents the activity vector. In terms of value, the counterpart of (1) is:

$$p'\mathbf{A} = p' \tag{2}$$

where p stands for the vector of prices. (By convention we use the term "vector" to denote column vectors. A prime is used to denote row vectors.) The implication of (1) and (2) is that matrix $(\mathbf{I} - \mathbf{A})$ is a singular matrix, and hence there is no unique solution of x or p.

In the open Leontief model a separate final demand vector is introduced. Consumption is no longer integrated into the input coefficients. Instead of (1) we now have:

$$\mathbf{A}x + d = x \tag{3}$$

where d stands for the final demand vector. Provided matrix $(\mathbf{I} - \mathbf{A})$ is regular, the activity levels which sustain the final demand are given by the solution:

$$x = (\mathbf{I} - \mathbf{A})^{-1}d \tag{4}$$

Under plausible conditions matrix $(\mathbf{I} - \mathbf{A})^{-1}$ exists and is semi-positive. This implies that any positive demand vector d can be satisfied by positive activity levels. Matrix $(\mathbf{I} - \mathbf{A})^{-1}$, which plays a crucial role in input–output analysis, is called the Leontief inverse. It also occurs when we look at the value side. The counterpart of (2) can be written as:

$$p'\mathbf{A} + v' = p' \tag{5}$$

where v stands for the value-added vector. The value-added represents what is paid to the primary factors such as labour and capital in the form of wages, profits, and so on. This leads to the following relation between value-added and prices:

$$p' = v'(\mathbf{I} - \mathbf{A})^{-1} \tag{6}$$

These relationships can be used to estimate the effects of exogenous changes in the economic system. For instance, let us suppose that the export of a particular good increases as a result of an increase in world demand. If the new final demand vector is $d + \Delta d$, we can use equation (4) to derive that the change in activity levels is equal to $\Delta x = (\mathbf{I} - \mathbf{A})^{-1}\Delta d$. This captures both the direct and indirect effects of the change in final demand.

The Dynamic Input–Output Model

So far we have concentrated on the flows of goods between sectors. But production also involves capital goods, which are stocks. Let us assume that for every unit of output in sector j we need k_{ij} units of good i ($i = 1, 2, \ldots, n$) as capital goods. These coefficients can be represented by the matrix of capital coefficients $\mathbf{K}$. As long as outputs remain the same, the capital stock must not be changed. However, when production increases, the capital stock must be expanded. Since the production of new capital goods requires time, a dynamic model must be formulated in order to take capital accumulation into account. Let us assume that new capital goods can be produced in one year's time. If the activity levels of period t are equal to x_t and those of period $t + 1$ equal to x_{t+1}, then clearly the amounts of new capital goods which must be produced are equal to $\mathbf{K}(x_{t+1} - x_t)$. It follows that instead of (3) we now have:

$$\mathbf{A}x_t + \mathbf{K}(x_{t+1} - x_t) + d_t = x_t \tag{7}$$

Rearranging terms, we obtain a system of recurrence equations linking the activity levels of different periods:

$$\mathbf{K}x_{t+1} = (\mathbf{I} - \mathbf{A} + \mathbf{K})x_t - d_t \tag{8}$$

Ideally, it is possible to solve (8) by calculating $x_{t+1} = \mathbf{K}^{-1}[(\mathbf{I} - \mathbf{A} + \mathbf{K})x_t - d_t]$, but obviously this only works if $\mathbf{K}^{-1}$ exists, which is far from certain. The reverse procedure, expressing x_t as a function of x_{t+1} and of d_t, i.e. $x_t = (\mathbf{I} - \mathbf{A} + \mathbf{K})^{-1}[\mathbf{K}x_{t+1} + d_t]$, might be considered as an alternative.

Monetary and Physical Models

In practice, input–output tables are usually expressed in values rather than in physical units. The available data are often limited to the values of the production in each sector (y_i, $i = 1, 2, \ldots, n$) and to the values of the deliveries between sectors (z_{ij}, $i, j = 1, 2, \ldots, n$). Each sector's revenue is equal to the sum of what it sells to other sectors (in other words, its intermediate demand) and what it sells to consumers, the government, and so on (its final demand). In matrix terms, this gives rise to the following system of equations:

$$\mathbf{Z}u + f = y \tag{9}$$

where u is a summation vector and f the vector of final demand values. Clearly, we have $f_i = d_i p_i$ and $y_i = x_i p_i$. The matrix of technical coefficients $\mathbf{A}$ expressed in monetary terms is derived from the matrix of interindustry transactions $\mathbf{Z}$ and from the vector of production values y by means of the transformation $a_{ij} = z_{ij}/y_j$. This means that system (9) leads to the following monetary version of system (3):

$$\mathbf{A}y + f = y \tag{10}$$

In what follows we will refer to the monetary rather than the physical version of the input–output model.

The Commodity-by-Industry Approach

Until now we have assumed that every sector is uniquely associated to a good: steel is produced only by the steel producing sector, and the steel producing sector produces nothing but steel. In reality, however, things are much more complicated: there are joint products, by-products, and so on. The commodity-by-industry approach is one way of dealing with these issues.

Let us assume there exist n industries which use and make m commodities. The $m \times n$ Use matrix $\mathbf{U}$ (also called the absorption or input matrix) describes how much each industry purchases (that is, uses) of each commodity. The $n \times m$ Make matrix $\mathbf{V}$ (also called the output matrix) represents how much each industry sells (that is, makes) of each commodity. These matrices are expressed in value terms, like matrix $\mathbf{Z}$.

The interpretation of these matrices is straightforward. Let us begin with the Use matrix, which is of the commodities-by-industries type. If we sum all the purchases of commodity i by the m industries and add to that the final demand f_i for this commodity, we obtain the total output q_i of commodity i (in value terms). By contrast, if we sum all the purchases of commodities by industry j and add to that the value added v_j created in this industry, we obtain the total output y_j of industry j. In an obvious matrix notation, this means:

$$\mathbf{U}u + f = q \tag{11}$$

$$u'\mathbf{U} + v' = y' \tag{12}$$

Just like $\mathbf{Z}$, the Use matrix $\mathbf{U}$ may also serve as a basis for the definition of a matrix of technical coefficients. Matrix $\mathbf{B}$ can be derived from $\mathbf{U}$ and y by the operation $b_{ij} = u_{ij}/y_j$. Equation (11) can then be rewritten as:

$$\mathbf{B}y + f = q \tag{13}$$

The Make matrix, on the other hand, is of the industries-by-commodities type. Instead of (11) and (12) we therefore have:

$$u'\mathbf{V} = q' \tag{14}$$

$$\mathbf{V}u = y \tag{15}$$

Matrix $\mathbf{V}$ can be used to define either the commodity output proportions matrix $\mathbf{D}$ by the operation $d_{ij} = v_{ij}/q_j$, or the industry output proportions matrix $\mathbf{C}$ by the operation $c_{ij} = v_{ij}/y_i$. It follows that we have:

$$\mathbf{D}q = y \tag{16}$$

$$\mathbf{C}y = q \tag{17}$$

Equation (16) allows us to transform total commodity outputs into total industry outputs, and equation (17) to do the opposite.

If we use (16) in conjunction with (13) we arrive at the following relation between commodity outputs and final demand:

$$q = (\mathbf{I} - \mathbf{B}\mathbf{D})^{-1}f \tag{18}$$

The matrix $(\mathbf{I} - \mathbf{BD})^{-1}$ is called a commodity-by-commodity total requirements matrix. It plays a role similar to the Leontief inverse in (4). If the number of commodities is equal to the number of industries, and if matrix $\mathbf{C}$ happens to be invertible, another expression can be obtained which links commodity outputs to final demand. In fact, in that case we can use (17) in conjunction with (13) to arrive at:

$$q = (\mathbf{I} - \mathbf{BC}^{-1})^{-1}f \qquad (19)$$

The matrix $(\mathbf{I} - \mathbf{BC}^{-1})^{-1}$ is also called a commodity-by-commodity total requirements matrix.

We therefore have two matrices which are akin to the technical coefficients matrix $\mathbf{A}$ in the basic input–output model: matrix $\mathbf{BD}$ and matrix $\mathbf{BC}^{-1}$. The first embodies the so-called industry-technology assumption. According to this interpretation, all commodities produced in a given industry have an identical input structure, equal to the corresponding column of matrix $\mathbf{B}$. The second embodies the commodity-technology assumption. The interpretation here is that irrespective of the industry in which it is produced, a commodity is always produced with the same input structure.

The commodity-by-industry approach has been introduced by Richard Stone (1913–1991) and his collaborators. It provides a solid framework to connect input–output analysis to systems of national accounting. In 1968 the United Nations proposed the approach as a standard for data collection and presentation. This is now known as the United Nations System of National Accounts (UNSNA or simply SNA), of which the latest version was issued in 2008. The European System of Accounts (ESA), of which the most recent version dates from 2010, is to a large extent the same.

One of the problems that may, and often will, occur if one adopts the commodity-technology assumption, is the occurrence of negative elements in the technical coefficients matrix $\mathbf{BC}^{-1}$. (Under the industry-technology assumption negative coefficients never occur.) Negative coefficients clearly have no sensible economic meaning. One solution of the problem consists of replacing the negative elements, which tend to be small, by zeroes. A more radical solution is to abandon the commodity-technology assumption altogether.

Updating Coefficients: The RAS Procedure

The construction of input–output tables requires massive amounts of information, often obtained by means of extensive – mostly also expensive – surveys. These surveys are usually not taken every year, but only every five or ten years. For the years in between, one usually has some information available. Updating techniques have been developed in order to estimate the technical coefficients for the years for which there is only limited information.

The best known technique is the RAS, or biproportional matrix balancing, technique. Assume that the complete matrix of technical coefficients of a given base year is known; let it be equal to $\mathbf{A}$. We want to obtain an estimate of the matrix of technical coefficients in year t, which we will designate as $\mathbf{A}(t)$. The information available for year t is: the total output of each sector, the total intermediate sales of each sector, and the total intermediate purchases of each sector. In technical terms, we know the output vector $y(t)$, and both the row and column sums of the matrix of intermediate deliveries $\mathbf{Z}(t)$. The vector of row sums is by convention designated as $u(t)$ and that of column sums as $v'(t)$.

To begin with, we simply assume that the matrix of technical coefficients has remained unchanged. Our initial estimate of $\mathbf{A}(t)$ is therefore:

$$\mathbf{A}(t)_{(0)} = \mathbf{A} \tag{20}$$

and the corresponding estimate of matrix $\mathbf{Z}(t)$ is $\mathbf{Z}(t)_{(0)} = \mathbf{A}(t)_{(0)}\hat{\mathbf{Y}}(t)$, where $\hat{\mathbf{Y}}(t)$ is a diagonal matrix of which the elements on the main diagonal are equal to the elements of vector $y(t)$. Next, we check whether the row and column sums of this matrix, i.e. $u(t)_{(0)}$ and $v'(t)_{(0)}$, are equal to $u(t)$ and $v'(t)$. If they are not, we proceed to a first stage of updating. Suppose that $u(t)_{(0)} \neq u(t)$. We then define coefficients $r_{i(1)} = u_i(t)/u_i(t)_{(0)}$, and construct a diagonal matrix $\hat{\mathbf{R}}_{(1)}$ with the elements $r_{i(1)}$ on the main diagonal. This is then used to obtain a new estimate of the matrix of technical coefficients:

$$\mathbf{A}(t)_{(1)} = \hat{\mathbf{R}}_{(1)}\mathbf{A}(t)_{(0)} \tag{21}$$

and a new estimate of matrix $\mathbf{Z}(t)$: $\mathbf{Z}(t)_{(1)} = \mathbf{A}(t)_{(1)}\hat{\mathbf{Y}}(t)$. By construction, the row sums of $\mathbf{Z}(t)_{(1)}$ are all equal to the row sums of $\mathbf{Z}(t)$, i.e. $u(t)_{(1)} = u(t)$. The column sums, however, are not necessarily equal to those of $\mathbf{Z}(t)$. If they are different, we proceed to a second stage of updating. Now we define coefficients $s_{j(2)} = v_j(t)/v_j(t)_{(1)}$, and construct a diagonal matrix $\hat{\mathbf{S}}_{(2)}$ with the elements $s_{j(2)}$ on the main diagonal. We use this to update our estimate of the matrix of technical coefficients to:

$$\mathbf{A}(t)_{(2)} = \mathbf{A}(t)_{(1)}\hat{\mathbf{S}}_{(2)} \tag{22}$$

and our estimate of matrix $\mathbf{Z}(t)$ to $\mathbf{Z}(t)_{(2)} = \mathbf{A}(t)_{(2)}\hat{\mathbf{Y}}(t)$. By construction, the column sums of $\mathbf{Z}(t)_{(2)}$ are all equal to the row sums of $\mathbf{Z}(t)$, i.e. $v'(t)_{(2)} = v'(t)$; the row sums, however, may be different.

As long as there are differences, the row and column updating procedures can be repeated, leading to updated estimates $\mathbf{A}(t)_{(3)}$, $\mathbf{A}(t)_{(4)}$, ... Usually, the algorithm converges and can be stopped if the estimated row and column sums approximate the given row and column sums. After q adjustments, we obtain the following matrix of technical coefficients:

$$\mathbf{A}(t)_{(q)} = \hat{\mathbf{R}}_{(q-1)}...\hat{\mathbf{R}}_{(3)}\hat{\mathbf{R}}_{(1)}\mathbf{A}\hat{\mathbf{S}}_{(2)}\hat{\mathbf{S}}_{(4)}...\hat{\mathbf{S}}_{(q)} = \mathbf{RAS} \tag{23}$$

Many variants of the basic RAS approach have been developed over the years.

Applications of Input–Output Analysis

Input–output models are versatile tools which can be adapted to study many different policy issues. We illustrate this by looking at interregional, international and environmental input–output models.

The interregional input–output model, originally developed by Walter Isard (1919–2010), is based on the assumptions that there exist several regions within a country, and that detailed data are available on the transactions between sectors located in the same region as well as on those between sectors located in different regions. Without loss of generality, we suppose there are just two regions, North and South. The matrix of inter-industry transactions can then be written as:

$$\mathbf{Z} = \begin{bmatrix} \mathbf{Z}^{NN} & \mathbf{Z}^{NS} \\ \mathbf{Z}^{SN} & \mathbf{Z}^{SS} \end{bmatrix} \tag{24}$$

where $\mathbf{Z}^{NN}$ and $\mathbf{Z}^{SS}$ represent the intraregional transactions in North and South, and $\mathbf{Z}^{NS}$ and $\mathbf{Z}^{NS}$ the interregional trade flows from North to South and from South to North, respectively. The technical coefficients are obtained by dividing all flows by the value of the output of the receiving sector, that is:

$$a_{ij}^{NN} = z_{ij}^{NN}/y_j^N, \ a_{ij}^{SS} = z_{ij}^{SS}/y_j^S \tag{25}$$

$$a_{ij}^{NS} = z_{ij}^{NS}/y_j^S, \ a_{ij}^{SN} = z_{ij}^{SN}/y_j^N \tag{26}$$

Given the final demand vector f, the system can then be written as:

$$(\mathbf{I} - \mathbf{A})y = f \tag{27}$$

where:

$$\mathbf{A} = \begin{bmatrix} \mathbf{A}^{NN} & \mathbf{A}^{NS} \\ \mathbf{A}^{SN} & \mathbf{A}^{SS} \end{bmatrix}, \ y = \begin{bmatrix} y^N \\ y^S \end{bmatrix}, \ f = \begin{bmatrix} f^N \\ f^S \end{bmatrix} \tag{28}$$

This decomposition allows us to study the interregional feedback effects of changes in final demand in one region. Suppose that final demand changes from to $f^N + \Delta f^N$ in the North, but remains the same in the South. This has direct effects on the production levels in the North, but indirectly also on those of the South, because part of the inputs of the North come from the South. This in turn has an influence on the production levels of the North, because the South also uses inputs from the North, and so forth. The overall effects on the production levels of the North and the South are equal to:

$$\Delta y^N = \mathbf{M}^{-1}\Delta f^N \tag{29}$$

$$\Delta y^S = (\mathbf{I} - \mathbf{A}^{SS})^{-1}\mathbf{A}^{SN}\mathbf{M}^{-1}\Delta f^N \tag{30}$$

where $\mathbf{M} = \mathbf{I} - \mathbf{A}^{NN} - \mathbf{A}^{NS}(\mathbf{I} - \mathbf{A}^{SS})^{-1}\mathbf{A}^{SN}$.

A full-blown interregional input–output model requires a lot of data, which are often not available. This has led to the development of alternative models which require less detailed data. These include the multiregional input–output model of Hollis B. Chenery

(1918–1994) and Leon N. Moses (1924–2013), and the balanced regional model of Leontief and others.

Many international input–output models closely resemble the regional input–output models, with import and export flows replacing the interregional trade flows. Several of such models have been developed for both Asian and European countries. In the 1970s Leontief himself took the lead in the development of a world model, with the support of the United Nations. This model was meant to be an instrument to promote economic development and to improve environmental policy.

In fact, a growing concern for environmental problems has been a driving force for the development of extended input–output models known as environmental input–output models. A simple way to proceed is to assume that it is possible to measure how much pollution is generated by each industry. Suppose this information is collected in matrix **E**, of which each row represents the amount of pollutants generated per unit of output of the corresponding industry. The total amount of pollutants which corresponds to the industry output vector y is therefore equal to:

$$e = \mathbf{E}y \tag{31}$$

Making use of (10) we can link the amount of pollutants to final demand by the expression:

$$e = \mathbf{E}(\mathbf{I} - \mathbf{A})^{-1}f \tag{32}$$

This allows us to estimate the total environmental impact of final demand or of a change of it. A more refined model is obtained when pollution abatement is also taken into account. This can be done by introducing pollution abatement industries among the sectors of production of the economy.

Social Accounting Matrices

In applied economic work one sometimes needs more detailed insights into the effects of economic policy on households, labour, social institutions, and so on, than what standard input–output analysis can provide. For this purpose the social accounting matrices (SAM) approach has been developed (see Pyatt 1985). It expands the input–output framework by means of several accounts, such as the household account, the government account and the rest-of-the-world account, which contain detailed information on the transactions and transfers occurring in the economic system. Since the information usually comes from different sources, this may lead to inconsistencies in the data. Balancing techniques have been developed to remove the inconsistencies. SAM models are often part of computable general equilibrium (CGE) models, the use of which has been propagated by the World Bank.

GUIDO ERREYGERS

See also:

Ladislaus von Bortkiewicz (I); British classical political economy (II); Richard Cantillon (I); Gustav Cassel (I); Vladimir Karpovich Dmitriev (I); Formalization and mathematical modelling (III); French Enlightenment (II);

General equilibrium theory (III); German and Austrian schools (II); Achilles-Nicolas Isnard (I); Wassily W. Leontief (I); Karl Heinrich Marx (I); Marxism(s) (II); Neo-Ricardian economics (II); John von Neumann (I); William Petty (I); François Quesnay and Physiocracy (I); Russian School of Mathematical Economics (II); Piero Sraffa (I); Robert Torrens (I); Marie-Esprit-Léon Walras (I).

References and further reading

Baumol, W. (2000), 'Leontief's great leap forward', *Economic Systems Research*, **12** (2), 141–52.
Bidard, C. and G. Erreygers (eds) (2010), *The Analysis of Linear Economic Systems: Father Maurice Potron's Pioneering Works*, London: Routledge.
Bjerkholt, O. and H.D. Kurz (eds) (2006), 'Special issue: the history of input–output analysis, Leontief's path and alternative tracks', *Economic Systems Research*, **18** (4).
Bortkiewicz, L. von (1906–07), 'Wertrechnung und Preisrechnung im Marxschen System', *Archiv für Sozialwissenschaft und Sozialpolitik*, **23** (1), 1–50, **25** (1), 10–51, **25** (2), 445–88.
Cantillon, R. (1755), *Essai sur la Nature du Commerce en Général*, reprinted 1952, Paris: Institut national d'études démographiques.
Charasoff, G. von (1910), *Das System des Marxismus: Darstellung und Kritik*, Berlin: H. Bondy.
Chenery, H.B. (1956), 'Interregional and international input–output analysis', in T. Barna (ed.), *The Structural Interdependence of the Economy*, New York: John Wiley, pp. 341–56.
Dmitriev, V.K. (1974), *Economic Essays on Value, Competition and Utility*, ed. with introduction by D.M. Nuti, Cambridge: Cambridge University Press.
European Commission (2013), *European System of Accounts – ESA 2010*, Luxembourg: Publications Office of the European Union.
European Commission, International Monetary Fund, Organisation for Economic Co-operation and Development, United Nations and World Bank (2009), *System of National Accounts 2008*, New York: United Nations.
Isard, W. (1951), 'Interregional and regional input–output analysis: a model of a space-economy', *Review of Economics and Statistics*, **33** (4), 318–28.
Isnard, A.-N. (1751), *Traité des Richesses*, London and Lausanne: François Grasset.
Kurz, H.D. (2011), 'Who is going to kiss Sleeping Beauty? On the "classical" analytical origins and perspectives of input–output analysis', *Review of Political Economy*, **23** (1), 25–47.
Kurz, H.D, E. Dietzenbacher and C. Lager (eds) (1998), *Input–Output Analysis*, 3 vols, Cheltenham, UK and Lyme, NH, USA: Edward Elgar.
Kurz, H.D. and N. Salvadori (2006), 'Input–output analysis from a wider perspective: a comparison of the early works of Leontief and Sraffa', *Economic Systems Research*, **18** (4, 373–90.
Kurz, H.D. and N. Salvadori (2010), '"Classical roots" of input–output analysis: a short account of a long history', *Economic Systems Research*, **12** (2), 153–79.
Leontief, W. (1928), 'Die Wirtschaft als Kreislauf', *Archiv für Sozialwissenschaft und Sozialpolitik*, **60** (3), 577–623.
Leontief, W. (1936), 'Quantitative input–output relations in the economic system of the United States', *Review of Economics and Statistics*, **18** (3), 105–25.
Leontief, W. (1941), *The Structure of American Economy, 1919–1939. An Empirical Application of Equilibrium Analysis*, Cambridge, MA: Harvard University Press.
Leontief, W. (1966), *Input–Output Economics*, Oxford: Oxford University Press.
Marx, K. (1867–94), *Das Kapital*, 3 vols, Hamburg: Meissner.
Miller, R.E. and P.D. Blair (2009), *Input–Output Analysis: Foundations and Extensions*, 2nd edn, Cambridge: Cambridge University Press.
Moses, L. (1955), 'The stability of interregional trading patterns and input–output analysis', *American Economic Review*, **45** (5), 803–32.
Neumann, J. von (1937), 'Über ein ökonomisches Gleichungssystem und eine Verallgemeinerung des Brouwerschen Fixpunktsatzes', *Ergebnisse eines Mathematischen Kolloquiums*, **8**, 73–83.
Petty, W. (1662), *A Treatise of Taxes and Contributions*, in C.H. Hull (ed.) (1899), *The Economic Writings of Sir William Petty*, vol. 1, Cambridge: Cambridge University Press, pp. 5–97.
Potron, M. (1911), 'Application aux problèmes de la "production suffisante" et du "salaire vital" de quelques propriétés des substitutions linéaires à coefficients ≥ 0', *Comptes Rendus de l'Académie des Sciences*, **153** (26), 1458–9.
Pyatt, G. (1995), 'Commodity balances and national accounts: A SAM perspective', *Review of Income and Wealth*, **31** (2), 155–69.
Quesnay, F. (1758), *Le Tableau Économique*, in C. Théré, L. Charles and J.-C. Perrot (eds) (2005), *Œuvres Économiques Complètes et Autres Textes*, vol. 1, Paris, Institut national d'études démographiques, pp. 391–403.

Remak, R. (1929), 'Kann die Volkswirtschaftslehre eine exakte Wissenschaft werden?', *Jahrbücher für Nationalökonomie und Statistik*, **131** (5), 703–35.

Sraffa, P. (1960), *Production of Commodities by Means of Commodities: Prelude to a Critique of Economic Theory*, Cambridge: Cambridge University Press.

Stone, R. (1961), *Input–Output and National Accounts*, Paris: Office of European Economic Cooperation.

Ten Raa, T. (2005), *The Economics of Input–Output Analysis*, Cambridge: Cambridge University Press.

Torrens, R. (1820), *An Essay on the Influence of the External Corn Trade upon the Production and Distribution of National Wealth*, 2nd edn, London: J. Hatchard and Son.

Institutional economics

The old American institutionalism was part of the pluralist mainstream of the interwar period, but declined for various reasons. After World War II, economics, particularly in the United States, became more formalized, technical and uniform, began to give importance to rational choice and testing of predictions and became focused on the analysis of markets, expanding it to other domains of social sciences. Tjalling Koopmans (1947) dismissed Wesley Mitchell's institutional work as nothing more than measures, and favoured the testing of theories. Milton Friedman's (1953) plea for testing predictions and neglecting the empirical basis of assumptions also ended the marginalist controversy. The scientific aspirations of institutionalism were undermined, its authors forgotten and (inaccurately) written off as anti-theoretical and purely descriptive. Institutionalism survived at the margins of economics, with authors such as Clarence Ayres, John Kenneth Galbraith, Simon Kuznets and Gunnar Myrdal.

However, the mainstream consensus was disrupted in the 1970s and new schools of thought, somehow related to institutionalist perspectives, emerged, such as radical economics, post-Keynesian economics, Austrian economics and social economics. This entry focuses on the schools labelled institutionalist after World War II; they are diverse and not always easily identifiable, but may be divided in two groups: new institutional economics and modern institutionalism.

The term new institutional economics (NIE) was coined by Williamson (1975), and its institutional existence was illustrated by the foundation of the International Society for New Institutional Economics in 1997. The theories included in this group have in common the use of economic analysis to study institutional change (following North 1990), governance structures (transaction costs economics), property rights (property rights theory), legal rules (economic analysis of law) and political processes (public choice). Consistent with methodological individualism, they view institutions as both equilibria resulting from interactions, and constraints to some form of rational choice. They also accept Friedmanian instrumentalism. In other words, they keep the core of neoclassical theory rejected by the old institutionalism. Probably as a consequence, they count a few laureates of the Sveriges Riksbank Prize in Economic Sciences in Memory of Alfred Nobel in their ranks: James Buchanan, Douglass North, Ronald Coase, Elinor Ostrom and Oliver Williamson.

The old institutionalist ideas, however, had resurfaced in the United States as early as the 1960s with the Association for Evolutionary Economics, founded in 1965 (originating from the Wardman group formed at the initiative of Allan Gruchy in 1959), and its *Journal of Economic Issues* in 1966. North American members of this second group include Ayres, Daniel Bromley, Joseph Dorfman, Galbraith, Herbert Liebhafsky, Gardiner Means, Marc Tool, Warren Samuels and Allan Schmid. Maybe because of the dominance of neoclassical economics in the US, old institutionalism moved towards Europe, around the European Association for Evolutionary Political Economy founded in 1988, the *Review of Political Economy*, and the *Cambridge Journal of Economics*. European institutionalists were also influenced by John Maynard Keynes, Karl Marx and Karl Polanyi, and were more interested in themes such as organizations and evolutionism: besides Kuznets or Myrdal, we can cite János Kornai, Giovanni Dosi, Brian Loasby, Geoffrey Hodgson and French regulationists Michel Aglietta and Robert

Boyer. Like the "old", this "modern" institutionalism abandons methodological individualism and substantive rationality, but stresses habits, routines, dynamics, learning and knowledge in a context of radical uncertainty. The individual is not exogenously given, but constructed by institutions: they shape preferences, means and ends, as well as power structures; causality between individuals and institutions is therefore reciprocal and mediated through habits (Hodgson 2000).

Coase occupies a special position in this division of the institutionalist world. He did not really know old institutionalism (which he nevertheless criticized). His major articles, "The nature of the firm" (Coase 1937) and "The problem of social cost" (Coase 1960), partly originated and shaped the renewal of interest in institutions. He is traditionally associated with NIE and is criticized by modern institutionalists (despite being credited as one of their sources) for his neoclassicism. He nevertheless rejected Richard Posner's imperialism or Williamson's stress on asset specificity, and a new look at his seminal contributions shows them to be closer to institutionalism than he (and others) believe (Medema 1996).

Even if NIE generally defines institutions as the "rules of the game" (North), while modern institutionalism views them as habits (in a Veblenian tradition), they share a common interest in studying institutions other than the market: they focus not only on the allocation of resources, but also on organization and control, albeit to different degrees; and the market itself is sometimes viewed as an institution. The firm, the market, the law and the state are the main institutions that these schools of thought study, even if some of them are also interested in macroeconomic aspects (see entries for financial economics and business cycles and growth). This entry will focus a bit more on law since (institutionalist) theories of the firm are treated in another entry of this volume. Institutionalist perspectives on law can be included in the vast "Law and Economics" movement, whose history, paralleling that of institutionalism, deserves to be separately dealt with in this introduction.

Economic–legal interactions had already been studied by, among others, the Scholastics, David Hume, Adam Smith, Jeremy Bentham, Henry Sidgwick, Arthur Pigou and German historicists. However, the "legal–economic nexus" became a central part of old institutionalism (John Commons, Robert Lee Hale, Walton Hamilton) and legal realism (Karl Lewellyn) in the 1920s and 1930s. Then, in the 1930s, at Chicago University, Henry Simons (a former student of Frank Knight) was appointed to the Economics Department and the Law School, to which he brought Aaron Director who founded the *Journal of Law and Economics* in 1958. In the meantime Knight was joined in the economics department by Friedman and George Stigler after the war. In the 1940s and 1950s this "Old (Chicago School of) Law and Economics" was applying economic theory to legal problems such as antitrust and labour law. The 1960s saw the rise of the "New (Chicago School of) Law and Economics", integrating into the old school Gary Becker's idea of applying economic tools to non-market behaviour. Other influences were the publication of "The problem of social cost", the consequences of which were drawn in a series of articles by Harold Demsetz (1964, 1967), as well as the seminal works of Armen Alchian (1961) and Guido Calabresi (1961). Coase was appointed to Chicago in 1964 and edited the *Journal of Law and Economics* for almost 20 years. The movement extended to lawyers in the 1970s, with the creation of Henry Manne's Institute for Law Professors in 1971, as well as the foundation of the *Journal of Legal Studies* and the publication of Richard Posner's *Economic Analysis of Law* the following year. This new Chicago school of law and economics, or economic analysis of law, applies neoclassical tools to the evaluation of legal rules. Nonetheless, new law and economics is not confined to Chicago: there are also the Yale tradition (Calabresi), Public Choice, institutional law and economics, Austrians, Marxians, critical legal studies and legal philosophy (see Mercuro and Medema 1997).

The history of institutional analyses of law and economics will be approached as that of specific schools of NIE (property rights theory and economic analysis of law) and modern institutionalism (institutional law and economics) since this entry is organized around these two groups. Our division is undoubtedly questionable; still, a fundamental gap remains between economists who study institutions as new objects for amended neoclassical economics (NIE broadly defined) and those who more radically alter this vision of the world to take into account how institutions shape individuals and their behaviours. Economists of the first group are concerned with the verifiability of their predictions, those of the second with the realism of their assumptions. One author, however, defies classification, and his role will be treated first.

The Central Role of Ronald Coase

Coase's role in post-war institutionalism is central in the two meanings of the term; both essential to its development, and positioned between the two schools of thought identified here. Coase criticizes standard microeconomics (including that of Becker and Posner) for its assumption of an agent who is just a logical collection of preferences, its focus on price theory and its neglect of the "institutional structure of production", namely, the firm, the market and the law. Coase

> showed in the "Nature of the firm" that, in the absence of transaction costs, there is no economic basis for the existence of the firm. What [he] showed in the "Problem of social cost" was that, in the absence of transaction costs, it does not matter what the law is, since people can always negotiate without cost to acquire, subdivide, and combine rights whenever this would increase the value of production. (Coase 1988: 14)

Transaction costs are therefore the missing element of economic theory: they explain the role of the institutions of the market (to diminish them), the existence of the firm (to avoid them) and the influence of the initial distribution of legal rights on the final allocation of resources. Similarly, economic policy should not be an abstract exercise on a blackboard, but should consist of choosing one institutional arrangement among others, all being costly: this is the comparative institutional method.

Coase's definition of the object of economics as explaining the economic system, rather than predicting the consequences of rational choices, links him to old institutionalist perspectives. His article on social cost (1960), expanding the role of transaction costs and the comparative institutional method (first introduced in his article on the firm in 1937), proved seminal for institutional economics and specifically for law and economics. It stressed that what is exchanged on the market are property rights on goods and services, determined by the law, and that they have to be clearly defined and allocated for the exchange to take place. It underlined the reciprocity of harms ("externalities") and the importance of the domain of torts and of common law for economics; and it put forward the idea of the economic efficiency of common law. While written in the old institutionalist style and cited as a source of modern institutionalism (Medema 1996), Coase's article and the issues it raised were also interpreted and extended using standard neoclassical analysis, as in NIE.

New Institutional Economics

Douglass North and institutional change

North's first works contributed to the rise of the new economic history, or cliometrics, but his subsequent works rejected neoclassical theory, which could not explain long-term change and only considered perfect markets. Neoclassical theory considers factors of growth – technical progress and growth of factors of production – to be exogenous, whereas, North argued, they *are* change. Following Coase and Demsetz, he claimed that institutions promoting growth were those that provided appropriate incentives, that is, structures of property rights that equalized private cost and social cost. The growth of the United States during the nineteenth century was interpreted with this theoretical framework, in which efficient institutions are put into place when their benefit is perceived to be greater than their cost (Davis and North 1971). North and Thomas (1973) extended the analysis to the rise of Western Europe over a longer period and endogenously explained its institutional structures as resulting from rational individual decisions. Facing the poor performances of some economies, North (1981) abandoned individual rationality and the thesis of the efficiency of institutions, and introduced the role of ideology and a theory of the state, close to public choice. His theoretical framework was again enriched when he stressed informal institutions, interactions between organizations and institutions, and the path dependency of institutional change (North 1990).

North mainly conceives institutions as constraints on (given) individuals, shaping their choice set and the structure of their incentives: "Institutions are the rules of the game in a society or, more formally, are the humanly devised constraints that shape human interaction" (North 1990: 3). They are formal or informal and result from the agents' interaction, often spontaneously (in the Hayekian sense). North's works have been criticized for being, almost paradoxically, ahistorical: institutions mechanically adjust to exogenous causes, and new institutional concepts such as transaction costs and property rights appear to have been plugged into a partial account of historical reality that lacks detailed knowledge of law.

Transaction costs economics

Following Commons, Williamson (1975, 1985) makes transaction the unit of analysis, which he defines as a transfer of the right to use a good or service between technologically separable activities. The concept of transaction costs is of course borrowed from Coase, but they are defined as "the comparative costs of planning, adapting, and monitoring task completion under alternative governance structures" (Williamson 1996: 58), the "governance structure" being the institutional matrix that governs the contract. Williamson takes the institutional environment as given and focuses on the choice of governance structure.

Four assumptions define the "world of governance": uncertainty, bounded rationality (borrowed from Herbert Simon), opportunism – "self-interest seeking with guile" (Williamson 1985: 47) – and asset specificity, which characterizes "durable investments that are undertaken in support of particular transactions, the opportunity cost of which investments is much lower in best alternative uses or by alternative users" (ibid.: 55). In this world, contracts are incomplete: they cannot be specified for every state of the world. And asset specificity implies bilateral dependence that generates a quasi-rent, part of which the partner may opportunistically appropriate. The problem is to design a contract that economizes on bounded rationality and safeguards against opportunistic behaviours. The institutionalist aspect of Williamson's theory is his focus on the differences of governance structures in their ability to adapt in an uncertain environment. The difference with Commons and Coase is that Williamson aims at "operationalizing" his theory, that is, providing refutable predictions. This comes to associate transactions differing in their attributes (frequency, uncertainty and asset specificity) with governance structures differing in their costs and advantages in a way that minimizes transaction costs, thereby providing testable predictions as to the organizational form of specific transactions.

Williamson makes a distinction between three types of contract, the legal aspects of which come from a reinterpretation of Macneil (1974)'s typology of contracts. At one end of the spectrum is the market exchange with its "classical" contract: short term, complete, decentralized, anonymous, resolution of disputes before the courts, incentives and adaptation through prices. At the other extreme are the unified structure and its hierarchical contract, with opposite characteristics: disputes resolved internally and incentives and adaptation through control. Between the two, the hybrid form corresponds to the "neoclassical" contract, and is defined by coordination between autonomous entities. As frequency, uncertainty and, above all, asset specificity increase, contracts are predicted to go from classical to neoclassical to hierarchical. Transaction costs economics is considered by Williamson to be "an empirical success story", early tests having been conducted since the beginning of the 1980s.

Williamson's position differs from old institutionalism in that there are no historical, social or political dimensions to institutions, which are viewed as contracts. The market itself is not viewed as an institution, as illustrated by the controversial sentence: "In the beginning there were markets" (Williamson 1975: 20), whereas the existence of markets presupposes the existence of law, rules, contracts, police, that is, of other institutions. Williamson formalized Coase's question of the emergence and choice of different governance structures, but consequently his theory remains an analysis of choice, with institutions viewed only as constraints. His four assumptions have no empirical support, but are formulated to design the problem of a choice of governance structure that comes down to a minimization of transaction costs. Commons's (1934) transaction has lost its interaction between individual and collective levels; Coase's opposition between market and hierarchy is blurred; Simon's (1955) bounded rationality is translated into a minimizing principle. Regarding law, Williamson bases his theory on a sociological analysis of law and focuses on private and incomplete ordering. He therefore neglects the real law of contracts and the role of the judge. Rather than analysing the interaction between law and economics, he separates the two dimensions and focuses on the latter. Real law, as well as real markets and real firms (as institutions), is eliminated.

Property rights theory
Property rights theory emerged in the 1960s following Coase's "Problem of social cost" (Alchian 1961, 1965; Demsetz 1964, 1967). It explicitly takes the individual as given and institutions and organizations as constraints on her rational choice, the aim being "to explain the behavior of the firm and other institutions by observing individual action *within* the organization"; therefore, "marginalism is not rejected, the standard techniques are merely extended to new applications" (Furubotn and Pejovich 1972: 1138, original emphasis). The differences with neoclassical economics come from the study of different structures of property rights (implicit and capitalist in classical and neoclassical theories), the introduction of transaction costs, and the assumption of maximization of utility by individual agents (managers, owners, workers) instead of maximization of profit by a firm. Property rights theory analyses how different systems of property rights determine individual behaviour and economic efficiency, asserts the superiority of private property rights over other forms of property, and argues that this more efficient form tends to prevail.

A property right over a good or service is defined as the socially enforced right to select use of this good or service. A private property right also encompasses the rights to raise revenue from the good and to sell this right; it is fractionable between these three different rights (to use, to raise revenue, and to sell), which can be owned by different persons, and is thus separable. The capitalist firm and the large corporation derive their efficiency from the exploitation of the partitionability, separability and alienability of private property (Alchian and Demsetz 1972).

The efficiency of private ownership is generally offered to argue against the communal property of a scarce resource, which entails overuse and negative externalities. Demsetz (1967) famously argued that the Labrador Peninsula evolved from communal property of forests to private ownership because of the development of the European fur trade at the end of the seventeenth century, which made animals scarce, increasing their value, and raising the advantages of private property rights over their costs. His thesis is that "property rights develop to internalize externalities when the gains of internalization become larger than the cost of internalization. Increased internalization ... results from changes in economic values, changes which stem from the development of new technology and the opening of new markets" (Demsetz 1967: 350).

Since private property rights are seldom perfect, someone other than the owner may use his good: this is an externality. If transaction costs were nil and property rights clearly defined, a negotiation would be possible, leading to an optimal outcome (Coase 1960). Property rights theory insists that remaining externalities are therefore due to positive transaction costs or ill-defined property rights, the two concepts being rather equivalent. Moreover, these transaction costs imply that the initial distribution of rights has an impact on the allocation of resources.

Economic analysis of law
Three early contributions were central to the development of economic analysis of law. First, Coase (1960) initiated a discussion of property rights from a market perspective, stressed the reciprocity of torts and introduced the criterion of efficiency for common-law judges. Second, Calabresi (1961, 1970) suggested allocating liability for accidents to

"the cheapest cost avoider". Third, Becker (1968) originated an economics of crime and punishment.

In 1972, Posner published the first edition of his *Economic Analysis of Law*, summing up the core of this theory. He applies rational choice theory to every domain of law (from property to contracts law, from torts to criminal law). Legal rules are studied from the point of view of their consequences in terms of economic efficiency. Posner's normative thesis, according to which the only objective of legal rules should be to maximize wealth, accompanies a positive thesis that common law actually does maximize wealth. The aim of the law is to promote efficiency through two means: "mimicking the market" (allocating the right to the person who would pay the most for it, since this person will use it in the way that maximizes the output value) and diminishing transaction costs. In other words, Posner equates justice with efficiency, itself defined as Kaldor–Hicks efficiency.

Posner's book (1972) was addressed to lawyers, explaining economic tools and applying them to all traditional fields of law. This approach was vehemently criticized by Coase as an example of economics invading other social sciences with its analysis of human choice. For his part, Coase (1960) was addressing economists and focused on the impact of the law on the economic system.

Economic analysis of law was also criticized for focusing on formal law and neglecting social norms or informal institutions that can be explained by contractual perspectives (see Greif 1989 or Ellickson 1991) or non-cooperative games of coordination (see Schotter 1981 or Sugden 1986).

The schools studied in this first group are deductive and formalized, far from the empiricism and pragmatism of old institutionalism, which a modern institutionalism tried to revive.

Modern Institutionalism

Old institutionalist perspectives were pursued after World War II by different authors: Ayres, in a Veblenian tradition (see the entry "Institutionalism"), and Galbraith, who added Keynesian to Veblenian economics. In *The Affluent Society*, Galbraith (1955) dismissed the encouragement of private consumption at the expense of public spending ("private affluence, public squalor") whereas the government has a role to play in economic success. *American Capitalism* (Galbraith 1952) argued that planning is also essential to the functioning of the private sector: the development of technology entails large investments and therefore important risks that only large corporations can take, and which they try to reduce by controlling their environment, including by involving themselves in political activities. Technical change and innovations through research and development departments of large corporations are also at the centre of *The New Industrial State* (Galbraith 1967), which developed another institutionalist theme: the shaping of preferences by institutions, here large corporations, through advertisement.

Since the 1970s, numerous and diverse authors have claimed old institutionalism as their inspiration, presenting their approach as complementary or opposed to neoclassical economics and NIE. They envisage the individual and his preferences not as given, but as resulting from learning, which involves dynamics and collective processes, and which is incorporated in habits or routines. They retain Knightian uncertainty and the impossibility to contract over judgement capacities. They view interactions as not only contractual, even in the case of a market exchange; the market itself is an institution, a set of rules, embedded in other institutions. Conflict is first; individuals and institutions interact in an evolutionary process; technology is decisive. Interdisciplinarity is conceived as importing into economics insights from social sciences rather than exporting neoclassical tools. Regarding economic policy, they, too, use the Coasean comparative institutional method, but with a criterion broader than the maximization of wealth, or even than economic efficiency. All this differentiates the authors of the second group from the first.

Modern institutionalism is evolutionary in the sense employed by Thorstein Veblen (1899) and Joseph Schumpeter (1911 [1934]). The work of Richard Nelson and Sidney Winter (1982) became central to its recent developments, even if it can be argued that this does not strictly belong to the lineage of old institutionalism. Nelson and Winter draw from Charles Darwin's process of evolution and selection, Alfred Marshall's focus on industry and dynamics, Schumpeter's view of innovation as disequilibrium and the source of growth, and Simon's theory of rationality. In their perspective, agents do not optimize, but follow habits, which depend on skills. A skill is a sequence of actions usually efficient in the same context; it is a tacit knowledge learnt from experience. A routine is an organizational skill, a collective habit, incorporating the memory of the organization. Routines are the equivalent of genes and are replicated; mutations result from research activities and exceptional events. Selection by the environment operates, since an organization with better performances tends to grow and replicates its routines rather than changing them, and vice versa. Consequently, better adaptive routines tend to be more frequent. This model allows the study of the evolution of a population of firms, and of the adaptation of a firm or industry to a shift in market conditions or a technical change. It endogenously explains industrial structure and its evolution. The diversity of capabilities, learning and innovative efforts explains the diversity and evolution of knowledge, institutions (including firms) and technologies, which become the object of analysis rather than being exogenously given (for example, Metcalfe 1994).

The firm and the market

Focusing on concepts such as knowledge, capacities, routines, and their evolution, institutionalist (or competence-based) theories of the firm are very different from new institutionalist (or contractual) theories of transaction costs economics and property rights theory. The production problem is viewed as distinct from the allocation of resources; technology is not given; the specificity of the employment contract is the object of study; firms are diverse and generate human learning and innovation in an uncertain environment. Reviving the Veblenian evolutionary view of economics, basing his work on a large panel of institutionalists and other social scientists, and claiming to complement NIE, Hodgson insisted in *Economics and Institutions* (1988) that firms and markets are two different institutions.

Hodgson's starting point is that fundamental uncertainty impedes decision, which therefore must rely on habits, routines, norms, procedures (Simon) and conventions (Keynes) that make perceptions and anticipations possible. Following Veblenian thought, stress is put on habits, which result from (collective) learning. Routines are defined as collective habits and they allow for coordination. Institutions, such as language, money, customs or firms, are systems of social rules, formal or not, but enforced.

As stressed by Veblen (1899) and Commons (1934), they constrain and enhance behaviour. They function because the rules are embedded in habits of thought and behaviour. Habits and institutions reinforce each other in a cumulative process: individuals change institutions and institutions shape their perceptions, preferences and behaviours. There is no such thing as a state of nature without institutions: individuals rely on norms or customs.

Among institutions, organizations, such as firms or families, are specific institutions with boundaries and chains of command. Like in Nelson and Winter, firms incorporate routines involving competences. Hodgson defines firms as specific organizations: they have a legal existence and are dedicated to production; they protect routines-competences in a durable structure, promote loyalty and trust and enhance innovations. A firm's durability creates norms and rules on a long-term basis. And these norms do not have a quantitative expression, which allows going without costs calculus.

Markets, on the contrary, are specific institutions that provide price norms through short-term contractual exchanges between numerous and ephemeral agents:

> Exchanges themselves take place in a framework of law and contract enforceability. Markets involve legal and other rules that help to structure, organize and legitimize exchange transactions. They involve pricing and trading routines that help to establish a consensus over prices, and often help by communicating information regarding products, prices, quantities, potential buyers or possible sellers. Markets, in short, are organized and institutionalized recurrent exchange. (Hodgson 2008: 327)

Finally there exist some exchanges of property rights that do not take place in a competitive situation with numerous buyers and sellers: they are long-term contractual relationships, such as "relational exchanges" (Goldberg 1980), which involve cooperation as against competition. Such non-market exchanges are no longer "hybrid forms" or quasi-firms. Hodgson argues that there is no continuum between firms and markets; rather, the firm, with its legal existence, is opposed to contractual exchanges, be they market or relational.

Institutional law and economics

Institutional law and economics originated from the works of Ayres (1944), Hale (1952) and Commons (1934), and is mainly represented by Samuels (1971, 1972, 1974, 1989), Schmid (1965, 1978), Liebhafsky (1987) and Bromley (1989).

Institutional law and economics authors criticize what they call "neoclassical law and economics", that is Chicago-style economic analysis of law, particularly Posner. They dismiss the assumptions of rational behaviour and given individuals, the absence of distribution issues (while they are at the core of a great part of legal decisions) and of notions such as justice and fairness. They reject the definition of efficiency as Kaldor–Hicks efficiency since it entails interpersonal comparisons of utility, gives more weight to the preferences of the wealthy, and since its normative application (giving the right to whoever is ready to pay the most) reinforces inequalities. They criticize the positive thesis of the efficiency of common law for various reasons: this thesis is not refutable; it is ahistorical and cannot explain changes in the law or the variety of legal systems; it does not account for the origin of the alleged criterion of efficiency; and judges pursue fairness or are subject to other types of influence.

Above all, institutional law and economics stresses the circularity of the normative claim that the law ought to maximize wealth, and particularly that a judge must attribute rights to the person who is ready to pay the most for it (Liebhafsky 1976; Samuels 1971, 1981). The reason is that each initial distribution of property rights determines the level of prices in which the output of this initial structure is measured, thus the outputs produced by different initial structures cannot be compared. Since to each structure of rights corresponds (at least) one allocation that maximizes wealth, choosing one structure amounts to choosing one efficient allocation among non-comparable others. Hence the choice of an allocation hides a choice of the distribution of rights at the origin of this allocation, which favours certain interests at the expense of others. This criticism stresses that the allocation of rights not only entails allocation considerations but also, more importantly, considerations of distribution. Therefore the choice of an efficient initial distribution of rights among others entails normative elements that are a matter of "selective perception". Finally, the recognition that to each initial distribution of rights corresponds an efficient allocation denies its relevance to the Posnerian positive efficiency thesis, which is reduced to an "empirical regularity" (Samuels 1981: 162).

The specificity of institutional law and economics comes from its not applying economic tools to study law, using instead, like Commons, an interdisciplinary approach to study the "legal–economic nexus": law is a function of economy (some legal issues have an economic component) and economy is a function of law (Samuels 1989). It is this last aspect that neoclassical theory cannot deal with: rights determine allocation of resources, distribution, opportunity sets and power structures (Liebhavsky 1976).

Institutional law and economics is a positive theory that analyses cumulative legal–economic processes and describes the consequences of different institutional arrangements, leaving normative choices to legal actors or citizens who are actually involved (Samuels and Schmid 1981). Since "optimal" solutions can be obtained from every rights structure, a choice between them is a matter of whose interests are to count; the economist does not decide this, and leaves it to the political process. These authors do not reject the efficiency criterion as such, but stress that it cannot be separated from distributional aspects: a particular efficient allocation entails a particular distribution. The government has to choose among different allocations of resources, all equally efficient, but each originating from a specific distribution of rights. It selectively perceives costs and advantages according to its ideology, and chooses a distribution of rights. Institutional law and economics authors do not want to answer the question of the best policy, but pose the question "better for whom?" Since values (costs and benefits) are not given independently of the law, choosing the law is choosing which values are to count; it is a choice between conflicting interests. As a consequence, they study the evolutionary change of the legal–economic nexus, rather than change of the law exogenously guided by efficiency considerations.

Another issue is that each right impedes actions from others, denying others some rights and entailing coercion: the dual nature of rights is recognized (an influence of Commons and Coase). Since externalities are ubiquitous and reciprocal, the law does not find an optimal solution, but sets out who is authorized to coerce whom. The economic system, which is not reduced to the market, is viewed as a structure of power, analysed from organization and control perspectives. The initial distribution of rights determines power structures and therefore influences allocation of resources, income levels and distribution of revenue. In the market, power generates coercion, and transactions are not perfectly voluntary.

Institutional law and economics indeed describes a world in which conflict is primary, and the law is designed and changed to maintain order. Rights are not given, but endogenously determined by government. Now, access to government is determined by power, unequally distributed. Since access to power gives access to government, which in turn gives access to rights, power is self-enforcing: "opportunities for gain, whether pecuniary profit or other advantage, accrue to those who can use government. . . If income distribution and risk allocation is a partial function of law (of property) then the law is an object of control for economic or other gain" (Samuels 1971: 444). The question of more or less government is irrelevant, since what may appear as a greater governmental intervention is only a redefinition of rights that were attributed beforehand by the government. The question is therefore: which type of regulation? Institutional law and economics does not distinguish between regulation, common law or statutory law: each defines rights.

With its descriptively historical and evolutionary analysis instead of a deductive one, institutional law and economics claims to go back to the sources of old institutionalism: "institutional law and economics is rather redundant language because institutional economics has never been anything but the nexus of law and economics" (Schmid 1994: 33).

Conclusion

To conclude, it is worthwhile noting that institutionalists, like old institutionalists and historicists before them, often have a rather relativistic view of economic theory, at the very least because economic systems and institutions evolve, and hence theories that describe them must evolve too. They have therefore been at the forefront of the defence of pluralism in economics. For example, in 1992, at the initiative of Hodgson, Uskali Mäki and Deirdre McCloskey, a plea for pluralism in economics was circulated, signed, and published as an advertisement in the *American Economic Review*. It is not by mere chance that prominent authors classified as or close to institutionalists have signed it: among others, Eirik Furubotn, Galbraith, Albert Hirschman, Kornai, Nelson and Simon. Similarly, institutionalists express a strong interest in the history of economic thought, from which they adopt and revive concepts.

ÉLODIE BERTRAND

See also:

Ronald Harry Coase (I); Economic sociology (III); Evolutionary economics (III); Institutionalism (II); Public choice (II); Theory of the firm (III).

References and further reading

Alchian, A.A. (1961), *Some Economics of Property*, Santa Monica, CA: RAND Corporation.
Alchian, A.A. (1965), 'Some economics of property rights', *Il Politico*, **30** (4), 816–29.
Alchian, A.A. and H. Demsetz (1972), 'Production, information costs, and economic organization', *American Economic Review*, **62** (5), 777–95.
Ayres, C.E. (1944), *The Theory of Economic Progress*, Chapel Hill, NC: University of North Carolina Press.
Becker, G. (1968), 'Crime and punishment: an economic approach', *Journal of Political Economy*, **76** (2), 169–217.
Bromley, D. (1989), *Economic Interests and Institutions*, New York: Basil Blackwell.

Calabresi, G. (1961), 'Some thoughts on risk distribution and the law of torts', *Yale Law Journal*, **70** (4), 499–553.

Calabresi, G. (1970), *The Cost of Accidents: A Legal and Economic Analysis*, New Haven, CT: Yale University Press.

Coase, R.H. (1937), 'The nature of the firm', *Economica*, New Series, **4** (16), 386–405.

Coase, R.H. (1960), 'The problem of social cost', *Journal of Law and Economics*, **3** (October), 1–44.

Coase, R.H. (1988), *The Firm, the Market and the Law*, Chicago, IL: University of Chicago Press.

Commons, J.R. (1934), *Institutional Economics. Its Place in Political Economy*, New York: Macmillan.

Davis, L. and D.C. North (1971), *Institutional Change and American Economic Growth*, Cambridge: Cambridge University Press.

Demsetz, H. (1964), 'The exchange and enforcement of property rights', *Journal of Law and Economics*, **7** (October), 11–26.

Demsetz, H. (1967), 'Toward a theory of property rights', *American Economic Review*, **57** (2), 347–59.

Ellickson, R.C. (1991), *Order without Law: How Neighbors Settle Disputes*, Cambridge, MA: Harvard University Press.

Friedman, M. (1953), 'The methodology of positive economics', in *Essays in Positive Economics*, Chicago, IL, University of Chicago Press, pp. 3–43.

Furubotn, E.G. and S. Pejovich (1972), 'Property rights and economic theory: a survey of recent literature', *Journal of Economic Literature*, **10** (4), 1137–62.

Galbraith, J.K. (1952), *American Capitalism*, Boston, MA: Houghton Mifflin.

Galbraith, J.K. (1955), *The Affluent Society*, Boston, MA: Houghton Mifflin.

Galbraith, J.K. (1967), *The New Industrial State*, Boston, MA: Houghton Mifflin.

Goldberg, V.P. (1980), 'Relational exchange: economics and complex contracts', *American Behavioral Scientist*, **23** (3), 337–52.

Greif, A. (1989), 'Reputation and coalitions in medieval trade: evidence on the Maghribi traders', *Journal of Economic History*, **49** (4), 857–82.

Hale, R.L. (1952), *Freedom Through Law*, New York: Columbia University Press.

Hodgson, G.M. (1988), *Economics and Institutions: A Manifesto for a Modern Institutional Economics*, Cambridge: Polity Press.

Hodgson, G.M. (2000), 'What is the essence of institutional economics?', *Journal of Economic Issues*, **34** (2), 317–29.

Hodgson, G.M. (2008), 'Markets', in S.N. Durlauf and L.E. Blume (eds), *The New Palgrave Dictionary of Economics*, vol. 5, 2nd edn, London: Palgrave Macmillan, accessed 27 January 2016 at http://www.dictionaryofeconomics.com/article?id=pde2008_M000402.

Koopmans, T.C. (1947), 'Measurement without theory', *Review of Economics and Statistics*, **29** (3), 161–72.

Liebhafsky, H.H. (1976), 'Price theory as jurisprudence: law and economics, Chicago style', *Journal of Economic Issues*, **10** (1), 23–43.

Liebhafsky, H.H. (1987), 'Law and economics from different perspectives', *Journal of Economic Issues*, **21** (December), 1809–36.

Macneil, I.R., (1974), 'The many futures of contracts', *Southern California Law Review*, **47** (3), 691–816.

Medema, S.G. (1996), 'Ronald Coase and American institutionalism', *Research in the History of Economic Thought and Methodology*, **14**, 51–92.

Mercuro, N. and S.G. Medema (1997), *Economics and the Law: From Posner to Post-Modernism*, Princeton, NJ: Princeton University Press.

Metcalfe, J.S. (1994), 'Competition, Fisher's principle and increasing returns in the selection process', *Journal of Evolutionary Economics*, **4** (4), 327–46.

Nelson, R.R. and S.G. Winter (1982), *An Evolutionary Theory of Economic Change*, Cambridge, MA: Harvard University Press.

North, D.C. (1981), *Structure and Change in Economic History*, New York: Norton.

North, D.C. (1990), *Institutions, Institutional Change, and Economic Performance*, Cambridge: Cambridge University Press.

North, D.C. and R.P. Thomas (1973), *The Rise of the Western World: A New Economic History*, Cambridge: Cambridge University Press.

Posner, R.A. (1972), *Economic Analysis of Law*, Boston, MA: Little, Brown.

Samuels, Warren J. (1971), 'Interrelations between legal and economic processes', *Journal of Law and Economics*, **14** (2), 435–50.

Samuels, W.J. (1972), 'Welfare economics, power and property', in G. Wunderlich and W.L. Gibson Jr (eds), *Perspectives of Property*, University Park, PA: Institute for Research on Land and Water Resources, Pennsylvania State University, pp. 61–127.

Samuels, W.J. (1974), 'The Coase theorem and the study of law and economics', *Natural Resources Journal*, **14** (1), 1–33.

Samuels, W.J. (1981), 'Maximization of wealth as justice: an essay on Posnerian law and economics as policy analysis', *Texas Law Review*, **60** (1), 147–72.
Samuels, W.J. (1989), 'The legal–economic nexus', *George Washington Law Review*, **57** (6), 1556–78.
Samuels, W.J. and A.A. Schmid (1981), *Law and Economics: An Institutional Perspective*, Boston, MA: Kluwer-Nijhoff.
Schmid, A.A. (1965), 'Property, power and progress', *Land Economics*, **41** (3), 275–9.
Schmid, A.A. (1978), *Property, Power and Public Choice: An Inquiry into Law and Economics*, New York: Praeger.
Schmid, A.A. (1994), 'Institutional law and economics', *European Journal of Law and Economics*, **1** (1), 33–51.
Schotter, A. (1981), *The Economic Theory of Social Institutions*, Cambridge: Cambridge University Press.
Schumpeter, J.A. (1911), *Theorie der wirtschaftlichen Entwicklung: eine Untersuchung über Unternehmergewinn, Kapital, Kredit, Zins und den Konjunkturzyklus*, Leipzig: Duncker & Humblot, English trans. R. Opie (1934), *The Theory of Economic Development, An Inquiry into Profits, Capital, Credit, Interest, and the Business Cycle*, London: Transaction.
Simon, H.A. (1955), 'A behavioral model of rational choice', *Quarterly Journal of Economics*, **69** (1), 99–118.
Sugden, R. (1986), *The Economics of Rights, Co-operation, and Welfare*, Oxford: Basil Blackwell.
Veblen, T.B. (1899), *The Theory of the Leisure Class: An Economic Study in the Evolution of Institutions*, New York: Macmillan.
Williamson, O.E. (1975), *Markets and Hierarchies, Analysis and Antitrust Implications: A Study in the Economics of Internal Organization*, New York: Free Press.
Williamson, O.E. (1985), *The Economic Institutions of Capitalism*, New York: Free Press.
Williamson, O.E. (1996), *The Mechanisms of Governance*, Oxford: Oxford University Press.

International trade

International trade is one of the oldest forms of globalization. Its motivations, advantages and possible drawbacks have been speculated on in the Western world for centuries by philosophers, businessmen, theologians and economists.

Greek Philosophers on the Causes and Advantages of Trade

The Greek philosophers wrote about how trade, within and among city-states, affected the welfare of their citizens. Aristotle among them advocated autarky or self-sufficiency as an ideal to be pursued by city-states. Others viewed trade as the only way a state can obtain the goods it lacks, and recognized that needed imports require exports in exchange. In Plato's words, in order for a state to create a commodity surplus it can exchange with other states, "home production must not merely suffice for themselves, but in quality and quantity meet the needs of those of whom they have need" (Plato 1963: 371a). Other writers were wary of "unnecessary exchange" and unregulated trade undertaken for the sake of money accumulation rather than the satisfaction of real needs. Aristotle asserted that "states which make themselves marts for the world only do it for the sake of revenue; and if a state ought not to indulge in this sort of profit-making, it follows that it ought not to be an exchange centre of that kind" (Aristotle 1946: 1327a). Rephrasing this in present-day terms, globalization may not be advantageous if it is undertaken purely for the sake of profit! Moreover, while the import of necessities may be justified, the Greeks regarded that of luxury goods with suspicion as it may lead to the corruption of morals.

In discussing the mutual gains from trade, the Greeks addressed the issue of whether the expertise in commodity production deployed by the parties to the trade is innate or induced by practice or training. Two millennia later Adam Smith leaned to the latter view, in line with his dictum that "the difference between the most dissimilar characters, between a philosopher and a common street porter, for example, seems to arise not so much from nature, as from habit, custom, and education" (Smith 1776 [1996], hereafter WN, I.ii.4). The Greeks instead believed people are born with different aptitudes. As Plato said in *The Republic*, "no two of us are born exactly alike. We have different natural aptitudes, which fit us for different jobs", so that "we do better to exercise one skill" than "to try to practice several". "Quantity and quality" – he concludes – "are . . . more easily produced when a man specializes appropriately on a single job for which he is naturally fitted, and neglects all others". According to Lowry, specialization in different tasks as described in Xenophon's *Cyropaedia* "suggests elements of the analysis of comparative advantage, or, at a minimum, reciprocal absolute advantage elaborated by nineteenth-century English economists", if "the latter notion [is extended] to geographic regions with different characteristics" (Lowry 1987: 65–6). We return to the rationale for trade starting with Smith and Ricardo's theories of trade discussed below.

Providence and Trade, Mercantilism, and the Eighteenth-Century Rule

The Greek views on self-sufficiency as regards individuals, families or entire city-states, and the role of trade in overcoming it, continued in the Christian era when it was given a religious dimension. The perceived need for a state to rely on other states for some of the commodities it requires was interpreted as part of a plan of divine providence to foster a spirit of mutual support and friendship among different peoples. Viner's *The Role of Providence in the Social Order* (1972) outlines a "providentialist" theory of trade where providence encourages different peoples to trade as a means of promoting solidarity among them, and creates the incentive for this by scattering resources unevenly throughout the globe. In the fourth century CE, Libanius, a pagan from Antioch who taught two of the earliest Church Fathers, St Basil and St John Chrysostom, claimed that:

> God did not bestow all products upon all parts of the earth, but distributed His gifts over different regions, to the end that men might cultivate a social relationship because one would have need of the help of another. And so he called commerce into being, that all might be able to have common enjoyment of the fruits of earth, no matter where produced. (Viner 1972: 36–7)

As was true of the Greek philosophers, some theologians warned about the less salubrious consequences of trade, such as the accumulation of money and wealth. In the Middle Ages Libanius' view continued to be supported by some scholastics, but was rejected by others for moral reasons based on the strictures against commercial transactions advanced by the Greek philosophers, and was corroborated by church teachings on the dangers to salvation arising from market transactions in general and foreign trade in particular. Some viewed self-sufficiency as preferable to economic dependence on foreigners and feared that the introduction of foreign goods could divert interest from the satisfaction of basic needs, channelling it toward ostentation, a taste for luxuries and money making, inequalities in wealth, envy and even wars. The greatest of the Scholastics, St Thomas Aquinas, took a more moderate and pragmatic view, realizing that self-sufficiency was a worthy ideal but unlikely to be achieved at times of harvest failures or merchants' needs to dispose of surpluses of commodities.

With the Enlightenment, the moral and religious view of trade espoused by the Scholastic writers gradually lost its appeal in favour of a more secular outlook. The mercantilist period is not noted for substantial theoretical contributions to trade theory, but the doctrine of mercantilism was rife with implications for trade policy. Mercantilist writers defined and calculated numbers for a country's balance of payments, identifying key components such as exports and imports. The difference between the values of exports and imports constitutes the "balance of trade", another important concept of that period of interest to policymakers. If its value is positive, the country sells more abroad than it buys, and the difference is paid to it in the form of bullion or precious metals. If instead it is negative, the country loses gold and silver to foreign creditors and consequently faces a decline in its money supply if its monetary system is based on the gold standard. Policymakers thus aimed at a positive balance of trade, in the awareness that they were playing a zero-sum game where one nation's gain implied another's loss. The futility of this policy was perceived by the more enlightened writers of the time who favoured instead a policy of free trade. They included Pierre de Boisguilbert and the Physiocrats in France, and David Hume, Henry Martyn, Sir Dudley North, Josiah Tucker and others in Britain.

Among the early critics of mercantilist policies, Pierre de Boisguilbert supported laissez-faire and free trade, as reflected in the slogan *laissez faire la nature et la liberté*. His economic reasoning earned him Marx's praise as one of the two founders (together with William Petty) of classical political economy. In his *Détail de la France* (1695) and subsequent writings, he criticized France's restrictive tax and trade policies, advocated competition among producers, and a price structure based on what he called "proportionate equilibrium". State-imposed impediments to the flows of commodities and money, such as internal barriers to trade, regulations in agriculture and manufacturing, export duties, and taxes such as the *taille*, should be abolished. Since he favoured the encouragement of agriculture over manufacturing, Boisguilbert opposed Colbert's edicts prohibiting wheat exports and advocated free trade and high domestic prices, first and foremost for the grain trade. He maintained that: "free competition, and particularly foreign trade, stabilises prices through the mechanisms of expectation and the price/quantity strategies". Unlike the claims of its opponents, Boisguilbert stressed that 'foreign' (provincial or national) trade is never damaging to the interests of the nation, and in terms of quantity it is ultimately very slight. Boisguilbert tried to lay to rest his contemporaries' overriding fear of a grain shortage (Faccarello 1999: 129).

Boisguilbert's writings inspired physiocracy, whose etymological meaning is "rule of nature". It was a notable manifestation of the French Enlightenment, and represents the first full-fledged school of political economy. Under the leadership of François Quesnay, who contributed several articles to the *Encyclopédie*, the Physiocrats launched a frontal attack against mercantilist doctrine and (following Boiguilbert's lead) they articulated a program of reforms for the French economy that included freedom of both domestic and foreign trade. During and after the short span of two decades (beginning in 1756) over which they were active, the Physiocrats influenced the British classical school and Adam Smith in particular, who spent three years in France from 1763 to 1766 and met several of them. Smith rejected their belief that agriculture is the sole productive sector of the economy in the sense of being the only one to yield a surplus over cost. Although agreeing with the Physiocrats' advocacy of free trade, Smith's system of economic thought departed from theirs in other significant respects.

The enduring legacies of physiocracy include the characterization of a competitive economy as one in which individuals pursuing their self-interest allow society's welfare to be maximized, and a depiction of the circular flow of commodities between the principal classes of society is described in Quesnay's *Tableau économique* (1759). Capital expenditures in the form of advances to farmer-entrepreneurs constituted an integral part of the process of production, and laid the foundations for the classical theory of capital. Given the Physiocrats' importance in the filiation of economic ideas, it is surprising and somewhat disappointing that they failed to take an interest in or contribute to the theory of international trade. While the mercantilists had given an overwhelming importance to a country's foreign trade because (*inter alia*) of its favourable effects on the pattern of economic activity, the Physiocrats regarded foreign trade as a "sterile" activity, on a par with domestic trade and manufacturing. They even argued that a large volume of foreign trade is harmful, although this was tempered with the belief that this volume was in any case likely to shrink as the economy developed. They did recognize the benefits of specialization, granting that "each country was considered as endowed with 'produits privilégiés' which, because of natural conditions or national aptitudes, it could produce more 'cheaply' than other countries" (Bloomfield 1938: 732). Moreover, they acknowledged the providentialist function of foreign trade in promoting international economic solidarity, and its usefulness in disposing of unwanted surpluses via exports, or offsetting through imports any shortfalls in production. However, these views were hardly novel or specific to them.

Despite their failure to advance the theory of international trade, the Physiocrats (following Boisguilbert) were staunch advocates of freedom in both internal and external trade. They regarded freedom in foreign trade as part of the natural order, going hand in hand with their doctrine of laissez-faire and their efforts to reduce all impediments to internal trade. They were especially strong advocates of the freedom to export grain. Stringent regulations had prevented grain exports until 1764 and had become the subject of heated debate. The export ban was one of the many mercantilist measures that the Physiocrats wanted to abolish as detrimental to the interests of the agricultural classes, with which their primary sympathies lay. The free export of grain would allow its price to maintain a satisfactory level (*bon prix*) even at times of abundant harvest, whereas an export ban would cause its price to fall, damaging both the profitability of agriculture and the nation's prosperity. As Vaggi (1987: 874) argues, "[the Physiocrats] looked to a positive balance of trade for French agriculture, since France should have become the granary of Europe . . . [and] . . . regarded foreign trade as necessary only because the French domestic market was too small and too poor to guarantee the profitable sale of French corn". Given the importance of agriculture in their system, it was the Physiocrats' enthusiastic advocacy of free grain exports that gave them no incentive to forge any analytical progress with a theory of international trade that embraces the other economic sectors they regarded as "sterile".

In 1752 the Scottish philosopher David Hume published a series of essays analysing a variety of commercial, developmental, monetary, fiscal and demographic issues relating to England, Scotland, France and other countries. Two more essays with an economic focus followed in 1758, including "Of the jealousy of trade" where he argued for free trade and against the petty mercantilist policies of that time where nation-states were concerned that competing economies would supplant them in world markets. Hume claimed instead that no country should worry that other countries could improve their production techniques to such an extent that they would no longer demand any of its products, seeing that "nature, by giving a diversity of geniuses, climates, and soils, to different nations, has secured their mutual intercourse and commerce, as long as they all remain industrious and civilized" (Hume 1955: 79). The diversity among nations implies that each can remain competitive in some economic sectors vis-à-vis its trading partners. Hume's mention of "a diversity of geniuses, climates, and soils" was later echoed by Smith, Ricardo and other classical economists, and has the merit of identifying diversity as an important reason for trade. Several of the trade models analysed below in fact postulate that trade arises from specific differences such as those in tastes, technology or factor endowments among countries.

In his earlier essay "Of commerce", Hume (1955: 14) had observed that "commerce with strangers . . . rouses men from their indolence" and that "imitation soon diffuses all those arts; while domestic manufactures emulate the foreign in their improvements, and work up every home commodity to the utmost perfection of which it is susceptible". In "Of the jealousy of trade", he argued (1955: 78–9) that:

> the encrease [*sic*] of riches and commerce in any one nation, instead of hurting, commonly promotes the riches and commerce of all its neighbours . . . Every improvement, which

we have since [two centuries ago] made, has arisen from our imitation of foreigners. . . . Notwithstanding the advanced state of our manufactures, we daily adopt, in every art, the inventions and improvements of our neighbours.

His contention that "imitation soon diffuses all those arts" was prescient, and two centuries later still reflects one of the chief benefits of international trade, the international diffusion of technology. Hume became even better known for his essay "Of the balance of trade" of 1752 where, utilizing the quantity theory of money, he depicted what became known as the price specie-flow mechanism, thanks to which any balance of trade surplus or deficit is automatically eliminated over time because of the impact of the resulting gold flows on the price levels and consequent trade flows between two trading countries. His point was that the mercantilist goal of maintaining a balance of trade surplus for an indefinite period of time was not just undesirable but impossible to attain. Hume's essay drove a nail into the coffin that soon encased the obsession of some mercantilist writers and policymakers with realizing a positive balance of trade as the prime goal of policy.

Hume and Josiah Tucker also engaged in what became known as the "rich country/poor country" debate, where they argued whether poor countries such as Scotland could catch up with or even surpass the standard of living of richer ones such as England. In opposition to Hume, Tucker maintained in a letter to Lord Kames (Rotwein 1955: 202–5) that the built-in advantages of rich countries are hard to reverse. Their argument is highly topical since one of the important issues that economists are still debating is whether present-day developed and developing countries are likely to converge in their per capita incomes over time, or destined to draw even further apart.

Although trade theory did not make much headway prior to the nineteenth century, several eighteenth-century writers speculated on how to conceptualize and measure the gains from trade. They made an important discovery that Jacob Viner dubbed the "eighteenth-century rule", according to which "it pays to import commodities from abroad whenever they can be obtained in exchange for exports at a smaller real cost than their production at home would entail" (Viner 1937: 440). In his *Considerations on the East-India Trade* of 1701, Henry Martyn presented the following illustration of this rule:

> If nine cannot produce above three Bushels of Wheat in *England*, if by equal Labour they might procure nine Bushels from another Country, to imploy these in agriculture at home, is to imploy nine to do no more work than might be done as well by three; . . . is the loss of six Bushels of Wheat; is therefore the loss of so much value. (Martyn 1701 [1954]: 583)

In his example wheat can be grown inefficiently at home, or the same labourers can be employed to produce an export commodity that can be exchanged for a lot more wheat on world markets. In France, three-quarters of a century later, A.-R.-J. Turgot also argued for free interregional trade within France by offering another instance of this rule. He pointed out that farmers in Brie "thought themselves thrifty by drinking bad wine from their own vineyards" (Turgot 1773 [1977]: 187) when they sacrificed good land suitable for wheat in order to grow vines. Had they devoted the land to wheat instead, they could easily have sold it in exchange for the best Burgundy. The eighteenth-century rule was subsequently used by both Smith and Ricardo to illustrate the gains from trade.

Adam Smith on the Benefits of Trade

Adam Smith's theory of foreign trade was found wanting by most economists until recent times. Unlike Ricardo's *Principles of Political Economy*, Smith's *Wealth of Nations* contains no chapter titled "On foreign trade". Smith's contributions to this area were called to the profession's attention by Arthur Bloomfield (1975), Hla Myint (1977), and recently by Paul Krugman:

> The long dominance of Ricardo over Smith – of comparative advantage over increasing returns – was largely due to the belief that the alternative was necessarily a mess. In effect, the theory of international trade followed the perceived line of least mathematical resistance. Once it was clear that papers on noncomparative-advantage trade could be just as tight and clean as papers in the traditional mold, the field was ripe for rapid transformation. (Krugman 1990: 4)

As noted below, Krugman's new trade theory has indeed some parallels with Smith's theory of foreign trade, though he expressed it in the mathematical terms that the economics profession is now accustomed to. Smith's most significant statements on foreign trade occur in the early chapters of Book IV of the *Wealth of Nations* where he launches his broadsides against mercantilism. The gains from foreign trade are highlighted in chapter 2 titled "Of restraints upon the importation from foreign countries of such goods as can be produced at home". Positive and normative elements of trade theory (with the emphasis on normative ones) are treated simultaneously by Smith who contends that:

> The natural advantages which one country has over another in producing particular commodities are sometimes so great, that it is acknowledged by all the world to be in vain to struggle with them. . . . Whether the advantages which one country has over another, be natural or acquired, is in this respect of no consequence. As long as the one country has those advantages, and the other wants them, it will always be more advantageous for the latter, rather to buy of the former than to make. (WN IV.ii.15)

Though he frequently uses the term "advantage" in this chapter, Smith never defines it rigorously. Most trade economists believe it stands for "absolute advantage" or a lower cost of production, a term to which I return below when comparing it to Ricardo's comparative advantage. One of Smith's goals for foreign trade is clearly the efficiency one of using it to minimize the overall cost of providing a given level of consumption by selling domestic commodities at the highest price and buying foreign ones at the lowest.

In certain cases Smith attributes advantages to the abundance of particular factors of production such as land in Britain's American colonies. Bloomfield (1975: 459) even claims that Smith anticipated the Heckscher–Ohlin theory of trade discussed below, arguing that Smith "lays down with remarkable clarity the elements of the proposition later to be made famous by Heckscher and Ohlin". But this is developed by example rather than in any systematic way. As Bloomfield himself recognizes, of greater importance to Smith than the causes of trade is its economic impact, or what has become known as the "gains from trade". As an important expression of the efficiency advantages just mentioned, Smith repeatedly applies the eighteenth-century rule to personal exchanges, exchanges between town and country, and international ones. As a secondary benefit he lists the gains that consumers enjoy beyond the purchase of cheaper goods, such as the availability of a greater variety of commodities, including some imported from America that were previously unknown. Unlike in the case of present-day mainstream trade theory, the third and most important gain occurs on the production, not the consumption, side: it is the stimulus to economic development occasioned by a widening of the market. According to Smith, the key to a nation's wealth is the division of labour, and this is limited by the extent of the market. When international trade enhances this extent by adding the foreign to the domestic market, it enables a greater division of labour and a gain in efficiency. An example of this followed from the discovery of America:

> By opening a new and inexhaustible market to all the commodities of Europe, it gave occasion to new divisions of labour and improvements of art, which, in the narrow circle of the ancient commerce, could never have taken place for want of a market to take off the greater part of their produce. The productive powers of labour were improved, and its produce increased in all the different countries of Europe, and together with it the real revenue and wealth of the inhabitants. (WN IV.i.32)

Myint (1977) called this Smith's "productivity theory of trade". It claims that the gains from trade are mainly dynamic rather than static, as they are in neoclassical trade theory where the economy moves along a given transformation curve in the direction of greater specialization, with no effect on technology or the "productive powers of labour". Other dynamic benefits that Smith mentions, possibly borrowing from his friend Hume's writings, are the incentive that the availability of foreign goods provides for greater work effort, and for the adoption and imitation of foreign technologies. A stimulus to economic development via import substitution and the activation of otherwise idle resources thanks to export demand are additional benefits of foreign trade that Smith emphasizes in the *Wealth of Nations*. In addition to Smith, other classical economists (including David Hume and John Stuart Mill) pointed out that international trade, in addition to its economic gains, also provides a set of non-economic benefits, such as the promotion of friendship and solidarity among nations, and even makes war among them obsolete.

David Ricardo and Comparative Advantage

Two years before Ricardo published his *Principles of Political Economy and Taxation* in 1817, Torrens hinted in literary terms at the concept of comparative advantage. In his *Essay on the External Corn Trade* (1815: 264–5), Torrens wrote that England would gain by exchanging its cloth for Polish corn even though English land "should be superior to the lands of Poland" and could be cultivated profitably. His reason was that "the capital which should be employed in manufacturing, would obtain a still greater excess of profit; and this greater excess of profit would determine the direction of our industry". Ricardo's formulation is generally regarded as superior to Torrens's since he expressed this concept in numerical terms, derived its policy implications and even quantified the gains from trade.

Chapter 7 of Ricardo's *Principles* contains the following paragraphs that relate to the exchange of cloth and wine by England and Portugal:

> The quantity of wine which she [Portugal] shall give in exchange for the cloth of England, is not determined by the respective quantities of labour devoted to the production of each, as it would be, if both commodities were manufactured in England, or both in Portugal.

England may be so circumstanced, that to produce the cloth may require the labour of 100 men for one year; and if she attempted to make the wine, it might require the labour of 120 men for the same time. England would therefore find it her interest to import wine, and purchase it by the exportation of cloth.

To produce the wine in Portugal, might require only the labour of 80 men for one year, and to produce the cloth in the same country, might require the labour of 90 men for the same time. It would therefore be advantageous for her to export wine in exchange for cloth. This exchange might even take place, notwithstanding that the commodity imported by Portugal could be produced there with less labour than in England. Though she could make the cloth with the labour of 90 men, she would import it from a country where it required the labour of 100 men to produce it, because it would be advantageous to her rather to employ her capital in the production of wine, for which she would obtain more cloth from England, than she could produce by diverting a portion of her capital from the cultivation of vines to the manufacture of cloth.

Thus England would give the produce of the labour of 100 men, for the produce of the labour of 80. (Ricardo 1817 [1951b]: 135)

These paragraphs contain Ricardo's famous numerical example of international trade according to comparative advantage, outlining both the reasons for trade and the gains that accrue to each trading country As Sraffa (1930) and Ruffin (2002) point out, Ricardo presents the number of workers that each country requires to produce the amounts of cloth or wine that it exports to the other and the number of workers it would require to produce the bundle of the commodity it imports in exchange. Thus England uses 100 men to produce the cloth it exchanges for an amount of wine that would require the labour of 120 Englishmen, so that its gains from trade are 20 men who can be employed in other pursuits. He makes a similar calculation for Portugal, finding that whereas 80 men can produce its wine exports, 90 would be required to produce the cloth it imports from England so that Portugal's gains from trade are 10 men. Each country's trade satisfies Viner's eighteenth-century rule for gains since its exports require a lower workforce than would be needed to produce its imports.

In Ricardo's example, comparative advantage is represented by the fact that in autarky (or the absence of trade) the relative price of each country's export commodity is lower than in the other country. To express this in algebraic terms, let a_{ji} be the amount of labour needed to produce one unit of commodity j in country i, w_i labour's wage in country i, r_i the profit rate paid on circulating capital in the form of advanced wages, and p_{ji} the price of commodity j in country i in autarky. The cost of producing commodity j in country i is the sum $a_{ji}w_i(1 + r_i)$ of the cost of labour $a_{ji}w_i$ and the profits $ra_{ji}w_i$ earned on circulating capital $a_{ji}w_i$. Since competition equates price and unit cost in each country, we obtain for any two commodities j and k:

$$p_{ji} = a_{ji}w_i(1 + r_i), \ p_{ki} = a_{ki}w_i(1 + r_i) \tag{1}$$

or

$$p_{ji} = a_{ji}y_i, \ p_{ki} = a_{ki}y_i \tag{2}$$

where $y_i = w_i(1 + r_i)$ is income per worker in country i. Dividing the first expression in (1) or (2) by the second we obtain country i's autarky price ratio of good j in terms of good k:

Table 7   Workers needed annually to produce one unit of cloth and wine in England and Portugal

Workers needed annually to produce	1 unit of C	1 unit of W
Portugal	$a_{CP} = \dfrac{90}{X}$	$a_{WP} = \dfrac{80}{Y}$
England	$a_{CE} = \dfrac{100}{X}$	$a_{WE} = \dfrac{120}{Y}$

$$\frac{p_{ji}}{p_{ki}} = \frac{a_{ji}}{a_{ki}} \tag{3}$$

Relative prices of commodities in autarky are proportional to the unit labour inputs in producing them, which is consistent with the labour theory of value that Ricardo adhered to in most of the *Principles*, including chapter 7 on foreign trade.

If England (country E) trades X of cloth (commodity C) for Y of wine (commodity W) with Portugal (country P), Portugal's terms of trade (defined as the price of wine in terms of cloth) are $\frac{X}{Y}$. Since Ricardo did not assign values to X and Y, these are left in algebraic form. If the production of each commodity is subject to constant unit costs, Table 7 shows the values of a_{ji} for each commodity in each country ($i = $ E, P; $j = $ C, W) derived from the passage quoted above.

Hence in autarky the relative prices of W in terms of C are given by (3) as $\frac{a_{WP}}{a_{CP}} = \frac{\frac{80}{Y}}{\frac{90}{X}} = 0.89\left(\frac{X}{Y}\right)$ in Portugal and $\frac{a_{WE}}{a_{CE}} = \frac{\frac{120}{Y}}{\frac{100}{X}} = 1.2\left(\frac{X}{Y}\right)$ in England. Since wine is cheaper in Portugal, Portugal has a comparative advantage in wine so that when trade opens it exchanges its wine for English cloth.

Let p_j ($j = $ C, W) be the after-trade price of commodity j in England and Portugal, which is set equal to unit cost in each country. If we assume zero transport costs, free trade, and complete specialization of each country in its export commodity, equations (2) are replaced by:

$$p_W = a_{WP}y_P, \quad p_C = a_{CE}y_E \tag{4}$$

which yield:

$$\frac{y_P}{y_E} = \left(\frac{a_{CE}}{a_{WP}}\right)\left(\frac{p_W}{p_C}\right) = \left(\frac{\pi_{WP}}{\pi_{CE}}\right)\left(\frac{p_W}{p_C}\right) \tag{5}$$

where the inverse of a_{ji} or $\pi_{ji} = \frac{1}{a_{ji}}$ is the productivity of labour in producing commodity j in country i ($i = $ E, P; $j = $ C, W). Equation (5) shows that relative income per worker is higher in Portugal as compared to England, the higher is Portuguese labour productivity in wine compared to English productivity in cloth, and the more favourable to Portugal are its terms of trade $\frac{p_W}{p_C}$. The positive linear relation between the factorial terms of trade $\frac{y_P}{y_E}$ and the commodity terms of trade $\frac{p_W}{p_C}$ over a certain range is illustrated by the segment BC of the broken line ABCD of Figure 6. Segments AB and CD of Figure 6 outline the

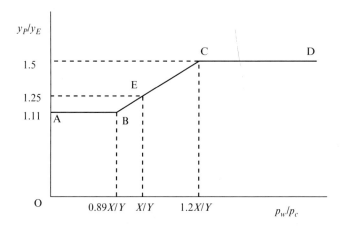

Figure 6   Relative per worker incomes in the Ricardian model

constant relative per worker incomes corresponding respectively to terms of trade equal to or below Portugal's autarky price ratio $0.89(X/Y)$, and equal to or above England's autarky price ratio $1.2(X/Y)$.

Substituting $\pi_{WP} = \frac{Y}{80}$ and $\pi_{CE} = \frac{X}{100}$ into (5), we obtain:

$$\frac{y_P}{y_E} = 1.25\left(\frac{X}{Y}\right)\left(\frac{p_W}{p_C}\right) \tag{6}$$

When $\frac{p_W}{p_C}$ is equal to the terms of trade X/Y, (6) yields $\frac{y_P}{y_E} = 1.25$ as shown by point E in Figure 6. We conclude that Portugal's absolute advantage in both wine and cloth causes its income per capita to be 25 per cent higher than England's.

Although comparative advantage is Ricardo's signal contribution to the theory of international trade, absolute advantage retains a fundamental importance in his trade model since it determines the relative standards of living in the two countries. Ricardo himself was fully aware of the power of absolute advantage in setting Portugal's standard of living relative to England's. In the last sentence of the passage from chapter 7 of the *Principles* quoted above, he stated "Thus England would give the produce of the labour of 100 men, for the produce of the labour of 80" (Ricardo 1817 [1951b]: 135). Since the produce of 100 Englishmen is exchanged for the produce of 80 Portuguese workers, the ratio of their per worker incomes is indeed 100/80 = 1.25 as shown by point E in Figure 6.

So far, unit labour costs have been assumed to be constant in each country. However, Ricardo's analysis of the determinants of rent and profits was an important foundation for the principal policy implication that flowed from both the *Essay on Profits* (Ricardo 1815 [1951a]) and the *Principles*: the repeal of Britain's Corn Laws leading to free trade in grain. The numerical examples that he used to illustrate his analysis of rent and profits are based on diminishing returns to labour when more labour is added to a fixed stock of land. These diminishing returns in the face of a constant real wage of labour cause the money wage to rise and the profit rate to fall.

Most of the examples of foreign trade found in the *Principles* concern trade in corn (Maneschi 1992). In chapter 7, Ricardo asserts that the two principal gains from trade for a country such as Britain are the efficiency gains arising from a reallocation of resources in line with comparative advantage, and a rise in the rate of profit:

> It is quite as important to the happiness of mankind, that our enjoyments should be increased by the better distribution of labour, by each country producing those commodities for which by its situation, its climate, and its other natural or artificial advantages, it is adapted, and by their exchanging them for the commodities of other countries, as that they should be augmented by a rise in the rate of profits. (Ricardo 1817 [1951b]: 132)

Ricardo went on to point out that one way for Britain to achieve the latter gain was to promote free trade in wage goods such as corn:

> It has been my endeavour to shew throughout this work, that the rate of profits can never be increased but by a fall in wages, and that there can be no permanent fall of wages but in consequence of a fall of the necessaries on which wages are expended. If, therefore, by the extension of foreign trade, or by improvements in machinery, the food and necessaries of the labourer can be brought to market at a reduced price, profits will rise. (Ibid.)

While Ricardo regarded technical change ("improvements in machinery") as adventitious and not amenable to public policy, he tied cheaper wage goods directly to the abolition of the trade policy responsible for the high price of corn: the Corn Laws.

Instead of an economy composed of two constant-cost sectors of the type analysed above, consider a Ricardian two-sector economy consisting of an agricultural sector subject to diminishing returns to labour and a manufacturing sector subject to constant returns. Each worker is paid a fixed subsistence wage s consisting of corn that is advanced at the beginning of the production period. Let L_j be the labour force in sector j, where j can denote a for agriculture or m for manufacturing, and $L = L_a + L_m$ be the total labour force. In line with Ricardo's reasoning in chapter 6 ("On profits") of the *Principles*, assume that agricultural (or "corn") production is given by a function $f(L_a)$ whose slope $f'(L_a)$ declines with the value of L_a but always exceeds s. The profit rate r is given by the excess over s of the marginal corn product of labour divided by s, or:

$$r = \frac{f'(L_a) - s}{s} = \frac{f'(L_a)}{s} - 1 \tag{7}$$

Although the profit rate is set in the corn sector, competition equalizes its value in both sectors. Assume that, when trade opens, the terms of trade p^*, defined as the relative price of corn in terms of cloth, are lower than the domestic relative price of corn which has risen over time because of diminishing marginal returns to labour in the corn sector. The consequence of trade for the sectoral allocation of the labour force is to increase manufacturing output at the expense of corn output, so that L_a falls and L_m rises if L is constant. As (7) shows, this raises both the marginal corn product of labour and the profit rate, and accomplishes the secondary benefit of trade that Ricardo mentioned above besides the primary benefit of a more efficient allocation of resources according to comparative advantage. A higher profit rate is expected to lead to greater investment and a higher growth rate, thus slowing down the economy's approach toward the stationary state. It provides a dynamic benefit from trade supplementary to the dynamic trade benefits to which, as was noted above, Adam Smith called attention in the *Wealth of Nations*.

S. Mountifort Longfield and John Stuart Mill

In nineteenth-century Britain, the principle of comparative advantage became an integral part of classical political economy based on Adam Smith's *Wealth of Nations* and Ricardo's *Principles of Political Economy*. Ricardo's principle was extended to more than two countries and more than two commodities. The first professor of political economy in Ireland, S. Mountifort Longfield, took the important step of generalizing the Ricardian model to many commodities by arguing that a commodity is exported by a country if and only if its labour productivity relative to the other country's exceeds their relative wages. In his words, "That kind of labour will succeed in each country which is more productive in proportion to its price" (Longfield 1835 [1971]: 56). Longfield noted the importance of reciprocal demand in determining the ranges of commodities exported and imported. He remarked (1835 [1971]: 69) that:

> if a nation enjoyed an immense superiority in the production of two or three articles of very general demand, the wages of her labourers might be, in consequence, so high that she could not compete with the rest of the world in any other manufacture, under a system of free trade.

To interpret the extension to more than two commodities pioneered by Longfield in present-day terms, consider two countries (A and B), and rank the commodities indexed $1, 2, \ldots, j, k, \ldots, n - 1, n$ in descending order of relative labour productivity $\frac{\pi_i^A}{\pi_i^B}$. When a trading equilibrium between A and B is established, select consecutive commodities j and k in the above range such that the factorial terms of trade (or ratios of income per worker in A and B) $\frac{y^A}{y^B}$ are smaller than $\frac{\pi_j^A}{\pi_j^B}$ but larger than $\frac{\pi_k^A}{\pi_k^B}$. This yields the chain of inequalities:

$$\frac{\pi_1^A}{\pi_1^B} > \frac{\pi_2^A}{\pi_2^B} > \ldots > \frac{\pi_j^A}{\pi_j^B} > \frac{y^A}{y^B} > \frac{\pi_k^A}{\pi_k^B} > \frac{\pi_{k+1}^A}{\pi_{k+1}^B} > \ldots > \frac{\pi_{n-1}^A}{\pi_{n-1}^B} > \frac{\pi_n^A}{\pi_n^B} \tag{8}$$

which imply that A produces commodities $1, 2, 3, \ldots, j$ more cheaply than B whereas B produces commodities $k, k + 1, \ldots, n - 1, n$ more cheaply than A. This so-called chain of comparative advantage for commodities 1 through n is broken by the factorial terms of trade $\frac{y^A}{y^B}$ such that commodities 1 through j are produced and exported by A while k through n are produced and exported by B. Each country exports commodities if its relative productivity in making them exceeds its relative per worker income. The borderline commodities j and k are such that j is the least competitive of A's commodities and k is the least competitive of B's given the factorial terms of trade. The location of these borderline commodities along the spectrum of commodities from 1 to n depends on an equilibrium condition similar to that in Mill's trade model discussed below, that the value of each country's imports is equal to the value of its exports.

The chain of inequalities (8) implies that the higher a country's wage compared to its trading partner's, the fewer the commodities it exports and the more it imports. This multi-commodity generalization of the Ricardian model is consistent with empirical cross-country studies of the relationship between relative wages and relative labour productivity across industries. Even if labour productivity in a poor country such as China is much lower than in the United States, its products can nevertheless be competitive on world markets because the wages it pays are proportionally lower compared to American wages. Hence China's unit labour costs in many manufacturing industries are lower than those in America despite its much lower labour productivity. Cross-country analyses of the relation between labour productivity and labour costs in manufacturing in a large sample of developed and developing countries have likewise found that wages and other labour costs are higher where labour productivity is higher and lower where productivity is lower, so that unit labour costs are roughly similar despite the significant productivity differences among countries (Irwin 2009: chs 2 and 6). The Ricardian model can thus offer empirically valid insights on the relation between productivity, trade competitiveness and real wages in the world economy.

In his *Principles of Political Economy* of 1848, a friend and admirer of Ricardo, John Stuart Mill, developed the theory of international trade based on comparative advantage in much greater detail and sophistication than Ricardo. He had published an earlier version in his *Essays on Some Unsettled Questions of Political Economy* (Mill 1844 [1948]) that he had written in 1829–30. Following the lead of his fellow economist Robert Torrens, Mill sought an answer to the question of what determines the equilibrium value of the commodity terms of trade that Ricardo had not specifically addressed. Equating the value of a country's imports to that of its exports, he found it in the strength of countries' reciprocal demand for each other's products, defined as the demand for alternative amounts of a country's import commodity in terms of the amount of exports it is willing to pay in exchange for them. The stronger a country's demand for imports, the higher the imports' price and hence the lower its terms of trade defined as the price of its exports in terms of its imports. Torrens extended his insights to commercial policy by insisting on reciprocity in tariffs rather than unconditional free trade with all countries as recommended by most classical economists. A trading partner's import tariff should be countered by a similar tariff if a country wishes to forestall a deterioration in its terms of trade. In his *Principles of Political Economy* John Stuart Mill expressed as follows what he named "the Equation of International Demand" or "law of International Values":

> The produce of a country exchanges for the produce of other countries, at such values as are required in order that the whole of her exports may exactly pay for the whole of her imports. . . So that supply and demand are but another expression for reciprocal demand: and to say that value will adjust itself so as to equalize demand with supply, is in fact to say that it will adjust itself so as to equalize the demand on one side with the demand on the other. (Mill 1848 [1920]: 592–3)

Mill observed that the two countries' autarky price ratios set the limits within which the equilibrium terms of trade must lie, and that the stronger a country's import demand, the closer the terms of trade are to its autarky terms of trade and hence the smaller its gains from trade.

Mill preceded this statement with a discussion of the demonstration effect of trade in stimulating a people in the early stages of economic development to work harder to enable them to import from abroad commodities they are newly aware of:

The opening of a foreign trade, by making them acquainted with new objects, or tempting them by the easier acquisition of things which they had not previously thought attainable, sometimes works a sort of industrial revolution in a country whose resources were previously undeveloped for want of energy and ambition in the people: inducing those who were satisfied with scanty comforts and little work, to work harder for the gratification of their new tastes, and even to save, and accumulate capital, for the still more complete satisfaction of those tastes at a future time. (Mill 1848 [1920]: 581)

Mill made this point with his customary eloquence, and his phrase that trade "sometimes works a sort of industrial revolution" is a memorable one. It contrasts with a trade theory that assumes that tastes are given and unchanged when an isolated society first opens to trade. His insight was not incorporated in the neoclassical trade theory that has dominated the field in the twentieth and twenty-first centuries (more details on the topics discussed in this chapter can be found in my entries on "comparative advantage" and "gains from trade" in Reinert and Rajan 2009).

The Protection of Infant Industries: Hamilton, Rae, List, Mill, Marshall and Taussig

The protection of infant industries was a commonplace in mercantilist times, and frequently advocated as a policy goal by authors and policymakers. In the typical words of a writer in the *Scots Magazine* of 1740:

All manufactures in their infancy require not only care, but considerable expense, to nurse them up to a state of strength and vigor. The original undertakers and proprietors are seldom able to lay down at once the necessary sums; but are obliged to take time, struggle with difficulties, and enlarge their bottoms by degrees. (Quoted by Viner 1937: 72)

Another writer in 1729 cautioned, however, that "if after their improvement [of manufactures] they can't push their own way, by being wrought so cheap as to sell at par with others of the same kind, it is in vain to force it" (ibid.).

Adam Smith was not impressed with the infant industry argument and contended instead:

By means of such regulations, indeed, a particular manufacture may sometimes be acquired sooner than it could have been otherwise, and after a certain time may be made at home as cheap or cheaper than in the foreign country. But though the industry of the society may be thus carried with advantage into a particular channel sooner than it could have been otherwise, it will by no means follow that the sum total, either of its industry, or of its revenue, can ever be augmented by any such regulation. (WN IV.ii.13)

His attitude toward infant industries was later contested by several influential writers as not applicable to countries that were beginning to develop their economies in competition with the superior technology and long manufacturing experience embodied in the products of the country where the Industrial Revolution began, Britain. Policies aimed at economic development and inspired by nationalistic considerations were proposed in contrast to the cosmopolitan economic language in which the *Wealth of Nations* was couched.

The founder of the school of national economists was Alexander Hamilton, Secretary of the Treasury to George Washington, who on 5 December 1791, submitted to Congress a "Report on manufactures" in which he noted the difficulties that beset investment in new enterprises in a country such as the newly independent United States:

> These have relation to – the strong influence of habit and the spirit of imitation – the fear of want of success in untried enterprises – the intrinsic difficulties incident to first essays towards a competition with those who have previously attained to perfection in the business to be attempted – the bounties premiums and other artificial encouragements, with which foreign nations second the exertions of their own Citizens in the branches, in which they are to be rivalled. (Hamilton 1791 [1964]: 140)

Investment in "untried enterprises" should be facilitated by government policies such as subsidies and premiums to innovation, which are preferable to protective duties and should be maintained for a limited length of time. The "temporary expense" that they entail is "more than compensated, by an increase of industry and Wealth, by an augmentation of resources and independence; & by the circumstance of eventual cheapness" (ibid.: 171).

Hamilton's arguments for infant industry protection and support were taken up by John Rae, a Scotsman who migrated to Canada and then to the US where he published *Statement of Some New Principles on the Subject of Political Economy, Exposing the Fallacies of the System of Free Trade, and of Some Other Doctrines Maintained in the "Wealth of Nations"* (Rae 1834). As the title promised, it was an extended critique of Smith's *Wealth of Nations*, and contained in addition a pioneering formulation of capital theory that subsequently impressed Mill and was further developed by Irving Fisher. Like Hamilton, Rae pinned his hopes for economic development on the encouragement of innovation in manufacturing and the transfer of foreign technologies.

After migrating to the US, the German economist Friedrich List became another admirer of Hamilton's "Report" and wrote *Outlines of American Political Economy* (List 1827). He then returned to Germany where in 1841 he published a book subsequently translated into English as *National System of Political Economy* (List 1856). List became the most influential advocate of infant industry protection in Germany, Europe and throughout the developing world. For him the main aim of protection was the generation and harnessing of a nation's "productive forces", an expression subsequently taken up by Karl Marx. The infant industry argument for protection was at first contested by the British classical school of political economy, probably under the influence of Smith's doubts about its validity. However, in his *Principles of Political Economy* of 1848, John Stuart Mill embraced John Rae's arguments as theoretically legitimate and worthy of cautious implementation. Mill's advocacy of infant industry protection (which he called "naturalizing a foreign industry") was instrumental in making this policy respectable in principle to economists and policymakers. Mill supported it in circumstances highlighted in book V of his *Principles* devoted to the role of the government, where he argued for policies designed to convert a potential comparative advantage into an actual comparative advantage:

> The superiority of one country over another in a branch of production often arises only from having begun it sooner. There may be no inherent advantage on one part, or disadvantage on the other, but only a present superiority of acquired skill and experience. A country which has this skill and experience yet to acquire, may in other respects be better adapted to the production than those which were earlier in the field: and besides, it is a just remark of Mr. Rae, that

nothing has a greater tendency to promote improvements in any branch of production than its trial under a new set of conditions . . . A protecting duty, continued for a reasonable time, might sometimes be the least inconvenient mode in which the nation can tax itself for the support of such an experiment. But it is essential that the protection should be confined to cases in which there is good ground of assurance that the industry which it fosters will after a time be able to dispense with it; nor should the domestic producers ever be allowed to expect that it will be continued to them beyond the time necessary for a fair trial of what they are capable of accomplishing. (Mill 1848 [1920]: 922)

The infant industry argument was subsequently given cautious approval by Alfred Marshall (1923 [1965]: 217–19) in the United Kingdom and Frank Taussig (1927) in the US, whose first book written when he was only 23 is titled *Protection to Young Industries as Applied in the United States* (Taussig 1883 [2000]). Both economists leaned toward free trade but respected the logic of infant industry protection. Taussig (1927: 179) noted that protection had promoted the growth of some American industries but not others. However, to a greater extent than the advocates of national systems considered above, he carefully related a country's success in creating new industries to the existence of potential comparative advantage, and attributed the latter to a complex interplay of natural and human factors.

Infant industry protection, according to its advocates, does not inherently conflict with eventual free trade. They all maintained that protection should be limited in time and specific to particular industries. However, they refused to believe that comparative advantage is predetermined by a country's geography or its natural and human resources, along the lines of the Heckscher–Ohlin trade model examined below. They aimed to develop a country's potential comparative advantage rather than exploit an exogenously given one. The distinction between present-day economists who accept the infant industry argument for protection and those who reject it parallels that between philosophers such as Plato, who believed that "one individual is naturally fitted for one task, and another for another" (Plato 1963: 370b), and those like Adam Smith who held such interpersonal differences to "arise not so much from nature, as from habit, custom, and education" (WN I.ii.4). Despite this view, as noted above Smith himself rejected the infant industry argument. The writings of the above-discussed "creators of comparative advantage" anticipated the field of economic development that evolved in the twentieth century.

Neoclassical Trade Theory: Barone, Haberler, Heckscher and Ohlin

In a long footnote inconspicuously embedded in a textbook of economic principles, the Italian economist Enrico Barone (1908: 88–90) created a diagram shown in Figure 7 consisting of a nonlinear production possibility frontier (PPF) and a map of community indifference curves to depict in general equilibrium terms the gains accruing to an economy as it passes from autarky to free trade. He thus anticipated similar diagrams presented some 25 years later by Jacob Viner, Abba Lerner, Wassily Leontief and Gottfried Haberler. In *The Theory of International Trade with its Application to Commercial Policy* (1936), the Austrian-born Haberler generalized Ricardian comparative advantage to an economy where price is defined by the opportunity cost of a commodity in terms of another, rather than the "real cost" of production utilized by Ricardo and the economists of the classical

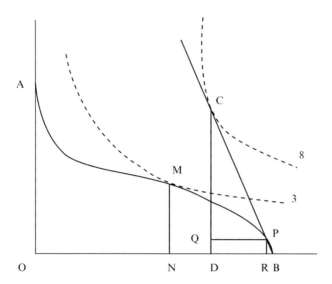

Figure 7   Barone's 1908 representation of the gains from trade

school. Whereas the PPF is linear in the textbook Ricardian case since real costs of production are assumed constant for any level of output, the neoclassical PPF depicting the menu of outputs that can be produced with the economy's factors of production given the available technology is concave to the origin. Its slope measures the opportunity cost of one commodity in terms of the other, and increases with the level of output because of increasing unit costs. In autarky the slopes of the two trading partners' PPFs are different and signal their comparative advantage in a particular commodity. Unlike in the textbook Ricardian case, this slope is no longer independent of demand considerations and the mix of factors used changes along the PPF together with its slope. Haberler thus generalized the comparative cost model while accepting most of the welfare conclusions reached by the Ricardian school.

In an article published in Swedish in 1919 and translated into English in 1949 as "The effect of foreign trade on the distribution of income", Eli Heckscher investigated the hitherto missing rationale in the Ricardian trade model for why comparative advantage differs across countries and how trade affects income distribution. The clue lies in the difference in the relative abundance of factors of production in various countries combined with differences in the intensities with which commodities use these factors. These features yield differences in commodity prices across countries that in turn lead to trade among them. With the additional assumption that techniques of production are identical across countries, Heckscher argued that trade causes the factor prices of trading partners to converge. They may even become equal if neither country becomes fully specialized, a result that was later proved rigorously by Paul Samuelson (1948, 1949) and became known as "factor price equalization". As in the case of Haberler's PPF, the difference between comparative costs in autarky is responsible for trade in the first place, but is subsequently erased by the very trade it engenders. After trade is established, and unlike the alleged Ricardian constant-cost case, the difference in comparative costs disappears since it is no longer needed to ensure continued trade.

In 1933 Heckscher's student Bertil Ohlin published a book-length critique of the Ricardian model and elaborated an alternative trade model based on neoclassical assumptions (Ohlin 1967). Together with Heckscher's 1919 article, it laid the foundations for what became the mainstream theory of international trade after World War II, the Heckscher–Ohlin or Heckscher–Ohlin–Samuelson theory. Ohlin accepted Heckscher's theory that trade derives from differences in relative factor endowments across countries. However, he believed that the Ricardian model was based on false assumptions that must be overthrown in order to reconstruct the theory of trade on the new foundations sketched by Heckscher and the neoclassical school represented by Gustav Cassel. He therefore rejected Heckscher's view that the Ricardian model could be reformed or generalized. The association of the term "comparative advantage" with the theory of comparative costs that Ohlin wished to discredit explains why this term does not even appear in the revised 1967 edition of his book.

The Heckscher–Ohlin–Samuelson Theory of Trade

It is somewhat ironic that, following Heckscher's lead and despite Ohlin's objection to the term comparative advantage, Ohlin ultimately provided the first book-length analysis of the causes of comparative advantage based on international factor endowment differences and differential factor intensities across commodities. The credit for the acceptance of the Heckscher–Ohlin (H–O) trade model by the economics profession and international trade economists in particular rests with Paul Samuelson. Thanks to some strategic simplifications of the theories of Heckscher and Ohlin, Samuelson and his followers rigorously elaborated the H–O theory that replaced the Ricardian or real cost theory as the mainstream trade theory after World War II. Samuelson's contributions to this development are so fundamental that his name is appropriately added to those of the two Swedish economists as the co-founder of the Heckscher–Ohlin–Samuelson (H–O–S) theory of trade. In an appendix to his book, Ohlin formulated a Walras–Cassel general equilibrium model of two trading regions with n commodities, r factors of production and s individuals. But his model was so general that it offered no simple insights into the factor-endowments theory itself, which was the main subject of the book, or the nature of comparative advantage, a term which Ohlin in any case studiously avoided.

The very general nature of Ohlin's formal trade model presented Samuelson (1948 and 1949, preceded by the Stolper and Samuelson paper of 1941) with a golden opportunity to create a scaled-down version capable of throwing greater light on the factor endowments theory. This was a two-by-two-by-two (or $2 \times 2 \times 2$) model featuring two countries, two commodities and two factors of production. Looking back on these contributions 50 years later, Samuelson interpreted his simplification of Ohlin's model as "bringing it out of the realm of n + m equations and n + m unknowns to the beautifully simple diagrams of land and labour, cloth and corn. Finally a *manageable* general equilibrium system – one with texture and content – was at hand" (Samuelson 1994: 345, original emphasis). Part of the workhorse appeal of the basic $2 \times 2 \times 2$ version of the H–O theory is that it is indeed a manageable general equilibrium model that is pedagogically suited to illustrate the concepts of comparative advantage and gains from trade when differential factor endowments are the main explanation of trade flows. However, on the theoretical side the H–O–S model is built on the following restrictive assumptions that are taken to be valid for both trading countries, and most of which would have been rejected by both Heckscher and Ohlin:

- its limited 2 × 2 × 2 structure, although extensions are possible with varying degrees of difficulty to more than two goods, factors or commodities;
- commodities and factors of production are qualitatively identical;
- production functions are identical and display constant returns to scale;
- commodities differ in their factor intensities so that one commodity uses intensively the same factor at all factor price ratios;
- there are zero transport costs, no trade impediments, and perfect competition in commodity and factor markets;
- factors of production are inelastically supplied, perfectly mobile among economic sectors, but internationally immobile;
- relative factor endowments (such as land–labour ratios) are unequal, so that one country is (say) relatively land-abundant while its trading partner is labour-abundant;
- demand functions are identical and homothetic, so that commodities are bought in the same proportions by all consumers at any given price ratio regardless of their income, in violation of Engel's law.

While some of these assumptions can be relaxed, others are much harder to generalize. The Samuelsonian strong factor-intensity assumption implies that there are no factor-intensity reversals, so that a commodity cannot be labour intensive at one set of factor prices and land intensive at another set. If trade is to equalize factor prices across countries (Samuelson's factor price equalization theorem), a further assumption is needed: that countries do not specialize in their export commodities.

Given these assumptions, the H–O–S theory yields four main propositions in the form of theorems initially proved for the 2 × 2 × 2 case, although some can be generalized to higher dimensions. The Heckscher–Ohlin theorem states that the country abundant in a particular factor exports the commodity that intensively uses that factor and imports the other commodity. According to the Stolper–Samuelson theorem, an increase in the relative price of a good increases the real wage of the factor used intensively in producing that good and lowers the real wage of the other factor. Provided that neither country specializes in its export commodity, the factor price equalization theorem states that trade equalizes both relative and real factor prices in the two countries. The Rybczynski theorem proves that if commodity prices are held constant and one factor expands, the output of the commodity that intensively uses that factor expands in a greater proportion, while the output of the other commodity actually declines.

These theorems constitute the four legs of the stool supporting the H–O model. Leontief (1954 [1968]) provided the first empirical test of the H–O theory using an input–output table of the US economy for 1947, and reached unexpected and disconcerting results. His test limited the factors of production to two, capital and labour, but extended to hundreds the number of export and import-competing commodities whose factor intensities he measured. Contrary to the general impression of economists and public opinion that the US immediately after World War II was the world's most capital-abundant economy, Leontief discovered that on average it exported labour-intensive and imported capital-intensive commodities! His finding became known as the Leontief paradox, and unleashed a torrent of papers that either attempted to explain what appeared to be a flagrant violation of the first theorem of the H–O model, or claimed that Leontief's test was invalid. Some economists argued that the undifferentiated labour and capital featured in Leontief's model were inadequate as the only factors he allowed for, and claimed they should be disaggregated into various categories of human capital or labour differentiated by skill level. Leontief himself provided what subsequently turned out to be a highly perceptive explanation for his paradoxical finding: that "one man year of American labor is equivalent to, say, three man years of foreign labor . . . [so that] the total number of American workers must be multiplied by three [to yield the number of] 'equivalent' foreign man years". This would imply that "the United States is rich in man power and poor in capital" (Leontief 1954 [1968]: 523–4).

Recent tests of the factor endowment model followed Leontief's suggestion and abandoned the H–O–S assumption that factors are qualitatively identical in different countries. The endowment of a given factor in a country is "corrected" by multiplying it by its estimated productivity so as to arrive at a stock labelled the country's "effective factor endowment". However, other serious concerns were voiced regarding the viability of even a modified H–O model as an explanation of most international trade flows. Despite the factor endowments of the industrialized countries being fairly similar, large and increasing amounts of trade were observed to occur among them rather than between industrialized and less developed countries with radically different relative factor endowments, as the H–O–S theory would predict. Economists began to search for alternative explanations of trade that incorporated features such as product differentiation and intra-industry trade. Their very existence could not be accommodated by the H–O–S theory, one of whose basic assumptions is that commodities and factors of production are homogeneous. The perceived inadequacies of a theory of trade crucially based on international factor endowment differences eventually gave birth to the new paradigms of trade explored next.

Alternatives to the H–O–S Theory of Trade

Given the formidable list of assumptions itemized above, and the unlikelihood that any one of them (let alone all of them) would be realized in practice, it is not surprising that deficiencies in the predictive power of the H–O–S framework soon became apparent when empirical tests of the model began, starting with the Leontief paradox and the inability of the H–O–S model to depict intra-industry trade. A particularly egregious assumption is that factors of production are homogeneous in quality and identical across countries. In Leontief's original test and subsequent ones, one of the two factors is "capital", and countries are differentiated according to whether they are "labour-abundant" or "capital-abundant". Since there is no homogeneous and measurable putty-like capital that can give substance to this empirical test, Leontief and others following him resorted to the market valuation of a heterogeneous bundle of capital goods. This meant that market prices as well as quantities, instead of pure quantities, had to be used from the outset in estimating countries' relative factor endowments. A similar critique applies to the assumed homogeneity of the factor "labour".

These and other critiques of the H–O–S model elicited a variety of responses among trade theorists. One was the birth of a "neo-Ricardian" theory of trade at the hands of Sergio Parrinello (1979), Ian Steedman (1979, 1987) and Lynn Mainwaring (1979, 1984), where the factors of production are homogeneous labour and a bundle of heterogeneous capital goods. Commodity prices in each trading country, both before and after trade, are determined by income distribution as well as technology. Since these models were inspired by the work of Sraffa (1960), they are sometimes referred to as "Sraffian". The profit component in total cost reflects the lag occurring between the application of inputs and the resulting output (a lag mostly ignored in neoclassical trade theory). One of the distributive variables, the wage or the profit rate, is assumed to be exogenously given. The advantages and limitations of neo-Ricardian models are well described in the "Introductory essay" (chapter 1) of Steedman (1979). The advantages claimed for them are the depiction of growing as opposed to stationary economies, and the allowance for the role of time and heterogeneous capital goods in the production of commodities. Their limitations are that they often focus on steady growth equilibria and do not allow for imperfections in competition. To ensure the attainment of steady growth, they omit inputs of land and other non-reproducible resources, a feature shared in common with neoclassical models whose authors are also mainly interested in elucidating the nature of steady-growth equilibria.

In considering the appropriateness of neo-Ricardian models as possible reflections of Ricardo's implicit trade model, recall that the primary aim of neo-Ricardian authors is rather to challenge the dominant H–O–S trade model. One of the basic issues they examine is whether the $2 \times 2 \times 2$ Heckscher–Ohlin model remains applicable when the factor of production "land", paired with "labour", is replaced by "capital" consisting of a heterogeneous bundle of goods. While this is not the place to review the heated controversies on the theory of capital of the 1960s and 1970s (Harcourt 1972), the inclusion of heterogeneous capital goods among a country's inputs is an important extension of the H–O–S theory in which capital is either ignored or assumed to be a putty-like substance on the same footing as land or labour. Neo-Ricardian authors do not claim to depict Ricardo's comparative cost example in chapter 7 of the *Principles* based on the labour theory of value, and in fact point out the errors implicit in Ricardo's procedure. Since positive profits usually cause prices to diverge from labour values, they show that, in contrast to Ricardo's assumption, countries may specialize in the "wrong" commodity (that in which they have a comparative disadvantage) and experience a lower welfare than under autarky. Consistency with Ricardo's conclusions about the causes and consequences of trade thus depends crucially on his assuming "all the great variations which take place in the relative value of commodities to be produced by the greater or less quantity of labour which may be required . . . to produce them" (1817 [1951b]: 36–7).

Another response to the inadequacies of the H–O trade model was to reject the assumption of perfect mobility of all factors among economic sectors, and assume instead that some are specific to the sectors in which they are located. This gave rise to the "Ricardo–Viner" or "specific-factors" model elaborated by Ronald Jones (1971), whose general features were suggested by Gottfried Haberler (1936: ch. 12). In Jones's simplest $2 \times 3 \times 2$ version of this model based on two sectors and three factors, each sector uses a type of capital (or land) specific to it as well as a "mobile" factor (taken to be homogeneous labour) common to both sectors.

The New Trade Theory

Another paradigm shift came with the emergence of the *new trade theory*, where the advances made in the theory of industrial organization were extended to the international trade arena by Paul Krugman, Elhanan Helpman, Gene Grossman, Wilfred Ethier, James Brander, Barbara Spencer, Kelvin Lancaster and others. For the pioneers of this new paradigm, the mainstream H–O–S theory symbolized the "homeostatic" view that "there is a natural pattern of specialization and trade, determined by underlying characteristics of countries, and that automatic forces tend to restore this natural pattern" (Krugman 1987: 41). The new theory instead invoked production based on increasing returns to scale, external economies, differentiated products and the associated imperfectly competitive market structures such as monopolistic competition, oligopoly and the existence of multinational corporations. Trade could be shown to arise even between economies that are identical with respect to factor endowments and technical knowledge, so that some of its models dispense altogether with the notion of comparative advantage.

One of the ironies underlying the new trade theory that challenged the ascendency of the mainstream Heckscher–Ohlin theory is that Ohlin himself anticipated it in his 1933 book. In chapter 3, titled "Another condition of interregional trade", he noted that "the economies of large-scale production make interregional division of labour profitable, irrespective of differences in the prices of the factors of production. In other words, the advantages of specialization resulting from large-scale production encourage interregional trade" (Ohlin 1967: 37). His anticipation of the new trade theory is remarkable for its details as well as its general thrust. Thanks to economies of scale, even regions with identical factor endowments gain from trade, and the particular industries in which each region specializes are arbitrary. In his words, "The character of this trade will be entirely a matter of chance if factor equipment is everywhere the same, for it doesn't matter whether a certain region specializes in one commodity or another, just as uniformly endowed individuals can with equal advantage specialize in any kind of work" (ibid.: 38). Ohlin also remarked on the importance of history and accident in moulding comparative advantage, a factor subsequently noted by Krugman. Some authors refer to this phenomenon as hysteresis, and provide examples such as the fact that production or research activity can become concentrated in the country that acquires a technological lead in an industry. According to Ohlin, "when certain industries have once been established in a place, there is a tendency for them to remain there. Friction of various kinds here is responsible" (ibid.: 39).

Unlike the H–O–S theory with its agreed list of underlying assumptions, the new trade theory is characterized by great heterogeneity in the models of its practitioners. This very diversity makes it difficult to generalize about the brave new world it opened for international trade theorists. An assessment of its implications for whether comparative advantage is still relevant to the explanation of trade flows and what forms it takes reveals a variety of viewpoints, including Krugman's quoted earlier that it provides a theoretical scaffolding for "noncomparative-advantage trade". An undoubted achievement was to provide a satisfactory explanation of the intra-industry trade that characterizes most of the advanced economies and many of the developing ones. In diametrical opposition to the prediction of the H–O–S theory where differential factor endowments lead to inter-industry trade, the volume of intra-industry trade has been shown to be greater, the more similar are the trading countries' factor endowments. Moreover, the new trade theory highlighted an important additional source of gains from trade: a greater variety of products and lower prices due to a higher scale of output. Because of the similarity of factor endowments, intra-industry trade softens the impact of trade on the gains or losses of particular factors of production, in contrast to inter-industry trade and the predictions of the Stolper–Samuelson theorem where one of the factors always loses from trade.

Some models of the new trade theory based on dynamic comparative advantage feature increases in productivity via a Smithian division of labour, depicted by learning-by-doing where cumulative past output determines current productivity. As Krugman (1987: 47) observes:

> Like a river that digs its own bed deeper, a pattern of specialization, once established, will induce relative productivity changes that strengthen the forces preserving that pattern. Clearly, history matters here even for the long run . . . Comparative advantage is "created" over time by the dynamics of learning, rather than arising from underlying national characteristics".

Such models of created comparative advantage are sophisticated versions of the infant industry argument reviewed above. Other models are hybrid ones that combine the novel insights into the determinants of trade with traditional explanations based on factor endowments and hence on comparative advantage, and allow room for policy intervention to garner for a country the advantages of specialization in high-technology goods.

In conclusion, some of the trade that characterizes the models of the new trade theory is intra-industry in nature and can indeed be described *à la* Krugman as non-comparative-advantage trade since it takes place even between countries with identical factor endowments. Other models accord an explicit role to the creation of comparative advantage via learning by doing, research and development (R&D) expenditure, or government policy. Unlike in the textbook presentations of the Ricardian and H–O–S models, comparative advantage is typically dynamic in nature and reminiscent of the way it was envisaged by Adam Smith and some of the "creators" of comparative advantage discussed above. The fact that the new trade theory often blends the insights of Smith and Ricardo shows, as argued in Maneschi (2002), that a suitably interpreted comparative advantage retains a vital role in trade theory, wherein both Smith and Ricardo should be accorded places of honour.

Epilogue

The theory of international trade has grown in extent and complexity since the days of mercantilism when pamphleteers like Henry Martyn presented examples of gains from trade and quantified them by means of what Jacob Viner named the eighteenth-century rule (see Maneschi 1998 for more details on topics covered in this entry). They viewed trade as an indirect method of production, where the commodities imported can be more cheaply obtained by means of exports than by attempting to produce them directly. The French Physiocrats, David Hume and Josiah Tucker also speculated about the reasons for and advantages of an international division of labour. Hume praised contact with foreigners as providing new commodities whose acquisition offers an incentive to work effort and a source of novel technology that can be profitably imitated. In the *Wealth of Nations* Adam Smith supplied further insights into the efficiency advantages of free trade in terms of the eighteenth century rule, the variety of commodities that it makes available, and the impetus to greater division of labour and productivity resulting from the widening of the extent of the market that trade secures.

Ricardo's discovery of comparative advantage in 1817 can be said to have established international trade as the first applied field of political economy. Ricardo's numerical example provided a quantitative expression for the gains from trade. John Stuart Mill made important additions to Ricardo's model by proving the existence and stability of a trade equilibrium in the case of two countries and two commodities. Following the lead of Robert Torrens, Mill highlighted the importance of reciprocal demand in determining the terms of trade. Neither Ricardo nor Mill speculated on the causes of comparative advantage, which they vaguely attributed to technological differences among countries and, in Ricardo's case, to a country's "situation, its climate, and its other natural or artificial advantages". The first thoroughgoing attempt to unearth these causes was made in the early twentieth century by Eli Heckscher and Bertil Ohlin in terms of differential factor endowments among countries coupled with an identical technology of production. The strategy adopted by these and subsequent innovators of trade theory was to discover a factor that differs among countries, hold everything else the same, and build a theory based on this difference. As the French put it, *c'est la différence qui compte* (it's the difference that counts). In addition to factor endowments, international differences were sought in terms of the availability of resources in some countries but not others, of tastes, technological expertise and human skills.

Although comparative advantage plays no role in some models of the new trade theory, where the industries that countries adopt are immaterial as long as they end up specializing and reaping economies of scale, differences among countries emerge once they specialize in the commodities that no other country can profitably produce. These models display irreversibility or hysteresis in their production patterns, in contrast to the more traditional trade models where changes in resource allocation are assumed to be reversible. Some of the new trade theory models combine economies of scale with traditional comparative advantage, as when a capital-abundant country specializes more heavily in increasing returns industries than a land-abundant one. Models of the Ricardian and neo-Ricardian types, based on differential technologies and exogenously given wage or profit rates, and of the Heckscher–Ohlin type based on differential factor endowments, endure as significant explanations of comparative advantage in the world economy.

Despite the role that actual and potential comparative advantage can play in mobilizing a country's resources for economic development, some economists and policymakers in less developed countries have regarded it with suspicion as a static concept that depends on exogenous variables such as the technology of production or a given endowment of factors of production. Some displayed an openly critical attitude towards the theory of comparative costs, viewing it as a rationalization for a frozen international division of labour in which their countries are assigned the role of "drawers of water and hewers of wood", or providers of primary products for the developed countries which end up garnering the lion's share of the gains from trade. This raises the issue of a possible "imperialism of free trade" (Robinson and Gallagher, 1953) that has attracted the attention of economists, political scientists and policymakers in developed and developing countries.

The drastic changes in the structure of world trade in the past half century, and the emergence of major new exporters such as China and the countries of the "East Asian miracle", present economists and policymakers with the task of keeping up with the rapid evolution of comparative advantage in the presence of multinational corporations, and of phenomena such as outsourcing and the rapid transmission of technological knowledge across frontiers. Whereas most textbooks in international economics are still subdivided into "international trade" and "international finance", entries in *The Princeton Encyclopedia of the World Economy* (Reinert and Rajan, 2009) add "international production" and "international economic development" to these as categories of equal importance. The limited scope of this entry did not allow the examination of these and many additional aspects relating to trade such as imperialism, unequal exchange and North–South trade relations. My aim has been to provide an introduction to the richness of the issues and models that have been proposed till now by international trade economists.

ANDREA MANESCHI

See also:

Antiquity (II); Enrico Barone (I); Pierre Le Pesant de Boisguilbert (I); British classical political economy (II); Cambridge School of Economics (II); Capital theory (III); Gustav Cassel (I); Economic thought in Scholasticism (II); Formalization and mathematical modelling (III); French Enlightenment (II); General equilibrium theory (III); David Hume (I); Income distribution (III); Industrial organization (III); International trade (III); Paul Robin Krugman (I); Labour and employment (III); Wassily W. Leontief (I); Friedrich List (I); Alfred Marshall (I); Karl Heinrich Marx (I); Mercantilism and the science of trade (II); John Stuart Mill (I); Neo-Ricardian economics (II); William Petty (I); François Quesnay and Physiocracy (I); David Ricardo (I); Paul Anthony Samuelson (I); Scottish Enlightenment (II); Adam Smith (I); Piero Sraffa (I); Technical change and innovation (III); Robert Torrens (I); Anne-Robert-Jacques Turgot (I); Marie-Esprit-Léon Walras (I); Welfare economics (III).

References and further reading

Aristotle (1946), *Politics*, Oxford: Clarendon Press.
Barone, E. (1908), *Principi di economia politica*, Rome: G. Bertero.
Bloomfield, A.I. (1938), 'The foreign-trade doctrines of the physiocrats', *American Economic Review*, **28** (December), 716–35.
Bloomfield, A.I. (1975), 'Adam Smith and the theory of international trade', in A.S. Skinner and T. Wilson (eds), *Essays on Adam Smith*, Oxford: Clarendon Press, pp. 455–81.
Boisguilbert, P. (1695), *Le détail de la France*, reprinted 1966 in *Pierre de Boisguilbert ou la Naissance de l'économie politique*, Paris: Institut National d'Etudes Demographiques.
Faccarello, G. (1999), *The Foundations of* Laissez-faire: *The Economics of Pierre de Boisguilbert*, London and New York: Routledge.
Haberler, G. (1936), *The Theory of International Trade*, Edinburgh: William Hodge.
Hamilton, A. (1791), 'Report on manufactures', reprinted in J.E. Cooke (ed.) (1964), *The Reports of Alexander Hamilton*, New York: Harper Torchbooks, pp. 115–205.
Harcourt, G.C. (1972), *Some Cambridge Controversies in the Theory of Capital*, Cambridge: Cambridge University Press.
Heckscher, E.F. (1949), 'The effect of foreign trade on the distribution of income', in H.S. Ellis and L.A. Metzler (eds), *Readings in the Theory of International Trade*, Homewood, IL: Irwin, pp. 272–300.
Hume, D. (1955), *Writings on Economics*, ed. E. Rotwein, Madison, WI: University of Wisconsin Press.
Irwin, D.A. (2009), *Free Trade Under Fire*, 3rd edn, Princeton, NJ: Princeton University Press.
Jones, R.W. (1971), 'A three-factor model in theory, trade, and history', in J.N. Bhagwati, R.W. Jones, R.A. Mundell and J. Vanek (eds), *Trade, Balance of Payments, and Growth*, Amsterdam: North-Holland, pp. 3–21.

Krugman, P.R. (1987), 'The narrow moving band, the Dutch disease, and the competitive consequences of Mrs. Thatcher: notes on trade in the presence of dynamic scale economies', *Journal of Development Economics*, **27** (1–2), 41–55.
Krugman, P.R. (1990), *Rethinking International Trade*, Cambridge, MA: MIT Press.
Leontief, W.W. (1954 [1968]), 'Domestic production and foreign trade: the American capital position re-examined', *Proceedings of the American Philosophical Society*, **97** (September), 331–49.
List, F. (1827), *Outlines of American Political Economy*, Philadelphia, PA: Samuel Parker.
List, F. (1856), *National System of Political Economy*, trans. G.A. Matile, Philadelphia, PA: J.B. Lippincott.
Longfield, M. (1835), *Three Lectures on Commerce, and One on Absenteeism*, reprinted 1971, New York: A.M. Kelley.
Lowry, S.T. (1987), *The Archaeology of Economic Ideas*, Durham, NC: Duke University Press.
Mainwaring, L. (1979), 'A neo-Ricardian analysis of international trade', in I. Steedman (ed.) *Fundamental Issues in Trade Theory*, New York: St Martin's Press, pp. 110–22.
Mainwaring, L. (1984), *Value and Distribution in Capitalist Economies: An Introduction to Sraffian Economics*, Cambridge: Cambridge University Press.
Maneschi, A. (1992), 'Ricardo's international trade theory: beyond the comparative cost example', *Cambridge Journal of Economics*, **16** (4), 421–37.
Maneschi, A. (1998), *Comparative Advantage in International Trade: A Historical Perspective*, Cheltenham, UK and Lyme, NH, USA: Edward Elgar.
Maneschi, A. (2002), 'How new is the "new trade theory" of the past two decades?', in S. Boehm, C. Gehrke, H.D. Kurz and R. Sturn (eds), *Is There Progress in Economics? Knowledge, Truth and the History of Economic Thought*, Cheltenham, UK and Northampton, MA, USA: Edward Elgar, pp. 240–55.
Marshall, A. (1923), *Money, Credit and Commerce*, reprinted 1965, New York: A.M. Kelley.
Martyn, H. (1701), *Considerations on the East-India Trade*, in J.R. McCulloch (ed.) (1954), *Early English Tracts on Commerce*, Cambridge: Cambridge University Press.
Mill, J.S. (1844), *Essays on Some Unsettled Questions of Political Economy*, reprinted 1948, London: London School of Economics and Political Science.
Mill, J.S. (1848), *Principles of Political Economy*, 7th edn 1920, ed. by W.J. Ashley, London: Longman, Green and Co.
Myint, H. (1977), 'Adam Smith's theory of international trade in the perspective of economic development', *Economica*, **44** (175), 231–48.
Ohlin, B. (1967), *Interregional and International Trade*, revised edn, Cambridge, MA: Harvard University Press.
Parrinello, S. (1979), 'Distribution, growth and international trade', in I. Steedman (ed.), *Fundamental Issues in Trade Theory*, New York: St Martin's Press, pp. 159–87.
Plato (1963), *Republic*, in E. Hamilton and H. Cairns (eds), *The Collected Dialogues of Plato*, Princeton, NJ: Princeton University Press.
Quesnay, F. (1759), *Tableau économique*, 3rd edn, English trans. M. Kuczynski and R. Meek (eds) (1972), *Quesnay's Tableau Economique*, London: Macmillan.
Rae, J. (1834), *Statement of Some New Principles on the Subject of Political Economy, Exposing the Fallacies of the System of Free Trade, and of Some Other Doctrines Maintained in the 'Wealth of Nations'*, Boston, MA: Hilliard, Gray, and Co.
Reinert, K.A. and R.S. Rajan (eds) (2009), *The Princeton Encyclopedia of the World Economy*, Princeton, NJ: Princeton University Press.
Ricardo, D. (1815), *An Essay on the Influence of a Low Price of Corn on the Profits of Stock*, in P. Sraffa (ed.) (1951a), *The Works and Correspondence of David Ricardo*, vol. IV, Cambridge: Cambridge University Press.
Ricardo, D. (1817), *On the Principles of Political Economy and Taxation*, in P. Sraffa (ed.) (1951b), *The Works and Correspondence of David Ricardo*, vol. I, Cambridge: Cambridge University Press.
Robinson, R. and R. Gallagher (1953), 'The imperialism of free trade', *Economic History Review*, 2nd Series, **6** (1), 1–15.
Rotwein, E. (1955), *David Hume: Writings on Economics*, Madison, WI: University of Wisconsin Press.
Ruffin, R.J. (2002), 'David Ricardo's discovery of comparative advantage', *History of Political Economy* **34** (4), 727–48.
Samuelson, P.A. (1948), 'International trade and the equalisation of factor prices', *Economic Journal*, **58** (230), 163–84.
Samuelson, P.A. (1949), 'International factor price equalisation once again', *Economic Journal*, **59** (234), 181–97.
Samuelson, P.A. (1994), 'Tribute to Wolfgang Stolper on the fiftieth anniversary of the Stolper–Samuelson theorem', in A.V. Deardorff and R.M. Stern (eds), *The Stolper–Samuelson Theorem: A Golden Jubilee*, Ann Arbor, MI: University of Michigan Press, pp. 343–9.

Smith, A. (1776), *An Inquiry into the Nature and Causes of the Wealth of Nations*, reprinted 1976, Oxford: Clarendon Press.

Sraffa, P. (1930), 'An alleged correction of Ricardo', *Quarterly Journal of Economics*, **44** (3), 727–48.

Sraffa, P. (1960), *Production of Commodities by Means of Commodities*, Cambridge: Cambridge University Press.

Steedman, I. (ed.) (1979), *Fundamental Issues in Trade Theory*, New York: St Martin's Press.

Steedman, I. (1987), 'Foreign trade', in J. Eatwell, M. Milgate and P. Newman (eds), *The New Palgrave: A Dictionary of Economics*, vol. 2, New York: Stockton Press, pp. 406–11.

Stolper, W.F. and P.A. Samuelson (1941), 'Protection and Real Wages', in H.S. Ellis and L.A. Metzler (eds) (1949), *Readings in the Theory of International Trade*, Homewood, IL: Irwin, pp. 333–57.

Taussig, F.W. (1883), *Protection to Young Industries as Applied in the United States*, reprinted in L. Magnusson (ed.) (2000), *Free Trade and Protectionism in America*, vol. 3, London: Routledge.

Taussig, F.W. (1927), *International Trade*, New York: Macmillan.

Torrens, R. (1815), *An Essay on the External Corn Trade*, London: Hatchard.

Turgot, A.-R.-J. (1773), *Letter on the 'Marque des Fers'*, in P.D. Groenewegen (ed. and trans.) (1977), *The Economics of A.R.J. Turgot*, The Hague: M. Nijhoff.

Vaggi, G. (1987), *The Economics of François Quesnay*, Durham, NC: Duke University Press.

Viner, J. (1937), *Studies in the Theory of International Trade*, New York: Harper.

Viner, J. (1972), *The Role of Providence in the Social Order*, Princeton, NJ: Princeton University Press.

Labour and employment

The problem of employment is a central topic in economic thought. Economists of all traditions and schools have always admitted short-run fluctuations in aggregate employment levels associated with the business cycle and explained them with reference to a variety of factors. Yet the central question is, of course, fluctuations around what long-run level of employment?

Concerning the replies to this question provided in the course of the history of economic thought, there is often a good deal of misapprehension among economists, to which John Maynard Keynes himself contributed, by attributing to all his predecessors from David Ricardo to Arthur Cecil Pigou (with few exceptions including Thomas Robert Malthus and Karl Marx) the view that both Say's law and full employment hold. Yet things are not so simple, and Keynes's definition of "classical" economists must be questioned in the light of recent developments in economic theory and the history of economic thought.

Keynes's definition is well suited to the approach he intended to attack, that is the marginalist theory of employment, particularly in the form put forward by Pigou in the 1930s. However, it is not representative of the approach of Ricardo and other classical economists (classical in the sense of Marx: from William Petty to Ricardo, including of course the French Physiocrats). Most of the old classical economists, particularly Ricardo, accepted Say's law and, on this basis, denied the possibility of "general gluts" in the economic system. Therefore they did not envisage the possibility of a fall in the employment level owing to a fall in aggregate demand. Even those who seemed to perceive the possibility and the importance of such phenomena (like Malthus) were unable to provide a consistent explanation of how this could come about.

However, in the classical economists, adherence to Say's law (that is, to the view that income is entirely spent, so that, on aggregate, the value of expenditure is equal to the value of production) did not entail the view that full employment prevails. Indeed, there is no sign of such a vision of the economic system, nor is there any reason for it to be present, since the tendency to full employment depends on a complex theoretical construction that began to emerge only after Ricardo's death with the (at the time highly controversial) wage fund theory. It was fully developed only with the emergence of the marginalist approach and the concept of the demand for a factor of production that is inversely related to its rate of remuneration.

Keynes's attack was in fact addressed to the marginalist (neoclassical) theory, and his positive contribution – albeit with some internal contradictions – was meant to demonstrate the normality of a level of employment below full employment not just in the short run, but also in a long-run equilibrium average position around which the economy fluctuates.

Shortly after the publication of *The General Theory* (1936) however, its conclusions were overturned by the neoclassical synthesis put forward by Hicks (1937) and Modigliani (1944), and involuntary unemployment was redefined as a short-run phenomenon, and/or a phenomenon necessarily caused by the existence of some nominal or real price and wage rigidity. Since then, mainstream debates on the theory of employment have substantially revolved around the legitimacy of assuming such rigidities (generally considered possible only in the short run), and their sources and consequences.

Outside the main stream, various strands of economic theory by contrast have developed analyses which incorporate and expand Keynes's contribution to employment theory, leading to quite different implications on a number of fundamental theoretical and policy issues.

The Classical Economists and Marx on Wages and Employment

The habit of conceiving of the working of an economic system in terms of demand and supply functions in commodity and factor markets is so deeply ingrained nowadays in economic thinking that many economists tend to consider such relations between price and quantity demanded or supplied as self-evident facts, rather than as elaborate theoretical constructions. This is not so however – and, as theoretical constructs, they have not always been there but were introduced only quite some time after the beginning of scientific enquiry in the field of economics. They were not part and parcel of economics in the classical and pre-classical period, so that the explanations of prices and distribution that we find in those economists are fundamentally different from the ones we find in the marginalist tradition.

One very important aspect of this difference, which is central to the theme under discussion here, is the determination of wages as the outcome of a social and institutional process. Fundamentally, in the classical approach wages (meaning here the wages of unqualified, adult male labour) are the result of power relations (affected by institutions and economic conditions) between parties with opposite interests, within limits set by the historically acquired living standards of the workers, which determine the subsistence minimum. In the words of Adam Smith:

> What are the common wages of labour, depends everywhere upon the contract usually made between those two parties, whose interests are by no means the same. The workmen desire to get as much, the masters to give as little as possible. The former are disposed to combine in order to raise, the latter in order to lower the wages of labour.
>
> It is not, however, difficult to foresee which of the two parties must, upon all ordinary occasions, have the advantage in the dispute, and force the other into a compliance with their terms. The masters, being fewer in number, can combine much more easily; and the law, besides, authorises, or at least does not prohibit their combinations, while it prohibits those of the workmen. . . . In all such disputes the masters can hold out much longer. A landlord, a farmer, a master manufacturer, or merchant, though they did not employ a single workman, could generally live a year or two upon the stocks which they have already acquired. Many workmen could not subsist a week, few could subsist a month, and scarce any a year without employment.
>
> . . . But though in disputes with their workmen, masters must generally have the advantage, there is however a certain rate below which it seems impossible to reduce, for any considerable time, the ordinary wages even of the lowest species of labour.
>
> . . . There are certain circumstances, however, which sometimes give the labourers an advantage, and enable them to raise their wages considerably above this rate; evidently the lowest which is consistent with common humanity.
>
> When in any country the demand for those who live by wages; labourers, journeymen, servants of every kind, is continually increasing; when every year furnishes employment for a greater number than had been employed the year before, the workmen have no occasion to combine in order to raise their wages. The scarcity of hands occasions a competition among masters, who bid against one another, in order to get workmen, and thus voluntarily break through the natural combination of masters not to raise wages. (Smith 1776 [1976], hereafter

WN, I.viii.11–15; see also Turgot 1766 [1973]: para. VI; Necker 1775 [1820–21]: 137–8 for similar statements)

The outcome of bargaining over wages is then affected by the institutional setting (the form of government, the degree of organization of the parties, the laws regulating the labour market) and by labour market conditions. The latter were regarded as the result, on the one hand, of demographic evolution, which determines the size of the working class population, and, on the other hand, of the rate of capital accumulation, which determines the employment level.

Wage differentials were seen as determined by a variety of factors, including the disagreeableness of jobs, the costs of acquiring the skills, the risks they involved or their social standing (WN I.x.b.1.116). An important factor is also the family role of the worker: typically adult male wages were seen to include, at a minimum, not only the subsistence of the labourer but also of his family, while this was not the case for female and child labour. Wage differentials across different types of labour employment were regarded as relatively stable over time, so that the wages of different types of work would tend to vary in the same proportion (Ricardo 1951–73, hereafter *Works*, I: 20–22, who quotes approvingly Smith on all this matter).

In the classical economists, employment levels were the result, given technology, of the level and composition of the social product. Composition depended on technology (determining the requirements of production) and the division of the product between different social groups, each characterized by historically and socially determined consumption habits (for a discussion of the analytical structure of the surplus approach, see Garegnani 1984). The level (scale) of production was the result of accumulation, with no constraints arising from the level of aggregate demand. As mentioned, most of the classics accepted Say's law, that is, they grasped the identity of the value of production and income, and, on the other hand, believed that the part of income not spent in consumption would directly or indirectly finance investments in the same period, so that the income deriving from production would be entirely spent either in consumption or investment goods: "No man produces, but with a view to consume or sell, and he never sells, but with an intention to purchase some other commodity, which may be immediately useful to him, or which may contribute to future production" (Ricardo *Works* I: 290; see also WN II.iii.15). This entailed that the economists who, like Ricardo, rigorously followed the implications of this proposition, would deny the possibility of general gluts, that is, a lack of aggregate demand causing a general underutilization of existing capital. They only saw the possibility of problems generated by a mismatch between production of and demand for individual commodities. Accordingly, there was no notion of the aggregate employment level being negatively affected by a lack of aggregate demand. However, it could be affected, and persistently reduced by changes in technology as well as changes in the structure of final consumption and output; as clearly maintained in Ricardo's chapter "On machinery" (*Works* I: 391–3). Indeed, adherence to Say's law and its implications should not be regarded as entailing a full employment economy. There were, in fact, no economic mechanisms in the theoretical approach of the classical economists such as to ensure that the employment level generated by the level and composition of output at any given stage of accumulation would be equal to the available labour force. There are several explicit indications that the economists of that period regarded underemployment or unemployment as a normal feature of the economy (Stirati 1994: 39 ff., 135 ff.). Hume, for example, saw the fear of unemployment as a major source of wage labour discipline: "the fear of punishment will never draw so much labour from a slave, as the dread of being turned off and not getting another service will from a freeman" (Hume 1752 [1955]: 116–17). On the other hand, the endogenous nature of labour supply through demographic change would in the very long run prevent the emerging of an indefinitely increasing gap between the available labour force and that employed.

As far as this secular tendency of labour supply to roughly adjust to the requirements of the accumulation process is concerned, while the classics tended to emphasize the role of population changes, earlier writers had focused on migration flows, and Marx on the constant re-creation of a reserve army of unemployed or underemployed workers as a result of capital accumulation itself (1887 [1954], I: 589–607).

Marx also differed from classical economists like Ricardo, among other things, in his criticism of Say's law. He saw that, in a monetary economy, part of the money income generated by production might be hoarded, thus generating a gap between the value of production and aggregate demand. This could generate realization problems and economic crises (Marx 1968: 492–543). In this respect Marx and the Marxists may be said to develop and systematize an issue around which there had been some earlier intuitions (though no precise theoretical analysis), such as hints that there could be "leakages" in the income-expenditure circuit causing lack of demand for products (for example, Quesnay 1767 [1962]: 236; Sismondi 1819 [1991]: 93, 101, 248), or Malthus's insistence on the possibility of general gluts.

In Marx therefore the employment level depends not only on technology and level and composition of income at a given stage of accumulation, but also on the volume of aggregate demand. However, a theory capable of determining a definite level of output and employment on the basis of aggregate demand, taking into account the interdependence between production, income and consumption expenditure, was advanced only by Keynes.

In the classical economists and Marx, changes in the employment level could affect the bargaining position of workers and hence the wage level – but a fall in wages caused by higher unemployment was not seen as favouring higher employment. Even before Marx, hints may rather be found at a possible negative effect on consumption demand and hence production (see, for instance, Turgot 1770 [1912–13], III: 288–9). With Marx, the tendency to keep wages low in the face of increasing productivity comes to be regarded as a distinctive inner contradiction of a capitalist system, which leads to realization problems and crises of over-production.

The surplus approach shared by the classical economists and Marx naturally leads to the perception of the existence of a conflict of interests over income distribution among social classes. Conversely, this perception disappears with the subsequent developments in the explanation of distribution. With the emergence of the notion of a decreasing relation between employment and real wage in the wage fund theory and later on of decreasing demand functions for production factors in marginalist theory, any attempt to increase the wage rate above its full employment equilibrium value, for example, owing to the action of trade unions, is regarded as causing a fall in the employment level. Thus, it is no longer true (as it was in the framework of the surplus approach) that a rise in wages will benefit a social group as a whole (the workers) at the expense of other social groups.

The Wage Fund Theory

The wage fund theory was clearly stated and consistently adhered to, after Ricardo's death, by influential economists such as McCulloch, J.S. Mill and Nassau Senior, though propositions reflecting wage fund notions can be found in only a few earlier writers, Malthus in particular. In 1869 Mill recanted the theory that ceased to be widely accepted. There were, however, some attempts to revive it, and some of its contents were passed on to the marginal theory.

The wage fund doctrine determines the general or average wage rate as equal in any period to the ratio between a given "wage fund" and the entire labour supply, usually identified with the labouring population (Mill 1848: 343–4; McCulloch 1864 [1965]: 316–17; Senior 1836 [1965]: 153). It is therefore the first instance, in the history of economic thought, of the notion of a necessarily inverse relationship between the real wage level and employment, which rests on the fixity of the "fund" destined to employ labour. Given such a relationship, competition among the workers and among the employers ensures that: "If the supply [of labour] is in excess of what capital can at present employ, wages must fall. If the labourers are all employed, and there is a surplus of capital still unused, wages will rise" (Mill 1869 [1965–82]: 643, also 1848 [1987]: 362). Equilibrium wage cannot be affected by anything but the ratio of the wage fund to the working-class population, and any attempt to increase the wage, which does not previously increase that ratio, is bound to fail (Mill 1848 [1987]: 344, 350, 360–62; McCulloch 1864 [1965]: 317, 320). The leading exponents of the theory were indeed favourable to the repeal of the "combination law" prohibiting workers' organizations, but this was precisely on the grounds that these organizations would be unable to persistently affect the equilibrium wage: combinations cannot keep wages above the full employment rate, as unemployment will cause competition among the workers; while if wages happen to be below that rate, combinations operate in the same direction as, and support, the workings of competition (see Mill 1848 [1987]: 934, 937).

Contrary to the view that wage fund theory is a short-run theory based on the fact that at the beginning of each production period there is a given amount of subsistence goods (food produced in the agricultural sector) available to be advanced in order to support the workers during the next "year" of production, the wage fund was conceived of as capital, or savings, destined to the support of the workers by the decisions of the capitalists:

> The distinction . . . between Capital and Not-capital does not lie in the kind of commodities, but in the mind of the capitalist . . . all property, however ill adapted in itself for the use of labourers, is a part of capital so soon as it, or the value received from it, is set apart for productive reinvestment. (Mill 1869 [1965–82]: 56; similar statements in McCulloch 1864 [1965]: 316, 318; Senior 1836 [1965]: 189–93)

As a consequence, it was a theory meant to explain the normal, long period equilibrium wage and employment (Stirati 1998).

The wage fund theory came under attack towards the end of the 1860s in the writings of

Longe (1866 [1904]) and Thornton (1870 [1971]). In his recantation Mill (1869 [1965–82]) accepted and developed some of the arguments that had been advanced against the theory. He admitted that there is no such thing as a given "wage fund" set aside by the capitalists, which will be paid for labour whatever its price and is a pre-determined portion of their entire income and wealth. The quantity of labour a capitalist employs depends on his expected sales, and these are not affected by changes in wages. Hence, argues Mill in his recantation, if workers accept to work for low wages, and the employers can have all the labour they need cheaply, they can and probably will choose to consume more of their income or wealth, rather than attempt to hire more workers. On the other hand, if wages are high (for example, because of a successful combination) employers will have to reduce their consumption to be able to obtain the labour they need.

Marginalist Theory

In marginalist (neoclassical) theory, the tendency to full employment rests on the two mirror constructs of demand functions in labour and capital markets. These factor demand functions are constructed on the basis of factor substitution in production and, indirectly, in consumption: a fall in the wage level was regarded as leading, in the long period, to a change of techniques in production which would entail, with the same quantity of capital incorporated in different capital goods, to a higher proportion of labour per unit of capital and output (see, for example, Hicks 1932 [1971]: 18–21). Such changes in production techniques would normally be accompanied by changes in consumption patterns also leading to a higher proportion of labour demanded with respect to capital: a fall in wages would cause, other things equal, a fall in the relative price of the commodities produced with higher labour intensity, and this in turn would cause an increased proportion of labour-intensive goods demanded by utility maximizing consumers. Both mechanisms underlie the construction of aggregate decreasing demand curves for factors of production and support the notion that, in the long period, these curves are relatively elastic (see, for example, Pigou 1933 [1968]: 40, 96–7). A reasonably high elasticity (that is, not far below one) of labour demand curves is necessary to make the explanation of distribution based on demand and supply curves plausible. With inelastic curves, large falls in wages would be needed to increase employment in order, for example, to match an increase in population, and this might cause social disruption and economic instability before full employment could be reached. In addition, it has recently been argued that, if demand curves are not very elastic (as suggested by several econometric studies), this would favour the emergence among the workers of social norms tending to prevent competition over wages, since the latter would prove damaging for the social group as a whole (Solow 1980).

In marginalist theory the decreasing relationship between the real wage and employment ensures that if wages are flexible, competition tends to bring the real wage rate to the full employment equilibrium level. Wages will be equal to the full employment marginal product of labour (or, even with fixed production coefficients, to the marginal contribution to consumers' utility). Where different types of labour exist, wage differentials will reflect different marginal contributions as determined by the interplay of labour endowments, consumer tastes and the costs of acquiring different skills, given technology and the amount of capital. Within this framework, human capital theory as an explanation of wage differentials simply adds that differences between types of labour may be brought about by education and training, which entail a cost that may be regarded as a form of investment. Wage differentials would thus reflect the return on such investments, which competition (arbitrage) ought to render equal to what can be obtained on other forms of investments, such as those in physical capital (a conclusion, however, that has not been confirmed by empirical evidence). In neoclassical models however decreasing returns on investment in education and training are assumed, so that the return on human capital does not depend only on the costs of acquiring the skill, but on its cost at the margin, and hence also on demand factors (that is, consumer's tastes) determining the relative scarcity of different types of labour (Becker 1975).

Decreasing labour demand curves and wage flexibility, however, are not enough to ensure that the economy will remain at full employment. The further condition is that "Say's law" applies, that is that, on aggregate, the volume of full employment output will be entirely sold, that is, the income derived from production will be entirely spent. This means that saving decisions at full employment output must be matched by an equal amount of aggregate investments. In the marginalist approach this actually rests on different premises than those found in the classical economists. It rests, that is, on a decreasing demand function for capital with respect to the interest rate. From this curve is derived a decreasing function of investments with respect to the same variable (equilibrium between demand and supply curves of capital as a stock requires that the changes in those stocks, that is the flows of investments and savings, are also brought to equilibrium). Thus in the marginalist theory, unlike in the classical approach, the so-called Say's law is based on an economic mechanism whereby the decisions to save and to invest, taken by different subjects, are brought to equilibrium by the interest rate owing to the fact that aggregate investments are a decreasing function of the latter. This was in fact the version of Say's law against which Keynes levelled his attack.

Before Keynes's *General Theory*, economic theory was characterized by the view that the economy would tend to be at, or close to, full employment in the long period, but this went along with the acknowledgement of economic cycles. Indeed, several interpretations of the business cycle and of temporary states of less than full employment were advanced. Of particular interest, owing to their similarities with recently advanced models and ideas, are the contributions by Pigou and Wicksell.

Writing in 1933, in the middle of the Great Depression and with unemployment peaking, Pigou still perceived the roots of unemployment as due to a lack of real wage flexibility, for which he provided various explanations. Wicksell saw the roots of economic fluctuations and episodes of price inflation and deflation in the existence, in a money economy, of a developed banking system capable of creating credit money. The endogeneity of credit money could cause (temporary) divergences between the actual and the equilibrium ("natural") interest rate, particularly following alterations of the latter such as could be caused by technical change. The divergence between actual and equilibrium interest rate could accordingly cause phases of over or under investment with respect to full employment savings, which however would soon be corrected by a return to the natural or equilibrium rate of interest thanks to the direct response of the banking system to such situations or, failing this, owing to the changes in bank reserves that would eventually determine the required adjustment (Wicksell 1934, II: 206–7).

Determination of Employment in Keynes's *General Theory*

All present discussions of employment theory cannot but take Keynes's *General Theory* as their starting point – and yet the interpretation of the latter remains highly controversial.

One point in particular calls for attention: textbook presentations of Keynes's theory of employment claim (1) that it is a short-run theory of cyclical fluctuations and/or that (2) it rests on the assumption of money wage rigidity. And yet it is possible to find in the *General Theory* very explicit statements to the contrary. In chapter 1 Keynes writes:

> I have called this book *The General Theory of Employment, Interest and Money*, placing the emphasis on the prefix *general* . . . I shall argue that the postulates of the classical theory are applicable to a special case only and are not the general case, the situation which it assumes being a limiting point of the possible positions of equilibrium. (Keynes 1936 [1978]: 3)

In the following chapter he explicitly acknowledges the existence of many theories dealing with the fluctuations in employment, but maintains that the fundamental theory, which assumes an underlying tendency towards the full employment of resources, has never been questioned (Keynes 1936 [1978]: 4–5, n. 1). The whole of chapter 19 is devoted to showing that the assumption of given money wages made in previous chapters is not necessary to his conclusions and to analysing the effects of downward wage flexibility. Hence textbook interpretations are at variance with Keynes's declared purposes and can be justified only by the claim that, whatever the intentions, Keynes's conclusions on employment theory can be given sound foundations only under the above listed conditions. As we shall see below, this is precisely the result arrived at by the so-called neoclassical synthesis initially proposed by Hicks (1937) and Modigliani (1944), which became the basis of all subsequent macroeconomic debates and developments in mainstream economics. This conclusion, though conflicting with Keynes's intentions, may be justified by certain weaknesses in Keynes's own analysis and assumptions.

Let us very briefly go through Keynes's theory of employment. As already mentioned, Keynes's criticism of received theory took as its point of attack Say's law, without however questioning the marginalist foundations of the theory, that is, the theoretical constructs of factor demand curves.

The positive kernel of his contribution is the principle of effective demand, showing that equilibrium between aggregate investments and savings can be reached through changes in output and employment levels, by which aggregate savings adjust to the level of aggregate investments, given the propensity to consume. The possibility of determining a definite equilibrium level of output and employment following a change in the components of aggregate demand by means of the multiplier represents an important progress with respect to earlier analyses recognizing a role of aggregate demand in the determination of employment, as in Marx and the Marxist tradition.

The principle of effective demand as formulated by Keynes, however, called for a determination of the interest rate that is alternative to the received one in terms of demand and supply functions of savings (as a flow) or demand and supply of capital (as a stock). This Keynes accomplished with his theory of a monetary determination of the interest rate. On the other hand, Keynes did not question the Marshallian foundation of economic theory, and retained both the notion of a decreasing curve of the marginal product of labour (yet hardly consistent with the existence of unused fixed capacity owing to a lack of effective demand) and of a decreasing function of aggregate investments with respect to the interest rate.

On these premises, Keynes's theory may be represented as a sequence, going from the determination of the interest rate in the money and financial market, to the amount of aggregate investments which, given the propensity to consume, determines output and employment. The price level would reflect marginal labour productivity and hence marginal costs at the level of employment thus determined and hence, with a given money wage, the real wage would tend to equal the marginal labour productivity via changes in the price level. This explains how in the *General Theory* the labour market only plays a passive role: both employment and real wage are in fact determined by effective demand.

It may be noted here that Keynes's analysis, precisely because it retains the notion of a decreasing marginal product of labour, entails the real wage being countercyclical: it falls when employment increases and vice versa. When confronted with the empirical results obtained by Dunlop (1938) and Tarshis (1938) which indicated pro-cyclical wage movements, Keynes (1939) wrote that those results, which appear to contradict the inverse relation between real wages and employment, would indeed provide further support for his analysis, though he was reluctant at the time to abandon the traditional Marshallian premises on the basis of that empirical evidence alone.

However, what if, when some involuntary unemployment exists, wages are flexible downward? First, Keynes observes that workers cannot bargain directly on real wages, but only on money wages. The natural question, within the framework outlined here, therefore is: can a fall in money wages lead to an increase in effective demand, that is, cause an increase in the propensity to consume and in the marginal efficiency of capital, or cause a fall in the interest rate? On these points chapter 19 of the *General Theory* offers very articulate arguments, leading to a negative answer concerning the possibility that unemployment can be overcome by means of wage flexibility. Of particular interest among these is the argument that a fall in wages, if it leads to real income redistribution away from labour incomes towards profits and other high incomes, will lead to a lower propensity to consume and hence have negative effects on aggregate demand and employment. On the other hand, if it is accompanied by price deflation and by expectation of a further fall in the price level (owing to the fall in monetary costs of production) it may cause a fall in aggregate demand owing to the decrease in expected returns from investment, the increase of debt burden, and the postponement of expenditure in durable consumption and investment goods. Given such negative effects, an increase in real money balances, which might lead to a fall in interest rates and hence in an improvement of aggregate investments, ought not to be pursued by means of wage and price deflation: monetary policy would definitely be better suited. However, according to Keynes, even monetary policy would hardly be capable of maintaining investments at the level required to keep the economy at full employment, owing to the difficulties it would encounter in regulating interest rates and, via them, aggregate investments. Among these, liquidity trap phenomena could be set in motion by attempts to lower interest rates below the expected or conventional level, or by the pessimistic expectations typical of a depressed economy. From this it follows that public expenditure management is a necessary tool to maintain high levels of employment in a market economy. In addition, since downward wage flexibility is shown to be unable to stimulate higher employment, and since it is likely to have adverse consequences on economic stability, Keynes concluded that the existence of money wage rigidity is desirable as it provides an anchor to money prices and thus prevents deflation and economic instability (Keynes 1936 [1978]: 270–71).

The Tendency towards Full Employment in the Neoclassical Synthesis

The neoclassical synthesis (the IS–LM model) re-established the pre-Keynesian idea that in a market economy with flexible money wages and prices endogenous mechanisms exist which establish a long-run tendency towards full employment: Keynesian outcomes are therefore a special case. This overturn of Keynes's conclusion, however, was achieved while apparently retaining his contribution in the theory of output and interest rate. This was accomplished by emphasizing the effect of wage and price deflation on the equilibrium interest rate, and of the latter on aggregate investment. The warnings about the negative effects of deflation were disregarded, and though obstacles to wage flexibility were largely recognized, the argument re-established in principle the self-adjusting nature of the economic system, while at the same time it was argued that in practice appropriate monetary policy would normally allow keeping the economy close to full employment. Such greater reliance on monetary policy than had been suggested by Keynes was itself linked to a different approach to the analysis of money demand and the determination of the interest rate. While Keynes's perspective had been "speculative" in the sense that he regarded the attitude towards the demand for money as a financial asset as mainly determined by expectations and the search for capital gains, the neoclassical synthesis regards the demand for money as part of a portfolio choice based on an evaluation of risks and returns, thus giving rise to much smoother changes and, at least in the long run, to the possibility for the central bank to control the interest rate and hence bring aggregate investments in line with full employment savings. More recently, increasing emphasis has been placed on the role of the so-called "real balance effect", that is, on the role of an increase in real money balances (following upon a fall in nominal wages and prices) in stimulating private consumption via an increase in the propensity to consume. Such increased emphasis may have been the result of growing uncertainty, on both empirical and theoretical grounds, over the effects of the interest rate on aggregate investments. Yet it is to be doubted that the real balance effect can, by itself, provide an endogenous mechanism leading to full employment, as recognized even by Patinkin (1987), one of the economists who contributed most to developing the analysis of such effect. In addition, money wage and price deflation may have serious adverse effects on aggregate demand by routes already suggested by Keynes in chapter 19 of *The General Theory*, among which is the increase of the debt burden, which may lead to defaults on the part of firms and households and, as a consequence, of banks.

Thus, it can be seen that at the basis of the neoclassical synthesis lies, on the one hand, a reference to those Marshallian elements, namely, the decreasing demand curves for labour and investment that Keynes did not criticize (and in fact could not at the time, since critical arguments concerning those theoretical foundations had not yet been developed). On the other hand, there are the inner contradictions of the *General Theory* between the objective of formulating a long-run, general theory of employment, and the short-run nature of some of the arguments put forward to maintain that the interest rate could not easily be established at the level consistent with full employment (Garegnani 1978–79).

Recent Developments in the Mainstream

Following the contributions by Hicks and Modigliani, the IS–LM model became the shared theoretical framework for all mainstream macroeconomic debates. Although quite heated and sometimes involving strong divergences concerning the appropriate short-run macroeconomic policy, these debates never addressed the theoretical foundations of the model and the associated tendency towards full employment (or towards the equilibrium unemployment rate determined by frictions and imperfections) in the long run. Debates initially centred on the elasticities of the IS and LM curves and hence the respective impact of monetary and fiscal policies as countercyclical policy tools. With the rise to dominance of monetarism the focus of debates has become the degree of flexibility of money wages and prices and their speed of adjustment (hence, the speed of adjustment towards potential output), which in turn depends on how expectations are formed. The possibility of "Keynesian" outcomes in the short run (that is, a role for aggregate demand in the determination of output and employment) has therefore come to depend on the assumptions about expectations. Fluctuations in output and employment, however, were still seen to depend on aggregate demand shocks, and hence the models required real wages to move counter-cyclically to remain consistent with decreasing marginal product for labour and profit-maximizing firms. Yet the labour market side of these analyses has encountered problems on empirical grounds. A number of empirical investigations have confirmed, with greater subtlety and sophistication of analysis, the results originally obtained by Dunlop and Tarshis, that is, that real wages are either moderately pro-cyclical or exhibit no consistent pattern over the cycle (see Brandolini 1995, for a survey). These results may be regarded as one of the factors that favoured the emergence and acceptance of real business cycle and new-Keynesian macroeconomic models.

The peculiarity of real business cycle models is that the labour market is continuously in equilibrium, so that the very concept of unemployment disappears from the analysis: cyclical fluctuations in the employment level reflect short-run voluntary changes in labour supply. These are the response of inter-temporally maximizing workers to short-run changes in real wages determined by (temporary) supply shocks, the nature of which is not usually discussed in any depth, but are generally associated with technical changes. While long-run labour supply is generally admitted to be inelastic with respect to permanent changes in wages, short-run changes in labour supply in these models are described as highly responsive to wage changes perceived as temporary, owing to the fact that agents maximize utility over the life-cycle and hence substitute labour and leisure inter-temporally. This could in principle render real business cycle models consistent with the observation that employment fluctuations are usually large, while real wages tend to be moderately pro-cyclical. Empirical analyses however, perhaps not surprisingly, have not confirmed the above short-run behaviour of labour supply (Altonji 1982, among others; see also Romer 2012: 228, 254–5).

On the other hand, the so-called new-Keynesian strand in mainstream macroeconomics purports to provide sound micro-foundations for real and nominal price rigidities which can explain, given the accepted theoretical framework, the existence of persistent involuntary unemployment and the short-run role of changes in aggregate demand in determining output and employment fluctuations. In their labour market analyses in particular, new-Keynesians have provided a large (perhaps too large) number of alternative or complementary models which could explain rigidity in real wages, thus explaining the possibility of some persistent, structural unemployment, the size of which ultimately depends on the institutional arrangements concerning unemployment benefits and employment protection. At the same time they have tried to provide foundations for price and/or money wage rigidities that could account for the temporary effects of aggregate demand on employment levels. With respect to consistency with observed facts, these models have the advantage that, since some structural unemployment exists, the short-run increase in labour supply does not require a movement along a standard labour supply curve (and hence strongly pro-cyclical real wages). Conversely, the assumption that firms do not necessarily change the price level over the cycle (even though marginal costs are changing) means that (in the short run) they are not moving along their labour demand curves (which would require countercyclical movements of real wages). The new-Keynesian approach therefore seems to have the advantage of greater flexibility in the analysis of the short-run and in rendering the models consistent with empirical observations of labour market and macroeconomic behaviour, though at the cost of losing clear theoretical foundations, particularly with regard to the theory of income distribution. In these models the macroeconomic equilibrium real wage turns out to be determined, not only by the marginal labour product, but also by the mark-up of the representative firm determined by the elasticity of its product demand curve, thus overlooking the input–output interdependence between firms and hence between prices and costs in the system as a whole. Labour market institutions in turn determine the equilibrium unemployment rate, that is, the unemployment required to keep the real wage at a level consistent with marginal labour product and the given mark-up.

During the late 1970s and the 1980s another approach to employment theory was influential, particularly in Europe, based on the introduction of wage and price rigidities in general equilibrium models. Within this approach, Malinvaud's "equilibria with rationing" proposed a taxonomy according to which unemployment could be either "Keynesian" or "Classical" (Malinvaud 1977). In the first case, price rigidity determines "low" real wages and households' consumption rationing which in turn causes underutilization of existing capacity and unemployment. Classical unemployment, on the other hand, features full utilization of capacity, with the latter unable to employ the available labour force. This situation is generally associated with exceedingly high wages, which discourage investment. The wage policies appropriate to deal with these two types of unemployment are therefore completely opposite, while in any given economy both may coexist in different industries or regions. Malinvaud's approach was criticized by some (mostly mainstream economists) on the grounds of the arbitrariness of the assumption of fixed wage and prices, while others (mostly non mainstream economists) expressed dissatisfaction both with the interpretation of Keynes and with the notion of classical unemployment and its roots in neoclassical assumptions (Kahn 1977; Schefold 1983).

Developments Outside the Mainstream

There are several streams of thought among critical, non-mainstream economists. A widely shared view, however, is the rejection of the supply and demand curve apparatus in factor markets, which is the foundation of the long-run tendency to full employment and the associated notion of distribution determined by full employment marginal products. The latter analytical framework has often been questioned on the grounds of its inability to describe and explain real-world phenomena. Such an inability, however, is connected to fundamental flaws in the theoretical construction that have emerged thanks to the results obtained by Sraffa (1960), Garegnani (1966, 1970) and Pasinetti (1966). These show that when heterogeneous capital goods exist, in an economic system with free competition and profit maximizing firms, a fall in wages will not necessarily lead to adopting techniques exhibiting a higher proportion of labour relative to the value of capital and/or a higher proportion of labour per unit of output: the cost-minimizing technique after the fall in the real wage may, on the contrary, turn out to exhibit a lower proportion of labour relative to capital and per unit of output. By the same token, it cannot be expected that the relative price of commodities produced with more labour intensive techniques will fall, thus inducing substitution in consumption and hence, indirectly, between factors of production.

These results therefore question the very foundations of factor demand curves (that is, for labour and capital and hence investments) and with them of the entire edifice of neoclassical theory.

From the point of view of the theory of employment, these criticisms lead to the rehabilitation of the principle of effective demand as the only sound theory of output and employment, and remove from the scene the endogenous mechanisms restoring full employment (or the equilibrium unemployment rate) put forward both by the pre-Keynesian versions of neoclassical theory and by subsequent mainstream macroeconomic models. The absence of a tendency towards full employment or equilibrium unemployment needs no longer to rest on any real or nominal rigidity in wages and prices. Downward flexibility of money prices and wages, even conceding that (as in the neoclassical synthesis) it would lead to a fall in the interest rate, would not by that route be able to stimulate investments, since a sound theoretical foundation of the inverse relation between interest and aggregate investment cannot be provided (Petri 2004: ch. 7), nor can it be supported by empirical evidence (Chirinko 1993). Nor would a fall in the real wage lead to higher employment by way of substitution mechanisms. On the contrary, by negatively affecting the propensity to consume, it may cause a fall in effective demand and employment. Keynes's statement about the desirability of money wage rigidity as a stability anchor for the economy is therefore vindicated and, in the light of the above criticisms, can now be extended also to real wages.

The traditional neoclassical foundations were still present in the *General Theory* and caused tensions between the intended generality and long-run nature of its main conclusions and the need for short-run assumptions (such as given expectations as to the normal level of the interest rate) in order to state them. The removal of the neoclassical elements provides the theory with theoretical robustness and generality. The principle of effective demand explains not only aggregate fluctuations of employment, but also its long-run level. The meaning of long run in this context requires some clarification, and is actually a twofold meaning. The first is that when a persistent change in effective demand (for example, in public spending) leads to a change in macroeconomic equilibrium output and employment, there is no endogenous mechanism in a market economy, which will restore the previous level of output. The second is that if there is no mechanism ensuring full utilization of capacity in any given period, it becomes natural to think that capacity creation over time through investment will reflect the degree of capacity utilization. That is, the main determinant of aggregate investments is the trend of effective demand. This implies that while in any given period effective demand determines aggregate output through the degree of utilization of existing capacity, in the long run it will determine potential output through capacity creation (Garegnani 1992). A parallel line of reasoning can be applied to the labour force: while in any given period effective demand will determine the unemployment rate, over longer periods of time it will tend to affect the size of the labour force available for wage labour. How this may come about had already been indicated by Marx when describing the creation of a reserve army of the unemployed as part of the accumulation processes. Consistently with that approach it may be recalled that, among other things, changes in the available labour force may be brought about in advanced economies also by migration flows and by changes in the activity rates of some sections of the population, particularly women, in response to persistent changes in employment opportunities. In less developed economies, effective demand and employment in the wage sector of the economy will affect the proportion of the population in low-income, pre-capitalist and informal activities and migration. Thus, evidence of a relative constancy of unemployment rates over very long periods of time may indicate endogeneity of labour supply in the very long run, rather than the adjustment of labour demand to the available labour supply, as would be predicted by mainstream analyses.

A rejection of the neoclassical foundations also requires an alternative approach to the theory of distribution. The traditional classical approach, which sees wages as resulting, within limits determined by the historically prevailing living standards and the institutional setting, from the relative bargaining power of the parties, naturally suggests itself as suitable for developments and integration with the theory of employment already outlined. Other streams in critical economic analysis tend to regard wages as residually determined by the mark-up charged by firms over costs. This in turn is explained by financial requirements and/or growth objectives by firms or the structure of the market for final products (for a critical assessment of these, see Pivetti 1992: 108–19; Steedman 1992). Some economists, following an initial suggestion by Sraffa, have highlighted the role of the interest rate in determining the return on capital required by firms and hence, by that route, the rate of profits (Pivetti 1992). This however should not be accepted mechanically, since distribution would ultimately depend also on the behaviour of money wages and prices, and thus be the outcome of actions undertaken by various parties and institutions, including the central bank (Stirati 2001).

These theories are consistent with, and can account for empirical evidence often found to be puzzling by mainstream macroeconomists, such as the wide fluctuations of employment accompanied by moderately pro-cyclical movements of real wages (Stirati 2015); or the downward sloping Phillips curve, which could very straightforwardly be interpreted as representing the influence of the unemployment rate on wage bargaining (Rothschild 1993), rather than reflect excess aggregate demand as in mainstream analyses; or the inability of labour market "rigidities" and institutions to account for the diversity of unemployment experiences (Baker et al. 2005, among others).

The approach to employment theory outlined above has very profound implications for economic policy, which are in many respects completely opposite to those that can be derived from mainstream models. According to this approach, long-term growth of output and employment can only be the result of growing aggregate demand, particularly of its autonomous and non-capacity-creating components, among which public spending has a very important role. On the other hand, labour market "reforms" aimed at greater flexibility have no direct impact on employment levels, and will be counterproductive if they have adverse effects on real wages and consequently on the propensity to consume.

ANTONELLA STIRATI

See also:

British classical political economy (II); British marginalism (II); Cambridge School of Economics (II); French classical political economy (II); John Maynard Keynes (I); Keynesianism (II); Karl Heinrich Marx (I); Marxism(s) (II); John Stuart Mill (I); Monetarism (II); Neo-Ricardian economics (II); New Classical Macroeconomics (II); New Keynesianism (II); Arthur Cecil Pigou (I); Post-Keynesianism (II); François Quesnay and Physiocracy (I); Adam Smith (I); Piero Sraffa (I); Anne-Robert-Jacques Turgot (I).

References and further reading

Altonji, J. (1982), 'The intertemporal substitution model of labor market fluctuations: an empirical analysis', *Review of Economic Studies*, **49** (5), 783–824.
Baker, D., A. Glyn, D.R. Howell and J Schmitt (2005), 'Labour market institutions and unemployment: assessment of the cross-country evidence', in D.R. Howell (ed.), *Fighting Unemployment. The Limits of Free Market Orthodoxy*, Oxford: Oxford University Press, pp. 72–118.
Becker, G. (1975), *Human Capital*, 2nd edn, New York: NBER.
Brandolini, A. (1995), 'In search of a stylised fact: do real wages exhibit a consistent pattern of cyclical variability?', *Journal of Economic Surveys*, **9** (2), 103–63.
Chirinko, R.S. (1993), 'Business fixed investment spending: modelling strategies, empirical results and policy implications', *Journal of Economic Literature*, **31** (4), 1875–911.
Dunlop, J.G. (1938), 'The movement of real and money wage rates', *Economic Journal*, **48** (September), 413–34.
Garegnani, P. (1966), 'Switching of techniques', *Quarterly Journal of Economics*, **80** (4), 554–67.
Garegnani, P. (1970), 'Heterogeneous capital, the production function and the theory of distribution', *Review of Economic Studies*, **37** (3), 407–36.
Garegnani, P. (1978–79), 'Notes on consumption, investments and effective demand', parts I and II, *Cambridge Journal of Economics*, pt I, **2**, 335–53; pt II, **3**, 68–82.
Garegnani, P. (1984), 'Value and distribution in the classical economists and Marx', *Oxford Economic Papers*, **36** (2), 291–325.
Garegnani, P. (1992), 'Some notes for an analysis of accumulation', in J. Halevi, D. Laibman and E. Nell (eds), *Beyond the Steady State*, London: Macmillan, pp. 47–72.
Hicks, J. (1932), *The Theory of Wages*, reprinted 1971, London: Macmillan.
Hicks, J. (1937), 'Mr Keynes and the classics: a suggested interpretation', *Econometrica*, **5** (2), 147–59.
Hume, D. (1752), *Of Commerce*, reprinted in E. Rotwein (ed.) (1955), *David Hume: Writings on Economics*, Edinburgh: Nelson.
Kahn, R. (1977), 'Malinvaud on Keynes – review article on Malinvad, the theory of unemployment reconsidered', *Cambridge Journal of Economics*, **1** (4), 375–88.
Keynes, J.M. (1936), *The General Theory of Employment, Interest and Money*, in E. Johnson and D. Moggridge (eds) (1978), *The Collected Writings of John Maynard Keynes*, vol. 7, Royal Economic Society, Cambridge: Cambridge University Press.
Keynes, J.M. (1939), 'Relative movements of real wages and output', in E. Johnson and D. Moggridge (eds) (1978), *The Collected Writings of John Maynard Keynes*, vol. 7, app. 3, Cambridge: Cambridge University Press, pp. 394–412.
Longe, F.D. (1866), *A Refutation of The Wage-Fund Theory of Modern Political Economy as Enunciated by Mr Mill and Mr Fawcett*, reprint of economic tracts 1904, ed. J.H. Hollander, Baltimore, MD: Johns Hopkins Press.
Malinvaud, E. (1977), *The Theory of Unemployment Reconsidered*, Oxford: Blackwell.
Marx, K. (1887), *Capital. A Critique of Political Economy*, reprinted 1954, London: Lawrence & Wishart.
Marx, K. (1968), *Theories of Surplus Value*, vol. 2, Moscow: Progress.
McCulloch, J.R. (1864), *Principles of Political Economy, with Some Inquiries Concerning Their Application*, reprints of economic classics, 5th edn 1965, New York: A.M. Kelley.
Mill, J.S. (1848), *Principles of Political Economy with Some of their Applications to Social Philosophy*, London: John W. Parker, reprinted 1987, New York: A.M. Kelley.

Mill, J.S. (1869), 'Thornton on labour and its claims', part I, *Fortnightly Review*, May, reprinted in J.M. Robson (ed.) (1965–82), *Collected Works of John Stuart Mill*, vol. V, Toronto: University of Toronto Press, pp. 633–68.

Modigliani, F. (1944), 'Liquidity preference and the theory of interest and money', *Econometrica*, **12** (1), 45–88.

Necker, J. (1775), *Sur la Législation et le Commerce des Grains*, in Baron de Stael (ed.) (1820–21), *Œuvres Complètes*, vol. 5, Paris: Treuttel & Wurtz.

Quesnay, F. (1767), 'General maxims', in R. Meek (ed.) (1962), *The Economics of Physiocracy – Essays and Translations*, London: Allen & Unwin, pp. 231–64.

Pasinetti, L. (1966), 'Changes in the rate of profit and switches of techniques', *Quarterly Journal of Economics*, **80** (4), 503–17.

Patinkin, D. (1987), 'Real balances', in J. Eatwell, M. Milgate, P. Newman (eds), *The New Palgrave. A Dictionary of Economics*, vol. 4, London: Macmillan, pp. 98–101.

Petri, F. (2004), *General Equilibrium, Capital and Macroeconomics*, Cheltenham, UK and Northampton, MA, USA: Edward Elgar.

Pigou, A.C. (1933), *The Theory of Unemployment*, reprinted 1968, New York: A.M. Kelley.

Pivetti, M. (1992), *An Essay on Money and Distribution*, Basingstoke: Macmillan.

Ricardo, D. (1951–73), *The Works and Correspondence of David Ricardo*, ed. P. Sraffa with the collaboration of M. Dobb, vols I–XI, Cambridge: Cambridge University Press.

Romer, D. (2012), *Advanced Macroeconomics*, New York: McGraw-Hill.

Rothschild, K.W. (1993), 'The Phillips curve and all that', in K.W. Rothschild (ed.), *Employment, Wages and Income Distribution*, London: Routledge, pp. 125–61.

Senior, N.W. (1836), *An Outline of the Science of Political Economy*, reprinted 1965, New York: A.M. Kelley.

Schefold, B. (1983), 'Kahn on Malinvaud', in J. Eatwell and M. Milgate (eds) *Keynes's Economics and the Theory of Value and Distribution*, London: Duckworth.

Sismondi, J.-C.J. (1819), *New Principles of Political Economy*, trans. R. Hyse (1991), London: Transaction.

Smith, A. (1776), *An Inquiry into the Nature and Causes of the Wealth of Nations*, in A.L. Macfie and D.D. Raphael (eds) (1976), *The Glasgow Edition of the Works and Correspondence of Adam Smith*, vols 2a–2b, Oxford: Oxford University Press.

Solow, R. (1980), 'On theories of unemployment', *American Economic Review*, **70** (1), 1–11.

Sraffa, P. (1960), *Production of Commodities by Means of Commodities*, Cambridge: Cambridge University Press.

Steedman, I. (1992), 'Questions for Kaleckians', *Review of Political Economy*, **2** (2), 125–51.

Stirati, A. (1994), *The Theory of Wages in Classical Economics. A Study of Adam Smith, David Ricardo and Their Contemporaries*, Aldershot, UK and Brookfield, VT, USA: Edward Elgar.

Stirati, A. (1998), 'Wage fund doctrine', in N. Salvadori and H. Kurz (eds), *The Elgar Companion to Classical Economics*, Cheltenham, UK and Lyme, NH, USA: Edward Elgar.

Stirati, A. (2001), Inflation, unemployment and hysteresis: an alternative view, *Review of Political Economy*, **13** (4), 427–51.

Stirati, A. (2015), 'Real wages in the business cycle and the theory of income distribution: an unresolved conflict between theory and facts in mainstream macroeconomics', *Cambridge Journal of Economics*, online advance publication 23 February, doi: 10.1093/cje/beu088.

Tarshis, L. (1938), 'Real wages in the United States and Great Britain', *Canadian Journal of Economics*, **4** (3), 362–76.

Thornton, W.T. (1870), *On Labour, Its Wrongful Claims and Rightful Dues, Its Actual Present and Possible Future*, 2nd edn, reprinted 1971, Shannon: Irish University Press.

Turgot, A.-R.-J. (1766), *Reflections on the Formation and Distribution of Wealth*, in R.L. Meek (ed.) (1973), *Turgot on Progress Sociology and Economics*, Cambridge: Cambridge University Press, pp. 119–82.

Turgot, A.-R.-J. (1770), *Lettre sur le Commerce des Grains*, in G. Schelle (ed.) (1913–23), *Œuvres de Turgot et document le concernant*, vol. 3, Paris: Librairie Félix Alcan, pp. 266–354.

Wicksell, K. (1934), *Lectures on Political Economy*, London: Routledge & Kegan Paul.

Macroeconomics

The aim of this entry is to introduce the reader to the main episodes that have marked the course of macroeconomics. It starts with an evocation of the emergence of modern macroeconomics as a new sub-discipline arising in the aftermath of John Maynard Keynes's *General Theory*. The bulk of the chapter consists of a presentation of the successive episodes that marked the history of macroeconomics. Keynesian macro-economics was the first of these, its heyday spanning the 1950s and 1960s. At the end of the 1960s, it came under attack, first from Milton Friedman and later, in a more radical way, from Robert Lucas and his associates such as Robert Barro, Thomas Sargent and Neil Wallace. These economists, new classical macroeconomists as they were called at the time, were able to dethrone Keynesian macroeconomics in a move that had all the trappings of a scientific revolution. In turn, Lucas's work triggered the rise of a series of new Keynesian models aimed at rebutting Lucas's claim, while adopting his neoclassical language. The next stage of the history of macroeconomics occurred when the baton was passed from new classical to real-business-cycle (RBC) theorists, in a move initiated by Finn Kydland and Edward Prescott. These economists transformed Lucas's qualitative model into a quantitative research programme into which they enrolled a large chunk of the macroeconomic profession. The latest stage in the history of macroeconomics is the internal evolution of RBC models towards a second generation of new Keynesian modelling, whereby central elements of Keynesian macroeconomics, in particular monopolistic competition and sluggishness, are reintroduced into the real business cycle framework.

Little space will be devoted to the content of the *General Theory* since this is fully covered in another entry. The same is true for macroeconomics as it existed before Keynes under the name of monetary theory (on this subject, we refer the reader to Laidler 1999 and Dimand 2008). In addition, the entry is limited to mainstream macro-economics (useful references for non-mainstream research lines are Snowdon and Vane 2005, King 2002, and Fine and Milonakis 2009).

The Emergence of Modern Macroeconomics

Without the Great Depression, Keynes's *The General Theory of Employment, Interest and Money* (1936) would not have seen the light of day. Keynes's aim in writing this book was to elucidate the causes of the mass unemployment that affected all major economies at that time, and to suggest policy measures that could be taken to solve the problem. This was a time of great disarray with no remedy at hand to fix the ailing economic system. In most countries, the unemployment rate was soaring and deflationary policies had failed. There was little room in economic theory for unemployment. The notion of frictional unemployment had started to be evoked but it had little theoretical content (see Batyra and De Vroey 2012). So, faced with the looming presence of the Great Depression, Keynes realised that monetary theory was blatantly wanting, and needed to be reformed.

The *General Theory* is a complex book, intertwining different types of arguments developed at distinct levels of abstraction. Most commentators agree that Keynes's aim in the book was to demonstrate the theoretical existence of involuntary unemployment. This, he recognised, was a phenomenon whose real-world existence was compelling, yet for which economic theory had, at that time, no room. The line he took to fill this lacuna was to state that involuntary unemployment resulted from a deficiency in aggregate demand, itself the result of insufficient investment.

Keynes's book got an enthusiastic reception, especially from young economists. Dissatisfied with the existing situation, they were crying out for a new theory that would justify abandoning the laissez-faire doctrine, and Keynes's work delivered. As Axel Leijonhufvud wrote, it was received as a "liberating revelation" (1968: 31). Dissenting views, focusing on the shortcomings of Keynes's reasoning, were expressed, but the pressure to produce a new theoretical framework that might account for the obvious dysfunctions in the market system was such that they were hardly listened to. Nevertheless, confusion over the central message of Keynes's book was great, even amongst his admirers.

Progress (although some readers of the *General Theory* considered it a step backwards) occurred when a session of the Econometric Society Conference was devoted to the book. James Meade (1937), Roy Harrod (1937) and John Hicks (1937) gave three separate papers aimed at bringing out the gist of Keynes's book (see Young 1987). All three took as their first task the reconstruction of what Keynes called the "classical model" in order to assess whether his model was more general than the classical one was sustainable. They all concluded that it was not. Although their interpretations were similar, one of them, Hicks's piece, was to have an extraordinary future, containing as it did the first version of what was to become the IS–LM model. In his attempt to compare Keynes's views with those of "classical economics", Hicks transformed Keynes's verbal presentation into a simple system of simultaneous equations. He also introduced an ingenious graph allowing the joint outcome of two different markets to be represented on a single diagram. The IS–LM model became the workhorse of Keynesian macroeconomics, to the point that one wonders what would have become of the *General Theory* had Hicks's interpretation never appeared.

The third and final stage in the emergence of macroeconomics consisted of transforming qualitative models into empirically testable ones. One person who played an important role in this respect was Jan Tinbergen. Like Keynes, he was a reformer, motivated by the desire to understand the Great Depression and to develop policies that would prevent it happening again. Tinbergen's (1939) League of Nations study of business fluctuations in the US from 1919 to 1932 can be pinpointed as the first econometric model bearing on a whole economy. However, Keynes was dismissive of Tinbergen's work, as he was of the opinion that little was to be gained from trying to test theoretical models empirically. Too much arbitrariness was involved in such an exercise, Keynes argued. Keynes's reservations were to no avail. Lawrence Klein was of the view that the *General Theory* "cried out for empirical verification", and under his influence a second wave of model construction began. In 1950, Klein published *Economic Fluctuations in the United States 1921–1941*, for the Cowles Commission. The main impetus, however, came from Klein and Goldberger's 1955 monograph, *An Econometric Model of the United States 1929–1952*, which introduced the celebrated Klein–Goldberger model.

This is how macroeconomics came into existence as a new sub-discipline of economics. It soon thrived. The offspring of the Great Depression, its overarching aim was to highlight market failures that could be remedied by state action. So, from the onset, it had a decidedly reformist flavour. Unemployment – and in particular involuntary unemployment – was its defining element.

The Heyday of Keynesian Macroeconomics

From the 1950s onwards, Keynesian macroeconomics established itself as a new sub-discipline of economics. It was taken up both in universities and in public institutions such as central banks. Modified by Franco Modigliani (1944) and popularised by Alvin Hansen (1953), the IS–LM model becomes its baseline tool. This model comprises two distinct sub-models, the Keynesian and the classical system. Hence, strictly speaking, it should not be considered Keynesian. But at the time of its dominance, most economists were convinced that the Keynesian variant corresponded to reality while the classical system was viewed as a foil.

One shortcoming of the elementary IS–LM model was its fixed prices assumption. The Phillips curve, drawn from Bill Phillips's study of the relationship between changes in wages and unemployment in the UK from 1861 to 1957 (Phillips 1958), did the job. It quickly found its place in the macroeconomic corpus. The fact that it was based on a solid empirical relationship, valid over a long period, was viewed as an advantage. Moreover, it had a Keynesian flavour since it incorporated the idea of wage sluggishness. An additional step taken by Paul Samuelson and Robert Solow (1960) was to suggest that the Phillips curve pointed to the possibility of a trade-off between inflation and unemployment – that is, government could "buy" a decrease in the level of unemployment by accepting an increase in the inflation rate.

The most impressive progress took place on the empirical side. As already noted, the appearance of the Klein–Goldberger model prompted the development of a new large-scale research programme. A model of an average size, in its first version it comprised 15 structural equations and five identities. The objective was, first, to make predictions about economic activity, and, second, to simulate the effects of alternative policy measures. Klein has always insisted that its inspiration came from the IS–LM model. However, significant transformations were needed. Above all, the static character of the initial model had to be replaced with a dynamic framework. Capital accumulation and technical progress had to be introduced. Some price and wage adjustments were also introduced, although only on a limited scale, so that states of general excess supply were always present. As a result, the models always encapsulated the economy as being in a Keynesian state (Deleau et al. 1984). Nonetheless the general architecture remained loose enough to allow a quasi-unlimited diversity of specifications. The hallmark of these models was their pragmatism. When it came to introducing additional specifications, this usually resulted from observations about reality rather than from theoretical considerations.

The next important stepping-stone was the Brookings model, which appeared in the middle of the 1960s. Its size was impressive, comprising close to 400 equations – at the time the view that the more complex a model, the better, prevailed. This development would of course have been impossible without the expansion of the computer industry. Supported by a wide consensus, these models reigned over the economic profession well beyond the dismissal of Keynesian theoretical macroeconomics.

The success of the IS–LM model cannot be due to mere luck. It has two main virtues.

The first is its ability to model economic interdependence in a simple and intuitive way. In this respect the IS–LM approach is unrivalled. Even in its most elementary form, it lends itself to drawing cogent real-world inferences. The second main virtue of the IS–LM model is its plasticity. It constitutes an architecture that is general enough to allow a more-or-less unlimited diversity of specifications. This plasticity also extends to policy implications, since friends and foes of Keynesian policy alike can use it to promote or refute policy prescriptions.

But the IS–LM model also has important shortcomings. First among these is its conceptual sloppiness. Macroeconomists never bothered to define the central notions of their paradigm, in particular involuntary unemployment and full employment, in any precise way. While Keynes himself liked to reason in terms of agents making choices, this microfoundational dimension received little emphasis. The initial IS–LM model was static and little attention was given to expectations. Later on, this state of affairs was slightly improved by taking the variables' past and present values as a proxy for future ones. The ability to capture the interdependence across sectors of the economy that characterised the elementary model was generally not transposed into empirical econometric models, which were therefore nothing more than half-baked general equilibrium models. Finally, the IS–LM model has been unable to achieve the proclaimed aim of Keynesian theory, to explain involuntary unemployment as a systemic market failure.

For some 25 years after the end of the Second World War, the IS–LM model dominated macroeconomics. With the advent of new classical macroeconomics in the early 1970s, that dominance was at first challenged and then broken. Yet the IS–LM model still lives on. While no longer central to the graduate training of most macroeconomists or to cutting-edge macroeconomic research, it continues to be a mainstay of undergraduate textbooks, finds wide application in areas of applied macroeconomics away from the front lines of macroeconomic theory, and, until the last decade, remained at the conceptual core of most government and macroeconometric models.

Disequilibrium and Non-Walrasian Equilibrium Modelling

While the IS–LM model with its pragmatic spirit dominated macroeconomics, some economists were nonetheless of the opinion that macroeconomics needed a stronger microfoundational anchor. The main names to be evoked here are those of Don Patinkin, Robert Clower and Leijonhufvud. Patinkin devoted two chapters of his book, *Money, Interest and Prices* (1956 [1965]) to casting Keynesian theory in a Walrasian framework, arguing that the only way in which involuntary unemployment could be introduced into a general equilibrium framework was by assuming that it was confined to the period of adjustment towards equilibrium. Clower (1965 [1984]), for his part, wrote an influential article introducing the "dual decision hypothesis", which he viewed as a new way of understanding Keynes's assumption that consumption is a function of income. According to this hypothesis, if labour suppliers happen to be rationed in the labour market, when participating in the goods market they will express a constrained (or "effective") demand that is lower than their "notional" (that is, Walrasian) demand. As to Leijonhufvud, he criticised traditional Keynesian macroeconomics for having lost the main message of the *General Theory*. To him, the "Keynesian Revolution got off on the wrong track and continued on it" (Leijonhufvud 1968: 388). Keynes's theory, he claimed, was different and richer from its IS–LM transmogrification; hence the need for a return to it. Moreover, while most of the interpreters of the *General Theory* have ended up viewing it as mingling incompatible theoretical claims, in contrast, Leijonhufvud strove to show that the various components of the *General Theory* were all pieces of a single jigsaw puzzle. Brilliantly written, his book was an instant, and well-deserved, success. Both the depth of Leijonhufvud's insights and his mastery of the intricacies of Keynes's argumentation were impressive. To Leijonhufvud, the central message of the *General Theory* was that the market system could fall prey to a failure of intertemporal coordination, an inability of the rate of interest to coordinate saving and investment, and that this was further compounded by the absence of any signal allowing this state of affairs to be detected. Clower soon joined forces with Leijonhufvud to propose a Marshallian general equilibrium approach focusing on the equilibrating process rather than the end state of the economy.

In the next stage, these pioneering works triggered "non-Walrasian equilibrium" models associated with Robert Barro and Herschel Grossman (1971, 1976), Jean-Pascal Benassy (1975), Jacques Drèze (1975) and Edmond Malinvaud (1977). Their aim was the same as that of their disequilibrium predecessors, that is, to vindicate Keynes's insight that the market system could experience market failures. However, to this end, these economists took Walrasian theory as their starting point, the "non-Walrasian" term being thus a misnomer. They wanted to produce rigorous mathematical demonstrations and to have their models based on Walrasian microfoundations, that is, describing situations where agents behave in an optimising way (although under special constraints). Therefore the change in label from "disequilibrium" to "non-Walrasian equilibrium" theory was anything but trivial.

However, after an enthusiastic beginning, the new approach subsided. While the pioneering articles succeeded in setting out a new framework, it seemed that there was no precise vision about what to do next, no specific research programme able to mobilise a wider group of economists. Many of the young researchers who started their career in this line of research soon moved to other areas.

The main reason for the downfall of non-Walrasian equilibrium models ought to be looked for in what happened in other areas of macroeconomics. The 1970s were years of high theory. The reappraisal of Keynesian theory led by disequilibrium and non-Walrasian equilibrium theorists was not the only new theoretical development in macroeconomics. At more or less the same time, the "rational expectations" school or "new classical macroeconomics" emerged under Lucas's lead, and it proved to be a daunting rival. It shared some features with non-Walrasian equilibrium modelling, such as the desire to base macroeconomics on choice-theoretical foundations, and the adoption of advanced mathematical methods. Although the two approaches both started from the Arrow–Debreu framework, their purposes were poles apart. While non-Walrasian equilibrium economists used neo-Walrasian theory as a foil, Lucas aimed to extend its domain of relevance to the business cycle. As will be seen, if this confrontation is pictured as one round in a wider battle about the course of macroeconomics, Lucas was the winner. The theoretical reorientation that he carved out won the day and succeeded in dethroning Keynesian macroeconomics. Non-Walrasian equilibrium macroeconomics was a collateral victim of this fall.

The Natural Rate of Unemployment

The Phillips curve had become a central piece of Keynesian macroeconomics; however, it took no time before it was attacked, with far-reaching consequences. Two economists, the veteran critic of Keynesian policy, Milton Friedman, and a younger economist, Edmund Phelps, were at the heart of the offensive. Although Phelps's two papers (1967, 1968) provided the most subtle and theoretically innovative argumentation, Friedman's Presidential Address to the American Economic Association in 1967 (Friedman 1968) got most of the fame for the new development. Both were honoured with the Sveriges Riksbank Prize in Economic Sciences in Memory of Alfred Nobel, Friedman in 1976, Phelps 30 years later. For lack of space, the discussion is limited to Friedman's paper.

Friedman's Presidential Address had a critical purpose. It attacked two central policy tenets of Keynesianism. The first was the view that governments should press central banks to keep the interest rate as low as possible, a prescription that Keynes made in chapter 24 of the *General Theory*. In Friedman's eyes such a policy cannot be sustained in the long term. His second target, the only one that we shall discuss, is the view that a trade-off exists between inflation and unemployment, that is, the idea that a government can durably decrease unemployment in a sustainable way by monetary activation. Such a trade-off requires a stable Phillips curve. Friedman readily admits that money supply has real effects in the short term. His claim is that no justification for a money creation policy ensues because these real effects only occur when the changes in money supply are unanticipated. To make his point, Friedman assumes a difference in perception between firms and workers. While firms' expectations are correct, those of workers are mistaken. Friedman shows that in such a context an increase in money supply is non-neutral. A displacement along the Phillips curve takes place. But this is only a short-run effect. In the next period of exchange, workers realise their earlier mistake, and integrate the rise in prices into their expectations. This triggers a displacement of the whole Phillips curve to the right. In order to maintain the rise in employment, the money supply needs to be increased at an accelerated rate, so that workers are fooled again. If this process continues, inflation is transformed into hyperinflation, a threat to the functioning of the monetary system, which compels the monetary authorities to abandon their expansionary policy. While the short-run Phillips curve is downwards sloping, in the long term it is vertical at a level of unemployment that Friedman dubbed the natural rate of unemployment, a terminology that became widely accepted. Friedman's conclusion is that it is useless to try to reduce unemployment below its natural level. His recurrent plea for monetary rules is thereby reinforced. Managing the money supply is not a task that should be left to the discretion of the central bank authorities, and even less to that of Ministers of Finance. On the contrary, they should function under strict monetary rules.

Friedman's argument was shrewd because he based his attack on Keynesian theory on one of its pillars, the Phillips relation. Keynesians could have retorted that his case against monetary policy rested on a situation in which there was no rationale for engaging in it to begin with. However, such a view was only brought out much later, after the main debate had moved to other topics. Moreover, while Friedman's argumentation was a mere sketch (and, for that matter, a rather sloppy one), the course of events, it has been widely claimed, verified its prediction. The emergence of the stagflation phenomenon (the joint existence of a high rate of inflation and a high rate of unemployment) came to be invoked as a quasi-real-world confirmation of the correctness of Friedman's claim.

Friedman's criticism of the Phillips curve was hardly a frontal attack on Keynesian macroeconomics. Unlike Lucas at a later date, Friedman had few qualms about Keynes's method; time and again, he praised Keynes for having adopted the Marshallian method. Likewise, Friedman had no problems with the IS–LM model per se, his target being rather the policy conclusion that Keynesian authors drew from it. The difference between Keynesians and monetarists, Friedman claimed, was mainly empirical. His plea was that the classical sub-system of the IS–LM model, assuming wage flexibility, was the "good" model and not the Keynesian sub-system, assuming wage rigidity.

At this juncture, it ought to be remarked that at the time the "Keynesian" adjective designated two distinct objects: a conceptual apparatus, the IS–LM model, on the one hand and a vision of the functioning of the economy on the other (the view that, for all its virtues, the market economy can exhibit market failures, which state intervention, in particular demand stimulation, can remedy). So, one may speak of "Keynesianism in the methodological sense" and of "Keynesianism in the policy-viewpoint sense". While Keynesian macroeconomics would be Keynesian on both scores, Friedman's theory turned out to be a hybrid combination of methodological Keynesianism and an anti-Keynesian policy standpoint.

The New Classical All-Out Attack on Keynesian Macroeconomics

Friedman had few qualms about the Marshallian–Keynesian conceptual apparatus. His anti-Keynesian offensive was mainly a matter of policy. This was no longer true for the next wave of attack against Keynesian theory led by Lucas and others, and inaugurating "new classical macroeconomics". While the new approach was evidently collective, Lucas was the leading character in the movement, and commandingly assumed the role of its methodological spokesperson.

The transition from Keynesian to new classical macroeconomics deserves to be viewed as a Kuhnian scientific revolution. This expression refers to an episode in the history of a discipline where a period of normal development is disturbed because of the persistence of unsolved puzzles which trigger a drive to change the agenda, the conceptual toolbox and the research methods in radical ways. This is often accompanied by thundering declarations of war (for example, Keynesian theory is "dead"), a confrontation between younger and older generations of researchers, the rise of new stars in the profession, and the eclipse of the previous stars.

Lucas's assessment of the *General Theory*

To Lucas, Keynes ought to be honoured for the role his ideas have played in the expansion of socialism rather than for his theoretical contribution. The latter, Lucas wrote, "is not Einstein-level theory, new paradigm, all this" (2004: 21). In Lucas's opinion macroeconomics started off on the wrong foot by being Keynesian. He regretted that Keynes did not try to make Walras's static model dynamic, as Hayek had suggested (before changing his mind). In Lucas's view, Keynes abandoned this line of research to tackle the easier task of demonstrating the existence of unemployment at one point in time, that is, in a static framework.

Lucas also criticised Keynes for having discarded what he called the "equilibrium discipline", a basic premise by which, he felt, economists should abide when constructing theories. It consists of two postulates: (1) that agents act in their own self-interest and (2) that markets clear (Lucas and Sargent 1979 [1994]: 15). These postulates are deemed to constitute a universal requirement, rather than being linked to the specific purposes of particular models. That is, they are viewed as constituent parts of neoclassical theory, which in turn is equated simply with economic theory. The counterpart of the equilibrium discipline is the rejection of the disequilibrium notion. According to Lucas, by betraying this equilibrium discipline, Keynes gave an example of "bad social science: an attempt to explain important aspects of human behaviour without reference either to what people like or what they are capable of doing" (1981: 4). Lucas accepted that Keynes's lapse from the equilibrium discipline was understandable in view of the apparent contradiction between cyclical phenomena and economic equilibrium, but it remains true, he claimed, that in retrospect it prompted a long detour in the progress of economic theory.

Turning now to Lucas's assessment of Keynesian economics, as distinct from the economics of Keynes, the following points should be brought out. First, Lucas praised Keynesian macroeconomics for having engaged in econometric modelling and empirical testing, in contrast to Keynes's reasoning in prose. The Keynesian macroeconomic models were the first to attain this level of explicitness and empirical accuracy; by doing so, they altered the meaning of the term "theory" to such an extent that the older business cycle theories could not really be viewed as "theories" at all (Lucas 1977 [1981]: 219).

Second, Lucas took a strong stance on the Phillips-curve controversy. The latter opposed Keynesians and monetarists *à la* Friedman: Keynesians defended the stable Phillips curve allowing for a trade-off between unemployment and inflation, while monetarists argued for the natural rate of unemployment hypothesis. Lucas's distinct contribution to the debate was to provide stronger foundations for Friedman's insight in his path-breaking article, "Expectations and the Neutrality of Money" (Lucas 1972 [1981]). The 1970s stagflation episode, Lucas claimed, demonstrated the failure of Keynesian activation policy, while confirming Friedman's predictions.

The most influential of Lucas's judgments about Keynesian theory is the famous "Lucas critique" (Lucas 1976 [1981]). It asserts that the econometric models of the time, all derivatives of the Klein–Goldberger model, could not serve their avowed purpose of comparing alternative economic policies because the coefficients of the models were estimated by econometric methods (rather than being derived from theory), and their numerical values were independent of any changes in institutional regime that might occur. Therefore, the model-builder will miss the fact that agents would change their decisions when faced with a policy change. As a result, a model of the economy estimated at a period during which a particular institutional regime held sway could not but provide inadequate information for assessing what might occur under a different regime. According to Lucas, only deeper, "structural models", that is, derived from the fundamentals of the economy, agents' preferences, and technological constraints, were able to provide a robust grounding for the evaluation of alternative policies.

Lucas's critique was part and parcel of the rational-behaviour hypothesis introduced by Muth (1961). It was meant to capture the idea that economic agents ought to be ascribed the ability of guessing (on average) the outcome of the market in which they are participating, conditional on the information available. That is, their subjective expectations about any coming event should coincide (on average) with the model-builder's objective expectations. The change involved is radical, a move away from a backward looking towards a forward-looking depiction of economic agents.

Kydland and Prescott's intertemporal inconsistency claim

One of Friedman's claims in his Presidential Address was that agents could not be fooled on a recurrent basis. In an influential article, Finn Kydland and Edward Prescott (1977) re-expressed this idea in a more rigorous way by building their argumentation on the rational expectations hypothesis. This article became an important element in the rules versus discretion debate, on the "rules" side. At stake was the issue of governments' policy declarations of intention. Kydland and Prescott's bold claim was that a benevolent well-informed government would repeatedly repudiate its promises unless it was constitutionally impeded from doing so. A standard example is that of a government aiming to boost investment and so announcing that an increase in the interest rate was going to occur in a year's time, thereby triggering firms to hasten their investment plans. The snag is that a year later it may well turn out that it is in the government's interest to forgo this increase because of its deflationary effects. However, if it does so, its credibility will be harmed, and its future announcements may no longer be taken seriously.

Kydland and Prescott's credibility argument was scarcely original – earlier versions can be found in the writings of dynamic games theorists – but they introduced it into the macroeconomic debate. Its implication is a drastic narrowing of governmental discretion. In effect, once the credibility dimension is taken on board, policy announcements will be deemed credible by private agents only if they can be sure that, when the proper time arises, the government will have a firm interest in (or no way out of) implementing the policy.

New Classical Macroeconomics: A Different Research Programme

The "new classical macroeconomics" term applies only to the works of Lucas and his associates. The paradigm that they had inaugurated soon underwent an inner evolution that led to the emergence of real business cycle modelling under Kydland and Prescott's stewardship. A further transformation, leading to the emergence of (second generation new Keynesian models) dynamic stochastic general equilibrium (DSGE) modelling, followed. These three modelling strategies should be considered as phases within the same research programme, the DSGE macroeconomics programme, the main features of which were present from the first instalment onwards. Drawing a contrast between two paradigms is a matter of selecting criteria against which they can be compared and assessing how they measure up to them. Table 8 summarises the results of such an exercise.

The first point to be stressed is the change in the research agenda that occurred. The central object of study of Keynesian macroeconomics was unemployment – in a wider sense, the search for the malfunctioning of markets. In the span of a few years, the unemployment theme ceased to be an important preoccupation of macroeconomists; the business cycle took its place at the top of the agenda. Of course, variations in economic activity are a central item in the study of economic fluctuations, but in the new paradigm

Table 8   Contrasting Keynesian and new classical macroeconomics

	Keynesian macroeconomics	New classical macroeconomics
1. The overarching aim of macroeconomics	Explaining unemployment	Explaining the business cycle
2. Basic model	The IS–LM model	The Lucas–Rapping supply function
3. Relative role of supply and demand	Emphasis on demand	Emphasis on supply
4. The wage–employment relationship	Stable Phillips curve allowing the policy exploitation of the inflation/unemployment inverse relation	No possibility of a policy exploitation of the inflation/unemployment inverse relation
5. Micro/macro relationship	Under the mantle of the neoclassical synthesis; macroeconomics is concerned with its disequilibrium short-period leg	Rejection of the neoclassical synthesis; its equilibrium long-period leg can provide all the explanation necessary
6. Expectations	Adaptive expectations	Rational expectations
7. Econometric modelling	Keynesian macroeconometric models are complex systems of equations, whose parameters are fixed by economically estimated coefficients	Models are simplified general equilibrium models which ought to be based on "deep structural" parameters based on the calibration method
8. Methodology	Marshallian	Walrasian
9. The nature of the business cycle and policy conclusions	The business cycle is viewed as a market failure – the policy aim is to bring the economy towards full employment through demand activation	Fluctuations express agents' optimising reaction to exogenous shocks – no activation policy should be undertaken

they are accounted for in terms of hours worked without consideration of the split between the employed and the unemployed.

Another stark difference concerns the way in which the business cycle issue is addressed. The challenge Lucas set himself was to construct an equilibrium theory of the business cycle, where the fluctuations of economic variables can be traced back to optimising decisions made by economic agents. Instead of entering into a detailed description of how he progressed in this enterprise, we shall just say the following. According to the Keynesian approach, variations in employment result from changes in aggregate demand. The underlying picture is that labour suppliers are passive, employment decisions being made unilaterally by firms. Moreover, this approach tended to consider the supply of labour and the labour force as the same thing, taking for granted that any difference between the total labour force and the level of employment is involuntary unemployment. Lucas's hunch (and Rapping's because the so-called Lucas supply function emerged in Lucas and Rapping's joint work (Lucas and Rapping 1969 [1981])) was that changes in the supply of labour, viewed as a result of optimising decision-making, play a central role in explaining fluctuations. His view, borrowed from neoclassical capital theory, is that the decision to participate in the labour market or to produce on a self-employed basis are a matter of allocating leisure (and hence labour) both within a given period of time and over time. Economic agents ought to be depicted as comparing the wage rate at one point in time with the wage rate they expect to prevail later in time, say today and tomorrow. If the former is more advantageous than the latter, they will decide to work more today and less tomorrow.

This intertemporal substitution phenomenon, Lucas contended, is decisive in explaining variations in the level of activity over time. On this insight, he constructed a model of the business cycle where variations in activity over time are due to two factors: exogenous monetary shocks, on the one hand, and agents' imperfect information, on the other. In this model, agents receive one signal incorporating two distinct pieces of information. On their own, these two pieces of information would trigger opposite reactions, changing or not changing the total hours worked. Needing to engage in signal extracting, the optimal solution agents will adopt is to mix the two opposite reactions in some weighted way. Hence the hours worked departs from what they would have been with perfect information. Here, Lucas claimed, rests the explanation of the variations in hours worked over the business cycle. Monetary shocks have real effects but, as argued by Friedman, the government cannot exploit them since they occur only when the changes in money supply are unanticipated.

A totally different picture of the business cycle emerged. Earlier, the business cycle was viewed as the disequilibrium phenomenon par excellence, the manifestation of a market failure. The mere assertion of its existence was seen as an invitation to the state to take steps to make it disappear. In the new approach, the business cycle expresses the optimising reactions of agents to outside shocks affecting the economy. That is, business fluctuations are no longer viewed as market failures, and governments should refrain from trying to prevent their occurrence. Nor is there any rationale for acting upon them.

The New Keynesian Counter-Offensive

Lucas's all out attack on Keynesianism was not left unanswered by those economists who, for one reason or another, felt that Keynes was right (and Lucas wrong). There were two types of reaction. The reaction of traditional Keynesians is typified by the observation made by Richard Lipsey that what occurred was the "replacement of messy truth by precise error" (Lipsey 2000: 76), thus claiming that the direction opened up by Lucas and his fellow economists should be radically rejected. In contrast, the other reaction amounted to admitting that many of Lucas's criticisms were well founded, and could not be dismissed with a sweep of the hand. This was the standpoint of the so-called "new Keynesian" economists. These wanted to re-habilitate Keynes's insights, in one way or another, while accepting the requirement that the analysis ought to rest on a choice-theoretical basis. Within a decade, several such new models blossomed. The main models, in the order of publication of their inaugural papers, were: implicit contract models (Baily 1974; Azariadis 1975); staggered wage-setting models (Fischer 1977; Phelps and Taylor 1977; Taylor 1979); search and coordination failure models (Diamond 1982); imperfect competition models (Hart 1982) efficiency wages models (Salop 1979; Shapiro and Stiglitz 1984); menu costs and near-rationality models (Mankiw 1985; Akerlof and Yellen 1985a, 1985b); coordination failures (Roberts 1987).

All these models shared the same purpose of amending, if not reversing, new classical conclusions, thereby reviving Keynes's mitigated view of the market system. The price to be paid for this endeavour was a stricter adherence to basic neoclassical principles and the abandonment of many traditional Keynesian notions. With a few exceptions, these models adopted the imperfect competition framework. Moreover, except for the staggered wage-setting model, they all were static models. These communalities aside, new Keynesian models developed in many different directions, to the effect that we can hardly speak of a new Keynesian school. Among the several dividing lines traversing new Keynesian models, the following two were central. The first is between the authors aiming to rescue the notion of involuntary unemployment from Lucas's stern attack by providing it with microfoundations, and those who had little interest in such a task preferring to react to Lucas and to Sargent and Wallace (1975) on the issue of the efficiency of monetary policy. Most of the models mentioned above followed the first of these two approaches, the exception being menu-costs and staggered-contract models. The second dividing line is between the theories pursuing the rigidity or stickiness line, be it real or nominal, and those whose builders felt the need to retain the flexibility of prices and wages assumption. The majority of new Keynesian models took the first line, the exception being Diamond's (1982) search model, Roberts's (1987) coordination model and Hart's (1982) imperfect competition model.

New Keynesian models were as conceptually innovative and technically clever as the new classical models they wished to refute. Nonetheless, they failed to alter the new course of macroeconomics which Lucas had initiated. As far as the defence of involuntary unemployment was concerned, the emergence of search and matching models vindicated Lucas's claim that the topic of unemployment could be sent back to labour economics instead of remaining at the centre of macroeconomics. Moreover, most of the new Keynesian models operated within a static framework while the dynamic stochastic perspective was becoming more and more dominant. Gradually, it dawned on new Keynesians that, if they wanted to have an impact on the development of the field, they needed to use the new language. This was to happen a few years later.

Real Business Cycle Models

While Keynesians were trying to challenge Lucas, others were trying to implement the research programme he had initiated. Kydland and Prescott's "Time to build and aggregate fluctuations" (1982) and John Long and Charles Plosser's "Real business cycles" (1983) are the two papers which started the real business cycle line of research. Both tried to model business fluctuations as the result of real shocks to the economy (rather than monetary shocks, as in Lucas's model). Kydland and Prescott's paper had the additional feature of wanting to move from the model to the facts, so inaugurating a new methodology by taking the neoclassical growth model to the computer.

Kydland and Prescott's model is, like Lucas's, neo-Walrasian. The equilibrium discipline, rational expectations, a dynamic-stochastic environment, and a central role for intertemporal substitution are all present in both types of model. But there are also striking differences. First, Kydland and Prescott shifted towards real technology shocks. Second, they abandoned the imperfect information line of research. Third, and most important, Kydland and Prescott's work was quantitative. In Michael Woodford's words:

> The real business cycle literature offered a new methodology, both for theoretical analysis and for empirical testing . . . It showed how such models [of the Lucas type] could be made *quantitative*, emphasising the assignment of realistic numerical parameter values and the computation of numerical solutions to the equations of the model, rather than being content with merely qualitative conclusions derived from more general assumptions. (Woodford 1999: 25–6, original emphasis)

Woodford was right. However, merely asserting that a qualitative model was transformed into a quantitative one may fail to convey the full measure of the change. While models *à la* Lucas could recruit only a tiny fraction of the macroeconomic profession, Kydland and Prescott were able to devise a research programme that became the bread and butter approach for legions of macroeconomists, both top-notch and average, for decades to come. This is the sign of a successful revolution.

The aim of Kydland and Prescott's 1982 model was to show that economic fluctuations could be explained as a consequence of economic agents' optimising adjustment to exogenous technological shocks. Their starting point was Ramsey's (1928) and Cass's (1965) models of optimal growth, which were extended to a stochastic economy by Brock and Mirman (1972). Ramsey studied the intertemporal optimising programme of a representative agent over an infinite horizon, subject to a budget and a technology constraint calculated by a benevolent and omniscient planner.

To the outside observer, what is striking in Kydland and Prescott's endeavour is the contrast between the model they build and its avowed purpose, to shed light on the development of the US economy from 1950 to 1975. Their model economy is summarised in one utility function and one production function. The production function is subject to stochastic technology shocks. The variables considered are, for production, capital, the level of employment (number of hours worked; not the number of people employed as opposed to those who are unemployed) and productivity, and for household preferences, consumption and investment. Two additional variables are involved: the hourly real wage and the real interest rate. Kydland and Prescott used two sources to parameterise the functional forms of the models: first, steady state conditions and, second, calibration. Calibration, a technique borrowed from computational general equilibrium analysis, consists of assigning values to the model's parameters by using information from panels, national accounts and other data banks. If such data are unavailable, the model-builder ascribes values based on theoretical reasoning.

The validation of the model occurs by comparing the moments (volatilities, correlations and auto-correlations) that summarise the actual experience of the US economy with the equivalent moments from the model economy. The model succeeds if the simulation mimics the empirical observations. To a large extent, this is true for Kydland and Prescott's model, which satisfactorily reproduces both the low variability of consumption and the high variability of investment. The same is true for the pro-cyclical character and persistence of most of the variables considered. However, as readily admitted by the authors, the model is wanting on two scores. It is unable to account for the variation in hours worked. In the real-world data, these hours are closely correlated with output, but they vary significantly less in the model. Another weakness concerns changes in the wage rate and the interest rate; in the model, these are pro-cyclical, but in reality wages are only weakly pro-cyclical (almost a-cyclical) while the interest rate is anti-cyclical.

Kydland and Prescott proved able to achieve their aim of constructing a model mimicking several important empirical traits of the fluctuations in the US economy over a quarter of a century, on the basis of the most rudimentary possible model. Before their paper appeared, the general opinion was that such an enterprise was impossible. Nevertheless, a large number of criticisms were levelled at Kydland and Prescott's model. Answering these led to a series of wide-ranging improvements, which we cannot enter into here. With time, Kydland and Prescott's initial real business cycle model grew into a simplified canonical model, the twin advantages of which were its parsimony and the purposes which it can serve.

New developments resulted from attempts to reply to the early criticisms, which pointed out insufficiencies and inconsistencies. New stylised facts were integrated into its successors. This led to a growth in the number and type of shocks considered. For example, in order to improve upon the anomalous correlation between productivity and hours worked, Christiano and Eichenbaum (1992) introduced a shock related to government consumption expenditures, which had a negative wealth effects on households. Another striking defect of the early real business cycle models was their lack of consideration of money. Kydland and Prescott had argued that monetary shocks played only a minor role in explaining business fluctuations. Accepting this conclusion was one thing, but the nagging stylized fact of the inverse evolution of the interest rate, on the one hand, and of inflation and output, on the other, was another. Monetary policy had thus to re-enter the picture. Woodford's (2003) book, *Interest and Prices*, blazed the trail.

Second-Generation New Keynesian Modelling

The mid-1990s saw a decline in real business cycle modelling and the concomitant emergence of a new type of models. This move should be seen as an endogenous change rather than a revolution. Ending their methodological fight, new Keynesians and real business cycle theorists came to agree upon adopting a workhorse model that both considered apposite – hence the "new neoclassical synthesis" label (Goodfriend and King 1997). Keynesians' contribution to the wedding was imperfect competition and sluggishness, as well as a focus on the role of the central bank. In exchange they accepted the basic components of real business cycle modelling (that is, exogenous shocks, the dynamic stochastic perspective, the equilibrium discipline, intertemporal substitution and rational expectations).

Monopolistic competition was integrated into DSGE modelling by borrowing the Dixit–Stiglitz aggregator from Dixit and Stiglitz's (1977) model of product differentiation. In the canonical version of this model, the economy comprises four types of goods: labour, a final all-purpose good, a continuum of intermediary goods, and money. The final good is a homogenous good produced using the intermediary goods. It is exchanged competitively. Intermediary goods are each produced by a monopolistic firm using Leontief technology based only on labour. These monopolistic firms are price-makers applying a mark-up on their marginal costs. If, for any reason, they are willing but unable to change their prices, it is in their interest to increase the quantity sold, until demand is fully satisfied.

As for sluggishness, at last, a satisfactory theoretical translation (that is, menu costs and staggering contracts) of its fact-of-life evidence seemed to have been found. It eventually became fixed in Calvo's (1983) price formation theory, a formulation close to the staggered contracts insight. It is assumed that at each period of exchange, firms are authorised to change their prices as soon as they receive a signal, occurring with a given probability. If, for instance, this probability is one in three, then on average, firms will reset their prices every three periods. While this price formation assumption can be criticised for being ad hoc, it has been more widely used than the earlier versions of sluggishness, as a result of its tractability.

Another development that emerged in the last decade of the twentieth century concerned monetary policy, in particular the rules that central banks should follow. Here a radical shift away from Friedman's vision took place as the rate of interest came to substitute the quantity of money as the leading control variable. Two economists, John Taylor and Michael Woodford played a prominent role in this development. Taylor devised a rule that became popular enough to be named the "Taylor rule". It originated in an article (Taylor 1993), which tried to provide an empirical assessment of the Federal Reserve System's (FED's) policy. The rule consists of fixing the rate of interest taking into account three objectives: (1) price stability, measured by the difference between the observed and the targeted rate of inflation; (2) the output gap, the deviation of effective from potential output (that is, the output level that would have occurred had the economy been competitive) and (3) an economic policy shock, a purely residual shock uncorrelated with either inflation or output. Woodford pursued the same idea in several contributions, ranging from a 1977 article (Rotemberg and Woodford 1997) to his 2003 book, *Interest and Prices: Foundations of a Theory of Monetary Policy*. This book quickly became a standard reference in the monetary policy literature. Woodford's approach was to address the problem at the level of principles by attempting to make a full link between macroeconomic stabilisation and economic welfare. Taking the stabilisation of inflation as the prominent aim of monetary policy, he nonetheless found ways to couple it with the Keynesian objective of a stabilisation of the output gap (Rotemberg and Woodford 1997). He also paid considerable attention to the credibility dimension:

> When choosing a policy to best serve the goal of stabilization, it is crucial to take account of the effects of the policy's systematic component on people's expectations of future policy. For this reason, my work has focused largely on the study of policy *rules*: this forces one to think about the systematic patterns that one can expect to be anticipated by sufficiently sophisticated market participants. (Woodford 2006: 2, original emphasis)

This perspective, Woodford further argues, has some counter-intuitive implications. For example, it makes policy inertia desirable or, in other words, purely forward-looking policy is seen to be harmful.

The end result of all these developments is that now economists holding opposite policy views have come to agree about the conceptual apparatus upon which to base their theoretical work. This state of affairs seems to be agreeable to both camps. Macroeconomists from the real business cycle tradition are happy because new Keynesians have yielded by adopting their language and toolbox. New Keynesians are content because they have been able to bring to the merger the concepts they were insisting upon in their more static days. Moreover, the admission that monetary policy can have real effects marks a reversal of the Friedman–Lucas view that had previously held the high ground. In other words, when it comes to policy, new Keynesians seem to be the winners.

Another milestone in the recent evolution of macroeconomics has been Christiano et al.'s (2005) article. This enriched the standard DSGE model, based on staggered wage and price contracts, with four additional ingredients: (1) habit formation in preferences for consumers; (2) adjustment costs in investment; (3) variable capital utilisation; and (4) the need for firms to borrow working capital in order to finance their wage bill. The ensuing (complex) model allows the authors to account for the inertia of inflation and persistence in output, two important features supporting the Keynesian standpoint on the real effects of monetary shocks.

The next step occurred when Smets and Wouters (2003) took up Christiano et al.'s model and estimated it for the euro zone viewed as a closed economy. Before this, central banks were still using models which, for all their sophistication, remained based on the Kleinian tradition. In contrast, the Smets–Wouters model was microfounded, specifying the preferences of households and the central bank. Smets and Wouters estimated seven variables (gross domestic product, consumption, investment, prices, real wages, employment and the nominal interest rate) under ten structural shocks (including productivity, labour supply, investment preferences, cost-push and monetary policy shocks). Having more shocks certainly gives a better fit. The flip side, however, is that none of them comes out as dominant. The model also embedded friction, which had the effect of slowing down the adjustment to shocks. Smets and Wouters's main contribution is technical, consisting of using Bayesian estimation methods in a DSGE setting for the first time. In a very short time, central banks around the world adopted the Smets–Wouters model for their policy analysis and forecasting, thus replacing "old" with "new" Keynesian modelling. However, one aspect of the old way of modelling remains: the distinctive trait of real business cycle models was their attempt to be as simple as possible. In effect, they comprised a limited number of equations. This parsimony is a feature no longer to be found in new models *à la* Smets–Wouters.

The Impact of the 2008–09 Financial Crisis on Macroeconomic Theory

How did macroeconomics stand in the wake of the so-called Great Recession (an analogy with the Great Depression of the 1930s)? These events brought out at least two blind spots in the dynamic stochastic approach to macroeconomics (that is, DSGE modelling in general). The first is the limited attention that had been given to the financial sector in these models, a dramatic blank once the Great Recession broke out in 2008. The second pertains to the limits of what can be done with equilibrium modelling, that is, using models premised on the view that, whatever the situation in which economic agents find themselves, they ought to be considered as having achieved their first best optimising plan. In other words, DSGE models exclude in advance the possibility of any pathology in the working of the market system, and certainly of any collapse in the trading system to the extent that we have recently encountered.

This marks a clear analogy with the situation faced by Keynes in the 1930s. Equilibrium models convey a Panglossian view, to borrow Keynes's characterisation (all is for the best in this best of all possible worlds), of the working of the economy as they rule out the possibility that markets can fail and that agents may find themselves in a state where they are unable to achieve their optimising plan (Keynes 1936: 33). When the economy is in a state of plain sailing, this neglect is admissible, but it is no longer justifiable when the economy shows signs of collapse. Whatever the virtues of the new-classical real business-cycle methodology, its limits are clear. To "old" Keynesians, this has the sweet smell of revenge. New voices have arisen proclaiming the need to return to Keynes's *General Theory*. Robert Skidelsky, Keynes's biographer and the author of *The Return of the Master* (Skidelsky 2009), and Paul Krugman – the 2008 laureate of the Sveriges Riksbank Prize in Economic Sciences in Memory of Alfred Nobel – (see, for example, Krugman 2010) are two prominent figures in this movement (not to mention Posner's rediscovery of Keynes's book – Posner 2009). In Krugman's words, "Keynesian economics remains the best framework we have for making sense of recessions and depressions" (2009: 8).

   The Great Recession will certainly have an impact on the course of macroeconomics. The clearest sign of this is the widespread admission that the loose integration of finance into macroeconomic models was a serious mistake, and the ensuing surge of work aiming to fill this gap. At this juncture, it is, however, still difficult to gauge whether a mere integration of the financial sector within the existing framework will suffice, or whether the Great Recession will trigger a more radical reorientation of macroeconomics.

MICHEL DE VROEY AND PIERRE MALGRANGE

See also:

Business cycles and growth (III); Growth (III); John Maynard Keynes (I); Keynesianism (II); Robert E. Lucas (I); Monetarism (II); New Classical Macroeconomics (II); New Keynesianism (II); Open economy macroeconomics (III); Post-Keynesianism (II); Robert Merton Solow (I); Joseph Eugene Stiglitz (I); James Tobin (I).

References and further reading

Akerlof, G. and J. Yellen (1985a), 'Can small deviations from rationality make significant differences to economic equilibria?', *American Economic Review*, **75** (4), 708–21.

Akerlof, G. and J. Yellen (1985b), 'A near-rational model of the business cycle with wage and price inertia', *Quarterly Journal of Economics, Supplement*, **100**, supplement, 823–38.

Azariadis, C. (1975), 'Implicit contracts and underemployment equilibria', *Journal of Political Economy*, **83** (6), 1183–2002.

Baily, M. (1974), 'Wages and employment under uncertain demand', *Review of Economic Studies*, **41** (1), 37–50.

Barro, R. and H. Grossman (1971), 'A general disequilibrium model of income and employment', *American Economic Review*, **61** (1), 82–93.

Barro, R. and H. Grossman (1976), *Money, Employment and Inflation*, Cambridge: Cambridge University Press.

Batyra, A. and M. De Vroey (2012), 'From one to many islands: the emergence of search and matching models', *Bulletin of Economic Research*, **64** (3), 393–414.

Benassy, J.-P. (1975), 'Neo-Keynesian disequilibrium theory in a monetary economy', *Review of Economic Studies*, **42** (4), 503–23.

Brock, W. and L. Mirman (1972), 'Optimal economic growth and uncertainty: the discounted case', *Journal of Economic Theory*, **4** (3), 479–513.

Buiter, W. (1980), 'The macroeconomics of Dr. Pangloss. A critical survey of the new classical macroeconomics', *The Economic Journal*, **90** (357), 34–50.

Calvo, G.-A. (1983), 'Staggered prices in a utility-maximizing framework', *Journal of Monetary Economics*, **12** (3), 383–98.

Cass, D. (1965), 'Optimal growth in an aggregate model of capital accumulation', *Review of Economic Studies*, **32** (3), 233–40.

Christiano, L. and M. Eichenbaum (1992), 'Current real business cycle theories and aggregate labour market fluctuations', *American Economic Review*, **82** (3), 430–50.

Christiano, L., M. Eichenbaum and C. Evans (2005), 'Nominal rigidities and the dynamic effects of a shock to monetary policy', *Journal of Political Economy*, **113** (1), 1–45.

Clower, R. (1965), 'The Keynesian counterrevolution: a theoretical appraisal', in D. Walker (ed.) (1984), *Money and Markets. Essays by Robert Clower*, Cambridge: Cambridge University Press, pp. 34–58.

Deleau, M., P. Malgrange and P.-A. Muet (1984), 'A study of short-run and long-run properties of macroeconometric dynamic models by means of an aggregative core model', in P. Malgrange and P.-A. Muet (eds), *Contemporary Macroeconomic Modelling*, Oxford: Basil Blackwell, pp. 215–24.

Diamond, P. (1982), 'Aggregate demand management in search equilibrium', *Journal of Political Economy*, **90** (5), 881–94.

Dimand, R. (2008), 'Macroeconomics, origins and history of', in N. Durlauf and L. Blume (eds), *The New Palgrave Dictionary of Economics*, 2nd edn, Basingstoke: Palgrave Macmillan.

Dixit, A.-K. and J. Stiglitz (1977), 'Monopolistic competition and optimum product diversity', *American Economic Review*, **67** (3), 297–308.

Drèze, J.H. (1975), 'Existence of equilibrium under price rigidities', *International Economic Review*, **16** (2), 301–20.

Fine, B. and D. Milonakis (2009), *From Economic Imperialism to Freakeconomics: The Shifting Boundaries between Economics and Other Social Sciences*, London: Routledge.

Fischer, S. (1977), 'Long-term contracts, rational expectations, and the optimal money supply rule', *Journal of Political Economy*, **85** (1), 191–295.

Friedman, M. (1968), 'The role of monetary policy', *American Economic Review*, **58** (2), 1–17.

Goodfriend, M. and R. King, (1997), 'The new neo-classical synthesis and the role of monetary policy', in B.S. Bernanke and J.J. Rotemberg (eds), *NBER Macroeconomics Annual 1997*, vol. 12, Cambridge, MA: NBER, pp. 231–83.

Hansen, A. (1953), *A Guide to Keynes*, New York: McGraw Hill.

Harrod, R.F. (1937), 'Mr Keynes and traditional theory', *Econometrica*, **5** (1), 74–86.

Hart, O. (1982), 'A model of imperfect competition with Keynesian features', *Quarterly Journal of Economics*, **97** (1), 109–38.

Hicks, J.R. (1937), 'Mr. Keynes and the classics', *Econometrica*, **2** (April), 147–59.

Keynes, J.M. (1936), *The General Theory of Employment, Interest, and Money*, London: Macmillan.

King, J. (2002), *A History of Post Keynesian Economics since 1936*, Cheltenham, UK and Northampton, MA, USA: Edward Elgar.

Klein, L.R. (1950), *Economic Fluctuations in the United States, 1921–1941*, New York: John Wiley.

Klein, L.R. and A. Goldberger (1955), *An Econometric Model of the United States, 1929–1952*, Amsterdam: North Holland.

Krugman, P. (2009), 'How did economists get it so wrong?', *New York Times Magazine*, 6 September, p. 8.

Kydland, F. and E. Prescott (1977), 'Rules rather than discretion: the inconsistency of optimal planes', *Journal of Political Economy*, **85** (3), 473–91.

Kydland, F. and E. Prescott (1982), 'Time to build and aggregate fluctuations', *Econometrica*, **50** (6), 1345–70.

Laidler, D. (1999), *Fabricating the Keynesian Revolution: Studies of the Inter-War Literature on Money, the Cycle, and Unemployment*, Cambridge: Cambridge University Press.

Leijonhufvud, A. (1968), *On Keynesian Economics and the Economics of Keynes*, Oxford: Oxford University Press.

Lipsey, R. (2000), 'IS–LM, Keynesianism, and the new classicism', in R. Backhouse and A. Salanti, (eds), *Macroeconomics and the Real World*, vol. 2, *Keynesian Economics, Unemployment and Policy*, Oxford: Oxford University Press, pp. 57–82.

Long, J. and C. Plosser (1983), 'Real business cycles', *Journal of Political Economy*, **94**, 39–69.

Lucas, R.E. Jr (1972), 'Expectations and the neutrality of money', reprinted in R.E. Lucas Jr (1981), *Studies in Business Cycle Theory*, Cambridge, MA: MIT Press, pp. 65–89.

Lucas, R.E. Jr (1976), 'Econometric policy evaluation: a critique', reprinted in R.E. Lucas Jr (1981), *Studies in Business Cycle Theory*, Cambridge, MA: MIT Press, pp. 104–30.

Lucas, R.E. Jr (1977), 'Understanding business cycles', reprinted in R.E. Lucas Jr (1981), *Studies in Business Cycle Theory*, Cambridge, MA: MIT Press, pp. 215–39.

Lucas, R.E. Jr (1981), *Studies in Business Cycle Theory*, Cambridge, MA: MIT Press.

Lucas, R.E. Jr (2004), 'My Keynesian education', in M. De Vroey and K. Hoover (eds), *The IS–LM Model: Its Rise, Fall, and Strange Persistence*, Durham, NC: Duke University Press, pp. 12–24.

Lucas, R.E. Jr and L. Rapping (1969), 'Real wages, employment, and inflation', *Journal of Political Economy*, **77** (5), 721–54.

Lucas, R.E. Jr and T. Sargent, (1979), 'After Keynesian macroeconomics' in P. Miller (ed.) (1994), *The Rational Expectations Revolution: Readings from the Front Line*, Cambridge, MA: MIT Press, pp. 5–30.

Malinvaud, E. (1977), *The Theory of Unemployment Reconsidered*, Oxford: Basil Blackwell.

Mankiw, N. (1985), 'Small menu costs and large business cycles: a macroeconomic modeling of monopoly', *Quarterly Journal of Macroeconomics*, **100** (2), 529–38.

Mankiw, N. and D. Romer (eds) (1991), *New Keynesian Economics*, 2 vols, Cambridge, MA: MIT Press.

Meade J. (1937), 'A simplified model of Keynes's system', *Review of Economic Studies*, **4** (2), 98–107.

Modigliani, F. (1944), 'Liquidity preference and the theory of interest and money', *Econometrica*, **12** (1), 44–88.

Muth, J. (1961), 'Rational expectations and the theory of price movements', *Econometrica*, **29** (3), 315–35.

Patinkin, D. (1956), *Money, Interest and Prices*, 2nd edn 1965, New York: Harper and Row.

Phelps, E. (1967), 'Phillips curves, expectations of inflation and optimal unemployment over time', *Economica*, **34** (135), 254–81.

Phelps, E. (1968), 'Money wage dynamics and labour market equilibrium', *Journal of Political Economy*, **76** (4), pt 2, 678–711.

Phelps, E. and J. Taylor (1977), 'Stabilizing powers of monetary policy under rational expectations', *Journal of Political Economy*, **85** (1), 163–90.

Phillips, W. (1958), 'The relationship between unemployment and the rate of change of money wages in the United Kingdom, 1861–1957', *Economica*, **25** (100), 283–99.

Posner, R. (2009), *A Failure of Capitalism. The Crisis of '98 and the Descent into Depression*, Cambridge, MA: Harvard University Press.

Ramsey, F. (1928), 'A mathematical theory of saving', *Economic Journal*, **38** (152), 543–59.

Roberts, J. (1987), 'An equilibrium model with involuntary unemployment at flexible, competitive prices and wages', *American Economic Review*, **77** (5), 856–74.

Rotemberg, J. and M. Woodford (1997), 'Interest rate rules in an estimated sticky price model', in J.B. Taylor (ed.) (1999), *Monetary Policy Rules*, Chicago, IL: University of Chicago Press, pp. 57–126.

Salop, S. (1979), 'A model of the natural rate of unemployment', *American Economic Review*, **69** (1), 117–25.

Samuelson, P.A. and R. Solow (1960), 'Analytical aspects of anti-inflationary policy', *American Economic Review*, **50** (2), 177–94.

Sargent, T. and N. Wallace (1975), 'Rational expectations, the optimal monetary instrument, and the optimal money supply rule', *Journal of Political Economy*, **83** (2), 241–54.

Shapiro, C. and J.E. Stiglitz (1984), 'Equilibrium unemployment as worker discipline device', *American Economic Review*, **74** (3), 433–44.

Skidelsky, R. (2009), *The Return of the Master*, London: Public Affairs.

Smets, F. and R. Wouters (2003), 'An estimated dynamic stochastic general equilibrium of the Euro Area', *Journal of the European Economic Association*, **5** (1), 1123–75.

Snowdon, B. and H. Vane, (2005), *Modern Macroeconomics. Its Origin, Development and Current State*, Cheltenham, UK and Northampton, MA, USA: Edward Elgar.

Solow, R. (1956), 'A contribution to the theory of economic growth', *Quarterly Journal of Economics*, **70** (1), 65–94.

Taylor, J.B. (1979), 'Estimation and control of an econometric model with rational expectations', *Econometrica*, **47** (5), 1267–86.

Taylor, J.B. (1993), 'Discretion versus policy rules in practice', *Carnegie-Rochester Conference Series on Public Policy*, **39** (December), 195–214.

Tinbergen, J. (1939), *Statistical Testing of Business-Cycle Theories*, vol. 2, *Business Cycles in the USA 1919–1932*, Geneva: League of Nations.

Usabiaga Ibanez, C. (1999), *The Current State of Macroeconomics: Leading Thinkers in Conversations*, Basingstoke: Macmillan.

Woodford, M. (1999), 'Revolution and evolution in twentieth century macroeconomics', mimeo, accessed 15 February 2015 at http://www.columbia.edu/~mw2230/.

Woodford, M. (2003), *Interest and Prices: Foundations of a Theory of Monetary Policy*, Princeton, NJ: Princeton University Press.

Woodford, M. (2006), 'Rules for monetary policy', *NBER Reporter: Research Summary*, Spring, accessed 15 February 2015 at http://www.nber.org/reporter/spring06/woodford.html.

Young, W. (1987), *Interpreting Mr. Keynes: The IS–LM Enigma*, Cambridge: Polity Press.

Methods in the history of economic thought

The practitioners of the history of economic thought engage frequently in discussion on issues relating to its subject-matter and method. It is because those who study this discipline like to feel firm ground beneath their feet that retrospective overviews and prospective considerations are presented cyclically, expressing concerns and hopes about the present and future situation of this field of knowledge. The places normally chosen for this purpose are the conferences promoted by the main international academic associations and scientific societies that each year bring together the members of this community. The testimonies of Donald Winch (2000), Heinz D. Kurz (2006) and E. Roy Weintraub (2007) are a clear illustration of this type of exhortation, while at the same time revealing quite different commitments and distinct ways of conceiving the existence of the history of economic thought or the history of economics. This contribution will be precisely devoted to clarify the methodological distinctions as well as the plurality and complementarity of methods practiced by historians of economic thought. Despite their differences of content and style, these approaches come together in their unequivocal defence of the rights acquired by a discipline that has already found a direction and sets great store in discussing its identity. Therefore, the next section will briefly refer to the key ontological question of the actual object itself that affords both autonomy and identity to this academic endeavour of revisiting the past of economics.

In Search of a Study Object

Those who engage in the study of a discipline are heirs to an accumulated knowledge whose origins cannot always be precisely identified. In the specific case under consideration here, those studying the history of economic thought, or the history of economics, know that the territory within which they operate has already been ploughed and furrowed by a wide range of different authors and that the history of the discipline is itself frequently confused with the very discipline whose history they seek to discover.

A first observation to be made is that, ever since the mid-eighteenth century, the authors usually credited as contributors to the foundation of modern political economy have themselves been subject to the attention of their contemporaries, making it possible to systematise, debate and criticise the theses that they have defended. It is widely known that the French Physiocrats wrote their own history (Dupont de Nemours 1768), thus recording what they understood to be the crucial moments of innovation introduced by François Quesnay and his followers. Equally well known are the references made by Adam Smith to the mercantile system and the physiocratic school in several chapters of book IV of *The Wealth of Nations*, explaining and criticising the approaches that his new system of political economy sought to supersede (Smith 1776), or the mentions made by Jean-Baptiste Say to different European approaches to economic issues in the preliminary remarks of his *Traité* (Say 1803). These examples, relating to the historical period during which political economy allegedly established itself as an autonomous science, represent a kind of prophecy of what would become an almost permanent attention to the history of the ways of thinking about and interpreting economic problems and phenomena. This is a history that pays homage, selects its own authoritative sources and questions views which are considered antiquated.

In the first half of the nineteenth century, at a time when the basic features of the classical tradition of political economy had already been established and consolidated, the historical overviews produced by J.A. Blanqui (1837–38), A. Villeneuve-Bargemont (1841) and J. R. McCulloch (1826, 1845) clearly showed the relationship that existed between the systematisation of concepts and instruments of analysis (which had merited greater attention in other works that they had written) and the efforts that they were making to arrive at a historical understanding of the processes involved in the emergence and progress of a science under construction. Or, in other words, the history of political economy was understood as an integral and explanatory part of the discipline's analytical content.

The authors mentioned above amount to nothing more than a few deliberately brief and early examples designed to illustrate a basic point. In a certain sense, it would not be inappropriate to consider that all the authors whose work has served as a pretext for producing the history of the science that they successfully attempted to cultivate also ended up themselves writing the history of that same science of which they were momentarily interpreters, even though this was not a priority in their plans. Also, in almost all of them, we can note the construction of causal views of the history of economic thought with the intention of being simultaneously critical and explanatory, thereby hoping to create for themselves an opportunity to subvert the prevailing orthodoxy and point out bright new paths for the future.

This does not mean that economics is a science that is condemned to permanently struggle with the tangled web of its own roots, even though the identification of our roots is generally a starting point for gaining a better knowledge of ourselves. The most sceptical will say that, over the past few decades, there have been no profound changes in the theoretical framework and analytical apparatus that economists have at their disposal. However, even they will agree that there have been developments and improvements that, even if they have not had the virtue of causing us to rethink the status of the science, have at least had the merit of making it more specific and instrumental.

For all of these reasons, it is easy to understand that researching into the history of economic thought does not represent a useless pastime, a mere ritual of digging up authors from the past in order to make them our accomplices in the present. There is, however, a terrible danger, of which all apprentice historians are aware, even if they have not always fully assimilated it, and this consists in transposing into the present more or less lucid views that were built on a historical reality that meanwhile has completely changed. When we say that present-day economic thought is largely derived from the past – or that the ways how economics developed and changed over time is a path-dependent process – we must guard against the mistake of interpreting such a claim as an invitation to blindly adopt rules and panaceas that have since lost any real support and foundation. The feeling that history repeats itself is always illusory, so that it is fundamental to recognise the existence of new problems that call for renewed solutions.

Not only is this warning important, but it does, in itself, have a meaning that could arouse certain attitudes of scorn towards those who write or study the history of economic thought. Doing it is not a symptom of some nostalgic yearning for the past, but, on the contrary, is a means of making the answers that the present requires from us better grounded and more understandable. Also, if the science in question has its object of study firmly situated within the sphere of human and social action, as is the case with economics, then there is all the more reason for the knowledge of its history to be considered even more urgent and essential; because those who have constructed it were responsible for leading movements of scientific divergence and discord, allowing themselves to be guided by convictions and beliefs, and being seduced by processes of change and reform, so that they cannot therefore be summarily judged on the basis of an abstract criterion of scientific validation.

Writing the history of economic thought is therefore a task that we consider to be indispensable, not so that we can make a positivist application to the present of the magical solution that history teaches us, but in order to discover the teachings that help us to re-encounter both the roots and the horizons of the world in which we now live.

What has just been said here about the history of economic thought may be similarly applied to other historiographical domains. It is therefore important to examine these remarks in greater depth and detail, and to clarify to what extent this interest aroused by the discipline is materialised in different methodological approaches.

Methodological Distinctions

There are various ways in which interest has been shown in researching into the possible forms for understanding economic mechanisms and problems from a historical perspective. The history of economic ideas and doctrines, the history of analysis and theory, the intellectual history of economics, the history of economic thought or economics, as well as the history of types of economic thought – these are just some of the possible combinations that obviously also reflect different ways of approaching the subject. However, these multiple varieties of interpretation are conventionally grouped together under two fundamental categories: on the one hand, there is a type of approach that can be described, in a more simplified form as internalist (or absolutist) in that it gives privilege to the repetitive process of creating a conceptual apparatus that is considered, above all, in terms of its formal internal logic; on the other hand, there is an externalist (or relativist) type of approach in which all the emphasis is laid on the external factors that condition the formulation of concepts.

Initially popularised by Mark Blaug (1962: 1–9), this division of methodological fields was later to be further enriched by the same author (Blaug 1990, 2001), through the application to the history of economics of a classification based on the scheme developed by Richard Rorty (1984) for the history of philosophy. According to the Rorty–Blaug scheme of things, there are four types of approach to be considered: (1) *Geistesgeschichte*, or histories of the spirit of a time; (2) historical reconstructions; (3) rational reconstructions; and (4) doxographies.

Under such a scheme, the extreme types are explicitly devalued, since it does not seem possible to accept a history of economics that is constructed solely on the basis of the themes or problems that have shown themselves to be central to the reflections undertaken by the economists from the past (*Geistesgeschichte*), nor even a mere composition of hymns of praise in which the texts and authors of the past are judged through the narrow filter of the current state of economics (doxographies). In this way, we can associate the operative notion of rational reconstruction with the internalist-absolutist methodological approach, and the notion of historical reconstruction with the externalist-relativist approach.

This binary opposition is necessarily reductionist and the distinction between methods of approaching the discipline does not fit into such a rigid divide (Klaes 2003). It is also worth stressing that within that dichotomous classification it is often difficult to decide to which of the categories belongs the same author (Davis 2013). Despite this caveat I think that for the sake of pedagogy these two great methodological sub-divisions may serve as a means to grasp the main practices developed by historians of economic thought.

Theoretical retrospect
According to the perspective of rational reconstructions, it is the objective contents of economics – that is, the structured group of concepts and relations between concepts that guarantee the cognitive capturing of the real world – that functions as the axis of historical retrospection. Taken individually, but without any concern for inserting them in their historical context other than that of establishing the dates between which they lived or the period when they wrote their works, the authors or schools are considered within the perspective of the contributions that they have successively made, whether to the development of instruments and techniques of analysis, or to the construction and improvement of a conceptual corpus that we wish to see increasingly refined, and preferably devoid of any ideological connotations. By following this type of procedure, it becomes possible not only to dissect the analytical scope of theoretical models created by past authors, but also to trace the evolution of particular concepts and, by extension, to chronicle the development of economics as a whole.

In such an avenue of research, there is always room for contradictions, changes, revolutions, which have in fact been thoroughly dissected through the application of the epistemological digressions of Popper, Kuhn or Lakatos to the concrete field of the history of economics (see Latsis 1976; Hausman 1984; De Marchi 1988). However, no matter how significant are the vicissitudes or conflicts that cause us to doubt the validity of scientific principles that are generally considered to be unquestionable, there always remains an axis around which the chronology of the successive advances recorded in the same field of research can be made to gravitate. This means that, if nowadays economics enjoys an undeniable citizenship, this is due to the trials and tribulations to which it has been subjected in the past. The result is clearly visible, and anyone who doubts this should simply consult any elementary university textbook in economics at random.

The great merit of this way of understanding and writing the history – or rather a retrospective – of economics lies precisely in the possibility that it provides for better understanding the interpretive models that we currently have available. It allows us to strengthen the capabilities of a science that, in order to achieve the level of suitability and performance that it is acknowledged to have, has had to experiment and to approximate, proceeding by trial and error, making successive conceptual elaborations, conjectures and refutations. It allows us to understand, for example, that the theorisation of the great economic aggregates and their relationships of functional dependence, or that the interpretation of the mechanisms of price formation in different types of markets, were successively tested before we reached our current point of arrival. In short, it serves a process of legitimisation of the present state of the science with the irrefutable arguments of the path that it has travelled and with the reflections made about the "mistakes" that have meanwhile been ironed out (see Blaug 1962; Pribram 1983; Negishi 1989; Niehans 1990; Dome 1994, to mention only texts whose subject-matter is the history of economic thought as a whole and not that of a particular period, theme or author). This historio-graphical genre seems appropriate to guarantee a fruitful dialogue between historians and economists, based on the premise that, in both groups, there are people interested in engaging in such dialogue, which unfortunately is not always the case.

However, we know how difficult this path has been, how many divergences there have been, how many contradictory analytical explanations have been constructed around the same research object. It would be as senseless as it is ingenuous to seek to give economics an image of irrepressible homogeneity. If we accept controversy as a sign of vitality – that is, if we consider that the fact of economists having access to distinct codes for the inter-pretation of reality does not represent an obstacle to the validation of their discourse nor establish the Manichean dichotomy of truth and falsehood – the exercise of performing rational reconstructions becomes equally essential, in so far as it allows us to detect the origins of the disagreements and the reasons for their continuing endurance. There is no one single theory of money, just as there is no one single theory of production, distribu-tion, well-being or equilibrium. There are, instead, different theoretical approaches, of greater or lesser convergence, that embody a scientific whole in which the right to differ does not prevent the establishment of basic principles (see Creedy and O'Brien 1984).

We may disagree with one or another of the postulates, but the arguments with which we attempt to refute them will be thrown back at us with the same level of commitment. For this reason, going back into the past of economic theory enables us to acquire an attitude of tolerance and humility towards a common inheritance that can withstand the emotion of its being divided up and shared out. This allows us to see that, among the self-confessed or implicit supporters of this way of understanding the virtues of rational reconstructions, we can find authors who openly declare themselves to be opposed to the mainstream theoretical thought and who do, in fact, use their study of the history of economic thought as an instrument for asserting the vitality and relevance of their heterodox and alternative conceptions.

The virtues of this retrospective procedure do not, however, prevent us from pointing out some limitations that arise both from the fact that only the interior dimension of the science is being considered, and, above all, from the concrete way in which this exercise is carried out. The first of these limitations is perfectly clear to the authors who devote themselves to the history of economic theory or analysis. In fact, they cannot be accused of understanding history more as an instrument than as an object of study, since they expressly and purposefully ensure that their motivations are devoid of any reflection that is exterior to the theoretical production in itself. The application of the concept of Whig history is, in this sense, perfectly appropriate (Samuelson 1987).

However, this openly a-historical point of view has inevitable repercussions when put to the concrete test of making rational reconstructions. The references to the past of economic theory are instrumentalised in accordance with a present state that one seeks to legitimise, thus resulting in two biases that even the most careful epistemological vigilance cannot avoid.

The first bias consists in the loyal devotion to theoretical currents in which authors place their absolute and exclusive trust, pouring scorn on the movements or schools that may oppose them. Given the multiplicity of themes that nowadays amount to study objects calling for the application of economics, given also the diversity of opinions that are issued about them, and given also the presence of value judgements that may determine the direction taken by such retrospection, the problem might be considered to be a simple phenomenon that is naturally inherent in the research undertaken in the realm of the social sciences. However, while the process of reconstructing the past from the present is not in question here, one cannot avoid pointing out the limitation that is involved in marginalising theoretical conceptions whose usefulness may be considered worthless.

The second bias derives from the type of language that is generally used to explain the contributions of the authors from the past. The instruments and techniques of analysis that we have available today are used for the purpose of modernising a language that is arrogantly considered to be out of date. Modern concepts, presented in the form of mathematical functions or diagrams, replace and subvert discourses in which the words were not expressed as algebraic symbols or in the form of graphs. While this procedure clearly has the great advantage of standardising the codes that apparently enshrine the scientific character of economic theory and making them understandable, it just as clearly leads to an emptying of their content and a limiting simplification of the theoretical legacies of the authors from the past, who never suspected that they would find themselves stripped of the forms of argument that they used. The danger is not that Adam Smith's theory of economic development is transformed into a mathematical model of endogenous growth; the danger is that we are thus led either to believe or infer that Adam Smith might have conceived such a model.

The conjugation of these two biases shapes a retrospective view of economics that invites the authors and schools of the past to sit in the dock. History is transformed into a courtroom in which those who have contributed, anticipated and forecast are absolved and applauded, while those who did not rise to the genial heights of authors who have been vested with the title of precursors are condemned and have scorn heaped upon them. Authors or schools become valued, not for what they effectively said and upheld, but for the prophetic flashes or naive omissions that, when seen from a distance, their work suggests.

Besides the references that have already been made to authors who have left their own indelible mark on the methodology that is centred upon rational reconstructions, we must also mention one of the authors who most contributed to its legitimisation. I am referring here to the work of Joseph A. Schumpeter (1954), who expressly wished to be associated with a vision that emphasised the objective contents of the science and its evolution over different periods. However, his book strays away from the narrow perspective of his confessed aims, and the great mine of historical information that he uses, revealing his extraordinary encyclopaedic knowledge, also shows a preference for an approach that is decidedly closer to the methodology that we define as historical reconstruction. That is, Schumpeter ended up accomplishing a different aim to the one that he stated that he wished to pursue.

History matters

The historiographical genre labelled as historical reconstructions, which was also previously classified in this entry as externalist or relativist, is characterised by the great care and precision taken in contextualising the process of conceptual elaboration, through the subordination of the scientific postulates to a network of conditioning factors that are seemingly external to it. What exactly are these conditioning factors?

First, the economic context: the factors related to the nature of the material and economic life of the period under research. How do economists respond to the changing material reality? How do they respond to the pressing economic problems? This means that, in the process of theoretical production, it is the very reality that is observed that influences the scope and limits for the formation of abstract conceptual categories. Thus, for example, it may be argued with some consistency that the Ricardian theory of diminishing returns derived directly from the negative consequences of the Napoleonic wars on English agriculture, or that the Keynesian general theory could only be developed because of the Great Depression that generally affected the western economies in the first half of the 1930s. The acceptance that these or other examples have merited should not, however, delude us about the validity of their generalisation.

The fact that, as a heuristic principle, we accept the existence of a relationship between the economic theory of an author, school or period and the accompanying set of contemporary problems, situations or economic and institutional conjunctures cannot be allowed to result in the adoption of single and immutable principles of causality. Relativising the theoretical and analytical procedures does not, therefore, signify their mere subordination to a deterministic dynamic of a material or economic nature. Other factors must necessarily also be taken into account.

The theorisation of economic life is riddled with elements that we might describe, in an abbreviated form, as doctrinal. The work of theoretical production maintains close ties with the institutional and intellectual frameworks within which the scientist operates, so that the authors who pioneered the emergence and development of economics as a science were inevitably influenced by the general conception of the world and the society that they lived in, by the spirit of their time, that Zeitgeist that made them the transmitters of norms and values that prevailed at a given moment.

It was not only at the political and legal level, but also at the ethical, philosophical and even religious level, that "the worldly philosophers" (Heilbroner 1953) adopted a series of principles that would shape a doctrine that, in a certain way, came before the process of interpreting the real world. In turn, these same principles were indissociable from their application, which leads us to establish a no less indissociable relationship between economic theory and policy making. In this way, a doctrine is to be considered both as an intellectual scenario of valuation and appraisal and as a practical guide to action.

Seen from this historiographical perspective, the authors and their works are treated as more or less conscious members of a school, or a family, in which invisible but unbreakable bonds of sharing and complicity are forged. Throughout history, there have successively been distinct coherences whose boundaries are defined not by the scientific postulates that they establish (which are sometimes identical), but, above all, by the doctrinal principles that they obey and which they attempt to make real.

Faced with this panorama, there is one question that must inevitably be asked: does this research perspective not lead to an emptying of the analytical content of economics, and to the painting of a picture of theoretical precariousness?

In fact, the risk of such an occurrence is a quite considerable one, in so far as there is a tendency to emphasise the dependence of economic principles on the historicity of the material context and doctrinal motivations that lie at their origin. This is a bias that results from the perspective that chooses the doctrines, ideas, institutions and economic processes as key study objects on the formation of economic reasoning. It should, however, be noted that the minimising of the conceptual apparatus may create an explanatory gap when an excessive relativism is applied to the study of the periods in which economics has acquired greater credibility as an established academic discipline.

The studies grounded on this methodological genre have tended to abandon the great narratives in order to give greater emphasis to particular approaches to specific authors and periods. But the group of essays produced by authors such as Warren Samuels (1992a, 1992b), Donald Winch (1996, 2009), Bob Coats (1992) and Jean-Claude Perrot (1992) have afforded a broad coverage to this historiographical perspective, which, it must be stressed, was the predominant view during the phase of affirmation of the history of economic thought as an acceptable subject of curricular study.

Among the most decisive recent contributions to the revitalisation of this approach based on historical reconstructions, mention should also be made of the works that undertake a comparative analysis of experiences in the history of economic thought, namely, those that have studied the processes for the dissemination and assimilation of ideas in distinct national settings (Colander and Coats 1989; Cardoso 2003), sometimes focusing on major authors (Tribe and Mizuta 2002, Faccarello and Izumo 2014), and those who have studied the processes for the institutionalisation of scientific knowledge that are performed by scientific journals, associations and societies, university and secondary-school textbooks and parliamentary debates (Augello and Guidi 2001, 2005).

Renewing historical approaches
For the current defenders of historical reconstructions, or of the writing of an intellectual, cultural and institutional history of economics, there is a commonly accepted presupposition: the uselessness of Whig history, or of historical narratives written for the purposes of justification, celebration and apology, through which the science is presented as a series of sustained advances, following an inexorable and cumulative march of progress towards the present. The mere analytical reconstruction is subject to strong criticism, in so far as historians should be interested, above all, in the processes of human creation inherent in the production of scientific knowledge. In order to understand the relevance of modern concepts we need to trace back the process of development that produce them and this exercise implies a historical reconstruction of that process. Thus, instead of studying the history of some "thing" that they have always been able to clearly identify (prices, markets, products, capital, money, you name it), the historians of economic thought turn their attention to the study of the way in which that "thing", without any permanent and transcendental identity, has been transformed into a historical object.

This leads to a broader vision of the craft and skills of the historian of economic thought, in terms of hermeneutics, that is, the process, principles and methods of interpretation of the contemporary and historical meanings of economic writings (Emmett 2003; Faccarello 2014). This may imply a new way of dealing with textual exegesis of the published works of past economists, inviting emphasis on the importance of biographical evidence, the relevance of archival materials, the role of the wider philosophical and political contexts and their interference in setting the economist's mind.

In this sense, the historian of economics penetrates into fields of interpretation that are also frequented by other historians of science: instruments, arguments, experiments, models, visual representations, laboratories, places of knowledge and power, laws and institutions. Also, frequently, historians are led to momentarily forget the science with which they are dealing, in order to focus on the environments of inspiration and conspiracy that spur economists into action (Mirowski 2002).

Such proximity in relation to the objects that are dealt with by the history of science in general certainly lay at the origin of the attempts to enlarge the community of scholars with whom historians of economics keep in company (Schabas 1992). The appeal for the inclusion of the history of economics within the analytical framework of the history of the social sciences with which economics is most closely engaged in dialogue (Backhouse and Fontaine 2010) is only one among a variety of different demonstrations of the permanent determination of the historians of economic thought to question the solidity of the very floor on which they stand.

Concluding Remarks

One of the most interesting aspects of this debate about methods lies in the question of knowing if it is either possible or desirable to choose between apparently opposite camps. Confronted with the different perspectives described earlier, it can easily be understood that what fundamentally separates them is the centre of interest, the point of view from which history is revisited.

History of economic thought aims at understanding ideas and concepts put forward by past thinkers and how and why they have developed and changed through time. In order to understand this complex process it is fundamental to acknowledge the existence and the legitimacy of an immense variety of approaches, styles and methods of doing the history of economic thought.

When considered in the abstract, the different perspectives complement each other for the construction of a history of economic thought of which they are themselves different forms of expression. While there is no disputing the claim that economic thought has undergone constant changes throughout history, and while there is similarly no argument about the presence of different families or schools of thought (whether or not from the same historical period), it must be accepted that the recognition of the validity of these statements presupposes the presentation of the history of economic thought as a complex intellectual endeavour that allows for different though complementary types of interpretation.

The ideal type of history of economic thought would therefore be the result of an eclectic compromise between variant approaches that contribute, albeit differently, to the construction of a common and global corpus of knowledge. This is a history that is also understood as a meeting place for disciplines and scholars from a wide variety of backgrounds, as a platform for interdisciplinary debates, and as a heuristic instrument for the study of history, economics and society.

The abstract option of choosing between one methodological perspective or another is therefore a false dilemma. The problem is not in discussing whether one is good and the other bad, but rather in recognising them as distinct and non-antagonistic ways of engaging in the study of the history of economic thought. The choice only makes sense when we move from the audience of historiography onto the stage where history is practised, or only by paying attention to the concrete object of study that we have chosen does it become pertinent to clarify the point of view adopted, in order to make both the aims and the methodology of the research to be undertaken quite explicit.

Thus, the coexistence of diversified methods does not represent either a factor of paralysis or a cause for lament. Instead, it should be seen as the reason that determines the dynamism and vitality of an eclectic community of researchers who both value and demonstrate the importance of the history of economic thought as an academic discipline.

José Luís Cardoso

See also:

Economic sociology (III); Economics and philosophy (III); Institutional economics (III); Joseph Alois Schumpeter (I).

References and further reading

Augello, M. and M. Guidi (eds) (2001), *The Spread of Political Economy and the Professionalisation of Economists. Economic Societies in Europe, America and Japan in the Nineteenth Century*, London and New York: Routledge.

Augello, M. and M. Guidi (ed.) (2005), *Economists in Parliament in the Liberal Age (1848–1920)*, Aldershot, UK: Ashgate.

Backhouse, R. and P. Fontaine (2010), 'Introduction: history of economics as history of social science', in R. Backhouse and P. Fontaine (eds), *The Unsocial Social Science? Economics and Neighboring Disciplines since 1945* (annual supplement to *History of Political Economy*, **34**), Durham, NC and London: Duke University Press, pp. 1–21.

Blanqui, J.A. (1837–38), *Histoire de l'économie politique en Europe, depuis les anciens jusqu'à nos jours, suivie d'une bibliographie raisonnée des principaux ouvrages d'économie politique*, Paris: Guillaumin, Libraire-editeur.

Blaug, M. (1962), *Economic Theory in Retrospect*, 5th edn 1997, Cambridge: Cambridge University Press.

Blaug, M. (1990), 'On the historiography of economic thought', *Journal of the History of Economic Thought*, **12** (1), 27–37.

Blaug, M. (2001), 'No history of ideas, please, we're economists', *Journal of Economic Perspectives*, **15** (1), 145–64.

Cardoso, J.L. (2003), 'The international diffusion of economic thought', in W. Samuels, J. Biddle and J. Davis (eds), *A Companion to the History of Economic Thought*, Oxford and New York: Blackwell, pp. 622–33.

Coats, A.W.B. (1992), *On the History of Economic Thought. British and American Economic Essays*, London and New York: Routledge.

Colander, D. and A.W.B. Coats (eds) (1989), *The Spread of Economic Ideas*, Cambridge and New York: Cambridge University Press.

Creedy, J. and D.P. O'Brien (1984), *Economic Analysis in Historical Perspective*, London: Butterworths.

Davis, J. (2013), 'Mark Blaug on the historiography of economics', *Erasmus Journal for Philosophy and Economics*, **6** (3), 44–63.

De Marchi, N. (ed.) (1988), *The Popperian Legacy in Economics*, Cambridge and New York: Cambridge University Press.

Dome, T. (1994), *History of Economic Theory. A Critical Introduction*, Aldershot, UK and Brookfield, VT, USA: Edward Elgar.

Dupont de Nemours, P.S. (1768), *De l'origine et des progrès d'une science nouvelle*, London and Paris: chez Dessaint, Libraire.

Emmet, R. (2003), 'Exegesis, hermeneutics and interpretation', in W. Samuels, J. Biddle and J. Davis (eds), *A Companion to the History of Economic Thought*, Oxford and New York: Blackwell, pp. 523–37.

Faccarello, G. (2014), 'In pursuit of the rarest of birds', interview in *Erasmus Journal for Philosophy and Economics*, **7** (1), 86–108.

Faccarello, G. and M. Izumo (eds) (2014), *The Reception of David Ricardo in Continental Europe and Japan*, London: Routledge.

Hausman, D.M. (ed.) (1984), *The Philosophy of Economics: An Anthology*, Cambridge and New York: Cambridge University Press.

Heilbroner, R. (1953), *The Worldly Philosophers: The Lives, Times and Ideas of the Great Economic Thinkers*, New York: Simon and Schuster.

Klaes, M. (2003), 'Historiography', in W. Samuels, J. Biddle and J. Davis (eds), *A Companion to the History of Economic Thought*, Oxford and New York: Blackwell, pp. 491–506.
Kurz, H.D. (2006), 'Whither the history of economic thought? Going nowhere rather slowly?', *European Journal of the History of Economic Thought*, **13** (4), 463–88.
Latsis, S. (ed.) (1976), *Method and Appraisal in Economics*, Cambridge and New York: Cambridge University Press.
McCulloch, J.R. (1826), *Historical Sketch of the Rise and Progress of the Science of Political Economy*, Edinburgh: A. Balfour & Co.
McCulloch, J.R. (1845), *The Literature of Political Economy: A Classified Catalogue of Select Publications in the Different Departments of that Science, with Historical, Critical, and Biographical Notices*, London: Longman.
Mirowski, P. (2002), *Machine Dreams: Economics becomes a Cyborg Science*, Cambridge and New York: Cambridge University Press.
Mitchell, W.C. (1967–69), *Types of Economic Theory: From Mercantilism to Institutionalism*, 2nd edn, first published 1935, New York: Augustus M. Kelly.
Negishi, T. (1989), *History of Economic Theory*, Amsterdam and New York: North Holland.
Niehans, J. (1990), *A History of Economic Theory. Classic Contributions*, Baltimore, MD and London: Johns Hopkins University Press.
Perrot, J.-C. (1992), *Une histoire intellectuelle de l'économie politique (XVIIe–XVIIIe siècle)*, Paris: Editions de l'EHESS.
Pribram, K. (1983), *A History of Economic Reasoning*, Baltimore, MD and London: Johns Hopkins University Press.
Rorty, R. (1984), 'The historiography of philosophy: four genres', in R. Rorty, J.B. Schneewind and Q. Skinner (eds), *Philosophy in History*, Cambridge and New York: Cambridge University Press, pp. 49–75.
Samuels, W. (1992a), *Essays in the History of Mainstream Political Economy*, London: Macmillan.
Samuels, W. (1992b), *Essays in the History of Heterodox Political Economy*, London: Macmillan.
Samuelson, P.A. (1987), 'Out of the closet. A program for the Whig history of economic science', *History of Economics Society Bulletin*, **9** (1), 51–60.
Say, J.-B. (1803), *Traité d'économie politique ou simple exposition de la manière dont se forment, se distribuent et se composent les richesses*, Paris: Crapelet.
Schabas, M. (1992), 'Breaking away: history of economics as history of science', *History of Political Economy*, **24** (1), 187–203.
Schumpeter, J.A. (1954), *History of Economic Analysis*, Oxford: Oxford University Press.
Smith, A. (1776), *Inquiry Into the Nature and Causes of the Wealth of Nations*, reprinted in R.H. Campbell and A.S. Skinner (eds) (1976), *The Glasgow Edition of the Works and Correspondence of Adam Smith*, 2 vols, Oxford: Clarendon Press.
Tribe, K. and H. Mizuta (eds) (2002), *A Critical Bibliography of Adam Smith*, London: Pickering & Chatto.
Villeneuve-Bargemont, A. (1841), *Histoire de l'économie politique, ou Études historiques, philosophiques et religieuses sur l'économie politique des peuples anciens et modernes*, Paris: Guillaumin.
Weintraub, E.R. (ed.) (2002), *The Future of the History of Economics*, annual supplement to *History of Political Economy*, **34**, Durham, NC and London: Duke University Press.
Weintraub, E.R. (2007), 'Economic science wars', *Journal of the History of Economic Thought*, **29** (3), 267–82.
Winch, D. (1996), *Riches and Poverty. An Intellectual History of Political Economy in Britain, 1848–1914*, Cambridge and New York: Cambridge University Press.
Winch, D. (2000), 'Does progress matter?', *European Journal of the History of Economic Thought*, **7** (4), 465–84.
Winch, D. (2009), *Wealth and Life. Essays on the Intellectual History of Political Economy in Britain, 1750–1834*, Cambridge and New York: Cambridge University Press.

Money and banking

Money and Banks from Aristotle to John Law

Money and interest

Money and banks did not go well together in philosophical and religious thought from Antiquity to the Renaissance. In his *Nicomachean Ethics* and *Politics*, Aristotle (384–322 BC) defines money as a measure of value, hence a medium of "justice in transactions" and of exchange, and as a store of value. On the other hand, he argues that reason condemns the lending of money for interest, because money in this case is no longer a means of economic activity, but its final end: "The most hated sort, and with the greatest reason, is usury, which makes a gain out of money itself, and not from the natural object of it. For money was intended to be used in exchange, but not to increase at interest" (Aristotle *Politics*, 1885: 19). Indeed, chrematistics properly speaking is what causes the unlimited desire of wealth that corrupts politics, according to Plato (425–347 BC). In addition, the Bible states God's prohibition of usury. Either through reasoning or revelation, the source of bank profit is condemned. However, God's order was the main cause of the hostility to banking activities prevailing in the Judeo-Christian world.

In AD 325, the Council of Nicaea prohibited priests from loaning money for interest; then Charlemagne extended the prohibition to lay people in 789, threatening those who exercised banking activities with excommunication. Five centuries later, in his *Summa Theologica* (1266–73), Thomas Aquinas drew his inspiration from Aristotle in order to reconcile faith with reason and argue in favour of God's prohibition. On the one hand, he condemned money if taken as an end in itself in exchanges, instead of as a means of exchange. On the other hand, he referred to Roman law and classified money not as a non-consumable good but as a consumable. It is important to recall that consumable goods, such as wheat or wine, unlike non-consumable goods, such as houses or land, cannot be lent for interest, because their use cannot be separated from their ownership.

In the same century, the bill of exchange emerged. This was a complex innovation, bringing several units of account into play and acting as a means of transaction that combines exchange and loan operations. The market pricing of bills of exchange was a source of bank profit, which may appear to be a commercial or arbitrage gain. In fact, it was an interest linked to the loan – a fact that was brought to light three centuries later (Davanzati in 1588). In the meantime, the scholastics began to legitimise the circumventing of usury laws by introducing risks and costs into the analysis of bills of exchange, arguing that the bills improve the functioning of markets, that is, that they favour the fixing of just prices. An additional argument touched on by Aquinas was formulated and developed by Calvin in 1545: interest is legitimate in so far as it is paid by the entrepreneur, out of the profit that he makes in an activity that would not have existed in the absence of the loan. Thus, the way was opened for legalising banking activity.

Money and prices

Paying interest on a debt is one thing, reimbursing the debt is quite another. For this purpose, money of account has to be distinguished from real money, that is, from the circulating medium. The former – the livre tournois and the pound sterling – were originally units of account in which prices, contracts and debts were denominated. The latter, real money – the louis d'or and the guinea – were specie coined in metal and used as means of exchange. The former were permanent, whereas the quantities of metal contained in the latter varied. In order to be legal tender, the specie had to have a legal price expressed in the money of account: for example, the louis d'or was worth 14 livres tournois. However, this price was established by the Prince, and its increase, as well as the coinage itself, provided sources of revenue known as seigniorage. Borrowing 10 louis d'or gave rise to a debt of 140 livres tournois and did not involve a promise to reimburse 10 louis d'or, but 140 livres tournois instead. A rise in the legal price of gold from 14 to 35 livres tournois would allow the debt to be reimbursed with 4 louis d'or. These were the practices that were under discussion.

This was the case with respect to the controversy between Jean Cherruyt de Malestroict, author of *Paradox on the Course of the Value of Money* (1566), and Jean Bodin, in his *Response to the Paradoxes of Malestroit* (1568), concerning rising prices during the sixteenth century. According to Malestroict, although the prices of goods had risen in the money of account, their specie prices were stable. He explained this paradox by the rise in the legal price of specie. Today, one would say that the money prices did not change, but the accounting prices did. Bodin responded that while this paradox is verified in the long run, it does not apply in the short run. To explain the short-run variations of money prices, Bodin argued that the quantity of money was one cause, an idea already present in Nicolas Oresme (1325–1382). This would have been a precursor of the quantity theory had Bodin neglected the effects on prices of real factors – demography, monopolies, trends and bad harvests – affecting the supply and demand of goods, just as the monetary manipulations mentioned by Malestroict did.

Monetary manipulations were criticised above all because they undermined political and financial confidence. Thomas Gresham (1519–1579) and Bodin (1529–1596) argued for the restoration of this confidence, in particular, in order to put an end to manipulations of the money-of-account price of legal tender coins. John Locke (1632–1704) also supported these arguments in *Some considerations of the consequences of the lowering of interest, and raising the value of money* (1692) and in his 1696 controversy with William Lowndes. Now, the stability between the legal price of legal tender specie and debt is essential for banking. If a lowering of the legal price of specie is anticipated, customers will hurry to the bank to deposit their gold in exchange for notes, which are labelled in the unit of account; on the contrary, if an increase in the legal price of specie is expected, they will hurry to withdraw their deposit in gold coins. This was first theorised by John Law in *Money and Trade Considered* (1705).

The Emergence of Paper Money and Quantity Theory

The emergence of banks and paper money
Private banking flourished as early as the twelfth century and banking institutions appeared from the beginning of the seventeenth century onwards. The Bank of Amsterdam was established in 1609. In the beginning, it was a municipal agency, without shareholders' funds, which had a monopoly on exchange operations. It did not take any liquidity risk, did not grant credit, did not issue banknotes but collected deposits expressed in florin banco. Their convertibility quickly became limited, and consequently their value fluctuated. The Bank of Stockholm was established in 1656, issued notes from

1661 and went bankrupt in 1664. The Bank of England was established in 1694, after three years of negotiations between an investors' group, the Chancellor of the Exchequer and the Parliament. They were not discussing the creation of a bank, but a new kind of Treasury debt that would be more liquid and less expensive. The issue was the intermediation of the Treasury debt through the establishment of a commercial joint company, with a large amount of shareholders' funds, authorised to issue banknotes payable at sight and to grant credit. The outstanding amount of banknotes and deposits was limited to the outstanding amount of shareholders' funds. However, there was no rule concerning the management of the cash reserve that was contributed by the shareholders when paying for their shares.

Although the establishment of the Bank of England seemed opportunistic, it emerged in an intellectual context that was favourable to banks. In England, at the beginning of the seventeenth century, there was a focus on providing credit to the poor, and the establishment of "banks of charity" in order to oust usurers. Dealing with credit risks, the mercantilists stressed the guarantees given by the borrowers – registration of property rights, solidarity mechanisms – insurance policies and bank shareholders' funds (J. Benbrigge 1646; J. Cooke 1648; H. Chamberlen 1649). Then the focus shifted towards the means of improving commercial credit risk, for example, with William Potter's *The Key of Wealth* (1650) or William Petty's *Quantulumcunque* (1682). The contributions were rich, but limited to the problem of bank solvency. There were no plans to create banks that would take liquidity risk. It was the same with land bank projects, which appeared in the 1690s (N. Barbon 1690; J. Biscoe 1694; H. Chamberlen 1695; J. Asgill 1696), whereby shareholders contributed property assets when paying their shares and where banknotes were convertible into, and backed by, property assets. This system appeared again in John Law's projects (1703–05), in which the bank would not have a cash reserve but would issue legal tender paper money. Law argued that such bank notes issued on demand and backed by property assets would be more stable in value than bank notes backed by precious metals whose value fluctuates according to changes in supply and demand. The hope that such a bank could lower interest rates was linked to the mercantilist view, as in Locke (1692), according to which an abundance of money would diminish the purchasing power of each unit of money and interest rates at the same time.

After Louis XIV's death, Law established in France a bank with very low shareholders' funds and which did not issue notes convertible into property assets but into specie. This bank was joined to a commercial company whose aim was to restructure the state debt (twice the level of national income). Law's scheme was that the company would issue shares payable with state notes and banknotes. In fact, at the end of 1719, Law's system turned into a speculative bubble where the bank granted loans and issued notes to speculators for buying the shares. At the peak of the speculation, the market value of the company was equal to six times the level of national income, and the outstanding amount of bank notes to three and half times. The system was illiquid and crashed during the following year. This failure contrasts with the success of the eighteenth century British financial revolution (Dickson 1967).

Indeed, from the start, the Bank of England succeeded in creating liquidity: although only 60 per cent of the capital was called up, the bank issued banknotes to up to 100 per cent of the authorised capital for financing a loan to the treasury, at 8 per cent, meaning that it was 400 basis points below the goldsmiths' interest rate. In 1697, it issued new shares payable with public debt, with a view to sustaining its price. To reduce the interest rate, it systemically and successfully intervened in the Exchequer bills market from 1707 on. For a century, until 1797, although its cash reserve fluctuated between 10 per cent and 40 per cent of the value of its outstanding issues, the bank succeeded in reimbursing its notes. England had invented the modern bank. Its note was not legal tender; it was a debt payable at sight issued against a credit debt payable at term. It created liquidity and helped to increase the liquidity of public debt and lower interest rates. The Bank of Scotland was established on the same model in 1695. Neither of the two banks had a monopoly on issuing notes, that is, creating liquidity. Private banks imitated them, and their banknotes circulated along with legal tender coins. The monetary debates during the eighteenth and nineteenth centuries inquired into the nature and effects of this paper money.

The quantity theory versus banknotes
The quantity theory with its corollary, the neutrality of money, was first expressed by William Potter in *The Key of Wealth* (1650): "an increase of money would occasion an increase in the price of commodities to such increase of money . . . consequently . . . would not occasion any increase in the sale of commodity: therefore not any increase of trade" (1650, in Hegeland 1951 [1969]: 31). However, Potter does not share this approach and believes that the quantity of money impacts on economic activity, by granting credit. His formulation of the quantity theory was rhetorical. Affirmation of the quantity theory, coupled with adherence to it, only appeared during the following century. It was present in the writings of authors who wished to demonstrate the uselessness and danger-ousness of banks: first Richard Cantillon, in the manuscript (1728–30) of his *Essay on the Nature of Trade in General* (1755), written after the South Sea and Mississippi bubbles (1719–20); second, David Hume, in the 1752 edition of *Moral, Political and Literary Essays*, at the time when the Scottish country banks began issuing banknotes.

Cantillon integrates the quantity theory into a representation of economic activity that predates Quesnay's *Tableau Économique* (1766 [1958]). Given the real proportions between production and real incomes, the level of nominal variables – prices of goods and nominal incomes – is determined by the quantity and velocity of specie: "the actual quantity in weight and fineness of the coins, taking into account the rapidity of circula-tion, is the base and regulator of values" (Cantillon 1755 [1959]: 299). Next, Cantillon introduced banks and the credit multiplier: the deposit of specie provides the bank with the cash that allows banknotes to be issued; loaning the specie leads to new deposits, then to new issues. According to Cantillon, the bank can issue a quantity of notes equal to ten times the level of its cash reserve, thus taking a liquidity risk. He then pondered the sustainability of banking activities. His answer was that private banking is desirable in small states and when it is limited to wealth management. On the contrary, it should be avoided in the case of a general bank in a great state which fuels speculation "with the complicity of a Minister" (ibid.: 323).

In fact, Cantillon was questioning the usefulness of paper money: issuing "ficti-tious" and "imaginary" money leads to an increase in the velocity of circulation of "real" money, or "ready cash" ("argent au comptant" in the French edition), which causes prices to increase, thereby bringing about a balance of trade deficit, then an exit of specie that endangers bank liquidity. The same conclusion was obtained by Hume, who formulated the *Price Specie Flow Mechanism* (hereafter referred to as PSFM), a mechanism already present in Malyne's book, *The Maintenance of Free Trade* (1622). The PFSM is an arbitrage based on the hypothesis that specie have the same value in neighbouring countries. This arbitrage brings about their international equilibrium distribution among countries. If economic activity grows in one country while it is stagnant in the others, the value of specie increases in this country – that is, the monetary price level decreases. This stimulates exports and discourages imports, resulting in a favourable balance of trade and an inflow of specie. The process operates smoothly until the value of specie reaches its international level. Inasmuch as the value and quantity of specie adjust themselves according to the needs of trade, issuing banknotes is useless. Symmetrically, if paper money were to expand in one country, prices would rise, resulting in a balance of trade deficit and an outflow of specie, thus endangering banks.

The quantity theory of Cantillon and Hume does not postulate the neutrality of money as Potter does. An increase in the quantity of money induces a change in the relative prices of goods. Depending on the channel through which additional money enters the economy, the money prices of some goods increase more or less, and some do not change. This is called the Cantillon effect. In any case, Cantillon and Hume's analysis is enough to conclude that variations in prices lead to adjustments of the quantity of specie according to the needs of trade, and that banks are both useless and dangerous. Cantillon and Hume are the originators of one of the two main trends in classic monetary and banking theory.

Monetary Stability and Banking Risks in Classical Theory

Banks as liquidity providers

Other main classical economists view banknotes favourably, starting in the eighteenth century with James Steuart in his *Enquiry into the Principles of Political Economy* (1767) and then Adam Smith in *An Inquiry into the Nature and Causes of the Wealth of Nations* (1776). According to Steuart, economic growth is a wealth transfer process between property owners and industrialists, which he called a "vibration of the balance of wealth". By granting mortgage credit, banks create new money, which makes property assets liquid, that is, it gives property owners the means to buy goods produced industrially, thereby allowing industrialists to make profits, then to buy the property assets. Now, while this view has been totally outshined by Smith's economics, we must nevertheless emphasise the influence of the former on the latter's banking theory. Steuart, in particular, shows very clearly how the cash reserve contributed by the shareholders creates the confidence necessary to allow the bank to grant credit by issuing notes in excess of the reserve. Smith sums up this approach, which links bank capital with credit and liquidity risks, just as he extends Steuart's analysis of the role played by the Bank of England in reducing interest rates by circulating Exchequer bills.

Smith integrates his banking theory into a theory of capital accumulation. Banks permit the substitution of bank notes for metallic money, without increasing the total amount. They make this substitution by discounting bills and granting credit or overdrafts (cash accounts). This reduces the maintenance costs of monetary circulation and releases a portion of capital that was previously unproductive. Banks create liquidity through lending because they have a fractional reserve ratio. They finance a part of merchants' circulating capital:

> It is not by augmenting the capital of the country, but by rendering a greater part of that capital active and productive than would otherwise be so, that the most judicious operations of banking can increase the industry of the country. That part of his capital which a dealer is obliged to keep by him unemployed, and in ready money for answering occasional demands, is so much dead stock, which, so long as it remains in this situation, produces nothing either to him or to his country. The judicious operations of banking enable him to convert his dead stock into active and productive stock. (Smith 1776 [1976]: 320)

Moreover, banks have to ensure that they are not lending to "projectors" who try to borrow in order to finance their whole capital, thus wasting capital. They verify that they loan money only to "prudent men", who borrow for the purpose of transactions. Normally they can monitor borrowers by observing their current accounts and repayments. However, according to Smith, because of informational asymmetries on the credit market, borrowers can cheat. This solvency risk could entail bank failures and as a result, systemic risk through contagion. A liquidity risk will also occur because, in this case, banks would have issued too much money. That is why Smith clearly advocates the creation of "fire walls" and a banking regulation system (the convertibility of notes to metal; a maximum limit for the rate of interest, since a rate that is too high would entail adverse selection in favour of "projectors"; prohibition on notes of small denominations; criticism of the "optional clause") and suggests that banks should be limited to short-term lending. It is said that these ideas are related to the real bills doctrine, according to which banks should only discount bills issued on commodities already produced. This signifies that the money supply is endogenous and adjusts to the demand for it. As a result, Smith is not in favour of the quantity theory. According to him, the level of monetary prices is determined by the ratio between the cost of production of commodities and the cost of production of precious metal.

Henry Thornton continues this tradition. He opens his book *An Inquiry into the Nature and the Effects of the Paper Credit of Great Britain* (1802) by considering trade to be facilitated by a circulation of claims and debts that have to be maintained in liquid form. Owing to their different liquidity features and interest rates, credit instruments have different velocities of circulation. However, this velocity may also vary in different periods depending on confidence. Banks are specific agents, "transforming" illiquid assets into less risky and therefore more liquid assets, for example, when a bank discounts a bill of exchange. Bank notes and deposits can be used in payments and can clear all other debts. The most liquid assets were Bank of England notes. They could be requested in case of "a flight to quality", a liquidity crisis, which is a systemic crisis. Therefore, in lending these notes to the banks, the central bank is a lender of last resort on the money market, as a special market for ultimate liquidity for banks, a notion that is introduced by Thornton. In so doing, it restores confidence and calms the panic. Following this line of thought, liquidity crises can be distinguished from solvency crises. Furthermore, there is no quantitative and rigid rule for monetary policy, rather a discretionary monetary policy that allows flexibility and breaks with the Smithian rule that adjusts the quantity of notes issued to variations in the gold reserves. The inconvertibility of Bank of England banknotes may even be necessary during a given period, to maintain a sufficient money supply if the Bank is losing its reserves.

Thornton criticised the real bills doctrine. Discounting real bills does not guarantee the borrower's solvency and it is a fallacy to think that it allows the issuing of money to be limited in the event that the rate of profit remains persistently above the rate of interest for borrowing. In the latter case, banks would constantly continue to discount and issue notes. This is why Thornton suggested that the central bank could raise its discount rate in order to control the credit demand that is at the root of the money supply.

The Banking School (Thomas Tooke, John Fullarton and John Stuart Mill) favoured a broad vision of payment instruments that included all sorts of credit instruments performing the functions of money, adhering to the tradition founded by Thornton. Notes and deposits thus have the same characteristic; both are bank debt issued through the medium of loans. They can substitute for each other. The quantity of credit and money is demand determined. However, as regards the real bills doctrine, the Banking School does not follow Thornton, but Smith. There cannot be an excess of issue because of the "law of reflux": any issue will return to banks as reimbursement of their credit, or for convertibility into coins or deposit. As a result, the Banking School does not adopt the quantity theory. Banks issue notes and create deposits by discounting bills.

For Tooke (*A History of Prices*, 1838–1856), economic cycles are not initiated by over-issue, but by speculation on commodities markets; however, they can be aggravated when the rate of interest on bank credit is too low or banks have been incautious in their advances. In this case of "overtrading and overbanking", banking crises can occur. This may have an impact on the possibility of maintaining the convertibility of notes into metal. That is why he advocates raising the bank rate at the start of the speculation. Tooke distinguishes these solvency crises from liquidity crises and contemplates the possibility of runs on banks through panic or distrust. In the latter case, the Bank of England must provide ultimate liquidity to banks and raise its bank rate to allow international capital flows to enter. Hence, the Banking School opposed the 1844 law whose aim was to transform the Bank of England in a currency board.

Price of gold, value of paper money and currency board
Joseph Schumpeter coined the phrase "a credit theory of money" to classify the analysis of Smith and Thornton, according to which a banknote is a kind of paper credit. David Ricardo abandoned this approach during the bullionist controversy (1797–1821), whose main analytical issue was to explain the causes of the rising market prices of silver and gold bullion in the context of the inconvertibility of Bank of England notes. Ricardo lost interest in the analysis of lender-of-last-resort function of the central bank, and rejected Adam Smith's anti-quantity theory and real bills doctrine as well as Thornton's approach of the balance of payments. He referred to Hume's PSFM to explain that the over-issue of banknotes was the one and only cause that could bring about an excess of the market price of bullion above its legal price. In so doing, he gave new insight into the quantity theory of money and banking. He formulated the foundations of the approach that Schumpeter called "a money theory of credit".

According to Ricardo, the banknote is not a kind of paper credit, but a kind of token money. It is a token money that is printed on paper instead of cheap metal. However, although it has the same characteristics as government-issued paper money, it is not issued by the government, but by banks. It is not a legitimate form of issue in so far as the seigniorage – that is, a tax equal to the difference between the value of the money and its production cost – does not benefit the state, but the banks which make a profit by financing credit with banknotes. Ricardo did not trust the directors of the Bank of England, particularly when they claimed that it was never in their interest to over-issue notes, so that they did not have any responsibility for the high price of bullion and the low exchange rate.

The core of Ricardo's bullionist argument – developed in *The High Price of Bullion* (1810) – is an analogy he establishes between inconvertible banknotes and debased coins. Both are token money, which circulate along with undebased coins. If the total quantity of money – debased coins, inconvertible banknotes and undebased coins – is low enough, the value of debased coins and inconvertible banknotes is equal to the value of the quantity of metal contained in the undebased coins, a value which is the same both within and outside England. Now, if the total quantity of money increases in England, the value of each component – debased coins, inconvertible banknotes and undebased coins – decreases inside the country but the value of undebased coins remains unchanged outside. According to Hume's PSFM, the exportation of undebased coins will diminish the quantity of money so that its value increases. If the quantity exported is high enough, the value of money, including the value of debased coins and inconvertible paper, will return to its previous level. The value of money does not depend on its intrinsic value, but on its quantity in relation to the quantity of goods to be traded.

Now, suppose that the quantity of money increases more than the quantity of goods to be traded, and that the exportation of all the outstanding undebased coins does not suffice to restore the previous value of money. In that case, the suspension of payments is unavoidable and there is no longer any form of mechanism to diminish the quantity of money. However, according to Ricardo, at this point, the value of gold bullion is higher outside England than inside, hence giving rise to an arbitrage opportunity. As a result of arbitrage, the London market price of bullion will rise above its mint price. Ricardo argues that the premium of the market price of bullion over the mint price occurs first, and then it makes the exchange rate fall, proving that the excess quantity of debased coins and inconvertible banknotes has brought about their depreciation. Ricardo wrote against Thornton's analysis of the gold premium, according to which the premium of the market price of gold was the effect of a fall in the exchange rate. Robert Malthus and Thomas Tooke were to reject Ricardo's view.

At the end of this debate, in the *Principles of Political Economy and Taxation* (1817) and *A Plan for the Establishment of a National Bank* (1824), Ricardo argued that the quantity of paper money in circulation determines its value, which "may be considered as seigniorage" (Ricardo 1817 [1951]: 353) belonging to the state. Therefore, the banknote must be a form of legal tender whose issue must be monopolised by a state bank. This bank would not be authorised to grant credit, but to buy and sell gold bullion at a fixed price, as well as public debt. In so far as the quantity of banknotes determines both its purchasing power and the market price of gold, the bank would stabilise both by reducing (increasing) this quantity when the market price of gold is above (below) the legal price. In this project, the convertibility of banknotes into legal tender coins becomes obsolete; convertibility into gold bullion is sufficient. This scheme relies on the idea that a fixed price for gold bullion is synonymous with stability of the purchasing power of money. Ricardo's *Plan* influenced the Currency School.

The currency principle, developed by Robert Torrens in *A Letter to the Right Honourable Lord Viscount Melbourne, on the Causes of the Recent Derangement in the Money Market and on the Bank Reform* (1837) and Samuel Jones-Loyd, Lord Overstone in *Thoughts on the Separation of the Department of the Bank of England, London, private edition* (1844), is based on the quantity theory of money and the PSFM, and relies on an exogenous view of money. There is a causal link from money to credit. Every form of credit instrument is a "multiple" of money (narrowly defined as "currency", which consists of notes and coins) previously deposited in a bank and loaned again (thus accelerating the velocity of money). In 1837 Torrens improved and developed the bank credit multiplier. Banks launch this money, which would have remained unused had they not intervened, back into circulation. However, they do not create new money, since it is the same money that circulates.

Bank credit is based on currency, meaning "legal tender" money, that is, Bank of England notes and coins. For the currency principle – banknotes being strictly linked to the quantity of bank reserves in metal – credit is automatically regulated by variations in currency, which is a strategic variable. The currency has to contract and expand consequently to the state of the balance of payments, meaning the outflows and inflows of bullion. Bank crises are the result of the over-issue of notes, because the Bank of England does not enforce this strict link between its issues and the variation of its reserves in metal.

In delaying the implementation of this principle, the bank's directors are thus obliged to "reign in" more severely later on. Therefore, it is necessary to make them restrict their issue immediately when they are losing metal.

This was the rationale of the 1844 Bank Charter Act, in favour of which the Currency School developed its argumentation and which divided the Bank of England into two separate departments (the Issue Department and the Banking Department). The activity of the Banking Department, which lends by discounting and is the source of the circulation of banknotes, is consequently controlled entirely by the quantity of banknotes it obtains from the Issue Department (in exchange for the gold it gives to this latter).

In fact, the currency principle proved itself capable of a degree of evolution. There is another cause of banking instability, which the Currency School identified from 1847 onward. They realised that the 1844 Act was incapable of regulating credit; it was only concerned with money. In 1858, Torrens stressed the "excessive and undue advances" by banks and their facilitating of an "undue diminution of their reserves" in notes, which could create panics. Nevertheless, he never advocated either a discretionary bank rate monetary policy or a relaxation of the 1844 Bank Charter Act.

Walter Bagehot, in *Lombard Street: A Description of the Money Market* (1873), introduced the concept of "lender of last resort" in an extension of the currency principle analysis, thus contributing to a renewal of its formulation that was to become British monetary orthodoxy, of which Bagehot was clearly a leading figure in 1870s. Bagehot developed this analysis by discussing the suspension of the reform in 1847, 1857 and 1866, stating that it was caused by the conduct of the Banking Department, when conditions were tight on the money market. According to him, the Bank of England's Banking Department had to be the lender of last resort, not the Issue Department. The former should increase its own capital, that is, its reserve so that it could lend to banks upon request. It would lend money exogenous to it – a loan of last resort did not equate to an issue of money. A liquidity crisis in the money market was a crisis of credit that should not be associated with a monetary crisis. The excess demand was for credit, not money.

The authors of the Free Banking School such as Henry Parnell, *Observations on Paper Money, Banking and Overtrading* (1827), and J.W. Gilbart, *The Laws of the Currency, as exemplified in the Circulation of Country Bank Notes in England since 1844* (1854), wanted to return to Smith and had an influence on Bagehot. They advocated that free competition between banks in issuing notes convertible into specie would provide limits to the issue through interbank clearing with settlements in gold, because a reflux of excess notes from a bank could be deposited in a rival bank, which would return the notes to the issuing bank and bring an end to over-issue. They invoked the experience of Scotland and criticised the Bank of England, saying that it needed to be controlled and divided in several competing banks (Parnell 1827). G.P. Scrope in *On Credit-Currency, and its Superiority to Coin, in Support of a Petition for the Establishment of a Cheap, Safe, and Sufficient Circulating Medium* (1830) was in favour of the abrogation of the legal status of the Bank of England that gave it a monopoly position. Cyclical fluctuations were due to errors of the Bank and the absence of a self-regulating mechanism. However, they lost their case on this point in Parliament.

Universal equivalent and finance capital

In *Capital. A Critique of Political Economy* (1867–94), Karl Marx distinguished himself from the classics in the way he integrated monetary theory into value theory. Smith defined money as a commodity, with an intrinsic value, which is used as a means of circulation to avoid the inconveniency of the lack of a double coincidence of wants. However, Smith commented that the exchange of a beaver for gold does not give rise to the circulation of two incomes as it does in the barter of a beaver for a deer, but only one income. He therefore emphasised that the "great wheel of circulation is altogether different from the goods which are circulated by means of it" (Smith 1776 [1976]: 289) and that it forms no part of the revenue of the society. However, he saves himself the bother of further inquiry into this topic and argues in favour of banknotes, which have negligible production cost, unlike coins. Thornton does not link money with commodities, but with credit. Ricardo, for his part, associates the value of money with seigniorage. Marx emphasises money has a value as a commodity.

According to Marx, prices of commodities are not accounting prices, but money prices. If a table is worth £2, this means that it is worth 2 sovereigns, that is, two times 7.322 grams of fine gold. £1 and a sovereign are names given to a quantity of gold. In fact, the price of the table is 14.644 grams of gold. Now, if the value of the table is expressed in gold, it is because gold is analogous to the table. Like the table, gold is a commodity that possesses an exchange value; the table and the two sovereigns have the same exchange value. Money is the commodity that officiates as a universal equivalent, that is, the exchange values of all the commodities are expressed in the commodity money. Whereas both market prices and natural prices are real prices according to Smith, the market price is a quantity of money for Marx.

Aristotle's influence is obvious when Marx distinguishes between two forms of circulation of money. In the first form, C–M–C (Commodity–Money–Commodity), money assumes the measure of value and the circulation of commodities; it "is in the end converted into a commodity, that serves as a use-value; it is spent once and for all" (Marx 1867 [1961]: 148). In the second form M–C–M', money is advanced and flows back to its point of departure. However, the reflux occurs together with an increment, a surplus value. Here, money circulates as interest-bearing capital. The surplus value is produced by labour power, but it belongs to the capitalist, who owns the money that allows labour power to be bought. This possibility for the capitalist to make surplus value may be transferred to the entrepreneur through credit. For Marx, a loan for interest is a very special kind of exchange between a money-capitalist and a functioning capitalist; through lending, interest-bearing capital becomes a commodity, whose price is the interest rate.

The interest rate is a very special kind of revenue and "there is no such thing as a natural rate of interest in the sense in which economists speak of a natural rate of profit and a natural rate of wages" (Marx 1894 [1962]: 355). The interest rates prevailing on the credit and financial markets do not deviate from any natural level, but are determined by the competition between lenders and borrowers; competition that shifts according to economic circumstances. Hence, during the upward phase of the cycle, commercial credit liquidity is high and clearing is easy, therefore entrepreneurs do not need bank credit to obtain means of payment; the interest rate is low. On the contrary, when a goods market crisis occurs, commercial credit becomes less liquid, the demand for means of payment increases, as does the interest rate. Influenced by the Banking School, Marx defined the banknote as "nothing but a draft upon a banker, payable at any time to the bearer, and given by the banker in place of private drafts" (ibid.: 395). He berated Overstone, calling him a "logician of usury" (ibid.: 314), but did not adhere to the real bills doctrine. In the event of a market glut, when the *salto mortale* of the commodities falls short, the bills lose their value, even if they had been issued to finance real production and transactions. The commercial crisis causes a money and banking crisis, a crisis "of the convertibility of bills of exchange into money" (ibid.: 478).

Apart from commercial credit, long-term investment is financed by the issue of shares. Again, there is no natural value. Prices are determined by the level, regularity and stability of the dividends, the capitalisation rate, speculation and all sorts of swindles, and the liquidity of markets. In his *Finance Capital* (1910), Rudolph Hilferding emphasised the intermediation function of banks in the process of issuing shares. After underlining that the regularity of dividends influences the risk premium of the capitalisation rates of the shares, he shows that the gap existing between the profit rate and the capitalisation rate brings about a leverage effect on the value of shares. The result is a financial profit, called "promoter's profit", a percentage of which is captured by banks. Thus, the banks acquire part of the capital of companies, which gives rise to "finance capital", that is, the oligopolistic merger between industrial, commercial and banking capital. "Finance capital" puts an end to the conflict between lenders and borrowers and to the anarchy of the markets, thereby stabilising capitalism.

From the Money Market to the Market for Money

At the end of the nineteenth century and the beginning of the twentieth, the analytical focus was on the role of credit and banks in the economic cycle, in a continuation of the classical tradition. For example, Henry Dunning MacLeod in *The Theory and Practice of Banking* (1892–93) and Hartley Withers in *The Meaning of Money* (1909) situated themselves within the Banking School tradition, stressing that money is a debt. However, later and progressively, the vision of the banking system as a liquidity provider regressed in economic analysis. The focus shifted from the money market as a special market for liquidity for banks onto the financial market and the concept of the market for money.

US debates regarding quantity theory and the elasticity of the banking system

Although in the United States of America, monetary and banking thought referred to Ricardo, Tooke and John Stuart Mill, it freed itself from British debates. The context and the problems to be solved were distinct. First, the balance of payments did not matter. Second, there were no central bank notes, but legal tender paper money issued by the Treasury, the greenback. Finally, the USA hesitated to give up bimetallism and adopt the gold standard. Two main events gave rise to lively controversies: first, the great deflation from 1873 to 1896; second, the recurrent crises of the national banking system (1873, 1884, 1890, 1893 and 1907). In both cases, bank credit analysis was linked to monetary analysis.

The explanation of the great deflation brought quantity theorists – namely, the very influential Francis Amasa Walker (1840–1897) – into conflict with the Credit School led by James Laurence Laughlin (1850–1897). According to Walker, the de facto demonetisation of silver – known as the crime of 1873 – had reduced the quantity of money. Quoting Stuart Mill, Walker defined the demand for money as "the amount of money-work to be done" (1888: 129), meaning the volume of goods to be exchanged against money, and argued that "the value of money, like the value of anything else, is purely a question of demand and supply" (ibid.: 128). As the supply of money – "the money-force available to do the money-work required to be done" (ibid.: 131) – was reduced, the demand for money increased and the value of money therefore increased, that is, the price level decreased. Since the deflation of prices increases the real value of debts, it impoverishes debtors, including farmers, and brings about a contraction of economic activity, in other words, a depression. The restoration of bimetallism would remove all of these disasters.

Opposing the inductive method to Walker's deductive methods, the Credit School showed that there was statistically absolutely no correlation between the general level of prices and the quantity of money for the period 1860–91, and then asserted that the quantity theory is refuted by facts, explaining that the banking system provides the means of circulation necessary for trade and concluding that deflation is not caused by a lack of money, but by technical innovations that bring about a decrease in the production and transport costs of goods. Firm supporters of "sound" money, they rejected any return to bimetallism.

After 1896, a new generation of quantity theorists opted for the gold standard and tried to validate the old theory statistically. In his PhD thesis, "Money and credit instruments in their relation to general prices" (1903), published in 1907, Edwin Walter Kemmerer statistically tested an equation – already present in one of Irving Fisher's articles published in 1897 – that Kemmerer understood as the equilibrium condition between monetary demand and the monetary supply, including credit: $PQ = MV + M'V'$. Eight years later, in his *Purchasing Power of Money* (1911), Fisher called this the "equation of exchanges" and improved its statistical verification. Furthermore, he provided an analysis of the real effects of the inherent, unpredictable and unavoidable changes in the value of money under the existing system of the gold standard. A falling value of money owing to the discovery of a new gold mine would lower the costs of borrowing, induce the development of bank credit financed by the issue of demand deposits, thus bringing about a rise in prices, but not in wages, that is, a cumulative process leading to the impoverishment of the workers and provoking bank illiquidity and then ending in a financial crisis. The symmetrical set of effects of the rising value of money due to a crisis, or associated with a trend in economic and trade growth, had already been described by the bimetallists. Fisher thought that changing the legal price of the ounce of gold every month – the "compensated dollar" plan – would correct the destabilising characteristics of the gold standard. But he did not convince his contemporaries.

There was more consensus among theorists in the analysis of the recurrent crises of the national banking system and the recurrent increases in the interest rate on the money market during periods of harvest. Quantity and anti-quantity theorists agreed that these situations were due to a periodical lack of elasticity in the issuing of banknotes. Both schools of thought believed that the supply of gold by the Treasury (deposits in banks) is insufficient to do away with liquidity banking crises and both argued for the creation of a central bank that could issue banknotes by discounting commercial credit. Concerning banking theory, it is worth noting that the distinction between insolvency and illiquidity had been well understood since the 1873 Coe Report, which was written to establish the rules for the issuing of clearing house loan certificates. Concerning monetary policy, at first, the Credit School's real bills view dominated. The establishment of the Federal Reserve in 1913 and the discovery of the open market tool in the 1920s shed new light on everything.

From Wicksell to Hayek

In *Interest and Prices* (1898), Knut Wicksell reformulated the quantity theory of money, introducing the market of credit and banking, in a desire to reconcile the former theory with cycle theory. He stressed a new transmission mechanism. He criticised Ricardo for not taking the relationship between the interest rate and the price level into account. "In other words, the real cause of the rise in prices is to be looked for, not in the expansion of the note issue as such, but in the provision by the Bank of easier credit, which is itself the cause of the expansion" (Wicksell 1898 [1936]: 87).

Wicksell introduced the role of the "bank discount rate", that is, a credit rate charged by banks to their borrowers on the credit market. He also called this "credit rate" a "money rate". This credit rate is compared with the "natural rate of interest", defined as the equilibrium rate between supply and demand of real capital, which also corresponds to the rate at which there is an equilibrium between the supply and demand for commodities. In a world with bank credit, there could be a difference between the "natural" rate and the "bank credit rate".

Wicksell assumed that the cycle was starting, because there was an increase in the natural rate. Entrepreneurs were to compare this rate of return on investment with the rate at which they borrow. If the discount rate is maintained at its previous level, this would alter the relationship between the supply and demand of commodities and would bring about a rise in all prices, until the rate of discount is realigned with the rate of return on investment. This occurs when the monetary system is a developed credit economy: in order to avoid liquidity difficulties, banks will increase their discount rate to reduce the demand for credit and the demand for cash. However, Wicksell (1898) introduced a system that he called the "organised credit economy", in which payments are only made by transfers between current accounts at banks, and loans are also centralised at banks. In this context, there is no longer any need for "cash". It is an "imaginary system" that was not entirely completed in reality in this form. It is worth underlining that banks do not take liquidity risk. Wicksell indicated that in this system, the dates on which deposits are owed always correspond to the periods for which the loans have been granted, because every withdrawal of a deposit automatically entails the deposit of an equal sum elsewhere, or the repayment of a loan of an equivalent size. So the aggregate of banks taken as a whole can lend any desired amount of money at any desired rate of interest. Edgeworth (1888) had established a new theory of banking showing that it is possible to economise on the volume of bank reserves by centralising them. According to Wicksell, the monetary system is elastic and the discrepancy between the two rates can be maintained; banks can raise the general level of prices to any desired amount. The effects of a low rate are not only permanent but cumulative, and the general price level is unstable. It can be said that in this case, the level of prices is indeterminate and that this echoes the "real bills fallacy". As a result, Wicksell was promoting a banking system policy that would bring the money rate into line with the natural rate.

The problem of the "power of banks" was later emphasised by Dennis Robertson and Friedrich von Hayek. In *Banking Policy and the Price Level* (1926), Robertson highlighted the fact that banks can lend, through their credit, more than what is available from saving. Hayek, in *Prices and Production* (1931), criticised Wicksell. According to Hayek, a good starting point for the explanation of the cycle is the discrepancy between the two rates of interest noted by Wicksell, but this analysis has to be clearly separated from the quantity theory of money and the variations in the general level of prices to which Wicksell confines his theory, the latter being an erroneous conclusion. On the contrary, this discrepancy (by maintaining an excessively low money rate of interest), which is a characteristic of the existence of a bank credit system, is the cause of the modification in the structure of relative prices and the structure of production. As a result, Hayek stressed that cycles are related to banks, permitting the financing of faster economic development and investment than that made possible only by voluntary saving, thus imposing "forced saving" on economic agents. Hayek's view was criticised by Piero Sraffa (1932), who argued that the "natural rate" is not independent of the money rate of interest and voluntary and forced savings cannot easily be discriminated. In disequilibrium there are as many natural or own rates of interest as there are commodities, and to ask banks to adjust the money rate to the natural rate makes no sense. Banks can influence income distribution by fixing the money rate.

From Hawtrey to Keynes
Between 1917 and 1930, the Cambridge School contributed to the evolution of the quantity theory. Alfred Marshall, Arthur Cecil Pigou and John Maynard Keynes, in *A Tract on Monetary Reform* (1923 [1971]), developed the analysis of incentives for the demand for cash balances. The general price level was then determined, corresponding to a given level of transactions, by the supply and demand for money. These authors wanted to

integrate money into the theory of choice. But their analysis of the demand for money had to free itself of Karl Helfferich's criticism (*Das Geld*, 1903) that we are arguing in a circle if we admit that money has an indirect utility that depends on its exchange value, because the former will vary with the latter. This means that the latter cannot be determined by the utility of money. Consequently, it is necessary to introduce the demand for money in real terms.

The demand for real money is first explained by a transaction motive that depends on long-term evolutions, such as the size of the real payments to be made and the degree of synchronisation between receipts and payments. There is also a precautionary motive, because of uncertainty concerning this possibility of synchronisation. Moreover, Marshall in *Money, Credit and Commerce* (1923) and Pigou in "The value of money" (1917) began to build tools for studying portfolio choices, which would later be refined. They considered the demand for money to be a function of the interest rate on financial assets, a function of the return gained from the ownership of physical capital and the utility resulting from the consumption of goods.

Hawtrey's cycle theory, developed in *Currency and Credit* (1919), is founded on the importance this author attributed to traders. Their activity is very elastic with respect to the short-term interest rate, because it is the cost at which they borrow to finance their stocks. At the macroeconomic level, traders will adjust their stocks in proportion to their expectations regarding demand for goods. However, if the bank interest rate is raised, traders will reduce their stocks and their demand to entrepreneurs. They contribute to a decrease in credit, income and demand, which will determine the cumulative decrease in output and prices. These reductions will cease, and a new expansion will begin once banks have replenished the reserves in their coffers and are again able to reduce their rate of interest.

Furthermore, Hawtrey also introduced the market for money in line with the Cambridge tradition, influencing Keynes's theory. The difference between consumers' income and spending is their "unspent margin". It is a demand for money for transactions (goods and assets, as in Marshall and Pigou). Traders and entrepreneurs also have a demand for money for transactions. The total cash balance of the two kinds of agents is compared to the total supply of cash balances.

According to Keynes in the *Treatise on Money* (1930), the role of the banking system is important. The demand for money is a demand for bank money. Keynes makes a distinction between "income deposits" (for the transaction motive) and "saving deposits", which are a kind of liquid asset. The interest rate is determined firstly but indirectly by the "bullishness" or "bearishness" of agents as regards the price of securities, and secondly by the behaviour of the banking system, depending on its money supply. As a result of their expectations regarding the price of securities, agents will choose to hold securities or to hold money. The decision of firms to buy new investment goods depends on their expected return compared with the interest rate, the latter not being determined by saving, but by decisions on portfolio composition of assets and by the "banking system policy".

That is why the *Treatise on Money* integrates the investment and liquidity preference theories to be found (but reformulated) in *The General Theory of Employment, Interest and Money* (1936). In the latter, Keynes wanted to separate the determination of the rate of return on investment from the price of debts or the interest rate. The prospective yields and the supply price of investment determine the marginal efficiency of capital goods.

Liquidity preference only determines the rate of interest, and investment is the result of a comparison between these two variables.

> Whilst liquidity-preference due to the speculative-motive corresponds to what in my *Treatise on Money*, I called "the state of bearishness", it is by no means the same thing. For "bearishness" is there defined as the functional relationship, not between the rate of interest (or price of debts) and the quantity of money, but between the price of assets and debts, taken together, and the quantity of money. This treatment, however, involved a confusion between results due to a change in the rate of interest and those due to a change in the schedule of the marginal efficiency of capital. (Keynes 1936 [1973]: 173)

In Keynes (1930), the central bank creates liquidity by lending to banks on the money market and through open market operations. It can influence the ability of banks to create liquidity. Banks supply liquid "saving deposits" and buy securities on the financial market. Therefore, banks take financial risks based on their own liquidity preference and their own "bullishness" or "bearishness". Three markets are taken into account: the money market, the market for money (income and saving deposits), and the financial market. In Keynes (1936 [1973]), the banking system is seen as a whole and the central bank intervenes with respect to the overall money supply. The market for money is the place where there is a confrontation between this money supply and the overall demand for money, first for the transaction and precautionary motives (related to income and which are not different from those of the Cambridge School) and secondly for the speculative motive (related to the interest rate), which stems from a choice between bonds and money with respect to the composition of all agents' financial portfolios. In *The General Theory*, liquidity preference is presented as a demand for money that determines the long-term interest rate, the most important variable for the investment function.

The importance of the role of banks and of the money market is reduced in this analysis. However, Keynes was primarily concerned with the impact of monetary policy on the financial market interest rate owing to the behaviour of banks, which may refuse to follow the central bank's lending policy and refuse to take risks by buying securities. In this case, fiscal policy must be introduced. This was to be described after Keynes in IS–LM models, through IS shifts.

From Keynes (1936) to the neoclassical synthesis

After Keynes, portfolio theory was developed, building microeconomic foundations of the demand for money, thus continuing the work of Hicks (1935) in his propositions for a research program designed to integrate money into the theory of choice. James Tobin (1958) sought to reformulate Keynes's demand for money, as he believed that it should not be related to speculation, but a way of diversifying a portfolio based on the return and risk of different kinds of securities, calculated on the probability that agents apply to the evolution of the interest rate, which is seen as a random variable. Holding money as a riskless asset will allow the total risk of a portfolio to be reduced. William Sharpe (1970) later defined these portfolio choices more clearly.

It is generally accepted that macroeconomic Keynesian models in the twentieth century were the first in the line of Hicks's IS–LM model (Hicks 1937). The central bank supply of money determines, with the public's demand for money, a long-term rate (bond rate) on the LM curve. This demand for money includes the three Keynesian motives: transaction, precaution and speculation. It is increasing with income and decreasing with the interest rate. The LM curve gives all the solutions (both income and interest rate) that correspond to the equilibrium of the market for money. Together with the IS curve (which describes equilibrium on the goods market), it determines the global macroeconomic equilibrium.

In the 1960s there was a revival of interest in the quantity theory of money. Milton Friedman (1956) reformulated this theory as a demand for money in the Cambridge style. Money is considered as a capital good. Any real or financial asset is a substitute for money within agents' wealth holdings. According to this new quantity theory, the velocity of circulation is no longer constant but a stable variable, because it is a function of stable factors. Friedman minimised the role of instable variables such as interest rates (returns on assets) in agents' choices that had been stressed by Keynesians and gave great impact to the stable new variable he introduced: permanent income. As a result, if the demand for money is stable, it is possible to rely on monetary policy to control economic variables.

However, this monetarist monetary policy is a rule that is imposed on the central bank. The latter has to increase its money supply with a fixed coefficient independently of the economic circumstances. Monetarists were to criticise the Phillips curve and introduce adaptive expectations. So, any increase in the money supply can only reduce unemployment (below its natural level) temporarily, before agents adjust their inflation expectations. As a result, it is better not to modify the monetary policy and to follow a quantitative and constant rule in order to attain an inflation target.

However, Keynesians criticised the stability of the monetarist demand for money in the 1970s as a result of empirical studies. Moreover, it became more and more difficult to define the quantity of money supply that could be the basis of monetary policy, because of constant financial innovations in liquid assets that are substitutes for money and encourage modifications of behaviour on the part of asset owners. The role of expectations was to be developed by the new classical economics, which introduced "rational expectations". Agents use all the information at their disposal in the best possible way. They cannot make systematic errors. Inflation is a function of the expected rate of growth of the money supply. So there is no possibility for a Phillips curve and no possibility to reduce (even in the short run) natural unemployment. Any discretionary monetary policy is useless.

Demand for Money and Value of Money

According to the Cambridge school, whereas the demand for nominal cash balance varies with the value of money, the demand for real cash balance does not; the demand functions for real money as for goods are homogeneous of degree zero in the price level of goods, and the demand for nominal money is homogeneous of degree one. In doing this, these authors thought they were solving Helfferich's vicious circle between utility and the value of money. In fact, as Oskar Lange (1942) and Don Patinkin (1948) demonstrated, they were confusing money prices with accounting prices. However, money prices, contrary to accounting prices, are relative prices, that is, the prices of goods expressed in money. Consider ($\tilde{P}_i$, $\tilde{P}_m$) the accounting prices respectively of good i and money. The money price of good i is equal to the accounting price of the good divided by the accounting price of money: $P_i = \frac{\tilde{P}_i}{\tilde{P}}$. As a consequence, whereas the budget constraint of households does not change with a proportional variation in the accounting prices of goods and money – leaving the money prices unchanged – it does with a non-proportional variation in these prices – which changes the money price level of goods. A rise in this level means a loss in the value of households' money supply. Households have to diminish their demand for goods, assets and real balance – their demand for nominal money increases less than the money price level of goods. The IS and LM curves shift to the left. Symmetrically, a fall in the money price level of goods means a rise in the value of households' money supply and results in a shift to the right of the IS and LM curves. Drawing the IS and LM curves supposes a given level of the money prices, that is, of the accounting prices of goods and money, and therefore of the value of money.

Although there is no dichotomy between the markets for goods, assets and money, when using an IS–LM model with flexible money prices, money wages and interest rate but a fixed level of real income, Patinkin demonstrated, in *Money, Interest and Prices, An Integration of Monetary and Value Theory* (1956 [1965]), that the quantity theory of money may be valid. Suppose an initial equilibrium that is disrupted by a 100 per cent increase in the quantity of money. Households are enriched and may demand more goods, assets and real money: the markets for goods and assets are in excess demand and the market for money in excess supply. This (positive) effect of the increase in the quantity of money on demand in the markets for goods, assets and money is called the real balance effect. It causes a rise in the money prices of consumption goods and assets, that is, a fall in the interest rate. The fall in the interest rate causes a rise in the demand for investment goods, therefore in their money prices. The rise in the money prices of goods means a decrease in the value of the cash balances; it causes a (negative) real balance effect on the markets for goods, assets and money. Because the level of real income is fixed, the supply of goods is fixed, so that the rise in prices lasts until the value of cash balances and the interest rate return to their initial levels. This will be the case when the money price level has doubled. So the 100 per cent increase in the quantity of money results in a proportionate rise in the money price level, leaving the value of the real balance unchanged. The value of money has diminished by 50 per cent.

Now, this demonstration of the quantity theory, the description of the adjustments, begins with an initial equilibrium in which the accounting price of money is positive: $\tilde{P}_m > 0$. But the real balance effect does not describe the existence of this equilibrium with a positive value of cash balances, but its stability. If the IS–LM model used by Patinkin contains as much independent equations as unknowns:

> equality between the number of unknowns and the number of independent equations is neither a necessary nor a sufficient condition for the existence of a solution. Nor does it insure that solutions, if they do exist, will be only finite in number. For our purposes, however, these highly complicated issues can be ignored. Instead, we shall accept such equality as justifying the reasonableness of the assumption that one and the same set of money prices can simultaneously create equilibrium in each and every market. We shall also assume that only one of such set exists. (Patinkin 1956 [1965]: 37)

Frank Hahn (1965), Robert W. Clower (1967) and Ross M. Starr (1974) investigate the difficulties in proving the existence of a general equilibrium with a positive accounting price of money. Hahn recalls that Walras's law does not imply that every good is scarce at equilibrium, that is, has a positive accounting price which clears its market. Some goods may be in excess supply and have a zero accounting price; these are free goods. Now, since the utility of money depends on its accounting price, a zero accounting price makes the money useless. In this case, there is no demand for money, so that a general equilibrium may be established although there is an excess supply on the market for money. It is a non-monetary equilibrium. This would be the case, for example, if the assets are liquid. This case is already mentioned by Patinkin: "the end result of making bonds completely liquid is to eliminate not the rate of interest but the use of money" (Patinkin 1956 [1965]: 109).

Clower underlines that the budget constraint of agents in Patinkin's model does not describe a monetary economy because it allows barter: "any commodity, whether a good or money, can be offered directly in trade for every other commodity" (Clower 1967 [1969]: 204). Clower suggests that a distinction should be made between an income constraint, where the agent sells goods and demands money, and an expenditure constraint, where he supplies money and demands goods. Starr highlights the fact that the demand for money in period t is a demand for money to be spent in period $t + 1$, so that the utility of money at the end of period t depends on its utility in period $t + 1$ and therefore also depends on its accounting price in $t + 1$. However, the horizon of both the agents and the model is finite, so that money has no utility at the end of the last period T; there is no period $T + 1$ for spending money. Then in T, money becomes a free good, its accounting price is zero. As a result of this zero price in T, the utility of money at the end of period $T - 1$ is also zero. Then in $T - 1$, money becomes a free good and its accounting price is zero. Then in $T - 2$, for the same reasons, money becomes a free good and its accounting price is zero. The same in $T - 3$, then in $T - 4$ and so on, in all periods. In the first period one then obtains a non-monetary equilibrium.

At the end of the twentieth century, the overlapping generations model initially developed by Maurice Allais (1947) and then Paul Samuelson (1958) to deal with the theory of capital appeared to be capable of solving the difficulties of the integration of monetary and value theory (Kareken and Wallace 1980). The model contains two generations of agents living two periods – the young and the old – so that the horizon of the model is infinite although the horizon of the agents is finite. The agents' initial endowments of goods and their intertemporal preferences make them want to sell goods when they are young and buy goods when they are old. Because the old cannot issue bonds (they will be dead in the following period and therefore cannot reimburse), the young cannot sell goods for bonds. Bonds cannot dominate money. Money is the unique means of transaction between young and old: the young sell goods for money to the old, who sell money for goods.

New Foundations for the Reintroduction of Banks

Introducing banks into the macroeconomic model
From the second half of the twentieth century, the role of banks in macroeconomics was neglected in Keynesian (IS–LM models) and later in monetarist models. Both approaches were concerned with money and bank liabilities, rather than with bank assets or bank credit, with the money supply process, rather than with the credit supply. The modelling of the banking system remained undeveloped. The neoclassical and rational

expectations model of the 1970s focused on the money–output correlation and did not take the financial system into account. It is only recently that bank lending and the importance of banks for the macroeconomic equilibrium and the means of transmission of monetary policy have once again become the object of studies.

John J. Gurley and Edward S. Shaw in *Money in a Theory of Finance* (1960) presented an analysis of the banking system through a general theory of the choice of optimum asset and debt portfolios by financial institutions of various kinds. They distinguished between "direct finance" and "indirect finance" as different ways for firms to be financed, and highlighted the role of financial intermediaries at the macroeconomic level, which cannot be substituted by markets. The intermediaries provide ultimate lenders with new types of securities and expand the borrowers' "financial capacity" (their balance sheets), which is an important determining factor of aggregate demand. They made the distinction between "inside money" (based on private domestic debt) and "outside money" (based on any other asset). Patinkin in *Money, Interest and Prices* (1956 [1965]) would later discuss the relevance of this distinction for the determination of the price level.

Other authors were to reformulate the macroeconomic model. The fact that, in a recession, the rate of interest will be stable or rise instead of diminishing cannot be explained by the "standard" theory at the root of the LM curve, but it can be explained if we introduce the credit supply curve.

Information asymmetries are at the root of the reintroduction of banks into economic theory. There will be macroeconomic consequences of imperfect information in financial markets. Supply of credit is based on a judgement regarding the debtor's solvency, a specific piece of information that is not transferable, and that is produced over a long-term relationship with banks. This customer relationship creates a "sunk cost" but reduces information costs later. Thus, bank credit and other market securities do not substitute for one another and some firms are dependent on banks; they cannot obtain funds on markets. The channel of monetary policy does not work solely through the demand for money, which involves the cash balance effect or the substitution effect in the portfolio choice between two types of assets: bonds and money. It also operates through the supply of credit by banks to agents who need to borrow from them (a credit availability effect). The credit market is introduced into the macroeconomic model. The bank lending rate is thus distinguished from the other market rates. This credit channel shows how a "monetary shock" will be transmitted to the real sector by banks through their credit supply. The central bank can affect the asset side of the banks' balance sheet (their credit supply), not only the liability side through their deposits. This was introduced into the IS–LM model (Bernanke and Blinder 1988) through a new kind of shift of the IS function, that is now called a CC (commodities and credit) function.

In this perspective, it is possible to describe the effects of a restrictive open market policy on the asset side of banks' balance sheets. Bank liquidity will diminish. Banks counteract this effect not by issuing debt securities, nor by selling short-term securities because they need to keep liquid assets, but by reducing the amount of loans. In this way, a reduction in economic activity could be possible without a change in market interest rates. However, monetary policy can have another effect, through a rise in the lending interest rate, which will damage balance sheets and the collateral of the firms that are borrowing. This will then reduce their direct or intermediated borrowing capability. It operates like a "financial accelerator" in the event of a shock.

A new microeconomics of banking and money market
These new macroeconomic developments were founded on a new microeconomics of banking which has been developed since 1970. The latter has allowed the analysis of the rationale of banks and bank risks to be reconsidered. As regards the consequences of informational asymmetries on the default risk, that is, the probability of default by borrowers, quoting Adam Smith, Stiglitz and Weiss (1981) show that banks must ration credit. Because they have an insufficient amount of information concerning their borrowers, banks are victims of adverse selection and moral hazard. That is why they are not interested in raising their credit rate too high when faced with an excess of credit demand, because this could result in a decrease in the rate of return on their loans, due to the resulting excess of risk taken by borrowers in the case of a higher interest rate. At fairly high levels of interest rates, low-risk borrowers may be inclined to stop borrowing and, on the contrary, only high-risk borrowers (who have a greater potential return on their project) may continue to borrow. Therefore, banks will limit the total loan amount to a level corresponding to the interest rate that they consider to be the maximum that can be paid by low-risk borrowers, and will not raise the interest rate, when there is an excess demand of credit.

Douglas Diamond (1984) stressed that it is optimal for final lenders to delegate the monitoring of borrowers to banks once they have deposited their funds in the bank and a loan has been granted to these borrowers by the bank itself. In this model, banks are now creating new kinds of securities, by establishing a credit contract with the borrower and a deposit contract with the individual lender who deposits his funds in the bank. Diamond showed that the total cost from this "delegated monitoring" operated by the bank (that is, the sum of the costs of the bank monitoring borrowers and of individual depositors monitoring the bank) is therefore inferior to the costs of individual lenders monitoring borrowers, when they are themselves in a direct financing relationship. The bank will benefit from scale economies in monitoring costs. Moreover, as banks hold bigger portfolios than individual lenders, they obtain a better diversification of their portfolio and, as a result, reduce the probability of default for ultimate lenders.

Contemporary economic theory also shows that it is possible to reduce informational asymmetries for banks by establishing long-term relationships between banks and their borrowers. This enables banks constantly to collect and accumulate data. The latter may be destroyed when banking crises occur. As a result, when banks are no longer able to lend, or when their informational capital has been destroyed, this will affect macroeconomic variables, because financial markets cannot replace them. This means that banking crises have an effect on the real sector of the economy not only by reducing the quantity of money, but also by destroying all the customer relationship and informational capital that banks have created and accumulated in lending (Bernanke 1983).

The microeconomics of banking also explores liquidity risks. Diamond and Dybvig (1983) showed how banks can provide a liquidity "insurance" for individual lenders that is different from the liquidity provided by financial markets, thanks to their supply of deposit contracts (which guarantees a fixed price) when this insurance cannot be provided through contracts between individual agents, owing to the fact that liquidity needs are "private" information that cannot be publicly verified. Banks will insure their depositors against random shocks that affect their intertemporal consumption preferences, while allowing them to benefit from the returns they obtain from investing their funds. The model shows that a bank is a means of improving agents' welfare, because it helps them to obtain a better consumption equilibrium than they could achieve on their own.

As long as these shocks are not perfectly correlated, the total quantity of liquid reserves required by a bank that is defined as a coalition of depositors rises less rapidly than the number of its deposits. As a result, the existence of a banking system with fractional reserves is possible, in which part of the deposits is used to finance illiquid investments.

However, this may create fragility for banks, and there is a limit to the provision of liquidity that can be obtained from them, since there may be a "bad" equilibrium, that is to say a bank run equilibrium. The latter is due to coordination failures between depositors. A given depositor's choice to "run" on a bank if he is not actually facing a liquidity shock is based on his anticipation of other depositors' behaviour. If he expects a great number of other depositors to withdraw early, he will be tempted to imitate them. Because of the deposit contract rule ("first come, first served"), if he seeks to withdraw his deposit too late, he will not obtain anything. When too many depositors share this feeling and withdraw early, they themselves cause the failure of the bank (even if its fundamental value is positive), which thus cannot repay all of its customers.

This model can also be used to study contagion between banks. When there is a bank failure, this can prompt other banks' depositors to modify their own expectations about the probability of failure of their own banks. That is why the model also shows the necessity of a deposit insurance. This takes the form of a tax on early withdrawals as a ratio of total withdrawals. As it penalises depositors, it will dissuade those who are not experiencing a liquidity shock from withdrawing early.

Liquidity problems may be solved through the interbank money market, which is used to pool such risks. Banks that have an excess of liquidity and are not experiencing early withdrawals can lend to other banks that are experiencing a run on withdrawals. On principle, when a bank cannot borrow on this market, this signifies that it is insolvent. However, for any bank, an asymmetry of information exists concerning the quality of the other banks' assets. Doubts about one bank's solvency may arise, even if it is perfectly sound. Moreover, in time of crisis, any bank may refuse to assist another bank if it lacks confidence in the latter's ability to assist it in turn should it itself experience such a need in the future (Freixas et al. 2000). As a result, the interbank money market may be the site of these coordination failures. Therefore the lender of last resort, namely the central bank, must intervene by lending to individual banks.

JÉRÔME DE BOYER DES ROCHES AND SYLVIE DIATKINE

See also:

Maurice Allais (I); Antiquity (II); Walter Bagehot (I); Balance of payments and exchange rates (III); Banking and currency schools (II); British classical political economy (II); Bullionist and anti-bullionist schools (II); Business cycles and growth (III); Cambridge School of Economics (II); Richard Cantillon (I); Chicago School (II); Economic thought in Scholasticism (II); Francis Ysidro Edgeworth (I); Financial economics (III); Irving Fisher (I); Milton Friedman (I); General equilibrium theory (III); Ralph George Hawtrey (I); Friedrich August von Hayek (I); John Richard Hicks (I); David Hume (I); Institutional economics (III); Institutionalism (II); International trade (III); Edwin Walter Kemmerer (I); John Maynard Keynes (I); Keynesianism (II); Oskar Ryszard Lange (I); John Law (I); Macroeconomics (III); Thomas Robert Malthus (I); Alfred Marshall (I); Karl Heinrich Marx (I); Marxism(s) (II); Mercantilism and the science of trade (II); John Stuart Mill (I); Monetarism (II); Robert Alexander Mundell (I); New Keynesianism (II); Open economy macroeconomics (III); Don Patinkin (I); Post-Keynesianism (II); David Ricardo (I); Paul Anthony Samuelson (I); Adam Smith

(I); James Steuart [James Denham-Steuart] (I); Joseph Eugene Stiglitz (I); Stockholm (Swedish) School (II); Theory of the firm (III); Henry Thornton (I); James Tobin (I); Thomas Tooke (I); Robert Torrens (I); Value and price (III); Knut Wicksell (I).

References and further reading

Allais, M. (1947), *Économie et intérêt*, Paris: Éd. Librairie des Publications Officielles.
Andreades, A. (1904), *Histoire de la Banque d'Angleterre*, ed. A. Rousseau, Paris, English trans. C. Meredith (1909), *History of the Bank of England*, Westminster: P.S. King & Son.
Aristotle (1885), *The Politics of Aristotle*, trans. B. Jowett, Oxford: Clarendon Press.
Arnon, A. (2011), *Monetary Theory and Policy from Hume and Smith to Wicksell: Money, Credit, and the Economy*, Cambridge: Cambridge University Press.
Bagehot, W. (1873), *Lombard Street, a Description of the Money Market*, ed. H. Withers 1915, London: John Murray.
Bernanke, B.S. (1983), 'Nonmonetary effects of the financial crisis in the propagation of the Great Depression', *American Economic Review*, **73** (3), 257–76.
Bernanke, B.S. and A.S. Blinder (1988), 'Credit, money and aggregate demand', *American Economic Review*, **78** (2), 435–9.
Boyer des Roches, J. de (2003), *La pensée monétaire, histoire et analyse*, Paris: Les Solos.
Boyer des Roches, J. de (2013), 'Bank liquidity risk from John Law (1705) to Walter Bagehot (1873)', *European Journal of the History of Economic Thought*, **20** (4), 547–71.
Capie, F. (1993), *History of Banking*, London: W. Pickering.
Cantillon, R. (1755), *Essai sur la nature du commerce en général*, ed. and trans. H. Higgs (1959), *Essay on the Nature of Trade in General*, London: Frank Cass.
Clapham, J. (1944), *The Bank of England*, Cambridge: Cambridge University Press.
Clower, R. (1967), 'A reconsideration of the microfoundations of monetary theory', *Western Economic Journal*, 6 (1), 1–9, republished in R. Clower (1969), *Monetary Theory, Selected Readings*, Harmondsworth: Penguin Education, pp. 202–11.
Coe Report (1873), 'Report of the Committee Appointed by the New York Clearing-House Association', 11 November, reproduced in O.M.W. Sprague, (1910), *History of Crises under the National Banking System, National Monetary Commission*, Washington, DC: Government Printing Office, pp. 91–103.
Diamond, D. (1984), 'Financial intermediation and delegated monitoring', *Review of Economic Studies*, 51 (3), 393–414.
Diamond, D. and P. Dybvig (1983), 'Bank runs, deposit insurance and liquidity', *Journal of Political Economy*, **91** (3), 401–19.
Diatkine, S. (1995), *Théories et politiques monétaires*, Paris: A. Colin.
Diatkine, S. (2002), *Les fondements de la théorie bancaire: des textes classiques aux débats contemporains*, Paris: Dunod.
Dickson, P.G.M. (1967), *The Financial Revolution in England*, London: Macmillan.
Edgeworth, F.Y. (1888), 'The mathematical theory of banking', *Journal of the Royal Statistical Society*, **51** (1), 113–27.
Fetter, F.W. (1965), *Development of British Monetary Orthodoxy, 1797–1875*, Cambridge, MA: Harvard University Press.
Fisher, I. (1897), 'The role of capital in economic theory', *The Economic Journal*, 7 (28), 511–37.
Fisher, I. (1911), *The Purchasing Power of Money. Its Determination and Relation to Credit, Interest and Crises*, New York: Macmillan.
Freixas, X., B. Parigi and J.C. Rochet (2000), 'Systemic risk, interbank relations and liquidity provision by the central bank', *Journal of Money, Credit and Banking*, **32** (3), 611–38.
Friedman, M. (1956), 'The quantity theory of money. A restatement', in M. Friedman (ed.), *Studies in the Quantity Theory of Money*, Chicago, IL: University of Chicago Press, pp. 3–21.
Gilbart, J.W. (1854), 'On the laws of the currency, as exemplified in the circulation of country bank notes in England since 1844', *Journal of the Statistical Society*, **18**, 289–321.
Gurley, J.J. and E.S. Shaw (1960), *Money in a Theory of Finance*, Washington, DC: Brookings Institution.
Hahn, F.H. (1965), 'On some problems of proving the existence of an equilibrium in a monetary economy', in F.H. Hahn and F. Brechling (eds), *The Theory of Interest Rates*, London: Macmillan, pp. 126–35.
Hawtrey, R.G. (1919), *Currency and Credit*, London: Longmans, Green.
Hayek, F. von (1931), *Prices and Production*, London: Routledge.
Hegeland, H. (1951), *The Quantity Theory of Money*, reprinted 1969, New York: A.M. Kelley.
Helfferich, K. (1903), *Das Geld*, Leipzig: C.L. Hirschfeld.
Hicks, J.R. (1935), 'A suggestion for simplifying the theory of money', *Economica*, **2** (5), 1–19.
Hicks, J.R. (1937), 'Mr Keynes and the classics. A suggested interpretation', *Econometrica*, **5** (2), 147–59.

Hilferding, R. (1910), *Das Finanzkapital. Eine Studie zur jüngsten Entwicklung des Kapitalismus*, Vienna: Wiener Volksbuchhandlung Ignaz Brand & Co, English trans. T. Bottomore (ed.) (1981), *Finance Capital. A Study of Latest Phase of Capitalist Development*, London: Routledge & Kegan Paul.

Horsefield, J.K. (1960), *British Monetary Experiments 1650–1710*, London: G. Bell and Sons.

Ito, S. (2011), 'The making of institutional credit in England, 1600 to 1688', *European Journal of the History of Economic Thought*, **18** (4), 487–519.

Kareken, J.H. and N. Wallace (1980), *Models of Monetary Economics*, Minneapolis, MN: Federal Reserve Bank of Minneapolis.

Kemmerer, E.W. (1907), *Money and Credit Instruments in their Relation to General Prices*, New York: Henry Holt.

Keynes, J.M. (1923), *A Tract on Monetary Reform*, in *The Collected Writings of John Maynard Keynes*, (1971), vol. 4, London: Macmillan and Cambridge University Press.

Keynes, J.M. (1930), *A Treatise on Money*, in *The Collected Writings of John Maynard Keynes*, (1971), vols 5 and 6, London: Macmillan and Cambridge University Press.

Keynes, J.M. (1936), *The General Theory of Employment, Interest and Money*, in *The Collected Writings of John Maynard Keynes*, (1973), vol. 7, London: Macmillan and Cambridge University Press.

Laidler, D. (1991), *The Golden Age of the Quantity Theory*, Princeton, NJ: Princeton University Press.

Laidler, D. (1999), *Foundations of Monetary Economics*, Cheltenham, UK and Northampton, MA, USA: Edward Elgar.

Lange, O. (1942), 'Say's law: a restatement and criticism', in O. Lange, F. McIntyre and T.O. Yntema (eds), *Studies in Mathematical Economics and Econometrics*, Chicago: University of Chicago Press, pp. 49–68.

Lloyd, S.J. (Lord Overstone) (1844), *Thoughts on the Separation of the Departments of the Bank of England*, London: Pelham Richardson.

MacLeod, H.D. (1892–93), *The Theory and Practice of Banking*, London: Longmans, Green and Co.

Marcuzzo, M.C. and A. Rosselli (1991), *Ricardo and the Gold Standard, the Foundations of the International Monetary Order*, London: Macmillan.

Marshall, A. (1923), *Money, Credit and Commerce*, London: Macmillan.

Marx, K. (1867), *Das Kapital – Kritik der politischen Oekonomie, Buch 1, Der Producktionsprocess des Kapitals*, Hamburg: Otto Meissner, English trans. F. Engels (ed.) (1887), *Capital – A Critical Analysis of Capitalist Production*, vol. 1, London: Swan Sonnenschein, Lowrey & Co., reprinted 1961, Moscow: Foreign Languages Publishing House.

Marx, K. (1885), *Das Kapital – Kritik der politischen Oekonomie, Buch 2, Der Circulationsprocess des Kapital*, ed. F. Engels, Hamburg: Otto Meissner, English trans. 1909, *Capital – The Process of Circulation of Capital*, vol. 2, Chicago, IL: Charles H. Kerr & Co., reprinted 1961, Moscow: Foreign Languages Publishing House.

Marx, K. (1894), *Das Kapital – Kritik der politischen Oekonomie, Buch 3, Der Gesamtprozess der Kapitalistischen Produktion*, ed. F. Engels, Hamburg: Otto Meissner, English trans. 1909, *Capital – The Process of Capitalist Production as a Whole*, vol. 3, Chicago, IL: Charles H. Kerr & Co., reprinted 1962, Moscow: Foreign Languages Publishing House.

Mints, L.W. (1945), *A History of Banking Theory in Great Britain and the United States*, Chicago, IL: University of Chicago Press.

Murphy, A. (1997a), *John Law, Economic Theorist and Policy-Maker*, Oxford: Clarendon Press.

Murphy, A. (1997b), *Monetary Theory, 1601–1758*, 6 vols, London and New York: Routledge.

O'Brien, D.P. (1994), *Foundations of Monetary Economics*, London: Pickering & Chatto.

Parnell, H. (1827), *Observations on Paper Money, Banking and Overtrading*, London: James Ridgway.

Patinkin, D. (1948), 'Relative prices, Say's law, and the demand for money', *Econometrica*, **16** (2), 135–54.

Patinkin, D. (1956), *Money, Interest and Prices, An Integration of Monetary and Value Theory*, 2nd edn 1965, New York: Harper & Row.

Pigou, A.C. (1917), 'The value of money', *Quarterly Journal of Economics*, **32** (1), 38–65.

Quesnay, F. (1766), *Analyse de la formule arithmétique du tableau économique, de la distribution des dépenses annuelles d'une nation agricole*, reprinted 1958, in *François Quesnay et la physiocratie*, Paris: INED, pp. 793–814.

Ricardo, D. (1810), *The High Price of Bullion*, in P. Sraffa (ed.) (1966), *The Works and Correspondence*, vol. 3, Cambridge: Cambridge University Press.

Ricardo, D. (1817), *On the Principles of Political Economy and Taxation*, ed. P. Sraffa (1951), Cambridge: Cambridge University Press.

Ricardo, D. (1824), *Plan for the Establishment of a National Bank*, in P. Sraffa (ed.) (1966), *The Works and Correspondence*, vol. 4, Cambridge: Cambridge University Press.

Rist, C. (1938), *Histoire des doctrines relatives au crédit et à la monnaie depuis John Law jusqu'à nos jours*, Paris: Sirey, English trans. J. Tabrisky Degras (1940), *History of Monetary and Credit Theory from John Law to the Present Day*, London: Macmillan.

Robertson, D. (1926), *Banking Policy and the Price Level*, London: P.S. King & Sons.

Samuelson, P. (1958), 'An exact consumption-loan model of interest with or without the social contrivance of money', *Journal of Political Economy*, **66** (December), 467–82.

Schumpeter, J. (1954), *History of Economic Analysis*, London, Allen & Unwin.

Scrope, G.P. (1830), *On Credit-Currency, and its Superiority to Coin, in Support of a Petition for the Establishment of a Cheap, Safe, and Sufficient Circulating Medium*, London: John Murray.

Sharpe, W. (1970), *Portfolio Theory and Capital Markets*, New York: McGraw Hill.

Smith, A. (1776), *An Inquiry into the Nature and Causes of the Wealth of Nations*, reprinted 1976, Liberty Classics, Oxford: Oxford University Press.

Sraffa, P. (1932), 'Dr Hayek on money and capital', *The Economic Journal*, **42** (March), 42–53.

Starr, R.M. (1974), 'The price of money in a pure exchange monetary economy with taxation', *Econometrica*, **42** (1), 45–54.

Stiglitz, J. and A. Weiss (1981), 'Credit rationing in markets with imperfect information', *American Economic Review*, **71** (3), 393–410.

Thornton, H. (1802), *An Enquiry into the Nature and Effects of the Paper Credit of Great Britain (1802): together with his evidence given before the Committees of Secretary of the two Houses of Parliament in the Bank of England, March and April, 1797, some manuscript notes, and his speeches on the bullion report, May 1811*, ed. and introduction by F.A. von Hayek 1939, London: Allen & Unwin.

Tobin, J. (1958), 'Liquidity preference as behaviour towards risk', *Review of Economic Studies*, **25** (2), 65–86.

Tooke, T. (1838–56), *A History of Prices and of the State of the Circulation from 1792 to 1856*, 5 vols, London: Longman, Brown, Green, and Longmans.

Tooke, T. (1848), *A History of Prices and of the State of the Circulation from 1839 to 1847 Inclusive*, London: Longman, Brown, Green, and Longmans.

Torrens, R. (1837), *A Letter to the Right Honourable Lord Viscount Melbourne, on the Causes of the Recent Derangement in the Money Market and on the Bank Reform*, London: Longmans.

Torrens, R. (1858), 'Lord Overstone on metallic and paper currency', *Edinburgh Review*, **107**, 248–93.

Walker, F.A. (1888), *Political Economy*, 3rd edn, revised and enlarged, New York: Henry Holt.

Wicksell, K. (1898), *Interest and Prices*, trans. R.F. Kahn (1936), London, Macmillan.

Withers, H. (1909), *The Meaning of Money*, London: John Murray.

Open economy macroeconomics

The Keynesian Approach

One line of thinking leading to the research field of international macroeconomics has been brought forward or at least initiated by John Maynard Keynes's theoretical work on war finance, on how the Bretton Woods/General Agreement on Tariffs and Trade (GATT) system might work, and on Britain's post-war loans (Vines 2003). In his work, Keynes laid the fundaments to and in many ways preceded the work of Mundell (1963) and Fleming (1962) and that of later studies on financial crises. He thereby used his earlier work published in the *Treatise on Money* (Keynes 1930) which he combined with the demand management from the *General Theory* (Keynes 1936). In his studies on war finance, Keynes has worked with an IS–LM–BP model in mind in a small open economy version and a two-country version. Yet, the open economy Keynesian model that we have been using had to wait until the 1960s to become popular and widely used (Vines 2003).

Open economy macroeconomics had been worked on and popularized particularly by the International Monetary Fund (IMF) where Mundell and Fleming worked in the Research Department which was headed by Polack at the beginning of the 1960s. Fleming's Keynesian tradition met Mundells view which had also been shaped by other influences: Meade's mathematical approach (Meade 1951), the discussion with Metzler on conditions of general equilibrium in an open economy (see Mundell 1961) and Samuelson's stability analysis (Samuelson 1947) have been important in developing Mundell's approach to the analysis of Open Economy Macroeconomics (Young and Darity 2004). Mundell looked for a way to analyse the difference between an economy with a fixed exchange rate and flexible prices and an economy with flexible exchange rates and fixed prices in a model with full-employment.

Given the low level of economic integration in the years of and immediately after the Great Depression, it is not surprising that Keynes's *General Theory* was presented and discussed in a closed economy framework. It has taken some time for the model for the open economy to be worked out, although there have been attempts from different directions. At the beginning of the 1960s, Mundell (1963) and Fleming (1962) succeeded in summarizing different attempts to achieve an open economy macroeconomics framework. Resulting from their work at the IMF, stabilization policy has been the focus of Mundell and Fleming's analyses. Since then, their framework has become the dominant paradigm for studying open-economy monetary and fiscal policy issues, which have gained in importance relative to closed-economy models because of the continuing integration of regions and countries to unprecedented levels.

International economic integration affects the ability to conduct domestic financial policies mainly through the capital flows that these policies induce. To stress this point, Mundell (1963) assumes an extreme degree of capital mobility that yields an identical interest rate in all countries in equilibrium. In combination with static exchange rate expectations, this assumption implies that all securities (which are restricted to government bonds) are perfect substitutes. These are certainly extreme assumptions, yet they bring out the policy implications as sharply as possible. In the presence of interest rate differences, perfect substitutability of the securities induces capital flows until the differences are eliminated. That does away with all financial policies conducted to stabilize the economy that work through a change in the interest rate. A stabilization policy that intends to lower the interest rate would induce capital outflows, which prevent the interest rate from falling.

The effectiveness of monetary and fiscal policies depends thereby on the choice of the exchange rate regime. Mundell (1963) and Fleming (1962) discuss the polar cases of flexible and fixed exchange rates showing that the two regimes generate strongly different effects of stabilization policies on an open economy's output. While flexible exchange rate regimes allow a priori for an active monetary policy, in fixed exchange rate regimes the money supply has to secure the exchange rate. Money supply becomes an endogenous variable, which cannot freely be used as a policy measure to affect the economic outcome. In flexible exchange rate regimes, in contrast, an autonomous monetary policy is in principle possible. Yet, it is strongly affected by the perfect substitutability of the securities. An expansionary monetary policy puts a downward pressure on the interest rate, which induces capital outflows. These outflows cause a depreciation of the exchange rate, which increases (under the assumption that the Marshall–Lerner–Robinson condition holds) the trade balance and thereby output and employment. The new equilibrium features a higher money stock, higher employment and output levels, and an improved trade balance and net foreign investment position, but the interest rate remains constant at the world interest rate level.

Fiscal policy, that is, an increase in government spending financed by government borrowing, is also affected by capital mobility. Government spending tends to raise incomes. Yet, this increases the money demand, which increases the interest rate and induces capital inflows. Capital inflows in turn appreciate the exchange rate, which depresses (a normal reaction assumed) the trade balance. The lower trade balance reduces incomes. This negative effect exactly equalizes the positive effect of government spending. Hence, with fixed interest rates, income is also fixed. "Fiscal policy thus completely loses its force as a domestic stabilizer when the exchange rate is allowed to fluctuate" (Mundell 1963: 478).

Under fixed exchange rates the results reverse: monetary policy cannot be used to affect incomes while fiscal policy can be an effective stabilizer. Increased government spending requires the central bank to increase money supply to defend the fixed exchange rate. Thus, income rises along with money stock. The government's budget deficit equals the trade deficit, which is balanced by an inflow of capital. The new equilibrium features an increase in foreign reserves which is the actual reason for the increase in money supply needed to defend the exchange rate. Income increases, unemployment falls, money supply expands and the government deficit increases as result of an expansionary fiscal policy under fixed exchange rates. The interest rate is unaffected.

The assumption that the securities of two countries are perfect substitutes, that is, that there are no information and transaction costs and no risk, is certainly too strong. Fleming (1962) includes imperfect substitutability of securities from different countries. While weakening Mundell's results, their tendency is supported by Fleming's findings. Monetary policy is effective under flexible exchange rates while fiscal policy is not. Under fixed exchange rates, fiscal policy is possible while monetary policy is not (always).

In the world of the Bretton Woods system the assumption of static exchange rate expectations might be acceptable. In the flexible exchange rate episode afterwards, it is certainly an odd assumption. Investors would make systematic mistakes, which contradicts rational expectations, an assumption that has become very prominent in macroeconomics. Dornbusch (1976) presented a version of the Mundell–Fleming framework augmented by rational exchange rate expectations, which are introduced through the uncovered interest parity. The long-run equilibrium supports the Mundell–Fleming results that (unanticipated) monetary policy is an effective tool of stabilization policy under flexible exchange rates. In the short run, Dornbusch found a depreciation of the exchange rate that exceeds its long-run level: the famous over-shooting result.

The over-shooting of the exchange rate results from sluggish price adjustments in the goods markets. Exchange rate expectations react faster and force the exchange rate to change in reaction to investors' shifts in the asset allocation. The goods market is not cleared until the price adjustment is completed. Output is determined by demand in the meantime. The trade balance may worsen or improve in the short run depending on the change in interest rates and their effect on absorption. In the long run, the trade balance improves and the Mundell–Fleming result applies.

The Mundell–Fleming–Dornbusch framework offers realistic predictions of long-run movements in the exchange rate, interest rate and output following drastic changes in monetary policy. Countries choosing drastic tightening almost always experience real appreciations. As a tool to predict systematic interest rates and exchange rate movements, however, the model does not perform as well (Meese and Rogoff 1983, 1988). Above all, however, the Mundell–Fleming–Dornbusch framework predicts sharp contrasts in the effectiveness of economic policy under different exchange rate regimes. Monetary policy shocks spill over to the real economy only in the flexible exchange rate regime, which led many economists to argue for fixed exchange rates to reduce volatility in real variables. While theoretically appealing, the effect of the chosen exchange rate regime on real variables in an economy is empirically rather limited (Baxter and Stockman 1989).

The strength of the Mundell–Fleming–Dornbusch framework lies in its close connection to policy debates. It is quite flexible and can be applied to various situations to advise necessary policy actions. Yet, as Obstfeld and Rogoff (1996) argue, the approach has several methodical drawbacks: (1) the lack of a micro-foundation particularly of aggregate demand, (2) the lack of private and government inter-temporal budget constraints which make it hard to analyse the dynamics of the current account, and (3) the lack of a natural welfare metric which would allow to compare alternative macroeconomic policies. Obstfeld and Rogoff (1995) have therefore presented a new theoretical framework that preserves the strengths of the Mundell–Fleming–Dornbusch approach but overcomes its limitations.

New Open Economy Macroeconomics

A new line of literature has started in the early 1990s that incorporates imperfect competition and sticky prices in infinite-horizon two-country models. This approach tackles all three shortcomings listed above: (1) all choices by individuals and firms can be clearly addressed; (2) the inter-temporal optimization of individuals, firms, and the government cares for the inter-temporal budget constraints, which are important in many policy contexts; and (3) the micro-foundation delivers a welfare metric to compare alternative policy measures. Obstfeld and Rogoff's "exchange rate dynamics redux" (1995) marks the start of this line of literature.

Obstfeld and Rogoff assume that individuals maximize their inter-temporal utility function with respect to their inter-temporal budget constraint. Utility is thereby positively affected by each period's consumption and non-interest bearing money holding, and negatively affected by the amount of time spent on working. In contrast to the traditional Keynesian models, the consumption bundle consists of a number of differentiated varieties, which include imported varieties from the foreign country. Each variety is produced by one single producer-household. In the production process which is the same for all varieties only labour is used. The horizontally differentiated varieties are supplied in monopolistic competition. The varieties are symmetric in their effect on utility. The composition index, on which utility depends, has the constant elasticity of substitution (CES) form which assumes an equal and constant elasticity of substitution between any two varieties. This elasticity is assumed to be the same in both countries.

Inter-temporal utility maximization of the representative individual relies on consumption shifting between the periods achieved by trading of a riskless asset on a perfectly integrated international financial market or by holding cash. This perfectly integrated financial market implies that the uncovered interest parity holds. Net trade in assets of both countries must be zero, thus total lending of the individuals from one country must equal total borrowing of the other country's individuals. Lending equals the country's current account surplus and leads to an increase in the net asset position of the country that enables the inhabitants to increase their consumption in the future above their period income. Borrowing equals the country's current account deficit and leads to a reduction in its net asset position.

The consumer-producer chooses his consumption level, money holding, and working time by equating his or her respective marginal utilities in the present period. In addition, all periods' marginal utility from consumption must be equalized. That is expressed in the Euler equation, which must hold. This inter-temporal consumption smoothing is the most important difference to the traditional Keynesian models. Consumption does not depend on current income alone but on lifetime income, that is, wealth. Changes in current income change the individual's wealth. The effect of a change in current income on consumption is spread over many periods. A wealth increase raises consumption and money holding but reduces labour input because the marginal utility of consumption and money holding falls, which requires the marginal utility of leisure (which is the time left after working) to fall too. Increasing wealth goes therefore along with reductions in output.

In the long run, prices adjust to their stationary equilibrium level. In the short run, however, prices are assumed to be fixed and pre-set in the previous period which can be motivated by menu costs. That requires demand to determine output if the shock that pushes the economy out of equilibrium is not too large. Because the monopolists set prices always above marginal costs, they can satisfy demand at their pre-set price. By assumption, prices are set in producer's currency. If the exchange rate changes, prices in the foreign country must therefore change with the exchange rate. The exchange rate, in turn, changes in reaction to both monetary and fiscal policy, because the uncovered interest parity holds. Moreover, the exchange rate reacts immediately despite pre-set prices. Hence, over-shooting as in the Dornbusch model does not result.

While the exchange rate behaves as in monetary models, economic policy is effective in the new open economy macroeconomics framework. For instance, a permanent expansion of money supply in the home country increases individuals' wealth, which raises consumption in the current period and in the long run. Output increases in the demand-driven short run and falls in the long run, when prices adjust. Increased consumption is partly satisfied by imports of foreign goods, as demand for all goods (including imports) rises. However, output rises even faster than consumption because inter-temporal utility optimization requires shifting some of the wealth gains to the future. The home country does therefore run a current account surplus in the short run. This surplus is administrated by the depreciation of the exchange rate. The falling exchange rate reduces the pre-set prices of home goods in terms of the foreign currency in the foreign country, which in turn induces foreign consumers to substitute home goods in the short run. In the long run, individuals in the home country realize higher consumption by enjoying net imports from the foreign country. Price adjustment raises prices at home even more than proportional to the money shock. Rising prices over-compensate the nominal exchange rate depreciation. Home's terms of trade improve relative to the initial situation. The rising prices induce the individuals to work less. Thus, monetary shocks have long-lasting real effects.

One great advantage of the new open economy macroeconomics approach is the welfare analysis, which is possible in this framework. The representative individuals in both the home country and the foreign country increase their inter-temporal utility if the home country conducts a small, unanticipated monetary expansion. This stems from the increase of world demand induced by the monetary expansion in the initial period, which is shared by both countries. The money shock reduces the inefficiency in production resulting from the fixed mark-up as in Blanchard and Kiyotaki (1987). The higher aggregate demand with pre-set prices forces higher work effort in the short run and pushes the economy closer to efficient production. That implies that the expenditure switching "beggar-thy-neighbour" effects of Mundell–Fleming–Dornbusch models might be overstated and the general inflationary effect that reduces the world interest rate is more important.

New Insights with Opposing Results

The new open economy macroeconomics framework led to several new insights on international welfare spillovers of monetary and fiscal policy. Yet, with its micro-foundation structure there are many more modelling choices to make which affect the results. In particular two issues are controversially debated: the source of the nominal rigidity and the pricing behaviour of exporters. Nominal rigidities might not necessarily stem from pre-set prices. They might also stem from sticky wages which are negotiated in advance (Obstfeld and Rogoff 2000; Corsetti and Pesenti 2001). Unfortunately, empirically there is no unambiguous answer where the rigidities stem from. Both distortions in wage setting and in price setting are possible. The same applies to the second issue: price setting by exporters is neither only conducted with respect to the home market (fixed mark-up in home currency) nor only with respect to the foreign market (fixed mark-up in foreign currency). Thus, both assumptions can be justified. Unfortunately, the choice of the assumption has non-trivial consequences for the resulting policy recommendation.

This is particularly nasty, since the new open economy macroeconomics aimed at providing a tractable tool for policy analysis.

If prices are pre-set and firms price in local currency as in Devereux and Engel (2001), nominal exchange rate changes have small or no short-run effects on international trade. This contrasts sharply with the traditional Keynesian view, with much of the policy advices, but also with the result from Obstfeld and Rogoff (1995) presented above. With local currency pricing the exchange rate pass-through, that is, the responsiveness of export prices to exchange rate changes, is zero instead of one as in the models assuming producer country's currency pricing. The consequence is that there is no expenditure switching effect in local currency pricing models. Without expenditure switching, the exchange rate moves stronger in the short run than in models relying on producer's currency pricing. Over-shooting is therefore possible in local currency pricing models.

An unanticipated monetary expansion in the home country improves home country's terms of trade in the short run, since home firm's export prices in home's currency increase with the nominal depreciation while the import prices at home are unaffected owing to local currency pricing. This is the opposite result to that in Obstfeld and Rogoff (1995). The consequence is that "beggar-my-neighbour" policy results from these models; not because of an expenditure switching effect but because the home country's monetary expansion reduces the terms-of-trade of the foreign country (Betts and Devereux 2000). A monetary expansion in such a setting induces a positive real wealth effect for individuals in the home country, which results from the improved terms of trade and increases output and consumption in the short run.

An interesting consequence of fixed prices in local currency is the deviation of the interest rate in both countries after an unanticipated monetary expansion in the home country. This deviation occurs despite a perfectly integrated asset market. Since the interest rate is directly linked to consumption growth, the interest rate at home falls relative to the initial rate and relative to the foreign interest rate. The reason is the diverging consumption pattern. While consumption grows proportionally to money in the initial period in the home country, foreign consumption is unaffected. Since future consumption at home is unchanged with pre-set prices for only one period, the interest rate at home must fall in the shock period because with rising prices in the future, shock period's savings are worth less in terms of consumption units. Foreign consumption is unchanged in all periods.

With no consumption smoothing in either country, there are no current account dynamics. The home country produces and consumes more in the initial period but does not spread the higher income to the following periods. The consumption path in the foreign country is completely unchanged. The monetary expansion does not create a trade imbalance with local currency pricing. The full effect of the expansionary policy occurs in the initial period. After this, money is neutral which stands in sharp contrast to the results of Obstfeld and Rogoff (1995).

It is the reaction of the current account following a major change in economic policy which leads Obstfeld and Rogoff to herald producer country's currency pricing (Obstfeld and Rogoff 2000). Although they admit that the pass-though is not one or not even close to one, they argue that improvements in the current account usually follow depreciations. Depreciations are empirically related to deteriorations and not to improvements of the term of trade (as the local currency pricing would predict). Yet, producers' currency pricing implies that the law of one price holds which is also not supported by the data (Froot et al. 1995). Both modelling strategies can however be tested in a nested empirical model which might be the appropriate jury in this debate.

Challenges

Empirical tests identify the two main challenges for further refinements of the new open economy macroeconomics (NOEM) approach. The results indicate direct and indirect support for both local currency pricing and producer currency pricing. That is troubling because the policy advice in both models differs a lot. Yet, the observed low pass-through might stem from other sources than local currency pricing (such as the distribution chain) and might therefore be compatible with expenditure switching effects. Moreover, currency invoicing of exports and imports should be endogenous (Bacchetta and van Wincoop 2005). Firms in countries with a stable monetary policy should opt for producer country pricing of their exports whereas exporters from countries with unstable monetary policies choose to stabilize their mark-ups by invoicing in importers currency. In addition, Goldberg and Tille (2008) present evidence for invoicing in a third (vehicle) currency, something that cannot arise in a two-country model. This vehicle currency denomination is well explained by industry characteristics as opposed to macroeconomic effects and the need of producers to match prices set by competitors located in other countries.

Overall, the models seem to overstate the effects of economic integration of countries. Even within the European Union, the cross-border transmission of shocks is by far smaller than the models would suggest. Obstfeld and Rogoff (2001) claim that the introduction of plausible iceberg trade costs in standard international macroeconomics models could explain the several – six – major puzzles, including the low-consumption-correlation puzzle, which expresses the observation that the high degree of consumption smoothing and therefore risk sharing implied in the models is not matched by consumers behaviour found in data.

Yet, the most severe challenge is posed by the failure of the models to predict exchange rate movements. Exchange rate movements are necessarily explained by fundamentals in the models. The models rely on both the law of one price and the uncovered interest parity, neither of which find overwhelming support in empirical studies. Even worse, empirically, the exchange rate is barely related to any macroeconomic variable in non-crisis situations. Note the large fraction of exogenous deviations from the purchasing power parity in explaining exchange rate movements in Lubik and Schorfheide (2006). This dissatisfactory phenomenon is found in so many studies that it even got a name: the exchange rate disconnect puzzle (Obstfeld and Rogoff 2001). For a theoretical framework that has been started to explain the transmission of monetary and exchange rate shocks between countries, exchange rate disconnect is frustrating and calls for more research.

Notwithstanding the poor performance in predicting exchange rate movements, central banks (which are usually mainly interested in domestic prices and output forecasts) all over the world have been using the framework for policy analyses (Smets and Wouters 2003, for example). They calibrate problem-tailored versions of NOEM models on specific situations of their economy to conduct quantitative policy analyses. NOEM models have thus become the workhorse of quantitative models to evaluate economic – and particularly monetary – policy.

The NOEM framework mainly concentrates on flexible exchange rate regimes. However, the debate about the appropriate exchange rate regime has not been spurred by the new framework. The small interest in fixed exchange rates has three roots: first, the main currencies float; second, there has been found little difference in the short-run behaviour of macroeconomic variables in countries with fixed relative to those in flexible exchange rate regime countries (exchange rate disconnect puzzle: Obstfeld and Rogoff 2000; Devereux and Engel 2002); and third, when studying fixed exchange rates using the small-economy version of the NOEM framework, very low welfare costs of exchange rate pegs have been found (Kollmann 2002; Galí and Monachelli 2005). The euro area with its within-pegged exchange rates has been changing this focus on flexible exchange rates (see Schmitt-Grohé and Uribe 2012). Given the continuing crisis in the European Monetary Union (EMU), a deeper understanding of the functioning of a currency union is desperately needed.

JOERN KLEINERT

See also:

Balance of payments and exchange rates (III); John Maynard Keynes (I); Keynesianism (II); Macroeconomics (III); Robert Alexander Mundell (I); New Keynesianism (II).

References and further reading

Bacchetta, P. and E. van Wincoop (2005), 'A theory of the currency denomination of international trade', *Journal of International Economics*, **67** (2), 295–319.

Baxter, M. and A. Stockman (1989), 'Business cycles and the exchange rate regime: some international evidence', *Journal of Monetary Economics*, **23** (May), 377–400.

Bergin, P. (2003), 'Putting the new open economy macroeconomics to a test', *Journal of International Economics*, **60** (1), 3–34.

Betts, C. and M. Devereux (2000), 'Exchange rate dynamics in a model of pricing-to-market', *Journal of International Economics*, **50** (1), 215–44.

Blanchard, O. and N. Kiyotaki (1987), 'Monopolistic competition and the effects of aggregated demand', *American Economic Review*, **77** (4), 647–66.

Corsetti, G. and P. Pesenti (2001), 'Welfare and macroeconomic interdependence', *Quarterly Journal of Economics*, **116** (2), 421–45.

Devereux, M. and C. Engel (2001), 'The optimal choice of the exchange rate regime: price-setting rules and internationalized production', in M. Blomstrom and L. Goldberg (eds), *Topics in Empirical International Economics: A Festschrift in Honor of Robert E. Lipsey*, Chicago, IL and London: University of Chicago Press, pp. 163–94.

Devereux, M. and C. Engel (2002), 'Exchange rate pass-through, exchange rate volatility, and exchange rate disconnect', *Journal of Monetary Economics*, **49** (5), 913–40.

Dornbusch, R. (1976), 'Expectations and exchange rate dynamics', *Journal of Political Economy*, **84** (6), 1161–76.

Fleming, M. (1962), 'Domestic financial policies under fixed and under floating exchange rates', *IMF Staff Papers*, **9**, 369–79.

Froot, K., M. Kim and K. Rogoff (1995), 'The law of one price over seven hundred years', NBER Working Paper no. 5132, National Bureau of Economic Research, Cambridge, MA.

Galí, J. and T. Monacelli (2005), 'Monetary policy and exchange rate volatility in a small open economy', *Review of Economic Studies*, **72** (3), 707–34.

Goldberg, L. and C. Tille (2008), 'Vehicle currency use in international trade', *Journal of International Economics*, **76** (2), 177–92.

Keynes, J.M. (1930), *A Treatise on Money*, reprinted in D. Moggridge (ed.) (1971), *The Collected Writings of John Maynard Keynes*, vols V and VI, London: Macmillan, and Cambridge: Cambridge University Press.

Keynes, J.M. (1936), *The General Theory of Employment, Interest and Money*, reprinted 1973 in *The Collected Writings of John Maynard Keynes*, vol. VII, London: Macmillan and St Martin's Press.

Kollmann, R. (2002), 'Monetary policy rules in the open economy: effects on welfare and business cycles', *Journal of Monetary Economics*, **49** (5), 989–1015.

Lubik, T. and F. Schorfheide (2006), 'A Bayesian look at new open economy macroeconomics', *NBER Macroeconomics Annual 2005*, **20**, 313–82.

Meade, J.E. (1951), *The Balance of Payment: Mathematical Supplement*, Oxford: Oxford University Press.

Meese, R. and K. Rogoff (1983), 'Empirical exchange rate models of the seventies: do they fit out of sample?', *Journal of International Economics*, **14** (1–2), 3–24.

Meese, R. and K. Rogoff (1988), 'Was it real? The exchange rate-interest differential relation over the modern floating-rate period', *Journal of Finance*, **43** (4), 933–48.

Mundell, R. (1961), 'The international disequilibrium system', *Kyklos*, **14** (2), 153–72.

Mundell, R. (1963), 'Capital mobility and stabilization policy under fixed and flexible exchange rates', *Canadian Journal of Economics and Political Science*, **29** (4), 475–85.

Obstfeld, M. and K. Rogoff (1995), 'Exchange rate dynamics redux', *Journal of Political Economy*, **102** (3), 624–40.

Obstfeld, M. and K. Rogoff (1996), *Foundations of International Macroeconomics*, Cambridge, MA: MIT Press.

Obstfeld, M. and K. Rogoff (2000), 'New directions for stochastic open economy models', *Journal of International Economics*, **50** (1), 117–53.

Obstfeld, M. and K. Rogoff (2001), 'The six major puzzles in international macroeconomics: is there a common cause?', *NBER Macroeconomics Annual 2000*, **15**, 339–90.

Samuelson, P. (1947), *Foundations of Economic Analysis*, Cambridge, MA: Harvard University Press.

Schmitt-Grohé, S. and M. Uribe (2012), 'Pegs and pain', mimeo, Columbia University.

Smets, F. and R. Wouters (2003), 'An estimated stochastic dynamic general equilibrium model of the euro area', *Journal of Economic Association*, **1** (5), 1123–75.

Vines, D. (2003), 'John Maynard Keynes 1937–1946: the creation of international macroeconomics: a review article on John Maynard Keynes 1937–1946: fighting for Britain by Robert Skidelsky', *The Economic Journal*, **113** (488), F338–F361.

Young, W. and W. Darity Jr (2004), 'IS–LM–BP: an inquest', *History of Political Economy*, **36** (Supplement 1), 127–64.

Political philosophy and economics: freedom and labour

The relationship between freedom and labour is a ground for reflection where political philosophy meets economics. A good point of departure in this regard is Georg Wilhelm Friedrich Hegel's well-known general reflection regarding freedom: "the East knew and to the present day knows only that One is Free; the Greek and Roman world, that some are free; the German World knows that All are free" (Hegel 1837 [2001]: 121). The concept of freedom is understood here in the sense of political freedom, that is, a social status recognized by the state, which allows the person to take part in the decisions concerning the future of the city. The evolution of the concept of political freedom through European history could be summarized as a general transition from what we can call, following Hegel, "freedom for some" to "freedom for all". This transition is essentially made possible by the recognition of labour as a fundamental dimension of man. In Europe, from the end of the sixteenth century, an increasingly ontological value was conferred on labour, to the point that Karl Marx in 1844 went so far as to say that "[Hegel] thus grasps the essence of labour and comprehends objective man – true, because real man – as the outcome of man's own labour (*als Resultat seinereignen Arbeit*)" (1844 [1975]: 332–3). Besides, it is highly significant that the disciples of Claude Henri de Saint-Simon, one of the most powerful thinkers regarding the transformation European society experienced in modern times, characterized the latter as the "reign of labour" (Bazard and Enfantin 1829 [1924]: 96). Further, in 1858, Pierre-Joseph Proudhon wrote that "who works prays" (1858 [1932]: 178), understanding by this that in modern times labour replaces religion. In this entry, a set of concepts will be invoked in order to analyse the transition from ancient Greece up to now. Consequently, it is this specific choice of concepts which dictates the selection of the authors canvassed in the reflections that follow. Such an exercise is not exhaustive, but lays emphasis on the internal consistency of the reasoning and some essential steps in the evolution of the idea.

In a world characterized by the first form of freedom, the exclusion of economic activities outside the city is the condition of the political freedom for some. Some men, deprived of freedom, have to work to allow others to be free. However, this exclusive opposition between freedom and labour – or more generally economic activities – evolved over time. Through European history, labour was progressively integrated into the sphere of political freedom. A new representation of freedom emerged progressively and supposed that you could not consider yourself as free in a society where some others were reduced to the rank of simple "animate tools" or simple objects. This new concept of freedom for all requested a positive conception of labour. The progressive integration of economic life into the city constituted, in Europe, a determining element of the conditions of modern freedom or freedom for all. Labour experienced a deep process of rehabilitation.

This entry first deals with the ancient world where the existence of politically non-free individuals was the condition for free individuals (Plato and Aristotle). Second, we set out the progressive emergence of the recognition of economic activities which is accompanied by a recognition of labour and of the workers (John Locke and Max Weber). Since the workers became citizens and were no more "outsiders", this second movement led to modern freedom for all. Third, the intuitive or immediate implications of the concept of freedom for all were formulated in terms of freedom of action, which puts the stress on the division of labour rather than on the role of the state. However, this third step does not lead to demanding conceptual reflection on political freedom (Bernard Mandeville, Scottish Enlightenment and, later, Friedrich Hayek). A fourth section presents a few political philosophers who questioned the concept of freedom for all. Their interrogation involves an examination of the conditions of the practice of freedom and of the role of the state. The authors under consideration include Jean-Jacques Rousseau, Immanuel Kant, Georg Wilhelm Friedrich Hegel, Karl Marx, John Rawls and Amartya Sen.

Freedom and Labour in the Ancient World

The concept of freedom emerges in the ancient world in a social context where the vision of labour as a condition incompatible with the freedom of man is in evidence. A free man, in the full sense of the term, that is, as a citizen, discharges the burden of efforts necessary to ensure his material existence onto politically non-free men. To put it differently, in the ancient world, political freedom, which confers to the individual the fully fledged status of citizen, is the condition of a person with private means, a "rentier", who has at his disposal sufficient labour force, that is, slaves, to be exempt from economic activity. Ancient society reduces a part of the population to the rank of objects, that is, to the rank of what Aristotle called a simple "animate tool" (Aristotle, 1885: 1253b 32), so that freedom existed for the rest of society. According to Moses I. Finley: "one aspect of Greek history . . . is the advance, hand in hand, of freedom *and* slavery" (1981: 115, original emphasis). In this world freedom does not exclude slavery; rather, the latter is a condition of the former.

In the fourth book of his *Republic*, Plato observes that in a just city three virtues must necessarily be present: wisdom, courage, temperance. For him, the first virtue belongs to the first class of the city, the guardians, the second characterizes the second class, that is, "the part which fights and goes out to war on the State's behalf". The reader would expect that the third virtue, "temperance", be expected from the rest of the population, that is, the part which works and produces. However, concerning temperance, Socrates underlines expressly that all of the members of the city share this virtue. In other words, the third part of the city does not have any specific virtue as do the other two classes. Jean-Pierre Vernant, commenting on this passage of *Republic*, stresses this significant asymmetry:

> This surprising asymmetry cannot be explained but by Plato's refusal to grant a positive virtue to those whose labour constitutes their social function. We can say that according to Plato labour remains unfamiliar to any human value and under certain aspects it appears to him as the antithesis of what in the human being is essential. (Vernant 1974: 12, our translation)

Through his profound knowledge of ancient Greece, Friedrich Nietzsche observes that in this world both labour and slavery were "a necessary disgrace, of which one feels *ashamed*, as a disgrace and a necessity at the same time" (Nietzsche 1911: 6, original emphasis). As much as possible the free man of the antique democratic state tries to get rid of the necessity of labour by passing it on to slaves. This does not mean that no free man works in this society. However, the condition of the real exercise of citizenship is incompatible with labour. A man who is forced to work could not be a good citizen able to dedicate himself entirely to the business of the city. One can say that in this society labour is rejected "outside the state" (ibid.: 122), out of the sphere of political freedom.

According to Aristotle and also to all the other thinkers of antiquity, to be free means essentially not to depend on the will of another person. A non-free man is a man who is forced to obey the orders of another's will. In this sense the producer or the labourer, from an exclusively economic point of view, is necessarily a non-free, dependent person because he or she obeys the will of the buyer who orders the work and pays for it. The difference between the free and non-free conditions can be specified by resorting to a conceptual difference, which was well known in ancient Greece, between *Poïesis* and *Praxis*. *Poïesis* is an activity, which gives birth to a product untied to its author. In this sense all activities of production, whatever they are, are considered as stemming from *Poïesis*. The product leaves its author and acquires an autonomous, exclusive existence. The agent has no control over his productive process when his activity is of *poïetic* type. The German philosophers of the nineteenth century describe this condition of becoming an outsider regarding one's own product by a reference to the notion of "estrangement" (*Entfremdung*). *Praxis* instead means an activity the finality of which does not escape its author. Sport, music, philosophy, science are these kind of activities. Through such activities the individual develops the force and the abilities of his body or his intellectual endowment and competences. The result of the activity does not leave its author. Consequently, activities which suit the free man are those which stem from *Praxis*. But when a *poïetic* activity is achieved freely, that is when the individual achieves it without being subjected to the constraint to work in order to ensure his subsistence, such an activity does not degrade him. In short, in this world, labour in its economic sense, that is, wage labour, degrades and enslaves its author. The salaried worker, whatever the particular activity he carries out, is necessarily in a demeaning situation.

The Emergence of Labour as a Positive Value

The main step towards modern freedom or freedom for all lies with the recognition of economic activity by political philosophers. This recognition comes along with that of labour and of the workers. Hence, if the workers are no longer considered as "outsiders", if they are allowed to take an active part in society, they acquire the status of full citizens and their political rights could no longer be ignored. Some major political philosophers participated in this movement, exemplified here by the two prominent figures of John Locke and Max Weber: although they are ages apart from one another, they correspond respectively to a rehabilitation of labour through the law of nature, or in reference to the emergence of a new spirituality in Europe. You cannot ignore the role played by Christianity in such a process of emergence.

Locke, labour and property
In particular with his *Two Treatises of Government* (1690 [2008]), Locke is traditionally seen as one of the founders of political liberalism. Indeed, his rejection of absolutism and his praise of representative government proceeds from man's natural liberty and natural equality. Locke (1690 [2008], s. 22: 283, original emphasis) writes: "the *Natural Liberty* of Man is to be free from any Superior Power on Earth, and not to be under the Will or Legislative Authority of Man, but to have only the Law of Nature for his rule". The law of nature is thus a key element in Locke since it defines the rights and the duties of every man in the state of nature. This state is not without law, in which everyone could

pursue his own ends without paying attention to others. On the contrary, each man has not only to preserve his life, freedom and possessions, but others' as well. Therefore, if men who are in the state of nature have the duty to obey the law of nature, they have as well the freedom to contravene it but must be punished in consequence. But Locke stresses that this "right to punish the offender" could go too far and lead to "confusion" and "disorder": "it is unreasonable for Men to be Judges in their own Cases . . . Self-love will make Men partial to themselves and their Friends. And on the other side, that Ill Nature, Passion and Revenge will carry them too far in punishing others" (ibid.: s. 13: 275). The solution proposed by Locke to alleviate the drawbacks of the state of nature is the constitution of a civil government. It is common to stress that Locke's description of the drawbacks of the state of nature – which leads to the state of war – has close links with Hobbes's "war of everyone against everyone". However, while Locke pleads for a civil government, which guarantees freedom and equality to everyone, Thomas Hobbes follows a very different path in *Leviathan* (1651 [1996]). According to Locke, the civil government must respect freedom, security and equality.

In addition to the protection of these three natural rights the civil government has to guarantee a fourth one: private property, which proceeds as well from the law of nature. At the beginning, property is common since "God . . . hath given the World to Men in common" (Locke 1690 [2008], s. 26: 286) but thanks to their work human beings are capable of translating this common property into a private one. Here lies one of the most original points of Locke's thought: by considering private property as a natural right Locke based its justification on labour:

> though the Earth, and all inferior Creatures be common to all Men, yet every Man has a *Property* in his own *Person*. This no Body has any Right to but himself. The *Labour* of his Body, and the *Work* of his Hands, we may say, are properly his. Whatsoever then he removes out of the State that Nature hath provided, and left it in, he hath mixed his *Labour* with, and joined to it something that is his own, and thereby makes it his *Property* . . . For this Labour being the unquestionable Property of the Labourer, no Man but he can have a right to what that is once joyned to, at least where there is enough, and as good left in common for others. (Ibid.: s. 27: 287–8)

You can clearly observe here that labour (and thus the labourer who enjoys the property of his own labour) plays a key role in Locke, since it makes it possible to distinguish between the things which are held in common and those which belong to the labourer. By "removing them out of that common state" (ibid.: s. 28: 289, original emphasis), the labourer acquires the right to own them. Locke thus states two major ideas: on the one hand, the property right is natural, it does not depend on someone else's or civil government's consent; on the other hand, the relationship between human beings and nature is defined through labour: men are not political animals, they are owners and labourers. Further, at first sight Locke establishes some limits to property rights: men could not take more than their shares – what they could use, eat, drink . . . before it goes bad – the rest belongs to others. It should be noted that these limits are also valid for the property of the land: "*the chief matter of* Property being . . . the *Earth it self*" (ibid.: s. 32: 290, original emphasis). However, with the invention of money Locke remarks that these limits do not apply anymore. By consent, men could amass wealth. At the same time, Locke seems to regret this situation but accepts its consequences, since it comes from a mutual agreement. Thus the subsequent inequalities could not be corrected. Finally, even if there is still some doubt about the way Locke sees the enlargement of somebody's possessions beyond his personal needs thanks to money, it remains that the philosopher shed light on labour and labourers as producers of value. This is a major step towards freedom for all.

Max Weber, labour and the new spirituality

Let us now turn to Max Weber's analyses – particularly his *Protestant Ethics and the Spirit of Capitalism* – which provide valuable conceptual elements for a better understanding of the process of recognition of labour. Weber expends great effort to conceptualize the modern attitude of the European individual regarding labour. He describes and analyses the radical transformation of the ethical and practical experience of labour in modern times.

The "spirit of capitalism" could not in any way be described by what in Latin is called *auri sacra fames*, "the greed for gold" (Weber 1904–05 [1958]: 56). On the contrary, the thirst for wealth is a human tendency, as old as humanity itself.

Capitalism requires rather a self-discipline to master this unlimited thirst of wealth, this "universal reign of absolute unscrupulousness" (Weber 1904–05 [1958]: 57). Weber starts his inquiry by quoting large extracts of Benjamin Franklin's *Advice to a Young Tradesman* (1748), where the American scientist and entrepreneur pronounces his famous advice: "Remember that time is money". However, even if the young tradesman is expressly invited to make money grow indefinitely, it is essential that this resolute will to earn "more and more money" be done in the frame of "legality", that is, under a strict ethical discipline. Earning money becomes one of the ultimate ends of ethical action and in this sense the Aristotelian perspective is radically reversed. However, this reversal is in no way a transgression of all ethical principles, in no way a complaisant settling in the "absolute reign of unscrupulousness". A new ethos governs human behaviour: an ethos which is neither "eudaemonistic" nor "hedonistic" (ibid.: 53). The major Weberian concept is *Beruf* which, as the word "calling", also relates back to the concept of vocation. Weber recalls that Luther preferred *Beruf* in his translation of the Bible, as an equivalent to the Hebraic word "work" – prior to Luther, in German versions of the Bible the same word was consistently translated as *Arbeit*. In his careful translation of Weber's book, Jean-Pierre Grossein proposed the term "profession-vocation" as equivalent to the concept of *Beruf* (Grossein 2002: 657).

Understanding Lutheran choice requires a reference to the well-known Protestant dogma of predestination (*Gnadenwahl*). According to this dogma, the destiny of the believer, that is his state of election beside the divinity, is decided independently of his will and his actions, even before his coming into the world. There is no possibility for a Protestant believer to have an influence on this decision: he has no chance to charm the divinity in order to obtain his benevolence or his favour. In such a religious context, the sacrifice, that is, all "techniques of salvation", the hope to "buy" his felicity through sacraments, becomes pure illusion, the "vanity of vanities"; this is a world of "disenchantment" (*Entzauberung*). Predestination pushes the believer necessarily into an "unprecedented pessimism". Therefore, in such an existence marked by vanity the only mode of non-illusory behaviour appears to be asceticism.

However, Weber distinguishes two types of asceticism: an otherworldly asceticism (*ausserweltliche Askese*) and a "worldly asceticism" (*innerweltliche Askese*) of a Protestant type. The former corresponds to the classical monastic type of asceticism, which is an asceticism that leads the believer to leave the world and to devote himself to meditation, avoiding as much as possible any worldly enjoyment or pleasure. Capitalism could not form and develop with such a passive and unproductive behaviour. The second type of asceticism is as rigorous as the first but the believer stays in the world and exercises a profession, a *Beruf*, that is, he produces while refraining from immediate enjoyment of the fruits of his labour. At first sight it is difficult to understand the reason why the individual would choose such a way in so far as he knows perfectly well that no possibility is granted to him to have any influence on the decision of the divinity. However, the work realized through his labour might bring another type of satisfaction to the believer: the more I perfect, develop and increase my work, the more it could function as the mirror of my state of election. If the work I undertake succeeds, this may be interpreted as the proof that my state of election is recognized by God since He is obviously helping me in my enterprise, and so the more I experience the good feeling of the divinity towards me. According to Weber the concept of "worldly asceticism" refers to this kind of ethical attitude: "the *summum bonum* of [this] ethics [is]: earning more and more money, combined with the strict avoidance of all spontaneous enjoyment of life" (1904–05 [1958]: 53). Franklin invites his young tradesman to adopt this ethic while reminding him expressly of one of the fundamental principles: "Beware of thinking all your own that you possess, and of living accordingly" (ibid.: 50). Weber recognizes in this "worldly asceticism" an ethical attitude ideally favourable to the development of capitalism.

Weberian analyses of the relations between Protestantism and capitalism clearly include certain idealistic, exaggerated, and even simplistic elements regarding the infinite complexity of what is called "capitalism" as a political, economic, sociological, scientific and technological phenomenon. The privilege conferred on the theological concepts of Protestantism particularly creates perplexity. Could not the same type of concepts or intuitions be found in other religions or value systems? The fundamental problem of Weber is in fact the genesis, that is, the conditions of the new vision of labour in modern society, the new relationship of the modern individual with labour. The Protestant concepts are appropriate analytical instruments in order to study this problem. In modern society labour is no longer a painful effort, a constraint, an unhappy necessity, a misfortune which descends upon man and tortures him. It is even less a degrading, demeaning, disgraceful condition than in the ancient world. From then on, labour as *Beruf* is conceived and lived as a calling, as an appeal originating from the divinity. It is conceived and lived as a duty, as a "categorical imperative", to employ Kantian terminology. This "categorical" character of labour became so oppressive, so absolute in the modern world that the modern individual assimilates it as a second nature:

> The capitalistic economy of the present day is an immense cosmos into which the individual is born, and which presents itself to him, at least as an individual, as an unalterable order of things in which he must live . . . In order that a manner of life so well adapted to the peculiarities of capitalism could be selected at all, that is, should come to dominate others, it had to originate somewhere, and not in isolated individuals alone, but as a way of life common to whole groups of men. (Weber 1904–05 [1958]: 54–5)

The necessity of working is settled in our unconscious, and becomes a "mass phenomenon" (ibid.: 57): each of us should work but nobody knows why and to what end. The more the ontological value of labour increases, the more the modern man lives and practices it as a natural necessity, the more individual actions are liberated from their ancient chains: all these issues give rise to further questions.

The "Spontaneous Order" as the Liberation of Individual Actions

Friedrich Hayek is the author who popularized the concept of "spontaneous order," which was frequently used throughout the nineteenth century. The tradition which represents the society as a spontaneous order is also named by Hayek "the tradition of the invisible hand". This means that Hayek considers the authors of the Scottish Enlightenment (Hume, Ferguson and Smith) as the fathers of the new and revolutionary vision of human society which the term "invisible hand" attempts to express. However, Hayek takes care to base the origin of this revolution on the work of Bernard Mandeville (Hayek 1966 [1967]: 134). However contestable that might seem, Hayek writes: "We owe to [Mandeville] the term of 'division of labour' and a clearer view of the nature of this phenomenon" (ibid.: 125). Even if the "term" is not an invention of Mandeville, the "nature" of the phenomenon is revealed, according to Hayek, by Mandeville. This "nature" lies in the capacity of the division of labour to coordinate a myriad of actions without any original planning in its capacity of self-regulation. The "spontaneous order" approach aims to prove the beneficial character of a society where all are free even if the concept of the state remains here unquestioned. Undoubtedly Hayek attaches undue importance to Mandeville concerning the advent of this new representation of the society as spontaneous order in the history of European thought. Such an order is largely conceptualized in the seventeenth century, in the Jansenist tradition, by authors such as Pierre Nicole and Pierre de Boisguilbert. However, as it is emphasized in the introduction, in the present entry what are privileged are the specific concepts which allow the analysis of the object of the enquiry and not the question of their authorship.

First you must refuse, says Hayek (1966 [1967]), to reduce *The Fable of the Bees* (Mandeville 1714 [1724]) to an exclusive ethical concern. The satiric poem, beyond its deliberately provocative style, reveals an interrogation of the nature and the organization of human society. Mandeville's discovery lies, according to Hayek, with his observation of the fundamental discontinuity between local and global orders. If you refer to Ferguson's well-known observation, Mandeville discovered that social "establishments . . . are indeed the result of human action, but not the execution of any human design" (Ferguson 1767 [1782]: 203). The gap between the individual design and the result of individual actions on the social level is Mandeville's real concern.

Hayek observes that until Mandeville a dichotomy between natural and artificial orders had repeatedly conditioned and governed political philosophy. Ancient Greeks called these two orders *physei* and *taxis*. Nature is governed by laws independent of the will of men. Contrary to this natural order, the human world is conceived as obeying the rules "which were the result of the deliberate arrangements of men" (Hayek [1966] 1967: 130), that is, *taxis*. Mandeville imagines a third kind of rule sharing both the necessity of the natural law and the artificiality of the human rule resulting from conscious and voluntary deliberations. In the Hayekian terminology this third kind of rule is called "abstract rules" and the order which they govern is designated by the term "spontaneous order". Abstract rules are those men obey and apply without any conscious knowledge of their content or even of their existence. The most illustrative examples of abstract rules are those which govern language. An overwhelming proportion of men make use of language without any conscious knowledge of the grammatical laws which govern it. The more the rules are integrated in the unconscious, the more their application is exact and perfect. Further, the abstract rules, in net opposition to the rules of an order as "taxis", do not aim at achieving particular ends. They are not teleological realities like the concrete rules, the justification and role of which are defined through their finality. Consequently, a deterministic logic governs individual behaviour when the latter strictly respect concrete rules. All the individuals are requested to conform to an archetypal model. Such a repetitive universe stifles greatly the capacity of innovation, since the novelty constitutes a threat for the stability of the social order governed by concrete rules. It can thus be argued that, through his *Fable*, Mandeville expresses his wish for the development of "abstract rules" in society, the emancipation of individual action from the determinism of concrete rules. This can explain why Mandeville's social analysis caused such scandal. The *Fable* totally opposes the traditional conception of ethics, which is based on the conviction of the existence of a natural and necessary positive relation between individual designs and their social result. According to traditional ethics, the condition of a good, positive, just, well-ordered society is the existence of morally good, just, honest individuals. However, such a conviction raises problems at two levels.

First, as observed above, concrete rules are governed by a teleological logic, that is, an essentially non-evolutionist logic, according to which, in the human case, the end to be reached is necessarily clearly foreseen and planned from the start. But this position is totally blind to what Smith attempts to conceptualize in his well-known remark concerning the division of labour:

> This division of labour, from which so many advantages are derived, is not originally the effect of any human wisdom, which foresees and intends that general opulence to which it gives occasion. It is the necessary, though very slow and gradual consequence of a certain propensity in human nature which has in view no such extensive utility; the propensity to truck, barter, and exchange one thing for another. (Smith 1776 [1976]: I.2.1)

In spite of the serious reservations Smith expresses regarding Mandeville's ethical position (Smith 1759 [1976]: VII, II, 98 ff.), he agrees totally with the author of the *Fable* regarding the progressive and non-teleological nature of human fact. The human edifice is built gradually, progressively, through a process of trial and error and not at the instigation of an omniscient will which defines at the origin the end the social process should necessarily reach. The evolution of societies is a process, the destination of which is necessarily unknown. The famous observation of the *Wealth of Nations* expresses the same idea: "[the individual] is in this, as in many other cases, led by an invisible hand to promote an end which was no part of his intention" (Smith 1776 [1976]: IV.2.9).

The second level is more important. The conviction relative to the continuity between local and global orders entails the danger of an authoritarian form of society, that is, a society governed exclusively by concrete rules. If the positivity of the social order depends on the nature of individual behaviours, political authorities would be perfectly within their rights to intervene forcefully and resolutely through a set of strong concrete rules in order to rectify individual behaviours according to the archetypal behavioural model they consider most appropriate. The logic called by Smith "the man of system" would invade the whole society and result in a negation of social diversity:

> The man of system . . . is apt to be very wise in his own conceit, and is often so enamoured with the supposed beauty of his own ideal plan of government, that he cannot suffer the smallest deviation from any part of it . . . he seems to imagine that he can arrange the different members of a great society with as much ease as the hand arranges the different pieces upon a chess-board. (Smith 1759 [1976]: VI.II.42)

Here the phrase "cannot suffer the smallest deviation" means the negation of the otherness as such. The man of system who is convinced of the so-called continuity between individual and collective orders regards a different behaviour – which does not conform to the one the archetypal model requires – only as a threat for the happiness of the whole: it must be eliminated. In fact what is really eliminated here is subjectivity as such since subjectivity is difference. Therefore the capacity to innovate and to create is denied in society.

Now the significance of the concept of the "invisible hand" can be understood. It does not mean simply the capacity of a society to spontaneously reach the desirable order. It refers, rather, to the motive of "confidence". The traditional vision of ethics could not adopt a positive attitude regarding the plurality of modes of existence, the plurality of actions. In the eyes of such an ethical conception the difference represents a danger and a threat. On the other hand, for the vision which points out a fundamental discontinuity between local and global orders, whatever the designs of individuals could be, there is a mechanism other than deliberate planning which coordinates individual actions and models and ensures the social order. The term "invisible hand" designates this mechanism. Therefore, the hypothesis of the invisible hand requires trust, a confidence in the beneficial character of the plurality of the individual actions even if many of the intentions which animate these actions could seem morally reprehensible. Society avoids the grip of the holistic domination of archetypical models thanks to the discovery of the beneficial effect of the infinite diversity of individual actions. In this context the concept of labour is subsumed in the concept of individual action. A society which tolerates the infinite diversity of individual actions logically recognizes the diversity of labours. The division of labour cannot develop indefinitely but by integrating the diversity of labours at its base. Such a process could be defined as a process of recognizing the positivity of *Poïesis*. In modern times *Poïesis* always acquires a more ontological value. In other terms, in modern society labour as spontaneous order becomes the driving force of the social dynamic. This observation amounts to saying that in modern times the recognizing of *Poïesis* and its infinite diversity are considered as the condition of real freedom. A free society is a society where labour and therefore the labourers are free. That means that the individual as labourer is integrated in society as a constituent part of it, on a footing of equality with all other members of the community. That is the fundamental conviction of the modern conception of the world. The tradition of the invisible hand shares unreservedly in this conviction.

Freedom for All: Freedom and its Conditions of Exercise

The great work of the Scottish Enlightenment tradition was the discovery of society as a spontaneous order. However, this tradition did not meditate sufficiently on the political dimension of the aforementioned process of recognizing and liberation. The thinkers of this tradition did not make sufficient effort to acknowledge that such a process could not be developed without a substantial role devoted to the state. The liberation of action, or the integration of the diversity of labours in the space of freedom, requires a complex process of recognition: recognition of the fundamental equality of individuals. The development of the division of labour, the formation of what Smith calls the "Great society", supposes the liberation of individual actions, hence the freedom of all individuals. However, men do not acquire freedom through a natural evolution, by virtue of the trial and error principle. Such an acquisition supposes a real and deep spiritual, economic and political mutation which definitively abolishes personal dependences, that is, the possibility of the submission of some to the will of others. Rousseau, Kant, Hegel and Marx and, later, Rawls and Sen could be considered as theoreticians who attempted to conceptualize the significance of this form of freedom and thus who contributed to this mutation.

The access to freedom for all requires an intervention. On the one hand, Rousseau and, on the other, Kant, the most rigorous follower of the French philosopher in political philosophy, through their concept of will, might allow the identification of the signification of such an intervention. Only the awareness of the equality of all and its implementation by specific laws can explain the advent of a modality of social existence as freedom for all. The transition from freedom for some to freedom for all presumes a resolution, a political act. Such a political act cannot but be the result of the "general will" in the case of Rousseau and the "good will" (Kant 1785 [1949]: 12) in the case of Kant. In this context one could claim that these two philosophers are the thinkers of the discontinuity in so far as the advent of the awareness of the equality of all cannot be conceived as the result of an evolutionary, a simple trial and error process.

Rousseau and the general will

For some commentators the main achievement of Rousseau's philosophical enquiry does not lie in his social contract hypothesis. As Vaughan (1962) and Derathé (1970) emphasize, the social contract theory is as old as European political thought, and as such it constitutes the weakest part of Rousseau's work. Rousseau's main achievement is his concept of "general will" and his analyses which present and develop the general will as the condition of freedom for all. "There is often a considerable difference between the will of all and the general will: the latter looks only to the common interest, the former looks to private interest, and is nothing but a sum of particular wills" (Rousseau 1762 [2007]: 60). In what sense is this concept of general will as expressing the common interest to be understood? For Rousseau the state of nature is the reign of absolute physical independence of beings who inhabit it. No constraint, no necessity exist there to compel them to submit themselves to the domination of another (Rousseau 1754 [1997]: 149). That is, there is no necessity to force the beings of the state of nature to abandon it in favour of the state of culture. In such a context only an unnatural cause could explain the transition to this state of culture. This motivation could not be imagined but as the "will". However, Rousseau thinks that a community could not wish to abandon a state where all enjoy physical independence to move into a state where this independence could be lost, at least for a part of the community. The new state could be desired only if it affords a superior mode of existence, only if the purely physical independence is promoted to the rank of freedom which is the cultural equivalent of physical independence, that is, "autonomy". The general will is thus the outcome of the will which allows the human beings of the state of nature to abandon the latter. Such a will could be a particular aptitude or tendency. It is to be supposed that it is a common aptitude, in other words it is a property inherent in human nature itself. We owe to Kant the remarkable analytical effort which brought a philosophical rigour to this difficult concept of will.

Kant and the good will
For Kant the problem of freedom or autonomy is not approached from the point of view of the problem of the transition from the state of nature to the state of culture, since such a transition is non representable. However, through his interrogation of the properties of the moral subject Kant observes that the condition of freedom lies, as for Rousseau, in a "will" each man as a man harbours within himself. The stress must be put here on the fact that the will, which is at stake in Kantian analyses, does not stem from desires or inclinations but from a feeling of "duty" the author calls the "categorical imperative". Also, this duty is not the product of a worldly experience; it is the product of reason in so far as a moral subject, whatever his specific conditions, is endowed with reason in the same way as he is endowed with instincts or sentiments. The will which obeys this duty is the will governed by reason, the "good will". Each moral subject as a member of the cogitable world wants, under the requisites of the categorical imperative, freedom and autonomy that is the cultural equivalent of physical independence in Rousseau's terminology. Here the concept of the social contract takes on its full meaning. Not an imaginary deliberation or negotiation which is supposed to lead the contractors to freedom, but a structure in which nobody can refuse to be free.

In the Kantian philosophical handling of Rousseau's political concepts and intuitions, the social contract theory loses all its positivist and arbitrary features and becomes the theory of the individual considered as the subject of moral law and as a rational being whose will is supposed to be necessarily "a universally legislating will". When Kant says that "we must use humanity in our own person as an end", he means that the human person, in his capacity as a member of the cogitable world, is equivalent to humanity and as such has to be considered as an absolute end. Such a conception of morality has nothing to do with any individualism. In line with Kant's reasoning, Hegel's concept of State represents the political community which recognizes the human person as an absolute end; as such the Hegelian state incarnates the general will. However, the question of the state is complex. The state, more exactly the states, always existed. The problem of Rousseau, Kant or Hegel is not so much to reach the essence of the state in general but to analyse the conditions of possibility of the state thanks to which all are free, to question the conditions of the abolition of "all personal dependence". Both Rousseau's "general will" and Kantian "good will" are above all attempts to conceptualize the political structure of freedom for all. However, on this matter Hegel goes further than Rousseau and Kant. His conception of the good and the general will is rigorously in line with

Rousseau's and Kant's, but concerning the modern state Hegel is attentive to the new social sphere through which labour is rehabilitated and the labourers recognized. This new social sphere is the "civil society". You could say that Hegel returns to the discovery of the Scottish Enlightenment through Rousseau and Kant.

Hegel, state and civil society

Hegel adopts and integrates the concept of "civil society" in his political and philosophical system under the name of *Bürgerliche Gesellschaft*. The main feature of this new vision of the society is that a new sphere obtains between the private and public spheres, which could be characterized as "social sphere", "between the family and the state" (Hegel 1821 [1967]: s. 182, addendum), where economic activity develops. However, Hegel emphasizes that the formation of civil society "follows later in time than that of the state" (ibid.). We must understand by this remark that civil society is a sphere based in the modern world thanks to a new conception of the state. The latter abolishes all personal dependence among individuals and so allows the liberation of individual actions. In this sense the modern state appears as the condition of civil society as a spontaneous order. The modern state, which learns progressively not to consider the subjectivity or the difference as a danger and a threat for its integrity, gives vent to the creative capacity of individual actions. In connection with this theme of subjectivity and individual creativeness, the praise directed by Marx to the Hegelian conception of man which is recalled in the introduction is highly meaningful:

> The outstanding achievement of Hegel's *Phänomenologie* and of its final outcome, the dialectic of negativity as the moving and generating principle, is thus first that Hegel conceives the self-creation (*Selbsterzeugung*) of man as a process . . . that he thus grasps the essence of labour and comprehends objective man – true, because real man – as the outcome of man's own labour (*als Resultat seinereignen Arbeit*). (Marx 1844 [1975]: 332–3)

According to Hegel, modern man, the member of civil society, is not only a simple labourer who creates goods and products. More profoundly, he is the product of his own labour. In other words, the civil society is the space of the recognizing and rehabilitation of the infinite value of labour as the essence of man. In Hegelian political and philosophical thought, freedom and labour are two concepts inseparably linked.

The originality of the Hegelian conception of modern society lies in its observation of the close complementarity between civil society and modern state, between the bourgeois and the citizen. The bourgeois is not seen exclusively in his negative face, as a purely egoistic individual, a mean-minded economic agent whose exclusive motivation is to maximize his private comfort. Obviously an individual who obeys such a motivation reduces necessarily all of his relations with others to instrumental ones and considers the other as a simple means at the disposal of his own interests. Yet Hegel is deeply aware of the negativity carried out by civil society; he calls it the "false infinite" (Hegel 1821 [1967]: s. 185 add). That is the reason why in the Hegelian system civil society could not pretend to a self-sufficient reality. Civil society abandoned to its logic of "false infinite" destroys itself necessarily. However, for Hegel, civil society is also the space of a highly positive phenomenon. The bourgeois represents the figure of an individual who is for himself his own end in the sense that he enjoys the juridical and material conditions of his own realization of himself, his subjectivity. Civil society allows individuals to achieve their specific potentialities by freeing them from the constraint of the personal dependence relations. More exactly, the removal of this constraint through the intervention of the modern state gives birth to the emergence of civil society. In Hegelian terminology there is a dialectical relation between civil society and modern state in the sense that each of them is the justification (*raison d'être*) of the other.

It is well known that Marx criticizes this Hegelian positive conception of the complementarity between civil society and modern state, between bourgeois and citizen, in particular in "Zur Judenfrage" (Marx 1843 [1963]) and *Zur Kritik der Hegelschen Rechtsphilosophie* (Marx 1843–44 [1994]). The Marxian critique also concerns the question of the freedom for all. In his analysis of the alienated labour, which finds its rigorous expression in his *Ökonomisch-philosophische Manuskripte aus dem Jahre 1844*, Marx stresses the violence which undermines civil society, a violence Hegel omits to face: the class struggle. On close examination, unbearable relations of exploitation of labour deform the beautiful space of the emancipation of the subjectivity. If Hegel refuses to face this tortured reality the reason lies, according to Marx, in his non-questioning of the issue of private property, especially the private property of the means of production. Marx considers that modern society is too far from achieving the conditions of freedom for all. Because of private property of the means of production, the overwhelming part of civil society is totally subjected to the will of the private owners of productive forces. The freedom of civil society is only a formal one, says Marx.

On the other hand, in his often relevant criticism of Hegelian political philosophy, Marx greatly misjudges the decisive philosophical importance of the difference between understanding (*Verstand*) and (dialectical) reason (*Vernunft*). It seems that this misjudgement could be explained by a certain "romanticism" Marx used to adopt as regards politics: he always distrusted the major operation of Hegelian philosophy, namely, the "mediation" (*Vermittelung*). Hegelian analysis shows admirably that modern man is the seat of a difficult tension between the particular and the universal. The romantic vision tries to overcome this tension. However, such a tension seems to be the condition of the development of subjectivity in society. Among the contemporary philosophers, one of the authors who best integrates in his reflection the importance of this tension through the Hegelian concept of "reconciliation" is John Rawls.

Rawls and Sen on formal and real freedom

On the same path as that paved by Rousseau, Kant and Hegel, some contemporary philosophers and economists have succeeded in defining the most advanced theories regarding the concept of freedom for all. These last philosophical developments correspond to a specific kind of liberalism called by Rawls "liberalism of freedom". According to him, the first principles of this kind of liberalism are "principles of political and civic freedoms, and these principles have a priority over other principles that may also be invoked" (Rawls 2000: 330). Rawls does not hesitate to stress also: "I see [Hegel] as an important exemplar in the history of moral and political philosophy of the *liberalism of freedom*. Other such exemplars are Kant and, less obviously, J.S. Mill. (*A Theory of Justice* is also a liberalism of freedom and learns much from them)" (ibid., fn. 3, original emphasis). According to Rawls, this new concept, the liberalism of freedom, contrasts with the liberalism of the classic utilitarians (Bentham, James Mill and Sidgwick) which he calls liberalism of happiness. This entry focuses on the way Rawls and another modern thinker, Amartya Sen, consider the effectiveness of the concept of freedom for all, that is, real freedom. Rawls in particular concurs with Hegel on this subject since both authors attempt to understand freedom together with its conditions: their works are more focused on the concrete meaning of freedom (Ege and Igersheim 2008). Hence, Rawls deals with an ambitious objective: to propose a theory which makes it possible to reconcile in a concrete way freedom, that is, the rational, the freedom of the moderns and Locke's tradition, with equality, that is, the reasonable, the freedom of the ancients and Rousseau's tradition. He claims that the conflict between the two types of traditions is solved within his "second" theory: political liberalism (Rawls 1993).

The reconciliation is ensured by the fact that the principles of justice apply to the basic structure of society and promote real freedoms, not just formal ones. The two principles of justice are described as follows (Rawls 1993: 291):

> (1) each person has an equal right to a fully adequate scheme of equal basic liberties which is compatible with a similar scheme of liberties for all. (2) Social and economic inequalities are to satisfy two conditions. First, they must be attached to offices and positions open to all under conditions of fair equality of opportunity; and second, they must be to the greatest benefit of the least advantaged members of society.

The first principle has priority over the second (equal basic rights and liberties) and the first part of the second principle (fair equality of opportunity) has priority over the second part (difference principle). It must be stressed that there is a change in the first principle of justice compared with what Rawls stated in *A Theory of Justice* (1971 [1999]): the phrase "a fully adequate scheme" replaces "the most extensive total system". What is the significance of this "new" first principle of justice? In the first place, the priority of liberties and of the first principle means that a basic liberty can be limited only for the sake of another basic liberty, but for no other kind of considerations. In the second place, granting a particular position to political liberties allows the basic liberties to be not merely formal. Indeed, if social and economic inequalities are too large, "those with greater responsibility and wealth can control the course of legislation to their advantage" (Rawls 1993: 325). Therefore, Rawls distinguishes basic liberties and their worth or usefulness. Thus, ignorance and poverty are not regarded as elements which limit individual freedom, but the worth of this liberty. Rawls moves from the opposition between formal freedom and effective or real freedom to the opposition between freedom and worth of freedom. The effective freedom or the worth of liberty of an individual can be "specified in terms of an index of the primary goods regulated by the second principle of justice" (ibid.: 326). Its effect is strengthened by a "fair value" of the political liberties for all: "this guarantee means that the worth of the political liberties to all citizens, whatever their social or economic positions, must be approximately equal, or at least sufficiently equal, in the sense that everyone has a fair opportunity to hold public office and to influence the outcome of political decisions" (ibid.: 327). In order to achieve such an aim, Rawls pleads in favour of a property-owning democracy. According to him, such an economic system is able to guarantee basic equal rights and liberties, fair value of political liberties as well as fair equality of opportunity. Indeed, "property-owning democracy avoids this, not by redistribution of income to those with less at the end of each period, so to speak, but rather by ensuring the widespread ownership of productive assets and human capital (that is, education and trained skills) at the beginning of each period, all this against a background of fair equality of opportunity" (Rawls 2001 [2003]: 139).

This clearly shows the Rawlsian theory is based on the idea that members of society have notably to work in a context of free choice of occupations to be able to fully cooperate. Therefore, it can be claimed that, according to Rawls, labour is one of the conditions of the emergence of real freedom.

Amartya Sen proposes to go one step further through appeal to the concept of capability. In some respects, Sen's capability approach attempts to answer a question raised by him in 1980: "equality of what?" (Sen 1980 [1982]). This question is central because of human diversity which leads to welfare inequalities. The capability approach combines many elements which seem essential to Sen: it takes into account some objective information regarding human beings' positions, human diversity and real freedom. The progressive development of his capability approach reflects these three afore-mentioned concerns. The set of opportunities of a person, that is his capability, corresponds to a choice set of different kinds of lives. A specific life is defined by a combination of functionings – "a functioning is an achievement of a person: what he or she manages to do or to be" (Sen 1985: 10) – which can be either basic (to be well-nourished, to be healthy, and so on) or complex (to be happy, to have a satisfying social life, and so on). Individual welfare is thus represented by a combination of functionings, while the capability of a person is the set of combinations of functionings he can reach depending on his personal circumstances (revenue, sex, health, skills, handicaps, and so on). Therefore, capabilities reflect the real freedoms that people might enjoy. If one must acknowledge that Sen's capability approach is subject to some limits (open-ended list of functionings, intrinsic value of freedom and so on), it sheds light on a central issue for economics and political philosophy: how to define a consistent concept of freedom for all, which encompasses both freedom and its conditions of exercise.

In this context, and even if the concept of labour is not deeply examined in Sen's theory, it is essential to ensure the promotion of extended capabilities: "the labour market can be a liberator in many different contexts" (Sen 1999: 116). Besides, "the development of free markets in general and of free seeking of employment in particular is a much appreciated fact in historical studies. Even that great critic of capitalism Karl Marx saw the emergence of freedom of employment as momentous progress" (ibid.: 113). As for Rawls, labour is thus understood by Sen as an indispensable way to promote freedom for all.

RAGIP EGE AND HERRADE IGERSHEIM

See also:

Antiquity (II); Jeremy Bentham (I); Economics and philosophy (III); French Enlightenment (II); Friedrich August von Hayek (I); Labour and employment (III); Karl Heinrich Marx (I); Scottish Enlightenment (II); Amartya Kumar Sen (I); Max Weber (I).

References and further reading

Aristotle (1885), *The Politics*, Oxford: Clarendon Press.
Bazard, S.-A., and P. Enfantin (1829), *Doctrine de Saint-Simon. Exposition. Première année*, reprinted 1924, Paris: Librairie des Sciences Politiques et Sociales Marcel Rivière.
Derathé, R. (1970), *Jean-Jacques Rousseau et la science politique de son temps*, Paris: Vrin.

Ege, R. and H. Igersheim (2008), 'Rawls with Hegel: the concept of liberalism of freedom', *European Journal of the History of Economic Thought*, **15** (1), 23–44.

Ferguson, A. (1767), *An Essay on the History of Civil Society*, 5th edn 1782, London: T. Cadell.

Finley, M.I. (1981), 'Was Greek civilisation based on slave labour', in M.I. Finley, *Economy and Society in Ancient Greece*, London: Chatto & Windus, pp. 97–115.

Grossein, J.-P. (2002), 'A propos d'une nouvelle traduction de *L'Ethique protestante et l'esprit du capitalisme*', *Revue Française de Sociologie*, **43** (4), 653–71.

Hayek, F.A. (1966), 'Lecture on a master mind. Dr. Bernard Mandeville', *Proceedings of the British Academy*, vol. 52, 1967, Oxford: Oxford University Press.

Hegel, G.W.F. (1821), *Grundlinien der Philosophie des Rechts oder Naturrecht und Staatswissenschaft im Grundrisse*, trans. J. Sibree (1967), *Foundations of the Philosophy of Right or Natural Right and Political Science in Outline*, Oxford: Oxford University Press.

Hegel, G.W.F. (1837), *Vorlesungen über die Philosophie der Weltgeschichte*, trans. S.W. Dyde (2001), *Lectures on the Philosophy of History*, Kitchener, ON: Batoche Books.

Hobbes, T. (1651), *Leviathan*, R. Tuck (ed.), 1996 edn, Cambridge: Cambridge University Press.

Kant, E. (1785), *Grundlegung zur Metaphysik der Sitten*, English trans.1949, *Groundwork of the Metaphysics of Morals*, New York: Bobbs-Merrill.

Locke, J. (1690), *Two Treatises of Government*, P. Laslett (ed.), 2008 edn, Cambridge: Cambridge University Press.

Mandeville, B. (1714), *The Fable of the Bees or Private Vices, Publick Benefits*, 3rd edn 1724, London: J. Tonson.

Marx, K. (1843), 'Zur Judenfrage', in K. Marx (1963), *Early Writings, on the Jewish Question*, London: Watts, pp. 1–40.

Marx, K. (1843–44), *Zur Kritik der Hegelschen Rechtsphilosophie*, in K. Marx (1994), *Early Political Writings, Critique of Hegel's Philosophy of Right*, Oxford: Cambridge University Press, pp. 57–70.

Marx, K. (1844), 'Ökonomisch-philosophische Manuskripte aus dem Jahre 1844', English trans. 1975, 'Economic & philosophic manuscripts of 1844', *Karl Marx Frederick Engels Collected Works*, vol. 3, New York: International, pp. 229–348.

Nietzsche, F. (1911), 'The Greek state: preface to an unwritten book', in F. Nietzsche, *Early Greek Philosophy and Other Essays*, Edinburgh: M.A. Mügge, pp. 1–18.

Proudhon, P.-J. (1858), *De la justice dans la révolution et dans l'Eglise, nouveaux principes de philosophie pratique adressés à Son Eminence Mgr Mathieu, cardinal-archevêque de Besançon*, vol. 3, reprinted 1932, Paris: Marcel Rivière.

Rawls, J. (1971), *A Theory of Justice*, reprinted 1999, Oxford: Oxford University Press.

Rawls, J. (1993), *Political Liberalism*, New York: Columbia University Press.

Rawls, J. (2000), *Lectures on the History of Moral Philosophy*, Cambridge, MA: Harvard University Press.

Rawls, J. (2001), *Justice as Fairness. A Restatement*, 2003 edn, Cambridge, MA: Harvard University Press.

Rousseau, J.-J. (1754), *Discours sur l'origine et les fondements de l'inégalité parmi les hommes*, in J.-J. Rousseau (1997), *The Discourses and Other Early Political Writings, Discourse on the Origin and Basis of Inequality Among Men*, Oxford: Cambridge University Press, pp. 113–88.

Rousseau, J.-J. (1762), *Du contrat social ou Principes du droit politique*, in J.-J. Rousseau (2007), *The Social Contract and Other Later Political Writings, Of the Social Contract or Principles of Political Right*, Cambridge: Cambridge University Press, pp. 39–152.

Sen, A.K. (1980), 'Equality of what?', reprinted in A.K. Sen (1982), *Choice, Welfare and Measurement*, Cambridge: Cambridge University Press, pp. 353–9.

Sen, A.K. (1985), *Commodities and Capabilities*, Amsterdam: North-Holland.

Sen, A.K. (1999), *Development as Freedom*, Oxford: Oxford University Press.

Smith, A. (1759), *The Theory of Moral Sentiments*, reprinted 1976, Oxford: Oxford University Press.

Smith, A. (1776), *An Inquiry Into the Nature and Causes of the Wealth of Nations*, reprinted 1976, Oxford: Oxford University Press.

Vaughan, C.E. (1962), 'Introduction', in C.E. Vaughan (ed.), *The Political Writings of Jean-Jacques Rousseau*, Oxford: Basil Blackwell, pp. 1–117.

Vernant, J.-P. (1974), *Mythe et pensée chez les grecs*, vol. 2, Paris: Maspéro.

Weber, M. (1904–05), *Die protestantische Ethik und der 'Geist' des Kapitalismus*, in M. Weber (1958), *The Protestant Ethic and the Spirit of Capitalism*, New York: Charles Scribner's Sons.

Population

Introduction

Reflections on population in economic analysis are rarely separated from comments on poverty, the prospects for economic development and, more generally, on well-being (Stangeland 1904; Overbeek 1974). In other words, the problem of population is discussed in the context of an inquiry into the causes and socio-economic consequences of demographic trends.

To reconstruct the general terms of economic analysis on the problem of population, two periods can be distinguished: the period up until the second half of the sixteenth century and the period thereafter. The main difference between the two is that while in the first period we encounter essentially only reflections and conjectures on the causes of demographic dynamics, from the mid-1650s onwards a coordinated body of knowledge and theoretical reflections on the topic of population gradually emerge.

It is possible to classify the different positions on population in three broad approaches. This does not mean that all the authors and economists considered can be rigidly grouped in this way. The three approaches rather serve the purpose of allowing us to distinguish between different types of theoretical and economic policy arguments. The three approaches are: (1) the populationist-macroeconomic approach; (2) the Malthusian-microeconomic approach; and (3) the "institutional" approach.

It should be added that the three main approaches overlap in the long period under consideration. This is for two main reasons. First, there is the fact that on the theme of population an extensive theoretical debate developed, concerning the conception of the causes and consequences in terms of the prospects for development and well-being of demographic change. The best known of these debates was triggered by the *Essay on the Principle of Population* by Thomas Robert Malthus (1798). It was the debate around Malthus's famous work that generated different positions and conflicting traditions on population.

The second cause can be traced back to the great paradigm shifts that affected the development of economic theories from mercantilism onwards. We can interpret the economic analysis of population looking at the great theoretical transformations that have taken place since mercantilist thinking. Each paradigm shift is accompanied by a transformation of the vision on population but, as we shall see below, we can trace in the history of economic analysis the continuity of the above mentioned three approaches which allow us to connect even very distant historical periods and theoretical contributions.

The Populationist-Macroeconomic Approach

According to this approach, the increase in population, when coupled with increasing investment and with technological and organizational improvements, leads to an increase in income and then, ultimately, to an improvement of material well-being for the entire society. This scheme is recognizable in the thought of the mercantilists and Adam Smith and, with reference to the analysis on increasing returns, even in Henry Charles Carey and Allyn Young.

As for the normative orientation resulting from this approach, this also belongs to those who, at the turn of the nineteenth and twentieth centuries, and until the Second World War, looked at the issue of population from a nationalistic perspective, and therefore moved away from a strictly analytical approach. These authors highlighted the strategic role of the demographic dynamics in the international balance of power. The analyses concerning strategic demography of Paul Leroy-Beaulieu, Corrado Gini and Roy Harrod (on the definition of strategic demography see Teitelbaum and Winter 1985: ch. 2; on the populationist demographic policies at the beginning of the nineteenth century see Glass 1967) fall into this category.

Returning to analytical issues, in this heterogeneous group of authors the common features which allow us to highlight a single scheme of reasoning are essentially two. First, population is considered as an aggregate variable that considerably influences the prospects of national economic development. In the case of the mercantilists, for example, the increase of population is considered a factor that, in itself, promotes economic growth, production capacity, the flow of taxes and, last but not least, the power of the state. According to Smith, on the other hand, population growth is inserted in the well-known dynamic development process, which ties the increase in productivity to the size of the market. In Smith's circuit of growth the population grows only through the processes allowing the development of production and the rise of wages but, at the same time, population growth contributes to the expansion of the market and thus reinforces the development process.

Secondly, and this is mainly related to normative aspects associated with the strategic role played by population, the growth of population, in a national comparative perspective, provides the opportunity for sustainable economic development, and it is an advantage from the perspective of colonial expansion. A tendency of this approach is linked to the pseudo-scientific studies of eugenics that developed along with the social sciences between the nineteenth and twentieth centuries.

Mercantilism

For Western European demographics the dividing line marking the change from a demographic regime of a mainly stationary population to a progressively growing one occurs in the second half of the 1600s. Then from the second half of the 1700s there was an unprecedented explosion in population growth, explained in terms of a gradual decline in the death rate, combined with a high birth rate, although the effect of these phenomena on each other is still not entirely clear.

Writers on this issue, starting from the seventeenth century, found themselves analysing a situation of considerable change, and this is probably partly why they expressed such a wide range of positions on the question of population. The basic position however remains that of general approval towards population growth and therefore towards policies that favoured it, through measures designed to encourage marriage and larger families, improve public health and limit emigration associated to incentives for the immigrant workforce, above all for qualified workers.

For the mercantilists, population growth essentially involved economic and political advantages. From the state's point of view, population growth meant not only an important element in the country's power policy but also, and above all, greater income and well-being for its citizens. The reason for this was that the population increase meant an increase in the labour force and, if the latter was employed in manufacturing, there would be a growth in productive capacity, exports and well-being. The emphasis on the nation's well-being did not make the slightest reference to the idea of per capita income or wealth. It was understood implicitly that the greater wealth produced would generate benefits for the whole population, but these were still analysed at an aggregate level.

These authors believed the increase in the state's wealth came about through a growth in production. To achieve this it was essential for the population to increase constantly so that the working population would also increase. The following passage from Daniel Defoe encapsulates this approach very well:

> Trade encourages manufacture, prompts invention, employs people, increases labour, and pays wages: as the people are employed, they are paid, and by that pay are fed, clothed, kept in heart, and kept together; that is, kept at home, kept from wandering into foreign countries to seek business, for where the employment is, the people will be. This keeping the people together is indeed the sum of the whole matter, for as they are kept together, they multiply together; and the numbers the wealth and strength of the nation, increase. (Defoe 1728 [1973]: 51)

Adam Smith

Smith's thoughts on population have their roots in the late-Mercantilist tradition. Despite their dealing with similar themes, namely the identification of a "natural" propensity in humankind to reproduce according to immutable laws, and the recognition of a connection between population growth and the availability of means of subsistence for the working class, Smith differs from the population analysis that preceded him on two points: first, on the question of the migration of work that, unlike the mercantilists, he did not believe was as decisive a factor in the development of nations, and secondly, in the emphasis placed on the relation between natural wages and demographic dynamics. The second point constitutes the heart of Smith's theory on the issues of population, wages and economic development, in other words, his theory of accumulation.

In the wage theory contained in chapter 8 of *The Wealth of Nations*, book I, Smith (1776 [1976]) explained the mechanism regulating demographic density and population growth rhythms in countries marked by different stages of economic development. For this purpose he used an effective analytical tool deduced from empirical observation: the subdivision of states into progressive, stationary, and regressive, applied to North America, China and Bengal respectively.

In Smith's analysis labour supply varied depending on the difference between the natural subsistence wage (which could be expressed in terms of a basket of subsistence goods for the worker and his family) and the market wage. When the natural wage dropped below subsistence level, the labour supply was reduced. The effects of this process were an increase in mortality and/or a lowering of the birth rate, and at times a rise in the migration rate, in the case of wage differences between regions, although for Smith this hypothesis was quite remote.

If, by contrast, the market wage was above the subsistence wage, then workers' living conditions could improve and the death rate, especially infant mortality, would fall. It needs to be pointed out, however, that in Smith's thought and in that of his successors, the value of the market wage systematically differed from its natural level due to casual factors that could not be foreseen, such as fluctuations in the labour market or price variations for subsistence goods. But the level towards which the market wage headed was that of the natural subsistence wage. The component of the wage theory that enabled Smith to use the tool of the differentiation between different kinds of countries was the demand for labour. If the availability of food for the working class constituted the prerequisite and the maximum limit for the expansion of the working population, it was the demand for labour that "regulated" wages, according to the following argument:

> The wages of the inferior classes of workmen . . . are every where necessarily regulated by two different circumstances; the demand for labour, and the ordinary or average price of provisions. The demand for labour, according as it happens to be either increasing, stationary, or declining, or to require an increasing, stationary, or declining population, regulates the subsistence of the labourer, and determines in what degree it shall be, either liberal, moderate, or scanty. The ordinary or average price of provisions determines the quantity of money which must be paid to the workman in order to enable him, one year with another, to purchase this liberal, moderate, or scanty subsistence. (Smith 1776 [1976]: 322)

From this it follows that the population grows only when the growing labour demand allows an increase in wages and a "liberal" level of subsistence. In thinking about this Smith had the case of North America in mind. In this situation there was no competition between workers, and wages were consequently on the increase (ibid.: 105). As for the necessary condition of sustaining the growing demand for labour, for Smith "it is not the actual greatness of national wealth, but its continual increase, which occasions a rise in the wages of labour" (ibid.).

In the progressive state a growing demand for labour corresponded to high wages and this did not necessarily mean a rising birth rate. Essentially, the population grew when there were the economic conditions to enable children to be brought up; the variation in population size was the result of a drop in death rates. In the stationary regime, labour demand is stationary, the level of wage and the level of population are constant, as in the case of China. Finally, in the regressive state of Bengal, the decreasing demand of labour is related to a decreasing level of wage and to a declining population.

In Smith's analysis, it did not follow that there was a direct relation between wages and population, valid for all countries. In other words there was no formulation of a "population law". This was because, especially in the progressive state, a wage increase and an increase in the means of subsistence could correspond not only to an increase in population but also, and at the same time, to a change in consumption habits which, once subsistence needs had been satisfied, would be directed towards the goods for which human desire "seems to have no limit or certain boundary" (Smith 1776 [1976]: 256). In conclusion, given an institutional context in which individual liberties were preserved, the human desire for improvement would not be threatened by an increase in population.

Henry Charles Carey and Allyn Young on increasing returns and population growth
In his *Principles of Social Science* Carey pointed out that there could not be a permanent imbalance between population and resources because, with the growth of population, other phenomena were triggered to counteract the initial phenomenon. In particular, as the population grows, there is an increase in "the power of association and combination". Through these processes, "man is enabled to control and direct the earth's forces, and to pass from the condition of nature's slave, to that of nature's master" (Carey 1859

[1963]: 313). The powers of association and combination supposedly derive from the human organizational capacity that develops only when the population grows.

The example given by Carey was the classical example of the transition from a primitive to a developed society, where it was the greater number of people that allowed the natural resources to be exploited more productively (Smith 1776 [1976]: 325). This process also gave rise to a greater power of accumulation due to the use of machinery in production (ibid.: 316, 325).

The elements of originality in Smith's approach, which, as we have seen, explain demographic dynamics as part of a general analysis on economic development and well-being, do not play an important role in the subsequent theoretical tradition. The long debate sparked off by Malthus's (1798) publication was a catalyst for all economic thought on the issue of the relation between demographic dynamics and economic development. At the same time it became important for every nineteenth century economist to adopt a position that was generally in favour of or opposed to that of Malthus, but which was in any case removed from Smith's thoughts on high wages and on the great potential for development generated by economic and social progress. Moreover, Smith's characteristic connection between increasing returns and population growth was not taken up either by the classical authors or later by the marginalists, and remained "hidden" until it again became relevant in the thought of Alfred Marshall and, above all, in that of Allyn Young.

Young's thoughts on increasing returns revolve around the concepts of "external economies" and "division of labour" deriving respectively from the analyses of Marshall and Smith. As for the question of population in relation to prospects of development, Young argues:

> It is a point of controversy, but I venture to maintain that under most circumstances, though not in all, the growth of population still has to be counted a factor making for a larger *per capita* product – although even that cautious statement needs to be interpreted and qualified. But just as there may be population growth with no increase of the average *per capita* product, so also . . . markets may grow and increasing returns may be secured while the population remains stationary. (Young 1928: 536)

The point is controversial, because in the 1920s both in the USA and in Europe the debate on the economic effects of demographic dynamics was very heated, owing to an increased awareness of the demographic transition. In other words, it had become clear that the population of advanced countries had ceased to grow and the debate had shifted to the "undesirable" effects of this trend, that is, the supposed presence of a eugenic selection opposed to development or even, in the so-called "race suicide" position, of the possible extinction of western civilization. Young evidently wants to stay well away from these subjects, and for this reason underlines that when increasing returns prevail, both a growing population and a stationary population are compatible with an increase in the per capita product; but he also wants to reiterate the validity of Smith's argument on population and increasing returns.

The Malthusian-Microeconomic Approach

The second approach, which we have called Malthusian-microeconomic, is probably the best known and most often referred to when it is necessary to connect economic analysis to the theory of population. We called this orientation Malthusian because, after the publication of Malthus's *Essay*, the long debate that took place in economic thinking right down to the present day, used Malthus's approach as its main theoretical reference point.

In the first edition of the *Essay*, Malthus's argument is directed to confuting the idea of progress and human perfectibility put forward by Condorcet and Godwin. Godwin defended the principle of the "substantial equality" of men, whereas Condorcet's conception of history saw mankind characterized by a perfectible nature. For both, the suffering of the lower classes derives from the structure of a society's government and of the institutions operating within it. According to Malthus, Godwin and Condorcet's theories had no scientific validity, since they were based on assumptions that could not be empirically verified. By contrast, he formulated two postulates:

> First, That food is necessary to the existence of man.
> Secondly, That the passion between the sexes is necessary and will remain nearly in its present state.
> These two laws, ever since we have had any knowledge of mankind, appear to have been fixed laws of our nature; and, as we have not hitherto seen any alteration in them, we have no right to conclude that they will ever cease to be what they now are . . . . Assuming then, my postulata as granted, I say, that the power of population is indefinitely greater than the power in the earth to produce subsistence for man. (Malthus 1798: 4)

In short, Malthus argued that when population grows there is a decrease in the amount of available resources for the sustenance of workers and, in parallel, through the reduction of wages that are pushed to subsistence level by the rising prices of essential goods, there is a decrease in per capita income and, as a result, in population. To summarize this process Malthus uses his famous progressions: geometrical for population growth and arithmetical for the increase of resources. If population growth is at its full potential, the population tends to increase according to a geometrical progression, which in absolute terms doubles the number of people every 25 years. Food production cannot keep up with this impetuous process of population growth, which means that population growth, when not hampered by preventive measures, is still reduced by repressive checks: hunger, disease, war, and so on.

This schema leaves no room for technical progress. For this reason, the modern representation of this argument is called the Malthusian population trap (see Todaro 2000: 224–9). The trap lies in the fact that individuals' higher income is compensated by the increase in population. This schema essentially represents a stable equilibrium characterized by low levels of income per capita and relatively high levels of population growth. The mechanism described by the trap is avoided when there are intervening changes that break up the interplay of action and reaction in the variables involved. At a micro level, this happens when the increase in income is not accompanied by an increase in population because individuals' reproductive behaviour has changed. At a macro level, the trap is avoided when continual technical progress raises the level of total production and, even with population increases, also the level of per capita income. This is the case described by Smith. In conclusion, seeing that Malthus does not consider technical progress to be a decisive factor in escaping from the trap, he relies on a micro level modification, suggesting in the *Essay* a "new" model of individual behaviour for workers.

The main objective of Malthus's *Essay* is to show that through the implementation of preventive checks, which are essentially abstinence from sex and the delay in marriage, what is called *moral restraint* starting from the second edition of 1803, it is possible to improve the condition of workers. This sense of responsibility can only arise from the perspective of poverty and, therefore, if public charity deletes this need it perpetuates the causes of the misery of the workers and population growth. Malthus wanted to show that the poverty of the workers did not depend on institutional and economic injustice, but was determined by individuals' decisions concerning reproduction. Only the transition from a biological reproductive model to a "conscious" reproductive model would lead to a reduction in population growth and an increase in income per capita.

In the general terms expressed by Malthus, this explanation of the causes of population growth and the reflections on the effects on the economy influenced the theoretical analysis of classical authors such as David Ricardo, John Ramsay McCulloch, Jean Baptiste Say and John Stuart Mill.

The aspect that most distinguishes this orientation is the microeconomic approach to the study of population and demographic dynamics. In other words, for Malthus and the authors cited, population increase is explained by the assumptions about the reproductive behaviour of individual family groups. The couple's decision to put children into the world, when it is not accompanied by a calculation on future disposable income, generates an overpopulation of the working poor.

As for the normative approach, referring to policies considered necessary to correct the tendency to overpopulation, there was more than one position. According to J.S. Mill, the solution to the problem of population growth over the limit set by available subsistence is birth control through the dissemination and the legalization of contraceptive methods. For the other authors, on the contrary, the state should not intervene in family planning through targeted policies because "modern" reproductive decisions must emerge spontaneously from the conduct of workers. Any policy, from the Poor Laws to birth control, which hindered the "moral" formation of workers, could only worsen the poverty of the working class.

Classical economists: toward the stationary state

As far as population theory is concerned, the period from the publication of the first edition of Malthus's *Essay* (1798) until the publication of John Stuart Mill's *Principles of Political Economy* (1848 [1963–91]) saw substantial support for Malthus's model from the major classical economists. What most influenced theoretical analysis in this period were the fundamental theoretical passages in the *Essay*. These can be summed up briefly in three points:

1. The size of the population was regulated by the availability of means of subsistence.
2. The population increased with the increase in the means of subsistence available for the feeding of wage earners.
3. Wage earners had the sole responsibility for their situation of need since they were the ones mainly responsible for population growth.

Taken together these three concepts are fundamental in the theory of Jean Baptiste Say, David Ricardo, John Ramsey McCulloch, and John Stuart Mill.

For Ricardo the workers' poverty could be attributed to the fact that population growth outpaced the growth of capital for investment and therefore the demand for labour. This position was different from that of Malthus, deriving from a different view of the effects that diminishing returns in agriculture had on development: for Ricardo diminishing returns raised the cost of producing wage goods and were therefore responsible for the slowing down of the process of capital accumulation, while for Malthus diminishing returns were fundamental in explaining the fact that the growth of means of subsistence did not proceed at the same pace as population growth.

By analysing Ricardo's *Principles of Political Economy* (1817 [1951–73]) we will try to show that the points shared by the theories of Malthus and Ricardo are, however, significant, above all in the aspects concerning the proposals to solve the problem of working-class poverty.

As we know, the basic aim of the work done by Ricardo in *Principles* is to examine the laws regulating the distribution of a country's production among the different classes of society, namely landowners, capitalists and workers.

In the chapter discussing Malthus's theory of rent, Ricardo introduced the argument by claiming that despite the criticisms levelled at it, Malthus's *Essay* was a fundamental work, which would in time reveal all its value. In the same way Ricardo argued for the important role played by Malthus' rent theory in economic debate, but he was ready to challenge its conclusions. He maintained that "the general progress of population is affected by the increase of capital, the consequent demand for labour, and the rise of wages; and that the production of food is but the effect of that demand" (Ricardo 1817 [1951–73]: 406). For Ricardo, Malthus was wrong to assert that the greater availability of food was the main factor encouraging new marriages and therefore the increase in population. The increase was caused by higher wages.

For Ricardo, as for Smith, the population grew *only after* a higher demand for labour had been manifested in the labour market. The repercussions of this event affected the economic system in the following way: "If wages rose, profits, and not rent, would fall. The rise of rent and wages, and the fall of profits, are generally the inevitable effects of the same cause–the increasing demand for food, the increased quantity of labour required to produce it, and its consequently high price" (Ricardo 1817 [1951–73]: 411).

Turning however to the practical implications, in the sense of remedies of political economy deriving from Ricardo's analysis on population, we again come up against the conclusions put forward by Malthus. For Ricardo in fact the Malthusian principle that the greater availability of resources for the worker meant an increase in the size of the family group, and therefore of the population, remained essentially valid, even though he did not agree with Malthus about the causes of the increase in the demand for food.

The increase of population, and the increase of food will generally be the effect, but not the necessary effect of high wages. The amended condition of the labourer, in consequence of the increased value which is paid him, does not necessarily oblige him to marry and take upon himself the charge of a family . . . but with the remainder he may, if it please him, purchase any commodities that may contribute to his enjoyments . . . But although this might be the consequence of high wages, yet so great are the delights of domestic society, that in practice it is invariably found that an increase of population follows the amended condition of the labourer; and it is only because it does so, that, with the trifling exception already mentioned, a new and increased demand arises for food. This demand then is the effect of an increase of capital and population, but not the cause. (Ricardo 1817 [1951–73]: 406–7)

Malthus's reasoning was therefore essentially confirmed. According to Ricardo, only in very few cases did the worker use the greater availability of income to improve his standard of living by consuming a wider range of goods. In most cases higher wages translated into an increase in population and in the demand for the food needed for its upkeep.

A further confirmation of the support for the Malthusian model came from Ricardo's rejection of the system of assistance of the Poor Laws. In concluding his chapter on wages in *Principles*, Ricardo states that the wage for work should not be subjected to any control by the legislative authority. Every intervention in the issue of regulating the income of the poor had the effect of generating a worsening of the initial situation because it precluded the operation of "stimuli" to "prudence and foresight". Only by acquiring these values could poor workers be sure that the higher income would not be "wasted" by a later increase in population.

In the period of classical economics another author who analyses the issue of population is McCulloch. At the level of theoretical economics McCulloch and Malthus have nothing in common. On the other hand, McCulloch's acceptance of Malthus' population theory was almost unconditional.

In his *Principles of Political Economy* McCulloch devoted an entire chapter to the issue of population, explaining that population was proportional to the means of subsistence (McCulloch 1825 [1995]: 227–30), and that thanks to the action of moral restraint a more advanced state of development and well-being could be achieved by the whole of society (ibid.: 230–31). The continuous increase in population was yet again seen as the strongest stimulus in the battle against natural human laziness and, as McCulloch underlined, also became a potent stimulus for research into new inventions. Population growth however became a positive factor of development only if it was associated with certain moral qualities in individuals.

A far more articulate position was taken by John Stuart Mill, not only towards Malthusian theory but, more particularly, towards the role played by population in a perspective of long-term growth, in other words, in the situation leading towards the stationary state.

For Mill the Malthusian principle contained a strong message which, if interpreted properly – namely, as a theoretical tool in support of human perfectibility – would lead to a decided improvement in the living conditions of the wage earning class.

In his *Principles of Political Economy* of 1848 Mill analysed the effects of excessive population growth on the economic system and adopted the scheme developed by Ricardo. When market wages were above their natural level then the population increased. At the same time, high wages discouraged investments and generated a drop in the demand for labour. As a result of this last effect, wages returned to subsistence level and the working population fell until there was another increase in the market wage.

Mill's study, especially the chapters on wages, therefore examines the conditions and the policies that can counteract population growth (Mill 1848 [1963–91] bk I: ch. 10; bk II: chs 11–12). It is on this point that Mill's analysis moves away from the approach of Malthus and Ricardo. He relied on state intervention to encourage the reduction of the number of members in workers' families, to raise the education level and, essentially, to guarantee that the stationary state would be characterized by a higher level of income per capita.

The only difference from the Malthusian approach came from considering the fact that the change in the workers' perspective did not derive exclusively from their individual growth and empowerment, but could actually be the result of a government policy. Overall, in his *Principles* the population issue was associated with three main aspects: (1) the limitation of family size had a significant effect on workers' income; (2) the reduction of the number of children was a fundamental aspect in the process of emancipation of women; and (3) population size regulated income level and therefore well-being in the stationary state. As for the last point, for Mill, approaching the stationary state was one of the typical features of the development of the capitalist system of production. The "natural" outcome of the process of accumulation, given the diminishing returns of agriculture and the progressively diminishing performance of capital, would be the situation of equilibrium where the same quantities would be reproduced over time and where, if the population remained stationary, a higher level of wealth could be achieved.

The "Institutional" Approach

Finally, the third approach is the one we decided to call "institutional". According to those who adhere to this view, the disproportion between population and resources does not derive either from natural laws or from the behaviour of workers. Each relationship between population and resources is mediated by the institutions in which it operates. The capitalist institutions, in other words, generate a relative surplus between population and available resources.

In the first half of the nineteenth century the debates over Malthus's principle were carried on in various contexts and were not limited to the strictly economic, demographic and statistical sphere of study. The economists, too, took part in the debate and were not insensitive to non-economic doctrines commonly held in the nineteenth century, such as, for example, the biological approach of Herbert Spencer (Spencer 1852). We have therefore tried to choose those contributions from the vast literature of the period that opposed Malthus's principle mainly on grounds of economic analysis, and above all were intent on confuting the theoretical and practical implications developed by classical economists, starting from an institutional approach.

In this heterogeneous group of critics of the "principle of population", we analyse the positions of Jean-Charles Léonard Simonde de Sismondi, the group of "Ricardian socialists" and Karl Marx.

Sismondi
Sismondi's position on population was considerably different from the formulation provided by Malthus. In his *New Principles of Political Economy* (1819) he argues against Malthus's vision, challenging the idea of the availability of resources as the element regulating population growth, placing the change in population size in a national institutional context, and declaring that "every nation very soon arrives at the degree of population which it can attain without changing its social institutions. It soon arrives at counting as many individuals as it can maintain with a revenue so limited, and so distributed" (Sismondi 1819 [1990]: 513).

What is fundamental for Sismondi is therefore the institutional context in which the demographic dynamic works, because it greatly affects the overall size and growth of the population. Sismondi argued that behind the individual's decision to create a family there was a rational calculation based on a trade-off between the benefits deriving respectively from marriage and celibacy. The benefits of marriage were represented by the "pleasures of conjugal life", by "parenthood" and by "reciprocal understanding". Celibacy on the other hand was generated by the consideration of "needs" and by "the fear of privation" (Sismondi 1819 [1990]: 513). According to Sismondi, the rational calculation about the choice of marriage applied only when workers did not impoverish. This happened because the size of the working population depended exclusively on income and if this relation became disproportioned, it was always due to the fact that society had deceived the workers on this point. The deception was due to the fact that workers could not determine the exact amount of their income. This came about because the demand for labour depended on events beyond their control. Wage-work in manufacturing was a clear example of this situation: the worker did not know the level of demand for the products he was making and, once employed, could only make calculations envisaging an income that, if there was a drop in demand, was denied to him if he was fired (or laid off, or worked less hours, became seriously ill or disabled, and so on). While for Malthus and the classical authors, poor workers were responsible for their own situation of indigence due to their thoughtless behaviour, for Sismondi, on the other hand, they lost their "moral capacities" owing to the way the system of production operated, leading them at best to take decisions based on erroneous forecasts or, when their income was extremely low, not to make any calculation at all.

The "Ricardian Socialists"
In the literature there is an extensive debate about the naming and recognition of the group of so-called "Ricardian socialists" (see, for example, Burkitt 1984; Kenyon 1997). In general these were often social scientists in the broad sense rather than economists, and can be considered a group of thinkers having in mind an alternative organization of the social system, more sensitive to workers' needs. In actual fact the thinker who had the greatest influence on this group was not so much Ricardo, as the main sources were John Locke, Adam Smith, Jeremy Bentham, William Godwin and Robert Owen. One feature that the theoretical formulations of the "Ricardian socialists" share is that they tried to reconcile the process of continual growth of production with a fairer distribution of the wealth produced (Kenyon 1997: v–vi). The "Ricardian socialists" include Piercy Ravenstone, Thomas Hodgskin, William Thompson and John Gray.

Ravenstone denied the validity of the Malthusian progressions because he argued that the population tended to grow constantly in every place and every nation and there could not be an imbalance between population and resources since "every man brings into the world the means of his own sustenance" (Ravenstone 1821 [1997]: 23).

Among the "Ricardian socialists", Thomas Hodgskin is considered the most liberal. He was firmly convinced that population growth was not an obstacle to the improvement of society but was in fact the main stimulus to human progress. This happened because the division of labour was explained as a consequence of population growth and therefore also indirectly of the growth of wealth produced (Kenyon 1997: xxxiii).

The eclectic William Thompson took up positions that were both liberal and socialist. He argued that population growth could be controlled in the cooperative society that he had theorized and that the reduction of the population, following Malthusian prescriptions, was not only hard to achieve but also counterproductive from the economic point of view (Kenyon 1997: ix–x).

Finally, John Gray also rejected Malthus's theory on the grounds that its basic principles were inapplicable and pointless. Gray maintained that, first, it was not possible to argue that the human reproductive instinct was unchangeable if this might result only in a calamity from the environmental and economic point of view. Secondly, he denied that all living beings tended to reproduce above the limits of survival. Lastly, like the other authors analysed so far, he challenged the validity of the Malthusian progressions (Gray 1825).

As we have seen, in the social models these four authors put forward as an alternative to the kind of production described by the classical authors, they did not believe there would be an excessive growth of population, because the social and economic reorganization would lead to a better organization of production. There would be a higher level of production and essentially a better social order. This would happen because population and resources were not regulated by forces "external" to the capitalist system, namely, by the principle of population and the law of diminishing returns, but by mechanisms "internal" to the system, determined over time, which set limits on production resulting in the population being relatively excessive.

Marx

A similar critical attitude towards the classical theoretical system can be found in Karl Marx. His position on the law of population was expressly anti-Malthusian. He rarely lost an opportunity to criticise or ridicule Malthus's theoretical contribution (see Meek 1953). In the *Grundrisse*, he rejected the idea that the laws of population were the same in all countries and in all moments of history, asserting that every stage of development had its own different law of population. In fact he writes that "in different modes of social production there are different laws of the increase of population and of overpopulation; the latter identical with pauperism. Only in the mode of production based on capital does pauperism appear as the result of labour itself, of the development of the productive force of labour" (Marx 1857 [1973]: 604).

The progressive impoverishment of wage earners was the condition that explained worker over-population; however, this could not be defined in absolute terms compared to the means of subsistence, but exclusively in relative terms.

> Never a relation to a *non-existent* absolute mass of means of subsistence, but rather relation to the conditions of reproduction, of the production of these means, including likewise the *conditions of reproduction of human beings*, of the total population, of relative surplus population. This surplus purely relative: in no way related to the *means of subsistence* as such, but rather to the mode of producing them. (Marx 1857 [1973]: 607–8, original emphases)

The mechanism causing relative overpopulation was therefore part of the process explaining capitalist accumulation. The problem could be unfolded in terms of a one-way process, expounded in *Capital* (1867), in which the workers became poorer and poorer, adding to the ranks of the industrial reserve army.

The progressive impoverishment of the workers was due to the increase in the organic composition of capital, in other words, to the relative increase in constant capital (machinery and raw materials) at the expense of variable capital (labour). The effect of this was the progressive reduction of necessary labour (to the mere reproduction of working capacity, that is, what was needed to feed a worker) compared to surplus labour (which was what produced surplus value) and a reduction in the demand for labour, which could be absolute or relative if it referred to the increase in overall capital.

The workers' situation was seriously compromised if there was also an increase in population. This happened because in this case there was an even more rapid increase in unemployment, that is, in the industrial reserve army. In other words, Marx, moving sharply away from the classical tradition, rejected the hypothesis of demographic movements as regulators of the ups and downs of the subsistence wage and the market wage and proclaimed the absolute general law of capitalist accumulation.

> The greater the social wealth, the functioning capital, the extent and energy of its growth, and, therefore, also the absolute mass of the proletariat and the productiveness of its labour, the greater is the industrial reserve-army. The same causes which develop the expansive power of capital, develop also the labour-power at its disposal. The relative mass of the industrial reserve-army increases therefore with the potential energy of wealth. (Marx 1867 [1978]: 594)

Keeping in mind that the working population can increase, not only due to demographic dynamics but above all because of the use of women and children in production processes, there will be too many workers compared to the needs of the labour market.

It was owing to this last aspect, according to Perrotta, that in Marx population growth was not considered essentially in demographic terms (unlike the positive difference between birth and death rates), but was mainly connected to the increase in the number of productive workers on the market (Perrotta 2000: 672). The demand for a greater number of productive workers occurred as a result of the capitalist process of accumulation deriving from the growth of industry, which with its increased productivity weakened the economic position of peasants and craftsmen and contributed to the process of "proletarianization" of the society.

Given these premises, for Marx it was inconceivable to talk about a "law of population" responsible for the excessive growth of the wage-earning class. The law he described as law of capitalist accumulation was a "social law" that "follows from the relationship of labour to capital" (Marx 1847 [1976], s. VI) and enabled Marx to explain why the wage-earning class was so numerous: "by replacing adults with children, modern industry places a veritable premium on the making of children" (ibid.).

While for Sismondi poor workers made no calculation about the future composition of their family, for Marx it was exactly the opposite. They were induced by the system of production to "choose" a bigger family group because, seeing that they were getting progressively poorer, they tried to counteract the negative effects produced by the process of accumulation on family income.

In conclusion, though Marx maintained the futility of treating the theory of population autonomously from the theory of accumulation, he managed to clearly show an aspect of the population/resources relation that was different from the previous tradition. It must, however, be pointed out that while on the one hand Marx makes it very clear that overpopulation is a phenomenon generated by capitalism itself, on the other there is no explanation of what would happen to the population after the collapse of capitalism. That is, the demographic dynamic in itself is not explained and it is not clear what effects population growth would have on economic development.

Veblen pointed out this anomaly in Marx, arguing that "the particular point at which the theory is most fragile, considered simply as a theory of social growth, is its implied doctrine of population, implied in the doctrine of a growing reserve of unemployed workmen" (Veblen 1906: 595). The weak point, according to Veblen, lay in the fact that the population in the Marxist system would keep growing regardless of the availability of means of subsistence. Empirical evidence gave "apparent support" to this theory given that poverty had never been an obstacle to population growth, but Marxist theory gave "no conclusive evidence in support of a thesis to the effect that the number of laborers must increase independently of an increase in the means of life. No one since Darwin would have the hardihood to say that the increase of the human species is not conditioned by the means of living" (ibid.).

On the issue of population, for all the authors considered in this section, the decisive fact is that modifications of the demographic dynamics must be considered in a precise institutional context before being studied in all their complexity. This is, above all, because it is also the institutional context that gives rise to the modifications in individual attitudes to reproductive behaviour. Apart from this initial consideration, however, the positions of the authors examined are totally diverse.

For Sismondi, for the Ricardian socialists and for Marx, it is not possible to appeal to a "population law" that is immutable and therefore foreign to capitalism. Furthermore, the fact of challenging the Malthusian principle and the role it played in the classical tradition leads, in different ways for the different authors, to the negation of capitalism itself.

This negation, for Sismondi, is expressed as the development of a society of "small owners" removed from the depersonalization resulting from the system of industrial production. For the Ricardian socialists the negation consists of plans for the reform of capitalism, ranging from the libertarian alternatives announced by Hodgskin to the cooperative scheme of Owen and to the egalitarian collectivist scenario proposed by Thompson. Finally, for Marx there could be no other outcome than the collapse of the entire capitalist system of production, because the very relations of capitalist production contained the innate elements that would lead to its downfall.

Concluding Remarks

Schumpeter, in his *History of Economic Analysis*, explains the "abandonment" of the theory of population, during the transition from the classical to the marginalist perspective, by mainly referring to the irrelevance of the theoreticians use of hypotheses on the size and dynamic of population. In other words, in a system of analysis based on the concept of marginal utility, there was no need of specific assumptions on the population's rate of growth and its total size, since the main aim was the explanation of the problem of the allocation of the given productive factors. Schumpeter sums up by setting out three explanations for the transition from classical to marginalist perspectives on population.

1. During the period of the consolidation of marginalist theory there was no immediate abandonment of the ideas on population. In this "interregnum" the leaders of the economic theory – Böhm-Bawerk, Marshall, Walras, and Wicksell – continued to consider, at least as a hypothetical starting point, the behaviour of the population variable "even though they no longer based upon it any part of their analytic structures" (Schumpeter 1954 [1997]: 890).
2. Around the end of the nineteenth century, partly through a more accurate collection of statistical data, the first evidence of demographic transition began to emerge, that is, the constant decline of birth and death rates. In the 1920s this event would orientate the economists' analysis towards research concentrated on the study of the effects of the gradual decline of the population.
3. Finally, specialization in the methods used to gather demographic data had led to the birth of demography as a discipline on the study of population behaviour, thus removing the subject from the spectre of those variables that were grist to the mill of economic analysis (ibid.).

On the first point, it has to be pointed out that the marginalist and neoclassical theoreticians, even though they did not develop any of their analyses starting from the behaviour of the population, nevertheless continued to study the effects of the demographic dynamic on economic development and well-being. In Marshall, for example, the demographic dynamic is placed within a long-term model of development in which, however, it is not possible to consider, independently of other variables, the effects of population on economic development (Rostow 1990: 164–70).

Wicksell develops a model of equilibrium growth based on the concept of the optimal population maximizing individual well-being, and hence starting precisely from the consideration of the behaviour of the relevant variable. In addition, Pareto too, taking Walras's approach as his starting point, develops a concept of "optimal population" with reference to a competitive system (see Boianovsky 2001: 117–49).

Concerning the second point, we would like to specify that the marginalist theoreticians, precisely because they were not interested in the direct study of the population, did not pay much attention to the evolution of demographic trends. In addition, when the economists became aware of the epoch-making changes in the demographic dynamic of the industrialized nations, they often reacted in excessively alarmed ways to the consequences of a presumed decline of the population (see Teitelbaum and Winter 1985).

Finally, and we are now dealing with point three, as far as the relationships between economics and demography are concerned, it is worth remembering that some economists, such as Wicksell and Pareto, applied methods of demographic enquiry to their economic models, and that the "permeability" between the two disciplines, around the end of the nineteenth century, was much more marked than in the early years of the following century.

We have tried to demonstrate that in the long process of the formation of economic ideas the demographic dynamic played an important role in explaining the prospects of well-being and long-term development of societies. Reconstructing the history of the analysis enabled us to highlight the main approaches in economic thought, starting from mercantilism, to explain and, through the tools of intervention of economic policy, to try to intervene in the demographic dynamic to attain specific objectives of growth. As we have seen in the case of the marginalists, the debate over population continued after the end of classical economics. The controversial "Malthusian-microeconomic" approach still plays a crucially important role in the recent literature on development (Birdsall 1988; Ahlburg and Cassen 2008) and in growth models (Kurz and Salvadori 2008), because it represents a watershed in the history of ideas. The point is not so much that of understanding whether Malthus's predictions were correct, but to place that model in the context of the historical period in which it was put forward and try to understand the reality it tried to explain. The "populationist-macroeconomic" approach linked population increase to benefits in terms of growth deriving from market creation and the intensification of trade. At the same time, the "institutional" model traced back to excessive population growth all those limits of a model of development in which the great majority of workers were left in poverty. In summary, the "Malthusian-microeconomic" approach tried to indicate, from a conservative perspective, how to attain a higher level of well-being for the entire population.

CLAUDIA SUNNA

See also:

British classical political economy (II); Development economics (III); Labour and employment (III); Mercantilism and the science of trade (II); Non-Marxian socialist ideas in Britain and the United States (II); Poverty (III).

References and further reading

Ahlburg, D. and R. Cassen (2008), 'Population and development', in A.K. Dutt and J. Ros (eds), *International Handbook of Development Economics*, vol. 1, Cheltenham, UK and Northampton, MA, USA: Edward Elgar, pp. 316–27.

Birdsall, N. (1988), 'Economic approaches to population growth', in H.B. Chenery and T.N. Srinivasan (eds), *Handbook of Development Economics*, vol. 1, Amsterdam: North Holland, pp. 477–543.

Boianovsky, M. (2001), 'Economists as demographers: Wicksell and Pareto on population', in G. Erreygers (ed.), *Economics and Interdisciplinary Exchange*, London: Routledge, pp. 117–49.

Burkitt, B. (1984), *Radical Political Economy: An Introduction to the Alternative Economics*, Brighton: Wheatsheaf.

Carey, H.C. (1859), *The Principles of Social Science*, vol. 3, reprinted 1963, New York: Kelley.

Charbit, Y. (2009), *Economic, Social and Demographic Thought in the XIXth Century. The Population Debate from Malthus to Marx*, Dordrecht, Heidelberg, London and New York: Springer.

Charbit, Y. (2011), *The Classical Foundations of Population Thought. From Plato to Quesnay*, Dordrecht, Heidelberg, London and New York: Springer.

Defoe, D. (1728), 'A plan of the English commerce', in N.L. Tranter (ed.) (1973), *Population and Industrialization*, London: A. & C. Black, pp. 51–6.

Glass, D. (1967), *Population Policies and Movements in Europe*, 2nd edn, New York: Kelley.

Gray, J. (1825), *A Lecture on Human Happiness*, reprinted 1931, London: London School of Economics and Political Science.

Kenyon, T.A. (1997), 'Introduction. Interpreting the thought of the Ricardian Socialists', in T.A. Kenyon, *The Ricardian Socialists*, 7 vols, London: Routledge/Thoemmes Press, pp. v–xlviii.

Kurz, H.D. and N. Salvadori (2008), 'New growth theory and development economics', in A.K. Dutt and J. Ros (eds), *International Handbook of Development Economics*, vol. 1, Cheltenham, UK and Northampton, MA, USA: Edward Elgar, pp. 207–22.

Livi Bacci, M. (1998), *Storia minima della popolazione del mondo*, Bologna: Il Mulino, English edn 1992, *A Concise History of World Population*, Cambridge: Blackwell.

Malthus, T.R. (1798), *An Essay on the Principle of Population as it Affects the Future Improvement of Society with Remarks on the Speculations of Mr. Godwin, M. Condorcet, and other Writers*, London: J. Johnson, accessed 12 December 2012 at at www.esp.org.

Marx, K. (1847), 'Wages', in *Marx and Engels Collected Works*, vol. VI, 1976 edn, London: Lawrence and Wishart, pp. 415–37, accessed 13 January 2013 at http://www.marx.org/archive/marx/works/1847/12/31.htm.

Marx, K. (1857), *Grundrisse: Foundations of the Critique of Political Economy*, M. Nicolaus (ed.), reprinted 1973, London: Penguin.

Marx, K. (1867), *Capital: A Critique of Political Economy*, vol. I, reprinted 1978, London: Penguin.

McCulloch, J.R. (1825), *The Principles of Political Economy*, Edinburgh: William and Charles Tait, reprint from the 4th edition in D.P. O'Brien (ed.) (1995), *The Collected Works of J. R. McCulloch*, vol. II, London: Routledge/Thoemmes Press.

McKeown, T. (1976), The Modern Rise of Population, New York: Academic Press.

Meek, R.L. (ed.) (1953), *Marx and Engels on the Population Bomb*, reprinted 1971, Berkeley, CA: Ramparts Press.

Mill, J.S. (1848), *Principles of Political Economy*, reprinted in J.M. Robson (ed.) (1963–91), *The Collected Works of John Stuart Mill*, vol. 2, Toronto: University of Toronto Press and London: Routledge & Kegan Paul.

Overbeek, J. (1974), *History of Population Theories*, Rotterdam: Rotterdam University Press.

Perrotta, C. (2000), 'Marx's deadlock on consumption', in V. Gioia and H. Kurz (eds), *Science, Institutions and Economic Development*, Milan: Giuffrè editore, pp. 669–88.

Ravenstone, P. (1821), *A Few Doubts as to the Correctness of Some Opinions Generally Entertained on the Subjects of Population and Political Economy*, London: John Andrews, reprinted 1997, London: Routledge-Thoemmes.

Ricardo, D. (1817), *On the Principles of Political Economy and Taxation*, in P. Sraffa and M. Dobb (eds) (1951–73), *The Works and Correspondence of David Ricardo*, vol. I, Cambridge: Cambridge University Press.

Rostow, W.W. (1990), *Theorists of Economic Growth from David Hume to the Present*, New York and Oxford: Oxford University Press.

Schumpeter, J.A. (1954), *History of Economic Analysis*, reprinted 1997, London: Routledge.

Sismondi, J.-C.L. Simonde de (1819), *New Principles of Political Economy*, English trans. 1990, Piscataway, NJ: Transaction.

Smith, A. (1776), *An Inquiry into the Nature and Causes of the Wealth of Nations*, in A.S. Skinner and R.H. Campbell (eds) (1976), *The Glasgow Edition of the Works and Correspondence of Adam Smith*, vol. III, Oxford: Oxford University Press.

Spencer, H. (1852), 'A theory of population deduced from the general law of animal fertility', *Westminster Review*, **57** (April), 468–501.

Stangeland, C.E. (1904), *Pre-Malthusian Doctrines of Population*, New York: Columbia University Press.

Teitelbaum, M.S. and J.M. Winter (1985), *The Fear of Population Decline*, Orlando, FL: Academic Press.

Todaro, M. (2000), *Economic Development*, 7th edn, London: Longman.

United Nations (1973), *The Determinants and Consequences of Population Trends*, vol. 1, New York: United Nations.

Veblen, T. (1906), 'The socialist economics of Karl Marx and his followers', *Quarterly Journal of Economics*, **20** (4), 575–95.

Young, A. (1928), 'Increasing returns and economic progress', *The Economic Journal*, **38** (152), 527–42.

Poverty

In the history of economic thought, poverty has been one of the most discussed problems. However, poverty did not mean the same thing for different authors. There are two main definitions of poverty: absolute and relative poverty. Traditionally, absolute poverty was the subject of attention but, in affluent societies, poverty is usually considered in the relative sense.

Definition

In classical political economy, poverty usually meant a standard of living lower than the subsistence level, which just maintains the population at its given size. The necessary goods which compose the subsistence can be different depending on time and place.

Adam Smith, in the *Wealth of Nations* (1776), implicitly used the definition of poverty of the standard of living lower than the subsistence level. For him, the subsistence level of living included goods regarded necessary by customs of the society. Towards the end of the eighteenth century, Jeremy Bentham distinguished poverty from indigence. He defined poverty as a state in which a person cannot sustain his or her life without labouring, and indigence as a state in which a person cannot obtain necessary means of subsistence owing to lack of ability to work or, even if he or she works, cannot obtain enough for subsistence (Bentham 2000, 2010). Poverty in Bentham's definition is the normal state of labourers who are the majority of people in any society, so indigence should be regarded poverty in usual terms. Then appeared Thomas Robert Malthus's *An Essay on the Principle of Population* (1798). Malthus studied the problem of poverty from the point of view of his principle of population. He examined the effects of the Poor Laws on the conditions of labourers, concluding that the Poor Laws had a tendency to increase poverty instead of reducing it. He seems to have implicitly defined poverty as a living below subsistence level. However, subsistence was not considered the biological minimum for survival. It included goods regarded as necessary for human life in the society of the time. This had already been argued by Adam Smith. Ricardo also explicitly regarded the subsistence wage rate as above the basket of goods the rate of wages required for biological survival.

Towards the end of the nineteenth century, Charles Booth investigated the state of life of the poor in London (*Life and Labour of the People in London*, 1902–04). He classified the people in eight groups (A, B, C, D, E, F, G, and H) in terms of labour conditions, income levels, and social positions. The group E which could get the lowest regular earnings (from 18 to 21 shillings per week) was regarded as "standard", just above the poverty line. The groups A (occasional labourers, loafers, semi-criminals) and B (those getting casual earnings) were classified as "very poor". The groups C getting "intermittent earnings" and D getting "small regular earnings" are regarded "poor". He showed the poverty line at the income level of 18 to 21 shillings a week, but he did not specify the consumption basket corresponding to that level of income.

Benjamin Seebohm Rowntree (*Poverty: A Study of the Tow Life*, 1922), following the study of Booth, made researches into the life conditions of labourers in York. He classified poverty into "primary poverty" and "secondary poverty". "Primary poverty" means the income level which cannot purchase the minimum requirements to maintain merely physical efficiency, whereas "secondary poverty" means the level of family income which is sufficient for living, but can be insufficient if not spent efficiently. His investigations revealed that nearly 10 per cent of the population was in "primary poverty" and more than 10 per cent in "secondary" poverty. His "primary poverty" can be understood as the level of living lower than needed for biological survival.

The subsistence or the socially lowest level of the standard of living which divided the poor from the non-poor was not absolutely fixed but relative to time and place, variable due to the social practices and ways of life and production. Peter Townsend, in his *Poverty in the United Kingdom* (1979), proposed the definition of poverty explicitly as "relative deprivations". He described the normal activities and amenities of the society and defined poverty as lack of a part of them, referring to it as "relative deprivations". For Townsend, poverty is a relative concept. In the relative sense, poverty is understood to exist in every society, and some authors have reduced the problem of poverty to inequality of income distribution. Following Townsend, there appeared many studies on poverty based on the relativist conception.

Amartya Kumar Sen (*Poverty and Famine*, 1981) contends that poverty should be distinguished from inequality. He recognizes that there is a relative aspect in the concept of poverty, but at the same time he points out that there should be an absolute meaning in the core of poverty, because hunger and famine must remain as the core of the concept of poverty in any definition. He defines poverty as the lack of the minimum capabilities of social life. A capability means a capacity to do something. There are various ways that provide for capabilities. In terms of capabilities, poverty is defined in an absolute sense, but the means that give the same capabilities (that is, commodities and services) can vary in time and place depending on climate, customs, ways of life and ways of production. Commodities give characteristics, which give capabilities, which give utility or pleasure. With this definition, Sen integrated the notions of absolute and relative poverty.

After World War II, there appeared many studies on the measurement of the extent of poverty of a society as a whole. The head-count measures and income ratio measures are often used, but these measures cannot reflect changes in income distribution among the poor people. As we have seen above, the relative position of an individual is important in understanding poverty (idea of relative deprivations). Sen proposed a measure which reflects relative deprivation and the distribution of income among the poor. For Sen, an unfavourable change of distribution among the poor may cause hunger and famine, which should be regarded as a rise of the extent of poverty of a society. Sen proposed a measure which is expressed by the formula $P = H\{I + [1 - I]G\}$ (*P*: measure of poverty, *H*: head-count ratio, I = income-gap ratio = percentage of short-fall of the average income of the poor from the poverty line, G = Gini coefficient of the distribution of income among the poor). His measure can reflect changes of income distribution among the poor.

Most authors in the history of economics have inquired into the nature and causes of poverty, and tried to find solutions for it. Especially for classical political economists, poverty was the most important problem they faced, because in their ages European countries including England were still in underdeveloped stages and the majority of people were poor. In the history of economics, economists sought to improve the living conditions of people not only below the poverty line but also of the people placed just a little bit above the line. This attitude vis-à-vis poverty is explicitly stated by

Alfred Marshall in chapter 1 of his *Principles of Economics* (1890). Most economists since Adam Smith had taken this position. Therefore, we will use below the term poverty meaning the state in which one's living standard is below or near the subsistence level in the society in which one lives.

Causes of Poverty and Types of Poverty

What are the causes of poverty? We find several types of poverty caused by different factors. Poverty can be classified into three types, depending on different causes: universal type of poverty, mass poverty, and poverty in affluent societies.

Universal type of poverty
This type of poverty can be found in every society and every age for universal causes such as old age, childhood without parents or family members who take care of them, diseases, lack of capabilities inborn or acquired, idleness, low wages, lack of employment, underemployment, and so on. The lack of employment is caused by different factors according to different stages of economic development. In underdeveloped economies, the major cause of unemployment is shortage of labour demand due to an insufficiency of capital. In developed economies, labour can be unemployed for insufficient demand for products and labour saving technical progress.

Mass poverty
This kind of poverty can often be seen in underdeveloped economies. The majority of people are poor in the early stages of economic development in every country owing to low productivity. In this case, the majority of poor people usually live in rural areas. We may call it rural poverty, but Galbraith calls it mass poverty because people are generally poor except only a few privileged members of society (*The Nature of Mass Poverty*, 1979).

In the early stages of economic development, the economy is a subsistence economy which cannot produce any economic surplus, or it is already above the subsistence level with some surplus, but the surplus is used up in population growth, or production and consumption of luxuries, or maintenance of unproductive classes, and cannot improve the average standard of living of common people. Even when a part of the population leaves the rural areas in order to work in manufactures in town, they are usually still poor.

Poverty in affluent societies
As economic development advances, mass poverty diminishes and we enter an affluent society such as the developed countries of today (Britain, Germany, France, Sweden, USA, Japan, Austria, Italy, Canada, Australia, and so on). However, even in affluent societies, there remains some poverty owing to inequality of income distribution and unemployment owing to insufficiency of demand for products and labour, or labour-saving technical progress, in addition to the universal type of poverty. Unemployment insurance, retirement pension and family allowance are main institutions established for relief of poverty. The welfare state is a system to relieve poverty and to improve the living conditions of common people in affluent societies.

Economic Surplus and Poverty

Economic surplus: definition

Economic surplus is the key concept to understand and to resolve the problem of poverty. It was a central concept of classical political economy for which mass poverty was a main issue.

For the definition of economic surplus, we here give a description of an economy in a very simple way as follows (Sraffa 1960):

$$A_a + B_a \rightarrow A \tag{1}$$

$$A_b + B_b \rightarrow B$$

A_a, A_b, B_a, B_b are inputs in sectors a and b which include the subsistence consumption of labourers. Their consumption is included in inputs, as it were, like materials or fodders. A and B are outputs. A combination of inputs (A_a, B_a) produces an output A. In another process or industry, a combination of inputs $(A_b$ and $B_b)$ produces output B.

A subsistence economy

A subsistence economy can be depicted simply as follows:

$$A_a + A_b = A \tag{2}$$

$$B_a + B_b = B$$

This economy is viable, but it has no possibility to grow, increase in population, no possibility of production and consumption of luxury goods and of the existence of unproductive classes. This economy is very vulnerable to natural disasters (bad weathers, floods, earthquakes, droughts, etc.) and human failures such as wrong policies. If natural disasters happen, some part of the population will die of hunger and the population will diminish. People live a life of mere subsistence (that is, the minimum standard of living that gives only the possibility to maintain the present size of population).

A system with a surplus

It is depicted simply as follows:

$$A_a + A_b < A \tag{3}$$

$$B_a + B_b < B$$

If we express the surplus in material terms:

$$A - (A_a + A_b) \tag{4}$$

$$B - (B_a + B_b)$$

In this economy, there are possibilities of economic growth, population growth, production and consumption of luxury goods and the existence of unproductive classes.

Even in a surplus economy, if the whole surplus is used up in increasing population, producing and consuming luxury goods, or maintaining unproductive classes, it cannot improve the living conditions of common people. It can grow only if part of the surplus it produces is invested in productive activities (maintenance of labourers that produce goods, production of machines, construction of factories, irrigation works, opening of new farm lands, and so on). Savings here mean the part of the surplus not devoted to unproductive consumption and used for investments that increase the productive capacity of the economy.

If the economic surplus is used in increasing population, the economy can realize economic growth in the sense of the size of production, but may not improve the living standard of people. If an economy uses its surplus in maintaining labourers that produce luxury goods only, the economy can grow but the growth cannot continue if there is no technological progress. In this case, the standard of living of the common people can be improved a little if the distribution is not so unequal that the whole luxury goods are consumed by only a privileged part of the population, because the luxury sector employs some labourers.

A continuous growth and improvement of the living conditions of common people can be realized only if a part (and possibly a substantial part) of the economic surplus is used continuously in maintaining additional productive labourers that produce necessary goods and in the production of means of production. We may need to reform political and social institutions and change the mind of people in order to make possible a continuous economic growth and a rise of the standard of living of people.

Poverty in the History of Economics

In the history of economics, most important economists have inquired into poverty, and sought to find solutions for it. For a long time, mass poverty has been the most important problem, even though the word, mass poverty, was not employed. Main authors in the history of economics tackled the mass poverty as their main issue, but at the same time they did not neglect the universal type of poverty.

Adam Smith

Adam Smith inquired into the nature of the market economy that was emerging at that time and argued about the increase of production of goods in the new system that would improve the living conditions of common people at large (*An Inquiry into the Nature and Causes of the Wealth of Nations*, 1776). If the larger proportion of the product is devoted to production, that is, to investment in material capital and in maintaining productive labourers, the rate of growth of the economy will be high. Smith argued that if people are left free to save, the rate of saving will become the highest possible because people have a natural desire to improve their living conditions. In other words, a larger proportion of surplus will be employed productively if the saving decisions are left in the hands of ordinary people, instead of in the hands of governments, which Smith regarded most extravagant, judging from the historical experiences. For Smith, economic growth was most important for the reduction of poverty. He believed that if the economy grows, even within unequal distribution of income, the gains from economic growth will trickle down to common people through the consumption of rich classes. Smith also emphasized the importance of human capital. Smith did not explicitly consider the Poor Laws in England, but he severely criticized the Law of Settlement that restricted the movement of people between parishes.

Thomas Robert Malthus

Malthus's idea was that the potential growth of population exceeds that of food production, but the actual rate of population growth is regulated by the actual rate of increase of food production. He recommended control of population growth by postponing the marriage age. In his view, by containing population growth, the average standard of living of common people could be raised and poverty could be diminished (*Essay on Population*, 1798). In the second edition of the *Essay on Population* (1803), Malthus introduced the moral restraint as a check to the increase of population; he regarded it as the only effective way to contain population growth in the long run.

He never recommended any artificial methods of birth control. In his view, the only efficient way to keep low the population increase and to improve the living conditions of labourers in the long run was the spread of moral constraint among the lower classes. Elementary education of common people, protection of private property, institution of laws which treat equally the lower classes and the higher classes, and some participation of labourers in politics were regarded necessary to spread moral constraint among the labouring classes.

In England there were the Poor Laws that had been established mainly in order to relieve the extreme poverty (indigence) in the time of Elizabeth I and were in force until 1948 when the establishment of the welfare state was proclaimed. Towards the end of the eighteenth century, Frederic Morton Eden made his inquiry into the state of the poor and the labouring classes under the Poor Laws (*The State of the Poor*, 1797). From the point of view of population growth, Malthus examined the effects of the Poor Laws. He argued that the Poor Laws had a tendency to increase population growth by weakening the preventive checks and that at the same time they would weaken the incentive of people to work by removing their fear of hunger. He concluded that the Poor Laws had a strong tendency to increase poverty in spite of their proclaimed intention to reduce it, and he proposed to abolish the Poor Laws and the Law of Settlement.

In his view, poverty cannot be eradicated completely, because it has its fundamental cause in a law of nature (the principle of population). Therefore, even if the labouring classes acquired the moral restraint, some poverty would remain. The remaining poverty should be relieved by charity, but charity should not be something that the labourers can rely on.

Malthus did not regard emigration as a good solution to excessive population and poverty. If population increases after emigrants leave the country, the excess of population will soon emerge again. For Malthus, population control by postponing the marriage age was essential in order to reduce poverty among the lower classes.

His abolitionist arguments of the Poor Laws had a big impact on the controversies around the Poor Laws in nineteenth-century England. His view of the Poor Laws, in fact, gave an important influence on the Poor Law reform in 1834, by which outdoor relief was, in principle, abolished. In 1909 the Royal Commission on the Poor Laws and Relief of Distress (1905–09), after investigations into poverty among labourers, published two reports: the majority report and the minority report. The majority report proposed to improve the existing system of Poor Laws, while the minority report edited by Beatrice Webb argued in favour of abolition of the Poor Laws for their failure of relieving poverty.

David Ricardo

Ricardo's main concern was with the improvement of the living conditions of the labouring classes, for which he emphasized the necessity of the free importation of corn (*On the Principles of Political Economy, and Taxation*, 1817). In his view, if the economy grows in a closed system, more and more of the economic surplus will be absorbed by rent, and the real wage rate and the profit rate will decline. In order to postpone the arrival of the stationary state of zero economic growth to a more distant future, he recommended developing industries by adopting the policy to import cheap food from abroad. This policy will distribute a larger part of the surplus to productive classes (labourers and capitalists), for which the income distribution becomes more equal and the majority of population will enjoy a higher living standard. The mass poverty will be reduced by that policy. His policy recommendation of the importation of cheap food from abroad is a means to prevent the deterioration of income distribution as between productive classes and to reduce mass poverty.

As to the extreme poverty and the effects of the Poor Laws, Ricardo basically agreed with the view of Malthus. However, he had a stronger abolitionist position of the Poor Laws than Malthus. He feared that the poor relief expenditures under the existing Poor Laws might absorb the whole economic surplus of the economy. Ricardo recognized the necessity of controlling the population growth. He admitted that trade unions can contribute to improving the living conditions of labourers. In his view, trade unions do not disturb the fair and free competition in markets (Ricardo 1951–55, VIII: 316, Ricardo's letter to McCulloch, 4 December 1820). For Ricardo, it was necessary to reform the Parliament dominated by landlords to realize the policy of free importation of corn (food) from abroad. He recognized the necessity of education of common people to reduce poverty, for which he maintained two schools for children of the poor. He advocated the establishment and running of savings banks for labourers to give them the incentive and the chances to make savings which would raise their living standard.

John Stuart Mill

For J.S. Mill, the capitalist system of Great Britain was able to generate a sufficient production for the whole population and lead to a sufficiently high standard of living. Therefore, for him the problem was to make the distribution of income more equal. In his view, the distribution of product or income can be separated from the process of production. He believed that at that time in Britain the economic development had already advanced so much that Britain could and should enter the stationary state before long (*Principles of Political Economy*, 1848).

For Mill, the stationary state was not considered the ultimate state of economic development in which the profit rate and the real wage rate were at their minimum level, and no population growth and no increase of production were any more possible. In Mill's stationary state, a sufficient economic surplus can be produced, but a part of it can be devoted to leisure time of people, which people may make use of to improve the quality of their life; for example, people can spend time in enjoying arts, or passing leisure time with friends. Mill recommended that we should employ the economic surplus in diminishing working hours and increasing leisure time.

Mill believed that the control of population growth was necessary in order to improve the living conditions of common people, for which he did not deny the use of artificial means of birth control. As to the Poor Laws, he contended to reform it to make the labouring classes have a mind of self-help and he supported the reform of the Poor Laws in 1834.

Karl Marx

According to Marx (*Das Kapital*, 1867), the social surplus gets exploited by the capitalist class. The wage rates are kept low by the existence of a reserve army (the stock of unemployed labourers) which capitalists intend to maintain by continuously adopting labour-saving technical progress. In order to improve the living conditions of common people, the capitalist system should be abolished. In Marx's view, the revolution by the labouring class is necessary in order to improve the standard of living. He did not see any possibility of improving the conditions of labourers within a capitalist economy.

Alfred Marshall, Knut Wicksell, and John Maynard Keynes

Marshall was motivated to study economics observing poverty among labourers in the East End of London. In chapter 1 of his *Principles of Economics* (1890), he states his object of studying economics. He found the primary cause of poverty of labourers in the low quality of their labour. Theoretically, this means a low productivity of labour, and the wage rate will become equal to the marginal productivity of labour. Usually it is assumed that the marginal productivity of labour is decreasing. In this view of distribution of income, a low wage rate is caused by low quality of labour or excessive supply of labour. His way to better the standard of life of labourers was to raise the productivity of labourers and to restrain population growth. He proposed to give them education, more leisure time and better living conditions (better food, better houses, a better environment, and so on), in short, to make the labourers more educated and more healthy.

Knut Wicksell in Sweden had a keen interest in the problem of poverty. He saw the main cause of poverty in an excessive population. He ardently supported neo-Malthusianism. In his main work, *Lectures on Political Economy* (original Swedish version, 1901), chapter 1 begins by discussing the population problem, although that chapter was not included in the English (1934) version.

As is well known, J.M. Keynes elaborated his theory of employment to show the fundamental cause of mass unemployment in the 1930s. Unemployment is one of the most serious causes of poverty in affluent societies (*The General Theory of Employment, Interest and Money*, 1936). He also had a profound interest in the population problem, because he believed that an excessive increase of population would lead to the decline of the standard of living of the people of the country by making the terms of trade in international trade worse for Britain. In his youth, Keynes was a neo-Malthusian and participated in the movement to promote the use of artificial birth control, but in the 1930s he changed his mind and became concerned with the decrease of population after there appeared forecasts of a future decline of the population in Britain (see Toye 2000).

Galbraith on Mass Poverty

John Kenneth Galbraith is well known for his analysis of affluent societies, especially of the United States (*The Affluent Society*, 1958). However, he made an inquiry into mass poverty in *The Nature of Mass Poverty* in 1979. He meant by mass poverty a phenomenon mainly in rural societies. In his view, in the early stages of development of the developed countries of today and in the present developing countries, the majority of the population lived and are living in rural areas under a minimum standard of living (life of subsistence). They are accustomed to that state of life and have no pronounced wish to improve the conditions of their life, Galbraith calls that state of mind "accommodation to poverty". If people are accommodated to the minimum standard of living, even if there is some economic surplus, they may consume it in drinking alcohol or in consumption of luxury goods, or they spend their time doing nothing useful, or consuming the economic surplus in increasing the population. Thus, people's standard of living remains as it is without any improvement whatever. Such a state of things Galbraith called equilibrium of poverty.

Economists often find causes of poverty in underdeveloped countries in a shortage of capital, a lack of technology and knowledge, but he thinks they are results of poverty, not causes. Mass poverty may arise from a low productivity of the economy. The most fundamental factor to preserve mass poverty is "accommodation to poverty". Therefore, an economy with mass poverty needs to break the accommodation in order to start improving the living conditions of common people. According to Galbraith, education of people is certainly necessary to break the accommodation. However, it takes time to instil in people's minds a wish to abandon their accustomed ways of life by general education. An efficient way to break accommodation is to find some leading persons with a positive mind and help them to get out of poverty. Their example will influence other members in the community. Other people in the community will have a wish to emulate them. They will want to get better living conditions and catch up with them.

After breaking the accommodation to poverty of people, Galbraith argues, effective ways to improve the standard of living of people are industrialization and emigration to foreign countries. Industrialization involves the process of movement of a part of the population from rural areas to towns. This transfer of population from agriculture to industry raises the productivity of the economy as a whole, because on the one hand it raises productivity in agriculture in which diminishing returns dominate and on the other hand it improves productivity in industry under increasing returns to scale. A rise in productivity increases the possibility of improving the standard of living of the labouring classes. Emigration of a part of the population from rural areas to foreign countries also has the effect of raising productivity in the agriculture of the country because in agriculture decreasing returns to scale operate.

Those who emigrate abroad will make up for the shortage of labour of the recipient countries where they settle down. The country that receives the emigrants can increase its product by adding a new labour force to the existing one. Galbraith says that the European countries benefited much from emigration in their past history. The representative examples are England, Scotland and Ireland. England developed its industries which absorbed many labourers from rural areas, but at the same time it sent out many emigrants to America, Australia, New Zealand, Canada, and so on. Ireland could not have survived if it had not reduced its population by sending out many of the nationals during the eighteenth and nineteenth centuries. England could realize a standard of living of its own people while it developed the industries in the country. The double benefits pointed out by Galbraith are apparent if we take into consideration that the European countries and the countries where the European emigrants settled are both the most developed and richest countries that are enjoying the highest standard of living in the world today.

A Japanese Example and Contemporary Studies

Galbraith's arguments are still applicable for developing countries in which mass poverty exists. For him, the most important factor for underdeveloped economies to escape mass poverty is a change of mind in people to believe in the possibility of bettering their living conditions. If people have a wish to better their own living conditions, they can find the capital and techniques necessary for the economic development.

It may be of interest here to mention the example of a farmer reformer called Kinjiro Ninomiya, who succeeded in restoring several hundred villages that had fallen into poverty in the Tohoku (North-East of Tokyo) regions in Japan towards the end of the Edo period just before the Meiji Revolution in 1868. He is very famous among the Japanese people as a person symbolizing diligence and parsimony, but he is more important as a reformer engaged in relieving the poverty of rural areas at that time. Ninomiya, in his restoration work of villages fallen into poverty, first made a meticulous inquiry into the state of the villages for about the previous ten years, examining each house's conditions, and then he proposed a detailed plan of restoration work to the feudal lords who asked him to do the restoration work. At the same time he demanded and persuaded the feudal lords to reduce the unfeasible official tax rates imposed on farmers to make room for saving and investment by the people. He concentrated his efforts on changing the minds of villagers accustomed to poverty as the destination given by Heaven (see Tomita 1912).

Among contemporary economists, Theodore William Schultz studied poverty in developing countries (*The Economics of Being Poor*, 1993). He pointed out that too much importance had been attached to endowments of natural resources, to land in particular. In his view, the most important thing in economic development is the quality of labour. He emphasized the importance of human capital for economic development, for which the people needed to be educated. A.K. Sen also examined poverty in developing countries. He studied famine and starvation as the core of poverty. For Sen, mere economic development is not sufficient to prevent famines and starvation: to achieve that, he contended that freedom of the people and democracy were essential (Sen 1981).

KATSUYOSHI WATARAI

See also:

Jeremy Bentham (I); British classical political economy (II); Development economics (III); Economic sociology (III); Growth (III); Income distribution (III); John Maynard Keynes (I); Labour and employment (III); Thomas Robert Malthus (I); Alfred Marshall (I); Karl Heinrich Marx (I); John Stuart Mill (I); Population (III); David Ricardo (I); Amartya Kumar Sen (I); Adam Smith (I); Technical change and innovation (III); Welfare economics (III); Knut Wicksell (I).

References and further reading

Bentham, J. (2001), *Writings on the Poor Laws*, vol. 1, ed. M. Quinn, Oxford: Clarendon Press.
Bentham, J. (2010), *Writings on the Poor Laws*, vol. 2, ed. M. Quinn, Oxford: Clarendon Press.
Booth, C. (1902–04), *Life and Labour of the People in London. First Series: Poverty*, reprinted 1970, New York: Ams Press.
Eden, F.M. (1797), *The State of the Poor: A History of the Labouring Classes in England with Parochial Reports*, London: J. Davis, abridged edn 1928, A.G.L. Rogers (ed.) and introduction, London: George Routledge.
Galbraith, J.K. (1958), *The Affluent Society*, London: Hamish Hamilton.
Galbraith, J.K. (1979), *The Nature of Mass Poverty*, New York: Harvard University Press.
Keynes, J.M. (1936), *The General Theory of Employment, Interest and Money*, London: Macmillan.
Malthus, T.R. (1789), *An Essay on the Principle of Population, As It Affects the Future Improvement of Society. With Remarks on the Speculations of Mr. Godwin, M. Condorcet, and Other Writers*, London: J. Johnson.
Malthus, T.R. (1803), *An Essay on Population or a View of its Past and Present Effects on Human Happiness, with an Inquiry into Our Prospects Respecting the Future Removal or Mitigation of the Evils which It Occasions*, 2nd edn, London: P. Johnson.
Marshall, A. (1890), *Principles of Economics*, 8th edn 1920, London: Macmillan.
Marx, K. (1867), *Das Kapital*, vol. 1, Hamburg: Verlag Otto Meister, first English trans. 1887, Moscow: Progress, another English edn 1954, London: Lawrence & Wishart.
Mill, J.S. (1848), *Principles of Political Economy, with Some of Their Applications to Social Philosophy*, 2 vols, London: John W. Parker, reprinted in J.M. Robson (ed.) (1965), *The Collected Works of John Stuart Mill*, vols II and III, Toronto: Toronto University Press.
Ricardo, D. (1817), *On the Principles of Political Economy and Taxation*, London: John Murray, reprinted in P. Sraffa (ed.) with the collaboration of M. Dobb (1951), *The Works and Correspondence of David Ricardo*, vol. I, Cambridge: Cambridge University Press.
Ricardo, D. (1951–55), *The Works and Correspondence of David Ricardo*, ed. P. Sraffa with the collaboration of M. Dobb, vols I–X, Cambridge: Cambridge University Press.
Rowntree, B.S. (1922), *Poverty: A Study of Town Life*, new edn, London: Longman, Green.
Royal Commission on the Poor Laws and Relief of Distress (1909a), *The Poor Law Report of 1909*, ed. H. Bosanquet, London: Macmillan.
Royal Commission on the Poor Laws and Relief of Distress (1909b), *The Minority Report of the Poor Law Commission*, ed. B. Webb, Clifton, NJ: A.M. Kelley.
Schultz, T.W. (1993), *The Economics of Being Poor*, Oxford: Blackwell.
Sen, A.K. (1981), *Poverty and Famine: An Essay on Entitlement and Deprivation*, Oxford: Clarendon Press.
Smith, A. (1776), *An Inquiry into the Nature and Causes of the Wealth of Nations*, London: W. Strahan & T. Cadell, Modern Library edn 1937, New York: Modern Library.
Sraffa, P. (1960), *Production of Commodities by Means of Commodities*, Cambridge: Cambridge University Press.
Tomita, K. (1912), *A Peasant Sage of Japan: The Life and Work of Sontoku Ninomiya* (trans. T. Yoshimoto from K. Tomita, *Hotokuki*), London: Longmans, Green.
Townsend, P. (1979), *Poverty in the United Kingdom: A Survey of Household Resources and Standard of Living*, Berkeley and Los Angeles, CA: University of California Press.
Toye, J. (2000), *Keynes on Population*, Cambridge: Cambridge University Press.
Wicksell, K. (1901), *Föreläsningar i Nationalekonomi*, Första delen: Teoritisk National-ekonomi, English edn 1934, *Lectures on Political Economy*, London: Routledge & Kegan Paul.

Public economics

A Paradoxical Subject

In his Palgrave entry on public economics, Serge-Christophe Kolm (1987: 1053), one of the pioneers of modern public economics, calls the subject "for many reasons the most paradoxical field of economics". Kolm explains those reasons in some detail, characterizing public economics as an interdisciplinary multi-level subject with a strong disciplinary core. Indeed, the history of public economics spans a vast area including philosophical speculations regarding the nature and purpose of the state as well as down-to-earth issues of an applied character, including institutional details and issues such as the legal definition of the base of a particular tax. Its multi-dimensionality renders public economics one of the most challenging fields of the history of economic thought. Kolm (1987: 1053) moreover argues that public economics "is one of the oldest fields in economics, yet it also is one of the newborns". This paradox is related to the multi-level character emphasized in his entry, offering ample opportunities for new combinations of tools and topics.

Richard Musgrave's (1987: 1055) informative entry on public finance is introduced by the observation that the latter "may well be the oldest branch of economics". This is substantiated by a historical account including cameralist, mercantilist and physiocratic authors as well as Thomas Hobbes, David Hume, Adam Smith, John Stuart Mill and the German language tradition. Kolm (1987), Musgrave (1987), and Creedy (1984) provide partially complementary and partially overlapping overviews of the field in historical perspective with a special focus on modern developments.

Diversity of roots

Those and other historically informed works on public economics include in-depth references to a highly diverse body of writers, apart from theorists primarily known as pioneers in public economics such as Adolph Wagner. First, we find the names of eminent philosophers dealing with political institutions in market societies based on private property rights and contracts, or with issues of tax justice and the normative architecture of government and state. This list of thinkers includes Hobbes, Hugo Grotius, Samuel von Pufendorf, John Locke, Charles Louis de Montesquieu, Jean-Jacques Rousseau, David Hume, Immanuel Kant, Jeremy Bentham, Henry Sidgwick, John Rawls and Robert Nozick. Notice, in particular, that the list of philosophers referred to in public economics is by no means restricted to the pre-history of the subject, when economic reasoning had not developed into a discipline of its own. Beginning with early modernity, it continues throughout the centuries of enlightenment and industrialization, including the very recent past.

Continuity throughout the centuries also applies to a second class of important references, consisting of pivotal figures in the history of economic analysis, including William Petty, François Quesnay, Adam Smith, David Ricardo, Jean-Baptiste Say, Alfred Marshall, Knut Wicksell, Vilfredo Pareto, Abba Lerner, Paul Samuelson and Kenneth Arrow. All of them are economists of outstanding importance and at the same time contributed in specific ways to key issues within public economics: Petty provided economic arguments in favour of excise taxes on consumption, already advocated by

Hobbes and others. In that context, recurrent issues in public finance such as double taxation and considerations regarding incentive effects of taxation came to the fore. *L'impôt unique* belongs to the core of physiocratic thought. Eleven out of 22 chapters of Ricardo's *Principles* (1951) are devoted to taxation, dealing with issues of incidence and the famous equivalence theorem regarding public debt. The incidence of product taxes was analysed by Marshall with the characteristic partial equilibrium emphasis on the elasticity of supply and demand curves – still to be found in any basic textbook. In the wake of Keynes's *General Theory* (1936), Lerner included macroeconomic considerations of stabilization in what he called functional finance. Samuelson (1954) formally derived the summation rule for the efficient provision of non-rival goods. Arrow inaugurated the general framework of social choice and wrote seminal pieces dealing with market failure related to the allocation of resources for invention and the provision of insurance under incomplete information, adverse selection, and moral hazard. And so on.

Third, there are names closely associated with problems of the public household and the practices of the public economy, such as, Jean-Baptiste Colbert, Sébastien Le Prêtre de Vauban, Johann Heinrich Gottlob von Justi, Joseph von Sonnenfels and other cameralists, or with problems of public utilities and public infrastructure from Jules Dupuit to Marcel Boiteux. Dupuit invented the user surplus criterion in the context of the evaluation of public projects, employing marginal reasoning and the summation rule for individual utilities. Boiteux dealt with the optimal pricing in cases of natural monopoly. This problem was also studied by Frank Ramsey and Harold Hotelling in the twentieth century.

Finally, some eminent contributors to public economics do not fall into any of those categories: John Stuart Mill, Arthur Cecil Pigou, James Buchanan, William Baumol, or Amartya Sen are economists concerned with issues of public economics at various levels throughout their careers, integrating advances at the conceptual, the normative, the technical, and the practical level of public economics. In that context, some nowadays less well-known currents suggesting encompassing visions of public economics deserve to be mentioned here for the sake of completion of this panoramic overview, including the French liberal school or some currents in Germany and in Italy, whose pertinent reasoning is driven by specific conceptualizations of society, state and politics: Those currents were informed by different pre-analytic visions: either by organic/romantic views and German Idealism, or by strong versions of private property individualism, or by a thoroughly strategic "Machiavellian" view of politics.

Diversity of topics

The heterogeneity of scholarly backgrounds reflected in the diversity of contributors to public economics indicates the intricacies of its subject matter. In so far as it studies the purposes and mechanisms of the public sector in a market economy, it has to deal with the logic, the virtues, the limits and failures of the market. Given the diagnosis of those limits and failures, it needs to transcend the borders of the private property-market economy and analyse collective choice, political mechanisms, public administration and public budgeting. Moreover, various types of interfaces between private and public sectors belong to the classical topics of public economics: taxation, regulation and public utilities are cases in point.

Given those multifarious dimensions, a contribution stressing characteristic challenges posed by public economics as a subject of the history of economic thought cannot aim at a sketch of all currents and topics that are somehow important. Consider the economics of taxation: concern with fiscal revenues is probably one of the oldest branches of positive economics. Theorists well before Adam Smith saw that in the absence of some understanding of market interdependences no systematic answer to crucial questions regarding taxation is possible: think, for instance, of tax incidence. The same applies to what is now called the "excess burden" of taxation, but also to socially desirable incentive effects captured by the concept of Pigovian taxes. Tax progression and the choice of tax base may be regarded as more narrowly technical issues, even though various definitions of income (as tax base) again presuppose assumptions which are by no means innocuous from the point of view of economic analysis. Arguments from social philosophy and ethics are invoked in the context of normative considerations regarding justifiability of patterns of taxation, such as horizontal equity, the leave-them-as-you-find-them rule (taxation should not change the relative wealth positions of households), ability-to-pay, or the benefit principle. Then there is a specific literature on issues such as personal taxation versus indirect taxation, company taxation, taxes on land, wealth and inheritance, local taxation, and taxation in an international setting. Finally, there is an important tradition in political economy regarding the conceptualization and implementation of tax reforms.

Each of these aspects, issues, or sub-subfields has a history of its own, sometimes commencing with thinkers such as Hobbes (for example, in the case of consumption taxes) or even earlier. The same applies to the expenditure side of the public budget and the functional core of governmental activity: thinkers such as Hobbes and Hume are renowned for emblematic statements and thought experiments regarding conditions where private coordination fails and life is solitary, poor, nasty, brutish, and short. Collective wants, public goods, social insurance, and the evaluation of public projects including cost–benefit analysis are further examples indicating the number and scope of conceptual histories covering the expenditure side. The list could be continued with public choice, or planning and budgeting. Mechanism design connotes profound issues regarding the way in which informational decentralization and incentive problems should be dealt with in the public sector.

Normative frameworks used in public economics include utilitarianism, contractualism and the natural law heritage. Studying the way in which those frameworks may be applied to typical problems of the public sector requires specific conceptualizations and is a demanding endeavour of its own, pursued by welfare economics: pertinent strands include Pigovian welfare economics, new welfare economics, social choice theory and subsequent developments such as welfare economics of the second-best and new approaches in normative economics integrating distributive criteria and non-utility information (such as, freedom, rights, capabilities and functionings).

Finally, there are some basic aspects regarding research methods and theoretical architecture: the question partial versus less partial ("general equilibrium") analysis is relevant for most of the above-mentioned issues. Depending on the research questions, it may be appropriate to analyse issues such as the pricing of public utilities or taxation either in a partial or a more encompassing framework. For some purposes, an integrated view of the revenue side and the expenditure side of the public budget is commendable. In important contexts, the tri-partite architecture – allocation, distribution, and stabilization – suggested by Musgrave is an expedient way of factorizing the problems of public economics. Its pre-history includes Wicksell's (1896) foundational treatise on optimal public good allocation as well as Wagner's distinction between distributive and allocative purposes of taxation.

However, one might try to integrate all those sub-currents and issues within a grandiose Whig story of progress in public economics. Accordingly, progress occurs as everything relevant known by earlier generations is also known by more recent generations of theorists – and something more. Here is a shorthand version of a Whig history of public economics as cumulative progress of what has become a tool-based science: the early and rude state of public finance was characterized by (1) a diversity of national strands and (2) a poorly systematized mixture of fragmentary economic insights, cooking recipes, rules of public accounting, and economic "principles" and "laws", supplemented by philosophical speculation regarding the purpose of government or the nature of the state. The more theoretical ingredients included the arguments supporting Wagner's law of the increasing relative importance of the public sector, Mill's anticipation of market failure theory, Ricardo's work on taxation and public debt, and the four principles of taxation as summarized by Smith (1776 V.ii.b):

I. The subjects of every state ought to contribute towards the support of the government, as nearly as possible . . . in proportion to their respective abilities; that is, in proportion to the revenue which they respectively enjoy under the protection of the state.

II. The tax which each individual is bound to pay ought to be certain, and not arbitrary. The time of payment, the manner of payment, the quantity to be paid, ought all to be clear and plain to the contributor, and to every other person.

III. Every tax ought to be levied at the time, or in the manner, in which it is most likely to be convenient for the contributor to pay it.

IV. Every tax ought to be so contrived as both to take out and keep out of the pockets of the people as little as possible, over and above what it brings into the public treasury of the state.

Indeed, Smith anticipated a broad range of concepts, from ability-to-pay and benefit principles to excess burden. In the twentieth century, public economics was more and more integrated into neoclassical economics, becoming a part of a globalized and cosmopolitan science based on a rigorously individualist theory of the public sector supported by formal modelling and quantitative research. National traditions became obsolete. Issues such as public spending or optimal taxation (once addressed by sets of principles, ad-hoc recipes, and philosophical speculations regarding the purpose of government) are now systematically integrated in a welfare-theoretic framework. The models of modern economics are the basis for quantitative analysis regarding the multifarious dimensions of public revenues, public expenditures, and public sector mechanisms. The optimization of goal-achievement in the public sector is made precise in an overarching welfare-theoretic framework, while paying due attention to the distortions caused by the intricate problems of public sector decision making: since the diffusion of public choice theory beginning in the 1960s, governmental behaviour is no longer conceptualized within the framework of the omniscient and benevolent planner – the implications of informational asymmetries and rent-seeking by interest groups are taken care of in micro-based models capturing agency problems in the public sector.

Some such kind of Whig story of progress does indeed capture an important aspect of the development of modern public economics, as summarized by works such as Atkinson and Stiglitz (1980) in the format of an advanced textbook. Progress in areas such as tax incidence, public debt, or externalities are clearly depending on advances in modelling interdependences in market economies. Indeed, model-based economic analysis is applied to specific problems of the public economy since the time of Ricardo. Specific advances in public economics are derived from the progress made with regard to economic modelling and econometric methods: general economics makes available theoretical tools and methods that subsequently are applied to problems of public economics. Today, progress in terms of tools and methods is a core element of substantial advances in public economics; think, for instance, of the role of game theory in areas such as (semi-)public goods.

That notwithstanding, the co-evolution of economics, public finance, and the public sector in modern market economies cannot be fully accounted for by the straightforward narratives suggested by a Whig perspective of cumulative progress. The overall history of public economics is far more complex. This should not be surprising, given the theoretical scope and the practical complexity of public economics. The multi-dimensional interfaces of public economics suggest that views of linear progress solely driven by ever more sophisticated economic theory and tools – plausible as they may seem at first sight – miss important aspects of advances, breakthroughs and vicissitudes in the theories and models of the public sector. The lacunae of a Whig perspective are reflected in two salient characteristics of the development of public economics:

1. In the politically and culturally diversified setting of post-Renaissance Europe, the way in which national traditions developed, interacted and eventually to some extent became merged, affected in important ways the development of the discipline at least until the 1960s. The late internationalization of public economics (late compared with general economics) indicates the scope of those influences.
2. Despite the undisputed role of analytical and empirical tools for twentieth-century advances in modern public economics, the evolution of public economics is to a remarkable extent based on conceptual and combinatorial progress even in the decades after World War II (probably to a higher degree than progress in general economics). That is, progress in the field is not solely driven by advances in technical tools and modelling. This is true even for the core of the theory of public economics and not merely for those parts of applied public finance and tax policy analysis which clearly hinge upon national traditions enshrined in tax codes or budgetary rules.

The next section summarizes some of the reasons for the specificities of progress in public economics, while the two sections following it expand on above observations (1) and (2).

The Character of the Subject in Historical Perspective

There is a straightforward prima facie explanation of the late internationalization of public economics: the nation-specific institutional features embedding public budgeting processes had a deep and lasting impact on the subject. However, this explanation does not capture the whole story. It applies to public finance as a technical discipline dealing with public sector accounting and public budgeting processes, while being of limited importance regarding public economics in general: as discussed in the above, some core parts of public economics (for example, tax incidence) evolve together with general economics. Any adequate analysis of taxation and public debt clearly must be based on the economic analysis of market interdependences. Moreover, the narrowly technical view of public finance is unsatisfactory for reasons which Joseph Schumpeter expressed as follows: "Public finance is never a special area but always the summary of all social, political, cultural, economic, and external relations and conditions of a nation" (Schumpeter 1926–27: 827; own translation). Indeed, Schumpeter's own fiscal sociology of the tax state highlights the deep-reaching tensions between private capitalism and the system of public revenues; those tensions are not easily resolved, as the development of modern societies is characterized by a co-evolution of private economy and the state.

Public finance should not be confined to a collection of technical tools to be handled by subaltern bureaucrats: this kind of public finance is "the most boring subject on earth", as Schumpeter puts it. Moreover, Schumpeter's emphasis on the scope of the interdependences embedding typical issues of public economics highlights the fact that the latter is not a discipline dealing only with technicalities in the context of public budgets in the sense of narrow cameralistic *Finanzwissenschaft*. Nor is it one of several sub-disciplines of applied economics, as some narrow view of the Anglo-Saxon tradition in public finance might have it. Only views of public finance steering clear of (1) the explanation and justification of public expenditures, (2) the logic of political mechanisms of collective choice, and (3) the co-evolution of the public sector within the dynamism of modern market economies could be thought of either as a sub-discipline or a narrowly technical exercise concerned with budgeting procedures.

Public economics and normative economics

Here are some elements of a broader view in an historical perspective. Public economics is interested in prescriptive knowledge regarding what the public sector should do and how. Unsurprisingly, the scope of the normative focus depends on the politico-economic context. In the feudal tradition, the household of the prince was framed as a quasi-private affair, implying the quest for expedient solutions on the revenue side while the expenditure side is not naturally regarded as a subject of analysis and justification. Yet a limited normative perspective regarding taxation is pursued from early on, for example, in the controversies on excise taxes in the times of Hobbes and Petty. In the writings of cameralists such as Justi, budgetary issues became framed by considerations on what the goals of policy should be. Compared with the comprehensive normative framework of welfare economics, the pre-history of public economics as an "art" is characterized by normative principles and perspectives associated with pragmatic and limited goals. The rationales and the ambiguities of the early normative concerns are vividly summarized in Fritz Karl Mann's "ideals of tax policy" (1937), commencing with ideas of equitable taxation in the context of natural law reasoning. In the course of the development of modern market economies of the past two centuries, the importance of the normative perspective evolved together with the growing public sector amounting to 30 to 60 per cent of gross domestic product (GDP) in the advanced economies of today. If the public sector is big, the patterns of revenue and expenditure more urgently require some kind of public justification. They require specific forms of justification if the political environment is a democracy cherishing individualist values: the pattern of public activities should demonstrably benefit all/most individuals. It cannot be justified in terms of some vague idea of the flourishing of the state (see Mann 1937: ch. 6). That is, the value of public economics as a socially useful subject depends on the availability of sustainable approaches of normative economics congruent with individual values. It is no coincidence that some of the greatest economists contributing to public economics (such as, Wicksell, Pigou, Samuelson, Arrow, or Sen) devoted substantial efforts to the development of a sustainable architecture of normative public economics.

Providing useful answers to the questions such as

1. Which are the properties of "good" tax bases and structures?
2. Which kinds of public institutions, public utilities, or public transfer schemes are solving the most salient problems emerging in the dynamism of market economies?
3. Which are the core properties of global institutions and workable mechanisms for controlling greenhouse gas emissions?

may be regarded as important fruits of seeking economic knowledge beyond the pure pleasure of truth. Such answers presuppose theorizations of social preference somehow integrated within economic analysis. Hence the analysis of social choice based on individual values is on the agenda of modern public economics.

A few simple observations indicate why economic reasoning on issues such as taxation is concerned with a complex interface of positive analysis and normative issues. Think, for instance, of tax policy. Suppose that we accept some normative principle of a "good" tax system, such as horizontal equity, requiring that taxpayers with the same ability-to-pay should pay the same amount of taxes. This principle must be implemented under real-world conditions. The process of implementation will require making operational normative concepts in a complex economic environment. This will entail assumptions (for example, regarding the definition of income) and specifications (is the individual or the household liable to pay the tax?) that are not innocuous from a normative perspective. Second, taxation is a good example for the coexistence of rights-based principles (such as horizontal equity) and utilitarian considerations, which easily get mixed up in an incoherent way in the absence of proper analytical frameworks. Third, ideals of a "good" tax system may be of questionable value if the underlying normative principles are not sustainable at a sufficiently general level. Finally, it cannot be taken for granted that positive analysis is independent of whether legally adopted normative principles are widely shared, or whether they are biased towards the special advantage of particular groups. For instance, tax compliance may be affected.

The quest for a sustainable normative perspective is complemented by a focus on the conditions of implementation and institutional design in the public economy, including the mechanisms of the public sphere and the choice of policies at various levels of government. The combination of normative stance, implementation, institutions, and market interdependencies is perhaps the most important general characteristic of public economics throughout its history. Hence public economics tends to employ a very broad class of research strategies. Issues of implementation include theoretical problems implied by analysis of markets and public institutions under non-ideal circumstances: it is no co-incidence that the economics of the second-best is an indispensable concept and tool of public economics. They also require the study of actual behaviour, institutions and history. Take, for instance, questions such as, "Why do we have the taxes that we have?" "Why did government grow as it has grown in the 150 years antedating the 1980s?" "How did the great transformation of capitalism culminating in the modern public sector using 30 to 60 per cent of GDP in the most advanced economies come about?" "How did institutions of taxation change in the wake of the emergence of modern statehood?" Answering such questions will involve the study of political mechanisms, of the civil service, of public education, of public utilities and regulation, of social security and welfare, and the history of war and peace (Peacock and Wiseman 2010). Consider the historical account of some tax system (for example, Brownlee 2004). Histories of tax systems will refer to institutional details as well as to legal and constitutional frameworks, modes of governance, or mechanisms for coping with tax evasion. The doctrinal history of taxation principles may play a role in explaining why certain systems of taxation are in place. For instance, Pigou's re-interpretation of the sacrifice principle (as equal marginal sacrifice) foreshadowed the trend towards historically unique high marginal income tax rates in the UK and the USA implemented in the 1940s (Pigou 1932a).

Beyond *homo oeconomicus*
In the context of public economics the importance of studying actual individual behaviour and motivations as opposed to the ideal type of *homo oeconomicus* is clear from early on. For Hume, the motivational mix of selfishness, limited generosity, limited foresight, and reciprocity is the key to understanding the basic architecture of the public realm. From Friedrich Benedikt Wilhelm Hermann (1832) onwards, German-language public economists stressed the role of communal preferences and fellow-feeling (*Gemeinsinn*) as a motivational ingredient in the public economy, complementing the selfishness dominating the marketplace. Eminent theorists such as Pareto suggested an explanatory sociology of fiscal decisions in which power and patron–client relations are looming large, thus establishing a kind of fiscal sociology explicitly transcending the methodological boundaries of individualistic economics (McLure 2003). This includes the sociology of taxation in the context of modern statehood as pursued by Rudolf Goldscheid, Schumpeter and Mann. Again, all this is not limited to the (pre)history of modern public economics: in the wake of the recent boom in behavioural and experimental economics, much of the interesting work is related to issues of public economics, notably to public good provision (see Fehr and Gächter 2000). Further behavioural and experimental work is dealing with issues of distribution and social security, regulation, and labour market institutions (see Shafir 2013). Experimental studies are providing evidence regarding systematic failures of individual rationality in choice settings such as the purchase of pension plans. This is relevant for assessing alternative frameworks of social insurance and the regulation of private insurance and retail finance. In general terms, this kind of work provides systematic evidence supporting conjectures that played a key role in Mill's (1848, bk V) arguments justifying public education and in Musgrave's (1959) "merit wants": some of the most important functions of the public sector are related to behavioural contexts where consumer sovereignty is not a credible assumption.

Nation-Specific Traditions

The importance of the historical, institutional and political background of nation-specific traditions in public economics has been repeatedly pointed out, for example, by von Stein (1875: 25–8), Creedy (1984: 89) and Kolm (2010: 689). The book by Musgrave and Peacock (1958) contains classic writings documenting the diversity of nation-specific traditions. Musgrave (1996–97) provides a systematic comparison between the British tradition of public finance and the German Finanzwissenschaft, focusing on the comparative achievements as well as the different ideological environments of the two. Musgrave's (1987) *Palgrave* entry on "Public finance" and Kolm's (1987) entry on "Public economics" provide systematic accounts of the subject in historical perspective, both paying due attention to national traditions. Faccarello and Sturn (2010) suggest that nation-specific traditions are not only a convenient expository device for presenting a vast range of material: their specific importance is closely related to what Kolm called the paradoxical character of public economics.

The co-evolution of theories and institutions
Analysis of differences between paradigmatic developments in Britain, Germany, France, and Italy may explain both late internationalization and the way in which combinations involving two or more national traditions eventually led to progress. To put the following in perspective, two more general aspects have to be kept in mind. (1) Regarding the historical context, the development of public economics may be thought of in terms of a co-evolution accompanying the emergence of modern statehood differing across Europe. In the feudal setting, taxation was conceptualized in framings not yet adapted to modern ideas of statehood and the public sphere. In older treatises on public finances, taxation is often viewed as an irregular source of revenue that should be tapped only in times of wars and emergencies (Mann 1937: ch. 3). The co-evolution of modern statehood and modern market economies coincides with the evolution of public finances and taxation, eventually triggering multifarious developments in public economics. (2) Different architectures of state and governance are developed by major thinkers of European modernity, influencing the discussions on the principles of public economy in different ways across the different eras and the different nations of modern Europe: Hobbes, Locke, Montesquieu, Kant, and Georg Wilhelm Friedrich Hegel. However, there are common elements too; public economics must deal with the coherence of the principles of governance and their implications for policies. The latter need to be analysed in an environment of complex market interdependences. Practical knowledge regarding "good" public institutions and mechanisms presupposes such analysis. Different sets of foundational principles were mapped into the conceptual space of public economics, including:

1. The voluntary-exchange theory of the state. This is related to the quid-pro-quo or benefit principle of taxation and the concept of a Lindahl equilibrium regarding the provision of public goods (see Foley 1967).
2. Locke's conception of the state as an expedient enforcement agency for pre-political private property rights. This is related to the view that the main task of the state is lowering the costs of private transactions, again gaining prominence in the wake of the Coase theorem.

3. Conceptualizations of the complementary functions of the state and the private property-market economy as emphasized in German idealism. This is related to conceptions of (re)productivity of the state and collective wants emerging in German language Public Economics (see Sturn 2006).

The range of influences on currents of thought includes such foundational reasoning along with nation-specific institutional features, policy challenges and ideologies. There is no one-to-one correspondence between nations and currents of thought: "national traditions" in public economics consist of combinations of elements whose origin is not always purely domestic. However, the specific mix of ideas and its evolution tends to be conditioned by institutional circumstances and political problems. In the nineteenth century, nation-specific developments and research strategies of public economics are influenced by historically specific forms of those two elements, that is:

1. *The theoretical background*, shaping thought regarding the role of the state in a market society. This includes public goods and market failure as well as the drawbacks of political mechanisms and the forces of self-regulation.
2. The political context, either putting public economics into the perspective of incremental reform in the context of an existing governance structure or else raising foundational issues of statehood pertinent to a more radical transformation of governance structures.

"National traditions" neither preclude the existence of common ingredients, nor of common problems, nor of cross-fertilization. For instance, theories capturing the self-regulating mechanisms of the market economy and the concomitant logic and potential of the spontaneous order had impacts across borders. The lessons of Smithian political economy were absorbed not only in France, but were taken up in Hegel's political philosophy (see Priddat 1990) and by the protagonists of German *Staatswirtschaftslehre* (economics of the state), whose theoretical architecture was influenced by theories of the state of German idealism. On the other hand, James Steuart was influenced by continental thought and influenced German nineteenth-century thought.

At a different level, some degree of thematic convergence occurred regarding specific issues of public finance across different national and theoretical contexts. Vauban and Pierre de Boisguilbert in France, Petty in England, and the cameralists often dealt with very similar problems. Examples include (1) the debates on excise taxes in early modernity, on income taxes in the nineteenth century (with important precursors), or recurrent debates on taxes on land from the eighteenth century onward; (2) ideals of governance without taxation that were promoted in liberal as well as in romantic circles; concerns related to (3) equitability of taxation (for example, ability to pay) and (4) exchange paradigms of taxation (for example, quid-pro-quo or insurance theories of taxation), both recurrent issues from the seventeenth century onward.

Nation-specific traditions should neither be considered as autochthonous currents nor as monolithic paradigms. They are influenced by the a-synchronic emergence of modern statehood and economy in Europe with all its institutional and ideological heterogeneity. They develop their specific profile as part of co-evolutionary processes contingent upon the interaction of modes of governance, pending policy-issues and ideas of statehood widely shared by influential elites and/or public opinion. Moreover, there may be more than one tradition responding to the politico-economic-ideological circumstances of one nation at the same time.

National traditions: an overview
This should be kept in mind in the context of the following overview of the broader background and the impact of some of the most important "national" traditions and schools, commencing with the British tradition. It supplied the general framework in which modern public economics developed after World War II: the framework of market failure. In the case of the market failure approach to governmental activities, the theoretical background is made up by the combination of the system of natural liberty established by Smithian political economy and the long-standing resistance to government in British thought (for example, Creedy 1984: 89–90), based on the presumption of incurable distortions in political and bureaucratic decision-making. The upshot of this is brilliantly expressed by Mill, moderate interventionist and foremost contributor to the market failure approach, in the long nineteenth century between Smith and Pigou:

> [F]ew will dispute the more than sufficiency of these reasons, to throw, in every instance, the burden of making out a strong case, not on those who resist, but on those who recommend government interference. Letting alone, in short, should be the general practice: every departure from it, unless required by some great good, is a certain evil. (Mill 1848 V.xi.7)

In the British tradition, the links between economics and public finance are very close from an early time onward. Regarding areas such as tax incidence or optimal taxation, dealing with issues of public finances as a specific chapter of the economic analysis of markets (rather than a field of its own) has obvious advantages. Notice that British public economics maintains that kind of conceptual affinity to economic analysis of markets also regarding the analysis of the tasks of the public sector: it developed the market failure approach to explain/justify government interference, thereby providing the basis for a natural extension of rigorous analyses of price systems to cases where some "real" interdependences are not mediated by "correct prices". The paradigmatic conceptualization of such coordination gaps was originally developed within the Marshallian partial equilibrium framework: an interdependence not properly mediated by a "correct price" is called an externality, conceptually pre-supposing the existence of a price system properly mediating all other interdependences. Useful as it is, this conceptualization is not without shortcomings. For decades, the conceptual relation between externalities and the price system rendered externalities "one of the most elusive concepts" in economics (Scitovsky 1954: 143; see Arrow and Scitovsky 1969: pt III). That elusiveness included the distinction between "Pareto relevant" technological externalities (to which the above definition applies) and pecuniary externalities (capturing impacts of my action on others operating through the price system that give rise to distributional concerns, but are neutral in terms of Pareto efficiency). Such conceptual ambiguities may have been dispatched now, but there is another difficulty. It has been observed that externalities tend to be seen as "freakish anomalies" in some versions of mainstream theory. Lagueux (2010) reviews discussions where concomitant problems with the "residual character of externalities" come to the fore. The function of the government is defined by a collection of prima facie unconnected specific cases of coordination gaps. Theorists such as William Baumol (1952) and Peter Hammond (1995) emphasize that in cases where coordination failures are pervasive throughout the economy, the theory of externalities becomes tricky, also in the sense that typical policy conclusions (according to which implementing a "correct price" on a previously missing market enhances efficiency) do not generally hold. In a more encompassing perspective, externalities may be ill suited to capture the strategic structure of public sector agenda which are related to the institutional foundations of the market rather than to particular coordination gaps (and their elimination by incremental reforms) within an otherwise well-ordered market system.

However, the Anglo-Saxon tradition inaugurating normative public economics as the theoretical underpinning of government intervention on a case-by-case basis was highly important for the development of the discipline. It included the systematic application of theoretical tools and empirical methods for a wide range of problems. The Pigovian programme (1932b, 1935) in particular promoted successfully the professional role for university-trained expert economists, whose command of analytical/empirical tools enables them to give theory-based technical advice.

The theoretical and political environment of nineteenth-century Germany with its history of political fragmentation and the national challenges posed by the Napoleonic wars sets the stage for a different agenda. Fundamental institutional questions of a "late nation state" are the topic of discussions for decades. In political philosophy, Kant and Hegel had come up with different versions of theories emphasizing the foundational interdependence between modern market society and modern state. Well-ordered institutions of the public sphere and private property were conceptualized as two complementary requirements of free welfare-enhancing exchange. That broader vision of the state and the tradition of cameralism came to be merged with basic insights of Smithian economics. Indeed, Prussia's Stein-Hardenberg reforms in the early nineteenth century (following Prussia's defeat by Napoleon) were inspired by German Smithians. In the same period, writers such as Adam Müller used Smith's thought as a critical reference point for their own Romantic thought, stressing organic conceptualizations of society. The combination of the historical setting and the various intellectual influences contributed to a framework in which foundational problems of the state were translated into a conceptual framework for the public economy. The state is seen as an institutional framework co-evolving with the market system. Rather than perceiving government as an agency in charge of amending market failure here and there, it is framed as an encompassing (re-)productive agency. All this is reflected in the conceptual histories of what now are called public goods and merit goods: Hermann's (1832) collective wants and the subsequent theorizations of the triad of German Finanzwissenschaft in its Golden Age – Lorenz von Stein (1875), Albert Schäffle (1867, 1880), Adolph Wagner (1876, 1886, 1891, 1893) – deserve to be mentioned. The marginalist transformation of that framework by Emil Sax, Friedrich von Wieser, Wicksell, Gustav Cassel, Erik Lindahl, and Italian economists such as Ugo Mazzola prepared the basis for modern public good theory. While the latter captures wants felt by individuals that are satisfied by collective goods/services, the concept of merit wants applies to cases where the sovereignty of the individual consumer is not a useful assumption: as emphasized by a number of authors in the German-language tradition (Sturn 2010, 2015), certain valuations (for example, regarding defence policy) make practical sense only when individuals perceive themselves as members of a pre-existing collective (for example, the state of France).

Compared with the British tradition, the German style of thought is much more geared towards institutional foundations and the characteristic mechanisms of the public sphere – and to a unified theory of taxation and expenditure. As indicated by the work of Sax (1887) and elaborated by Wicksell's (1896) collective choice mechanism regarding the provision of tax-financed public goods, the concept of public goods is a more expedient starting point for analysing the logic of collective action and the economic functions of the state – which are not limited to correcting specific distortions of the price system in an otherwise well-ordered society. Notice that the public sectors of "late nation states" were engaged in encompassing co-ordination problems and corresponding big issues of institutional design and nation building. Large-scale problems were in the focus of the agenda, not "local" co-ordination gaps here and there in an otherwise well-ordered market economy. By contrast, Pigou explicitly assumes reasonably well-ordered public institutions and organizations, providing the background for conceptions related to piecemeal incremental reform in order to eliminate the residual inefficiencies diagnosed as externalities. All this may be related to the stability and efficiency of British institutions in Pigou's formative years (see Pigou 1935).

In France, the political system was characterized by a high degree of centralization, beginning with very early modernity (fifteenth century) and accelerating in the seventeenth century when administrators such as Vauban began to deal with problems of governance and taxation in a systematic fashion, setting the stage for a prominent role of the public sector in economic development (infrastructure, industrial policy). The French philosophical landscape is diverse throughout the centuries, including currents which tend to prepare the ground for interventionist rationalism, but also currents emphasizing the ruse of spontaneous processes. Seen together, the range of foundational concepts pertinent to normative public economics is extraordinarily wide, including (1) utilitarian reasoning, (2) various versions of natural rights (with different stances vis-à-vis "possessive individualism"), and (3) emphasis on non-homogeneous interests based on class structures. At any rate, the French brand of a sensationist approach and "enlightenment rationalism" is specifically important for thinkers such as Condorcet and Turgot: their contributions include pivotal conceptualizations, including non-rivalry as a distinct characteristic of public goods as well as elaborate reflections regarding the normative dimensions of public economics under the premises of enlightenment. The latter is also the background of early normative reasoning on the logic of collective choice, famously culminating in Condorcet's voting paradox. The nineteenth century saw the coexistence of three important strands: (1) seminal contributions by engineer economists such as Dupuit, who adapted the metric suggested by utilitarian philosophy in the context of optimizing solutions to practical problems regarding the evaluation of public projects; (2) associationist/socialist thinkers such as Pierre-Joseph Proudhon or Jean-Charles Léonard Simonde de Sismondi whose contributions include arguments in favour of tax progression based on the differential incidence of the benefits of public goods in a class society; and (3) various strands of liberal/libertarian economists in the wake of Say whose writings deal with the question of how to justify government and its limits in an individualist market society, based on private property (see Faccarello 2010). This resulted in reflections on the productivity of government spending, the insurance premium-concept of taxation, and different versions of non-utilitarian conceptualizations of distributive justice (see Sigot 2010). The latter are reflected in Leon Walras's *économie sociale*, to be distinguished from *économie appliquée* (under which the work of the engineer economists guided by the metric of *utilité* may be subsumed) and *économie pure*.

In centres such as Florence, Renaissance Italy saw the earliest forms of proto-capitalism in Europe. In terms of politics, Italy is notorious for its pronounced fragmentation, leaving it as the second important late nation state in the nineteenth century. Fragmentation set the stage for politics as a specific game of private interests, epitomized by Niccolò Machiavelli's prince, including the Condottiere as private entrepreneur supplying military power. Influential treatises such as Giambattista Vico's *Scienza Nuova* (1725) developed visions different from optimistic perspectives of rational reform promoted by enlightenment. So, Italy has a certain tradition of disenchanted perspectives emphasizing strategic aspects of the political business. From the point of view of historical challenges, foundational issues of public sector economics related to the task of nation building came to be high on the agenda in the second half of the nineteenth century. Together with more coincidental circumstances, this may explain that Italian economists such as Mazzola congenially interacted with German language theorists regarding conceptualization and analysis of public goods. Indeed, the kind of public good theory that was exported to Anglo-Saxon economics mainly by economists with continental intellectual roots such as Musgrave, was a German-Austrian-Italian-Swedish co-production. Buchanan was particularly fond of a specific Italian twist of that kind of theory, triggered by the sceptical view of politics: the Italian literature soon began to develop lucidly "realistic" economic model-sketches of public decision making with its distortions. Pareto was critical of that literature, arguing that political power games cannot be captured by economic models but instead require a kind of fiscal sociology to account for irrational forces. Notice that disenchanted views of politics gained some ground in France in the second half of the nineteenth century: a case in point is Paul Leroy-Beaulieu's "positive" account of distortive tendencies in public choice (Faccarello 2010).

Crossing Traditions, Combinatorial Progress

The Sax–Mazzola–Wicksell–Lindahl theorization of public goods is itself one of the finest examples for the combination of heterogeneous elements, and cross-fertilization across different strands: it is based on the combination of the optimizing calculus of marginal utility theory and conceptualizations of collective wants in the German tradition from Hermann to Wagner. But there are several other examples for advances in public economics that were realized by some combination of foundational, methodological, conceptual, and technical aspects. As mentioned, Dupuit combined the metric provided by utilitarianism with the engineer-approach of economic evaluation of public projects, exemplified by projects related to the development of the network of waterway infrastructure in the 1820s (see Kolm 2010: 695). The logic of Marshallian economics and the normative thrust of utilitarianism were combined in the development of Pigou's (1932a) economics of welfare, transforming those foundations into a method for designing and evaluating public policies.

The impact of nation-specific traditions is not confined to the prehistory of public economics. It extends well into the twentieth century: while international interaction between the various strands of neo-classical economic theory after the rise of marginalism in the late nineteenth century contributed to the dynamism of the new paradigm, the large-scale internationalization of what is now perceived as predominantly Anglo-Saxon public economics took off only well after World War II.

As has been repeatedly pointed out, earlier Anglo-Saxon public economics, notably including Pigou's (1928, 1932a) comprehensive conceptual framework of public finance and market failure on the basis of Marshallian economics, completely overlooked the continental literature on public goods and political provision mechanisms. In particular, early marginalist contributions to public economics by Austrian, Italian and Swedish authors remained largely unknown. Wicksell (1896) – whose general economics contributions were fairly well known in the Anglo-Saxon world – is no exception. As Musgrave and Peacock (1958: vii) put it, the neglect of continental theory "has meant that Anglo-Saxon economics has suffered in consequence". (For other contributions making visible the importance of what Musgrave called "crossing traditions", see Buchanan 1952, Baumol 1952; Musgrave 1996–97.)

It remains to summarize some of the ways in which heterogeneous traditions were combined in the post-World War II era when globalized modern public economics began to emerge. The foundational texts of modern globalized public economics published in the 1950s and 1960s explicitly reflect the multifarious background of modern public economics. Examples include Baumol (1952), Musgrave (1959), Buchanan and Tullock (1962), Kolm (1964), Mancur Olson (1965), and an essay by Duncan Foley (1967), which is seminal in terms of its formal treatment of equilibrium concepts related to public good provision, associated with the names of Lindahl and Wicksell. Finally, the group of economists associated with the Cowles Commission (many of them European émigrés with a good command of mathematics) must be mentioned in the context of paradigmatic changes beyond the Pigovian framework. Three keywords must suffice to indicate the directions and the background of that change: general equilibrium economics, mechanism design, and social choice theory. All three currents include systematic analyses of mechanisms and choice procedures of the public sector as well as frameworks for less partial analysis compared with Marshallian/Pigovian partial equilibrium.

The texts mentioned above and some parts of the surrounding literature provide incisive insights into the history of the subject and its importance in the formative period of modern public economics. The broad spectrum of contributions in the post-World War II era marking the emergence of modern internationalized public economics indicates the relevance of national traditions as well as the role of combinatorial progress. Those contributions are related to the achievements of different eras, different national traditions, and different horizons of theorizing. For instance, Samuelson's (1954) formal paper on the summation rule for the optimal provision of public goods reveals an acute awareness regarding the importance of conceptual issues and their historical backgrounds. Another example can be found in a recently published text from the 1950s: Peacock and Wiseman (2010: 572) stress the conceptual dimension of progressive research strategies: "Progress must come from a widening of conceptions of government behaviour from which the study begins, rather than from further analysis of logically clear but practically barren 'welfare' situations".

Further interdisciplinary perspectives including legal, political, behavioural, and normative theory are part of this picture. The discussions in the wake of the Coase theorem (1960) enhanced developments emphasizing (1) transaction costs as a crucial category defining the role of public sector institutions in a market society and/or (2) well-defined private property rights as the essential starting point for market exchange, thereby triggering modes of governance that aim at curing market failures preferably not by means of public institutions, but by making the system of private property rights ever more perfect. Another paradigm gaining ground in the 1960s puts agency in the public sector centre stage, emphasizing systematic distortions of public decision making and coining the notion of government failure: the Virginia School of Public Choice with its neo-Hobbesian and contractarian thrust popularized models of politics "as if it were market exchange". The seminal work by Buchanan and Tullock (1962) set a specific agenda and provided a foundational frame for modelling the public sector. The implications of the assumption of self-interest seeking with guile (that is, ubiquitous selfish opportunism including the public sector) were elaborated in various contexts, such as the Leviathan approach modelling a revenue-maximizing state.

As the practical perspective of public economics hinges upon a broadly acceptable and consistently applicable metric of social preference in terms of which public policies and institutions are evaluated, the combination of developments in economics and ethics are still on the agenda, as is illustrated by the combination of optimal taxation theory with the Rawlsian difference principle (which implies that reforms are seen as desirable if and only if they benefit the worst off) or the recent debate on non-utility information, freedoms, rights, capabilities, and issues of responsibility (Fleurbaey 2008). The basic architecture of the public sector – its goals, purposes, and principles – is a genuinely interdisciplinary problem, involving political philosophy as well as economics. At the applied and explanatory levels, there are important interdisciplinary interfaces including fiscal sociology and fiscal psychology. To summarize, interdisciplinary perspectives along with "national traditions" are setting the stage for combinatorial progress.

The importance of conceptual and methodological foundations for key issues in public economics is also highlighted by the conception of merit wants (or merit goods), introduced by Musgrave (for example, 1959) for areas of public activity where consumer sovereignty is not useful as an assumption. More recently, advances in behavioural economics re-invigorate foundational discussions related to merit wants, even though this terminology is rarely used in that literature (see Shafir 2013). Further examples illustrating the importance of conceptual issues and the interdisciplinary dimension include the economics of fiscal federalism and of (semi-)public institutions beyond the nation state, from common property institutions (famously brought to the fore by political scientist Elinor Ostrom 1990, largely arguing in a semi-public good framework) to issues of global governance. Interdisciplinary work in those fields brings together game-theoretic work on (semi-)public goods, behavioural economics, institutional economics, and political science.

All that should not come as a surprise. The core issues of public finance as envisaged by Schumpeter cannot be dealt with by merely applying methods and models provided by general economic theory. Those issues (1) sometimes require autonomous conceptual developments, as exemplified by concepts such as "public goods" or "merit wants", (2) sometimes entail an immediate relationship to foundational issues regarding the problems of a science aiming at both "light and fruit", and (3) sometimes suggest a specifically straightforward quest for interaction with other disciplines. This notably includes positive political theory (public choice can be seen as a specific strand of it) and fiscal sociology emphatically endorsed by eminent economists such as Pareto and Schumpeter. In a nutshell, all this crops up in the early version of the famous displacement effect hypothesis suggested by Peacock and Wiseman, stressing the importance of history, environment and "attitudes" (that are more commonly theorized in political science and sociology). Straightforward interdisciplinary horizons also include political philosophy: think of issues such as tax justice. Or think of "property rights" that gained prominence in the wake of Coase (1960) and developments in "law and economics", but have a long tradition including nineteenth-century strands of public economics influenced by natural law thought.

Concluding Remarks

Given the variety of possible impacts on theoretical development, the shadow of specific institutional traditions is only one among several factors contributing to the late homogenization and internationalization of public economics. Some of the reasons for the persistence of "national" specificities were the result of differences in the theoretical architecture (for example, social/public wants according to the German tradition versus externalities according to the Marshallian tradition). Others include (1) a broad understanding of the role and function of the state according to its historical tasks in the era under consideration (for example, mere administration versus national development versus nation building) and (2) basic issues in political philosophy and method.

The diversity of foundational influences suggests that some knowledge of the history of public economics would be beneficial for the further development of contemporary research programs, as it enhances the awareness of unexploited combinatorial opportunities. The twentieth-century history of public economics was a process in which predominantly Anglo-Saxon public economics absorbed continental influences in a specific way. This process has been conditioned by historically specific developments within and beyond the profession. It also has been influenced by historical circumstances of the twentieth century, such as a wave of emigration of economists with Jewish, liberal, and left-wing political backgrounds from Europe to the USA.

Analysis of particular episodes within the emergence of modern public economics together with the broader panorama facilitates re-thinking the role of basic concepts in new combinations. For instance, work related to the conceptual history of merit wants may put recent discussions on "nudges" and "libertarian paternalism" (triggered by the boom in behavioural economics) into a more general perspective.

Public economics is not, at least not only, an applied subfield of economics. As it is employing economic methods all over the place, it is neither a discipline of its own nor simply an inter- or trans-disciplinary subject. It is economics interacting with other disciplines studying the interfaces of two sub-systems: the private market economy and the public sphere. Despite the fact that public economics studies the public economy, that is, the economic side of the public sphere, positive analysis of the public sphere needs to go beyond pure economics. Normative public economics will rely on principles that are not derivable from models of pure economics. This is the background against which some distinguishing features in the history of public economics are understandable: the first and foremost of those properties is that progress in public economics is to an extraordinary degree combinatorial and conceptual. The second aspect is the important role of national traditions linked to historically specific forms of statehood. Not least for those specific reasons, it should come as no surprise that the Whig concept of progress applies only in a carefully qualified sense to public economics.

RICHARD STURN

See also:

Richard Abel Musgrave (I); Arthur Cecil Pigou (I); Public choice (II); Adolph Heinrich Gotthilf Wagner (I); Friedrich von Wieser (I).

References and further reading

Arrow, K.J. and T. Scitovsky (eds) (1969), *Readings in Welfare Economics*, American Economic Association Series, vol. 12, London: George Allen & Unwin.
Atkinson, A.B. and J.E. Stiglitz (1980), *Lectures on Public Economics*, New York: McGraw-Hill.
Baumol, W. (1952), *Welfare Economics and the Theory of the State*, London: Bell.
Brownlee, W.E. (2004), *Federal Taxation in America: A Short History*, Cambridge: Cambridge University Press.
Buchanan, J.M. (1952), 'Wicksell on fiscal reform', *American Economic Review*, **42** (4), 599–602.
Buchanan, J.M. and G. Tullock (1962), *The Calculus of Consent*, Ann Arbor, MI: University of Michigan Press.
Cassel, G. (1918), *Theoretische Sozialökonomie*, Leipzig: C.F. Winter, English trans. 1923, *Theory of Social Economy*, London: T.F. Unwin and New York: Harcourt, Brace & Co., new revised edn 1932, London: E. Benn.
Coase, R. (1960), 'The problem of social cost', *Journal of Law and Economics*, **3** (October), 1–44.
Creedy, J. (1984), 'Public finance', in J. Creedy and D.P. O'Brien, *Economic Analysis in Historical Perspective*, London: Butterworths, pp.48–116.
Creedy, J. and D.P. O'Brien (1984), *Economic Analysis in Historical Perspective*, Butterworths Advanced Economics Texts, London: Butterworths.
Faccarello, G. (2006), 'An "Exception culturelle"? French sensationist political economy and the shaping of public economics', *European Journal of the History of Economic Thought*, **13** (1), 1–38.
Faccarello, G. (2010), 'Bold ideas. French liberal economists and the state: Say to Leroy-Beaulieu', *European Journal of the History of Economic Thought*, **17** (4), 719–58.
Faccarello, G. and R. Sturn (2010), 'Introduction: the challenge of the history of public economics', *European Journal of the History of Economic Thought*, **17** (4), 537–42.
Fehr, E. and S. Gächter (2000), 'Cooperation and punishment in public goods experiments', *American Economic Review*, **90** (4), 980–94.
Fleurbaey, M. (2008), *Fairness, Responsibility, and Welfare*, Oxford: Oxford University Press.
Foley, D. (1967), 'Resource allocation and the public sector', *Yale Economic Essays*, **7** (1), 45–98.
Hammond, P. (1995), 'Four characterizations of constrained Pareto efficiency in continuum economies with widespread externalities', *Japanese Economic Review*, **46** (2), 103–24.
Hermann, F.B.W. (1832), *Staatswirtschaftliche Untersuchungen*, Munich: Anton Weber'sche Buchhandlung.
Keynes, J.M. (1936), *The General Theory of Employment, Interest and Money*, New York: Harcourt Brace.
Kolm, S.-C. (1964), *Les fondements de l'économie publique*, Paris: IFP.
Kolm, S.-C. (1987), 'Public economics', *The New Palgrave. A Dictionary of Economics*, vol. 3, London: Macmillan, pp.1042–55.
Kolm, S.-C. (2010), 'History of public economics: the historical French school', *European Journal of the History of Economic Thought*, **17** (4), 687–718.
Lagueux, M. (2010), 'The residual character of externalities', *European Journal of the History of Economic Thought*, **17** (4), 957–73.
Lindahl, E. (1919), *Die Gerechtigkeit der Besteuerung*, Lund: Gleerupska Universitets-Bokhandeln.
Lindahl, E. (1928), 'Einige strittige Fragen der Steuertheorie', in H. Mayer (ed.), *Die Wirtschaftstheorie der Gegenwart*, vol. 4, Vienna: Springer, pp.282–304.
Mann, F.K. (1937), *Steuerpolitische Ideale*, Jena: Gustav Fischer.
Mazzola, U. (1890), *I dati scientifici della finanza pubblica*, Rome: Loescher.
McLure, M. (2003), 'Fiscal sociology', Discussion Paper 03.16, School of Economics and Commerce, University of Western Australia, Perth.
Mill, J.S. (1848), *Principles of Political Economy*, 2 vols, London: John W. Parker.
Mongin, P. (2006), 'Value judgments and value neutrality in economics', *Economica*, **73** (290), 257–86.
Musgrave, R.A. (1959), *The Theory of Public Finance*, New York: Mc Graw-Hill.

Musgrave, R.A. (1987), 'Public finance', *The New Palgrave. A Dictionary of Economics*, vol. 3, London: Macmillan, pp. 1055–60.

Musgrave, R.A. (1996–97), 'Public finance and Finanzwissenschaft: traditions compared', *Finanzarchiv*, New Series, **53** (2), 145–93.

Musgrave, R.A. and A.T. Peacock (1958), *Classics in the Theory of Public Finance*, London: Macmillan.

Olson, M. (1965), *The Logic of Collective Action*, Cambridge, MA: Harvard University Press.

Ostrom, E. (1990), *Governing the Commons: The Evolution of Institutions for Collective Action*, Cambridge: Cambridge University Press.

Peacock, A. and J. Wiseman (2010), 'Two unpublished papers from the 1950s', *European Journal of the History of Economic Thought*, **17** (4), 559–77.

Pigou, A.C. (1928), *A Study in Public Finance*, London: Macmillan.

Pigou, A.C. (1932a), *Economics of Welfare*, 4th edn, London: Macmillan.

Pigou, A.C. (1932b), *Theory of Public Finance*, London: Macmillan.

Pigou, A.C. (1935), *Economics in Practice*, London: Macmillan.

Priddat, B.P. (1990), *Hegel als Ökonom*, Volkswirtschaftliche Schriften No. 403. Berlin: Duncker & Humblot.

Ricardo, D. (1951), *On the Principles of Political Economy and Taxation*, ed. P. Sraffa with the collaboration of M. Dobb, Cambridge: Cambridge University Press.

Samuelson, P. (1954), 'The pure theory of public expenditure', *Review of Economics and Statistics*, **36** (November), 387–89.

Sax, E. (1887), *Grundlegung der theoretischen Staatswirthschaft*, Vienna: Alfred Hölder.

Schäffle, A. (1867), *Das gesellschaftliche System der menschlichen Wirtschaft*, 2nd edn, Tübingen: Laupp'sche Buchhandlung.

Schäffle, A. (1880), *Die Grundsätze der Steuerpolitik*, Tübingen: Laupp'sche Buchhandlung.

Schumpeter, J.A. (1926–27), 'Finanzpolitik', *Der deutsche Volkswirt*, **1** (2), 827–30.

Scitovsky, T. (1954), 'Two concepts of external economies', *Journal of Political Economy*, **62** (2), 143–51.

Shafir, E. (ed.) (2013), *The Behavioral Foundations of Public Policy*, Princeton, NJ and Oxford: Princeton University Press.

Sigot, N. (2010), 'Utility and justice: French liberal economists in the nineteenth century', *European Journal of the History of Economic Thought*, **17** (4), 759–92.

Smith, A. (1776), *An Inquiry into the Nature and Causes of the Wealth of Nations*, London: Strahan.

Stein, L. von (1875), *Lehrbuch der Finanzwissenschaft*, 3rd improved edn, Leipzig: Brockhaus.

Sturn, R. (2006), 'Subjectivism, joint consumption and the state: public goods in Staatswirtschaftslehre', *European Journal of the History of Economic Thought*, **13** (1), 39–67.

Sturn, R. (2010), 'Public goods before Samuelson: Interwar Finanzwissenschaft and Musgrave's synthesis', *European Journal of the History of Economic Thought*, **17** (2), 279–312.

Sturn, R. (2015), 'The merits of merit wants', in C. Binder, G. Codognato, M. Teschl and Y. Xu (eds), *Individual and Collective Choice and Social Welfare. Essays in Honor of Nick Baigent*, Heidelberg, New York, Dordrecht and London: Springer, pp. 289–308.

Vico, G. (1725), *Scienza Nuova*, F. Nicolini, Giusta l'edizione del 1730, Bari: Laterza.

Wagner, A. (1876), *Allgemeine oder theoretische Volkswirthschaftslehre. Erster Theil. Grundlegung, Mit Benutzung von Rau's Grundsätzen der Volkswirthschaftslehre*, K.H. Rau (ed.), completely reworked by A. Wagner and E. Nasse, *Lehrbuch der politischen Oekonomie*, vol. 1, Leipzig and Heidelberg: C.F. Winter'sche Verlagshandlung.

Wagner, A. (1886), 'Wagner on the present state of political economy', *Quarterly Journal of Economics*, **1** (1), 113–33.

Wagner, A. (1891), 'Marshall's principles of economics', *Quarterly Journal of Economics*, **5** (3), 319–38.

Wagner, A. (1893), *Grundlegung der politischen Oekonomie. Erster Theil. Grundlagen der Volkswirtschaft*, 2. Halbband, Books 4–6, substantially reworked and enlarged 3rd edn, A. Wagner et al. (eds), *Lehr- und Handbuch der politischen Oekonomie*, vol. 1, Hauptabtheilung, Leipzig and Heidelberg: C.F. Winter'sche Verlagshandlung.

Wicksell, K. (1896), *Finanztheoretische Untersuchungen*, Jena: Gustav Fischer.

Wieser, F. von (1884), *Über den Ursprung und die Hauptgesetze des Wirthschaftlichen Werthes*, Vienna: Alfred Hölder.

Wieser, F. von (1889), *Der Natürliche Werth*, Vienna: Alfred Hölder.

Resource and environmental economics

The purpose of this entry is to provide an overview of the development of environmental and resource economics and its present situation. Although resource and environmental constraints were not clearly recognized by early economists, setting aside some notable exceptions, it was gradually considered explicitly by economists and analysed in economic models in the middle of the twentieth century. Yet, economic studies on resources and the environment were not regarded as independent branches of economics. It was after the experience of heavy pollution in the 1960s–1970s that they came to be established as branches of economics. Indeed, resources and environmental economics has developed very quickly since then, and has derived a number of useful policy implications and options.

The structure of this entry is as follows. We first provide a precise definition of "resources". The definition is rather broad, so that any substance in natural environment can be included as part of resources in this essay. Next we deal briefly with the early economists' view on resource and environmental constraints. It is shown that despite their pessimism about endless economic growth, they were rather optimistic as regards the exhaustion of natural resources. Then we review the development of studies on reproducible and non-reproducible natural resources. Next, Pigou's study of external diseconomy is reinterpreted from the point of view of resource use, and the generalization of his theory is briefly explained. Then the contributions to environmental and resource studies made by non-economists are discussed. It is shown how they had an impact on economists. A survey of the development of environmental and resource economics up to the present time follows. It is emphasized that contemporary research is concerned with its applicability to real environmental issues. A few remarks conclude the entry.

Concepts

The word "resources" has multiple meanings, being understood differently by various people. It means natural resources such as oil, coal, ores, and so on when used in daily conversation or in the media. On the other hand, researchers use the word in a slightly different way, and the usage may differ among disciplines and even within a discipline itself. In order to avoid possible misunderstandings, we first explain how the word has been interpreted in economics so far, and how it is defined here.

In modern mainstream economics, represented by a general equilibrium theory, resources refer to materials and services required for production; primary resources such as labour, land, and natural resources, as well as produced means of production such as capital goods. When one refers to, say, efficiency of resource allocation in a general equilibrium analysis, the word means the resource just mentioned.

In this usage, natural resources are merely a part of resources broadly defined in modern economics. In the following I speak of resources in a broad sense, on the one hand, and natural resources or resources in a narrow sense, on the other.

In whichever way the word is defined or interpreted, there is a common nature in resources defined or interpreted in either way: they are objects of market transaction, so that their cost of production or their scarcity is reflected in prices. The higher their cost of production or their scarcity, the higher is their price.

It was quite natural for the early economists to have focused their analysis mainly on resources which can be sold and bought in markets, since materials or services with positive value were their primary concern: materials without value or price were not regarded as an object of economic analysis. Consequently, in so far as resources are transacted with positive prices in markets, they could be analysed within a framework of traditional economics, with minor modification, if any, regardless of the difference of definition.

There are, however, materials or services whose scarcity is not reflected in prices, despite their essential contribution to human economic activities. The natural environment, such as air, rivers, lakes, oceans, ground (differentiated from land which can be transacted in markets), wilderness, the ecosystem, and so on, are bases for all creatures including human beings. Without these, human beings cannot sustain their lives and engage in economic activities.

Owing to the indispensable characters of these environmental elements for our lives and economic activities, they may be considered resources, even though their scarcity is not directly reflected in markets, on which they are traded and priced. Let us call them environmental resources. Actually, by so defining it, the natural environment has come to be analysed by extending conventional economics, and, furthermore, the results can be interpreted in the scope of resources economics.

In the following, when the word "resources" is referred to, it means both resources in a broad sense and environmental resources in most cases. Yet, occasionally, the word must have a specific meaning and, in that case, expressions such as "resources in a broad sense" or "environmental resources" are used.

Early Economists' Views on Resources

It might look a little odd to start the explanation of resources economics from the Physiocrats, since they paid attention mostly to land, although they occasionally referred to other resources such as mines. The core of their argument is that the wealth of a nation comes from agricultural production and not from the acquisition of precious metals.

Yet, it must be noted that both resources in a broad sense and environmental resources were the basis of their argument, however implicit it might have been. Their fundamental idea is that the order of nature prevails and controls an economy. They were convinced that human beings cannot create value via economic activities against the natural order.

The primary result of this thinking is that land is the ultimate resource, which is able to produce surplus, and the basis of all the wealth owned by people. Hence, the value of all the produced materials was considered to intrinsically come from land and labour, not from precious metals as the mercantilists had contended. Agricultural activities were, therefore, the only source of value for them.

They were also interested in how the surplus produced by agricultural activities was distributed among social classes. In the exploration of the distribution process, Quesnay, the leading Physiocrat, analysed the interdependency of economic sectors by means of an economic table. This idea is akin to a study of reproducibility of an economy, which was inherited by classical economists as well as modern classical ones represented by Sraffa (1960). Reproducibility of an economy based upon land and labour as the essential sources of value is nothing but sustainability in a modern sense.

The classical economists started from the basic idea of value of the Physiocrats, but developed it in certain directions so that they could take into account the development of the industrial sector. They understood that both in agriculture and in manufacturing labour is needed to generate a gross and net product, as social surplus. As the importance of labour in production was recognized, labour was elevated to the sole source of value. This is quite natural, since most of the classical economists lived in the midst of the Industrial Revolution, and witnessed the extraordinary development of industrial sectors.

For the classical economists and the Physiocrats, neither environmental nor natural resources were as important as land or labour as the source of value. For those economists in the early days, the natural environment as well as natural resources, apart from land, appeared to be available in abundance. Only a few economists contemplated the finiteness of the natural environment (see below).

The classical economists saw essentially only one natural resource as constraining production and population growth: arable land. Diminishing returns in agriculture were seen to put a limit to economic development and growth, which could only be overcome by improvement, that is, technical change, as it was contemplated by Ricardo in the *Principles* (1817 [1951]: ch. 2). Diminishing returns in agriculture were reflected in terms of differential rents paid to the proprietors of the more fertile plots of all the different qualities of land cultivated, whereas on the least fertile plot amongst them (so-called "marginal land") no rent was paid.

If agricultural production was subject to diminishing returns, the limited amount of arable land would not sustain a growing population. This was the main point made by Malthus (1798). He derived from casual empirical observations that agricultural production did not grow as fast as population tended to grow, so that there was a tendency of overpopulation and misery. Malthus's view was however proved wrong: agricultural production began to increase faster than population, thanks to improvements in agricultural technology. While Malthus was a technological pessimist, Ricardo saw no stationary state around the corner (see Kurz 2010).

Some aspects of Malthus's pessimistic view, which led to the definition of economics as "the dismal science" (Carlyle 1849), were adopted by J.S. Mill (1848). He clearly noticed the exhaustible nature of some natural resources, although he somehow optimistically considered this as not causing any problem due to technical progress. At the same time he did not consider that an economy would grow forever: he argued that it was bound to eventually arrive at a stationary state someday, owing to the constraints of resources in a broad sense, whatever they might be. One of his remarkable views was that such a stationary economy was not necessarily a bad thing, but might bring about real wellbeing of people. He thus dispensed with vulgar materialism, which became prominent in the course of the Industrial Revolution.

Another author who saw limits to economic growth was William S. Jevons (1865). In the midst of the Industrial Revolution, Jevons (1865) stressed that the economic prosperity of Britain at that time depended heavily upon consumption of coal as an energy source (see Martinez-Alier 1987). Interestingly, he noticed that the Industrial Revolution presupposed essentially an energy revolution (see Wrigley 1988). Based upon this observation, he opined that economic growth would be constrained by the production of coal, an exhaustible resource. His anticipation turned out to be wrong, also: coal has not been exhausted since his time and other natural resources have been found that can replace it. Contrary to his anticipation, coal is supposed to be available for the next 300 years.

In short, population growth, a lack of agricultural products owing to diminishing returns or a shortage of coal have not brought economic growth and development to a standstill. This is one of the reasons why resource and environmental constraints have not been taken into account in most economic analyses for a long time.

Also, Karl Marx (1894) did not worry about the natural environment as a potential constraint of economic development and expansion. Although he critically pointed out the environmental destruction, which a capitalist economy necessarily brought about, he seemed optimistic about a new classless society in which such destruction was supposed to be prevented, unlike in a capitalist economy. Furthermore, he believed that the progress of science would relieve human beings from environmental and resource constraints (Robinson 1989; Kula 1998).

A common feature of economists in the early days is that they were first and foremost concerned with the reproduction of a capitalist economy at a constant or upward-spiralling trajectory. Thus, income distribution and price formation, which guarantee reproducibility of an economy, were fully explored. In conditions of free competition, profits would be obtained according to a uniform rate on the capital invested in each sector. This idea can be generalized to cover the modern concept of sustainability in which environmental resources are explicitly taken into account.

Theory of Reproducible and Non-Reproducible Resources

Until the mid-twentieth century, most economists shared the classical economists' optimism. Only then did some economists begin to worry about the possibility of running out of natural resources and others about destruction of the natural environment. In this section, I deal with the progress of studies on natural resources. The development of economic analyses of environmental destruction is taken up in the next section.

Natural and environmental resources are classified into two categories: one is reproducible resources, and the other non-reproducible resources. Reproducible resources are those which can be reproduced after extraction by nature itself or by human beings, and thus the stock of relevant resources is constant or even increases. Fish, biomass, livestock, water, wind, and so on, are examples. On the other hand, non-reproducible resources are those which cannot be reproduced after extraction, so that the stock cannot be increased and may run out someday. Oil, coal, and mineral resources are examples.

Non-reproducible resources: Hotelling and after

It was not until Hotelling's seminal work (1931) that resource problems were explicitly and rigorously analysed by means of an economic model. In the process of the rapid development of a capitalist economy in industrial countries, particularly in the United States, people became more concerned with the possibility of exhaustion of some natural resources. Hotelling's contribution was the start of publication of numerous papers on non-reproducible natural resources.

The basic Hotelling model (see Halvorsen and Smith 1991) is the following (see also Krautkraemer 1998). Denote the production function as:

$$y = f(x^p, t, n(x^e, Z, t)) \tag{1}$$

with y, x^p, x^e, Z, t, and $n(\cdot)$ as output, reproducible inputs used in processing activities and extraction of natural resources, cumulative extraction, time, and an extraction sub-production function, respectively. Denoting also S as the total stock of the resource, the constraint can be written as:

$$Z \le S \text{ and } \dot{Z} = n \tag{2}$$

Maximization of profits $p^q q(x^p, t, n) - p x^p - c^e(n, p^e, Z, t)$ subject to the above constraints leads to:

$$\dot{\mu} = r\mu - \frac{\partial c^e}{\partial Z} \tag{3}$$

where p^q, p, p^e, c^e, μ and r denote prices of an output and inputs for processing as well as for extraction, an extraction cost function obtained by the function $n(\cdot)$, scarcity rent (resource *in situ* price, or user cost), and the interest rate. Obviously, $q(\cdot)$ is another expression of y.

Equation (3) implies that the increase in scarcity rent equals the forgone interest, $r\mu$, minus the increase in costs for extracting the marginal unit in the future, $\frac{\partial c^e}{\partial Z}$. If the last term is supposed to be zero, the simplest form of the Hotelling rule is obtained:

$$\frac{\dot{\mu}}{\mu} = r \tag{4}$$

which implies that the price of a non-reproducible resource will rise at the interest rate. When the price arrives at a certain level, the technology which uses the non-reproducible resource is replaced with a backstop technology: a technology which substitutes relatively abundant resources in a broad sense for non-reproducible resources. Solar power generation is an example for a backstop technology of power generation by fossil fuels.

Although the rule is extremely simple and attractive, a serious problem was found with it. There was a gap between theory and reality: contrary to the anticipation of the simple rule (4), prices of almost all non-reproducible resources such as coal, oil, minerals and so on decreased for a long time.

Since the extraction cost cannot be ignored, the fundamental principle of the change in scarcity rents should be (3) instead of (4). Considering this, even if the scarcity rents increased, one may see that resource prices might decrease possibly due to technical progress, substitution among resources and so on, so that the Hotelling rule, if it is formulated by (3), could be correct. Some studies to confirm whether movement of the scarcity rents followed formula (3) or not have been published (see Neumayer 2000). Some (Stollery 1983; Miller and Upton 1985) are more affirmative upon certain conditions, and others (Slade 1982; Farrow 1985; Halvorsen and Smith 1991) are rather negative.

There are two different but related points on this controversy. One is on an academic matter, which is about whether Hotelling's formulation, not the formulation represented by the narrowly defined Hotelling rule (4) but that represented by the broadly defined rule (3) or a more general formulation (Dasgupta and Heal 1979), is theoretically and empirically supported. To answer this question, elements such as (1) substitutability among natural resources, (2) recycling, (3) man-made capital, (4) technical progress, (5) exploration costs, (6) uncertainty, and so on must be taken into account in the model and empirically tested by the relevant data.

The other point is on a practical matter. Is the resource optimism justified, and, if so, can the Malthusian spectre be dismissed? If so, serious attention does not have to be paid to the natural resource constraint, regardless of fluctuation of prices of natural resources.

Neo-Ricardian contribution to the theory of non-reproducible resources

While a few mainstream economists have contributed to the theory of exhaustible resources, extending and generalizing the Hotelling rule, alternative theories of non-renewable resources have been developed by non-mainstream economists, particularly economists called neo-Ricardian. Presumably, Parrinello (1983) is the first neo-Ricardian who tries to accommodate the theory of non-renewable resources in the Sraffian framework. Parrinello's work induced quite a few researchers such as Salvadori (1987), Schefold (1989), Kurz and Salvadori (1995: ch. 12, 1997, 2014: chs 14–16), and Parrinello (2004) to develop the theory of non-exhaustible resources, based upon the neo-Ricardian tradition. Furthermore, in the special issue of *Metroeconomica*, Hosoda (2001), Kurz and Salvadori (2001), Lager (2001a), Parrinello (2001) and Schefold (2001) debate on the corn-guano model presented by Bidard and Erreygers (2001a, 2001b), critically assessing it, and demonstrating that the Sraffian approach is fruitful in developing the theory of non-renewable resources.

The focal point of the neo-Ricardian theory of non-renewable resources is how to deal with dynamic aspects caused by the use of non-renewable resources in a Sraffian type of multi-sectoral model. Although there are slight differences among those economists in solving the long-run equilibrium problem, they are successful in making a consistent model, deducing a dynamic equilibrium path.

It must be noted that the neo-Ricardian interpretation of a non-renewable resource is different from that of mainstream economics. In the latter, it is assumed that the resource is homogenous, and that extraction of the resource is only constrained by the amount of the resource stock left from the former period. On the other hand, the former considers that various mines with different productivity are extracted at the same time, and that extraction at each period is subject to a capacity constraint. Thus, a Ricardian rent appears in the extraction of the mine.

Yet, neo-Ricardian economists also adopt the Hotelling rule, which is interpreted as the rule showing a change of royalties for conservation of the resource *in situ*. Interestingly, it can be shown that the prices of commodities produced by means of the non-renewable resource do not change on certain conditions, although the royalties and thus the price of the resource increase according to the Hotelling rule (Kurz and Salvadori 2014: ch. 15). This is because the increase in the royalties may possibly be cancelled out by the decrease in the rent. Clearly, this treatment reflects reality, since an increase in prices of non-renewable resources does not always mean a change of prices of the commodities produced by means of those resources.

Finally, I refer to an interesting application of the corn-guano model to waste management and recycling. Hosoda (2001) demonstrates how a waste disposal technique is switched to a recycling technique by taking the constraint of landfill space as a non-renewable resource into account. This shows how fertile the neo-Ricardian analyses of non-renewable resources are.

Reproducible resources: open-access problems

Each reproducible and renewable resource has a specific character. Some are marketable, while others are not. Property rights are defined for some reproducible resources, but not for others. Theoretical and empirical studies have been developed for each type of resource with its specific character (see Kneese and Sweeney 1985). The case of a fishery may be used as an illustration, since it has a very interesting feature from the viewpoint of sustainable use of common resources.

Consider a static equilibrium analysis, following the pioneering work of Gordon (1954). Suppose that a fishing ground is a common property, so that any fisherman can have access to it. For simplicity, assume that there is only one input to fishery called fishing effort, which is denoted as e, and its unit cost is denoted as w. Marginal and average productivities are denoted as $MP(e)$ and $AP(e)$ respectively.

The total rent from this fishing ground at the fishing effort level e is expressed as $p \int_0^e MP(\varepsilon) d\varepsilon - we$, where p denotes the price of fish. Consequently, the rent is maximized at the fishing effort level e^* such that $pMP(e^*) = w$ holds. This is formally the same as profit maximization of production, apart from the fact that the fishing ground is in fixed supply and not variable as input.

Yet, notice that the fishing ground is a common property, so that open-access prevails. When the average rent is positive, it is likely that there will be an additional gain for a fisherman if he increases the fishing effort. Since every fisherman thinks in the same way, fishing effort is increased until the average rent (thus the total rent) disappears. Consequently, in an open-access equilibrium, $pAP(e^{**}) = w$ holds. Since as the "first come, first served" principle is applicable to the fishing ground, there should be new entry as far as there is positive rent. Therefore, rent is squeezed and finally disappears in equilibrium.

This type of inefficiency more or less occurs in almost all common properties unless carrying capacities are so large that marginal productivity does not decline. There may be an exception: population explosion does not affect production of oxygen in the atmosphere, which is an indispensable input in human activity, since the carrying capacity of the atmosphere is large enough. This is, however, a mere exception, which is not applicable to other natural or environmental resources.

Although a static equilibrium explains the aforementioned interesting characteristics of a common property, it does not tell about stocks of reproducible resources, which is sometimes essential, particularly from the viewpoint of sustainable resource use. This can be shown with reference to Gould (1972).

In addition to the variables defined above, define the stock of fish in a fishing ground as S. It is usual to assume that the natural growth rate of the stock depends upon itself, and is expressed by $f(S)$, where there exist S^* and $\overline{S}(0 < S^* < \overline{S})$ such that $f(\overline{S}) = 0$, $f'(S) > 0$ for $S \in [0, S^*)$, and $f'(S) < 0$ for $S \in (S^*, \overline{S}]$ holds. Obviously, $f(S)$ is maximized at the stock level S^*. It is the maximum yield of fish which can make the fishery stock

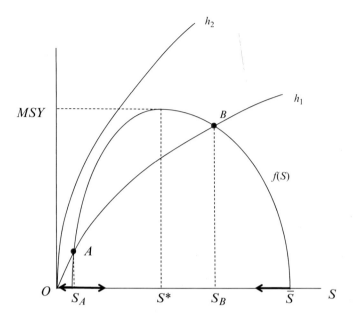

Note: The highest point of the curve is *MSY*. The equilibrium catches are given by *A* and *B*, the former being unstable and the latter stable.

Figure 8   *The relationship between fish stock and its growth*

constant, so that $f(S^*)$ is called the maximum sustainable yield (MSY) (see Figure 8). A simple example of the function is:

$$f(S) = aS\left(1 - \frac{S}{\overline{\overline{S}}}\right),$$ (5)

where $S^* = \frac{\overline{S}}{2}$ and $MSY = \frac{a\overline{S}}{4}$ hold.

Suppose that the yield of fish depends upon fishing effort as well as the fishery stock as $y = g(e, S)$, where $\frac{\partial g}{\partial e} > 0$, $\frac{\partial g}{\partial S} > 0$, and the second order conditions hold. Hence, as fishing effort and/or the fishery stock increases, the yield of fish increases less than proportionately. It is easy to see that $\frac{\partial g}{\partial e}$ is essentially the same as $MP(e)$ defined above.

Since the growth rate of the fishery stock is the natural growth rate less the yield of fish, the following holds:

$$\frac{\partial S}{\partial t} \equiv \dot{S} = f(S) - y,$$ (6)

where t denotes time. As explained above, rent is squeezed and finally disappears in an open-access fishing ground, so that:

$$py = we \text{ or } e = \frac{py}{w},$$ (7)

must hold, where p denotes the market price of fish. Substituting (4) into $y = g(e, S)$, and solving the equation with respect to y, we obtain $y = h(S)$, where h is an increasing function of S. This, coupled with (3), leads us to the following dynamic equation:

$$\dot{S} = f(S) - h(S) \tag{8}$$

It can easily be seen that, by construction, location and shape of the curve obtained by $h(\cdot)$ depend upon the market price of fish (p) and the real wage rate (or the fishing-effort price) (w). As the market price increases (decreases) and/or the fishing effort price decreases (increases), the curve shifts upward (downward).

How the dynamic system works and an equilibrium obtains is explained by Figure 8. Two h curves are drawn in it. Consider h_1 first. There are two equilibria shown as A and B. In the intervals of $[0, S_A)$ and $(S_B, \overline{S}]$, clearly $f(S) < h(S)$ holds, so that the fishery stock decreases due to (5). On the other hand, in the interval of (S_A, S_B), it increases, since $f(S) > h(S)$ holds. Consequently, S_B is a stable equilibrium, while S_A is an unstable equilibrium. If the initial fishery stock is smaller than S_A, it decreases continually and converges to zero. Hence, in the long run, the fishery stock vanishes.

Next, look at the curve h_2. For all the stock levels S, an inequality $f(S) < h(S)$ holds. This implies that the fishery stock decreases, starting from any stock level. The final state is that of the extinction of the fish. As the price of fish is sufficiently high and/or the wage rate is sufficiently low, the curve h may possibly be located in a rather high position, and thus, the possibility of extinction becomes high in such a situation. This partly explains how the rising price of caviar has accelerated the crisis of extinction of sturgeon in the Caspian Sea. Yet it must be noted that extinction is not a problem peculiar to open-access resources, and could occur in non-open-access resources as well (Peterson and Fisher 1977).

Externalities as Resource Problems

Environmental problems such as air pollution, soil pollution, water pollution and so on are often described as externality problems, being analysed in terms of external diseconomies. This tradition goes back to A.C. Pigou. His analysis was very timely after the Industrial Revolution: the railway network in Britain was extended rapidly, and steam locomotives emitted smoke and soot without any restriction, damaging woods along the tracks. Seeing that the costs of the damages were never reflected in tariffs, Pigou (1932) formulated this problem as a gap between social and private benefits. The gap is nothing but the external diseconomy.

Those problems can be treated as resource problems as well without changing the essence of Pigou's argument. In the above example of steam locomotives, the problem may be formulated as whether to allocate the right of use of the atmosphere along the railways to railway companies or owners of woods, and how to do so. This is nothing but a resource allocation problem, although atmosphere, one of the environmental resources defined here, is not marketable, so that its scarcity is not realized in a price.

Consider a representative consumer, who has a utility function $U = U(y, E)$, where y and E denote a consumption good and clean atmosphere surrounding this person respectively. We assume $\frac{\partial U}{\partial y} \equiv U_y > 0$, $U_{yy} < 0$, $\frac{\partial U}{\partial E} \equiv U_E > 0$, $U_{EE} < 0$, $U_{yE} = U_{Ey} < 0$, and concavity of the function as well.

On the other hand, a firm's production function is assumed to be $y = f(x, e)$, where x and e denote a vector of inputs of ordinary resources and an input of environmental resource, that is, the use of the atmosphere as a disposal place for smoke. Considering the total amount of the total environmental resource given $(\bar{E} = E + e)$, it must be considered how $\bar{E}$ is allocated to a consumer and a firm. Assume the ordinary assumptions on derivatives of f to hold, that is, $\frac{\partial f}{\partial x} \equiv f_x > 0$, $\frac{\partial f}{\partial e} \equiv f_e > 0$, $f_{xx} < 0$, $f_{yy} < 0$, $f_{xy} = f_{yx} > 0$, and concavity of the function as well.

The market price of the product and the wage rate being denoted as p and w, the profit π is expressed as $\pi = py - wx$. Suppose that e is a given parameter temporarily. Then, profit maximization leads us to $\frac{w}{p} = f_x(x^*, e)$, from which $x^* = \psi(e, \frac{w}{p})$ is obtained. Then, the maximized profits are expressed as:

$$\pi^* \equiv \pi^*\left(e, \frac{w}{p}\right) = pf\left(\psi\left(e, \frac{w}{p}\right), e\right) - w\psi\left(e, \frac{w}{p}\right). \tag{9}$$

We get $\frac{\partial \pi^*}{\partial e} = pf_e$ and $\frac{\partial^2 \pi^*}{\partial e^2} < 0$. Assume that there exists e_{max} such that $\frac{\partial \pi^*}{\partial e}\big|_{e=e_{max}} = 0$. Then, the amount $e_{max} - e(\equiv b)$ means reduction of an environmental resource input. Since $\pi^*(e_{max}) - \pi^*(e) = \pi^*(e_{max}) - \pi^*(e_{max} - b)$ is a profit loss due to reduction of emission by the amount of b, it is nothing but the abatement costs. Its derivative with respect to b is often called the marginal abatement costs, denoted $MAC(b)$. Clearly, $MAC(b) = pf_e$ holds.

Without any restriction on the use of an environmental resource, a firm uses it up to the point where $MAC(b) = 0$ or $e = e_{max}$ holds. Obviously, this situation is not optimal from a social welfare viewpoint. The optimal point is obtained by maximizing $U(y, E)$ subject to $y = f(x, e)$. By optimization, $U_y = \lambda$ and $U_E = \lambda f_e$ are obtained, where λ is a Lagrangian multiplier. From these,

$$U_E = U_y f_e \tag{10}$$

is obtained. Notice U_E equals $-\frac{\partial U}{\partial e}$, which is marginal damages, denoted as $MD(e)$. If U_y is equalized to p somehow, (10) means $MD(e) = MAC(b)$, which is often seen in textbooks of environmental economics: marginal damages are equal to marginal abatement costs in the optimal situation. Denote b and e that satisfy this equation as b^* and e^* respectively. An important question is how to attain this allocation in a market.

Suppose that an omnipotent authority knows this allocation and imposes a tax t^* per unit of emission as $t^* \equiv MD(e^*)$. Then, a firm's profit function is modified to $\pi \equiv py - wx - t^*e$. From the profit maximization, $MD(e^*) \equiv t^* = pf_e \equiv MAC(b^*)$ holds, so that the optimal allocation is realized in a market. This is Pigouvian taxation.

The remarkable nature of this scheme is demonstrated when there are many potential polluters in a market. Suppose that there are n firms with a representative consumer. Subscript i ($i = 1, 2, \ldots, n$) is supposed to identify a firm. Then, the total emission is $e = \sum_1^n e_i$, where $e_i = e_{imax} - b_i$. The same procedure as above leads us to the optimal condition $MD(e^*) = MAC_i(b_i^*)$. The so-called equi-marginal principle must hold.

Again, setting $MD(e^*) = t^*$ as a tax per unit of emission, the authority can achieve the goal where $MD(e^*) = t^* = MAC_i(b_i^*)$ holds in a market. The equi-marginal principle prevails not by command-and-control, but by individual incentives.

Four remarks are apposite. First, the applicability of a Pigouvian tax, at least at an abstract level, is based upon the condition that the authority knows the optimal allocation of resources. Otherwise she cannot set the optimal tax rate correctly. Yet this does not seem probable in reality. At best, she can guess aggregate functions of marginal damages and abatement costs. If the authority, obtaining as much information as possible, can deduce the data on the emission level which is sufficiently close to the optimal one, Pigouvian tax may work well even if it does not exactly hit the target.

Secondly, there may be situations in which the authority cannot obtain any information on aggregate functions of marginal damages and abatement costs. An emission tax, though it is not exactly a Pigouvian tax, can achieve the least cost for reduction of emissions even in such a case. This is because the equi-marginal principle holds when a tax rate is given. Although the total amount of emission reduction at the tax rate is not the optimal level, except by a fluke, the reduction is made with the least cost, being cost effective.

Third, on the condition that there is no new entry, it can be shown that a subsidy fulfils the optimality conditions. Suppose the omnipotent authority subsidizes polluters by s^* per unit of reduction of emission from a business-as-usual level, where $s^* \equiv MD(e^*)$. Again, $s^* \equiv MD(e^*) = MAC_i(b_i^*)$ is achieved. This is called Pigouvian subsidy. If there is a new entry of potential polluters, however, the optimal conditions collapse, since the subsidy is originally planned on the supposition that there are fixed numbers of polluters, so that the optimal conditions are different before and after the entry.

Finally, it can be shown that the above analytical framework can be generalized within a general equilibrium framework (Baumol and Oates 1988: ch. 4). It is not easy to implement a Pigouvian tax or subsidy in a rigorous sense, since, as already shown, the authority cannot generally be expected to obtain sufficient information to do so. This does not, however, imply that the underlying ideas to real policies based upon individual incentives cannot somehow be applied. So-called environmental tax or carbon tax may be regarded as a variation of a Pigouvian tax. Furthermore, its basic idea can be interpreted as the basis of the polluter pays principle (PPP), which says that dischargers of pollutants should pay for prevention costs of pollution. PPP has now been introduced into quite a few countries as an anti-pollution policy.

Impacts of Pollution on Economics

Although, as has been shown in the preceding two sections, economic researchers sporadically took up issues on natural resources and the environment as important themes of economics, it can hardly be said that resources and environmental economics were established as proper fields of economics before the high-growth era which came soon after World War II. Studies of those issues might be regarded as a mere application of ordinary economic principles. Economic researchers were first and foremost concerned with economic growth and development. Natural and environmental resources were still considered to be of secondary importance.

At the very time of growth and development after the war, however, heavy pollution arose in most of the advanced countries. Air in big cities such as London and Tokyo was polluted not only by smoke and soot emitted from smokestacks of plants, but by exhaust gas from automobiles. Rivers were contaminated by waste water from plants and houses. People came to notice that environmental resources are not limitless.

The tragedy of the commons

Drastic economic changes for solving environmental problems were required, meaning that a deeper and more practical analysis of resources and the environment was called for. Yet, it seems that a response from orthodox economists was delayed, partly owing to their trust in the market mechanism, and partly owing to their ignorance of the seriousness of the problems. Rather, unorthodox economists such as Marxists or non-economists responded to the problems in a timely manner. Among them, Garret Hardin became the symbolic figure of an environmental study: his paper entitled "The tragedy of the commons" (Hardin 1968) attracted the attention of many researchers in various fields, and had a deep and lasting impact on them.

Hardin's explanation is extremely simple: suppose there is pastureland which is open to every herdsman. A herdsman may possibly consider that he or she would be able to get more profits by increasing the number of his or her cattle. Yet every herdsman will think in the same way, so that the total number of cattle will increase. As far as herdsmen can have free-access to the pastureland, overgrazing of pastureland cannot be avoided. This is how the tragedy of the commons occurs.

He insists that the same logic can be applied to overuse of the atmosphere such as in air pollution: factories consider that they can use freely the atmosphere (commons) as a disposal place for smoke and soot, paying no attention to the behaviour of others. Although the profits of each factory may be maximized by that behaviour, the social benefits will not be due to the deterioration of air quality. Again, the tragedy of the commons makes an appearance.

The tragedy of the commons says that a shared resource, like pastureland, fishing grounds, the atmosphere, or whatever it may be, will be depleted by the myopic behaviour of independent individuals even though the depletion of the resource and the inefficient utilization of the resource in the long-run are clear to all individuals. To stop it, Hardin proposes the allocation of property rights to those resources with coercive measures by the authorities.

Despite the simplicity of his logic, it is dubious whether the nature of common resources is the real cause of the tragedy. We can find many examples in which common pool resources are utilized and controlled well by communities without any tragedy in history (Ostrom 2008). A typical example is Japan's *iriaichi* (communal land), which are commons of local communities. With rather strict rules implemented, those commons are considered to have been utilized in a sustainable way by members of the communities, particularly in the Edo period (1603–1868).

Then, what is the real reason for the tragedy? Notice that the logical structure of Hardin's argument is almost the same as that explained in an open-access problem of a fishery (see above). Recall why common resources of fish are overexploited in fishing grounds. It is clear that the overexploitation is caused by open access to fishermen. If entry to fishing grounds is regulated somehow, rent does not disappear and the stock of fish may not vanish. The same argument applies to the use of the atmosphere as a disposal place for smoke and soot.

Consequently, the tragedy that Hardin described may correctly be called the tragedy of open access, instead of the tragedy of commons.

There is an important point here: even if property rights are assigned to common resources, and even if coercive measures are adopted for proper use of those resources, as Hardin suggested, there is still the possibility of running out of them in a dynamic process. If a high discount rate is adopted, the optimal planning of the resource use may imply exhaustive use in a short period, leaving nothing for future generations. To solve this intergenerational problem, another institutional consideration is required, as shown in the sustainability argument presented below.

The limits to growth: the Malthusian spectre again?
Another important challenge to resources and environmental problems from non-economic researchers came from the Club of Rome. *The Limits to Growth* (Meadows et al. 1972) had a deep impact not only on researchers but also business leaders, who shared the feeling of an environmental crises, represented by population explosion, pollution, exhaustion of natural resources and so on.

Using a system dynamics approach, which was the newest analytical technique at that time, the authors, D.H. Meadows et al., explored whether human beings could maintain the economic growth and development enjoyed by people in advanced countries. On the presupposition that the world population would increase and capital accumulation would continue, they arrived at the conclusion that economic growth could not be sustained and that a catastrophe would hit the world, in which business-as-usual continued, owing to heavy pollution, exhaustion of natural resources, lack of food, and so on. This is nothing but the Malthusian spectre in a new guise.

The scholars involved were pessimistic as regards the development of technology: according to their model, further technical progress could not solve the problems. Consequently, to save human beings from disaster they proposed to stop both population increase and capital accumulation. Since, in addition to the heavy pollution in the 1960s–1970s, the first oil crisis struck the world in 1973 just after the publication of their book, curbing economic growth in advanced countries, the book became widely accepted.

After the two oil crises, however, increases in prices of energy and other natural resources drastically reduced demands for energy and resources on the one hand, and accelerated development of new technologies which contributed to savings of energy and natural resources on the other. Thanks to these, advanced countries experienced again moderate economic growth and development.

Furthermore, strict regulations against pollution were introduced in almost all advanced countries, inducing development of pollution prevention technology. As the PPP was adopted as the basic concept of anti-pollution policies, pollution came to be felt as a cost by firms, so that pollution prevention became a priority for them. In big cities, such as London and Tokyo, air quality was greatly improved.

Exhaustion of energy and other natural resources was avoided, and pollution problems were solved, at least in advanced countries. Despite the prophecy of the Club of Rome, the Malthusian spectre fortunately did not make itself felt (Nordhaus 1974).

It turned out that the price mechanism works much better than Meadows et al. had thought: actors in markets respond flexibly to the increases in scarcity of energy and natural resources. Pollution prevention policies triggered the development of new techniques that helped to fight the problems under consideration.

Yet it cannot be denied that the Club of Rome as well as Hardin had an important effect on economics. Particularly, around the time when the transboundary environmental problems such as climate change (global warming), depletion of the ozone layer, soil erosion, destruction of rain forests, and so on became a world concern in the late 1980s and the early 1990s, another Malthusian spectre loomed, and we could not help but remember their warnings. Yet, this time, economists were well prepared for pioneering environmental studies, establishing resources and environmental economics as fields of economics.

Modern Economics on Resources and Environment

One typical example of environmental economics as an established field can be seen in a standard textbook written by Baumol and Oates (1988), a result of the orthodox economics which analyses systematically allocation of environmental resources almost in the same way as that of other ordinary resources, generalizing Pigou's idea. Scarcity of those resources are analysed by means of general and partial equilibrium analyses, with applicability to real environmental policies.

Mainstream environmental economics extended and advanced the basic framework of environmental analysis to the extent that more realistic and substantial environmental issues became subjects of analyses. As applicability of those analyses was greatly enhanced, many important policy implications were deduced.

One good example is an analysis of trade of emission permits or entitlements. The idea of this policy scheme became popular among economists after Dales (1968), being regarded as an alternative policy to Pigouvian taxation. The idea was given a rigorous theoretical base by Montgomery (1972), and the workings of an economy under the scheme have been explored rigorously by means of a general equilibrium analysis since then.

It is easy to show that trade of emission permits has the same effect on the allocation of resources as a Pigouvian taxation in the purely hypothetical case in which the environmental authority is omnipotent and omniscient, that is, it has complete information on marginal damages (MD) and marginal abatement costs (MAC).

Weitzman (1974) showed that two schemes have different effects on reduction of targeted pollutants if there is uncertainty. Suppose that the environmental authority does not know how a MAC curve is located, but knows that of a MD curve. If the absolute value of the slope of a MD curve is larger than that of a MAC curve in the neighbourhood of an equilibrium point, trade of emission permits is preferred to Pigouvian taxation, since the former scheme hits at a point nearer to the optimal one than the latter, and vice versa.

The same analytical method as Baumol and Oates's has been applied to a policy analysis of waste management and recycling as well as utilization of secondary resources, which is one of the most fundamental issues in recent environmental policy. Fullerton and Kinnaman's seminal paper (1995) demonstrates, by means of a matchbox general equilibrium model, how alternative policies for waste management and recycling work. Many studies on waste management and recycling follow them (Calcott and Walls 2000; Eichner and Pethig 2001). One of the most important contributions of those researches is that an upstream policy such as the extended producer responsibility (EPR), which was proposed as a policy concept by the Organisation for Economic Co-operation and Development (OECD) for reduction of waste and promotion of recycling, is theorized and justified by rigorous economic analysis.

Sustainable development is another important issue related closely to real environmental policies. The concept of "sustainable development" first appeared in *Our Common Future* written by the United Nations World Commission on Environment and Development (1987), better known as the Brundtland Report. As global environmental problems such as climate change (global warming), depletion of the ozone layer, desertification, destruction of rainforests, acid rain and so on came to be recognized as impending crises for human beings, sustainability became the key concept for environmental policies.

Related to this, it is worth pointing out that maximization of the discounted sum of future streams of net benefits does not necessarily guarantee sustainability. According to the conventional optimization theory, it is quite possible that the present generations will not leave resources in a narrow sense for future generations, giving less weight to their descendant's welfare than to their own. That is, the optimal path determined at present is different from the sustainable path.

Then, the question is how to find and implement the sustainable path. One of the most lucid answers was given by Hartwick (1977). He showed that an economy can be sustainable if all the profits obtained from the use of non-reproducible resources (natural capital, S) are invested for accumulation of man-made capital (K_M), which can be substituted for the former resources. This idea is called the Hartwick rule. The path that guarantees constant utilities for all future generations can be attained by this rule.

On the path implemented by the rule, the following equation holds:

$$p_S \Delta S + p_M \Delta K_M = 0 \qquad (11)$$

Here p_S and p_M are prices of natural resources (natural capital) and man-made capital, respectively. If the left-hand side of (11) is positive, an economy can possibly leave more resources to future generations, satisfying sustainability. Actually, the left-hand side is called genuine savings, which are used as an index to measure sustainability by the World Bank.

An interesting result related to the sustainability argument, which is about Green Net National Product (NNP), is the following. Denoting the consumption of non-renewable resources (natural capital) as R, Green NNP is defined as:

$$GreenNNP \equiv C + p_M \Delta K - p_S R. \qquad (12)$$

Based upon Weitzman's idea of NNP (Weitzman 1976), it is shown that Green NNP is "the stationary equivalent of future consumption". Notice that Green NNP defined above may not be feasible. Onuma (1999) shows that increasing Green NNP is a necessary condition for maximum sustainable consumption, which satisfies feasibility.

For the Hartwick rule to hold, and for the concept of Green NNP to be justified, an important assumption must be satisfied: natural resources (natural capital) can be substituted by man-made capital or human capital. Otherwise, sustainable development cannot be realized. Sustainability based upon substitutability is called weak sustainability.

This notion of sustainability is, however, criticized by non-mainstream economists such as ecological economists, who argue that some natural resources can be substituted neither by man-made capital nor by human capital. The notion of strong sustainability is based upon the presupposition of restricted substitutability among different types of capital. Yet, strong sustainability can be considered to be fulfilled in a steady-state economy, where reproducible resources must be used within the regenerative capacity and non-reproducible resources be used as far as they are substituted by reproducible resources at least in the same amount (Daily 1991). The steady state, which ecological economists have in their minds, may be quite akin to the idea of the classical economists represented by Mill. In this context, it is worth pointing out that some ecological economists are sceptical about economic development or growth, since neither of them is compatible with the second law of thermodynamics (see Martinez-Alier 1987).

This is too short a discussion in my view. Another similarity to the classical economists' viewpoint is found in the works of researchers in the tradition of Sraffa (1960). As already shown, the classical economists focused their analysis on the reproducibility of a capitalist economy, where natural prices or production prices prevail. Modern classical economists analyse the reproducible nature of an economy from the viewpoints of income distribution and inter-industrial relationships, using Sraffa's analytical framework.

Beginning in the early 1980s they have developed their basic models by explicitly introducing environmental resources. Giving up the free-disposal assumption, and considering uses of environmental resources as joint products, they demonstrate how natural prices of discommodities (bads) as well as of commodities (goods) are formed (Schefold 1988, 2006; Lager 2001b; Parrinello 2001; Hosoda 2010b). Although those models are abstract, an interesting application to a real issue of waste management and recycling is made based upon them. Extended producer responsibility (EPR) can be justified in a case where waste treatment service has the same nature as a non-basic commodity in Sraffa's sense. Hence, EPR is justified for household waste only, not for industrial waste (Hosoda 2010a).

Conclusion

With few exceptions, the classical economists did not consider resource and environmental constraints as posing severe problems, although they considered that an economy would arrive at a stationary state sooner or later. They considered that limitation of economic growth was basically attributed to exponential population growth and diminishing returns in agriculture. Their idea of reproducibility of an economy exhibits some similarity to that of sustainability in modern terms. Actually, the idea is rehabilitated and applied to resource and environmental problems by modern classical economists.

Although Hotelling anticipated theoretically an increase in scarcity of non-renewable resources, resource prices decreased for rather a long time after the Industrial Revolution. This might have made economists optimistic as regards constraints due to natural resources. Actually, economic growth and development were their main concern after World War II. Experiencing the two oil crises in the 1970s and heavy pollution in the1960s–1970s, however, economists noticed that resource and environmental constraint became much tighter than they had anticipated. Around these periods, economics on resources and the environment came to be established as a branch of economics.

Resources and environmental economics is not merely an application of theoretical economics. Researchers engaged in resources and environmental studies are required to respond to social problems that follow from tighter constraints of natural and environmental resources.

Diversity of economics is indispensable for solving diverse environmental problems. Whichever analytical method may be adopted, a new idea on the value and scarcity of environmental resources must be developed. Such an endeavour to explore the scarcity of environmental resources can be found in Simpson et al. (2005).

EIJI HOSODA

See also:

Thomas Robert Malthus (I); John Stuart Mill (I); Neo-Ricardian economics (II); Arthur Cecil Pigou (I); François Quesnay and Physiocracy (I); David Ricardo (I); Piero Sraffa (I).

References and further reading

Baumol, W.J. and W.E. Oates (1988), *The Theory of Environmental Policy*, 2nd edn, Cambridge: Cambridge University Press.
Bidard, C. and G. Erreygers (2001a), 'The corn-guano model', *Metroeconomica*, **52** (3), 243–53.
Bidard, C. and G. Erreygers (2001b), 'Further reflections on the corn-guano model', *Metroeconomica*, **52** (3), 254–67.
Calcott, K. and M. Walls (2000), 'Can downstream waste disposal policies encourage upstream "design for environment"?', *American Economic Review*, **90** (2), 233–7.
Daily, H. (1991), *Steady-State Economics: Second Edition with New Essays*, Washington, DC: Island Press.
Dales, J.H. (1968), *Pollution, Property and Prices*, Toronto: University of Toronto Press.
Dasgupta, P.S. and G.M. Heal (1979), *Economic Theory and Exhaustible Resources*, Cambridge: Cambridge University Press.
Eichner, T. and R. Pethig (2001), 'Product design and efficient management of recycling and waste treatment', *Journal of Environmental Economics and Policy Studies*, **41** (1), 109–34.
Farrow, S. (1985), 'Testing the efficiency of extraction from a stock resource', *Journal of Political Economy*, **93** (3), 452–87.
Fullerton, D. and T. Kinnaman (1995), 'Garbage, recycling, and illicit burning or dumping', *Journal of Environmental Economics and Policy Studies*, **29** (1), 78–91.
Gordon, H.S. (1954), 'Theory of a common property resource', *Journal of Political Economy*, **62** (2), 124–42.
Gould, J.R. (1972), 'Extinction of fishery by commercial exploitation: a note', *Journal of Political Economy*, **80** (5), 1031–8.
Halvorsen, R. and T.R. Smith (1991), 'A test of the theory of exhaustible resources', *Quarterly Journal of Economics*, **106** (1), 123–40.
Hardin, G. (1968), 'The tragedy of the commons', *Science*, **162** (3859), 1243–8.
Hartwick, J.M. (1977), 'Intergenerational equity and the investing of rents from exhaustible resources', *American Economic Review*, **67** (5), 972–74.
Hosoda, E. (2001), 'Recycling and landfilling in a dynamic Sraffian model: application of the corn-guano model to a waste treatment problem', *Metroeconomica*, **52** (3), 268–81.
Hosoda, E. (2010a), 'Malfunction of a market in a transaction of waste. A reason for the necessity of an upstream policy in waste management', in J. Vint, J.S. Metcalfe, H.D. Kurz, N. Salvadori and P.A. Samuelson (eds), *Economic Theory and Economic Thought. Essays in Honour of Ian Steedman*, London: Routledge, pp. 234–53.
Hosoda, E. (2010b), 'Bads as joint products in a linear production system', in A. Birolo, D.K. Foley, H.D. Kurz, B. Schefold and I. Steedman (eds), *Production, Distribution and Trade*, London: Routledge, pp. 33–61.

Hotelling, H. (1931), 'The economics of exhaustible resources', *Journal of Political Economy*, **39** (2), 137–75.

Jevons, W.S. (1865), *The Coal Question: An Inquiry Concerning the Progress of the Nation and the Probable Exhaustion of our Coal Mines*, London: Macmillan.

Kneese, A.V. and J.L. Sweeney (1985), *Handbook of Natural Resource and Energy Economics*, The Hague: North-Holland.

Krautkraemer, J.A. (1998), 'Non-renewable resource scarcity', *Journal of Economic Literature*, **36** (4), 2065–107.

Kula, E. (1998), *History of Environmental Economic Thought*, London: Routledge.

Kurz, H.D. (2010), 'Technical change, capital accumulation and income distribution in classical economics: Adam Smith, David Ricardo and Karl Marx', *European Journal of the History of Economic Thought*, **11** (5), 1183–222.

Kurz, H.D. and N. Salvadori (1995), *Theory of Production. A Long-Period Analysis*, Cambridge, Melbourne and New York: Cambridge University Press.

Kurz, H.D. and N. Salvadori (1997), 'Exhaustible resources in a dynamic input–output model with "classical" resources', *Economic Systems Research*, **9** (3), 235–51.

Kurz, H.D. and N. Salvadori (2001), 'Classical economics and the problem of exhaustible resources', *Metroeconomica*, **52** (3), 282–96.

Kurz, H.D. and N. Salvadori (2014), *Revisiting Classical Economics*, Abingdon and New York: Routledge.

Lager, C. (2001a), 'Joint production with "restricted free disposal"', *Metroeconomica*, **52** (1), 49–78.

Lager, C. (2001b), 'A note on non-stationary prices', *Metroeconomica*, **52** (3), 297–300.

Malthus, R.T. (1798), *An Essay on the Principle of Population as it Affects the Future Improvement of Society*, 3rd edn 1890, London: Ward Lock.

Martinez-Alier, J. (1987), *Ecological Economics*, Oxford: Basil Blackwell.

Marx, K. (1894), *Das Kapital, Third Volume*, trans. S. Moor, London: Lawrence and Wishart.

Meadows, D.H., D.L. Meadows, J. Randers and W.W. Behrens III (1972), *The Limits to Growth*, London: Universe Books.

Mill, J.S. (1848), *Principles of Political Economy*, New York: Appleton.

Miller, M.H. and C.W. Upton (1985), 'A test of the Hotelling valuation principle', *Journal of Political Economy*, **93** (1), 1–25.

Montgomery, W.E. (1972), 'Markets in licenses and efficient pollution control programs', *Journal of Economic Theory*, **5** (3), 395–418.

Neumayer, E. (2000), 'Scarce or abundant? The economics of natural resource availability', *Journal of Economic Surveys*, **14** (3), 307–35.

Nordhaus, W.D. (1974), 'Resources as a constraint on growth', *American Economic Review*, **64** (2), 22–16.

Onuma, A. (1999), 'Sustainable consumption, sustainable development, and green net national product', *Environmental Economics and Policy Studies*, **2** (3), 187–98.

Ostrom, E. (2008), *Governing the Commons*, Cambridge: Cambridge University Press.

Parrinello, S. (1983), 'Exhaustible natural resources and the classical method of long-period equilibrium' in J. Kregel (ed.), *Distribution, Effective Demand and International Economic Relations*, London: Macmillan, pp. 186–99.

Parrinello, S. (2001), 'The price of exhaustible resources', *Metroeconomica*, **52** (3), 301–15.

Parrinello, S. (2004), 'The notion of effectual supply and the theory of normal prices with exhaustible resources', *Economic Systems Research*, **16** (3), 319–30.

Peterson, F.M. and A.C. Fisher (1977), 'The exploitation of extractive resources', *Economic Journal*, **87** (348), 681–721.

Pigou, A.C. (1932), *The Economics of Welfare*, London: Macmillan.

Ricardo, D. (1817), *On the Principles of Political Economy and Taxation*, reprinted in P. Sraffa (ed.) with the collaboration of M.H. Dobb (1951), *The Works and Correspondence of David Ricardo*, vol. 1, Cambridge: Cambridge University Press.

Robinson, T.J.C. (1989), *Economic Theories of Exhaustible Resources*, London and New York: Routledge.

Salvadori, N. (1987), 'Les ressources naturelles rares dans la theorie de Sraffa', in G. Bidard (ed.), *La rente, acutalite de l'approche classique*, Paris: Economica, pp. 161–76.

Schefold, B. (1988), 'The dominant technique in joint production systems', *Cambridge Journal of Economics*, **12** (1), 97–123.

Schefold, B. (1989), *Mr. Sraffa on Joint Production and Other Essays*, London: Macmillan.

Schefold, B. (2001), 'Critique of the corn-guano model', *Metroeconomica*, **52** (3), 316–28.

Schefold, B. (2006), 'Joint production: triumph of economic over mathematical logic?', *European Journal of the History of Economic Thought*, **12** (3), 525–52.

Simpson, R.D., M.A. Toman and R.U. Ayres (eds) (2005), *Scarcity and Growth Revisited: Natural Resources and the Environment in the New Millennium*, Washington, DC: Resources for the Future.

Slade, M.E. (1982), 'Trends in natural-resource commodity prices: an analysis of the time domain', *Journal of Environmental Economics and Management*, **9** (2), 122–37.

Sraffa, P. (1960), *Production of Commodities by Means of Commodities*, Cambridge: Cambridge University Press.

Stollery, K.R. (1983), 'Mineral depletion with cost as the extraction limit: a model applied to the behavior of prices in the nickel industry', *Journal of Environmental Economics and Management*, **10** (2), 151–65.

United Nations World Commission on Environment and Development (1987), *Our Common Future*, Oxford: Oxford University Press.

Weitzman, M.L. (1974), 'Price vs. quantities', *Review of Economic Studies*, **41** (1), 477–91.

Weitzman, M.L. (1976), 'On the welfare significance of national product in a dynamic economy', *Quarterly Journal of Economics*, **90** (1), 156–62.

Wrigley, E.A. (1988), *Continuity, Chance and Change*, Cambridge: Cambridge University Press.

Social choice

Social choice in its modern guise is a young subject that can be dated back to the end of the 1940s and the beginning of the 1950s in the works of Duncan Black (1948), Kenneth Arrow (1950, 1951) and Georges-Théodule Guilbaud (1952). This is nowadays considered as a rebirth, the (first) birth being generally attributed to Jean-Charles de Borda (1784) and Marie-Jean-Antoine-Nicolas Caritat de Condorcet (1785). However, as will be clear in this entry, there are other earlier precursors.

Social choice is concerned with the selection of options on the basis of the opinions of individuals over these options. Note that there is an analogy with the choice by an individual of, say, an object, in the presence of multiple criteria. However, this entry is restricted to the multi-individual framework. The selection procedures have been studied either from a rather abstract point of view or from a more practical point of view. In the former, one considers notions such as aggregation functions, social choice functions and their properties, and in the latter one considers voting rules, voting games, and so on. It is interesting to note that this dichotomy has a historical origin, the abstract aspect being generally associated with the utilitarian tradition from Jeremy Bentham to Abram Bergson and Paul Samuelson, and with welfare economics and the practical aspect being associated with questions related to elections, be they elections in small committees or in larger organizations.

The precursors (this phrase will be used for authors living before the eighteenth century) dealt mostly with voting. The eighteenth century saw also an upsurge of interest under both aspects in the contributions of Borda and Condorcet. It is surprising that during the nineteenth century the interest in voting rather faded away in spite of the emergence of democratic societies. However, there has been some work on proportional representation (or the equivalent apportionment methods) by European scholars rediscovering what some founding fathers of American democracy previously did, with the brilliant exception to this lack of interest of Charles Lutwidge Dodgson, better known as Lewis Carroll.

The rebirth of social choice theory in the twentieth century offers the same dichotomy. Although both Black and Arrow are economists, the former obviously belongs to the voting tradition and the latter to the welfare economics tradition. Even though voting aspects are not absent in the founding book by Arrow, *Social Choice and Individual Values* (1951), a significant part is devoted to discussions of the compensation tests debate between John Hicks, Nicholas Kaldor and Tibor Scitovsky and of the Bergson–Samuelson social welfare functions. A large part of this entry will be devoted to Arrow's theorem and its descendants and to other major results that form the cornerstone of the domain.

The Precursors

Several major classics were collected in an excellent anthology by Iain McLean and Arnold Urken (1995). Furthermore, McLean and Urken wrote a remarkable introduction that is one of the main sources of this entry as far as pre-Arrovian social choice is concerned.

Even if both Plato and Aristotle's views regarding the goodness of the various political systems could have been discussed here, since it seems that, for them, the ideal would be some authoritarian regime – oligarchy for Plato and monarchy with some kind of benevolent dictator for Aristotle with as objective the maximization of the happiness of the state as a whole, a theme related to both Bentham and Arrow – the standard (but quite recent) usage to consider Pliny the Younger as the first author to deal with a social choice problem is followed.

Pliny the Younger

Caius Caecilius – the younger Pliny (AD 61 or 62–113) – was born in a Roman high society family in Como. His uncle (his mother's brother) was Pliny the Elder, a naturalist, natural philosopher, naval and army commander, and friend of the emperor Vespasian. Pliny the Elder died during the Vesuvius eruption that destroyed Pompeii and Herculaneum in August 79 while he was trying to rescue friends. The younger Pliny was the heir of his uncle and the change of name – Caius Plinius Luci filius Caecilius Secundus – indicates his adoption by will as a son (his father, Lucius Caecilius had died while he was very young). Pliny started his career at the Roman bar at the age of 18. He moved through the regular offices in a senator's career, even becoming consul in 100 under Emperor Trajan. On this occasion he delivered the speech of thanks known as the *Panegyricus*. However, he is better known for his letters that are considered to be a social document of his times and are praised for the quality of their prose.

The letter that interests us is Letter 14 in Book VIII (Pliny 1969) and was brought to the attention of social choice theorists by Robin Farquharson (1969) in his exceptional book on strategic voting (on Farquharson see Dummett 2005). Farquharson's book includes a 1752 translation by John, Earl of Orrery, of Pliny's letter. According to Riker (1986: 88), the translator "did not seem to understand the parliamentary issues involved and therefore did not see what happened at the end of the event". There is, fortunately, a new translation by Betty Radice in Pliny (1969).

Pliny's letter is to Titius Aristo, a pre-eminent jurist. After a long digression praising the addressee, Pliny explains that "the case at issue concerned the freedmen of the consul Afranius Dexter, who had been found dead; it was not known whether he had killed himself or his servants were responsible, and, if the latter, whether they acted criminally or in obedience to their master." Three kinds of decisions were then suggested: acquittal, banishment or death penalty. (Pliny also suggests that some people were in favour of banishment for the freedmen and death for the slaves, although there is no further mention of slaves.) Pliny wished to have a plurality voting system in this case: "my own proposal was that the three sentences should be reckoned as three, and that two should not join forces under a temporary truce" (Pliny 1969: 39). He feared the formation of a coalition of senators in favour of death with those in favour of banishment, defeating those who were in favour of acquittal. He even imagined a run-off with a vote on death against banishment. Although the letter does not explain this, we can infer from it that the banishment penalty would have defeated both acquittal and death penalty in pairwise majority voting, being what is now called a Condorcet winner. Pliny succeeded in his request to have a (one round) plurality vote. Then:

> the proposer of the death sentence was convinced by the justice of my request . . ., dropped his own proposal, and supported that of banishment. He was afraid, no doubt, that if the sentences were taken separately (which seemed likely if he did not act) the acquittal would

have a majority, for there were many more people in favour of this than either of the other two proposals. Then, when those who had been influenced by him found themselves abandoned by his crossing the floor and the proposal thrown over by its author, they dropped it too, and deserted after their leader. So the three sentences became two, and the second carried the day by elimination of the third which could not defeat both the others, and therefore chose to submit to one. (Pliny 1969: 45)

It seems clear in Radice's translation that the senate voted for the banishment penalty. According to Riker (1986) Pliny proposed the plurality rule because he thought that voters would vote sincerely. He tried to manipulate the Roman Senate by promoting a rule that would generate the decision he was in favour of: acquittal. However, he did not understand clearly that those in favour of the death penalty would manipulate the voting rule by voting strategically. The 1752 translation is unclear on this and a French translation by Annette Flaubert (Pliny 2002) has a footnote in which it is said that acquittal carried the day!

It remains that Pliny describes a situation that is manipulable (by a coalition) in the modern sense of Gibbard and Satterthwaite: a group of individuals by voting strategically forces the voting rule to generate an outcome that the members of the group prefer to the outcome that would have prevailed if they had not voted strategically.

Ramon Lull

Ramon Lull (*c.* 1233–1316) was born in Mallorca into a wealthy family. As a young man, he was a troubadour writing poetry and songs. At the age of about 30, while he was writing a song to a lady he loved, he saw Jesus Christ on the cross and from then on devoted his life to religion – abandoning his wife and his two children. He believed to have three missions: writing books against the errors of the unbelievers, founding schools for teaching foreign languages and converting Jews and Moslems. He wrote about 290 books (260 reached us), some of them in Arabic, on a variety of subjects, including, of course, religion, but also logic and mathematics, astrology and alchemy.

Social choice theorists first heard of Lull (also, for that matter, of Nicholas Cusanus) from a paper by McLean and London (1990). McLean and London identified two sources: a novel entitled *Blanquerna* and another text whose title is *De Arte Eleccionis*. Since then a third text, *Artificium Electionis Personarum*, was called to our attention by scholars from Augsburg, in particular Friedrich Pukelsheim (see Hägele and Pukelsheim 2001, 2008). It is remarkable that *Blanquerna* is considered as one of the first novels ever written (in Catalan) in Europe. In *Artificium Electionis Personarum*, the first published among the three texts as well as in *Blanquerna* and the later *De Arte Eleccionis*, Lull recommends systems based on pair-wise (majority) voting. In both works all pair-wise comparisons are done. There is however a difference, since in *Blanquerna*, the ballot is organized in two stages. The set of voters and the set of possible elected persons are identical. At a first stage, voters have to reduce the size of these two sets. Lull considers a set of 20 voters to be reduced to seven. He describes a method to reach these seven: each voter is asked to select seven among 19 (this probably means that voters are not permitted to vote for themselves), and the seven collectively chosen are those who have the most votes. The next step, pair-wise (majority) voting is among some also reduced set of candidates, but this set is not identical to the reduced set of voters as Lull in his example considers nine candidates (why nine and from where are they coming, it is impossible to know). The winner is the candidate who is victorious in most of the pair-wise contests. This method is known today as the Copeland method and more sophisticated versions are used in tournaments, in particular in sports. (Copeland was a mathematician at the University of Michigan. His paper, "A reasonable social welfare function" 1951, has never been published.) McLean and Urken (1995) hesitate to provide a clear-cut interpretation as they mention that Lull's description could be Borda's rule. Lull was conscious that the method could generate ties. He then proposed a tie-breaking rule that, to say the least, is rather obscure: "The art recommends that these two or three or more should be judged according to art alone. It should be found out which of these best meets the four aforementioned conditions, for she [the reference is to a nun] will be the one who is worthy to be elected" (McLean and Urken 1995: 72).

These four conditions are: which of them best loves and knows God; which of them best loves and knows the virtues; which of them knows and hates most strongly the vices; and which is the most suitable person. Since ties would happen, given an odd number of voters and strict preferences (linear orderings), in case of a top cycle, the only way to break this would be to organize a deliberation among voters and proceed to a new ballot among tied candidates. It is not clear whether this corresponds to what Lull had in mind.

In *De Arte Eleccionis*, the procedure is quite different even though it is still based on (majority) pair-wise voting. It is based on successive eliminations. This rule is often known as the parliamentary procedure since it imitates the successive votes on bill proposals and amendments. It seems that Lull did not see that this method is highly agenda-manipulable (the outcome is strongly linked to the order in which the pair-wise contests are organized) and that it can select a candidate who is Pareto dominated (that is, a candidate could be elected even though all voters prefer another candidate). Donald Saari (2008) gives an example of "electing Fred" even though Fred is Pareto dominated by three out of five other candidates. One of the only virtues of the rule is probably that it will not select a Condorcet loser (a candidate that is beaten by all the other candidates in pair-wise contests) since the elected candidate won the last confrontation.

Nicholas of Cusa

Nicholas of Cusa – also known as Nicholas Cusanus or Nikolaus von Kues – was born in Kues in 1401 into a wealthy family. Kues is a small town on the Mosel valley situated between Trier and Koblenz. He studied at the universities of Heidelberg, Padua and Cologne, had a very successful ecclesiastical career, becoming a cardinal, and died in Todi (Umbria) in 1464. He is generally considered as one of the greatest polymaths of the fifteenth century. He participated in the Council of Basel in 1433–34. It is during these years that he wrote his first major work *De Concordantia Catholica* (Nicholas of Cusa 1433) – an English translation, *The Catholic Concordance*, was published in 1991.

In it, Cusanus devotes some paragraphs to the description of a voting method for the election of the Emperor of the Holy Roman Empire. He considers an example with ten candidates. He assumes that each voter ranks the candidates without ties from the least preferred to the most preferred, giving marks from 1 to 10 on the basis of this ranking. He writes: "the teller must add up the numbers by each name, and the candidate who has collected the highest total will be emperor" (McLean and Urken 1995: 78). This is clearly Borda's rule as it is now known. Cusanus adds:

By this method innumerable malpractices can be avoided, and indeed no malpractice is possible. In fact, no method of election can be conceived which is more holy, just, honest, or free. For by this procedure, no other outcome is possible, if the electors act according to conscience, than the choice of that candidate adjudged best by the collective judgment of all present. (McLean and Urken 1995: 78)

Cusanus does not mention the possibility of ties (whose probability is not negligible when the set of voters is small).

Samuel von Pufendorf
Samuel von Pufendorf was born in 1632. He studied in Leipzig, Jena and Leiden and held professorships in Heidelberg (1661) and Lund (1670). He left Lund for Stockholm to become a political-jurisprudential councillor at the courts of Sweden. He then wrote a monumental history of Sweden. He spent the last years of his life in Brandenburg-Prussia as appointed historian. He died in 1694. The book of interest to social choice theorists and economists in general is *De Jure Naturae et Gentium* (*The Law of Nature and of Nations*). It was published in 1672. Among the translations, the French one with many additional comments by Jean de Barbeyrac (*Le droit de la nature et des gens*) played an important role in the French Enlightenment, in particular it influenced both Diderot and Rousseau. Wulf Gaertner (2005) describes in some detail Pufendorf's contributions to voting and economics. In book VII, chapter II, section 18, one can read:

Thus those who fix a fine upon a man, at twenty units of value, may be united with those who fix it at ten units, against such as would acquit him altogether, and the defendant will be fined ten units, because this is agreeable to the majority of judges, in view of the fact that those in favour of the twenty, are included with those in favour of the ten. (Gaertner 2005: 237)

Pufendorf insists on the difference between quantitative options (fines) and qualitative options (here acquittal). According to Gaertner, this can be viewed as single-peaked preferences, with preference orderings from most preferred to least preferred being either 20, ten, acquittal, or acquittal, ten, 20, or ten, 20, acquittal. Of course, in this case, the median option, here ten, is selected by the majority rule. Another possibility would be to consider this example as analogous to Pliny's example: the judges in favour of a fine of 20 join those in favour of a fine of ten to defeat the acquittal option which is the option they ranked last. This possibility could justify a reference to Pliny's letter in Pufendorf's work as indicated by Gaertner.

The Founding Fathers

Even if Cusanus proposed Borda's rule more than 300 years before Borda, and Lull's description of elections are generally based on pair-wise majority voting anticipating, maybe, Condorcet, their works cannot be compared with those of Borda and Condorcet. Borda was a great applied scientist of his time and Condorcet's contribution to human knowledge is still probably underestimated. What they left us on voting is not commensurate with what Cusanus or Lull left. A third founding father should be added because of his influence on later thinkers: Bentham, who might well be the father of the utilitarian social welfare function.

Jean-Charles de Borda

Borda was born in Dax in the South West of France in 1733 in a family of little nobility – he was Chevalier, that is knight and not Count as written in Mathias Risse (2005) even though the pun "Count de Borda"/"Borda count" opposed to the "Marquis de Condorcet" was amusing and clever. He studied at the Collège Royal Henry-le-Grand (a College of Jesuits at that time) in La Flèche, a small town near Le Mans. The most famous pupil of this Collège was Descartes and La Flèche is also well known for being the city where David Hume settled while in France and where he wrote most of *A Treatise of Human Nature*. Borda became a member of the military engineering corps, worked on ballistics and became a member of the Académie Royale des Sciences. He participated in the American war of independence as a French Navy officer but was taken prisoner by the British. Later, he worked on the metric system as chairman of the Commission des Poids et Mesures (Committee of Weights and Measures). He died in 1799.

Borda's work in social choice is rather limited: nine pages in *Histoire de l'Académie Royale des Sciences pour 1781*, published in 1784. In his "Mémoire sur les élections au scrutin", Borda presents his system: the so-called Borda count. Each voter ranks the candidates without ties: one point is attributed to the candidate ranked last in the voter's ranking, two points are attributed to the candidate ranked just before the last one, and so on, the top candidate obtaining a number of points that is equal to the number of candidates. Note that we could start from zero up to the number of candidates minus one, or even, as indicated by Borda, start from any number and add the same fixed number when we go from one rank to the rank that is just above it. The points obtained by a candidate are added and the winner(s) is (are) the candidate(s) who has (have) obtained the greatest number. However, there is more in these nine pages. First, an example is given where a plurality winner is a Condorcet loser. This demonstrates that, in Borda's view, the plurality rule is flawed. On the other hand, there is no proof that, in non-trivial cases, a Borda winner cannot be a Condorcet loser. However, Borda derives simple inequalities for the case when there is a Borda winner that coincides with a plurality winner.

Marie-Jean-Antoine-Nicolas Caritat, Marquis de Condorcet

Condorcet was born in 1743 in Ribemont near Saint-Quentin (North-East of Paris). He was also educated by the Jesuits, first privately and then at the Collège des Jésuites in Reims. He studied mathematics in Paris and at 26 he entered the Académie Royale des Sciences. He was a friend of Turgot and, as such, was interested in economics but also in politics and in the theory of elections. He was elected to the Legislative Assembly in 1791, and then at the Convention in 1792. He contested in vain the Assembly's right to judge the King and voted against capital punishment. He wrote the famous *Esquisse d'un Tableau Historique des Progrès de l'Esprit Humain* while he was hiding. Finally, he was arrested and died on 7 April 1794, of poisoning or exhaustion.

The 1785 *Essai sur l'application de l'analyse à la probabilité des décisions rendues à la pluralité des voix* is an impressive piece of work. It has nearly 500 pages if we include the "Discours préliminaire". While it is the most important book Condorcet devoted to elections, it is not the only one. Other important works include, among others, the *Lettres d'un bourgeois de New Heaven à un citoyen de Virginie, sur l'inutilité de partager le pouvoir législatif entre plusieurs corps*, and the *Essai sur la constitution et les fonctions des assemblées provinciales*, both published in 1788 (see Condorcet 1986). Most scholars have focused their attention on the "Discours préliminaire" for several reasons, an obvious one being that some pages of the main text are covered with long probability calculations that are very similar, at first sight, to expressions we find today in works about the probability of pathologies for specific voting rules (see, for instance, Gehrlein and Lepelley 2011). However, according to Bernard Bru and Pierre Crépel (1994), the main part of the *Essai* cannot be eschewed. In particular, according to them, how could we explain why some crucial parts gave rise to contradictory interpretations?

The basic theme of the 1785 *Essai* concerns the probability of taking a correct decision. This is the now famous Condorcet's jury theorem, where we have members of a jury for whom the probability to have the correct opinion is given by v and to be in error is given by e ($= 1 - v$). If v is greater than 0.5, majorities are more likely to select the correct opinion and this likelihood will increase with the number of voters. However, Condorcet was not certain that $v > e$, and, since with $e > v$, the result would be inversed, he was rather prudent. He wrote:

> The assumption that $e > v$ is not absurd. For many important questions either complex or under the influence of prejudices or passions, it is likely that a poorly educated man will have an erroneous opinion. There are, consequently, a great number of points for which, the more we increase the number of voters, the more we can fear to obtain, with plurality, a decision in contradiction with truth so that a purely democratic constitution would be the worst of all for all these objects on which the people would not know the truth. (English translation of Condorcet 1785: 6–7)

Condorcet then recommended that only enlightened men be attributed the prerogatives to make proposals of law. The popular assemblies would not be asked to vote on whether the law is useful or dangerous, but only if it is against justice or against the primary rights of men. A "pure" democracy could only be good for a very well educated people, so well educated that there had never been such a people.

Condorcet is most known now for the example showing that majority rule could generate a cycle. Suppose there are 60 voters and three candidates A, B and C. The rankings are given by the following – 23 voters: ABC, meaning A ranked first, B, second and C third; 17 voters: BCA; 2 voters: BAC; 10 voters: CAB; 8 voters: CBA. A majority of voters (33) can be seen to prefer A to B, a majority (35) prefer C to A and a majority (42) prefer B to C. Of course one can also obtain a cycle very simply with three voters whose rankings are respectively ABC, BCA and CAB.

In the main text of the *Essai*, Condorcet proposed a method to deal with this problem. This method, rather obscure in Condorcet's words, has been the object of a reconstruction by, among others, Young (1988) and Monjardet (1990).

Condorcet also alluded to Borda and gave an example showing that Borda's rule could select another candidate than the Condorcet winner. Suppose 81 voters have the following rankings over three candidates A, B and C – 30 voters: ABC; 1 voter: ACB; 10 voters: CAB; 29 voters: BAC; 10 voters: BCA; 1 voter: CBA.

Candidate A is a Condorcet winner (he beats B only by 41 against 40), but B is the Borda winner. That A is a better candidate than B seems obvious to Condorcet. This was the beginning of a long debate which still goes on today (see, for instance, Dummett 1984, 1997; Saari 1995, 2006; Risse 2005; Emerson 2007). Of course, again, a very simple example is possible, for instance, with 19 voters. 10 voters: ABC and 9 voters: BCA.

Candidate *A* is a Condorcet winner (and a plurality winner) but *B* is the Borda winner. On page clxxix, Condorcet (1785) alluded to some kind of strategic voting indicating that Borda's rule is not immune to this possible voters' behaviour.

In *Lettres d'un bourgeois de New Heaven*, Condorcet proposed that the Condorcet winner be selected if there is one, and, if there is none, he proposed to select the candidate that won the most pair-wise confrontations (again, this is Copeland's method suggested by Lull long before). For the selection of committees of *k* members to be chosen in a set of 3*k* candidates, Condorcet recommended in 1792 that each voter partitions the set of candidates in three sets of *k* candidates and ranks the three sets (a set of *k* most-preferred candidates, a set of *k* intermediately-preferred candidates, and a set of *k* least pre-ferred candidates). Each voter indicates his *k* most-preferred candidates and, as a supple-mentary list, the *k* "intermediate" candidates. If at least *k* candidates obtain a majority, this is done by selection of the *k* candidates who have obtained the most votes. If not, one considers the supplementary lists. It is at the same time original and unorthodox, but still to be formally studied.

The works of Condorcet prompted a number of studies by Pierre-Simon Laplace, Simon Antoine Jean Lhuillier, Sylvestre-François Lacroix, José Isidore Morales and Pierre-Claude-François Daunou (see McLean and Urken 1995).

Jeremy Bentham

Bentham's (1748–1832) role on the development of social choice was rather indirect. Even though the paternity of utilitarianism cannot be attributed to Bentham, he did popularize it, in particular through the publication in 1789 of *An Introduction to the Principles of Morals and Legislation*. Utilitarianism belongs to the sphere of individual, not social, ethics. However, from the utilitarian basic principles, in David Wiggins's words (2006), "the new moral philosophy of Jeremy Bentham, James Mill, and James's son, John Stuart, came to be linked with a stupendous programme of social and politi-cal reform" (Wiggins 2006: 144). The search for the "greatest happiness of the greatest number" is the utilitarian motto, generally attributed to Bentham – but Hutcheson used this phrase before. It is unclear whether this means that Bentham had in mind some kind of utilitarian social welfare function. However, one can read, at the very beginning of his book: "The community is a fictitious *body*, composed of the individual persons who are considered as constituting as it were its *members*. The interest of the community then is, what? – the sum of the interests of the several members who compose it" (Bentham 1789 [1970]: 12, original emphases).

We can take this as a somewhat vague definition of a utilitarian social welfare func-tion and Bentham can then be viewed as an ancestor of Bergson and Samuelson. Arrow's contribution was obviously prompted by Bergson's paper (Arrow 1951 [1963]: 22) and Arrow also alludes to Bentham.

Social Choice during the Nineteenth Century

During the nineteenth century, in spite of the development of democratic institutions, the theory of social choice has been rather dormant, save for a few exceptions.

A basic question that had to be solved in the USA was the apportionment ques-tion: given a state with its population, what is the correct number of representatives that would respect the principle of equality of the citizens across the various states? The equality here means that each representative should represent the same number of people. Although this looks simple, and maybe secondary, the difficulty arises from the fact that the numbers of representatives are integers. The problem of apportionment is identical to the problem of proportional representation. A number of methods have been devised, in particular by some of the founding fathers of American democracy, especially Thomas Jefferson and Alexander Hamilton, and rediscovered later by Europeans generally in the context of proportional representation. The definitive book on this topic is Michel Balinski and Peyton Young (1982). It includes many historical developments.

Two scholars have to be mentioned. The first is C.L. Dodgson (Lewis Carroll) (1832–1898) and the second is Edward John Nanson (1850–1936). Dodgson was a logician at Oxford University. He wrote some pamphlets that are reproduced in Black (1958). Through time, he proposed various voting methods. For instance, even though he apparently knew neither Borda nor Condorcet, he proposed the use of Borda's rule and a run-off between the two top candidates. Later, he proposed selection of the Condorcet winner if there is one, and, if not, to have recourse to Borda's rule, a rule that is generally associated with Duncan Black.

Nanson spent most of his life in Australia as a professor of mathematics at the University of Melbourne. He knew the French literature on voting – Condorcet as well as Borda. He wanted to promote procedures that select the Condorcet winner when there is one. He eventually proposed a method based on Borda's rule, used in an iterative way. At each stage the candidates who failed to obtain an average Borda score are eliminated. Then, the procedure starts again on the basis of the modified rankings and is repeated until only one candidate remains (who must be the Condorcet winner, if there is one).

Arrovian Social Choice

A standard view of the British economists at the end of the nineteen century and the beginning of the twentieth century was that welfare, utility, satisfaction, and so on had a money measure (Pigou 1932). It seems clear that in this case a utilitarian social welfare function could be used where the social welfare is the addition of the individual welfares. Since individual utility was measured in monetary terms, the problems of scales, origin, comparability, and so on were assumed to have already been solved. Maximizing social welfare amounted to finding a maximum for the utilitarian social welfare function, given that individual utility functions were fixed, the variables being the social states, whatever the term of social state covers. However, at the same time under the influence of Léon Walras and, above all, Vilfredo Pareto, economists wanted to get rid of the measurement of utility problem. The solution was to use ordinal utility or even the underlying preference relation. With ordinal utility functions, still numerical functions, the real numbers/utilities could only be meaningfully compared according to the relation $\geq$. All the other mathematical properties defining the field of real numbers were rejected. A kind of corollary to the ordinalism thesis was that interpersonal comparisons have to be excluded too, even when these comparisons are limited to the relation $\geq$, that is, it could not be asserted that the utility of individual i in state x is, say, greater than the utility of individual j in state y. On this basis, the only possible concept relative to the social goodness of a social state was Pareto optimality: a social state x is optimal if there is no other feasible social state y such that all individual utilities are greater for y than for x (or in its strong version: all individual utilities are at least as great for y than for x and one is greater).

In the 1930s, interpersonal comparisons were, however, reintroduced as (virtual) compensations by Hicks, Kaldor, Harrod and Scitovsky (see Arrow and Scitovsky 1969; Baumol and Wilson 2001). The principle of compensation is that in a change of social states, say from x to y, individuals who gain in the change could virtually compensate those who lose, making the change a Pareto improvement, that is, after compensation every individual has a greater utility due to the change. It is obvious that this procedure entails interpersonal comparisons. Furthermore, it has been shown that it was not immune to paradoxes. It is in this context that Bergson proposed the new notion of social welfare function in 1938. The form of the function has been modified by Samuelson (1947) and it is in this form proposed by Samuelson that the function is generally presented. In Samuelson's version, the social welfare function, say f, associates a real number to a list of individual utilities $u_1, \ldots, u_n$ of individuals $1, \ldots, n$ for some social state belonging to a fixed set of social states. The individual utility functions are fixed. For instance, if we have a Cobb–Douglas utility function defined over the positive orthant of a k-dimensional Euclidean space for individual i, say, $u_i(x) = (3/5)\, x_1^{1/k}\, x_2^{1/k} \ldots x_k^{1/k}$, the parameters 3/5 and $1/k$ are fixed, whatever the variables $x_1, \ldots, x_k$ are. To impose upon such a social welfare function a Paretian property is to assume that $\partial f/\partial u_i > 0$ (loosely speaking, social welfare increases, or decreases, when individual i's utility increases, or decreases, all other things being equal). The purpose of the function is then to select some Pareto-optimal social state through classical maximization, and this for public policy. However, it remains to be known how and who will construct the function. In some sense, Arrow provided a reply to this question, doubly negative, with his impossibility theorem. Arrow's analysis marks the birth of modern social choice theory.

Formal preliminaries

The standard social choice framework is the following. Consider a set X of social states (or states of the world). These social states must be interpreted as extremely detailed descriptions of a-temporal situations. In particular, a given social state will include descriptions of characteristics pertaining to agents. Preferences over X are binary relations that are assumed to be complete. The preference relation for social states x and y will be denoted by $x \succsim y$ and it will mean x is at least as good as y. The asymmetric part (strict preference), x is better than y, will be denoted by $x \succ y$ and defined, given completeness, by not $y \succsim x$, and the symmetric part (indifference) will be denoted by $x \sim y$ and defined by $x \succsim y$ and $y \succsim x$. The preference $\succsim$ is said to be complete if, for all x and y in X, either $x \succsim y$ or $y \succsim x$; x and y are always comparable. The set of agents will be denoted by N. Each individual (agent) has a preference that is a complete preorder over X. Her preference is a transitive binary relation. If she finds x as least as good as y and y at least as good as z, then she must find x at least as good as z. One should note that in this case both the strict preference relation and the indifference relation are also transitive. Individual i's preference will be denoted by $\succsim_i$. In the following analysis, the social preference, denoted by $\succsim_S$, will be assumed to be complete, and will satisfy some rationality conditions. We will consider three different conditions:

1. Transitivity: for all x, y and z in X, $x \gtrsim_S y$ and $y \gtrsim_S z \Rightarrow x \gtrsim_S z$.
2. Quasi-transitivity: for all x, y and z in X, $x >_S y$ and $y >_S z \Rightarrow x >_S z$.
3. $>$-acyclicity: there is no finite subset of X, $\{x_1, \ldots, x_k\}$, for which $x_1 >_S x_2$, $x_2 >_S x_3, \ldots, x_{k-1} >_S x_k$ and $x_k >_S x_1$.

A complete binary relation satisfying transitivity is a complete preorder. In this case the social preference has the same characteristics as the individual preferences. When the set of social states X is finite, it means that the social states can be ranked from a top element to a bottom element with possible ties.

Let $\mathbb{P}$ be the set of complete preorders over X. The agents' preferences are given by a profile π which is a function from the set of individuals N into $\mathbb{P}$. This is a kind of labelling operation. It assigns a complete preorder to each individual. When N is finite of size n, we have the usual list of individual preferences $(\gtrsim_1, \ldots, \gtrsim_n)$. We will consider two types of aggregation rules. They will be called respectively aggregation functions and social choice functions (the definition of a social choice function will be given in the sub-section devoted to the Gibbard–Satterthwaite theorem).

An aggregation function is a function f which associates to each possible profile π a social preference $\gtrsim_S$ over X. When the social preference $\gtrsim_S$ is a complete preorder, the aggregation function is the classical Arrovian "social welfare function" (Arrow 1951). In the double finite case (the set of individuals and the set of social states being finite), given a complete ranking of the social states by each individual, a social welfare function gives a complete ranking of the social states at the social/collective level. Individual and social rationalities are identical. When $\gtrsim_S$ is complete and satisfies $>$-acyclicity, the aggregation function, following Sen (1970b), will be called a "social decision function" and, when it satisfies quasi-transitivity, it will be called a "QT-social decision function".

Arrow's impossibility theorem
The conditions introduced by Arrow do not concern a particular class of aggregation functions. Their definitions never necessitate a condition of transitivity or other collective rationality property. They are valid for all aggregation functions.

Condition U (universality)   A profile π may include any individual complete preorder.

This means that the individual preferences are not restricted; they are complete preorders, but no extra rationality conditions are postulated, as it is the case, for instance, with Black's single-peakedness. For instance, with three social states, there are 13 complete preorders. Each of these 13 is feasible.

Condition I (independence of irrelevant alternatives)   Consider two social states a and b and two profiles π^1 and π^2. If, for each individual, the preference regarding a and b is the same in profile π^1 and profile π^2, then the social preference regarding a and b must be identical for both profiles.

This means that the information used in the aggregation is myopic, and, given the definition in terms of preferences, ordinal. For instance, when there is a set of ten social states, the fact that individual j ranks a first and b tenth will have the same effect as if she had ranked a first and b second. Also, one should remark that this condition uses two profiles; it is a multi-profile condition. Since preferences could be represented by ordinal utility functions, this means that the individual utility functions are possibly different so that an Arrovian social welfare function is quite different from a Bergson–Samuelson social welfare function where the utility functions were fixed.

Condition P (Pareto principle) Let a and b be two social states and π be a profile in which every individual prefers a to b (for all $i \in N$, $a >_i b$); then a is socially preferred to b ($a >_s b$).

This is simply a unanimity principle. As a consequence, if individuals can either prefer a to b or b to a so that there is a tiny diversity among the feasible profiles (which is the case, of course, under Condition U), then it is impossible that the aggregation function f is a constant function. Are functions then excluded that would be based on a moral or religious code, independently of the individuals constituting the society, since such functions will always generate the same social preference whatever the profiles of individual preferences are?

A dictator would be an individual i such that for any social states x and y, the aggregation function would generate $x >_s y$ whenever $x >_i y$. One can see that a dictator imposes his strict preferences on the society – in Arrow's framework, the dictator does not impose his indifferences.

Condition D (no-dictatorship) There is no dictator.

Arrow's impossibility theorem If N is finite and includes at least two individuals, and if there are at least three social states, there is no social welfare function satisfying conditions U, I, P and D.

Dishonest comments were made about the impossibility of democracy. First, the theorem is about transitivity, whose violation entails that there are three social states. With only two, there is no problem. Furthermore, we can challenge the conditions. Condition U was in fact challenged in Black (1948), that is, before the publication of Arrow's first paper. But it is condition I that has been contested most often – among others by Sen (1970b) and by Saari (1995) – mainly because it excludes intra- and inter-personal comparisons of the intensities of preferences. We can also consider a weakening of the condition of transitivity to quasi-transitivity of the social preference. In this case, that is, for QT-social decision function, Gibbard showed that if the function satisfied conditions U, I and P, we obtained an oligarchy. An oligarchy is a group of individuals who have the power of a dictator when they agree and where each member has a veto power (that is, loosely speaking, a power sufficient to preclude that the social preference be the inverse of his preference). If the number of oligarchs is small, we are not so far from dictatorship. As was shown by Mas-Colell and Sonnenschein (1972), there is not much to gain from a further weakening to acyclicity of the asymmetric part of the social preference, that is, in considering social decision functions.

Independently of the beauty of Arrow's result, it is most remarkable that it was developed in an elegant framework that became the framework of the whole subject (for the origin of this framework, see Suppes 2005).

Sen and the Paretian liberal paradox
In a six-page article Sen (1970a) introduces a notion of individual rights within the Arrovian framework of social choice. These six pages had a fundamental importance on the development of studies on non-welfaristic aspects of normative economics. At about the same time, Kolm (1972, 1997) introduced the notions of fairness, equity and social justice using rather standard microeconomics models (for instance, Edgeworth boxes).

Sen introduced two conditions of liberalism, or individual freedom, the second one being a weakening of the first that turns out to be sufficient to get the result.

Condition L (liberalism)   For each individual $i \in N$, there are two social states a_i and b_i such that we get $a_i >_s b_i$ whenever $a_i >_i b_i$ and $b_i >_s a_i$ whenever $b_i >_i a_i$.
The second condition states that at least two individuals enjoy liberalism as defined above.

Condition ML (minimal liberalism)   There exist two individuals i and j, two social states a and b for i and two social states c and d for j such that $a >_s b$ whenever $a >_i b$, $b >_s a$ whenever $b >_i a$, $c >_s d$ whenever $c >_j d$ and $d >_s c$ whenever $d >_j c$.

Sen's impossibility theorem   If there are at least two individuals and two social states, there is no social decision function satisfying conditions U, P and ML.

We can note that there is no need of the finiteness of N and of condition I and that the result already holds for two social states. To understand the power of this result – which, incidentally, has no real meaning in a voting context since this would mean that two individuals have a partial dictatorship power – one has to consider that social states are descriptions of the states of the world as detailed as one wishes with possible personal elements. The following example is adapted from Salles (2011).

There are two individuals i and j. The social states a and b are identical except that in a individual i eats legs of lamb with garlic and in b without garlic. Individual i is a garlic addict and, accordingly, strongly prefers a to b. The social states c and d are also identical except that in c individual j puts some Guerlain's "L'Instant Magic" perfume before going to sleep and, in d, does not. Individual j has a passion for "L'Instant Magic" and so strongly prefers c to d. Now imagine that j is i's wife and that she hates garlic as much as her husband hates perfume in general and "L'Instant Magic" in particular. On this basis, let us suppose that the two individuals' preferences are the following: $d >_i a >_i b >_i c$ and $b >_j c >_j d >_j a$.

Since there is nothing more personal than culinary tastes or tastes related to smells, the social states a and b perfectly fit J.S. Mill's notion of personal sphere regarding individual i, and likewise for individual j, concerning states c and d (Mill 1859). This illustration exemplifies the difficulty one can encounter with this notion of personal sphere in the presence of what the economists call externalities. We will assume that our society is only composed of i and j. It is in fact very easy to consider a general profile π with appropriate preferences for the other individuals. By Condition P, since both individuals prefer d to a, we have $d >_s a$, and since they both prefer b to c, $b >_s c$. Now, since i prefers a to b, by condition ML, $a >_s b$. Since individual j prefers c to d, then by condition ML, $c >_s d$. We have accordingly a cycle: $a >_s b$, $b >_s c$, $c >_s d$, $d >_s a$.

A major by-product of Sen's paper is the tremendous development of the freedom of choice literature (see, for instance, Dowding and van Hees 2009).

The Gibbard–Pattanaik–Satterthwaite theorem

As previously noted the problem identified by Pliny was the problem of strategic voting. The general result on this topic was obtained independently by Allan Gibbard (1973) and Mark Satterthwaite (1975). A fundamental contribution due to Dummett and Farquharson (1961), more than ten years before, in spite of being published in *Econometrica* went rather unnoticed. The major contributions of Prasanta Pattanaik (1973, 1978) have been neglected because Pattanaik's framework was the traditional Arrovian framework of aggregation functions and, accordingly, strategic voting had to be defined in a more complicated way than in the framework chosen by Gibbard and Satterthwaite.

We will assume that X, the set of social states, here, say, candidates, is finite and, for reasons of simplicity, that individual preferences are given by linear orders, denoted by $>_i$. This means that individuals rank the candidates without ties. A profile π will then be a list of individual rankings $(>_1, \ldots, >_n)$. A social choice function is a function f from the set of profiles into X. This means that rather than selecting a social preference as in the case of aggregation functions, a social choice function selects, given a profile, a candidate.

We will say that individual i manipulates the social choice function f in profile $\pi = (>_1, \ldots, >_n)$ if there is a profile π' which is identical to profile π except for the preference of individual i such that $f(\pi') >_i f(\pi)$. For simplicity, imagine that the profile π is a profile of sincere individual preferences. Individual i manipulates f if, by misrepresenting her preference (lying), she can force the function to generate a result that she prefers to the result that would have been obtained otherwise. We will assume that the social choice function is surjective: for any candidate x, there is a profile π such that $x = f(\pi)$. This basically means that there is no fictitious candidate. A consequence is, of course, that if there are at least two candidates, the function cannot be a constant function.

A dictator for a social choice function f will be an individual i such that for all profiles π, $f(\pi) >_i x$, for all $x \neq f(\pi)$.

Gibbard–Satterthwaite theorem Suppose that there are at least two individuals and three candidates, that all linear orderings (individual preferences) are permissible and that f is surjective and non-manipulable. Then there is a dictator.

This theorem has been at the origin of a tremendous number of contributions in social choice theory, but also in public economics, and is strongly related to implementation theory (Jackson 2001; Maskin and Sjöström 2002).

Black, single-peakedness and majority rule

In 1948, that is, even slightly before Arrow, Duncan Black (1908–1991), a British economist, introduced the notion of single-peaked preference (Black 1948). He studied the effects of this assumption on the outcomes generated by majority rule. He proved among other results what is now called the "median voter" theorem. He used a kind of geometrical setting. Assume that the set of options (candidates, social states or whatever) is a closed interval $[a, b]$. Furthermore, assume that individuals have ordinal continuous

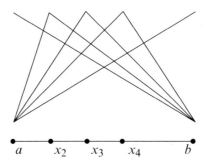

Figure 9   Black's single-peakedness

utility functions u_i that are increasing until they reach a maximum, and then decreasing until they reaches b. In Figure 9, we have the curves of five functions representing preferences.

In Figure 9, u_1 reaches its maximum for option a, u_2 for option x_2 and so on. Individual 3 is the median individual and the option selected by the majority rule is x_3. In the figure, the functions are strictly concave, but the definition allows strict quasi-concavity. When the space of options is no longer one-dimensional, difficulties arise (see Austen-Smith and Banks 1999; Schofield 2008).

Black's analysis will now be presented in a discrete setting. The discrete version of single-peakedness is due to Arrow (1951). First let us define majority rule. Assume that individual preferences are given by complete preorders. Majority rule is an aggregation function such that for all (distinct) options x and y, $x >_s y$ if and only if the number of individuals i for whom $x >_i y$ is > than the number of individuals for whom $y >_i x$, and $y \gtrsim_s x$ otherwise. The following definition of single-peakedness is adapted from Sen (1966).

A set of complete preorders over X satisfies the condition of single-peakedness over $\{a,b,c\} \subseteq X$ if either $a \sim b$ and $b \sim c$, or there is an option among the three options, say, b, such that $b > a$ or $b > c$. We will say that a set of complete preorders satisfies the condition of single-peakedness if it satisfies the condition of single-peakedness over all $\{x,y,z\} \subseteq X$. Figure 10 is a geometrical representation of this condition over $\{a,b,c\}$.

Black's theorem   Let us assume that there are at least two individuals and three options, and that all individual preferences belong to a set of complete preorders satisfying the condition of single-peakedness. Let us assume further that the number of individuals who are not indifferent between x, y, z is odd for any $\{x,y,z\} \subseteq X$. Then the majority rule is a social welfare function satisfying conditions I, P and D.

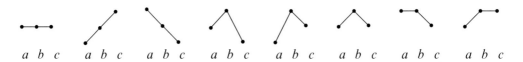

Figure 10   Black's single-peakedness over $\{a, b, c\}$

Since the majority rule obviously satisfies condition *I*, *P* and *D*, this simply means that $\succsim_S$ is transitive. The specific condition on the number of non-indifferent individuals can appear as problematic, but it is not so problematic since if we drop it we still get a QT-social decision function ($\succ_S$ is then transitive). The literature of this sort, where individual preferences are restricted by some kind of super-rationality, is abundant and has been excellently surveyed in Gaertner (2001). A special kind of restriction refers to the so-called economic domains and is, of course, related to Black's analysis since in the standard microeconomic framework, individual preferences are continuous, convex or strictly convex, and so on (see Le Breton and Weymark 2010).

Harsanyi and utilitarianism
John Harsanyi (1920–2000), in two papers (1953, 1955; see also Harsanyi 1976), considers social choice in risky environments. In his 1955 paper, he presents a major result that, in some sense, justifies utilitarianism, more precisely a weighted version of utilitarianism, from a technical perspective. The set of social states is supposed to be a set of lotteries, that is, the probability distributions over a finite set of prizes. If all probabilities are permitted, this set is infinite and uncountable. Individuals have a preference over this set of lotteries given by a complete preorder and representable by a utility function. In the lotteries setting, rather than using ordinal utility functions, economists generally adopt a framework developed by John von Neumann and Oskar Morgenstern (1953) for dealing with risky situations in game theory, the so-called von Neumann–Morgenstern utility functions. In fact, given appropriate assumptions on the set of lotteries and the set of complete preorders over the set of lotteries (some of these assumptions are topological assumptions), it can be shown that there exists a utility function representing the complete preorder and having the so-called expected utility property. If we assume that a lottery x is given by k prizes $x_1, \ldots, x_k$ and a probability distribution $p_1, \ldots, p_k - p_i$ being the probability of receiving prize x_i – the utility function u is said to satisfy the expected utility property if:

$$u(x) = \sum_{j=1}^{k} p_j u(x_j).$$

This means that the utility associated with the lottery x is the sum of the utilities associated to the prizes, weighted by the probabilities of receiving these prizes. An important consequence of this property is that the utility function is not only unique up to an increasing transformation, as in the case of ordinal utility functions, but unique up to a specific form of the increasing transformation: a positive affine transformation; if u is a von Neumann–Morgenstern utility function representing a complete preorder $\succsim$, then $v = \alpha u + \beta$, where α and β are real numbers and $\alpha > 0$, is also a von Neumann–Morgenstern utility function representing this same $\succsim$. As a major consequence, the differences of utilities can be compared according to the relation $\geq$, which was not possible for ordinal utility functions. Such functions are said to be cardinal. In the following presentation which is essentially due to Weymark (1991) three conditions are introduced. Since the prizes are fixed, a lottery will be assimilated to the associated probability distribution $p = (p_1, \ldots, p_k)$.

Condition P-I (Pareto indifference)   Let p and q be two lotteries. If for all $i \in N$, $p \sim_i q$, then $p \sim_S q$.

  If all individuals are indifferent between two lotteries, so is the society.

Condition S-P (strong Pareto)   Let p and q be two lotteries. If for all $i \in N$, $p \gtrsim_i q$, and for some $i \in N$, $p >_i q$, then $p >_S q$.

Condition I-P (Independent prospects)   For each $i \in N$, there exist two lotteries p^i and q^i such that $p^i >_i q^i$ and for all $j \neq i$ $p^i \sim_j q^i$.

  For instance, let x_1 be a piece of cheesecake and x_2 a piece of chocolate cake. Assume that $x_1 >_i x_2$ and for all $j \neq i$ $x_1 \sim_j x_2$, then i will prefer lottery (1,0,0,. . .,0.) to lottery (0,1,0,0. . .,0), but all the other individuals are going to be indifferent between the two lotteries.

  In Harsanyi's theorem, both individual utility functions and the social welfare function w are supposed to be von Neumann–Morgenstern utility functions. The theorem is then the following (this presentation follows Weymark).

Harsanyi–Weymark's Theorem   (1) If condition *P-I* is satisfied, then there exist real numbers a_i such that $\gtrsim_S$ is represented by $w = \Sigma a_i u_i$. (2) if condition *S-P* is also satisfied, the real numbers a_i are positive. (3) If condition *I-P* is also satisfied, the a_is are unique up to a positive factor of proportionality.

In (1), it is not said that the weights attached to the individual utility functions are positive. With a negative weight, an increase in individual utility would decrease social welfare. The result in (3) can be considered as the theorem about weighted utilitarianism.

  A number of authors have challenged the use of von Neumann–Morgenstern utility functions. Diamond (1967) in particular has criticized the assumption that the social preference could satisfy the assumptions introduced by von Neumann and Morgenstern. Furthermore, some authors have criticized Harsanyi by arguing that his utilitarianism could not be associated with classical utilitarianism, mainly because of the von Neumann–Morgenstern framework (see Sen 1976; Roemer 1996; and contributions in Fleurbaey et al. 2008).

Conclusion

Regarding Arrovian social choice, and given the limited space, the results that were selected are results which are well established and had an important descent. More recent major trends such as judgement aggregation (see List and Puppe 2009), freedom of choice, or empirical social choice have not been taken into account. John Nash's epoch-making contribution to bargaining theory (1950) and voting games, in particular Nakamura's theorem (1979), were left out. The real difficulty is that social choice has some rather fuzzy boundaries. The overlap with political economy, public economics, game theory, political philosophy, formal political science, welfare economics, normative economics, social ethics, and some other areas is quite large, as exemplified by Sen's book (2009) as far as social justice is concerned. To get a good view of the present state of the subject, see Arrow et al. (2002, 2010), Anand et al. (2009) and the introductory text by Gaertner (2009).

MAURICE SALLES

See also:

Kenneth Joseph Arrow (I); Jeremy Bentham (I); Abram Bergson [Abram Burk] (I); James M. Buchanan (I); Marie-Jean-Antoine-Nicolas Caritat de Condorcet (I); Economics and philosophy (III); Formalization and mathematical modelling (III); Game theory (III); John Stuart Mill (I); Arthur Cecil Pigou (I); Political philosophy and economics: freedom and labour (III); Public choice (II); Paul Anthony Samuelson (I); Amartya Kumar Sen (I); Utilitarianism and anti-utilitarianism (III); Welfare economics (III).

References and further reading

Anand, P., P.K. Pattanaik and C. Puppe (eds) (2009), *The Handbook of Rational and Social Choice*, Oxford: Oxford University Press.

Arrow, K.J. (1950), 'A difficulty in the concept of social welfare', *Journal of Political Economy*, **58**, 328–46.

Arrow, K.J. (1951), *Social Choice and Individual Values*, 2nd edn 1963, New York: Wiley.

Arrow, K.J. and T. Scitovsky (eds) (1969), *Readings in Welfare Economics*, Homewood, IL: Irwin.

Arrow, K.J., A.K. Sen and K. Suzumura (eds) (2002), *Handbook of Social Choice and Welfare*, vol. 1, Amsterdam: Elsevier.

Arrow, K.J., A.K. Sen and K. Suzumura (eds) (2010), *Handbook of Social Choice and Welfare*, vol. 2, Amsterdam: Elsevier.

Austen-Smith, D. and J.S. Banks (1999), *Positive Political Theory I, Collective Preference*, Ann Arbor, MI: University of Michigan Press.

Balinski, M. and H.P. Young (1982), *Fair Representation. Meeting the Ideal of One Man, One Vote*, New Haven, CT: Yale University Press.

Baumol, W.J. and C.A. Wilson (eds) (2001), *Welfare Economics*, vol. 1, Cheltenham, UK and Northampton, MA, USA: Edward Elgar.

Bentham, J. (1789), *An Introduction to the Principles of Morals and Legislation*, reprinted 1970, Oxford: Oxford University Press.

Bergson, A. (1938), 'A reformulation of certain aspects of welfare economics', *Quarterly Journal of Economics*, **52** (3), 310–34, and in K.J. Arrow and T. Scitovsky (eds) (1969), *Readings in Welfare Economics*, Homewood, IL: Irwin, pp. 7–38.

Black, D. (1948), 'On the rationale of group decision making', *Journal of Political Economy*, **56** (1), 23–34.

Black, D. (1958), *The Theory of Committees and Elections*, Cambridge: Cambridge University Press, revd 2nd edn, I. Mac Lean, A. McMillan and B.L. Monroe (eds), Boston, MA: Kluwer.

Borda, J.-C. de (1784), 'Mémoire sur les élections au scrutin', in *Histoire de l'Académie des Sciences pour 1781*, Paris: Imprimerie Royale, pp. 657–65.

Bru, B. and P. Crépel (eds) (1994), *Condorcet. Arithmétique politique: Textes rares et inédits*, Paris: Institut National d'Etudes Démographiques.

Condorcet, M.J.A.-N. de C., Marquis de (1785), *Essai sur l'application de l'analyse à la probabilité des décisions rendues à la pluralité des voix*, Paris: Imprimerie Royale.

Condorcet, M.J.A.-N. de C., Marquis de (1986), *Sur les Élections et Autres Textes*, Paris: Fayard.

Diamond, P. (1967), 'Cardinal welfare, individualistic ethics, and interpersonal comparisons of utility: comment', *Journal of Political Economy*, **75** (5), 765–6.

Dowding, K. and M. van Hees (2009), 'Freedom of choice', in P. Anand, P.K. Pattanaik and C. Puppe (eds), *The Handbook of Rational and Social Choice*, Oxford: Oxford University Press, pp. 374–92.

Dummett, M. (1984), *Voting Procedures*, Oxford: Oxford University Press.

Dummett, M. (1997), *Principles of Electoral Reform*, Oxford: Oxford University Press.

Dummett, M. (2005), 'The work and life of Robin Farquharson', *Social Choice and Welfare*, **25** (2–3), 475–83.

Dummett, M. and R. Farquharson (1961), 'Stability in voting', *Econometrica*, **29** (1), 33–43.

Emerson, P. (ed.) (2007), *Designing an All-Inclusive Democracy*, Heidelberg: Springer.

Farquharson, R. (1969), *Theory of Voting*, Oxford: Blackwell.

Fleurbaey, M., M. Salles and J.A. Weymark (eds) (2008), *Justice, Political Liberalism, and Utilitarianism. Themes from Harsanyi and Rawls*, Cambridge: Cambridge University Press.

Gaertner, W. (2001), *Domain Conditions in Social Choice Theory*, Cambridge: Cambridge University Press.

Gaertner, W. (2005), 'De jure naturae et gentium: Samuel von Pufendorf's contribution to social choice theory and economics', *Social Choice and Welfare*, **25** (2–3), 231–41.

Gaertner, W. (2009), *A Primer in Social Choice Theory*, Oxford: Oxford University Press.

Gehrlein, W.V. and D. Lepelley (2011), *Voting Paradoxes and Group Coherence*, Heidelberg: Springer.
Gibbard, A. (1973), 'Manipulation of voting schemes: a general result', *Econometrica*, **41** (4), 587–601.
Guilbaud, G.-T. (1952), 'Les théories de l'intérêt général et le problème logique de l'agrégation', *Economie Appliquée*, **5** (4), 501–51.
Hägele, G. and F. Pukelsheim (2001), 'Llull's writings on electoral systems', *Studia Lulliana*, **41** (1), 3–38.
Hägele, G. and F. Pukelsheim (2008), 'The electoral systems of Nicholas of Cusa in the *Catholic Concordance* and beyond', in G. Christianson, T.M. Izbicki and C.M. Bellito (eds), *The Church, the Councils, & Reform: The Legacy of the Fifteenth Century*, Washington, DC: Catholic University of America Press, pp. 229–49.
Harsanyi, J.C. (1953), 'Cardinal utility in welfare economics and in the theory of risk-taking', *Journal of Political Economy*, **61** (5), 434–5.
Harsanyi, J.C. (1955), 'Cardinal utility, individualistic ethics, and interpersonal comparisons of utility', *Journal of Political Economy*, **63** (4), 309–21.
Harsanyi, J.C. (1976), *Essays on Ethics, Social Behavior, and Scientific Explanation*, Dordrecht: Reidel.
Jackson, M.O. (2001), 'A crash course in implementation theory', *Social Choice and Welfare*, **18** (4), 655–708.
Kolm, S.-C. (1972), *Justice et Équité*, Paris: Editions du C.N.R.S.
Kolm, S.-C. (1997), *Justice and Equity*, Cambridge, MA: MIT Press.
Le Breton, M. and J.A. Weymark (2010), 'Arrovian social choice theory on economic domains', in K.J. Arrow, A.K. Sen and K. Suzumura (eds), *Handbook of Social Choice and Welfare*, vol. 2, Amsterdam: Elsevier, pp. 191–299.
List, C. and C. Puppe (2009), 'Judgment aggregation', in P. Anand, P.K Pattanaik and C. Puppe (eds), *The Handbook of Rational and Social Choice*, Oxford: Oxford University Press, pp. 457–82.
Mas-Colell, A. and H. Sonnenschein (1972), 'General possibility theorems for group decisions', *Review of Economic Studies*, **39** (2), 185–92.
Maskin, E. and T. Sjöström (2002), 'Implementation theory', in K.J. Arrow, A.K. Sen and K. Suzumura (eds), *Handbook of Social Choice and Welfare*, vol. 1, Amsterdam: Elsevier, pp. 237–88.
McLean, I. and J. London (1990), 'The Borda and Condorcet principles: three medieval applications', *Social Choice and Welfare*, **7** (2), 99–108.
McLean, I. and A.B. Urken (eds) (1995), *Classics of Social Choice*, Ann Arbor, MI: University of Michigan Press.
Mill, J.S. (1859), *On Liberty*, London: Longman, Roberts and Green, in J. Gray (ed.) (1991), *John Stuart Mill, On Liberty and Other Essays*, Oxford: Oxford University Press, pp 5–128.
Monjardet, B. (1990), 'Sur diverses formes de la "règle de Condorcet" d'agrégation des préférences', *Mathématiques, Informatique et Sciences Humaines*, **111**, 61–71.
Nakamura, K. (1979), 'The vetoers in a simple game with ordinal preferences', *International Journal of Game Theory*, **8** (1), 55–61.
Nash, J.F. (1950), 'The bargaining problem', *Econometrica*, **18** (2), 155–62.
Nicholas of Cusa (1433), *The Catholic Concordance*, ed. and trans. P.E. Sigmund (1991), Cambridge: Cambridge University Press.
Pattanaik, P.K. (1973), 'On the stability of sincere voting situations', *Journal of Economic Theory*, **6** (6), 558–74.
Pattanaik, P.K. (1978), *Strategy and Group Choice*, Amsterdam: North-Holland.
Pigou, A.C. (1932), *The Economics of Welfare*, London: Macmillan.
Pliny (1969), *Letters, Books VIII–X, Panegyricus*, trans. by B. Radice, Cambridge, MA: Harvard University Press (Loeb Classical Library).
Pliny (2002), *Lettres, Livres I à X*, trans. by A. Flaubert, Paris: Flammarion.
Riker, W.H. (1986), *The Art of Political Manipulation*, New Haven, CT: Yale University Press.
Risse, M. (2005), 'Why the count de Borda cannot beat the Marquis de Condorcet', *Social Choice and Welfare*, **25** (1), 95–113.
Roemer, J.E. (1996), *Theories of Distributive Justice*, Cambridge, MA: Harvard University Press.
Saari, D.G. (1995), *Basic Geometry of Voting*, Heidelberg: Springer.
Saari, D.G. (2006), 'Which is better: the Condorcet or Borda winner?', *Social Choice and Welfare*, **26** (1), 107–29.
Saari, D.G. (2008), *Disposing Dictators, Demystifying Voting Paradoxes: Social Choice Analysis*, Cambridge: Cambridge University Press.
Salles, M. (2011), 'On rights and social choice', in R. Ege and H. Igersheim (eds), *Freedom and Happiness in Economic Thought and Philosophy*, Abingdon: Routledge, pp. 227–42.
Samuelson, P.A. (1974), *Foundations of Economic Analysis*, Cambridge: MA: Harvard University Press.
Satterthwaite, M.A. (1975), 'Strategy-proofness and Arrow's conditions: existence and correspondence theorems for voting procedures and social welfare functions', *Journal of Economic Theory*, **10** (2), 187–217.
Schofield, N. (2008), *The Spatial Model of Politics*, Abingdon: Routledge.
Sen, A.K. (1966), 'A possibility theorem on majority decisions', *Econometrica*, **34** (2), 491–9.
Sen, A.K. (1970a), 'The impossibility of a Paretian liberal', *Journal of Political Economy*, **78** (1), 152–7.

Sen, A.K. (1970b), *Collective Choice and Social Welfare*, San Francisco, CA: Holden-Day.

Sen, A.K. (1976), 'Welfare inequalities and Rawlsian axiomatics', *Theory and Decision*, **7** (4), 243–62.

Sen, A.K. (2009), *The Idea of Justice*, London: Allen Lane.

Suppes, P. (2005), 'The pre-history of Kenneth Arrow's social choice and individual values', *Social Choice and Welfare*, **25** (2–3), 319–26.

Von Neumann, J. and O. Morgenstern (1953), *Theory of Games and Economic Behavior*, Princeton, NJ: Princeton University Press.

Weymark, J.A. (1991), 'A reconsideration of the Harsanyi–Sen debate on utilitarianism', in J. Elster and J.E. Roemer (eds), *Interpersonal Comparisons of Well-Being*, Cambridge: Cambridge University Press, pp. 255–320.

Wiggins, D. (2006), *Ethics. Twelve Lectures on the Philosophy of Morality*, Cambridge, MA: Harvard University Press.

Young, H.P. (1988), 'Condorcet's theory of voting', *American Political Science Review*, **82** (4), 1231–44.

Technical change and innovation

The problem of technical change, its causes, forms and effects, has been high on the agenda of economic analysis ever since its systematic inception in the second half of the seventeenth century and its full blooming at the time of the French and English classical political economists. This is hardly surprising, since around the same time Western Europe experienced the Industrial Revolution and in its wake the take-off on a path of sustained growth of income per capita. Technical change was discussed in the writings of François Quesnay and the Physiocrats, who emphasized the importance of education, learning and knowledge. It played a particularly important role in the works of Adam Smith and David Ricardo and an even more important one in that of Karl Marx, who saw the capitalist economic system incessantly in travail because of deep reaching and all spheres of life encompassing technical and organizational revolutions. The concern with economic dynamics and its prime mover, technical progress, lost momentum towards the end of the nineteenth century with the rise to dominance of Marginalism and its focus on the static problem of the allocation of given resources to alternative uses. The issue of innovations – "new combinations" – resurged with Joseph A. Schumpeter's explanation of the restlessness of capitalism at the beginning of the twentieth century. While Schumpeter, like the classical economists and Marx, understood technical change as an endogenous phenomenon, coming from within the economic system, neoclassical growth theory championed by Robert Solow and Trevor Swan in the late 1950s treated it as exogenous. This was criticized in the 1980s both by advocates of an evolutionary approach to the problem under consideration, especially Richard Nelson and Sidney Winter, and by protagonists of what became known as "new" or "endogenous" growth theory, especially Paul Romer. In more recent times the concepts of "general purpose technologies" and "national systems of innovation" gained prominence in theoretical and applied research on technical change and innovation.

Adam Smith: Technical Change and the Division of Labour

Smith defined the task of *The Wealth of Nations* (1776 [1976], hereafter WN) as consisting of an investigation into "[t]he causes of this improvement, in the productive powers of labour, and the order, according to which its produce is naturally distributed among the different ranks and conditions of men in the society" (WN I.5). Smith saw a virtuous circle at work: the increase in labour productivity is the result of a deepening of the social division of labour, which is propelled forward by a growth of markets. The growth of markets, in turn, is seen to depend on the speed with which capital accumulates; this is why the "frugal man" is the hero in Smith's story. Higher labour productivity, in turn, implies higher incomes and profits and therefore more capital accumulation, and so on and so forth. According to Young (1928: 529), Smith's "theorem" is "one of the most illuminating and fruitful generalizations which can be found anywhere in the whole literature of economics".

This story encompasses a major theme of classical economic thinking; namely, that in addition to the intended consequences of human activities there are typically also non-intended ones, some positive, some negative. These, in turn, induce further activities and thus engender further consequences. There emerges the picture of an incessant flow of technical and organizational change, which on the one hand solves imminent problems, but on the other creates new ones. These changes are both a source and an effect of the continual transformation to which the market system is subjected: the process is characterized by cumulative causation.

According to Smith technical change is economy wide: it affects not only all producing sectors – primary production (agriculture, and so on), manufactures, trade and services (commerce) (see WN I.x.b.43) – but also banking (WN II.ii.39). The division of labour is a catch-all concept comprising all forms of technical and organizational change. Smith (and others before him) argued that labour productivity increases because of (1) improvements in the dexterity of workers as a gain from specialization; (2) the time saved through avoidance of shifts from one activity to another and the related better utilization of ever more costly plant and equipment; and (3) the invention of machines that replace labour in an increasingly complex labour process (see WN I.i.6–8).

Smith pointed out that some activities that were originally a part of the division of labour within the firm may eventually become a different "trade" or "business", so that the division of labour within the firm is but a step towards the division of labour among firms. This process of subdividing the labour process ever more deeply engenders also what today is called research and development (R&D). In describing this process Smith used the combinatory metaphor:

> Many improvements have been made by the ingenuity of the makers of the machines, when to make them became the business of a peculiar trade; and some by that of those who are called philosophers or men of speculation [that is, scientists], whose trade it is, not to do anything, but to observe every thing; and who, upon that account, are often capable of combining together the powers of the most distant and dissimilar objects. (WN I.i.9)

Interestingly, the productivity and well-being of society, Smith insisted, depends first and foremost on the "quantity of science" applied in the economy (WN I.i.9).

While Smith saw that successful innovations give rise to "extra profits" of the innovating firm and introduce some temporary monopoly elements into the system, free competition would, in the long run, establish a tendency towards a uniform rate of profits. Smith's argument is thus implicitly based on the hypothesis that each single firm operates under constant returns, while total social production is subject to increasing returns. Smith's analysis foreshadows the concepts of learning by doing (Kenneth Arrow), learning by using (Nathan Rosenberg) and of dynamically increasing returns (Allyn Young). Technical change is endogenously generated from within the economic system; it is not exogenously given from the outside as in some later theories.

David Ricardo: Technical Change and Income Distribution

The role of the manufacturing sector as the engine of growth had largely escaped Smith's attention, who still lived in an "age of corn". In Ricardo we glimpse the transition to an age of "coal and iron", with machine power gradually replacing labour power. He began to sense what was not yet to be openly seen, that is, the process of incessant technological and organizational change that had seized the Western European economies. He elaborated analytical concepts and tools that allow us to describe and analyse almost any form of technical progress and its implications.

The arguably most important analytical tool Ricardo forged formed the basis of what he called the "fundamental law of income distribution", that is, the inverse relationship between the general rate of profits, r, and the real wage rate (or, alternatively, the share of wages), w, given the system of production actually in use, $r = \phi(w)$, where $\phi'(w) < 0$. Ricardo in fact maintained: "The greater the portion of the result of labour that is given to the labourer, the smaller must be the rate of profits, and vice versa" (Ricardo 1951–73, hereafter *Works*, VIII: 194). Technical change affects $\phi(w)$ and moves the corresponding wage curve over time in $w - r$ space. We owe Ricardo the following findings:

1. In the case in which technical improvements are set aside and less and less fertile plots of land have to be cultivated in order to produce a growing amount of wheat, the profit rate, given w, is bound to fall. This is Ricardo's version of the falling tendency of the rate of profits. The reason for this fall is the "niggardliness of nature".
2. In the case of technical progress new methods of production replace old ones and new commodities and the methods to produce them enter the system. If technical change affects the production of wage goods ("necessaries") or capital goods needed directly or indirectly in the production of wage goods, then for a given real wage rate (a given rate of profits) the rate of profits (the wage rate) will increase. As early as in the *Essay on Profits* of 1815, Ricardo stressed that "it is no longer questioned" that improved machinery "has a decided tendency to raise the real wage of labour" (*Works* IV: 35). This is possible without a fall in the general rate of profits, because improved machinery reduces the quantity of labour needed directly and indirectly in the production of the various commodities: it reduces "the sacrifices of labour" (*Works* IV: 397).
3. If technical change affects only "luxuries", the general rate of profits will not change, given the real wage rate; only the prices of luxuries will fall relative to that of necessaries.
4. Ricardo was convinced that technical progress reduces the amount of labour needed directly and indirectly to produce the commodity under consideration. According to the particular shift of the wage curve, one may distinguish between different forms of technical progress. In chapter 2 of the *Principles* Ricardo distinguishes between direct labour saving, capital (that is, indirect labour) saving and land saving forms of progress. These affect income distribution, employment and growth differently.
5. In the newly added chapter 31, "On machinery", in the third edition of the *Principles* (1821), Ricardo discussed a particular form of technical progress, which, he insisted, "is often very injurious to the interests of the class of labourers" (*Works*, I: 388). The case under consideration is "the substitution of machinery for human labour" that reduces the gross produce. It is characterized by an increase in labour productivity and in the capital–output ratio, and thus a decrease in the maximum rate of profits: it is both labour saving and (fixed) capital using. The gross produce reducing mechanization entails what was later called "technological unemployment", which might exert a downward pressure on real wages, viz. its injurious effect on workers.
6. Ricardo also had a clear understanding of induced technical change. A newly invented machine, for example, may not be introduced by cost-minimizing producers, because at the given real wage rate and prices it would not be profitable to do so; it is born into an environment that is inimical to it. In Schumpeter's words,

there would be an "invention" but no "innovation", because the new knowledge would not be applied. However, as capital accumulates and the population grows, in conditions without any further technical progress wage goods would rise in price relative to manufactured products (such as machines), and for a given real wage rate nominal wages would have to follow suit. This situation is at the back of Ricardo's statement: "Machinery and labour are in constant competition and the former can frequently not be employed until labour rises" (*Works* I: 395).

Karl Marx: A Rising Organic Composition of Capital

Marx had access to a much larger illustrative material than Ricardo as regards the technological dynamism of capitalism. There could no longer be any doubt that it revolutionized continually the system of production from within. This is well reflected in Marx's notebooks on technology and technical change.

Marx's system of accounting, like Ricardo's, is in terms of (labour) values. In *Capital* he started from the premise that commodities are produced by means of commodities, that is, he started from an input–output scheme. This is reflected by a "constant capital" (produced means of production) needed in each line and at each stage of production. The important implication of this is that the maximum rate of profits of the system, R, is finite. R informs about the capacity of the economic system to generate a surplus product over and above what is being used up in production. The organic composition, κ, is equal to the ratio of "dead" (C) and "living labour" (L): $\kappa = C/L$, and thus equals the inverse of the maximum rate of profits: $\kappa = R^{-1}$. The actual rate of profits, r, is given by:

$$r = \frac{S/L}{(C/L) + (V/L)} = \frac{1 - \omega}{(1/R) + \omega} = \frac{R(1 - \omega)}{1 + R\omega} \tag{1}$$

where S designates surplus labour (profits), V "variable capital" and κ the share of wages. The long run trend of the rate of profits thus depends on two magnitudes, one referring to distribution, the other to the socio-technical conditions of production: ω and $\kappa = R^{-1}$.

Marx characterized the stages of economic history in terms of a sequence of phases, each of which had its own dominant pattern of technical and structural change; namely, (1) cooperation; (2) division of labour and manufacture; and (3) machinery and modern industry (see Marx 1954: pt IV). He also distinguished between different forms of technical change. He discussed not only the case he took to dominate capitalist development and which in his view implied a falling rate of profits, but also cases in which it "may remain the same" or "could even rise" (Marx 1959: 230), given the real wage rate. In this context he mentioned what later was called Harrod-neutral technical change, which moves the wage curve clockwise, with a given and constant R as its pivot.

While Marx admitted that these latter forms cannot be excluded on a priori grounds, he was convinced that κ was bound to rise and thus R to fall as capitalism develops. The features of this case are precisely those Ricardo had investigated in his chapter on machinery. The endogenous mechanism that according to Marx favours this bias of technical change reflects the inherent logic of capitalism. Labour saving and capital using technical progress, he insisted, was "*just another expression peculiar to the capitalist mode of production*" (Marx 1959: 213, Engels's (ed.) 1894 edition emphasis). It is the antagonism between capital and wage labour that directs technical change towards a rising organic composition. In the conflict over the distribution of the product, capitalists seek to replace the element that cannot be fully controlled and disciplined, the worker, by the element that can, the machine. Marx apparently counted upon a ruse of history. By replacing labour power by machine power, capitalists in the short run are able to ward off threats to their profit position. However, in the long run they thereby unconsciously undermine that very position because profits come out of (surplus) labour, which is progressively made redundant. "Behind capitalists' backs" the system's nemesis is taking shape: the general rate of profits, the key to the whole system, tends to fall. Hence in Marx, as opposed to Ricardo, the rate of profits is assumed to fall, not because there is insufficient technical change to counteract the "niggardliness of nature", but because there is a particular bias to technical change. Alas, Marx's reasoning regarding a falling tendency of the profit rate cannot be sustained (see Kurz 2010).

For a rigorous elaboration of the tool of the wage curve, see Sraffa (1960); see also, for example, Kurz and Salvadori (1995). For a discussion of the classical approach to technical progress, see Schefold (1976) and Kurz (2010). See also Piketty (2014), who sees a long-term rise in the capital–output ratio and thus a falling maximum rate of profits. The labour displacing effects of new technologies and their possible compensation by capital accumulation gave rise to a big debate to which contributed, among others, Ricardo, Marx, Wicksell, Hicks and Leontief. Dynamic input–output analysis was used to study the diffusion of new technologies; see Leontief and Duchin (1986) and Kalmbach and Kurz (1990).

With the rise of Marginalism, the classical economists' concern with the problem of technical change and economic dynamics gave way to a concern with static allocation problems. If technical change was discussed at all, it was in terms of an exogenous change of production techniques. This type of approach one encounters, for example, in Gustav Cassel at the beginning of the twentieth century and then several decades later in Solow (1956). A noteworthy exception is Alfred Marshall who in some of his analysis entertained an evolutionary perspective. Another and perhaps even more important exception is Joseph A. Schumpeter, who considered innovations and technical change as a dynamic process of "creative destruction" generated from within the economic system.

Joseph A. Schumpeter: Innovation and Creative Destruction

The starting point of Schumpeter's analysis of the causes and effects of technical change is the "circular flow", where the economy is in a stationary state and technical change is absent. In studying the dynamic behaviour of economies, Joseph A. Schumpeter (1912 [1934]) drew a distinction between three stages: invention, innovation and diffusion (that is, the Schumpeterian trilogy). He thereby emphasized that there is no automatism that links these three stages and that changes at any stage have different sources and implications: (1) An invention means the availability of new technical knowledge and thus new production possibilities, but in itself it has no significant economic effects. (2) An innovation means the actual use of an invention in economic life by some firm that becomes a "pioneer" or technological leader. The innovation exploits the economic potential of the invention. Schumpeter's hero is the "entrepreneur", who introduces "new combinations". (3) The successful introduction of novelties is the basis for a change in the economy, but it is the process of diffusion by which innovations gain economic weight and are absorbed into the system. Through this process of "adaptation" overall productivity improves. The diffusion of different types of innovations, according to Schumpeter, changes the economic system from within and is the engine of economic development. These dynamics involve a process of "creative destruction":

> The opening up of new markets, foreign or domestic, and the organizational development from the craft shop and factory to such concerns as U.S. Steel illustrate the same process of industrial mutation – if I may use that biological term – that incessantly revolutionizes the economic structure from within, incessantly destroying the old one, incessantly creating a new one. This process of Creative Destruction is the essential fact about capitalism. (Schumpeter 1942 [2010]: 73)

Innovations are responsible for the cyclicity of economic development, the leaps and bounds of economic expansion – business cycles on the one hand and long waves or growth cycles, so-called "Kondratieffs", on the other. Depending on the size, scope and clustering of innovations, the process of absorbing the new gives rise to cycles of different length and amplitude.

Schumpeter's ideas fell on fertile ground in studies of long waves of economic development, in evolutionary economics and in parts of new growth theory. However, for a long time the discussion was surprisingly dominated by a theory that treated technical change as exogenous.

Neoclassical Growth Theory: Technical Change as "Manna from Heaven"

In the neoclassical growth model, growth results from increasing amounts of employment of factors of production and from increasing productivity of these factors. The approach relies on a distinction between (1) a movement along and (2) a shift of the postulated macro production function:

$$Q = f(K, L; t), \tag{2}$$

where total output Q is a function of the capital stock K, total employment L and time t; see, in particular, Solow (1956, 1957). As time goes by the system miraculously becomes more productive.

Solow assumed technical change to be Hicks neutral. In this case the production function can be written as:

$$Q = A(t)f(K, L) \tag{3}$$

with $A(t)$ measuring the overall effect of shifts over time. Total output growth splits into employment growth of input factors and the rate of technical change. The latter is computed as a *residual* contribution to growth not explained by the growth of inputs. This so-called Solow residual $\dot{A}/A$ is derived from the fundamental equation of "growth accounting":

$$\frac{\dot{A}}{A} = \frac{\dot{Q}}{Q} - w_K\frac{\dot{K}}{K} - w_L\frac{\dot{L}}{L} \tag{4}$$

Assuming a Cobb–Douglas production function $Q = A(t)K^\alpha L^{1-\alpha}$ with constant returns to scale and production factors paid according to their marginal productivities in conditions of perfect competition, w_K is equal to the share of profits and w_L is equal to the share of wages. Given the data on the growth rates of output, capital and labour and the income shares, the contribution of technical change to growth can be estimated.

Empirical studies by Solow (1957) and others showed the overwhelming importance of "technical progress" for growth (see Felipe 1999), but how is one to interpret the Solow residual? According to Solow, the shift factor $A(t)$ – dubbed total factor productivity by John Kendrick (1956) – is a catch-all term for the unexplained and includes not only the effect of new technology, but also economies of scale, skill improvements, better health and so on. Moses Abramovitz (1956: 11) therefore spoke aptly of "some sort of measure of our ignorance about the causes of economic growth". Besides the ambiguity of interpretation, the conceptualization of technical change as disembodied, that is, completely separated from the process of capital formation, and as an exogenously given exponential function of time – "manna from heaven" – invited criticism and further developments.

Embodied technical change is explored in the so-called vintage capital approach, in which "capital" cannot be treated as a homogenous entity, since new machines are typically better than old ones. In contrast to disembodied technical change, which evenly affects the whole stock of capital, here the age-profile of the collection of different kinds of pieces of capital determines productivity. As a change in the age-profile of the capital stock is pivotal to increases in productivity, (gross) investment is the key vehicle to foster technical change. The idea that investment carries new technologies into the system has been explored *inter alia* in works of Leif Johansen, Robert E. Solow, Wilfred E.G. Salter and a paper by Nicholas Kaldor and James A. Mirrlees in the 1960s. Compared with the Solow model, "now the manna of technical progress falls only on the latest machines" (Hahn and Matthews 1964: 837–8).

Linear and Non-Linear Models of Innovation

Making use of Schumpeter's trilogy, and based on the neoclassical approach, linear models of innovation were developed in the mid-twentieth century. A characteristic feature of linear models is that the innovation process is formalized into sequential stages. Within this modelling framework in particular the interdependency between the invention and the innovation stage is studied (Nelson 1959). Focusing on both a micro and a macro perspective, an early example is the technology-push model. It revolves around the idea that technology is supply driven and that the innovation process starts with basic research, followed by applied research and finally the production and diffusion of an innovation (see Rothwell and Zegveld 1985). Contrary to this, Schmookler (1966) developed the demand-pull linear model of innovation, postulating that innovation is a demand-driven process where demand conditions and market needs are key factors.

Arrow (1962a, 1962b) contributed to linear models by focusing on the supply side and introducing knowledge and learning as two essential ingredients of the innovation process. Since the production of knowledge is risky and not (perfectly) predictable, future payoffs of R&D are uncertain. This together with the fact that private benefits are smaller than social benefits (especially with respect to basic research) may result in underinvestment, creating the necessity of government intervention. Arrow also argued that competition propels innovation: a monopolist innovates less since he has less to gain from innovation than firms under competitive pressure.

Arrow (1962b) introduced increasing returns to investment in physical capital in a Solow-type growth model. In this context, uncertainty exists only with regard to innovations, but not the diffusion process, where learning effects prevail. Once knowledge is created, it is irreversible, that is, if workers change jobs they take with them their experience, which renders them more productive irrespective of where they work. In other words, knowledge once created is directly incorporated in the firm's workers and costless to move between firms. The greater the experience workers and firms have accumulated the more productive they are. The process of "learning by doing" makes firms produce more efficiently and at lower unit cost. Moving along the learning curve thus entails a competitive advantage of existing firms over new ones.

Applied to international specialization, Arrow's argument implies that there are "first mover advantages": late movers have difficulties making up for the experience first movers have already acquired. The involved aspect of path dependency played an important role in the contributions of Paul A. David, Douglass C. North and Brian Arthur.

Linear models suffer from a lack of feedback effects in the innovation chain. In criticizing Arrow for concentrating solely on the role of the innovator, Rosenberg (2000: 62) emphasized the role of imitators for technological change: imitators are "the essential carriers of an improvement process". Moreover, Rosenberg (1982) stressed that R&D is a complex learning process involving many actors which is clouded by uncertainties. In this process both forward and backward linkages as well as the institutional structure of research systems matter (Mowery and Rosenberg 1989). In early non-linear models, the utilization of innovations and their commercial applicability during the diffusion phase are the focus of attention. Uncertainty turns out to be not only present at the innovation stage, but also during diffusion. Rosenberg (1982) also introduced the concept of "learning by using": users report their experience with a new machine back to the engineers, who constructed it and who then improve it; a case in point is the aviation industry. As a result, the firm cannot be treated as a "black box" whose internal organization and structure are irrelevant to technological change.

Induced Innovations and Directed Technical Change

The question of how a change of the economic environment acts upon the process of technical change revolved around the idea that relative factor prices, conceived of as scarcity indexes, do have a significant impact on the rate and bias of innovations and technical change. John R. Hicks (1932) proposed the so-called induced innovation hypothesis:

The real reason for the predominance of labour saving inventions is surely that . . . [a] change in the relative prices of factors of production is itself a spur to invention, and to invention of a particular kind – directed to economizing the use of a factor which has become relatively expensive. (Hicks 1932: 124)

Salter (1960) criticized the hypothesis and argued that firms implement innovations that reduce total costs and are not concerned with a particular innovation bias. In a similar vein Samuelson (1965: 354–5) stressed that "since at minimum-cost equilibrium all inputs are equally marginally dear or productive, the simplest theory of induced innovation is ill-founded."

Despite these objections the induced innovation hypothesis found its way into growth theory in the 1960s (Kennedy 1964; von Weizsäcker 1965; Samuelson 1965). Central to these models is the innovation possibility frontier (IPF), introduced by Kennedy (1964). The IPF describes technological restrictions on innovation possibilities. It is assumed to have the properties of a neoclassical transformation function and thus poses a fundamental trade-off between the rate of reducing labour and capital requirements for unit production. Based on this concept, Kennedy showed that firms, seeking to maximize overall unit cost reduction, choose a combination of capital and labour saving innovations that depends on relative factor shares.

Nordhaus (1973) questioned the usefulness of Kennedy's model, because it assumes (1) that innovating is a costless activity and (2) that the IPF is exogenously imposed and static such that the rate of reducing capital requirements does not depend on the level of reduction of labour requirements. The model, Nordhaus (1973: 208) concluded, is "too defective to be used in serious economic analysis".

About 30 years later, Daron Acemoglu (2002) revived the idea of induced innovations within an endogenous growth model. He investigates the determinants and consequences of directed technical change: innovative activities, responding to profit incentives, are biased towards different factors of production. This is so because firms are likely to invest in the development of the most promising type of innovation (embodied in an intermediate good, for example, a machine) in terms of profitability. The latter is determined by two forces working in opposite directions: (1) the price effect, that is, the incentives to invest in a specific technology increase with the price of the good in whose production the technology is deployed; thus, the price effect implies technical change to be biased towards scarce factors of production; (2) the market size effect, that is, the larger the supply of a specific production factor, the more likely the development of a new technology that embodies a relatively large amount of this factor. This effect is similar to the market forces at work in the demand-pull model by Schmookler (1966), except that innovative activities are driven by factor markets, since the market size effect promotes technical change in favour of the (relatively) abundant factors.

Which of the two effects ultimately prevails depends on the substitutability between the different technologies (respective factors). For a sufficiently large elasticity of substitution, the demand curve for an abundant factor might even be upward sloping. This was the case with regard to skilled labour in the US in the second half of the twentieth century, Acemoglu contended: the increase in qualified workers was a strong incentive to develop a technology that embodies a lot of human capital (and not the other way round). The resulting rate of skill-biased technical change induced a rise in the skill premium, outweighing the usual substitution effect between skilled and unskilled workers owing to this change in the relative price of the two kinds of labour. The model, also entailing the innovation possibility frontier, is said to also contribute to an explanation of income disparities between rich and poor countries and the potential innovation bias triggered by international trade.

Innovation in an Evolutionary Framework

Based on Schumpeter's invention–innovation–diffusion trilogy, evolutionary economics tackles three basic questions. (1) How is technological variety generated? (2) How, at which rate and in which direction do innovations spread through the system? (3) How do innovation activities and diffusion processes shape the evolution of firms, of industries and of the economy as a whole?

The formal application of evolutionary thinking to economics by Nelson and Winter (1982) is inspired by Schumpeter's theory and is concerned with the mechanisms involved in the process of technical change. The approach relies on explicit micro-foundations with heterogeneous, bounded-rational agents who do not engage in optimizing behaviour but follow routines. Further, the economy is not in equilibrium but constitutes the environment in which evolutionary processes of stochastic variety generation and competitive selection interact. Based on this, Nelson and Winter investigated the processes of searching for new production methods and imitation, the dynamics of selection and the consequences for aggregate growth and industry concentration.

According to this "bottom-up" approach, technical change at the aggregate level is the outcome of ongoing "search and selection" of firms and can be measured by what is called "evolutionary accounting": "The fundamental evolutionary idea is that distributions . . . change as a result of (1) learning by incumbent entities; (2) differential growth (that is, a form of selection) of incumbent entities themselves; (3) death (indeed, a different and more radical form of selection); and (4) entry of new entities" (Dosi and Grazzi 2006: 194–5). See Metcalfe (1997) for the connection between innovation, diffusion and the aggregate measure of total factor productivity. Silverberg and Lehnert (1993) adopted the Nelson–Winter approach and explain the empirical evidence of long waves generated by the introduction and gradual diffusion of new energy technologies. For an extensive discussion of evolutionary models of innovation-driven growth, see Dawid (2006).

In evolutionary selection models diffusion of new techniques is effectuated via differential firm growth: cost and profit rate differentials translate into growth differentials. Similar to the vintage approach, investment is necessary in order to exploit the economic potential of innovations. The formalization of selection dynamics adopts the replicator equation and Fisher's principle, taken from population theory, and provides insights into the determinants of the direction and velocity of technical change as well as into the impact of diffusion processes on aggregate dynamics (see Metcalfe 1998).

Evolutionary diffusion models provide an explanation of the stylized facts of the diffusion process, namely, that it is a time-consuming process and typically follows an S-shaped curve. Early empirical diffusion studies dating back to the 1940s and 1950s led to the development of a variety of technology diffusion models which are not based on the mechanism of differential growth but on imitation and adoption decisions, including epistemic and probit models (see Stoneman 2002). The evolutionary framework of Nelson and Winter (1982) laid the basis for the development of various further concepts concerned with Schumpeter's trilogy seen as a non-linear process.

Technical Change in New Growth Theory

New Growth Theory seeks to provide endogenous explanations of technical change. The most prominent contributions came from Romer (1986, 1990) and Lucas (1988). Their models are neoclassical in spirit and developed on the basis of the following concepts: a macro production function, representative agents and maximizing behaviour (representing rationality).

In these endogenous growth models economic change is driven by the production and accumulation of technological and scientific knowledge. Lucas (1988) introduced human capital in the macro production function. Since the presence of human capital makes both physical capital and simple labour more productive, the growth rate depends on how workers allocate their time between work and studying. Romer (1990) highlights the specific nature of knowledge and its impact on the economy: The non-rivalry of ideas implies spillovers and increasing returns, whereas the partial excludability of new designs (for example, by patenting) gives market power to the inventor and leads to monopolistic competition among innovating firms. It is these characteristics that distinguish knowledge from other goods and essentially drive sustained economic expansion: owing to its partial excludability, each design generates a new intermediate good for the production of the output, while non-rivalry leads to a rise in the total stock of knowledge and an increase in the productivity of human capital in the R&D sector. Thus, the (endogenously) expanding variety of products as the outcome of innovation processes prevents growth from vanishing (see also Grossman and Helpman 1991).

Pervasive Technical Change Driven by "General Purpose Technologies"

A more comprehensive discussion regarding the effects of innovations for the economy is provided in the literature on general purpose technologies (GPTs), which spur sustained growth via their pervasive use in the economy. General purpose technologies are characterized by the following three features (see Jovanovic and Rousseau 2005): (1) pervasiveness, (2) scope of improvement and (3) innovational complementarities between the sector supplying the GPT and the sectors that apply it.

Introduced by Bresnahan and Trajtenberg (1995), the initial focus was on the problems of coordinating innovation activities between up- and downstream sectors in a partial equilibrium model. The lack of technological information flowing between the GPT-providing sectors and the user sectors prevent externalities from coming to full play. Not last in an attempt to explain the productivity slowdown in the US in the 1980s, models were developed around the notion of GPTs emphasizing the impact of major technological change on economic structure and long-term growth. The general content of this discussion was not new, but had close links to previous concepts, such as techno-economic paradigms or macro inventions seeking to explain radical technological change in an evolutionary framework (see Lipsey et al. 2005 for a review of GPT models and related theories). Nevertheless, the notion of GPTs is by no means re-inventing the wheel, not least because of its emphasis on the generality of purpose of a technological breakthrough.

At the theoretical level, the approach by Helpman and Trajtenberg (1998), embedded in a model of expanding product variety (Romer 1990; Grossman and Helpman 1991), and the Schumpeterian framework of Aghion and Howitt (1998), became the workhorse models in this strand of research: its broad applicability ensures a new GPT to be demanded in a wide range of sectors, but the crudity in design hampers its adoption immediately upon arrival (characteristics 1 and 2). Thus, firms need to engage in the development of complementary components required for the efficient utilization of the technology (characteristic 3).

The shift of resources from the manufacturing sector towards R&D therefore may cause a slump in output as an "integral feature" (Helpman and Trajtenberg 1998: 71) of this type of technological change. Sooner or later, productivity grows due to the increasing variety of complementary components available for the new GPT. Other approaches draw on quality-ladder models to explain the cyclical productivity pattern.

The GPT models extend those of Lucas and Romer by explicitly considering the interaction between technological breakthroughs and complementary (sub-)technologies. However, in all these theories the GPT enters the economy in the form of a productivity parameter, the technology itself and innovations in GPTs being left out of the picture. Furthermore, the focus on the development of new technical solutions to the efficient utilization of the GPT implies a rather simple view of the complex process of adoption of a radically different technology across heterogeneous agents. Yet it is their inherent potential to diffuse over the whole economic system that assigns to GPTs a crucial role in spurring long-term growth. Addressing some of these criticisms, a comprehensive, evolutionary framework for dealing with the variety and coexistence of GPTs was proposed by Carlaw and Lipsey (2011). Focusing more on a meso-macro level, one popular framework – building partly on evolutionary economics – is the "systems of innovation" approach.

Systems of Innovation: A Policy-Orientated View on Innovation

The system of innovation (SI) approach, notwithstanding its Schumpeterian roots (in particular the invention–innovation–diffusion trilogy), can be traced back to Friedrich List's book *Das nationale System der politischen Ökonomie* (1841 [1959]). Defining a "system" as a set of interrelated units, in the SI framework, innovation is considered as the outcome of an interactive learning process in which many different elements are involved (see Lundvall 1992 [2010]: 2). The elements pivotal to the innovation process are firms, private and public institutions, universities, research laboratories as well as other educational institutions and organizations. The emphasis is on the generation, dissemination and use of new, economically useful knowledge. The interaction of elements in a SI proceeds through both formal and informal activities and will typically involve some uncertainty. While the former include, for example, innovative and research activities as well as financing aspects of the innovation process, the latter refer, for instance, to "learning by doing" or "learning by using" and other learning mechanisms which help to turn an invention into an innovation, and thus into new and economically useful knowledge.

All SI approaches share the view that innovations and technological change are essential determinants of the long-term development of economies. While the focus was initially on the national level of analysis, globalization and an increased internationalization of the innovation process necessitated transcending a purely national perspective. Several other non-linear concepts evolved, regarding also the regional, the local and the sectoral levels. These different approaches do reflect, first, differences in the geographical dimension, contrasting the national level with a sub-national or supra-national level, and second, conceptual differences (see Carlsson et al. 2002). The performance-orientated view on SI in terms of economic growth and productivity gains made the concept popular with policy-makers. For instance, the Organisation for Economic Co-operation and Development (OECD) and several national organizations involved in technology and innovation policy used the concept as a policy-orientated framework (for some case studies, see Nelson 1993).

From a more theoretical perspective, the SI framework contains evolutionary elements. This can be seen, for instance, in the fact that a SI is considered as a historically grown system and is shaped by the specific cultural and social patterns with which it co-evolved. Different types of innovations are considered as endogenous variables emerging through the dynamic interaction of the elements within a SI. And these dynamics involve continuous change arising from within the system.

The SI framework was also exposed to several criticisms. It was particularly objected that the approach lacks clarity and does not constitute a unifying theory. Yet, the pluralistic perspective underlying the study of SI can be regarded as an advantage. Lundvall (2007: 872) in this context stressed the wide-ranging scientific relevance of the SI concept within the academic community: "Economists, business economists, economic historians, sociologists and, not least, economic geographers have utilized the concept in their attempts to explain and understand phenomena related to innovation and competence building."

Concluding Remarks

"Technical change", one commentator remarked, "is like God. It is much discussed, worshipped by some, rejected by others, but little understood" (Thompson 1984: 243). While this is still somewhat true, the efforts of several generations of economists have not been in vain. Today we know a great deal more about technical change and innovations than previous generations did, but we also have a better idea of how much we don't know yet. As is quite common in research, while the number of old questions we can answer increases, the number of new questions we cannot as yet increases more rapidly.

DAVID HAAS, HEINZ D. KURZ, NICOLE KATHRIN PALAN, ANDREAS RAINER,
MARLIES SCHÜTZ AND RITA STROHMAIER

See also:

British classical political economy (II); Business cycles and growth (III); Competition (III); Economic dynamics (III); Evolutionary economics (III); Growth (III); Input–output analysis (III); Nicholas Kaldor (I); Wassily W. Leontief (I); Friedrich List (I); Karl Heinrich Marx (I); Neo-Ricardian economics (II); David Ricardo (I); Joseph Alois Schumpeter (I); Adam Smith (I); Robert Merton Solow (I); Arthur Spiethoff (I); Thorstein Bunde Veblen (I).

References and further reading

Abramovitz, M. (1956), 'Resource and output trends in the United States since 1870', *American Economic Review*, **46** (2), 5–23.

Acemoglu, D. (2002), 'Directed technical change', *Review of Economic Studies*, **69** (4), 781–809.

Aghion, P. and P. Howitt (1998), 'On the macroeconomic effects of major technological change', in E. Helpman (ed.), *General Purpose Technologies and Economic Growth*, Cambridge: MIT Press, pp. 121–44.

Arrow, K.J. (1962a), 'Economic welfare and the allocation of resources for invention', in R. Nelson (ed.), *The Rate and Direction of Inventive Activity*, Princeton, NJ: Princeton University Press.

Arrow, K.J. (1962b), 'The economic implications of learning by doing', *Review of Economic Studies*, **29** (3), 155–73.

Bresnahan, T. and M. Trajtenberg (1995), 'General purpose technologies: "engines of growth"?', *Journal of Econometrics*, **65** (1), 83–108.

Carlaw, K. and R. Lipsey (2011), 'Sustained endogenous growth driven by structured and evolving general purpose technologies', *Journal of Evolutionary Economics*, **21** (4), 563–93.

Carlsson, B., S. Jacobsson, M. Holmén and A. Rickne (2002), 'Innovation systems: analytical and methodological issues', *Research Policy*, **31** (2), 233–45.

Dawid, H. (2006), 'Agent-based models of innovation and technological change', in L. Tesfatsion and K. Judd (eds), *Handbook of Computational Economics, Vol. 2: Agent-Based Computational Economics*, Amsterdam: Elsevier, pp. 1235–72.

Dosi, G. and M. Grazzi (2006), 'Technologies as problem-solving procedures and technologies as input–output relations: some perspectives on the theory of production', *Industrial and Corporate Change*, **15** (1), 173–202.

Felipe, J. (1999), 'Total factor productivity growth in East Asia: a critical survey', *Journal of Development Studies*, **35** (4), 1–41.

Grossman, G. and E. Helpman (1991), *Innovation and Growth in the Global Economy*, Cambridge: MIT Press.

Hahn, F. and R. Matthews (1964), 'The theory of economic growth: a survey', *The Economic Journal*, **74** (296), 779–902.

Helpman, E. and M. Trajtenberg (1998), 'A time to sow and a time to reap: growth based on general purpose technologies', in E. Helpman (ed.), *General Purpose Technologies and Economic Growth*, Cambridge: MIT Press, pp. 55–83.

Hicks, J. (1932), *The Theory of Wages*, London: Macmillan.

Jovanovic, B. and P. Rousseau (2005), 'General purpose technologies', in P. Aghion and N. Durlauf (eds), *Handbook of Economic Growth*, vol. 1B, Amsterdam: Elsevier, pp. 1181–224.

Kalmbach, P. and H.D. Kurz (1990), 'Micro-electronics and employment: a dynamic input–output study of the West German economy', *Structural Change and Economic Dynamics*, **1** (2), 371–86.

Kendrick, J. (1956), 'Productivity trends: capital and labor', *Review of Economics and Statistics*, **38** (3), 248–57.

Kennedy, C. (1964), 'Induced bias in innovation and the theory of distribution', *The Economic Journal*, **74** (295), 541–7.

Kurz, H.D. (2010), 'Technical progress, capital accumulation and income distribution in classical economics: Adam Smith, David Ricardo and Karl Marx', *European Journal of the History of Economic Thought*, **17** (5), 1183–222.

Kurz, H.D. and N. Salvadori (1995), *Theory of Production. A Long-Period Analysis*, Cambridge, New York and Melbourne: Cambridge University Press.

Leontief, W. and F. Duchin (1986), *The Future Impact of Automation on Workers*, New York: Oxford University Press.

Lipsey, R., K. Carlaw and C. Bekar (2005), *Economic Transformations. General Purpose Technologies and Long-Term Economic Growth*, New York: Oxford University Press.

List, F. (1841), *Das nationale System der politischen Ökonomie*, reprinted 1959, Basel: Kyklos-Verlag.

Lucas, R.E. (1988), 'On the mechanics of economic development', *Journal of Monetary Economics*, **22** (1), 3–42.

Lundvall, B.-Å. (ed.) (1992), *National Systems of Innovation: Towards a Theory of Innovation and Interactive Learning*, reprinted 2010, London, New York and Delhi: Anthem Press.

Lundvall, B.-Å. (2007), 'National innovation systems: from List to Freeman', in H. Hanusch and A. Pyka (eds), *Elgar Companion to Neo-Schumpeterian Economics*, Cheltenham, UK and Northampton, MA, USA: Edward Elgar, pp. 872–81.

Marx, K. (1954), *Capital*, vol. 1, Moscow: Progress.

Marx, K. (1959), *Capital*, vol. 3, Moscow: Progress.

Metcalfe, S. (1997), 'The evolutionary explanation of total factor productivity growth: macro measurement and micro process', *Revue d'économie industrielle*, **80** (1), 93–114.

Metcalfe, S. (1998), *Evolutionary Economics and Creative Destruction*, London: Routledge.

Mowery, D.C. and N. Rosenberg (1989), *Technology and the Pursuit of Economic Growth*, Cambridge: Cambridge University Press.

Nelson, R. (1959), 'The economics of invention: a survey of the literature', *Journal of Business*, **32** (2), 101–27.

Nelson, R. (ed.) (1993), *National Innovation Systems: A Comparative Analysis*, Oxford: Oxford University Press.

Nelson, R. and S. Winter (1982), *An Evolutionary Theory of Economic Change*, Cambridge: Belknap Press.

Nordhaus, W. (1973), 'Some skeptical thoughts on the theory of induced innovation', *Quarterly Journal of Economics*, **87** (2), 208–19.

Piketty, T. (2014), *Capital in the 21st Century*, Cambridge, MA: Harvard University Press.

Ricardo, D. (1951–73), *The Works and Correspondence of David Ricardo*, 11 vols, ed. P. Sraffa with collaboration of M.H. Dobb, Cambridge: Cambridge University Press.

Romer, P. (1986), 'Increasing returns and long-run growth', *Journal of Political Economy*, **94** (5), 1002–37.

Romer, P. (1990), 'Endogenous technological change', *Journal of Political Economy*, **98** (5), 71–102.

Rosenberg, N. (1982), *Inside the Black Box: Technology and Economics*, Cambridge: Cambridge University Press.

Rosenberg, N. (2000), *Schumpeter and the Endogeneity of Technology, Some American Perspective*, London: Routledge.

Rothwell, R. and W. Zegveld (1985), *Reindustrialization and Technology*, Harlow: Longman.

Salter, W. (1960), *Productivity and Technical Change*, Cambridge: Cambridge University Press.

Samuelson, P. (1965), 'A theory of innovation along Kennedy–Weizsäcker lines', *Review of Economics and Statistics*, **47** (4), 343–56.

Schefold, B. (1976), 'Different forms of technical progress', *Economic Journal*, **86** (344), 806–19.

Schmookler, J. (1966), *Invention and Economic Growth*, Cambridge, MA: Harvard University Press.

Schumpeter, J.A. (1912, *The Theory of Economic Development: An Inquiry Into Profits, Capital, Credit, Interest, and the Business Cycle*, reprinted 1934, London: Transaction Books.

Schumpeter, J.A. (1942), *Capitalism, Socialism, and Democracy*, reprinted 2010, London and New York: Routledge.

Silverberg, G. and D. Lehnert (1993), 'Long waves and "evolutionary chaos" in a simple Schumpeterian model of embodied technical change', *Structural Change and Economic Dynamics*, **4** (1), 9–37.

Smith, A. (1776), *An Inquiry into the Nature and Causes of the Wealth of Nations*, 2 vols, in R.H. Campbell and A.S. Skinner (eds) (1976), *The Glasgow Edition of the Works and Correspondence of Adam Smith*, Oxford: Oxford University Press.

Solow, R. (1956), 'A contribution to the theory of economic growth', *Quarterly Journal of Economics*, **70** (1), 65–94.

Solow, R. (1957), 'Technical change and the aggregate production function', *Review of Economics and Statistics*, **39** (3), 312–20.

Sraffa, P. (1960), *Production of Commodities by Means of Commodities. Prelude to a Critique of Economic Theory*, Cambridge: Cambridge University Press.

Stoneman, P. (2002), *The Economics of Technological Diffusion*, Oxford: Blackwell.

Thompson, E.A. (1984), *Studies in the Theory of Ideology*, Berkeley, CA: University of California Press.

von Weizsäcker, C.-C. (1965), 'Tentative notes on a two sector model with induced technical progress', *Review of Economic Studies*, **33** (3), 245–51.

Young, A.A. (1928), 'Increasing returns and economic progress', *The Economic Journal*, **38** (152), 527–42.

Theory of the firm

The marginalist or neoclassical theory of the firm conceptualizes it as a producer and analyses its behaviour similarly to that of the consumer: maximization (of profit) under constraint (of the production function). In particular, industrial organization focuses on firm equilibrium in different market structures, focusing more on the market than on the firm itself. From the 1970s onwards, "recent theories of the firm" opposed this view and claimed to answer questions such as the existence, boundaries, performance, internal organization or financing structure of the firm, referring to seminal works of the twentieth century, and especially to Ronald Coase (1937). However, not only had some of these issues already been addressed by economists since the eighteenth century, but the ascendancy of the marginalist theory of the firm since the 1930s has always been paralleled by critical alternative or complementary approaches. When Coase (and others) opened the "black box" of the neoclassical firm, the box itself was only recent and had been conceptualized by splitting away from the theory of the entrepreneur, de facto eliminating this central figure of classical economics.

Three periods can be distinguished. From the end of the nineteenth century to the 1930s, economists dealing with firm-related issues increasingly concentrated on questions of equilibrium, putting aside the entrepreneur. They constructed a marginalist theory of the firm that would then become dominant. From the 1930s to the end of the 1960s, the marginalist controversy (see, for example, Mongin 1997) and other works – such as those by Coase, Joseph Schumpeter and Edith Penrose – questioned this theory and highlighted some essential aspects, including uncertainty, innovation and growth. They contributed to view the firm as an organization, and to reveal the different roles of the entrepreneur. The more recent development, since the 1970s, is ambiguous: two groups of recent theories of the firm, grounded on the contributions of the second period, can be identified. On the one hand, contractual theories of the firm explain the firm and its size by the need to facilitate transactions; ever more formalized, they have increasingly neglected the entrepreneur figure. On the other hand, evolutionary and competence-based theories, built on a fundamental questioning of rationality in a radically uncertain world, focus on the routines developed by firms and on the sphere of production in which the entrepreneur's role is central.

From Theories of the Entrepreneur to the Marginalist Theory of the Firm

The "entrepreneur" was a central figure of the works by Richard Cantillon (1755) – "undertaker" in the English translation – and Jean-Baptiste Say (1803). From Cantillon's farmer to Karl Marx's industrial capitalist, from Adam Smith's (1776) manufacturer to Say's innovator, different functions of the entrepreneur are identified: he refrains from consuming and engages capital (where the entrepreneur is also the capitalist), takes some risks, organizes the production, buys and sells, and also innovates. The nature and determination of the remuneration of these different activities are discussed: wage, interest or profit (residual or not). Regarding the firm, it is conceived as the locus of the division of labour (for Smith or John Stuart Mill (1848)) and of exploitation (for Marx).

Building the marginalist theory of the firm

The marginalist theory of the firm was built upon Alfred Marshall's work, retaining one aspect only of his twofold view of the firm. On the one hand, in his *Principles* (1890), the owner-entrepreneur is considered a decision-maker, and the emphasis is on short-period and long-period equilibria of industries and representative firms. Since manufacturing firms have a finite life cycle of expansion and decline, the long-period supply of an industry is provided by different firms at specific moments of their lives, and the "representative" firm is a fictitious average. This approach leads to an elaborate discussion of the firm's behaviour, of its costs and returns and thus of its optimal size. Here, the "undertaker" is the capitalist-owner-manager who provides "the supply of business power in command of capital [which] may be regarded as consisting of three elements, the supply of capital, the supply of the business power to manage it, and the supply of the organization by which the two are brought together and made effective for production" (*Principles* VI, 7). The first function is rewarded by "interest", the others by "earnings of management".

On the other hand, Marshall also conceived the firm from a more dynamic perspective, as a source of growth. The entrepreneur-founder of the firm is now an innovator, who obtains a quasi-rent that disappears in the long run. The discussions of the advantages of the division of labour in *Industry and Trade* (1919) and in the *Principles* follow Smith and Charles Babbage. In this approach, the Marshallian firm is not a passive player but interacts with its environment (Loasby 1999).

The cost controversy of the 1920s focused the attention on Marshall's equilibrium approach. His concept of "external economies", and its reinterpretation by Arthur Pigou in his *Wealth and Welfare* (1912), gave rise to a controversy on the forms of costs. One of the results of this debate was the refinement of Marshall's analysis on the optimal size of the firm (Pigou 1932) and on the theory of costs and production (Viner 1931).

In the same vein, Joan Robinson (1933) generalized the Marshallian behaviour of firms to monopolistic situations: each firm is characterized by a production function and confronted with a demand curve, and it maximizes its profits. While introducing the fictitious Marshallian firm into the core of microeconomics, Robinson lost sight of the firm as an organization. Edward Chamberlin (1933), through his general theory of market structure (monopolistic competition), was the first to insist on the multi-dimensionality of the strategy of the firm: price, differentiation and advertisement. Formalizing some of Marshall's insights, but disregarding others, Robinson's and Chamberlin's works mark the birth of industrial organization and of the neoclassical theory of the firm, emerging at the same time as consumer theory (Hicks and Allen 1934). The neoclassical theory of the firm soon became and would remain dominant. Since this theory assumes perfect information and focuses on static equilibrium, it leaves no role for an entrepreneur making decisions under uncertainty, reacting to and causing change. Paradoxically, this is a theory of the firm in which there is no firm: the "firm" is an optimization process, with given technology. This is in fact a theory of prices, so the issue at hand is the allocation of resources and not the process of their production, with its creation and use of knowledge. The increasing formalization of economics no doubt favoured this neglect of the entrepreneur, production and organization. But there were also some seminal critical works, more or less at the margins of mainstream economics.

Questioning the Neoclassical Theory of the Firm

Institutionalist perspectives

American institutionalism proposed some alternatives to the views of the firm offered by classical and neoclassical economics. In his historical analysis of capitalism, Thorstein Veblen (1904, 1923) saw institutions, including firms, as mental habits evolving in a cumulative sequence. In the first, industrial, era of capitalism, owners, led by the instinct of workmanship, became individual entrepreneurs and promoted social progress. However, from the 1870s onwards, the institution of property took the form of the business enterprise: the absentee owners returned to the leisure class, since they were only interested in the pecuniary aspects of the firm and not in the direction of production, which they delegated to managers. They thus constituted large financial trusts with monopoly power.

In John Commons's typology (1934), the managerial transaction describes the relationship between employers and employees inside the firm as superior-inferior, seeking efficiency and based upon the negotiational psychology of command and obedience. Therefore, even if the firm also involves the two other types of transaction (bargaining and rationing), its focus is not on exchange or distribution but on wealth creation, not on allocation but on production.

The role of the entrepreneur in capitalist growth was central for Joseph Schumpeter (1911). As distinct from the capitalist who lends money and bears the risk, the entrepreneur is crucial for the process of innovation and responsible for business and other cycles. The innovation of the successful entrepreneur gains him an extra profit, but he is imitated by other entrepreneurs and the system returns to a new state of equilibrium. Here, the entrepreneur is viewed as an innovative individual, whereas in Schumpeter's subsequent work (1942), innovations result from the research routines of specialist departments in large corporations trying to secure transitory monopoly power.

In Frank Knight's theory (1921), the entrepreneur interacts with an uncertain world (inputs, outputs and production functions are not exogenously given), and must make decisions and exercise control. He owns certain capacities of "judgement" that help him to deal with uncertainty, but that cannot be transferred or evaluated. Since this judgement cannot be contracted, it is used inside the firm and gives rise to a profit. The entrepreneurial firm hence develops along the lines of the specific entrepreneur's competence. Workers are more risk-averse and their competences can be assessed, which is why they are paid wages.

The non-contractible aspect of the Knightian entrepreneur's competence was not understood by Coase, who rejected the involved explanation of the firm. His "The nature of the firm" (1937) initially went unnoticed, gaining fame only after the success of "The problem of social cost" (Coase 1960) and Oliver Williamson's use of the concept of transaction costs (1979). Coase's 1937 article was celebrated for the question it posed: if coordination by the market was as efficient as some economists argued, why would this alternative mode of coordination by hierarchy exist? This was the very same issue that was stressed by Smith or Marx: there is division of labour inside the firm, that is, another form of coordination than the market. But Coase linked it to the planning debate of the 1930s: why is there planning in our market economies if planning is as inefficient as its opponents claimed? Coase's answer was based on the costs of the operation of the market, "marketing costs" that consist in "discovering what the relevant prices are" and "negotiating and concluding a separate contract for each exchange transaction" (Coase 1937: 390–91). Inside the firm, multiple short-term contracts are replaced by a unique long-term contract which does not need to specify all contingencies; details are given later by the entrepreneur-coordinator. Coase was worried about the unrealistic assumptions underlying the neoclassical firm, but still wanted to use the Marshallian tool of substitution at the margin. He therefore carried on with the issue of the optimal size of the firm and explained its boundaries as a result of a trade-off between the costs of the market and the costs of hierarchy (mainly due to the cognitive limits of the entrepreneur).

Coase's article oscillates between an institutionalist and a neoclassical perspective, which explains its influential role for recent theories issued from both traditions (Foss 1994). On the one hand, he places hierarchy and the market in opposition, and views the entrepreneur as facing uncertainty and adapting to unforeseen contingencies. On the other, he keeps the analysis of equilibrium and optimality; he views the firm as playing the same role as the market – coordination – and the line between the two gets increasingly blurred (Coase 1988). Like in marginalist theory, the firm passively adapts to its environment and to the market instead of changing them.

The successes of the organization and the competences of the firm were put forward by Penrose in 1959 in a book that was at first neglected, but nevertheless became a fertile ground for evolutionary and competence-based theories of the firm. She defines "a firm [as] more than an administrative unit; it is a collection of productive resources the disposal of which between uses and over time is determined by administrative decision" (Penrose 1959: 24), these resources being physical and human. Her interest was in the internal organization of the firm, specifically in management, whose capacities were limited and therefore constrained the growth of the firm, but which constantly pushed against these limits. The specificity of each firm results not from the individual entrepreneur, but from the managerial personnel, learning both to manage and to work together. This learning inside the firm creates specific competences and path-dependency, which explains the diversity of firms.

The marginalist controversy

The neoclassical theory of the firm was, at least temporarily, more shaken by the marginalist controversy than by these isolated contributions. The assumption of maximization of profit was questioned not only by empirical studies (Hall and Hitch 1939; Lester 1946), but also by behaviourist and managerial theories.

Behaviourism was concerned about the empirical validity of neoclassical assumptions and was searching for laws to describe the behaviours and decision processes of businessmen. Herbert Simon (1955) more realistically considered that their rationality was bounded, referring to the cognitive limitations of the decision makers, that is, limits in their knowledge and computation capacities. Behaviourists mainly see the firm as a means of compensating for the limits of rationality, and composed of different self-interested groups in conflict (March and Simon 1958). Richard Cyert and James March (1963) viewed the firm as a collection of individual members each with different goals (production, sales, market share, and so on) and seeking compromises out of the resulting conflict.

The conflict between owners and managers, neglected by the marginalist theory, is the main problem addressed by managerial theories. This is the problem identified by Adolf Berle and Gardiner Means (1932) as "the separation of ownership from control" in the modern corporation. In their analysis, inspired by Veblen, power moves away from the owners to managers in large business enterprise. These managers are very different from the heroic Schumpeterian entrepreneurs: they are engaged in maximizing their own rewards, which may clash with ownership interests. This separation of ownership and control goes hand in hand with the extension of large corporations, that is, of administered sectors that fix prices and reduce the interaction of supply and demand on the market. In the 1960s, managerialists pursued this analysis of managers' objectives (beyond profit maximization). William Baumol (1959) assumes that managers maximize revenue (sales). Williamson (1964), also influenced by the behavioural group, conceives managers as agents who are not controlled by owners and have preferences over staff count and emoluments. Robin Marris (1964) sees the aim of managers as increasing corporate growth, while the shareholders weigh up the costs of reduced wealth with the costs of controlling managers.

Facing all these criticisms, the champions of the profit maximization assumption defended it by citing the process of selection and the necessity of unrealistic assumptions (Machlup 1946; Alchian 1950; Friedman 1953). Fritz Machlup (1967: 9, 27) explicitly asserted that the marginalist firm was only a "mental construct", "an imaginary reactor to environmental changes" with no "empirical counterpart". However, new waves of criticisms of and alternatives to this view, based on the contributions mentioned above, emerged during the 1970s.

Recent Theories of the Firm

Contractual theories of the firm

Stemming from managerial theories, property rights theory rejected the idea of a firm as an entity who maximizes profits and assumed instead individuals, each maximizing their own utility, under different property rights structures, and with positive transaction costs. Armen Alchian and Harold Demsetz (1972) start from the incentive problem of team production (non-separable output) among the owners of resources. It is resolved by the introduction of a monitor, whose incentive is guaranteed by giving him the right to negotiate the contracts of the team, the right to the residual income and the right to sell both these rights. This bundle of rights defines the owner-manager of the capitalist firm, and actually results in its efficiency. Attenuation of at least one of these rights diminishes efficiency, as it is the case in cooperative or not-for-profit firms. However, there is no problem of separation of ownership (right to residual income) and control. On the contrary, the large corporation exploits the separability of private property rights: it enhances specialization in decision-making, and managers are competitively controlled by the markets for control and ownership. These authors view the firm as a collection of resources related by contracts. The firm as an organization does not exist and the employment contract is not specific: the firm "has no power of fiat, no authority, no disciplinary action any different in the slightest degree from ordinary market contracting between any two people" (Alchian and Demsetz 1972: 777).

Managerial theories were also integrated into neoclassical theory with the reinterpretation of the conflict between shareholders and managers in terms of agency theory, initially developed to analyse tenancy problems (Stiglitz 1974). Relations inside the firm, between owners and managers, monitors and workers, are formalized by designing complete contracts (specifying all contingencies) as optimal solutions to agency problems. Studying different forms of financing (equity and debt), Michael Jensen and William Meckling (1976: 310) define firms as "simply legal fictions which serve as a nexus for a set of contracting relationships among individuals". They extend Alchian and Demsetz's focus on the residual claimant beyond the team problem: "contractual relations are the essence of the firm, not only with employees but with suppliers, customers, creditors, and so on" (ibid.). The specific problems of the corporation are thoroughly analysed: ownership structures (ibid.), markets for managers inside firms (Fama 1980), separation of the moments of decision (Fama and Jensen 1983). Again, the firm is not distinguished from the market, and the figure of the entrepreneur eventually disappears (Fama 1980). The firm is a pacific and efficient space of resolution of conflicts by contracts between free and equal wills.

Building on managerial and behavioural theories, Williamson (1975) rejected Alchian and Demsetz's explanation of the firm using Coase and Simon: bounded rationality prevents agents from designing contracts that would specify all future contingencies; contracts are therefore "incomplete". He detailed the relative advantages of hierarchy: it extends the domain of rationality through specialization of decisions and reduced communication costs, has control mechanisms and enhances coordination. In contrast to market contracts, the firm contract (hierarchical and incomplete) allows adaptation by authority and internal resolution of disputes. But the loss of incentives through prices and cognitive limits lie at the origin of the organizational costs. The firm's boundaries are therefore explained by a trade-off between the powerful incentives of the market and the protection and coordination of the firm. This explanation of the firm had an important consequence for antitrust policies: mergers may not aim at gaining monopoly power, but at minimizing transaction costs, in which case they may be favourable to growth. Williamson (1975) also focused on the internal organization of the firm: he reinterpreted Chandler's (1962) historical account of the passage from the functional or unitary form of capitalist enterprise to multidivisional as evidence of the superiority of the latter over the former. Transaction costs theory would later insist on the role of asset specificity: specific investment *ex post* locks partners of the exchange into a bilateral monopoly; since the contract is incomplete, there is a risk of one party behaving opportunistically to appropriate the quasi-rent of the investment. Vertical integration protects against this risk of hold-up (Klein et al. 1978; Williamson 1985). Williamson (1979, 1985) then introduced hybrid forms between the two polar cases of firm and market, such as franchises or joint ventures. The theory of the firm here became the theory of organizations, also including intermediate forms. Since production is divided into multiple transactions analysed as contracts, the firm is viewed as a contract.

Still in this contractual perspective, the "new property rights" or "incomplete contracts" theory (Grossman and Hart 1986; Hart and Moore 1990) was derived from property rights theory, but, following Williamson, added that contracts were necessarily incomplete due to transaction costs and bounded rationality. Ownership of an asset is defined as giving the owner the right to determine the use of the asset that is not contractually determined, namely, the right of residual control, whose allocation determines behaviour and performance. The firm is a collection of owned physical resources, and the best allocation of residual control rights depends on the size and specificity of investments over these assets.

These contractual theories of the firm, pertaining to new institutional economics, conceive the firm as a set of exchanges and in this sense they do not really distinguish it from the market. Because uncertainty is not so radical and rationality not so bounded, and because technology and preferences are given, there is no role for the entrepreneur, whose non-specific services can be contracted. Simon (1991: 42) himself rejected this view: "the attempts of the new institutional economics to explain organizational behavior solely in terms of agency, asymmetric information, transaction costs, opportunism, and other concepts drawn from neoclassical economics ignore key organizational mechanisms like authority, identification, and coordination, and hence are seriously incomplete". In contrast, competence-based theories have focused on the successes of firms, which exist in the first place, instead of having a firm substituting for a defective market.

Competence-based theories of the firm
The figure of the entrepreneur, and with him the variety and evolution of firms, returned with institutionalist views of the firm, called "competence-based", "resources-based", "capabilities" or "evolutionary" theories. They built on the tradition interested in dynamics and the role of the entrepreneur that included writers such as Smith, Marx, Marshall, Schumpeter, Knight, Austin Robinson (1931) and Penrose, adding the Austrian idea of tacit knowledge. These views were developed, among others, by George Richardson (1972), David Teece (1982), Richard Nelson and Sydney Winter (1982), Geoffrey Hodgson (1988) and Richard Langlois (1992).

Considering truly the limits of rationality, they view decisions as based on learning and habits, and the firm as a stock of knowledge or a set of competences, which are incorporated in non-transferable and tacit routines, routines that are therefore specific to the firm (and not to the transaction). These competences – organizational, managerial, technological or reputational – are dynamic and cumulative, and are therefore path dependent and differ among firms, accounting for their diversity in terms of internal organization or strategies. The differences with contractual theories are numerous: these theories study problems of coordination other than incentive conflicts, reintroduce technology and innovation, and explain variety among firms, their historical evolution and strategy; they study the process of production and take into account the specificity of the employment contract; they give a role to the entrepreneur, with competences that are specific and cannot be contracted (Hodgson 1998).

Influenced by Schumpeter, Marshall, Darwin, the behavioural and managerial schools, and Alchian (1950), the work of Nelson and Winter (1982) is central for evolutionary economics. It claims that, owing to the problems of rationality, firms operate with organizational routines (in production, price setting, research, and so on), the diversity of which explains the diversity of behaviours and therefore of performances. Firms inherit routines (genes); they can copy existing routines or develop new ones (mutation, which can also result from exceptional events); and the environment selects successful firms, and thus routines. The pluralism of environments of selection also accounts for the variety of trajectories. In line with Smith's and Marshall's positions, the firm is viewed as an instrument of dynamic progress since it generates and protects knowledge (which is not individual but embodied in collective structures). The firm is defined as a repository of routines, which "are the skills of an organization" (Nelson and Winter 1982: 124). Works by Giovanni Dosi and Teece (1992) added that the evolution of the firm is path-dependent and focused on its coherence and "core competence".

These evolutionary theories of the firm stress the firm's cognitive aspects at the expense of its social or historical dimensions, and disregard conflict, even if routines are themselves at the core of conflicts. Other institutionalist perspectives on the firm, which are also evolutionary, see conflict and power as central, as illustrated by Harvey Leibenstein (1987) or Hodgson (1988), as well as Marxian-radical theories in which the firm develops to exert power on the market (Marglin 1974). Hodgson insists on the durable character of the firm in relation to the market, which protects routines and competences, essential to production, against destruction through competition or simply the changing environment. Continuity of the firm also allows for innovations. It makes the firm a corporate culture, shaping preferences toward trust and cooperation and building a common culture (a common framework for the perception and interpretation of information) and common motives. This facilitates learning and reduces opportunism and cognitive or communicative distortions, and eventually enhances production, but also encourages inertia and conformism. The firm therefore has specific advantages over the market. Hodgson also insists that the firm has a legal existence, which makes it essentially different from hybrid forms (Williamson 1985) or networks (Powell 1990). These latter forms are better reinterpreted as a form of exchange beyond market exchange, "relational exchange", involving cooperation as opposed to competition.

The neoclassical view of the firm as a black box, which emerged in the 1930s after a century of economic analysis and gave a central role to the entrepreneur and the firm as factors of change, was continuously challenged, even if until the 1970s alternative views were too isolated to be heard. Recent theories of the firm have either integrated these insights into a neoclassical framework, viewing the firm as a contractual equilibrium, or have more radically rejected neoclassical tools, thus returning to the role of the entrepreneur and the firm in evolution.

ÉLODIE BERTRAND

See also:

Ronald Harry Coase (I); Evolutionary economics (III); Industrial organization (III); Institutional economics (III); Institutionalism (II); Labour and employment (III); Alfred Marshall (I); Technical change and innovation (III).

References and further reading

Alchian, A.A. (1950), 'Uncertainty, evolution and economic theory', *Journal of Political Economy*, **58** (3), 211–12.
Alchian, A.A. and H. Demsetz (1972), 'Production, information costs, and economic organization', *American Economic Review*, **62** (5), 777–95.
Baumol, W.J. (1959), *Business Behavior, Value and Growth*, New York: Macmillan.
Berle, A.A. and G.C. Means (1932), *The Modern Corporation and Private Property*, New York: Macmillan.
Cantillon, R. (1755), *Essai sur la Nature du Commerce en Général*, reprinted 1931, H. Higgs (ed.), London: Macmillan.
Chamberlin, E.H. (1933), *The Theory of Monopolistic Competition; A Re-Orientation of the Theory of Value*, Cambridge, MA: Harvard University Press.
Chandler, A. (1962), *Strategy and Structure*, Cambridge, MA: Harvard University Press.

Coase, R.H. (1937), 'The nature of the firm', *Economica*, **4** (16), 386–405.

Coase, R.H. (1960), 'The problem of social cost', *Journal of Law and Economics*, **3** (October), 1–44.

Coase, R.H. (1988), 'The nature of the firm: origin, meaning, influence', *Journal of Law, Economics, and Organization*, **4** (1), 3–47.

Commons, J.R. (1934), *Institutional Economics. Its Place in Political Economy*, New York: Macmillan.

Cyert, R.M. and J.G. March (1963), *A Behavioral Theory of the Firm*, Englewood Cliffs, NJ: Prentice Hall.

Dosi, G., D.J. Teece and S.G. Winter (1992), 'Towards a theory of corporate coherence: preliminary remarks', in G. Dosi, R. Giannetti and P.A. Toninelli (eds), *Technology and Enterprise in a Historical Perspective*, Oxford: Oxford University Press, pp. 185–211.

Fama, E.F. (1980), 'Agency problems and the theory of the firm', *Journal of Political Economy*, **88** (2), 288–307.

Fama, E.F. and M.C. Jensen (1983), 'Separation of ownership and control', *Journal of Law and Economics*, **26** (2), 301–25.

Foss, N.J. (1994), 'The two Coasian traditions', *Review of Political Economy*, **6** (1), 37–61.

Friedman, M. (1953), 'The methodology of positive economics', *Essays in Positive Economics*, Chicago, IL: University of Chicago Press, pp. 3–43.

Grossman, S.J. and O.D. Hart (1986), 'The costs and benefits of ownership: a theory of vertical and lateral integration', *Journal of Political Economy*, **94** (4), 691–719.

Hall, R.L. and C.J. Hitch (1939), 'Price theory and business behaviour', *Oxford Economic Papers*, **2** (1), 12–45.

Hart, O. and J. Moore (1990), 'Property rights and the nature of the firm,' *Journal of Political Economy*, **98** (6), 1119–58.

Hicks, J.R. and R.G.D. Allen (1934), 'A reconsideration of the theory of value', *Economica*, **1** (1), 52–76.

Hodgson, G.M. (1988), *Economics and Institutions: A Manifesto for a Modern Institutional Economics*, Cambridge: Polity Press.

Hodgson, G.M. (1998), 'Competence and contract in the theory of the firm', *Journal of Economic Behavior and Organization*, **35** (2), 179–201.

Jensen, M.C. and W.H. Meckling (1976), 'Theory of the firm: managerial behaviour, agency costs and ownership structure', *Journal of Financial Economics*, **3** (4), 305–60.

Klein, B., R.A. Crawford and A.A. Alchian (1978), 'Vertical integration, appropriable rents, and the competitive contracting process', *Journal of Law and Economics*, **21** (2), 297–326.

Knight, F.H. (1921), *Risk, Uncertainty, and Profit*, New York: August M. Kelley.

Langlois, R. (1992), 'External economies and economic progress: the case of the microcomputer industry', *Business History Review*, **66** (1), 1–50.

Leibenstein, H. (1987), *Inside the Firm*, Cambridge, MA: Harvard University Press.

Lester, R.A. (1946), 'Shortcomings of marginal analysis for wage-employment problems', *American Economic Review*, **36** (1), 63–82.

Loasby, B.J. (1999), 'Marshall's theory of the firm', in R.E. Backhouse and J. Creedy (eds), *From Classical Economics to the Theory of the Firm: Essays in Honour of D.P. O'Brien*, Cheltenham, UK and Northampton, MA, USA: Edward Elgar, pp. 175–93.

Machlup, F. (1946), 'Marginal analysis and empirical research', *American Economic Review*, **36** (4), 519–54.

Machlup, F. (1967), 'Theories of the firm: marginalist, behavioral, managerial', *American Economic Review*, **57** (1), 1–33.

March, J.G. and H.A. Simon (1958), *Organizations*, New York: Wiley.

Marglin, S. (1974), 'What do bosses do? The origins and functions of hierarchy in capitalist production', *Review of Radical Political Economics*, **6** (2), 60–112.

Marris, R. (1964), *The Economic Theory of 'Managerial' Capitalism*, London: Macmillan.

Marshall, A. (1890), *Principles of Economics*, 9th edn 1961, G.W. Guillebaud (ed.), London: Macmillan.

Marshall, A. (1919), *Industry and Trade*, 4th edn 1923, London: Macmillan.

Mill, J.S. (1848), *Principles of Political Economy*, 7th edn 1909, W.J. Ashley (ed.), London: Longmans, 1909.

Mongin, P. (1997), 'The marginalist controversy', in J. Davis, W. Hands and U. Mäki (eds), *Handbook of Economic Methodology*, Cheltenham, UK and Lyme, NH, USA: Edward Elgar, pp. 558–62.

Nelson, R.R. and S.G. Winter (1982), *An Evolutionary Theory of Economic Change*, Cambridge, MA: Harvard University Press.

Penrose, E.T. (1959), *The Theory of the Growth of the Firm*, Oxford: Blackwell.

Pigou, A.C. (1912), *Wealth and Welfare*, London: Macmillan.

Pigou, A.C. (1932), *The Economics of Welfare*, 4th edn, London: Macmillan.

Powell, W.W. (1990), 'Neither market nor hierarchy: network forms of organization', *Research in Organizational Behavior*, **12**, 295–336.

Richardson, G.B. (1972), 'The organisation of industry', *Economic Journal*, **82** (327), 883–96.

Robinson, E.A.G. (1931), *The Structure of Competitive Industry*, Cambridge: Cambridge University Press.

Robinson, J. (1933), *The Economics of Imperfect Competition*, 2nd edn 1969, London: Macmillan.

Say, J.-B. (1803), *Traité d'Economie Politique ou Simple Exposition de la Manière dont se Forment, se*

Distribuent ou se Consomment les Richesses, English trans. 1964, *A Treatise on Political Economy: or the Production, Distribution and Consumption of Wealth*, New York: A.M. Kelley.

Schumpeter, J.A. (1911), *The Theory of Economic Development*, trans. R. Opie (1934), Cambridge: Harvard University Press.

Schumpeter, J.A. (1942), *Capitalism, Socialism and Democracy*, New York: Harper.

Simon, H.A. (1955), 'A behavioral model of rational choice', *Quarterly Journal of Economics*, **69** (1), 99–118.

Simon, H.A. (1991), 'Organization and markets', *Journal of Economic Perspectives*, **5** (2), 25–44.

Smith, A. (1776), *An Inquiry into the Nature and Causes of the Wealth of Nations*, 2 vols, reprinted 1976, R.H. Campbell, A.S. Skinner and W.B. Todd (eds), Oxford: Oxford University Press.

Stiglitz, J.E. (1974), 'Incentives and risk sharing in sharecropping', *Review of Economic Studies*, **41** (2), 219–55.

Teece, D.J. (1982), 'Towards an economic theory of the multi-product firm', *Journal of Economic Behavior and Organization*, **3** (1), 39–64.

Veblen, T.B. (1904), *The Theory of Business Enterprise*, New York: Charles Scribners.

Veblen, T.B. (1923), *Absentee Ownership and Business Enterprise in Recent Times: The Case of America*, New York: Huebsch.

Viner, J. (1931), 'Cost curves and supply curves', *Zeitschrift für Nationalökonomie*, **3** (1), 23–46.

Williamson, O.E. (1964), *The Economics of Discretionary Behavior: Managerial Objectives in a Theory of the Firm*, Englewood Cliffs, NJ: Prentice-Hall.

Williamson, O.E. (1975), *Markets and Hierarchies: Analysis and Antitrust Implications*, New York: Free Press.

Williamson, O.E. (1979), 'Transaction-cost economics: the governance of contractual relations', *Journal of Law and Economics*, **22** (2), 233–61.

Williamson, O.E. (1985), *The Economic Institutions of Capitalism*, New York: Free Press.

Uncertainty and information

Uncertainty and information are ideas that have a central role in contemporary economics in the domain of decision theory. The expected utility hypothesis is a powerful instrument widely used in theoretical and empirical analysis. However, the leading role in this story is not played by utility, as is usual in the traditional reconstructions of historians of economic thought, but by probability. Uncertainty is in fact a multifaceted concept. It refers to a subjective condition or a mental status of an agent not knowing for certain the consequences of a present or a future event (subjective uncertainty). It refers also to an objective status of things that may results in different outcomes (frequency of occurrences), or are knowable only through careful measurements subject to errors (objective uncertainty). In order for the modern developments to happen, two conditions were required: both objective and subjective uncertainty needed to be treated with the device of probability. Both these recognitions slowly emerged between the seventeenth and the twentieth centuries.

From the Origins to the St Petersburg Paradox

The idea of probability originates with gambling. The so-called "classical theory of probability" was developed in order to deal with the particular objective uncertainty in the games of chance. Its history was masterfully reconstructed by Ian Hacking (1975). Mathematical theory of probability is generally taken to begin in 1654 with a correspondence between Blaise Pascal and Pierre de Fermat where some gambling problems were analysed. In 1657 Christiaan Huygens published a *Libellus de Ratiociniis in Ludo Aleae* (*On Calculations in the Game of Dice*) that "for nearly half a century . . . was the unique introduction to the theory of probability" (David 1962: 115). In this *Libellus* the notion of expectation in gambling was clearly defined in reference to the problem of the fair price for a gamble. The notion of fair price or of a fair entry fee for a game of chance was of practical importance for gamblers deciding to participate in a bet; or for when it was necessary to divide a stake because the gamble was interrupted before its conclusion; or again for when a gambler was asked by another to sell his or her place in the gamble. The mixture of money and chance was considered a natural idea, and the basic tenet of "equi-possibility", as it was called later by Pierre-Simon de Laplace, was based on the symmetry (fairness) of the device used for a gamble. It was therefore possible to consider only games with even chance (even lay). The interest for these problems most likely originated from a robust economic incentive. The rough technology used for the construction of the gambling machine (dice, roulette wheels, and so on) allowed professional gamblers to systematically gain if they made their bets after having discovered the odds realized in a single device. The alternative reference point is the law of chance governing an ideally fair device. The notion of the expected value of a game of chance is the value of a game in a fair device. The fair price is then equated to the expected value of a fair game. This is Huygens's postulate:

> That my Chance or Expectation to win any thing is worth just such a Sum, as wou'd procure me in the same Chance an Expectation at a fair Lay. As for Example, if any one shou'd put 3 Shillings in one Hand, without letting me know which, and 7 in the other, and give me Choice

of either of them; I say, it is the same thing as if he shou'd give me 5 Shillings; because with 5 Shillings I can, at a fair Lay, procure the same even Chance or Expectation to win 3 or 7 Shillings. (Huygens 1657: 1)

At around the same time Pascal formulated a problem now considered as the first appearance of decision theory under uncertainty. The question "Either God is or he is not" is considered similar to the tossing of a (fair) coin which will come down head or tail; and "you must wager":

Let us weigh up the gain and the loss involved in calling heads that God exists. Let us assess the two cases: if you win you win everything, if you lose you lose nothing. Do not hesitate then; wager that he does exist . . . here there is an infinity of infinitely happy life to be won. (Pascal 1670 [1985]: 154)

Pascal's wager testified for the first time that it is possible in the calculation of the expected value of a game to exchange monetary value with the happiness derived from winning the game. This is the first conceptual step toward Daniel Bernoulli's solution of the St Petersburg paradox.

In 1738 Daniel Bernoulli published in Latin his "Specimen Theoria Nova de Mensura Sortis" ("Exposition of a new theory on the measurement of risk"). In fact, the general problem tackled by Bernoulli is the classical one about the fair price of a gamble. Contrary to Huygens' approach – the fair price of a game is its expected value – Bernoulli proposed to replace money with the advantage (Latin word: *emolumentum*) derived from money. So, the fair price of the game became the emolumentum medium of the game. In the first English translation (1954) "emolumentum" became "utility", and "emolumentum medium" became "moral expectation" giving a modern flavour to Bernoulli's intuition:

If the utility of each possible profit expectation is multiplied by the number of ways in which it can occur, and we then divide the sum of these products by the total number of possible cases, a mean utility [moral expectation] will be obtained, and the profit which corresponds to this utility will equal the value of the risk in question. (Bernoulli 1738 [1954]: 24)

All of the three cited authors lacked the explicit reference to the notion of probability. This is not surprising because they used the more basic idea of odds ratio. They had in mind something corresponding to the aleatory notion of possibility: in the ideal model of the game of chance it is possible to list all possible outcomes and to count the favourable outcomes. In the definition of expectation there was not probability, but the ratio of favourable to total possible outcomes. According to Hacking (1975), the idea of possible outcome was interpreted in terms of a physical possibility, or the physical propensity of each outcome to happen. The application of this kind of analysis was therefore confined to cases where it was possible to list all possible outcomes; each outcome having the same physical propensity to happen.

Laplace accomplished the treatment of these questions in terms of probability for good (Laplace 1812: 432–45). It was through Laplace's work that the distinction between *fortune physique* (physical advantage) and *fortune morale* (moral advantage) became common in nineteenth-century probability treatises (Todhunter 1865). Since then, the notions of the expected value of a game and of expected utility may be written in its modern notation, replacing odds ratios with probability. Let x_i be the monetary value – the Laplacean *fortune physique* – of the *i*-th outcome of a gamble and p_i its probability; then the expected value of the gamble is $E = \sum_{i=1}^{n} p_i x_i$. If we let $u(x_i)$ be the moral advantage derived – that is, the subjective evaluation in terms of utility or satisfaction – from the monetary value x_i, it is possible to calculate the expected utility of the gamble as $EU = \sum_{i=1}^{n} p_i u(x_i)$.

Bernoulli's memoir is universally known for containing the St Petersburg paradox – so called because it was published in the *Commentarii* of the St Petersburg Academy. When the fair price of a gamble is equated to its expected value, and a particular gamble is considered, the following paradox emerges (the seminal contribution on this is Samuelson 1977): the particular gamble consists in repeatedly tossing a coin in the air; if heads comes up on the first toss, the gambler will receive 2 shillings; if it does not come up until the second toss, he will receive 4 shillings; heads only on the third toss will pay 8 shillings, and so on. The expected value for the *n*-th toss is $\frac{1}{2^n} 2^n$ shillings; if the game continues indefinitely, the expected value of the game is infinite, given that $E = \sum_{i=1}^{\infty} \frac{1}{2^n} 2^n = \infty$. The fair price of the game is then infinite, but simple observation tells us that "no one would be willing to purchase it at a moderately high price" (Bernoulli 1738 [1954]: 31). If, according to Bernoulli, the expected value is replaced by a bounded expected utility, the paradox vanishes. Bernoulli proposed the following model where a person possessing a certain quantity of money w, receives an additional quantity dw. Bernoulli maintained that the relative value of this increase is directly proportional to dw and inversely proportional to w, that is $du = k\frac{dw}{w}$ where k is a constant. From this derives the logarithmic function of the *fortune morale*, that is, $u = a + k \log w$. When this formula is used, the fair price of the St Petersburg game becomes finite; a reasonable result for thought experiments with gambling agents.

Subjective Probability and Mercantile Speculations

Despite Laplace's advancement, the applicability of expectations (mathematical or moral) continued to be limited to gambling or to situations where it was possible to define probability as in games of chance. In fact, the classical theory of probability was developed from the systematic study of gambling and it turned out to be impossible to use it for a theory of choice applied to domains different from gambling. The limits of probability semantics narrowed the boundaries of its practical application. The passage from this domain to the application of probability to more general problems of choice under uncertainty – the extensions of Pascal's wager to everyday problems – happened sometime in the first part of nineteenth century. This development was determined by a change in the philosophical interpretation of probabilities.

Antoine-Augustin Cournot (1843) in the *Exposition de la Théorie des Chances et des Probabilités* developed a pluralist view of probabilities. He maintained the notion of "mathematical probability", traditionally associated with gambling, defined as the ratio of favourable outcomes to total outcomes, and put it side by side to a strictly subjective interpretation of probability, depending on the status of imperfect knowledge of an individual (Cournot 1843: 438). This kind of probability governs the rules regarding the stakes in a "marché aléatoire" (aleatory market). He explicitly introduced, perhaps for the first time, the modern notion of lottery as the general device to treat problems of choice under uncertainty (Cournot 1843: 89–90). He suggested that in a lottery where the prize is a generic good, every ticket may be considered as an "eventual right" over the good. Every ticket obviously may be sold in a market and its fair price ("valeur vénale") is its mathematical expectation, where probability is defined in reference to the subjective status of knowledge of agents. At the same time, Cournot, having rejected utility in the theory of demand (Fry and Ekelund 1971), also strongly rejected the idea of expected utility, considering it as "arbitrary" and "without real applications". Considering utility and not probability as the main problem for the development of the expected utility framework is an idea that emerged probably for the first time with Cournot. It is the story that, from this time on, characterizes all historical reconstructions of this problem made by economists.

In the same time period in England Augustus de Morgan explicitly used mathematical expectation as a device to model "mercantile speculations" and "every species of affair in which no absolute certainty exists" (De Morgan 1838: 98). For de Morgan the nature of probability was also very different from the one proposed in classical theory: "Probability is the feeling of the mind, not the inherent property of a set of circumstances" (De Morgan 1838: 7), and this probability is different for different persons depending on the status of their knowledge and "impressions". This enlargement of the notion of probability paved the way to its rigorous application to all "questions involving loss and gain" (De Morgan 1838: 103): that is, not only to gambling but also to matters of "commercial speculation" (De Morgan 1847: 404) and principally to problems regarding insurance offices. The passage from the notion of mathematical expectation to that of "moral expectation" involves, according to De Morgan, a supplementary problem concerning "the temperament of the individual", that is, in modern jargon, the question of risk propensity and aversion:

> different persons will look forward in the same circumstances with different degrees of hope. One man will consider himself better off than before when he has bartered one pound certain for an even chance of two; a second will contemplate loss more strongly than gain, and will consider himself damnified by the exchange. (De Morgan 1847: 409)

Indeed, according to De Morgan the main problem in practical applications arises not from the side of utility, but from the side of probability: when the probability of an outcome is very small, and benefits depend upon this vanishing probability, then "the mathematical expectation is not a sufficient approximation to the actual phenomenon of the mind, even when the fortune of the player forms no part of the consideration" (De Morgan 1847: 409). In the St Petersburg paradox, for example, neither mathematical expectation nor moral expectation may be considered as the fair price of the game, because both depend on very small probabilities. This intuition is similar to the notion of weight of probability in prospect theory (see below).

Marginalist Expected Utility and the Frequentist Dead End

Cournot and De Morgan laid the basis for modern choice under uncertainty, and both underlined the conceptual problems related to the use of utility and probability for this purpose. Schlee (1992) documented that during the so-called marginalist revolution, the expected utility was used to analyse a variety of decisions made under uncertainty, a result ascribed to the definition of a sound notion of marginal (decreasing) utility.

From the point of view adopted here this explanation is only partial. A more correct one requires a distinction between scholars that in the last 30 years of the nineteenth century discussed these questions in reference to treatises on probability, ethics, psychology and philosophy in general, and those who considered the problem as exclusively belonging, so to speak, to the economic profession. William S. Jevons and Francis Y. Edgeworth are examples of the first kind of approach, Alfred Marshall and Arthur Cecil Pigou of the second.

Bernoulli's hypothesis was "self-evident" for Jevons who took its application not only to gambling but also to commerce for granted (Jevons 1879: 173–4). The basic structure of human reasoning "in selecting a course of action which depends on uncertain events, as, in fact, does everything in life", consists in multiplying

> the quantity of feeling attaching to every future event by the fraction denoting its probability. A great casualty, which is very unlikely to happen, may not be so important as a slight casualty which is nearly sure to happen. Almost unconsciously we make calculations of this kind more or less accurately in all the ordinary affairs of life; and in systems of life, fire, marine, or other insurance, we carry out the calculations to great perfection. In all industry directed to future purposes, we must take similar account of our want of knowledge of what is to be. (Jevons 1879: 36)

Behind all this there was not only a new idea of utility, but also a logical theory of probability developed in *The Principles of Science* (Jevons 1874). According to Jevons, probability is the "noblest creation of the intellect" (Jevons 1874: 200), in that it "deals with quantity of knowledge, an expression of which a precise explanation and measure can presently be given. An event is only probable when our knowledge of it is diluted with ignorance, and exact calculation is needed to discriminate how much we do and do not know" (Jevons 1874: 199). According to Jevons, the idea that probability "belongs wholly to the mind" (Jevons 1874: 198) does not signify that it is personalistic, as in De Morgan. On the contrary, it is the basis of "rational expectation" obtained "by measuring the comparative amounts of knowledge and ignorance" (Jevons 1874: 200). The principal value of the theory is normative, consisting "in correcting and guiding our belief, and rendering our states of mind and consequent actions harmonious with our knowledge of exterior conditions" (Jevons 1874: 199).

Marshall's *Principles of Economics* (Marshall 1890 [1961]) professionalized the question of choice under uncertainty; it was treated in a footnote in chapter 6 of book 3 and in note 9 of the mathematical appendix. Marshall cited the introductory chapter of Jevons as his main reference. He used expected utility to solve truly economic problems. In particular:

> to measure numerically the present value of a future pleasure, on the supposition that we know, (i) its amount, (ii) the date at which it will come, if it comes at all, (iii) the chance that it will come, and (iv) the rate at which the person in question discounts future pleasures. (Marshall 1890 [1961]: 135)

Its present value is the value of future expected utility (ibid.: 840). He then discussed the problem that the maximization of the expected utility of wealth is inconsistent with gambling at fair odds, introducing the idea that gambling may be explained if the pleasure of gambling is separately considered (Schlee 1992).

Marshall's treatment paved the way to the (moderate) diffusion of expected utility hypothesis in economics – almost always associated with the assumption of diminishing marginal utility. Scholars applied it in order to explain advantages of fair insurance or the necessity of a reward for risk bearing (Schlee 1992: 737). Pigou (1924) treated risk or "uncertainty bearing" as a factor of production. On the whole, uncertainty in the post-Marshallian tradition was treated routinely and in a soft manner, probably following Marshall's statement that the measurement of expected utility "belongs to Hedonics, and not properly to Economics" (Marshall 1890 [1961]: 840).

Edgeworth adopted a radically divergent view since he was completely engaged in the traditional vision according to which probability theory was the main problem (Baccini 2009: 2011). His reference point was the frequentist approach to probability, presented in the epoch-making work of John Venn *The Logic of Chance* (1888). Both Edgeworth and Venn agreed that a coherent frequentist theory prevented the cogent use of probability for choice under uncertainty for logical and philosophical reasons. From a logical point of view, frequentist probability is objective, it is defined as relative frequency, and may be applied properly only to a particular class of things: series. Probability serves to construct assertions such as, "The relative frequency of individuals with property R in population P is x". If probability is not a property of individual events constituting the series, then it is invalid to infer from the preceding one an assertion such as "The probability that individual i, who belongs to population P, enjoys property R is x". This has relevant effects for decision theory: if choices are exercised essentially around single events, probability can be of no help in the choice of actions, being unable to say anything at all about those events. As a consequence, probability cannot be used as a decision-making instrument other than in extremely rare cases where some very peculiar conditions hold (Baccini 2001). The second point in the argumentation was related to the nineteenth-century debate on the theory of human action. According to the philosopher Alexander Bain (1859), belief is preparedness to act, a necessary condition for human action. In order to apply probability to decision theory, the relations between belief and probability had to be defined properly. At the end of different strategies of reasoning, Venn and Edgeworth concluded that probability is not a direct measurement of belief, that it does not necessarily give rise to belief, and, as a consequence, that it is not useful for a theory of human choice (Baccini 1997, 2001, 2007).

At the turn of the nineteenth century two roads are clearly delineated for uncertainty in economics. The first shuts out uncertainty and expected utility from the professional toolbox of economists, limiting its use to the narrow problems of gambling and insurance. The second road, inherited by the secular tradition of probabilists and philosophers, faces the frequentist dead end.

Keynes's *Treatise on Probability*

This is the context in which John Maynard Keynes wrote his doctoral dissertation that he discussed in 1908 and published much later in a revised form as *A Treatise on Probability* (Keynes 1921). Bradley W. Bateman (1996) argues that Keynes's *Treatise* found its origin in reflections on George E. Moore's *Principia Ethica* (1903) and, in particular, in his intuition that the weak point of Moore's argument lay in the use of a naive version of frequentist probability. When Keynes began to study probability theory, he discovered the logical and practical limitations of the frequentist tradition. Keynes's problem became, therefore, not so much that of criticising Moore's probability, but rather of finding an alternative theory that made it possible to consider probability as a guide to action (Baccini 2004). Indeed, according to Keynes:

> the importance of probability can only be derived from the judgement that it is rational to be guided by it in action; and a practical dependence on it can only be justified by a judgement that in action we *ought* to act to take some account of it. It is for this reason that probability is to us the "guide of life". (Keynes 1921: 323, original emphasis)

The *Treatise* contains the development of a new logical theory of probability: it is concerned with the "degree of belief" which is *rational* to entertain in given conditions of knowledge, and not, as in De Morgan, merely with the actual beliefs of particular individuals "which may or may not be rational" (Keynes 1921: 4). According to Keynes, there is a direct connection between probability, rational belief and action: to have a belief signifies being disposed to act on the basis of it: "the probable is the hypothesis on which it is rational for us to act" (Keynes 1921: 307).

However, the question is not so simple "for the obvious reason that of two hypotheses it may be rational to act on the less probable if it leads to the greater good" (Keynes 1921: 307). Mathematical expectation and expected utility maximization are not the right tools to solve these kinds of problems. Keynes raised three formidable objections to the theory of mathematical expectation, all from the side of probability. The first was that probability is not fully measurable; the second, that in mathematical expectation the weight of the argument, that is, the amount of evidence upon which probability is based, is not considered; the third, that the element of "risk" is completely ignored, assuming that "an even chance of heaven or hell is precisely as much to be desired as the certain attainment of a state of mediocrity" (Keynes 1921: 312). To overcome these objections, Keynes proposed a "conventional coefficient", substituting the probability value in the mathematical expectation formula, and considering together the probability of "goodness", the risk associated with it and the weight of evidence, that is, the degree of unreliability or ambiguity of the information on which the probability value is based (Brady 1993). The Keynesian coefficient may be formulated as $c = \frac{2pw}{(1 + q)(1 + w)}$ where p is probability, $q = 1 - p$ is the risk coefficient and $0 \leq w \leq 1$ the weight of the argument. The introduction of this coefficient generalizes the expected value formula by transforming it, according to Keynes, into a useful tool guiding actions in conditions of uncertainty. In the Keynesian formulation, the standard case – when an agent makes her choice using the expected value of different outcomes – becomes a very particular case. In this case the agent maintains that the information at her disposal is unambiguous and certain, that is, $w = 1$; and at the same time she is risk neutral, in the particular sense that she prefers not to consider the risk value of her choice, and then she drops q from the Keynesian coefficient.

Keynes added to this exposition a paragraph containing a famous disclaimer regarding the usefulness of mathematics in moral sciences that attracted the attention of posterity. As a consequence, Keynes's rejection of expected utility was categorized, starting at least from Shackle (1952), as a by-product of a general scepticism about the possibility to apply mathematical tools to economic problems. Instead, his contribution may be better understood as an escape from both utilitarianism (the refusal of the use of utility value) and frequentism, and as an anticipation of a modern approach to choice under uncertainty focusing on the problem of weighting probability values with the measures of the reliability of information on which probability values are based.

Von Neumann and Morgenstern's Utility

According to Ellsberg, "it was the feeling that the emphasis on mathematical expectation was arbitrary and unrealistic which led to the decline of the concept even before doubt arose that a measurable utility could be discovered to make it meaningful" (1954: 537). The decline of the Bernoulli–Marshallian tradition (Marschak 1938; Tintner 1942; Friedman and Savage 1948; Arrow 1951) was stopped by the appearance of von Neumann and Morgenstern's book (1944), containing a complete and, to professional economists, satisfactory axiomatic treatment of choice under uncertainty. It represented a dramatic break in continuity and opened the way to a central field in twentieth-century economic analysis.

Von Neumann and Morgenstern's discussion of the question of utility was "mainly opportunistic" (von Neumann and Morgenstern 1953: 8). They needed a cardinal measure of utility to be considered "identical" to "money or a single monetary commodity" (unrestrictedly divisible, substitutable and transferable) (von Neumann and Morgenstern 1953: 8). Their goal was to define a cardinal notion of utility without following the unsatisfactory patterns of their predecessors. In particular they were interested in a cardinality not based on a more or less introspective measure of pleasure or satisfaction derived from goods. They tried also to divorce their approach from cardinality based on the comparability of preference differences (Fishburn 1989: 131). The solution consisted in the definition of numerical utility "as being that thing for which the calculus of mathematical expectation is legitimate" (von Neumann and Morgenstern 1953: 28). The basic operation in deriving a cardinal utility index is the analysis of a situation where an agent is choosing between a sure outcome and two possible outcomes with given probabilities. In order to fix the origin and unit of the utility index, arbitrary numbers are assigned to the two outcomes A and B, with an order respecting the order of preference of the agent. For the sake of simplicity, set the utility of the worst outcome A to $U_A = 0$, and of the best B to $U_B = 1$. Consider now a third outcome C which the agent ranks between the first two. The utility index of C is the probability p at which the agent is indifferent between having C with certainty or participating in a lottery with a probability p of winning B, and $(1 - p)$ of winning A. Thus $U_C = pU_B + (1 - p)U_A = p$. The same reasoning may be applied to define other utility numbers reflecting other choices consistent with this last one for other intermediate outcomes. If, for example, an alternative outcome D which the agent ranks between C and B is considered, the utility index is $U_D = q$ where q is the probability for which the agent is indifferent between having D with certainty or participating in a lottery with a probability q of winning B and $(1 - q)$ of winning C. The only consistency requirement is that $U_B > U_D > U_C$. It is therefore possible to elicit the entire utility function of the agent (for modern expositions, see Binmore 2009; Gilboa 2009); the utility index so defined is unique up to a linear transformation that is a cardinal measure of utility. It is defined directly through the observation of choices of agents in risk situations, and it allows us to describe agents with different patterns of behaviours in risk situations. Von Neumann and Morgenstern derived this operational result from an "axiomatic treatment of numerical utilities". A "controversial" axiom is also introduced, according to which the agent is indifferent between two possible outcomes which are derivable from each other according to the rules of probability. On this basis it is possible to reduce systematically to a simple lottery lotteries in which prizes are other lotteries. The controversial nature of this axiom rests on the fact that it constrains the agent to be indifferent about the number of steps of the gamble, since the interest lies only in the final possible outcome, and not in intermediate possible winnings (Ellsberg 1954: 543). Now it is finally possible to calculate the expected utility of different possible outcomes as $EU = \sum p_i U(x_i)$, where $U(x_i)$ are the utility values constructed with the operations described above regarding possible outcomes (x_i), and not the utility values of riskless outcome, as in the Bernoulli–Marshallian tradition. Consider two even lotteries with prizes respectively A and D, and C and D, as defined above. The expected utility of the first one is $EU_1 = 0.5 \times U_A + 0.5 \times U_D = 0.5p$, and of the second one $EU_2 = 0.5 \times U_C + 0.5 \times U_D = 0.5p + 0.5q$; the two lotteries can be ordered in relation to their expected utilities $EU_2 > EU_1$; the rational agents choose respecting this order. The choice of agents can be described as they are maximizing their expected utility.

From our point of view, the nature of probability must still be discussed. Von Neumann and Morgenstern's construction used probability as an individual numerical estimate of utility. They therefore stated clearly that a "subjective concept" of probability "would not serve" their purpose. They insisted "upon the alternative, perfectly well founded interpretation of probability as frequency in long runs. This gives directly the necessary numerical foothold" (von Neumann and Morgenstern 1953: 19). Moreover they did not cite any authors on this point. It is therefore possible to conjecture that they were unaware of, or considered irrelevant, the discussion about the proper domain and applicability of frequentist probability. They evidently considered the discussion on the nature of probability involved in their theory as a minor point. This interpretation is supported also by a footnote in which they suggested that it is possible to make a joint axiomatization of probability and utility (von Neumann and Morgenstern 1953: 19, fn 2), without resorting to statistical probability.

Von Neumann and Morgenstern's book opened a lively discussion among economists in the course of which emerged the complete professionalization of the theme. The first question was that of cardinal utility: Von Neumann and Morgenstern were accused of taking economics back to the pre-Pareto and Hicksian era (Baumol 1951). The second concerned the kind of probability assumed. This probability, as underlined by Savage, "can apply fruitfully only to repetitive events" and cannot be used to elicit "which of several actions is the most promising" because probability is not assigned to the truth of propositions (Savage 1954 [1972]: 4). It was through searching for a solution to this last problem that Savage generalized the structure of the von Neumann and Morgenstern utility.

The Emergence of Subjective Expected Utility as the Mainstream Paradigm

As we have seen, von Neumann and Morgenstern derived utility given the notion of statistical probability. Some years earlier, Bruno de Finetti (1937) had developed a notion of subjective probability starting from the choice problem of an individual maximizing an expected monetary value. Frank P. Ramsey (1926 [1931]), in discussing Keynes's probability, developed a subjective view of probability and utility without assuming any of these concepts as primitive. Savage adopted also this strategy. He "virtually copied" (Savage 1954 [1972]: 97) the treatment reserved by von Neumann and Morgenstern to utility by developing the idea of a subjective probability. Savage's model includes two primitive concepts: outcomes, as usual, and states, as the list of all scenarios that may happen. The outcome is the conjoined result of the agent's choice of an act and of the unfolding of a state of the world. When the agent makes her choice over acts, she does not reason in terms of numbers, utility and probabilities; but on a very simple framework containing the description of possible states and the unique outcome resulting from the choice of every act in every state (that is, when an act has been chosen by an agent, and a state of the world has been unfolded, only an outcome is necessarily verified). With this simple structure and seven axioms, Savage demonstrated that both a (bounded) utility function and probability measure exist in such a way that decisions are made as if the agent is maximizing the expectation of the utility relative to the probability measure (for a presentation, see Gilboa 2009: 94–112). More precisely, the subjective expected utility hypothesis is equivalent to the joint hypothesis that the agent possesses a subjective probabilistic belief about the states of the world $\mu(s_i)$, and a von Neumann and Morgenstern utility function over outcomes $U(x_i)$; and she evaluates acts according to a preference function (for a finite state space) of the form $W = \sum_{i=1}^{n} U(x_i)\mu(s_i)$. Savage restricted the applicability of his theory to what he called a "small world". In a small world it is always possible for an agent to "look . . . before you leap" given that it is possible to have a description so complete that the consequences of every action would be known. This idea can be expressed from another point of view: an agent in a small world can take account in advance of the impact of all future possible information on his or her subjective beliefs about the state of the world. The consistency of an agent's choices are guaranteed if his or her personal degrees of belief are coherent in such a way that a Dutch book – a system of bets which guarantee that anyone who takes them all on will lose no matter what happens – could not be made against him or her.

Savage's results reinforced the von Neumann and Morgenstern construction, and the subjective expected utility became the major paradigm in decision making in the second half of the twentieth century. According to this view the expected utility maximization with respect to a subjective probability is the only rational way of behaviour suitable for cogently treating every kind of economic problem characterized by the presence of uncertainty. The Arrow–Pratt measure of risk aversion provided a powerful operative tool (Pratt 1964; Arrow 1965). Since then applications of the expected utility model flowered in problems of optimal savings, international trade, portfolio selection, environmental economics, and economic analysis of law.

Contemporary Developments and Prospect Theory

The success of the von Neumann and Morgenstern model was not overshadowed by research results documenting that expected utility maximization is not a good predictor of real choices. Maurice Allais (1953) provided the first evidence that people tend to violate axioms of von Neumann and Morgenstern, by placing more weight on certainty than the standard theory predicts. Daniel Ellsberg (1961) showed that people behave in a way that cannot be described by Savage's subjective probability. In particular people tend to be "ambiguity averse", that is people prefer situations where probabilities are known to situations where probabilities are unknown, thus violating one of the Savage's axioms, the so called sure thing principle. (An excellent review of this literature may be found again in Schoemaker 1982).

Contemporary developments try to cope with these kinds of problems by adopting different strategies. The first strategy is probably the more conservative, because it maintains the subjective notion of probability. It consists in generalizations of the expected utility model by removing linearity in the probabilities and by positing non-linear functional forms for the preference function. Several such forms have been formally proposed and axiomatized, most are capable of generating well known features, such as risk aversion and violations of independence axioms (Machina 2008). A second strategy consists in replacing probability with alternative notions of belief able to describe the way that people make decisions, or the way they can be convinced to make rational decisions when standard probabilities cannot be defined. The basic intuition may be grasped by the following example. Consider two coins. The experience of repeated flips of the first coin suggest that it is a fair one; therefore, it is reasonable to give probability 0.5 to head and 0.5 to tail. Suppose that the other coin is completely unknown; you have no reason to prefer one side to the other (symmetric information). If we decide to give probability 0.5 to both head and tail, then this assignment is very different from the preceding one based on frequency experience. This last kind of assignment does not necessarily respect the additive rule for probability. For example: we can legitimately assign, respecting symmetric lack of information, a non-additive probability $v(H) = v(T) = 0.4$; nonetheless it is true that $v(H < T) = 1$. Building on this intuition, in the so-called Choquet expected utility the standard probability is replaced by a capacity or a non-additive probability. These models explain most of the observed paradoxes but they also offer simple but flexible representations, and allow for more diversified patterns of behaviour under uncertainty (Schmeidler 1989). A third strategy consists in considering explicitly how beliefs are constructed. In the case-based decision theory (Gilboa and Schmeidler 1995), cases are considered primitive and a system of axiom was construed permitting the choice of the best act based on its past performance in similar cases. Each act is evaluated by the sum of the utility levels that resulted from using this act in past cases, each weighted by the similarity of that past case to the problem at hand.

Probably, the most innovative contributions to this stream of literature came from Daniel Kahneman and Amos Tversky. From the early 1960s they developed a systematic study of several violations of the standard assumptions of stability of preferences, and of invariance of choices with respect to the particular kind of description of risky prospects. Their laboratory experiments and those of their followers appear to be "a knockdown refutation of the claim that the von Neumann and Morgenstern theory is usually a good predictor of how ordinary people behave" (Binmore 2009: 58). In their approach, the so-called prospect theory, the von Neumann and Morgenstern utility is replaced by the psychological values of gain and loss. This psychological value is similar to the Edgeworthian notion of utility as experienced pleasure, objectively measurable by means of a technical device called "hedonimeter" (Baccini 2011). Also "the decision weights that people assign to outcomes are not identical to the probabilities of these outcomes, contrary to the expectation principle. . . . The expectation principle, by which values are weighted by their probability, is poor psychology" (Kahneman 2011). In this case the line of reasoning recalls Keynes's notion of the weight of an argument. In particular

Kahneman and Tversky (1979) documented the following: (1) a psychophysics of value according to which people are risk averse in the domain of gains and risk seeking in the domain of losses; (2) a psychophysics of chance in which people overweight sure things and improbable events, relative to events of moderate probability; and (3) that decision problems can be described or framed in multiple ways that give rise to different preferences, contrary to the invariance criterion of rational choice.

Prospect theory is considered as the best available description of how people evaluate risk in experimental settings. Despite this, there are relatively few broadly accepted applications to economics (for a review see Barberis 2013). A probable explanation may be that prospect theory represents a paradigm shift in the theory of choice under uncertainty and therefore it is not easily adaptable to the problems discussed in the domain of normal economics.

ALBERTO BACCINI

See also:

Maurice Allais (I); Daniel Bernoulli (I); British marginalism (II); Economics and philosophy (III); Francis Ysidro Edgeworth (I); John Maynard Keynes (I); Frank H. Knight (I); Alfred Marshall (I); John von Neumann (I); Frank Plumpton Ramsey (I); Utilitarianism and anti-utilitarianism (III).

References and further reading

Allais, M. (1953), 'Le Comportement de l'Homme Rationnel devant le Risque: Critique des Postulats et Axiomes de l'Ecole Americaine', *Econometrica*, **21** (4), 503–46.
Arrow, K.J. (1951), 'Alternative approaches to the theory of choice in risk-taking situations', *Econometrica*, **19** (4), 404–37.
Arrow, K.J. (1965), *Aspects of the Theory of Risk-Bearing*, Helsinki: Yrjö Jahnssonin Säätiö.
Baccini, A. (1997), 'Edgeworth on the fundamentals of choice under uncertainty', *History of Economic Ideas*, **5** (2), 27–51.
Baccini, A. (2001), 'Frequentist probability and choice under uncertainty', *History of Political Economy*, **33** (4), 743–72.
Baccini, A. (2004), 'High pressure and black clouds: Keynes and the frequentist theory of probability', *Cambridge Journal of Economics*, **28** (5), 653–66.
Baccini, A. (2007), 'Edgeworth on the foundations of ethics and probability', *European Journal of the History of Economic Thought*, **14** (1), 79–96.
Baccini, A. (2009), 'F.Y. Edgeworth's treatise on probabilities', *History of Political Economy*, **41** (1), 143–62.
Baccini, A. (2011), 'Francis Ysidro Edgeworth on the regularity of law and the impartiality of chance', in T. Boylan, R. Prendergast and J. Turner (eds), *A History of Irish Economic Thought*, London: Routledge, pp. 233–48.
Bain, A. (1859), *The Emotions and the Will*, London: J.W. Parker and Son.
Barberis, N.C. (2013), 'Thirty years of prospect theory in economics: a review and assessment', *Journal of Economic Perspectives*, **27** (1), 173–95.
Bateman, B.W. (1996), *Keynes's Uncertain Revolution*, Ann Arbor, MI: University of Michigan Press.
Baumol, W.J. (1951), 'The Neumann–Morgenstern Utility Index – an ordinalist view', *Journal of Political Economy*, **59** (1), 61–6.
Bernoulli, D. (1738), 'Specimen Theoria Nova de Mensura Sortis', English trans. 1954, 'Exposition of a new theory on the measurement of risk', *Econometrica*, **22** (1), 23–36.
Binmore, K.G. (2009), *Rational Decisions*, Princeton, NJ: Princeton University Press.
Brady, M.E. (1993), 'J.M. Keynes's theoretical approach to decision-making under conditions of risk and uncertainty', *British Journal for the Philosophy of Science*, **44** (2), 357–76.
Cournot, A.A. (1843), *Exposition de la Théorie des Chances et des Probabilités*, Paris: Hachette.
David, F.N. (1962), *Games, Gods and Gambling. A History of Probability and Statistical Ideas*, London: Charles Griffin.
De Finetti, B. (1937), 'La prévision: ses lois logiques, ses sources subjectives', *Annales de l'Institute Henry Poincaré*, **7** (1), 1–68.
De Morgan, A. (1838), *An Essay on Probabilities, and Their Application to Life Contingencies and Insurance Offices*, new edn, The Cabinet Cyclopædia vol. 13, London: Longman, Orme, Brown, Greens & Longmans).

De Morgan, A. (1847), 'Theory of probabilities', *The Encyclopaedia of Pure Mathematics forming part of the Encyclopaedia Metropolitana*, Glasgow: Griffin, pp. 393–490.

Ellsberg, D. (1954), 'Classic and current notions of "measurable utility"', *The Economic Journal*, **64** (255), 528–56.

Ellsberg, D. (1961), 'Risk, ambiguity, and the savage axioms', *Quarterly Journal of Economics*, **75** (4), 643–69.

Fishburn, P.C. (1989), 'Retrospective on the utility theory of von Neumann and Morgenstern', *Journal of Risk and Uncertainty*, **2** (2), 127–57.

Friedman, M. and L.J. Savage (1948), 'The utility analysis of choices involving risk', *Journal of Political Economy*, **56** (4), 279–304.

Fry, C.L. and R.B. Ekelund Jr (1971), 'Cournot's demand theory: a reassessment', *History of Political Economy*, **3** (1), 190–97.

Gilboa, I. (2009), *Theory of Decision under Uncertainty*, Econometric Society monographs, Cambridge and New York: Cambridge University Press.

Gilboa, I. and D. Schmeidler (1995), 'Case-based decision theory', *Quarterly Journal of Economics*, **110** (3), 605–39.

Hacking, I. (1975), *The Emergence of Probability: A Philosophical Study of Early Ideas about Probability, Induction and Statistical Inference*, London and New York: Cambridge University Press.

Huygens, C. (1657), *De Ratiociniis in Ludo Aleae (The Value of all Chances in Games of Fortune; Cards, Dice, Wagers, Lotteries & C. Mathematically Demonstrated)*, English trans. 1714, London: Keimer and Woodward.

Jevons, W.S. (1874), *The Principles of Science: A Treatise on Logic and Scientific Method*, 2 vols, London: Macmillan.

Jevons, W.S. (1879), *The Theory of Political Economy*, 3rd edn, London: Macmillan.

Kahneman, D. (2011), *Thinking, Fast and Slow*, New York: Farrar, Straus and Giroux.

Kahneman, D. and A. Tversky (1979), 'Prospect theory: an analysis of decision under risk', *Econometrica*, **47** (2), 262–91.

Keynes, J.M. (1921), *A Treatise on Probability*, London: Macmillan.

Laplace, P.S. (1812), *Théorie analytique des probabilités*, Paris and Brussels: Culture et civilisation.

Machina, M.J. (2008), 'Non-expected utility theory', in S.N. Durlauf and L.E. Blume (eds), *The New Palgrave Dictionary of Economics*, Basingstoke: Palgrave Macmillan.

Marschak, J. (1938), 'Money and the theory of assets', *Econometrica*, **6** (4), 311–25.

Marshall, A. (1890), *Principles of Economics*, 2 vols, 9th variorum edn 1961, London and New York: Macmillan for the Royal Economic Society.

Moore, G.E. (1903), *Principia Ethica*, Cambridge, Cambridge University Press.

Pascal, B. (1670), *Pensées*, Paris: Guillaume Depriez, reprinted 1985, Oxford: Oxford University Press.

Pigou, A.C. (1924), *The Economics of Welfare*, 2nd edn, London: Macmillan.

Pratt, J.W. (1964), 'Risk aversion in the small and in the large', *Econometrica*, **32** (1/2), 122–36.

Ramsey, F.P. (1926), 'Truth and probability', *The Foundations of Mathematics and other Logical Essays*, reprinted 1931, London: Kegan Paul, pp. 156–98.

Samuelson, P.A. (1977), 'St. Petersburg paradoxes: defanged, dissected, and historically described', *Journal of Economic Literature*, **15** (1), 24–55.

Savage, L.J. (1954), *The Foundations of Statistics*, 2nd revised edn 1972, New York: Dover Publications.

Schlee, E.E. (1992), 'Marshall, Jevons, and the development of the expected utility hypothesis', *History of Political Economy*, **24** (3), 729–44.

Schmeidler, D. (1989), 'Subjective probability and expected utility without additivity', *Econometrica*, **57** (3), 571–87.

Schoemaker, P.J.H. (1982), 'The expected utility model: its variants, purposes, evidence and limitations', *Journal of Economic Literature*, **20** (2), 529–63.

Shackle, G.L.S. (1952), *Expectation in Economics*, 2nd edn, Cambridge: Cambridge: University Press.

Tintner, G. (1942), 'A contribution to the non-static theory of choice', *Quarterly Journal of Economics*, **56** (2), 274–306.

Todhunter, I. (1865), *History of the Mathematical Theory of Probability from the Time of Pascal to that of Laplace*, Cambridge and London: Macmillan.

Venn, J. (1888), *The Logic of Chance. An Essay on the Foundations and Province of the Theory of Probability, with Especial Reference to Its Application to Moral and Social Science*, 3rd edn, first published 1866, London and Cambridge: Macmillan.

Von Neumann, J. and O. Morgenstern (1944), *Theory of Games and Economic Behavior*, Princeton, NJ: Princeton University Press.

Von Neumann, J. and O. Morgenstern (1953), *Theory of Games and Economic Behavior*, 3rd edn, Princeton, NJ: Princeton University Press.

Utilitarianism and anti-utilitarianism

While there is wide variation in utilitarian approaches to ethics, they are united by their endorsement of the following general principle: the morally right action is judged through the goodness of its outcomes for society, and, conversely, what is good for society is based on what is good for individuals.

Utilitarianism, as a family of philosophical theories, has been the most powerful and pervasive approach in the development of economics since the marginalist revolution. Utilitarianism was developed in the eighteenth century and then fully articulated in the nineteenth, designed to do good to the world not from the point of view of the Christian church or any religion, but rather from a secular point of view based on rational thought. It was conceived as a way to think about the legal system, and to improve it on the basis of a single coherent rational and acceptable principle, that of the utility principle. It hence may be used to think about the constitution, about civil and penal laws, and, last but not least, any kind of policy judgment whether economic or social. Economics has endorsed some important aspects of utilitarianism ever since the 18th century. In particular, welfare economics, and hence virtually every public policy recommendation formulated by economists, has for years been influenced by utilitarianism in some manner, albeit not always explicitly recognized. The efforts to get away from utilitarianism may even explain aspects of the evolution of welfare economics.

Utilitarianism is not only a moral and political philosophy, however; it is also a philosophy of action. As an ethical theory, it sets down what individuals should do to improve their own situation, and what should be done by every individual and by the collectivity to improve collective welfare. As a theory of action, utilitarianism claims that individuals seek to promote their own utility, such that utility appears as both an explanation of and a guide for human action. Notice that utilitarianism is sometimes claimed to be rooted in a consideration of strictly selfish actions, with no attention paid to the utility of others: but this is merely an exaggerated caricature of the theory. Being motivated by one's own pleasure does not require that this pleasure be exclusively self-oriented. There certainly exist extra-regarding pleasures, functioning as truly motivating factors, such that seeking one's own self-interest does not imply that one disregards the fate of others. The ideational evolution in the utilitarian philosophy of action is exactly parallel to that in utilitarian moral philosophy. In the classical versions of utilitarianism, pleasure guides human actions, as a psychological hedonistic law would suggest. The theory has then moved away from hedonism to consider that the psychological law at stake is the search for the satisfaction of preferences, no matter what these preferences are made of, and no matter what their substantive cause. Other aspects of the utilitarianist philosophy of action shall not be discussed in this entry, in so far as this is closely connected to standard rational choice theory as used in economics: the interested reader might want to refer to decision theory and the associated heterodox literature.

As a way of setting out the diversity of utilitarian approaches, this entry has chosen the following as a key idea. Utility has a plural nature: it is both positive and normative, and it is normative not only for every individual, but normative also for the collectivity. This plurality generates tensions. The effort to reconcile these tensions explains the diversity of utilitarian doctrines as well as their evolution, both within classical utilitarian theories and contemporary theories, and even the development from hedonist utilitarianism to preference utilitarianism.

As shall be recalled in the next section, classical utilitarianism mostly retained a hedonistic interpretation of utility. It is a doctrine that, in its standard nineteenth century formulation, meant the promotion of the greatest happiness for the greatest number.

Contemporary utilitarianism can be defined as the combination of act consequentialism, welfarism, and a principle of sum-ranking (Sen 1979c). Consequentialism implies that an action is moral if, and only if, the social outcome of the resulting state of the world is good. Welfarism is the principle that the goodness of an outcome depends solely on individual utilities and on no other information. Sum-ranking says that the appropriate method of aggregation is to add individual utilities. As described in the following section, contemporary approaches in utilitarianism develop refinements of preferences utilitarianism.

There are also a wide range of anti-utilitarian theories which do not in general question the premiss that more goodness is better than less, but rather question the ethical implications of monism (the exclusive focus on utility as opposed to other values), the priority of goodness over fairness, or the democratic failures of utilitarianism. In the economics literature, the alternative to utilitarianism is often supposed to be represented by the Rawlsian theory, as generally encapsulated in the famous Bentham–Rawls opposition. Rawls has indeed been important in making it acceptable to call into question the assertion of an all-powerful and uncontested utilitarianism. The diversity of critiques and alternatives to utilitarianism is presented in the final section.

Early and Classical Utilitarianism

The proto-history of utilitarianism goes back to the British moralists of the seventeenth century, including Richard Cumberland and John Gay, who defended the link between individual morality and the general good. The early utilitarians were influenced by the materialist Helvétius, who claimed that interest dictates judgements, and stressed the importance of education in the formation of human souls; as well as by Francis Hutcheson and David Hume, who held that a kind of common-sense morality is generally compatible with public utility. (For more details on the precursors of utilitarianism, see, for example, Rosen 2003; Driver 2009). Our aim in this section is to present the historical stages of classical utilitarianism, defined as follows: "The utilitarian doctrine is, that happiness is desirable, and the only thing desirable, as an end; all other thing being only desirable as means to that end" (Mill 1861 [1987]: 307).

Utilitarian hedonism

Jeremy Bentham (1748–1832) is generally considered the father of actual utilitarianism. The principle of utility – the "greatest happiness principle" or "the greatest happiness for the greatest number" – is the fundamental utilitarian principle, as expressed in this famous passage:

> Nature has placed mankind under the governance of two sovereign masters, pains and pleasure. It is for them alone to point out what we ought to do, as well as to determine what we shall do. On the one hand the standard of right and wrong, on the other the chain of causes and effects, are fastened to their throne. They govern us in all we do, in all we say, in all we think . . . The

principle of utility recognizes this subjection, and assumes it for the foundation of that system, the object of which is to rear the fabric of felicity by the hands or reason and of law. (Bentham 1789 [1967]: 1–2)

Bentham sometimes alludes to the sum of individual utility, but the commitment of classical utilitarianism to the principle of the sum does not seem as robust and important as that of two other essential principles: impartiality and welfarism. Impartiality means that everyone counts for one and none for more than one. Welfarism is the focus on individual utility. Utility is conceived as a mental state representing happiness, the positive result of a balance between pains and pleasures or any personal valuable feelings. Individual utilities are calculated in three stages (Baujard 2009). First, Bentham lists the different classes of elementary pleasures or pains. Second, the value of utility is assessed according to different criteria including intensity, duration, certainty or uncertainty, propinquity or remoteness, fecundity, purity and extent – the three latter criteria refer to secondary effects of actions, likely to concern different persons, or induce other actions whose consequences should be assessed. Finally, the result of this calculation is adjusted to each individual on the basis of the circumstances that influence her sensitivity. Since the idea of measuring pleasures and comparing them raises many practical problems, Bentham proposes to use some proxy for estimating it, and money may be able to provide the needed measuring rod – this being the ancestor of the idea of the willingness to pay or to accept. More generally, there is a global assumption according to which everyone shares vital concerns including security of expectations, subsistence, abundance and equality, such that rights are associated to all these goals.

A tension lies in the duality of utility, which is supposed both to explain and justify actions. Why would an action that is desired by an individual always be good for her? Moreover, why would it be good for society? Is vice really undesirable and virtue desirable? Should individuals sacrifice their happiness for that of others? There can be tensions between the reach of the individual's happiness and that of society, which utilitarianism needs to reconcile.

Bentham recognizes there may be mistakes, cognitive limits, or more fundamentally what we would call now external effects – as introduced by the criteria of fecundity, purity and extent – that are likely to hamper the ideal conjunction of individual interests. Whenever utility is likely not to be maximized, Bentham designs external punishments and rewards, and appeals to various kinds of influence (such as peer pressure) to make sure that individuals are incited to revert to a better action, so that egoistic people, or people who might be wrong, bad at calculating, or insufficiently informed, will eventually act to maximize social utility.

John Stuart Mill's utilitarianism (1806–1873), influenced by perfectionist intuitions, is also meant to answer objections such as those levelled at Bentham's theory. Among other insights, he recognizes that all pleasures do not seem equally valuable, as evoked in a celebrated passage: "It is better to be a human being dissatisfied than a pig satisfied; better to be Socrates dissatisfied than a fool satisfied. And if the fool, or the pig, are of a different opinion, it is because they only know their own side of the question" (Mill 1861 [1998]: 37). Mill's utilitarianism is able to discriminate higher moral and aesthetic sentiments from sources of swinish pleasure. His proof for his principle of ranking is based on the fact that those who have experienced both kinds of pleasures know which is more valuable; this is why we speak of Mill's qualitative utilitarianism.

The details of the consideration of different sources of pleasure as set out in Mill's view has led certain authors to regret Mill's "naturalist fallacy" (Moore 1903). In order to distinguish between different kinds of pleasures, we need to suppose there exists another value, other than utility, which has intrinsic importance, such that some specific actions are good by their nature rather than by their actual consequences.

From utilitarianism to economics

Henry Sidgwick's (1838–1900) *The Methods of Ethics* (1874) has been influential in the clarification of important features of utilitarianism and as regards some developments of the marginalist literature in economics. First, he shows that utilitarianism can resolve any conflicts of values or rules, at least under the principle that an ethical agent must be impartial between one person's pleasures and another's. Sidgwick, though, made an important case for criticizing the hedonist approach in utilitarianism: a problem of "dualism of practical reason" occurs when it seems better on utilitarian grounds to sacrifice one's own interests for others'. Some economists, notably Jevons (1871), and more recently Skyrms (1996) among many others, have answered this problem by defending the claim that utility was made a moral norm through socio-evolutionary explanations of the emergence and reinforcement of utilitarian rules, so that the existence of a link between the normative and the positive approaches to utility does not seem implausible. Second, Sidgwick discusses the impact of time and population on utilitarianism. He tackles the problem of the sacrifice of a present pleasure for a greater one in the future, seeing this as parallel to the sacrifice of a person's own pleasure for somebody else's. Francis Ysidro Edgeworth (1845–1926) assumed that natural units of pleasure and pain can in principle be ascertained and aggregated over varying populations and time horizons. The population issue later came to be the subject of extensively study (Blackorby et al. 2005). In modern utilitarianism, social welfare is optimized when the sum of individual cardinal utilities is maximized. Derek Parfit (1984) showed that sum utilitarianism was exaggeratedly populationist, because it implies what he called "the repugnant conclusion": that a numerous and miserable population is to be judged better off than a sparse and happy one. Conversely, average utilitarianism would be Malthusian because new inhabitants provide a distinct value according to whether they are more or less happy.

Third, Sidgwick stressed the need for developing formal models of a utilitarian calculus under ideal conditions so that the implications of quantitative hedonistic utilitarian reasoning could be clarified. The utilitarian economists have gone beyond his original intentions. They have assumed that the utility numbers are known with precision, which allows them to compute properly interpersonal comparisons of utilities and the sum of utilities in every situation. An issue is thus raised as to who shall be responsible for performing and enforcing the utilitarian calculations. Edgeworth and others have considered it best to trust a utilitarian elite for this delicate task. Along the same line, Sidgwick made a point of insisting that the utilitarian theory should not be publicized, because uneducated people, those incapable of moral reflection, may misuse it. Utilitarian rules should thus rather be applied by educated people, while the laymen should be content to be governed by the utilitarian elite. This corresponds to the colonial elitism of Sidgwick's times, which Bernard Williams (1973) derisively called "Government House

Utilitarianism". It is hard to deny that utilitarianism in this sense utterly contradicts individual sovereignty, at least that of allegedly uneducated persons.

Contemporary Utilitarianism

The ordinalist revolution that affected economic science from Pareto to the 1930s watershed has totally modified the definition of utility in economics: in order to secure economics' status as a science, it was necessary to exclude the hedonist interpretation of utility and favour the preference interpretation; this move was completed by the revealed preference theory. A similar evolution occurred in the utilitarian philosophical litera-ture, especially in the second part of the twentieth century. Both in economics and in philosophy, the model of utility as a measure of pleasure has now been replaced by the preference model (on the comparison of the two models, see, for example, Haslett 1990). Preference utilitarianism also corresponds to a preference view of welfare: if you prefer x to y, it also follows you are better off in x than in y.

Harsanyi's rational choice utilitarianism

John Harsanyi's (1953, 1955) articles are both leading contributions to modern utilitari-anism. The 1953 paper offers a philosophical reconstruction of the notion of utilitarian impartiality. Harsanyi imagines that an impartial spectator compares the utility of two populations. The fiction ought to help derive a function of social welfare from individual utilities, capturing the fact that social utility is based on the individuals' personal assess-ment of their situation. A primary requirement is that the spectator should be impartial, that is to say, he should not favour the situation of one individual over another, whatever their differences. For instance, a poorer person should not be favoured over a richer one, nor the converse. Everyone is hence given a strictly equal weight. Harsanyi's innovative idea was to extract this reasoning from the context of risk theory. Suppose you were to become one person in a given population: you have as much chance of becoming one person as any other – as much chance of being rich as poor. From outside, and not knowing who you end up eventually to be, you have no reason to favour one person over another in revealing your preference, so that you should consider being any person in the society with equal chance. You therefore want to maximize the sum of all indi-vidual utilities – for a given population, equivalently, the average utility. Impartiality is enforced by the fiction of a (thin) veil of ignorance.

In his 1955 article, Harsanyi provides an axiomatic justification of the criterion of the sum. Based on the von Neumann and Morgenstern characterization of utility under risk, Harsanyi treats the individual reasoning under the veil of ignorance described above. For any weights a_i, and for utility u_i of all the individuals i of the society composed of N individuals, he obtains the following characterization of weighted utilitarianism:

$$W = \sum_{i \in N} a_i u_i \qquad (1)$$

This "construction" of what utility should be under impartiality entails that there exist two definitions of utility, whether actual or ethical. Actual utility refers to subjective utility as it is, capturing the individual's personal interest, including egoistic or altruistic views; it corresponds to a numerical indicator of preferences, which is revealed by actual choice behaviour. Such utilities are ordinal, and neither cardinal measures nor comparisons of utility in this sense are meaningful. By contrast, ethical utility corresponds to what utilities should be on the basis of impartial and impersonal considerations alone; they are cardinal and interpersonally comparable. The identification of ethical utility requires certain conditions to enforce impartiality. This is the task of the veil of ignorance. Furthermore, imagine that *i* is an altruistic person, whose utility is increasing with *j*'s utility. Then *j*'s utility is likely to be counted twice, in contravention of the impartiality criterion. Other-regarding preferences should therefore be excluded in order to avoid such double-counting (Dworkin 1978).

Since their publication, however, the implications of Harsanyi's results have spilled over into diverse issues: the interpretation of possible negative weights, problems of distribution, cardinality, difficulty with the introduction of subjective and heterogeneous utility, inconsistencies, and so on. The rich debate between Rawls and Harsanyi is one of its most famous outcomes (for example, Rawls 1974; Harsanyi 1975). The reasoning under uncertainty on which Harsanyi's utilitarian social welfare function is based relies heavily on the specifics of his choices regarding risk aversion.

By contrast, John Rawls (1971) proposes a thicker veil of ignorance. As he thinks impartiality requires that less information is available to each individual, he conceives the following fiction. Individual *i* does not know any more the list of all possible situations: *i* then faces a situation of uncertainty rather than a risky situation. *i* can hardly weight all the possible situations equally, while *i* may fear falling into the worst situation. Any individual *i* under this veil is interested in improving the worst situation, such that the maximin criterion is more suitable. In the end, utilitarian impartiality implies the maximization of the sum of utilities, while the Rawlsian theory of justice as fairness entails devoting all attention to the most disfavoured group in society. As a consequence, the former ignores all distributive issues while the latter is fundamentally egalitarian.

Preference utilitarianism

Most modern contributions to utilitarianism retain the preference model of utility, such that utility is simply the satisfaction of preferences. The "strong preference" model is the one that is most commonly used in social sciences: individual preferences are revealed in the actual choices of individuals. Specifically, utilities are the numerical representation of preferences as revealed by choices. If I choose wine when I could drink tea, my preference is for wine over tea. In terms of utility, the numerical value of the utility that I associate with wine is therefore greater than the numerical value of the utility that I associate with tea. For example, I can capture either the choice situation or the preference by the following utility numbers: $U(\text{Wine}) = 10$ and $U(\text{Tea}) = 0$ or, equivalently, 4 and -2.67 respectively. In this context, ordinal measures of utility are all that counts, but cardinal utility is meaningless – such that summing and comparison are impossible. Arrow and Hahn, Debreu, Hicks and Samuelson, among many others, had been convinced of the primacy of this model for economic science since the forties. The revealed preference model is the basis for the interpretation of the utilities found in our microeconomic textbooks. Nevertheless, the same model of utility is likely to be used in other chapters of these textbooks, those which tackle issues of welfare economics, and even applied public economics. In this context, social welfare is hence supposed to depend on individual utilities alone, which only represent individual choices. The use of this model in welfare economics is heavily criticized for several reasons (for example, Hausman 2012). For one thing, it ignores the fact that individuals may act against their own interests: for instance, a knowledgeable person who continues to smoke, or a penniless young man who prefers to work for a low wage rather than concentrate on his studies. More generally, we cannot distinguish actions by interest, lack of information, whether they are based on false beliefs or lack of will, constrained by social norms, and so on. As a consequence, it is difficult to interpret the concept of utility corresponding to the strong preference model as the well-being of the person, and even more as relevant information to compute social welfare.

While the strong model of preferences –that is, revealed preference theory – is mostly retained in economics, most philosophers prefer to retain a weak model of preferences. They claim that utility stands for specific kinds of preferences: they should be rational, informed, and based on true beliefs (for example, Hare 1981; Griffin 1986; Sumner 1996). The introduction of these conditions has two consequences. First, this model answers most of the criticisms that plagued utilitarianism both in its hedonist version and in the strong preference model. Second, it implies that, for utilitarianism, the relevant preferences are not actual preferences but some kind of ethical preferences: actual preferences should be "laundered" (Goodin 1986) – notice that the issue of who should be entitled to perform the actual task of laundering preferences when utilitarian policies are implemented remains open so far.

Further, if you suppose we know the rational and informed preferences, and if you can transform each individual utility by any positive monotonic function $f(.)$, then you can design some ordinalist utilitarianism where:

$$W = \sum_{i \in N} f(u_i(x)) \tag{2}$$

It has been shown that the Rawlsian ranking is a special case of all utilitarian ordinalist functions, where the concavity of f is extreme (Arrow 1973).

Anti-Utilitarianism

The scope of criticism of utilitarianism is wide, whether on ethical grounds or on practical issues. Such criticism can be accommodated by utilitarianism with refinements. These refinements constitute the focus of this section. However, this critical movement has also induced a sort of "non-utility revolution", both in political philosophy and normative economics. Notice that most alternative approaches would not call themselves anti-utilitarian – though a notable exception is the Mouvement Anti-Utilitariste dans les Sciences Sociales (MAUSS) project (see, for example, Caillé 2006) – but at most post-welfarist.

Ethical limits of utilitarianism

The principle of aggregation has been criticized for being a mere sum of utilities which rules out any distributive considerations. Indeed, in a crude version of utilitarianism, it is considered socially equivalent to give a large amount of money either to one rich person or to a myriad of poor people who would be able to change their quality of life thanks to it. This example runs against moral intuitions and should induce the rejection of the theory. Yet it seems implausible to claim that equality has never been a concern of utilitarian thinkers. In an old and standard assumption that goes back not only to the precursors of the marginalists, but also to the first utilitarians, the marginal utility of money is decreasing. In order to maximize the sum of individual utility, it is therefore socially better to give an extra euro to a poor person than to give the same extra euro to a rich one: for the former act is a bigger producer of utility than the latter. A way of representing the egalitarian functions of social welfare is specifically to retain a utilitarian utility function with concave individual utility functions. In this sense, the criticism over the issue of distribution holds only for crude versions of utilitarianism where 1 euro is supposed to provide the same amount of utility to any person; yet this case is more important than we might think at first sight, in view of Robbins's claim that the assumption of decreasing marginal utility was a normative assumption and should consequently be kept away from economic science. Nevertheless, even with some given concave utility function, the choice of the criterion of sum (or average) may have consequences that collide with distributive concerns. Utilitarianism can judge certain inequalities as socially better in so far as they contribute to increasing the sum of utilities. For example, it may be appropriate to give subsidies to a rich businessperson rather than using the same amount of money to improve the fate of worse-off children if the extra utility associated with the grant is higher than that associated with assistance. Some utilitarians are comfortable with this criticism since it implies, after all, an increase in the sum of utilities: the decisions of the businessperson, they say, may provide more jobs and wealth in a wide area, increasing the welfare of numerous families in a way likely to compensate for the low quality of the children's lives. Opponents of utilitarianism then return with another example, where the unquestioned new increase of welfare only accrues to families that were already well-off. While the choice of examples in this vigorous debate seems crucial to determine which side is more convincing, it remains that there exist cases where the utilitarian criteria favour the rich over the poor, the well-off to the needy. In the end, it remains that distributive issues may be important in utilitarianism, yet only on instrumental bases. This dependency on utility as the sole intrinsic value still generates unquestionable violations of equality concerns.

Beyond the issue of equality, the utility principle is likely to justify the sacrifice of minorities. In a famous example, utilitarianism underwrites the Roman spectacle of the circus. In the arena, a few Christian martyrs suffer a great deal, while each spectator derives a little pleasure from observing their suffering. If the spectators are sufficiently numerous, the sum of their low positive utilities shall compensate for the pain of the few Christians.

More generally, the focus on utility implies possible violations of any liberal rights. According to an interpretation of Sen's (1970) theorem of the Paretian liberal, it is impossible to attribute an intrinsic importance to utility while simultaneously endorsing a specific concept of freedom. This interpretation has been generalized on the basis of other results pertaining to utility and other values.

Sen has called "welfarism" the doctrine according to which social welfare only depends on utility and on no other values or information (Sen 1979b, 1979c). All versions of utilitarianism are fundamentally welfarist. However, welfarism is a problem, first, because it implies the rejection of any other values (or at least it subsumes them). Some alternative theories consider that a plurality of values should be at stake for welfare issues: they make a case for a multidimensional account of welfare, such as quality of life or capabilities (Nussbaum and Sen 1993) and complex equality (Walzer 1983). Secondly, utility may not be the suitable information for gauging social welfare, because it entails counterintuitive consequences. After Sen's famous paper "Equality of what?" (Sen 1979a), it has been common to consider alternative informational bases of justice such as primary goods (Rawls 1971), resources (Dworkin 1981a, 1981b), access to advantages (Cohen 1989), welfare opportunities (Arnerson 1989), opportunities (Roemer 1999), etc.

Utilitarianism considers that utility, which is important for individuals, is also the relevant information for resolving issues of justice. Some regret the confusion of justice and morality in utilitarianism, where goodness is prior to fairness. Conversely, in other traditions – mainly political liberalism – morality focuses on every individual's judgement of what is good or bad; justice concerns all society and tackles the issue of living together, no matter what the individuals' differences, and even considering divergences in their moral views. Consider the usual case of conflict of interests: utility, even if perfect for one individual, is hardly suitable for improving social welfare. The redefinition of welfare imposed in utilitarianism in order to circumvent the absence of a natural conjunction of interests raises fundamental problems regarding the integrity and the autonomy of persons. First, utilitarianism may force individuals to sacrifice something to benefit others, including total strangers. For instance, utilitarianism is likely to justify the execution of innocent people to prevent rioting and consequent numerous deaths, where raising the general welfare is presented as a serious justification for the innocents' deaths. Secondly, utilitarianism imposes negative responsibilities. Individuals are as responsible for what they do not do as for what they do: people have the responsibility to pursue better social consequences, and not just better consequences for themselves (Williams 1973). It is debatable, however, on what basis utilitarianism can impose upon people a goal that is not a priori supposed to be theirs. Thirdly, Rawls (1971: 26–7) claims that utilitarian neutrality implies the loss of the essential separateness of individuals, such that some human beings may be used as a means to the welfare of others.

> On [a utilitarian] conception of society separate individuals are thought of as so many different lines along which rights and duties are to be assigned and scarce means of satisfaction allocated in accordance with rules so as to give the greatest fullfilment of wants. . . . The correct decision is essentially a question of efficient administration. . . . Utilitarianism does not take seriously the distinction between persons. (Rawls 1971: 27)

This argument quickly become famous within the debates over utilitarianism, and has been greatly discussed and refined (see, for example, Parfit 1984). Rawlsian political liberalism, in which fairness is prior to goodness, constitutes the most famous alternative to utilitarianism. Fourthly, another family of ethical criticisms concerns the democratic failures of utilitarianism when its implementation is at stake.

Practical limits of utilitarianism
Though welfarism, and especially welfarism based on subjective utility, is widely used in normative economics, the empirical facts hardly confirm that people are indeed utilitarian. Nozick (1974 [1988]) imagined an "experience machine", which has been fatal to hedonist utilitarianism. Individuals are offered the chance to be plugged into a

machine for life. The latter would feed signals into their brain so that they felt wonderful experiences, irrespective of what was actually happening in the world. Since people do not (in general) prefer the happiness machine to their actual life, it seems to follow that the mental state of happiness is not everything that is valued by these people. The preference model does not do better in this regard. In their seminal article on normative experimental economics, based on a survey, Yaari and Bar-Hillel (1984) highlighted in particular that the assessment of income distributions turned on needs rather than on tastes or beliefs, as utilitarians would claim. According to an important and robust result of normative experimental economics, the way people judge the fairness of situations depends on contextual circumstances and not on the mere description of individual utilities. For example, for similar utility levels, an even split of a resource between two persons is not judged as being equal when survey respondents learn that one recipient is hard working and disabled while the other is lazy and already in receipt of benefits. Utility thus does not seem in fact to be the sole important value, and nor is it the sole relevant source of information in people's eyes.

Notably defended by J. Austin (1832 [1954]), rule utilitarianism had been clearly formulated by S.E. Toulmin (1950), J.O. Urmson (1953) and R.B. Brandt (1959). It supposes that the consequences of rules are assessed, and that actions – and also therefore classes of actions – are judged, according to rules. Harrod (1936) raised an important problem with rule utilitarianism on the basis of a famous example. A lie is a bad thing, and a good rule should be not to lie. However, in special cases a lie is likely to induce better outcomes – although it would be judged negatively by rule utilitarianism, contrary to a priori intuition. Accordingly, act utilitarianism, where every action is assessed through its actual consequences, is favoured. This other version of utilitarianism was defended originally by Bentham, Sidgwick and Moore. Against act utilitarianism, however, some have complained that it is unable to guide practical decision making: because of lack of information, because gathering such information would be too tedious and costly, because mistakes are more likely to be made when there are so many calculations to be made, and because existing rules or norms could not be used to build expectations nor in particular to trust others' promises. In short, rule utilitarianism requires approximations and generalizations which are likely to conflict with the utility principle in certain concrete cases, while act utilitarianism requires unworkable computations.

Notice that the possibility of measuring utility and implementing utilitarian policies depends on the choice of the utility model. If utility were a mental state, it would be quite difficult to consider the different natures of pleasures on a common scale, in so far as many a priori seem incommensurable. The model of experience in play here also entails some counter-intuitive consequences. For example, as long as Mary does not know that she has been ruined on Black Tuesday of the 1929 Crash, she has not experienced her misfortune. Whereas it is impossible to deny that her utility – as experienced happiness – remains as high as when she was a wealthy lady, it is also hard to accept that she remains as well off as before. Moreover, it is impossible – or, rather, difficult – to measure, compare, and add feelings, that is, subjective utilities. As was already underlined, the preference model supposes individual ordinal rankings that are not easier to compare nor to add. This again hampers actual implementation of utilitarian policies.

A famous criticism of utilitarianism is based on Michel Foucault's (1975) analysis of Bentham's Panopticon. The Panopticon is a "simple idea of architecture" (Bentham

1791: 5), which determines the organization of life in a prison as a first step. Bentham's project was to apply this in many other areas of social life, such as homes for the poor, schools, hospitals, public administration, and factories. The prison cells are arranged concentrically around a central building where an inspector is located: he personifies the otherwise fictitious impartial spectator. He can observe each person's action, and everything that happens. Prisoners are kept separate from the others and from the spectator, of whom they know only they might be being observed. "Hence the major effect of the Panopticon: to induce in the inmate state a conscious and permanent visibility that assures the automatic functioning of power" (Foucault 1975: 234).

The inspector reflects the behavioural expectations of the whole society, and the prisoners feel in their flesh the pressure of the utility principle: hence their own autonomous desires are transformed now so as to feel and act in order to improve the greatest happiness for the greatest number; individuals gradually become their own jailer. As all that is needed here is the thought that there might be an inspector, who may be anybody: he may be changeable or even absent, such that the system seems free from any drift towards tyranny – precisely in accordance with the requirement of impartiality. It remains that individual autonomy is here being totally neglected in favour of social utility: the disciplinary system organized by the Panopticon guarantees the total submission of individuality to the collectivity, as in an authoritarian regime.

This democratic failure may be seen in the preference model as well. In theory, an impartial spectator properly computes utilities and suggests which policy will best improve social welfare. In practice, utilitarian policies suppose that some experts have made the utility computation in the name of the other individuals. In the ideal preference model, the computation also supposes they launder individual utilities. What is the actual legitimacy of such experts? How can we be sure that such a utilitarian elite may desire and succeed in promoting the good for the mass of people? The problem would not arise if a normative demarcation of the scope of expertise were possible. Under such a demarcation, experts could be contracted within a well-defined area in which they are responsible solely for making factual observations and computations. The citizens would have previously decided that the policy should be utilitarian, such that the experts would use utilitarian models to derive their prescriptions. As a consequence, expert decisions based on utilitarianism would legitimately proceed from the will of individuals, although in fact implemented by an expert. The possibility of such a demarcation is, however, doubtful (Baujard 2013). In the end, this objection again recalls the issue of the lack of democracy in the elaboration of actual policy recommendations and the implementation of utilitarian policies. An alternative to utilitarianism hence supposes the introduction of theories of democracy within welfare economics, for example, following Sen's more recent ideas (Sen 2009).

Conclusion

In seeking to deepen her understanding of this subject, the reader will quickly find herself within a wide arena of impressively numerous primary and secondary references on utilitarianism and its criticism. Glover's introduction to and collection of utilitarian texts (Glover 1990), as well as his thematic bibliography (Glover 1990: 251–5), provide a useful guide within this otherwise daunting literature.

Unquestionably, utilitarianism has evolved and developed since its appearance in the eighteenth century. In order to retain the essential kernel of the theory – that what is important for society is that individuals have high utility – authors have sought creative responses to the tensions raised by the opposition between positive and normative definitions of utility, and individual and collective definitions of welfare. Utilitarianism has consequently been permanently modified and refined. This constant adaptation has made utilitarianism into the most important ethical theory in the Anglo-Saxon world, and in particular within the evolution of welfare economics.

Whenever the theory has been modified to repel strong criticism, it has increased its theoretical stability while aggravating its practical fragility. It hardly appears possible to answer both the practical and ethical objections raised against the utilitarian – or at least welfarist – bases of welfare economics. The ethical criticism returns when the theory is to be applied and implemented in concrete settings, that is, when the formulation of actual policy recommendations is at stake. Conceived and reconstructed on the bases of the most refined versions of contemporary utilitarianism, a welfarist welfare economics may be bound to remain a beautiful but vain theory, as is presaged by the news of the death of welfare economics. Considering the practical stakes, going beyond utilitarianism, and even beyond welfarism, in welfare economics may now prove to be an absolute necessity.

ANTOINETTE BAUJARD

See also:

Behavioural and cognitive economics (III); Jeremy Bentham (I); Economics and philosophy (III); Francis Ysidro Edgeworth (I); William Stanley Jevons (I); John Stuart Mill (I); Amartya Kumar Sen (I); Henry Sidgwick (I); Social choice (III); Uncertainty and information (III); Welfare economics (III).

References and further reading

Arneson, R.J. (1989), 'Equality and equal opportunity for welfare', *Philosophical Studies*, **56** (1), 77–93.
Arrow, K.J. (1973), 'Some ordinalist-utilitarian notes on Rawls's theory of justice', *Journal of Philosophy*, **70** (9), 254.
Austin, J. (1832), *The Province of Jurisprudence Determined*, reprinted 1954, ed. H.L.A. Hart, London: Weidenfeld.
Baujard, A. (2009), 'A return to Bentham's felicific calculus. From moral welfarism to technical non-welfarism', *European Journal of the History of Economic Thought*, **16** (3), 431–53.
Baujard, A. (2013), 'Value judgments and economics expertise', Working Paper GATE L-SE, WP 1314, accessed 1 February 2016 at url: ftp://ftp.gate.cnrs.fr/RePEc/2013/1314.pdf.
Bentham, J. (1789), *Introduction to the Principles of Morals and Legislation*, reprinted 1967, Oxford's Political Texts, Oxford: Blackwell.
Bentham, J. (1791), *Panoptique: Mémoire sur un nouveau principe pour construire des maisons d'inspection, et nommément des maisons de force*, reprinted 2002, Paris: Mille et une nuits.
Blackorby, C., W. Bossert and D. Donaldson (2005), *Population Issues in Social Choice Theory, Welfare Economics, and Ethics*, Econometric Society Monographs No. 39, Cambridge: Cambridge University Press.
Brandt, R.B. (1959), *Ethical Theory*, Englewood Cliffs, NJ: Prentice-Hall.
Caillé, A. (ed.) (2006), *De l'anti-utilitarisme. Anniversaire, bilan et controversies*, *Revue du MAUSS*, special issue, no. 27.
Cohen, G.A. (1989), 'On the currency of egalitarian justice', *Ethics*, **99** (4), 906–44.
Driver, J. (2009), 'The history of utilitarianism', in E.N. Zalta (ed.), *The Stanford Encyclopedia of Philosophy*, 27 March, accessed 10 February 2016 at http://plato.stanford.edu/entries/utilitarianism-history/.
Dworkin, R. (1978), *Taking Rights Seriously*, Cambridge, MA: Harvard University Press.
Dworkin, R. (1981a), 'What is equality? Part 1: Equality of welfare', *Philosophy and Public Affairs*, **10** (3), 185–246.
Dworkin, R. (1981b), 'What is equality? Part 2: Equality of resources', *Philosophy and Public Affairs*, **10** (4), 283–345.
Foucault, M. (1975), *Surveiller et punir*, Paris: Gallimard.

Glover, J. (1990), *Utilitarianism and Its Critics*, New York: Macmillan.
Goodin, R.E. (1986), 'Laundering preferences', in J. Elster and A. Hylland (eds), *Foundations of Social Choice Theory*, Cambridge: Cambridge University Press, pp. 75–101.
Griffin, J. (1986), *Well-Being: Its Meaning, Measurement, and Moral Importance*, Oxford: Clarendon Press.
Hare, R.M. (1981), *Moral Thinking: Its Levels, Method and Point*, Oxford: Clarendon Press.
Harrod, R.F. (1936), 'Utilitarianism revisited'. *Mind*, **45** (178), 137–56.
Harsanyi, J.C. (1953), 'Cardinal utility in welfare economics and in the theory of risk-taking', *Journal of Political Economy*, **61** (5), 434–5.
Harsanyi, J.C. (1955), 'Cardinal welfare, individual ethics, and interpersonal comparisons of utility', *Journal of Political Economy*, **63** (4), 309–21.
Harsanyi, J.C. (1975), 'Can the maximin principle serve as a basis for morality? A critique of John Rawls theory', *American Political Science Review*, **59** (2), 594–606.
Haslett, D. (1990), 'What is utility?', *Economics and Philosophy*, **6** (1), 65–94.
Hausman, D.M. (2012), *Preferences, Value, Choice, and Welfare*, Cambridge: Cambridge University Press.
Jevons, W.S. (1871), *The Theory of Political Economy*, London: Macmillan.
Mill, J.S. (1861), 'Utilitarianism', in John Stuart Mill and Jeremy Bentham, *Utilitarianism and Other Essays*, edited by A. Ryan (1987), London: Penguin Books, pp. 272–338.
Moore, G.E. (1903), *Principia Ethica*, Cambridge: Cambridge University Press.
Nozick, R. (1974), *Anarchy, State and Utopia*, New York: Basic Books.
Nussbaum, M.C. and A.K. Sen (1993), *The Quality of Life*, Oxford: Clarendon Press.
Parfit, D. (1984), *Reasons and Persons*, Oxford: Oxford University Press.
Rawls, J. (1971), *A Theory of Justice*, Cambridge, MA: The Belknap Press of Harvard University Press.
Rawls, J. (1974), 'Reply to Alexander and Musgrave', *Quarterly Journal of Economics*, **88** (4), 633–55.
Roemer, J.E. (1999), *Equality of Opportunity*, Cambridge, MA: Harvard University Press.
Rosen, F. (2003), *Classical Utilitarianism from Hume to Mill*, London: Routledge.
Sen, A.K. (1970), 'The impossibility of a Paretian liberal', *Journal of Political Economy*, **78** (1), 152–7.
Sen, A.K. (1979a), 'Equality of what?', in S. McMurrin (ed.), *The Tanner Lectures on Human Values*, vol. 1. Cambridge: Cambridge University Press, as cited in A.K. Sen (1982), *Choice, Welfare and Measurement*, Cambridge, MA: MIT Press, pp. 365–6.
Sen, A.K. (1979b), 'Personal utilities and public judgements: or what's wrong with welfare economics?', *The Economic Journal*, **89** (355), 537–58.
Sen, A.K. (1979c), 'Utilitarianism and welfarism', *Journal of Philosophy*, **76** (9), 463–89.
Sen, A.K. (2009), *The Idea of Justice*, Cambridge, MA: Harvard University Press.
Sidgwick, H. (1874), *The Methods of Ethics*, London: Macmillan.
Skyrms, B. (1996), *Evolution of the Social Contract*, Cambridge: Cambridge University Press.
Sumner, L.W. (1996), *Welfare Happiness and Ethics*, Oxford: Oxford University Press.
Toulmin, S. (1950), *The Place of Reason in Ethics*, Cambridge: Cambridge University Press.
Urmson, J.O. (1953), 'The interpretation of the moral philosophy of J.S. Mill', *Philosophical Quarterly*, **3** (10), 33–9.
Walzer, M. (1983), *Spheres of Justice. A Defense of Pluralism and Equality*, New York: Basic Books, New York, French edn 1997, *Sphères de justice. Une défense du pluralisme et de l'égalité*, Paris: Le Seuil.
Williams, B. (1973), 'A critique of utilitarianism', in J. Smart and B. Williams (eds), *Utilitarianism: For and Against*, Cambridge: Cambridge University Press, pp. 75–150.
Yaari, M. and M. Bar-Hillel (1984), 'On dividing justly', *Social Choice and Welfare*, **1** (1), 1–24.

Value and price

Basic Concepts

Transactions in which an individual, household, firm, government, or other economic entity ("the buyer") purchases something (usually with money) from another economic entity ("the seller") are widespread and familiar events in many societies. Economic theory describes the exchanged "thing" or "item" variously as a "good", an "asset", or a "commodity". The term "good" emphasizes the usefulness of the thing exchanged to the buyer or some ultimate purchaser of the item in a chain of transactions. The term "asset" emphasizes the fact that the seller owns and controls the item, and has the legal right to transfer ownership to the buyer. The term "commodity" has a narrower sense of a good produced with the intention of selling it in a system of production organized through exchange.

"Price" is the commonly used term for the amount of money exchanged in such a transaction for the item. By extension, the term "price" is often used to describe a standing offer to make such transactions, whether there is an actual transaction or not. In the rarer case of barter transactions, in which one non-money item is exchanged for another, the ratio in which the items are exchanged is often described as the "relative price". Economic arguments that abstract from the mediation of money in exchange are often couched in terms of relative prices.

Price derives through Middle English and Old French from the Latin *pretium*, which translates as both price and value; value derives also through Middle English and Old French from the Latin *valere*, meaning "be strong, be worth". The dictionary definition of value (omitting senses deriving from ethics, and applications to people) is a rich one with a number of meanings:

> **I.** 1. That amount of some commodity, medium of exchange, etc., which is considered to be an equivalent for something else; a fair or adequate equivalent or return. 2. The material or monetary worth of a thing; the amount at which it may be estimated in terms of some medium of exchange or other standard of a like nature. 3. The equivalent (in material worth) of a specified sum or amount. The extent or amount of a specified standard or measure of length, quantity, etc. **II.** The relative status of a thing, or the estimate in which it is held, according to its real or supposed worth, usefulness or importance. (Little et al. 1973: 2449)

That of price is narrower:

> **I.** Money, or the like, paid for something. The money (or other equivalent) for which anything is bought or sold; the rate at which this is done or proposed. . . Payment of money in purchase of something. **II.** Value, worth (obsolete, archaic). (Little et al. 1973: 1667)

In the light of these definitions and usages, it is not surprising that in political economy the relation between value and price is contested and prone to confusion. The term "value" in both ordinary and technical economic language is used in a bewildering array of senses, including as a synonym for "price", as the "value" of a collection of items calculated by multiplying the quantity of each by a corresponding price, in particular as "value added", as the value of a collection of produced items net of the costs of the non-labour inputs required to produce them, as the relation between the underlying quality or usefulness of the item and the price ("good" or "bad value for money"), as the general social usefulness of the item, and, by the classical political economists such as Adam Smith and David Ricardo and their critic Karl Marx, in the sense of the quantity of labour time necessary to produce a commodity. This last, more technical, sense of the term "value" will be the main focus of our discussion.

Broadly speaking, in classical economics value is a substance of something; it is expressed in money as a price, and being a substance, some "productive" activities produce it and other "unproductive" activities use it up. This chapter elaborates the development of this perspective.

The Economy as an Organic Mechanism

In European medieval society, all economic and social relationships were interpreted through the prism of Christian theology and Aristotelian "natural law". These relationships were regarded as both "natural" and divinely inspired, and were regulated by the church. People's horizons were local (and rural), with trade and commerce limited by time (market day) and place (marketplace). Where there was trade, transactions were supposed to take place at "just prices", sufficient to compensate sellers for costs of acquisition and transport and to allow them to maintain their customary status, but no higher or lower.

Gradually, over some centuries, this society of custom and tradition disintegrated. The forces of disintegration were various (for example, the commutation of feudal services for a monetary rent, technological progress in agriculture and the expansion of trade), and their effects were to widen the sphere and scope of monetary transactions. This process tended to break down the religious bonds of society, encouraging the growth of individualism in order to take advantage of the opportunities offered by the growth of markets for material advancement. The development of early forms of capitalism, based on the individual pursuit of monetary gain, accelerated these tendencies. However, the growth of individualism posed a problem: if society was not held together by divine providence, by what, if anything, was it held together?

Hobbes's answer, written in the mid-seventeenth century against the background of the English Civil War, was that society was held together by a "social contract", whereby the people transfer some of their rights to a strong central authority in order to guarantee their protection. Otherwise, in the natural state of mankind characterized by no strong central authority, war would ensure that:

> there is no place for industry; because the fruit thereof is uncertain: and consequently no culture of the earth; no navigation, nor use of the commodities that may be imported by sea; no commodious building; no instruments of moving, and removing, such things as require much force; no knowledge of the face of the earth; no account of time; no arts; no letters; no society; and which is worst of all, continual fear, and danger of violent death; and the life of man, solitary, poor, nasty, brutish, and short. (Hobbes 1651 [2010]: ch. 13, para. 9)

The drive to war was part of human nature; the human instinct of acquisitiveness, greed or selfishness expressed through competition "maketh men invade for gain" (Hobbes 1651 [2010]: ch. 13, para. 7). So what holds society together in the face of such human nature, averting anarchy, is the politics of a social contract.

In the early eighteenth century the emphasis changed when Mandeville (in his *Fable of the Bees*, in a variety of editions between 1714 and 1724) argued that "vice" rather than "virtue" was the foundation of prosperity. By "virtue" he meant cooperative behaviour in conscious pursuit of the good of others, in contrast to "vice", which was the selfish pursuit of greed. This latter, if wisely channelled by skilful politicians, would generate public benefits. In contrast to the Hobbesian view that human nature was vicious and could only lead to anarchy unless politically controlled, Mandeville proposed that the greed of human nature, provided it was politically guided, constituted the fabric of social intercourse and progress. It was then a short intellectual step, after another 50 years, for Adam Smith to advocate the removal of political guidance and to focus on the benefits of a laissez-faire state to the operation of an invisible hand.

Political philosophers and nascent "political economists" in this period gave a great deal of attention to the problem of understanding how decentralized pursuit of self-interest might lead to organized and socially beneficial outcomes. In particular, political economic discourse of this period evolved the idea that self-regulating standards were latent in the competitive hurly-burly of the marketplace. Behind the constantly fluctuating market prices at which commodities actually exchanged lay "natural prices" or "values" to which market prices were tethered and around which they "gravitated". To the degree that these natural prices represented socially beneficial guides to allocation of resources (such as land, other non-labour inputs, and labour), this process of competitive gravitation would act as an "invisible hand" in regulating social production.

The idea that order emerges from spontaneity was a powerful "grand narrative" that was not confined to political economy. However, Smith's intuition that the innumerable actions of competing individuals in pursuit of self-interest could generate something other than chaotic anarchy set an intellectual agenda that remains contemporary. Since trading activity in decentralized markets appeared to characterize the process of the invisible hand, it threw a particular focus on what was brought to the market, what was taken from the market, and the prices at which these trades took place. It was therefore critical to give an account of the forces influencing both market prices and natural prices, which poses the questions a theory of value has to answer.

Value and Price in Smith

Smith's invisible hand is a metaphor for how prices organize a complex social division of labour. Within the factory, the division of labour is completely planned, and its purpose is to increase labour productivity. For Smith this occurred for three reasons. Specialization of tasks increased dexterity and reduced the time otherwise needed to move between tasks; these two reasons are more or less specific to handicraft production. Thirdly, and historically overwhelmingly the most important, the division of labour was extended and productivity increased through the use of specialized machinery. However, outside the factory it is a different story. Rather than planned and hierarchically organized, the division of labour is (in principle) completely unplanned and spontaneous, emerging as the outcome of profit-seeking producers responding to price fluctuations, and limited only by the extent of the market. Thus Adam Smith famously wrote,

[M]an has almost constant occasion for the help of his brethren, and it is in vain for him to expect it from their benevolence only. He will be more likely to prevail if he can interest their self-love in his favour, and show them that it is for their advantage to do for him what he requires of them. Whoever offers to another a bargain of any kind, proposes to do this. Give me that which I want, and you shall have this which you want, is the meaning of every such offer; and it is in this manner that we obtain from one another the far greater part of those good offices which we stand in need of. It is not from the benevolence of the butcher, the brewer, or the baker that we expect our dinner, but from their regard to their own interest. We address ourselves, not to their humanity, but to their self-love, and never talk to them of our own necessities, but of their advantages. (Smith 1776, hereafter WN, I.ii.2)

As well as depending upon what Smith called "a certain propensity in human nature . . . to truck, barter and exchange one thing for another" (WN, I.ii.1), this market determination depended upon mobility of inputs. Since the accumulation of wealth depended upon the labour productivity increases brought about by the division of labour (restricted only by the overall size of the market), it seemed obvious then to relate the price of a product to the labour performed in its production. Certainly if a production process required labour alone, such as hunting deer and beaver on common land with no produced implements, then deer and beaver would exchange in a ratio measuring the relative times spent in hunting each. For if they did not, labour would reallocate itself to the more profitable activity in terms of labour time expended. So labour mobility is an important presupposition of a theory of value.

Although the Industrial Revolution was in its early stages during Adam Smith's lifetime, in most major sectors of production labour had come to be organized along capitalist lines, in which direct producers did not own the means of production, but sold their capacity to labour (in Marx's terms, "labour-power") to a capitalist, who did own means of production, in exchange for a wage. The capitalist's profit per time period, for example, a year, is $\Pi = R - C - W$, where R is the sales revenue per year, C is the cost of other purchased inputs per year, and W is the wage payment per year, all in money units. If the capitalist in pursuit of profit on average ties up money, or "capital" worth K, the profit rate is $r = \frac{\Pi}{K}$, a pure number per unit of time like an interest rate. Using "capital" to refer to the total money sum invested by the capitalist, irrespective of what inputs it is used to purchase, Smith and the other classical political economists argued that because the motivation of capitalist producers was the expansion of their wealth, they would tend to seek out sectors of production with the highest profit rate, withdrawing capital (and with it labour) from sectors with lower than average profit rates and moving capital (and labour) to sectors with higher than average profit rates.

Smith thus argued that a crucial feature of capitalist society was the mobility of capital. For he supposed that the long run level of price was determined through competition among capitalists by whatever level would generally equalize the rate of profit across all activities. This he called the "natural price", contrasting it with the day-to-day fluctuations of the "market price" caused by all sorts of ephemeral and contingent factors. For Smith, the problem of the theory of value was to explain what determined the natural prices of commodities. In his "early and rude state of society which precedes both the accumulation of stock and the appropriation of land" (WN, I.vi.1), natural prices were determined primarily by labour hours required for the production of each commodity.

However, when means of production are appropriated (through the accumulation of "stock", which is Smith's technical term for the non-labour means of production) the determination of natural prices must also be influenced by the mobility of capital in search of higher profit rates. More generally, once the organization of the hunting process took a capitalist form, with the capitalist hiring hunters and supplying them with hunting implements, Smith's simple labour theory of value became problematic. This is because the revenues from production have to cover more than wages: the capitalist requires a return on his or her capital, which has been invested in both labour and non-labour inputs, in the form of profit, and the landlord requires a return on his or her ownership of land in the form of rent. Faced with the need to include rent, wages, and profit in his account, Smith abandoned his labour-embodied theory for an adding-up theory of value based on the idea of explaining the natural price of commodities by adding up labour costs, land costs, and capital costs at natural wage, rent, and profit levels. This then required an independent determination of natural wage, rent and profit levels.

Smith did have some idea of a subsistence wage, and that wage determination was affected by employers ("masters") being fewer in number than the workers they hired, more able to hold out longer in disputes, and more favoured by institutions and politics. He also had some idea that profits and rents were deductions from the product of labour, although he had no systematic theoretical account of any inverse relationships between distributive variables. Indeed Smith did not have any systematic account of the independent determination of natural levels of rent, wages and profit, and, without these, his adding-up theory remained enmeshed in circularity.

While he did not manage to work out a natural price interpretation of rent, wages and profit, Smith was very clear that differences between market price and natural price called forth quantity adjustments in an arbitrage process, and that this process was endless. Smith thus had an account of market price fluctuations around levels determined by natural prices, for the invisible hand process was one of continual adjustment (towards an equalized rate of profit) combined with continual displacement (as technology and demand evolved). Natural price was in effect the value substance underpinning market price, but once Smith had abandoned his embodied labour theory of value, he had no satisfactory theory of natural price levels.

Smith is therefore the father of modern economics in at least two ways. First, while he did not invent it but built on his predecessors, he had a clear vision of a decentralized market economy as an organic self-organized system that produced a roughly orderly and comprehensible result rather than chaotic anarchy. When an individual pursues private profit, "he is . . . led by an invisible hand to promote an end which was no part of his intention. . . . By pursuing his own interest he frequently promotes that of the society more effactually than when he really intends to promote it" (WN, IV.ii.9).

Second, his two theories of price were the ancestral foundations of all subsequent theories of price. Contemporary neoclassical economics traces its genealogy back to Smith's adding-up theory, while Smith's immediate successors focused on developing his embodied labour theory of value, with both theories holding to the presumptions of labour and capital mobility.

Value and Price in Ricardo

Smith had supposed that, when producers could freely shift from one line of commodity production to another, natural prices would tend to adjust to equalize the "whole of the advantages and disadvantages of the different employments of labour" in the production of commodities (WN, I.x.1). If the main component of the "advantages and disadvantages" is the labour time required to produce commodities, natural prices will tend to be proportional to required labour times. Ricardo generalized this conception to an economy in which "stock" had been accumulated, so that prices were determined by the sum of the labour actually performed (direct or living labour) and the labour embodied in the means of production (indirect or dead labour). Ricardo assumed that the various different types of labour (because of different skills and intensities of work) could all be reduced to a common standard unit (although he paid little attention to how this might be done). Then, measuring in this common standard, relative prices were determined by embodied labour ratios.

These relative prices were Smith's natural prices. Thus Ricardo wrote:

> In making labour the foundation of the value of commodities, and the comparative quantity of labour which is necessary to their production, the rule which determines the respective quantities of goods which shall be given in exchange for each other, we must not be supposed to deny the accidental and temporary deviations of the actual or market price of commodities from this, their primary and actual price . . . In the 7th chap. of the Wealth of Nations, all that concerns this question is most ably treated. Having fully acknowledged the temporary effects which, in particular employments of capital, may be produced on the prices of commodities, as well as on the wages of labour, and the profits of stock, by accidental causes, without influencing the general price of commodities, wages or profits, since these effects are equally operative in all stages of society, we will leave them entirely out of our consideration, whilst we are treating of the laws which regulate natural prices, natural wages and natural profits, effects totally independent of these accidental causes. In speaking then of the exchangeable value of commodities, or the power of purchasing possessed by any one commodity, I mean always that power which it would possess, if not disturbed by any temporary or accidental cause, and which is its natural price. (Ricardo 1821 [1951]: 88, 91–2)

However, Ricardo soon discovered that simultaneously determining prices by embodied labour, and considering these prices as the "natural prices" at which profit rates were competitively equalized, was not logically possible.

To see this, suppose a current production process has direct labour per unit of output L_1 working with means of production, and suppose these means of production were produced one period previously, and only with direct labour per unit of output L_2. So a capitalist must advance wL_2 at the beginning of the previous period, to earn $(1 + r)wL_2$ at the end of that period, and must advance $wL_1 + (1 + r)wL_2$ at the beginning of the current period, to earn $(1 + r)[wL_1 + (1 + r)wL_2]$ at the end of the current period. Now consider two production processes, one producing commodity A and the other commodity B. Given the simple technology, the price equations are:

$$p_A = (1 + r)[wL_{A1} + (1 + r)wL_{A2}]$$

$$p_B = (1 + r)[wL_{B1} + (1 + r)wL_{B2}]$$

Suppose A and B are each produced by identical quantities of embodied labour, $(L_{A1} + L_{A2}) = (L_{B1} + L_{B2})$, so that they have identical values and hence natural prices. However, also suppose their production processes are differently divided as between direct and indirect labour. The time when the labour was embodied makes no difference to the quantity of labour embodied, which remains the same for the two commodities, but it matters a great deal to the capitalists concerned. If commodity A has more indirect labour embodied than commodity B, then the capital invested in the production of commodity A is tied up for longer than the capital invested in commodity B, and consequently the rate of profit accruing to each capitalist cannot be the same. The rate of profit on the capital invested in the production of commodity B will be higher, and this contradicts the definition of natural price as supporting an equalized rate of profit. Conversely, if the rates of profit are equalized, then the prices that bring this about cannot reflect the total labour embodied in the production of each commodity. The natural price of commodity A must be higher, and this contradicts the embodied labour theory of value.

Simple inspection of the price equations shows that the embodied labour theory of value and the equalization of the rate of profit are only compatible in two cases. The first case requires a zero profit rate (strongly reminiscent of Smith's "early and rude state of society"). The second case requires the additional and highly special assumption that the time structure of embodiment is the same, so that $L_{A1} = L_{B1}$ and $L_{A2} = L_{B2}$, and the ratio of indirect to direct labour is the same in each production process. Whenever these ratios differ (which will normally be the case), prices at which the rate of profit is equalized cannot be formed out of the sum of direct and indirect labour. The embodied labour theory of value cannot explain natural prices because it ignores the structure of production, and natural prices depend upon the structure of production.

Ricardo never resolved this difficulty. Partly, he thought that it would not matter very much in practice, provided that differences in the structure of production were not too great (perhaps not too unreasonable an approximation in the early years of industrialization). Writing to Mill in December 1818, Ricardo contrasted his view with that of Adam Smith:

> [I]t is not because capital accumulates, that exchangeable value varies, but it is in all stages of society, owing only to two causes: one the more or less labour quantity required, the other the greater or less durability of capital: – that the former is never superseded by the latter, but is only modified by it. (Ricardo 1821 [1951]: xxxvii)

And writing to Malthus in October 1820, he remarked,

> You say that my proposition "that with few exceptions the quantity of labour employed on commodities determines the rate at which they will exchange for each other, is not well founded" I acknowledge that it is not rigidly true, but I say that it is the nearest approximation to truth, as a rule for measuring relative value, of any I have ever heard. (Ricardo 1821 [1951]: xl)

As well as acknowledging the difficulty of combining an embodied labour theory of value with the competitive equalization of the rate of profit but insisting that the incompatibility would not be large, Ricardo also tried a different approach. Since the incompatibility was produced by different structures of production, perhaps he could find some commodity with an "average" structure of production in some sense, so that its value would be determined only by the total labour directly and indirectly embodied in it. It could then be used as an "invariable standard of value", invariable that is to changes in the wage, so that distributional relations could be then analysed independently of prices. Otherwise, if the wage rate rose, the fall in the profit rate would entail effects on prices determined by the structure of production, and these in turn would alter the magnitude of the net product and hence wages and profits. Ricardo speculated that any particular commodity, such as gold, might not serve as an exact invariable standard:

> Neither gold then, nor any other commodity, can ever be a perfect measure of value for all things; but I have already remarked, that the effect on the relative prices of things, from a variation of profits, is comparatively slight; that by far the most important effects are produced by the varying quantities of labour required for production; and therefore, if we suppose this important cause of variation removed from the production of gold, we shall probably possess as near an approximation to a standard measure of value as can be theoretically conceived. (Ricardo 1821 [1951]: 45)

However, this was clearly theoretically unsatisfactory, and Ricardo never found the "average" commodity he wanted.

This turned out to be a very complicated problem. For a given technique of production, Sraffa's "standard commodity" (Sraffa 1960) solves the analytical problem, but across different techniques no such invariable standard of value has been discovered (Kurz and Salvadori 1995: ch. 4, ss 3–5). Further, modern investigations based on data on average prices of commodities and their structure of production tend to support Ricardo's conjecture that differences between natural prices and embodied labour ratios are not very large (for example, Shaikh 1998). Any such investigation, however, rests on some particular measure of the deviations of one relative price system from another, and empirical political economists have not reached agreement on any one method for measuring these differences.

Value and Price after Ricardo: The Bifurcation

Three intellectual responses were possible to the Ricardian difficulty in combining a labour theory of value with capitalist competition and the equalization of the rate of profit. The first was simply to abandon the idea that there was a competitive tendency towards the equalization of the rate of profit. Typically, this was not pursued. Not only did it appear to run counter to an evident empirical tendency; at a deeper level it ran counter to the notion of a decentralized economy that was (self-)organized by competitive behaviour rather than merely anarchic. The second was to separate the theory of value from its dependence on labour performed, a path taken by neoclassical economics after the 1870s. The third was to recast the labour theory of value, which was attempted by Marx.

Value and Price in Neoclassical Economics

Around the 1870s, William Stanley Jevons, Carl Menger and Léon Walras all took the classical political economy Ricardian method of determining rent (as, in the case of the "extensive margin", the difference between the productivity of a given plot of land and the productivity of the worst equal-size plot in cultivation, or, more generally in the case of the "intensive margin", as the difference in the productivities of plots as more labour and complementary inputs are applied to them) and applied it to the determination of the prices of other "factors of production" – hence the terminology "neoclassical".

In so doing, they developed a distinct alternative to the classical approach, in which the wage, for example, depends not on the conditions of the supply and reproduction of the labour force, but on its short-term scarcity. Instead of starting with the problem of the determination of long-period prices of production (and then considering the market price fluctuations around them), technological change and the reproduction of the economy, the neoclassical starting point was the problem of finding equilibrium prices with given stocks of input resources such as land, labour, and means of production. Consequently, the term "capital" came to have a generally narrower reference than in classical political economy, meaning either the sum of money invested in non-labour means of production or the physical inputs so purchased, depending on the context. Rather than considering the turbulent mobility of labour, on the one hand, and capital as invested money, on the other, as in classical political economy, the neoclassical vision was based on a given state of allocation of resources, in which, for any given technology, endowments and preferences, all firms and households optimized on the basis of parametric prices and all markets cleared. Instead of contingent demand and supply fluctuations causing actual market prices to fluctuate around their long period equilibrium, in the neoclassical approach those demand and supply fluctuations are understood as being themselves the immediate determinants of equilibrium prices. Underlying demand are the choices of the utility-maximizing consumer households, but choices restricted by the equilibrium prices and incomes, and supply is in the first instance restricted to the actions of the same consumer households in selling less wanted endowments in order to purchase a more desired bundle of commodities. Hence the neoclassical initial focus was on an exchange economy, in which the individual as consumer was sovereign. The subsequent addition to the picture of producing firms that passively choose input and output levels to minimize costs and maximize profit at equilibrium prices is something of an afterthought, requiring no fundamental change in the theory of determination of equilibrium prices (as long as technology is assumed to be characterized by non-increasing returns).

From the neoclassical point of view, the classical political economy distinctions among the categories of value, price of production, and market price are subsumed under the general category of equilibrium price. Once equilibrium prices are explained, there is no theoretical role for the concept of value in the neoclassical framework. As a result neoclassical economists tend to use the term "value" either in the sense of the value of a bundle of commodities (the sum of the quantities of each commodity in the bundle multiplied by the corresponding price), or simply as a synonym for "price".

By the 1950s, Debreu (1959) could call his study of neoclassical general equilibrium theory *The Theory of Value*, and Koopmans could define "value theory" as "the theory of prices as guides to allocation of resources and of the relation of these prices to the technology" (Koopmans 1957: 148). The theory of value has no content for neoclassical economics other than as an ontology of consumer sovereignty with exogenous preferences, and the theory of price becomes an atemporal theory of market-clearing equilibrium prices.

Both internal and external critics of the neoclassical framework have noted several lacunae in the neoclassical theory of prices. If all agents are price-takers, it is not obvious how any price is ever changed. The institutions of households and firms are emptied of any substantive sociological content (as indeed are markets) and become purely mathematical abstractions in the form of utility and production functions. Despite heroic efforts of mathematical economists, the uniqueness and stability of a general equilibrium system of market-clearing prices cannot be assured without restrictive special assumptions. Trading at disequilibrium prices and the resulting path-dependence of final allocations has not been addressed effectively. The attempt to apply the theory of market-clearing equilibrium prices to produced means of production gives rise to paradoxes discovered by Piero Sraffa, including the phenomena of "reverse capital deepening" (a fall in the value of capital at lower profit rates), and "re-switching of techniques" (cost-minimizing firms adopting the same technique of production at high and low profit rates and a different technique for intermediate profit rates), which are incompatible with the notion that the profit rate is an index of the scarcity of capital. The attempts of neoclassical economics to circumvent these problems by generalizing the framework from atemporal equilibrium to intertemporal equilibrium have foundered on problems of incompleteness of markets, the formation of expectations, the constant introduction of novel commodities as a result of technological change and the exogeneity and stability of preferences over time. (On these points see Kirman 2006; Foley 2010; and references cited therein.)

As a result, the neoclassical theory of market-clearing equilibrium resource allocation has become increasingly disconnected from economic reality. For example, in the later years of the twentieth century the existence of unemployment was attributed by many neoclassical economists to the intertemporal substitution of leisure for labour by forward-looking perfectly rational workers, a logically necessary implication of the presumption of market-clearing prices in the labour market, but a conclusion that struck many others as absurd.

Value and Price in Marx

All theories, however abstractly formulated, have associated preconceptions, or visions, which determine what it is that the theory is supposed to explain. Often this larger vision is implicit, having to be teased out; generally it is based on a set of priors involving beliefs, a world view, which shapes what the theory can and cannot explain. Marx's world view was based on his "historical materialism", that purposive activity by cooperating human beings transforms the physical and social environment within which that activity occurs, and that those transformations alter the human beings themselves. "Cooperating" might not be voluntary; indeed, in all of known human history following the invention of settled agriculture, it generally entailed elements of coercion. Those who owned and/or controlled the means of production necessary for realizing purposive activities could compel those who did not to work for them rather than with them. Societies, that is, were class societies, and classes existed in antagonistic relations to each other.

Smith and Ricardo had talked in terms of social classes. Smith had often emphasized the role of power in determining the distribution of income as wages, rent and profits, and Ricardo had seen the interests of landowners and capitalists as opposed to one another (the protective tariffs known as the Corn Laws were a dominating theme in British politics in the first half of the nineteenth century). However, Smith and Ricardo had no conception of class other than defined through the receipt of a type of income. Neither had seen the antagonistic relation between those who owned and controlled the means of production and those who did not as the overarching perspective it assumed in Marx.

How was such antagonism compatible with the notion that society was non-anarchically self-organized? In one way, Marx followed in the footsteps of Smith, although he put it in different terms.

> [T]he amounts of products corresponding to the differing amounts of needs demand differing and quantitatively determined amounts of society's aggregate labour. It is **self-evident** that this *necessity* of the *distribution* of social labour in specific proportions is certainly not abolished by the *specific form* of social production; it can only change *its form of manifestation*. Natural laws cannot be abolished at all. The only thing that can change, under historically differing conditions, is the *form* in which those laws assert themselves. And the form in which this proportional distribution of labour asserts itself in a state of society in which the interconnection of social labour expresses itself as the *private exchange* of the individual products of labour, is precisely the *exchange value* of these products. (Marx 1868 [1988]: 68, bold and emphases in original)

However, at the same time, Marx considered that there would be periodic ruptures in the social fabric. For class relations were defined in terms of property relations, and the development of technology (which he called the "forces of production") by these class relations periodically rendered existing property relations redundant. A social revolution then occurred, overthrowing the basis of existing class relations, and establishing new relations more compatible with the forces of production. An analogy might be a landscape which appears peaceful, harmonious and at rest; and yet if this landscape rests on tectonic plates moving remorselessly against each other, then, irregularly and unpredictably, these movements result in earthquakes which violently recast the landscape. So Marx both retained the eighteenth-century vision of society and its economy as a social organism, but at the same time he also transformed it into something with evolutionary and path-dependent dynamics, by changing the focus from self-seeking individuals to antagonistic classes.

This transformation presents a challenge. For while slave societies and feudal societies were characterized by explicitly coercive structures for maintaining and enforcing their class relations, this was not evident in capitalist societies. Indeed, the opposite appeared to be the case. For such societies were based on the universalization of markets:

> [A] very Eden of the innate rights of man. It is the exclusive realm of Freedom, Equality, Property and Bentham. Freedom, because both buyer and seller of a commodity . . . are determined only by their own free will. They contract as free persons, who are equal before the law. Their contract is the final result in which their joint will finds a common legal expression. Equality, because each enters into relation with the other, as with a simple owner of commodities, and they exchange equivalent for equivalent. Property because each disposes only of what is his own. And Bentham because each looks only to his own advantage. The only force bringing them together, and putting them into relation with each other, is the selfishness, the gain and the private interest of each. Each pays heed to himself only, and no one worries about the others. And precisely for that reason . . . they all work together to their mutual advantage, for the common weal, and in the common interest. (Marx 1867 [1976]: 280)

This vision is extraordinarily powerful, indeed so powerful that the distance between it and the vision underlying contemporary economic theory more than a century later, for all its formalization, is negligible.

Marx's approach to this Eden of unfettered free markets was not to begin with the chaotic appearances of actual markets, but rather to establish a set of abstract general analytical relations (drawn from the detailed observation of real historical processes). This he called "the method of inquiry", whose purpose was "to appropriate the material in detail, to analyze its different forms of development and to track down their inner connection" (Marx 1867 [1976]: 102). Proof of success in this process is determined by the ability to develop these inner connections so that they can encapsulate reality "not as the chaotic conception of a whole but as a rich totality of many determinations and relations" (Marx 1973: 100). This is delicate; if the concrete is understood as some manifestation of the abstract, the abstract itself has to be concretely grounded. Otherwise, theory becomes an idealist construction, creating the material world instead of being created by it.

Exchange value, value and price were Marx's organizing abstractions, abstractions that were developed on the basis of their concrete reality in the universalization of commodity purchase and sale. For Marx, as for his predecessors, it was through exchange value, value and price that the "anarchy of the market" organized the distribution of the labour resources of society. However, it did this via antagonistic class relations. Marx's approach to the Eden of appearances was to develop the abstract relations of exchange value, value and price to show that capitalism's "Freedom, Equality, Property and Bentham" were all founded on coercive class relations. In this, individuals were only treated explicitly in so far as they could be considered the "bearers" of capitalist relations.

The commodity law of exchange

Marx, like his predecessors in political economy, distinguished "value in use" from "value in exchange". Value in use, or "use-value", derives from the qualitative properties of a product that make it desirable for someone to consume. Thus a chair, for example, has use-value because one can sit on it; by contrast, a two-legged chair has no use-value (except possibly as firewood). It is their different use-values that constitute objects as different from each other, and so objects with use-value, or use-values, are inherently heterogeneous. One way producers can meet their own needs is to consume the use-values they themselves create.

Value in exchange, or exchange-value, on the other hand, derives from the fact that when each producer has the power to exchange his or her own products for those of other producers, it is possible to acquire use-values in the marketplace by offering something equivalent in exchange. Our own produced use-value is therefore "worth" so many units of some other use-value produced by someone else. In an economy where produced use-values are exchangeable as commodities, producers can meet their own needs by exchanging the use-values they themselves create for other use-values produced by other producers.

In a money economy exchanges of commodities are typically transacted indirectly through money: the producer of a commodity sells it for money and then uses the money to buy other commodities. A commodity is worth so many units of money, which is its price. Because units of money are homogeneous, qualitatively identical and differing only in quantity, so too are exchange-values expressed as prices. A theory of commodity exchange is simultaneously a theory of production, a theory of prices, and a theory of money.

Confining attention to objects that are produced to be exchanged, that is, to commodities, the problem of the theory of value is to explain what determines the exchange-value of a typical or representative commodity. Because any commodity can be transformed into any other through sale and purchase, regarded purely as exchange-values all commodities are homogeneous, differing only in quantity.

For Marx, the homogeneity of commodities as exchange-values reflects the fact that the production of any commodity requires a certain fraction of the total labour time of society. This labour time at any moment takes many different concrete forms, but labour has the capacity to adapt through training and practice to the requirements of various productive activities. It is fungible in a way that non-labour inputs are not. Underlying exchange-value is thus an amount of potentially homogeneous social labour time, social labour considered only as a quantity of (standardized or "socially necessary") hours. That labour time is always employed in particular ways, with particular tasks required to produce particular commodities. It is this heterogeneity that produces particular use-values, and Marx called "concrete labour" the labour involved from this perspective. That same labour considered as producing a quantity of homogeneous exchange-value expressed in terms of money, Marx called "abstract labour". This was then the substance of value, and was measured in units of "socially necessary labour time". Exchange-value is the form in which abstract labour appears, and since prices are expressed in monetary units, money expresses abstract labour.

Consider an equation of exchange, such as x units of commodity i are worth y units of commodity g. This is only possible because both i and g require amounts of society's total labour; so that the value of i is expressed in terms of g. This entails that i's value is expressed relatively in g, and g's value is the equivalent of that of i. However, g is some particular use-value, so that it is this use-value that expresses the value of i. Hence the concrete labour producing g represents the abstract labour that produces i. This inversion was part of what Marx called the "peculiarities of the equivalent form" (Marx 1867 [1976]: ch. 1, s. 3; also Marx 1867 [1994]) on which he also based his theory of ideology, which he attributed to the "fetishism of the commodity" (Marx 1867 [1976]: ch. 1, s. 4).

Following such inversion, social development selects some particular g (that has properties of homogeneity of units, portability, divisibility, storage without deterioration and so on) to act as the equivalent form of value of all other commodities, to act, that is, as the money commodity. The money commodity (for example, gold) has, like other commodities, particular use-values (as a conducting medium in electronic circuits or for capping teeth in dentistry) and acquires an additional use-value in serving as the universal equivalent form of value. With the development of a money commodity, the exchange-value of a unit of i is its price (p_i^*), and its price is defined as the ratio of its natural price or value (λ_i) to the natural price or value of the money commodity g (λ_g).

$$p_i^* = \frac{\lambda_i}{\lambda_g} \tag{1}$$

Equation (1) is formulated on the basis that commodities exchange as equivalents at natural prices: equivalent exchange implies that natural prices or values are proportional to social labour times required to produce commodities, with the common factor of proportionality being the inverse of the value of the money commodity, sometimes called the monetary expression of labour time (MELT) $m = \frac{1}{\lambda_g}$. Retaining this presumption for the present, then equation (1) applies to every commodity (and obviously therefore to every aggregate of commodities). Because of this universality, it could be called the commodity law of exchange. In particular, the commodity law of exchange applies to labour-power and to aggregate value added. It is through these aggregates that Marx explained the mechanism of exploitation in capitalist production. Consider each in turn.

The commodity law of exchange and labour-power
The distinction between labour and labour-power is one of the defining characteristics of the Marxian approach. By labour-power Marx meant the capacity to work. When an individual is in possession of (sufficient) means of production, she can exercise her capacity to work, and the work then done is her labour, which eventuates in a produced use-value, to be directly consumed and/or traded for other use-values. However, if an individual has to access means of production through the market, and has negligible non-labour resources with which to trade, then effectively the only asset that individual has to sell is her capacity to work, or her labour-power. Of course, logically some individuals might choose to sell non-labour inputs to purchase means of subsistence, but historically the typical case was that most individuals had nothing with which to trade except their capacity to work. The historical process that separates people from the means of production (typically a separation from land, enforced either economically, or juridically or through extra-legal violence) is called "primitive accumulation" (Marx 1867 [1976]: pt 8).

In these circumstances labour-power is commoditized, with, like any other commodity, a use-value, a value and a price. Its use-value is straightforward, for the purchaser of labour-power can set it to work in a production process, producing value of greater amount than the value of labour-power. This excess is called surplus-value, and it accrues to the purchaser of labour-power (just as the use-value of a loaf of bread accrues to its purchaser, who can consume it or throw it to the ducks, or whatever). The existence of surplus-value requires that the capitalist purchaser of labour-power can extract from the worker labour producing more value than he paid for it. Hence the value of labour-power requires careful specification.

Labour-power is a peculiar commodity, because it is a human attribute, and the (re)production of people takes place outside of capitalist relations of production, which lends some analytical complexity to the concept of the value of labour-power. By definition, the value of labour-power, like any other commodity, is the socially necessary labour time required to produce it. Marx hypothesized that this was equivalent to the value of the subsistence wage-bundle of commodities, although he modified the Malthusian perspective with a focus on social norms. Hence, continuing the presumption of equivalent exchange, and if H is the total number of hours worked, then, at the prevailing value of money, the value of labour-power (λ_{lp}) per hour of hire is the hourly wage rate (w), which in turn is spent on the (hourly) wage bundle of commodities (b/H) at prices p^*_b:

$$\frac{\lambda_{lp}}{\lambda_g} = w = \frac{\lambda_b}{\lambda_g}\frac{b}{H} = p_b^* \frac{b}{H} \tag{2}$$

However, it is not only equivalent exchange that underpins equation (2); it is also that people are perfectly mobile and that labour-power is fungible across all potential and actual employments. Only then could there be a uniform value of labour-power, or, equivalently, a uniform wage rate.

The importance of the distinction between labour and labour-power cannot be overemphasized. The seller of labour-power meets the purchaser in the marketplace as a juridical equal, and sellers and purchasers contract over only what is their own property. Exchanges only take place if they are mutually advantageous, and sellers and purchasers are free to walk away if this does not obtain. However, sellers of labour-power are not only free to walk away from unsatisfactory contract proposals. They are also "free" of possession of the means of production (and of resources through which to possess them) via the historical processes of dispossession that created a property-less working class. Thus they must strike a bargain with some (capitalist) owner of means of production or withdraw from the social division of labour altogether in circumstances in which relying on their own use-value production was tantamount to destitution and starvation. This dual freedom is summarized in the notion of perfect labour mobility: while workers are free to sell their labour-power to whomever they choose, they are compelled to sell it to someone in order to participate in the social division of labour. And the purchaser of labour-power is free to enjoy its use-value by consuming it, which means putting it to work in a production process, creating more value than labour-power possesses. In capitalist society, freedom in exchange, with exchange of equivalents, is the precondition of exploitation in production.

The commodity law of exchange and total value added
For Marx, following Ricardo, the value of a single commodity comprises the value embodied in the means of production with which labour works (transferred through concrete labour to the product of the production process) and the socially necessary labour time worked by living labour. If A is a matrix of input–output coefficients, a_{ij} expressing the amount of commodity i required to produce one unit of commodity j, and l is a vector whose components l_j express the number of hours of labour required to produce one unit of commodity j, then the vector of values is:

$$\lambda = \lambda A + l \tag{3}$$

Under equivalent exchange at natural prices proportional to labour times required for the production of commodities, the relationship "price equals value divided by the value of money" obviously holds for any aggregate of commodities. In particular, it holds for value added (H).

In physical terms, gross outputs (x) and net outputs (y) are related by:

$$x = Ax + y \tag{4}$$

Postmultiplying equation (3) by x, premultiplying equation (4) by λ and subtracting yields:

$$lx = \lambda y \tag{5}$$

where $lx \equiv H$. Hence:

$$p^*y = \frac{\lambda y}{\lambda_g} = \frac{H}{\lambda_g} \tag{6}$$

or net output aggregated in price terms is proportional to total value added.

However, equation (6) is more than a trivial proportionality relation. For the total number of hours worked in various concrete activities can also be regarded as the total potential abstract social labour of society, which expresses itself in the money price of commodities. This social abstract labour is distributed across different production processes that together produce net outputs y. So prices can be thought of as the means by which this distribution is effected. Equation (6) determines prices as the bearers of social labour time, which is obvious when all prices are proportional to labour values.

If the wage is w, the profit a capitalist appropriates from the production of a unit of commodity j when commodities exchange at prices p^* is $\pi_j = p_j^* - \sum_i p_i^* a_{ij} - wl_j$. Aggregating these profits, we see that:

$$s = \sum_j \pi_j x_j = p(I - A)x - wlx = p^*y - wH = (m - w)H \tag{7}$$

Thus the capitalist who employs labour-power to produce a commodity appropriates a profit, or surplus-value equal to the excess of the value added by the expenditure of labour in production over the wage paid for the labour-power. By virtue of equivalent exchange at natural prices or values proportional to the labour time required to produce commodities, total profits must be proportional to total surplus-value in terms of labour time, and total wages to total variable capital in terms of labour time. In this manner, aggregate profits accruing to the capitalist class are determined as the unpaid labour of the working class.

The capitalist law of exchange

On this basis of equivalent exchange, Marx analysed with considerable historical and contemporary detail how capital (any sum of money invested in order to make more money) creates surplus-value in the production process, and then how surplus-value creates capital as an accumulation process. In essence this was what now would be called a macroeconomic approach. All individual capitals are treated qualitatively as identical, differing only in quantity. Any individual capital in these terms is representative of all capitals, and Marx talked in terms of "capital in general". As long as his focus was on the economic categories representing class, this was sufficient for his purpose of exposing and analysing the deepest determinations.

However, it was only a first step. The freedom of markets entails competition, for each individual capital pursues the highest profit on its investment, and this entails mobility of capital in addition to the previously presumed mobility of labour. If capitals are perfectly mobile, then competition must ensure an equalized rate of profit on average over repeated production periods. Thus, in an economy where capitalists as employers allocate social labour, the principle of the equalization of the rate of profit determines natural prices, while the principle of the equalization of the advantages of production tends to equalize wages, or more generally rates of exploitation (ratios of unpaid to paid labour, because workers are still free to move from sectors where they are more exploited to sectors where they are less exploited). There is no reason to presume that the equalization of the profit rate is actually achieved – rather it is a tendency, whose long run achievement is continually disrupted by empirical contingency. Marx called the prices at which the rate of profit is equalized prices of production: they are Smith's natural prices when capitalist employers determine the distribution of labour among branches of commodity production. Such a determination is the capitalist law of exchange.

Prices of production in general are different from the natural prices-proportional-to-labour time required of equations (1), (2) and (6). For once capital-in-general is individuated into competing capitals, those competing capitals will have production processes that typically differ in technology. There will be a whole spectrum of ratios of non-labour to labour inputs, from highly mechanized almost completely automated technologies to those that are very labour-intensive. Highly automated capitals employ very little labour; very labour-intensive industries employ a lot. With perfect labour mobility enforcing a uniform rate of surplus-value, highly automated capitals produce very little new value and very labour-intensive industries a lot. Therefore the prices at which each capital would earn the same rate of profit cannot be prices-proportional-to-values. Hence capitalist exchange (except under very special analytical assumptions) *must* be non-equivalent exchange. This entails that value is realized at prices of production in different sectors from where it was produced. The competition among capitalist firms that enforces the tendency for rates of profit on invested capital to be equalized effectively redistributes surplus-value among the sectors of commodity production.

In principle, this does not affect equation (6), for in the aggregate value added is invariant to where it is produced: the total number of hours of labour remains the same. Hence writing p for the vector of prices of production:

$$py = \frac{H}{\lambda_g} \tag{8}$$

Equations (6) and (8) have the same interpretation: prices distribute social labour across net output. They differ in that distribution according to whether commodity exchange or capitalist exchange is considered, but for prices to be bearers of social labour time, what matters is only that there is a distribution. The social division of labour allocates portions of social labour to production processes, and it does this through a decentralized price mechanism. Prices, qualitatively, are always the bearers of social labour, and, quantitatively, total net output, evaluated at whatever prices are, must always equal total hours worked at the prevailing value of money. Because of this, equation (8) also serves to define the value of money in a world of capitalist exchange and allows for a more general notion of money than the commodity gold.

The redistribution of surplus-value through competition also does not affect the sale of labour-power for a wage, because there is no capitalist production process of labour-power, no rate of profit earned on its production and no technology of production to consider. Hence the left-hand side of equation (2) is not affected by the difference between commodity exchange and capitalist exchange:

$$\frac{\lambda_{lp}}{\lambda_g} = w \tag{9}$$

where, as in equation (8), the value of money is understood more generally than the value of the commodity gold. However, the wage cannot be proportional to the labour value of the wage bundle of commodities (which means that the latter does not determine the value of labour-power under capitalist exchange), and it is also unnecessarily restrictive to presume the whole wage is always spent, so that budget constraint part of equation (2) can be dropped. Equations (8) and (9) together imply that the value of labour-power is the wage share of money value added, so that, however prices are conceived, profits remain the measure of unpaid labour, the rate of surplus-value is the profit–wage ratio, and capitalist exchange is founded on exploitation.

We have emphasized that, equations (8) and (9) apart, the capitalist law of exchange entails that value appears in places other than where it is produced, and that this is not contingent or accidental but systemic. This feature of Marx's account is particularly important, and its implications are under-recognized. For unequal or non-equivalent exchange implies that surplus-value is redistributed. In principle, the magnitude of these redistributions can be calculated by multiplying each capital's wage bill by the uniform rate of exploitation, and comparing the resulting surplus-value produced in each firm or sector with the actual profits accruing there. However, in practice this is complicated by another factor.

For non-equivalent exchange is a more general phenomenon than just the requirements made of prices by different technological structures. Consider again the equivalent exchanges of commodity exchange and of capital in general. Once a commodity has been produced, it has to be sold, and this requires human activity. Similarly, it takes human activity to assemble labour and non-labour inputs ready to commence production. However, selling an already produced commodity changes the form in which value exists (from a commodity form to a money form), but it does not change its amount. Similarly, using a sum of money to purchase labour and non-labour inputs again changes the form in which value exists (from a money form to a productive form), but it does not change its amount. Marx called the labour that is actually value-creating "productive labour", and the labour that alters only the form in which value exists but not its amount (typically commercial and financial labour) "unproductive labour". He also called "unproductive" the pure labour of supervision. However, all of these activities must be paid for, and the only source for their payment is the production of new value. Hence a more careful specification of what labour is to count as value-creating requires a further elaboration of unequal or non-equivalent exchange.

Unequal exchange means that Marx's analysis has deep and in some dimensions very non-intuitive implications. Even very large productive capitalist firms are small relative to the whole system of capitalist production, the division of labour it creates, and the enormous resulting pool of surplus-value in the whole world capitalist economy. Thus each capitalist firm makes a negligible contribution to the pool of surplus-value through the exploitation of its own workers. The profitability of any firm rests on its ability to secure a share of the pool of surplus-value through its competitive strategy. In extreme cases, such as land rents and intellectual property royalties and rents, the appropriators of surplus-value may make no contribution at all to the pool of surplus-value through production and the direct exploitation of workers. In many cases strategies that increase a productive firm's share of the pool of surplus-value, such as cost reduction through technical change or shifting to lower-wage labour-power, also do contribute to enlarging the global pool of surplus-value. However, the contribution any particular firm makes to this pool is bound to be small compared to the effects of its competitive strategy on its share of the pool.

The resulting apparent disconnection between the realization of surplus-value in particular firms or sectors and the expenditure of productive labour in actual production leads to widespread illusions and misconceptions in understanding the capitalist economic system. The most common misconception, which Marx's detailed analyses in volume III of *Capital* (1894 [1981]) were aimed at dispelling, is that value and surplus-value are not actually produced by the expenditure of labour at all. Victims of this misconception (which include everyone educated to look at the world through the lenses of neoclassical price theory) will be led to one or another of the fallacious theories of value anatomized in Marx's *Theories of Surplus-Value*, such as the idea that value is the "economic (consumer) surplus" realized from the transfer of assets from agents who subjectively value them less to agents who subjectively value them more through exchange. From these points of view the distinction between productive and unproductive labour, which was fundamental to the classical political economists and Marx, becomes incomprehensible.

Similarly, the perennial flourishing of enthusiasms for imaginary economies based on completely automated production of goods, services such as information processing, intellectual property creation, or financial manipulations that seem to involve negligible labour expenditure rests on the same misunderstanding. The dreamers of these alternative economic universes confuse the mode of appropriation of surplus-value with the conditions of production of surplus-value. From the point of view of a software seller with a powerful monopoly of a proprietary system subject to network externalities, who can sell the same software over and over again with negligible costs of production, the pool of surplus-value does indeed seem to be limited only by the software seller's own imagination and competitive ruthlessness. In these cases (which are more and more prominent in the contemporary globalized economy) there can be very high degrees of increasing returns to scale and diminishing average costs to the appropriation of surplus-value. However, the core lesson of the theory of value of the classical political economists is that the actual source of value and surplus-value lies in the expenditure of productive labour.

"Dual system" interpretations of the theory of value and the "transformation problem"
The interpretation of Marx's theory of value we have offered in the last section is sometimes called a "single-system" theory, because it emphasizes the relationship between the theoretical categories of value and price and real-world money prices. Another influential body of work on the theory of value takes a different, "dual-system", approach, based on a system of "values" proportional to embodied labour coefficients that coexists with the phenomenal system of money prices. These embodied labour-coefficient

values are determined according to the principles we have called the commodity law of exchange, in which mobility of labour leads to natural long-period prices of commodities proportional to the labour time required to produce them. Dual-system theorists identify Marxian categories such as the value of labour-power and the rate of exploitation in terms of this underlying, but not directly observable, system of values. In the dual-system framework, the question arises as to the relation between the system of values and the system of observable prices of production. The study of this relation constitutes the "problem of the transformation of values into prices of production" or, more compactly, "the transformation problem".

The discussion of the transformation problem revolves around the mathematical investigation of the relation between equation (3), which is taken as defining values proportional to embodied labour coefficients, and the representation of profit-rate equalizing prices derived from Sraffa's work:

$$\boldsymbol{p} = (1 + r)\boldsymbol{p}A + w\boldsymbol{l} \tag{10}$$

where $\boldsymbol{p}$ is a vector of relative prices and the other symbols have the meanings we have assigned already. The main difficulty encountered in the transformation problem is in reproducing the invariance claimed by Marx in chapter 10 of Volume III of *Capital* (1894 [1981]) for the total value of production, variable capital, surplus-value, and hence the rate of surplus-value and profit rate between the value and price of production schemes. This difficulty has led theorists in this tradition either to assert a meaning to value and its significance which, because of its detachment from the prices of equation (10), is vulnerable to the charge of arbitrariness (for example, Sweezy 1942); or it has led them to abandon a labour theory of value altogether, to concentrate on the analysis and implications of equation (10) (for example, Steedman 1977).

From the point of view of the single-system approach, it is more natural to pose these issues in terms of an "inverse transformation problem", which takes observed prices, output, and productive labour inputs as given and seeks to recover the abstract labour time embodied in commodities produced in each line of production. One way to solve this problem is to assume that rates of exploitation of productive labour are equalized across different sectors by the mobility of labour, which determines the abstract labour time imputed to each sector of production, and identifies the redistribution of surplus-value between sectors in a pattern that is consistent with the economy-wide rate of surplus-value defined earlier in our discussion.

Value and Price in Classical Economics: A Summary

Smith, Ricardo and Marx all understood the economy as a decentralized social organism which was self-organized through markets and the prices they established. All three presumed labour mobility and capital mobility. For all three, the relevant prices for political economic analysis were "natural" prices (Smith and Ricardo), or "prices of production" (Marx), prices at which the rate of profit was equalized. None considered at any moment of time that the rate of profit was actually equalized, so that explanation of prices required a "long period" approach, in which economic laws were laws of tendency.

For Smith the social division of labour was organized through the profit-seeking actions of selfish individuals. In the absence of private property in land and means of production, labour mobility implied that a labour theory of value explained natural prices. However, Smith never worked out how a labour theory of value could be applied to the property relations of a capitalist economy to explain rent and profits, and he quickly abandoned it in favour of his adding-up theory.

Ricardo shared Smith's general vision, but extended the labour theory of value to the determination of natural prices in a capitalist economy in which there was private property both in land and in other non-labour inputs. However, he was unable to do this precisely, and his specification of the labour theory of value must therefore be considered incomplete.

Marx took the vision of a decentralized social organism self-organized through markets and transformed it through a focus on antagonistic class relations in production rather than the individualistic exchange relations of avaricious traders. This he achieved through the development of the distinction between labour and labour-power, which emerged out of the contrast between "commodity exchange" and "capitalist exchange". Commodity exchange combined with input mobility entailed an exact labour theory of value. Capitalist exchange combined with input mobility entailed a labour theory of value that was exact only in the labour market and for total value added. However, this was sufficient to explain the fact of exploitation, the rate of exploitation and the overall level of profits as unpaid labour. Individual prices remained qualitatively the bearers of social labour, but quantitatively diverged from labour values because capitalist exchange entailed systemic unequal or non-equivalent exchange.

The distinctions the classical political economists discovered, and Marx elaborated, between the phenomena of market prices, the underlying regularity of natural prices, and their connection with the emergent decentralized allocation of labour time enforced by commodity production have far-reaching implications. The distinction between value and price is the window through which we can understand the inner nature of the capitalist economy, and this remains the enduring feature of the classical approach to value and price as it culminated in the work of Marx.

DUNCAN FOLEY AND SIMON MOHUN

See also:

Eugen von Böhm-Bawerk (I); Ladislaus von Bortkiewicz (I); British classical political economy (II); Competition (III); Vladimir Karpovich Dmitriev (I); General equilibrium theory (III); German and Austrian schools (II); Hermann Heinrich Gossen (I); Alfred Marshall (I); Karl Heinrich Marx (I); Neo-Ricardian economics (II); Vilfredo Pareto (I); David Ricardo (I); Adam Smith (I); Piero Sraffa (I); Mikhail Ivanovich Tugan-Baranovsky (I); Anne-Robert-Jacques Turgot (I); Marie-Esprit-Léon Walras (I).

References and further reading

Debreu, G. (1959), *Theory of Value*, Cowles Foundation Monograph 17, New York: John Wiley.
Foley, D.K. (2010), 'What's wrong with the fundamental existence and welfare theorems?', *Journal of Economic Behavior & Organization*, **75** (2), 115–31.
Hobbes, T. (1651), *Leviathan*, reprinted 2010, London: Andrew Cooke, accessed 10 March 2012 at http://www.gutenberg.org/files/3207/3207-h/3207-h.htm.
Kirman, A. (2006), 'Demand theory and general equilibrium: from explanation to introspection, a journey down the wrong road', *History of Political Economy*, **38** (Supplement 1), 246–80.
Koopmans, T.C. (1957), *Three Essays on the State of Economic Science*, New York and London: McGraw-Hill.
Kurz, H.D. and N. Salvadori (1995), *Theory of Production*, Cambridge: Cambridge University Press.

Little, W., H.W. Fowler, J. Coulson and G.W.S. Friedrichsen (1973), *The Shorter Oxford English Dictionary on Historical Principles*, Oxford: Oxford University Press.
Mandeville, B. (1724), *The Fable of the Bees or Private Vices, Publick Benefits*, 2 vols, London: J. Tonson, vol. 1 with a commentary critical, historical, and explanatory by F.B. Kaye, accessed 10 March 2012 at https://books.google.co.uk/books?id=ISFWAAAAYAAJ&printsec=frontcover&dq=Mandeville+Fable+of+the+Bees&hl=en&sa=X&redir_esc=y#v=onepage&q=Mandeville%20Fable%20of%20the%20Bees&f=false.
Marx, K. (1867), *Capital*, vol. I, reprinted 1976, Harmondsworth: Penguin.
Marx, K. (1867), *The Value Form*, in S. Mohun (ed.) (1994), *Debates in Value Theory*, London: Macmillan.
Marx, K. (1868), Letter to Kugelman 11 July 1868, in K. Marx and F. Engels (1988), *Collected Works*, vol. 43. London: Lawrence and Wishart.
Marx, K. (1894), *Capital*, vol. III, reprinted 1981, Harmondsworth: Penguin.
Marx, K. (1973), *Grundrisse*, Harmondsworth: Penguin.
Ricardo, D. (1821), *On the Principles of Political Economy and Taxation*, in P. Sraffa (ed.) with the collaboration of M.H. Dobb (1951), *The Works and Correspondence of David Ricardo*, vol. 1, Cambridge: Cambridge University Press.
Shaikh, A. (1998), 'The empirical strength of the labour theory of value', R. Bellofiore (ed.), *Marxian Economics: A Reappraisal*, vol. 2, London: Macmillan, pp. 225–51.
Smith, A. (1776), *An Inquiry into the Nature and Causes of the Wealth of Nations*, London: W. Strahan and T. Cadell, accessed 10 March 2012 at https://www.gutenberg.org/ebooks/3300.
Sraffa, P. (1960), *Production of Commodities By Means of Commodities*, Cambridge: Cambridge University Press.
Steedman, I. (1977), *Marx After Sraffa*, London: New Left Books.
Sweezy, P.M. (1942), *The Theory of Capitalist Development*, New York: Monthly Review Press.

Welfare economics

Welfare economics is the economic study of the definition and the measure of the social welfare; it offers the theoretical framework used in public economics to help collective decision making, to design public policies, and to make social evaluations. Questions usually tackled by welfare economics are the following: what is social welfare? Is there a reliable and satisfying way to measure it? If social welfare is based on individual preferences, can we derive a social preference from the preferences of individuals? Are competitive equilibrium outcomes optimal in the sense that they lead to the highest social welfare? Can any optimal outcome be achieved by a modified market mechanism? Can we really formulate recommendations for public policies on the basis of such welfare analyses?

In spite of the uncontroversial importance of all these issues, some have been overshadowed while others have drawn enormous attention. The exclusion of normative information was justified in a bid to scientific rigour, until the oblivion of the prescriptive role of welfare economics. From then on, the death of welfare economics has been often foretold (Hicks 1939: 697; Chipman and Moore 1978: 548; Mishan 1981; Hausman and MacPherson 1996: 96). Setting out the history of welfare economics implies, first, to recall its evolution, secondly to discuss the reasons why it has almost missed its project. Thirdly, there are strong reasons to hope: welfare economics is back (Sen 1999; Fleurbaey and Mongin 2005), yet at the cost of accepting the normative nature of (welfare) economics.

This entry defends that the driving forces of the evolution of welfare economics through the last century are the role of interpersonal comparisons of utility, the interpretation of utility, and the status of value judgements. Interpersonal comparisons of utility concern the trade-offs between different persons' welfares; their existence requires these trade-offs to be meaningful. This entry recalls they have been more or less accepted. The interpretation of utility may be objective or subjective. Utility is subjective if it captures the individual's personal judgement or degree of satisfaction. It differs from other interpretations of utility capturing some mere description of a state of affairs, including revealed preferences or objective utility. This entry shows that when utility is subjective or based on revealed preferences, it can just be measured ordinally; in such a case the numerical value of utility captures mere comparisons but no computations are allowed. This is one reason to question whether interpersonal comparisons are meaningful. Value judgements refer to the incorporation of a particular set of values, regarding the rightness, goodness, usefulness or fairness in judgements, for instance, regarding the trade-offs between different persons' welfares. Consequently, the exclusion of values from the scope of welfare economics is another reason why interpersonal comparisons can hardly be made meaningful.

The evolution of welfare economics marks up different periods and types of contributions. According to Philippe Mongin (2002, 2006), its history may be divided in at least four successive stages.

The pre-history of welfare economics is as old as political economics: classical and neo-classical economists were studying the efficiency and equity of productive systems, more specifically wondering how to value commodities or labour, and to assess the best allocation of goods and of tasks for the society (Myint 1965). Utilitarianism which, since

Jeremy Bentham, aimed at providing tools to measure and improve individual and collective well-being, may be considered as one genuine root of welfare economics.

In the first stage, the creation of the first tool of welfare economics goes back to Alfred Marshall (or, even earlier, to the works of Jules Arsène Dupuit): the introduction of the notion of consumer surplus is meant to provide a method to measure relative change in consumers' utility generated by some evolution of the environment, for example, by a variation of price induced by a fiscal policy. Assuming a link between welfare and demand, it uses the information on the shape of the demand functions to infer the utility variations. Policy recommendations may be derived from the surplus analyses. However, welfare economics was more clearly born with Arthur Cecil Pigou's book published in 1920, *The Economics of Welfare*, in which he has among others developed the famous distinction between private and social marginal cost or productivity, the role of the size and the distribution of the "national dividend" in measuring economic welfare, and his defence of the transfer principle. Pigou defends the distinction between private and social costs when there are what can now be called external effects. National dividend is somewhat the ancestor of our gross domestic product. Pigou claims that not only is welfare increased when the size of the dividend increases, but welfare also increases when its distribution among the rich and the poor is more equal. To capture the notion of equality, Pigou developed the principle of transfer according to which a distribution of income X is more equal than another distribution Y if the only difference between X and Y is that one individual transferred $\delta€$ to a poorer person than her – who remains not as rich after transfers. In other words, X is more equal according to the Pigou criterion of transfers if the rich are less rich and the poor are not as poor. The definition of welfare was not really unified at this stage: it could be the "national dividend" or a mix between the amount of the dividend and the distribution of income, and even something else. The specificity of this early stage of welfare economics is its deliberate account for value judgements, and as a consequence, its use of interpersonal comparisons of utility.

In the second stage, the new welfare economics established a clear separation between the optimality conditions based on the Paretian condition and their applications to the market. A social state X is better than Y according to the Pareto criterion if X is better than Y for every individual; X is Pareto optimal if it is not possible to improve the situation of any individual without injuring the situation of at least one individual. There exist other Pareto conditions considering the possibility of transfers. At this stage, the definition of welfare was uniformly based on strictly ordinal and subjective individual utilities. The best-known applications are the fundamental theorems of welfare economics. The question of income distribution, including when applying the principle of compensation, was then mostly left aside.

In the third stage, after the Arrovian negative result tolled the death knell in the 1950s, social choice theory, public economics and the theories of inequality and poverty have been kept separate for decades. The only noteworthy element of continuity and unity is that most contributions were then welfarist, that is, the only relevant information for social welfare or public decision was individual utilities.

In the fourth stage, some post-welfarist economic theories of justice or fairness have been developed recently. Some economists suggest redirecting their research, for example, to analyse rights, or to integrate information such as talents and handicaps, opportunities and capabilities among others.

This entry is organized as followed. The Paretian watershed exposed in the next section marks the evolution from the first to the second stage of welfare economics and the formulation of the two fundamental theorems of welfare economics. The problems raised with both approaches of the new welfare economics described in the following section provide some clues to understand the disintegration of the third stage. Recent and promising avenues for researches are developed in the last section.

The Paretian Watershed

The old and the new welfare economics

At the turn of the century, Vilfredo Pareto introduced the concept of ophelimity in economics. Ophelimity differs from utility, which is a richer sociological concept that may be hard to tackle with scientific rigor. On the basis of scientific criteria, Pareto encouraged narrowing the amount of information we could derive from it: it should be an ordinal concept, and interpersonal comparisons of ophelimity ought to be ruled out.

Had the term "ophelimity" not been retained afterwards, this watershed would have been confirmed by the publication of Lionel Robbins's famous 1932 book, *An Essay on the Nature and Significance of Economic Science*, in which he disputed the meaning of interpersonal comparisons of utility and the material definition of economics. As far as a subjective account of utility holds, there exists no way, whether by introspection or by observation, to compare the intensity of satisfactions of two different persons (Cooter and Rappoport 1984). If assertions implying the meaning of cardinal utility or of comparisons, such as the rule of decreasing marginal utility, are formulated, they necessarily derive from a value judgement. Notwithstanding, if economics claims to remain a science, hence to be value neutral, such comparisons should be absolutely avoided.

Paul Anthony Samuelson (1947: 249) draws the consequences of the ban of interpersonal comparisons of utility, as well as of the restrictions of utility to the scientific theory of demand, by distinguishing the old from the new welfare economics:

> While in a real sense there is only one all-inclusive welfare economics, which reaches its most complete formulation in the writings of Bergson, it is possible to distinguish between the New Welfare Economics . . . which makes no assumptions concerning interpersonal comparability of utility, and the Old Welfare Economics which starts out with such assumptions.

The Pareto criterion

The only uncontroversial normative criterion at the collective level for the new welfare economics relies on individual utilities, as far as comparing utilities among individuals is not required nor even allowed. According to Pareto (1906 [1909]: 261):

> [T]he members of a collectivity enjoy maximum ophelimity in a certain position when it is impossible to find a way of moving from that position very slightly in such a manner that the ophelimity enjoyed by each of the individuals of that collectivity increases or decreases. That is to say, any small displacement in departing from that position necessarily has the effect of increasing the ophelimity which certain individuals enjoy, and decreasing that which others enjoy, of being agreeable to some, and disagreeable to others.

A social state is hence said to be Pareto optimal if it is not possible to improve the situation of certain individuals without making the situation of at least one other individual worse off.

Let us consider how to use this criterion. Compare different social states for a given population, where everyone has monotonous preferences over the commodities x and y. In state S1, the allocation of resources among individuals is fully equal for each commodity. Now, if individuals' tastes are heterogeneous – some prefer to have more x while others want relatively more y – they will find opportunities for exchange between x and y. In the social state S2, the situation of individuals who saw an interest in the exchange has improved while the situation of others did not deteriorate from S1 to S2. S2 is better than S1 according to the Pareto criterion as the situation of some has improved without damaging the situations of others. Nobody has a vested interest to go back from S2 to S1 and, at most, some are indifferent. The fundamental theorems of welfare economics characterize this optimum, and specify the conditions of its existence (see below). The choice among different Pareto-optimal equilibria, notably on the basis of explicit value judgements, is the task devoted to the Bergson–Samuelson version of welfare economics.

Imagine now that, in state S3, resources entirely belong to a single rich individual, while the others are totally deprived. The Pareto criterion does not help to compare S1 and S3. May the unequal distribution of S3 be repellent, the rich individual's satisfaction would drop from S3 to S1, which implies that at least one person would suffer a downturn. As the Pareto criterion does not apply, no ranking between S1 and S3, or S3 and S2 may be derived. Hence a strict Paretian welfare economics is mute as to whether or not public policies should go towards state S1 or S2 while in S3. More generally, it cannot disentangle situations in which trade-offs among the satisfactions of different individuals are required. However, most policies are likely to hurt some individuals or groups of individuals in order to improve the situation of another significant group of people. They imply trade-offs at the end, hence they rely on some kinds of interpersonal comparisons of utility. That is why, after Robbins's attack against the normative aspects of economics and especially against the use of interpersonal comparisons, welfare economics was likely to become silent for any policy recommendations and could have lost its *raison d'être*.

The British version of the Paretian welfare economics provides some tricks to generate recommendations without, so they claim, involving any value judgements. The new approaches to welfare economics such as the capability approach and the equity theory succeed in considering these situations and formulate explicit normative criteria to justify the trade-offs.

The fundamental theorems of welfare economics
The social optimum is well described through the fundamental theorems of welfare economics, which formalize some ideas already present in Pareto's works (especially for the first theorem) and in Walras's works (especially for the latter).

Oskar Lange (1942), Abba Lerner (1934), and Harold Hotelling (1938) have provided the first order conditions for economic efficiency, and the primary proofs of the first theorem. The problem of maximizing overall welfare amounts to maximizing the utility of each individual under the constraints of others' utility, possible allocation and transformation functions, which has up to three conditions. First, individual utilities are maximized if the marginal rates of substitution for two given commodities between two different individuals are equal. Second, the aggregate output and the optimal allocation of goods among individuals are obtained by equalizing the marginal rates of substitution with the marginal rates of transformation between the two given commodities. Finally, the marginal rates of transformation of the different firms among any two commodities must be equal to guarantee the efficiency of production for the various technologies. Notice these results, now rigorously established, resume some economic laws previously discovered by the precursors of the marginalists, such as Hermann Heinrich Gossen in 1854, and by the marginalists themselves, such as William Stanley Jevons in 1871.

Kenneth Arrow (1951), Gérard Debreu (1951), and then the two together (Arrow and Debreu 1954) have generalized the proofs and these results. In formal terms, they have overcome the use of calculus, though intuitive to use for demonstrations related to optimization problems, by now using set theory. They have shown, with very few conditions, that the optimum more fundamentally derives from the price system. That is how they have formulated what is now called the two fundamental theorems of welfare economics.

The first theorem of welfare economics states that competitive equilibria are Pareto-optimal, if individual preferences are monotonic and if there are complete markets.

The second fundamental theorem of welfare economics states that one can achieve any Pareto-optimal allocation in a competitive equilibrium when the social planner undertakes an appropriate redistribution of endowments. Among several Pareto optima, some are probably more satisfactory than others. The theorem points out that the preferred social optimum can be achieved by a competitive equilibrium if accompanied by proper redistribution policy which shall establish the new "initial" allocations. An important consequence of this theorem is that it is not necessary to alter the competitive system to obtain Pareto optimality. A trade-off between efficiency vs. equity is not any more required; however, the issue of the redistribution is pregnant.

The New Welfare Economics

Two types of approaches of the new welfare economics were developed in the 1930s and the 1940s, which we may call the British approach and the American approach.

The British approach to the new welfare economics

As far as the only uncontroversial normative criterion is the Pareto criterion, welfare economics establishes a clear test: a situation is economically efficient if it could not be better for the individuals without decreasing some people's satisfaction, which implies unanimity to justify any change. If it were nonetheless confined to such unanimous improvements, its object would be far too restrictive. The British approach, particularly represented by the works of Nicholas Kaldor (1939), John Hicks (1941) and Tibor Scitovsky (1941), essentially coming from the London School of Economics, developed a new concept of Pareto improvements in order to reach a decision and bypass the problem of comparisons. They propose a "Pareto efficiency criterion" which considers the possibility of hypothetical compensations, and then applies the test of unanimity. Because the compensations are just hypothetical, they claim their consideration does not imply any value judgements.

Imagine a single individual i loses x by a new public policy, while all others gain. The strict version of Pareto criterion cannot conclude that this policy should be implemented. Imagine now that others gain an amount that is greater than x. If the winners compensate Mrs. i by transferring to her the amount x, they would still gain from the new policy, while Mrs. i would now be, at least, indifferent. The change would be a Pareto-improvement, that is, would be unanimously better, if such compensation were made. In all cases, this change passes the test of hypothetical compensations and is considered to be "Pareto efficient", and then could be recommended. Economists are however not entitled to decide whether or not these transfers should eventually be made; such responsibility should be left to politicians on a second and distinct stage. This division of tasks between the economist as a scientist and the policymaker as a politician allows compliance with Robbins's contentions, yet formulation of public policy recommendations. From then on, this general framework rehabilitated surplus analyses and paved the way to the widespread use of cost–benefit analysis.

Extremely serious and sceptic criticisms have been raised against this approach by leading experts in the field (Arrow 1963; Sen 1979c; Boadway and Bruce 1984, among others). First, the internal consistency of the model is challenged because there are two criteria, and each of them is valid for a different reference state. Imagine you apply compensating variations, that is, you compare project state and status quo according to the status quo reference. You may prefer the project state to the status quo. Now apply the criterion of equivalent variations, that is, compare the project state and the status quo according to the project state reference. You may now prefer the status quo. At the end, this welfare criteria "could not escape the possibility of giving rise to an inconsistent sequence of policy recommendations, unless either the distribution of income and wealth or the forms and degree of dissimilarity of consumers' preferences were assumed to be suitably restricted" (Chipman and Moore 1978: 578). Secondly, the normative aspects of this approach are strongly contested: even though it pretends to avoid interpersonal comparisons of utilities, it operates exactly on the basis of their existence (Cooter and Rappoport 1984; Blackorby and Donaldson 1990). Yet it does prevent any discussion of the value judgements involved in such analysis. Thirdly, beyond the problem of aggregation, these tests are more generally blamed because they are "welfarist". A social welfare evaluation is called welfarist when it relies on subjective individual utilities only (Sen 1979a, 1979b). Amartya K. Sen and many others have shown the logical, pragmatic and normative limits of such an account of individual welfare in the context of designing or assessing public policies. Chipman and Moore concluded in 1978: "judged in relation to its basic objective of enabling economists to make welfare prescriptions without having to make value judgements and, in particular, interpersonal comparisons of utility, the New Welfare Economics must be considered a failure" (Chipman and Moore 1978: 548). In spite of such an acknowledgement, the success of this approach in occupying a leading position in most contemporary works of public economics, industrial economics or international economics remains today unchallenged.

The American approach to the new welfare economics

What shall be called here "the American approach" is associated with the position of Abram Bergson, from the Massachusetts Institute of Technology (MIT), and Paul Samuelson, from Harvard University, that is, both coming from Cambridge, Massachusetts in the United States. Bergson formalized the concept of social welfare in

1938 (Burk [Bergson] 1938). He defines it as a function of all the elements relevant for welfare: all products, consumer's goods, the amount of work of each type, non-labour factors, characteristics of the environment, and so on. Through the application of the Pareto criterion, the function may emphasize the "fundamental value of individual preference." The social welfare function, as eventually formulated by Samuelson (1947), is defined as a function of the individual utility functions that each individual derives from the social state. The shape of these functions captures some value judgements that are explicitly formulated.

How can we legitimately decide which would be the right social welfare function? What does a "social preference" even mean? The question was notably asked by the logician Olaf Helmer to Kenneth Arrow when both were working at the Rand Corporation in 1948. Consistently, this function should rely on the individuals' views, yet without resorting to interpersonal comparisons of utility. Arrow (1963) provides a first answer in 1950. He shows that, under certain conditions, it is impossible to aggregate the preferences of at least three rational individuals in a single collective preference, which would itself be rational (that is, represented by a complete and transitive relation over social states). These conditions are the following: we must not exclude any combination of individual preferences (no restriction domain); we do not wish to resort to dictatorial decision (non-dictatorship); the collective decision should not contradict the unanimous preferences (Pareto principle). Arrow also imposes an independence to non-relevant alternatives condition, which he interpreted as a ban on interpersonal comparisons of utility. This impossibility is at the very least annoying: we cannot derive a collective judgement on the basis of individual preferences unless it is dictatorial. It is hence questionable whether the notion of collective welfare would at all make sense. For this reason, the new welfare economics seemed bound to a failure again. Fortunately, this prediction did not materialize.

A Promising Future for Welfare Economics

Different challenges indeed need to be taken up to restore a future for welfare economics: it should be possible to make recommendations of public policies; either interpersonal comparisons of utility are impossible and not required, or their meaning and their status should be clearly defended; a framework to make explicit which value judgements are at stake is needed; and it is necessary to go beyond the Arrovian impossibility to legitimate the use of social welfare function. While the economics of happiness has provided some positive evidences of the necessity to challenge the notion of welfare, the comparative approach and the theory of equity lead us to expect a promising future for a normative welfare economics.

Economics of happiness

In the 1950s, Richard Easterlin examined whether income promoted happiness in the population on the basis of opinion surveys. In his famous article published in 1974, he has observed that, in a given country, people with higher incomes are more likely to claim to be happy. However, in international comparisons, at least for countries with income high enough to meet basic needs, the expressed level of happiness does not vary much with the national per capita income. Finally, although the per capita income increased steadily in the United States between 1946 and 1970, expressed happiness recorded no upward trend in the long run, and even decreased between 1960 and 1970. Facing the Easterlin paradox, the standard public policies, which are based exclusively on economic growth, seem to be missing their target. If growth and wealth are not what count, the primary goal should be to identify the factors for happiness. The "economics of happiness" is essentially a positive, interdisciplinary, and empirical literature. It describes what is, but does not study what ought to be. Happiness studies are interdisciplinary in the sense that they belong to economics, cognitive sciences, humanities and social sciences. Notice it constitutes an alternative to the standard economic model. First, it moves away from the revealed preference model and from the usual assumptions of rationality. Then the overall satisfaction of individuals is at stake, rather than just the satisfaction they derive from the consumption of market goods. It consists in conducting econometric studies of happiness, emotion, subjective well-being, quality of life, life satisfaction – in so far as those terms are, in this specific context, interchangeable – to identify their factors. Measurement of happiness often relies on self-assessment scales, based on responses to questionnaires in which participants express how happy they feel.

Since the Easterlin paradox, many studies have tried to explain why, at the aggregate level, growth of national income did not necessarily enhance well-being. The results of the economics of happiness reveal that poverty reduces happiness more than wealth increases it; an increase of income for a poor person is more likely to increase his or her happiness than an increase in income for a rich person. Happiness can be enhanced by reducing inequalities, improving working conditions, the reduction of working time and, in some cases, neutralizing the negative effects of unemployment and some school reforms. Besides, we learn that the influence of purely economic factors in the happiness of people is generally overestimated in our representations as compared with factors. However, unemployment and labour relations can have considerable influence in the lives of people. Unemployment kills happiness, even after individuals get their jobs back. Some think happiness may constitute a yardstick, and that it is possible to transcribe it in money measures, which allow cost–benefit analysis to be completed.

Gathering information on the factors to enhance or to avoid decreasing of happiness, as well as on the measure of happiness, most likely may be of great help for policymakers. It appears to be a particularly innovative and important contribution to understanding the determinants of happiness, for making *ex post* evaluation of certain public policies, and to complete the data needed by policymakers who should not be satisfied with economic data. Nevertheless, the analyses of surveys have given rise to many criticisms, at the methodological and the normative level. Some highlight difficulties in interpreting the replies, challenge their reliability, and doubt that cross-country comparisons are meaningful. More generally, the very status of subjective data is discussed. If individuals are happy with what they have and what they do, they may be happy out of adaptation. This becomes highly problematic if adaptation is nothing but resignation. Beyond the methodological criticisms, some question its ability to formulate policy recommendations. At a pinch this research could justify the administration of tranquilizers to everyone, as in Layard (2005). Although hardly anybody would seriously defend this view, this counter-intuitive example invites us to beware of any possible manipulations of happiness indicators. Furthermore, economics of happiness describes what could be the target of a benevolent policymaker – as did classical utilitarianism. However, it disregards any justifications of the relevance of the happiness criterion as it pretends to be a pure positive science. Happiness may be important for individuals, yet this does not imply governments are responsible for enhancing it.

Lucie Davoine (2009: 905) concludes: "happiness is a useful criterion to evaluate society's state, but should not be the only one: happiness data can allow avoiding paternalism and ethnocentrism, but happiness economics face several and serious challenges that should prevent researchers from transforming satisfaction scores into the only barometer of public action".

The comparative approach

Throughout his critical analysis of the welfarist approach (see, in particular, Sen 1979a, 1979b), Amartya Sen suggested assessing social situations by considering quality of life rather than just utility or wealth. He developed the bases for the "comparative approach" in general and the illustration of what it could be, the capability approach, notably in his first Tanner lectures published in 1980 and his Hennipman lecture published in 1985 (see also Sen 1987, 1992, 1993). It constitutes an intermediate response to the debate on "equality of what?" which opposes welfarist approaches to resourcist theories. It provides rankings of situations based on explicit criteria of justice, and considers objective descriptions of life situations as relevant information to capture quality of life, that is, an index of individual welfare as an "individual basis for justice". On the one hand, utility, says Sen among many other critics, is too sensitive to adaptation, and, on the other hand, resources do not pay attention to the particular individual ability to transform commodities into well-being. Quality of life may hence be better captured with functionings, which Sen (1985: 6–7) defines as "what the person succeeds in doing with the commodities and characteristics at his or her command. . . . It is an achievement of a person: what he or she manages to do or to be".

At any moment, according to his or her situation, tastes, or life plans, a person may choose some particular functioning among the capability set. Capabilities are "the various combinations of possible functionings a person can achieve and from which he or she can choose one collection" (Sen 1985: 9). The wider this set is, the more the individual is free to choose between different lifestyles. The use of capabilities as an informational basis to assess quality of life therefore focuses not only on the role of commodities in generating well-being, taking into account individual's specific ability to transform commodities into well-being, but also values for itself the freedom to choose their lifestyle.

There remain two technical remarks and one further discussion. First, as far as this information is objective in the sense that they are observable and measurable on a common scale, interpersonal comparisons are meaningful (Baujard 2011) so that the latter are justified and well accepted in this context. Secondly, the assessment of capabilities is based on some valuation of lists of different functionings, themselves being a vector of achieved doings and beings. Such multi-dimensionality is likely to cause moral dilemmas in certain situations, hence to generate substantial incompleteness. For instance, what if I have more health but less education or social relations? A possible answer, specific to Sen, is to accept that rankings of social states may be incomplete. He does not consider incompleteness as a relevant problem in the context of normative issues (see, notably, Sen 2009). Another approach is to gather the functionings into an index by weighting them according to their importance (Robeyns 2005a). Thirdly, the crux of the debate opposing these two different philosophical capability approaches lies in the question of operationalization (on this opposition, see Robeyns 2005b; Baujard 2007). Following Aristotle, Martha Nussbaum believes that there is a single notion of the human good, virtues and flourishing life (Nussbaum 1988, 1993). This leads to the proposition of a concrete and comprehensive list of functionings, so that the approach belongs to fundamental universalism. Operational applications are therefore implementable for scientists (Alkire 2002; Robeyns 2006). The fact that values and weighting are determined by scientists rather than by the individuals themselves explains why this approach is often criticized for its paternalism. In contrast, Sen's position meets certain relativism, in order to give to public deliberation the main role in a democracy. Therefore, he refuses to provide a clear list of functionings which could measure well-being for everyone on a common scale. It is therefore difficult to implement a mere application of Sen's capability approach since it fundamentally relies on public debate. The latter is the only legitimate place to decide which moral values should be at stake, hence the retention of specific lists of functionings and, eventually, measurement of capabilities.

The extremely extensive literature on the capability approach, at least since the 2000s, is but a multi-dimensional analysis of living conditions, for which the United Nations Development Programme (UNDP) human development index (HDI) is only one very rough illustration. As the approach was generalizing, it has lost its specificity, which was to pay special attention to the value of freedom, understood as the possibility for everyone to live the life they have reasons to value.

Equity theory

The theory of fairness or equity theory, including fair allocations theory and even applications to public economics, borrowed the axiomatic methods from social choice theory and the theory of bargaining to study the implications of equity criteria in the framework of the Arrow–Debreu general equilibrium model.

Different fairness criteria can be contemplated for division rules. The idea of "no envy" was independently introduced by Jan Tinbergen (1953), Duncan Foley (1967) and developed by Serge-Christophe Kolm (1971), Allan Feldman and Alan Kirman (1974). An allocation is "envy free" if no individual would like better anybody else's basket. A fundamental result of equity theory is such that the competitive equilibrium with equal endowments, that is, equal budgets, satisfies both the criteria of "no envy" and Pareto. Refinements of such analyses were first conducted in the context of distribution of a consumption economy without production, then to study equal opportunities, incentives and optimal taxation, division of a single divisible good with single-peaked or monotonic preferences, the allocation of several commodities, the properties of a production economy, and so on.

The no-envy criterion, however, may conflict with the criterion of efficiency. This was proved by Elisha Pazner and David Schmeidler in 1974: no allocation respects Pareto efficiency and fairness (as no envy) in the context of production with unequal skills – that is, with production handicaps. This impossibility result can be interpreted as the incompatibility between a principle of reward and a principle of compensation. The no-envy test indeed requires that the allocation of individuals with identical preferences is on the same indifference curve. According to the principle of reward, individuals with similar talents should not envy each other, since there should not be any different treatment for different preferences. Also, according to the principle of compensation, individuals who have identical preferences should have the same benefit, eliminating the inequalities due to talents.

The same authors proposed in 1978 another test of fairness based on egalitarian equivalent allocations. An allocation is egalitarian-equivalent when each one is indifferent between the basket of goods in the allocation and the basket she would have in an egalitarian economy. In this perspective, Marc Fleurbaey and François Maniquet (2005) – among other similar contributions – considered the introduction of skills heterogeneity, and studied the consistency between compensation of skills inequalities and the condition of equal access to resources for all preferences. For a deeper understanding of the subject of responsibility and unequal handicaps, see Fleurbaey (2008) and, for a comprehensive presentation of the economic theory of fairness, see Fleurbaey and Maniquet (2011).

The theory of equity took up the different challenges welfare economics was facing. First, it is worth noticing it eventually overcame the Arrovian impossibility. Second, it did reject interpersonal comparisons of utility. Unlike standard economics which relies on the model of subjective revealed preferences, welfare is here described as an index of resources; and unlike the comparative approach, they still keep some account of individual ordinal preferences, which avoids the risk of paternalism. Third, the theory of fairness accepts the challenge of value judgements transparency in making clear the criteria of justice.

Conclusion

Public policies are expected to increase social welfare. Welfare economics aims to provide the framework to accomplish such a goal, developing a wide range of techniques to adapt different situations. However, looking carefully, this wonderful textbook world may be gloomier than it seems at first sight. Is welfare economics bound to die because of its difficulty in handling value judgements? Recommendations are always linked with some normative involvement, even through the undebated Pareto criterion. Beyond this, welfare economics suffers from the fact that a necessary discussion on the very definition of welfare had been avoided for too long. What is welfare? How can we justify this or that meaning of welfare for public policy? Pareto or Pigou acknowledge that, overall, welfare is much more than, or even different from, economic welfare. Yet Pareto developed a pure theory of ophelimity which was afterwards used by economists, although not under this name. Pigou eventually focused on economic welfare, and especially on the national dividend; from then on gross domestic product (GDP) appeared as an acceptable approximation of welfare for decades. These assumptions are increasingly debated.

It now seems generally accepted that GDP is a questionable goal, and the definition of welfare has become a topic of discussion. The theory of fairness and social welfare, which took over all challenges faced by welfare economics, now provides a unified approach of social choice theory, the theory of fair allocations and public economics. Sen's capability approach rehabilitates the role of public debate and reintroduces democracy in economics. All is in place to expect a promising future for (welfare) economics.

ANTOINETTE BAUJARD

See also:

Kenneth Joseph Arrow (I); Jeremy Bentham (I); Abram Bergson [Abram Burk] (I); British marginalism (II); Development economics (III); Economic sociology (III); Economics and philosophy (III); Hermann Heinrich Gossen (I); John Richard Hicks (I); Institutional economics (III); William Stanley Jevons (I); Nicholas Kaldor (I); Oskar Ryszard Lange (I); Abba Ptachya Lerner (I); Alfred Marshall (I); Vilfredo Pareto (I); Arthur Cecil Pigou (I); Poverty (III); Public choice (II); Public economics (III); Lionel Charles Robbins (I); Paul Anthony Samuelson (I); Tibor Scitovsky (I); Amartya Kumar Sen (I); Social choice (III); Jan Tinbergen (I); Utilitarianism and anti-utilitarianism (III); Marie-Esprit-Léon Walras (I).

References and further reading

Alkire, S. (2002), *Valuing Freedoms. Sen's Capability Approach and Poverty Reduction*, Oxford: Oxford University Press.

Arrow, K.J. (1950), 'A difficulty in the concept of social welfare', *Journal of Political Economy* **58** (4), 328–46.

Arrow, K.J. (1951), 'An extension of the basic theorems of classical welfare economics', in J. Neyman (ed.), *Proceedings of the Second Berkeley Symposium on Mathematical Statistics and Probability*, Berkeley and Los Angeles, CA: University of California Press, pp. 507–32.

Arrow, K.J. (1963), *Social Choice and Individual Values*, 2nd edn, New Haven, CT and London: Yale University Press.

Arrow, K.J. and G. Debreu (1954), 'Existence of an equilibrium for a competitive economy', *Econometrica*, **22** (3), 265–90.

Baujard, A. (2007), 'Commensurable freedoms in the capability approach. A discussion of Pattanaik and Xu's "Minimal relativism, dominance, and standard of living comparisons based on functionings"', Working Papers CREM 2007-03, 'Public Economics and Social Choice' series, accessed 18 February 2016 at http://crem.univ-rennes1.fr/wp/2007/200703.pdf.

Baujard, A. (2011), 'L'économie du bien-être est morte. Vive l'économie du bien-être!', Working Papers CREM 2011-02, 'Public Economics and Social Choice' series, June, accessed 18 February 2016 at http://crem.univ-rennes1.fr/wp/2011/201102.pdf.

Blackorby, C. and D. Donaldson (1990), 'A review article: the case against using the sum of compensating variations in cost–benefit analysis', *Canadian Journal of Economics*, **23** (3), 471–94.

Boadway, R. and N. Bruce (1984), *Welfare Economics*, Oxford: Blackwell.

Burk [Bergson], A. (1938), 'A reformulation of certain aspects of welfare economics', *Quarterly Journal of Economics*, **52** (2), 310–34.

Chipman, J.S. and J.C. Moore (1978), 'The new welfare economics, 1939–1974', *International Economic Review*, **19** (3), 547–84.

Cooter, R. and P. Rappoport (1984), 'Were the ordinalists wrong about welfare economics', *Journal of Economic Literature*, **22** (2), 507–30.

Davoine, L. (2009), 'L'économie du bonheur', *Revue économique*, **60** (4), 905–26.

Debreu, G. (1951), 'The coefficient of resource utilization', *Econometrica*, **19** (3), 273–92.

Easterlin, R.A. (1974), 'Does economic growth improve the human lot?', in P.A. David and M.W. Reder (eds), *Nations and Households in Economic Growth: Essays in Honor of Moses Abramovitz*, New York: Academic Press.

Feldman, A. and A. Kirman (1974), 'Fairness and envy', *American Economic Review*, **64** (6), 995–1005.

Fleurbaey, M. (2008), *Fairness, Responsibility and Welfare*, Oxford: Oxford University Press.

Fleurbaey, M. and F. Maniquet (2005), 'Fair social orderings when agents have unequal production skills', *Social Choice and Welfare*, **24** (1), 93–127.

Fleurbaey, M. and F. Maniquet (2011), *A Theory of Fairness and Social Welfare*, Cambridge: Cambridge University Press.

Fleurbaey, M. and P. Mongin (2005), 'The news of the death of welfare economics is greatly exaggerated', *Social Choice and Welfare*, **25** (1), 381–418.

Foley, D. (1967), 'Resource allocation and the public sector', *Yale Economic Essays*, **7** (1), 45–98.

Gossen, H.H. (1854), *Entwickelung der Gesetze des menschlichen Verkehrs, und der daraus fließenden Regeln für menschliches Handeln*, Braunschweig: F. Vieweg.

Hausman, D.M. and M.S. MacPherson (1996), *Economic Analysis and Moral Philosophy*, Cambridge: Cambridge University Press.

Hicks, J.R. (1939), 'The foundations of welfare economics', *The Economic Journal*, **49** (December), 696–712.

Hicks, J.R. (1941), 'The rehabilitation of consumer's surplus', *Review of Economic Studies*, **8** (2), 108–16.

Hotelling, H. (1938), 'The general welfare in relation to problems of taxation and of railway and utility rates', *Econometrica*, **6** (3), 242–69.

Jevons, W.S. (1871), *The Theory of Political Economy*, London: Macmillan.

Kaldor, N. (1939), 'Welfare propositions of economics and interpersonal comparisons of utility', *The Economic Journal*, **49** (195), 549–52.

Kolm, S.-C. (1971), *Justice et équité*, Paris: CEPREMAP.

Lange, O. (1942), 'The foundations of welfare economics', *Econometrica*, **10** (3–4), 215–28.

Layard, R. (2005), *Happiness. Lessons from a new science*, London: Penguin Books.

Lerner, A.P. (1934), 'The concept of monopoly and the measurement of monopoly power', *Review of Economic Studies*, **1** (3), 157–75.

Mishan, E.J. (1981), *Economic Efficiency and Social Welfare. Selected Essays on Fundamental Aspects of the Economic Theory of Social Welfare*, London: G. Allen and Unwin.

Mongin, P. (2002), 'Is there progress in normative economics?', in S. Boehm, C. Gehrke, H.D. Kurz and R.Sturn (eds), *Is There Progress in Economics?*, Cheltenham, UK and Northampton, MA, USA: Edward Elgar, pp. 145–69.

Mongin, P. (2006), 'A concept of progress in normative economics?', *Economics and Philosophy*, **22** (1), 19–54.

Myint, H. (1965), *Theories of Welfare Economics*, New York: Augustus M. Kelley, published for the London School of Economics and Political Science.

Nussbaum, M.C. (1988), 'Nature, function and capability: Aristotle on political distribution', *Oxford Studies in Ancient Philosophy*, **6**, supplement, 145–84.

Nussbaum, M.C. (1993), 'Non-relative virtues: an Aristotelian approach', in M.C. Nussbaum and A.K. Sen (eds), *The Quality of Life*, Oxford: Clarendon Press, pp. 242–76.

Pareto, V. (1906), *Manual of Political Economy*, in Italian, French trans. 1909, Paris: M. Giard and E. Brière, English trans. 1971 of the 1906 original.

Pazner, E. and D. Schmeidler (1974), 'A difficulty in the concept of fairness', *Review of Economic Studies*, **41** (3), 441–3.

Pazner, E. and D. Schmeidler (1978), 'Egalitarian equivalent allocations: a new concept of economic equity', *Quarterly Journal of* Economics, **92** (4), 671–87.

Pigou, A.C. (1912), *Wealth and Welfare*, London: Macmillan.

Pigou, A.C. (1920), *The Economics of Welfare*, London: Macmillan.

Robbins, L. (1932), *An Essay on the Nature and Significance of Economic Science*, 3rd edn, London: Macmillan. See also excerpts in D.M. Hausman (ed.) (1984), *The Philosophy of Economics. An Anthology*, Cambridge: Cambridge University Press, pp. 113–40.

Robeyns, I. (2005a), 'The capability approach: a theoretical survey', *Journal of Human Development*, **6** (1), 93–114.

Robeyns, I. (2005b), 'Selecting capabilities for quality of life measurement', *Social Indicators Research*, **74** (1), 191–215.

Robeyns, I. (2006), 'The capability approach in practice', *Journal of Political Philosophy*, **14** (3), 351–76.

Samuelson, P.A. (1947), *Foundations of Economic Analysis*, Cambridge, MA: Harvard University Press.

Scitovsky, T. (1971), 'A note on welfare propositions in economics', *Review of Economic Studies*, **9** (1), 92–5.

Sen, A.K. (1979a), 'Personal utilities and public judgements: or what's wrong with welfare economics?', *The Economic Journal*, **89** (355), 537–58.

Sen, A.K. (1979b), 'Utilitarianism and welfarism', *Journal of Philosophy*, **76** (9), 463–89.

Sen, A.K. (1979c), 'The welfare basis of real income comparisons: a survey', *Journal of Economic Literature*, **17** (1), 1–45.

Sen, A.K. (1980), 'Equality of what?', in S. McMurrin (ed.), *The Tanner Lectures on Human Values*, vol. 1, Cambridge: Cambridge University Press, pp. 185–220.

Sen, A.K. (1985), *Commodities and Capabilities*, Oxford: Oxford University Press.

Sen, A.K. (1987), *The Standard of Living*, Cambridge: Cambridge University Press.

Sen, A.K. (1992), *Inequality Re-Examined*, Oxford: Clarendon Press.

Sen, A.K. (1993), 'Capability and well-being', in M.C. Nussbaum and A.K. Sen (eds), *The Quality of Life*, Oxford: Clarendon Press, pp. 30–53.

Sen, A.K. (1999), 'The possibility of social choice', *American Economic Review*, **89** (3), 349–78.

Sen, A.K. (2009), *The Idea of Justice*, Cambridge, MA: Harvard University Press.

Tinbergen, J. (1953), *Redelijke Inkomensverdeling*, 2nd edn, Haarlem: N. DeGuiden Pers.

Index